sixth edition

Understanding Psychology

Robert S. Feldman

University of Massachusetts at Amherst

Boston   Burr Ridge, IL   Dubuque, IA   Madison, WI   New York   San Francisco   St. Louis
Bangkok   Bogotá   Caracas   Kuala Lumpur   Lisbon   London   Madrid   Mexico City
Milan   Montreal   New Delhi   Santiago   Seoul   Singapore   Sydney   Taipei   Toronto

McGraw-Hill Higher Education

A Division of The McGraw-Hill Companies

UNDERSTANDING PSYCHOLOGY, SIXTH EDITION

Published by McGraw-Hill, a business unit of The McGraw-Hill Companies, Inc., 1221 Avenue of the Americas, New York, NY 10020. Copyright © 2002, 1999, 1996, 1993, 1990, 1987 by The McGraw-Hill Companies, Inc. All rights reserved. No part of this publication may be reproduced or distributed in any form or by any means, or stored in a database or retrieval system, without the prior written consent of The McGraw-Hill Companies, Inc., including, but not limited to, in any network or other electronic storage or transmission, or broadcast for distance learning.

Some ancillaries, including electronic and print components, may not be available to customers outside the United States.

This book is printed on acid-free paper.

2 3 4 5 6 7 8 9 0 VNH/VNH 0 9 8 7 6 5 4 3 2 1

ISBN 0–07–242297–1
ISBN 0–07–112104–8 (ISE)

Editorial director: *Jane E. Karpacz*
Senior sponsoring editor: *Melissa Mashburn*
Editorial coordinator: *Cheri Dellelo*
Editorial assistant: *Libby Putman*
Senior marketing manager: *Chris Hall*
Project manager: *Vicki Krug*
Production supervisor: *Enboge Chong*
Coordinator of freelance design: *Michelle D. Whitaker*
Freelance cover/interior designer: *Christopher Reese*
Cover images: *ibid*
Spine image: *Sharon Hoogstraten*
Senior photo research coordinator: *Carrie K. Burger*
Photo research: *Toni Michaels*
Senior supplement producer: *Brenda A. Ernzen*
Media technology senior producer: *Sean Crowley*
Compositor: *GTS Graphics, Inc.*
Typeface: *10/12 Times Roman*
Printer: *Von Hoffmann Press, Inc.*

The credits section for this book begins on page Ak.1 and is considered an extension of the copyright page.

Library of Congress Cataloging-in-Publication Data

Feldman, Robert S. (Robert Stephen), 1947–
    Understanding psychology / Robert S. Feldman. — 6th ed.
        p.   cm.
    Includes bibliographical references and indexes.
    ISBN 0–07–242297–1 (alk. paper)
    1. Psychology. I. Title.

    BF121 .F34   2002
    150—dc21   2001030337
                                                                CIP

INTERNATIONAL EDITION ISBN 0–07–112104–8
Copyright © 2002. Exclusive rights by The McGraw-Hill Companies, Inc., for manufacture and export. This book cannot be re-exported from the country to which it is sold by McGraw-Hill. The International Edition is not available in North America.

www.mhhe.com

About the Author

Robert S. Feldman is a Professor in the Department of Psychology at the University of Massachusetts at Amherst, where he is Director of Undergraduate Studies. Professor Feldman, who is a Hewlett Teaching Fellow and winner of the College Distinguished Teacher award at UMass, has also taught courses at Mount Holyoke College, Wesleyan University, and Virginia Commonwealth University. As Director of Undergraduate Studies he initiated the Minority Mentoring Program, and he also teaches introductory psychology in the Talent Advancement Program to classes of 20 to 500 students.

A Fellow of both the American Psychological Association and the American Psychological Society, Professor Feldman received a B.A. from Wesleyan University and an M.S. and Ph.D. from the University of Wisconsin-Madison. He is a winner of a Fulbright Senior Research Scholar and Lecturer award, and he has written more than 100 books, book chapters, and scientific articles. His books, which have been translated into many languages, including Spanish, French, Chinese, and Albanian, include *Fundamentals of Nonverbal Behavior, Development of Nonverbal Behavior in Children, Social Psychology, Development Across the Life Span,* and *P.O.W.E.R. Learning: Strategies for Success in College and Life.* His research interests encompass the development of nonverbal behavior in children and the social psychology of education and have been supported by grants from the National Institute of Mental Health and the National Institute on Disabilities and Rehabilitation Research.

Professor Feldman's spare time is most often devoted to serious cooking and earnest, but unpolished, piano playing. He has three children and lives with his wife, also a psychologist, overlooking the Holyoke mountain range in Amherst, Massachusetts.

To

Jonathan, Joshua, Sarah,

and Kathy

Contents in Brief

Preface xx | Using *Understanding Pschology:* A Guide for Students xxxi

Chapter One	Introduction to Psychology	2
Chapter Two	Psychological Research	28
Chapter Three	The Biology Underlying Behavior	52
Chapter Four	Sensation and Perception	88
Chapter Five	States of Consciousness	130
Chapter Six	Learning	164
Chapter Seven	Memory	197
Chapter Eight	Thought and Language	226
Chapter Nine	Intelligence	258
Chapter Ten	Motivation and Emotion	286
Chapter Eleven	Sexuality and Gender	318
Chapter Twelve	Development: The Beginnings of Life	352
Chapter Thirteen	Development: Adolescence to the End of Life	386
Chapter Fourteen	Personality	412
Chapter Fifteen	Health Psychology: Stress, Coping, and Well-Being	442
Chapter Sixteen	Psychological Disorders	468
Chapter Seventeen	Treatment of Psychological Disorders	502
Chapter Eighteen	Social Psychology	528
Appendix	Going by the Numbers: Statistics in Psychology	A

Glossary	G.1
References	R.1
Acknowledgments	AK.1
Name Index	NI.1
Subject Index	SI.1

Contents

Preface xx | Using *Understanding Psychology:* A Guide for Students xxxi

---

Prologue: Snatched from the Grave 3
Looking Ahead 4

Psychologists at Work 5
The Subfields of Psychology: Psychology's Family Tree 5
Working at Psychology 8

Psychology at Work
Carolyn Cupper, Government Analyst 10

A Science Evolves: The Past, the Present, and the Future 11
The Roots of Psychology 12
Today's Perspectives 14

Applying Psychology in the 21st Century
Psychology and the Reduction of Violence 17

Psychology's Key Issues 18
EXPLORING DIVERSITY
Understanding How Culture, Ethnicity, and Race Influence Behavior 20
Psychology's Future 21
BECOMING AN INFORMED CONSUMER OF PSYCHOLOGY
Thinking Critically About Psychology: Distinguishing Legitimate Psychology from Pseudo-Psychology 22
Looking Back 24 | Key Terms and Concepts 25 | Psychology on the Web 25 | OLC Preview 26
Epilogue 25

Chapter One

Introduction to Psychology 2

Prologue: Why Was No Help Offered? 29
Looking Ahead 30

The Scientific Method 30
Theories: Specifying Broad Explanations 31
Hypotheses: Crafting Testable Predictions 32

Psychological Research 33
Archival Research 33
Naturalistic Observation 34
Survey Research 34
The Case Study 34

Applying Psychology in the 21st Century
Web Surveys 35
Correlational Research 36
Experimental Research 37

Research Challenges: Exploring the Process 43
The Ethics of Research 43

Psychology at Work
Mary Garrett, AIDS Researcher 44

EXPLORING DIVERSITY
Choosing Participants Who Represent the Scope of Human Behavior 44
Should Animals Be Used in Research? 46
Threats to Experiments: Experimenter and Participant Expectations 47

Chapter Two

Psychological Research 28

BECOMING AN INFORMED CONSUMER OF PSYCHOLOGY
Thinking Critically About Research 47

Looking Back 49 | Key Terms and Concepts 50 | Psychology on the Web 50 | OLC Preview 51
Epilogue 50

Chapter Three

The Biology Underlying Behavior 52

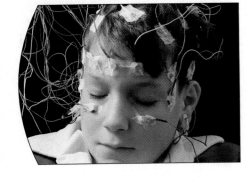

Prologue: The Fight of His Life 53
Looking Ahead 54

Neurons: The Elements of Behavior 55
The Structure of the Neuron 55
Firing the Neuron 57
Where Neurons Meet: Bridging the Gap 58
Neurotransmitters: Multitalented Chemical Couriers 60

The Nervous System 62
Central and Peripheral Nervous Systems 62
The Evolutionary Foundations of the Nervous System 65
Behavioral Genetics 66

The Brain 67
Studying the Brain's Structure and Functions: Spying on the Brain 67

Applying Psychology in the 21st Century
Mind over Cursor: Using Brain Waves to Overcome Physical Limitations 69

The Central Core: Our "Old Brain" 69
The Limbic System: Beyond the Central Core 71
The Cerebral Cortex: Our "New Brain" 73
Mending the Brain 76
The Specialization of the Hemispheres: Two Brains or One? 77
EXPLORING DIVERSITY
Human Diversity and the Brain 78
The Split Brain: Exploring the Two Hemispheres 80

The Endocrine System: Of Chemicals and Glands 80
BECOMING AN INFORMED CONSUMER OF PSYCHOLOGY
Learning to Control Your Heart—and Mind—Through Biofeedback 82

Looking Back 84 | Key Terms and Concepts 85 | Psychology on the Web 86 | OLC Preview 86
Epilogue 86

Chapter Four

Sensation and Perception 88

Prologue: Now Hear This! 89
Looking Ahead 90

Sensing the World Around Us 90
Absolute Thresholds: Detecting What's Out There 91
Difference Thresholds: Noticing Distinctions Between Stimuli 92
Sensory Adaptation: Turning Down Our Responses 92

Vision: Shedding Light on the Eye 93
Illuminating the Structure of the Eye 94
Sending the Message from the Eye to the Brain 96
Processing the Visual Message 97
Color Vision and Color Blindness: The Seven-Million-Color Spectrum 98

Applying Psychology in the 21st Century
Bringing Sight to People with Blindness 101

Hearing and the Other Senses   102
    Sensing Sound   102
    Smell and Taste   107
    The Skin Senses: Touch, Pressure, Temperature, and Pain   108

Psychology at Work
Julia A. Mennella, Taste Researcher   110

    BECOMING AN INFORMED CONSUMER OF PSYCHOLOGY
    Managing Pain   111

Perceptual Organization: Constructing Our View of the World   113
    The Gestalt Laws of Organization   113
    Feature Analysis: Focusing on the Parts of the Whole   114
    Top-Down and Bottom-Up Processing   116
    Perceptual Constancy   118
    Depth Perception: Translating 2-D to 3-D   118
    Motion Perception: As the World Turns   119
    Perceptual Illusions: The Deceptions of Perceptions   120
    EXPLORING DIVERSITY
    Culture and Perception   121
    Subliminal Perception   123
    Looking Back   125 | Key Terms and Concepts   127 | Psychology on the Web   127 | OLC Preview   128
    Epilogue   128

    Prologue: A Deadly Binge   131
    Looking Ahead   132

Sleep and Dreams   133
    The Stages of Sleep   134
    REM Sleep: The Paradox of Sleep   135
    Why Do We Sleep, and How Much Sleep Is Necessary?   136
    The Function and Meaning of Dreaming   137
    Sleep Disturbances: Slumbering Problems   141
    Circadian Rhythms: Life Cycles   142
    Daydreams: Dreams Without Sleep   143
    BECOMING AN INFORMED CONSUMER OF PSYCHOLOGY
    Sleeping Better   143

Hypnosis and Meditation   145
    Hypnosis: A Trance-Forming Experience?   145
    Meditation: Regulating Our Own State of Consciousness   147
    EXPLORING DIVERSITY
    Cross-Cultural Routes to Altered States of Consciousness   147

Drug Use: The Highs and Lows of Consciousness   149
    Stimulants: Drug Highs   150

Applying Psychology in the 21st Century
Just Say No—to D.A.R.E.? Finding Antidrug Programs That Work   151

    Depressants: Drug Lows   154
    Narcotics: Relieving Pain and Anxiety   157
    Hallucinogens: Psychedelic Drugs   158
    BECOMING AN INFORMED CONSUMER OF PSYCHOLOGY
    Identifying Drug and Alcohol Problems   159
    Looking Back   161 | Key Terms and Concepts   162 | Psychology on the Web   162 | OLC Preview   163
    Epilogue   163

Chapter Five

States of Consciousness
130

Chapter Six

Learning 164

Prologue: A Friend Named Ike   165
Looking Ahead   166

Classical Conditioning   167
   The Basics of Classical Conditioning   167
   Applying Conditioning Principles to Human Behavior   169
   Extinction   170
   Generalization and Discrimination   170
   Beyond Traditional Classical Conditioning: Challenging Basic Assumptions   171

Operant Conditioning   173
   Thorndike's Law of Effect   173
   The Basics of Operant Conditioning   174
   Positive Reinforcers, Negative Reinforcers, and Punishment   175
   The Pros and Cons of Punishment: Why Reinforcement Beats Punishment   176
   Schedules of Reinforcement: Timing Life's Rewards   177
   Discrimination and Generalization in Operant Conditioning   180
   Superstitious Behavior   180
   Shaping: Reinforcing What Doesn't Come Naturally   180
   Biological Constraints on Learning: You Can't Teach an Old Dog Just Any Trick   181

Psychology at Work
Lynn Calero, Dolphin Researcher   182

Cognitive-Social Approaches to Learning   183
   Latent Learning   183
   Observational Learning: Learning Through Imitation   185
   Violence on Television and in Movies: Does the Media's Message Matter?   186

Applying Psychology in the 21ˢᵗ Century
Does Virtual Aggression Lead to Actual Aggression?   187

   EXPLORING DIVERSITY
   Does Culture Influence How We Learn?   187
   The Unresolved Controversy of Cognitive-Social Learning Theory   189
   BECOMING AN INFORMED CONSUMER OF PSYCHOLOGY
   Using Behavior Analysis and Behavior Modification   189
   Looking Back   192 | Key Terms and Concepts   193 | Psychology on the Web   193-194 | OLC Preview   194
   Epilogue   194

Chapter Seven

Memory 196

Prologue: The Man Who Vanished into His Past   197
Looking Ahead   198

Encoding, Storage, and Retrieval of Memory   198
   The Three Systems of Memory: Memory Storehouses   199
   Contemporary Approaches to Memory: Working Memory, Memory Modules, and
      Associative Models of Memory   204

Recalling Long-Term Memories   208
   Retrieval Cues   208
   Levels of Processing   209
   Flashbulb Memories   210
   Constructive Processes in Memory: Rebuilding the Past   211
   Memory in the Courtroom: The Eyewitness on Trial   211

Applying Psychology in the 21ˢᵗ Century
Repressed Memories: Truth or Fiction?   213

Autobiographical Memory: Where Past Meets Present   214
EXPLORING DIVERSITY
Are There Cross-Cultural Differences in Memory?   214

Forgetting: When Memory Fails   215
Proactive and Retroactive Interference: The Before and After of Forgetting   217
The Biological Bases of Memory   217
Memory Dysfunctions: Afflictions of Forgetting   219
BECOMING AN INFORMED CONSUMER OF PSYCHOLOGY
Improving Your Memory   220
Looking Back   222 | Key Terms and Concepts   223 | Psychology on the Web   223 | OLC Preview   224
Epilogue   224

Prologue: House Call in Space   227
Looking Ahead   228

Thinking and Reasoning   228
Mental Images: Examining the Mind's Eye   229
Concepts: Categorizing the World   230
Reasoning: Making Up Your Mind   232

Problem Solving   234
Preparation: Understanding and Diagnosing the Problem   234
Production: Generating Solutions   237
Judgment: Evaluating the Solutions   240
Impediments to Solutions: Why Is Problem Solving Such a Problem?   241
Creativity and Problem Solving   243
BECOMING AN INFORMED CONSUMER OF PSYCHOLOGY
Thinking Critically and Creatively   244

Applying Psychology in the 21st Century
Can Computers Think Creatively?   245

Language   246
Grammar: Language's Language   246
Language Development: Developing a Way with Words   247
Understanding Language Acquisition: Identifying the Roots of Language   248
The Influence of Language on Thinking: Do Eskimos Have More Words for Snow Than Texans Have?   249
Do Animals Use Language?   250

Psychology at Work
Rose Sevcik, Language Researcher   252

EXPLORING DIVERSITY
Teaching with Linguistic Variety: Bilingual Education   251
Looking Back   254 | Key Terms and Concepts   255 | Psychology on the Web   255 | OLC Preview   256
Epilogue   256

Chapter Eight

Thought and Language   226

Prologue: Mindie Crutcher and Greg Smith   259
Looking Ahead   260

Defining Intelligent Behavior   260
Measuring Intelligence   261
Are There Different Kinds of Intelligence?   267

Applying Psychology in the 21st Century
When a High IQ Keeps You from Getting a Job: Are You Too Smart for the Job You Want?   268

The Biological Basis of Intelligence: Finding the Site of IQ   271

Chapter Nine

Intelligence 258

Practical Intelligence and Emotional Intelligence: Toward a More Intelligent View of
    Intelligence   271
    BECOMING AN INFORMED CONSUMER OF PSYCHOLOGY
    Scoring Better on Standardized Tests   274

Variations in Intellectual Ability   275
Mental Retardation   275
The Intellectually Gifted   276

Psychology at Work
Rob Davies, Advocate for the Mentally Retarded   278

Individual Differences in Intelligence: Hereditary and Environmental Determinants   278
EXPLORING DIVERSITY
The Relative Influence of Heredity and Environment: Nature, Nurture, and IQ   279
Placing the Heredity-Environment Question in Perspective   281
Looking Back   283 | Key Terms and Concepts   284 | Psychology on the Web   284 | OLC Preview   285
Epilogue   284

Chapter Ten

Motivation and Emotion   286

Prologue: Tour de Lance   287
Looking Ahead   288

Explaining Motivation   288
Instinct Approaches: Born to Be Motivated   289
Drive-Reduction Approaches: Satisfying Our Needs   289
Arousal Approaches: Beyond Drive Reduction   289
Incentive Approaches: Motivation's Pull   289
Cognitive Approaches: The Thoughts Behind Motivation   292
Maslow's Hierarchy: Ordering Motivational Needs   292
Applying the Different Approaches to Motivation   293

Human Needs and Motivation: Eat, Drink, and Be Daring   295
The Motivation Behind Hunger and Eating   295
Eating Disorders   298
BECOMING AN INFORMED CONSUMER OF PSYCHOLOGY
Dieting and Losing Weight Successfully   299
The Need for Achievement: Striving for Success   301
The Need for Affiliation: Striving for Friendship   301
The Need for Power: Striving for Impact on Others   302

Understanding Emotional Experiences   303
The Functions of Emotions   304
Determining the Range of Emotions: Labeling Our Feelings   304

The Roots of Emotions   305
The James-Lange Theory: Do Gut Reactions Equal Emotions?   306
The Cannon-Bard Theory: Physiological Reactions as the Result of Emotions   306
The Schachter-Singer Theory: Emotions as Labels   307
Contemporary Perspectives on Emotions   308

Applying Psychology in the 21st Century
The Truth About Lies: Do Lie Detectors Work?   309

Nonverbal Behavior and the Expression of Emotions   310
EXPLORING DIVERSITY
Do People in All Cultures Express Emotion Similarly?   310
The Facial-Feedback Hypothesis: Smile, Though You're Feeling Blue   312
Looking Back   314 | Key Terms and Concepts   315 | Psychology on the Web   315–316 | OLC Preview   316
Epilogue   316

Prologue: From Boy to Girl and Back   319
Looking Ahead   320

Gender and Sex   320
Gender Roles: Society's Expectations for Women and Men   320
Gender Differences: More Similar Than Different   324
Sources of Gender Differences: Where Biology and Society Meet   326

Understanding Human Sexual Response: The Facts of Life   329
The Basic Biology of Sexual Behavior   329
Psychological Aspects of Sexual Excitement: What Turns People On?   330
The Phases of Sexual Response: The Ups and Downs of Sex   331
EXPLORING DIVERSITY
Female Circumcision: A Celebration of Culture—or Genital Mutilation?   332

The Varieties of Sexual Behavior   335
Approaches to Sexual Normality   335
Surveying Sexual Behavior: What's Happening Behind Closed Doors?   336
Masturbation: Solitary Sex   336
Heterosexuality   337
Homosexuality and Bisexuality   339

Sexual Difficulties: When Sex Goes Wrong   341
Rape   341

Psychology at Work
Pat Unger, Crisis Center Counselor   342

Childhood Sexual Abuse   343
Sexually Transmitted Diseases (STDs)   343
Sexual Problems   345
BECOMING AN INFORMED CONSUMER OF PSYCHOLOGY
Lowering the Risks of Date Rape   346

Applying Psychology in the 21st Century
Bringing Sexual Dysfunction into the Open: The Newest Sexual Revolution   347

Looking Back   348 | Key Terms and Concepts   349 | Psychology on the Web   350 | OLC Preview   350
Epilogue   350

Prologue: The Brave New World of Childhood   353
Looking Ahead   354

Nature and Nurture: The Enduring Developmental Issue   354
Determining the Relative Influences of Nature and Nurture   356
Specific Research Approaches   357

Prenatal Development: From Conception to Birth   357
The Basics of Genetics   357
Development from Zygote to Birth   358

Applying Psychology in the 21st Century
Cloning, Gene Therapy, and the Coming Medical Revolution   359

Chapter Eleven

Sexuality and Gender   318

Chapter Twelve

Development: The Beginnings of Life   352

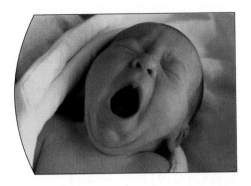

The Extraordinary Newborn   364
  Reflexes   364
  Development of the Senses: Taking in the World   364

The Growing Child: Infancy Through Middle Childhood   367
  Physical Development   367
  Development of Social Behavior: Taking on the World   368
  Cognitive Development: Children's Thinking About the World   374

Psychology at Work
Michael J. Morrier, Preschool Coordinator   380

  EXPLORING DIVERSITY
  Supporting Children's School Achievement: The Asian Success Story   381
  BECOMING AN INFORMED CONSUMER OF PSYCHOLOGY
  Maximizing Children's Competence   381
  Looking Back   383 | Key Terms and Concepts   384 | Psychology on the Web   385 | OLC Preview   385
  Epilogue   385

Chapter Thirteen

Development: Adolescence to the End of Life
386

Prologue: Life Goes On   387
Looking Ahead   388

Adolescence: Becoming an Adult   388
  Physical Development: The Changing Adolescent   389
  Moral and Cognitive Development: Distinguishing Right from Wrong   390
  Social Development: Finding Oneself in a Social World   392
  EXPLORING DIVERSITY
  Rites of Passage: Coming of Age Around the World   396

Early and Middle Adulthood: The Middle Years of Life   397
  Physical Development: The Peak of Health   398
  Social Development: Working at Life   398
  Marriage, Children, and Divorce: Family Ties   399

Applying Psychology in the 21st Century
The Changing Institution of Marriage: Is Marriage Declining?   401

The Later Years of Life: Growing Old   403
  Physical Changes in Late Adulthood: The Aging Body   403
  Cognitive Changes: Thinking About—and During—Old Age   404
  The Social World of Late Adulthood: Old but Not Alone   406
  BECOMING AN INFORMED CONSUMER OF PSYCHOLOGY
  Adjusting to Death   407
  Looking Back   409 | Key Terms and Concepts   410 | Psychology on the Web   410 | OLC Preview   410
  Epilogue   410

Chapter Fourteen

Personality
412

Prologue: Good Guy or Good Fella?   413
Looking Ahead   414

Psychoanalytic Approaches to Personality   414
  Freud's Psychoanalytic Theory   414
  The Neo-Freudian Psychoanalysts   419

Other Major Approaches to Personality: In Search of Human Uniqueness   421
  Trait Approaches: Placing Labels on Personality   421
  Learning Approaches: We Are What We've Learned   424
  Biological and Evolutionary Approaches: Are We Born with Personality?   426

Applying Psychology in the 21st Century
Can Unjustified High Self-Esteem Lead to Violence? 427

Humanistic Approaches: The Uniqueness of You   428

Comparing Approaches to Personality   430

Assessing Personality: Determining What Makes Us Special   431

EXPLORING DIVERSITY

Should Norms Be Based on Race and Ethnicity?   432

Self-Report Measures of Personality   433

Projective Methods   434

Behavioral Assessment   436

BECOMING AN INFORMED CONSUMER OF PSYCHOLOGY

Assessing Personality Assessments   436

Looking Back   438 | Key Terms and Concepts   439 | Psychology on the Web   439 | OLC Preview   440

Epilogue   439

Prologue: So Much to Do, So Little Time to Do It   443

Looking Ahead   444

Stress and Coping   444

Stress: Reacting to Threat and Challenge   445

Psychology at Work

Alan Benner, Police Psychologist   450

Coping with Stress   450

BECOMING AN INFORMED CONSUMER OF PSYCHOLOGY

Effective Coping Strategies   453

Psychological Aspects of Illness and Well-Being   454

The A's and B's of Coronary Heart Disease   454

Psychological Aspects of Cancer   456

Smoking   457

EXPLORING DIVERSITY

Hucksters of Death: Promoting Smoking Throughout the World   459

Well-Being and Happiness   460

Applying Psychology in the 21st Century

If You Won the Lottery, Would You Be Happier?   461

Psychological Factors Related to Physical Illness: Going to the Doctor   462

Physician–Patient Communication   462

Complying with Physicians' Recommendations   463

BECOMING AN INFORMED CONSUMER OF PSYCHOLOGY

Speaking with Your Physician   464

Looking Back   466 | Key Terms and Concepts   467 | Psychology on the Web   467 | OLC Preview   467

Epilogue   467

Chapter Fifteen

Health Psychology: Stress, Coping, and Well-Being 442

Prologue: Lori Schiller   469

Looking Ahead   470

Normal Versus Abnormal: Making the Distinction   470

Defining Abnormality   470

Psychology at Work

Margaret H. Coggins, Senior Research Psychologist   472

Perspectives on Abnormality: From Superstition to Science   472

Classifying Abnormal Behavior: The ABCs of the *DSM*   475

Chapter Sixteen

Psychological Disorders 468

Major Disorders   478
  Anxiety Disorders   478
  Somatoform Disorders   482

Applying Psychology in the 21ˢᵗ Century
Internet Addiction: Real or Virtual?   483

  Dissociative Disorders   483
  Mood Disorders   485
  Schizophrenia   488
  Personality Disorders   492

Beyond the Major Disorders: Abnormal Behavior in Perspective   495
  EXPLORING DIVERSITY
  The DSM and Culture—and the Culture of the DSM   *495*
  The Prevalence of Mental Disorders: The Mental State of the Union   496
  BECOMING AN INFORMED CONSUMER OF PSYCHOLOGY
  Deciding When You Need Help   *497*
  Looking Back   499 | Key Terms and Concepts   500 | Psychology on the Web   500-501 | OLC Preview   501
  Epilogue   *501*

Chapter Seventeen

Treatment of Psychological Disorders   502

Prologue: Breaking the Silence   *503*
Looking Ahead   504

Psychotherapy: Psychological Approaches to Treatment   504
  Psychodynamic Approaches to Therapy   504
  Behavioral Approaches to Therapy   507
  Cognitive Approaches to Therapy   510
  Humanistic Approaches to Therapy   512
  Group Therapy   514
  Evaluating Psychotherapy: Does Therapy Work?   515

Applying Psychology in the 21ˢᵗ Century
Virtual Therapy: Is the World Wide Web a Good Place to Get Treatment?   517

  EXPLORING DIVERSITY
  Racial and Ethnic Factors in Treatment: Should Therapists Be Color-Blind?   *517*

Biomedical Therapy: Biological Approaches to Treatment   519
  Drug Therapy   519
  Electroconvulsive Therapy (ECT)   522
  Psychosurgery   523
  Biomedical Therapies in Perspective: Can Abnormal Behavior Be Cured?   523
  Community Psychology: A Focus on Prevention   524
  BECOMING AN INFORMED CONSUMER OF PSYCHOLOGY
  Choosing the Right Therapist   *524*
  Looking Back   526 | Key Terms and Concepts   527 | Psychology on the Web   527 | OLC Preview   527
  Epilogue   *527*

Chapter Eighteen

Social Psychology   528

Prologue: A Modern Lynching   *529*
Looking Ahead   530

Attitudes and Social Cognition   530
  Persuasion: Changing Attitudes   530

Psychology at Work
Ann Altman, Advertising Executive   534

  Social Cognition: Understanding Others   534

EXPLORING DIVERSITY
Attributions in a Cultural Context: How Fundamental Is the Fundamental Attribution Error? *538*

Social Influence 539
  Conformity: Following What Others Do 539
  Compliance: Submitting to Direct Social Pressure 539
  Obedience: Obeying Direct Orders 542

Applying Psychology in the 21st Century
Reading Your Mind, Reaching Your Wallet: Using Computer Technology to Increase
  Compliance 543

Prejudice and Discrimination 545
  The Foundations of Prejudice 546
  Working to End Prejudice and Discrimination 546

Positive and Negative Social Behavior 548
  Liking and Loving: Interpersonal Attraction and the Development of Relationships 548
  Aggression and Prosocial Behavior: Hurting and Helping Others 551
  BECOMING AN INFORMED CONSUMER OF PSYCHOLOGY
  Dealing with Anger Effectively 555

  Looking Back 557 | Key Terms and Concepts 558 | Psychology on the Web 559 | OLC Preview 559
  Epilogue 559

Prologue: Selma Vorwerk A
Looking Ahead A.1

Descriptive Statistics A.1
  The Mean: Finding the Average A.2
  The Median: Finding the Middle A.3
  The Mode: Finding What Is Most Frequent A.3
  Comparing the Three M's: Mean Versus Median Versus Mode A.3

Measures of Variability A.5
  The Range: Highest Minus Lowest A.5
  The Standard Deviation: Differences from the Mean A.5

Using Statistics to Answer Questions: Inferential Statistics and Correlation A.7
  The Correlation Coefficient: Measuring Relationships A.8
  Looking Back A.12 | Key Terms and Concepts A.12

Appendix

Going by the Numbers: Statistics in Psychology   A

Glossary G.1
References R.1
Acknowledgments AK.1
Name Index NI.1
Subject Index SI.1

Preface

Estella Ramirez gained a better understanding of her mother's lifelong battle with major depression after learning about its possible causes in her introductory psychology course. She also developed a new appreciation for the struggles her mother faced in coping with this disorder.

* * *

As a new father, Phil Westport realized that he didn't know very much about infants, including his own daughter. He decided to take introductory psychology in part to learn more about child development. Applying what he learned in the course, Phil gained new insights into his daughter's behavior and more confidence in his ability to be a good parent.

* * *

Although he enrolled in introductory psychology because it was the only class that fit conveniently into his schedule, Jacob Rakovitch found himself increasingly interested in the subject matter. He became fascinated by the relationship between the brain and behavior, and by the end of the term he was seriously thinking about majoring in psychology.

* * *

Joanne Chu was planning to become a special education teacher after graduating from college. Her aspirations were fueled while studying, in her introductory psychology course, how people learn and how psychologists explain variations in intelligence.

Psychology speaks with many voices to the diversity of students we teach, offering a personal message to each one. To some, the discipline is a vehicle that can provide a better understanding of others' behavior; to others it is a pathway to self-understanding. To some, psychology offers the potential of a future career; others are drawn to psychology because it gives them an opportunity for intellectual discovery.

Understanding Psychology, sixth edition, is designed to present the discipline of psychology in a way that engages and excites students about the field of psychology—no matter what led them to take the introductory course or what level of motivation they initially bring to the course. It is designed to draw them into its way of looking at the world and to inform their understanding of psychological issues. The book provides a broad, comprehensive introduction to the field of psychology, covering basic theories and research findings, as well as highlighting current applications outside the laboratory.

Revising *Understanding Psychology*

Over its lifetime, hundreds of thousands of students have used *Understanding Psychology* in forms ranging from traditional print versions to e-books. The book has been adopted at colleges and universities throughout the United States, as well as in Asia, Europe, Australia, and Africa. It has been translated into French, Spanish, Chinese, and several other languages. Students at community colleges, state schools, and Ivy League campuses have used the book, and it has been used in distance learning courses as well as traditional, lecture-based courses.

How does one maintain and improve the quality of a book that has served the needs of students through five editions? As a research psychologist, I responded to this challenge by doing empirical research to determine what instructors were looking for in the new edition. My editors and I collected and analyzed an enormous amount of data to identify the changes and improvements that needed to be made.

To begin the research process, we asked more than a hundred professors who teach introductory psychology to complete extensive questionnaires. In addition, we individually interviewed scores of instructors through their participation in focus groups in a variety of locations, including California, Texas, and Florida. Students were also included in the review

process: Over the course of a semester I met weekly with a panel of students, systematically examining each chapter, and hundreds of other student users provided written comments about the previous edition. Finally, we solicited reviews of the prior edition from dozens of instructors who teach the introductory course.

After I had drafted the manuscript for the revision in response to this feedback, a large panel of instructors, the majority of whom were using other texts, reviewed each chapter. The second draft also benefited from an extensive review process. Ultimately, every chapter was reviewed by at least twenty instructors. *No introductory psychology text has involved more extensive prepublication research than Understanding Psychology, sixth edition.*

What did we learn from this prepublication research? Instructors wanted the revision of *Understanding Psychology,* like previous editions, to provide a contemporary, accurate, and lively introduction to the discipline. They wanted to build on the previous editions' history of strong pedagogy, which ensured that students could read and understand the text on their own. Instructors—and students—wanted the text to have an inviting design and be of a manageable length.

Furthermore, instructors wanted the book to be able to address a broad range of students, including those whose interest and motivation in the subject area was initially low. To accomplish this, they wanted the text to contain (and be accompanied by) the most sophisticated instructional pedagogy available, giving students the tools to master the complex material that make up an introduction to the discipline of psychology. Finally, they wanted *Understanding Psychology* to help students move beyond what was in the text and into the information age, encouraging students to search Web-based as well as traditional sources of information relating to psychology and to be able to critically evaluate the material they found.

As a result of the exhaustive research process and the enthusiastic endorsements received from reviewers, I am confident that the new edition reflects what instructors want and need: a book that motivates students to understand and apply psychology to their own lives. *Understanding Psychology* is a book designed not only to expose readers to the content—and promise—of psychology, but to do so in a way that will nurture students' excitement about psychology and keep that excitement alive for a lifetime.

Overview of *Understanding Psychology*

Understanding Psychology, sixth edition, was written to accomplish the following goals:

- To provide broad coverage of the field of psychology, introducing the theories, research, and applications that constitute the discipline
- To arouse intellectual curiosity and build an appreciation of the relevance of psychology, motivating and engaging students
- To serve as an impetus for readers to think critically about psychological phenomena, particularly those that have an impact on their everyday lives
- To illustrate the substantial diversity both within the field of psychology and in society by presenting material that reflects the discipline's increasing concern with cultural, gender, racial, and ethnic issues

Understanding Psychology includes extensive coverage of both the traditional areas of psychology and applied topics, including the biological foundations of behavior, sensation and perception, states of consciousness, learning, memory, cognition, human development, personality, abnormal behavior and treatment, and social psychology. Moreover, it features more applications-oriented chapters, such as gender and sexuality and health psychology. Ultimately, the book reflects a combination of traditional core topics and contemporary applied subjects, providing a broad and extremely current view of the field of psychology.

The flexibility of the book's organizational structure, a hallmark of this text, is

Prepare

Organize

Work

Evaluate

Rethink

considerable. Each chapter is divided into three or four manageable, self-contained units, allowing instructors to choose and omit sections in accordance with their syllabus.

Building on its strong tradition of facilitating student learning, the new edition of *Understanding Psychology* contains several new and improved features:

- **The option of using a systematic study strategy built into the book—the *P.O.W.E.R. Learning* system.** The new edition of *Understanding Psychology* provides students with the option of using *P.O.W.E.R. Learning,* a systematic approach to learning and studying based on five key steps (***P**repare, **O**rganize, **W**ork, **E**valuate, and **R**ethink.)* Based on empirical research, *P.O.W.E.R. Learning* systematizes the acquisition of new material by providing a learning framework. The system stresses the importance of learning objectives, self-evaluation, and critical thinking. The elements of *P.O.W.E.R. Learning* can also be used in conjunction with other learning systems, such as *SQ3R.* (A more detailed description of the use of the *P.O.W.E.R. Learning* system follows in the Student Guide section of the Preface.)
- **Addition of Web-based exercises.** New to this edition, every chapter includes several exercises that require students to use the World Wide Web to identify and research information related to psychology.
- **Inclusion of additional thought-provoking examples.** Great care has been taken to select relevant and high-interest examples that motivate students to read as well as to explain key concepts.
- **Addressing diverse student learning styles.** Our prepublication research revealed that an increasing number of instructors find that the presentation of material in multiple modalities facilitates student mastery of material. Consequently, this edition includes several features that speak to the diverse learning styles of students. These include:

    1. *More and improved figures.* The number of figures has been increased, and each figure has been drawn to maximize clarity and pedagogical value. Many figures include annotations that draw attention to major points in the illustrations.
    2. *More photos and captions that directly support learning.* Photos have been carefully chosen to support learning of key concepts, as well as for their visual impact. Captions have been improved and expanded, and many now include questions designed to promote critical thinking.

- **Fine-tuning of definitions.** Definitions of key terms and concepts introduced in the text, which appear in the margins and in the end-of-book glossary, have been revised and made more precise.
- **Addition of new and updated material.** The sixth edition incorporates a significant amount of new and updated information, reflecting the advances in the field and the suggestions of reviewers. *Overall, more than a thousand new citations have been added, with most of those from articles and books published within the last three years.*

Advances in such areas as evolutionary perspectives, brain and behavior, mapping the human genome, cognition, emotions, and cultural approaches to psychological phenomena receive expanded and new coverage. In addition to the extensive updating, a broad range of new topics have been incorporated. The following sample of new and revised topics featured in this edition provides a good indication of the currency of this revision:

- Evolutionary perspectives (Chapter 1)
- Using the Web for research (Chapter 2)
- The Human Genome Project and behavioral genetics (Chapter 3)
- Cochlear implants (Chapter 4)
- PET scan data and psychoanalytic explanations of dreaming (Chapter 5)
- "Date rape" drugs (Chapter 5)

- Effects of violent video games (Chapter 6)
- Spreading activation and associative models of memory (Chapter 7)
- Critical periods (Chapter 8)
- Bilingual education (Chapter 8)
- Brain scans and intelligence (Chapter 9)

- Being too smart for a job (Chapter 9)
- Intrinsic motivation (Chapter 10)
- Erectile dysfunction and Viagra (Chapter 11)
- Gene therapy (Chapter 12)
- Teratogens (Chapter 12)
- Child-care effects (Chapter 12)
- Estrogen replacement therapy (Chapter 13)
- Self-esteem (Chapter 14)

- The preconscious (Chapter 14)
- Self-efficacy (Chapter 14)
- Well-being and happiness (Chapter 15)
- Depression, ADHD (Chapter 16)
- Virtual therapy (Chapter 17)
- St. John's wort (Chapter 17)
- Industrial/organizational psychology (Chapter 18)
- Psychographics (Chapter 18).

The Learning Features of
Understanding Psychology

Understanding Psychology, sixth edition, contains many features designed to help students learn, study, and master the text's content. These include the following:

- **Prologue.** Each chapter starts with an account of a real-life situation that demonstrates the relevance of basic principles and concepts of psychology to pertinent issues and problems. These prologues depict well-known people and events, such as Michael J. Fox's fight against Parkinson's disease, Lance Armstrong's motivation to win the Tour de France, and the racially motivated murder of James Byrd, Jr.
- **Looking Ahead.** These sections follow each prologue, expressing the key themes and issues discussed within the chapter.
- **Prepare and Organize.** Each major section of the chapter incorporates the first two steps of the *P.O.W.E.R. Learning* system: *Prepare* and *Organize*. The *Prepare* section includes several broad questions designed to orient students to the major topics of the chapter. The *Organize* section provides an outline of the material. Together, they offer a framework for conceptualizing and organizing the material that follows.
- **Applying Psychology in the 21st Century.** These boxes—which highlight the relevance of psychology—illustrate applications of current psychological theory and research findings to real-world problems, focusing on current advances and future possibilities. For example, these discussions explore such topics as the use of brain waves to command computers, the consequences of playing violent video games on actual aggressive behavior, cloning and gene therapy, and Internet addiction.
- **Psychology at Work.** These interviews provide biographical sketches of people working in professions that make use of the findings of psychology. Some of the individuals profiled are psychologists, some work in other fields; all of them draw on psychological principles on a daily basis. For example, there are interviews with a police psychologist, a preschool teacher, and a psychologist who works for the Secret Service evaluating threats against the president of the United States.
- **Exploring Diversity.** In addition to a substantial amount of material relevant to diversity integrated throughout the text, every chapter also includes at least one special section devoted to an aspect of racial, ethnic, gender, or cultural diversity. These sections highlight the way in which psychology informs (and is informed by) issues relating to the increasing multiculturalism of our global society. The *Exploring Diversity* topics include cross-cultural differences in memory, cross-cultural similarities in emotional expression, cultural perspectives on female circumcision, and the use of race to establish test norms.
- **"PsychLinks"** are marginal icons providing brief descriptions of websites relevant to the text discussion. Each "PsychLink" includes a URL that leads to a hot-link on the *Understanding Psychology* website.

- **Becoming an Informed Consumer of Psychology.** Every chapter includes material designed to make readers more informed consumers of psychological information by giving them the ability to evaluate critically what the field of psychology offers. These discussions also provide sound, useful guidance concerning common problems. These unique sections discuss such topics as how to assess research claims, identify drug and alcohol problems, lose weight successfully, assess personality assessments, and choose a therapist.

- **Evaluate and Rethink.** Every major chapter section concludes with an *Evaluate* and *Rethink* section as part of the *P.O.W.E.R. Learning* system. The *Evaluate* sections test recall of the material, assessing the degree of initial learning. The *Rethink* sections provide thought-provoking questions designed to engage critical thinking about the material.

- **Running Glossary.** Key terms are highlighted in boldface type within the text where they are introduced and are defined in the margin of the page, with pronunciation guides for difficult words. There is also an end-of-book glossary.

- **Looking Back.** To facilitate both review and synthesis of the information covered, a number of end-of-chapter features reinforce student learning. First, a *chapter summary* emphasizes the key points of the chapter and is organized according to the *Prepare* questions posed at the beginning of every major section. Second, a list of key terms and concepts, including the page numbers where they are introduced, encourages student review. Third, *Psychology on the Web* takes students online to analyze psychological issues relevant to the chapter content. Fourth, the *OLC Preview* suggests that students visit the book website for self quizzes, activities, and, additional information.

- **Epilogue.** Each chapter ends with an epilogue that incorporates critical thinking questions relating to the *Prologue* at the opening of the chapter. These thought-provoking questions provide a way to tie the chapter together and illustrate how the concepts addressed in the chapter apply to the real-world situation described in the *Prologue*.

The Research–Driven Supplements Package

The sixth edition of *Understanding Psychology* is accompanied by an extensive, integrated set of supplemental materials designed to support the teaching of both new and veteran instructors. The utility and value of each part of the supplements package were assessed through the same comprehensive development process used for the text itself. This research has ensured that the supplement package is state-of-the-art and reflects the needs of students and of instructors teaching through both traditional and electronic instruction. The supplements listed here may accompany *Understanding Psychology*, sixth edition. Please contact your local McGraw-Hill representative for details concerning policies, prices, and availability, as some restrictions may apply.

FOR THE INSTRUCTOR

Instructor's Manual (ISBN 0-07-245066-5)
By Saundra Ciccarelli, Gulf Coast Community College
This thoroughly revised manual provides instructors of introductory psychology with all the tools and resources they need to present and enhance their course. The Instructor's Manual includes detailed chapter outlines, learning objectives, chapter maps, ideas for lectures, activities, and student projects, ready-to-use handouts, overhead masters, and multimedia references. Fully integrated with the *P.O.W.E.R. Learning* system, this manual has tips and activities that have a usefulness beyond any particular teaching approach.

Test Bank (ISBN 0-07-245073-8)

By Jeffrey Kaufmann and Beverly Knoernschild, Muscatine Community College
The Test Bank has been thoroughly upgraded to reflect the new content in *Understanding Psychology*, sixth edition. The Test Bank contains more than 2,000 multiple-choice items, classified by cognitive type and level of difficulty, and keyed to the appropriate learning objective and section in the textbook. Items that test knowledge of material in the textbook's boxes are indicated for easy reference. Essay questions are provided for all chapters, and grading suggestions make the Test Bank easy to use.

Computerized Test Bank, Macintosh/Windows compatible (ISBN 0-07-245065-7)

Available in a cross-platform format, this CD-ROM makes all the items from the Test Bank easily available to instructors to create their own tests. The test-generating program facilitates the selection of questions from the Test Bank and the printing of tests and answer keys, and also allows instructors to import questions from other sources.

Online Learning Center (ISBN 0-07-245075-4)

The Online Learning Center for Instructors houses downloadable versions of the Instructor's Manual and Powerpoint slides, a variety of other text-specific instructor resources, including a bank of 146 images and a newsletter written by Robert Feldman, and access to our acclaimed customized website creation tool, Page Out! Instructors in need of assistance can contact their McGraw-Hill sales representative via e-mail from the Online Learning Center. Visit us at http://www.mhhe.com/feldmanup6/.

New! Distance Learning Integration Guide (ISBN 0-07-250863-9)

By Christopher R. Poirier and Robert Feldman, University of Massachusetts–Amherst
The Distance Learning Integration Guide is an effective manual for instructors who teach (or wish to teach) via the Internet and use *Understanding Psychology*, sixth edition, as the main text and supplements. The guide will give instructors the information and resources they need to plan their online curriculum and teach a distance learning course.

New! *Understanding Psychology* Orientation Video

Available through your publisher's representative, this detailed overview provides a videotaped walkthrough of the book and the total learning package accompanying *Understanding Psychology*, sixth edition. The orientation video is particularly useful for rapidly acquainting instructors, teaching assistants, and adjunct faculty with the most effective use of the book and its supplements.

Instructor's Resource CD-ROM (ISBN 0-07-245072-X)

This CD-ROM contains every key instructor's resource in one flexible format. The Instructor's Manual, the Test Bank, Powerpoint presentations, and a 145-item Image Bank are included along with an easy-to-use interface for the design and delivery of multimedia classroom presentations.

Powerpoint Slides (ISBN 0-07-245071-1)

For instructors using a computer monitor for demonstrations in the classroom, Powerpoint slides downloadable from the Online Learning Center were specially created by John Story of Lexington Community College to support the use of *Understanding Psychology*, sixth edition. Chapter-by-chapter Powerpoint presentations including illustrations from the Image Bank allow instructors to deliver their lectures in an effective manner.

Image Bank

Over 145 illustrations can be downloaded from the Image Bank on the Online Learning Center and used on your course website or in Powerpoint presentations.

Overhead Transparencies (ISBN 0-07-245074-6)

A set of acetate transparencies containing key illustrations, graphs, and tables complements *Understanding Psychology*, sixth edition, package for instructors using projectors to deliver their lectures.

In-Class Activities Manual for Instructors of Introductory Psychology
(ISBN 0-07-238431-X)

By Patricia A. Jarvis, Cynthia R. Nordstrom, and Karen B. Williams, Illinois State University
Geared to instructors of large introductory psychology courses, this activities manual covers every major topic in introductory psychology. Nineteen chapters include 58 separate activities, all of which have been used successfully in the authors' introduction to psychology classes. Each activity includes a short description of the demonstration, the approximate time needed to complete the activity, the materials needed, step-by-step procedures, practical tips, and suggested readings related to the activity. The manuual also includes advice and teaching tips for the novice and experienced instructor, on how to prepare an effective syllabus, what to consider when structuring your large section, how to select and manage a teaching assistant, and other key topics.

Annual Editions Online: Psychology (ISBN 0-07-234602-7)

By Karen G. Duffy, SUNY at Geneseo, New York
With Annual Editions Online: Psychology, you'll have online access to current, carefully selected articles from the public press. This abridged version contains 20 online readings that are supported with well-researched links of interest and built-in assessment in the form of online quizzes and article reviews. An online search engine to connect with additional articles and an online Instructor's Resource Guide are also included. If you are interested in packaging Annual Editions Online with a McGraw-Hill textbook, contact your sales representative for details.

Annual Editions: Psychology 01/02, 31/e (ISBN 0-07-243377-9)

By Karen G. Duffy, SUNY at Geneseo, New York
This reader of public press articles explores the science of psychology; biological bases of behavior; perceptual processes; learning and remembering; cognitive processes; emotion and motivation; development: personality processes; social processes; psychological disorders; and psychological treatments. Annual Editions is supported by Dushkin Online (www.dushkin.com/online/), a student website that provides study support tools and links to related websites.

Taking Sides: Clashing Views on Controversial Psychological Issues, 11/e (ISBN 0-07-237142-0)

By Brent Slife, Brigham Young University, Utah
This debate reader is designed to introduce students to controversies in psychology. The readings, which represent the arguments of leading psychologists and commentators, reflect a variety of viewpoints and have been selected for their liveliness and substance and because of their value in a debate framework. By requiring students to analyze opposing viewpoints and reach considered judgements, Taking Sides actively develops critical thinking skills.

Sources: Notable Selections in Psychology, 3/e (ISBN 0-07-303187-9)

By Terry F. Pettijohn, Ohio State University–Marion
This volume contains approximately 40 selections of enduring intellectual value—classic articles, book excerpts, and research studies—that have shaped the study of psychology and our contemporary understanding of it.

FOR THE STUDENT

Study Guide (ISBN 0-07-245063-0)

By Barbara Radigan, Community College of Allegheny County, Pennsylvania
The Study Guide integrates the *P.O.W.E.R. Learning* system into a comprehensive review of the text material. Multiple-choice practice tests and essay questions allow students to gauge their understanding of the material. An answer key provides answers to all of the chapter's exercises, including feedback for all multiple-choice items. A list of activities and projects that encourage students to apply psychology to their daily lives is also included. New to this edition is additional information created by Dr. Sheryl Hartman of Miami-Dade Community College that is designed to aid non-native speakers of English in understanding and retaining key course information.

Online Learning Center (ISBN 0-07-245075-4)

The Student Online Learning Center houses an array of chapter-by-chapter study tools, including detailed chapter outlines, concepts and learning objectives, key works, self-quizzes, essay questions, activities and projects, explanations of American idiomatic expressions for ESL students, answers to the *Epilogue* questions in the textbook, crossword puzzles, interesting Web links, and interactive exercises. Visit us at http://www.mhhe.feldmanup6/.

Making the Grade Student CD-ROM (ISBN 0-07-245070-3)

Packaged free with each copy of the text, this CD-ROM is designed to help students perform at their best. It contains practice quizzes for each text chapter, a learning style assessment, study skills primer, guide to electronic research, and link to the text website.

New! In-Psych Student CD-ROM (ISBN 0-07-247689-3)

In-Psych sets a new standard for introductory psychology multimedia. Every **In-Psych** CD-ROM is organized according to the textbook the CD accompanies and features 70 interactive exercises chosen to illustrate especially difficult core introductory psychology concepts. Each exercise showcases one of three types of media assets—an audio clip, a video clip, or a simulation—and includes a pre-test, follow-up assignments, and Web resources. **In-Psych** also includes chapter quizzes, a student research guide, and an interactive timeline that puts events, key figures, and research in psychology in historical perspective. A learning style assessment tool helps students identify what kind of learners they are—kinesthetic, auditory, or visual—and then provides them with study tips tailored to their own particular learning style.

WebQuester: Psychology (ISBN 0-07-240850-2)

By Terry F. Pettijohn, Ohio State University–Marion

WebQuester is a series of online interactive exercises covering approximately 20 core topics in psychology. Each website includes 1 to 3 multiple-choice questions, short-answer questions, and essay questions. A 150-page Guidebook to the Web provides practical information and tips; topic areas include Searching the Web, Evaluating Information, Thinking Critically in a World of Information, and Computer Ethics.

Acknowledgments

One of the central features of *Understanding Psychology* is the involvement of both professionals and students in the review process. The sixth edition of *Understanding Psychology* has relied heavily—and profited substantially—from the advice of instructors and students from a wide range of backgrounds.

I am especially grateful to members of the focus groups, who provided extensive evaluations of the previous edition and ancillary package, and shared their insights into the introductory psychology course of the future. I am also grateful to those who responded to a pre-revision questionnaire. Members of various panels and questionnaire participants included the following:

Richard Baiardo
Evergreen Valley College, California

Manolya Bayar
Harford Community College, Maryland

Kathleen Bey
Palm Beach Community College, Central Campus, Florida

Theresa Botts
Eastern Kentucky University

Dominic Brucato
Miami-Dade Community College–North Campus, Florida

Shirin Khosropour
Austin Community College, Pinnacle Campus, Texas

Linda Chaparro
Oxnard College, California

Carolyn Cohen
Massachusetts Bay Community College

Bob Conkright
Austin Community College, Cypress Campus, Texas

Natividad DeAnda
Los Medanos College, Pittsburg, California

Giselle Diaz
Palm Beach Community College, Florida

Karen Douglas
San Antonio College, Texas

Todd Farrar
Virginia College, Alabama

Aaron Fielder
Virginia College, Alabama

Stanley Fitch
El Camino College, California

Classie Foat
Skyline College, California

Tracy Forte
Potomac College, District of Columbia

Christopher Frost
Southwest Texas State University

Rod Gillis
University of Miami, Florida

Anthony Gordon
Contra Costa College, California

Joseph Hanak
Corning Community College, New York

Sarah Harrison
Evergreen Valley College, California

Milton Hatcher
Arkansas State University

Toni Haynes
Palm Beach Community College, South Campus, Florida

Alylene Hegar
Eastfield College, Texas

Kerry Hinkel
Valdosta State University, Georgia

Wayne Hren
Los Angeles Pierce College, California

Robert Hutchison
Modesto Junior College, California

Barbara Lusk
Collin Country Community College, Texas

Leslie Martin
La Sierra University, California

Michael T. Miles
Palm Beach Community College, Central Campus, Florida

Gwen Murdock
Missouri Southern State College

Glen Musgrove
Broward Community College Central Campus, Florida

Glenda Nichols
Tarrant County Junior College South Campus, Texas

Sonya Nieves
Broward Community College South Campus, Florida

Carol Ponday
Los Angeles Pierce College, California

Ben Price
San Jose City College, California

Kimberly Rector
Academy of Business College, Arizona

George Riday
Citrus College, California

MaryLou Robbins
San Jacinto College South Campus, Texas

Harry Saterfield
Foothill College, California

Bishop Scott
College of Alameda, California

Sharon Scott
South Plains College, Texas

Elizabeth Shaw
Texarkana College, Texas

Charlotte Simon
Montgomery College–Rockville, Maryland

Jean Spaulding
Northwest College HCC, Texas

Mary Helen Spear
Prince George's Community College, Maryland

Brian Spillane
Antelope Valley College, California

Patricia Stephenson
Miami-Dade Community College–Kendall Campus, Florida

Janet Stubbs
Salem State College, Massachusetts

Robert Templeton
Palm Beach Community College, Central Campus, Florida

Donald Thompson
Troy State University–Montgomery, Alabama

Joe Tinnin
Richland College, Texas

Richard Townsend
Miami-Dade Community College South Campus, Florida

Barbara Turner
Pasadena City College, California

Robin Vallacher
Florida Atlantic University, Florida

Jean Volckmann
Pasadena City College, California

Gwen Walker
Los Angeles Mission College, California

Sandra Wilcox
California State University–Dominguez Hills, California

Stephen Wurst
State University of New York at Oswego

Andrea Zabel
Midland College, Texas

Both the previous edition of *Understanding Psychology* and the manuscript of the sixth edition were evaluated by a large number of psychologists who served in their capacity as content experts and teachers of introductory psychology. These reviewers helped to ensure that this new edition is accurate and incorporates state-of-the-art research findings in psychology. I am extraordinarily grateful to the following:

Marilyn Andrews
Hartnell College, California

Richard Baiardo
Evergreen Valley College, California

Louis Banderet
Northeastern University, Massachusetts

Carol Batt
Sacred Heart University, Connecticut

Steven L. Berman
Florida International University, Florida

Kathleen Bey
Palm Beach Community College, Florida

David Bjorklund
Florida Atlantic University, Florida

Don Borden
Corning Community College, New York

Deb Brihl
Valdosta State University, Georgia

Richard Cavasina
California University of Pennsylvania

Natividad DeAnda
Los Medanos College, California

Karen T. Douglas
San Antonio College, Texas

Stanley K. Fitch
El Camino College, California

Linda Flickinger
St. Clair County Community College, Michigan

Dave Harrison
Virginia Polytechnic Institute and State University, Virginia

Sara Hart Harrison
Evergreen Valley College, California

Lisa M. Henry
Loyola Marymount University, California

Judith M. Horowitz
Medaille College, New York

Loreen Huffman
Missouri Southern State College

Robert Hynes
Limestone College, South Carolina

Robert Jensen
California State University–Sacramento

Norman E. Kinney
Southeast Missouri State University

W. Richard Krall
Gateway Community College, Arizona

Len Larsen
Eastfield College, Texas

Joe Manganello
Gloucester County College, New Jersey

Michael R. Markham
Florida International University, Florida

Leslie R. Martin
La Sierra University, California

John Mastenbrook
Del Mar College, Texas

Dorothy L. Mercer
Eastern Kentucky University

Michael Miles
Palm Beach Community College, Florida

Richard Miller
Navarro College, Texas

Mindy Miserendino
Sacred Heart University, Connecticut

Glenn J. Musgrove
Broward Community College–Central Campus, Florida

Jerry Newell
Citrus Community College, California

Geri Olson
Sonoma State University, California

Dan Quinn
Northeastern University, Massachusetts

Barbara Radigan
Community College of Allegheny County, Pennsylvania

Christopher K. Randall
Troy State University–Montgomery, Alabama

Karen Pitts Saenz
Houston Community College–Southeast, Texas

Nicole Schnopp-Wyatt
Pikeville College, Kentucky

Norman Schorr
Montgomery College–Rockville, Maryland

Sharon Scott
South Plains College, Texas

Ann Shaver
Fairmont State College, West Virginia

Debjani Sinha
University of Cincinnati, Ohio

Nathan Slaughter
Merritt College, California

Jeanne Spaulding
Houston Community College, Texas

William Vasquez
Palo Alto College, California

Charles Verschoor
Miami-Dade Community College, Florida

Sandra G. Wilcox
California State University–Dominguez Hills

Matthew P. Winslow
Eastern Kentucky University

Andrea Zabel
Midland College, Texas

The second group of reviewers consisted of a panel of four students who had used the previous edition of *Understanding Psychology* in their introductory psychology class. Over the course of a subsequent semester, they reviewed the entire manuscript, literally line by line. Their insights, suggestions, and sometimes all-too-enthusiastic criticism were invaluable to me as I prepared this revision. The student review panel consisted of Cherilyn Johnson, Louis Meunier, Stacey Whitbourne, and Phil Zetye.

Finally, hundreds of students read parts or all of the manuscript to ensure that the material was clear and engaging. Their suggestions are incorporated throughout the text.

I am grateful to all of these reviewers, who provided their time and expertise to help ensure that *Understanding Psychology* reflects the best that psychology has to offer.

Many teachers along my educational path have shaped my thinking. I was introduced to psychology at Wesleyan University, where several committed and inspiring teachers—in particular Karl Scheibe—conveyed their sense of excitement about the field and made its relevance clear to me. Karl epitomizes the teacher-scholar combination to which I aspire, and I continue to marvel at my good fortune in having such a role model.

By the time I left Wesleyan I could envision no other career but that of psychologist. Although the University of Wisconsin, where I did my graduate work, could not have been more different from much smaller Wesleyan, the excitement and inspiration were similar. Once again, a cadre of excellent teachers—led, especially, by the late Vernon Allen—molded my thinking and taught me to appreciate the beauty and science of the discipline of psychology.

My colleagues and students at the University of Massachusetts at Amherst provide ongoing intellectual stimulation, and I thank them for making the University a fine place to work. Several people also provided extraordinary research and editorial help. In particular, I am grateful to my superb students, past and present, including Erik Coats, Sara Levine, Jim Forrest, Darren Spielman, Dan Hrubes, and Chris Poirier. Dan and Chris, in particular,

The student review panel, who reviewed every chapter of Understanding Psychology *in depth, consisted of Phil Zetye, Cherilyn Johnson, Louis Meunier, and Stacey Whitbourne.*

provided a good deal of help and advice on this edition of the book. Edward Murphy helped in a variety of important ways, providing highly useful and intelligent editorial input and advice. Finally, I am extremely grateful to John Graiff, whose hard work and dedication helped immeasurably on just about everything involving this book.

The Burrston House team, led by Glenn and Meg Turner, provided as much feedback and good advice as any author could wish for. Their work, and constant push for quality, provided the impetus for the major changes that characterize this edition. I thank them for their extraordinary work.

I also offer thanks to the McGraw-Hill editorial team which included Hélène Greenwood, Sharon Geary, and Jane Vaicunas. I also thank Vice President and Editor-in-Chief Thalia Dorwick, whose hands-on interest in the project helped it along at every critical juncture. Melissa Mashburn, sponsoring editor for this edition, has brought a thoughtful, creative energy and strong commitment to the book, and I am grateful for her support. Finally, every reader of this book owes a debt to Rhona Robbin, developmental editor on prior editions of *Understanding Psychology.* Her relentless pursuit of excellence helped form this book, and she taught me a great deal about the craft and art of writing.

Other people at McGraw-Hill were central to the design and production process, including project manager Vicki Krug and designer Michelle Whitaker. I am also appreciative of marketing manager Chris Hall, whose savvy I'm counting on. I am proud to be a part of this world-class team.

Finally, I remain completely indebted to my family. My parents, Leah Brochstein and the late Saul D. Feldman, provided a lifetime foundation of love and support, and I continue to see their influence in every corner of my life. My extended family also plays a central role in my life. They include, more or less in order of age, my nieces and nephews, my brother, assorted brothers- and sisters-in-law, Ethel Radler, and Harry Brochstein. Finally, my mother-in-law, the late Mary Evans Vorwerk, had an important influence on this book, and I remain ever grateful to her.

Ultimately, my children, Jonathan, Joshua, and Sarah, and my wife, Katherine, remain the focal point of my life. I thank them, with immense love.

Robert S. Feldman
Amherst, Massachusetts

Using *Understanding Psychology:* A Guide for Students

If you're reading this passage, you're probably taking an introductory psychology course. Maybe you're studying psychology because you've always been interested in what makes people tick. Or perhaps you've had a friend or family member who has sought assistance for a psychological disorder. Or maybe you have no idea of what psychology is all about, but you know that taking an introductory psychology course would fulfill a degree requirement.

Whatever your motivation for taking the course and reading this book, here's my commitment to you: by the time you finish this text, you will have a better understanding of why people—including you—behave the way they do. You will know how, and why, psychologists conduct research, and you'll have an understanding of the theories that guide their research. You will become acquainted with the breadth of the field, and you'll obtain practical, useful information. In short, you'll gain a wealth of knowledge that, I hope, will excite your curiosity and increase your understanding of people's behavior.

To meet this commitment, *Understanding Psychology* has been written with you, the reader, in mind. At every step in the development of this book, students and instructors have been consulted extensively in an effort to identify the combination of learning tools that would maximize your ability to learn and retain the subject matter of psychology. The result is a wealth of features that will not only help you understand psychology, but also make the discipline of psychology a part of your life.

Now it's your turn; you'll need to take several steps to maximize the effectiveness of the learning tools in this book. These steps include familiarizing yourself with the scope and structure of the book, using the built-in learning aids, and employing a systematic study strategy.

Familiarize Yourself with the Scope and Organization of *Understanding Psychology*

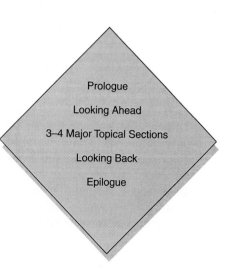

Prologue

Looking Ahead

3–4 Major Topical Sections

Looking Back

Epilogue

Begin by reading the list of chapters and skimming the detailed table of contents. From this you will get a sense of the topics covered and the logic of the sequence of chapters. Then take some time to flip through the book. Choose a chapter that sounds particularly interesting to you, skim it, and see for yourself how it is laid out. Note that every chapter follows the same diamond-shaped pattern, illustrated at the right.

The heart of each chapter consists of several self-contained units that provide logical starting and stopping points for reading and studying. You can plan your studying around the three or four major sections of each chapter. For instance, if your instructor assigns a chapter to read over the course of a week, you might plan to read and study one major section each day, using later days in the week to review the material.

Use the Built-in Learning Aids

Once you have acquired a broad overview of *Understanding Psychology,* you are ready to begin reading and learning about psychology. Each chapter contains learning aids that will help you master the material. In addition, the book incorporates the *P.O.W.E.R. Learning* system. As we'll discuss in further detail later, the *P.O.W.E.R. Learning* system is based on a series of five steps: *P*repare, *O*rganize, *W*ork, *E*valuate, and *R*ethink. Each major section of a chapter starts with a *P*repare and *O*rganize segment, and—after you do the *W*ork of reading the section—ends with an *E*valuate and *R*ethink segment. Making use of the *P.O.W.E.R. Learning* system and the other built-in features will help you study more easily and effectively.

❶ **Prologue and Epilogue**

Each chapter begins with a Prologue and ends with an Epilogue. The Prologue sets the stage for the chapter, providing a brief account of a real-life event that is relevant to the chapter content, and demonstrating why the material in the chapter is important. The Epilogue refers back to the Prologue, seeking to place it in the context of the chapter subject matter and asking questions designed to encourage you to think critically about what you've read.

❷ **Looking Ahead**

The Looking Ahead section, which follows the Prologue, identifies the key themes and issues addressed in the chapter. It alerts you to what you'll have learned after reading and studying the chapter.

❸ **PsychLinks**

These marginal icons provide links to websites relevant to the material being discussed in the chapter. Use them to find additional information about important topics.

❹ **Prepare and Organize segments**

The Prepare section consists of learning objectives to help focus your thinking about the chapter content. (The same questions are used to organize the chapter summary at the end of the chapter.) The Organize section provides an outline of the material to orient you to the topics that will be covered.

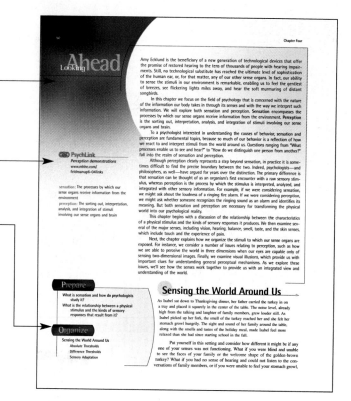

❺ **Applying Psychology in the 21st Century**

These boxes describe psychological research that is being applied to everyday problems. Read them to understand how psychology promises to improve the human condition, in ways ranging from new approaches to treating psychological disorders to using brain waves to overcome physical disabilities.

❻ **Exploring Diversity**

Every chapter includes at least one section devoted to an aspect of racial, ethnic, gender, or cultural diversity. These features illustrate the contributions of psychology to a better understanding of multicultural issues that are so central a part of our global society.

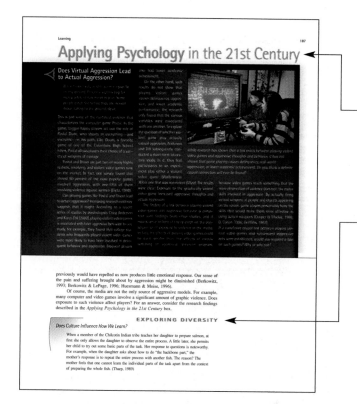

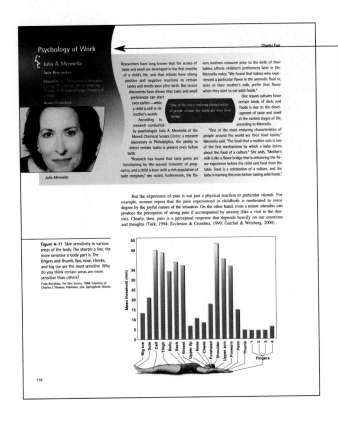

❼ Psychology at Work

These boxes present interviews with psychologists and other professionals who draw on psychological principles and findings in their work. These biographical sketches provide a glimpse into the broad range of professions that use psychology. They can help answer your questions on how to use your knowledge of psychology as you follow your own career path.

❽ Running Glossary

When a key term or concept appears in the text, it appears either in boldface or italics. Boldfaced words are of primary importance; italicized words are of secondary importance. Terms and concepts in bold are defined in the text where they are introduced, in the text margins, and in the end-of-book glossary. In addition, boldfaced terms are included in the page-referenced list of Key Terms and Concepts at the end of every chapter. You might want to highlight these terms with a marker.

❾ Becoming an Informed Consumer of Psychology

One of the major goals of *Understanding Psychology* is to make readers more informed, critical consumers of information relating to psychological issues. These discussions, found in every chapter, give you the tools to evaluate information concerning human behavior that you might hear or read about in the media or on the Web.

Daydreams: Dreams Without Sleep

It is the stuff of magic: Our past mistakes can be wiped out and the future filled with noteworthy accomplishments. Fame, happiness, and wealth can be ours. In the next moment, though, the most horrible of tragedies can occur, leaving us devastated, alone, and penniless.

The source of these scenarios is **daydreams**, fantasies that people construct while awake. Unlike dreaming that occurs while sleeping, daydreams are more under people's control. Therefore their content is often more closely related to immediate events in the environment than is the content of the dreams that occur during sleep. Although they might include sexual content, daydreams also pertain to other activities or events that are relevant to a person's life.

Daydreams are a typical part of waking consciousness, even though our awareness of the environment around us declines while we are daydreaming. People vary considerably in the amount of daydreaming they do. For example, around 2 to 4 percent of the population spend at least half their free time fantasizing. Although most people daydream much less frequently, almost everyone fantasizes to some degree. Studies that ask people to identify what they are doing at random times during the day have shown that they are daydreaming about 10 percent of the time. As for the content of fantasies, most concern such mundane, ordinary events as paying the telephone bill, picking up the groceries, or solving a romantic problem (Singer, 1975; Lynn & Rhue, 1988; Lynn et al., 1996).

Frequent daydreaming might seem to suggest psychological difficulties, but there appears to be little relationship between psychological disturbance and daydreaming. Except in those rare cases in which a daydreamer is unable to distinguish a fantasy from reality (a mark of serious problems, as we discuss in Chapter 12), daydreaming seems to be a normal part of waking consciousness. Indeed, fantasy can contribute to the psychological well-being of some people by enhancing their creativity and by permitting them to use their imagination to understand what other people are experiencing (Lynn & Rhue, 1988; Pihlgren, Gidycz, & Lynn, 1993; Lynn et al., 1996).

Daydreams are fantasies that people construct while they are awake. What are the similarities and differences between daydreams and night dreams?

daydreams: Fantasies that people construct while awake

BECOMING AN INFORMED CONSUMER OF PSYCHOLOGY

Sleeping Better

Do you have trouble sleeping? You're not alone—almost 40 million people in the United States have chronic difficulty sleeping, and 30 million others have occasional sleep problems. For those of us who spend hours tossing and turning in bed, psychologists studying sleep disturbances have a number of suggestions for overcoming insomnia (National Institutes of Health, 1996b; Kupfer & Reynolds, 1997; Scharf, 1999), including these:

- *Exercise during the day (at least six hours before bedtime) and avoid naps.* Not surprisingly, it helps to be tired before going to sleep! Moreover, learning systematic relaxation techniques and biofeedback (see Chapter 2) can help you unwind from the day's stresses and tensions (Lehrer, 1996).
- *Choose a regular bedtime and stick to it.* Adhering to a habitual schedule helps your internal timing mechanisms regulate your body more effectively.
- *Don't use your bed as an all-purpose area.* Leave studying, reading, eating, watching TV, and other recreational activities to some other part of your living quarters. If you follow this advice, your bed will become a cue for sleeping.
- *Avoid drinks with caffeine after lunch.* The effects of beverages such as coffee, tea, and some soft drinks can linger for as long as 8 to 12 hours after they are consumed.
- *Drink a glass of warm milk at bedtime.* (Your grandparents were right when they dispensed this advice: Milk contains the chemical tryptophan, which helps people fall asleep.)

⑩ Evaluate and Rethink

Every major section ends with an Evaluate and Rethink segment. Evaluate sections provide a series of questions on the chapter content that ask for concrete information, in a multiple choice, fill-in, or true-false format. The Rethink questions are designed to encourage you to think critically about a topic or issue, and they often have more than one correct answer.

Answer Evaluate and Rethink questions! Your responses will indicate both the degree of your mastery of the material and the depth of your knowledge. If you have no trouble with the questions, you can be confident that you are studying effectively. Use the questions you have difficulty with as a basis for further study.

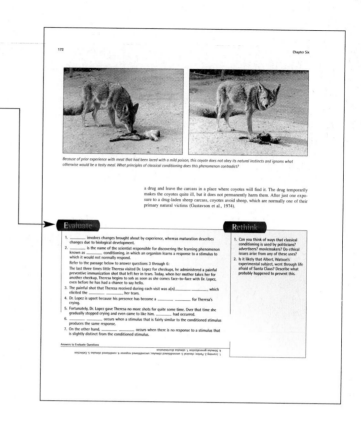

Because of prior experience with meat that had been laced with a mild poison, this coyote does not obey its natural instincts and ignores what otherwise would be a tasty meal. What principles of classical conditioning does this phenomenon contradict?

⑪ Looking Back

These end-of-chapter sections include four parts: a chapter summary, a list of key terms and concepts, *Psychology on the Web,* and *OLC Preview.* The summary is organized around the *Prepare* questions from each major section. The key terms and concepts list includes a page number where the term is first introduced in the chapter. To find its definition, you have two choices: turn to the margin of the page where the term is introduced, or consult the end-of-book Glossary, which contains every key term and concept. *Psychology on the Web* exercises take you online to help you learn more about topics covered in the chapter. The *OLC Preview* points you to the book website, where you can test your knowledge, do additional activities, and find interesting resources.

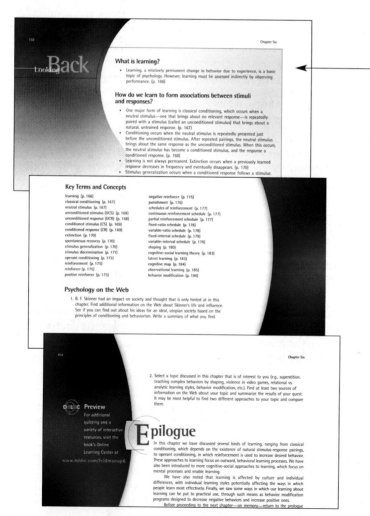

You'll find the same set of features in every chapter. Consequently, the book provides a set of familiar landmarks to help you chart your way through new material. This structure will help you organize each chapter's content, as well as learn and remember the material.

One final note: This text uses a variation on the reference citation style endorsed by the American Psychological Association (APA). According to APA style, citations include a name and date, typically set off in parentheses at the end of a sentence specifying the author of the work being cited and the year of publication. An example: (Anderson & Dill, 2000). Each of these "author-date" citations refers to a book or article listed in the References section at the end of this book.

Using *P.O.W.E.R. Learning,* a Proven Strategy for Effective Study and Critical Thinking

Now that you are acquainted with the special features of *Understanding Psychology* that are designed to help you understand and master this book's content, you should consider consistently applying the *P.O.W.E.R. Learning* system incorporated in the book. By using *P.O.W.E.R. Learning,* you can increase your ability to learn and retain information and to think critically, not only in your psychology course but in all your academic subjects.

As noted earlier, the *P.O.W.E.R. Learning* strategy includes five key steps: **P**repare, **O**rganize, **W**ork, **E**valuate, and **R**ethink. *P.O.W.E.R. Learning* systematizes the acquisition of new material by providing a learning framework. It stresses the importance of learning objectives and appropriate preparation prior to beginning to study, as well as the significance of self-evaluation and the incorporation of critical thinking into the learning process. Specifically, use of the *P.O.W.E.R. Learning* system entails the following steps:

❶ **Prepare**   Before starting any journey, we need to know where we are headed. Academic journeys are no different; we need to know what our goals are. The *Prepare* stage consists of thinking about what we hope to attain from reading a particular section of the text by identifying specific goals that we seek to accomplish. In *Understanding Psychology,* these goals are presented in the form of broad questions that start each major section.

❷ **Organize**   Once we know what our goals are, we need to develop a route to accomplish those goals. The *Organize* stage involves developing a mental roadmap of where we are headed. *Understanding Psychology* highlights the organization of each upcoming section. Read the outline to get an idea of what topics are covered and how they are organized.

❸ **Work**   The heart of the *P.O.W.E.R. Learning* system entails actually reading and studying the material presented in the book. In some ways *Work* is the easy part, because, if you have carried out the steps in the preparation and organization stage, you'll know where you're headed and how you'll get there. Of course it's not so simple—you'll need the motivation to conscientiously read and think about the material presented in the chapter. And remember, the main text isn't the only material that you need to read and think about. It's also important to read the boxes, the marginal glossary terms, and the special sections in order to gain a full understanding of the material, so be sure to include them as part of the *Work* of reading the chapter.

❹ **Evaluate**   The fourth step, *Evaluate,* provides you with the opportunity to determine how effectively you have mastered the material. *Understanding Psychology* has a series of questions at the end of each section that permit a rapid check of your understanding of the material. Evaluating your progress is essential to assessing your degree of mastery of the material.

❺ **Rethink** The final step in *P.O.W.E.R. Learning* involves critical thinking, which entails reanalyzing, reviewing, questioning, and challenging assumptions. It provides the opportunity to look at the big picture by thinking about how material fits with other information that you have already learned. Every major section of *Understanding Psychology*, sixth edition, ends with a *Rethink* section that contains thought-provoking questions. Answering them will help you understand the material more fully and at a deeper level.

If you want to maximize your potential to master the material in *Understanding Psychology*, sixth edition, use *P.O.W.E.R. Learning!* Taking the time and effort to work through the steps of the system is a proven technique for understanding and learning the material.

Supplementing *P.O.W.E.R.* Learning with *SQ3R*

Although *P.O.W.E.R. Learning* is the learning strategy that is built into the book and consequently is the easiest to use, it is not the only system compatible with the book. For example, some readers may wish to supplement the *P.O.W.E.R. Learning* system with the *SQ3R* method, which includes a series of five steps, designated by the initials S-Q-R-R-R. The first step is to *survey* the material by reading the chapter outlines, chapter headings, figure captions, recaps, and Looking Ahead and Looking Back sections, providing yourself with an overview of the major points of the chapter. The next step—the Q in *SQ3R*—is to *question*. Formulate questions about the material—either aloud or in writing—prior to actually reading a section of the material. The queries posed in the *Prepare* sections and the *Evaluate* and *Rethink* questions that end each part of the chapter are also a good source of questions.

The next three steps in *SQ3R* ask you to *read, recite,* and *review* the material. *Read* carefully and, even more importantly, read actively and critically. While you are reading, answer the questions you have asked yourself. Critically evaluate material by considering the implications of what you are reading, thinking about possible exceptions and contradictions, and examining underlying assumptions. The *recite* step involves describing and explaining to yourself (or to a friend) the material you have just read and answering the questions you have posed earlier. Recite aloud; the recitation process helps to identify your degree of understanding of the material you have just read. Finally, *review* the material, looking it over, reading the Looking Back summaries, and answering the in-text review questions.

Some Final Comments

The *P.O.W.E.R. Learning* system (as well as *SQ3R*) provides a proven means of increasing your study effectiveness. Yet you need not feel tied to a particular strategy. You might want to combine other elements into your own study system. For example, learning tips and strategies for critical thinking will be presented throughout *Understanding Psychology*, such as in Chapter 7 when the use of mnemonics (memory techniques for organizing material to help its recall) are discussed. If these tactics help you to successfully master new material, stick with them.

By using a systematic study strategy, you will maximize your understanding of the material in this book and will master techniques that will help you learn and think critically in all of your academic endeavors. More importantly, you will optimize your understanding of the field of psychology. It is worth the effort: the excitement, challenges, and promise that psychology holds for you are significant.

Understanding Psychology

Chapter One

Introduction to Psychology

Prologue: Snatched from the Grave

Looking Ahead

Psychologists at Work

The Subfields of Psychology: Psychology's Family Tree

Working at Psychology

Psychology at Work: Carolyn Copper

A Science Evolves: The Past, the Present, and the Future

The Roots of Psychology

Today's Perspectives

Applying Psychology in the 21ˢᵗ Century: Psychology and the Reduction of Violence

Psychology's Key Issues

Exploring Diversity: Understanding How Culture, Ethnicity, and Race Influence Behavior

Psychology's Future

Becoming an Informed Consumer of Psychology: Thinking Critically About Psychology: Distinguishing Legitimate Psychology from Pseudo-Psychology

Looking Back

Key Terms and Concepts

Psychology on the Web

OLC Preview

Epilogue

The devastating earthquake in India, which left over 30,000 people dead, raised a variety of psychological issues and concerns.

Prologue

Snatched from the Grave

It was only by chance that the two British rescue workers, taking a break from hours of combing over the rubble of houses, apartments, and businesses after a devastating earthquake in India, found themselves in front of the pink and cream seven-story building that had collapsed around Viral Dalal.

Dalal, a 24-year-old student studying computer science at Fairleigh Dickinson University in New Jersey, was home on vacation, visiting his parents and brother in Bhuj, India, when the earthquake struck. The monstrous quake, which killed an astounding 30,000 people, left Dalal trapped in a small area near the bottom of the building's ruins, with 30 feet of rubble on top of him and only a foot of breathing space.

When the rescue workers heard Dalal's voice, weak and shaking, they began chipping away at the mountain of concrete above him. Using a flame cutter that could slice through iron rods, they carefully made their way closer to him, until they were able to make a small hole above him. Pulling Dalal through the hole, they first saw his toes, then his body, and finally his head.

Miraculously, Dalal did not have a scratch on him. He had survived more than one hundred hours before being rescued.

But Dalal's happiness over being saved turned to despair when he found that the rest of his family had not been so lucky. They were all dead, victims of one of the most destructive earthquakes in modern times (Dugger, 2001).

Looking Ahead

Although it originated as a geological event far beneath the surface of the earth, the consequences of the Indian earthquake are primarily psychological in nature. Consider, for example, the ways in which different kinds of psychologists would look at the disaster:

- Psychologists who study the biology underlying behavior would examine changes in the functioning of the body in individuals who dealt with the emergency situation.
- Psychologists who specialize in learning and memory would examine what people later remember about the disaster.
- Psychologists who study thinking processes would consider how people view risks such as living in an area prone to earthquakes and how they calculate how such risks apply to them personally.
- Developmental psychologists who study children might consider whether there is a relationship between the stress experienced by earthquake victims and subsequent child abuse.
- Health psychologists would examine how experiencing the disaster might be linked to later illness.
- Clinical and counseling psychologists, who provide therapy for psychological disorders, might help earthquake survivors deal with the guilt they may experience because they survived when many others did not.
- Social psychologists, who study interpersonal interaction, would try to understand the reasons behind the helpfulness and heroism of some individuals and the uncaring, violent behavior of others.

Although the approaches taken by different types of psychologists in studying the impact of the earthquake are diverse, there is a common link: each represents a specialty area within the general field of study of **psychology,** the scientific study of behavior and mental processes.

Since the first stirrings of the discipline, psychologists have debated what the scope of the field should be. Should psychologists limit themselves to the study of outward, observable behavior? Is it possible to study thinking scientifically? Should the field encompass the study of such diverse topics as physical and mental health, perception, dreaming, and motivation? Is it appropriate to focus solely on human behavior, or should the behavior of nonhumans be included?

Most psychologists have answered these questions with the argument that the field should be receptive to a variety of viewpoints and approaches. Consequently, the phrase *behavior and mental processes* in the definition of psychology must be understood to mean many things: It encompasses not just what people do, but also their thoughts, feelings, perceptions, reasoning processes, memories, and even the biological activities that maintain bodily functioning.

When we speak of the "study" of behavior and mental processes, psychology's perspective is equally broad. Psychologists try to describe, predict, and explain human behavior and mental processes, as well as help change and improve the lives of people and the world in which they live. The use of scientific methods allows psychologists to find answers that are far more valid and legitimate than those resulting from mere intuition and speculation. And what a variety and range of questions psychologists seek to answer! Consider these examples: How long can we live without sleep? What is the best way to study? What is intelligence? What is normal sexual behavior? Can people change their dysfunctional behavior? Can aging be delayed? How does stress affect our lives? How can we reduce violence?

These questions provide just a hint of the various topics that we will encounter as we explore the field of psychology. Our discussions will take us through the range of what is known about behavior and mental processes. At times, we will explore animal behavior because it provides important clues about human behavior. Many psychologists study nonhuman species in order to determine general laws of behavior that pertain to *all* organisms. But we will always return to the everyday problems that confront human beings.

This book incorporates several features that illustrate how psychology can affect each of our lives. You will see how psychologists are applying what they have learned to resolve practical problems of daily life (*Applying Psychology in the 21st Century* boxes).

psychology: The scientific study of behavior and mental processes.

 **PsychLink**

Psychology Organization Home Pages
www.mhhe.com/
feldmanup6-01links

You will meet people who have experienced firsthand how valuable a background in psychology can be in their professional lives (*Psychology at Work* boxes). You will learn how psychology contributes to our understanding of the multicultural world in which we live (Exploring Diversity sections). And you will find material in each chapter that is intended to help you incorporate psychology into your everyday life (*Becoming an Informed Consumer of Psychology*).

This introductory chapter presents several topics central to an understanding of psychology. We begin our journey through the field of psychology by describing the different types of psychologists and the various roles they play. Next, we examine the major perspectives that guide the work psychologists do. Finally, we identify the major issues that underlie psychologists' views of the world and human behavior.

Psychologists at Work

A month after losing his arm in an industrial accident, Henry Washington sits with his eyes closed as Hector Valdez, a research psychologist who studies the perception of touch, dribbles warm water on his cheek. Washington is startled as he reports feeling the water not only on his cheek, but running down his missing arm. The sensation is so strong that he checks to be sure that the arm is still missing.

***

Evelyn Poirier welcomes to her lab the Chow brothers, a pair of identical twins who were adopted by different families just after they were born. They have come to participate in her study examining similarities in the behavioral and personality traits of twins. By comparing twins who have lived together virtually all their lives to those who have been separated from birth, Poirier is seeking to determine the relative influence of heredity and experience on human behavior.

***

Methodically—and painfully—recounting events that occurred in his youth, the college student discloses a childhood secret that he has revealed previously to no one. The listener, psychologist Jonnetta Pennybaker, responds with support, suggesting to him that his concern is in fact shared by many people.

Although the last scene might be the only one that fits your image of the practice of psychology, each of these episodes describes work carried out by contemporary psychologists. Psychologists address extraordinarily different types of behavior, ranging from the most basic biological processes to how people are affected by their culture.

Prepare

What is the science of psychology?
What are the major specialties in the field of psychology?
Where do psychologists work?

Organize

Psychologists at Work
The Subfields of Psychology
Working at Psychology

The Subfields of Psychology: Psychology's Family Tree

The diversity of topical areas within psychology has resulted in the development of a number of subfields (described in Table 1-1). The subfields of psychology can be likened to an extended family, with assorted nieces and nephews, aunts and uncles, and cousins who, although they might not interact on a day-to-day basis, are related to one another because they share a common goal: understanding behavior. Several basic questions about behavior that are addressed by key subfields include the following:

What Are the Biological Foundations of Behavior?

In the most fundamental sense, people are biological organisms. *Biopsychology* is the subfield of psychology that specializes in the biological bases of behavior. While they study a broad range of topics, biopsychologists focus on the operation of the brain and nervous system, considering how our body influences our behavior. For example, they might examine the link between specific sites in the brain and the muscular tremors of

Table 1-1   The Major Subfields of Psychology

Subfield	Description
Biopsychology	*Biopsychology* examines how biological structures and functions of the body affect behavior.
Clinical psychology	*Clinical psychology* deals with the study, diagnosis, and treatment of psychological disorders.
Clinical neuropsychology	*Clinical neuropsychology* unites the areas of biopsychology and clinical psychology, focusing on the relationship between biological factors and psychological disorders.
Cognitive psychology	*Cognitive psychology* focuses on the study of higher mental processes.
Counseling psychology	*Counseling psychology* focuses primarily on educational, social, and career adjustment problems.
Cross-cultural psychology	*Cross-cultural psychology* investigates the similarities and differences in psychological functioning in and across various cultures and ethnic groups.
Developmental psychology	*Developmental psychology* examines how people grow and change from the moment of conception through death.
Educational psychology	*Educational psychology* is concerned with teaching and learning processes, such as the relationship between intelligence and school performance and the development of better teaching techniques.
Environmental psychology	*Environmental psychology* considers the relationship between people and their physical environment, including how our physical environment affects our emotions and the amount of stress we experience in a particular setting.
Evolutionary psychology	*Evolutionary psychology* considers how behavior is influenced by our genetic inheritance from our ancestors.
Experimental psychology	*Experimental psychology* studies the processes of sensing, perceiving, learning, and thinking about the world.
Forensic psychology	*Forensic psychology* focuses on legal issues, such as deciding on criteria for determining whether a defendant was legally sane at the time a crime was committed.
Health psychology	*Health psychology* explores the relationship between psychological factors and physical ailments or disease.
Industrial/organizational psychology	*Industrial/organizational psychology* is concerned with the psychology of the workplace.
Personality psychology	*Personality psychology* focuses on the consistency in people's behavior over time and the traits that differentiate one person from another.
Program evaluation	*Program evaluation* focuses on assessing large-scale programs, such as the Head Start preschool program, to determine whether they are effective in meeting their goals.
Psychology of women	*Psychology of women* focuses on issues such as discrimination against women, structural differences in women's and men's brains, and the causes of violence against women.
School psychology	*School psychology* is devoted to counseling children in elementary and secondary schools who have academic or emotional problems.
Social psychology	*Social psychology* is the study of how people's thoughts, feelings, and actions are affected by others.
Sport psychology	*Sport psychology* applies psychology to athletic activity and exercise.

people affected by Parkinson's disease (discussed in Chapter 3) or attempt to determine how our emotions are related to physical sensations (Chapter 10).

How Do People Sense, Perceive, Learn, and Think About the World?

If you have ever wondered why you are susceptible to optical illusions, how your body registers pain, or how you can study with the greatest effectiveness, an experimental psychologist can answer your questions. *Experimental psychology* is the branch of psychology that studies the processes of sensing, perceiving, learning, and thinking about the world. (The term *experimental psychologist* is somewhat misleading: As we'll see in Chapter 2, psychologists in every specialty area use experimental techniques, and experimental psychologists do not use only experimental methods.)

Several subspecialties of experimental psychology have become specialties in their own right. One example is *cognitive psychology*, which focuses on higher mental processes, including thinking, memory, reasoning, problem solving, judging, decision making, and language (as we will discuss in Chapters 7 and 8).

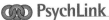 **PsychLink**
Journey through Biopsychology
www.mhhe.com/
feldmanup6-01links

What Are the Sources of Change and Stability in Behavior Across the Life Span?

A baby producing her first smile . . . taking her first step . . . saying her first word. These universal milestones in development are also singularly special and unique for each person. *Developmental psychology* studies how people grow and change from the moment of conception through death (Chapters 12 and 13). *Personality psychology* focuses on the consistency in people's behavior over time and the traits that differentiate one person from another (Chapter 14).

How Do Psychological Factors Affect Physical and Mental Health?

If you are frequently depressed, feel constant stress, or seek to overcome a fear that prevents you from carrying out your normal activities, your problems would interest a health psychologist. *Health psychology* explores the relationship between psychological factors and physical ailments or disease. For example, health psychologists are interested in how long-term stress (a psychological factor) can affect physical health and in identifying ways to promote behavior that brings about good health (Chapter 15).

Clinical psychology deals with the study, diagnosis, and treatment of psychological disorders. Clinical psychologists are trained to diagnose and treat problems ranging from the everyday crises of life, such as unhappiness over the breakup of a relationship, to more extreme conditions, such as profound, lingering depression. Some clinical psychologists also research and investigate issues that range from identifying the early signs of psychological disturbance to studying the relationship between family communication patterns and psychological disorders (Chapters 16 and 17).

How Do Our Social Networks Affect Behavior?

The complex networks of social interrelationships that are part of our world are the focus of study for a number of subfields of psychology. For example, *social psychology* is the study of how people's thoughts, feelings, and actions are affected by others. Social psychologists focus on such diverse topics as human aggression, liking and loving, persuasion, and conformity.

Cross-cultural psychology investigates the similarities and differences in psychological functioning in and across the various cultures and ethnic groups of the world. For example, cross-cultural psychologists examine how cultures differ in their use of punishment during child rearing, or why certain cultures view academic success as being determined mostly by hard work while others see it as being determined mostly by innate ability (J. G. Miller, 1999; Rosenzweig, 1999; Aycan, 2000).

Expanding Psychology's Frontiers

As a science, psychology's boundaries are constantly growing. Two newer members of the field's family tree—clinical neuropsychology and evolutionary psychology—have sparked particular excitement, and debate, within psychology.

Experimental psychologists study how people sense the world. How do you think researchers adapt their experimental techniques when working with children?

PsychLink
Health Psychology
www.mhhe.com/
feldmanup6-01links

Counseling psychologists who staff college centers advise students on career choices, methods of study, and strategies for coping with everyday problems.

Clinical neuropsychology unites the areas of biopsychology and clinical psychology: It focuses on the relationship between biological factors and psychological disorders. Building on advances in our understanding of the structure and chemistry of the brain, the specialty is leading to promising new treatments for psychological disorders, as well as debates over the use of medication to control behavior.

Evolutionary psychology considers how behavior is influenced by our genetic inheritance from our ancestors. The evolutionary approach suggests that the chemical coding of information in our cells not only determines such traits as hair color and race, but also holds the key to understanding a broad variety of behaviors that helped our ancestors survive and reproduce (Geary & Bjorklund, 2000).

Evolutionary concepts have been used to explain similarities in behavior across cultures, such as the qualities desired in potential mates. However, such explanations have stirred up controversy by suggesting that many significant behaviors are wired into the human species as a result of evolution and occur automatically.

Working at Psychology

Help Wanted: Assistant professor at a small liberal arts college. Teach undergraduate courses in introductory psychology and courses in specialty areas of cognitive psychology, perception, and learning. Strong commitment to quality teaching and student advising necessary. The candidate must also provide evidence of scholarship and research productivity.

Help Wanted: Industrial-organizational consulting psychologist. International firm is seeking psychologists for full-time career positions as consultants to management. Candidates must have the ability to establish a rapport with senior business executives and to help them find innovative, practical, and psychologically sound solutions to problems concerning people and organizations.

***

Help Wanted: Clinical psychologist. Ph.D., internship experience, and license required. Comprehensive clinic seeks psychologist to work with children and adults providing individual and group therapy, psychological evaluations, crisis intervention, and development of behavior treatment plans on multidisciplinary team. Broad experience with substance-abuse problems is desirable.

PsychLink

Industrial/organizational psychology
www.mhhe.com/
feldmanup6-01links

As these advertisements suggest, psychologists are employed in a variety of settings. Most doctoral-level psychologists are employed by institutions of higher learning (universities and colleges) or are self-employed, usually working as private practitioners treating clients (see Figure 1-1). Other work sites include hospitals, clinics, mental health centers, counseling centers, government human-services organizations, and schools (APA, 1996, 2000).

Why do so many psychologists work in academic settings? Because these are effective settings for the three major roles played by psychologists in society—teacher, scientist, and clinical practitioner. Many psychology professors are also actively involved in research or in

Figure 1-1 A breakdown of where U.S. psychologists (who have a Ph.D. or Psy.D. degree) work (APA, 1999). Why do you think so many psychologists work in university and college settings?

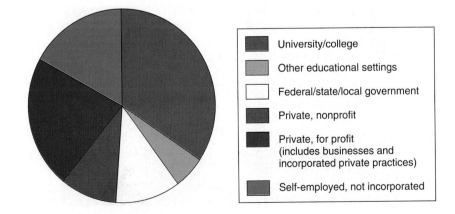

- University/college
- Other educational settings
- Federal/state/local government
- Private, nonprofit
- Private, for profit (includes businesses and incorporated private practices)
- Self-employed, not incorporated

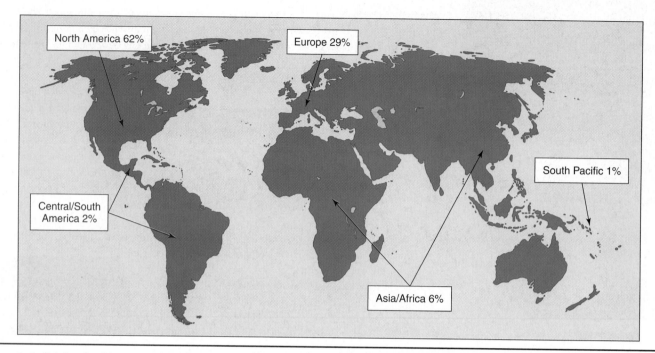

Figure 1-2 Origin of published research (APA, 1999). How do you think the heavy concentration of psychologists in North America impacts the field of psychology?

serving clients. Whatever their particular job site, however, psychologists share a commitment to improving individual lives as well as society in general. (For the perspective of someone who uses psychology in her work on a daily basis, see the *Psychology at Work* box.)

Psychologists: A Statistical Portrait

Is there an "average" psychologist in terms of personal characteristics? Probably not. About half of U.S. psychologists are men and about half are women. It is predicted that by the year 2010 the number of women in the field will exceed the number of men (Pion et al., 1996).

Although most psychologists today are found in the United States, about one-third of the world's 500,000 psychologists are found in other parts of the world (see Figure 1-2). Psychologists outside the United States are increasingly influential in adding to the knowledge base and practices of psychology (Mays, Rubin, Sabourin, & Walker, 1996; Pawlik & d'Ydewalle, 1996).

One issue of great concern is the relative lack of racial and ethnic diversity among psychologists in the United States. According to figures compiled by the American Psychological Association (APA), of those psychologists who identify themselves in surveys by race and ethnic origin—four-fifths of respondents—the vast majority are white. Past educational and occupational discrimination and a lack of encouragement for minorities to enter the field have resulted in only 6 percent of psychologists being members of minority groups. This percentage is lower than the proportion of minorities in society at large. Although the numbers of minority psychologists and graduate students of psychology have increased, they have not kept up with the growth of the minority population at large (Tomes, 1998; Waters, 2000).

The underrepresentation of racial and ethnic minorities among psychologists is significant for several reasons. First, the field of psychology is diminished by a lack of the diverse perspectives and talents provided by minority group members. Furthermore, minority-group psychologists serve as role models for members of minority communities; their lack of representation within the profession might deter other minority group members from seeking to enter the field. Finally, because members of minority groups frequently prefer to receive psychological therapy from treatment providers of their own

Psychology at Work

Carolyn Copper

**Government Analyst
National Security and International
Affairs, U.S. Government**

Education: B.A. in psychology, Ohio University, Athens, Ohio; M.A., Ph.D., Syracuse University, Syracuse, New York

Home: Arlington, Virginia

Carolyn Copper

When Carolyn Copper entered college with the dream of addressing social problems, she soon learned that psychology could provide the path to achieving her goals.

"After taking the first few introductory courses in psychology, I thought it was the best avenue to get the skills I needed to perform research and deal effectively with social problems and issues," says Copper, a senior social science analyst with the National Security and International Affairs office of the federal government.

Copper has investigated numerous federal programs. For instance, she examined the factors that contributed to the success of Operation Desert Storm, the military action that involved U.S. forces fighting in Iraq.

"In my work, I design research, collect data, conduct interviews and statistical analyses, review and synthesize literature, interpret data, and prepare reports of study procedures and findings. My training in psychology is critical for the work that I do, and especially useful for trying to make my work meaningful for the public and members of Congress," she explains.

The research on Operation Desert Storm required more than a hundred interviews, as well as analysis of scores of background documents. According to Copper, her psychology background was excellent preparation for getting people to open up during the interviews, as well as for interpreting what people were saying. Furthermore, it let her present her findings in a way that could guide future decisions.

"There is a unique satisfaction and a special challenge associated with serving the public," she adds.

> "After taking the first few introductory courses in psychology, I thought it was the best avenue to get the skills I needed to perform research and deal effectively with social problems and issues."

> "My training in psychology is critical for the work that I do, and especially useful for trying to make my work meaningful for the public and members of Congress."

race or ethnic group, the rarity of minority psychologists can discourage some members of minority groups from seeking treatment (King, 1993; Chamberlin, 1998).

The Education of a Psychologist

How do people become psychologists? The most common route is a long one. Most psychologists have a doctorate, either a *Ph.D.* or (less frequently) a *Psy.D.* The Ph.D. is a research degree, requiring a dissertation based on an original investigation. The Psy.D. is obtained by psychologists who wish to focus on the treatment of psychological disorders. Both the Ph.D. and the Psy.D. typically take four or five years of work past the bachelor's level. Some fields of psychology involve education beyond the doctorate. For instance, doctoral-level clinical psychologists, who deal with people with psychological disorders, typically spend an additional year on an internship.

About a third of people working in the field of psychology have a master's degree as their highest degree, which is earned following two or three years of graduate work. Master's-level psychologists teach, conduct research under the supervision of a doctoral-level psychologist, or work in specialized programs dealing with drug abuse or crisis intervention. Some work in universities, government, and business, collecting and analyzing data.

An undergraduate major in psychology provides good preparation for a variety of occupations, although it does not allow professional work in psychology per se. For instance, many people in business, nursing, law, social work, and other professions report that an undergraduate background in psychology has proven invaluable in their careers. Some 20 percent of recipients of bachelor's degrees in psychology work in the social services or in some other form of public affairs. Furthermore, undergraduates who specialize in psychology typically have good analytical skills, are trained to think critically, and are able to synthesize and evaluate information well—skills that are held in high regard by employers in business, industry, and the government (APA, 2000).

Evaluate

1. Match each subfield of psychology with an issue or question posed below.

a. Biopsychology

b. Experimental psychology

c. Cognitive psychology

d. Developmental psychology

e. Personality psychology

f. Health psychology

g. Clinical psychology

h. Counseling psychology

i. Educational psychology

j. School psychology

k. Social psychology

l. Industrial/organizational psychology

1. Joan, a college freshman, is panicking. She needs to learn better organizational skills and study habits to cope with the demands of college.

2. At what age do children generally begin to acquire an emotional attachment to their fathers?

3. It is thought that pornographic films that depict violence against women can prompt aggressive behavior in some men.

4. What chemicals are released in the human body as a result of a stressful event? What are their effects on behavior?

5. Luis is unique in his manner of responding to crisis situations, with an even temperament and a positive outlook.

6. The teachers of 8-year-old Jack are concerned that he has recently begun to withdraw socially and show little interest in schoolwork.

7. Janetta's job is demanding and stressful. She wonders if her lifestyle is making her more prone to certain illnesses, such as cancer and heart disease.

8. A psychologist is intrigued by the fact that some people are much more sensitive to painful stimuli than others are.

9. A strong fear of crowds leads a young woman to seek treatment for her problem.

10. What mental strategies are involved in solving complex word problems?

11. What teaching methods most effectively motivate elementary school students to successfully accomplish academic tasks?

12. Jessica is asked to develop a management strategy that will encourage safer work practices in an assembly plant.

Answers to Evaluate Questions

1. a-4, b-8, c-10, d-2, e-5, f-7, g-9, h-1, i-11, j-6, k-3, l-12

Rethink

1. Why might the study of twins who were raised together and twins who were not be helpful in distinguishing the effects of heredity and environment?

2. Suppose you know a 7-year-old child who is having problems learning to read and you want to help. Imagine that you can consult as many psychologists as you want to. How might each type of psychologist approach the problem?

A Science Evolves: The Past, the Present, and the Future

Some half-million years ago, people assumed that psychological problems were caused by evil spirits. To allow these spirits to escape the person's body, ancient healers performed an operation called trephining. Trephining consisted of chipping away at a patient's skull with crude stone instruments until a hole was cut through the bone. Because archaeologists have found skulls with signs of healing around the opening, it's a fair guess that some patients survived the cure.

* * *

Prepare

What are the historical roots of the field of psychology?

What are the major approaches used by contemporary psychologists?

Organize

A Science Evolves

The Roots of Psychology

Today's Perspectives

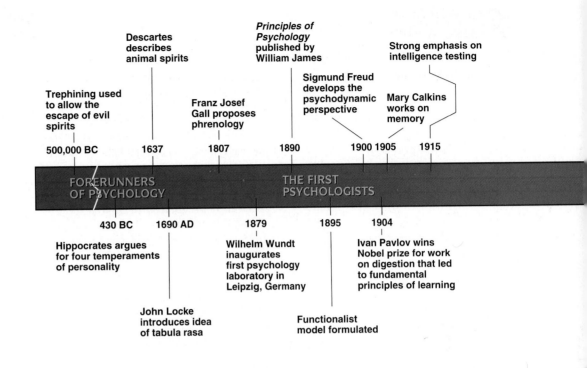

Figure 1-3 The timeline highlights the major landmarks in the development of psychology.

first psychology is laboratory in 1879

structuralism: Wundt's approach, which focuses on the basic elements that form the foundation of thinking, consciousness, emotions, and other kinds of mental states and activities.

 **PsychLink**

History of Psychology
www.mhhe.com/
feldmanup6-01links

Wilhelm Wundt

According to the seventeenth-century philosopher Descartes, nerves were hollow tubes through which "animal spirits" conducted impulses in the same way that water is transmitted through a pipe. When a person put a finger too close to a fire, heat was transmitted into the brain through the tubes.

***

Franz Josef Gall, an eighteenth-century physician, argued that a trained observer could discern intelligence, moral character, and other basic personality characteristics from the shape and number of bumps on a person's skull. His theory gave rise to the "science" of phrenology, employed by hundreds of devoted practitioners in the nineteenth century.

Though these explanations might sound far-fetched, in their own times they represented the most advanced thinking regarding what might be called the psychology of the era. Our understanding of behavior has advanced tremendously since these earlier views were formulated, yet most of the advances have been recent—for, as sciences go, psychology is one of the "new kids on the block." (For some of the highlights in the development of the field, see Figure 1-3.)

Psychology's roots can be traced back to the ancient Greeks and Romans, and philosophers argued for hundreds of years about some of the questions psychologists grapple with today. However, the formal beginning of psychology as a science is generally set at 1879, when Wilhelm Wundt established in Leipzig, Germany, the first experimental laboratory devoted to psychological phenomena. At about the same time, William James was setting up his laboratory in Cambridge, Massachusetts.

The Roots of Psychology

When Wilhelm Wundt set up the first psychology laboratory in 1879, his aim was to study the building blocks of the mind. He considered psychology to be the study of conscious experience, and he developed a perspective that came to be known as structuralism. **Structuralism** focused on the basic elements that constitute the foundation

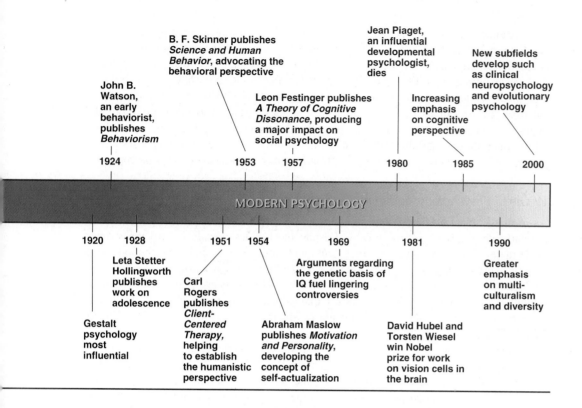

B. F. Skinner publishes *Science and Human Behavior*, advocating the behavioral perspective

Jean Piaget, an influential developmental psychologist, dies

New subfields develop such as clinical neuropsychology and evolutionary psychology

John B. Watson, an early behaviorist, publishes *Behaviorism*

Leon Festinger publishes *A Theory of Cognitive Dissonance*, producing a major impact on social psychology

Increasing emphasis on cognitive perspective

1924   1953   1957   1980   1985   2000

MODERN PSYCHOLOGY

1920   1928   1951   1954   1969   1981   1990

Leta Stetter Hollingworth publishes work on adolescence

Arguments regarding the genetic basis of IQ fuel lingering controversies

Greater emphasis on multi-culturalism and diversity

Gestalt psychology most influential

Carl Rogers publishes *Client-Centered Therapy,* helping to establish the humanistic perspective

Abraham Maslow publishes *Motivation and Personality,* developing the concept of self-actualization

David Hubel and Torsten Wiesel win Nobel prize for work on vision cells in the brain

of perception, consciousness, thinking, emotions, and other kinds of mental states and activities.

To come to an understanding of how basic sensations combined to produce our perception of the world, Wundt and other structuralists used a procedure called **introspection** to study the mind. In introspection, people were presented with a stimulus—such as a bright green object or a sentence printed on a card—and were asked to describe, in their own words and in as much detail as they could manage, what they were experiencing. Wundt argued that, by analyzing the reports people offered of their reactions, psychologists could come to better understand the structure of the mind.

Over time, psychologists challenged Wundt's structuralism. They became increasingly dissatisfied with the assumption that introspection could unlock the fundamental elements of the mind. Introspection was not a truly scientific technique. There were few ways an outside observer could confirm the accuracy of others' introspections. Moreover, people had difficulty describing some kinds of inner experiences, such as emotional responses. Such drawbacks led to the evolution of new approaches, which largely supplanted structuralism.

However, the heritage of structuralism still exists. As we will see in Chapter 8, there has been a renewed interest in people's descriptions of their inner experience. Cognitive psychologists, who focus on higher mental processes such as thinking, memory, and problem solving, have developed innovative techniques that help us understand people's conscious experience and that overcome many of the difficulties inherent in introspection.

The main perspective that came to replace structuralism as psychology evolved is known as functionalism. Rather than focusing on the mind's components, **functionalism** concentrated on what the mind *does* and how behavior *functions*. Functionalists, whose perspective became prominent in the early 1900s, asked what roles behavior plays in allowing people to better adapt to their environments. Led by the American psychologist William James, the functionalists examined how behavior allows people to satisfy their needs. The famous American educator John Dewey used functionalism to develop the field of school psychology, proposing ways to best meet students' educational needs.

introspection: A procedure used to study the structure of the mind, in which subjects are asked to describe in detail what they are experiencing when they are exposed to a stimulus.

functionalism: An early approach to psychology that concentrated on what the mind does—the functions of mental activity—and the role of behavior in allowing people to adapt to their environments.

William James

Mary Whiton Calkins

gestalt (geh SHTALLT) psychology: An approach to psychology that focuses on the organization of perception and thinking in a "whole" sense, rather than on the individual elements of perception.

Another important reaction to structuralism was the development of gestalt psychology in the early 1900s. **Gestalt psychology** is a perspective focusing on how perception is organized. Instead of considering the individual parts that make up thinking, gestalt psychologists took the opposite tack, concentrating on how people consider individual elements together as units or wholes. Their credo was "The whole is different from the sum of its parts," meaning that, when considered together, the basic elements that compose our perception of objects produce something greater and more meaningful than those individual elements alone. As we will see in Chapter 4, gestalt psychologists have made substantial contributions to our understanding of perception.

Women in Psychology: Founding Mothers

As in many scientific fields, societal constraints hindered women's participation during the early development of psychology. Despite the hurdles they faced, several women made major contributions to psychology, although until recently their contributions were largely overlooked. For example, Leta Stetter Hollingworth was one of the first psychologists to focus on child development and on women's issues. She collected data to refute the view, popular in the early 1900s, that women's abilities regularly declined during parts of the menstrual cycle (Benjamin & Shields, 1990; Hollingworth, 1943/1990; Denmark & Fernandez, 1993).

Mary Calkins, who studied memory in the early part of the twentieth century, became the first female president of the American Psychological Association. Karen Horney (pronounced "HORN-eye") focused on the social and cultural factors behind personality, and June Etta Downey spearheaded the study of personality traits and became the first woman to head a psychology department at a state university. Anna Freud (daughter of Sigmund Freud) also made notable contributions to the treatment of abnormal behavior (Horney, 1937; Stevens & Gardner, 1982).

Today's Perspectives

The women and the men who worked to build the foundations of psychology shared a common goal: to explain and understand behavior, using scientific methods. Seeking to achieve this same goal, the tens of thousands of psychologists who followed these early pioneers embraced—and often rejected—a variety of broad perspectives (Benjamin, 1997; Robins, Gosling, & Craik, 1999).

The various perspectives offer distinct outlooks and emphasize different factors. Just as we can use more than one map to find our way around a particular region—for instance, a map that shows roads and highways and another map that shows major landmarks—psychologists developed a variety of approaches to understanding behavior. When considered jointly, the different perspectives provide the means to explain behavior in its amazing variety.

Today, the field of psychology involves five major perspectives (summarized in Figure 1-4). Each of these broad perspectives emphasizes different aspects of behavior and mental processes, and each takes our understanding of behavior in somewhat different directions.

The Biological Perspective: Blood, Sweat, and Fears

biological perspective: The approach that views behavior from the perspective of biological functioning.

When we get down to the basics, human beings are animals made of skin and bones. The **biological perspective** considers how people and nonhumans function biologically: how individual nerve cells are joined together, how the inheritance of certain characteristics from parents and other ancestors influences behavior, how the functioning of the body affects hopes and fears, which behaviors are instinctual, and so forth. Even more complex kinds of behaviors, such as a baby's response to strangers, are viewed as having critical biological components by psychologists using the biological perspective. This perspective includes the study of heredity and evolution, and how heredity might influence behavior.

The Major Perspectives of Psychology

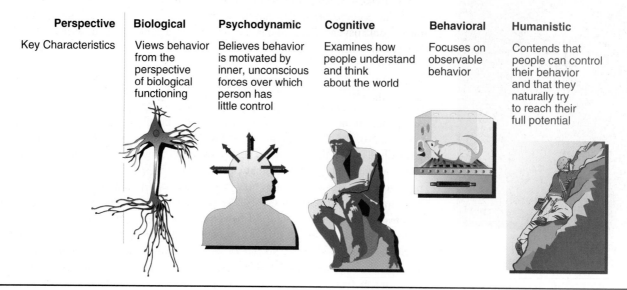

Perspective	Biological	Psychodynamic	Cognitive	Behavioral	Humanistic
Key Characteristics	Views behavior from the perspective of biological functioning	Believes behavior is motivated by inner, unconscious forces over which person has little control	Examines how people understand and think about the world	Focuses on observable behavior	Contends that people can control their behavior and that they naturally try to reach their full potential

Figure 1-4 The major perspectives used by psychologists.

Because every behavior can at some level be broken down into its biological components, the biological perspective has broad appeal. Psychologists who subscribe to this perspective have made major contributions to the understanding and betterment of human life, ranging from developing cures for certain types of deafness to identifying medications to treat people with severe mental disorders.

The Psychodynamic Perspective: Understanding the Inner Person

To many people who have never taken a psychology course, psychology begins and ends with the psychodynamic perspective. Proponents of the **psychodynamic perspective** believe that behavior is motivated by inner forces and conflicts about which we have little awareness or control. Dreams and slips of the tongue are viewed as indications of what a person is truly feeling within a seething cauldron of unconscious psychic activity.

The psychodynamic view is intimately linked with one individual: Sigmund Freud. Freud was a Viennese physician in the early 1900s whose ideas about unconscious determinants of behavior had a revolutionary effect on twentieth-century thinking, not just in psychology but in related fields as well. Although some of the original principles of psychodynamic thinking have been roundly criticized, contemporary use of the perspective has provided a means not only to understand and treat some kinds of psychological disorders, but also to understand everyday phenomena such as prejudice and aggression.

The Cognitive Perspective: Identifying the Roots of Understanding

The route to understanding behavior leads some psychologists straight into the mind. Evolving in part from structuralism, the **cognitive perspective** focuses on how people think, understand, and know about the world. The emphasis is on learning how people comprehend and represent the outside world within themselves, and how our ways of thinking about the world influence our behavior.

Psychologists using the cognitive perspective often compare human thinking to the workings of a computer, considering how information is input, transformed, stored, and retrieved. In this view, thinking is *information processing*.

psychodynamic perspective: The approach based on the belief that behavior is motivated by unconscious inner forces over which the individual has little control.

cognitive perspective: The approach that focuses on how people think, understand, and know about the world.

Sigmund Freud

John B. Watson

behavioral perspective: The approach that suggests that observable behavior should be the focus of study.

Psychologists relying on the cognitive perspective ask questions ranging from how people make decisions to whether a person can watch television and study at the same time. The common elements that link cognitive approaches are an emphasis on how people understand and think about the world and a concern to describe the patterns and irregularities in the operation of our minds.

The Behavioral Perspective: Observing the Outer Person

Whereas the biological, psychodynamic, and cognitive approaches look inside the organism to determine the causes of its behavior, the behavioral perspective takes a very different approach. The **behavioral perspective** grew out of a rejection of psychology's early emphasis on the inner workings of the mind, suggesting instead that the field should focus on observable behavior that can be measured objectively.

John B. Watson was the first major American psychologist to advocate a behavioral approach. Working in the 1920s, Watson was adamant in his view that one could gain a complete understanding of behavior by studying and modifying the environment in which people operated. In fact, he believed rather optimistically that it was possible to elicit any desired sort of behavior by controlling a person's environment. This philosophy is clear in his own words: "Give me a dozen healthy infants, well-formed, and my own specified world to bring them up in and I'll guarantee to take any one at random and train him to become any type of specialist I might select—doctor, lawyer, artist, merchant-chief, and yes, even beggar-man and thief, regardless of his talents, penchants, tendencies, abilities, vocations and race of his ancestors" (Watson, 1924). The behavioral perspective was later championed by B. F. Skinner, who until his death in 1990 was probably the best-known psychologist. Much of our understanding of how people learn new behaviors is based on the behavioral perspective.

As we will see, the behavioral perspective crops up along every byway of psychology. Along with its influence in the area of learning processes, this perspective has also made contributions in such diverse areas as treating mental disorders, curbing aggression, resolving sexual problems, and ending drug addiction.

The Humanistic Perspective: The Unique Qualities of Homo Sapiens

humanistic perspective: The approach that suggests that all individuals naturally strive to grow, develop, and be in control of their lives and behavior.

Rejecting the views that behavior is determined largely by automatic biological forces, by unconscious processes, or by the environment, the **humanistic perspective** instead suggests that all individuals naturally strive to grow, develop, and be in control of their lives and behavior. Humanistic psychologists maintain that each of us has the capacity to seek and reach fulfillment.

According to Carl Rogers and Abraham Maslow, who were central figures in the development of the humanistic perspective, people will strive to reach their full potential if given the opportunity. The emphasis of the humanistic perspective is on *free will*, the ability to freely make decisions about one's own behavior and life. The notion of free will stands in contrast to *determinism,* which sees behavior as caused, or determined, by things beyond a person's control.

The humanistic perspective assumes that people have the ability to make their own choices about their behavior rather than rely on societal standards. More than any other approach, it stresses the role of psychology in enriching people's lives and helping them to achieve self-fulfillment. The humanistic perspective has had an important influence on psychologists, reminding them of their commitment to the individual person in society.

It is important not to let the abstract qualities of the broad approaches we have discussed lull you into thinking that they are purely theoretical: These perspectives underlie ongoing work of a practical nature, as we will discuss throughout this book. As a start in seeing this, read the *Applying Psychology in the 21st Century* box.

Applying Psychology in the 21st Century

Psychology and the Reduction of Violence

A 6-year-old boy brings a gun to school and shoots a classmate with whom he had a playground dispute the previous day.

An elderly woman is killed by two teenage muggers during a robbery; she had less than $2 for them to steal.

Three white men tie a black man to a truck and drag him at high speed down a country road; he dies a gruesome death.

Violence in the United States has reached epidemic levels, and there are few signs that it will let up. Surveys consistently reveal that violence and crime rank near the top of the list of social problems that concern Americans most (Stone & Kelner, 2000; Taylor, 2000).

Yet violence has not gone unchallenged, and the field of psychology is playing a key role in efforts to reduce this social ill. Psychologists specializing in diverse areas and employing the major perspectives of the field are making a concerted effort to answer key questions relating to violence. These are some examples:

- *Does watching violence on television and in movies lead viewers to be violent?* Most social and developmental psychologists agree that observation of aggression in the media enhances the likelihood that viewers will act aggressively. Furthermore, it desensitizes viewers to displays of aggression, leading them to react with passivity to actual incidents of aggression, and it makes the world seem to be a more dangerous place (Seppa, 1997; American Academy of Pediatrics, 1999).
- *What is the effect of extremely violent video games on the people who play them?* Playing violent video games has consequences similar to watching violence in the media: an increase in subsequent aggression, desensitization to actual

violence, and a view of the world as being more hostile (Anderson & Dill, 1999).
- *How can youth violence be reduced?* Cultural, societal, and individual psychological factors—including parental neglect, frequent observation of violence, poverty, prejudice, and discrimination—are associated with higher rates of violence. Successful training programs have been designed to teach inner-city students with a history of

The role of guns in American culture is a widely discussed and controversial topic. What can psychologists add to the discussion?

aggression to respond to provocative situations without violence (Staub, 1996; Spielman & Staub, 2000; Enserink, 2000).
- *How can rape be prevented?* According to some estimates, one in four women in the United States stands a chance of being raped at some point during her lifetime (Koss, 1993). Psychologists from different subfields of the field—including clinical psychology, developmental psychology, and the psychology of women—have been

working to reduce sexually aggressive behavior by teaching values that make aggression, of any kind, less likely (Hall & Barongan, 1997).
- *Is there a "cycle of violence" that extends violence from one generation to another?* Many child abusers were victims of abuse in their own childhood. According to the "cycle of violence" explanation, abuse and neglect during their childhood make people more likely to abuse and neglect their own children. On the other hand, developmental psychologists who study growth and change throughout the life span have found that being abused does not inevitably lead to abusing one's own children. Why some people are able to break the cycle of violence, while others succumb to it, remains a key question for psychologists (Wileman & Wileman, 1995; Peled, Jaffe, & Edleson, 1995).
- *What role do biological factors play in aggression?* Some psychologists have considered whether aggression is linked to biological factors. For instance, biopsychologists and social psychologists have found a link between aggressive behavior and the presence of certain hormones in the body. These findings suggest the possibility that medical treatments might reduce violence in perpetrators (Dabbs, Hargrove, & Heusel, 1996; Davidson, Putnam, & Larson, 2000).

Clearly, psychologists are taking a variety of approaches to combating violence. And violence is not the only societal problem to which psychologists are contributing their expertise in an effort to alleviate human suffering. As we will explore in the Applying Psychology in the 21st Century boxes in every chapter, psychology's basic principles help address and solve a wide range of social problems.

Assuming that the research on video games is confirmed, should violent video games be restricted to certain age groups? Should they be banned entirely? Why or why not?

Evaluate

1. Wundt described psychology as the study of conscious experience, a perspective he called _____.

2. Early psychologists studied the mind by asking people to describe what they were experiencing when exposed to various stimuli. This procedure was known as _____.

3. The statement, "In order to study human behavior, we must consider the whole of perception rather than its component parts" might be made by a person subscribing to the _____ perspective.

4. Jeanne's therapist asks her to recount a violent dream she recently experienced in order to gain insight into the unconscious forces affecting her behavior. Jeanne's therapist is working from a _____ perspective.

5. "We should study observable behavior, not the suspected inner workings of the mind." This statement was most likely made by someone with which perspective:

   a. cognitive perspective

   b. biological perspective

   c. humanistic perspective

   d. behavioral perspective

6. "My therapist is wonderful! She always points out my positive traits. She dwells on my uniqueness and strength as an individual. I feel much more confident about myself—as if I'm really growing and reaching my potential." The therapist being described most likely practices from a _____ perspective.

Answers to Evaluate Questions

1. structuralism 2. introspection 3. gestalt 4. psychodynamic 5. d 6. humanistic

Rethink

1. How might today's major perspectives of psychology be related to the earliest perspectives, such as structuralism, functionalism, and gestalt psychology?

2. Select one of the five major perspectives in use today (biological, psychodynamic, cognitive, behavioral, or humanistic), and describe the sorts of research questions and studies that researchers using that perspective might pursue.

Prepare

What are psychology's key issues and controversies?

What is the future of psychology likely to hold?

Organize

Psychology's Key Issues

Psychology's Future

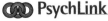 **PsychLink**

Nature vs. Nurture
www.mhhe.com/
feldmanup6–01links

Psychology's Key Issues

As you consider the many topics and perspectives that make up psychology, which range from a narrow focus on minute biochemical influences on behavior to a broad focus on social behaviors, you might find yourself thinking that the discipline lacks cohesion. Yet the field is actually more unified than a first glimpse might suggest. For one thing, no matter what topical area a psychologist specializes in, he or she will rely on one of the five major perspectives. For example, a developmental psychologist who specializes in the study of children could make use of the cognitive perspective *or* the psychodynamic perspective *or* any of the other major perspectives.

Psychologists also agree on what the key issues of the field are. Although major arguments exist regarding how to best address and resolve these, psychology is a unified science because of this collective acknowledgment that these issues must be addressed in order for the field to advance.

As you contemplate these key issues (described below and summarized in Table 1-2), try not to think of them in "either/or" terms. Instead, consider the opposing viewpoints on each issue as opposite ends of a continuum, with the positions of individual psychologists typically falling somewhere between the two ends.

- *Nature (heredity) versus nurture (environment).* How much of our behavior is due to heredity (or "nature") and how much is due to environment ("nurture"), and what is the interplay between the two forces? This question has deep philosophical and historical roots and it is a factor in many topics of psychology.

  A psychologist's take on this issue depends partly on which major perspective she or he subscribes to. For example, developmental psychologists, whose focus is on how people grow and change throughout the course of their

Table 1-2 Positions Taken by Psychologists Using the Major Perspectives of Psychology

Issue	PERSPECTIVE				
	Biological	**Psychodynamic**	**Cognitive**	**Behavioral**	**Humanistic**
Nature (heredity) vs. nurture (environment)	Nature (heredity)	Nature (heredity)	Both	Nurture (environment)	Nurture (environment)
Conscious vs. unconscious determinants of behavior	Unconscious	Unconscious	Both	Conscious	Conscious
Observable behavior vs. internal mental processes	Internal emphasis	Internal emphasis	Internal emphasis	Observable emphasis	Internal emphasis
Free will vs. determinism	Determinism	Determinism	Free will	Determinism	Free will
Individual differences vs. universal principles	Universal emphasis	Universal emphasis	Individual emphasis	Both	Individual emphasis

lives, might be most interested in learning more about hereditary influences if they were employing a biological perspective. On the other hand, developmental psychologists who are proponents of the behavioral perspective would be more likely to focus on environment.

- *Conscious versus unconscious causes of behavior.* How much of our behavior is produced by forces of which we are fully aware, and how much is due to unconscious activity—mental processes that are not accessible to the conscious mind? This question represents one of the great controversies in the field of psychology. For example, clinical psychologists adopting a psychodynamic perspective argue that much of abnormal behavior is motivated by unconscious factors, whereas others employing the cognitive perspective suggest that abnormal behavior is largely the result of faulty thinking processes. The specific approach taken has a clear impact on how abnormal behavior is diagnosed and treated.

- *Observable behavior versus internal mental processes.* Should psychology concentrate solely on behavior that can be seen by outside observers? Or should it focus on unseen thinking processes? Some psychologists, particularly those relying on the behavioral perspective, contend that the only legitimate source of information for psychologists is behavior that can be observed directly. Other psychologists, building on the cognitive perspective, argue that what goes on inside a person's mind is critical and that we cannot understand behavior without concerning ourselves with mental processes.

- *Free will versus determinism.* How much of behavior is a matter of *free will* (choices made freely by an individual), and how much is subject to *determinism,* the notion that behavior is largely produced by factors beyond people's willful control? An issue long debated by philosophers, the free-will/determinism argument is also central to the field of psychology (Kimble, 1989; Hoeller, 1990). For example, some psychologists specializing in psychological disorders argue that people make intentional choices and that those who display so-called "abnormal behavior" should be considered responsible for their actions. Other psychologists disagree and contend that such individuals are the victims of forces beyond their control. The position psychologists take on this issue has important implications for how they will treat abnormal behavior, especially in deciding whether treatment should be forced on individuals who reject it.

- *Individual differences versus universal principles.* How much of our behavior is a consequence of our unique and special qualities and how much reflects the culture and society in which we live? How much of our behavior is universally human? Psychologists relying on the biological perspective tend to look for universal principles of behavior, such as how our nervous system operates or the way

certain hormones automatically prime us for sexual activity. Such psychologists concentrate on the similarities in our behavioral destinies despite vast differences in our upbringing. In contrast, psychologists employing the humanistic perspective focus more on the uniqueness of every individual. They consider how every person's behavior is a reflection of distinct and special qualities.

The question of the degree to which psychologists can identify universal principles that apply to all people has taken on new significance in light of the tremendous demographic changes now occurring in the United States. For instance, the proportion of people of Hispanic descent in the United States by 2050 is projected to be more than twice what it is today. Soon after that, non-Hispanic whites will be a numerical minority in the United States. Similar demographic changes are slated to occur across the world. As we discuss next, these and other changes raise new and critical issues for the discipline of psychology in the twenty-first century.

EXPLORING DIVERSITY

Understanding How Culture, Ethnicity, and Race Influence Behavior

A mother in Burr Ridge, Illinois, helps her son with his math assignment. After he complains that he is "terrible at math," she tries to cheer him up by saying, "Don't feel bad; some people are born to do well in math, and others have a lot of trouble with it. It's just the way things are." At the same time, on the other side of the world in Taipei, Taiwan, a mother is helping her daughter with her math homework. When the daughter complains that she's no good at math, the mother tells her to keep at it because everyone has pretty much the same ability in math, and it is hard work that guarantees success.

These two apparently simple parent-child exchanges reveal a deep difference in perspectives on the world. People in Europe and North America are far more likely to attribute success to unchanging causes, such as intelligence, than are people in Asia, who are more likely to attribute school performance to temporary, situational factors such as the amount of effort expended.

These different perspectives might help explain the fact that Asian students often outperform U.S. students in international comparisons of student achievement. Asian students are taught that hard work and increased effort lead to academic success, so they might be readier to put in effort to achieve success. In contrast, North American students tend to believe that their ability is fixed at birth and largely determines their success, and so they might be less willing to work hard (Chen & Stevenson, 1995; Hall, 1997; Chao, 2000).

Members of different cultures attribute academic success to different factors. How might different cultural perspectives affect the performance of Asian versus North American students?

Our knowledge that people in different cultures can have very different views of the world underlines the importance of moving beyond North America and examining other cultural groups in order to identify universal principles of behavior. Furthermore, broad cultural differences are not the only ones taken into account by psychologists seeking to identify general principles of behavior. Subcultural, ethnic, racial, and socioeconomic differences are increasingly important targets of study by psychologists.

Although the discipline is growing more aware of the importance of taking cultural and subcultural factors into account, progress has not been rapid in actual practice. As we will discuss in Chapter 2, the amount of research conducted in the U.S. on groups other than white middle-class college students is woefully small. Furthermore, progress has been slowed by disagreement on what constitutes a culture or subculture. There isn't even universal agreement on the use of terms such as *race* and *ethnic group,* which sometimes have been used inappropriately. *Race,* for instance, is a biological concept that, technically, should be used only to refer to classifications based on physical characteristics of an organism or species. In contrast, *ethnic group* and *ethnicity* are broader terms that refer to cultural background, nationality, religion, and language.

The notion of race has been particularly difficult to address. Despite the formal definition, which revolves around biological factors, *race* has been used to denote anything from skin color to culture. As a concept, it has remained quite imprecise. For example, depending on the definition one uses, anywhere from 3 to 300 races exist. In addition, no race is "pure" in a biological sense (Betancourt & Lopez, 1993; Winkler, 1997).

To compound the difficulty, there are no universally acceptable names for races and ethnic groups. Psychologists—like other members of society—are divided on whether they should use the label *African American* (which focuses on geographical origins) or *black* (which focuses on skin color), just as they disagree on whether to use *Caucasian* or *white, Hispanic* or *Latino,* and *Native American* or *American Indian* (Jones, 1994; Phinney, 1996).

Psychologists also know that the consequences of race as a biological factor cannot be understood without taking into account environmental and cultural factors. Whatever aspects of people's behavior are based on race are a joint product of race, per se, and of the treatment they receive from others because of their race. In sum, only by examining behavior across ethnic, cultural, and racial lines can psychologists differentiate principles that are universal from those that are culture-bound (Fiske et al., 1998).

Psychology's Future

We've examined psychology's foundations. But what does the future hold for the discipline? Although the course of scientific development is difficult to predict, several trends do seem likely to emerge in the near future:

- As its knowledge base grows, psychology will become increasingly specialized and new perspectives will evolve (Robins, Gosling, & Craik, 1999).
- More psychologists will focus on the prevention of psychological disorders rather than just on their treatment. Psychological treatment will become more available and socially acceptable as the number of psychologists increases (APA, 1999).
- Psychology's influence on issues of public interest will grow. The major problems of our time—such as violence, racial and ethnic prejudice, poverty, and environmental and technological disasters—have important psychological aspects, and it is likely that psychologists will make important practical contributions toward their resolution (Cialdini, 1997; Lerner, Fisher, & Weinberg, 2000).
- As the population of the United States becomes more diverse, issues of diversity—embodied in the study of racial, ethnic, linguistic, and cultural factors—will become more critical to psychologists providing services and doing research. The result will be a field that can provide an understanding of *human* behavior in its broadest sense (J. G. Miller, 1999; Rosenzweig, 1999; Leong & Blustein, 2000).

 **PsychLink**

Cross-cultural psychology
www.mhhe.com/
feldmanup6-01links

BECOMING AN INFORMED CONSUMER OF PSYCHOLOGY

Thinking Critically About Psychology:
Distinguishing Legitimate Psychology from Pseudo-Psychology

- An advertisement in a national magazine proclaims a cure for a major psychological problem: "The 8-week Phobia Treatment: A Complete Home-Treatment Guide to Phobia and Stress Relief." For only $29.95 (plus $3.05 for postage), a reader is furnished with an "amazing" book covering topics such as "why pills and medication won't help," "your own tests," and "much, much more."
- An advertisement selling computer software proclaims in bold type, "Announcing the new hi-tech program that gives you a short-cut to success."
- A World Wide Web site invites visitors to submit by e-mail confidential questions regarding their relationships, which will be answered by "cybershrinks."

From advertisements, to television and radio talk shows, to the World Wide Web, we are daily subjected to a barrage of information about psychology. We are told that we can become better-adjusted, smarter, more insightful, and happier individuals by learning secrets that psychologists allegedly have revealed.

Yet such promises are usually empty. If self-improvement were this easy, we would live in a country of happy-go-lucky, fully satisfied individuals. Obviously life is not quite so simple, and the quality of advice provided by self-styled "experts"—and even, on occasion, by some less-than-reputable psychologists—varies widely.

How can we separate accurate information from pseudo-psychology? The best approach is to employ critical thinking techniques. Developed by psychologists who specialize in learning, memory, cognition, intelligence, and education, critical thinking procedures provide the tools to scrutinize assumptions, evaluate assertions, and think with greater precision (Coats, Feldman, & Schwartzberg, 1994).

We'll be considering ways to boost critical thinking skills in the *Becoming an Informed Consumer of Psychology* sections in each chapter. To get started, let's consider what you need to know to evaluate information of a psychological nature, whether the source is an advertisement, a television show, a magazine article, or even a book as seemingly reliable as a college textbook.

- For starters, know who is offering the information and advice. Are the purveyors of the information trained psychologists? What kinds of degrees do they have? Are they licensed? Are they affiliated with a particular institution? Before seriously relying on the advice of "experts," check out their credentials.
- Keep in mind that there's no free ride. If it is possible to solve major psychological ills through the purchase of a $29.95 book, then why do many people who suffer from such problems typically expend large amounts of time and money before they can be helped? If a computer program would really "unlock the hidden truths" about others, wouldn't it be in widespread use? Be wary of simple, glib "solutions" to major difficulties.
- Be aware that few universal cures exist for humankind's ills. No method or technique works for everyone. The range of difficulties attached to the human condition is so broad that any procedure that purports to resolve all problems is certain to disappoint anyone who tries it.
- Finally, remember that no source of information or advice is definitive. The notion of infallibility is best left to religious realms, and you should approach psychological information and advice from a critical and thoughtful perspective.

Despite these cautions, remember that the field of psychology has contributed a wealth of information we can draw upon for suggestions about every phase of our lives. One of the major

goals of this book is to make you an informed consumer of psychological knowledge by enhancing your ability to evaluate what psychologists have to offer. Ultimately, this book will give you the tools you need to analyze critically the theories, research, and applications psychologists have developed. As a result, you will be able to appreciate the real contributions the field of psychology has made to improving human life.

Evaluate

1. What perspective suggests that abnormal behavior is largely the result of unconscious forces?
2. "Psychologists should worry only about behavior that is directly observable." This statement would most likely be made by a person using which psychological perspective?
3. Psychology is currently moving toward increased specialization. True or false?

Answers to Evaluate Questions

1. psychodynamic 2. behavioral 3. True

Rethink

1. "The fact that some businesses now promote their ability to help people 'expand their mind beyond virtual reality' shows the great progress psychology has made lately." Criticize this statement in light of what you know about professional psychology and pseudo-psychology.
2. How do some of the key issues identified in this chapter relate to law enforcement and criminal justice?

Looking Back

What is the science of psychology?

- Psychology is the scientific study of behavior and mental processes, encompassing not just what people do, but their biological activities, feelings, perceptions, memory, reasoning, and thoughts. (p. 4)

What are the major specialties in the field of psychology?

- Biopsychologists focus on the biological basis of behavior, whereas experimental psychologists study the processes of sensing, perceiving, learning, and thinking about the world. (p. 5)
- Cognitive psychology, an outgrowth of experimental psychology, studies higher mental processes, including memory, knowing, thinking, reasoning, problem solving, judging, decision making, and language. (p. 6)
- Developmental psychologists study how people grow and change throughout the life span. (p. 7)
- Personality psychologists consider the consistency and change in an individual's behavior as he or she moves through different situations, as well as the individual differences that distinguish one person's behavior from another's when each is placed in the same situation. (p. 7)
- Health psychologists study psychological factors that affect physical disease; clinical psychologists consider the study, diagnosis, and treatment of psychological disorders. (p. 7)
- Social psychology is the study of how people's thoughts, feelings, and actions are affected by others. (p. 7)
- Cross-cultural psychology examines the similarities and differences in psychological functioning across various cultures. The psychology of women concentrates on psychological factors relating to women's behavior and development. (p. 7)

Where do psychologists work?

- Psychologists are employed in a variety of settings. Although the primary sites of employment are universities and colleges, many psychologists are found in hospitals, clinics, community mental health centers, and counseling centers. (p. 8)

What are the historical roots of the field of psychology?

- The foundations of psychology were established by Wilhelm Wundt in Germany in 1879. (p. 12)
- Early perspectives that guided the work of psychologists were structuralism, functionalism, and gestalt theory. (p. 12)

What are the major approaches used by contemporary psychologists?

- The biological approach focuses on the biological functioning of people and animals, considering the most basic components of behavior. (p. 14)
- The psychodynamic perspective suggests that there are powerful, unconscious inner forces and conflicts that people have little or no awareness of and that are primary determinants of behavior. (p. 15)
- Cognitive approaches to behavior consider how people know, understand, and think about the world. (p. 15)
- The behavioral perspective deemphasizes internal processes and concentrates instead on observable behavior, suggesting that an understanding and control of a person's environment is sufficient to fully explain and modify behavior. (p. 16)

- The humanistic perspective emphasizes that people are uniquely inclined toward psychological growth and higher levels of functioning and that they will strive to reach their full potential. (p. 16)

What are psychology's key issues and controversies?

- Among the key issues are the questions of nature versus nurture, conscious versus unconscious determinants of behavior, observable behavior versus internal mental processes, free will versus determinism, and individual differences versus universal principles. (p. 18)

What is the future of psychology likely to hold?

- Psychology will become increasingly specialized, will pay increasing attention to prevention instead of just treatment, will become increasingly concerned with the public interest, and will take the growing diversity of the nation's population into account more fully. (p. 21)

Key Terms and Concepts

psychology (p. 4)

structuralism (p. 12)

introspection (p. 13)

functionalism (p. 13)

gestalt psychology (p. 14)

biological perspective (p. 14)

psychodynamic perspective (p. 15)

cognitive perspective (p. 15)

behavioral perspective (p. 16)

humanistic perspective (p. 16)

Psychology on the Web

1. Practice using several search strategies to find out more information on the Internet about one of the key issues in psychology (e.g., free will versus determinism, nature versus nurture, or conscious versus unconscious determinants of behavior):
   a. Go to a "general purpose" search engine (such as Alta Vista at www.altavista.com).
   b. Go to a more specialized search engine (such as Yahoo's Psychology section, under the "Social Science" heading, at www.yahoo.com).
   c. Go to one of the more specialized psychology websites listed in PsychLinks on the *Understanding Psychology* website (www.mhhe/feldman/up6).
   Summarize and then compare the kind of information you have found through each strategy. List any useful websites you encounter in your searches.
2. Search the Internet for discussions of video games and violence and try to find
   a. an article in the general news media,
   b. information from a psychological perspective (e.g., experimental information or recommendations for parents from a professional organization), and
   c. political opinion or debate about how to address the issue of video game violence.
   Identify and briefly evaluate in writing the kind of information you have read, mentioning why you consider it trustworthy or not.

# Epilogue

As we have seen, the field of psychology is broad and diverse. It encompasses many different subfields and specialties practiced in a variety of settings, with new subfields arising and coming to prominence all the time.

Preview

For additional
quizzing and a
variety of interactive
resources, visit the
Understanding
Psychology Online
Learning Center at
www.mhhe.com/feldmanup6

We have also seen that even within the various subfields of the field, it is possible to adopt several different approaches, including the biological, psychodynamic, cognitive, behavioral, and humanistic perspectives.

For all its diversity, though, psychology focuses on certain key issues that unify the field along common lines and shared findings. These issues will reappear as themes throughout this book, as we discuss the work and accomplishments of psychologists in the many subfields of the discipline.

Before we turn to the methods psychologists use to study behavior, return for a moment to the opening prologue of this chapter, which discusses the rescue of Viral Dalal, the college student who was trapped under rubble for a hundred hours following a massive earthquake. In light of what you've learned about the subfields and perspectives of psychology, consider the following questions:

1. What kinds of factors might psychologists who use the biological perspective focus on to explain people's reactions to the earthquake?
2. How would the approach taken by a psychologist using the biological perspective differ from the approach taken by a cognitive psychologist?
3. Assume that two developmental psychologists are studying how being a survivor of a natural disaster will affect a young child's future development. One employs the psychodynamic perspective and the other takes the behavioral perspective. What kinds of questions would they ask themselves?

Chapter Two

Psychological Research

Prologue: Why Was No Help Offered?

Looking Ahead

The Scientific Method

Theories: Specifying Broad Explanations

Hypotheses: Crafting Testable Predictions

Psychological Research

Archival Research

Naturalistic Observation

Survey Research

Applying Psychology in the 21st Century: Web Surveys

The Case Study

Correlational Research

Experimental Research

Psychology at Work: Mary Garrett, AIDS Researcher

Research Challenges: Exploring the Process

The Ethics of Research

Exploring Diversity: Choosing Participants Who Represent the Scope of Human Behavior

Should Animals Be Used in Research?

Threats to Experiments: Experimenter and Participant Expectations

Becoming an Informed Consumer of Psychology: Thinking Critically About Research

Looking Back

Key Terms and Concepts

Psychology on the Web

OLC Preview

Epilogue

Prologue

Why Was No Help Offered?

The 30-year-old male Haitian immigrant named Abner Louima was <u>hustled in</u>to a New York City police station lobby. There some police officers <u>stripped</u> him naked from the waist down and took him in handcuffs to the station bathroom, where one police officer, wearing a pair of protective gloves he borrowed from another officer, raped Louima with a toilet plunger. He then thrust the plunger into Louima's mouth, breaking several teeth. The immigrant was then taken to a holding cell. Only because other occupants of the cell noticed that Louima was bleeding was an ambulance called an hour later. He was eventually transported to a hospital, where he lay near death for several days.

Despite the extreme violence of the attack on Abner Louima, no one came forward to help him. How might researchers study this phenomenon?

The bathroom where the assault took place was in the center of the police station, and it is difficult to imagine that no one heard Louima's screams of pain while he was being attacked. In fact, several days later some officers admitted that they had witnessed the incident. Yet no one offered any help to the victim, and for several days other officers refused to admit that they had any knowledge of the attack.

The question remains: Why did no one come to Louima's aid?

Were this an isolated incident, we might be able to attribute the bystanders' inaction to something specific about the situation. However, events such as this one are all too common.

For example, in another infamous case, a woman named Kitty Genovese was attacked by a man near an apartment building in New York City in the mid 1960s. At one point during the assault, which lasted thirty minutes, she managed to free herself and screamed, "Oh, my God, he stabbed me. Please help me!" In the stillness of the night, no fewer than thirty-eight neighbors heard her screams. Windows opened and lights went on. One couple pulled chairs up to the window and turned off the lights so they could see better. Someone called out, "Let that girl alone." But shouts were not enough to scare off the killer. He chased her, stabbing her eight more times, and sexually molested her before leaving her to die. And how many of those thirty-eight witnesses came to her aid? As with Abner Louima, not one person helped (Rogers & Eftimiades, 1995).

The cases of Abner Louima and Kitty Genovese both remain dismaying—and puzzling—examples of "bad Samaritanism." Most people (not just the general public, but also psychologists) found it difficult to explain how so many people could stand by without coming to the aid of the victims.

Editorial writers suggested that the incidents could simply be attributed to the basic shortcomings of "human nature." But such an assumption is woefully inadequate. Many people have risked their own lives to help others in dangerous situations, so "human nature" encompasses a wide range of both negative and positive responses.

Psychologists puzzled over the problem for many years. After much research they finally reached an unexpected conclusion: Abner Louima and Kitty Genovese probably would have been better off if only a few people, rather than many, had heard their cries for help. In fact, had there been only one bystander present in each instance, the chances of that person intervening might have been fairly high. For it turns out that the *fewer* the witnesses to an assault, the *better* the victim's chances of getting help.

How did psychologists come to such a curious conclusion? After all, logic and common sense clearly suggest that *more* bystanders would produce a greater likelihood that someone would help a person in need. This seeming contradiction—and the way psychologists resolved it—illustrates a central task for the field of psychology: the challenge of asking and answering questions of interest.

In this chapter, we examine how psychologists reach conclusions about the unknown. We begin by examining the scientific method used to pose and answer questions of psychological interest. We describe how psychologists develop suppositions and theories that can be tested through research. We then consider the specific means of doing research, using as one example psychologists' investigations into bystander helping behavior. We discuss the major techniques used in carrying out research, considering the benefits and limitations of each. Finally, we examine the ethics of research and how we can become knowledgeable and critical consumers of research findings.

 **PsychLink**

Guide for beginning researchers
www.mhhe.com/
feldmanup6-02links

Prepare

What is the scientific method, and how do psychologists use theory and research to answer questions of interest?

Organize

The Scientific Method
    Theories
    Hypotheses

The Scientific Method

Birds of a feather flock together . . . or do opposites attract? Two heads are better than one . . . or if you want a thing done well, do it yourself? The more the merrier . . . or two's company, three's a crowd?

If we were to rely on "common sense" to understand behavior, we'd have considerable difficulty—especially because commonsense views are often contradictory. In fact, one of the major undertakings for the field of psychology is to determine which suppositions about behavior are accurate, and to develop those suppositions in the first place.

The challenge of posing appropriate questions and properly answering them has been met through reliance on the scientific method. The **scientific method** is the approach used by psychologists to systematically acquire knowledge and understanding about behavior and other phenomena of interest. As illustrated in Figure 2-1, it consists of three main steps: (1) identifying questions of

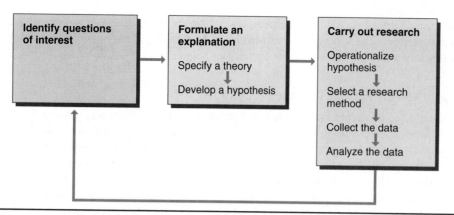

Figure 2-1 The scientific method, which encompasses the process of identifying, asking, and answering questions, is used by psychologists, and by researchers from every other scientific discipline, to come to an understanding about the world. What do you think are the advantages of this method?

interest, (2) formulating an explanation, and (3) carrying out research designed to lend support to or refute the explanation.

Theories: Specifying Broad Explanations

In using the scientific method, psychologists start with the kinds of observations about behavior we are all familiar with. If you have ever asked yourself why a particular teacher is so easily annoyed, why a friend is always late for appointments, or how your dog understands your commands, you have been formulating questions about behavior. Psychologists, too, ask questions about the nature and causes of behavior, and this questioning is the first step in the scientific method: identifying questions of interest.

Once a question has been identified, the next step in the scientific method involves developing theories to explain the phenomenon that has been observed. **Theories** are broad explanations and predictions concerning phenomena of interest. They provide a framework for understanding the relationships among a set of otherwise unorganized facts or principles.

All of us have developed our own informal theories of human behavior, such as "People are basically good" or "People's behavior is usually motivated by self-interest." However, psychologists' theories are more formal and focused. They are established on the basis of a careful study of the psychological literature to identify relevant research conducted and theories formulated previously, as well as psychologists' general knowledge of the field (Sternberg, 1990; Sternberg & Beall, 1991; McGuire, 1997).

Growing out of the diverse models of psychology described in Chapter 1, theories vary both in their breadth and in the level of detail they employ. For example, one theory might seek to explain and predict as broad a phenomenon as emotional experience in general. A narrower theory might purport to predict how people display the emotion of fear nonverbally after receiving a threat. An even more specific theory might attempt to explain how the muscles of the face work together to produce expressions of fear.

Psychologists Bibb Latané and John Darley, responding specifically to the Kitty Genovese case, developed a theory based on a phenomenon they called *diffusion of responsibility* (Latané & Darley, 1970). According to their theory, the greater the number of bystanders or witnesses to an event that calls for helping behavior, the more the responsibility for helping is perceived to be shared by all the bystanders.

scientific method: The approach used by psychologists to systematically acquire knowledge and understanding about behavior and other phenomena of interest.

theories: Broad explanations and predictions concerning phenomena of interest.

Because of this sense of shared responsibility, then, the more people present in an emergency situation, the less personal responsibility each person feels—and the less likely it is that any single person will come forward to help.

Hypotheses: Crafting Testable Predictions

Although such a theory makes sense, it represented only the beginning phase of Latané and Darley's investigative process. Their next step was to devise a way of testing their theory. To do this, they needed to create a hypothesis. A **hypothesis** is a prediction stated in a way that allows it to be tested. Hypotheses stem from theories; they help to test the underlying validity of theories.

> **hypothesis:** A prediction, stemming from a theory, stated in a way that allows it to be tested.

In the same way as we develop our own broad theories about the world, we also construct hypotheses about events and behavior. They can range from trivialities (such as why our English instructor wears those weird shirts) to more meaningful matters (such as what is the best way to study for a test). Although we rarely test these hypotheses systematically, we do try to determine whether they are right. Perhaps we try comparing two strategies: cramming the night before an exam versus spreading out our study over several nights. By assessing which approach yields better test performance, we have created a way to compare the two strategies.

Latané and Darley's hypothesis was a straightforward prediction from their more general theory of diffusion of responsibility: The more people who witness an emergency situation, the less likely it is that help will be given to a victim. They could, of course, have chosen another hypothesis (for instance, that people with greater skills related to emergency situations will not be affected by the presence of others), but their initial formulation seemed to offer the most direct test of the theory.

Psychologists rely on formal theories and hypotheses for many reasons. For one thing, theories and hypotheses allow psychologists to make sense of unorganized, separate observations and bits of information by permitting them to place the pieces within a structured and coherent framework. In addition, theories and hypotheses offer psychologists the opportunity to move beyond already known facts and principles and make deductions about as yet unexplained phenomena. In this way, theories and hypotheses provide a reasoned guide to the direction that future investigation ought to take.

In sum, then, theories and hypotheses help psychologists pose appropriate questions. But how are such questions answered? As we shall see, the answers come from research.

Evaluate

1. An explanation about a phenomenon of interest is known as a ___Theory___.
2. To test this explanation, it must be stated in terms of a testable question known as a ___hypothesis___

Rethink

1. Starting with the theory that diffusion of responsibility causes responsibility for helping to be shared among bystanders, Latané and Darley derived the hypothesis that the more people who witness an emergency situation, the less likely it is that help will be given to a victim. How many other hypotheses can you think of based on the same theory of diffusion of responsibility?

2. Is it possible to formulate testable hypotheses from the theories behind the headlines in popular tabloid newspapers (e.g., about UFOs, Elvis's survival, or other popular notions)? Why or why not?

Answers to Evaluate Questions

1. theory 2. hypothesis

Psychological Research

Research, systematic inquiry aimed at the discovery of new knowledge, is a central ingredient of the scientific method in psychology. It provides the key to understanding the degree to which theories and hypotheses are accurate.

Just as we can apply different theories and hypotheses to explain the same phenomena, we can use a number of alternative methods to conduct research on the same problem (Ray, 2000). First, though, the hypothesis must be restated in a way that will allow it to be tested, a procedure known as operationalization. **Operationalization** is the process of translating a hypothesis into specific, testable procedures that can be measured and observed.

There is no single way to go about operationalizing a hypothesis; it depends on logic, the equipment and facilities available, the psychological model being employed, and ultimately the creativity of the researcher. For example, one researcher might develop a hypothesis in which she operationalizes "fear" as an increase in heart rate. In contrast, another psychologist might operationalize "fear" as a written response to the question, "How much fear are you experiencing at this moment?"

We will consider several of the major tools in the psychologist's research kit. As we discuss these research methods, keep in mind that their relevance extends beyond testing and evaluating theories and hypotheses in psychology. Even people who do not have degrees in psychology, for instance, often carry out elementary forms of research on their own. For example, a supervisor might need to evaluate an employee's performance; a physician might systematically test the effects of different dosages of a drug on a patient; a salesperson might compare different persuasive strategies. Each of these situations calls for the use of the research practices we are about to discuss.

Furthermore, a knowledge of the research methods used by psychologists permits us to better evaluate the research that others conduct. The media constantly bombard us with claims about research studies and findings. Knowledge of research methods allows us to sort out what is credible from what should be ignored. Finally, there is evidence that by studying some kinds of research methods in depth, people learn to reason more critically and effectively. Understanding the methods by which psychologists conduct research can enhance our ability to analyze and evaluate the situations we encounter in our everyday lives (Lehman, Lempert, & Nisbett, 1988; Shaughnessy, Zechmeister, & Zechmeister, 2000; Shadish, Cook, & Campbell, 2002).

Archival Research

Suppose that, like psychologists Latané and Darley, you were interested in finding out more about emergency situations in which bystanders did not provide help. One of the first places you might turn to would be historical accounts. By using newspaper records, for example, you might find support for the notion that a decrease in helping behavior historically has accompanied an increase in the number of bystanders.

Using newspaper articles is an example of archival research. In **archival research,** existing data, such as census documents, college records, or newspaper clippings, are examined to test a hypothesis. For example, college records might be used to determine if there are gender differences in academic performance.

Archival research is a relatively inexpensive means of testing a hypothesis because someone else has already collected the basic data. Of course, the use of existing data has several drawbacks. For one thing, the data might not be in a form that allows the researcher to test a hypothesis fully. The information could be incomplete, or it could have been collected haphazardly (Stewart & Kamins, 1993).

Most archival research is hampered by the simple fact that records with the necessary information do not exist. In these instances, researchers often turn to another research method: naturalistic observation.

Prepare

What are the different research methods employed by psychologists?

How do psychologists establish cause-and-effect relationships in research studies?

Organize

Psychological Research

Archival Research

Naturalistic Observation

Survey Research

The Case Study

Correlational Research

Experimental Research

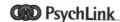 **PsychLink**

Research methods

www.mhhe.com/
feldmanup6-02links

operationalization: The process of translating a hypothesis into specific, testable procedures that can be measured and observed.

archival research: Research in which existing data, such as census documents, college records, or newspaper clippings, are examined to test a hypothesis.

Dian Fossey, a pioneer in the study of gorillas in their native habitat, relied on naturalistic observation for her research. What are the advantages of this approach?

naturalistic observation: Research in which an investigator simply observes some naturally occurring behavior and does not make a change in the situation.

survey research: Research in which people chosen to represent some larger population are asked a series of questions about their behavior, thoughts, or attitudes.

case study: An in-depth, intensive investigation of an individual or small group of people.

Naturalistic Observation

In **naturalistic observation,** the investigator simply observes some naturally occurring behavior and does not make a change in the situation. For example, a researcher investigating helping behavior might observe the kind of help given to victims in a high-crime area of a city. The important point to remember about naturalistic observation is that the researcher is passive and simply records what occurs (Erlandson et al., 1993; Adler & Adler, 1994; Schmidt, 1999).

Although the advantage of naturalistic observation is obvious—we get a sample of what people do in their "natural habitat"—there is also an important drawback: the inability to control any of the factors of interest. For example, we might find so few naturally occurring instances of helping behavior that we would be unable to draw any conclusions. Because naturalistic observation prevents researchers from making changes in a situation, they must wait until appropriate conditions occur. Furthermore, if people know that they are being watched, they might alter their reactions, producing behavior that is not truly representative of the group in question.

Survey Research

There is no more straightforward way of finding out what people think, feel, and do than asking them directly. For this reason, surveys are an important research method. In **survey research,** a *sample* of people chosen to represent some larger group of interest (a *population*) are asked a series of questions about their behavior, thoughts, or attitudes. Survey methods have become so sophisticated that even with a very small sample researchers are able to infer with great accuracy how a larger group would respond. For instance, a sample of just a few thousand voters is sufficient to predict within one or two percentage points who will win a presidential election—if the representative sample is chosen with care (Weisberg, Krosnick, & Bowen, 1996; Fink & Kosecoff, 1998).

Researchers investigating helping behavior might conduct a survey by asking people to complete a questionnaire in which they indicate their reasons for not wanting to come forward to help another individual. Similarly, researchers interested in learning about sexual practices have carried out surveys to learn which practices are common and which are not, and to chart changing notions of sexual morality over the past several decades (as we consider in Chapter 11).

Asking people directly about their behavior seems in some ways the most straightforward approach to understanding what people do, but survey research has several potential drawbacks. For one thing, people might give inaccurate responses because of memory lapses or because they don't want the researcher to know what they really believe about a particular issue. Moreover, people sometimes offer responses they think the researcher wants to hear—or, in just the opposite instance, responses they assume the researcher *doesn't* want to hear. Finally, if the sample of people who are surveyed are not representative of the broader population of interest, the results of the survey have little meaning—as we consider in the *Applying Psychology in the 21st Century* box (Schwarz, 1999).

The Case Study

When the police officers who participated in Abner Louima's assault were arrested, many people wondered what it was about the officers' personalities or backgrounds that might have led to their behavior. To answer this question, psychologists might conduct a case study. In contrast to a survey, in which many people are studied, a **case study** is an in-depth, intensive investigation of an individual or a small group of people. Case studies often include *psychological testing,* a procedure in which a carefully designed set of questions is used to gain some insight into the personality of the individual or group being studied (Kvale, 1996; Sommer & Sommer, 1997; Gass et al., 2000).

"This is the New York 'Times' Business Poll again, Mr. Landau. Do you feel better or worse about the economy than you did twenty minutes ago?"

Applying Psychology in the 21st Century

Web Surveys

Q. Who is the greatest warrior and statesman of the 20th century?

A. Mustafa Kemal Ataturk.

Q. And who is the greatest entertainer and artist of the 20th century?

A. Mustafa Kemal Ataturk.

Who? In case you don't know, M. K. Ataturk is the founding father of modern Turkey. Ataturk is apparently held in high regard by the people who responded to a *Time* poll on the magazine's website that sought to identify the greatest people of the twentieth century. During the three-year period preceding the turn of the millennium, Ataturk was at the top of several of the lists for a good part of the time.

The case of the omnipresent Ataturk illustrates the dangers of surveys conducted on the Internet. Another example comes from the period during which President Bill Clinton was being impeached by the U.S. Congress. Although every traditional scientific survey showed that the majority of U.S. citizens were against impeachment, polls on the Internet showed that 70 percent of respondents supported impeachment (Witt, 1998).

Why are Web surveys so unreliable? The answer is that they do not provide a clear, rep-

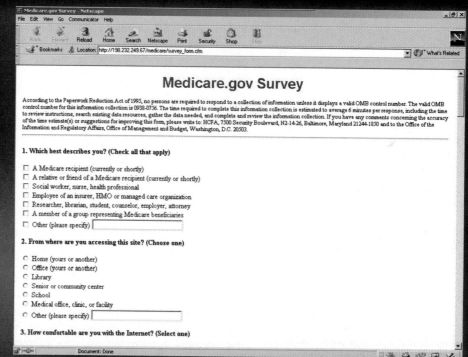

Medicare.gov Survey

According to the Paperwork Reduction Act of 1995, no persons are required to respond to a collection of information unless it displays a valid OMB control number. The valid OMB control number for this information collection is 0938-0756. The time required to complete this information collection is estimated to average 6 minutes per response, including the time to review instructions, search existing data resources, gather the data needed, and complete and review the information collection. If you have any comments concerning the accuracy of the time estimate(s) or suggestions for improving this form, please write to: HCFA, 7500 Security Boulevard, N2-14-26, Baltimore, Maryland 21244-1850 and to the Office of the Information and Regulatory Affairs, Office of Management and Budget, Washington, D.C. 20503.

1. Which best describes you? (Check all that apply)

☐ A Medicare recipient (currently or shortly)
☐ A relative or friend of a Medicare recipient (currently or shortly)
☐ Social worker, nurse, health professional
☐ Employee of an insurer, HMO or managed care organization
☐ Researcher, librarian, student, counselor, employer, attorney
☐ A member of a group representing Medicare beneficiaries
☐ Other (please specify)

2. From where are you accessing this site? (Choose one)

○ Home (yours or another)
○ Office (yours or another)
○ Library
○ Senior or community center
○ School
○ Medical office, clinic, or facility
○ Other (please specify)

3. How comfortable are you with the Internet? (Select one)

Mustafa Kemal Ataturk. Statesman and entertainer?

resentative sample of any particular group. No one knows who the respondents are and what groups they represent. Because the kind of people who use the Web hardly are representative of the population at large—we know that women are less likely to be on line than men, and that minority group members are less likely to have access to and use computers—the results of Web polls could pertain to only a small (and unidentifiable) segment of the general population (Dillman, 2000).

Furthermore, because most Internet polls permit multiple responses, the same people can repeatedly respond to a survey. Consequently, a relatively small group of people with an extreme point of view can bias the results considerably. (That's what led to Ataturk's popularity in the *Time* poll.)

Finally, Web surveys rarely are carefully constructed, which is a problem because polling results are extremely sensitive to the specific wording of the question being asked. For example, one survey of college students posed this question: "How much special consideration should black students receive in college admissions?" The results showed that more than 70 percent of those surveyed thought that African American students should receive

at least some special consideration. However, when the question was stated in terms of whether affirmative action in college admissions *should be abolished,* 50 percent of those surveyed responded yes. Because the two questions were getting at essentially the same thing, the two findings are clearly inconsistent (Shea, 1996a).

Supporters of Web surveys claim that because tens of thousands of people sometimes respond to Web polls, the huge numbers must make their polls meaningful. However, this is an unsound argument: Even when large numbers of people respond to a question, there is still no way of knowing whether those respondents represent a reasonable sample of the general population—or even a reasonable sample of people who use the Internet. In short, when it comes to survey research, traditional findings are considerably more reliable than research conducted on the Web.

If 500,000 people responded to a survey on the Web, would you feel that the large number of respondents would give the findings validity? Why or why not? What if the amazingly high number of 260 million responses—a number roughly corresponding to the population of the United States—were received?

When case studies are used as a research technique, the goal is often not only to learn about the few individuals being examined, but to use the insights gained from the study to improve our understanding of people in general. Sigmund Freud built his theories through case studies of individual patients. Similarly, case studies of the two killers in the Columbine High School shootings might help identify other adolescents who are prone to violence.

Correlational Research

In using the research methods that we have described, researchers often wish to determine the relationship between two variables. **Variables** are behaviors, events, or other characteristics that can change, or vary, in some way. For example, we might want to find out if there is a relationship between the variable of religious service attendance and the variable of helpfulness in emergency situations. If we did find such a relationship, we could say that there was an association—or correlation—between attendance at religious services and helpfulness in emergencies.

In **correlational research,** the relationship between two sets of variables is examined to determine whether they are associated, or "correlated." The strength and direction of the relationship between the two variables is represented by a mathematical score, known as a *correlation* (or, more formally, a *correlation coefficient*), that can range from $+1.0$ to -1.0.

A *positive correlation* indicates that as the value of one variable increases, we can predict that the value of the other variable will also increase. For example, if we predict that the more that students study for a test, the higher their subsequent grades on the test will be, and that the less they study, the lower their test scores will be, we are expecting to find a positive correlation. (Higher values of the variable "amount of study time" would be associated with higher values of the variable "test score," and lower values of "amount of study time" would be associated with lower values of "test score.") The correlation, then, would be indicated by a positive number, and the stronger the association between studying and test scores, the closer the number would be to $+1.0$. For example, we might find a correlation of $+.85$ between test scores and amount of studying time, indicating a strong positive association.

On the other hand, a *negative correlation* tells us that as the value of one variable increases, the value of the other decreases. For instance, we might predict that as the number of hours spent studying increases, the number of hours spent in partying decreases. Here, we are expecting a negative correlation, ranging between 0 and -1.0. More studying is associated with less partying, and less studying is associated with more partying. The stronger the association between study and partying, the closer the correlation would be to -1.0. For instance, a correlation of $-.85$ would indicate a strong negative association between partying and studying.

Of course, it's quite possible that little or no relationship exists between two variables. For instance, we would probably not expect to find a relationship between number of study hours and height. Lack of a relationship would be indicated by a correlation close to 0. For example, if we found a correlation of $-.02$ or $+.03$, it would indicate that there is virtually no association between the two variables; knowing how much someone studies does not tell us anything about how tall he or she is. (You can read more about the concept of correlation, and how statistics in general are used by psychologists, in the Appendix at the end of this book.)

When we find that two variables are strongly correlated with one another, it is tempting to presume that one variable causes the other. For example, if we find that more study time is associated with higher grades, we might guess that more studying *causes* higher grades. Although this is not a bad guess, it remains just a guess—because finding that two variables are correlated does not mean that there is a causal relationship between them. Although the strong correlation suggests that knowing how much a person studies can help us predict how she or he will do on a test, it does not mean that the studying caused the test performance. It might be, for instance, that people who are interested in

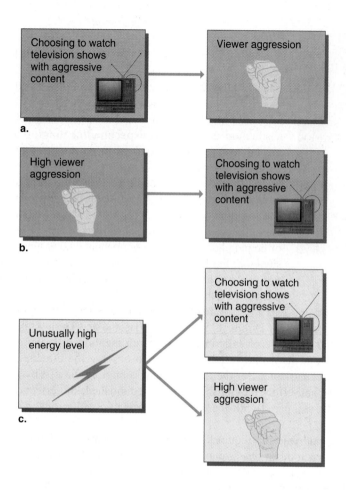

a.

b.

c.

Figure 2-2 If we find that frequent viewing of television programs having aggressive content is associated with high levels of aggressive behavior, we might cite several plausible causes, as suggested in this figure. For example, choosing to watch shows with aggressive content could produce aggression (a); or being a highly aggressive person might cause one to choose to watch televised aggression (b); or having a high energy level might cause a person to *both* choose to watch aggressive shows and act aggressively (c). Correlational findings, then, do not permit us to determine causality. Can you think of a way to study the effects of televised aggression on aggressive behavior that is not correlational?

experiment: The investigation of the relationship between two (or more) variables by deliberately producing a change in one variable in a situation and observing the effects of that change on other aspects of the situation.

the subject matter tend to study more than those who are less interested, and that the amount of interest, not the number of hours spent studying, predicts test performance. The mere fact that two variables occur together does not mean that one causes the other.

Another example illustrates the critical point that correlations tell us nothing about cause and effect but only provide a measure of the strength of a relationship between two variables. We might find that children who watch a lot of television programs featuring high levels of aggression are likely to demonstrate a relatively high degree of aggressive behavior, and that those who watch few television shows that portray aggression are apt to exhibit a relatively low degree of such behavior (see Figure 2-2). But we cannot say that the aggression is *caused* by the TV viewing, because several other explanations are possible.

For instance, it could be that children who have an unusually high level of energy seek out programs with aggressive content *and* are more aggressive. The children's energy level, then, could be the true cause of the children's higher incidence of aggression. Finally, it is also possible that people who are already highly aggressive choose to watch shows with high aggressive content *because* they are aggressive. Clearly, then, any number of causal sequences are possible—none of which can be ruled out by correlational research.

The inability of correlational research to demonstrate cause-and-effect relationships is a crucial drawback to its use. There is, however, an alternative technique that does establish causality: the experiment.

Experimental Research

The *only* way psychologists can establish cause-and-effect relationships through research is by carrying out an experiment. In a formal **experiment,** the relationship between two (or more) variables is investigated by deliberately producing a change in one variable in

Many studies show that the observation of violence in the media is associated with aggression in viewers. Can we conclude that the observation of violence causes aggression?

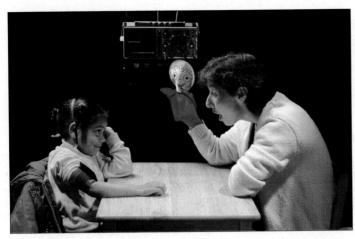

In this experiment, preschoolers' reactions to the puppet are monitored. Can you think of a hypothesis that might be tested in this way?

experimental manipulation: The change that an experimenter deliberately produces in a situation.

treatment: In an experiment, the manipulation implemented by the experimenter.

experimental group: Any group receiving a treatment in an experiment.

control group: A group that receives no treatment in an experiment.

 **PsychLink**

Two-group randomized experiment
www.mhhe.com/
feldmanup6–02links

a situation and observing the effects of that change on other aspects of the situation. In an experiment, then, the conditions required to study a question of interest are created by an experimenter, who deliberately makes a change in those conditions in order to observe the effects of that change.

The change that an experimenter deliberately produces in a situation is called the **experimental manipulation.** Experimental manipulations are used to detect relationships between different variables.

Several steps are involved in carrying out an experiment, but the process typically begins with the development of one or more hypotheses for the experiment to test. Recall, for example, the hypothesis derived by Latané and Darley to test their theory of helping behavior: The more people who witness an emergency situation, the less likely it is that any of them will help the victim. We can trace the way these researchers designed an experiment to test this hypothesis.

Their first step was to operationalize the hypothesis by conceptualizing it in a way that could be tested. Doing so required that Latané and Darley take into account the fundamental principle of experimental research mentioned earlier. Experimenters must manipulate at least one variable in order to observe the effects of the manipulation on another variable. But the manipulation cannot be viewed by itself, in isolation; if a cause-and-effect relationship is to be established, the effects of the manipulation must be compared with the effects of no manipulation or a different kind of manipulation.

Experimental research requires, then, that the responses of at least two groups be compared with each other. One group will receive some special **treatment**—the manipulation implemented by the experimenter—and another group will receive either no treatment or a different treatment. Any group receiving a treatment is called an **experimental group;** a group that receives no treatment is called a **control group.** (In some experiments there are multiple experimental and control groups, each of which is compared with another.)

By employing both experimental and control groups in an experiment, researchers are able to rule out the possibility that something other than the experimental manipulation produced the results observed in the experiment. With no control group, we couldn't be sure that some other variable, such as the temperature at the time we were running the experiment, the color of the experimenter's hair, or even the mere passage of time, wasn't causing the changes observed.

For example, consider a medical researcher who thinks she has invented a medicine that cures the common cold. To test her claim, she gives the medicine one day to a group of twenty people who have colds, and finds that ten days later all of them are cured. Eureka? Not so fast. An observer viewing this flawed study might reasonably argue that the people would have gotten better even without the medicine. What the researcher obviously needed was a control group consisting of people with colds who *don't* get the medicine, and whose health is also checked ten days later. Only if there is a difference between experimental and control groups can the effectiveness of the medicine be assessed. Through the use of control groups, then, researchers can isolate specific causes for their findings—and draw cause-and-effect inferences.

Returning to Latané and Darley's experiment, we note that the researchers needed a means of operationalizing their hypothesis in order to proceed. They decided they would create a false emergency situation that would appear to require the aid of a bystander. As their experimental manipulation, they decided to vary the number of bystanders present. They could have had just one experimental group with, say, 2 people present, and a control group for comparison purposes with just 1 person present. Instead, they settled on a more complex procedure involving three groups—consisting of 2, 3, and 6 people—that could be compared with one another.

Latané and Darley had now identified what is called the experimenter's independent variable. The **independent variable** is the variable that is manipulated by an experimenter. (You can think of the independent variable as being independent of the actions of those taking part in an experiment; it is controlled by the experimenter.) In the case of the Latané and Darley experiment, the independent variable was the number of people present, manipulated by the experimenters.

The next step was to decide how they were going to determine the effect that varying the number of bystanders had on behavior of those in the experiment. Crucial to every experiment is the **dependent variable,** the variable that is measured and is expected to change as a result of changes caused by the experimenter's manipulation of the independent variable. The dependent variable is dependent on the actions of the *participants* or *subjects,* the people taking part in the experiment.

Latané and Darley had several possible choices for their dependent measure. One might have been a simple yes/no measure of the participants' helping behavior. But the investigators also wanted a more precise analysis of helping behavior. Consequently, they also measured the amount of time it took for a participant to provide help.

Latané and Darley now had all the necessary components of an experiment. The independent variable, manipulated by them, was the number of bystanders present in an emergency situation. The dependent variable was the measure of whether bystanders in each of the groups provided help and the amount of time it took them to do so. Consequently, like all experiments, this one had both an independent and a dependent variable. (To remember the difference, recall that a hypothesis predicts how a dependent variable *depends* on the manipulation of the independent variable.) *All* true experiments in psychology fit this straightforward model.

Bibb Latané and John Darley

The Final Step: Random Assignment of Participants

To make the experiment a valid test of the hypothesis, the researchers needed to add a final step to the design: properly assigning participants to receive a particular treatment.

The significance of this step becomes clear when we examine various alternative procedures. For example, the experimenters might have assigned just males to the group with 2 bystanders, just females to the group with 3 bystanders, and both males and females to the group with 6 bystanders. Had they done so, however, any differences they found in helping behavior could not be attributed with any certainty solely to group size, because the differences might just as well be due to the composition of the group. A more reasonable procedure would be to ensure that each group had the same composition in terms of gender; then the researchers would be able to make comparisons across groups with considerably more accuracy.

Participants in each of the experimental groups ought to be comparable, and it is easy enough to create groups that are similar in terms of gender. The problem becomes a bit more tricky, though, when we consider other participant characteristics. How can we ensure that participants in each experimental group will be equally intelligent, extroverted, cooperative, and so forth, when the list of characteristics—any one of which could be important—is potentially endless?

The solution is a simple but elegant procedure called **random assignment to condition:** Participants are assigned to different experimental groups or "conditions" on the basis of chance and chance alone. The experimenter might, for instance, put the names of all potential participants into a hat and draw names to make assignments to specific groups. The advantage of this technique is that participant characteristics have an equal chance of being distributed across the various groups. By using random assignment, chances are that each of the groups will have approximately the same proportion of intelligent people, cooperative people, extroverted people, males and females, and so on.

Figure 2-3 provides another example of an experiment. Like all experiments, it includes the following set of key elements, which are important to keep in mind as you consider whether a research study is truly an experiment:

PsychLink

Random assignment explained
www.mhhe.com/
feldmanup6-02links

independent variable: The variable that is manipulated by an experimenter.
dependent variable: The variable that is measured and is expected to change as a result of changes caused by the experimenter's manipulation.
random assignment to condition: A procedure in which participants are assigned to different experimental groups or "conditions" on the basis of chance and chance alone.

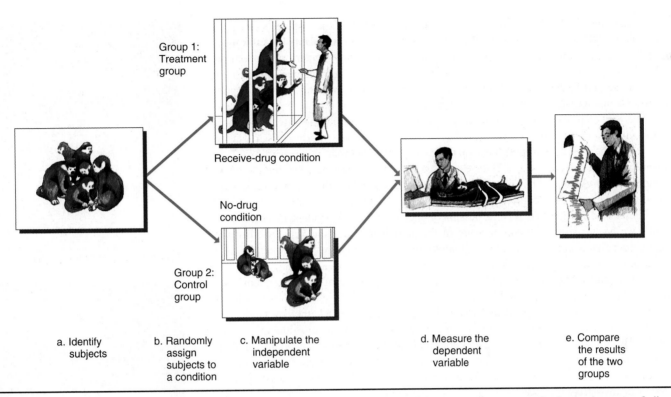

Group 1:
Treatment
group

Receive-drug condition

No-drug
condition

Group 2:
Control
group

a. Identify
   subjects

b. Randomly
   assign
   subjects to
   a condition

c. Manipulate the
   independent
   variable

d. Measure the
   dependent
   variable

e. Compare
   the results
   of the two
   groups

Figure 2-3 In this depiction of a study investigating the effects of the drug propranolol on stress, we can see the basic elements of all true experiments. The subjects of the experiment were monkeys, who were randomly assigned to one of two groups. Monkeys assigned to the treatment group were given a drug, propranolol, hypothesized to prevent heart disease, whereas those in the control group were not given the drug. Administration of the drugs, then, was the independent variable.

All the monkeys were given a high-fat diet that was the human equivalent of two eggs with bacon every morning, and they were occasionally reassigned to different cages to provide a source of stress. To determine the effects of the drug, the monkeys' heart rates and other measures of heart disease were assessed after 26 months. These measures constituted the dependent variable. (The results? As hypothesized, monkeys who received the drug showed lower heart rates and fewer symptoms of heart disease than those who did not.) (Based on a study by Kaplan & Manuck, 1989).

- An independent variable, the variable that is manipulated by the experimenter
- A dependent variable, the variable that is measured by the experimenter and expected to change as a result of the manipulation of the independent variable
- A procedure that randomly assigns participants to different experimental groups or "conditions" of the independent variable
- A hypothesis that predicts what effect the independent variable will have on the dependent variable.

Only if each of these elements is present can a research study be considered a true experiment in which cause-and-effect relationships can be determined. (For a summary of the different types of research we've discussed, see Table 2-1.)

Were Latané and Darley Right?

By now, you must be wondering whether Latané and Darley were right when they hypothesized that increasing the number of bystanders in an emergency situation would lower the degree of helping behavior.

According to the results of the experiment they carried out, their hypothesis was right on target. To test the hypothesis, they used a laboratory setting in which participants were told that the purpose of the experiment was to hold a discussion about personal problems associated with college. The discussion was to be held over an intercom, supposedly to avoid the potential embarrassment of face-to-face contact. Chatting about personal problems was not, of course, the true purpose of the experiment, but participants

Table 2-1 Research Strategies

	Correlational Research	Experimental Research
General Process	Researcher observes a previously existing situation but does not make a change in the situation	Researcher manipulates a situation in order to observe the outcome of the manipulation
Intended Result	Identifies associations between factors	Learns how changes in one variable cause changes in another variable
Type	Archival research (examines records to confirm hypothesis)	Experiment (investigator produces a change in one variable to observe the effects of that change on other variables)
	Naturalistic observation (observation of naturally occurring behavior, without making a change in the situation)	
	Case study (intensive investigation of an individual or small group)	

were told that it was as a way of keeping their expectations about the experiment from biasing their behavior. (Consider how they would have been affected if they had been told that their helping behavior in emergencies was being tested. The experimenters could never have gotten an accurate assessment of what the participants would actually do in an emergency. By definition, emergencies are rarely announced in advance.)

The sizes of the discussion groups were 2, 3, and 6 people, which constituted the manipulation of the independent variable of group size. Participants were randomly assigned to these groups upon their arrival at the laboratory.

As the participants in each group were holding their discussion, they suddenly heard through the intercom one of the other participants (in reality a trained *confederate,* or employee, of the experimenters) having what sounded like an epileptic seizure and calling for help.

The participants' behavior was now what counted. The dependent variable was the time that elapsed from the start of the "seizure" to the time a participant began trying to help the "victim." If six minutes went by without a participant's offering help, the experiment was ended.

As predicted by the hypothesis, the size of the group had a significant effect on whether a participant provided help (Latané & Darley, 1970). In the 2-person group (in which participants thought they were alone with the victim), the average elapsed time was 52 seconds; in the 3-person group (the participant, the victim, and one other person), the average elapsed time was 93 seconds; and in the 6-person group (the participant, the victim, and four others), the average time was 166 seconds. Considering a simple yes/no measure of whether help was given confirms the elapsed-time pattern. Eighty-five percent of the participants in the 2-person-group condition helped; 62 percent in the 3-person-group condition; and only 31 percent helped in the 6-person-group condition (see Figure 2-4).

Because these results are so straightforward, it seems clear that the original hypothesis was confirmed. However, Latané and Darley could not be sure that the results were truly meaningful until they determined whether the results represented a **significant outcome.** Through various statistical analyses—discussed further in the Appendix at the end of this book—researchers can determine whether a numeric difference is meaningful or trivial. Only when differences between groups are large enough that statistical tests show them to be significant is it possible for researchers to confirm a hypothesis (Estes, 1997; Cwikel, Behar, & Rabson-Hare, 2000).

significant outcome: Meaningful results that make it possible for researchers to feel confident that they have confirmed their hypotheses.

Figure 2-4 The results of the Latané and Darley experiment showed that as the size of the group witnessing an emergency increased, helping behavior decreased.

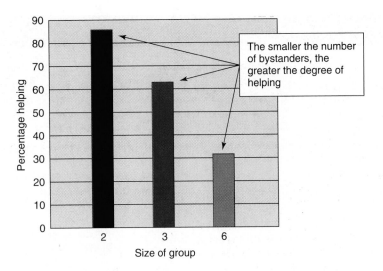

The smaller the number of bystanders, the greater the degree of helping

Moving Beyond the Study

The Latané and Darley study contains all the elements of an experiment: an independent variable, a dependent variable, random assignment to conditions, and multiple experimental groups. Consequently, we can say with some confidence that group size *caused* changes in the degree of helping behavior.

Of course, one experiment alone does not forever resolve the question of bystander intervention in emergencies. Psychologists require that findings be **replicated,** or repeated, sometimes using other procedures, in other settings, with other groups of participants, before full confidence can be placed in the validity of any single experiment. A procedure called *meta-analysis* permits psychologists to combine the results of many separate studies into one overall conclusion (Hunt, 1999).

In addition to replicating experimental results, psychologists need to test the limitations of their theories and hypotheses in order to determine under which specific circumstances they do and do not apply. It seems unlikely, for instance, that increasing the number of bystanders *always* results in less helping. Therefore it is critical to understand the conditions in which exceptions to this general rule occur. For example, we might speculate that in cases in which onlookers believe that a victim's difficulties could later affect them in some way, they will be more willing to help (Aronson, 1988). Testing this hypothesis (for which, in fact, there is some support) requires additional experimentation.

Like any science, then, psychology increases our understanding in small, incremental steps, with each step building upon previous work. The work is carried out on many fronts and involves many people—individuals such as Mary Garrett, who is doing research on AIDS as she studies to become a psychologist (see the *Psychology at Work* box on page 44).

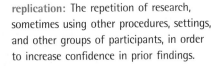

replication: The repetition of research, sometimes using other procedures, settings, and other groups of participants, in order to increase confidence in prior findings.

Evaluate

1. An experimenter is interested in studying the relationship between hunger and aggression. He defines aggression as the number of times a participant will hit a punching bag. What is the process of defining this variable called?

2. Match the following forms of research to their definition:

   1. Archival research

   2. Naturalistic observation

   3. Survey research

   4. Case study

   a. Directly asking a sample of people questions about their behavior (3)

   b. Examining existing records to test a hypothesis (1)

   c. Looking at behavior in its true setting without intervening in the setting (2)

   d. In-depth investigation of a person or small group (4)

Rethink

1. Can you describe how a researcher might use naturalistic observation, case study methods, and survey research to investigate gender differences in aggressive behavior at the workplace? First state a hypothesis, then describe your research approaches. What positive and negative features does each method have?

3. Match each of the following research methods with a problem basic to it:

1. Archival research

2. Naturalistic observation

3. Survey research

4. Case study

a. Might not be able to generalize to the population at large. (4)

b. People's behavior could change if they know they are being watched. (2)

c. The data might not exist or might be unusable. (1)

d. People might lie in order to present a good image. (3)

4. A friend tells you,"Anxiety about speaking in public and performance are negatively correlated. Therefore, high anxiety must cause low performance." Is this statement true or false, and why? False

5. A psychologist wants to study the effect of attractiveness on willingness to help a person with a math problem. Attractiveness would be the _independent_ variable, while amount of helping would be the _dependent_ variable.

6. The group in an experiment that receives no treatment is called the _control_ group.

Answers to Evaluate Questions

1. Operationalization; 2. 1. b; 2. c; 3. a; 4. d; 3. 1. c; 2. b; 3. d; 4. a; 4. False. Correlation does not imply causation. Just because two variables are related does not mean that one causes the other. Poor performance might cause people to become more anxious, or a third variable might cause both of these effects. 5. independent; dependent; 6. control

2. Tobacco companies have frequently asserted that no experiment has ever proved that tobacco use causes cancer. Can you explain this claim in terms of the research procedures and designs discussed in this chapter? What sort of research would establish a cause-and-effect relationship between tobacco use and cancer? Is such a research study possible?

Prepare

What major issues underlie the process of conducting research?

Organize

Research Challenges

The Ethics of Research

Should Animals Be Used in Research?

Threats to Experiments

Research Challenges: Exploring the Process

It is probably apparent by now that there are few simple formulas psychologists can follow as they carry out research. They must make choices about the type of study to conduct, the measures to take, and the most effective way to analyze the results. Even after they make these essential decisions, they must still consider several critical issues. We turn first to the most fundamental of these issues: ethics.

The Ethics of Research

Put yourself in the place of one of the participants in the Latané and Darley experiment. How would you feel when you learned that the person you thought was having a seizure was, in reality, a paid accomplice of the experimenter?

Although you might at first experience relief that there had been no real emergency, you might also feel some resentment that you had been deceived by the experimenter. And you might also experience concern that you had been placed in an unusual situation—one that might have dealt a blow to your self-esteem, depending on how you had behaved.

Most psychologists argue that the use of deception is sometimes necessary to prevent participants from being influenced by what they think the study's true purpose is. (If you knew that Latané and Darley were actually studying your helping behavior, wouldn't you automatically have been tempted to intervene in the emergency?) To avoid such outcomes, researchers must occasionally use deception.

Nonetheless, because research has the potential to violate the rights of participants, psychologists are expected to adhere to a strict set of ethical guidelines aimed at protecting participants (American Psychological Association [APA], 1992). These guidelines advocate the following:

- Protection of participants from physical and mental harm
- The right of participants to privacy regarding their behavior
- The assurance that participation in research is completely voluntary
- The necessity of informing participants about the nature of procedures prior to their participation in the experiment

PsychLink

Ethics in research
www.mhhe.com/
feldmanup6-02links

Psychology at Work

Mary Garrett

San Francisco State College, San Francisco, California

Education: A.A., City College of San Francisco; B.A., San Francisco State College; enrolled in M.A. program, San Francisco State College

Home: San Francisco, California

Mary Garrett

Most high school students have only a vague idea of what they will do with their lives, but for Mary Garrett there was absolutely no question what she wanted: She yearned to be a psychologist.

In her forties, Garrett finally began to make her dream come true. After a gap of many years in her education, she enrolled in a graduate program in research psychology at San Francisco State College.

> "I've always been interested in people, in people's behavior, and why they do what they do."

"I've always been interested in people, in people's behavior, and why they do what they do," she says. "Even when I was in high school I wanted to be a psychologist, and now I plan to teach and do research in psychology at the college level."

As part of her graduate studies, Garrett is working on an innovative and potentially significant study of African American women with the AIDS virus. "The study is intended to increase our knowledge about the nature of the effects of stress on the mental and physical health of African American women with HIV and AIDS, and the coping processes that mediate these effects, in order to design effective psychosocial intervention," she says.

The impetus for the study was a similar project conducted by one of her professors. He had done an initial study on coping with AIDS, using only men in his sample. Garrett became interested in comparing how women and men deal with the disease.

"I want to find out if the coping strategies and processes are different for women. Women do have different stressors than men, such as being single mothers or being a black female in this society," she says.

The research, according to Garrett, will involve three phases: an initial exploratory study, in-depth interviews, and a written questionnaire. She attributes much of her ability to design the study to her undergraduate training as

> "All of my undergraduate work in psychology was instrumental in preparing for this current study."

a psychology major. "It was in my methods class that I learned how to develop and give surveys. I'll also be using material I've learned from classes in statistics, methods, and aging and adult development," Garrett adds. "All of my undergraduate work in psychology was instrumental in preparing for this current study."

Although the guidelines do allow the use of deception, all experiments involving deception must be reviewed by an independent panel before their use—as must all research that uses human beings as participants (Rosnow et al., 1993; Rosenthal, 1994; Fisher & Fyrberg, 1994; Gurman, 1994; Bersoff, 1995; Kimmel, 1996).

One of the key ethical principles followed by psychologists is **informed consent.** Before participating in an experiment, participants must sign a document affirming that they have been told the basic outlines of the study and are aware of what their participation will involve, what risks the experiment may hold, and the fact that their participation is purely voluntary and may be terminated at any time. Furthermore, following participation in a study, participants must be given a *debriefing* in which they receive an explanation for the study and the procedures involved. The only time informed consent and a debriefing can be eliminated is in experiments in which the risks are minimal, as in a purely observational study on a street corner or in another public location (Koocher & Keith-Spiegel, 1998; Chastain & Landrum, 1999).

informed consent: A document signed by participants affirming that they have been told the basic outlines of a research study and are aware of what their participation will involve.

EXPLORING DIVERSITY

Choosing Participants Who Represent the Scope of Human Behavior

When Latané and Darley, both college professors, decided who should be used as participants in their experiment, they turned to the people who were most readily accessible to them: college students. In fact, college students are used so frequently in experiments that psychology has been called—somewhat contemptuously—the "science of the behavior of the college sophomore" (Rubenstein, 1982).

While readily available and widely used as research subjects, college students may not represent the population at large. What are some advantages and drawbacks of using college students as subjects?

The use of college students as participants has both advantages and drawbacks. The big benefit is their availability. Because most research occurs in university settings, college students are readily available. Typically, they participate for either extra course credit or a relatively small monetary payment, making the cost to the researcher minimal.

The problem with relying on college students for participants is that they might not adequately represent the general population. College students tend to be younger and better educated than a significant percentage of the rest of the population of the United States. Moreover, their attitudes are likely to be less well formed, and they are apt to be more susceptible than older adults to social pressures from authority figures and peers (Sears, 1986).

Furthermore, college students are disproportionately white and middle class. In fact, even research that does not employ college students tends to use white, middle-class participants. In particular, the use of African Americans, Latinos, Asians, and other minorities as participants is low (Graham, 1992; Guthrie, 1998).

When a science that purports to explain human behavior in general disregards a significant proportion of the population in drawing conclusions, something is amiss. Consequently, psychological researchers have become increasingly sensitive to the importance of using participants who are fully representative of the general population (Rogler, 1999).

Researchers are increasingly sensitive to the importance of using participants in experiments who represent the general population.

Research involving animals is controversial, but, when conducted within ethical guidelines, yields significant benefits for humans.

Should Animals Be Used in Research?

Like those who work with humans, researchers who use animals in experiments have their own set of exacting guidelines to ensure that the animals do not suffer. Specifically, researchers must make every effort to minimize discomfort, illness, and pain, and procedures subjecting animals to distress may be used only when an alternative procedure is unavailable and when the research is justified by its prospective value. Moreover, there are federal regulations specifying how animals are to be housed, fed, and maintained. Not only must researchers strive to avoid physical discomfort in the animals, they are also required to promote the *psychological* well-being of some species of animals—such as primates—that are used in research (Novak & Petto, 1991; APA, 1993).

Why should animals be used for research in the first place? Is it really possible to learn about human behavior from the results of research employing rats, gerbils, and pigeons? The answer is that psychological research that does employ animals has a different focus and is designed to answer different questions than research that uses humans. For example, the shorter life span of animals (rats live an average of two years) allows researchers to learn about the effects of aging in a much more rapid time frame than if they studied aging using human participants. Moreover, the very complexity of human beings can obscure information about fundamental phenomena that can be more plainly identified in animals. Finally, some studies require large numbers of participants who share similar backgrounds or who have been exposed to particular environments—conditions that could not practically be met with human beings (Gallagher & Rapp, 1997; Mukerjee, 1997).

Research using animals has provided psychologists with information that has profoundly benefited humans. For instance, animal research furnished the keys to detecting eye disorders in children early enough to prevent permanent damage, communicating more effectively with severely retarded children, and reducing chronic pain in people, to name just a few results (APA, 1988; Botting & Morrison, 1997).

Despite the value of research that uses animals as participants, their use in psychological research is highly controversial. For example, some critics believe that animals have rights no less significant than those of humans, and that because animals are unable to consent to participation in studies, their use is unethical. Others object to the use of animals on methodological grounds, saying it is impossible to generalize from findings on nonhuman species to humans.

Because the issues involve complex moral and philosophical concerns, they are not easily resolved. As a consequence, review panels, which must approve all research before it is carried out, are particularly careful to ensure that research involving animals is conducted ethically (Plous, 1996a, 1996b; Barnard & Kaufman, 1997).

 **PsychLink**

Ethical research using animals
www.mhhe.com/
feldmanup6-02links

Threats to Experiments: Experimenter and Participant Expectations

Even the best-laid experimental plans are susceptible to **experimental bias**—factors that distort how the independent variable affects the dependent variable in an experiment. One of the most common forms of experimental bias is *experimenter expectations:* An experimenter unintentionally transmits cues to participants about the way they are expected to behave in a given experimental condition. The danger is that these expectations will bring about an "appropriate" behavior—one that might not have otherwise occurred (Blanck, 1993; Rosnow & Rosenthal, 1994, 1997).

A related problem is *participant expectations* about appropriate behavior. If you have ever been a participant in an experiment, you know that you quickly develop guesses about what is expected of you. In fact, it is typical for people to develop their own hypotheses about what the experimenter hopes to learn from the study. If participants form their own hypotheses, it might no longer be the experimental manipulation, but rather the participant's expectations, producing an effect.

To guard against participant expectations biasing the results of an experiment, the experimenter may try to disguise the true purpose of the experiment. Participants who do not know that helping behavior is being studied, for example, are more apt to act in a "natural" way than they would if they knew.

In some experiments it is impossible to hide the actual purpose of the research. In cases such as these, other techniques are available. For example, suppose you were interested in testing the ability of a new drug to alleviate the symptoms of severe depression. If you simply gave the drug to half your participants and not to the other half, participants given the drug might report feeling less depressed merely because they knew they were getting a drug. Similarly, the participants who got nothing might report feeling no better because they knew that they were in a no-treatment control group.

To solve this problem, psychologists typically use a procedure in which all participants receive a treatment, but those in the control group receive only a **placebo,** a false treatment, such as a pill, "drug," or other substance, that has no significant chemical properties or active ingredient. Because members of both groups are kept in the dark as to whether they are getting a real or a false treatment, any differences that are found can be attributed to the quality of the drug and not to the possible psychological effects of being administered a pill or other substance (Kirsch, 1999; Enserink, 1999, 2000a).

But there is still one more safeguard that a careful researcher must apply in an experiment such as this. To overcome the possibility that experimenter expectations will affect the participant, the person who administers the drug shouldn't know whether it is actually the true drug or the placebo. By keeping both the participant and the experimenter who interacts with the participant "blind" as to the nature of the drug that is being administered, researchers can more accurately assess the effects of the drug. This method is known as the *double-blind procedure*.

experimental bias: Factors that distort how the independent variable affects the dependent variable in an experiment.

placebo: A false treatment, such as a pill, "drug," or other substance, that has no significant chemical properties or active ingredient.

BECOMING AN INFORMED CONSUMER OF PSYCHOLOGY

Thinking Critically About Research

If you were about to purchase an automobile, it is unlikely that you would stop at the nearest car dealership and drive off with the first car a salesperson recommended. Instead, you would probably mull over the purchase, read about automobiles, consider the alternatives, talk to others about their experiences, and ultimately put in a fair amount of thought before you made such a major purchase.

In contrast, many of us are considerably less conscientious when we expend our intellectual, rather than financial, assets. People often jump to conclusions on the basis of incomplete and inaccurate information, and only rarely do they take the time to critically evaluate the research and data to which they are exposed.

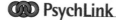 **PsychLink**

Links to ongoing research
www.mhhe.com/
feldmanup6-02links

Because the field of psychology is based on an accumulated body of research, it is crucial for psychologists to scrutinize thoroughly the methods, results, and claims of researchers. Yet it is not just psychologists who need to know how to evaluate research critically; all of us are constantly exposed to the claims of others. Knowing how to approach research and data can be helpful in areas far beyond the realm of psychology.

Several basic questions can help us sort through what is valid and what is not. Among the most important questions to ask are the following:

- *What was the purpose of the research?* Research studies should evolve from a clearly specified theory. Furthermore, we must take into account the specific hypothesis that is being tested. Unless we know what hypothesis is being examined, it is not possible to judge how successful a study has been.
- *How well was the study conducted?* Consider who the participants were, how many were involved, what methods were employed, and what problems in collecting the data the researcher encountered. There are important differences, for example, between a case study that reports the anecdotes of a handful of respondents and a survey that collects data from several thousand people.
- *Are the results presented fairly?* It is necessary to assess statements based on the actual data they reflect and their logic. For instance, when the manufacturer of car X boasts that "no other car a has a better safety record than car X," this does not mean that car X is safer than every other car. It just means that no other car has been proved safer, though many other cars could be just as safe as car X. Expressed in the latter fashion, the finding doesn't seem worth bragging about.

These three basic questions can help you assess the validity of research findings you come across—both within and outside the field of psychology. The more you know how to evaluate research in general, the better you will be able to assess what the field of psychology has to offer.

Evaluate

1. Ethical research begins with the concept of informed consent. Before signing up to participate in an experiment, participants should be informed of
   a. The procedure of the study, stated generally
   b. The risks that may be involved
   c. Their right to withdraw at any time
   d. All of the above
2. List three benefits of using animals in psychological research.
3. Deception is one means experimenters can use to try to eliminate participants' expectations. True or false?
4. A procedure in which neither participants nor experimenter knows whether participants are or are not receiving an actual treatment is known as the ___double blind___ procedure.
5. According to a report, a study has shown that men differ from women in their preference for ice cream flavors. This study was based on a sample of 2 men and 3 women. What might be wrong with this study? *The number of person.*

Rethink

1. A pollster studies people's attitudes toward welfare programs by circulating a questionnaire via the Internet. Is this study likely to accurately reflect the views of the general population? Why or why not?
2. A researcher strongly believes that college professors tend to show female students less attention and respect in the classroom than they show male students. She sets up an experimental study involving observation of classrooms in different conditions. In explaining the study to the professors and students who will participate, what steps should the researcher take to eliminate experimental bias based on both experimenter expectations and participant expectations?

Answers to Evaluate Questions

1. d; 2. (1) We can study some phenomena in animals more easily than we can in people, because with animal subjects we have greater control over environmental and genetic factors. (2) Large numbers of similar participants can be easily obtained. (3) We can look at generational effects much more easily in animals, because of their shorter life span, than we can with people. 3. True; 4. double-blind; 5. There are far too few participants. Without a larger sample, no valid conclusions can be drawn about ice cream preferences based on gender.

What is the scientific method, and how do psychologists use theory and research to answer questions of interest?

- The scientific method is an approach psychologists use to understand the unknown. It consists of three steps: identifying questions of interest, formulating an explanation, and carrying out research that is designed to support the explanation. (p. 30)
- Research in psychology is guided by theories (broad explanations and predictions of phenomena of interest) and hypotheses (derivations of theories that are predictions stated in a way that allows them to be tested). (p. 31)

What are the different research methods employed by psychologists?

- Archival research uses existing records, such as old newspapers or other documents, to test a hypothesis. In naturalistic observation, the investigator acts mainly as an observer, making no change in a naturally occurring situation. In survey research, people are asked a series of questions about their behavior, thoughts, or attitudes. The case study is an in-depth interview and examination of one person. (p. 33)
- These methods rely on correlational techniques, which describe associations between various variables but cannot determine cause-and-effect relationships. (p. 36)

How do psychologists establish cause-and-effect relationships in research studies?

- In a formal experiment, the relationship between variables is investigated by deliberately producing a change—called the experimental manipulation—in one of them and observing changes in the other. (p. 37)
- For a hypothesis to be tested, it must be operationalized: A researcher must translate the abstract concepts of the hypothesis into the actual procedures used in the study. (p. 37)
- In an experiment, at least two groups must be compared with each other to assess cause-and-effect relationships. The group receiving the treatment (the special procedure devised by the experimenter) is the experimental group; the second group (which receives no treatment) is the control group. There also may be multiple experimental groups; each of which is subjected to a different procedure and then compared with the others. (p. 38)
- The variable that experimenters manipulate is the independent variable. The variable that they measure and expect to change as a result of manipulation of the independent variable is called the dependent variable. (p. 39)
- In a formal experiment, participants must be assigned to treatment conditions randomly so that participant characteristics are evenly distributed across the different conditions. (p. 39)

What major issues underlie the process of conducting research?

- One of the key ethical principles followed by psychologists is that of informed consent. Participants must be informed, prior to participation, about the basic outline of the experiment and the risks and potential benefits of their participation. (p. 44)
- Although the use of college students as participants has the advantage of easy availability, there are drawbacks too. For instance, students do not necessarily represent the population as a whole. The use of animals as participants also has costs in terms of generalizability, although the benefits of using animals in research have been profound. (p. 44)

- Experiments are subject to a number of threats, or biases. Experimenter expectations can produce bias when an experimenter unintentionally transmits cues to participants about her or his expectations regarding their behavior in a given experimental condition. Participant expectations can also bias an experiment. To help eliminate bias, researchers use placebos and double-blind procedures. (p. 47)

Key Terms and Concepts

scientific method (p. 31)
theories (p. 31)
hypothesis (p. 32)
operationalization (p. 33)
archival research (p. 33)
naturalistic observation (p. 34)
survey research (p. 34)
case study (p. 34)
variables (p. 36)
correlational research (p. 36)
experiment (p. 37)
experimental manipulation (p. 38)

treatment (p. 38)
experimental group (p. 38)
control group (p. 38)
independent variable (p. 39)
dependent variable (p. 39)
random assignment to condition (p. 39)
significant outcome (p. 41)
replication (p. 42)
informed consent (p. 44)
experimental bias (p. 47)
placebo (p. 47)

Psychology on the Web

1. Identify a product or service that is advertised on the Internet using broad, unspecific claims, such as a weight loss formula or body-building method. Find at least two advertisements on the Internet for that product or service and evaluate the claims they make according to the principles discussed in this chapter. Summarize the evidence that is presented for those claims, and describe a method that might be used to confirm the claims using actual research.

2. Find a website that focuses on an important social issue (e.g., urban violence, gender differences in hiring or promotion, poverty) and locate descriptions of a research study about the issue. Evaluate the study by identifying the hypotheses that were tested, the methods used to test them, and the validity of the results reported.

Epilogue

In this chapter we have discussed ways in which psychologists seek to understand phenomena and answer questions of interest. We've examined the scientific method and its reliance on posing good questions, creating productive theories, and crafting testable hypotheses. We have also looked at the basic methods psychologists use to conduct research studies and compared correlational methods and experimental methods. Finally, we've explored some of the major challenges that psychologists have to deal with when conducting research, including ethical considerations, the use of animals in research, and potential bias.

Before we turn to the biology of behavior, return for a moment to the opening prologue of this chapter. Consider the case of Abner Louima, who was attacked in a police station, and reflect on the following questions in light of what you now know about conducting psychological research.

1. Suppose that, instead of studying helping behavior in the Abner Louima case, you were interested in studying aggressive behavior among police officers. Can you formulate a theory that would provide an explanation for the behavior of the police officers who participated in the beating?

2. What hypotheses (testable predictions) can you construct to test your theory?

3. Can you design a *correlational* study to test one of your hypotheses? Which correlational method(s) (archival research, naturalistic observation, survey research, case study) would you use in your study?

4. Can you design an *experimental* study to test the same or another hypothesis? Describe the experiment, including the participants, the experimental manipulation, the treatment, and the independent and dependent variables.

Preview

For additional quizzing and a variety of interactive resources, visit the Understanding Psychology Online Learning Center at www.mhhe.com/feldmanup6

Chapter Three

The Biology Underlying Behavior

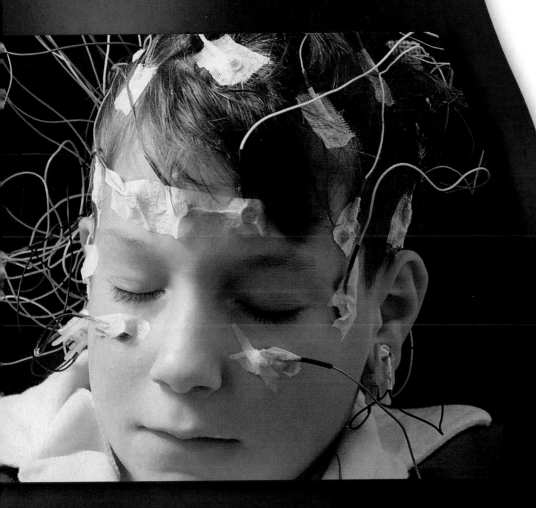

Prologue: The Fight of His Life

Looking Ahead

Neurons: The Elements of Behavior

The Structure of the Neuron

Firing the Neuron

Where Neurons Meet: Bridging the Gap

Neurotransmitters: Multitalented Chemical Couriers

The Nervous System

Central and Peripheral Nervous Systems

The Evolutionary Foundations of the Nervous System

Behavioral Genetics

The Brain

Studying the Brain's Structure and Functions: Spying on the Brain

Applying Psychology in the 21st Century: Mind over Cursor: Using Brain Waves to Overcome Physical Limitations

The Central Core: Our "Old Brain"

The Limbic System: Beyond the Central Core

The Cerebral Cortex: Our "New Brain"

Mending the Brain

The Specialization of the Hemispheres: Two Brains or One?

Exploring Diversity: Human Diversity and the Brain

The Split Brain: Exploring the Two Hemispheres

The Endocrine System: Of Chemicals and Glands

Becoming an Informed Consumer of Psychology: Learning to Control Your Heart—and Mind— Through Biofeedback

Looking Back

Key Terms and Concepts

Psychology on the Web

OLC Preview

Epilogue

Michael J. Fox is free for the moment of the worst symptoms of Parkinson's, following an operation called a thalamotomy.

Prologue

The Fight of His Life

Michael J. Fox simply could not get out of the limousine. He and actress wife Tracy Pollan had just pulled up to the Beverly Hilton for the Golden Globe Awards last January, and the actor realized he was in serious trouble. Outside, reporters and photographers stood poised to greet the star of ABC's hit sitcom *Spin City*, but Fox, 37, was in no shape to greet them. Like so many times before, his left arm and leg were shaking uncontrollably. Behind the limo's darkened windows, Pollan began squeezing Fox's hand and massaging his foot. But she could provide only temporary relief. For the tremors to fully subside, the couple would have to wait for his medication to kick in. Fox asked the driver to circle the block once. Then a second time. And a third. "He probably thought I was nuts," says Fox with a faint smile. "But I just couldn't get out of the car and let my arm go, or mumble, or shuffle." (Schneider & Gold, 1998, p. 136)

Looking Ahead

Fox's symptoms were produced by Parkinson's disease, a disorder marked by varying degrees of muscular rigidity and shaking. Parkinson's afflicts about a million people in the United States alone (including former Attorney General Janet Reno and Muhammad Ali), strikes for no known reason, and typically progresses with age.

Happily, though, Fox is free for the moment of the worst symptoms of the disease, following a painstaking four-hour operation called a thalamotomy. In this procedure, surgeons bored a hole into Fox's brain and located and destroyed misfiring brain cells.

The ability of surgeons to identify damaged portions of the brain and carry out repairs is little short of miraculous. But the greater miracle is the brain itself. As we shall see in this chapter, the brain, an organ roughly half the size of a loaf of bread, controls our behavior through every waking and sleeping moment. The brain and the nerves that extend throughout the body constitute the human nervous system. Our movements, thoughts, hopes, aspirations, dreams—our very awareness that we are human—are all intimately related to this system.

Because of the importance of the nervous system in controlling behavior, and because humans at their most basic level are biological beings, psychologists and researchers from other fields as diverse as computer science, zoology, and medicine have paid special attention to the biological underpinnings of behavior. These experts are collectively called *neuroscientists* (Beatty, 2000).

Psychologists who specialize in considering the ways in which biological structures and functions of the body affect behavior are known as **biopsychologists** (or **behavioral neuroscientists**). These specialists seek to answer questions such as these: What are the bases for voluntary and involuntary functioning of the body? How are messages communicated to and from the brain to other parts of the body? What is the physical structure of the brain, and how does this structure affect behavior? Can the causes of psychological disorders be traced to biological factors, and how can such disorders be treated?

This chapter addresses such questions, focusing on the biological structures of the body that are of interest to biopsychologists. Initially, we discuss nerve cells, called neurons, which allow messages to travel through the brain and body; we learn that through their growing knowledge of neurons and the nervous system, psychologists are increasing their understanding of human behavior and are uncovering important clues in their efforts to cure certain kinds of diseases. Then we turn to the structure and main divisions of the nervous system, explaining how they work to control voluntary and involuntary behaviors. In the process we also examine how the various parts of the nervous system operate together in emergency situations to produce lifesaving responses to danger.

Next, we consider the brain itself, examining its major structures and how these affect behavior. We see how the brain controls movement, our senses, and our thought processes. We also consider the fascinating notion that the two halves of the brain might have different specialties and strengths. Finally, we examine the chemical messenger system of the body, the endocrine system.

As we discuss these biological processes, it is important to keep in mind the rationale for doing so: Our understanding of human behavior cannot be complete without knowledge of the fundamentals of the brain and the rest of the nervous system. As we'll see in future chapters, biological factors have an important impact on our sensory experiences, states of consciousness, motivation and emotion, development throughout the life span, and physical and psychological health. Advances in biopsychology have paved the way for the creation of drugs and other treatments for psychological and physical disorders. In short, we cannot understand behavior—the moods, motivations, goals, and desires that are central to the human condition—without an understanding of our biological makeup.

biopsychologists (or behavioral neuroscientists): Psychologists who specialize in considering the ways in which biological structures and functions of the body affect behavior

 **PsychLink**

Description of neuropsychology
www.mhhe.com/
feldmanup6-03links

Neurons: The Elements of Behavior

If you have ever watched the precision with which a well-trained athlete or dancer executes a performance, you may have marveled at the complexity—and wondrous abilities—of the human body. But even the most everyday tasks, such as picking up a pencil, writing, and speaking, require a sophisticated sequence of events that is itself truly impressive. For instance, the difference between saying the words *dime* and *time* rests primarily on whether the vocal cords are relaxed or tense during a period lasting no more than one one-hundredth of a second. Yet it is a distinction that almost everyone can make with ease.

The nervous system provides the pathways that permit us to carry out such precise activities. To understand how it is able to exert such exacting control over our bodies, we must begin by examining neurons, the most basic parts of the nervous system, and considering how nerve impulses are transmitted throughout the brain and body.

Prepare

Why do psychologists study the brain and nervous system?

What are the basic elements of the nervous system?

How does the nervous system communicate electrical and chemical messages from one part to another?

Organize

Neurons

   The Structure of the Neuron

   Firing the Neuron

   Where Neurons Meet

   Neurotransmitters

The Structure of the Neuron

The ability to play the piano, drive a car, or hit a tennis ball depends, at one level, merely on muscle coordination. But if we consider *how* the muscles involved in such activities are activated, we see that there are more fundamental processes involved. It is necessary for the body to provide messages to the muscles and to coordinate those messages, for the muscles to be able to produce the complex movements that characterize successful physical activity.

Such messages—as well as those that enable us to think, remember, and experience emotion—are passed through specialized cells called neurons. **Neurons,** or nerve cells, are the basic elements of the nervous system. Their quantity is staggering—perhaps as many as one *trillion* neurons throughout the body are involved in the control of behavior. Although there are several types of neurons, they all have a similar basic structure, as illustrated in Figure 3-1. Like all cells in the body, neurons have a cell body, containing a nucleus. The nucleus incorporates the inherited material that establishes how the cell will function. Neurons are physically held in place by *glial cells,* which provide nourishment and insulate them (Bear, Connors, & Paradiso, 2000).

In contrast to most other cells, however, neurons have a distinctive feature: the ability to communicate with other cells and transmit information, sometimes across relatively long distances. As you can see in Figure 3-1, neurons have clusters of fibers called **dendrites** at one end. These fibers, which look like the twisted branches of a tree, receive messages from other neurons. At the opposite end, neurons have a long, slim, tubelike extension called an **axon,** the part of the neuron that carries messages destined for other neurons. The axon is considerably longer than the rest of the neuron. Although most axons are several millimeters in length, some can be as long as three feet. Axons end in small bulges called **terminal buttons** that send messages to other neurons.

The messages that travel through the neuron are purely electrical in nature. Although there are exceptions, these electrical messages generally move across neurons as if they were traveling on a one-way street. They follow a route that begins with the dendrites, continues into the cell body, and leads ultimately down the tubelike extension, the axon. Dendrites, then, *d*etect messages from other neurons; *a*xons carry signals *a*way from the cell body.

To prevent messages from short-circuiting one another, axons must be insulated in some fashion (just as electrical wires must be insulated). In most axons, this is done with a **myelin sheath,** a protective coating of specialized fat and protein cells that wrap themselves around the axon.

The myelin sheath also serves to increase the velocity with which the electrical impulses travel through the axons. Those axons that carry the most important and most urgently required information have the greatest concentrations of myelin. If your hand

neurons: Nerve cells, the basic elements of the nervous system

dendrites: A cluster of fibers at one end of a neuron that receive messages from other neurons

axon: The part of the neuron that carries messages destined for other neurons

terminal buttons: Small bulges at the end of axons that send messages to other neurons

myelin sheath: Specialized cells of fat and protein that wrap themselves around the axon, providing a protective coating

Figure 3-1 The primary components of the specialized cell called the neuron, the basic element of the nervous system (Van de Graaff, 2000). What advantages does the treelike structure of the neuron provide?

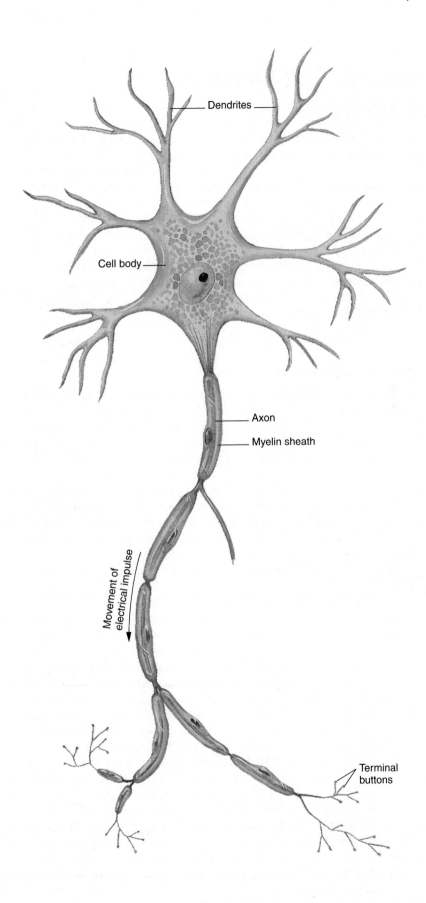

Dendrites

Cell body

Axon

Myelin sheath

Movement of electrical impulse

Terminal buttons

touches a painfully hot stove, for example, the information regarding the pain is passed through axons in the hand and arm that have a relatively thick coating of myelin, speeding the message of pain to the brain. In certain diseases, such as multiple sclerosis, the myelin sheath surrounding the axon deteriorates, exposing parts of the axon that are normally covered. This short-circuits messages between the brain and muscles and results in symptoms such as the inability to walk, vision difficulties, and general muscle impairment.

Firing the Neuron

Like a gun, neurons either fire or don't fire; there is no in-between stage, just as pulling harder on a gun trigger doesn't make the bullet travel faster or move more surely. Similarly, neurons follow an **all-or-none law:** they are either on or off, with nothing in between the on or off state. Once triggered beyond a certain point, a neuron fires.

Before a neuron is triggered—that is, when it is in a **resting state**—it has a negative electrical charge of about −70 millivolts (a millivolt is one one-thousandth of a volt). This charge is caused by the presence of more negatively charged ions (a type of molecule) within the neuron than outside it. You might think of the neuron in terms of a miniature car battery, with the inside of the neuron representing the negative pole and the outside of the neuron the positive pole.

However, when a message arrives, the cell walls in the neuron allow positively charged ions to rush in, at rates as high as 100 million ions per second. The sudden arrival of these positive ions causes the charge within that part of the cell to change momentarily from negative to positive. When the charge reaches a critical level, the "trigger" is pulled, and an electrical nerve impulse, known as an **action potential,** travels down the axon of the neuron (see Figure 3-2).

The action potential moves from one end of the axon to the other like a flame moving across a fuse toward an explosive. As the impulse travels along the axon, the movement of ions causes a sequential change in charge from negative to positive (see Figure 3-3). After the passage of the impulse, positive ions are pumped out of the axon, and the neuron charge returns to negative.

Just after an action potential has passed, the neuron cannot fire again immediately, no matter how much stimulation it receives. It is as if the gun has to be painstakingly reloaded after each shot. There then follows a period in which, though it is possible for the

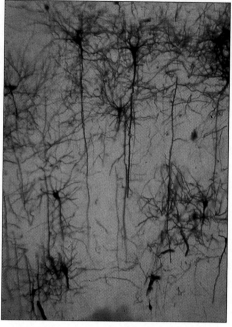

Taken with the aid of an electron microscope, this photograph shows cell bodies, dendrites, and axons in a cluster of neurons.

all-or-none law: The rule that neurons are either on or off

resting state: The state in which there is a negative electrical charge of about −70 millivolts within the neuron

action potential: An electric nerve impulse that travels through a neuron when it is set off by a "trigger," changing the neuron's charge from negative to positive

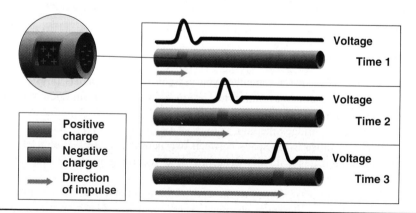

Figure 3–2 Movement of an action potential across an axon. Just prior to time 1, positively charged ions enter the cell walls, changing the charge within that part of the cell from negative to positive. The action potential is thus triggered, traveling down the axon, as illustrated in the changes occurring from Time 1 to Time 3 (from top to bottom in this drawing). Following the passage of the action potential, positive ions are pumped out of the axon, restoring its charge to negative. The change in voltage illustrated at the top of the axon can be seen in greater detail in Figure 3-3 on page 58 (Stevens, 1979).

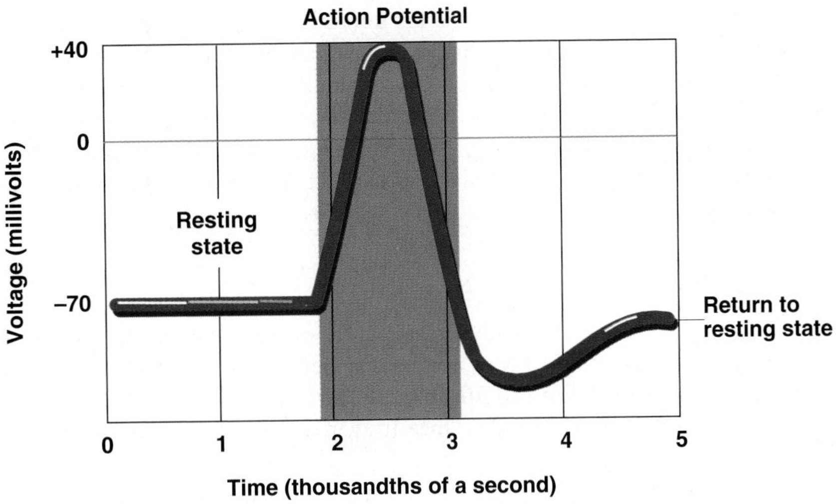

58

Figure 3-3 Changes in the electrical charge of a neuron during the passage of an action potential. In its normal resting state, a neuron has a negative charge of around −70 millivolts. When an action potential is triggered, however, the cell charge becomes positive, increasing to about +40 millivolts. Following the passage of the action potential, the charge becomes even more negative than it is in its typical state. It is not until the charge returns to its resting state that the neuron will be fully ready to be triggered once again.

Action Potential

(Graph) Voltage (millivolts) plotted against Time (thousandths of a second). Y-axis values: +40, 0, −70. Labels: "Resting state", "Return to resting state". X-axis: 0, 1, 2, 3, 4, 5. X-axis label: **Time (thousandths of a second)**

PsychLink

The Myelin Project
www.mhhe.com/
feldmanup6–03links

synapse: The space between two neurons where the axon of a sending neuron communicates with the dendrites of a receiving neuron using chemical messages

neurotransmitters: Chemicals that carry messages across the synapse to the dendrite (and sometimes the cell body) of a receiver neuron

PsychLink

All about synapses
www.mhhe.com/
feldmanup6–03links

neuron to fire, a stronger stimulus is needed than would be needed if the neuron had reached its normal resting state. Eventually, though, the neuron is ready to be fired once again.

These complex events can occur at dizzying speeds, although there is great variation among different neurons. The particular speed at which an action potential travels along an axon is determined by the axon's size and the thickness of its myelin sheath. Axons with small diameters carry impulses at about 2 miles per hour; longer and thicker ones can average speeds of more than 225 miles per hour.

Neurons differ not only in terms of how quickly an impulse moves across the axon, but in their potential rate of firing. Some neurons have the potential to fire as many as a thousand times per second; others have a maximum potential rate that is much lower. The intensity of a stimulus that provokes a neuron determines how much of this potential rate is reached. A strong stimulus, such as a bright light or a loud sound, leads to a higher rate of firing than a less intense stimulus does. Thus, even though all impulses move at the same strength or speed across a particular axon—because of the all-or-none law—there is variation in the frequency of impulses, providing a mechanism by which we can distinguish the tickle of a feather from the weight of someone standing on our toe.

The structure, operation, and functions of the neuron illustrate how fundamental biological aspects of the body underlie several primary psychological processes. Our understanding of the way we sense, perceive, and learn about the world would be greatly restricted without the information about the neuron that biopsychologists and other researchers have acquired.

Where Neurons Meet: Bridging the Gap

If you've ever looked inside a computer, you've seen that each part is physically connected to another. In contrast, evolution has produced a neural transmission system that at some points has no need for a structural connection between its components. Instead, a chemical connection bridges the gap, known as a synapse, between two neurons (see Figure 3-4). The **synapse** is the space between two neurons where the axon of a sending neuron communicates with the dendrites of a receiving neuron using chemical messages.

When a nerve impulse comes to the end of the axon and reaches a terminal button, the terminal button releases a chemical courier called a neurotransmitter. **Neurotransmitters** are chemicals that carry messages across the synapse to the dendrite (and sometimes the cell body) of a receiver neuron. Like a boat that ferries passengers across a river, these chemical messengers move toward the shorelines of other neurons. The chemical mode of message transmission that occurs between neurons is strikingly different from the means by which communication occurs inside neurons. It is important

(a)

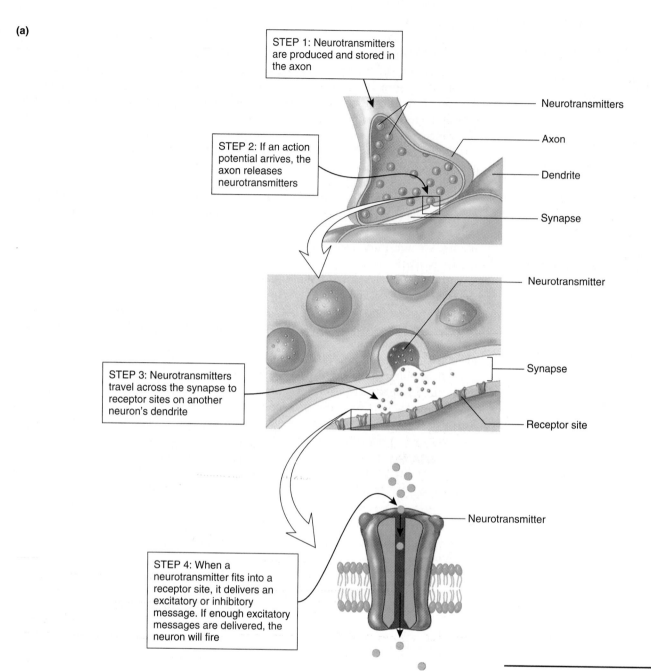

STEP 1: Neurotransmitters are produced and stored in the axon

Neurotransmitters

Axon

STEP 2: If an action potential arrives, the axon releases neurotransmitters

Dendrite

Synapse

Neurotransmitter

Synapse

STEP 3: Neurotransmitters travel across the synapse to receptor sites on another neuron's dendrite

Receptor site

Neurotransmitter

STEP 4: When a neurotransmitter fits into a receptor site, it delivers an excitatory or inhibitory message. If enough excitatory messages are delivered, the neuron will fire

(b)

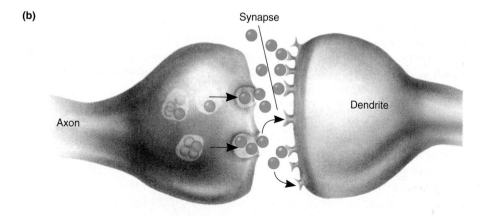

Synapse

Axon

Dendrite

Figure 3–4 *(a)* A synapse is the junction between an axon and a dendrite. The gap between the axon and the dendrite is bridged by chemicals called neurotransmitters (Mader, 2000). *(b)* Just as the pieces of a jigsaw puzzle can fit in only one specific location in a puzzle, each kind of neurotransmitter has a distinctive configuration that allows it to fit into a specific type of receptor cell (Johnson, 2000). Why is it advantageous for axons and dendrites to be linked by temporary chemical bridges rather than by the hard wiring typical of a radio connection or telephone hookup?

to remember, then, that although messages travel in electrical form *within* a neuron, they move *between* neurons through a chemical transmission system.

There are several types of neurotransmitters, and not all receiver neurons are capable of making use of the chemical message carried by a particular neurotransmitter. In the same way as a jigsaw puzzle piece can fit in only one specific location in a puzzle, so each kind of neurotransmitter has a distinctive configuration that allows it to fit into a specific type of receptor site on the receiving neuron (see Figure 3-4b). It is only when a neurotransmitter fits precisely into a receptor site that successful chemical communication is possible.

If a neurotransmitter does fit into a site on the receiving neuron, the chemical message it delivers is basically one of two types: excitatory or inhibitory. **Excitatory messages** make it more likely that a receiving neuron will fire and an action potential will travel down its axon. **Inhibitory messages,** in contrast, do just the opposite; they provide chemical information that prevents or decreases the likelihood that the receiving neuron will fire.

Because the dendrites of a neuron receive both excitatory and inhibitory messages simultaneously, the neuron must integrate the messages by using a kind of chemical calculator. If the concentration of excitatory messages is greater than the concentration of inhibitory ones, the neuron fires. On the other hand, if the inhibitory messages outweigh the excitatory ones, nothing happens, and the neuron remains in its resting state (Thomson, 1997; Miles, 2000).

If neurotransmitters remained at the site of the synapse, receptor neurons would be awash in a continual chemical bath, producing constant stimulation of the receptor neurons—and effective communication across the synapse would no longer be possible. To solve this problem, neurotransmitters are either deactivated by enzymes or—more frequently—reabsorbed by the terminal button in an example of chemical recycling called **reuptake.** Like a vacuum cleaner sucking up dust, neurons reabsorb the neurotransmitters that are now clogging the synapse. All this activity occurs at lightning speed, with the process taking just several milliseconds (Helmuth, 2000).

Neurotransmitters: Multitalented Chemical Couriers

Neurotransmitters are a particularly important link between the nervous system and behavior. Not only are they important for maintaining vital brain and body functions, but a deficiency or an excess of a neurotransmitter can produce severe behavior disorders. More than a hundred chemicals have been found to act as neurotransmitters, and biopsychologists believe that more may ultimately be identified (Purves et al., 1997; Penney, 2000).

Neurotransmitters vary significantly in terms of how strong their concentration must be to trigger a neuron to fire. Furthermore, the effects of a given neurotransmitter vary, depending on the area of the nervous system in which it is produced. The same neurotransmitter, then, can cause a neuron to fire when it is secreted in one part of the brain and can inhibit the firing of neurons when it is produced in another part. (The major neurotransmitters are described in Table 3-1.)

One of the most common neurotransmitters is *acetylcholine* (or *ACh,* its chemical symbol), which is found throughout the nervous system. ACh is involved in our every move, because—among other things—it transmits messages relating to our skeletal muscles. ACh is also involved in memory capabilities, and a diminished production of ACh might be related to Alzheimer's disease (Selkoe, 1997).

Another common excitatory neurotransmitter, *glutamate,* plays a role in memory. As we'll discuss in Chapter 7, memories appear to be produced by specific biochemical changes at particular synapses, and glutamate, along with other neurotransmitters, plays an important role in this process (Gibbs et al., 1996; Li et al., 1999; Bennett, 2000).

Gamma-amino butyric acid (GABA), found in both the brain and the spinal cord, appears to be the nervous system's primary inhibitory neurotransmitter. It moderates a

excitatory message: A chemical message that makes it more likely that a receiving neuron will fire and an action potential will travel down its axons

inhibitory message: A chemical message that prevents a receiving neuron from firing

reuptake: The reabsorption of neurotransmitters by a terminal button

Table 3-1 Some Major Neurotransmitters

Name	Location	Effect	Function
Acetylcholine (ACh)	Brain, spinal cord, peripheral nervous system, especially some organs of the parasympathetic nervous system	Excitatory in brain and autonomic nervous system; inhibitory elsewhere	Muscle movement; cognitive functioning
Glutamate	Brain, spinal cord	Excitatory	Memory
Gamma-amino butyric acid (GABA)	Brain, spinal cord	Main inhibitory neurotransmitter	Eating, aggression, sleeping
Dopamine (DA)	Brain	Inhibitory or excitatory	Muscle disorders, mental disorders, Parkinson's disease
Serotonin	Brain, spinal cord	Inhibitory	Sleeping, eating, mood, pain, depression
Endorphins	Brain, spinal cord	Primarily inhibitory, except in hippocampus	Pain suppression, pleasurable feelings, appetites, placebos

variety of behaviors, ranging from eating to aggression. Several common substances, such as the tranquilizer Valium and alcohol, are effective because they permit GABA to operate more efficiently (Tabakoff & Hoffman, 1996).

Another major neurotransmitter is *dopamine (DA)*. The discovery that certain drugs can have a marked effect on dopamine release has led to the development of effective treatments for a wide variety of physical and mental ailments. For instance, Parkinson's disease, from which actor Michael J. Fox suffers, is caused by a deficiency of dopamine in the brain. Techniques for increasing the production of dopamine in Parkinson's patients are proving effective (Schapira, 1999; LeWitt, 2000).

In other instances, *over*production of dopamine produces negative consequences. For example, researchers have hypothesized that schizophrenia and some other severe mental disturbances are affected or perhaps even caused by the presence of unusually high levels of dopamine. Drugs that block the reception of dopamine reduce the symptoms displayed by some people diagnosed with schizophrenia, as we will examine further in Chapters 16 and 17 (Kahn, Davidson, & Davis, 1996).

Another neurotransmitter, *serotonin*, is associated with the regulation of sleep, eating, mood, and pain. A growing body of research points toward a broader role for serotonin, suggesting its involvement in such diverse behaviors as coping with stress, alcoholism, depression, suicide, impulsivity, and aggression (Smith, Williams, & Cowen, 2000).

Endorphins, another class of neurotransmitters, are a family of chemicals produced by the brain that are similar in structure to painkilling drugs such as morphine. The production of endorphins seems to reflect the brain's effort to deal with pain. For instance, people who are afflicted with diseases that produce long-term, severe pain often develop large concentrations of endorphins in their brains—suggesting an effort by the brain to control the pain. Endorphins can also produce the euphoric feelings that runners sometimes experience after long runs. The exertion and perhaps even the pain involved in a long run stimulate the production of endorphins—ultimately resulting in what has been called "runner's high" (Kremer & Scully, 1994; Dishman, 1997).

Endorphin release might also explain other phenomena that have long puzzled psychologists. For example, acupuncture and placebos (pills or other substances that contain no actual drugs but that patients *believe* will make them better) might induce the release of endorphins, leading to the reduction of pain (Mikamo et al., 1994; Murray, 1995).

Evaluate

1. The _Neuron_ is the fundamental element of the nervous system.
2. Neurons receive information through their _____ and they send messages through their _____.
3. Just as electrical wires have an outer coating, so axons are insulated by a coating called the _____ _____.
4. The gap between two neurons is bridged by a chemical connection called a _____.
5. Endorphins are one kind of _____, the chemical "messengers" between neurons.

Answers to Evaluate Questions

1. neuron 2. dendrites; axons 3. myelin sheath 4. synapse 5. neurotransmitter

Rethink

1. Can you use your knowledge of psychological research methods to suggest how researchers can study the effects of neurotransmitters on human behavior?
2. In what ways might endorphins help produce the placebo effect? Is there a difference between believing that one's pain is reduced and actually experiencing reduced pain? Why or why not?

Prepare

In what way are the structures of the nervous system tied together?

Organize

The Nervous System
   Central and Peripheral Nervous Systems
   The Evolutionary Foundations of the Nervous System
   Behavioral Genetics

The Nervous System

Given the complexity of individual neurons and the neurotransmission process, it should come as no surprise that the connections and structures formed by the neurons are complicated. Because just one neuron can be connected to 80,000 other neurons, the total number of possible connections is astonishing. For instance, estimates of the number of neural connections within the brain fall in the neighborhood of 1 quadrillion—a 1 followed by 15 zeros; some experts put the number even higher (McGaugh, Weinberger, & Lynch, 1990; Estes, 1991; Eichenbaum, 1993).

Whatever the actual number of neural connections, the human nervous system has both a logic and an elegance. We turn now to its basic structures.

Central and Peripheral Nervous Systems

As you can see from the schematic representation in Figure 3-5, the nervous system is divided into two main parts: the central nervous system and the peripheral nervous system. The **central nervous system (CNS)** is composed of the brain and spinal cord. The **spinal cord,** about the thickness of a pencil, contains a bundle of nerves that leaves the brain and runs down the length of the back (see Figure 3-6, p. 64). It is the primary means for transmitting messages between the brain and the body.

However, the spinal cord is not just a communications conduit. It also controls some simple kinds of behaviors on its own, without any involvement of the brain. One example is the way your knee jerks forward when it is tapped with a rubber hammer. Such behaviors, called **reflexes,** are automatic, involuntary responses to incoming stimuli. Similarly, when you touch a hot stove and immediately withdraw your hand, a reflex is at work. Although the brain eventually analyzes and reacts to the situation ("Ouch—hot stove—pull away!"), the initial withdrawal is directed only by neurons in the spinal cord.

Three sorts of neurons are involved in reflexes. **Sensory (afferent) neurons** transmit information from the perimeter of the body to the central nervous system. **Motor (efferent) neurons** communicate information from the nervous system to muscles and glands of the body. **Interneurons** connect sensory and motor neurons, carrying messages between the two.

The importance of the spinal cord and reflexes is illustrated by the outcome of accidents in which the cord is injured or severed. Actor Christopher Reeve, who was injured in a horse-riding accident, suffers from *quadriplegia,* a condition in which voluntary muscle movement below the neck is lost. In a less severe but still debilitating condition, *paraplegia,* people are unable to voluntarily move any muscles in the lower half of their body.

central nervous system (CNS): The system that includes the brain and spinal cord
spinal cord: A bundle of nerves that leaves the brain and runs down the length of the back and is the main means for transmitting messages between the brain and the body
reflexes: Automatic, involuntary responses to incoming stimuli
sensory (afferent) neurons: Neurons that transmit information from the perimeter of the body to the central nervous system
motor (efferent) neurons: Neurons that communicate information from the nervous system to muscles and glands of the body
interneurons: Neurons that connect sensory and motor neurons, carrying messages between the two

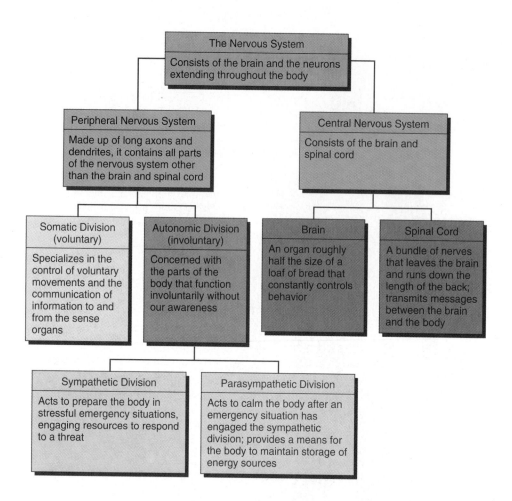

The Nervous System

Consists of the brain and the neurons extending throughout the body

Peripheral Nervous System

Made up of long axons and dendrites, it contains all parts of the nervous system other than the brain and spinal cord

Central Nervous System

Consists of the brain and spinal cord

Somatic Division (voluntary)

Specializes in the control of voluntary movements and the communication of information to and from the sense organs

Autonomic Division (involuntary)

Concerned with the parts of the body that function involuntarily without our awareness

Brain

An organ roughly half the size of a loaf of bread that constantly controls behavior

Spinal Cord

A bundle of nerves that leaves the brain and runs down the length of the back; transmits messages between the brain and the body

Sympathetic Division

Acts to prepare the body in stressful emergency situations, engaging resources to respond to a threat

Parasympathetic Division

Acts to calm the body after an emergency situation has engaged the sympathetic division; provides a means for the body to maintain storage of energy sources

Figure 3-5 A schematic diagram of the relationship of the parts of the nervous system.

As suggested by its name, the **peripheral nervous system** branches out from the spinal cord and brain and reaches the extremities of the body. Made up of long axons and dendrites, the peripheral nervous system encompasses all parts of the nervous system other than the brain and spinal cord. There are two major divisions, the somatic division and the autonomic division, both of which connect the central nervous system with the sense organs, muscles, glands, and other organs. The **somatic division** specializes in the control of voluntary movements—such as the motion of the eyes to read this sentence or of the hand to turn this page—and the communication of information to and from the sense organs. On the other hand, the **autonomic division** is concerned with the parts of the body that keep us alive—the heart, blood vessels, glands, lungs, and other organs that function involuntarily without our awareness. As you are reading at this moment, the autonomic division of the peripheral nervous system is pumping blood through your body, pushing your lungs in and out, overseeing the digestion of the meal you had a few hours ago, and so on—all without a thought or care on your part.

Activating the Divisions of the Autonomic Nervous System

The autonomic division plays a particularly crucial role during emergency situations. Suppose as you are reading you suddenly sense that a stranger is watching you through the window. As you look up, you see the glint of something that just might be a knife. As confusion races through your mind and fear overcomes your attempts to think rationally, what happens to your body? If you are like most people, you react immediately on a physiological level. Your heart rate increases, you begin to sweat, and you develop goose bumps all over your body.

peripheral nervous system: The part of the nervous system that includes the autonomic and somatic subdivisions; made up of long axons and dendrites, it branches out from the spinal cord and brain and reaches the extremities of the body

somatic division: The part of the nervous system that specializes in the control of voluntary movements and the communication of information to and from the sense organs

autonomic division: The part of the nervous system that controls involuntary movement (the actions of the heart, glands, lungs, and other organs)

Figure 3-6 The central nervous system—consisting of the brain and spinal cord—and the peripheral nervous system.

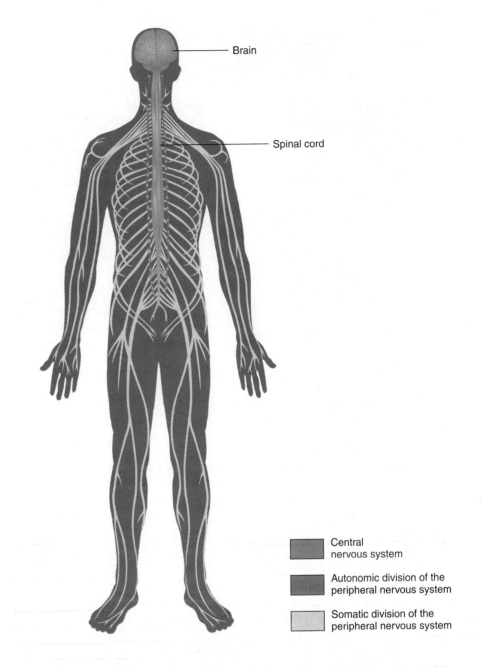

Brain

Spinal cord

Central nervous system

Autonomic division of the peripheral nervous system

Somatic division of the peripheral nervous system

sympathetic division: The part of the autonomic division of the nervous system that acts to prepare the body in stressful emergency situations, engaging all the organism's resources to respond to a threat

parasympathetic division: The part of the autonomic division of the nervous system that acts to calm the body after the emergency situation is resolved

The physiological changes that occur result from the activation of one of the two parts that make up the autonomic division: the **sympathetic division.** The sympathetic division acts to prepare the body in stressful emergency situations, engaging all of the organism's resources to respond to a threat. This response often takes the form of "fight or flight." In contrast, the **parasympathetic division** acts to calm the body after the emergency situation is resolved. When you find, for instance, that the stranger at the window is actually your roommate who has lost his keys and is climbing in the window to avoid waking you, your parasympathetic division begins to predominate, lowering your heart rate, stopping your sweating, and returning your body to the state it was in prior to your fright. The parasympathetic division also provides a means for the body to maintain storage of energy sources such as nutrients and oxygen. The sympathetic and parasympathetic divisions work together to regulate many functions of the body (see Figure 3-7). For instance, sexual arousal is controlled by the parasympathetic division but sexual orgasm is a function of the sympathetic division.

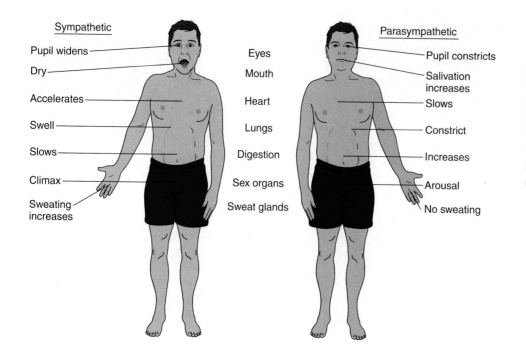

Sympathetic

Pupil widens

Dry

Accelerates

Swell

Slows

Climax

Sweating increases

Eyes

Mouth

Heart

Lungs

Digestion

Sex organs

Sweat glands

Parasympathetic

Pupil constricts

Salivation increases

Slows

Constrict

Increases

Arousal

No sweating

Figure 3-7 The major functions of the autonomic nervous system. The sympathetic division acts to prepare certain organs of the body for stressful emergency situations, and the parasympathetic division acts to calm the body after the emergency situation is resolved. Can you explain why each response of the sympathetic division might be useful in an emergency?

The Evolutionary Foundations of the Nervous System

The complexities of the nervous system can be understood only by taking the course of evolution into consideration. The forerunner of the human nervous system is found in the earliest simple organisms to have a spinal cord. Basically, these organisms were simple input-output devices: When the upper side of their spinal cord was stimulated by for instance, being touched, they reacted with a simple response, such as jerking away. Such responses were completely a consequence of the organism's genetic makeup.

Over millions of years, the front end of the spinal cord became more specialized, and organisms became capable of distinguishing between different kinds of stimuli and responding appropriately to them. Ultimately, the front end of the spinal cord evolved into what we would consider a primitive brain. At first, it had just three parts, devoted to close stimuli (such as smell), more distant stimuli (such as sights and sounds), and the ability to maintain balance and bodily coordination. In fact, many animals, such as fish, still have a nervous system that is structured in roughly similar fashion today. In contrast, the human brain evolved from this three-part configuration into an organ that is far more complex and differentiated (Merlin, 1993).

Furthermore, the nervous system is *hierarchically organized,* meaning that relatively newer (from an evolutionary point of view) and more sophisticated regions of the brain regulate the older, and more primitive, parts of the nervous system. As we move up along the spinal cord and continue upward into the brain, then, the functions controlled by various regions become progressively more advanced.

Why should we care about the evolutionary background of the human nervous system? The answer comes from researchers working in the area of **evolutionary psychology,** the branch of psychology that seeks to identify how behavior is influenced and produced by our genetic inheritance from our ancestors, They argue that the course of evolution is reflected in the structure and functioning of the nervous system, and that evolutionary factors consequently have a significant influence on our everyday behavior. Their work, and that of other scientists, has led to the development of a new field: behavioral genetics.

evolutionary psychology: The branch of psychology that seeks to identify behavior patterns that result from our genetic inheritance from our ancestors

PsychLink

Human behavioral genetic data
www.mhhe.com/
feldmanup6–03links

behavioral genetics: The study of the
effects of heredity on behavior

PsychLink

The Human Genome Project
www.mhhe.com/
feldmanup6–03links

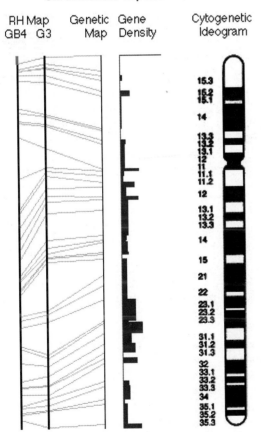

Chromosome 5: pTEL-D5S678

Part of the human DNA sequence, identified by the
Human Genome Project, which has mapped the
specific location and sequence of every gene.

Behavioral Genetics

Our evolutionary heritage manifests itself not only through the structure and functioning of the nervous system, but through our behavior as well. In the view of a blossoming new area of study, people's personality and behavioral habits are affected in part by their genetic heritage. **Behavioral genetics** studies the effects of heredity on behavior. Behavioral genetics researchers are finding increasing evidence that cognitive abilities, personality traits, sexual orientation, and psychological disorders are determined to some extent by genetic factors (Funder, 1997; Craig et al., 2000).

Behavioral genetics gets to the heart of the nature-nurture issue that we first discussed in Chapter 1. Although no one would argue that our behavior is *solely* determined by inherited factors, evidence collected by behavioral geneticists does suggest that our genetic inheritance predisposes us to respond in particular ways to our environment, and even to seek out particular kinds of environments. For instance, research indicates that genetic factors might be related to such diverse behavior as level of family conflict, schizophrenia, learning disabilities, and general sociability (Elkins, McGue, & Iacono, 1997; Berrettini, 2000).

Furthermore, important human characteristics and behaviors are related to the presence (or absence) of particular *genes,* the genetic material that controls the transmission of traits. For example, researchers have found evidence that novelty-seeking behavior is determined, at least in part, by a certain gene.

Researchers have identified some 30,000 individual genes, each of which appears in a specific sequence on particular chromosomes. Scientists only recently succeeded in mapping these genes as part of a massive, multibillion-dollar project known as the Human Genome Project, which, after a decade of effort, identified the sequence of the three billion chemical pairs that make up the DNA in genes. By understanding the basic structure of the human *genome,* the "map" of humans' total genetic makeup, scientists are a giant step closer to understanding the biochemical recipes that direct human functioning (Human Genome Project, 2000; Pennisi, 2000).

Despite its relative infancy, the field of behavioral genetics has already made substantial contributions. By understanding the relationship between our genetic heritage and the structures of the nervous system, we are gaining new knowledge about the development of various behavioral difficulties, such as the psychological disorders we'll discuss in Chapter 16. Perhaps more importantly, behavioral genetics holds the promise of developing new treatment techniques to remedy genetic deficiencies that can lead to physical and psychological difficulties. For example, analysis of a drop of blood might tell a woman whether she has a form of breast cancer that is likely to be deadly or is treatable, and scientists might be able to analyze our children's genes to determine if they are susceptible to heart disease, as we'll discuss in detail in Chapter 12 (Risch & Merikangas, 1996; Haseltine, 1997; Begley, 2000).

We turn now to a consideration of the particular structures of the brain and the primary functions to which they are related. However, a caution is in order. Although we'll be discussing how specific brain areas are tied to specific behaviors, this approach is an oversimplification. No simple one-to-one correspondence between a distinct part of the brain and a particular behavior exists. Instead, behavior is produced by complex interconnections among sets of neurons located in many areas of the brain: Our behavior, emotions, thoughts, hopes, and dreams are produced by a variety of neurons throughout the nervous system, working in concert (Grillner, 1996; Joseph, 1996; Sharma, Angelucci, & Sur, 2000).

Evaluate

1. If you should put your hand on a red-hot piece of metal, the immediate response of pulling it away would be an example of a(n) _reflex_
2. The central nervous system is composed of the _Brain_ and _Spinal Cord_
3. In the peripheral nervous system, the _somatic_ division controls voluntary movements, whereas the _autonomic_ division controls organs that keep us alive and function without our awareness.
4. Maria saw a young boy run into the street and get hit by a car. When she got to the fallen child, she was in a state of panic. She was sweating and her heart was racing. Her biological state resulted from the activation of what division of the nervous system?

   a. Parasympathetic

   b. Central

   c. Sympathetic

5. The increasing complexity and hierarchy of the nervous system over millions of years is the subject of study for researchers working in the field of _evolutionary psychology_
6. The emerging field of _behavioral genetics_ studies how our genetic inheritance predisposes us to behave in certain ways.

Answers to Evaluate Questions

1. reflex 2. brain; spinal cord 3. somatic; autonomic 4. c 5. evolutionary psychology 6. behavioral genetics

Rethink

1. How might communication within the nervous system result in human consciousness?
2. How is the "fight or flight" response helpful to organisms in emergency situations?

The Brain

It is not much to look at. Soft, spongy, mottled, and pinkish-gray in color, it can hardly be said to possess much in the way of physical beauty. Despite its physical appearance, however, it ranks as the greatest natural marvel we know of and possesses a beauty and sophistication all its own.

The object to which this description applies? The human brain. Our brain is responsible for our loftiest thoughts—and our most primitive urges. It is the overseer of the intricate workings of the human body. If one were to attempt to design a computer to mimic the range of capabilities of the brain, the task would be nearly impossible; in fact, it has proved difficult even to come close. The sheer quantity of nerve cells in the brain is enough to daunt even the most ambitious computer engineer. Many billions of nerve cells make up a structure weighing just three pounds in the average adult. However, the most astounding thing about the brain is not its number of cells but its ability to allow human intellect to flourish as it guides our behavior and thoughts.

Studying the Brain's Structure and Functions: Spying on the Brain

The brain has posed a continual challenge to those wishing to study it. For most of history, its examination was possible only after an individual was dead. Only then could the skull be opened and the brain cut into without serious injury. Although this was informative, such a limited procedure could hardly tell us much about the functioning of the healthy brain.

Today, however, important advances have been made in the study of the brain through the use of brain-scanning techniques. Using brain scanning, investigators can take a snapshot of the internal workings of the brain without having to cut surgically into a person's skull. The major scanning techniques, described below, are illustrated in Figure 3-8 on the next page.

Prepare

How do researchers identify the major parts and functions of the brain?

What are the major parts of the brain, and for what behaviors is each part responsible?

How do the two halves of the brain operate interdependently?

How can an understanding of the nervous system help us find ways to relieve disease and pain?

Organize

The Brain

　Studying the Brain's Structure and Functions

　The Central Core

　The Limbic System

　The Cerebral Cortex

　Mending the Brain

　The Specialization of the Hemispheres

　The Split Brain

The Endocrine System

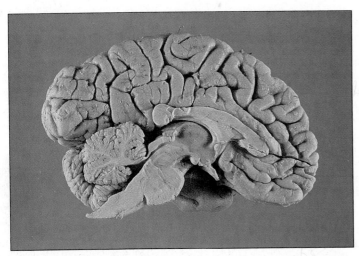

The brain may not be much to look at but it represents one of the great marvels of human development. Why do most scientists believe that it will be difficult, if not impossible, to duplicate the brain's abilities?

PsychLink

Numerous brain scans
www.mhhe.com/
feldmanup6-03links

PsychLink

Information about NMR
www.mhhe.com/
feldmanup6-03links

- The *electroencephalogram (EEG)* records electrical activity in the brain through electrodes placed on the outside of the skull. Although traditionally the EEG could produce only a graph of electrical wave patterns, new techniques are now able to transform the brain's electrical activity into a pictorial representation of the brain that allows the diagnosis of such problems as epilepsy and learning disabilities.
- The *computerized axial tomography (CAT) scan* uses a computer to construct an image of the structures of the brain by combining thousands of separate X rays taken at slightly different angles. It is very useful for showing abnormalities in the structure of the brain, such as swelling and enlargement of certain parts, but does not provide information about brain activity.
- The *magnetic resonance imaging (MRI) scan* provides a detailed, three-dimensional computer-generated image of brain structures and activity by aiming a powerful magnetic field at the body. For example, it is capable of producing vivid images of individual bundles of nerves, opening the way for improved diagnosis of such ailments as chronic back pain.
- The *superconducting quantum interference device (SQUID)* is sensitive to tiny changes in magnetic fields that occur when neurons fire. Using SQUID, researchers can pinpoint the location of neural activity.
- The *positron emission tomography (PET) scan* shows biochemical activity within the brain at a given moment in time. PET scans begin by injecting into the bloodstream a radioactive (but safe) liquid that makes its way to the brain. By locating radiation within the brain, a computer can determine which are the more active regions, providing a striking picture of the brain at work.

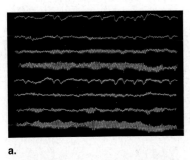
a.

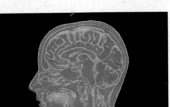
c.

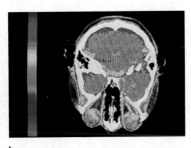
b.

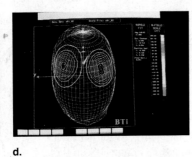
d.

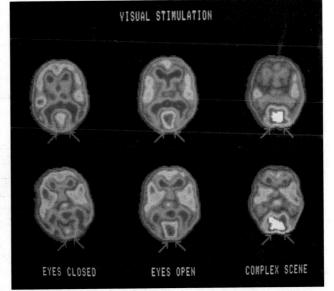
e.

Figure 3–8 Brain scans produced by different techniques. *(a)* A computer-produced EEG image. *(b)* This CAT scan shows the structures of the brain. *(c)* The MRI scan uses a magnetic field to detail the parts of the brain. *(d)* The SQUID scan shows the neural activity of the brain *(e)* The PET scan displays the functioning of the brain at a given moment and is sensitive to the person's activities.

Applying Psychology in the 21st Century

Mind over Cursor: Using Brain Waves to Overcome Physical Limitations

For four years, Hans-Peter Balzmann, a lawyer suffering from Lou Gehrig's disease, was locked within his own body. Paralyzed by the disease and unable to eat, speak, or even breathe on his own, he had relied on a respirator and feeding tube to survive. Although his mind functioned normally, he was unable to communicate with the outside world.

All that changed, however, after Balzmann obtained an experimental device that allows brain waves to be translated into written communication. Using EEG scanning techniques that react to the pattern of brain waves originating in the brain, Balzmann learned to boost and curtail certain types of brain waves. After hundreds of hours of practice, he was able to select letters that appear on a video screen. By stringing letters

together, he could spell out messages. The process, which makes use of brain waves called "slow cortical potentials," permitted Balzmann to communicate effectively for the first time in years. Although the method is slow and tedious—Balzmann can produce only about two characters per minute—it holds great promise (Birbaumer et al., 1999).

Other increasingly sophisticated procedures may permit faster communication with brain waves in the future. For example, neurosurgeon Philip Kennedy of Emory University is experimenting with a procedure in which he implants electrodes into a paralyzed patient's motor cortex. When the patient thinks about moving her hands, tongues, or eyes, the brain produces electrical signals that are amplified by the implant and translated into the movement of a cursor. Using this system, the patient can spell out words and hit icons (such as "I'm cold") on the computer screen ("Mind over Matter," 1999).

Technological advances offer the possibility of treating other brain disorders. For example, an experimental system is being tested to treat seizures due to epilepsy. The system consists of a pacemaker-like device, implanted into the chest, that sends signals to the brain to block seizures. When patients feel that a seizure is about to occur, they can activate the system, short-circuiting the seizure (Forest, 1997).

Ultimately, systems such as these might be useful not just for people with illnesses and disabilities, but for anyone. For instance, it is conceivable that one day you will be able to control your computer's cursor by simply thinking about moving it. Mind-over-cursor could be in everyone's future.

Can you think of a mechanism that would permit brain-wave communication between two people? What implications would there be if people gained the ability to communicate with each other in this way?

Each of these techniques offers exciting possibilities not only for the diagnosis and treatment of brain disease and injuries, but also for an increased understanding of the normal functioning of the brain. In addition, researchers are developing ways to combine separate scanning techniques (such as integrated, simultaneous PET and MRI scans) to produce even more effective portraits of the brain, such as three-dimensional reconstructions of the brain that can be used during surgery (Grimson et al., 1999).

Advances in brain scanning are also aiding the development of new methods for harnessing the brain's neural signals. We consider some of these intriguing findings in the *Applying Psychology in the 21st Century* box.

The Central Core: Our "Old Brain"

Even though the capabilities of the human brain far exceed those of the brain of any other species we know of, it is not surprising that the basic functions that we share with more primitive animals, such as breathing, eating, and sleeping, are directed by a relatively primitive part of the brain. The portion of the brain known as the **central core** (see Figure 3-9) is quite similar to that found in all vertebrates (species with backbones). The central core is sometimes referred to as the "old brain" because its evolutionary underpinnings can be traced back some 500 million years to primitive structures found in nonhuman species.

If we were to move up the spinal cord from the base of the skull to locate the structures of the central core of the brain, the first part we would come to would be the *hindbrain*, which contains the medulla, pons, and cerebellum (see Figure 3-10). The *medulla* controls a number of critical body functions, the most important of which are breathing and heartbeat. The *pons* comes next, joining the two halves of the cerebellum, which lies adjacent

central core: The "old brain," which controls such basic functions as eating and sleeping and is common to all vertebrates

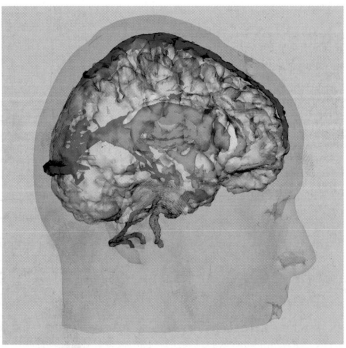

To get a better view of the brain, researchers are experimenting with various scanning techniques; this photo combines PET and MRI scans.

Figure 3-9 The major divisions of the brain: the cerebral cortex and the central core (Seeley, Stephens, & Tate, 2000).

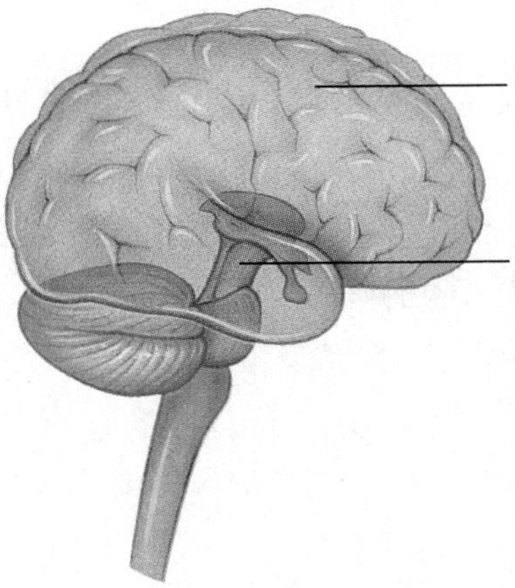

Cerebral cortex (the "new brain")

Central core (the "old brain")

cerebellum (ser uh BELL um): The part of the brain that controls bodily balance

reticular formation: The part of the brain from the medulla through the pons made up of groups of nerve cells that can immediately activate other parts of the brain to produce general bodily arousal

to it. Containing large bundles of nerves, the pons acts as a transmitter of motor information, coordinating muscles and integrating movement between the right and left halves of the body. It is also involved in the control of sleep.

The **cerebellum** is found just above the medulla and behind the pons. Without the help of the cerebellum we would be unable to walk in a straight line without staggering and lurching forward, for it is the job of the cerebellum to control bodily balance. It constantly monitors feedback from the muscles to coordinate their placement, movement, and tension. In fact, drinking too much alcohol seems to depress the activity of the cerebellum, leading to the unsteady gait and movement characteristic of drunkenness. The cerebellum is also involved in several intellectual functions, ranging from analysis of sensory information to problem solving (Gao et al., 1996; Wickelgren, 1998a).

The **reticular formation** extends from the medulla through the pons, passing through the middle section of the brain—or *midbrain*—and into the front-most part of the brain, called the *forebrain*. Like an ever-vigilant guard, the reticular formation is made up of groups of nerve cells that can immediately activate other parts of the brain to produce general bodily arousal. If you are startled by a loud noise, for example, your reticular formation can put you into a heightened state of awareness so you can determine whether

Figure 3-10 The major structures in the brain (Johnson, 2000).

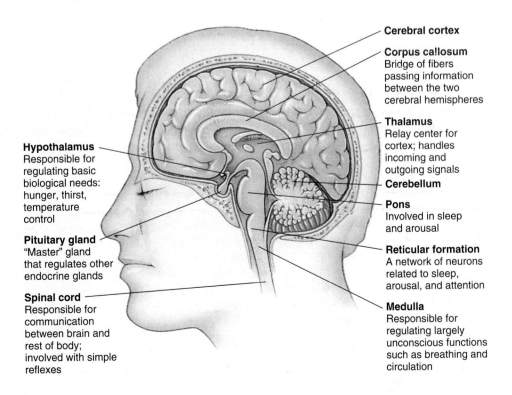

Cerebral cortex

Corpus callosum
Bridge of fibers passing information between the two cerebral hemispheres

Thalamus
Relay center for cortex; handles incoming and outgoing signals

Cerebellum

Pons
Involved in sleep and arousal

Reticular formation
A network of neurons related to sleep, arousal, and attention

Medulla
Responsible for regulating largely unconscious functions such as breathing and circulation

Hypothalamus
Responsible for regulating basic biological needs: hunger, thirst, temperature control

Pituitary gland
"Master" gland that regulates other endocrine glands

Spinal cord
Responsible for communication between brain and rest of body; involved with simple reflexes

While the cerebellum is involved in several intellectual functions, its main duty is to control balance, constantly monitoring feedback from the muscles to coordinate their placement, movement, and tension. Do you think the cerebellum is under conscious or automatic control as people negotiate difficult balancing tasks?

a response is necessary. In addition, the reticular formation serves a different function when we are sleeping, seeming to filter out background stimuli to allow us to sleep undisturbed.

Hidden within the forebrain, the **thalamus** acts primarily as a busy relay station, mostly for information concerning the senses. Messages from the eyes, ears, and skin travel to the thalamus to be communicated upward to higher parts of the brain. The thalamus also integrates information from higher parts of the brain, sorting it out so that it can be sent to the cerebellum and medulla.

The **hypothalamus** is located just below the thalamus. Although tiny—about the size of a fingertip—the hypothalamus plays an inordinately important role. One of its major functions is to maintain *homeostasis,* a steady internal environment for the body. As we'll discuss further in Chapter 10, the hypothalamus helps maintain a constant body temperature and monitors the amount of nutrients stored in the cells. A second major function is equally important: It produces and regulates behavior that is critical to the basic survival of the species, such as eating, self-protection, and sex.

thalamus: The part of the brain located in the middle of the central core that acts primarily as a busy relay station, mostly for information concerning the senses

hypothalamus: A tiny part of the brain, located below the thalamus of the brain, that maintains homeostasis and produces and regulates vital, basic behavior such as eating, drinking, and sexual behavior

The Limbic System: Beyond the Central Core

In an eerie view of the future, some science fiction writers have suggested that people will someday routinely have electrodes implanted in their brains. These electrodes will permit them to receive tiny shocks that produce the sensation of pleasure by stimulating certain centers of the brain. When they feel upset, people will simply activate their electrodes to achieve an immediate high.

Although farfetched, and ultimately improbable, such a futuristic fantasy is based on fact. The brain does have pleasure centers in several areas, including some in the **limbic system.** Consisting of a series of doughnut-shaped structures including the *amygdala, hippocampus,* and *fornix,* the limbic system borders the top of the central core and has connections with the cerebral cortex (see Figure 3-11).

The structures of the limbic system jointly control a variety of basic functions relating to emotions and self-preservation, such as eating, aggression, and reproduction. Injury to the limbic system can produce striking changes in behavior. It can turn animals that are usually docile and tame into belligerent savages. Conversely, those that are usually wild and uncontrollable might become meek and obedient (Bedard & Parsinger, 1995).

Research examining the effects of mild electric shocks to parts of the limbic system and other parts of the brain have produced some thought-provoking findings (Olds & Milner, 1954; Olds & Fobes, 1981). In one experiment, rats who pressed a bar received mild electric stimulation through an electrode implanted in their brain, which produced pleasurable feelings. Even starving rats on their way to food would stop to press the bar as many times as they could. Some rats would actually stimulate themselves literally thousands of times an hour—until they collapsed with fatigue (Routtenberg & Lindy, 1965).

limbic system: The part of the brain located outside the "new brain" that controls eating, aggression, and reproduction

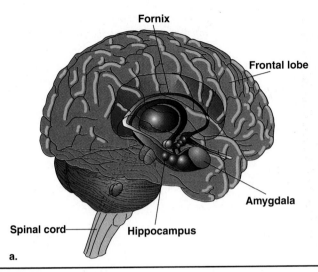

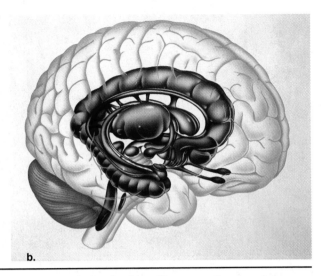

Figure 3-11 *(a)* The limbic system consists of a series of doughnut-shaped structures that are involved in self-preservation, learning, memory, and the experience of pleasure. *(b)* This computer-generated image provides another view of the limbic system (Courtesy of Dr. Robert B. Livingston, University of California-San Diego, and Philip J. Mercurio, Neurosciences Institute).

The extraordinarily pleasurable quality of certain kinds of stimulation has also been experienced by humans, who, as part of treatment for certain kinds of brain disorders, have received electrical stimulation to certain areas of the limbic system. Although at a loss to describe just what it feels like, these people report the experience to be intensely pleasurable, similar in some respects to sexual orgasm.

The limbic system also plays an important role in learning and memory, a finding demonstrated in patients with epilepsy. In an attempt to stop their seizures, such patients have had portions of the limbic system removed. One unintended consequence of the surgery is that these individuals sometimes have difficulty learning and remembering new information. In one case (discussed again when we focus on memory in Chapter 7), a patient who had undergone surgery was unable to remember where he lived, although he had resided at the same address for eight years. Further, even though the patient was able to carry on animated conversations, he was unable, a few minutes later, to recall what had been discussed (B. Milner, 1966).

The limbic system, then, is involved in several important functions, including self-preservation, learning, memory, and the experience of pleasure. These functions are hardly unique to humans; in fact, the limbic system is sometimes referred to as the "animal brain" because its structures and functions are so similar to those of other mammals. To identify the part of the brain that provides the complex and subtle capabilities that are uniquely human, we need to turn to another structure—the cerebral cortex.

Evaluate

1. _____ _____ is a procedure whereby a picture of the brain can be taken without opening the skull.
2. Match the name of each brain scan with the appropriate description:
   a. EEG 2
   b. CAT b
   c. PET 1

   1. By locating radiation within the brain, a computer can provide a striking picture of brain activity.
   2. Electrodes placed around the skull record the electrical signals transmitted through the brain.
   3. A computer image combines thousands of X-ray pictures into one.

Rethink

1. How would you answer the argument that "psychologists should leave the study of neurons and synapses and the nervous system to biologists"?
2. Before sophisticated brain-scanning techniques were developed, biopsychologists' understanding of the brain was largely based on the brains of people who had died. What limitations would this pose, and in what areas would you expect the most significant advances once brain-scanning techniques were possible?

3. Control of such functions as breathing and sleep is located in the _brains old_.
4. Match the portion of the brain with its function:

   a. medulla
   b. pons
   c. cerebellum
   d. reticular formation

   1. Maintains breathing and heartbeat _a_
   2. Controls bodily balance _c_
   3. Coordinates and integrates muscle movements _b_
   4. Activates other parts of the brain to produce general bodily arousal _d_

5. The _cerebellum_, a fingertip-sized portion of the brain, is responsible for the regulation of the body's internal environment.

Answers to Evaluate Questions

1. Brain scanning 2. a-2; b-3; c-1 3. central core or "old brain" 4. a-1; b-3; c-2; d-4 5. hypothalamus

The Cerebral Cortex: Our "New Brain"

As we have proceeded up the spinal cord and into the brain, our discussion has centered on areas of the brain that control functions similar to those found in less sophisticated organisms. But where, you may be asking, are the portions of the brain that enable humans to do what they do best, and that distinguish humans from all other animals? Those unique features of the human brain—indeed, the very capabilities that allow you to come up with such a question in the first place—are embodied in the ability to think, evaluate, and make complex judgments. The principal location of these abilities, along with many others, is the **cerebral cortex.**

The cerebral cortex is referred to as the "new brain" because of its relatively recent evolution. It consists of a mass of deeply folded, rippled, convoluted tissue that amounts to some 80 percent of the brain's total mass. Although only about one-twelfth of an inch thick, it would, if flattened out, cover an area of more than two feet square. This configuration allows the surface area of the cortex to be considerably greater than if it were smoother and more uniformly packed into the skull. The uneven shape also permits a high level of integration of neurons, allowing sophisticated processing of information.

The cortex has four major sections, called **lobes.** If we take a side view of the brain, the *frontal lobes* lie at the front center of the cortex, and the *parietal lobes* lie behind them. The *temporal lobes* are found in the lower center of the cortex, with the *occipital lobes* lying behind them. These four sets of lobes are physically separated by deep grooves called sulci. Figure 3-12 shows the four areas.

Another way of describing the brain is by considering the functions associated with a given area. Figure 3-12 also shows the specialized regions within the lobes related to specific functions and areas of the body. Three major areas have been discovered: the motor areas, the sensory areas, and the association areas. Although we will discuss these areas as though they were separate and independent, keep in mind that this is an oversimplification. In most instances, behavior is influenced simultaneously by several structures and areas within the brain, operating interdependently. Furthermore, even within a given area, additional subdivisions exist. Finally, when people suffer certain kinds of brain injury, uninjured portions of the brain can sometimes take over the functions that were previously handled by the damaged area. In short, the brain is extraordinarily adaptable (Gibbons, 1990; Sharma, Angelucci, & Sur, 2000).

The Motor Area of the Cortex

If you look at the frontal lobe in Figure 3-12, you will see a shaded portion labeled the **motor area.** This part of the cortex is largely responsible for the voluntary movement of particular parts of the body. Every portion of the motor area corresponds to a specific locale within the body. If we were to insert an electrode into a particular part of the motor area of the cortex and apply mild electrical stimulation, there would be involuntary movement in the corresponding part of the body. If we moved to another part of the motor area and stimulated it, a different part of the body would move.

distinguish human from animal

cerebral cortex: The "new brain," responsible for the most sophisticated information processing in the brain; contains the lobes

lobes: The four major sections of the cerebral cortex: frontal, parietal, temporal, and occipital

motor area: The part of the cortex that is largely responsible for the voluntary movement of particular parts of the body

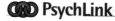 **PsychLink**

Information about lobes
www.mhhe.com/
feldmanup6-03links

Figure 3–12 The cerebral cortex of the brain. The major physical *structures* of the cerebral cortex are called lobes. This figure also illustrates the *functions* associated with particular areas of the cerebral cortex. Are any areas of the cerebral cortex present in nonhuman animals?

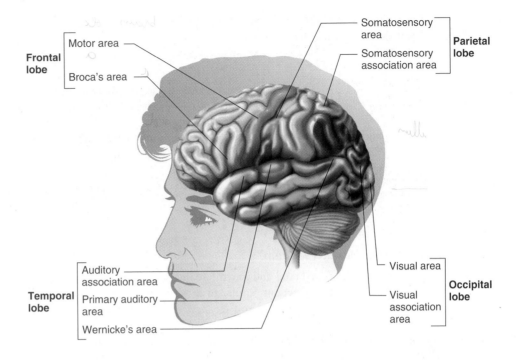

The motor area is so well mapped that researchers have identified the amount and relative location of cortical tissue used to produce movement in specific parts of the human body. For example, the control of body movements that are relatively large scale and require little precision, such as movement of a knee or a hip, is centered in a very small space in the motor area. In contrast, movements that must be precise and delicate, such as facial expressions and finger movements, are controlled by a considerably larger portion of the motor area.

In short, the motor area of the cortex provides a guide to the degree of complexity and the importance of the motor capabilities of specific parts of the body. Keep in mind, however, that behavior is produced by multiple sets of neurons in the nervous system, linked in elaborate ways. Like other behavior, movement is produced through the coordinated firing of a complex variety of neurons, working together but not necessarily lined up neatly in the motor area of the cortex (Sanes et al., 1995; Batista et al., 1999; Kakei, Hoffman, & Strick, 1999).

The Sensory Area of the Cortex

Given the one-to-one correspondence between motor area and body location, it is not surprising to find a similar relationship between specific portions of the cortex and the senses. The **sensory area** of the cortex includes three regions: one that corresponds primarily to body sensations (including touch and pressure), one relating to sight, and a third relating to sound. For instance, the *somatosensory area* encompasses specific locations associated with the ability to perceive touch and pressure in a particular area of the body. As with the motor area, the amount of brain tissue related to a particular location on the body determines the degree of sensitivity of that location. The greater the space within the cortex, the more sensitive that area of the body. As you can see from the weird-looking individual in Figure 3-13, parts such as the fingers are related to proportionally more space in the somatosensory area and are the most sensitive.

The senses of sound and sight are also represented in specific areas of the cerebral cortex. An *auditory area* located in the temporal lobe is responsible for the sense of hearing. If the auditory area is stimulated electrically, a person will hear sounds such as clicks or hums. It also appears that particular locations within the auditory area respond to specific pitches (deCharms, Blake, & Merzenich, 1998; Klinke et al., 1999).

sensory area: The site in the brain of the tissue that corresponds to each of the senses, with the degree of sensitivity relating to the amount of tissue

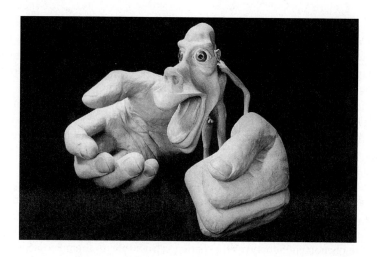

Figure 3-13 The greater the amount of tissue in the somatosensory area of the brain that is related to a specific body part, the more sensitive is that body part. If the size of our body parts reflected the corresponding amount of brain tissue, we would look like this strange creature.

The *visual area* in the cortex, located in the occipital lobe, operates analogously to the other sensory areas. Stimulation by electrodes produces the experience of flashes of light or colors, suggesting that the raw sensory input of images from the eyes is received in this area of the brain and transformed into meaningful stimuli. The visual area also provides another example of how areas of the brain are intimately related to specific areas of the body: Particular areas of the eye's retina are related to a particular part of the cortex—with, as you might guess, more space in the brain given to the most sensitive portions of the retina (Martin et al., 1995; Miyashita, 1995).

The Association Areas of the Cortex

Consider the following case:

> Twenty-five-year-old Phineas Gage, a railroad employee, was blasting rock one day in 1848 when an accidental explosion punched a 3-foot-long spike, about an inch in diameter, completely through his skull. The spike entered just under his left cheek, came out the top of his head, and flew into the air. Gage immediately suffered a series of convulsions, yet a few minutes later was talking with rescuers. In fact, he was able to walk up a long flight of stairs before receiving any medical attention. Amazingly, after a few weeks his wound healed, and he was physically close to his old self again. Mentally, however, there was a difference: Once a careful and hard-working person, Phineas now became enamored with wild schemes and was flighty and often irresponsible. As one of his physicians put it, "Previous to his injury, though untrained in the schools, he possessed a well-balanced mind, and was looked upon by those who knew him as a shrewd, smart businessman, very energetic and persistent in executing all his plans of operation. In this regard his mind was radically changed, so decidedly that his friends and acquaintances said he was 'no longer Gage'" (Harlow, 1869, p. 14).

association areas: One of the major areas of the brain; the site of the higher mental processes such as thought, language, memory, and speech

What had happened to the old Gage? Although there is no way of knowing for sure—science being what it was in the 1800s—we can speculate that the accident injured the association areas of Gage's cerebral cortex. The **association areas** are generally considered to be the site of higher mental processes such as thinking, language, memory, and speech (Rowe et al, 2000).

The association areas take up a large proportion of the cerebral cortex. Most of our understanding of the association areas comes from patients who have suffered some type of brain injury. In some cases the injury stemmed from natural causes such as a tumor or a stroke, either of which would block certain blood vessels within the cerebral cortex. In other cases, accidents were the culprits, as was true with Phineas Gage. In any event, damage to these areas can result in unusual behavioral changes, indicating the importance of the association area to normal functioning (Herholz, 1995; Gannon et al., 1998).

A model of the injury sustained by Phineas Gage.

Gage's case provides evidence that there are specialized areas for making rational decisions. When this area is damaged, people undergo personality changes that affect their ability to make moral judgments and process emotions. At the same time, people with damage in this area can still be capable of reasoning logically, performing calculations, and recalling information (Damasio et al., 1994).

Injuries to other parts of the association areas can produce a condition known as apraxia. *Apraxia* occurs when an individual is unable to integrate activities in a rational or logical manner. The disorder is most evident when people are asked to carry out a sequence of behaviors requiring a degree of planning and foresight, suggesting that the association areas act as "master planners," or organizers of actions.

Injuries to the association areas of the brain can also produce *aphasia,* problems with language. In *Broca's aphasia* (caused by damage to the part of the brain first identified by a French physician, Paul Broca, in 1861), speech becomes halting, laborious, and often ungrammatical. The speaker is unable to find the right words, in a kind of tip-of-the-tongue phenomenon that we all experience from time to time. People with aphasia, though, grope for words almost constantly, eventually blurting out a kind of "verbal telegram." A phrase like "I put the book on the table" comes out as "I . . . put . . . book . . . table" (Cornell, Fromkin, & Mauner, 1993; Goodglass, 1993; Kirshner, 1995).

Wernicke's aphasia is a disorder named for Carl Wernicke, who identified it in the 1870s. Wernicke's aphasia produces difficulties both in understanding others' speech and in the production of language. The disorder is characterized by speech that sounds fluent but makes no sense. For instance, one patient, asked what brought him to a hospital, gave this rambling reply: "Boy, I'm sweating, I'm awful nervous, you know, once in a while I get caught up, I can't mention the tarripoi, a month ago, quite a little, I've done a lot well, I impose a lot, while, on the other hand, you know what I mean, I have to run around, look it over, trebbin and all that sort of stuff" (Gardner, 1975, p. 68).

Brain injuries, such as those that result in aphasia, and brain disorders due to disease and illness have given new impetus to scientists who are seeking to map the neural circuitry of the brain. Using sophisticated computer technology, researchers are seeking to create a database encompassing every facet of the brain (see Figure 3-14). Such efforts are producing significant innovations in the study of the brain.

Mending the Brain

Shortly after he was born, Jacob Stark's arms and legs started jerking every 20 minutes. Weeks later he could not focus his eyes on his mother's face. The diagnosis: uncontrollable epileptic seizures involving his entire brain.

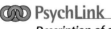

PsychLink

Description of aphasia
www.mhhe.com/
feldmanup6-03links

Figure 3-14 A sample computer screen from BrainMap, a computerized data base designed to make every aspect of the brain accessible.

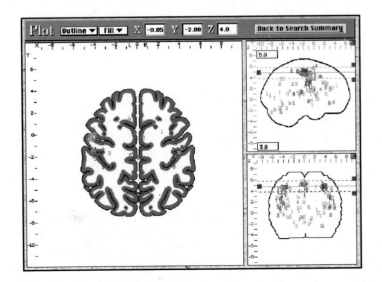

aphasia problem with language

His mother, Sally Stark, recalled: "When Jacob was two and a half months old, they said he would never learn to sit up, would never be able to feed himself. Nothing could be done to prevent profound retardation. They told us to take him home, love him and find an institution." (Blakeslee, 1992a, C3).

Instead, the Starks brought Jacob to the University of California at Los Angeles for brain surgery when he was five months old. Surgeons removed 20 percent of his brain. The operation was a complete success. Three years later, Jacob seems normal in every way, with no sign of seizures.

Jacob's surgery is representative of increasingly daring approaches in the treatment of brain disorders. It also illustrates how our growing understanding of the processes that underlie brain functioning can be translated into solutions to difficult problems.

The surgery that helped Jacob was based on the premise that the diseased part of his brain was producing seizures throughout the entire brain. Surgeons reasoned that if they removed the misfiring portion, the remaining parts of the brain, which appeared intact in PET scans, would take over. They bet that Jacob could still lead a normal life following surgery, particularly because the surgery was being done at so young an age. Clearly, the gamble paid off.

The success of such surgery is in part related to new findings about the regenerative powers of the brain and nervous system. Although it has been known that the brain has the ability to shift functions to different locations following injury to a specific area or in cases of surgery, it had been assumed for decades that the neurons of the spinal cord and brain could never be replaced.

However, new evidence is beginning to suggest otherwise. For instance, researchers have found that the cells from the brains of adult mice can produce new neurons, at least in a test tube environment. Similarly, researchers have reported partial restoration of movement in rats who had a 1/5-inch-long gap in their spinal cords and, as a result, were unable to move their hind limbs. The researchers transplanted neurons from the peripheral nervous system into the gap, and subsequently the rats were able to flex their legs. One year after the operation, they were able to support themselves and move their legs, and examination of the neurons in the spinal cord showed significant regeneration around the area of the transplantation (Cheng, Cao, & Olson, 1996; McDonald, 1999; Blakeslee, 2000).

The future also holds promise for people who, like Michael J. Fox, suffer from the tremors and loss of motor control produced by Parkinson's disease. Because Parkinson's is caused by a gradual loss of cells that stimulate the production of dopamine in the brain, investigators reasoned that a procedure that increases the supply of dopamine might be effective. They seem to be on the right track. When certain cells from human fetuses are injected directly into the brains of Parkinson's sufferers, they seem to take root, stimulating dopamine production. For most of those who have undergone this procedure, the preliminary results are promising, with some patients showing great improvement. On the other hand, the technique remains experimental, and it also raises some thorny ethical issues, given that the source of the implanted fetal tissue is aborted fetuses (HMHL, 2000; Pollack, 2000).

The Specialization of the Hemispheres: Two Brains or One?

The most recent development, at least in evolutionary terms, in the organization and operation of our brain probably occurred in the last million years: a specialization of the functions controlled by the two sides of the brain, which has symmetrical left and right halves.

Specifically, the brain can be divided into two roughly similar mirror-image halves—just as we have two arms, two legs, and two lungs. Because of the way nerves are connected from the brain to the rest of the body, these two symmetrical left and right halves, called **hemispheres,** control the side of the body opposite to their location. The left hemisphere of the brain, then, generally controls the right side of the body, and the right hemisphere controls the left side of the body. Thus damage to the right side of the brain is typically indicated by functional difficulties in the left side of the body.

hemispheres: The two symmetrical left and right halves of the brain; each controls the side of the body opposite to it

*difficulties language aphasia
left part of the brain endogamed*

lateralization: The dominance of one
hemisphere of the brain in specific
functions

Despite the appearance of similarity between the two hemispheres of the brain, they are involved in somewhat different functions. It appears that certain activities are more likely to occur in one hemisphere than in the other. Early evidence for the functional differences between halves of the brain came from studies of people with aphasia. Researchers found that people with the speech difficulties characteristic of aphasia tended to have physical damage to the left hemisphere of the brain. In contrast, physical abnormalities in the right hemisphere of the brain tended to produce far fewer problems with language. This finding led researchers to conclude that for most people, language is **lateralized,** or located more in one hemisphere than in the other—in this case, in the left side of the brain (Grossi et al., 1996).

It now seems clear that the two hemispheres of the brain are somewhat specialized in terms of the functions they carry out. The left hemisphere concentrates more on tasks that require verbal competence, such as speaking, reading, thinking, and reasoning. The right hemisphere has its own strengths, particularly in nonverbal areas such as the understanding of spatial relationships, recognition of patterns and drawings, music, and emotional expression (Ornstein, 1998; Robertson & Ivry, 2000).

In addition, information is processed somewhat differently in the two hemispheres. The left hemisphere tends to consider information sequentially, one bit at a time; the right hemisphere tends to process information globally, considering it as a whole (Turkewitz, 1993; Banich & Heller, 1998).

On the other hand, it is important to keep in mind that the differences in specialization between the hemispheres are not great, and the degree and nature of lateralization vary from one person to another. If you are right-handed, control of language is probably concentrated more in your left hemisphere. If you are among the 10 percent of people who are left-handed or are ambidextrous (you use both hands interchangeably), it is much more likely that the language centers of your brain are located more in the right hemisphere or are divided equally between left and right hemispheres.

Researchers have also unearthed evidence that there may be subtle differences in brain lateralization patterns between males and females. In fact, some scientists have suggested that there are slight differences in the structure of the brain according to gender and culture. As we see next, such findings have led to a lively debate in the scientific community.

EXPLORING DIVERSITY

Human Diversity and the Brain

The interplay of biology and environment is particularly clear when we consider evidence suggesting that there are both sex and cultural differences in brain structure and function. Let's consider sex first. According to accumulating evidence, females and males show some intriguing differences in brain lateralization and weight, although the nature of those differences—and even their very existence—is a matter of considerable controversy (Kimura, 1992; Dorion et al., 2000).

We can be reasonably confident about some differences. For instance, most males tend to show greater lateralization of language in the left hemisphere. For them, language is clearly relegated largely to the left side of the brain. In contrast, women display less lateralization, with language abilities apt to be more evenly divided between the two hemispheres (Gur et al., 1982; Shaywitz et al., 1995; Kulynych et al., 1994). Such differences in brain lateralization could account, in part, for female superiority on certain measures of verbal skills, such as the onset and fluency of speech, and the fact that far more boys than girls have reading problems in elementary school (Kitterle, 1991).

Other research suggests that men's brains are somewhat bigger than women's brains, even after taking into account differences in body size. On the other hand, part of the *corpus callosum,* a bundle of fibers that connects the hemispheres of the brain, is proportionally larger in women than in men. Furthermore, some research suggests that women's brains have a higher proportion of the neurons that are actually involved in thinking than men's brains do (Witelson, 1995; Falk et al., 1999; Gur et al., 1999).

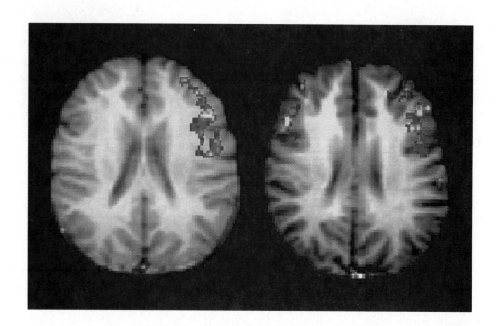

Figure 3-15 These composite MRI brain scans show the distribution of active areas in the brains of males *(left)* and females *(right)* during a verbal task involving rhyming. In males, activation is more lateralized, or confined, to the left hemisphere, while in females, activation is bilateralized, that is, occurring in both hemispheres of the brain.

(Source: B.A. Shaywitz et al., 1995. NMR/Yale Medical School)

Men and women also might process information differently. For example, MRI brain scans of men sounding out words show activation of a small area of the left side of the brain, whereas women use areas on both sides of the brain (Shaywitz et al., 1995; see Figure 3-15). Similarly, PET brain scans of men and women while they are not engaged in mental activity show differences in the use of glucose (Gur et al., 1995; Gur, 1996).

The meaning of such sex differences is far from clear. Consider one possibility related to the differences that have been found in the proportional size of the corpus callosum: Its increased proportion in women might permit stronger connections to develop between those parts of the brain that control speech. In turn, this would explain why speech tends to emerge slightly earlier in girls than in boys.

Before we rush to such a conclusion, though, it is important to consider an alternative hypothesis: It is plausible that the earlier emergence of verbal abilities in girls is due to the fact that infant girls receive greater encouragement to verbalize than infant boys do. This greater early experience could foster growth of certain parts of the brain. Hence, physical brain differences might be a *reflection* of social and environmental influences, rather than a *cause* of the differences in men's and women's behavior. At this point, it is impossible to confirm which of these two alternative hypotheses is correct.

The culture in which we are raised also might give rise to differences in brain lateralization. For example, native speakers of Japanese seem to process information regarding vowel sounds primarily in the brain's left hemisphere. In contrast, North and South Americans, Europeans, and individuals of Japanese ancestry who learn Japanese later in life handle vowel sounds principally in the right hemisphere.

The reason for this cultural difference in lateralization? One explanation could be that certain characteristics of the Japanese language, such as the ability to express complex ideas using only vowel sounds, result in the development of a specific type of brain lateralization in native speakers. Differences in lateralization could account for other dissimilarities between the ways native Japanese speakers and Westerners think about the world (Tsunoda, 1985).

In general, scientists are just beginning to understand the extent, nature, and meaning of sex and cultural differences in lateralization and brain structure. Furthermore, in evaluating the research on brain lateralization, it is important to keep in mind that the two hemispheres of the brain function in tandem. It is a mistake to think of particular kinds of information as being processed solely in the right or the left hemisphere. The hemispheres work interdependently in deciphering, interpreting, and reacting to the world.

In addition, people who suffer injury to the left side of the brain and lose linguistic capabilities often recover the ability to speak. In such cases, the right side of the brain often pitches in and takes over some of the functioning of the left side. This shift is especially true in young

children; the earlier the injury occurs, the greater the extent of recovery. Overall, then, the brain is remarkably adaptable. It can significantly modify its functioning in response to adverse circumstances, and, despite earlier beliefs that no new brain cells appear after childhood, recent evidence suggests that new brain cells are created during adulthood in certain parts of the brain such as the hippocampus (Kempermann & Gage, 1999; Gould et al., 1999).

The Split Brain: Exploring the Two Hemispheres

> The patient, V.J., had suffered severe seizures. By cutting her corpus callosum, the fibrous portion of the brain that carries messages between the hemispheres, surgeons hoped to create a firebreak to prevent the seizures from spreading. The operation did decrease the frequency and severity of V.J.'s attacks. But V.J. developed an unexpected side effect: She lost the ability to write at will, although she could read and spell words aloud. (Strauss, 1998, p. 287).

People like V.J., whose corpus callosum has been surgically cut to stop seizures and who are therefore called **split-brain patients,** offer a rare opportunity for researchers investigating the independent functioning of the two hemispheres of the brain. For example, psychologist Roger Sperry—who won the Nobel Prize for his work—developed a number of ingenious techniques for studying how each hemisphere operated (Sperry, 1982; Baynes et al., 1998; Gazzaniga, 1998).

In one experimental procedure, blindfolded subjects were allowed to touch an object with their right hand and were asked to name it. Because the right side of the body is connected to the left side of the brain—the hemisphere that is most responsible for language—the split-brain patient was able to name it. But if the blindfolded subjects touched the object with their left hand, they were not able to name it aloud. However, the information had registered: When the blindfold was taken off, subjects could pick out the objects that they had touched. Information can be learned and remembered, then, using only the right side of the brain. (By the way, unless you've had a split-brain operation, this experiment won't work with you, because the bundle of fibers connecting the two hemispheres of a normal brain immediately transfer the information from one hemisphere to the other.)

It is clear from experiments like this one that the right and left hemispheres of the brain specialize in handling different sorts of information. At the same time, it is important to realize that they are both capable of understanding, knowing, and being aware of the world, albeit in somewhat different ways. The two hemispheres, then, should be regarded as different in terms of the efficiency with which they process certain kinds of information, rather than as two entirely separate brains. Moreover, in people with normal, nonsplit brains, the hemispheres work interdependently to allow the full range and richness of thought of which humans are capable.

The Endocrine System: Of Chemicals and Glands

One aspect of the biopsychology of behavior that we have not yet considered is the **endocrine system,** a chemical communication network that sends messages throughout the nervous system via the bloodstream. Although not a structure of the brain itself, the endocrine system is intimately tied to the hypothalamus. The job of the endocrine system is to secrete **hormones,** chemicals that circulate through the blood and affect the functioning or growth of other parts of the body (Crapo, 1985; Kravitz, 1988).

Like neurotransmitters, hormones communicate chemical messages throughout the body, although the speed and mode of transmission are quite different. Whereas neural messages are measured in thousandths of a second, hormonal communications can take minutes to reach their destination. Furthermore, neural messages move across neurons

split-brain patient: A person who suffers from independent functioning of the two halves of the brain, as a result of which the sides of the body work in disharmony

tie to the hypothalamus → secret hormone

endocrine system: A chemical communication network that sends messages throughout the nervous system via the bloodstream

hormones: Chemicals that circulate through the blood and affect the functioning or growth of other parts of the body

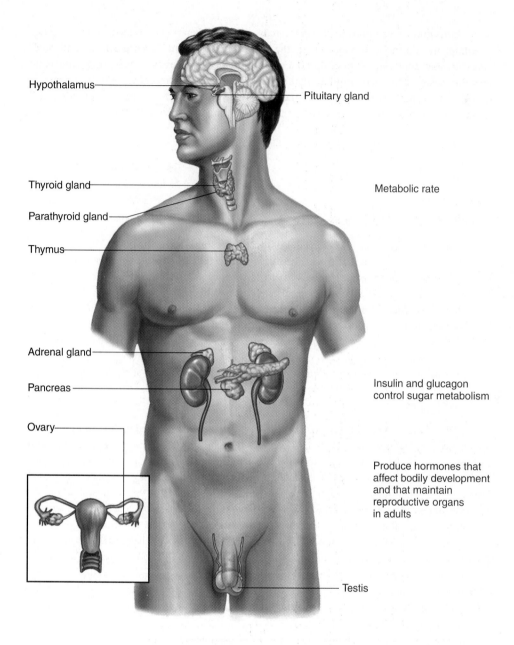

Hypothalamus

Pituitary gland

Thyroid gland

Parathyroid gland

Thymus

Metabolic rate

Adrenal gland

Pancreas

Insulin and glucagon
control sugar metabolism

Ovary

Produce hormones that
affect bodily development
and that maintain
reproductive organs
in adults

Testis

Figure 3-16 Location and function of
the major endocrine glands (Mader,
2000).

in specific lines (as with wires strung along telephone poles), whereas hormones travel
throughout the entire body, similar to the way radio waves transmit across the entire
landscape. Just as radio waves evoke a response only when a radio is tuned to the correct station, so hormones flowing through the bloodstream activate only those cells that
are receptive and "tuned" to the appropriate hormonal message.

A major component of the endocrine system is the **pituitary gland,** found near—
and regulated by—the hypothalamus. The pituitary gland has sometimes been called the
"master gland," because it controls the functioning of the rest of the endocrine system.
But the pituitary gland is more than just the taskmaster of other glands; it has important
functions in its own right. For instance, hormones secreted by the pituitary gland control growth. Extremely short people and unusually tall ones usually have pituitary gland
abnormalities. Other endocrine glands, shown in Figure 3-16, affect emotional reactions,
sexual urges, and energy levels.

Despite its designation as the "master gland," the pituitary is actually a servant of
the brain, because the brain is ultimately responsible for the endocrine system's functioning. The brain regulates the internal balance of the body, ensuring that homeostasis
is maintained through the hypothalamus.

pituitary gland: The "master gland," the
major component of the endocrine system,
which secretes hormones that control
growth

Individual hormones can wear many hats, depending on circumstances. For example, the hormone oxytocin is at the root of many of life's satisfactions and pleasures. In new mothers, oxytocin produces an urge to nurse newborn offspring. The same hormone also seems to stimulate cuddling between species members. And, at least in rats, it encourages sexually active males to seek out females more passionately, and females to be more receptive to males' sexual advances (Angier, 1991).

BECOMING AN INFORMED CONSUMER OF PSYCHOLOGY

Learning to Control Your Heart—and Mind—Through Biofeedback

biofeedback: A procedure in which a person learns to control through conscious thought internal physiological processes such as blood pressure, heart and respiration rate, skin temperature, sweating, and constriction of particular muscles

On a June evening in 1985, Tammy DeMichael was cruising along the New York State Thruway with her fiancé when he fell asleep at the wheel. The car slammed into the guardrail and flipped, leaving DeMichael with what the doctors called a "splattered C-6, 7"—a broken neck and crushed spinal cord.

After a year of exhaustive medical treatment, she still had no function or feeling in her arms and legs. "The experts said I'd be a quadriplegic for the rest of my life, able to move only from the neck up," she recalls. . . . But DeMichael proved the experts wrong. Today, feeling has returned to her limbs, her arm strength is normal or better, and she no longer uses a wheelchair. "I can walk about 60 feet with just a cane, and I can go almost anywhere with crutches," she says. (Morrow & Wolf, 1991, p. 64)

The key to DeMichael's astounding recovery: biofeedback. **Biofeedback** is a procedure in which a person learns to control through conscious thought internal physiological processes such as blood pressure, heart and respiration rate, skin temperature, sweating, and constriction of particular muscles. Although it had traditionally been thought that the heart, respiration rate, blood pressure, and other bodily functions were under the control of parts of the brain over which we have no influence, psychologists have discovered that these responses are actually susceptible to voluntary control (Rau et al., 1996; Grimsley & Karriker, 1996; Bazell, 1998).

In biofeedback, a person is hooked up to electronic devices that provide continuous feedback relating to particular physiological responses. For instance, a person interested in controlling headaches through biofeedback might have electronic sensors placed on certain muscles on her head and learn to control the constriction and relaxation of those muscles. Later, after she mastered this training, when she felt a headache starting she could relax the relevant muscles and end the pain.

In DeMichael's case, biofeedback was effective because not all of the nervous system's connections between the brain and her legs were severed. Through biofeedback, she learned how to send messages to specific muscles, "ordering" them to move. Although it took more than a year, DeMichael was successful in restoring a large degree of her mobility.

Learning to control physiological processes through the use of biofeedback is not easy, but biofeedback has been employed with success in a variety of ailments, including emotional problems (such as anxiety, depression, phobias, tension headaches, insomnia, and hyperactivity); physical illnesses with a psychological component (such as asthma, high blood pressure, ulcers, muscle spasms, and migraine headaches); and physical problems (such as DeMichael's injuries, strokes, cerebral palsy, and, as we see in Figure 3-17, curvature of the spine).

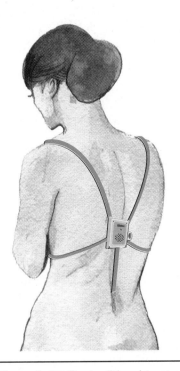

Figure 3-17 The traditional treatment for curvature of the spine employs an unsightly, cumbersome brace. In contrast, biofeedback treatment employs an unobtrusive set of straps attached to a small electronic device that produces tonal feedback when the patient is not standing straight. The person learns to maintain a position that gradually decreases the curvature of the spine until the device is no longer needed (Source: Miller, 1985a). What other disorders might biofeedback devices like this one help to treat?

Evaluate

1. A surgeon places an electrode on a portion of your brain and stimulates it. Immediately, your right wrist involuntarily twitches. The doctor has most likely stimulated a portion of the _left_ area of your brain.

2. The _sensory cortex_ its corresponding space within the cortex, the more sensitive an area of the body is.

3. Each hemisphere controls the _opposite_ side of the body.

4. Nonverbal realms, such as emotions and music, are controlled primarily by the _right hemisphere_ hemisphere of the brain, whereas the _left_ hemisphere is more responsible for speaking and reading.

5. The left hemisphere tends to consider information _sequentially_, whereas the right hemisphere tends to process information _left globally_

6. As studies with split-brain patients have shown, information can be learned and remembered using only the nonverbal side of the brain. True or False?

Answers to Evaluate Questions

1. motor 2. greater 3. opposite 4. right; left 5. sequentially; globally 5. True

Rethink

1. Suppose that abnormalities in an association area of the brain were linked through research to serious criminal behavior. Would you be in favor of mandatory testing of individuals and surgery to repair or remove those abnormalities? Why or why not?

2. Could personal differences in people's specialization of right and left hemispheres be related to occupational success? For example, might an architect who relies on spatial skills have a different pattern of hemispheric specialization than a writer?

Looking**Back**

Why do psychologists study the brain and nervous system?

- A full understanding of human behavior requires knowledge of the biological influences underlying that behavior. This chapter reviews what biopsychologists (psychologists who specialize in studying the effects of biological structures and functions on behavior) have learned about the human nervous system. (p. 55)

What are the basic elements of the nervous system?

- Neurons, the most basic elements of the nervous system, allow nerve impulses to pass from one part of the body to another. Information generally follows a route that begins with the dendrites, continues into the cell body, and leads ultimately down the tubelike extension, the axon. (p. 55)

How does the nervous system communicate electrical and chemical messages from one part to another?

- Most axons are protected by a coating called the myelin sheath. When an axon receives a message to fire, it releases an action potential, an electrical charge that travels through the neuron. Neurons operate according to an all-or-none law: Either they are at rest or an action potential is moving through them. There is no in-between state. (p. 55)
- Once a neuron fires, nerve impulses are carried to other neurons through the production of chemical substances, neurotransmitters, that bridge the gaps—known as synapses—between neurons. Neurotransmitters are either excitatory (telling other neurons to fire), or inhibitory (preventing or decreasing the likelihood of other neurons firing). The major neurotransmitters include acetylcholine (ACh), which produces contractions of skeletal muscles, and dopamine, which has been linked to Parkinson's disease and certain mental disorders such as schizophrenia. (p. 57)
- Endorphins, another type of neurotransmitter, are related to the reduction of pain. Endorphins aid in the production of natural painkillers and are probably responsible for creating the kind of euphoria that joggers sometimes experience after running. (p. 61)

In what way are the structures of the nervous system tied together?

- The nervous system is made up of the central nervous system (the brain and spinal cord) and the peripheral nervous system (the remainder of the nervous system). The peripheral nervous system is made up of the somatic division, which controls voluntary movements and the communication of information to and from the sense organs, and the autonomic division, which controls involuntary functions such as those of the heart, blood vessels, and lungs. (p. 62)
- The autonomic division of the peripheral nervous system is further subdivided into the sympathetic and parasympathetic divisions. The sympathetic division prepares the body in emergency situations, and the parasympathetic division helps the body return to its typical resting state. (p. 63)
- Evolutionary psychology, the branch of psychology that seeks to identify behavior patterns that are a result of our genetic inheritance, has led to increased understanding of the evolutionary basis of the structure and organization of the human nervous system. Behavioral genetics extends this study to include the evolutionary and hereditary bases of human personality traits and behavior. (p. 65)

How do researchers identify the major parts and functions of the brain?

- Brain scans take a "snapshot" of the internal workings of the brain without having to cut surgically into a person's skull. Major brain-scanning techniques include the electroencephalogram (EEG), computerized axial tomography (CAT), the functional magnetic resonance imaging (MRI) scan, the superconducting quantum interference device (SQUID), and the positron emission tomography (PET) scan. (p. 68)

What are the major parts of the brain, and for what behaviors is each part responsible?

- The central core of the brain is made up of the medulla (which controls such functions as breathing and the heartbeat), the pons (which coordinates the muscles and the two sides of the body), the cerebellum (which controls balance), the reticular formation (which acts to heighten awareness in emergencies), the thalamus (which communicates sensory messages to and from the brain), and the hypothalamus (which maintains homeostasis, or body equilibrium, and regulates basic survival behaviors). The functions of the central core structures are similar to those found in other vertebrates. This part of the brain is sometimes referred to as the "old brain." Increasing evidence also suggests that female and male brains might differ in structure in minor ways. (p. 69)
- The cerebral cortex—the "new brain"—has areas that control voluntary movement (the motor area); the senses (the sensory area); and thinking, reasoning, speech, and memory (the association area). The limbic system, found on the border of the "old" and "new" brains, is associated with eating, reproduction, and the experiences of pleasure and pain. (p. 73)

How do the two halves of the brain operate interdependently?

- The brain is divided into left and right halves, or hemispheres, each of which generally controls the opposite side of the body. Each hemisphere can be thought of as specialized in the functions it carries out: The left is best at verbal tasks, such as logical reasoning, speaking, and reading; the right is best at nonverbal tasks, such as spatial perception, pattern recognition, and emotional expression. (p. 77)
- The endocrine system secretes hormones, allowing the brain to send messages throughout the nervous system via the bloodstream. A major component is the pituitary gland, which affects growth. (p. 80)

How can an understanding of the nervous system help us find ways to relieve disease and pain?

- Biofeedback is a procedure by which a person learns to control internal physiological processes. By controlling what were previously considered involuntary responses, people are able to relieve anxiety, tension, migraine headaches, and a wide range of other psychological and physical problems. (p. 82)

Key Terms and Concepts

biopsychologists (behavioral neuroscientists) (p. 54)

neurons (p. 55)

dendrites (p. 55)

axon (p. 55)

terminal buttons (p. 55)

myelin sheath (p. 55)

all-or-none law (p. 57)

resting state (p. 57)
action potential (p. 57)
synapse (p. 58)
neurotransmitters (p. 58)
excitatory message (p. 60)
inhibitory message (p. 60)
reuptake (p. 60)
central nervous system (CNS) (p. 62)
spinal cord (p. 62)
reflexes (p. 62)
sensory (afferent) neurons (p. 62)
motor (efferent) neurons (p. 62)
interneurons (p. 62)
peripheral nervous system (p. 63)
somatic division (p. 63)
autonomic division (p. 63)
sympathetic division (p. 64)
parasympathetic division (p. 64)
evolutionary psychology (p. 65)

behavioral genetics (p. 66)
central core (p. 69)
cerebellum (p. 70)
reticular formation (p. 70)
thalamus (p. 71)
hypothalamus (p. 71)
limbic system (p. 71)
cerebral cortex (p. 73)
lobes (p. 73)
motor area (p. 73)
sensory area (p. 74)
association areas (p. 75)
hemispheres (p. 77)
lateralization (p. 78)
split-brain patient (p. 80)
endocrine system (p. 80)
hormones (p. 80)
pituitary gland (p. 81)
biofeedback (p. 82)

Preview

For additional quizzing and a variety of interactive resources, visit the *Understanding Psychology* Online Learning Center at

www.mhhe.com/feldmanup6

Psychology on the Web

1. Biofeedback research is continuously changing and being applied to new areas of human functioning. Find at least two websites that discuss recent research on biofeedback and summarize the research and any findings it has produced. Include in your summary your own best estimate of future applications of this technique.
2. Find one or more websites on Parkinson's disease and learn more about this topic. Specifically, find reports of new treatments for Parkinson's that do not involve the use of fetal tissue. Write a summary of your findings.

Epilogue

This chapter has traced the ways in which biological structures and functions of the body affect behavior. Starting with neurons, we considered each of the components of the nervous system, culminating in an examination of how the brain permits us to think, reason, speak, recall, and experience emotions—the hallmarks of being human.

Before we proceed to the next chapter, where we put our knowledge of the biology of behavior to use in a look at sensation and perception, turn back for a moment to the prologue of this chapter, involving television and movie star Michael J. Fox. Consider the following questions.

1. Using what you now know about brain structures and functioning, can you explain what might have produced Fox's Parkinson's disease in the first place?
2. The operation used to treat Fox's disorder destroyed certain cells of his brain. Speculate about what part of the brain the operation might have involved.
3. Do you think biofeedback techniques could be used to control the symptoms of Parkinson's disease? Why or why not?

Chapter Four

Sensation and Perception

Prologue: Now Hear This!

Looking Ahead

Sensing the World Around Us

Absolute Thresholds: Detecting What's Out There

Difference Thresholds: Noticing Distinctions Between Stimuli

Sensory Adaptation: Turning Down Our Responses

Vision: Shedding Light on the Eye

Illuminating the Structure of the Eye

Color Vision and Color Blindness: The Seven-Million-Color Spectrum

Applying Psychology in the 21st Century: Bringing Sight to People with Blindness

Hearing and the Other Senses

Sensing Sound

Smell and Taste

The Skin Senses: Touch, Pressure, Temperature, and Pain

Psychology at Work: Julia A. Mennella, Taste Researcher

Becoming an Informed Consumer of Psychology: Managing Pain

Perceptual Organization: Constructing Our View of the World

The Gestalt Laws of Organization

Feature Analysis: Focusing on the Parts of the Whole

Top-Down and Bottom-Up Processing

Perceptual Constancy

Depth Perception: Translating 2-D to 3-D

Motion Perception: As the World Turns

Perceptual Illusions: The Deceptions of Perceptions

Exploring Diversity: Culture and Perception

Subliminal Perception

Looking Back

Key Terms and Concepts

Psychology on the Web

OLC Preview

Epilogue

Prologue

Now Hear This!

Amy Ecklund

You'd almost think Amy Ecklund is a contestant on a game show called *Guess That Sound.* "That's a glass!" she proudly exclaims as she hears a clinking noise in the New Haven pub where she's having lunch. "Silverware!" she cries at the clang of a fork. When a hammer bangs, Ecklund gets really excited. "Wow!" she says, "that is loud!"

Life's everyday clatter is a symphony to Ecklund, 29, who for four years has played deaf hospital administrator Abigail Bauer on the CBS soap *Guiding Light.* Hearing-impaired since age 6 (doctors never determined the cause), Ecklund no longer has to read lips to do scenes. Last January she had a Nucleus 24 cochlear implant put in her right ear, thus becoming one of the 2,000 people in the U.S. to have benefited from the revolutionary hearing device...[which] has allowed Ecklund to hear nearly normally, dramatically changing her life. "It's like watching a child being born," says Michael O'Leary, who plays her husband, Dr. Rick Bauer, on *Guiding Light.* (Ecklund, 1999, p. 68)

Looking Ahead

Amy Ecklund is the beneficiary of a new generation of technological devices that offer the promise of restored hearing to the tens of thousands of people with hearing impairments. Still, no technological substitute has reached the ultimate level of sophistication of the human ear, or, for that matter, any of our other sense organs. In fact, our ability to sense the stimuli in our environment is remarkable, enabling us to feel the gentlest of breezes, see flickering lights miles away, and hear the soft murmuring of distant songbirds.

In this chapter we focus on the field of psychology that is concerned with the nature of the information our body takes in through its senses and with the way we interpret such information. We will explore both sensation and perception. **Sensation** encompasses the processes by which our sense organs receive information from the environment. **Perception** is the sorting out, interpretation, analysis, and integration of stimuli involving our sense organs and brain.

To a psychologist interested in understanding the causes of behavior, sensation and perception are fundamental topics, because so much of our behavior is a reflection of how we react to and interpret stimuli from the world around us. Questions ranging from "What processes enable us to see and hear?" to "How do we distinguish one person from another?" fall into the realm of sensation and perception.

Although perception clearly represents a step beyond sensation, in practice it is sometimes difficult to find the precise boundary between the two. Indeed, psychologists—and philosophers, as well—have argued for years over the distinction. The primary difference is that sensation can be thought of as an organism's first encounter with a raw sensory stimulus, whereas perception is the process by which the stimulus is interpreted, analyzed, and integrated with other sensory information. For example, if we were considering sensation, we might ask about the loudness of a ringing fire alarm. If we were considering perception, we might ask whether someone recognizes the ringing sound as an alarm and identifies its meaning. But both sensation and perception are necessary for transforming the physical world into our psychological reality.

This chapter begins with a discussion of the relationship between the characteristics of a physical stimulus and the kinds of sensory responses it produces. We then examine several of the major senses, including vision, hearing, balance, smell, taste, and the skin senses, which include touch and the experience of pain.

Next, the chapter explains how we organize the stimuli to which our sense organs are exposed. For instance, we consider a number of issues relating to perception, such as how we are able to perceive the world in three dimensions when our eyes are capable only of sensing two-dimensional images. Finally, we examine visual illusions, which provide us with important clues for understanding general perceptual mechanisms. As we explore these issues, we'll see how the senses work together to provide us with an integrated view and understanding of the world.

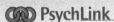

PsychLink

Perception demonstrations
www.mhhe.com/
feldmanup6-04links

sensation: The processes by which our sense organs receive information from the environment
perception: The sorting out, interpretation, analysis, and integration of stimuli involving our sense organs and brain

Prepare

What is sensation and how do psychologists study it?
What is the relationship between a physical stimulus and the kinds of sensory responses that result from it?

Organize

Sensing the World Around Us
    Absolute Thresholds
    Difference Thresholds
    Sensory Adaptation

Sensing the World Around Us

As Isabel sat down to Thanksgiving dinner, her father carried the turkey in on a tray and placed it squarely in the center of the table. The noise level, already high from the talking and laughter of family members, grew louder still. As Isabel picked up her fork, the smell of the turkey reached her and she felt her stomach growl hungrily. The sight and sound of her family around the table, along with the smells and tastes of the holiday meal, made Isabel feel more relaxed than she had since starting school in the fall.

Put yourself in this setting and consider how different it might be if any one of your senses was not functioning. What if you were blind and unable to see the faces of your family or the welcome shape of the golden-brown turkey? What if you had no sense of hearing and could not listen to the conversations of family members, or if you were unable to feel your stomach growl,

smell the dinner, or taste the food? Clearly, you would experience the dinner very differently from someone whose sensory apparatus was intact.

Moreover, the sensations mentioned above barely scratch the surface of sensory experience. Although perhaps you were taught, as I was, that there are just five senses—sight, sound, taste, smell, and touch—this enumeration is too modest. Human sensory capabilities go well beyond the basic five senses. It is well established, for example, that we are sensitive not merely to touch, but to a considerably wider set of stimuli—pain, pressure, temperature, and vibration, to name a few. In addition, vision has two subsystems—relating to day and night vision—and the ear is responsive to information that allows us not only to hear but also to keep our balance. Psychologists now believe there are at least a dozen distinct senses, all of which are interrelated.

To consider how psychologists understand the senses, and, more broadly, sensation and perception, we first need a basic working vocabulary. In formal terms, if any passing source of physical energy activates a sense organ, the energy is known as a stimulus. A **stimulus,** then, is energy that produces a response in a sense organ.

Stimuli vary in both type and intensity. Different types of stimuli activate different sense organs. For instance, we can differentiate light stimuli (which activate our sense of sight and allow us to see the colors of a tree in autumn) from sound stimuli (which, through our sense of hearing, permit us to hear the sounds of an orchestra).

Each sort of stimulus that is capable of activating a sense organ can also be considered in terms of its strength, or *intensity*. How intense a light stimulus needs to be before it is capable of being detected, or how much perfume a person must wear before it is noticed by others, are questions related to stimulus intensity.

The issue of how the intensity of a stimulus influences our sensory responses is considered in a branch of psychology known as psychophysics. **Psychophysics** is the study of the relationship between the physical aspects of stimuli and our psychological experience of them. Psychophysics played a central role in the development of the field of psychology, and many of the first psychologists studied issues related to psychophysics (Baird, 1997; Gescheider, 1997).

Absolute Thresholds: Detecting What's Out There

Just when does a stimulus become strong enough to be detected by our sense organs? The answer to this question requires an understanding of the concept of absolute threshold. An **absolute threshold** is the smallest intensity of a stimulus that must be present for it to be detected. Consider the following examples of absolute thresholds for the various senses (Galanter, 1962):

- *Sight:* A candle flame can be seen from 30 miles away on a dark, clear night.
- *Hearing:* The ticking of a watch can be heard 20 feet away under quiet conditions.
- *Taste:* Sugar can be tasted when 1 teaspoon is dissolved in 2 gallons of water.
- *Smell:* Perfume can be detected when one drop is present in a three-room apartment.
- *Touch:* A bee's wing falling from a distance of 1 centimeter can be felt on the cheek.

Such thresholds permit our sensory apparatus to detect a wide range of sensory stimulation. In fact, the capabilities of our senses are so fine-tuned that we might have problems if they were any more sensitive. For instance, if our ears were just slightly more acute, we would be able to hear the sound of air molecules in our ears knocking into our eardrum—a phenomenon that would surely prove distracting and might even prevent us from hearing sounds outside our bodies.

Of course, the absolute thresholds we have been discussing are measured under ideal conditions. Normally our senses cannot detect stimulation quite as well because of the presence of noise. *Noise,* as defined by psychophysicists, is background stimulation that interferes with the perception of other stimuli. Hence, noise refers not just to

stimulus: Energy that produces a response in a sense organ

psychophysics: The study of the relationship between the physical aspects of stimuli and our psychological experience of them

absolute threshold: The smallest intensity of a stimulus that must be present for the stimulus to be detected

 **PsychLink**

International Society for Psychophysics
www.mhhe.com/
feldmanup6-04links

Crowded conditions, sounds, and sights can all be considered as noise that interferes with sensation. Can you think of other examples of noise that is not auditory in nature?

auditory stimuli, the most obvious example, but also to stimuli that affect the other senses. Picture a talkative group of people crammed into a small, crowded, smoke-filled room at a party. The din of the crowd makes it hard to hear individual voices, and the smoke makes it difficult to see, or even taste, the food. In this case, the smoke and crowded conditions would both be considered "noise" because they are both preventing sensation at more discriminating levels.

Difference Thresholds: Noticing Distinctions Between Stimuli

Suppose you wanted to choose the six best apples from a supermarket display—the biggest, reddest, and sweetest apples. One approach would be to systematically compare one apple with another until you were left with a few so similar that you could not tell the difference between them. At that point, it wouldn't matter which ones you chose.

Psychologists have discussed this comparison problem in terms of the **difference threshold,** the smallest level of stimulation required to sense that a *change* in stimulation has occurred. Put another way, the difference threshold is the minimum stimulation required to detect the difference between two stimuli, or a **just noticeable difference.**

The stimulus value that constitutes a just noticeable difference depends on the initial intensity of the stimulus. For instance, when the moon is visible during the late afternoon, it appears relatively dim—yet against a dark night sky, it seems quite bright.

The relationship between changes in the original value of a stimulus and the degree to which the change will be noticed forms one of the basic laws of psychophysics: Weber's law. **Weber's law** (with *Weber* pronounced "vay-ber") states that a just noticeable difference is a constant proportion of the intensity of an initial stimulus. For example, Weber found that the just noticeable difference for weight is 1:50. Consequently, it takes a 1-ounce increase in a 50-ounce weight to produce a noticeable difference, and it would take a 10-ounce increase to produce a noticeable difference if the initial weight were 500 ounces. In both cases, the same proportional increase is necessary to produce a just noticeable difference—1:50 = 10:500.

Similarly, the just noticeable difference distinguishing changes in loudness between sounds is larger for sounds that are initially loud than for sounds that are initially soft. This principle explains why a person in a quiet room is more apt to be startled by the ringing of a telephone than a person in an already-noisy room. To produce the same amount of reaction in a noisy room, a telephone ring might have to approximate the loudness of cathedral bells.

Sensory Adaptation: Turning Down Our Responses

You enter a bar, and the odor of cigarettes assaults you. A few minutes later, though, you barely notice the smell.

The reason you acclimate to the odor is sensory adaptation. **Adaptation** is an adjustment in sensory capacity following prolonged exposure to stimuli. Adaptation occurs as people become accustomed to a stimulus and change their frame of reference. In a sense, our brains mentally turn down the volume of the stimulation they're experiencing.

One example of adaptation is the decrease in sensitivity that occurs after repeated exposure to a strong stimulus. If you were to hear a loud tone over and over again, eventually it would begin to sound softer. Similarly, although jumping into a cold lake might be temporarily unpleasant, eventually we probably will get used to the temperature.

This apparent decline in sensitivity to sensory stimuli is due to the inability of the sensory nerve receptors to constantly fire off messages to the brain. Because these receptor cells are most responsive to *changes* in stimulation, constant stimulation is not effective in producing a reaction.

Judgments of sensory stimuli are also affected by the context in which the judgments are made. This is because judgments are made, not in isolation from other stimuli, but in terms of preceding sensory experience.

---

difference threshold: The smallest level of stimulation required to sense that a *change* in stimulation has occurred

just noticeable difference: The minimum stimulation required to detect the difference between two stimuli

Weber's law: One of the basic laws of psychophysics, that a just noticeable difference is in constant proportion to the intensity of an initial stimulus

PsychLink

The fading dot
www.mhhe.com/
feldmanup6-04links

adaptation: An adjustment in sensory capacity following prolonged exposure to stimuli

You can demonstrate this for yourself by trying a simple experiment. Take two envelopes, one large and one small, and put fifteen nickels in each. Now lift the large envelope, put it down, and lift the small one. Which seems to weigh more? Most people report that the small one is heavier, although, as you know, the weights are nearly identical. The reason for this misconception is that the physical context of the envelope interferes with the sensory experience of weight. Adaptation to the context of one stimulus (the size of the envelope) alters responses to another stimulus (the weight of the envelope) (Coren & Ward, 1989).

Evaluate

1. _Perception_ is the stimulation of the sense organs; _____ is the sorting out, interpretation, analysis, and integration of stimuli by our sense organs.
2. The term *absolute threshold* refers to the _smallest_ intensity of a stimulus that must be present for the stimulus to be detected.
3. Weber discovered that in order for a difference between two stimuli to be perceptible, the stimuli must differ by at least a _constant_ proportion.
4. After completing a very difficult rock climb in the morning, Carmella found the afternoon climb unexpectedly easy. This case illustrates the phenomenon of _adaptation_.

Answers to Evaluate Questions

1. Sensation; perception 2. smallest 3. constant 4. adaptation

Rethink

1. Do you think it is possible to have sensation without perception? Is it possible to have perception without sensation?
2. Do you think sensory adaptation is essential for everyday psychological functioning?

Vision: Shedding Light on the Eye

If, as poets say, the eyes provide a window to the soul, they also provide us with a window to the world. Our visual capabilities permit us to admire and react to scenes ranging from the beauty of a sunset to the configuration of our lover's face to the words written on the pages of a book.

Vision starts with light, the physical energy that stimulates the eye. Light is a form of electromagnetic radiation waves, which, as shown in Figure 4-1, are measured in wavelengths. The sizes of wavelengths correspond to different types of energy. The range of wavelengths that humans are sensitive to—called the *visual spectrum*—is relatively small. Many nonhuman species have different capabilities. For instance, some reptiles and fish sense energies of longer wavelengths than humans do, and certain insects sense energies of shorter wavelengths than humans do.

Light waves coming from some object outside the body (imagine the light reflected off the flower in Figure 4-2) are sensed by the only organ that is capable of responding to the visual spectrum: the eye. Our eyes shape light into a form that can be used by the neurons that serve as messengers to the brain. The neurons themselves take up a relatively small percentage of the total eye. In other words, most of the eye is a mechanical device, analogous in many respects to a camera without film, as you can see in Figure 4-2.

Despite the similarities between the eye and a camera, vision involves processes that are far more complex and sophisticated than those of any camera. Furthermore, once the image reaches the neuronal receptors of the eye, the eye/camera analogy ends, for the processing of the visual image in the brain is more reflective of a computer than a camera.

Prepare

What basic processes underlie the sense of vision?
How do we see colors?

Organize

Vision
    Illuminating the Structure of the Eye
    Sending the Message from the Eye to the Brain
    Processing the Visual Message
    Color Vision and Color Blindness

PsychLink

Visual perception
www.mhhe.com/
feldmanup6–04links

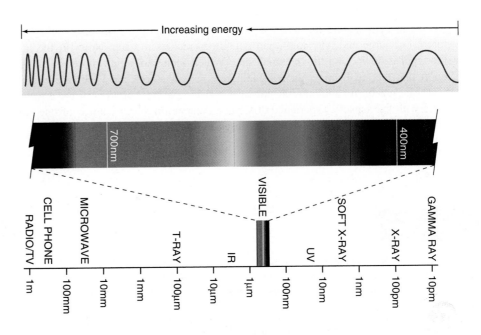

Illuminating the Structure of the Eye

The ray of light we are tracing as it is reflected off the flower first travels through the *cornea,* a transparent, protective window. The cornea bends (or *refracts*) light as it passes through in order to more sharply focus it. After moving through the cornea, the light traverses the pupil. The *pupil* is a dark hole in the center of the *iris,* the colored part of the eye, which in humans ranges from a light blue to a dark brown. The size of the pupil opening depends on the amount of light in the environment. The dimmer the surroundings, the more the pupil opens in order to allow more light to enter.

Why shouldn't the pupil be opened completely all the time, thereby allowing the greatest amount of light into the eye? The answer relates to the basic physics of light. A small pupil greatly increases the range of distances at which objects are in focus. With a wide-open pupil, the range is relatively small, and details are harder to discern. The eye takes advantage of bright light by decreasing the size of the pupil and thereby becoming more discerning. In dim light the pupil expands to enable us to view the situation better—but at the expense of visual detail. (Perhaps one reason candlelight dinners are thought of as romantic is that the dim light prevents one from seeing the details of a partner's physical flaws.)

Once light passes through the pupil, it enters the *lens,* which is located directly behind the pupil. The lens acts to bend the rays of light so they are properly focused on the rear of the eye. The lens focuses light by changing its own thickness, a process called *accommodation.* The lens becomes flatter when viewing distant objects and rounder when looking at closer objects.

Like the automatic lighting system on a camera, the human eye dilates to let in more light (left), and contracts to block out light (right). Can humans adjust their ears to let in more or less sound in a similar manner?

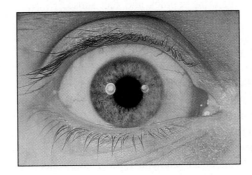
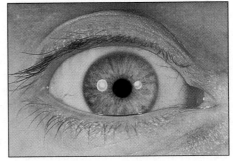

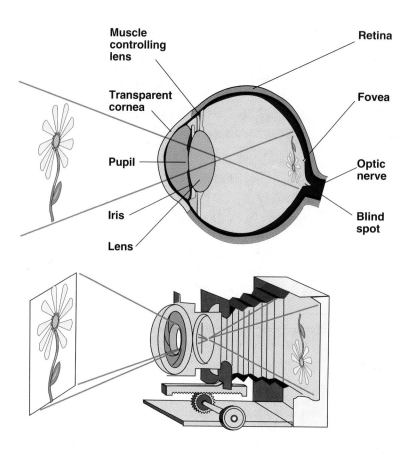

Figure 4–2 Although human vision is far more complicated than the most sophisticated camera, in some ways basic visual processes are analogous to those used in photography.

Reaching the Retina

Having traveled through the pupil and lens, our image of the flower finally reaches its ultimate destination in the eye—the **retina.** Here the electromagnetic energy of light is converted into the neural codes used by the brain. It is important to note that because of the physical properties of light, the image has reversed itself in traveling through the lens, and it reaches the retina upside down (relative to its original position). Although it might seem that this reversal would cause difficulties in understanding and moving about the world, this is not the case. The brain interprets the image in terms of its original position.

The retina consists of a thin layer of nerve cells at the back of the eyeball (see Figure 4-3). There are two kinds of light-sensitive receptor cells found in the retina. The names they have been given describe their shapes: rods and cones. **Rods** are thin, cylindrical receptor cells highly sensitive to light. **Cones** are cone-shaped, light-sensitive receptor cells that are responsible for sharp focus and color perception, particularly in bright light. The rods and cones are distributed unevenly throughout the retina. The greatest concentration of cones is on the part of the retina called the *fovea* (refer back to Figure 4-2). The fovea is a particularly sensitive region of the retina. If you want to focus in on something of particular interest, you will automatically try to center the image from the lens onto the area of the fovea to see it more sharply.

The density of cones declines just outside the fovea, although cones are found throughout the retina in lower concentrations. On the other hand, there are no rods in the very center of the fovea, but the density is greatest outside the fovea and then gradually declines toward the edges of the retina. Because the fovea covers only a small portion of the eye, there are fewer cones (about 7 million) than there are rods (about 125 million).

retina: The part of the eye that converts the electromagnetic energy of light into useful information for the brain

rods: Thin, cylindrical receptor cells in the retina that are highly sensitive to light

cones: Cone-shaped, light-sensitive receptor cells in the retina that are responsible for sharp focus and color perception, particularly in bright light

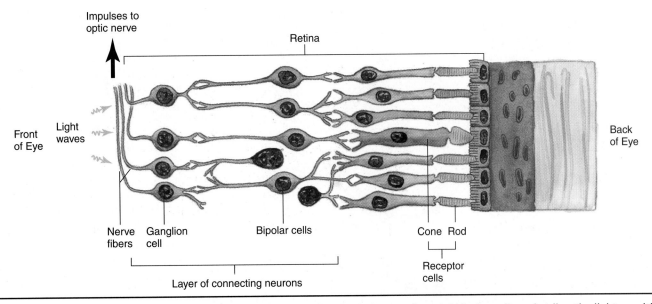

Figure 4–3 The basic cells of the eye. Light entering the eye travels through the ganglion and bipolar cells and strikes the light-sensitive rods and cones located at the back of the eye. The rods and cones then transmit nerve impulses to the brain via the bipolar and ganglion cells (Shier, Butler, & Lewis, 2000).

The rods and cones are not only structurally dissimilar, but they play distinctly different roles in vision. Cones are primarily responsible for the sharply focused perception of color, particularly in brightly lit situations; rods are related to vision in dimly lit situations and are largely insensitive to color and to details as sharp as those the cones are capable of recognizing. The rods play a key role in *peripheral vision*—seeing objects that are outside the main center of focus—and in night vision.

Rods and cones also are involved in *dark adaptation,* the phenomenon of adjusting to dim light after being in brighter light. (Think of the experience of walking into a dark movie theater and groping your way to a seat, but a few minutes later seeing the seats quite clearly.) The speed at which dark adaptation occurs is a result of the rate of change in the chemical composition of the rods and cones. Although the cones reach their greatest level of adaptation in just a few minutes, the rods take 15 minutes to reach the maximum level. The opposite phenomenon—*light adaptation,* or the process of adjusting to bright light after exposure to dim light—occurs much faster, taking only a minute or so.

The distinctive abilities of rods and cones make the eye analogous to a camera that is loaded with two kinds of film. One type is a highly sensitive black-and-white film (the rods). The other type is a somewhat less sensitive color film (the cones).

Sending the Message from the Eye to the Brain

When light energy strikes the rods and cones, it starts a chain of events that transforms light into neural impulses that can be communicated to the brain. Even before the neural message reaches the brain, however, some initial coding of the visual information takes place.

What happens when light energy strikes the retina depends in part on whether it encounters a rod or a cone. Rods contain *rhodopsin,* a complex, reddish-purple substance whose composition changes chemically when energized by light. The substance found in cone receptors is different, but the principles are similar. Stimulation of the nerve cells in the eye triggers a neural response that is transmitted to other nerve cells, called *bipolar cells* and *ganglion cells,* leading to the brain.

Bipolar cells receive information directly from the rods and cones. This information is then communicated to the ganglion cells. Ganglion cells collect and summarize

Figure 4-4 To find your blind spot, close your right eye and look at the haunted house with your left eye. You will see the ghost on the periphery of your vision. Now, while staring at the house, move the page toward you. When the book is about a foot from your eye, the ghost will disappear. At this moment, the image of the ghost is falling on your blind spot.

But also notice how, when the page is at that distance, not only does the ghost seem to disappear, but the line seems to run continuously through the area where the ghost used to be. This shows how we automatically compensate for missing information by using nearby material to complete what is unseen. That's the reason you never notice the blind spot. What is missing is replaced by what is seen next to the blind spot. Can you think of any advantages that this tendency to provide missing information gives humans as a species?

visual information, which is gathered and moved out of the back of the eyeball through a bundle of ganglion axons called the **optic nerve.**

Because the opening for the optic nerve passes through the retina, there are no rods or cones in the area, which creates a blind spot. Normally, however, this absence of nerve cells does not interfere with vision, because you automatically compensate for the missing part of your field of vision (Ramachandran, 1995; Churchland & Ramachandran, 1995). (To find your blind spot, see Figure 4-4.)

Once beyond the eye itself, the neural signals relating to the image move through the optic nerve. As the optic nerve leaves the eyeball, its path does not take the most direct route to the part of the brain right behind the eye. Instead, the optic nerves from each eye meet at a point roughly between the two eyes—called the *optic chiasm*—where each optic nerve then splits.

When the optic nerves split, the nerve impulses coming from the right half of each retina are sent to the right side of the brain, and the impulses arriving from the left half of each retina are sent to the left side of the brain. Because the image on the retinas is reversed and upside down, however, those images coming from the right half of each retina actually originated in the field of vision to the person's left, and images coming from the left half of each retina originated in the field of vision to the person's right (see Figure 4-5). In this way, our nervous system ultimately produces the phenomenon introduced in Chapter 3, in which each half of the brain is associated with the functioning of the opposite side of the body.

Processing the Visual Message

By the time a visual message reaches the brain, it has passed through several stages of processing. One of the initial sites is the ganglion cells. Each ganglion cell gathers information from a group of rods and cones in a particular area of the eye and compares the amount of light entering the center of that area with the amount of light in the area around it. Some ganglion cells are activated by light in the center (and darkness in the surrounding area). Other ganglion cells are activated when there is darkness in the center and light in the surrounding areas. The ultimate effect of this process is to maximize the detection of variations in light and darkness. The neural image that is passed on to the brain, then, is an enhanced version of the actual visual stimulus outside the body.

The ultimate processing of visual images takes place in the visual cortex of the brain, and it is here that the most complex kinds of processing occur. Psychologists David Hubel and Torsten Wiesel won the Nobel Prize for their discovery that many neurons in the cortex are extraordinarily specialized, being activated only by visual stimuli of a particular shape or pattern—a process known as **feature detection.** They found that some cells are activated only by lines of a particular width, shape, or orientation. Other cells are activated only by moving, as opposed to stationary, stimuli (Hubel & Wiesel, 1979; Patzwahl, Zanker, & Altenmuller, 1994).

optic nerve: A bundle of ganglion axons that carry visual information

PsychLink
Anatomy of the eye
www.mhhe.com/
feldmanup6-04links

feature detection: The activation of neurons in the cortex by visual stimuli of specific shapes or patterns

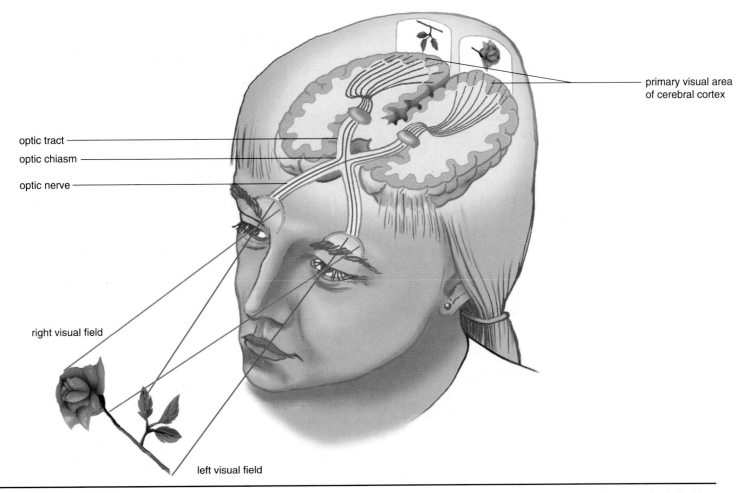

optic tract

optic chiasm

optic nerve

primary visual area
of cerebral cortex

right visual field

left visual field

Figure 4-5 Because the optic nerve coming from each eye splits at the optic chiasm, the image to a person's right is sent to the left side of the brain, and the image to the person's left is transmitted to the right side of the brain.

More recent work has added to our knowledge of the complex ways in which visual information coming from individual neurons is combined and processed. Different parts of the brain seem to process nerve impulses in several individual systems simultaneously. For instance, one system relates to shapes, one to colors, and others to movement, location, and depth (Moutoussis & Zeki, 1997).

If separate neural systems exist for processing information about specific aspects of the visual world, how are all these data integrated by the brain? Although the exact process is not yet well understood, it seems likely that the brain makes use of information regarding the frequency, rhythm, and timing of the firing of particular sets of neural cells. Furthermore, it appears that the brain's integration of visual information does not occur in any single step or location in the brain, but instead is a process that occurs on several levels simultaneously. The ultimate outcome, though, is indisputable: a vision of the world around us (Macaluso, Frith, & Driver, 2000; deGelder, 2000).

PsychLink

Explanation of color blindness
www.mhhe.com/
feldmanup6-04links

Color Vision and Color Blindness: The Seven-Million-Color Spectrum

Although the range of wavelengths to which humans are sensitive is relatively narrow, at least in comparison with the entire electromagnetic spectrum, the portion to which we are capable of responding still allows us great flexibility in sensing the world. Nowhere is this clearer than in terms of the number of colors we can discern. A person with normal color vision is capable of distinguishing no less than seven million different colors (Bruce, Green, & Georgeson, 1997).

a.   b.   c.

Figure 4.6 *(a)* To someone with normal vision, these hot-air balloons appear like this. *(b)* A person with red-green color blindness would see the scene like this, in hues of blue and yellow. *(c)* A person who is blue-yellow blind, conversely, would see it in hues of red and green.

Although the variety of colors that people are generally able to distinguish is vast, there are certain individuals whose ability to perceive color is quite limited—the color-blind. Interestingly, the condition of these individuals has provided some of the most important clues for understanding how color vision operates (Neitz, Neitz, & Kainz, 1996).

Before continuing, though, look at the photos shown in Figure 4-6. If you have difficulty seeing the differences among the series of photos, you may well be one of the 1 in 50 men or 1 in 5,000 women who are color-blind.

For most people with color-blindness, the world looks quite dull. Red fire engines appear yellow, green grass seems yellow, and the three colors of a traffic light all look yellow. In fact, in the most common form of color blindness, all red and green objects are seen as yellow. There are other forms of color blindness as well, but they are quite rare. In yellow-blue blindness, people are unable to tell the difference between yellow and blue, and in the most extreme case an individual perceives no color at all. To such a person the world looks something like the picture on a black-and-white television set.

To understand why some of us are color-blind, it is necessary to consider the basics of color vision. There appear to be two processes involved. The first process is explained by the **trichromatic theory of color vision.** This theory suggests that there are three kinds of cones in the retina, each of which responds primarily to a specific range of wavelengths. One is most responsive to blue-violet colors, one to green, and the third to yellow-red (Brown & Wald, 1964). According to trichromatic theory, perception of color is influenced by the relative strength with which each of the three kinds of cones is activated. If we see a blue sky, the blue-violet cones are primarily triggered, and the others show less activity. The trichromatic theory provides a straightforward explanation of color-blindness. It suggests that one of the three cone systems malfunctions, and colors covered by that range are perceived improperly (Nathans et al., 1989).

However, there are phenomena that the trichromatic theory is less successful at explaining. For example, the theory does not explain what happens after you stare at something like the flag shown in Figure 4-7 for about a minute. Try this yourself, and then look at a blank white page: You'll see an image of the traditional red, white, and blue U.S. flag. Where there was yellow, you'll see blue, and where there were green and black, you'll see red and white.

The phenomenon you have just experienced is called an *afterimage*. It occurs because activity in the retina continues even when you are no longer staring at the

trichromatic theory of color vision: The theory that there are three kinds of cones in the retina, each of which responds primarily to a specific range of wavelengths

Figure 4–7 Stare at the dot in this flag for about a minute, and then look at a piece of plain white paper. What do you see? Most people see an afterimage that converts the colors in the figure into the traditional red, white, and blue U.S. flag. If you have trouble seeing it the first time, blink once and try again.

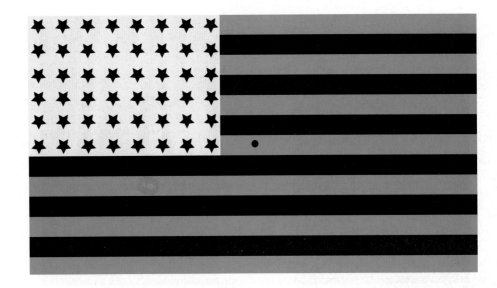

opponent-process theory of color vision: The theory that receptor cells are linked in pairs, working in opposition to each other

original picture. However, it also demonstrates that the trichromatic theory does not explain color vision completely. Why should the colors in the afterimage be different from those in the original?

Because trichromatic processes do not provide a full explanation of color vision, alternative explanations have been proposed. According to the **opponent-process theory of color vision,** receptor cells are linked in pairs, working in opposition to each other. Specifically, there is a blue-yellow pairing, a red-green pairing, and a black-white pairing. If an object reflects light that contains more blue than yellow, it will stimulate the firing of the cells sensitive to blue, simultaneously discouraging or inhibiting the firing of receptor cells sensitive to yellow—and the object will appear blue. If, on the other hand, a light contains more yellow than blue, the cells that respond to yellow will be stimulated to fire while the blue ones are inhibited, and the object will appear yellow.

The opponent-process theory provides a good explanation for afterimages. When we stare at the yellow in the figure, for instance, our receptor cells for the yellow component of the yellow-blue pairing become fatigued and are less able to respond to yellow stimuli. On the other hand, the receptor cells for the blue part of the pair are not tired, because they are not being stimulated. When we look at a white surface, the light reflected off it would normally stimulate both the yellow and the blue receptors equally. But the fatigue of the yellow receptors prevents this from happening. They temporarily do not respond to the yellow, which makes the white light appear to be blue. Because the other colors in the figure do the same thing relative to their specific opponents, the afterimage produces the opponent colors—for a while. The afterimage lasts only a short time, because the fatigue of the yellow receptors is soon overcome, and the white light begins to be perceived more accurately.

Both opponent processes and trichromatic mechanisms are at work in allowing us to see color. However, they operate in different parts of the visual sensing system. Trichromatic processes work within the retina itself, whereas opponent mechanisms operate both in the retina and at later stages of neuronal processing (Leibovic, 1990; Gouras, 1991; de Valois & de Valois, 1993).

As we have gained more understanding of the processes that permit us to see, some psychologists have begun to develop new techniques to help overcome visual deficiencies in people with serious problems such as visual impairment or total blindness. One of the most promising devices is discussed in the *Applying Psychology in the 21st Century* box.

Applying Psychology in the 21st Century

Bringing Sight to People with Blindness

At first sight, it looks like an off-center ponytail flopping at the back of the head of a 62-year-old man named Jerry. But a closer look reveals that it is actually a bundle of wires entering Jerry's skull.

The purpose of the wires is to link a computer directly into Jerry's brain. The computer responds to a tiny pinhole camera mounted on one lens of a pair of sunglasses Jerry is wearing, along with an ultrasonic rangefinder mounted on the other lens. The camera and rangefinder send minute electrical charges through 68 electrodes implanted in a small area of the surface of Jerry's brain, allowing Jerry to perceive specks of light.

Admittedly, the kind of vision Jerry experiences is greatly limited. He is able to locate a mannequin in a room, find a black cap that is hanging on a wall, and place it on the head of the mannequin. He can also recognize two-inch-tall letters from five feet away.

Jerry (whose last name has not been divulged) is using an experimental device that may someday bring close to normal vision to people with blindness. Although in its current version the device permits Jerry to see only specks of flickering light, it is still sophisticated enough to permit him to perceive differences between light and dark areas (Dobelle, 2000).

Technological advances are providing other approaches to helping the blind. For instance, sensory perception psychologist Jack Loomis and colleagues are developing what they call a "personal guidance system" to help people with vision limitations move through their environment (Loomis et al., 1993; Golledge et al., 1998; Loomis, Golledge, & Klatzky, in press).

The system uses a positioning device linked to navigation satellites overhead that are able to map the ground with an accuracy of several feet. Geographic information from the satellites is

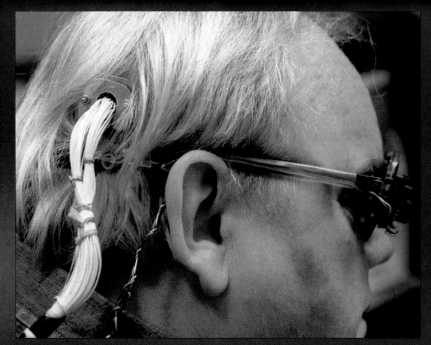

Jerry, a 62-year-old man with blindness, is able to see as the result of electrodes implanted in his brain and connected to a camera mounted on a pair of glasses. A small computer on his hip permits him to read large letters and move around large objects in a room. Do you think modern technology will ever duplicate the functions of the human eye?

transmitted to an on-ground receiver and computer strapped to a person's back. The computer translates the geographic information into acoustic stimulation that is sent to one earphone or the other. The stimulation, which for now is just a code word, becomes softer or louder, depending on the direction the person is supposed to turn.

Klatzky and Loomis predict that future versions will go beyond a single code word to provide complete verbal directions, such as "go forward ten feet, and then turn to the right." In addition, the computer will identify landmarks the person is passing by ("I'm the post office, and I'm 20 feet to your left"). Furthermore, the size of the backpack should shrink significantly, perhaps fitting into a pack around the waist.

Researchers predict that devices such as Jerry's electrodes and the personal guidance system will be commercially available within the next few years. Next on the horizon are electronic retinal implants, a kind of bionic eye, that will restore sight to people with damaged retinas. Some experts feel that such devices can be developed well before the end of the decade (Marcus, 1998; Eisenberg, 1999; Dobelle, 2000).

What psychological adjustments might be necessary when sight is restored for people who have been blind for their entire lives? Can you think of any disadvantages of the restoration of sight and why some blind individuals might decide not to have their sight restored?

Evaluate

1. Light entering the eye first passes through the _____, a protective window.
2. The structure that converts light into usable neural messages is called the _____.
3. A woman with blue eyes could be described as having blue pigment in her _____.
4. What is the process by which the thickness of the lens is changed in order to focus light properly?
5. The proper sequence of structures that light passes through in the eye is the _____, _____, _____, and _____.
6. Match each type of visual receptor with its function.

   a. Rods   1. Used for dim light, largely insensitive to color.
   b. Cones   2. Detect color, good in bright light.

7. Paco was to meet his girlfriend in the movie theater. As was typical, he was late and the movie had begun. He stumbled down the aisle, barely able to see. Unfortunately, the woman he sat down beside and attempted to put his arm around was not his girlfriend. He sorely wished he had given his eyes a chance and waited for _____ adaptation to occur.
8. _____ theory states that there are three types of cones in the retina, each of which responds primarily to a different color.

Answers to Evaluate Questions

1. cornea 2. retina 3. iris 4. Accommodation 5. cornea, pupil, lens, retina 6. a-1, b-2 7. dark 8. Trichromatic

Rethink

1. If the eye were constructed with a second lens that "unreversed" the image hitting the retina, do you think there would be changes in the way people perceive the world?
2. From an evolutionary standpoint, why might the eye have evolved so that the rods, which we rely on in low light, do not provide sharp images? Are there any advantages to this system?

Prepare

What role does the ear play in the senses of sound, motion, and balance?

How do smell and taste function?

What are the skin senses, and how do they relate to the experience of pain?

Organize

Hearing and the Other Senses
  Sensing Sound
  Smell and Taste
  The Skin Senses

Hearing and the Other Senses

The blast-off was easy compared with what the astronaut was experiencing now: space sickness. The constant nausea and vomiting were enough to make him wonder why he had worked so hard to become an astronaut. Even though he had been warned that there was a two-thirds chance that his first experience in space would cause these symptoms, he wasn't prepared for how terribly sick he really felt.

Whether or not the astronaut turns his rocket around and heads back to earth, his experience, a major problem for space travelers, is related to a basic sensory process centered in the ear: the sense of motion and balance. This sense allows people to navigate their bodies through the world and maintain an upright position without falling. Along with hearing, which is the process by which sound waves are translated into understandable and meaningful forms, the senses of motion and balance are the major functions of the ear.

Sensing Sound

Although many of us think primarily of the *outer ear* when we consider hearing, this part functions simply as a reverse megaphone, designed to collect and bring sounds into internal portions of the ear (see Figure 4-8). However, the location of the outer ears on different sides of the head helps with *sound localization,* the process by which we identify the location from which a sound is originating. Wave patterns in the air enter each ear at a slightly different time, permitting the brain to use the discrepancy to locate the sound's point of origin. In addition, the two outer ears delay or amplify sounds of particular frequencies to different degrees (Middlebrooks & Green, 1991; Yost, 1992; Konishi, 1993).

Sound is the movement of air molecules brought about by the vibration of an object. Sounds travel through the air in wave patterns similar in shape to those made

sound: The movement of air molecules brought about by the vibration of an object

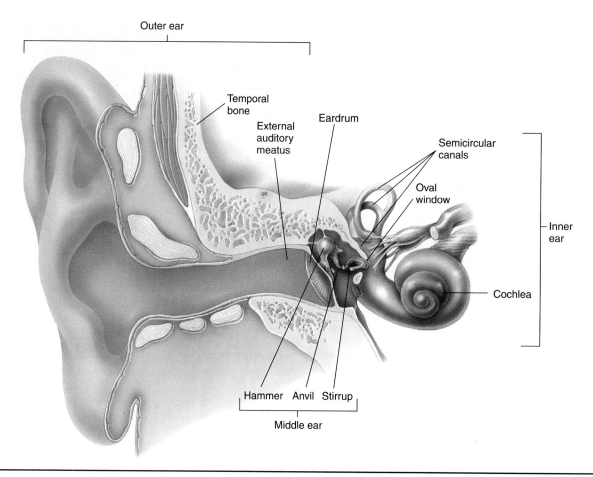

Figure 4–8 The ear (Seeley, Stephens, & Tate, 2000).

in water when a stone is thrown into a still pond. Sounds, arriving at the outer ear in the form of wave vibrations, are funneled into the *auditory canal,* a tubelike passage that leads to the eardrum. The **eardrum** is aptly named because it operates like a miniature drum, vibrating when sound waves hit it. The more intense the sound, the more the eardrum vibrates. These vibrations are then transferred into the *middle ear,* a tiny chamber containing three bones (the *hammer,* the *anvil,* and the *stirrup*) that transmit vibrations to the *oval window,* a thin membrane leading to the inner ear. Because the hammer, anvil, and stirrup act as a set of levers, they not only transmit vibrations but increase their strength. Moreover, because the opening into the middle ear (the eardrum) is considerably larger than the opening out of it (the oval window), the force of sound waves on the oval window becomes amplified. The middle ear, then, acts as a tiny mechanical amplifier.

The *inner ear* is the portion of the ear that changes the sound vibrations into a form that allows them to be transmitted to the brain. It also contains the organs that allow us to locate our position and determine how we are moving through space. When sound enters the inner ear through the oval window, it moves into the **cochlea,** a coiled tube that looks something like a snail and is filled with fluid that can vibrate in response to sound. Inside the cochlea is the **basilar membrane,** a structure that runs through the center of the cochlea, dividing it into an upper and a lower chamber. The basilar membrane is covered with **hair cells.** When these hair cells are bent by the vibrations entering the cochlea, a neural message is transmitted to the brain (Cho, 2000).

Although sound typically enters the cochlea via the oval window, there is an additional method of entry: bone conduction. Because the ear rests on a maze of bones within the skull, the cochlea is able to pick up subtle vibrations that travel across the

eardrum: The part of the ear that vibrates when sound waves hit it

cochlea (KOKE lee uh): A coiled tube in the ear filled with fluid that vibrates in response to sound

basilar membrane: A vibrating structure that runs through the center of the cochlea, dividing it into an upper and a lower chamber, and containing sense receptors for sound

hair cells: Tiny cells covering the basilar membrane that, when bent by vibrations entering the cochlea, transmit neural messages to the brain

The eardrum is aptly named because it operates like a miniature drum, vibrating when sound waves hit it.

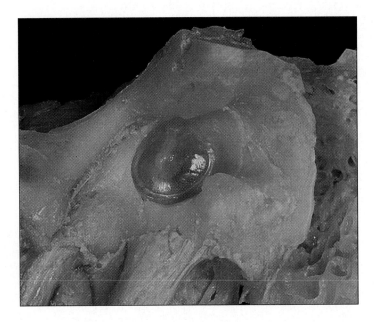

bones from other parts of the head. For instance, one of the ways you hear your own voice is through bone conduction. This explains why you sound different to yourself than to other people who hear your voice. (Listen to yourself on a tape recorder sometime to hear what you *really* sound like!) The sound of your voice reaches you both through the air and via bone conduction and therefore sounds richer to you than to everyone else.

The Physical Aspects of Sound

As we mentioned earlier, what we refer to as sound is actually the physical movement of air molecules in regular, wavelike patterns caused by the vibration of an object (see Figure 4-9). Sometimes it is even possible to view these vibrations, as in the case of a stereo speaker that has no enclosure. If you have ever seen one, you know that, at least when the lowest notes are playing, you can see the speaker moving in and out. What is less obvious is what happens next: The speaker pushes air molecules into waves with the same pattern as its movement. These wave patterns soon reach your ear, although their strength has been weakened considerably during their travels. All other stimuli that produce sound work in essentially the same fashion, setting off wave patterns that move through the air to the ear. Air—or some other medium, such as water—is necessary to make the vibrations of objects reach us. This explains why there can be no sound in a vacuum.

We are able to see the stereo speaker moving when low notes are played because of a primary characteristic of sound called frequency. *Frequency is the number of wave cycles that occur in a second*. With very low frequencies there are relatively few, and therefore slower, up-and-down wave cycles per second. These are visible to the naked eye as vibrations in the speaker. Low frequencies are translated into a sound that is very low in pitch. (*Pitch* is the characteristic that makes sound "high" or "low.") For example, the lowest frequency that humans are capable of hearing is 20 cycles per second. Higher frequencies translate into higher pitch. At the upper end of the sound spectrum, people can detect sounds with frequencies as high as 20,000 cycles per second.

Intensity is a feature of wave patterns that allows us to distinguish between loud and soft sounds. Intensity is produced by the difference between the peaks and valleys of air pressure in a sound wave as it travels through the air. Waves with small peaks and valleys produce soft sounds; those that are relatively large produce loud sounds.

PsychLink

Sound waves
www.mhhe.com/
feldmanup6–04links

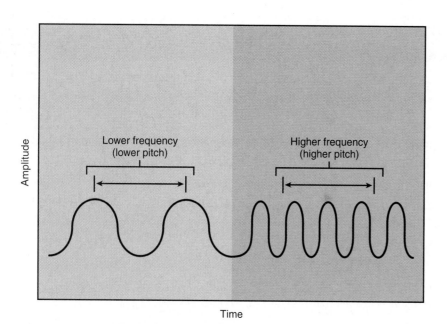

Figure 4-9 The waves produced by different stimuli are transmitted—usually through the air—in different patterns, with lower frequencies indicated by fewer peaks and valleys per second.

We are sensitive to a broad range of sound intensity. The loudest sounds we are capable of hearing are about 10 million times as intense as the very weakest sound we can hear. This range is measured in *decibels*. When sounds get higher than 120 decibels, they become painful to the human ear.

Hearing Loss and Deaf Culture

The delicacy of the organs involved in hearing makes the ear vulnerable to damage. For instance, exposure to intense levels of sound—coming from events ranging from rock concerts to overly loud headphones—can eventually result in hearing loss, as the hair cells of the basilar membrane lose their elasticity and bend and flatten (see Table 4-1). Such hearing loss is often permanent.

Even without actual injury, many people eventually lose hearing acuity over the course of their lives. Ultimately, almost 10 percent of all individuals have some degree of hearing impairment.

Although minor hearing impairment can be treated with hearing aids that increase the volume of sounds reaching the ear, more drastic measures are necessary in more severe cases. Certain forms of deafness, produced by damage to the hair cells, can be treated through a *cochlear implant,* like that received by Amy Ecklund, whose case was discussed in the chapter prologue. Implants consist of a tiny receiver inside the ear and an electrode that stimulates hair cells, controlled by a small external sound processor worn behind the ear.

Although the restoration of hearing to a deaf person may seem like an unquestionably positive achievement, some advocates for the deaf suggest otherwise, especially when it comes to deaf children who are not old enough to provide informed consent. These critics suggest that deafness represents a legitimate culture—no better nor worse than the hearing culture—and that providing even limited hearing to deaf children robs them of their natural cultural heritage. It is, without doubt, a controversial position.

Sorting Out Theories of Sound

How are our brains able to sort out wavelengths of different frequencies and intensities? One clue comes from studies of the basilar membrane, the area within the cochlea that translates physical vibrations into neural impulses. It turns out that sounds affect different areas of the basilar membrane, depending on the frequency of the sound wave. The part of the basilar membrane nearest the oval window is most sensitive to high-frequency

Table 4-1 Now Hear This

Various sounds, their decibel levels, and the amount of exposure that results in hearing damage

Sound	Decibel Level	Exposure Time Leading to Damage
Whispering	25 dB	
Library	30 dB	
Average home	50 dB	
Normal conversation	60 dB	
Washing machine	65 dB	
Car	70 dB	
Vacuum cleaner	70 dB	
Busy traffic	75 dB	
Alarm clock	80 dB	
Noisy restaurant	80 dB	
Average factory	85 dB	16 hours
Live rock music (moderately loud)	90 dB	8 hours
Screaming child	90 dB	8 hours
Subway train	100 dB	2 hours
Jackhammer	100 dB	2 hours
Helicopter	105 dB	1 hour
Sandblasting	110 dB	30 minutes
Auto horn	120 dB	7.5 minutes
Live rock music (loud)	130 dB	3.75 minutes
Air raid siren	130 dB	3.75 minutes
THRESHOLD OF PAIN	140 dB	Immediate damage
Jet engine	140 dB	Immediate damage
Rocket launching	180 dB	Immediate damage

place theory of hearing: The theory that different areas of the basilar membrane respond to different frequencies

frequency theory of hearing: The theory that the entire basilar membrane acts like a microphone, vibrating as a whole in response to a sound

sounds, and the part nearest the cochlea's inner end is most sensitive to low-frequency sounds. This finding has led to the **place theory of hearing,** which says that different areas of the basilar membrane respond to different frequencies.

On the other hand, place theory does not tell the full story of hearing, because very low frequency sounds trigger neurons across such a wide area of the basilar membrane that no single site is involved. Consequently, an additional explanation for hearing has been proposed: frequency theory. The **frequency theory of hearing** suggests that the entire basilar membrane acts like a microphone, vibrating as a whole in response to a sound. According to this explanation, the nerve receptors send out signals that are tied directly to the frequency (the number of wave crests per second) of the sounds to which we are exposed, with the number of nerve impulses being a direct function of the sound's frequency. Thus, the higher the pitch of a sound (and therefore the greater the frequency of its wave crests), the greater the number of nerve impulses that are transmitted up the auditory nerve to the brain.

Neither place theory nor frequency theory provides the full explanation for hearing (Luce, 1993; Hirsh & Watson, 1996). Place theory provides a better explanation for the sensing of high-frequency sounds, whereas frequency theory explains what happens when low-frequency sounds are encountered. Medium-frequency sounds incorporate both processes.

After an auditory message leaves the ear, it is transmitted to the auditory cortex of the brain through a complex series of neural interconnections. As the message is transmitted, it is communicated through neurons that respond to specific types of sounds. Within the auditory cortex itself, there are neurons that respond selectively to very specific sorts of sound features, such as clicks or whistles. Some neurons respond only to a specific pattern of sounds, such as a steady tone but not an intermittent one. Furthermore, specific neurons transfer information about a sound's location through their particular pattern of firing (Ahissar et al., 1992; Middlebrooks et al., 1994).

If we were to analyze the configuration of the cells in the auditory cortex, we would find that neighboring cells are responsive to similar frequencies. The auditory cortex, then, provides us with a "map" of sound frequencies, just as the visual cortex furnishes a representation of the visual field.

Balance: The Ups and Downs of Life

Several structures of the ear are related more to our sense of balance than to our hearing. The **semicircular canals** of the inner ear consist of three tubes containing fluid that sloshes through them when the head moves, signaling rotational or angular movement to the brain. The pull on our bodies caused by the acceleration of forward, backward, or up-and-down motion, as well as the constant pull of gravity, is sensed by the **otoliths,** tiny, motion-sensitive crystals. When we move, these crystals shift like sands on a windy beach. The brain's inexperience in interpreting messages from the weightless otoliths is the cause of the space sickness commonly experienced by two-thirds of all space travelers (Flam, 1991; Stern & Koch, 1996).

semicircular canals: Three tubelike structures of the inner ear containing fluid that sloshes through them when the head moves, signaling rotational or angular movement to the brain

otoliths: Tiny, motion-sensitive crystals within the semicircular canals that sense body acceleration

Smell and Taste

Until he bit into a piece of raw cabbage on that February evening in 1997, Dr. Raymond Fowler had not thought much about the sense of taste.

The cabbage, part of a pasta dish he was preparing for his family's dinner, had an odd, burning taste, but he did not pay it much attention. Then a few minutes later, his daughter handed him a glass of cola, and he took a swallow. "It was like sulfuric acid," he said. "It was like the hottest thing you could imagine boring into your mouth." (Goode, 1999b, p. D1-D2)

It was clear that something was very wrong with Fowler's sense of taste. After extensive testing, it became clear that he had damaged the nerves involved in his sense of taste, probably because of a viral infection or medicine he was taking. (Luckily for him, a few months later his sense of taste returned to normal.)

Even without disruptions in our ability to perceive the world such as those experienced by Fowler, we all know the important roles that taste and smell play. We'll consider these two senses next.

Smell

Although many animals have keener abilities to detect odors than we do, our sense of smell *(olfaction)* permits us to detect more than 10,000 separate smells. We also have a good memory for smells, and long-forgotten events and memories can be brought back with the mere whiff of an odor associated with the memory (Schab, 1991; Bartoshuk & Beauchamp, 1994; Gillyatt, 1997).

Results of "sniff tests" have shown that women generally have a better sense of smell than men (Engen, 1987). People also seem to have the ability to distinguish males from females on the basis of smell alone. In one experiment, blindfolded students, asked to sniff the breath of a female or male volunteer who was hidden from view, were able

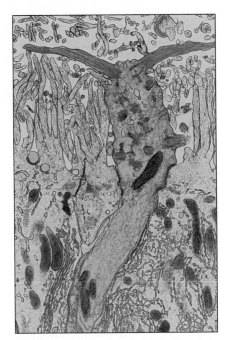

More than 1000 receptor cells, known as olfactory cells, are spread across the nasal cavity. The cells are specialized to react to particular odors. Do you think it is possible to "train" the nose to pick up a greater number of odors?

PsychLink

Taste and smell
www.mhhe.com/
feldmanup6-04links

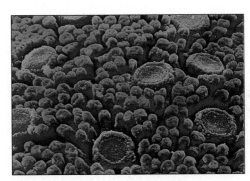

There are 10,000 taste buds spread across the tongue and other parts of the mouth. Taste buds wear out and are replaced every 10 days. What would happen if taste buds were not regenerated?

to distinguish the sex of the donor at better than chance levels. People can also distinguish happy from sad emotions by sniffing underarm smells (Doty et al., 1982; Haviland-Jones & Chen, 1999).

Our understanding of the mechanisms that underlie the sense of smell is just beginning to emerge. We do know that the sense of smell is sparked when the molecules of a substance enter the nasal passages and meet *olfactory cells,* the receptor cells of the nose, which are spread across the nasal cavity. More than 1,000 separate types of receptor cells have been identified so far. Each of these cells is so specialized that it responds only to a small band of different odors. The responses of the separate olfactory cells are then transmitted to the brain, where they are combined into recognition of a particular smell (Buck & Axel, 1991; Katz & Rubin, 1999).

There is increasing evidence that smell can also act as a hidden means of communication for humans. It has long been known that nonhumans release *pheromones,* pollen-like chemicals that produce a reaction in other members of a species, permitting the transmission of such messages as sexual availability. For instance, certain substances in the vaginal secretions of female monkeys contain pheromones that stimulate sexual interest in male monkeys (Holy, Dulac, & Meister, 2000).

Although it seems reasonable that humans might also communicate through the release of pheromones, the evidence is still scanty. Women's vaginal secretions contain chemicals similar to those found in monkeys, but in humans the smells do not seem to be related to sexual activity. On the other hand, the presence of these substances might explain why women who live together for long periods of time tend to start their menstrual cycles on the same day. In addition, women are able to identify their babies solely on the basis of smell just a few hours after birth (Porter, Cernich, & McLaughlin, 1983; Engen, 1987; Grammer, 1996).

Taste

Unlike smell, which employs more than a thousand separate types of receptor cells, the sense of taste *(gustation)* seems to make do with only a handful of fundamental types of receptors. Most psychologists believe that there are just four basic receptor cells, which specialize in either sweet, sour, salty, or bitter flavors. Every other taste is simply a combination of these four basic qualities, in the same way that the primary colors blend into a vast variety of shades and hues (McLaughlin & Margolskee, 1994).

The receptor cells for taste are located in roughly 10,000 *taste buds,* which are distributed across the tongue and other parts of the mouth and throat. The taste buds wear out and are replaced every ten days or so. That's a good thing, because if our taste buds weren't constantly reproducing, we'd lose the ability to taste after we'd accidentally burned our tongues.

The sense of taste differs significantly from one person to another, determined largely by genetic factors. Some people, dubbed "supertasters," are highly sensitive to taste; they have twice as many taste receptors as "nontasters," who are relatively insensitive to taste. Supertasters (who, for unknown reasons, are more likely to be female than male) find sweets sweeter, cream creamier, and spicy dishes spicier, and weaker concentrations of flavor are enough to satisfy any cravings they may have. On the other hand, because they aren't so sensitive to taste, nontasters may seek out relatively sweeter and fattier foods in order to maximize the taste. As a consequence, they may be prone to obesity (Bartoshuk & Drewnowski, 1997; Bartoshuk, 2000).

To determine your own taste sensitivity, try the test in Figure 4-10. And to learn more about research being done on taste and smell, see the *Psychology at Work* box on page 110.

The Skin Senses: Touch, Pressure, Temperature, and Pain

It started innocently, when Jennifer Darling hurt her right wrist during gym class. At first it seemed like a simple sprain. But even though the initial injury healed, the excruciating, burning pain accompanying it did not go away. Instead, it spread

TAKE A TASTE TEST

1. Taste Bud count

Punch a hole with a standard hole punch in a square of wax paper. Paint the front of your tongue with a cotton swab dipped in blue food coloring. Put wax paper on the tip of your tongue, just to the right of center. With a flashlight and magnifying glass, count the number of pink, unstained circles. They contain taste buds.

2. Sweet taste

Rinse your mouth with water before tasting each sample. Put 1/2 cup sugar in a measuring cup, and then add enough water to make 1 cup. Mix. Coat front half of your tongue, including the tip, with a cotton swab dipped in the solution. Wait a few moments. Rate the sweetness according to the scale shown below.

3. Salt taste

Put 2 teaspoons of salt in a measuring cup and add enough water to make 1 cup. Repeat the steps listed above, rating how salty the solution is.

4. Spicy taste

Add 1 teaspoon of Tabasco sauce to 1 cup of water. Apply with a cotton swab to first half inch of the tongue, including the tip. Keep your tongue out of your mouth until the burn reaches a peak, then rate the burn according to the scale.

TASTE SCALE

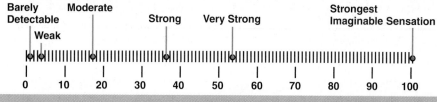

	SUPERTASTERS	NONTASTERS
No. of taste buds	25 on Average	10
Sweet rating	56 on Average	32
Tabasco	64 on Average	31

Average tasters lie in between supertasters and nontasters. Bartoshuk and Lucchina lack the data at this time to rate salt reliably, but you can compare your results with others taking the test.

Figure 4-10 All tongues are not created equal, according to taste researchers Linda Bartoshuk and Laurie Lucchina. Instead, they suggest that the intensity of a flavor experienced by a given person is determined by their genetic background. This taste test can help determine if you are a Nontaster, Average Taster, or Supertaster (Bartoshuk & Lucchina, 1997).

to her other arm, and then to her legs. The pain, which Jennifer described as similar to "a hot iron on your arm," was unbearable—and never stopped.

The source of Darling's pain turned out to be a rare condition known as "reflex sympathetic dystrophy syndrome," or RSDS for short. For a victim of RSDS, a stimulus as mild as a gentle breeze or the touch of a feather can produce agony. Even bright sunlight or a loud noise can trigger intense pain.

Pain like Darling's can be devastating. Yet a lack of pain can be equally bad. If you never experienced pain, for instance, you might not notice that your arm had brushed against a hot pan, and you would suffer a severe burn. Similarly, without the warning sign of abdominal pain that typically accompanies an inflamed appendix, your appendix might eventually rupture, spreading a fatal infection throughout your body.

In fact, all our **skin senses**—touch, pressure, temperature, and pain—play a critical role in survival, making us aware of potential danger to our bodies. Most of these senses operate through nerve receptor cells located at various depths throughout the skin, distributed unevenly throughout the body. For example, some areas, such as the fingertips, have many more receptor cells sensitive to touch and as a consequence are notably more sensitive than other areas of the body (Kreuger, 1989; see Figure 4-11).

Probably the most extensively researched skin sense is pain, and with good reason: People consult physicians and take medication for pain more than for any other symptom or condition (Langreth, 1996; Price, 2000).

Pain is a response to a great variety of different kinds of stimuli. A light that is too bright can produce pain, and sound that is too loud can be painful. One explanation is that pain is an outcome of cell injury; when a cell is damaged, regardless of the source of damage, it releases a chemical called *substance P* that transmits pain messages to the brain.

skin senses: The senses that include touch, pressure, temperature and pain

Psychology at Work

Julia A. Mennella

Taste Researcher

Education: B.S., biology, Loyola University, Chicago; M.S., biology, DePaul University, Chicago; Ph.D., biopsychology, University of Chicago.

Home: Philadelphia

Julia Mennella

Researchers have long known that the senses of taste and smell are developed in the first months of a child's life, and that infants have strong positive and negative reactions to certain tastes and smells soon after birth. But recent discoveries have shown that taste and smell preferences can start even earlier—while a child is still in its mother's womb.

According to research conducted by psychologist Julia A. Mennella of the Monell Chemical Senses Center, a research laboratory in Philadelphia, the ability to detect certain tastes is present even before birth.

"Research has found that taste pores are functioning by the second trimester of pregnancy, and a child is born with a rich population of taste receptors," she noted. Furthermore, the fla-

> "One of the most enduring characteristics of people around the world are their food habits."

vors mothers consume prior to the birth of their babies affects children's preferences later in life. Mennella notes, "We found that babies who experienced a particular flavor in the amniotic fluid or, later, in their mother's milk, prefer that flavor when they start to eat solid foods."

One reason cultures favor certain kinds of diets and foods is due to the development of taste and smell at the earliest stages of life, according to Mennella.

"One of the most enduring characteristics of people around the world are their food habits," Mennella said. "The food that a mother eats is one of the first mechanisms by which a baby learns about the food of a culture." She adds, "Mother's milk is like a flavor bridge that is enhancing the flavor experience before the child eats food from the table. Food is a celebration of a culture, and the baby is learning this even before tasting solid foods."

But the experience of pain is not just a physical reaction to particular stimuli. For example, women report that the pain experienced in childbirth is moderated to some degree by the joyful nature of the situation. On the other hand, even a minor stimulus can produce the perception of strong pain if accompanied by anxiety (like a visit to the dentist). Clearly, then, pain is a perceptual response that depends heavily on our emotions and thoughts (Turk, 1994; Eccleston & Crombez, 1999; Gatchel & Weisberg, 2000).

Figure 4–11 Skin sensitivity in various areas of the body. The shorter a line, the more sensitive a body part is. The fingers and thumb, lips, nose, cheeks, and big toe are the most sensitive. Why do you think certain areas are more sensitive than others?

From Kenshalo, *The Skin Senses,* 1968. Courtesy of Charles C Thomas, Publisher, Ltd., Springfield, Illinois.

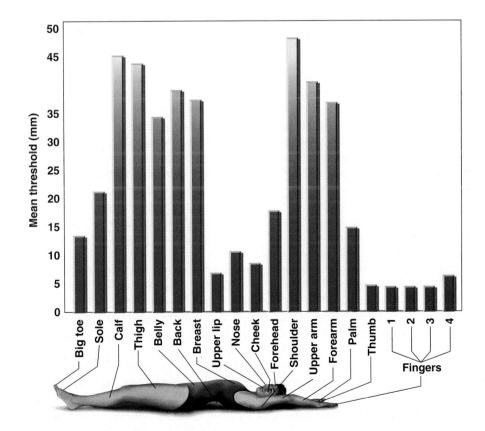

According to the **gate-control theory of pain,** particular nerve receptors in the spinal cord lead to specific areas of the brain related to pain. When these receptors are activated because of some injury or problem with a part of the body, a "gate" to the brain is opened, allowing us to experience the sensation of pain.

However, another set of neural receptors is able, when stimulated, to close the "gate" to the brain, thereby reducing the experience of pain. The gate can be shut in two different ways. First, other impulses can overwhelm the nerve pathways relating to pain, which are spread throughout the brain. In this case, non-painful stimuli compete with and sometimes displace the neuronal message of pain, thereby shutting off the painful stimulus. This explains why rubbing the skin around an injury helps reduce pain. The competing stimuli from the rubbing can overpower the painful ones (Wall & Melzack, 1989; Kakigi, Matsuda, & Kuroda, 1993).

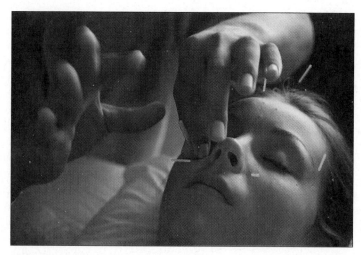

The ancient practice of acupuncture is still used in the 21st century. How does the gate-control theory of pain explain how acupuncture works?

Psychological factors account for the second way a gate can be shut. Depending on an individual's current emotions, interpretation of events, and previous experience, the brain can close a gate by sending a message down the spinal cord to an injured area, producing a reduction in or relief from pain. Thus soldiers who are injured in battle might experience no pain—the surprising situation in more than half of all combat injuries. The lack of pain probably occurs because a soldier experiences such relief at still being alive that the brain sends a signal to the injury site to shut down the pain gate (Turk, 1994; Gatchel & Weisberg, 2000).

gate-control theory of pain: The theory that particular nerve receptors lead to specific areas of the brain related to pain

Gate-control theory might also explain cultural differences in the experience of pain. Some of these variations are astounding. For example, in India people who participate in the "hook-swinging" ritual, to celebrate the power of the gods, have steel hooks embedded under the skin and muscles of their backs. During the ritual, they swing from a pole, suspended by the hooks. What would seem likely to induce excruciating pain instead produces a state of celebration and near-euphoria. In fact, when the hooks are later removed, the wounds heal quickly, and after two weeks almost no visible marks remain (Kosambi, 1967).

Gate-control theory suggests that the lack of pain is due to a message from the participant's brain, which shuts down the pain pathways. Gate-control theory might also explain the effectiveness of *acupuncture,* an ancient Chinese technique in which sharp needles are inserted into various parts of the body. The sensation from the needles might close the gateway to the brain, reducing the experience of pain. It is also possible that the body's own painkillers, the endorphins (discussed in Chapter 3), as well as positive and negative emotions, can play a role in opening and closing the gate (Murray, 1995; Bromm & Desmedt, 1995).

BECOMING AN INFORMED CONSUMER OF PSYCHOLOGY

Managing Pain

Pain—whether it is a pounding, aching, stinging soreness or a burning feeling—is one sensation that cannot be easily overlooked. To fight pain, psychologists and medical specialists have devised several strategies. Among the most important approaches are these (Gatchel & Turk, 1996; Bazell, 1998; Keefe & France, 1999):

- *Medication.* Painkilling drugs are the most popular treatment in fighting pain. Drugs range from those that directly treat the source of the pain—such as reducing swelling in painful joints—to those that work on the symptoms of the pain. Medication can be in the form of pills, injections, or liquids. In a recent innovation, drugs are pumped directly into the spinal cord.

- *Nerve and brain stimulation.* Pain can sometimes be relieved when a low-voltage electric current is passed through the specific part of the body that is in pain. In even more severe cases, electrodes can be surgically implanted directly into the brain, and a handheld battery pack can stimulate nerve cells to provide direct relief (Garrison & Foreman, 1994; Walsh, et al., 1995). This process is known as *transcutaneous electrical nerve stimulation,* or *TENS.*

- *Hypnosis.* For people who can be hypnotized, this method can greatly relieve pain (Holroyd, 1996; Spiegel, 1996c).

- *Biofeedback and relaxation techniques.* As we discussed in Chapter 3, biofeedback is a process through which people learn to control such "involuntary" functions as heartbeat and respiration. If the pain involves muscles, such as in tension headaches or back pain, biofeedback can be helpful when people are trained to relax their bodies systematically (Hermann, Kim, & Blanchard, 1995; National Institutes of Health, 1996a).

- *Surgery.* In one of the most extreme methods, surgery can be used to cut certain nerve fibers that carry pain messages to the brain. Still, because of the danger that other bodily functions will be affected, surgery is a treatment of last resort, used most frequently with dying patients.

- *Cognitive restructuring.* People who continually say to themselves, "This pain will never stop," "The pain is ruining my life," or "I can't take it any more" are likely to make their pain even worse. As we'll discuss in Chapter 13, by substituting more positive ways of thinking, people can increase their sense of control—and actually reduce the degree of pain they experience. Teaching people to rewrite the "script" that controls their reaction to pain through therapy can result in significant reductions in the perception of pain (Turk & Nash, 1993; Mufson, 1999).

If you wish to learn more about chronic pain, you can consult the American Pain Society (847-375-4715; www.ampainsoc.org) or the American Chronic Pain Association (916-632-0922; www.theacpa.org). In addition, many hospitals have pain clinics that specialize in the treatment of pain. Be sure, though, that the clinic you use is approved by the Commission for the Accreditation of Rehabilitative Facilities or the Joint Commission on the Accreditation of Health-Care Organizations.

Evaluate

1. The tubelike passage leading from the outer ear is known as the _____ _____.

2. The purpose of the eardrum is to protect the sensitive nerves underneath it. It serves no purpose in actual hearing. True or false?

3. The three middle ear bones transmit their sound to the _____.

4. The _____ theory of hearing states that the entire basilar membrane responds to a sound, vibrating more or less, depending on the nature of the sound.

5. The three fluid-filled tubes in the inner ear that are responsible for our sense of balance are known as the _____ _____.

6. The _____-_____theory states that when certain skin receptors are activated as the result of an injury, a "pathway" to the brain is opened, allowing pain to be experienced.

Rethink

1. Much research is being conducted on repairing faulty sensory organs through such devices as personal guidance systems, eyeglasses, and so forth. Do you think that researchers should attempt to improve normal sensory capabilities beyond their "natural" range (e.g., make human visual or audio capabilities more sensitive than normal)? What benefits might this bring? What problems might it cause?

2. Why might sensitivity to pheromones have evolved differently in humans than in other species? What cultural factors might have played a role?

Answers to Evaluate Questions

5. semicircular canals 6. gate-control

1. auditory canal 2. False; it vibrates when sound waves hit it, and transmits the sound. 3. oval window 4. frequency

Perceptual Organization: Constructing Our View of the World

Consider the vase shown in Figure 4-12a for a moment. Or is it a vase? Take another look, and instead you might see the profiles of two people.

Now that an alternative interpretation has been pointed out, you will probably shift back and forth between the two interpretations. Similarly, if you examine the shapes in Figure 4-12b and 4-12c long enough, you will probably experience a shift in what you're seeing. The reason for these reversals is this: Because each figure is two-dimensional, the usual means we employ for distinguishing the *figure* (the object being perceived) from the *ground* (the background or spaces within the object) do not work.

The fact that we can look at the same figure in more than one way illustrates an important point. We do not just passively respond to visual stimuli that happen to fall on our retinas. Instead, we actively try to organize and make sense of what we see.

We turn now from a focus on the initial response to a stimulus (sensation) to what our minds make of that stimulus—perception. Perception is a constructive process by which we go beyond the stimuli that are presented to us and attempt to construct a meaningful situation (Haber, 1983; Kienker et al., 1986).

Prepare

What principles underlie our organization of the visual world, allowing us to make sense of our environment?

How are we able to perceive the world in three dimensions when our retinas are capable of sensing only two-dimensional images?

What clues do visual illusions give us about our understanding of general perceptual mechanisms?

Organize

Perceptual Organization: Constructing Our View of the World
The Gestalt Laws of Organization
Feature Analysis
Top-Down and Bottom-Up Processing
Perceptual Constancy
Depth Perception
Motion Perception
Perceptual Illusions
Subliminal Perception

The Gestalt Laws of Organization

Some of the most basic perceptual processes operate according to a series of principles that describe how we organize bits and pieces of information into meaningful wholes. These are known as **gestalt laws of organization,** set forth in the early 1900s by a group

gestalt laws of organization: A series of principles that describe how we organize bits and pieces of information into meaningful wholes

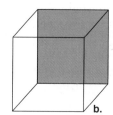

Figure 4-12 When the usual cues we use to distinguish figure from ground are absent, we might shift back and forth between different views of the same figure. If you look at each of these objects long enough you'll probably experience a shift in what you're seeing. In *a*, you can see either a vase or the profiles of two people. In *b*, the shaded portion of the figure, called a Necker cube, can appear to be either the front or the back of the cube. Finally, in *c*, you'll be able to see a face of a woman if you look at the drawing long enough.

Figure 4-13 How we organize these bits and pieces of information into meaningful wholes is one of the most basic processes of perception known as the gestalt laws of organization. Do you think any other species share this organizational tendency? How might we find out?

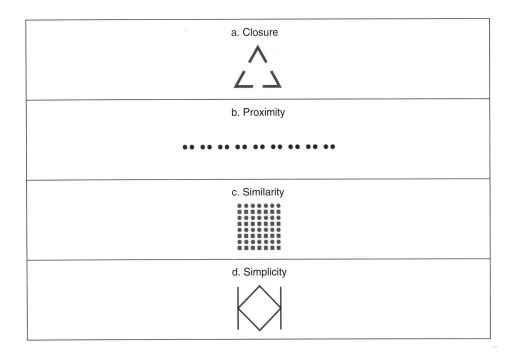

a. Closure

b. Proximity

c. Similarity

d. Simplicity

AND FOR MY NEXT TRICK...

of German psychologists who studied patterns, or *gestalts* (Wertheimer, 1923). They discovered a number of important principles that are valid for visual (as well as auditory) stimuli, illustrated in Figure 4-13:

*   *Closure*. Groupings are usually made in terms of enclosed or complete figures rather than open ones. We tend to ignore the breaks in Figure 4-13a and concentrate on the overall form.
*   *Proximity*. Elements that are closer together are grouped together. As a result, we tend to see pairs of dots rather than a row of single dots, as in Figure 4-13b.
*   *Similarity*. Elements that are similar in appearance are grouped together. We see, then, horizontal rows of circles and squares in Figure 4-13c instead of vertical mixed columns.
*   *Simplicity*. In a general sense, the overriding gestalt principle is simplicity: When we observe a pattern, we perceive it in the most basic, straightforward manner that we can. For example, most of us see Figure 4-13d as a square with lines on two sides, rather than as the block letter *W* on top of the letter *M*. If we have a choice of interpretations, we generally opt for the simpler one.

Although gestalt psychology no longer plays a prominent role in contemporary psychology, its legacy endures. For instance, one fundamental gestalt principle that remains influential is that two objects considered together form a whole that is different form the simple combination of the objects. Gestalt psychologists argued, quite convincingly, that the perception of stimuli in our environment goes well beyond the individual elements that we sense. Instead, it represents an active, constructive process carried out within the brain. There, bits and pieces of sensations are put together to make something more meaningful than the separate elements (Kriz, 1995; Humphreys & Muller, 2000; see Figure 4-14).

Feature Analysis: Focusing on the Parts of the Whole

feature analysis: A theory of perception according to which we perceive a shape, pattern, object, or scene by reacting first to the individual elements that make it up

A more recent approach to perception, **feature analysis,** considers how we perceive a shape, pattern, object, or scene by reacting first to the individual elements that make it up. These individual components are then used to understand the overall nature of what we are perceiving. Feature analysis begins with the evidence that individual neurons in the

Figure 4-14 Although at first it is difficult to distinguish anything in this drawing, keep looking, and eventually you'll probably be able to see the figure of a dog (James, 1966). The dog represents a *gestalt,* or perceptual whole, which is something greater than the sum of the individual elements.

brain are sensitive to specific spatial configurations, such as angles, curves, shapes, and edges, as discussed earlier in the chapter. The presence of these neurons suggests that any stimulus can be broken down into a series of component features. For example, the letter *R* is a combination of a vertical line, a diagonal line, and a half circle (see Figure 4-15).

According to feature analysis, when we encounter a stimulus—such as a letter—our brain's perceptual processing system initially responds to its component parts. Each of these parts is compared with information about components that is stored in memory. When the specific components we perceive match up with a particular set of components that we have encountered previously, we are able to identify the stimulus (Spillmann & Werner, 1990; Ullman, 1996).

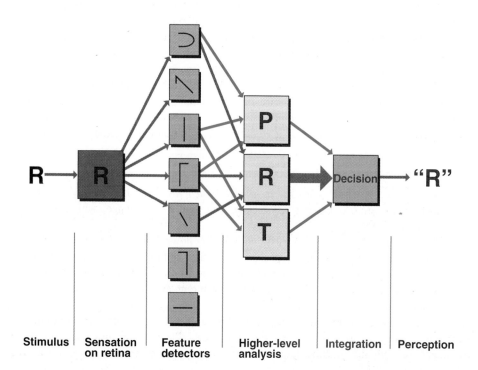

Stimulus | Sensation on retina | Feature detectors | Higher-level analysis | Integration | Perception

Figure 4-15 According to feature analysis approaches to perception, we break down stimuli into their component parts and then compare these parts to information that is stored in memory. When we find a match, we are able to identify the stimulus. In this example, the process by which we recognize the letter *R* is illustrated (Goldstein, 1984).

Figure 4-16 Components and simple objects created from them (Adapted from Biederman, 1990).

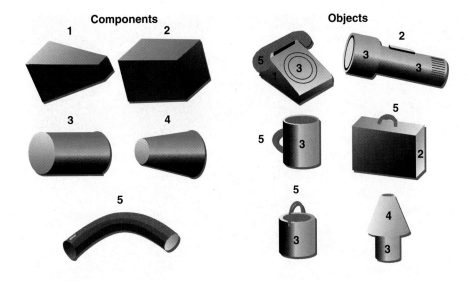

According to some research, the way we perceive complex objects is similar to how we perceive simple letters—viewing them in terms of their component elements. For instance, just 36 fundamental components seem to be capable of producing over 150 million objects—more than enough to describe the 30,000 separate objects that the average person can recognize (see Figure 4-16). Ultimately, these component features are combined into a representation of the whole object in the brain. This representation is compared to existing memories, thereby permitting us to identify the object (Biederman, 1987, 1990).

Psychologist Anne Treisman has a different perspective. She suggests that the perception of objects is best understood in terms of a two-stage process. In the *preattentive stage,* we focus on the physical features of a stimulus, such as its size, shape, color, orientation, or direction of movement. This initial stage takes little or no conscious effort. In the *focused-attention stage,* we pay attention to particular features of an object, choosing and emphasizing features that were initially considered separately (Treisman, 1988, 1993).

For example, take a look at the two upside-down photos in Figure 4-17. Probably, your first impression is that you're viewing two similar photos of the Mona Lisa. But now look at them rightside up, and you'll be surprised to note that one of the photos has distorted features. In Treisman's terms, your initial scanning of the photos took place at the preattentive stage. When you turned them over, however, you immediately progressed into the focused-attention stage, where you were able to more carefully consider the actual nature of the stimuli.

Treisman's perspective and other approaches to feature analysis raise a puzzling question about the fundamental nature of perceptual processes: Is perception based mainly on consideration of the component parts of a stimulus, or is it grounded primarily in perception of the stimulus as a whole? This is the issue to which we turn next.

Top-Down and Bottom-Up Processing

Ca- yo- re-d t-is -en-en-e, w-ic- ha- ev-ry -hi-d l-tt-r m-ss-ng? It probably won't take you too long to figure out that it says, "Can you read this sentence, which has every third letter missing?"

If perception were based primarily on breaking down a stimulus into its most basic elements, understanding the sentence, as well as other ambiguous stimuli, would not be possible. The fact that you were probably able to recognize such an imprecise stimulus illustrates that perception proceeds along two different avenues, called top-down processing and bottom-up processing.

In **top-down processing,** perception is guided by higher-level knowledge, experience, expectations, and motivations. You were able to figure out the meaning of the sentence with the missing letters because of your prior reading experience, and

top-down processing: Perception that is guided by higher-level knowledge, experience, expectations, and motivations

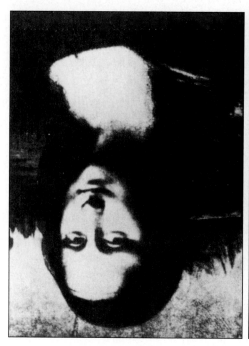 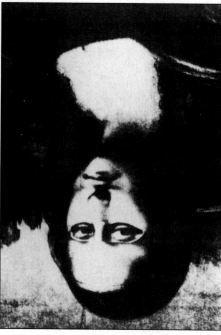

Figure 4–17 Double Mona Lisas? These pictures appear similar at first glance because only our preattentive process is active. When the pictures are seen upright, the true detail in the two faces is revealed (From Julesz, 1986).

because written English contains redundancies. Not every letter of each word is necessary to decode its meaning. Moreover, your expectations played a role in your being able to read the sentence. You were probably expecting a statement that had *something* to do with psychology, and not the lyrics to an Eminem song.

Top-down processing is illustrated by the importance of context in determining how we perceive objects (Biederman, 1981). Look, for example, at Figure 4-18. Most of us perceive that the first row consists of the letters *A* through *F*, while the second contains the numbers 10 through 14. But take a more careful look, and you'll see that the "B" and the "13" are identical. Clearly, our perception is affected by our expectations about the two sequences—even though the two stimuli are exactly the same.

Yet top-down processing cannot occur on its own. Even though top-down processing allows us to fill in the gaps in ambiguous and out-of-context stimuli, we would be unable to perceive the meaning of such stimuli without bottom-up processing. **Bottom-up processing** consists of recognizing and processing information about the individual components of the stimuli. We would make no headway in our recognition of the sentence without being able to perceive the individual shapes that make up the letters. Some perception, then, occurs at the level of the patterns and features of each of the separate letters.

It should be apparent that top-down and bottom-up processing occur simultaneously, and interact with each other, in our perception of the world around us. Bottom-up processing permits us to process the fundamental characteristics of stimuli, whereas top-down processing allows us to bring our experience to bear on perception. And as we learn more about the complex processes involved in perception, we are developing a better understanding of how our brain continually interprets information from our senses and permits us to make responses appropriate to the environment (Egeth & Yantis, 1997; Rees, Frith, & Lavie, 1997).

bottom-up processing: Perception that consists of recognizing and processing information about the individual components of the stimuli

A B C D E F

10 11 12 13 14

Figure 4–18 The power of context is shown in this figure. Note how the B and the 13 are identical (Coren & Ward, 1989).

When the moon is near the horizon, we do not see it by itself and perceptual constancy leads us to take into account a misleading sense of distance.

Perceptual Constancy

Consider what happens as you finish a conversation with a friend and she begins to walk away from you. As you watch her walk down the street, the image on your retina becomes smaller and smaller. Do you wonder why she is shrinking?

Of course not. Despite the very real change in the size of the retinal image, you factor into your thinking the knowledge that your friend is moving further away from you due to perceptual constancy. *Perceptual constancy* is a phenomenon in which physical objects are perceived as unvarying and consistent, despite changes in their appearance or in the physical environment.

One of the most dramatic examples of perceptual constancy involves the rising moon. When the moon first appears at night, close to the horizon, it seems to be huge—much larger than when it is high in the sky later in the evening. You may have thought that the apparent size of the moon was caused by the moon's being physically closer to the earth when it first appears. In fact, though, this is not the case at all.

Instead, the moon appears to be larger when it is close to the horizon primarily because of a misapplication of perceptual constancy. When the moon is near the horizon, the perceptual cues of intervening terrain and objects such as trees on the horizon produce a misleading sense of distance. Because perceptual constancy leads us to take that distance into account when we view the moon, we perceive the moon as relatively large. On the other hand, when the moon is high in the sky, we see it by itself, and perceptual constancy leads us to perceive it as relatively small. To prove this, try looking at the moon when it is relatively low on the horizon through a paper-towel tube; the moon will suddenly appear to "shrink" back to normal size (Coren & Aks, 1990; Coren, 1992b).

Although other factors help account for the moon illusion, perceptual constancy appears to be a primary ingredient in our susceptibility to the illusion. Furthermore, perceptual constancy occurs not just in terms of size (as with the moon illusion) but with shape and color as well. Despite the varying images on our retina as a plane approaches, flies overhead, and disappears, we do not perceive the plane as changing shape (Coren & Aks, 1990; Suzuki, 1991).

Depth Perception: Translating 2-D to 3-D

As sophisticated as the retina is, the images projected onto it are flat and two-dimensional. Yet the world around us is three-dimensional, and we perceive it that way. How do we make the transformation from 2-D to 3-D?

The ability to view the world in three dimensions and to perceive distance—a skill known as *depth perception*—is due largely to the fact that we have two eyes. Because there is a certain distance between the eyes, a slightly different image reaches each retina. The brain then integrates these two images into one composite view. But it does not

Anyone who has ever seen railroad tracks that seem to join together in the distance knows that distant objects appear to be closer together than nearer ones, a phenomenon called linear perspective.

ignore the difference in images, which is known as *binocular disparity.* The disparity allows the brain to estimate the distance of an object from us.

You can get a sense of binocular disparity for yourself. Hold a pencil at arm's length and look at it first with one eye and then with the other. There is little difference between the two views relative to the background. Now bring the pencil just 6 inches away from your face, and try the same thing. This time you will perceive a greater difference between the two views.

The fact that the discrepancy between the images in the two eyes varies according to the distance of objects that we view provides us with a means of determining distance. If we view two objects, and one is considerably closer to us than another, the retinal disparity will be relatively large and we will have a greater sense of depth between the two. On the other hand, if the two objects are a similar distance from us, the retinal disparity will be minor, and we will perceive them as being a similar distance from us.

In some cases, certain cues permit us to obtain a sense of depth and distance with just one eye (Burnham, 1983). These cues are known as *monocular cues.* One monocular cue—*motion parallax*—is the change in position of an object on the retina due to movement of the head. The brain is able to calculate the distance of the object by the amount of change in the retinal image. Similarly, experience has taught us that if two objects are the same size, the one that makes a smaller image on the retina is farther away than the one that provides a larger image—an example of the monocular cue of *relative size.*

Finally, anyone who has ever seen railroad tracks that seem to join together in the distance knows that distant objects appear to be closer together than nearer ones, a phenomenon called linear perspective. People use *linear perspective* as a monocular cue in estimating distance, allowing the two-dimensional image on the retina to record the three-dimensional world (Bruce, Green, & Georgeson, 1997; Dobbins et al., 1998).

Motion Perception: As the World Turns

When a batter tries to hit a pitched ball, the most important factor is the motion of the ball. How is a batter able to judge the speed and location of a target that is moving at some 90 miles per hour?

The answer rests, in part, on several cues that provide us with relevant information about the perception of motion (Movshon & Newsome, 1992). For one thing, the movement of an object across the retina is typically perceived relative to some stable, unmoving background. Moreover, if the stimulus is heading toward us, the image on the retina will expand in size, filling more and more of the visual field. In such cases, we assume that the stimulus is approaching—and not that it is an expanding stimulus viewed at a constant distance.

Figure 4-19 In building the Parthenon, the Greeks constructed an architectural wonder that looks perfectly straight, with right angles at every corner, as in *a*. However, if it had been built with completely true right angles, it would have looked as it does in *b*, due to the visual illusion illustrated in *c*. To compensate for this illusion, the Parthenon was designed to have a slight upward curvature, as shown in *d* (Coren & Ward, 1989, p. 5).

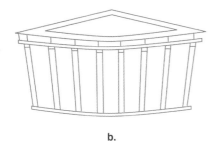

b.

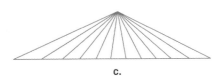

c.

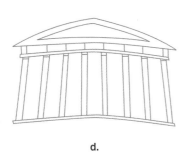

d.

 **PsychLink**

Optical and sensory illusions
www.mhhe.com/
feldmanup6-04links

visual illusions: Physical stimuli that consistently produce errors in perception

It is not, however, just the movement of images across the retina that brings about the perception of motion. If it were, we would perceive the world as moving every time we moved our heads. Instead, one of the critical things we learn about perception is to factor information about head and eye movements along with information about changes in the retinal image.

Perceptual Illusions: The Deceptions of Perceptions

If you look carefully at the Parthenon, one of the most famous buildings of ancient Greece and still standing at the top of an Athens hill, you'll see that it was built with a bulge on one side. If it didn't have that bulge—and quite a few other "tricks" like it, such as columns that incline inward—it would look as if it were crooked and about to fall down. Instead, it appears to stand completely straight, at right angles to the ground.

The fact that the Parthenon appears to be completely upright is the result of a series of visual illusions. **Visual illusions** are physical stimuli that consistently produce errors in perception. In the case of the Parthenon, the building appears to be completely square, as illustrated in Figure 4-19a. However, had it been built that way, it would look to us as it does in Figure 4-19b. The reason for this is the illusion illustrated in 4-19c, which makes angles placed above a line appear as if they were bent. To offset the illusion, the Parthenon was constructed as in Figure 4-19d, with a slight upward curvature.

Such perceptual insights did not stop with the Greeks. Modern-day architects and designers also take visual distortions into account in their planning. For example, the New Orleans Superdome makes use of several visual tricks. Its seats vary in color throughout the stadium to give the appearance, from a distance, that there is always a full house. The carpeting in some of the sloping halls has stripes that make people slow their pace by producing the perception that they are moving faster than they actually are. The same illusion is used at toll booths on superhighways. Stripes painted on the pavement in front of the toll booths make drivers feel that they are moving more rapidly than they actually are and cause them to decelerate quickly.

The implications of visual illusions go beyond the attractiveness of buildings. For instance, suppose you were an air traffic controller watching a radar screen like the one shown in Figure 4-20a. You might be tempted to sit back and relax as the two planes, whose flight paths are indicated in the figure, drew closer and closer together. If you did,

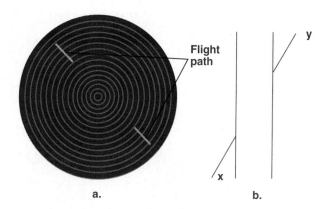

a.

b.

Figure 4-20 *(a)* Put yourself in the shoes of a flight controller and look at the flight paths of the two planes on this radar screen. A first glance suggests that they are headed on different courses and will not hit each other. But now take a ruler and lay it along the two paths. Your career as a flight controller might well be over if you were guiding the two planes and you allowed them to continue without a change in course (Coren, Porac, & Ward, 1984, p. 7). *(b)* The Poggendorf illusion, in which the two diagonal lines appear (incorrectly) as if they would not meet if extended toward each other.

however, the result might be an air disaster. Although it looks as if the two planes will miss each other, they are headed for a collision. Investigation has suggested that some 70 to 80 percent of all airplane accidents are caused by pilot errors of one sort or another (O'Hare & Roscoe, 1990; Baker et al., 1993).

The flight-path illustration provides an example of a well-known visual illusion called the *Poggendorf illusion*. As you can see in Figure 4-20b, the Poggendorf illusion, when stripped down to its basics, gives the impression that line X would pass *below* line Y if it were extended through the pipelike figure, instead of heading directly toward line Y as it actually does.

The Poggendorf illusion is just one of many that consistently fool the eye (Perkins, 1983; Greist-Bousquet & Schiffman, 1986). Another, illustrated in Figure 4-21, is called the *Müller-Lyer illusion*. Although the two lines are the same length, the one with the arrow tips pointing inward (Figure 4-21a, top) appears to be longer than the one with the arrow tips pointing outward (Figure 4-21a, bottom).

Although all kinds of explanations for visual illusions have been suggested, most concentrate either on the physical operation of the eye or on our misinterpretation of the visual stimulus. For example, one explanation for the Müller-Lyer illusion is that eye movements are greater when the arrow tips point inward, making us perceive the line as longer than when the arrow tips face outward. In contrast, a different explanation for the illusion suggests that we unconsciously attribute particular significance to each of the lines (Gregory, 1978; Redding & Hawley, 1993). When we see the top line in Figure 4-21a, we tend to perceive it as if it were the inside corner of a room extending away from us, as illustrated in Figure 4-21b. On the other hand, when we view the bottom line in Figure 4-21a, we perceive it as the relatively close outside corner of a rectangular object such as the building corner in Figure 4-21c. Because previous experience leads us to assume that the outside corner is closer than the inside corner, we make the further assumption that the inside corner must therefore be larger.

Despite the complexity of the latter explanation, a good deal of evidence supports it. For instance, cross-cultural studies show that people raised in areas where there are few right angles—such as the Zulu in Africa—are much less susceptible to the illusion than people who grow up where most structures are built using right angles and rectangles (Segall, Campbell, & Herskovits, 1966).

EXPLORING DIVERSITY

Culture and Perception

As the example of the Zulu indicates, the particular culture in which we are raised has clear consequences for how we perceive the world. Consider the drawing in Figure 4-22. Sometimes called the "devil's tuning fork," it is likely to produce a mind-boggling effect, as the center tine of the fork alternates between appearing and disappearing.

a.   b.   c.

Figure 4-21 In the Müller-Lyer illusion *(a)*, the upper horizontal line appears longer than the lower one. One explanation for the Müller-Lyer illusion suggests that the line with arrow points directed inward is to be interpreted as the inside corner of a rectangular room extending away from us *(b)*, and the line with arrow points directed outward is viewed as the relatively close corner of a rectangular object, such as the building corner in *(c)*. Our previous experience with distance cues leads us to assume that the outside corner is closer than the inside corner and that the inside corner must therefore be longer.

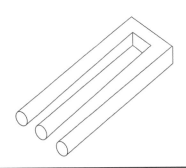

Figure 4-22 The "devil's tuning fork" has three prongs... or does it have two?

Now try to reproduce the drawing on a piece of paper. Chances are that the task is nearly impossible for you—unless you are a member of an African tribe with little exposure to Western cultures. For such individuals, the task is simple; they have no trouble reproducing the figure. The reason seems to be that Western people automatically interpret the drawing as something that cannot exist in three dimensions, and they are therefore inhibited from reproducing it. The African tribal members, on the other hand, do not make the assumption that the figure is "impossible" and instead view it in two dimensions, which enables them to copy the figure with ease (Deregowski, 1973).

Cultural differences are also reflected in depth perception. A Western viewer of Figure 4-23 would interpret the hunter in the drawing as aiming for the antelope in the foreground, while an elephant stands under the tree in the background. A member of an isolated African tribe, however, interprets the scene very differently by assuming that the hunter is aiming at the elephant. Westerners use the difference in sizes between the two animals as a cue that the elephant is farther away than the antelope (Hudson, 1960).

The misinterpretations created by visual illusions are ultimately due, then, to errors in both fundamental visual processing and the way the brain interprets the information it receives. But visual illusions, by illustrating something fundamental about perception, become more than mere psychological curiosities. There is a basic connection between our prior knowledge, needs, motivations, and expectations about how the world is put together and the way we perceive it. Our view of the world is very much a function, then, of fundamental psychological factors. Furthermore, each person perceives the environment in a way that is unique and special—a fact that allows each of us to make our own special contribution to the world.

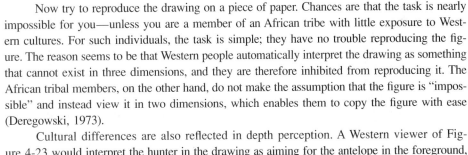

Figure 4-23 Is the man aiming for the elephant or the antelope? Westerners assume that the differences in size between the two animals indicate that the elephant is farther away, and therefore the man is aiming for the antelope. On the other hand, members of some African tribes, not used to depth cues in two-dimensional drawings, assume that the man is aiming for the elephant. (The drawing is based on Deregowski, 1973.) Do you think Westerners, who view the picture in three dimensions, could explain what they see to someone who views the scene in two dimensions and eventually get them to view it in three dimensions?

Subliminal Perception

Can stimuli that we're not even aware we've been exposed to change our behavior in a significant way? Probably not.

Subliminal perception refers to the perception of messages about which we have no awareness. The stimulus could be a word, a sound, or even a smell that activates the sensory system, but that is not intense enough for a person to report having experienced it. For example, in some studies people are exposed to a descriptive label—called a *prime*—about a person (such as the word *smart* or *happy*) so briefly that they cannot report seeing the label. Later, however, they form impressions that are influenced by the content of the prime. Somehow, they have been influenced by the prime that they say they couldn't see, providing some evidence for subliminal perception (Bargh & Pietromonaco, 1982; Greenwald, Draine, & Abrams, 1996).

Yet does this mean that subliminal messages can actually lead to significant changes in attitudes or behavior? Most research suggests not. Although we are able to perceive at least some kinds of information of which we are unaware, no evidence demonstrates that subliminal messages can change our attitudes or behavior in any substantial way (Greenwald et al., 1991).

Extrasensory Perception (ESP)

Given the lack of evidence for subliminal perception, psychologists are even more skeptical of reports of *extrasensory perception,* or *ESP*—perception that does not involve our known senses. Most psychologists reject the existence of ESP, asserting that there is no sound documentation that the phenomenon exists (Swets & Bjork, 1990; Hyman, 1994).

However, an ongoing debate in the last decade in one of the most prestigious psychology journals, *Psychological Bulletin,* has heightened interest in the area. According to proponents of ESP, reliable evidence exists for an "anomalous process of information transfer," or *psi* (Bem & Honorton, 1994). These researchers, who painstakingly reviewed considerable evidence, argue that a cumulative body of research shows reliable support for the existence of psi.

However, their conclusion has been challenged on several counts. For example, critics suggest that the research methodology was inadequate, and that the experiments supporting psi are flawed (Hyman, 1994; Milton & Wiseman, 1999).

PsychLink

Analysis of subliminal influence
www.mhhe.com/
feldmanup6-04links

PsychLink

Extrasensory perception
www.mhhe.com/
feldmanup6-04links

Because of questions about the quality of the research, as well as a lack of any credible theoretical explanation for how extrasensory perception might take place, most psychologists continue to believe that there is no reliable scientific support for ESP. Still, the exchanges in *Psychological Bulletin* are likely to heighten the debate. More importantly, the renewed interest in ESP among psychologists is likely to inspire more research, which is the only way that the issue can be resolved.

Evaluate

1. Match each of the following organizational laws with its meaning:

   a. Closure

   b. Proximity

   c. Similarity

   d. Simplicity

   1. Elements close together are grouped together.
   2. Patterns are perceived in the most basic, direct manner possible.
   3. Groupings are made in terms of complete figures.
   4. Elements similar in appearance are grouped together.

2. _____ analysis deals with the way in which we break an object down into its component pieces in order to understand it.

3. Processing that involves higher functions such as expectations and motivations is known as _____, while processing that recognizes the individual components of a stimulus is known as _____.

4. When a car passes you on the road and appears to shrink as it gets farther away, the phenomenon of _____ permits you to realize that the car is not in fact getting smaller.

5. _____ is the ability to view the world in three dimensions instead of two.

6. The eyes use a technique known as _____, which makes use of the differing images each eye sees to give three dimensions to sight.

7. Match the monocular cues with their definitions.

   a. Relative size

   b. Linear perspective

   c. Motion parallax

   1. Straight lines seem to join together as they become more distant.
   2. An object changes position on the retina as the head moves.
   3. If two objects are the same size, the one producing the smaller retinal image is farther away.

Rethink

1. Can you think of examples of the combined use of top-down and bottom-up processing in everyday life? Is one type of processing superior to the other?

2. In what ways do painters represent three-dimensional scenes in two dimensions on a canvas? Do you think artists in non-Western cultures use the same or different principles to represent three-dimensionality? Why?

Answers to Evaluate Questions

1. a-3; b-1; c-2; d-4 2. Feature 3. top-down; bottom-up 4. perceptual constancy 5. Depth perception 6. binocular disparity 7. a-3; b-1; c-2

What is sensation, and how do psychologists study it?

- Sensation is the stimulation of the sense organs that comes from our initial encounter with stimuli (forms of energy that activate a sense organ). In contrast, perception is the process by which we sort out, interpret, analyze, and integrate stimuli to which our senses are exposed. (p. 90)

What is the relationship between a physical stimulus and the kinds of sensory responses that result from it?

- The absolute threshold is the smallest amount of physical intensity at which a stimulus can be detected. Although under ideal conditions absolute thresholds are extraordinarily sensitive, the presence of noise (background stimuli that interfere with other stimuli) reduces detection capabilities. (p. 91)
- Difference thresholds relate to the smallest level of stimulation required to sense that a change in stimulation has occurred, with a just noticeable difference being the minimum stimulation required to detect the difference between two stimuli. According to Weber's law, a just noticeable difference is a constant proportion of the intensity of an initial stimulus. (p. 92)
- Sensory adaptation occurs when we become accustomed to a constant stimulus and change our evaluation of it. Repeated exposure to a stimulus results in an apparent decline in sensitivity to it. (p. 92)

What basic processes underlie the sense of vision?

- Human sensory experience goes well beyond the traditional five senses, although most is known about just two: vision and hearing. Vision depends on sensitivity to light, electromagnetic waves that are reflected off objects outside the body. The eye shapes the light into an image that is transformed into nerve impulses and interpreted by the brain. (p. 93)
- When light first enters the eye, it travels through the cornea and then traverses the pupil, a dark hole in the center of the iris. The size of the pupil opening adjusts according to the amount of light entering the eye. Light then enters the lens, which, by a process called accommodation, acts to focus light rays onto the rear of the eye. On the rear of the eye is the retina, composed of light-sensitive nerve cells called rods and cones. Because of the phenomenon of adaptation, it takes time to adjust to situations that are darker than the previous environment. (p. 94)
- The visual information gathered by the rods and cones is transferred via bipolar and ganglion cells through the optic nerve, which leads to the optic chiasm— the point where the optic nerve splits. Because the image on the retina is reversed and upside down, images from the right half of the retina actually originated in the field of vision to the left of the person, and vice versa. (p. 96)

How do we see colors?

- Color vision seems to be based on two processes described by the trichromatic theory and the opponent-process theory. The trichromatic theory suggests that there are three kinds of cones in the retina, each of which is responsive to a certain range of colors. The opponent-process theory presumes pairs of different types of cells in the eye. These cells work in opposition to each other. (p. 98)

What role does the ear play in the senses of sound, motion, and balance?

- Sound, motion, and balance are centered in the ear. Sounds, in the form of vibrating air waves, enter through the outer ear and travel through the auditory

canal until they reach the eardrum. The vibrations of the eardrum are transmitted into the middle ear, which consists of three bones: the hammer, the anvil, and the stirrup. These bones transmit vibrations to the oval window. In the inner ear, vibrations move into the cochlea, which encloses the basilar membrane. Hair cells on the basilar membrane change the mechanical energy of sound waves into nerve impulses that are transmitted to the brain. The ear is also involved in the sense of balance and motion. (p. 102)

- Sound has a number of important characteristics, including frequency and intensity. The place theory of hearing and the frequency theory of hearing explain the processes by which we distinguish sounds of varying frequency and intensity. (p. 104)

How do smell and taste function?

- Smell employs olfactory cells (the receptor cells of the nose), and taste is centered in the tongue's taste buds. (p. 107)

What are the skin senses, and how do they relate to the experience of pain?

- The skin senses are responsible for the experiences of touch, pressure, temperature, and pain. Gate-control theory suggests that particular nerve receptors lead to specific areas of the brain related to pain. When these receptors are activated, a "gate" to the brain is opened, allowing the sensation of pain to be experienced. In addition, another set of receptors closes the gate when stimulated, thereby reducing the experience of pain. Endorphins might also affect the operation of the gate. (p. 109)
- Among the techniques used most frequently to alleviate pain are administration of drugs, hypnosis, biofeedback, relaxation techniques, surgery, nerve and brain stimulation, and psychotherapy. (p. 111)

What principles underlie our organization of the visual world, allowing us to make sense of our environment?

- Work on figure-ground distinctions shows that perception is a constructive process in which people go beyond the stimuli that are physically present and try to construct a meaningful situation. Perception follows the gestalt laws of organization, a series of principles by which we organize bits and pieces of information into meaningful wholes, known as gestalts. Among the most important laws are closure, proximity, similarity, and simplicity. (p. 113)
- Feature analysis pertains to how we consider a shape, pattern, object, or scene in terms of the individual elements that make it up. These component features are then combined into a representation of the whole object in the brain. Finally, this combination of features is compared against existing memories, permitting identification of the object. (p. 114)
- Processing of perceptual stimuli occurs in both a top-down and a bottom-up fashion. In top-down processing, perception is guided by higher-level knowledge, experience, expectations, and motivations. In bottom-up processing, perception involves recognizing and processing information about the individual components of stimuli. (p. 116)
- Perceptual constancy permits us to perceive stimuli as unvarying and consistent, despite changes in the environment or the appearance of the objects being perceived. Perceptual constancy occurs in terms of size, shape, and color constancy. (p. 118)

How are we able to perceive the world in three dimensions when our retinas are capable of sensing only two-dimensional images?

- Depth perception is the ability to perceive distance and to view the world in three dimensions, even though the images projected on our retinas are two-dimensional. We are able to judge depth and distance as a result of binocular disparity and monocular cues, such as motion parallax, the relative size of images on the retina, and linear perspective. (p. 118)
- Motion perception depends on several cues. They include the perceived movement of an object across our retina and information about how the head and eyes are moving. (p. 119)

What clues do visual illusions give us about our understanding of general perceptual mechanisms?

- Visual illusions are physical stimuli that consistently produce errors in perception, causing judgments that do not accurately reflect the physical reality of the stimulus. Two of the best-known illusions are the Poggendorf illusion and the Müller-Lyer illusion. (p. 120)
- Visual illusions are usually the result of errors in the brain's interpretation of visual stimuli. Furthermore, culture clearly affects how we perceive the world. (p. 121)
- Subliminal perception refers to the perception of messages about which we have no awareness. The reality of the phenomenon, as well as of ESP, is open to question and debate. (p. 123)

Key Terms and Concepts

sensation (p. 90)
perception (p. 90)
stimulus (p. 91)
psychophysics (p. 91)
absolute threshold (p. 91)
difference threshold (p. 92)
just noticeable difference (p. 92)
Weber's law (p. 92)
adaptation (p. 92)
retina (p. 95)
rods (p. 95)
cones (p. 95)
optic nerve (p. 97)
feature detection (p. 97)
trichromatic theory of color vision (p. 99)
opponent-process theory of color vision (p. 100)

sound (p. 102)
eardrum (p. 103)
cochlea (p. 103)
basilar membrane (p. 103)
hair cells (p. 103)
place theory of hearing (p. 106)
frequency theory of hearing (p. 106)
semicircular canals (p. 107)
otoliths (p. 107)
skin senses (p. 109)
gate-control theory of pain (p. 111)
gestalt laws of organization (p. 113)
feature analysis (p. 114)
top-down processing (p. 116)
bottom-up processing (p. 117)
visual illusions (p. 120)

Psychology on the Web

1. Select one topic of personal interest to you that was mentioned in this chapter (e.g., psi, cochlear implants, visual/optical illusions). Find one "serious" or scientific website and one "popular" or commercial website with information about your chosen topic. Compare the type, level, and reliability of the information that you find on each site. Write a summary of your findings.
2. Are there more gestalt laws of organization than the four discussed in this chapter (i.e., closure, proximity, similarity, and simplicity)? Find the answer to this question on the Web and write a summary of any additional gestalt laws you find.

Epilogue

In this chapter we have noted the important distinction between sensation and perception, and we have examined the processes that underlie both of them. We've seen how external stimuli evoke sensory responses, and how our different senses process the information contained in those responses. We also have focused on the physical structure and internal workings of the individual senses, including vision, hearing, balance, smell, taste, and the skin senses, and we've explored how our brains organize and process sensory information to construct a consistent, integrated picture of the world around us.

Before we proceed to a discussion of consciousness in the next chapter, let's return to the opening prologue of this chapter. Consider the story of Amy Ecklund and answer the following questions, using your knowledge of sensation and perception.

1. What do you think happens when a formerly deaf person such as Amy Ecklund first hears a sound that is new to her, like the "chirping" of a modern cell telephone? What differences would there be in her *sensation* of the sound and her *perception* of it?
2. Do you think that Ecklund's cochlear implant is capable of sensory adaptation—a decrease in sensitivity after repeated exposure to a strong stimulus? If it is not, how would this affect her experience of the world?
3. Do you think Ecklund will gradually lose her ability to read lips? Will she necessarily lose her sense of belonging in the culture of the deaf? What disadvantages would this have for her?

Preview

For additional quizzing and a variety of interactive resources, visit the *Understanding Psychology* Online Learning Center at

www.mhhe.com/feldmanup6

Chapter Five

States of Consciousness

Prologue: A Deadly Binge

Looking Ahead

Sleep and Dreams

The Stages of Sleep

REM Sleep: The Paradox of Sleep

Why Do We Sleep, and How Much Sleep Is Necessary?

The Function and Meaning of Dreaming

Sleep Disturbances: Slumbering Problems

Circadian Rhythms: Life Cycles

Daydreams: Dreams Without Sleep

Becoming an Informed Consumer of Psychology: Sleeping Better

Hypnosis and Meditation

Hypnosis: A Trance-Forming Experience?

Meditation: Regulating Our Own State of Consciousness

Exploring Diversity: Cross-Cultural Routes to Altered States of Consciousness

Drug Use: The Highs and Lows of Consciousness

Stimulants: Drug Highs

Applying Psychology in the 21ˢᵗ Century: Just Say No—to D.A.R.E.? Finding Antidrug Programs That Work

Depressants: Drug Lows

Narcotics: Relieving Pain and Anxiety

Hallucinogens: Psychedelic Drugs

Becoming an Informed Consumer of Psychology: Identifying Drug and Alcohol Problems

Looking Back

Key Terms and Concepts

Psychology on the Web

OLC Preview

Epilogue

Prologue

A Deadly Binge

Scott Krueger

The Massachusetts Institute of Technology is known as a demanding school, and Scott Krueger was ready for it. He had graduated near the top of his high-school class classes with early-morning crew practice. But in Boston, there is another side to MIT: its 30 fraternities are a magnet for whiz kids who like to party.

Scott Krueger wasn't ready for that. During a Greek Week celebration, the Phi Gamma Delta pledge passed out after downing the equivalent of 16 shots in an hour. His frat brothers carried him back to his basement room in their stately Boston mansion, then noticed he wasn't breathing well. Rescue workers found Krueger comatose. His blood-alcohol level was a staggering .41; the state's legal driving limit is .08. Either Krueger's blood got so thick from alcohol that the oxygen wasn't able to reach his brain or he choked on his own vomit. Days later, his anguished parents took their son off life support (Rosenberg & Bai, 1997, p. 69).

Looking Ahead

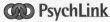 **PsychLink**

Information on consciousness
www.mhhe.com/
feldmanup6-05links

Binge drinking—defined as five drinks in a row for men, and four for women—is commonplace on college campuses. Although most binge drinkers are luckier than Krueger, all put themselves at serious risk. In fact, each year thousands of people die from complications of alcohol and drug overdoses, and many more are addicted to various kinds of drugs.

What leads people to use alcohol and other types of drugs to alter their normal states of consciousness? More generally, what *is* consciousness, and how does normal waking consciousness relate to states of consciousness such as sleep, hypnotic trances, or drug-induced experiences? In this chapter, we consider these questions.

Consciousness is the awareness of the sensations, thoughts, and feelings being experienced at a given moment. Consciousness is our subjective understanding of both the environment around us and our private internal world, unobservable to outsiders.

Consciousness is generally divided into two broad states: waking consciousness and altered states of consciousness, although the boundary between the two types is not always clear. In *waking consciousness,* we are awake and aware of our thoughts, emotions, and perceptions. In more active states of waking consciousness, we systematically carry out mental activity, focusing our thoughts and absorbing the world around us. In more passive states of waking consciousness, thoughts and images come to us more spontaneously; we might drift from one thought to another (Velmans, 2000).

When we enter an *altered state of consciousness,* our mental state differs significantly from waking consciousness. Some altered states of consciousness, such as sleeping and dreaming, occur naturally. Others, such as those induced by drug use or hypnosis, are triggered by deliberate attempts to alter one's state of consciousness.

Because consciousness is so personal a phenomenon, psychologists have sometimes been reluctant to study it. After all, who can say that your consciousness is similar to or, for that matter, different from anyone else's? In fact, early psychologists suggested that the study of consciousness was out of bounds for the discipline. They argued that because consciousness could be understood only by relying on the "unscientific" introspections of experimental participants about what they were experiencing at a given moment, its study was best left to disciplines such as philosophy. Proponents of this view suggested that philosophers could speculate at their leisure on such knotty issues as whether consciousness is separate from the physical body, how people know they exist, how the body and mind are related to each other, and how we identify what state of consciousness we are in at any given moment in time (Rychlak, 1997).

However, contemporary psychologists reject the view that the study of consciousness is unsuitable for the field of psychology. Instead, they argue that several approaches permit the scientific study of consciousness. For example, biopsychologists can measure brain-wave patterns under conditions of consciousness ranging from sleep to waking to hypnotic trances. Moreover, new understanding of the chemistry of drugs such as marijuana and alcohol has provided insights into the way they produce their pleasurable—as well as adverse—effects (Shear, 1997; Damasio, 1999; Sommerhof, 2000).

Another impetus for the study of consciousness is the realization that people in many different cultures routinely seek ways to alter their states of consciousness. Across a variety of cultures, variations in states of consciousness share some basic characteristics (Ludwig, 1969; Martindale, 1981). One is an alteration in thinking, which may become shallow, illogical, or otherwise different from normal. In addition, people's sense of time can become disturbed, and their perceptions of the world and of themselves might be changed. They might experience a loss of self-control, doing things that they would never otherwise do. Finally, they might feel a sense of *ineffability*—the inability to understand an experience rationally or describe it in words.

This chapter considers several states of consciousness, beginning with two that we have all experienced: sleeping and dreaming. Next, we turn to states of consciousness found under conditions of hypnosis and meditation. Finally, we examine drug-induced states of consciousness.

Sleep and Dreams

The crowd roared as running back Donald Dorff, age 67, took the pitch from his quarterback and accelerated smoothly across the artificial turf. As Dorff braked and pivoted to cut back over a tackle, a huge defensive lineman loomed in his path. One hundred twenty pounds of pluck, Dorff did not hesitate. But let the retired grocery merchandiser from Golden Valley, Minnesota, tell it:

"There was a 280-pound tackle waiting for me, so I decided to give him my shoulder. When I came to, I was on the floor in my bedroom. I had smashed into the dresser and knocked everything off it and broke the mirror and just made one heck of a mess. It was 1:30 a.m." (Long, 1987, p. 787)

Dorff, it turned out, was suffering from a rare condition (called *REM sleep behavior disorder*) where the mechanism that usually shuts down bodily movement during dreams does not function properly. People with the malady have been known to hit others, smash windows, punch holes in walls—all while fast asleep.

Luckily, Dorff's problem had a happy ending. With the help of clonazepam, a drug that suppresses movement during dreams, his malady vanished, permitting him to sleep through the night undisturbed.

Despite the success of Dorff's treatment, many unanswered questions about sleep remain, along with a considerable number of myths. (Try testing your own knowledge of sleep and dreams by answering the questions in the sleep quiz below.)

Prepare

What are the different states of consciousness?

What happens when we sleep, and what are the meaning and function of dreams?

What are the major sleep disorders and how can they be treated?

How much do we daydream?

Organize

Sleep and Dreams
   The Stages of Sleep
   REM Sleep
   Why Do We Sleep, and How Much Sleep Is Necessary?
   The Function and Meaning of Dreaming
   Sleep Disturbances
   Circadian Rhythms
   Daydreams

SLEEP QUIZ

Although sleeping is something we all do for a significant part of our lives, myths and misconceptions about the topic abound. To test your own knowledge of sleep and dreams, try answering the following questions before reading further.

_____ 1. Some people never dream. *True or false?*

_____ 2. Most dreams are caused by bodily sensations such as an upset stomach. *True or false?*

_____ 3. It has been proved that people need eight hours of sleep to maintain mental health. *True or false?*

_____ 4. When people do not recall their dreams, it is probably because they are secretly trying to forget them. *True or false?*

_____ 5. Depriving someone of sleep will invariably cause the individual to become mentally imbalanced. *True or false?*

_____ 6. If we lose some sleep, we will eventually make up all the lost sleep the next night or another night. *True or false?*

_____ 7. No one has been able to go for more than 48 hours without sleep. *True or false?*

_____ 8. Everyone is able to sleep and breath at the same time. *True or false?*

_____ 9. Sleep enables the brain to rest, because little brain activity takes place during sleep. *True or false?*

_____ 10. Drugs have been proved to provide a long-term cure for sleeping difficulties. *True or false?*

Scoring: This is an easy set of questions to score, for every item is false. But don't lose any sleep if you missed them; they were chosen to represent the most common myths regarding sleep.

The Stages of Sleep

Most of us consider sleep a time of tranquility, as we set aside the tensions of the day and spend the night in uneventful slumber. However, a closer look at sleep shows that a good deal of activity occurs throughout the night, and that what at first appears to be a unitary state is, in fact, quite diverse.

Much of our knowledge of what happens during sleep comes from the *electroencephalogram,* or *EEG,* a measurement of electrical activity within the brain (see Chapter 2). When probes from an EEG machine are attached to the surface of a sleeping person's scalp and face, it becomes clear that the brain is active throughout the night. It produces electrical discharges with systematic, wavelike patterns that change in height (or amplitude) and speed (or frequency) in regular sequences. Instruments that measure muscle and eye movements also reveal a good deal of physical activity.

People progress through four distinct stages of sleep during a night's rest, moving through the stages in cycles lasting about 90 minutes. Each of these four sleep stages is associated with a unique pattern of brain waves, as shown in Figure 5-1. Moreover, there are specific biological indicators of dreaming.

When people first go to sleep, they move from a waking state in which they are relaxed with their eyes closed into **stage 1 sleep,** which is characterized by relatively rapid, low-voltage brain waves. This is actually a stage of transition between wakefulness and sleep. During stage 1, images sometimes appear, as if we were viewing still photos. However, true dreaming does not occur during the initial entry into this stage, although it does happen during subsequent periods of stage 1 sleep that occur later in the night.

As sleep becomes deeper, people enter **stage 2 sleep,** which is characterized by a slower, more regular wave pattern. However, there are also momentary interruptions of sharply pointed, spiky waves that are called *sleep spindles* because of their configuration. It becomes increasingly difficult to awaken a person from stage 2 sleep, which makes up about half of the total sleep of those in their early twenties.

As people drift into **stage 3 sleep,** the next stage of sleep, the brain waves become slower, with higher peaks and lower valleys in the wave pattern. By the time sleepers arrive at **stage 4 sleep,** the pattern is even slower and more regular, and people are least responsive to outside stimulation.

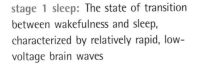

stage 1 sleep: The state of transition between wakefulness and sleep, characterized by relatively rapid, low-voltage brain waves

stage 2 sleep: A sleep deeper than that of stage 1, characterized by a slower, more regular wave pattern, along with momentary interruptions of "sleep spindles"

stage 3 sleep: A sleep characterized by slow brain waves, with greater peaks and valleys in the wave pattern

stage 4 sleep: The deepest stage of sleep, during which we are least responsive to outside stimulation

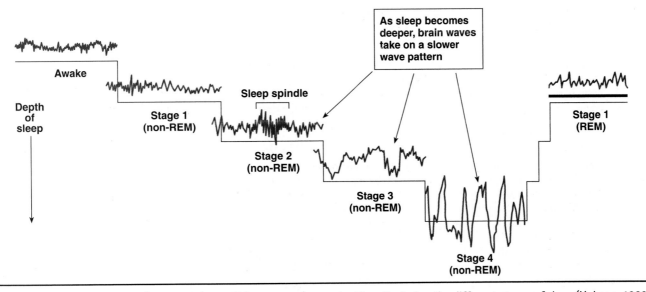

Figure 5-1 Brain-wave patterns (measured by an EEG apparatus) vary significantly during the different stages of sleep (Hobson, 1989). As sleep moves from stage 1 through stage 4, brain waves become slower.

  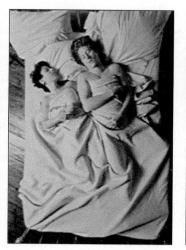 

People progress through four distinct stages of sleep during a night's rest spread over cycles lasting about 90 minutes. REM sleep, which occupies only 20 percent of adults' sleeping time, occurs in stage 1 sleep. These photos, taken at different times of night, show the synchronized patterns of a couple accustomed to sleeping in the same bed.

As you can see in Figure 5-2, stage 4 sleep is most likely to occur during the early part of the night. In the first half of the night, our sleep is dominated by stages 3 and 4. The last half is characterized by lighter stages of sleep—as well as the phase of sleep during which dreams occur, as we discuss next (Dement & Wolpert, 1958). In addition to passing through regular transitions between stages of sleep, then, people tend to sleep less and less deeply over the course of the night.

REM Sleep: The Paradox of Sleep

Several times a night, while sleepers are in stage 1 sleep, something curious happens. Their heart rate increases and becomes irregular, their blood pressure rises, their breathing rate increases, and males—even male infants—have erections. Most characteristic of this period is the back-and-forth movement of their eyes, as if they were watching an action-filled movie. This period of sleep is called **rapid eye movement,** or **REM, sleep,** and contrasts with stages 1 through 4, which are grouped together under the label of *non-REM* (or *NREM*) sleep. REM sleep occupies a little over 20 percent of adults' total sleeping time.

rapid eye movement (REM) sleep: Sleep occupying 20 percent of an adult's sleeping time, characterized by increased heart rate, blood pressure, and breathing rate; erections; eye movements; and the experience of dreaming

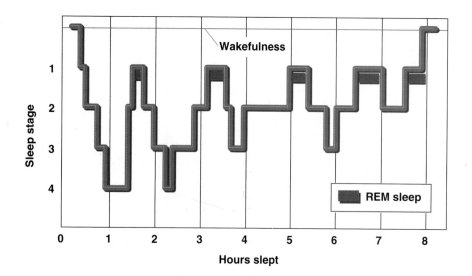

Figure 5-2 During the night, the typical sleeper passes through all four stages of sleep and several REM periods.

From E. Hartmann, *The Biology of Dreaming*, 1967. Courtesy of Charles C Thomas, Publisher, Ltd., Springfield, Illinois.

Paradoxically, while all this activity is occurring, the major muscles of the body appear to be paralyzed—except in rare cases such as Donald Dorff's. In addition, REM sleep is usually accompanied by dreams, which—whether or not people remember them—are experienced by *everyone* during some part of the night.

One possible explanation for rapid eye movements is that the eyes follow the action that is occurring in the dream (Dement, 1979; Kelly, 1991b). For instance, people who have reported dreaming about watching a tennis match just before they were awakened showed regular right-left-right eye movements, as if they were observing the ball flying back and forth across the net.

There is good reason to believe that REM sleep plays an important role in every-day human functioning. People deprived of REM sleep—by being awakened every time they begin to display the physiological signs of the stage—show a *rebound effect* when allowed to rest undisturbed. With this rebound effect, REM-deprived sleepers spend significantly more time in REM sleep than they normally would. It is as if the body requires a certain amount of REM sleep in order to function properly.

Why Do We Sleep, and How Much Sleep Is Necessary?

Sleep is a requirement for normal human functioning, although, surprisingly, we don't know exactly why. It is reasonable to expect that our bodies would require a tranquil "rest and relaxation" period in order to revitalize themselves, and experiments with rats show that total sleep deprivation results in death. Some researchers, using an evolutionary perspective, suggest that sleep permitted our ancestors to conserve energy at night, a time when food was relatively hard to come by. Still, this explanation is speculative, and although we know that *some* sleep is necessary, we don't fully know why we must sleep (Webb, 1992; Porkka-Heiskanen et al., 1997).

Scientists have been unable to establish just how much sleep is absolutely required. For instance, today most people sleep seven to eight hours each night, but they sleep three hours a night *less* than people did a hundred years ago. In addition, there is wide variability among individuals, with some people needing as little as three hours. Sleep requirements also vary over the course of a lifetime: As they age, people generally need less and less sleep (see Figures 5-3 and 5-4).

People who participate in sleep deprivation experiments, in which they are kept awake for stretches as long as 200 hours, show no lasting effects. It's no fun—they feel weary and irritable, can't concentrate, and show a loss of creativity, even after only minor deprivation. They also show a decline in logical reasoning ability. However, after being allowed to sleep normally, they bounce back quickly and are able to

PsychLink

Basics of sleep behavior
www.mhhe.com/
feldmanup6-05links

Figure 5-3 Although most people report sleeping between eight and nine hours per night, the amount varies a great deal (Dorbely, 1996). Where would you place yourself on this graph, and why do you think you need more or less sleep than others?

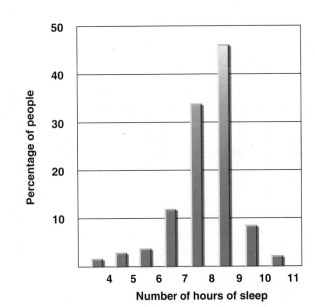

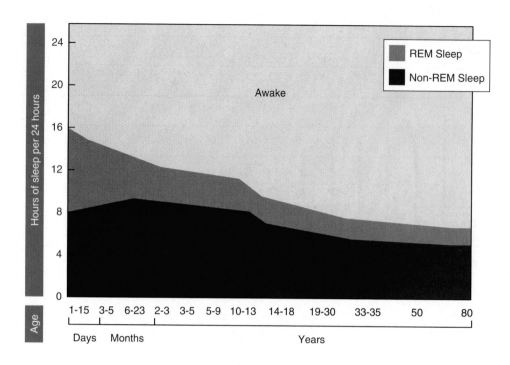

Figure 5-4 Over the course of their life span, people sleep less (Roffwarg, Muzio, & Dement, 1996). In addition, the proportion of REM sleep increases.

Reprinted with permission from H.P. Roffwarg, J.N. Munzio and W.C. Dement, "Ontogenic Development of the Human Sleep–Dream Cycle," *Science*, 152, 1996, p. 604–619. Copyright 1996 American Association for the Advancement of Science.

perform at predeprivation levels after just a few days (Dement, 1976; Webb, 1992; Dinges et al., 1997).

Those of us who worry, then, that long hours of study, work, or perhaps partying are ruining our health should feel heartened. As far as anyone can tell, most people suffer no permanent consequences of such temporary sleep deprivation. At the same time, though, a lack of sleep can make us feel edgy, slow our reaction time, and lower our performance on academic tasks. In addition, we put ourselves, and others, at risk when we carry out routine activities, such as driving, when we're very sleepy.

The Function and Meaning of Dreaming

> I was sitting at my desk when I remembered that this was the day of my chemistry final! I was terrified, because I hadn't studied a bit for it. In fact, I had missed every lecture all semester. In a panic, I began running across campus desperately searching for the classroom, to which I'd never been. It was hopeless; I knew I was going to fail and flunk out of college.

If you have had a similar dream—a surprisingly common dream among people involved in academic pursuits—you know how utterly convincing are the panic and fear that the events in the dream can bring about. *Nightmares,* unusually frightening dreams, occur fairly often. In one survey, almost half of a group of college students who kept records of their dreams over a two-week period reported having at least one nightmare. This works out to some twenty-four nightmares per person each year, on average (Wood & Bootzin, 1990; Berquier & Ashton, 1992; Tan & Hicks, 1995).

On the other hand, most of the 150,000 dreams the average person experiences by the age of 70 are much less dramatic (Snyder, 1970; Webb, 1992). They typically encompass such everyday events as going to the supermarket, working at the office, or preparing a meal. Students dream about going to class; professors dream about lecturing. Dental patients dream of getting their teeth drilled;

PsychLink

Comprehensive information on dreams

www.mhhe.com/ feldmanup6-05links

THE FAR SIDE   By GARY LARSON

"I've got it again, Larry . . . an eerie feeling like there's something on top of the bed."

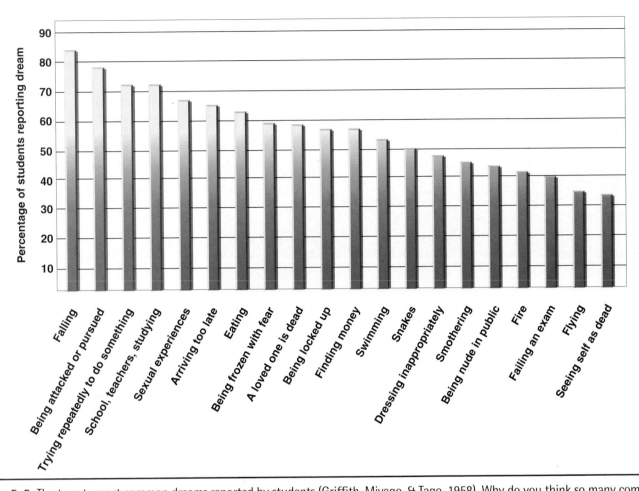

Figure 5-5 The twenty most common dreams reported by students (Griffith, Miyago, & Tago, 1958). Why do you think so many common dreams are unpleasant and so few pleasant? Do you think this tells us anything about the function of dreams?

dentists dream of drilling the wrong tooth. The English take tea with the Queen in their dreams; in the United States, people go to a bar with the president (Solomon, 1993; Potheraju & Soper, 1995; Domhoff, 1996; see Figure 5-5 for the most common dreams).

But what, if anything, do all these dreams mean? Whether dreams have a specific significance and function is a question that scientists have considered for many years, and they have developed several alternative theories.

Do Dreams Represent Unconscious Wish Fulfillment?

Sigmund Freud viewed dreams as a guide to the unconscious (Freud, 1900). In his **unconscious wish fulfillment theory,** he proposed that dreams represented unconscious wishes that dreamers desire to see fulfilled. However, because these wishes are threatening to the dreamer's conscious awareness, the actual wishes—called the **latent content of dreams**—are disguised. The true subject and meaning of a dream, then, may have little to do with its overt story line, which Freud called the **manifest content of dreams.**

To Freud, it was important to pierce the armor of a dream's manifest content to understand its true meaning. To do this, Freud tried to get people to discuss their dreams, associating symbols in the dreams to events in the past. He also suggested that certain common symbols with universal meanings appear in dreams. For example, to Freud, dreams in which the person is flying symbolize a wish for sexual intercourse. (See Table 5-1 for other common symbols.)

Today many psychologists reject Freud's view that dreams typically represent unconscious wishes and that particular objects and events in a dream are symbolic.

unconscious wish fulfillment theory: Sigmund Freud's theory that dreams represent unconscious wishes that dreamers desire to fulfill

latent content of dreams: According to Freud, the "disguised" or real meanings of dreams, hidden by more obvious subjects

manifest content of dreams: According to Freud, the overt story line of dreams

Table 5-1 Dream Symbolism, According to Freud

Symbol (Manifest Content of Dream)	Interpretation (Latent Content)
Climbing up a stairway, crossing a bridge, riding an elevator, flying in an airplane, walking down a long hallway, entering a room, train traveling through a tunnel	Sexual intercourse
Apples, peaches, grapefruits	Breasts
Bullets, fire, snakes, sticks, umbrellas, guns, hoses, knives	Male sex organs
Ovens, boxes, tunnels, closets, caves, bottles, ships	Female sex organs

Instead, they believe that the direct, overt action of a dream is the focal point of its meaning. For example, a dream in which we are walking down a long hallway to take an exam for which we haven't studied does not relate to unconscious, unacceptable wishes. Instead, it simply might mean we are concerned about an impending test. Even more complex dreams can often be interpreted in terms of everyday concerns and stress (Domhoff, 1996; Nikles et al., 1998).

Moreover, we now know that some dreams reflect events occurring in the dreamer's environment as he or she is sleeping. For example, sleeping participants in one experiment were sprayed with water while they were dreaming. These unlucky volunteers reported more dreams involving water than a comparison group of participants who were left to sleep undisturbed (Dement & Wolpert, 1958). Similarly, it is not unusual to wake up to find that the doorbell that was being rung in a dream is actually an alarm clock telling us it is time to get up.

Dreams-for-Survival Theory

According to the **dreams-for-survival theory,** dreams permit information that is critical for our daily survival to be reconsidered and reprocessed during sleep. Dreaming is seen as an inheritance from our animal ancestors, whose small brains were unable to sift sufficient information during waking hours. Consequently, dreaming provided a mechanism that permitted the processing of information twenty-four hours a day.

According to this theory, dreams represent concerns about our daily lives, illustrating our uncertainties, indecisions, ideas, and desires. Dreams are seen, then, as consistent with everyday living. Rather than being disguised wishes, as Freud suggested,

dreams-for-survival theory: The theory that dreams permit information that is critical for our daily survival to be reconsidered and reprocessed during sleep

Freud suggested that certain common symbols with universal meanings appear in dreams. According to his symbolism, a plane flying across the sky might represent the dreamer's wish for sexual intercourse. Can this claim be proved?

they would represent key concerns growing out of our daily experiences (Pavlides & Winson, 1989; Winson, 1990).

Research supports the dreams-for-survival theory, suggesting that certain dreams permit people to focus on and consolidate memories, particularly dreams that pertain to "how-to-do-it" memories related to motor skills. For instance, in one experiment, participants learned a visual memory task late in the day. They were then sent to bed, but awakened at certain times during the night. When they were awakened at times that did not interrupt dreaming, their performance on the memory task typically improved the next day. But when they were awakened during rapid eye movement (REM) sleep—the stage of sleep when people dream—their performance declined. The conclusion: Dreaming can play a role in helping us remember material to which we have been previously exposed (Karni et al., 1992, 1994).

Activation-Synthesis Theory

activation–synthesis theory: Hobson's theory that the brain produces random electrical energy during REM sleep that stimulates memories lodged in various portions of the brain

According to psychiatrist J. Allan Hobson, who proposed **activation-synthesis theory,** the brain produces random electrical energy during REM sleep, possibly due to changes in the production of particular neurotransmitters. This electrical energy randomly stimulates memories lodged in various portions of the brain. Because we have a need to make sense of our world, even while asleep, the brain takes these chaotic memories and weaves them into a logical story line, filling in the gaps to produce a rational scenario (Hobson, 1996; Porte & Hobson, 1996).

Yet Hobson does not entirely reject the view that dreams reflect unconscious wishes. He suggests that the particular scenario a dreamer produces is not just random but instead is a clue to the dreamer's fears, emotions, and concerns. Hence, what starts out as a random process culminates in something meaningful.

Dream Theories in Perspective

The range of theories about dreaming (summarized in Table 5-2) clearly illustrates that dream researchers have yet to agree on the fundamental meaning of dreams. Furthermore, new research is suggesting that the different approaches might be closer together than originally thought.

For instance, according to work by Allen Braun and colleagues, the parts of the brain associated with emotions and visual imagery are strongly activated during REM sleep. Using PET scans that show brain activity, Braun's research team found that the limbic and paralimbic regions of the brain, which are associated with emotion and motivation, are particularly active during REM sleep. At the same time, the association areas of the prefrontal cortex, which control logical analysis and attention, are inactive during REM sleep (Braun et al., 1998; see Figure 5-6).

Table 5-2 Three Views of Dreams

Theory	Basic Explanation	Meaning of Dreams	Is Meaning of Dream Disguised?
Unconscious wish fulfillment theory (Freud)	Dreams represent unconscious wishes the dreamer wants to fulfill	Latent content reveals unconscious wishes	Yes, by manifest content of dreams
Dreams-for-survival theory	Information relevant to daily survival is reconsidered and reprocessed	Clues to everyday concerns about survival	Not necessarily
Activation-synthesis theory	Dreams are the result of random activation of various memories, which are tied together in a logical story line	Dream scenario that is constructed is related to dreamer's concerns	Not necessarily

The results can be viewed as consistent with several aspects of Freudian theory. For example, the high activation of emotional and motivational centers of the brain during dreaming makes it more plausible that dreams might reflect unconscious wishes and instinctual needs, just as Freud suggested. Similarly, the fact that the areas of the brain responsible for emotions are highly active, while the brain regions responsible for rational thought are offline during REM sleep, suggests that the ego and superego are dormant, permitting unconscious thoughts to dominate.

On the other hand, critics of Freudian explanations for dreams disagree that the new research findings necessarily support Freud. There is still is no evidence that the meaning of dreams is hidden behind symbols found in the storyline of the dream. Furthermore, just because areas of the brain involved with motivation and emotion are activated during REM sleep does not prove that dreams relate to hidden motivations and emotions of the dreamer.

One thing is clear: Despite the advances in our understanding of the biological aspects of dreaming, the debate about the meaning of dreams is not yet resolved. But Freud would probably take satisfaction in the fact that almost a hundred years after he published his first book on the meaning of dreams, scientists are still debating his theory.

Sleep Disturbances: Slumbering Problems

At one time or another, almost all of us have difficulty sleeping—a condition known as *insomnia.* It could be due to a particular situation, such as the breakup of a relationship, concern about a test score, or the loss of a job. Some cases of insomnia, however, have no obvious cause. Some people are simply unable to fall asleep easily, or they go to sleep readily but wake up frequently during the night. Insomnia is a problem that afflicts about a quarter of the population of the United States (Hauri, 1991; Pressman & Orr, 1997).

Interestingly, some people who *think* they have sleeping problems are mistaken. For example, researchers in sleep laboratories have found that some people who report being up all night actually fall asleep in thirty minutes and stay asleep all night. Furthermore, some people with insomnia accurately recall sounds that they heard while they were asleep, which gives them the impression that they were actually awake during the night. In fact, some researchers suggest that future drugs for insomnia could function by changing people's *perceptions* of how much they have slept, rather than by making them sleep more (Engle-Friedman, Baker, & Bootzin, 1985; Klinkenborg, 1997).

Other sleep problems are less common than insomnia, although they are still widespread. For instance, some 20 million people suffer from *sleep apnea,* a condition in which a person has difficulty breathing while sleeping. The result is disturbed, fitful sleep, as the person is constantly reawakened when the lack of oxygen becomes great enough to trigger a waking response. Some people with apnea wake as many as 500 times during the course of a night, although they might not even be aware that they have wakened. Not surprisingly, such disturbed sleep results in complaints of fatigue the next day. Sleep apnea might also account for *sudden infant death syndrome (SIDS),* a mysterious killer of seemingly normal infants who die while sleeping (Ball et al., 1997).

Narcolepsy is uncontrollable sleeping that occurs for short periods while awake. No matter what the activity—holding a heated conversation, exercising, or driving—the narcoleptic will suddenly fall asleep. People with narcolepsy go directly from wakefulness to REM sleep, skipping the other stages. The causes of narcolepsy are not known, although there could be a genetic component because narcolepsy runs in some families (Siegel, 2000).

We know relatively little about sleeptalking and sleepwalking, two sleep disturbances that are usually harmless. Both occur during stage 4 sleep and are more frequent in children than in adults. Sleeptalkers and sleepwalkers usually have a vague consciousness of the world around them, and a sleepwalker might be able to walk with agility around obstructions in a crowded room. Unless a sleepwalker wanders into a dangerous environment, sleepwalking typically poses little risk (Hobson & Silverstri, 1999).

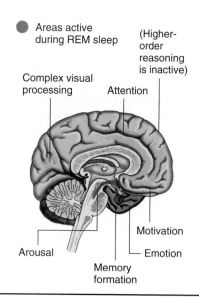

Figure 5-6 New research has found that those parts of the brain that are associated with emotions and visual imagery are strongly activated during REM sleep. Why might this be the case?

 **PsychLink**

Sleep disorders information
www.mhhe.com/
feldmanup6-05links

Figure 5-7 These are the times of day that people report feeling the sleepiest (during periods when they are normally awake and trying to stay alert). What implications does this information have for the workplace? For schools and colleges? (Dement, 1989).

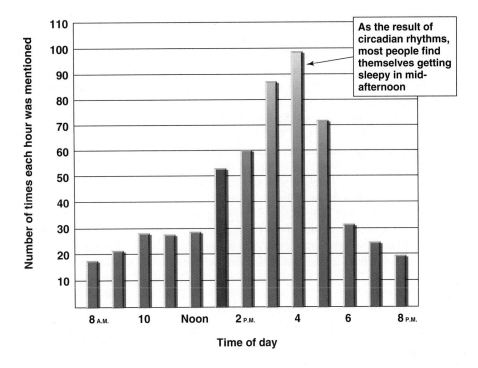

As the result of circadian rhythms, most people find themselves getting sleepy in mid-afternoon

circadian rhythms: Biological processes that occur repeatedly on approximately a twenty-four-hour cycle

 **PsychLink**

Circadian rhythms
www.mhhe.com/
feldmanup6-05links

Circadian Rhythms: Life Cycles

The fact that we cycle back and forth between wakefulness and sleep is one example of our body's circadian rhythms. **Circadian rhythms** (from the Latin *circa diem,* or "around a day") are biological processes that occur repeatedly on approximately a 24-hour cycle. Sleep and waking, for instance, occur naturally to the beat of an internal pacemaker that works on a cycle of about 24 hours. Several other bodily functions, such as body temperature and the female menstrual cycle, also work on circadian rhythms (Oren & Terman, 1998; Czeisler et al., 1999; Young, 2000).

Circadian cycles are complex. For instance, sleepiness occurs not just in the evening, but throughout the day in regular patterns. As you can see in Figure 5-7, most of us tend to get drowsy in midafternoon—regardless of whether we have eaten a heavy lunch. By making an afternoon siesta part of their everyday habit, people in several cultures take advantage of the body's natural inclination to sleep at this time (Dement, 1989; Ogilvie & Harsh, 1994).

The brain's hypothalamus controls the beat of circadian rhythms. However, the relative amount of light and darkness, which differs with the seasons of the year, also plays a role in determining circadian rhythms. In fact, some people experience *seasonal affective disorder,* a form of severe depression in which feelings of despair and hopelessness increase during the winter and lift during the rest of the year. The disorder appears to be a result of the brevity and gloom of winter days. Psychologists have found that several hours of daily exposure to bright lights is sometimes sufficient to improve the mood of those with the disorder (Sack et al., 1990; Roush, 1995; Oren & Terman, 1998).

Circadian rhythms explain the difficulty people have in flying through multiple time zones—the phenomenon of *jet lag.* Pilots, as well as others who must work on constantly changing time shifts (police officers and physicians), must fight their internal clocks. The result can be fatigue, irritability, and, even worse, outright error. In fact, an analysis of major disasters caused by human error finds that many, such as the Exxon *Valdez* oil spill in Alaska and the Chernobyl nuclear reactor accident, occurred late at night (Mapes, 1990; Moore-Ede, 1993).

Daydreams: Dreams Without Sleep

It is the stuff of magic: Our past mistakes can be wiped out and the future filled with noteworthy accomplishments. Fame, happiness, and wealth can be ours. In the next moment, though, the most horrible of tragedies can occur, leaving us devastated, alone, and penniless.

The source of these scenarios is **daydreams,** fantasies that people construct while awake. Unlike dreaming that occurs while sleeping, daydreams are more under people's control. Therefore their content is often more closely related to immediate events in the environment than is the content of the dreams that occur during sleep. Although they might include sexual content, daydreams also pertain to other activities or events that are relevant to a person's life.

Daydreams are a typical part of waking consciousness, even though our awareness of the environment around us declines while we are daydreaming. People vary considerably in the amount of daydreaming they do. For example, around 2 to 4 percent of the population spend at least half their free time fantasizing. Although most people daydream much less frequently, almost everyone fantasizes to some degree. Studies that ask people to identify what they are doing at random times during the day have shown that they are daydreaming about 10 percent of the time. As for the content of fantasies, most concern such mundane, ordinary events as paying the telephone bill, picking up the groceries, or solving a romantic problem (Singer, 1975; Lynn & Rhue, 1988; Lynn et al., 1996).

Frequent daydreaming might seem to suggest psychological difficulties, but there appears to be little relationship between psychological disturbance and daydreaming. Except in those rare cases in which a daydreamer is unable to distinguish a fantasy from reality (a mark of serious problems, as we discuss in Chapter 12), daydreaming seems to be a normal part of waking consciousness. Indeed, fantasy can contribute to the psychological well-being of some people by enhancing their creativity and by permitting them to use their imagination to understand what other people are experiencing (Lynn & Rhue, 1988; Pihlgren, Gidycz, & Lynn, 1993; Lynn et al., 1996).

Daydreams are fantasies that people construct while they are awake. What are the similarities and differences between daydreams and night dreams?

daydreams: Fantasies that people construct while awake

BECOMING AN INFORMED CONSUMER OF PSYCHOLOGY

Sleeping Better

Do you have trouble sleeping? You're not alone—almost 40 million people in the United States have chronic difficulty sleeping, and 30 million others have occasional sleep problems. For those of us who spend hours tossing and turning in bed, psychologists studying sleep disturbances have a number of suggestions for overcoming insomnia (National Institutes of Health, 1996b; Kupfer & Reynolds, 1997; Scharf, 1999), including these:

- *Exercise during the day (at least six hours before bedtime) and avoid naps.* Not surprisingly, it helps to be tired before going to sleep! Moreover, learning systematic relaxation techniques and biofeedback (see Chapter 2) can help you unwind from the day's stresses and tensions (Lehrer, 1996).

- *Choose a regular bedtime and stick to it.* Adhering to a habitual schedule helps your internal timing mechanisms regulate your body more effectively.

- *Don't use your bed as an all-purpose area.* Leave studying, reading, eating, watching TV, and other recreational activities to some other part of your living quarters. If you follow this advice, your bed will become a cue for sleeping.

- *Avoid drinks with caffeine after lunch.* The effects of beverages such as coffee, tea, and some soft drinks can linger for as long as 8 to 12 hours after they are consumed.

- *Drink a glass of warm milk at bedtime.* (Your grandparents were right when they dispensed this advice: Milk contains the chemical tryptophan, which helps people fall asleep.)

- *Avoid sleeping pills.* Although some prescription pills can be temporarily effective, in the long run they can cause more harm than good because they disrupt the normal sleep cycle (Haimov & Lavie, 1996; Zhdanova, Lynch, & Wurtman, 1997).
- *Try* not *to sleep.* This approach works because people often have difficulty falling asleep because they are trying so hard. A better strategy is to go to bed only when you feel tired. If you don't get to sleep within ten minutes, leave the bedroom and do something else, returning to bed only when you feel sleepy. Continue this process all night if necessary. But get up at your usual hour in the morning, and don't take any naps during the day. After three or four weeks, most people become conditioned to associate their beds with sleep—and fall asleep rapidly at night (Seltzer, 1986; Ubell, 1993; Sloan et al., 1993).

For long-term problems with sleep, you might consider visiting a sleep disorders center. For a list of accredited clinics, send a self-addressed, stamped envelope to: American Sleep Disorders Association, 6301 Bandel Road, Suite 101, Rochester, Minnesota 55901, or go to their website at http://www.asda.org.

Evaluate

1. _____ is the term used to describe our understanding of the world external to us, as well as our own internal world.
2. A great deal of neural activity goes on during sleep. True or false?
3. Dreams occur in _____ sleep.
4. _____ _____ are internal bodily processes that occur on a daily cycle.
5. Freud's theory of unconscious _____ _____ states that the actual wishes that an individual expresses in dreams are disguised because they are threatening to the person's conscious awareness.
6. Match the theory of dreaming with its definition.

1. Activation-synthesis theory	a. Dreams permit important information to be reprocessed during sleep.
2. Dreams-for-survival theory	b. The manifest content of dreams disguises the latent content of the dreams.
3. Dreams as wish fulfillment	c. Electrical energy stimulates random memories, which are woven together to produce dreams.

7. Match the sleep problem with its definition.

1. Insomnia	a. Condition that makes breathing while sleeping difficult
2. Narcolepsy	b. Difficulty in sleeping
3. Sleep apnea	c. Uncontrollable need to sleep during the day

Rethink

1. How would studying the sleep patterns of nonhuman species potentially help us figure out which of the theories of dreaming provides the best account of the functions of dreaming?

2. Suppose that a new "miracle pill" is developed that will allow a person to function with only one hour of sleep per night. However, because a night's sleep is so short, a person who takes the pill will never dream again. Knowing what you do about the functions of sleep and dreaming, what would be some advantages and drawbacks of such a pill from a personal standpoint? Would you take such a pill?

Answers to Evaluate Questions

1. Consciousness 2. True 3. REM 4. Circadian rhythms 5. wish fulfillment 6. 1-c; 2-a; 3-b 7. 1-b; 2-c; 3-a

Hypnosis and Meditation

Prepare

Are hypnotized people in a different state of consciousness?

What are the effects of meditation?

Organize

Hypnosis and Meditation
Hypnosis
Meditation

You are feeling relaxed and drowsy. You are getting sleepier and sleepier. Your body is becoming limp. Now you are starting to become warm, at ease, more comfortable. Your eyelids are feeling heavier and heavier. Your eyes are closing; you can't keep them open any more. You are totally relaxed.

Now, as you listen to my voice, do exactly as I say. Place your hands above your head. You will find they are getting heavier and heavier—so heavy you can barely keep them up. In fact, although you are straining as hard as you can, you will be unable to hold them up any longer.

An observer watching the above scene would notice a curious phenomenon occurring. Many of the people listening to the voice would, one by one, drop their arms to their sides, as if they were holding heavy lead weights. The reason for this strange behavior? The people have been hypnotized.

It is only recently that hypnotism has become an area considered worthy of scientific investigation. In part, the initial rejection of hypnosis relates to its bizarre eighteenth-century origins: Franz Mesmer's arguing that a form of "animal magnetism" could influence people and cure their illnesses. After a commission headed by Benjamin Franklin discredited the phenomenon, it fell into disrepute, only to rise again to respectability in the nineteenth century. But even today, as we will see, the nature of hypnosis is a matter of controversy.

Hypnosis: A Trance–Forming Experience?

People under **hypnosis** are in a trancelike state of heightened susceptibility to the suggestions of others. In some respects, it appears that they are asleep. Yet other aspects of their behavior contradict this notion, for these people are attentive to the hypnotist's suggestions and might carry out bizarre or silly suggestions.

Despite their compliance when hypnotized, people do not lose all will of their own. They will not suddenly become antisocial or self-destructive. They will not reveal hidden truths about themselves, and they are capable of lying when hypnotized. Moreover, people cannot be hypnotized against their will—despite popular misconceptions (Gwynn & Spanos, 1996).

There are wide variations in people's susceptibility to hypnosis. About 5 to 20 percent of the population cannot be hypnotized at all, and some 15 percent are very easily hypnotized. Most people fall somewhere in between. Moreover, the ease with which a person is hypnotized is related to a number of other characteristics. People who are readily hypnotized are also easily absorbed while reading books or listening to music, becoming unaware of what is happening around them, and they often spend an unusual amount of time daydreaming. In sum, then, they show a high ability to concentrate and to become completely absorbed in what they are doing (Rhue, Lynn, & Kirsch, 1993; Weitzenhoffer, 1999).

hypnosis: A trancelike state of heightened susceptibility to the suggestions of others

Despite common misconceptions, people such as these cannot be hypnotized against their will, nor do they lose all will of their own. In what ways is hypnosis beneficial?

 **PsychLink**

*Comprehensive hypnosis
information*
www.mhhe.com/
feldmanup6-05links

A Different State of Consciousness?

The question of whether hypnosis is a state of consciousness that is qualitatively different from normal waking consciousness is controversial. Psychologist Ernest Hilgard presented one side of the argument when he argued convincingly that hypnosis is a state of consciousness that differs significantly from other states. He contended that particular behaviors clearly differentiate hypnosis from other states, including higher suggestibility, increased ability to recall and construct images, and the acceptance of suggestions that clearly contradict reality. Moreover, changes in electrical activity in the brain are associated with hypnosis, supporting the position that hypnosis is a state of consciousness different from normal waking (Hilgard, 1975; Graffin, Ray, & Lundy, 1995).

On the other side of the controversy were theorists who rejected the notion that hypnosis is a significantly different state of consciousness from normal waking consciousness. They argued that altered brain-wave patterns are not sufficient to demonstrate a qualitative difference, given that no other specific physiological changes occur when a person is in a trance. Furthermore, little support exists for the contention that adults can accurately recall memories of childhood events while hypnotized. Such evidence suggests that there is nothing qualitatively special about the hypnotic trance (Spanos et al., 1993; Kirsch & Lynn, 1998).

There is increasing agreement that the controversy over the nature of hypnosis has led to extreme positions on both sides of the issue (Kirsch & Lynn, 1995). More recent approaches suggest that the hypnotic state might best be viewed as lying along a continuum, in which hypnosis is neither a totally different state of consciousness nor totally similar to normal waking consciousness.

As arguments about the true nature of hypnosis continue, though, one thing is clear: Hypnosis has been successfully used to solve practical human problems. In fact, psychologists working in many different areas have found hypnosis to be a reliable, effective tool (Rhue, Lynn, & Kirsch, 1993). Among the range of applications are the following:

- *Controlling pain.* Patients suffering from chronic pain might be given the suggestion, while hypnotized, that their pain is eliminated or reduced. They might also be taught to hypnotize themselves to relieve pain or to gain a sense of control over their symptoms. Hypnosis has proved to be particularly useful during childbirth and dental procedures (Oster, 1994; Mairs, 1995; Barber, 1996).
- *Reducing smoking.* Although it hasn't been successful in stopping drug and alcohol abuse, hypnosis sometimes helps people stop smoking through hypnotic suggestions that the taste and smell of cigarettes are unpleasant (Erickson, Hershman, & Secter, 1990; Spiegel et al., 1993).
- *Treating psychological disorders.* Hypnosis sometimes is used during treatment for psychological disorders. For example, hypnosis may be employed to heighten relaxation, reduce anxiety, increase expectations of success, or modify self-defeating thoughts (Fromm & Nash, 1992).
- *Assisting in law enforcement.* Witnesses and victims are sometimes better able to recall details of a crime when hypnotized. In one case, a witness to the kidnapping of a group of California schoolchildren was placed under hypnosis and was able to recall all but one digit of the license number on the kidnapper's vehicle (Geiselman et al., 1985). On the other hand, sometimes hypnotic recollections are inaccurate, and the legal status of hypnosis is unresolved (Gibson, 1995; Lynn et al., 1997; Baker, 1998).
- *Improving athletic performance.* Athletes sometimes turn to hypnosis to improve their performance. For example, baseball player Rod Carew used hypnotism to increase his concentration when batting, with considerable success (Udolf, 1981; Stanton, 1994; Edgette & Edgette, 1995).

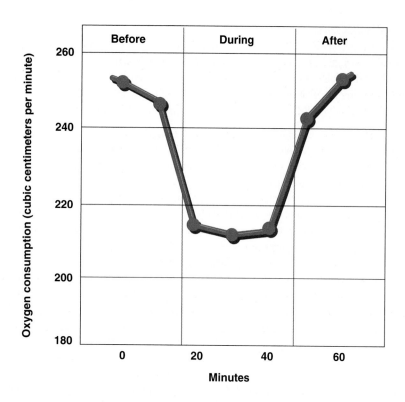

Figure 5-8 The body's use of oxygen declines significantly during meditation (Benson, 1993).

Meditation: Regulating Our Own State of Consciousness

When traditional practitioners of the ancient eastern religion of Zen Buddhism want to achieve greater spiritual insight, they turn to a technique that has been used for centuries to alter their state of consciousness: meditation.

Meditation is a learned technique for refocusing attention that brings about an altered state of consciousness. Meditation often consists of the repetition of a *mantra*— a sound, word, or syllable—over and over. In other forms of meditation, the focus is on a picture, flame, or specific part of the body. Regardless of the nature of the particular initial stimulus, the key to the procedure is concentrating on it so thoroughly that the meditator becomes unaware of any outside stimulation and reaches a different state of consciousness.

Following meditation, people report feeling thoroughly relaxed. They sometimes relate that they have gained new insights into themselves and the problems they are facing. The long-term practice of meditation can even improve health due to the biological changes it produces. For example, oxygen usage decreases, heart rate and blood pressure decline, and brain-wave patterns can change (Wallace & Benson, 1972; Holmes, 1985; Jevning et al., 1996; Zamarra et al., 1996; see Figure 5-8).

Anyone can meditate by using a few simple procedures. The fundamentals include sitting in a quiet room with eyes closed, breathing deeply and rhythmically, and repeating a word or sound—such as the word *one*—over and over. Practiced twice a day for 20 minutes, the technique is effective in bringing about relaxation (Benson & Friedman, 1985; Benson, 1993; Benson et al., 1994).

 **PsychLinks**

Transcendental meditation research
www.mhhe.com/
feldmanup6-05links

meditation: A learned technique for refocusing attention that brings about an altered state of consciousness

EXPLORING DIVERSITY

Cross-Cultural Routes to Altered States of Consciousness

• A group of Native American Sioux sit naked in a steaming sweat lodge, as a medicine man throws water on sizzling rocks to send billows of scalding steam into the air.

- Aztec priests smear themselves with a mixture of crushed poisonous herbs, hairy black worms, scorpions, and lizards. Sometimes they drink the potion.
- During the sixteenth century, a devout Hasidic Jew lies across the tombstone of a celebrated scholar. As he murmurs the name of God repeatedly, he seeks to be possessed by the soul of the dead wise man's spirit. If successful, he will attain a mystical state, and the deceased's words will flow out of his mouth.

Each of these rituals has a common goal: suspension from the bonds of everyday awareness and access to an altered state of consciousness (Furst, 1977; Fine, 1994). Although they might seem exotic from the vantage point of many Western cultures, these rituals represent an apparently universal effort to alter consciousness.

Some scholars suggest that the quest to alter consciousness represents a basic human desire (Siegel, 1989). Whether or not one accepts such an extreme view, it is clear that different cultures have developed their own unique forms of consciousness-altering activities. Similarly, when we discuss psychological disorders in Chapter 12, we will see that what is deemed "abnormal" behavior varies considerably from one culture to another.

Of course, realizing that efforts to produce altered states of consciousness are widespread throughout the world's societies does not answer a fundamental question: Is the experience of *un*altered states of consciousness similar across different cultures?

There are two possible responses to this question. Because humans share basic biological commonalties in the ways their brains and bodies are wired, we might assume that the fundamental experience of consciousness is similar across cultures. As a result, we could suppose that consciousness shows some basic similarities across cultures.

On the other hand, cultures can differ greatly in how they interpret and view certain aspects of consciousness. For example, people in different cultures might experience the passage of time differently: One study found that Mexicans view time as passing more slowly than other North Americans do (Diaz-Guerrero, 1979).

Whatever the true nature of consciousness and why people seek to alter it, it is clear that people often seek the means to alter their everyday experience of the world. In some cases that need becomes overwhelming, as we see next when we consider the use of drugs.

Evaluate

1. _____ is a state of heightened susceptibility to the suggestions of others.
2. A friend tells you, "I once heard of a person who was murdered by being hypnotized and then told to jump from the Golden Gate Bridge!" Could such a thing have happened? Why or why not?
3. _____ is a learned technique for refocusing attention to bring about an altered state of consciousness.
4. Leslie repeats a unique sound, known as a _____, when she engages in meditation.

Answers to Evaluate Questions

1. Hypnosis 2. No; people who are hypnotized cannot be made to perform self-destructive acts; 3. Meditation 4. mantra

Rethink

1. What sorts of mental functioning does hypnosis appear to affect most strongly? Do you think it might have more effect on the left or right hemisphere of the brain, or would it affect both equally? Why?
2. Meditation produces several physical and psychological benefits. Does this suggest that we are physically and mentally burdened in our normal state of waking consciousness? Why?

Drug Use: The Highs and Lows of Consciousness

Green Bay Packers quarterback Brett Favre can tell you exactly when he changed his life, even if he doesn't remember it. It was 6 p.m. on February 27, and Favre was in his room at Bellin Hospital in Green Bay, Wisconsin, recovering from ankle surgery. A nurse was about to reinsert his IV, and the oft-injured quarterback was rolling his eyes in resignation at his longtime girlfriend, Deanna Tynes, and their 7-year-old daughter, Brittany. Then suddenly he went into convulsions. "His whole body was jerking around, his lip was folded under," says Deanna, 27, who screamed to the nurse to stop him from swallowing his tongue. Asked a terrified Brittany: "Mom, is he going to die?"

In a sense, just the opposite happened. When Favre, 26, regained consciousness minutes later, he awakened to a central fact of his life: He was an addict in need of help. For the previous five months, Favre had been taking the painkiller Vicodin—first to help him deal with a season's worth of injuries and then as a crutch for coping with fame. Doctors could not pinpoint the cause of the seizure, but it seemed clear to Favre that it was related to his dependency on the prescription drug. Three months later he checked into the Menninger Clinic in Topeka, Kansas, for six weeks of rehab. (Plummer & Pick, 1996, p. 129)

Brett Favre was successful in his personal war on drugs: He became free of painkillers and later was able to lead his team to triumph in the Super Bowl. Others, though, are not so lucky. Each year, thousands of people die from complications of drug overdoses, and many more are addicted to various kinds of drugs.

Drugs are a part of almost everyone's life. From infancy on, most people take vitamins, aspirin, cold-relief medicine, and the like, and surveys find that 80 percent of adults in the United States have taken an over-the-counter pain reliever in the past six months. However, these drugs rarely produce an altered state of consciousness (Dortch, 1996).

On the other hand, some substances, known as psychoactive drugs, lead to an altered state of consciousness. **Psychoactive drugs** influence a person's emotions, perceptions, and behavior. Yet even these drugs are common in most of our lives. If you have ever had a cup of coffee or sipped a beer, you have taken a psychoactive drug.

A large number of individuals have used more potent— and dangerous—psychoactive drugs than coffee and beer (see Figure 5-9). For instance, surveys find that 40 percent of U.S. high school seniors have used an illegal drug within the last year, and over 60 percent report having been drunk on alcohol. The figures for the adult population are even higher (Johnston, Bachman, & O'Malley, 1999).

Of course, drugs vary widely in the effects they have on users, in part because they affect the nervous system in very different ways. Some drugs alter the limbic system, others affect the operation of specific neurotransmitters across the synapses of neurons (see Chapter 3). For example, some drugs block or enhance the release of neurotransmitters, some block the receipt or the removal of a neurotransmitter, and still others mimic the effects of particular neurotransmitters (see Figure 5-10).

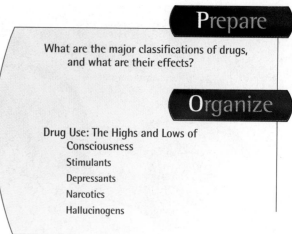

Prepare

What are the major classifications of drugs, and what are their effects?

Organize

Drug Use: The Highs and Lows of Consciousness
Stimulants
Depressants
Narcotics
Hallucinogens

psychoactive drugs: Drugs that influence a person's emotions, perceptions, and behavior

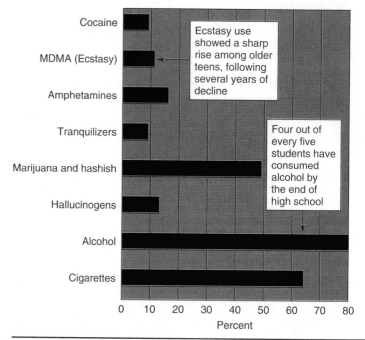

Figure 5-9 How many teenagers use drugs? Results of the most recent comprehensive survey of 14,000 high school seniors across the United States show the percentage of respondents who have used various substances for nonmedical purposes at least once (Johnston, Bachman, & O'Malley, 1999). Can you think of any reasons why teenagers—as opposed to older people—might be particularly likely to use drugs?

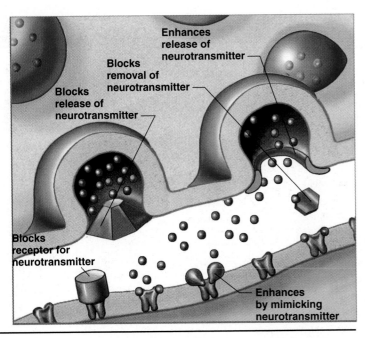

Figure 5-10 Different drugs affect different parts of the nervous system and brain and each drug functions in one of these specific ways.

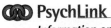 **PsychLink**

Information on addiction
www.mhhe.com/
feldmanup6-05links

addictive drugs: Drugs that produce a biological or psychological dependence in the user; withdrawal from them leads to a craving for the drug that in some cases can be nearly irresistible

stimulants: Drugs that affect the central nervous system by causing a rise in heart rate, blood pressure, and muscular tension

The most dangerous drugs are addictive. **Addictive drugs** produce a biological or psychological dependence in the user, and withdrawal from them leads to a craving for the drug that, in some cases, can be nearly irresistible. Addictions can be *biologically based,* in which case the body becomes so accustomed to functioning in the presence of a drug that it cannot function in its absence. Or addictions can be *psychologically based,* in which case people believe that they need the drug in order to respond to the stresses of daily living. Although we generally associate addiction with drugs such as heroin, everyday sorts of drugs like caffeine (found in coffee) and nicotine (found in cigarettes) have addictive aspects as well.

We know surprisingly little about the underlying causes of addiction. One of the problems in identifying the causes is that different drugs (such as alcohol and cocaine) affect the brain in very different ways—and yet can be equally addicting. Furthermore, it takes longer to become addicted to some drugs than to others, even though the ultimate consequences of addiction can be equally grave (Wickelgren, 1998b; Thombs, 1999).

Why do people take drugs in the first place? There are many reasons, ranging from the perceived pleasure of the experience itself, to the escape a drug-induced high affords from the everyday pressures of life, to an attempt to achieve a religious or spiritual state. But other factors, ones that have little to do with the nature of the experience itself, also lead people to try drugs (McDowell & Spitz, 1999).

For instance, the alleged drug use of well-known role models (such as baseball player Darryl Strawberry and film star Robert Downey, Jr.), the easy availability of some illegal drugs, and peer pressure all play a role in the decision to use drugs. In some cases, the motive is simply the thrill of trying something new. Finally, the sense of helplessness experienced by poor, unemployed individuals trapped in lives of poverty might lead them to try drugs as a way of escaping the bleakness of their lives. Regardless of the forces that lead a person to begin using drugs, drug addiction is among the most difficult of all behaviors to modify, even with extensive treatment (Dupre et al., 1995; Tucker, Donovan, & Marlatt, 1999).

Because of the difficulty in treating drug problems, there is little disagreement that the best hope for dealing with the overall societal problem of substance abuse is to prevent people from becoming involved with drugs in the first place. However, there is little accord on how to accomplish this goal. In fact, as we consider in the *Applying Psychology in the 21st Century* box, the effectiveness of even the most popular antidrug program is questionable.

Stimulants: Drug Highs

It's one o'clock in the morning, and you still haven't finished reading the last chapter of the text on which you will be tested in the morning. Feeling exhausted, you turn to the one thing that might help you stay awake for the next two hours: a cup of strong, black coffee.

If you have ever found yourself in such a position, you have been relying on a major **stimulant,** caffeine, to stay awake. *Caffeine* is one of a number of stimulants that affect the central nervous system by causing a rise in heart rate, blood pressure, and muscular tension. Caffeine is present not only in coffee; it is an important ingredient in tea, soft drinks, and chocolate as well (see Figure 5-11).

Caffeine produces several reactions. The major behavioral effects of caffeine are an increase in attentiveness and a decrease in reaction time. Caffeine can also bring about an improvement in mood, most likely by mimicking the effects of a natural brain chemical, adenosine. Too much caffeine, however, can result in nervousness and insomnia. People

Applying Psychology in the 21st Century

Just Say No—to D.A.R.E.? Finding Antidrug Programs That Work

The two eighth-graders in a classroom in New York City's Spanish Harlem can barely suppress their giggles. "You are sitting on a stalled, crowded bus," their teacher tells them. "Start up a conversation." Esther, petite and ponytailed, begins. "Well, this bus is really crowded!" "Yeah," says Luis. "I can't wait to get outta here—I'm gonna suffocate." Pause. Esther: "Nice day, isn't it? Where are you going?" Luis: "To take my girlfriend to the movies." Esther: "I have a date too." Painful pause. Luis: "The bus is certainly . . . stopped." The class cracks up, and the two scamper back to their desks. (Van Biema, 1996)

This dialogue might not sound like it has much to do with helping adolescents avoid getting hooked on drugs, but in fact it is part of a new approach to drug prevention called Life Skills Training. Unlike previous efforts, this program focuses on teaching a broad range of social skills that adolescents need to deal with the range of pressures they face.

The Life Skills program contrasts sharply with D.A.R.E. (Drug Abuse Resistance Education), currently the most popular antidrug program in the United States. Used in more than 80 percent of school districts in the United States, D.A.R.E. consists of a series of seventeen lessons on the dangers of drugs, alcohol, and gangs, taught to fifth- and sixth-graders by a police officer. The program is highly popular with school officials, parents, and politicians.

The problem: Several well-controlled evaluations have been unable to demonstrate that the D.A.R.E. program is effective in reducing drug use over the long term. In fact, one study even showed that D.A.R.E. graduates were *more* likely to use marijuana than a comparison group of nongraduates (Clayton et al., 1996; Lynan et al., 1999).

Because of problems in identifying long-term positive effects of D.A.R.E., researchers have sought to develop alternative strategies, such as the Life Skills Training program. Instead of focusing on long-term dangers, Life Skills Training concentrates on immediate negative consequences. During 15 sessions, students are taught to be more assertive and confident, and to assess more accurately the communications they receive from their peers and popular culture. The notion is that by learning general social skills, students will be better equipped to deal with perceived peer pressure to use drugs, alcohol, and cigarettes (Botvin & Botvin, 1992; Dusenbury & Botvin, 1992).

Analysis of the Life Skills Training approach suggests that it is successful in reducing adolescent drug use. For example, an evaluation of several thousand students in Newark, New Jersey, who had participated in Life Skills Training in seventh grade and were tracked until they graduated from high school, showed that the students used drugs, tobacco, and alcohol at half the rate of their peers who had not been in the program (Botvin et al., 1994; Botvin et al., 1995; Van Biema, 1996).

An alternative to the popular D.A.R.E. program, Life Skills Training concentrates on immediate negative consequences instead of long-term dangers. Why might this approach be more effective?

Whether the D.A.R.E. program will win continued support or be replaced by other programs, such as Life Skills Training, remains to be seen. What is clear is that teenage drug use remains a considerable social problem, and that effective approaches to stem the use of drugs are sorely needed.

Why do you think the D.A.R.E. program is so popular among the police and school boards? Do you think the students who go through the training are as supportive as the adults who sponsor its use?

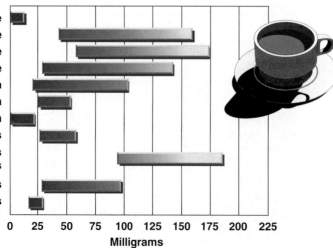

Decaffeinated coffee	
Percolated coffee	
Drip-brewed coffee	
Instant coffee	
Brewed tea	
Instant tea	
Cocoa	
Many soft drinks	
Weight-loss drugs, diuretics and stimulants	
Pain relievers	
Cold/allergy remedies	

0   25   50   75   100   125   150   175   200   225
Milligrams

Figure 5-11 How much caffeine are you eating and drinking? This chart shows the range of caffeine found in common foods and drinks (*The New York Times*, 1991). The average person in the U.S. consumes about 200 milligrams of caffeine each day.

can build up a biological dependence on the drug. If they suddenly stop drinking coffee, they might experience headaches or depression. Many people who drink large amounts of coffee on weekdays have headaches on weekends because of a sudden drop in the amount of caffeine they are consuming (Silverman et al., 1992; Silverman, Mumford, & Griffiths, 1994; James, 1997).

Nicotine, found in cigarettes, is another common stimulant. The soothing effects of nicotine help explain why cigarette smoking is addictive. Smokers develop a dependence on nicotine, and those who suddenly stop smoking develop strong cravings for the drug. This is not surprising: nicotine activates neuronal mechanisms similar to those activated by cocaine, which, as we see next, is also highly addictive (Murray, 1990; Pich et al., 1997). (We will discuss smoking in greater detail in Chapter 15 when we consider health psychology.)

Cocaine

Although its use has declined over the last decade, the stimulant *cocaine* and its derivative, crack, are still a serious concern. Cocaine is inhaled or "snorted" through the nose, smoked, or injected directly into the bloodstream. It is rapidly absorbed into the body and takes effect almost immediately.

When used in relatively small quantities, cocaine produces feelings of profound psychological well-being, increased confidence, and alertness. Cocaine produces this "high" through the neurotransmitter dopamine. As you'll recall from Chapter 2, dopamine is one of the chemicals that transmit between neurons messages related to ordinary feelings of pleasure. Normally when dopamine is released, excess amounts of the neurotransmitter are reabsorbed by the releasing neuron. However, when cocaine enters the brain, it blocks reabsorption of leftover dopamine. As a result, the brain is flooded with dopamine-produced pleasurable sensations (Landry, 1997; Bolla, Cadet, & London, 1998; see Table 5-3 for a summary of the effects of cocaine and other illegal drugs.)

However, there is a steep price to be paid for the pleasurable effects of cocaine. The drug is psychologically and physically addictive, and users can grow obsessed with obtaining it. Cocaine addicts indulge in binge use, administering the drug every ten to thirty minutes if it is available. During these binges, they think of nothing but cocaine; eating, sleeping, family, friends, money, and even survival have no importance. Their lives become tied to the drug. Over time, users deteriorate mentally and physically. In extreme cases, cocaine can cause hallucinations—a common one is of insects crawling over one's body. Ultimately, an overdose of cocaine can lead to death (Pottieger et al., 1992; Crits-Christoph et al., 1999).

Almost 2.5 million people in the United States are occasional cocaine users, and as many as 1.5 million use the drug regularly. Given the strength of cocaine, withdrawal from

During the late 19th century, and even into the early 20th century, cocaine was used in numerous home remedies and medicines.

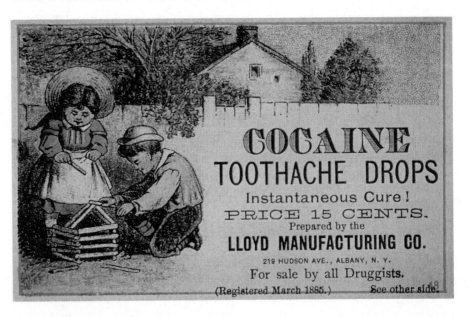

Table 5-3 Drugs and Their Effects

Drug	Street Name	Effects	Withdrawal Symptoms	Adverse/Overdose Reactions
Stimulants				
Cocaine	Coke, blow, snow, lady, crack	Increased confidence, mood elevation, sense of energy and alertness, decreased appetite, anxiety, irritability, insomnia, transient drowsiness, delayed orgasm	Apathy, general fatigue, prolonged sleep, depression, disorientation, suicidal thoughts, agitated motor activity, irritability, bizarre dreams	Elevated blood pressure, increase in body temperature, face-picking, suspiciousness, bizarre and repetitious behavior, vivid hallucinations, convulsions, possible death
Amphetamines Benzedrine Dexedrine	Speed Speed			
Depressants				
Alcohol	Booze	Anxiety reduction, impulsiveness, dramatic mood swings, bizarre thoughts, suicidal behavior, slurred speech, disorientation, slowed mental and physical functioning, limited attention span	Weakness, restlessness, nausea and vomiting, headaches, nightmares, irritability, depression, acute anxiety, hallucinations, seizures, possible death	Confusion, decreased response to pain, shallow respiration, dilated pupils, weak and rapid pulse, coma, possible death
Barbiturates Nembutal Seconal Phenobarbital	Yellowjackets, yellows Reds			
Rohypnol	Roofies, rope, "date-rape drug"	Muscle relaxation, amnesia, sleep	Seizures	Seizures, coma, incapacitation, inability to resist sexual assault
Narcotics				
Heroin	H, hombre, junk, smack, dope, crap, horse,	Anxiety and pain reduction, apathy, difficulty in concentration, slowed speech, decreased physical activity, drooling, itching, euphoria, nausea	Anxiety, vomiting, sneezing, diarrhea, lower back pain, watery eyes, runny nose, yawning, irritability, tremors, panic, chills and sweating, cramps	Depressed levels of consciousness, low blood pressure, rapid heart rate, shallow breathing, convulsions, coma, possible death
Morphine	Drugstore dope, cube, first line, mud			
Hallucinogens				
Cannabis Marijuana Hashish Hash oil	Bhang, kif, ganja, dope, grass, pot, smoke, hemp, joint, weed, bone, Mary Jane, herb, tea	Euphoria, relaxed inhibitions, increased appetite, disoriented behavior	Hyperactivity, insomnia, decreased, appetite, anxiety	Severe reactions are rare but include panic, paranoia, fatigue, bizarre and dangerous behavior, decreased testosterone over long term; immune-system effects
MDMA	Ecstasy	Heightened sense of oneself and insight, feelings of peace, empathy, energy	Not reported	Increase in body temperature, possible memory difficulties
LSD	Acid, quasey, microdot, white lightning	Heightened aesthetic responses; vision and depth distortion; heightened sensitivity to faces and gestures; magnified feelings; paranoia; panic; euphoria	Not reported	Nausea and chills; increased pulse, temperature, and blood pressure; slow, deep breathing; loss of appetite; insomnia; bizarre, dangerous behavior

the drug is difficult, and people pass through several distinct phases (see Figure 5-12). Although the use of cocaine among high school students has declined in recent years, the drug is still a major problem (Johnston, Bachman, & O'Malley, 1999).

Amphetamines

Amphetamines are strong stimulants, such as Dexedrine and Benzedrine, popularly known as "speed." When their use soared in the 1970s, the phrase "speed kills" became prevalent as the drugs caused an increasing number of deaths. Although amphetamine use has declined from its 1970s peak, many drug experts believe that speed would quickly resurface in large quantities if cocaine supplies were interrupted.

 **PsychLink**

Factline on cocaine
www.mhhe.com/
feldmanup6-05links

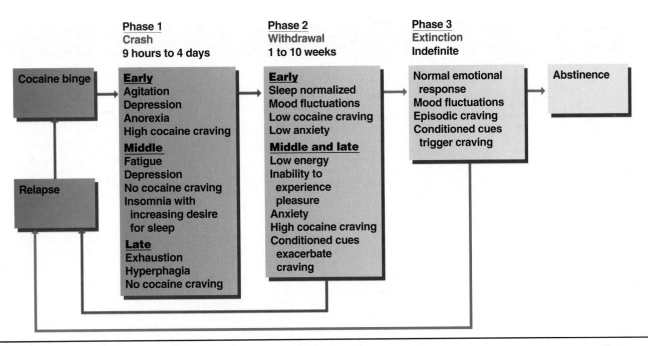

Phase 1
Crash
9 hours to 4 days

Phase 2
Withdrawal
1 to 10 weeks

Phase 3
Extinction
Indefinite

Figure 5-12 Phases of cocaine deprivation. In the first phase, users crave cocaine, feel depressed and agitated, and experience increasing anxiety. In the second phase, which begins from nine hours to four days later, heavy users begin the process of "withdrawal." If addicts are able to pass through the withdrawal phase, they move into the third phase, in which craving for cocaine is further reduced. However, they remain highly sensitive to cues related to cocaine use, and relapses are common. (Based on Gawin, 1991.)

In small quantities, amphetamines—which stimulate the central nervous system—bring about a sense of energy and alertness, talkativeness, heightened confidence, and a mood "high." They increase concentration and reduce fatigue. Amphetamines also cause a loss of appetite, increased anxiety, and irritability. When taken over long periods of time, amphetamines can cause feelings of being persecuted by others, as well as a general sense of suspiciousness. People taking amphetamines can lose interest in sex. If taken in too large a quantity, amphetamines overstimulate the central nervous system to such an extent that convulsions and death can occur.

Depressants: Drug Lows

depressants: Drugs that slow down the nervous system

In contrast to the initial effect of stimulants, which is an increase in arousal of the central nervous system, the effect of **depressants** is to impede the nervous system by causing neurons to fire more slowly. Small doses result in at least temporary feelings of *intoxication*—drunkenness—along with a sense of euphoria and joy. When large amounts are taken, however, speech becomes slurred and muscle control becomes disjointed, making motion difficult. Ultimately, heavy users can lose consciousness entirely.

Alcohol

The most common depressant is *alcohol,* which is used by more people than any other drug. Based on liquor sales, the average person in the United States over the age of 14 drinks 2½ gallons of pure alcohol over the course of a year. This works out to more than 200 drinks per person. Although alcohol consumption has declined steadily over the last decade, surveys show that more than three-fourths of college students indicate that they have had a drink within the last thirty days (Carmody, 1990; National Center on Addiction and Substance Abuse, 1994; Johnston, Bachman, & O'Malley, 1999).

Amphetamines (shown here greatly magnified) are strong stimulants that increase alertness and energy and provide a sense of heightened confidence.

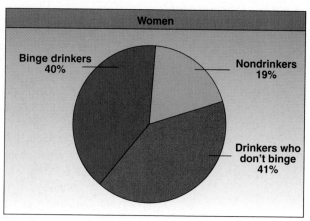
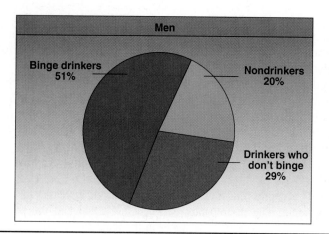

Figure 5-13 Drinking habits of college students (Wechsler et al., 2000). For men, binge drinking was defined as consuming five or more drinks in one sitting; for women, the total was four or more.

One of the more disturbing trends is the high frequency of binge drinking among college students, the practice that led to the death of Scott Krueger (described in the chapter prologue). For men, *binge drinking* is defined as drinking five or more drinks in one sitting; for women, who generally weigh less than men and whose body absorbs alcohol less efficiently, binge drinking is defined as having four or more drinks at one sitting.

As shown in Figure 5-13, some 50 percent of male college students and 40 percent of female college students responding to a nationwide survey said they had engaged in binge drinking within the prior two weeks. Some 17 percent of female students and 31 percent of male students admitted drinking on ten or more occasions during the past thirty days. Furthermore, even light drinkers were affected by the high rate of alcohol use: Two-thirds of lighter drinkers said that they had had their studying or sleep disturbed by drunk students, and around one-third had been insulted or humiliated by a drunk student. A quarter of the women said they had been the target of an unwanted sexual advance by a drunk classmate (Wechsler et al., 1994; Wechsler et al., 2000).

Although alcohol consumption is widespread, there are significant gender and cultural variations in its use. For example, women are typically somewhat lighter drinkers than men—although the gap between the sexes is narrowing for older women and has

Although most alcohol consumers are casual users, there are more than 14 million alcoholics in the United States. The effects of alcohol vary significantly, depending on who is drinking it and the setting in which they are drinking. If alcohol were a newly discovered drug, do you think its sale would be legal?

closed completely for teenagers. In addition, women are usually more susceptible to the effects of alcohol, because of differences in blood volume and body fat that permit more alcohol to go directly into the bloodstream (Galanter, 1995; National Center on Addiction and Substance Abuse, 1996; Blume, 1998).

There are also ethnic differences in alcohol consumption. For example, people of East Asian backgrounds who live in the United States tend to drink significantly less than Caucasians or African Americans, and their incidence of alcohol-related problems is lower. It could be that physical reactions to drinking, which can include sweating, a quickened heartbeat, and flushing, are more unpleasant for East Asians than for other groups (Akutsu et al., 1989; Smith & Lin, 1996; Garcia-Andrade, Wall, & Ehlers, 1997).

Although alcohol is a depressant, most people claim that it increases their sense of sociability and well-being. The discrepancy between the actual and the perceived effects of alcohol lies in the initial effects it produces in the majority of individuals who use it: release of tension and stress, feelings of happiness, and loss of inhibitions (Steele & Southwick, 1985; Josephs & Steele, 1990; Steele & Josephs, 1990; Sayette, 1993). As the dose of alcohol increases, however, the depressive effects become more pronounced (see Figure 5-14). People might feel emotionally and physically unstable. They also show poor judgment and might act aggressively. Moreover, their memories are impaired, brain processing of spatial information is diminished, and speech becomes slurred and incoherent. Eventually they might fall into a stupor and pass out. If they drink enough alcohol in a short time, they can die of alcohol poisoning (Bushman, 1993; Matthews et al., 1996; Chin & Pisoni, 1997).

Although most people fall into the category of casual users, there are some 14 million alcoholics in the United States. *Alcoholics,* people with alcohol-abuse problems, come to rely on alcohol and continue to drink even though it causes serious difficulties. In addition, they become increasingly immune to the effects of alcohol. Consequently, alcoholics must drink progressively more in order to experience the initial positive feelings that alcohol produces (Galanter & Kleber, 1999).

Some alcoholics must drink constantly in order to feel well enough to function in their daily lives. Other alcoholics drink inconsistently, but occasionally go on sporadic binges in which they consume large quantities of alcohol.

It is not clear why certain people become alcoholics and develop a tolerance for alcohol, while others do not. Some evidence suggests a genetic cause, although the question of whether there is a specific inherited gene that produces alcoholism is controversial. What is clear is that the chances of becoming alcoholic are considerably higher if there are alcoholics in earlier generations of a person's family. On the other hand, not all alcoholics have close relatives who are alcoholics. In these cases, environmental stressors are suspected of playing a larger role (Pennisi, 1997a; McGue, 1999).

PsychLink

Alcohol and alcoholism information
www.mhhe.com/
feldmanup6–05links

Barbiturates

Barbiturates, which include such drugs as Nembutal, Seconal, and Phenobarbital, are another form of depressant. Frequently prescribed by physicians to induce sleep or to reduce stress, barbiturates produce a sense of relaxation. Yet they also are psychologically and physically addictive, and the combination of barbiturates with alcohol can be deadly because it relaxes the muscles of the diaphragm to such an extent that the user stops breathing.

Rohypnol

Rohypnol is frequently called the "date rape drug," because when it is mixed with alcohol it can prevent victims from resisting sexual assault. Sometimes people who are unknowingly given the drug are so incapacitated that they have no memory of the assault.

Even legal drugs, when used improperly, can lead to addiction.

Number of drinks consumed in 2 hours		Alcohol in blood, percentage	Typical effects
	2	0.05	**Judgment, thought, and restraint weakened; tension released, giving carefree sensation**
	3	0.08	**Tensions and inhibitions of everyday life lessened; cheerfulness**
	4	0.10	**Voluntary motor action affected, making hand and arm movements, walk, and speech clumsy**
	7	0.20	**Severe impairment—staggering, loud, incoherent, emotionally unstable,100 times greater traffic risk; exuberance and aggressive inclinations magnified**
	9	0.30	**Deeper areas of brain affected, with stimulus-response and understanding confused; stuporous; blurred vision**
	12	0.40	**Incapable of voluntary action, sleepy, difficult to arouse; equivalent of surgical anesthesia**
	15	0.50	**Comatose; centers controlling breathing and heartbeat anesthetized; death increasingly probable**

Figure 5-14 The effects of alcohol. The quantities represent only rough benchmarks; the effects vary significantly depending on an individual's weight, height, recent food intake, genetic factors, and even a person's psychological state.

Note: A drink refers to a typical 12-ounce bottle of beer, a 1.5-ounce shot of hard liquor, or a 5-ounce glass of wine.

Narcotics: Relieving Pain and Anxiety

Narcotics are drugs that increase relaxation and relieve pain and anxiety. Two of the most powerful narcotics, *morphine* and *heroin,* are derived from the poppy seed pod. Although morphine is used medically to control severe pain, heroin is illegal in the United States. This has not prevented its widespread use.

Heroin users usually inject the drug directly into their veins with a hypodermic nee-dle. The immediate effect has been described as a "rush" of positive feeling, similar in some respects to a sexual orgasm—and just as difficult to describe. After the rush, a heroin user experiences a sense of well-being and peacefulness that lasts three to five hours. When the effects of the drug wear off, however, the user feels extreme anxiety and a desperate desire to repeat the experience. Moreover, larger amounts of heroin are needed each time to pro-duce the same pleasurable effect. This leads to a cycle of biological and psychological

narcotics: Drugs that increase relaxation and relieve pain and anxiety

addiction: The user is constantly either shooting up or attempting to obtain ever-increasing amounts of the drug. Eventually, the life of the addict revolves around heroin.

Because of the powerful positive feelings the drug produces, heroin addiction is particularly difficult to cure. One treatment that has shown some success is the use of methadone. *Methadone* is a synthetic chemical that satisfies a heroin user's physiological cravings for the drug without providing the "high" that accompanies heroin. When heroin users are placed on regular doses of methadone they might be able to function relatively normally. The use of methadone has one substantial drawback, however. Although it can eliminate the psychological dependence on heroin, it replaces the biological addiction to heroin with a biological addiction to methadone. Researchers are attempting to find nonaddictive chemical substitutes for heroin, as well as substitutes for other addictive drugs, that do not replace one addiction with another (Waldrop, 1989; Sinclair, 1990; Pulvirenti & Koob, 1994).

Hallucinogens: Psychedelic Drugs

What do mushrooms, jimsonweed, and morning glories have in common? Besides being fairly common plants, each can be the source of a powerful **hallucinogen,** a drug that is capable of producing hallucinations, or changes in the perceptual process.

The most common hallucinogen in widespread use today is *marijuana,* whose active ingredient—tetrahydrocannabinol (THC)—is found in a common weed, cannabis. Marijuana is typically smoked in cigarettes or pipes, although it can be cooked and eaten. Almost 40 percent of high school seniors and more than a third of eighth-graders report having used marijuana within the past year. Furthermore, these figures have been steadily increasing since the early 1990s (Johnston, Bachman, & O'Malley, 1999; see Figure 5-15).

The effects of marijuana vary from person to person, but they typically consist of feelings of euphoria and general well-being. Sensory experiences seem more vivid and intense, and a person's sense of self-importance seems to grow. Memory can be impaired, causing the user to feel pleasantly "spaced out." On the other hand, the effects are not universally positive. Individuals who use marijuana when feeling depressed can end up even more depressed, because the drug tends to magnify both good and bad feelings.

There are clear risks associated with long-term, heavy marijuana use. Although marijuana does not seem to produce addiction by itself, some evidence suggests that there are similarities in the way marijuana and drugs such as cocaine and heroin affect the brain.

The use of heroin creates a cycle of biological and physical dependence. Combined with the strong positive feelings produced by the drug, this makes heroin addiction especially difficult to cure.

hallucinogen: A drug that is capable of producing hallucinations, or changes in the perceptual process

Figure 5-15 Marijuana use continues at high levels. For instance, almost 40 percent of high school seniors, and more than one-third of eighth graders, say they have used the drug within the previous year.

(Source: Johnston, Bachman, & O'Malley, 1999.)

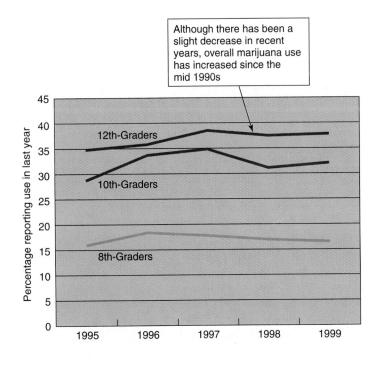

Although there has been a slight decrease in recent years, overall marijuana use has increased since the mid 1990s

Furthermore, there is some evidence that heavy use at least temporarily decreases the production of the male sex hormone testosterone, potentially affecting sexual activity and sperm count (DiChiara et al., 1997; Iversen, 2000).

In addition, marijuana smoked during pregnancy has lasting effects on children who are exposed prenatally. Heavy use also diminishes the ability of the immune system to fight off germs and increases stress on the heart, although it is unclear how strong these effects are. There is one unquestionably negative consequence of smoking marijuana: The smoke damages the lungs much the way cigarette smoke does, producing an increased likelihood of developing cancer and other lung diseases (Julien, 1995; "Marijuana as Medicine," 1997).

Despite the possible dangers of marijuana use, there is little scientific evidence for the popular belief that users "graduate" from marijuana to more dangerous drugs. Furthermore, the use of marijuana is routine in certain cultures. For instance, some people in Jamaica habitually drink a marijuana-based tea for religious purposes. In addition, marijuana has several medical uses; it can prevent nausea from chemotherapy, treat some AIDS symptoms, and relieve muscle spasms for people with spinal cord injuries. In a controversial move, several states have made the use of the drug legal if it is prescribed by a physician—although it remains illegal under U.S. federal law (Brookhiser, 1997; Iverson, 2000).

What are the effects of a hallucinogen on thinking? Artists have tried to depict the hallucinogenic experience, as in this yarn painting.

MDMA (Ecstasy) and LSD

MDMA ("Ecstasy") and *lysergic acid diethylamide* (LSD, or "acid") fall into the category of hallucinogens. Both drugs affect the operation of the neurotransmitter serotonin in the brain, altering brain-cell activity and perception (Aghajanian, 1994; Cloud, 2000).

Ecstasy users report a sense of peacefulness and calm, increased empathy and connection with others, and feeling relaxed yet energetic. Although the data are not conclusive, some researchers have found declines in memory and performance on intellectual tasks for Ecstasy users, and such findings suggest that there can be long-term changes in serotonin receptors in the brain (McCann et al., 1999).

LSD produces vivid hallucinations. Perceptions of colors, sounds, and shapes are altered so much that even the most mundane experience—such as looking at the knots in a wooden table—can seem moving and exciting. Time perception is distorted, and objects and people might be viewed in a new way, with some users reporting that LSD increases their understanding of the world. For others, however, the experience brought on by LSD can be terrifying, particularly if users have had emotional difficulties in the past. Furthermore, people can experience flashbacks—hallucinations that start suddenly, long after they stopped using the drug.

PsychLink

Information on marijuana
www.mhhe.com/
feldmanup6-05links

BECOMING AN INFORMED CONSUMER OF PSYCHOLOGY

Identifying Drug and Alcohol Problems

In a society bombarded with commercials for drugs that are guaranteed to do everything from cure the common cold to give new life to "tired blood," it is no wonder that drug-related problems are a major social issue. Yet many people with drug and alcohol problems deny they have them, and even close friends and family members can fail to realize when occasional social use of drugs or alcohol has turned into abuse.

Certain signs, however, indicate when use becomes abuse (Archambault, 1992; National Institute on Drug Abuse, 2000). Among them:

- Always getting high to have a good time
- Being high more often than not
- Getting high to get oneself going
- Going to work or class while high

- Missing or being unprepared for class or work because you were high
- Feeling bad later about something you said or did while high
- Driving a car while high
- Coming in conflict with the law because of drugs
- Doing something while high that you wouldn't otherwise do
- Being high in nonsocial, solitary situations
- Being unable to stop getting high
- Feeling a need for a drink or a drug to get through the day
- Becoming physically unhealthy
- Failing at school or on the job
- Thinking about liquor or drugs all the time
- Avoiding family or friends while using liquor or drugs

Any combination of these symptoms should be sufficient to alert you to the potential of a serious drug problem. Because drug and alcohol dependence are almost impossible to cure on one's own, people who suspect that they have a problem should seek immediate attention from a psychologist, physician, or counselor.

You can also get help from national hotlines. For alcohol difficulties, call the National Council on Alcoholism at (800) 622-2255. For drug problems, call the National Institute on Drug Abuse at (800) 662-4357. You can also check your telephone book for a local listing of Alcoholics Anonymous or Narcotics Anonymous. Finally, you can write to the National Council on Alcoholism and Drug Dependence, 12 West 21st Street, New York, NY 10010, or consult their website at http://www.ncadd.org, for help with alcohol and drug problems.

Evaluate

1. Drugs that affect a person's consciousness are referred to as _____.
2. Match the type of drug to an example of that type.

   1. Narcotic—a pain reliever   a. LSD
   2. Amphetamine—a strong stimulant   b. Heroin
   3. Hallucinogen—capable of producing   c. Dexedrine or speed
      hallucinations

3. Classify each drug listed as a stimulant (S), depressant (D), hallucinogen (H), or narcotic (N).

   1. Nicotine _____
   2. Cocaine _____
   3. Alcohol _____
   4. Morphine _____
   5. Marijuana _____

4. The effects of LSD can recur long after the drug has been taken. True or false?
5. _____ is a drug that has been used to cure people of heroin addiction.

Answers to Evaluate Questions

1. psychoactive 2. 1–b; 2–c; 3–a 3. 1–S; 2–S; 3–D; 4–N; 5–H 4. True 5. Methadone

Rethink

1. Why do you think people in almost every culture use psychoactive drugs and search for altered states of consciousness?

2. People often use the word *addiction* loosely, speaking of an addiction to candy or a television show. Can you explain the difference between this type of "addiction" and a true physiological addiction? Is there a difference between this type of "addiction" and a psychological addiction?

What are the different states of consciousness?

- Consciousness is a person's awareness of the sensations, thoughts, and feelings at a given moment. It can vary from more active to more passive states. (p. 132)

What happens when we sleep, and what are the meaning and function of dreams?

- Using the electroencephalogram, or EEG, to study sleep, scientists have found that the brain is active throughout the night, and that sleep proceeds through a series of stages identified by unique patterns of brain waves. (p. 134)
- REM (rapid eye movement) sleep is characterized by an increase in heart rate, a rise in blood pressure, an increase in the rate of breathing and, in males, erections. Dreams occur during this stage. (p. 135)
- According to Freud, dreams have both a manifest content (their apparent story line) and a latent content (their true meaning). He suggested that the latent content provides a guide to a dreamer's unconscious, revealing unfulfilled wishes or desires. (p. 138)
- The dreams-as-survival theory suggests that information relevant to daily survival is reconsidered and reprocessed in dreams. Finally, the activation-synthesis theory proposes that dreams are a result of random electrical energy that stimulates different memories, which are then woven into a coherent story line. (p. 139)

What are the major sleep disorders and how can they be treated?

- Insomnia is a sleep disorder characterized by difficulty sleeping. Sleep apnea is a condition in which people have difficulty sleeping and breathing at the same time. People with narcolepsy have an uncontrollable urge to sleep. Sleepwalking and sleeptalking are relatively harmless. (p. 141)
- Psychologists and sleep researchers advise people with insomnia to increase exercise during the day, avoid caffeine and sleeping pills, drink a glass of warm milk before bedtime, and avoid *trying* to go to sleep. (p. 143)

How much do we daydream?

- Daydreaming may occur 10 percent of the time, although wide individual differences exist in the amount of time devoted to it. (p. 143)

Are hypnotized people in a different state of consciousness?

- Hypnosis produces a state of heightened susceptibility to the suggestions of the hypnotist. Under hypnosis, significant behavioral changes occur, including increased concentration and suggestibility, heightened ability to recall and construct images, lack of initiative, and acceptance of suggestions that clearly contradict reality. (p. 145)

What are the effects of meditation?

- Meditation is a learned technique for refocusing attention that brings about an altered state of consciousness. (p. 147)
- Different cultures have developed their own unique ways to alter states of consciousness. (p. 147)

What are the major classifications of drugs, and what are their effects?

- Drugs can produce an altered state of consciousness. However, they vary in how dangerous they are and in whether or not they are addictive, producing a physical or psychological dependence. Drug addiction is one of the most difficult behaviors to modify. (p. 149)
- Stimulants cause arousal in the central nervous system. Two common stimulants are caffeine (found in coffee, tea, and soft drinks) and nicotine (found in cigarettes). More dangerous are cocaine and amphetamines, or "speed." In large quantities they can overload the central nervous system, leading to convulsions and death. (p. 150)
- Depressants decrease arousal in the central nervous system, causing the neurons to fire more slowly. They can cause intoxication along with feelings of euphoria. The most common depressants are alcohol and barbiturates. (p. 154)
- Alcohol is the most frequently used depressant. Its initial effects of released tension and positive feelings yield to depressive effects as the dose of alcohol increases. Both genetic causes and environmental stressors can lead to alcoholism. (p. 154)
- Morphine and heroin are narcotics, drugs that produce relaxation and relieve pain and anxiety. Because of their addictive qualities, morphine and heroin are particularly dangerous. (p. 157)
- Hallucinogens are drugs that produce hallucinations or other changes in perception. The most frequently used hallucinogen is marijuana, which has several long-term risks. Two other hallucinogens are LSD and Ecstasy. (p. 158)
- A number of signals indicate when drug use becomes drug abuse. A person who suspects that he or she has a drug problem should get professional help. People are almost never capable of solving drug problems on their own. (p. 159)

Key Terms and Concepts

consciousness (p. 132)
stage 1 sleep (p. 134)
stage 2 sleep (p. 134)
stage 3 sleep (p. 134)
stage 4 sleep (p. 134)
rapid eye movement (REM) sleep (p. 135)
unconscious wish fulfillment theory (p. 138)
latent content of dreams (p. 138)
manifest content of dreams (p. 138)
dreams-for-survival theory (p. 139)
activation-synthesis theory (p. 140)

circadian rhythms (p. 142)
daydreams (p. 143)
hypnosis (p. 145)
meditation (p. 147)
psychoactive drugs (p. 149)
addictive drugs (p. 150)
stimulants (p. 150)
depressants (p. 154)
narcotics (p. 157)
hallucinogen (p. 158)

Psychology on the Web

1. Find a resource on the Web that interprets dreams, and another that reports the results of scientific dream research. Compare the nature and content of the two sites in terms of the topics covered, reliability of information provided, and promises made about the use of the site and its information. Write a summary of what you found.
2. There is considerable debate about the effectiveness of D.A.R.E., the Drug Abuse Resistance Education program. Find a discussion of both sides of the issue on the Web and summarize the arguments on each side. State your own preliminary conclusions about the D.A.R.E. program.

Epilogue

In this chapter we discussed consciousness in its full range from active states to passive states. We focused especially on factors that affect consciousness, from natural factors like sleep, dreaming, and daydreaming, to more intentional ways of altering consciousness, including hypnosis, meditation, and drugs. We examined some of the reasons people seek to alter their consciousness, considered both uses and abuses of consciousness-altering strategies, and attempted to address some of the most dangerous ways people alter their consciousness.

Before we turn to the subject of learning in the next chapter, return briefly to the prologue of this chapter, about Scott Krueger's death from binge drinking. Consider the following questions in light of your understanding of alcohol use and abuse.

1. What do you think might have caused Krueger's excessive drinking the evening he overdosed on alcohol?
2. Do you believe Krueger should have been considered an alcoholic? Was he addicted either physiologically or psychologically to alcohol?
3. How does alcohol affect the state of consciousness of users such as Krueger?
4. Why do you think the incidence of binge drinking is so high?

O L C Preview

For additional quizzing and a variety of interactive resources, visit the *Understanding Psychology* Online Learning Center at

www.mhhe.com/feldmanup6

Chapter Six

Learning

Prologue: A Friend Named Ike

Looking Ahead

Classical Conditioning

The Basics of Classical Conditioning

Applying Conditioning Principles to Human Behavior

Extinction

Generalization and Discrimination

Beyond Traditional Classical Conditioning: Challenging Basic Assumptions

Operant Conditioning

Thorndike's Law of Effect

The Basics of Operant Conditioning

Positive Reinforcers, Negative Reinforcers, and Punishment

The Pros and Cons of Punishment: Why Reinforcement Beats Punishment

Schedules of Reinforcement: Timing Life's Rewards

Discrimination and Generalization in Operant Conditioning

Superstitious Behavior

Shaping: Reinforcing What Doesn't Come Naturally

Biological Constraints on Learning: You Can't Teach an Old Dog Just Any Trick

Psychology at Work: Lynne Calero

Cognitive-Social Approaches to Learning

Latent Learning

Observational Learning: Learning Through Imitation

Violence on Television and in Movies: Does the Media's Message Matter?

Applying Psychology in the 21st Century: Does Virtual Aggression Lead to Actual Aggression?

Exploring Diversity: Does Culture Influence How We Learn?

The Unresolved Controversy of Cognitive-Social Learning Theory

Becoming an Informed Consumer of Psychology: Using Behavior Analysis and Behavior Modification

Looking Back

Key Terms and Concepts

Psychology on the Web

OLC Preview

Epilogue

Prologue

A Friend Named Ike

Elizabeth Twohy, who had polio as a child, needs to use a wheelchair most of the day, and the list of little things that are hard to do in a wheelchair is just about endless. But she has a friend, Ike, who helps out.

He picks up things she drops, turns light switches on and off, puts clothes in the dryer and takes the dishes out of the dishwasher, sorts the recyclables and brings her the telephone.

"The only thing that Ike can't do that would be really nice would be to drive the car," said Ms. Twohy, director of disability services for Brookdale Community College in Lincroft, N.J. Ike does have a license, but it's a dog license (O'Neil, 1999, p. D6).

Learning, a permanent change in behavior brought on by experience, plays a central role in practically every specialty area of psychology.

Looking Ahead

Ike's helpfulness did not just happen, of course. It is the result of painstaking training procedures—the same ones that are at work in each of our lives, illustrated by our ability to read a book, drive a car, play poker, study for a test, or perform any of the numerous activities that make up our daily routine. Like Ike, each of us must acquire and then refine our skills and abilities through learning.

Learning is a fundamental topic for psychologists and plays a central role in almost every specialty area of psychology, as we will see throughout this book. For example, a psychologist studying perception might ask, "How do we learn that people who look small from a distance are far away and not simply tiny?" A developmental psychologist might inquire, "How do babies learn to distinguish their mothers from other people?" A clinical psychologist might wonder, "Why do some people learn to be afraid when they see a spider?" A social psychologist might ask, "How do we learn to believe that we've fallen in love?" Each of these questions, although drawn from very different fields of psychology, can be answered only through an understanding of basic learning processes.

What do we mean by learning? Although psychologists have identified a number of different types of learning, a general definition encompasses them all: **Learning** is a relatively permanent change in behavior brought about by experience.

To understand learning, we need to return to the nature-nurture issue we first discussed in Chapter 1. Specifically, we must distinguish between performance changes due to *maturation* and changes brought about by experience. (Maturation is the nature part of the nature-nurture question; experience is the nurture part.) For instance, children become better tennis players as they grow older partially because their strength increases with their size—a maturational phenomenon. Maturational changes need to be differentiated from improvements due to practice, which indicate that learning has taken place.

Similarly, we must distinguish short-term changes in behavior that are due to factors other than learning, such as declines in performance resulting from fatigue or lack of effort, from performance changes that are due to actual learning. For example, if Venus Williams performs poorly in a tennis game because of tension or fatigue, this does not mean that she has not learned to play correctly or has forgotten how to play well.

The distinction between learning and performance is critical, and not always easy to make (Druckman & Bjork, 1994). To some psychologists, we can examine learning only indirectly, by observing changes in performance. Because there is not always a one-to-one correspondence between learning and performance, understanding when true learning has occurred is difficult—as someone who has done poorly on an exam due to fatigue, but who really does know the material, can well understand.

On the other hand, some psychologists have approached learning from a very different perspective. By considering learning simply as any change in behavior, they maintain that learning and performance are the same thing. Such an approach tends to dismiss the thinking that can be involved with learning by focusing only on observable performance. As we will see, the degree to which learning can be understood without considering mental processes is one of the major areas of disagreement among learning theorists of varying orientations.

In short, we begin this chapter by examining the type of learning that explains responses ranging from a dog salivating when it hears its owner opening a can of dog food to the emotions we feel when our national anthem is played. We then discuss other theories that consider how learning is a consequence of rewarding circumstances. Finally, we examine approaches that focus on the cognitive aspects of learning.

learning: A relatively permanent change in behavior brought about by experience

PsychLink

Theories on learning
www.mhhe.com/
feldmanup6-06links

Classical Conditioning

Does the mere sight of the golden arches in front of McDonald's make you feel pangs of hunger and think about hamburgers? If it does, then you are displaying an elementary form of learning called classical conditioning. Classical conditioning helps explain such diverse phenomena as crying at the sight of a bride walking down the aisle, fearing the dark, and falling in love.

The Basics of Classical Conditioning

Ivan Pavlov, a Russian physiologist, never intended to do psychological research. In 1904 he won the Nobel Prize for his work on digestion, testimony to his contribution to that field. Yet Pavlov is remembered not for his physiological research, but for his experiments on basic learning processes—work that he began quite accidentally (Windholz, 1997).

Pavlov had been studying the secretion of stomach acids and salivation in dogs in response to the ingestion of varying amounts and kinds of food. While doing so, he observed a curious phenomenon: Sometimes stomach secretions and salivation would begin in the dogs when they had not yet eaten any food. The mere sight of the experimenter who normally brought the food, or even the sound of the experimenter's footsteps, was enough to produce salivation in the dogs. Pavlov's genius was his ability to recognize the implications of this discovery. He saw that the dogs were responding not only on the basis of a biological need (hunger), but also as a result of learning—or, as it came to be called, classical conditioning. **Classical conditioning** is a type of learning in which a neutral stimulus (such as the experimenter's footsteps) comes to bring about a response after it is paired with a stimulus (such as food) that naturally brings about that response.

To demonstrate and analyze classical conditioning, Pavlov conducted a series of experiments (Pavlov, 1927). In one, he attached a tube to the salivary gland of a dog, which would allow him to measure precisely the dog's salivation. He then rang a bell and, just a few seconds later, presented the dog with meat. This pairing occurred repeatedly and was carefully planned so that each time exactly the same amount of time elapsed between the presentation of the bell and the meat. At first the dog would salivate only when the meat itself was presented, but soon it began to salivate at the sound of the bell. In fact, even when Pavlov stopped presenting the meat, the dog still salivated after hearing the sound. The dog had been classically conditioned to salivate to the bell.

As you can see in Figure 6-1, the basic processes of classical conditioning that underlie Pavlov's discovery are straightforward, although the terminology he chose is not simple. Consider first the diagram in Figure 6-1a. Before conditioning, there are two unrelated stimuli: the ringing of a bell and meat. We know that normally the ringing of a bell does not lead to salivation but to some irrelevant response, such as perking up the ears or perhaps a startle reaction. The bell is therefore called the **neutral stimulus** because it is a stimulus that, before conditioning, does not naturally bring about the response we are interested in. We also have meat, which, because of the biological makeup of

Prepare

What is learning?
How do we learn to form associations between stimuli and responses?

Organize

Classical Conditioning
    The Basics of Classical Conditioning
    Applying Conditioning Principles to Human Behavior
    Extinction
    Generalization and Discrimination
    Beyond Traditional Classical Conditioning

classical conditioning: A type of learning in which a neutral stimulus comes to bring about a response after it is paired with a stimulus that naturally brings about that response
neutral stimulus: A stimulus that, before conditioning, does not naturally bring about the response of interest

Ivan Pavlov (center), developed the principles of classical conditioning.

Figure 6-1 The basic process of classical conditioning. *(a)* Prior to conditioning, the ringing of a bell does not bring about salivation—making the bell a neutral stimulus. On the other hand, meat naturally brings about salivation, making the meat powder an unconditioned stimulus and salivation an unconditioned response. *(b)* During conditioning, the bell is rung just before the presentation of the meat. *(c)* Eventually, the ringing of the bell alone brings about salivation. We can now say that conditioning has been accomplished: The previously neutral stimulus of the bell is now considered a conditioned stimulus that brings about the conditioned response of salivation.

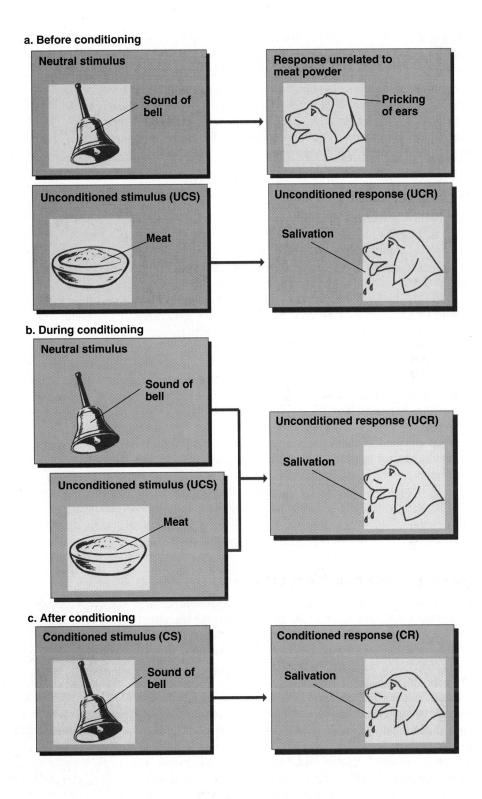

a. Before conditioning

b. During conditioning

c. After conditioning

unconditioned stimulus (UCS): A stimulus that brings about a response without having been learned

unconditioned response (UCR): A response that is natural and needs no training (e.g., salivation at the smell of food)

the dog, naturally leads to salivation—the response that we are interested in conditioning. The meat is considered an **unconditioned stimulus,** or **UCS,** because food placed in a dog's mouth automatically causes salivation to occur. The response that the meat elicits (salivation) is called an **unconditioned response,** or **UCR**—a natural, innate response that is not associated with previous learning. Unconditioned responses are always brought about by the presence of unconditioned stimuli.

Figure 6-1b illustrates what happens during conditioning. The bell is rung just before each presentation of the meat. The goal of conditioning is for the bell to become

associated with the unconditioned stimulus (meat) and therefore to bring about the same sort of response as the unconditioned stimulus. During this period, salivation gradually increases each time the bell is rung, until the bell alone causes the dog to salivate.

When conditioning is complete, the bell has evolved from a neutral stimulus to what is now called a **conditioned stimulus,** or **CS.** At this time, salivation that occurs as a response to the conditioned stimulus (bell) is considered a **conditioned response,** or **CR.** This situation is depicted in Figure 6-1c. After conditioning, then, the conditioned stimulus evokes the conditioned response.

The sequence and timing of the presentation of the unconditioned stimulus and the conditioned stimulus are particularly important (Rescorla, 1988; Wasserman & Miller, 1997). Like a malfunctioning warning light at a railroad crossing that goes on after the train has passed by, a neutral stimulus that *follows* an unconditioned stimulus has little chance of becoming a conditioned stimulus. On the other hand, just as a warning light works best if it goes on right before a train passes, a neutral stimulus that is presented *just before* the unconditioned stimulus is most apt to result in successful conditioning. Research has shown that conditioning is most effective if the neutral stimulus (which will become a conditioned stimulus) precedes the unconditioned stimulus by between a half-second and several seconds, depending on what kind of response is being conditioned.

Although the terminology Pavlov used to describe classical conditioning might at first seem confusing, the following summary rules can help make the relationships between stimuli and responses easier to understand and remember:

- An *un*conditioned stimulus leads to an *un*conditioned response.
- *Un*conditioned stimulus–*un*conditioned response pairings are *un*learned and *un*trained.
- During conditioning, a previously neutral stimulus is transformed into the conditioned stimulus.
- A conditioned stimulus leads to a conditioned response, and a conditioned stimulus–conditioned response pairing is a consequence of learning and training.
- An unconditioned response and a conditioned response are similar (such as salivation in the example described earlier), but the conditioned response is learned, whereas the unconditioned response occurs naturally.

Applying Conditioning Principles to Human Behavior

Although the initial conditioning experiments were carried out with animals, classical conditioning principles were soon found to explain many aspects of everyday human behavior. Recall, for instance, the earlier illustration of how people might experience hunger pangs at the sight of McDonald's golden arches. The cause of this reaction is classical conditioning: The previously neutral arches have become associated with the food inside the restaurant (the unconditioned stimulus), causing the arches to become a conditioned stimulus that brings about the conditioned response of hunger.

Emotional responses are particularly likely to be learned through classical conditioning processes. For instance, how do some of us develop fears of mice, spiders, and other creatures that are typically harmless? In a now-famous case study designed to show that classical conditioning was at the root of such fears, an 11-month-old infant named Albert, who initially showed no fear of rats, heard a loud noise just as he was shown a rat (Watson & Rayner, 1920). The noise (the unconditioned stimulus) evoked fear (the unconditioned response). After just a few pairings of noise and rat, Albert began to show fear of the rat by itself. The rat, then, had become a CS that brought about the CR, fear. Similarly, the pairing of the appearance of certain species (such as mice or spiders) with the fearful comments of an adult may cause children to develop the same fears their parents have. (By the way, we don't know what happened to the unfortunate Albert, and Watson, the experimenter, has been condemned for using ethically questionable procedures.)

Learning via classical conditioning also occurs during adulthood. For example, you might not go to a dentist as often as you should because of prior associations of dentists

conditioned stimulus (CS): A once-neutral stimulus that has been paired with an unconditioned stimulus to bring about a response formerly caused only by the unconditioned stimulus

conditioned response (CR): A response that, after conditioning, follows a previously neutral stimulus (e.g., salivation at the ringing of a bell)

 **PsychLink**

Information on classical conditioning
www.mhhe.com/
feldmanup6-06links

and pain. Or you might have a particular fondness for the smell of a certain perfume or aftershave lotion because the feelings and thoughts of an early lover come rushing back whenever you encounter it. Classical conditioning, then, explains many of the reactions we have to stimuli in the world around us (Woodruff-Pak, 1999).

Extinction

What do you think would happen if a dog who had become classically conditioned to salivate at the ringing of a bell never again received food when the bell was rung? The answer lies in one of the basic phenomena of learning: extinction. **Extinction** occurs when a previously conditioned response decreases in frequency and eventually disappears.

To produce extinction, one needs to end the association between conditioned and unconditioned stimuli. For instance, if we had trained a dog to salivate at the ringing of a bell, we could produce extinction by ceasing to provide meat after the bell was rung. At first the dog would continue to salivate when it heard the bell, but after a few such instances, the amount of salivation would probably decline, and the dog would eventually stop responding to the bell altogether. At that point, we could say that the response had been extinguished. In sum, extinction occurs when the conditioned stimulus is repeatedly presented without the unconditioned stimulus. We should keep in mind that extinction can be a helpful phenomenon. Consider, for instance, what it would be like if the fear you experienced while watching *The Blair Witch Project* never was extinguished. You might well tremble with fright every time you entered any wooded area.

As we will describe in Chapter 17, psychologists have treated people with irrational fears, or phobias, by using a form of therapy called systematic desensitization. The goal of *systematic desensitization* is to bring about the extinction of the phobia. For example, a therapist using systematic desensitization for a client who is afraid of dogs might repeatedly expose the client to dogs, starting with a less frightening aspect (a photo of a cute dog) and moving toward more feared ones (such as an actual encounter with an unfamiliar dog). As the anticipated negative consequences of exposure to the dog (e.g., being jumped on or bitten) do not occur, the fear eventually becomes extinguished.

Once a conditioned response has been extinguished, has it vanished forever? Not necessarily. Pavlov discovered this when he returned to his dog a few days after the conditioned behavior had seemingly been extinguished. If he rang a bell, the dog once again salivated—an effect known as **spontaneous recovery,** or the reemergence of an extinguished conditioned response after a period of rest.

Spontaneous recovery helps explain why it is so hard to overcome drug addictions. For example, cocaine addicts who are thought to be "cured" could experience an irresistible impulse to use the drug again if they are subsequently confronted by a stimulus with strong connections to the drug, such as a white powder (O'Brien et al., 1992; Drummond et al., 1995).

Generalization and Discrimination

Despite differences in color and shape, to most of us a rose is a rose is a rose. The pleasure we experience at the beauty, smell, and grace of the flower is similar for different types of roses. Pavlov noticed a similar phenomenon. His dogs often salivated not only at the ringing of the bell that was used during their original conditioning but at the sound of a buzzer as well.

Such behavior is the result of stimulus generalization. **Stimulus generalization** takes place when a conditioned response follows a stimulus that is similar to the original conditioned stimulus. The greater the similarity between the two stimuli, the greater the likelihood of stimulus generalization. Baby Albert, who, as we mentioned earlier, was conditioned to be fearful of rats, was later found to be afraid of other furry white things as well. He was fearful of white rabbits, white fur coats, and even a white Santa

---

extinction: The decrease in frequency, and eventual disappearance, of a previously conditioned response; one of the basic phenomena of learning

spontaneous recovery: The reemergence of an extinguished conditioned response after a period of rest

stimulus generalization: A response to a stimulus that is similar to but different from a conditioned stimulus; the more similar the two stimuli, the more likely generalization is to occur

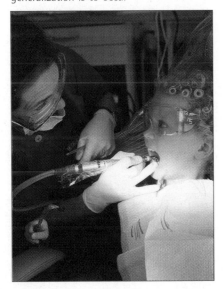

Because of a previous unpleasant experience, a person may expect a similar occurrence when faced with a comparable situation in the future, a process known as stimulus generalization. Can you think of ways this process is used in everyday life?

Claus mask. On the other hand, according to the principle of stimulus generalization, it is unlikely that he would have been afraid of a black dog, because its color would differentiate it sufficiently from the original fear-evoking stimulus.

The conditioned response elicited by the new stimulus is usually not as intense as the original conditioned response, although the more similar the new stimulus is to the old one, the more similar the new response will be. It is unlikely, then, that Albert's fear of the Santa Claus mask was as great as his learned fear of a rat. Still, stimulus generalization permits us to know, for example, that we ought to brake at all red lights, even if there are minor variations in size, shape, and shade.

If two stimuli are sufficiently distinct from one another so that one evokes a conditioned response but the other does not, we can say that stimulus discrimination has occurred. **Stimulus discrimination** is the ability to differentiate between stimuli. For example, the ability to discriminate between a red and a green traffic light prevents us from getting mowed down by oncoming traffic at intersections.

stimulus discrimination: The ability to differentiate between stimuli

Beyond Traditional Classical Conditioning: Challenging Basic Assumptions

Although Pavlov hypothesized that all learning is nothing more than long strings of conditioned responses, this notion has not been supported by subsequent research. It turns out that classical conditioning provides us with only a partial explanation of how people and animals learn and that Pavlov was wrong in some of his basic assumptions (Rizley & Rescorla, 1972; Hollis, 1997).

For example, according to Pavlov, the process of linking stimuli and responses occurs in a mechanistic, unthinking way. In contrast to this perspective, learning theorists influenced by cognitive psychology have argued that learners actively develop an understanding and expectancy about which particular unconditioned stimuli are matched with specific conditioned stimuli. A ringing bell, for instance gives a dog something to think about: the impending arrival of food (Rescorla, 1988; Clark & Squire, 1998; Woodruff-Pak, 1999).

Traditional explanations of how classical conditioning operates have also been challenged by learning psychologist John Garcia, whose research was initially concerned with the effects of exposure to nuclear radiation on laboratory animals. In the course of his experiments, he realized that rats placed in a radiation chamber drank almost no water, even though in their home cage they drank eagerly. The most obvious explanation—that it had something to do with the radiation—was soon ruled out. Garcia found that even when the radiation was not turned on, the rats still drank little or no water in the radiation chamber (Garcia, Hankins, & Rusiniak, 1974; Garcia, 1990).

Initially puzzled by the rats' behavior, Garcia eventually figured out that the drinking cups in the radiation chamber were made of plastic, thereby giving the water an unusual, plastic-like taste. In contrast, drinking cups in the home cage were made of glass and left no abnormal taste.

As a result, the plastic-tasting water had become repeatedly paired with illness brought on by exposure to radiation, and that had led the rats to form a classically conditioned association. The process began with the radiation acting as an unconditioned stimulus evoking the unconditioned response of sickness. With repeated pairings, the plastic-tasting water had become a conditioned stimulus that evoked the conditioned response of sickness.

This finding violated one of the basic rules of classical conditioning—that an unconditioned stimulus should *immediately* follow a conditioned stimulus for optimal conditioning to occur. Instead, Garcia's findings showed that conditioning could occur even when there was an interval of as long as eight hours between exposure to the conditioned stimulus and the response of sickness. Furthermore, the conditioning persisted over very long periods and sometimes occurred after just one exposure to water that was followed later on by illness.

These findings have had important practical implications. For example, to prevent coyotes from killing their sheep, some ranchers now routinely lace a sheep carcass with

Because of prior experience with meat that had been laced with a mild poison, this coyote does not obey its natural instincts and ignores what otherwise would be a tasty meal. What principles of classical conditioning does this phenomenon contradict?

a drug and leave the carcass in a place where coyotes will find it. The drug temporarily makes the coyotes quite ill, but it does not permanently harm them. After just one exposure to a drug-laden sheep carcass, coyotes avoid sheep, which are normally one of their primary natural victims (Gustavson et al., 1974).

Evaluate

1. _____ involves changes brought about by experience, whereas maturation describes changes due to biological development.

2. _____ is the name of the scientist responsible for discovering the learning phenomenon known as _____ conditioning, in which an organism learns a response to a stimulus to which it would not normally respond.

   Refer to the passage below to answer questions 3 through 6:

   The last three times little Theresa visited Dr. Lopez for checkups, he administered a painful preventive immunization shot that left her in tears. Today, when her mother takes her for another checkup, Theresa begins to sob as soon as she comes face-to-face with Dr. Lopez, even before he has had a chance to say hello.

3. The painful shot that Theresa received during each visit was a(n)_____ _____, which elicited the _____ _____, her tears.

4. Dr. Lopez is upset because his presence has become a _____ _____ for Theresa's crying.

5. Fortunately, Dr. Lopez gave Theresa no more shots for quite some time. Over that time she gradually stopped crying and even came to like him. _____ had occurred.

6. _____ _____ occurs when a stimulus that is fairly similar to the conditioned stimulus produces the same response.

7. On the other hand, _____ _____ occurs when there is no response to a stimulus that is slightly distinct from the conditioned stimulus.

Rethink

1. Can you think of ways that classical conditioning is used by politicians? advertisers? moviemakers? Do ethical issues arise from any of these uses?

2. Is it likely that Albert, Watson's experimental subject, went through life afraid of Santa Claus? Describe what probably happened to prevent this.

Answers to Evaluate Questions

1. Learning 2. Pavlov; classical 3. unconditioned stimulus; unconditioned response 4. conditioned stimulus 5. Extinction 6. Stimulus generalization 7. stimulus discrimination

Operant Conditioning

Prepare

What is the role of reward and punishment in learning?

Organize

Very good. . . . What a clever idea. . . . Fantastic. . . . I agree. . . . Thank you. . . . Excellent. . . . Super. . . . Right on. . . . This is the best paper you've ever written; you get an A. . . . You are really getting the hang of it. . . . I'm impressed. . . . Let me give you a hug. . . . You're getting a raise. . . . Have a cookie. . . . You look great. . . . I love you. . . .

Operant Conditioning

  Thorndike's Law of Effect

  The Basics of Operant Conditioning

  Positive Reinforcers, Negative Reinforcers, and Punishment

  The Pros and Cons of Punishment

  Schedules of Reinforcement

  Discrimination and Generalization in Operant Conditioning

  Superstitious Behavior

  Shaping

  Biological Constraints on Learning

Few of us mind being the recipient of any of the above comments. But what is especially noteworthy about them is that each of these simple statements can be used, through a process known as operant conditioning, to bring about powerful changes in behavior and to teach the most complex tasks. Operant conditioning is the basis for many of the most important kinds of human, and animal, learning.

Operant conditioning is learning in which a voluntary response is strengthened or weakened, depending on its favorable or unfavorable consequences. Unlike classical conditioning, in which the original behaviors are the natural, biological responses to the presence of some stimulus such as food, water, or pain, operant conditioning applies to voluntary responses, which an organism performs deliberately, to produce a desirable outcome. The term *operant* emphasizes this point: The organism *operates* on its environment to produce some desirable result. For example, operant conditioning is at work when we learn that toiling industriously can bring about a raise, or that studying hard results in good grades.

As with classical conditioning, the basis for understanding operant conditioning was laid by work with animals. We turn now to some of that early research, which began with a simple inquiry into the behavior of cats.

operant conditioning: Learning in which a voluntary response is strengthened or weakened, depending on its favorable or unfavorable consequences

Thorndike's Law of Effect

If you placed a hungry cat in a cage and then put a small piece of food outside of it, just beyond the cat's reach, chances are the cat would eagerly search for a way out of the cage. The cat might first claw at the sides or push against an opening. Suppose, though, that you had rigged things so that the cat could escape by stepping on a small paddle that released the latch to the door of the cage (see Figure 6-2). Eventually, as it moved around the cage, the cat would happen to step on the paddle, the door would open, and the cat would eat the food.

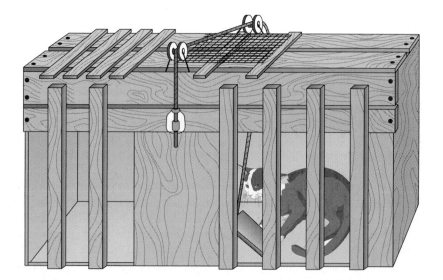

Figure 6-2 Edward L. Thorndike devised this puzzle box to study the process by which a cat learns to press a paddle to escape the box and receive food. Do you think Thorndike's work has relevance to the question of why humans voluntarily solve puzzles, such as crossword puzzles and jigsaw puzzles? Do they receive any rewards?

Figure 6-3 A Skinner box, used to study operant conditioning. Laboratory animals learn to press the lever in order to obtain food, which is delivered in the tray.

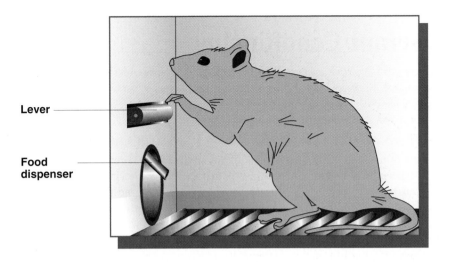

Lever

Food dispenser

What would happen if you then returned the cat to the box? The next time, it would probably take a little less time for the cat to step on the paddle and escape. After a few trials, the cat would deliberately step on the paddle as soon as it was placed in the cage. What would have occurred, according to Edward L. Thorndike (1932), who studied this situation extensively, was that the cat would have learned that pressing the paddle was associated with the desirable consequence of getting food. Thorndike summarized that relationship by formulating the *law of effect:* that responses that lead to satisfying consequences are more likely to be repeated, and responses followed by negative outcomes are less likely to be repeated.

Thorndike believed that the law of effect operated as automatically as leaves fall off a tree in autumn. It was not necessary for an organism to understand that there was a link between a response and a reward. Instead, Thorndike believed, over time and through experience the organism would make a direct connection between the stimulus and the response without any awareness that the connection existed.

The Basics of Operant Conditioning

Thorndike's early research served as the foundation for the work of one of the century's most influential psychologists, B. F. Skinner, who died in 1990. You may have heard of the Skinner box (shown in one form in Figure 6-3), a chamber with a highly controlled environment used to study operant conditioning processes with laboratory animals. Whereas Thorndike's goal was to get his cats to learn to obtain food by leaving the box, animals in a Skinner box learn to obtain food by operating on their environment within the box. Skinner became interested in specifying how behavior varied as a result of alterations in the environment.

Skinner, whose work went far beyond perfecting Thorndike's earlier apparatus, is considered the inspiration for a whole generation of psychologists studying operant conditioning (Delprato & Midgley, 1992; Bjork, 1993; Keehn, 1996). To illustrate Skinner's contribution, let's consider what happens to a pigeon in the typical Skinner box.

Suppose you want to teach a hungry pigeon to peck a key that is located in its box. At first the pigeon will wander around the box, exploring the environment in a relatively random fashion. At some point, however, it will probably peck the key by chance, and when it does, it will receive a food pellet. The first time this happens, the pigeon will not learn the connection between pecking and receiving food and will continue to explore the box. Sooner or later the pigeon will again peck the key and receive a pellet, and in time the frequency of the pecking response will increase. Eventually, the pigeon will peck the key continually until it satisfies its hunger, thereby demonstrating that it has learned that the receipt of food is contingent on pecking the key.

B. F. Skinner, who was the founding father of operant conditioning, developed what came to be called the "Skinner box." In what ways has Skinner's research contributed to the study of learning?

Reinforcing Desired Behavior

Skinner called the process that leads the pigeon to continue pecking the key "reinforcement." **Reinforcement** is the process by which a stimulus increases the probability that a preceding behavior will be repeated. In other words, pecking is more likely to occur again due to the stimulus of food.

In a situation such as this one, the food is called a reinforcer. A **reinforcer** is any stimulus that increases the probability that a preceding behavior will occur again. Hence, food is a reinforcer because it increases the probability that the behavior of pecking the key (formally referred to as the *response* of pecking) will take place.

What kind of stimuli can act as reinforcers? Bonuses, toys, and good grades can serve as reinforcers—if they strengthen the probability of the response that occurred before their introduction. In each case, it is critical that the organism learn that the delivery of the reinforcer is contingent on the response occurring in the first place.

Of course, we are not born knowing that 75 cents can buy us a candy bar. Rather, through experience we learn that money is a valuable commodity because of its association with stimuli, such as food and drink, that are naturally reinforcing. This fact suggests a distinction between primary reinforcers and secondary reinforcers. A *primary reinforcer* satisfies some biological need and works naturally, regardless of a person's prior experience. Food for the hungry person, warmth for the cold person, and relief for the person in pain would all be classified as primary reinforcers. A *secondary reinforcer,* in contrast, is a stimulus that becomes reinforcing because of its association with a primary reinforcer. For instance, we know that money is valuable because we have learned that it allows us to obtain other desirable objects, including primary reinforcers such as food and shelter. Money thus becomes a secondary reinforcer.

What makes something a reinforcer depends on individual preferences. Though a Hershey bar could act as a reinforcer for one person, an individual who dislikes chocolate might find 75 cents more desirable. The only way we can know if a stimulus is a reinforcer for a given organism is to observe whether the frequency of a previously occurring behavior increases after the presentation of the stimulus.

Positive Reinforcers, Negative Reinforcers, and Punishment

In many respects, reinforcers can be thought of in terms of rewards; both a reinforcer and a reward increase the probability that a preceding response will occur again. But the term *reward* is limited to *positive* occurrences, and this is where it differs from a reinforcer—for it turns out that reinforcers can be positive or negative.

A **positive reinforcer** is a stimulus *added* to the environment that brings about an increase in a preceding response. If food, water, money, or praise is provided following a response, it is more likely that that response will occur again in the future. The paycheck that workers get at the end of the week, for example, increases the likelihood that they will return to their jobs the following week.

In contrast, a **negative reinforcer** refers to an unpleasant stimulus whose *removal* from the environment leads to an increase in the probability that a preceding response will occur again in the future. For example, if you have cold symptoms (an unpleasant stimulus) that are relieved when you take medicine, you are more likely to take the medicine when you experience such symptoms again. Taking medicine, then, is negatively reinforcing, because it removes the unpleasant cold symptoms. Similarly, if the radio volume is so loud that it hurts your ears, you are likely to find that turning it down relieves the problem. Lowering the volume is negatively reinforcing and you are more apt to repeat the action in the future. Negative reinforcement, then, teaches the individual that taking an action removes a negative condition that exists in the environment. Like positive reinforcers, negative reinforcers increase the likelihood that preceding behaviors will be repeated.

"Oh, not bad. The light comes on, I press the bar, they write me a check. How about you?"

reinforcement: The process by which a stimulus increases the probability that a preceding behavior will be repeated

reinforcer: Any stimulus that increases the probability that a preceding behavior will occur again

 **PsychLink**

Positive and negative reinforcers
www.mhhe.com/
feldmanup6-06links

positive reinforcer: A stimulus added to the environment that brings about an increase in a preceding response

negative reinforcer: An unpleasant stimulus whose removal leads to an increase in the probability that a preceding response will occur again in the future

Table 6-1 Types of Reinforcement and Punishment

	EFFECT ON BEHAVIOR	
Procedure	**Increases**	**Decreases**
Presentation of Stimulus	*Positive reinforcement* *Example:* Giving a raise for good performance *Result: Increase* in frequency of response (good performance)	*Positive punishment* *Example:* Giving a spanking following misbehavior *Result: Decrease* in frequency of response (misbehavior)
Removal of Stimulus	*Negative reinforcement* *Example:* Terminating a headache by taking aspirin *Result: Increase* in frequency of response (taking aspirin)	*Negative punishment* *Example:* Removal of favorite toy after misbehavior *Result: Decrease* in frequency of response (misbehavior)

punishment: A stimulus that decreases the probability that a previous behavior will occur again

It is important to note that negative reinforcement is not the same as punishment. **Punishment** refers to a stimulus that *decreases* the probability that a prior behavior will occur again. Unlike negative reinforcement, which produces an *increase* in behavior, punishment reduces the likelihood of a prior response. If we receive a shock that is meant to decrease a certain behavior, then, we are receiving punishment; but if we are already receiving a shock and do something to stop that shock, the behavior that stops the shock is considered to be negatively reinforced. In the first case, the specific behavior is apt to decrease because of the punishment; in the second, it is likely to increase because of the negative reinforcement.

There are two types of punishment: positive punishment and negative punishment, just as there is positive and negative reinforcement. (In both cases, "positive" means adding something, whereas "negative" means removing something.) *Positive punishment* weakens a response through the application of an unpleasant stimulus. For instance, spanking a child for misbehaving or ten years in jail for committing a crime is positive punishment. In contrast, *negative punishment* consists of the removal of something pleasant. For instance, when a teenager is told she is "grounded" and will no longer be able to use the family car because of her poor grades, or when an employee is informed that he has been demoted with a cut in pay because of poor job evaluations, negative punishment is being administered. Both positive and negative punishment result in a decrease in the likelihood that a prior behavior will be repeated.

The distinctions between the two types of punishment, as well as positive and negative reinforcement, might seem confusing initially, but the following rules (and the summary in Table 6-1) can help you to distinguish these concepts from one another:

- Reinforcement *increases* the frequency of the behavior preceding it; punishment *decreases* the frequency of the behavior preceding it.
- The *application* of a *positive* stimulus brings about an increase in the frequency of behavior and is referred to as positive reinforcement; the *application* of a *negative* stimulus decreases or reduces the frequency of behavior and is called positive punishment.
- The *removal* of a *negative* stimulus that results in an increase in the frequency of behavior is termed negative reinforcement; the *removal* of a *positive* stimulus that decreases the frequency of behavior is called negative punishment.

PsychLink

Numerous articles on punishment
www.mhhe.com/
feldmanup6-06links

The Pros and Cons of Punishment: Why Reinforcement Beats Punishment

Is punishment an effective way to modify behavior? Punishment often presents the quickest route to changing behavior that, if allowed to continue, might be dangerous to an individual. For instance, a parent might not have a second chance to warn a child not to

run into a busy street, so punishing the first incidence of this behavior might prove to be wise. Moreover, the use of punishment to suppress behavior, even temporarily, provides the opportunity to reinforce a person for subsequently behaving in a more desirable way.

There are some rare instances in which punishment can be the most humane approach to treating certain severe disorders. For example, some children suffer from *autism,* a psychological disorder that can lead them to abuse themselves by tearing at their skin or banging their heads against the wall, injuring themselves severely in the process. In such cases—and when all other treatments have failed—punishment in the form of a quick but intense electric shock has been used to prevent self-injurious behavior. Such punishment, however, is used only to keep the child safe and to buy time until positive reinforcement procedures can be initiated (Lovaas & Koegel, 1973; Linscheid et al., 1990; Siegel, 1996b).

Several disadvantages make the routine use of punishment questionable. For one thing, punishment is frequently ineffective, particularly if it is not delivered shortly after the undesired behavior or if the individual is able to leave the setting in which the punishment is being given. An employee who is reprimanded by the boss might quit; a teenager who loses the use of the family car might borrow a friend's instead. In such instances, the initial behavior that is being punished might be replaced by one that is even less desirable.

Even worse, physical punishment can convey to the recipient the idea that physical aggression is permissible and perhaps even desirable. A father who yells at and hits his son for misbehaving teaches the son that aggression is an appropriate, adult response. The son might soon copy his father's behavior by acting aggressively toward others. In addition, physical punishment is often administered by people who are themselves angry or enraged. It is unlikely that individuals in such an emotional state will be able to think through what they are doing or control carefully the degree of punishment they are inflicting. Ultimately, those who resort to physical punishment run the risk that they will grow to be feared. Punishment can also reduce the self-esteem of recipients unless they can understand the reasons for it.

Finally, punishment does not convey any information about what an alternative, more appropriate behavior might be. To be useful in bringing about more desirable behavior in the future, punishment must be accompanied by specific information about the behavior that is being punished, along with specific suggestions concerning a more desirable behavior. Punishing a child for staring out the window in school could merely lead her to stare at the floor instead. Unless we teach her appropriate ways to respond, we have merely managed to substitute one undesirable behavior for another. If punishment is not followed up with reinforcement for subsequent behavior that is more appropriate, little will be accomplished.

In short, reinforcing desired behavior is a more appropriate technique for modifying behavior than using punishment. Both in and out of the scientific arena, then, reinforcement usually beats punishment (Sulzer-Azaroff & Mayer, 1991; Seppa, 1996).

Schedules of Reinforcement: Timing Life's Rewards

The world would be a different place if poker players never played cards again after their first losing hand, fishermen returned to shore as soon as they missed a catch, or door-to-door salespeople turned in their samples after their first experience of being turned away. The fact that such unreinforced behaviors continue, often with great frequency and persistence, illustrates that reinforcement need not be received continually in order for behavior to be learned and maintained. In fact, behavior that is reinforced only occasionally can ultimately be learned better than behavior that is always reinforced.

When we refer to the frequency and timing of reinforcement following desired behavior, we are talking about **schedules of reinforcement.** Behavior that is reinforced every time it occurs is said to be on a **continuous reinforcement schedule;** if it is reinforced some but not all of the time, it is on a **partial reinforcement schedule.** Although

schedules of reinforcement: The frequency and timing of reinforcement following desired behavior

continuous reinforcement schedule: Reinforcement of behavior every time it occurs

partial reinforcement schedule: Reinforcement of behavior some but not all of the time

learning occurs more rapidly under a continuous reinforcement schedule, behavior lasts longer after reinforcement stops when it is learned under a partial reinforcement schedule.

Why should partial reinforcement schedules result in stronger, longer-lasting learning than continuous reinforcement schedules? We can answer the question by examining how we might behave when using a candy vending machine compared with a Las Vegas slot machine. When we use a vending machine, prior experience has taught us that every time we put in the appropriate amount of money, the reinforcement, a candy bar, ought to be delivered. In other words, the schedule of reinforcement is continuous. In comparison, a slot machine offers a partial reinforcement schedule. We have learned that after putting in our cash, most of the time we will not receive anything in return. At the same time, though, we know that we will occasionally win something.

Now suppose that, unbeknownst to us, both the candy vending machine and the slot machine are broken, so that neither one is able to dispense anything. It would not be very long before we stopped depositing coins into the broken candy machine. Probably at most we would try only two or three times before leaving the machine in disgust. But the story would be quite different with the broken slot machine. Here, we would drop in money for a considerably longer time, even though there would be no payoff.

In formal terms, we can see the difference between the two reinforcement schedules: Partial reinforcement schedules (such as those provided by slot machines) maintain performance longer than continuous reinforcement schedules (such as those established in candy vending machines) before extinction—the disappearance of the conditioned response—occurs.

Certain kinds of partial reinforcement schedules produce stronger and lengthier responding before extinction than others (King & Logue, 1990). Although many different partial reinforcement schedules have been examined, they can most readily be put into two categories: schedules that consider the *number of responses* made before reinforcement is given, called fixed-ratio and variable-ratio schedules, and those that consider the *amount of time* that elapses before reinforcement is provided, called fixed-interval and variable-interval schedules.

Fixed- and Variable-Ratio Schedules

fixed-ratio schedule: A schedule whereby reinforcement is given only after a certain number of responses are made

In a **fixed-ratio schedule,** reinforcement is given only after a certain number of responses. For instance, a pigeon might receive a food pellet every tenth time it pecked a key; here, the ratio would be 1:10. Similarly, garment workers are generally paid on fixed-ratio schedules: They receive several dollars for every blouse they sew. Because a greater rate of production means more reinforcement, people on fixed-ratio schedules are apt to work as quickly as possible (see Figure 6-4).

variable-ratio schedule: A schedule whereby reinforcement occurs after a varying number of responses rather than after a fixed number

In a **variable-ratio schedule,** reinforcement occurs after a varying number of responses rather than after a fixed number. Although the specific number of responses necessary to receive reinforcement varies, the number of responses usually hovers around a specific average. A good example of a variable-ratio schedule is a telephone salesperson's job. She might make a sale during the third, eighth, ninth, and twentieth calls without being successful during any call in between. Although the number of responses that must be made before making a sale varies, it averages out to a 20 percent success rate. Under these circumstances, you might expect that the salesperson would try to make as many calls as possible in as short a time as possible. This is the case with all variable-ratio schedules, which lead to a high rate of response and resistance to extinction.

Fixed- and Variable-Interval Schedules: The Passage of Time

In contrast to fixed- and variable-ratio schedules, in which the crucial factor is the number of responses, fixed-*interval* and variable-*interval* schedules focus on the amount of *time* that has elapsed since a person or animal was rewarded. One example of a fixed-interval schedule is a weekly paycheck. For people who receive regular, weekly paychecks, it typically makes relatively little difference exactly how much they produce in a given week.

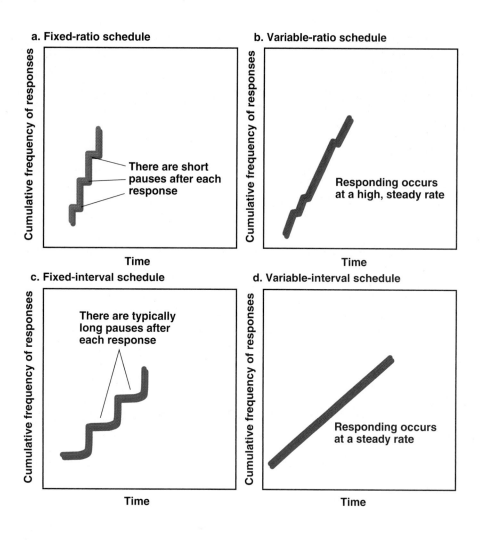

Figure 6–4 Typical outcomes of different reinforcement schedules. *(a)* In a fixed-ratio schedule, short pauses occur following each response. Because the more responses, the more reinforcement, fixed-ratio schedules produce a high rate of responding. *(b)* In a variable-ratio schedule, responding also occurs at a high rate. *(c)* A fixed-interval schedule produces lower rates of responding, especially just after reinforcement has been presented, since the organism learns that a specified time period must elapse between reinforcement. *(d)* A variable-interval schedule produces a fairly steady stream of responses.

Because a **fixed-interval schedule** provides reinforcement for a response only if a fixed time period has elapsed, overall rates of response are relatively low. This is especially true in the period just after reinforcement when the time before another reinforcement is relatively great. Students' study habits often exemplify this reality. If the periods between exams are relatively long (meaning that the opportunity for reinforcement for good performance is fairly infrequent), students often study minimally or not at all until the day of the exam draws near. Just before the exam, however, students begin to cram for it, signaling a rapid increase in the rate of their studying response. As you might expect, immediately following the exam there is a rapid decline in the rate of responding, with few people opening a book the day after a test.

One way to decrease the delay in responding that occurs just after reinforcement, and to maintain the desired behavior more consistently throughout an interval, is to use a variable-interval schedule. In a **variable-interval schedule,** the time between reinforcements varies around some average rather than being fixed. For example, a professor who gives surprise quizzes that vary from one every three days to one every three weeks, averaging one every two weeks, is using a variable-interval schedule. Compared to the study habits we observed with a fixed-interval schedule, students' study habits under such a variable-interval schedule would most likely be very different. Students would be apt to study more regularly since they would never know when the next surprise quiz would be coming. Variable-interval schedules, in general, are more likely to produce relatively steady rates of responding than fixed-interval schedules, with responses that take longer to extinguish after reinforcement ends.

fixed–interval schedule: A schedule that provides reinforcement for a response only if a fixed time period has elapsed, making overall rates of response relatively low

variable–interval schedule: A schedule whereby the time between reinforcements varies around some average rather than being fixed

Nomar Garciaparra, like many baseball players, goes through a ritual of superstitious behaviors before batting. How can his actions be explained in terms of the principles of reinforcement?

 **PsychLink**

Psychology of superstition
www.mhhe.com/
feldmanup6-06links

shaping: The process of teaching a complex behavior by rewarding closer and closer approximations to the desired behavior

Discrimination and Generalization in Operant Conditioning

It does not take a child long to learn that a red light at an intersection means stop and a green light indicates that it is permissible to continue. Just as in classical conditioning, then, operant learning involves the phenomena of discrimination and generalization.

The process by which people learn to discriminate stimuli is known as stimulus control training. In *stimulus control training,* a behavior is reinforced in the presence of a specific stimulus, but not in its absence. For example, one of the most difficult discriminations many people face is determining when someone's friendliness is not mere friendliness, but a signal of romantic interest. People learn to make the discrimination by observing the presence of certain nonverbal cues—such as increased eye contact and touching—that indicate romantic interest. When such cues are absent, people learn that no romantic interest is indicated. In this case, the nonverbal cue acts as a discriminative stimulus, one to which an organism learns to respond during stimulus control training. *A discriminative stimulus* signals the likelihood that reinforcement will follow a response. For example, if you wait until your roommate is in a good mood before you ask to borrow her favorite compact disc, your behavior can be said to be under stimulus control because you can discriminate between her moods.

Just as in classical conditioning, the phenomenon of stimulus generalization, in which an organism learns a response to one stimulus and then applies it to other stimuli, is also found in operant conditioning. If you have learned that being polite produces the reinforcement of getting your way in a certain situation, you are likely to generalize your response to other situations. Sometimes, though, generalization can have unfortunate consequences, such as when people behave negatively toward all members of a racial group because they have had an unpleasant experience with one member of that group.

Superstitious Behavior

When my son, a college senior, takes an exam, he puts on a tie. The reason: Early in his college career, he took an exam wearing a tie (because he had an interview later in the day), and he got an A. From that time on, he wore a tie to every exam.

To learning psychologists, such a ritual is an example of *superstitious behavior.* Superstitious behavior can be explained in terms of learning and reinforcement. As we have seen, behavior that is followed by a reinforcer tends to be strengthened. Occasionally, however, the behavior that occurs prior to the reinforcement is entirely coincidental. Still, an association is made between the behavior and reinforcement.

Imagine, for instance, that a baseball player taps his bat against the ground three times in a row just prior to getting a single. The hit is, of course, coincidental to the batter's tapping the ground, but the player might see it as somehow related. Because the player makes this association, he might tap the ground three times every time he is at bat in the future. And because he will be at least partially reinforced for this behavior— batters usually get a hit 25 percent of the time—his tapping behavior will be maintained, as a superstitious behavior (Van Ginkel, 1990; Matute, 1994, 1995).

Shaping: Reinforcing What Doesn't Come Naturally

Consider the difficulty of using operant conditioning to teach people to repair an automobile transmission. If you had to wait until they chanced to fix a transmission perfectly before you provided them with reinforcement, the Model T might be back in style long before they mastered the repair process.

There are many complex behaviors, ranging from auto repair to zoo management, that we would not expect to occur naturally as part of anyone's spontaneous behavior. For such behaviors, for which there might otherwise be no opportunity to provide reinforcement (because the behavior would never occur in the first place), a procedure known as shaping is used. **Shaping** is the process of teaching a complex behavior by rewarding closer and closer approximations of the desired behavior. In shaping, you start by reinforcing any behavior that is at all similar to the behavior you want the person to learn. Later, you reinforce only responses that are closer to the behavior you ultimately

want to teach. Finally, you reinforce only the desired response. Each step in shaping, then, moves only slightly beyond the previously learned behavior, permitting the person to link the new step to the behavior learned earlier.

Shaping allows even lower animals to learn complex responses that would never occur naturally, ranging from lions jumping through hoops to dolphins rescuing divers lost at sea. Shaping also underlies the learning of many complex human skills. For instance, the organization of most textbooks is based on the principles of shaping. Typically, information is presented so that new material builds on previously learned concepts or skills. Thus the concept of shaping could not be presented in this chapter until we had discussed the more basic principles of operant learning. (For a further discussion of the applications of psychological approaches to learning, see the *Psychology at Work* box.)

Biological Constraints on Learning: You Can't Teach an Old Dog Just Any Trick

Psychologists Keller and Marian Breland were pleased with their idea: As consultants to a professional animal trainer, they came up with the notion of having a pig place a wooden disk into a piggy bank. With their experience in training animals through operant conditioning, they thought the task would be easy to teach, given that it was certainly well within the range of the pig's physical capabilities. Yet every time they tried out the procedure, it failed. Upon viewing the disk, the pigs were willing to do nothing but root the wooden disk along the ground. Apparently, the pigs were biologically programmed to push stimuli in the shape of disks along the ground.

Their lack of swine success led the Brelands to substitute a raccoon. Although the procedure worked fine with one disk, when two disks were used, the raccoon refused to deposit either of them and instead rubbed the two together, as if it were washing them. Once again, it appeared that the disks evoked biologically innate behaviors that were impossible to replace through even the most exhaustive training (Breland & Breland, 1961).

The Brelands' difficulties illustrate an important point: Not all behaviors can be trained in all species equally well. Instead, there are *biological constraints,* built-in limitations, in the ability of animals to learn particular behaviors. In some cases, an organism will have a special predisposition that will aid in its learning a behavior (such as pecking behaviors in pigeons); in other cases, biological constraints will act to prevent or inhibit an organism from learning a behavior. In either instance, it is clear that animals have specialized learning mechanisms that influence how readily both classical and operant conditioning influence their behavior, and each species is biologically primed to develop particular kinds of associations and to have a difficult time in learning others (Hollis, 1984).

Biological constraints make it nearly impossible for animals to learn certain behaviors. Here, psychologist Marian Bailey attempts to overcome the natural limitations that inhibit the success of conditioning in this rooster.

Psychology at Work

Lynne Calero

Dolphin Research Center, Grassy Key, Florida

Education: B.A. in psychology, George Washington University

Home: Big Pine Key, Florida

Lynne Calero

Many people have read about the possible connections between dolphins and humans in terms of both behavior and intellect, but for more than a decade Lynne Calero has seen these similarities firsthand.

An employee of the Dolphin Research Center in Grassy Key, Florida, Calero received her primary exposure to psychology as an undergraduate major at George Washington University in Washington, D.C. "Our facility is a research education facility in which we do training to educate the public, as well as monitoring individual animals' health," she says.

In training dolphins, Calero makes use of the basic principles of learning. "The whole basis of the training done with dolphins and sea lions is operant conditioning and positive reinforcement," she notes.

For instance, one specific type of training aims at getting dolphins to present their tail flukes, thereby permitting medical tests that require blood samples. "All the animals first learn the basics, such as responding to a whistle. The whistle becomes connected with feeding, giving attention, or a back rub.

"From there we gradually get them to position alongside of the dock," she explains, "followed by a series of approximations, as in training with any behavior. With each step we get closer to the tail flukes until the dolphin allows us to hold onto the flukes above the water surface."

Younger dolphins are easier to train, and it takes only a month of training before they will present their flukes.

To Calero, this is one example of the unusual intelligence of dolphins. "Certainly their brain anatomy is very complicated. Overall, my impression is that dolphins are incredibly intelligent, as well as being intensely intuitive."

> "Our facility is a research education facility in which we do training to educate the public, as well as monitoring individual animals' health."

> "Overall, my impression is that dolphins are incredibly intelligent, as well as being intensely intuitive and wise."

Evaluate

1. _____ conditioning describes learning that occurs as a result of reinforcement.
2. Match the type of operant learning with its definition:

   1. An unpleasant stimulus is presented to decrease behavior
   2. An unpleasant stimulus is removed to increase behavior
   3. A pleasant stimulus is presented to increase behavior
   4. A pleasant stimulus is removed to decrease behavior

   a. Positive reinforcement
   b. Negative reinforcement
   c. Positive punishment
   d. Negative punishment

3. Sandy had had a rough day, and his son's noisemaking was not helping him relax. Not wanting to resort to scolding, Sandy told his son in a serious manner that he was very tired and would like the boy to play quietly for an hour. This approach worked. For Sandy, the change in his son's behavior was

   a. positively reinforcing.
   b. negatively reinforcing.

4. In a_____ reinforcement schedule, behavior is reinforced some of the time, while in a_____ reinforcement schedule, behavior is reinforced all the time.
5. Match the type of reinforcement schedule with its definition.

   1. Reinforcement occurs after a set time period
   2. Reinforcement occurs after a set number of responses
   3. Reinforcement occurs after a varying time period

   a. Fixed-ratio
   b. Variable-interval
   c. Fixed-interval

Rethink

1. How might operant conditioning be used to address serious personal concerns, such as smoking and unhealthy eating?
2. How might you go about "curing" superstitious behavior, such as the rituals people engage in before examinations or athletic competitions? Should we try to extinguish such behavior?

4. Reinforcement occurs after a   d. Variable-ratio
   varying number of responses

6. Fixed reinforcement schedules produce greater resistance to extinction than variable
   reinforcement schedules. True or false?

Cognitive-Social Approaches to Learning

Prepare

What is the role of cognition and thought in learning?

What are some practical methods for bringing about behavior change, both in ourselves and in others?

Organize

Cognitive-Social Approaches to Learning
  Latent Learning
  Observational Learning
  Violence on Television and in Movies
  The Unresolved Controversy of Cognitive-Social Learning Theory

Consider what happens when people learn to drive a car. They don't just get behind the wheel and stumble around until they randomly put the key into the ignition, and later, after many false starts, accidentally manage to get the car to move forward, thereby receiving positive reinforcement. Instead, they already know the basic elements of driving from prior experience as passengers, when they more than likely noticed how the key was inserted into the ignition, the car was put in drive, and the gas pedal was pressed to make the car go forward.

Clearly, not all learning is due to operant and classical conditioning. In fact, examples like learning to drive a car imply that some kinds of learning must involve higher-order processes in which people's thoughts and memories and the way they process information account for their responses. Such situations argue against regarding learning as the unthinking, mechanical, and automatic acquisition of associations between stimuli and responses, as in classical conditioning, or the presentation of reinforcement, as in operant conditioning.

Instead, some psychologists view learning in terms of the thought processes, or cognitions, that underlie it—an approach known as **cognitive-social learning theory.** Although psychologists using the cognitive-social learning perspective do not deny the importance of classical and operant conditioning, they have developed approaches that focus on the unseen mental processes that occur during learning, rather than concentrating solely on external stimuli, responses, and reinforcements.

In its most basic formulation, cognitive-social learning theory suggests that it is not enough to say that people make responses because there is an assumed link between a stimulus and a response due to a past history of reinforcement for the response. Instead, according to this point of view, people—and even animals—develop an *expectation* that they will receive a reinforcer upon making a response. Support for this point of view comes from several quarters.

cognitive-social learning theory: The study of the thought processes that underlie learning

Latent Learning

Some of the most direct evidence regarding cognitive processes comes from a series of experiments that revealed a type of cognitive-social learning called latent learning. In **latent learning,** a new behavior is learned but not demonstrated until reinforcement is provided for displaying it (Tolman & Honzik, 1930). In the studies, psychologists examined the behavior of rats in a maze such as the one shown in Figure 6-5a. In one representative experiment, a group of rats was allowed to wander around the maze once a day for seventeen days without ever receiving any reward. Understandably, these rats made many errors and spent a relatively long time reaching the end of the maze. A second group, however, was always given food at the end of the maze. Not surprisingly, these rats learned to run quickly and directly to the food box, making few errors.

A third group of rats started out in the same situation as the unrewarded rats, but only for the first ten days. On the eleventh day, a critical experimental manipulation was

latent learning: Learning in which a new behavior is acquired but is not demonstrated until reinforcement is provided

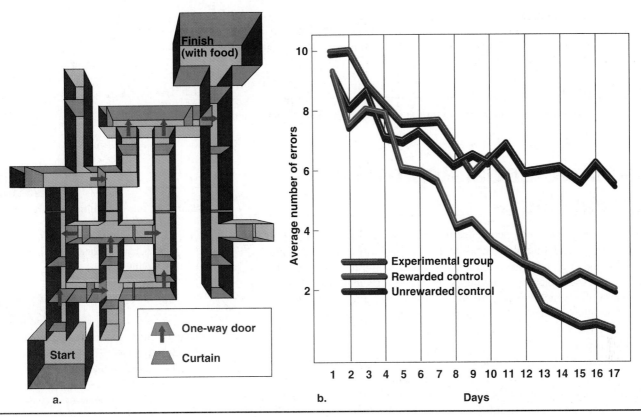

a.   b.

Figure 6-5 *(a)* In an attempt to demonstrate latent learning, rats were allowed to roam through a maze of this sort once a day for seventeen days. *(b)* Those rats that were never rewarded (the unrewarded control condition) consistently made the most errors, whereas those that received food at the finish every day (the rewarded control condition) consistently made far fewer errors. But the results also showed latent learning: Rats that were initially unrewarded but began to be rewarded only after the tenth day (the experimental group) showed an immediate reduction in errors and soon became similar to the error rate of the rats that had been consistently rewarded. According to cognitive-social learning theorists, the reduction in errors indicates that the rats had developed a cognitive map—a mental representation—of the maze (Tolman & Honzik, 1930). Can you think of other examples of latent learning?

cognitive map: A mental representation of spatial locations and directions

introduced: From that point on, the rats in this group were given food for completing the maze. The results of this manipulation were dramatic, as you can see from the graph in Figure 6-5b. The previously unrewarded rats, who had earlier seemed to wander about aimlessly, showed such reductions in running time and declines in error rates that their performance almost immediately matched that of the group that had received rewards from the start.

To cognitive-social theorists, it seemed clear that the unrewarded rats had learned the layout of the maze early in their explorations; they just never displayed their latent learning until the reinforcement was offered. Instead, the rats seemed to develop a **cognitive map** of the maze—a mental representation of spatial locations and directions.

People, too, develop cognitive maps of their surroundings, based primarily on particular landmarks. When they first encounter a new environment, their maps tend to rely on specific paths—such as the directions we might give someone unfamiliar with an area: "Turn right at the stop sign, make a left at the bridge, and then go up the hill." However, as people become more familiar with an area, they develop an overall conception of it, which has been called an abstract cognitive map. Using such a map, they are eventually able to take shortcuts as they develop a broad understanding of the area (Garling, 1989; Gale et al., 1990; Plumert et al., 1995).

The possibility that we develop our cognitive maps through latent learning presents something of a problem for strict operant conditioning theorists. If we consider the results of Tolman's maze experiment, for instance, it is unclear what the specific reinforcement was that permitted the rats that initially received no reward to learn about the layout of the maze, because there was no obvious reinforcer present. Instead, the results support a cognitive-social view of learning, in which learning might have resulted in changes in unobservable mental processes.

Observational Learning: Learning Through Imitation

Let's return for a moment to the case of a person learning to drive. How can we account for instances in which an individual with no direct experience in carrying out a particular behavior learns the behavior and then performs it? To answer this question, psychologists have proposed another form of cognitive-social learning: observational learning.

According to psychologist Albert Bandura and colleagues, a major part of human learning consists of **observational learning,** which they define as learning through observing the behavior of another person called a *model* (Bandura, 1977). Bandura and his colleagues demonstrated rather dramatically the ability of models to stimulate learning. In what is now considered a classic experiment, young children saw a film of an adult wildly hitting a 5-foot-tall inflatable punching toy called a Bobo doll (Bandura, Ross, & Ross, 1963a, 1963b). Later the children were given the opportunity to play with the Bobo doll themselves and, sure enough, most displayed the same kind of behavior, in some cases mimicking the aggressive behavior almost identically.

Not only negative behaviors are acquired through observational learning. In one experiment, for example, children who were afraid of dogs were exposed to a model—dubbed the Fearless Peer—playing with a dog (Bandura, Grusec, & Menlove, 1967). Following exposure, childern who had observed the model were considerably more likely to approach a strange dog than children who had not viewed the Fearless Peer.

According to Bandura, observational learning takes place in four steps: (1) paying attention and perceiving the most critical features of another person's behavior; (2) remembering the behavior; (3) reproducing the action; and (4) being motivated to learn and carry out the behavior. Instead of learning occurring through trial and error, then, with successes being reinforced and failures punished, many important skills are learned through observational processes (Bandura, 1986).

Observational learning is particularly important in acquiring skills for which shaping is inappropriate. Piloting an airplane and performing brain surgery, for example, are behaviors that could hardly be learned using trial-and-error methods without grave cost—literally—to those involved in the learning.

Not all behavior that we witness is learned or carried out, of course. One crucial factor that determines whether we later imitate a model is the consequences of the model's behavior. If we observe a friend being rewarded for putting more time into her studies by receiving higher grades, we are more likely to imitate her behavior than if her behavior only results in her being stressed and tired. Models who are rewarded for behaving in a particular way are more apt to be mimicked than models who receive punishment. Interestingly, though, observing the punishment of a model does not necessarily stop observers from learning the behavior. Observers can still describe the model's behavior—they are just less apt to perform it (Bandura, 1977, 1986, 1994).

Observational learning is central to a number of important issues relating to the extent to which people learn by simply watching the behavior of others. For instance, the degree to which observation of aggression in the media produces subsequent aggression on the part of viewers is a crucial—and controversial—question, as we discuss next.

As this boy watches his father, he is using observational learning. How does observational learning contribute to defining gender roles?

 **PsychLink**

Social learning theory
www.mhhe.com/
feldmanup6-06links

observational learning: Learning through observing the behavior of another person called a *model*

Illustrating observational learning, this infant observes an adult on the television and then is able to imitate his behavior. Learning has obviously occurred through the mere observation of the television model.

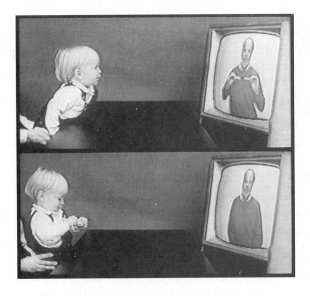

PsychLink

Violence in the media
www.mhhe.com/
feldmanup6–06links

Albert Bandura examined the principles of observational learning.

Violence on Television and in Movies: Does the Media's Message Matter?

The daughter of a judge from a politically prominent family runs off with her ne'er-do-well boyfriend. They drop LSD and watch, over and over, the ultraviolent Oliver Stone movie "Natural Born Killers," about a young couple who take drugs and kill people for pleasure. One afternoon, out joyriding in rural Mississippi, the boy suggests [according to the girl] "finding an isolated farmhouse and doing a home invasion, robbing a family and killing them, leaving no witnesses . . . as if he was fantasizing from the movie 'Natural Born Killers'." At a cotton gin on a lonely highway, the boyfriend guns down an innocent citizen, a devoted husband of 40 years, just for the thrill of it. . . . The next day the boy says to the girl, "It's your turn." That night, wearing a hooded poncho, she shoots a convenience-store clerk in cold blood, leaving the mother of three children paralyzed below the neck. (A. G. Miller, 1999, p. 42)

The aftermath of the killers' shooting spree may have a profound effect not just on the individuals directly involved, but on the motion picture industry, because the family of one of the victims is suing Oliver Stone, the director of *Natural Born Killers* and Warner Brothers, which released the film, for millions of dollars. Although legal experts suggest that the lawsuit is unlikely to succeed, it raises a critical issue: Does observation of violence and antisocial acts in the media lead viewers to behave in similar ways? Because research on modeling shows that people frequently learn and imitate the aggression that they observe, this question is among the most important being addressed by social psychologists.

Certainly, the amount of violence in the mass media is enormous. Between the ages of 5 and 15, the average American child is exposed to no fewer than 13,000 violent deaths on television; the number of fights and aggressive sequences that children view is still higher. Adult television shows also contain significant violence, with cable television leading the way with such shows as *When Animals Attack* and *World's Scariest Police Shootouts* (Liebert & Sprafkin, 1988; Mifflin, 1998).

Most experts agree that watching high levels of media violence make viewers more susceptible to acting aggressively—for several reasons. For one thing, viewing violence seems to lower inhibitions against the performance of aggression—watching television portrayals of violence makes aggression seem a legitimate response to particular situations. Viewing violence also can distort our understanding of the meaning of others' behavior, predisposing us to view even nonaggressive acts by others as aggressive. Finally, a continual diet of aggression can leave us desensitized to violence, and what

Applying Psychology in the 21st Century

Does Virtual Aggression Lead to Actual Aggression?

Blood flows freely as still-warm corpses lie on the ground. Potential victims beg for mercy, while others moan in pain. Some people catch fire before they are mowed down, falling to the ground, dead.

This is just some of the continual violence that characterizes the computer game Postal. In the game, trigger-happy players act out the role of Postal Dude, who shoots at everything—and everyone—in his path. Like Doom, a favorite game of one of the Columbine High School killers, Postal allows players their choice of a variety of weapons of carnage.

Postal and Doom are just two of many highly realistic, involving, and violent video games now on the market. In fact, one survey found that almost 80 percent of the most popular games involved aggression, with one-fifth of them involving violence against women (Dietz, 1998).

Can playing games like Postal and Doom lead to actual aggression? Increasing research evidence suggests that it might. According to a recent series of studies by psychologists Craig Anderson and Karen Dill (2000), playing violent video games is associated with later aggressive behavior. In one study, for example, they found that college students who frequently played violent video games were more likely to have been involved in delinquent behavior and aggression. Frequent players also had lower academic achievement.

On the other hand, such results do not show that playing violent games *causes* delinquency, aggression, and lower academic performance; the research only found that the various variables were *associated with* one another. To explore the question of whether violent game play actually caused aggression, Anderson and Dill subsequently conducted a short-term laboratory study. In it, they had participants in an experiment play either a violent video game (Wolfenstein 3D) or one that was nonviolent (Myst). The results were clear: Exposure to the graphically violent video game increased aggressive thoughts and actual aggression.

The finding of a link between playing violent video games and aggressive behavior is consistent with findings from other studies, and it makes sense in light of the research on the consequences of exposure to violence in the media. In fact, the effects of playing video games could be even greater than the effects of merely watching an aggressive television program,

While research has shown that a link exists between playing violent video games and aggressive thoughts and behavior, it has not shown that game playing causes delinquency, real-world aggression, or lower academic achievement. Do you think a definite causal connection will ever be found?

because video games teach something that the mere observation of violence does not: the motor skills involved in aggression. By actually firing virtual weapons at people and objects appearing on the screen, game players presumably hone the skills that would make them more effective in using actual weapons (Cooper & Mackie, 1986; D. Cohen, 1996; Griffiths, 1997).

If a conclusive causal link between playing violent video games and subsequent aggressive acts were established, would you support a ban on such games? Why or why not?

---

previously would have repelled us now produces little emotional response. Our sense of the pain and suffering brought about by aggression might be diminished (Berkowitz, 1993; Berkowitz & LePage, 1996; Huesmann & Moise, 1996).

Of course, the media are not the only source of aggressive models. For example, many computer and video games involve a significant amount of graphic violence. Does exposure to such violence affect players? For an answer, consider the research findings described in the *Applying Psychology in the 21ˢᵗ Century* box.

EXPLORING DIVERSITY

Does Culture Influence How We Learn?

When a member of the Chilcotin Indian tribe teaches her daughter to prepare salmon, at first she only allows the daughter to observe the entire process. A little later, she permits her child to try out some basic parts of the task. Her response to questions is noteworthy. For example, when the daughter asks about how to do "the backbone part," the mother's response is to repeat the entire process with another fish. The reason? The mother feels that one cannot learn the individual parts of the task apart from the context of preparing the whole fish. (Tharp, 1989)

Table 6-2 Learning Styles

Relational Style	Analytical Style
1. Perceive information as part of total picture	1. Able to dis-embed information from total picture (focus on detail)
2. Exhibit improvisational and intuitive thinking	2. Exhibit sequential and structured thinking
3. More easily learn materials that have a human, social content and are characterized by experiential/cultural relevance	3. More easily learn materials that are inanimate and impersonal
4. Have a good memory for verbally presented ideas and information, especially if relevant	4. Have a good memory for abstract ideas and irrelevant information
5. Are more task-oriented concerning nonacademic areas	5. Are more task-oriented concerning academics
6. Are influenced by authority figures' expression of confidence or doubt in students' ability	6. Are not greatly affected by the opinions of others
7. Prefer to withdraw from unstimulating task performance	7. Show ability to persist at unstimulating tasks
8. Style conflicts with the traditional school environment	8. Style matches most school environments

It should not be surprising that children raised in the Chilcotin tradition, which stresses instruction that starts by communicating the entire task, might have difficulty with traditional Western schooling. In the approach to teaching most characteristic of Western culture, tasks are broken down into their component parts. Only after each small step is learned is it thought possible to master the complete task.

Do the differences in teaching approaches between cultures affect how people learn? According to one school of thought, learners develop *learning styles,* characteristic ways of approaching material, based on their cultural background and unique pattern of abilities (Anderson & Adams, 1992; Milgram, Dunn, & Price, 1993; Chi-Ching & Noi, 1994; Furnham, 1995; Sternberg & Grigorenko, 1997).

Learning styles differ along several dimensions. For example, one central dimension is analytic versus relational approaches to learning (Anderson, 1988; Tharp, 1989). As illustrated in Table 6-2, people with a relational learning style master material best through exposure to a full unit or phenomenon. Parts of the unit are comprehended only by understanding their relationship to the whole.

In contrast, people with an analytical learning style do best when they can carry out an initial analysis of the principles and components underlying a phenomenon or situation. By developing an understanding of the fundamental principles and components, they are best able to understand the full picture. (In certain respects, the distinction between relational and analytic learning styles is similar to the distinction between top-down and bottom-up perception that we discussed in Chapter 4.)

Although research findings are mixed, some evidence suggests that particular minority groups within Western societies display characteristic learning styles. For instance, James Anderson and Maurianne Adams (1992) argue that Caucasian females and African American, Native American, and Hispanic American males and females are more apt to use a relational style of learning than Caucasian and Asian American males, who are more likely to employ an analytical style.

The conclusion that members of particular ethnic and gender groups have similar learning styles is controversial. Because there is so much diversity within each particular racial and ethnic group, critics argue that generalizations about learning styles cannot be used to predict the style of any single individual, regardless of group membership. Many psychologists contend that a discussion of group learning styles is a misguided undertaking. (This argument echoes a controversy about the usefulness of IQ tests that we will examine in Chapter 9.) Instead, they suggest that it is more fruitful to concentrate on determining each individual's particular learning style and pattern of academic and social strengths.

Still, it is clear that values about learning, which are communicated through a person's family and cultural background, have an impact on how successful students are in school. For instance, one theory suggests that members of minority groups who were voluntary immigrants are more apt to be successful in school than those who were brought into a majority culture against their will. Korean children in the United States, for example—the sons and daughters of voluntary immigrants—perform quite well, as a group, in school. But Korean children in Japan—often the sons and daughters of people who were forced to immigrate during World War II, essentially as forced laborers—tend to do poorly in school. Presumably, children in the forced immigration group are less motivated to succeed than those in the voluntary immigration group (Ogbu, 1992; Gallagher, 1994).

The Unresolved Controversy of Cognitive-Social Learning Theory

The degree to which learning is based on unseen internal factors rather than on external factors remains one of the major issues dividing learning theorists today. Both classical conditioning and operant conditioning theories consider learning in terms of external stimuli and responses—a kind of "black box" analysis in which all that matters are the observable features of the environment, not what goes on inside a person's head. To the cognitive-social learning theorists, such an analysis misses the mark. Instead, they argue that what is crucial is the mental activity—the thoughts and expectations—that takes place inside the head.

Regardless of how the theoretical controversies are resolved, research on learning has allowed psychologists to make important advances in such areas as the treatment of psychological disorders (discussed in Chapter 17), and—as we see next—in suggesting solutions to everyday problems.

BECOMING AN INFORMED CONSUMER OF PSYCHOLOGY

 **PsychLink**

Journal of Applied Behavior Analysis
www.mhhe.com/
feldmanup6-06links

Using Behavior Analysis and Behavior Modification

A couple who had been living together for three years began to fight more and more frequently. The issues of disagreement ranged from the seemingly petty, such as who was going to do the dishes, to the more profound, such as the quality of their love life and whether they found each other interesting. Disturbed about this increasingly unpleasant pattern of interaction, the couple went to a behavior analyst, a psychologist who specialized in behavior-modification techniques. After interviewing each of them alone and then speaking to them together, he asked them to keep a detailed written record of their interactions over the next two weeks—focusing in particular on the events that precede their arguments.

When they returned two weeks later, he carefully went over the records with them. In doing so, he noticed a pattern that the couple themselves had observed after they had started keeping their records: Each of their arguments had occurred just after one or the other had left some household chore undone. For instance, the woman would go into a fury when she came home from work and found that the man, a student, had left his dirty lunch dishes on the table and had not even started dinner preparations. The man would get angry when he found the woman's clothes draped on the only chair in the bedroom. He insisted it was her responsibility to pick up after herself.

Using the data that the couple had collected, the behavior analyst devised a system for the couple to try out. He asked them to list all of the chores that could possibly arise and assign each one a point value depending on how long it took to complete. Then he had them divide the chores equally according to total points and agree in a written contract to fulfill the ones assigned to them. If either failed to carry out one of the assigned chores, he or she would have to place $1 per point in a fund for the other to spend. They also agreed to a program of verbal praise, promising to verbally reward each other for completing a chore.

Although skeptical about the value of such a program, the couple agreed to try it for a month and to keep careful records of the number of arguments they had during this period. To their surprise, the number of arguments declined rapidly, and even the more basic issues in their relationship seemed on the way to being resolved.

The case described above provides an illustration of **behavior modification,** a formalized technique for promoting the frequency of desirable behaviors and decreasing the incidence of unwanted ones. Using the basic principles of learning theory, behavior-modification techniques have proved to be helpful in a variety of situations. People with severe mental retardation have learned the rudiments of language and, for the first time in their lives, have started dressing and feeding themselves. Behavior modification has also helped people lose weight, give up smoking, and behave more safely (Bellack, Hersen, & Kazdin, 1990; Sulzer-Azaroff & Mayer, 1991; Malott, Whaley, & Malott, 1993; Walter, Vaughan, & Wynder, 1994).

The techniques used by behavior analysts are as varied as the list of processes that modify behavior. These include reinforcement scheduling, shaping, generalization training, discrimination training, and extinction. Participants in a behavior-change program do, however, typically follow a series of similar basic steps. These steps include:

- *Identify goals and target behaviors.* The first step is to define "desired behavior." Is it an increase in time spent studying? a decrease in weight? an increase in the use of language? a reduction in the amount of aggression displayed by a child? The goals must be stated in observable terms and lead to specific targets. For instance, a goal might be "to increase study time," with the target behavior "to study at least two hours per day on weekdays and an hour on Saturdays."
- *Design a data-recording system and record preliminary data.* To determine whether behavior has changed, it is necessary to collect data before any changes are made in the situation. This information provides a baseline against which future changes can be measured.
- *Select a behavior-change strategy.* The most crucial step is to select an appropriate strategy. Because all the principles of learning can be employed to bring about behavior change, a "package" of treatments is normally used. This might include the systematic use of positive reinforcement for desired behavior (verbal praise or something more tangible, such as food), as well as a program of extinction for undesirable behavior (ignoring a child who throws a tantrum). Selecting the right reinforcers is critical; it could be necessary to experiment a bit to find out what is important to a given individual. It is best for participants to avoid threats, because these are merely punishing and ultimately not very effective in bringing about long-term changes in behavior.
- *Implement the program.* The next step is to institute the program. Probably the most important aspect of program implementation is consistency. It is also important to make sure that one is reinforcing the behavior one wants to reinforce. For example, suppose a mother wants her daughter to spend more time on her homework, but as soon as the child sits down to study, she asks for a snack. If the mother gets one for her, she is likely to be reinforcing her daughter's delaying tactic, not her studying. Instead, the mother might tell her child that she will provide her with a snack after a certain time interval has gone by during which she has studied—thereby using the snack as a reinforcement for studying.

behavior modification: A formalized technique for promoting the frequency of desirable behaviors and decreasing the incidence of unwanted ones

 **PsychLink**

Behavioral analysis issues
www.mhhe.com/
feldmanup6-06links

- *Keep careful records after the program is implemented.* Another crucial task is record keeping. If the target behaviors are not monitored, there is no way of knowing whether the program has been successful. Participants are advised not to rely on memory, because memory lapses are all too frequent.
- *Evaluate and alter the ongoing program.* Finally, the results of the program should be compared with baseline, pre-implementation data to determine its effectiveness. If successful, the procedures employed can gradually be phased out. For instance, if the program called for reinforcing every instance of picking up one's clothes from the bedroom floor, the reinforcement schedule could be modified to a fixed-ratio schedule in which every third instance was reinforced. On the other hand, if the program has not been successful in bringing about the desired behavior change, consideration of other approaches might be advisable.

Behavior-change techniques based on these general principles have enjoyed wide success and have proved to be one of the most powerful means of modifying behavior (Greenwood et al., 1992). Clearly, it is possible to employ the basic notions of learning theory to improve our own lives.

Evaluate

1. Cognitive-social learning theorists are concerned only with overt behavior, not with its internal causes. True or false?
2. In cognitive-social learning theory, it is assumed that people develop an_____ about receiving a reinforcer when they behave a certain way.
3. In_____ learning, a new behavior is learned but is not shown until appropriate reinforcement is presented.
4. Bandura's theory of_____ learning states that people learn through watching a_____—another person displaying the behavior of interest.
5. A man wishes to quit smoking. Upon the advice of a psychologist, he begins a program in which he sets goals for his withdrawal, carefully records his progress, and rewards himself for not smoking during a certain period of time. What type of program is he following?

Rethink

1. What is the relationship between a model (in Bandura's sense) and a role model (as the term is used popularly)? Celebrities often complain that their actions should not be scrutinized closely because they do not want to be role models. How would you respond?
2. The relational style of learning sometimes conflicts with the traditional school environment. Could a school be created that takes advantage of the characteristics of the relational style? How? Are there types of learning for which the analytical style is clearly superior?

Answers to Evaluate Questions

1. False; cognitive-social learning theorists are primarily concerned with mental processes 2. expectation 3. latent 4. observational; model 5. Behavior modification

Looking Back

What is learning?

- Learning, a relatively permanent change in behavior due to experience, is a basic topic of psychology. However, learning must be assessed indirectly by observing performance. (p. 166)

How do we learn to form associations between stimuli and responses?

- One major form of learning is classical conditioning, which occurs when a neutral stimulus—one that brings about no relevant response—is repeatedly paired with a stimulus (called an unconditioned stimulus) that brings about a natural, untrained response. (p. 167)
- Conditioning occurs when the neutral stimulus is repeatedly presented just before the unconditioned stimulus. After repeated pairings, the neutral stimulus brings about the same response as the unconditioned stimulus. When this occurs, the neutral stimulus has become a conditioned stimulus, and the response a conditioned response. (p. 168)
- Learning is not always permanent. Extinction occurs when a previously learned response decreases in frequency and eventually disappears. (p. 170)
- Stimulus generalization occurs when a conditioned response follows a stimulus that is similar to, but not the same as, the original conditioned stimulus. The converse phenomenon, stimulus discrimination, occurs when an organism learns to distinguish between stimuli. (p. 170)

What is the role of reward and punishment in learning?

- A second major form of learning is operant conditioning. According to B. F. Skinner, the major mechanism underlying learning is reinforcement, the process by which a stimulus increases the probability that a preceding behavior will be repeated. (p. 173)
- Primary reinforcers involve rewards that are naturally effective without prior exposure because they satisfy a biological need. Secondary reinforcers begin to act as if they were primary reinforcers through frequent pairings with a primary reinforcer. (p. 175)
- Positive reinforcers are stimuli that are added to the environment and lead to an increase in a preceding response. Negative reinforcers are stimuli that remove something unpleasant from the environment, leading to an increase in the preceding response. (p. 175)
- Punishment decreases the probability that a prior behavior will occur. Positive punishment weakens a response through the application of an unpleasant stimulus, while negative punishment weakens a response by the removal of something positive. In contrast to reinforcement, in which the goal is to increase the incidence of behavior, punishment is meant to decrease or suppress behavior. (p. 176)
- Schedules and patterns of reinforcement affect the strength and duration of learning. Generally, partial reinforcement schedules—in which reinforcers are not delivered on every trial—produce stronger and longer-lasting learning than continuous reinforcement schedules. (p. 176)
- Among the major categories of reinforcement schedules are fixed- and variable-ratio schedules, which are based on the number of responses made, and fixed- and variable-interval schedules, which are based on the time interval that elapses before reinforcement is provided. (p. 176)
- Generalization and discrimination operate in operant conditioning as well as classical conditioning. (p. 180)

- Superstitious behavior results from the mistaken belief that particular ideas, objects, or behavior will cause certain events to occur. (p. 180)
- Shaping is a process for teaching complex behaviors by rewarding closer and closer approximations of the desired final behavior. (p. 180)
- There are biological constraints, or built-in limitations, on the ability of an organism to learn. Because of these constraints, certain behaviors will be relatively easy to learn, whereas other behaviors will be either difficult or impossible to learn. (p. 181)

What is the role of cognition and thought in learning?

- Cognitive-social approaches consider learning in terms of thought processes or cognition. Phenomena such as latent learning—in which a new behavior is learned but not performed until reinforcement is provided for its performance—and the apparent development of cognitive maps support cognitive-social approaches. Learning also occurs through observation of the behavior of models. (p. 183)
- The major factor that determines whether an observed behavior will actually be performed is the nature of reinforcement or punishment a model receives. (p. 185)
- Learning styles are characteristic ways of approaching material, based on a person's cultural background and unique pattern of abilities. One major dimension relates to analytic versus relational approaches to learning. (p. 185)

What are some practical methods for bringing about behavior change, both in ourselves and in others?

- Behavior modification is a method for formally using the principles of learning theory to promote the frequency of desired behaviors and to decrease or eliminate unwanted ones. (p. 190)

Key Terms and Concepts

learning (p. 166)
classical conditioning (p. 167)
neutral stimulus (p. 167)
unconditioned stimulus (UCS) (p. 168)
unconditioned response (UCR) (p. 168)
conditioned stimulus (CS) (p. 169)
conditioned response (CR) (p. 169)
extinction (p. 170)
spontaneous recovery (p. 170)
stimulus generalization (p. 170)
stimulus discrimination (p. 171)
operant conditioning (p. 173)
reinforcement (p. 175)
reinforcer (p. 175)
positive reinforcer (p. 175)

negative reinforcer (p. 175)
punishment (p. 176)
schedules of reinforcement (p. 177)
continuous reinforcement schedule (p. 177)
partial reinforcement schedule (p. 177)
fixed-ratio schedule (p. 178)
variable-ratio schedule (p. 178)
fixed-interval schedule (p. 179)
variable-interval schedule (p. 179)
shaping (p. 180)
cognitive-social learning theory (p. 183)
latent learning (p. 183)
cognitive map (p. 184)
observational learning (p. 185)
behavior modification (p. 190)

Psychology on the Web

1. B. F. Skinner had an impact on society and thought that is only hinted at in this chapter. Find additional information on the Web about Skinner's life and influence. See if you can find out about his ideas for an ideal, utopian society based on the principles of conditioning and behaviorism. Write a summary of what you find.

2. Select a topic discussed in this chapter that is of interest to you (e.g., superstition, teaching complex behaviors by shaping, violence in video games, relational vs. analytic learning styles, behavior modification, etc.). Find at least two sources of information on the Web about your topic and summarize the results of your quest. It may be most helpful to find two different approaches to your topic and compare them.

Epilogue

In this chapter we have discussed several kinds of learning, ranging from classical conditioning, which depends on the existence of natural stimulus-response pairings, to operant conditioning, in which reinforcement is used to increase desired behavior. These approaches to learning focus on outward, behavioral learning processes. We have also been introduced to more cognitive-social approaches to learning, which focus on mental processes and enable learning.

We have also noted that learning is affected by culture and individual differences, with individual learning styles potentially affecting the ways in which people learn most effectively. Finally, we saw some ways in which our learning about learning can be put to practical use, through such means as behavior modification programs designed to decrease negative behaviors and increase positive ones.

Before proceeding to the next chapter—on memory—return to the prologue of this chapter and consider the following questions in relation to Ike, the helpful dog who served Elizabeth Twohy.

1. Is Ike's learning primarily an example of classical conditioning, operant conditioning, or cognitive-social learning? Why?
2. Do you think punishment would be an effective teaching strategy for Ike? Why?
3. In what way would shaping have been used to teach Ike some of his more complex behaviors, such as sorting the recyclables and removing dishes from the dishwasher?

Chapter Seven

Memory

Prologue: The Man Who Vanished into His Past

Looking Ahead

Encoding, Storage, and Retrieval of Memory

The Three Systems of Memory: Memory Storehouses

Contemporary Approaches to Memory: Working Memory, Memory Modules, and Associative Models of Memory

Recalling Long-Term Memories

Retrieval Cues

Levels of Processing

Flashbulb Memories

Constructive Processes in Memory: Rebuilding the Past

Memory in the Courtroom: The Eyewitness on Trial

Applying Psychology in the 21st Century: Repressed Memories: Truth or Fiction?

Autobiographical Memory: Where Past Meets Present

Exploring Diversity: Are There Cross-Cultural Differences in Memory?

Forgetting: When Memory Fails

Proactive and Retroactive Interference: The Before and After of Forgetting

The Biological Bases of Memory

Memory Dysfunctions: Afflictions of Forgetting

Becoming an Informed Consumer of Psychology: Improving Your Memory

Looking Back

Key Terms and Concepts

Psychology on the Web

OLC Preview

Epilogue

Prologue

The Man Who Vanished into His Past

Terry Dibert got up from his desk in the school district headquarters in Bedford, Pennsylvania, and vanished into his past.

That sounds like an opening line to a thriller. But for Mr. Dibert, who left his computer running and his jacket on the back of his chair, it was literally true.

Six days after his disappearance, Terry Dibert was found wandering aimlessly in a wildfire, 800 miles from home, and thinking it was 11 years earlier.

Six days later and 800 miles away, Mr. Dibert, the district's business manager, reappeared near dawn in the midst of a natural disaster. Police officers from Daytona Beach, Florida, found him ... wandering on Interstate 95 through the blinding smoke from the wildfires that had shut the highway and forced the evacuation of much of the area.

Mr. Dibert told the police he was a 23-year-old sergeant trying to rejoin his Army unit at Fort Bragg. He was worried about being separated from his wife, who was pregnant with their first child (Sherman, 1999, p. F8).

Looking Ahead

Terry Dibert was accurate—except for one thing: His account was 11 years out of date. When police called Fort Bragg, they found that he had been discharged almost a dozen years earlier, and his wife, whom he thought was pregnant, had delivered the child ten years earlier.

The source of Dibert's strange memory loss proved to be a brain cyst that was pressing against part of the brain that helps store memories. Following surgery to drain the cyst, Dibert's memory returned to normal.

Stories like this illustrate not only the important role memory plays in our lives, but also its fragility. Memory allows us to retrieve a vast amount of information. We are able to remember the name of a friend we haven't talked with for years and to recall details of a picture that hung in our childhood bedroom. At the same time, though, memory failures are common. We forget where we left the keys to the car and fail to answer an exam question about material we studied only a few hours earlier.

In this chapter, we consider the nature of memory. We examine how information is stored and retrieved. We discuss approaches that suggest there are several separate types of memory, and we explain how each type is believed to function in a somewhat different fashion. We examine the problems of retrieving information from memory, the accuracy of memories, and the reasons information is sometimes forgotten. We also consider the biological foundations of memory. Finally, we discuss some practical means of increasing memory capacity.

Prepare

What is memory?
Are there different kinds of memory?

Organize

Encoding, Storage, and Retrieval of Memory
 The Three Systems of Memory
 Contemporary Approaches to Memory

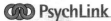 PsychLink

Reports on memory
www.mhhe.com/
feldmanup6-07links

memory: The process by which we encode, store, and retrieve information

Encoding, Storage, and Retrieval of Memory

You are playing a game of Trivial Pursuit, and winning the game comes down to one question: On what body of water is Bombay located?

As you rack your brain for the answer, several fundamental processes relating to memory come into play. Perhaps you have never been exposed to information regarding Bombay's location, or if you have been exposed to it, perhaps it didn't register in a meaningful way. In other words, your difficulty in answering the question might be traced to the initial encoding stage of memory. *Encoding* refers to the process by which information is initially recorded in a form usable to memory.

On the other hand, even if you had been exposed to the information and originally knew the name of the body of water, you might still be unable to recall it during the game because of a failure in the retention process. Memory specialists speak of *storage,* the maintenance of material saved in the memory system. If the material is not stored adequately, it cannot be recalled later.

Memory also depends on a third process: retrieval. In *retrieval,* material in memory storage is located, brought into awareness, and used. Your failure to recall Bombay's location, then, could rest on your inability to retrieve information that you learned earlier.

In sum, psychologists consider **memory** as the process by which we encode, store, and retrieve information (see Figure 7-1). Each of the three parts of this definition—encoding, storage, and retrieval—represents a different process. You can think of these processes as analogous to the functions of a computer's keyboard (encoding), disk (storage), and screen (retrieval). Only if all three processes have operated will you experience success and be able to recall the body of water on which Bombay is located: the Arabian Sea.

However, before continuing, we should keep in mind the value of memory *failures.* Forgetting is essential to the proper functioning of memory. The ability to forget inconsequential details about experiences, people, and objects helps us to avoid being burdened and distracted by immense stores of meaningless data. Furthermore, forgetting permits us to form general impressions and recollections. For example, the reason our friends consistently look familiar to us is because of our ability to forget their clothing, facial blemishes, and other transient features that change from one occasion to the next. Instead,

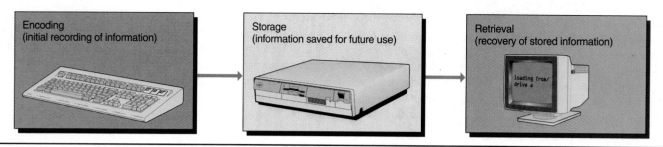

Figure 7–1 Memory is built on three basic processes—encoding, storage, and retrieval—that are analogous to the functions of a computer's keyboard, disk, and screen. The analogy is not perfect, however, because human memory is less precise than a computer's. How might you modify the analogy to make it more accurate?

our memories are based on a summary of various critical features—a far more economical use of our memory capabilities. Forgetting unnecessary information, then, is as essential to the proper functioning of memory as is remembering more important material.

The Three Systems of Memory: Memory Storehouses

Although the processes of encoding, storing, and retrieving information are necessary for memory to operate successfully, they do not describe *how* information enters into memory. Many psychologists studying memory suggest that there are different systems or stages through which information must travel if it is to be remembered.

According to one of the most influential and enduring theories, based on the cognitive perspective we first discussed in Chapter 1, there are three kinds of memory storage systems. These storehouses vary in terms of their function and the length of time they retain information (Atkinson & Shiffrin, 1968, 1971).

As shown in Figure 7-2, **sensory memory** refers to the initial, momentary storage of information, lasting only an instant. Information is recorded by the person's sensory system as an exact replica of the stimulus. In a second stage, **short-term memory** holds information for 15 to 25 seconds and stores it according to its meaning rather than as mere sensory stimulation. The third type of storage system is **long-term memory.** Information is stored in long-term memory on a relatively permanent basis, although it might be difficult to retrieve.

sensory memory: The initial, momentary storage of information, lasting only an instant

short-term memory: Memory that holds information for 15 to 25 seconds

long-term memory: Memory that stores information on a relatively permanent basis, although it might be difficult to retrieve

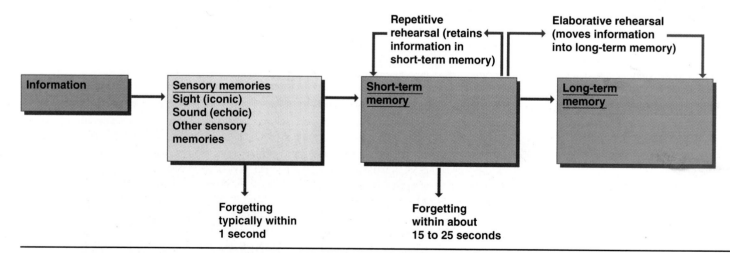

Figure 7–2 In this three-stage model of memory, information initially recorded by the person's sensory system enters sensory memory, which momentarily holds the information. It then moves to short-term memory, which stores the information for 15 to 25 seconds. Finally, the information can move into long-term memory, which is relatively permanent. Whether the information moves from short-term to long-term memory depends on the kind and amount of rehearsal of the material that is carried out. (After Atkinson & Shifrin, 1968).

PsychLink

Theory of sensory memory
www.mhhe.com/
feldmanup6-07links

iconic memory: Memory of information from our visual system

echoic memory: Memory of auditory information coming from the ears

Although we'll be discussing the three types of memory as separate memory stores, keep in mind that these are not mini-warehouses located in particular portions of the brain. Instead, they represent three different types of memory systems with different characteristics. Furthermore, although the three-part model of memory dominated the field of memory research for several decades, recent studies have suggested several newer models, as we'll discuss later. Still, considering memory in terms of three major kinds of stores provides us with a useful framework for understanding how information is both recalled and forgotten.

Sensory Memory

A momentary flash of lightning, the sound of a twig snapping, and the sting of a pinprick all represent stimulation of exceedingly brief duration, but they might nonetheless provide important information that can require some response. Such stimuli are initially—and briefly—stored in sensory memory, the first repository of the information that the world presents to us. Actually, the term *sensory memory* denotes several types of sensory memories, each related to a different source of sensory information. There is **iconic memory,** which reflects information from our visual system; **echoic memory,** which stores auditory information coming from the ears; and corresponding memories for each of the other senses.

Regardless of the individual subtypes, sensory memory in general is able to store information for only a very short time. If information does not pass to short-term memory, it is lost for good. For instance, iconic memory seems to last less than a second, although if the initial stimulus is very bright, the image might last a little longer. Echoic memory typically fades within two or three seconds. However, despite the brief duration of sensory memory, its precision is high: Sensory memory can store an almost exact replica of each stimulus to which it is exposed (Darwin, Turvey, & Crowder, 1972; Long & Beaton, 1982; Sams et al., 1993).

If the storage capabilities of sensory memory are so limited and information stored within sensory memory so fleeting, it would seem almost impossible to find evidence for its existence; new information would constantly be replacing older information, even before a person could report its presence. Not until psychologist George Sperling (1960) conducted a series of clever and now-classic studies was sensory memory well understood. Sperling briefly exposed people to a series of twelve letters arranged in the following pattern:

$$
\begin{array}{cccc}
\text{F} & \text{T} & \text{Y} & \text{C} \\
\text{K} & \text{D} & \text{N} & \text{L} \\
\text{Y} & \text{W} & \text{B} & \text{M}
\end{array}
$$

When exposed to this pattern of letters for just one-twentieth of a second, most people could accurately recall only four or five of the letters. Although they knew that they had seen more, the memory of these letters had faded by the time they reported the

A momentary flash of lightning leaves a sensory visual memory, a fleeting but exact replica of the stimulus that fades rapidly.

first few letters. It was possible, then, that the information had initially been accurately stored in sensory memory, but during the time it took to verbalize the first four or five letters the memory of the other letters faded.

To test that possibility, Sperling conducted an experiment in which a high, medium, or low tone sounded just after a person had been exposed to the full pattern of letters. People were told to report the letters in the highest line if a high tone were sounded, the middle line if the medium tone occurred, or the lowest line at the sound of the low tone. Because the tone occurred after the exposure, people had to rely on their memory to report the correct row.

The results of the study clearly showed that people had been storing the complete pattern in memory. They were accurate in their recollection of the letters in the line that had been indicated by the tone, regardless of whether it was the top, middle, or bottom line. Obviously, *all* the lines they had seen had been stored in sensory memory. Despite its rapid loss, then, the information in sensory memory was an accurate representation of what people had seen.

By gradually lengthening the time between the presentation of the visual pattern and the tone, Sperling was able to determine with some accuracy the length of time that information was stored in sensory memory. The ability to recall a particular row of the pattern when a tone was sounded declined progressively as the period between visual exposure and tone increased. This decline continued until the period reached about one second in duration, at which point the row could not be recalled accurately at all. Sperling concluded that the entire visual image was stored in sensory memory for less than a second.

In sum, sensory memory operates as a kind of snapshot that stores information—of a visual, auditory, or other sensory nature—for a brief moment in time. But it is as if each snapshot, immediately after being taken, is destroyed and replaced with a new one. Unless the information in the snapshot is transferred to some other type of memory, it is lost.

An artist must repeatedly view the subject of a painting in order to capture the image as viewed, using both short-term and long-term memory. Why do you think people tend to close their eyes when recalling a scene or picture?

Short-Term Memory: Giving Memory Meaning

Because the information that is stored briefly in our sensory memory consists of representations of raw sensory stimuli, it is not meaningful to us. For us to make sense of it and to allow for the possibility of long-term retention, the information must be transferred to the next stage of memory, short-term memory. Short-term memory is the memory store in which information first has meaning, although the maximum length of retention there is relatively short.

The specific process by which sensory memories are transformed into short-term memories is not yet clear. Some theorists suggest that the information is first translated into graphical representations or images, and others hypothesize that the transfer occurs when the sensory stimuli are changed to words (Baddeley & Wilson, 1985). What is clear, however, is that unlike sensory memory, which holds a relatively full and detailed—if short-lived—representation of the world, short-term memory has incomplete representational capabilities.

In fact, the specific amount of information that can be held in short-term memory has been identified as seven items, or "chunks," of information, with variations up to plus or minus two chunks. A **chunk** is a meaningful grouping of stimuli that can be stored as a unit in short-term memory. According to George Miller (1956), it could be individual letters or numbers, permitting us to hold a seven-digit phone number (like 226-4610) in short-term memory.

But a chunk might also consist of larger categories, such as words or other meaningful units. For example, consider the following list of twenty-one letters:

P B S F O X C N N A B C C B S M T V N B C

Because the list exceeds seven chunks, it is difficult to recall the letters after one exposure. But suppose they were presented to you as follows:

PBS FOX CNN ABC CBS MTV NBC

 **PsychLink**

Short-term memory demonstration
www.mhhe.com/
feldmanup6–07links

chunk: A meaningful grouping of stimuli that can be stored as a unit in short-term memory

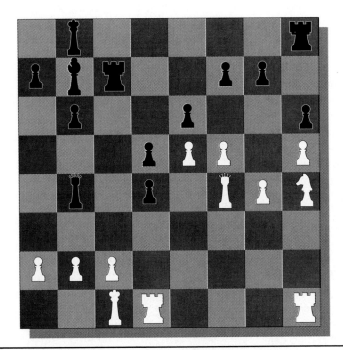

Figure 7-3 Examine the chessboard containing the chess pieces for about five seconds. Then, after covering up the board, try to reproduce the position of the pieces on the blank chessboard. Unless you are an experienced chess player, you are likely to have great difficulty carrying out such a task. Yet chess masters—the kind who win tournaments—do quite well (deGroot, 1966). They are able to reproduce correctly 90 percent of the pieces on the board. In comparison, inexperienced chess players are typically able to reproduce only 40 percent of the board properly. The chess masters do not have superior memories in other respects; they generally test normally on other measures of memory. What they can do better than others is see the board in terms of chunks or meaningful units and reproduce the position of the chess pieces by using these units.

In this case, even though there are still twenty-one letters, you'd be able to store them in short-term memory, because they represent only seven chunks.

Chunks can vary in size from single letters or numbers to categories that are far more complicated. The specific nature of what constitutes a chunk varies according to one's past experience. You can see this for yourself by trying an experiment that was first carried out as a comparison between expert and inexperienced chess players, illustrated in Figure 7-3 (deGroot, 1966; Schneider et al., 1994; Gobet & Simon, 1996).

Although it is possible to remember seven or so relatively complicated sets of information entering short-term memory, the information cannot be held there very long. Just how brief is short-term memory? Anyone who has looked up a telephone number at a pay phone, struggled to find coins, and forgotten the number at the sound of the dial tone knows that information in short-term memory does not remain there very long. Most psychologists believe that information in short-term memory is lost after 15 to 25 seconds—unless it is transferred to long-term memory.

Rehearsal

rehearsal: The repetition of information that has entered short-term memory

The transfer of material from short- to long-term memory proceeds largely on the basis of **rehearsal,** the repetition of information that has entered short-term memory. Rehearsal accomplishes two things. First, as long as the information is repeated, it is maintained in short-term memory. More important, however, rehearsal allows us to transfer the information into long-term memory.

Whether the transfer is made from short- to long-term memory seems to depend largely on the kind of rehearsal that is carried out. If the information is simply repeated over and over again—as we might do with a telephone number while we rush from the phone book to the phone—it is kept current in short-term memory, but it will not necessarily be

placed in long-term memory. Instead, as soon as we stop punching in the phone numbers, the number is likely replaced by other information and will be completely forgotten.

On the other hand, if the information in short-term memory is rehearsed using a process called elaborative rehearsal, it is much more likely to be transferred into long-term memory (Craik & Lockhart, 1972). *Elaborative rehearsal* occurs when the information is considered and organized in some fashion. The organization might include expanding the information to make it fit into a logical framework, linking it to another memory, turning it into an image, or transforming it in some other way. For example, a list of vegetables to be purchased at a store could be woven together in memory as items being used to prepare an elaborate salad; they could be linked to the items bought on an earlier shopping trip; or they could be thought of in terms of the image of a farm with rows of each item.

By using organizational strategies such as these—called *mnemonics*—we can vastly improve our retention of information. Mnemonics (pronounced "neh MON ix") are formal techniques for organizing information in a way that makes it more likely to be remembered. For instance, when a beginning musician learns that the spaces on the music staff spell the word *FACE,* or when we learn the rhyme "Thirty days hath September, April, June, and November . . . ," we are using mnemonics (Mastropieri & Scruggs, 1991; Bellezza, Six, & Phillips, 1992; Schoen, 1996; Goldstein et al., 1996; Carney et al., 2000).

Long-Term Memory: The Final Storehouse

Material that makes its way from short-term memory to long-term memory enters a storehouse of almost unlimited capacity. Like a new file we save on our hard drive, the information in long-term memory is filed and coded so that we can retrieve it when we need it.

Evidence of the existence of long-term memory, as distinct from short-term memory, comes from a number of sources. For example, people with certain kinds of brain damage have no lasting recall of new information following the damage, although information about people and events stored in memory prior to the injury remains intact (Milner, 1966). Because information that was encoded and stored before the injury can be recalled and because short-term memory following the injury appears to be operational—new material can be recalled for a very brief period—we can infer that there are two distinct types of memory, one for short-term and one for long-term storage.

Results from laboratory experiments are also consistent with the notion of separate short- and long-term memories. For example, in one set of studies people were asked to recall a relatively small amount of information (such as a set of three letters). Then, to prevent practice of the initial information, participants were required to recite some extraneous material aloud, such as counting backward by threes (Brown, 1958; Peterson & Peterson, 1959). By varying the amount of time between presentation of the initial material and the need for its recall, investigators found that recall was quite good when the interval was very short but declined rapidly thereafter. After 15 seconds had gone by, recall hovered at around 10 percent of the material initially presented.

Apparently the distraction of counting backward prevented almost all the initial material from reaching long-term memory. Initial recall was good because it was coming from short-term memory, but these memories were lost at a rapid rate. Eventually, all that could be recalled was the small amount of material that had made its way into long-term storage despite the distraction of counting backward.

PsychLink

Long-term memory article
www.mhhe.com/
feldmanup6-07links

Contemporary Approaches to Memory: Working Memory, Memory Modules, and Associative Models of Memory

So far, we have relied on the traditional model of memory, which suggests that the processing of information in memory proceeds in three sequential stages: starting with sensory memory, advancing to short-term memory, and potentially ending in long-term memory. However, many contemporary approaches suggest that this traditional model provides an incomplete account of memory. For instance, rather than information being processed sequentially from sensory to short-term to long-term memory stores (a *serial* process), increasing evidence suggests that the brain processes information simultaneously in different memory components (a *parallel* process). These views are exemplified by approaches to short- and long-term memory that we consider next.

Working Memory

working memory: An active "workspace" in which information is retrieved and manipulated, and in which information is held through rehearsal

Rather than seeing short-term memory as an independent way-station through which memories travel, some theorists conceive of short-term memory as an information-processing system known as working memory. **Working memory** is an active "workspace" in which information is retrieved and manipulated, and in which information is held through rehearsal (Baddeley, 1992, 1993, 1995a, 1995b; see Figure 7-4).

In this view, working memory contains a *central executive* processor, which is involved in reasoning and decision making. The central executive coordinates two distinct storage-and-rehearsal systems: the visual store and the verbal store. The *visual store* specializes in visual and spatial information, and the *verbal store* is responsible for holding and manipulating material relating to speech, words, and numbers (Della Sala et al., 1995; Baddeley, 1996; Logie & Gilhooly, 1998).

Working memory permits us to briefly maintain information in an active state so that we can do something with the information. For instance, we use working memory when we're doing a multistep arithmetic problem in our heads, storing the result of one calculation while getting ready to move to the next stage. (I make use of my working memory when I figure a 20 percent tip in a restaurant by first calculating 10 percent of the total bill, then doubling it.)

Some researchers suspect that a breakdown in the central executive might result in the memory losses that are characteristic of Alzheimer's disease, the progressively degenerative disorder that produces loss of memory and confusion (Cherry, Buckwalter, & Henderson, 1996). (We'll discuss Alzheimer's disease and other memory disorders at greater length later in this chapter.)

Figure 7-4 Working memory is an active "workspace" in which information is retrieved and manipulated, and in which information is held through rehearsal (Gathercole & Baddeley, 1993). It consists of a "central executive" that coordinates the visual store (which concentrates on visual and spatial information) and the verbal store (concentrating on speech, words, and numbers).

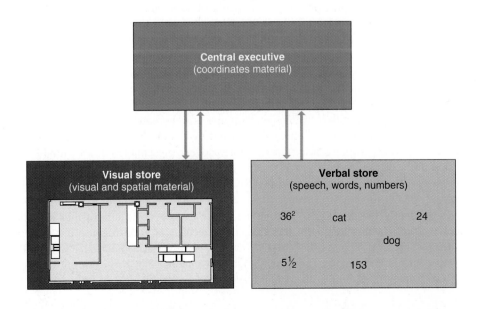

Central executive
(coordinates material)

Visual store
(visual and spatial material)

Verbal store
(speech, words, numbers)

36^2 cat   24

dog

$5\frac{1}{2}$ 153

Long-Term Memory Modules

Just as short-term memory is often viewed in terms of working memory, many contemporary researchers now see long-term memory as made up of several different components, or memory modules. Each of these modules is related to a separate memory system in the brain.

For instance, one major distinction within long-term memory is between declarative and procedural memory. **Declarative memory** is memory for factual information: names, faces, dates, and facts such as a bike has two wheels. In contrast, **procedural memory** (sometimes referred to as "nondeclarative memory") refers to memory for skills and habits, such as how to ride a bike or hit a baseball. Information *about* things is stored in declarative memory; information regarding *how to do* things is stored in procedural memory (Eichenbaum, 1997; Schacter, Wagner, & Buckner, 2000).

The facts in declarative memory can be further subdivided into semantic and episodic memory (Tulving, 1993; Nyberg & Tulving, 1996). **Semantic memory** is memory for general knowledge and facts about the world, as well as memory for the rules of logic that are used to deduce other facts. Because of semantic memory, we remember that $2 \times 2 = 4$, that the ZIP code for Beverly Hills is 90210, and that *memoree* is a misspelling. Thus, semantic memory is somewhat like a mental almanac of facts.

In contrast, **episodic memory** is memory for the biographical details of our individual lives. Memories of what we have done and the kinds of experiences we have had constitute episodic memory. Consequently, our recall of the first time we rode a bike or our first date is based on episodic memories. (To help your long-term memory keep straight the distinctions between the different types of long-term memory, study Figure 7-5.)

Episodic memories can be surprisingly detailed. Consider, for instance, how you'd respond if you were asked to identify what you were doing on a specific day two years ago. Impossible? You might think otherwise as you read the following exchange between a researcher and a participant in a study who was asked, in a memory

The ability to remember specific skills and the order in which they are used is known as procedural memory. If driving involves our procedural memory, is it safe to use a cell phone while driving?

declarative memory: Memory for factual information: names, faces, dates, and the like

procedural memory: Memory for skills and habits, such as riding a bike or hitting a baseball, sometimes referred to as "nondeclarative memory"

semantic memory: Memory for general knowledge and facts about the world, as well as memory for the rules of logic that are used to deduce other facts

episodic memory: Memory for the biographical details of our individual lives

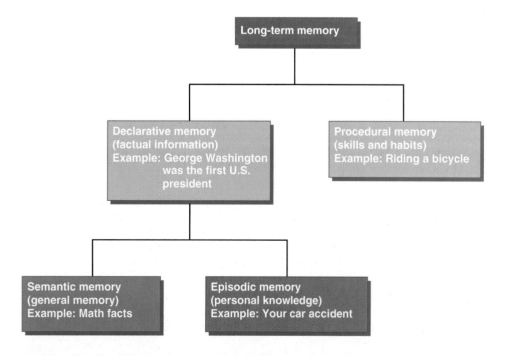

Figure 7-5 Long-term memory can be subdivided into several different types. What type of long-term memory is involved in your recollection of the moment you first arrived on your campus at the start of college?

In addition to procedural memory, driving a car also involves what is known as declarative or explicit memory, which permits us to remember how to get to our destination.

experiment, what he was doing "on Monday afternoon in the third week of September two years ago."

> PARTICIPANT: Come on. How should I know?
> EXPERIMENTER: Just try it anyhow.
> PARTICIPANT: OK. Let's see: Two years ago . . . I would be in high school in Pittsburgh. . . . That would be my senior year. Third week in September—that's just after summer—that would be the fall term. . . . Let me see. I think I had chemistry lab on Mondays. I don't know. I was probably in chemistry lab. Wait a minute—that would be the second week of school. I remember he started off with the atomic table—a big fancy chart. I thought he was crazy trying to make us memorize that thing. You know, I think I can remember sitting . . .
> (Lindsay & Norman, 1977)

Episodic memory, then, can provide information from events that happened long in the past (Reynolds & Takooshian, 1988). But semantic memory is no less impressive, permitting us to dredge up tens of thousands of facts ranging from the date of our birthday to the knowledge that $1 is less than $5.

Associative Models of Memory

Our ability to recall detailed information has led some memory researchers to view memory primarily in terms of associations between different pieces of information. **Associative models of memory** suggest that memory consists of mental representations of clusters of interconnected information (e.g., Collins & Quillian, 1969; Collins & Loftus, 1975).

Consider, for example, Figure 7-6, which shows some of the relationships in memory relating to the concept "animal." Associative memory models suggest that thinking about a particular concept leads to recall of related concepts. For example, seeing a bird in the distance could activate our recollections of "robin," which in turn might activate recall of related concepts such as "eats worms" and "has a red breast." Activating one memory triggers the activation of related memories in a process known as *spreading activation*.

Associative memory models help account for **priming,** a phenomenon in which exposure to a word or concept (called a *prime*) later makes it easier to recall related information. Priming effects occur even when people have no conscious memory of the original word or concept (Tulving & Schacter, 1990; Toth & Reingold, 1996; Schacter, 1998).

The typical experiment designed to illustrate priming helps clarify the phenomenon. In priming experiments, participants are rapidly exposed to a stimulus such as a word, an object, or perhaps a drawing of a face. The second phase of the experiment is held after an interval ranging from several seconds to several months. At that point, participants are exposed to incomplete perceptual information that is related to the first stimulus, and they are asked whether they recognize it. For example, the new material might consist of the first letter of a word that had been presented earlier, or a part of a face that had been shown earlier. If participants are able to identify the stimulus more readily than they identify stimuli that have not been presented earlier, priming has taken place.

Priming occurs even when participants report no conscious awareness of having been exposed to a stimulus earlier. For instance, studies have found that people who are anesthetized during surgery can sometimes recall snippets of information that they heard during surgery—even though they have no conscious recollection of the information (Kihlstrom et al., 1990; Sebel, Bonke, & Winogard, 1993).

The discovery that people have memories about which they are unaware has been an important one. It has led to speculation that two forms of memory, explicit and implicit, might exist side-by-side. **Explicit memory** refers to intentional or conscious recollection of information. When we try to remember a name or date that we have

associative models of memory: Models suggesting that memory consists of mental representations of clusters of interconnected information

priming: A phenomenon in which exposure to a word or concept (called a *prime*) later makes it easier to recall related information, even when one has no conscious memory of the word or concept

explicit memory: Intentional or conscious recollection of information

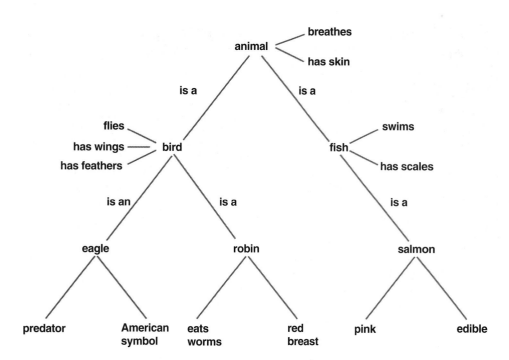

Figure 7-6 Associative models suggest that semantic memory consists of relationships between pieces of information, such as those relating to the concept of "animal," shown in this figure. (After Collins & Quillian, 1969.)

encountered or learned about previously, we are using explicit memory. In contrast, **implicit memory** refers to memories people are not consciously aware of, but that can affect their subsequent performance and behavior. Skills that operate automatically and without thinking, such as jumping out of the path of an automobile coming toward us as we walk down the side of a road, are stored in implicit memory. Similarly, a feeling of vague dislike for an acquaintance, when we don't know why we have that feeling, could be a reflection of implicit memories. In short, when an event that we are unable to consciously recall affects our behavior, implicit memory is at work (Graf & Masson, 1993; Schacter, Chiu, & Ochsner, 1993; Schacter, 1994b, 1995; Underwood, 1996; Tulving, 2000).

implicit memory: Memories people are not consciously aware of, but that can affect their subsequent performance and behavior

The Multiple Models of Memory

We've seen that the way that memory is viewed has been expanded from the three-stage model of memory. Although the traditional view of memory has not been rejected, contemporary views take a broader approach, considering memory in terms of multiple interdependent systems, operating simultaneously, that are responsible for different types of recall. Moreover, greater emphasis has been placed on working memory, in an effort to determine how different types of information can be simultaneously stored and processed.

You might be asking which of these views of memory is most accurate. It's a fair question, but one that is not easily answered at this point. More than most areas of psychology, memory has attracted a great deal of theorizing, and it is probably too early to tell—let alone remember—which of the multiple models proposed by different memory psychologists gives us the most accurate characterization of memory (Collins et al., 1993; Searleman & Herrmann, 1994; Wolters, 1995; Bjork & Bjork, 1996; Conway, 1997).

 **PsychLink**

Implicit memory issues
www.mhhe.com/
feldmanup6-07links

Evaluate

1. Match the type of memory with its definition:
   1. Long-term memory   a. Holds information 15 to 25 seconds
   2. Short-term memory   b. Can be difficult to retrieve
   3. Sensory memory   c. Direct representation of a stimulus
2. A _____ is a meaningful group of stimuli that can be stored together in short-term memory.
3. _____ are strategies used to organize information for retrieval.
4. There appear to be two types of long-term memory: _____ memory, for knowledge and facts, and _____ memory, for personal experiences.
5. _____ models of memory state that long-term memory is stored as associations between pieces of information.

Answers to Evaluate Questions

1. 1-b; 2-a; 3-c 2. chunk 3. Mnemonics 4. semantic; episodic 5. Associative

Rethink

1. It is a truism that "you never forget how to ride a bicycle." Why might this be so? Where is information about bicycle riding stored? What happens when a person has to retrieve that information after not using it for a long time?
2. Priming often occurs without conscious awareness. How might this effect be used by advertisers and others to promote their products? What ethical principles are involved? Can you think of a way to protect yourself from unethical advertisers?

Prepare

What causes difficulties and failures in remembering?

Organize

Recalling Long-Term Memories
    Retrieval Cues
    Levels of Processing
    Flashbulb Memories
    Constructive Processes in Memory
    Memory in the Courtroom
    Autobiographical Memory

Recalling Long-Term Memories

An hour after his job interview, Ricardo was sitting in a coffee shop, telling his friend Laura how well it had gone, when the woman who had interviewed him walked in. "Well, hello, Ricardo. How are you doing?" Trying to make a good impression, Ricardo began to make introductions, but suddenly realized he could not remember the name of the interviewer. Stammering, he desperately searched his memory, but to no avail. "I *know* her name," he thought to himself, "but here I am, looking like a fool. I can kiss this job goodbye."

Have you ever tried to remember someone's name, convinced that you knew it, but were unable to recall it no matter how hard you tried? This common occurrence—known as the **tip-of-the-tongue phenomenon**—exemplifies the difficulties that can occur in retrieving information stored in long-term memory (Smith, 1994; Riefer, Keveri, & Kramer, 1995; Schwartz et al., 2000).

Retrieval Cues

One reason recall is not perfect is the sheer quantity of recollections stored in long-term memory. Although the issue is far from settled, many psychologists have suggested that the material that makes its way to long-term memory is relatively permanent (Tulving & Psotka, 1971). If they are correct, this suggests that the capacity of long-term memory is vast, given the broad range of people's experiences and educational backgrounds. For instance, if you are like the average college student, your vocabulary includes some 50,000 words, you know hundreds of mathematical "facts," and you are able to conjure up images—such as the way your childhood home looked—with no trouble at all. In fact, simply cataloging all your memories would probably take years of work.

How do we sort through this vast array of material and retrieve specific information at the appropriate time? One of the major ways is through the use of retrieval cues. A *retrieval cue* is a stimulus that allows us to recall more easily information that is located in long-term memory (Tulving & Thompson, 1973; Ratcliff & McKoon, 1989). It could be a word, an emotion, a sound; whatever the specific cue, a memory will suddenly come

The tip-of-the-tongue phenomenon is especially frustrating in situations in which a person cannot recall the name of someone he or she has just met. Can you think of ways to avoid this common occurrence?

to mind when the retrieval cue is present. For example, the smell of roasting turkey might evoke memories of Thanksgiving or family gatherings (Schab & Crowder, 1995).

Retrieval cues guide people through the information stored in long-term memory in much the same way as the cards in an old-fashioned card catalog guided people through a library, or a search engine like Yahoo! guides people through the World Wide Web. They are particularly important when we are making an effort to *recall* information, as opposed to being asked to *recognize* material stored in memory. In *recall,* a specific piece of information must be retrieved—such as that needed to answer a fill-in-the-blank question or write an essay on a test. In contrast, *recognition* occurs when people are presented with a stimulus and asked whether they have been exposed to it previously, or are asked to identify it from a list of alternatives.

As you might guess, recall is generally a more difficult task than recognition (the task in Figure 7-7 is more difficult than the task in Figure 7-8). Recall is more difficult because it consists of a series of processes: a search through memory, retrieval of potentially relevant information, and then a decision regarding whether or not the information you have found is accurate. If the information appears correct, the search is over, but if it does not, the search must continue. On the other hand, recognition is simpler because it involves fewer steps (Anderson & Bower, 1972; Miserando, 1991).

Levels of Processing

One determinant of how well memories are recalled is the way in which material is first perceived, processed, and understood. **Levels-of-processing theory** emphasizes the degree to which new material is mentally analyzed (Craik & Lockhart, 1972; Craik, 1990). Levels-of-processing theory suggests that the amount of information processing that occurs when material is initially encountered is central in determining how much of the information is ultimately remembered. According to this approach, the depth of information processing during exposure to material—meaning the degree to which it is analyzed and considered—is critical; the greater the intensity of its initial processing, the more likely we are to remember it.

Because we do not pay close attention to much of the information to which we are exposed, typically only scant mental processing takes place, and we forget new material almost immediately. However, information to which we pay greater attention is processed more thoroughly. Therefore, it enters memory at a deeper level—and is less apt to be forgotten than information processed at shallower levels.

The theory goes on to suggest that there are considerable differences in the ways information is processed at various levels of memory. At shallow levels, information is processed merely in terms of its physical and sensory aspects. For example, we might pay attention only to the shapes that make up the letters in the word *dog.* At an intermediate level of processing, the shapes are translated into meaningful units—in this case, letters of the alphabet. These letters are considered in the context of words, and specific phonetic sounds might be attached to the letters.

At the deepest level of processing, information is analyzed in terms of its meaning. We might see it in a wider context and draw associations between the meaning of the information and broader networks of knowledge. For instance, we might think of dogs not merely as animals with four legs and a tail, but in terms of their relationship to cats and other mammals. We could form an image of our own dog, thereby relating the concept to our own lives. According to the levels-of-processing approach, the

Figure 7-7 Try to recall the names of these characters. Because it is a recall task, it is relatively difficult.

tip-of-the-tongue phenomenon: The inability to recall information that one realizes one knows—a result of the difficulty of retrieving information from long-term memory

levels-of-processing theory: The theory of memory that emphasizes the degree to which new material is mentally analyzed

---

Answer this recognition question:

Which of the following are the names of the seven dwarfs in the Disney movie *Snow White and the Seven Dwarfs*?

Goofy	Bashful
Sleepy	Meanie
Smarty	Doc
Scaredy	Happy
Dopey	Angry
Grumpy	Sneezy
Wheezy	Crazy

Figure 7-8 The recognition problem posed above is considerably easier than the recall task in the previous figure.

deeper the initial level of processing of specific information, the longer the information will be retained.

Levels-of-processing theory has considerable practical implications. For example, the depth at which information is processed is critical when learning and studying course material. Rote memorization of a list of key terms for a test is unlikely to produce long-term recollection of information, because it involves only a shallow level of processing. In contrast, thinking about the meanings of the terms and reflecting on how they relate to other information you know is a far more effective route to long-term retention.

Flashbulb Memories

Where were you on October 3, 1995? You will most likely draw a blank until this piece of information is added: October 3, 1995, was the day the O. J. Simpson verdict of not guilty was announced by the jury.

You probably have little trouble recalling your exact location and a variety of trivial details about your surroundings when you heard the news, even though the incident happened years ago. The reason is a phenomenon known as flashbulb memory. **Flashbulb memories** are memories of a specific, important, or surprising event that are so vivid, they are like a snapshot of the event.

Several types of flashbulb memories are common among college students, including involvement in a car accident, meeting one's roommate for the first time, and the night of high school graduation (Rubin, 1985; see Figure 7-9).

Of course, flashbulb memories do not contain every detail of an original scene. For instance, I remember vividly that some four decades ago I was sitting in Mr. Sharp's tenth-grade geometry class when I heard that President John Kennedy had been shot.

flashbulb memories: Memories of a specific, important, or surprising event that are so vivid, they are like a snapshot of the event

PsychLink

Role of flashbulb memories
www.mhhe.com/
feldmanup6-07links

Figure 7-9 These are the most common flashbulb memories, based on a survey of college students (Rubin, 1985). What are some of your flashbulb memories?

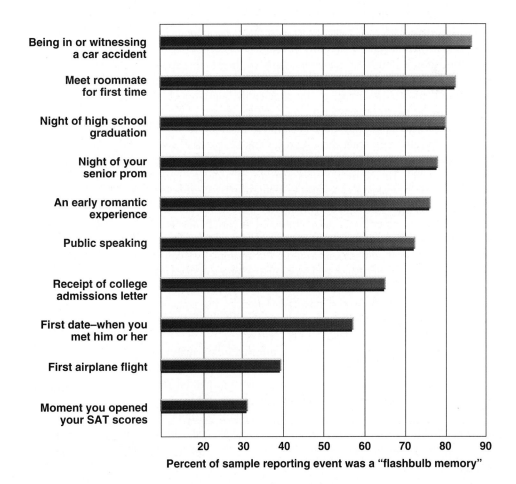

Percent of sample reporting event was a "flashbulb memory"

However, although I recall where I was sitting and how my classmates reacted to the news, I do not recollect what I was wearing or what I had for lunch that day.

Furthermore, the details recalled in flashbulb memories are often inaccurate. For example, three days after the O. J. Simpson verdict was announced, a group of college students were asked how they had heard the news. When the same people were asked the identical question 15 months later, half the recollections were highly accurate, with only 11 percent containing major errors. But after 32 months, less than a third of the recollections were highly accurate, and over 40 percent had major distortions (Schmolck, Buffalo, & Squire, 2000; Winningham, Hyman & Dinnel, 2000).

Flashbulb memories illustrate a more general phenomenon about memory: Memories that are exceptional are more easily retrieved (although not necessarily accurately) than those relating to events that are commonplace. The more distinctive a stimulus, then, the more likely we are to recall it later (von Restorff, 1933; Winningham, Hyman, & Dinnel, 2000).

Constructive Processes in Memory: Rebuilding the Past

As we have seen, although it is clear that we can have detailed recollections of significant and distinctive events, it is difficult to gauge the accuracy of such memories. In fact, it is apparent that our memories reflect, at least in part, **constructive processes,** processes in which memories are influenced by the meaning that we give to events. When we retrieve information, then, the memory that is produced is affected not just by the direct prior experience we have had with the stimulus, but by our guesses and inferences about its meaning as well.

The notion that memory is based on constructive processes was first put forward by Sir Frederic Bartlett, a British psychologist. He suggested that people tend to remember information in terms of **schemas,** organized bodies of information stored in memory that bias the way new information is interpreted, stored, and recalled (Bartlett, 1932). Our reliance on schemas means that memories often consist of a general reconstruction of previous experience. Bartlett argued that schemas are based not only on the specific material to which people are exposed, but also on their understanding of the situation, their expectations about the situation, and their awareness of the motivations underlying the behavior of others.

One of the earliest demonstrations of schemas came from a classic study that involved a procedure similar to the children's game of "telephone," in which information from memory is passed sequentially from one person to another. In the study, a participant viewed a drawing of a variety of people of differing racial and ethnic backgrounds on a subway car, one of whom—a white person—was shown with a razor in his hand (Allport & Postman, 1958). The first participant was asked to describe the drawing to someone else without looking back at it. Then that person was asked to describe it to another person (without looking at the drawing), and then the process was repeated with still one more participant.

The report of the last person differed in significant, yet systematic, ways from the initial drawing. Specifically, many people described the drawing as depicting an African American with a knife—an incorrect recollection. The transformation of the Caucasian's razor into an African American's knife clearly indicates that participants held a schema that included the unwarranted prejudice that African Americans are more violent than Caucasians and thus more apt to be holding a knife.

In short, our expectations and knowledge affect the reliability of our memories (Katz, 1989; Ross & Newby, 1996; McDonald & Hirt, 1997). Sometimes the imperfections of people's recollections can have profound implications, as we see when we consider memory in the legal realm.

Memory in the Courtroom: The Eyewitness on Trial

For William Jackson, the inadequate memories of two people cost him five years of his life. Jackson was the victim of mistaken identity when two witnesses picked him out of a lineup as the perpetrator of a crime. On that basis, he was convicted and sentenced to serve fourteen to fifty years in jail.

constructive processes: Processes in which memories are influenced by the meaning we give to events

schemas: Organized bodies of information stored in memory that bias the way new information is interpreted, stored, and recalled

Five years later the actual criminal was identified, and Jackson was released. For Jackson, though, it was too late. In his words, "They took away part of my life, part of my youth. I spend five years down there, and all they said was 'we're sorry' " (*Time*, 1982).

Unfortunately, Jackson is not the only victim to whom apologies have had to be made; there have been many cases of mistaken identity that have led to unjustified legal actions. Research on eyewitness identification of suspects, as well as on memory for other details of crimes, has shown that witnesses are apt to make substantial errors when they try to recall details of criminal activity (Miller, 2000; Wells et al., 2000).

One reason is the impact of weapons used in crimes. When a criminal perpetrator displays a gun or knife, it acts like a perceptual magnet attracting the eyes of the witnesses. As a consequence, witnesses pay less attention to other details of the crime and are less able to recall what actually occurred (Loftus, Loftus, & Messo, 1987; Steblay, 1992).

Even when weapons are not involved, eyewitnesses are prone to errors relating to memory. For instance, viewers of a twelve-second film of a mugging that was shown on a New York City television news program were later given the opportunity to pick out the assailant from a six-person lineup (Buckhout, 1975). Of some two thousand viewers who called the station after the program, only 15 percent were able to pick out the right person—a percentage similar to random guessing.

One reason eyewitnesses are prone to memory-related errors is that the specific wording of questions posed to them by police or attorneys can affect the way they recall information, as a number of experiments illustrate. For example, in one experiment participants were shown a film of two cars crashing into each other. Some were then asked the question, "About how fast were the cars going when they *smashed* into each other?" On average, they estimated the speed to be 40.8 miles per hour. In contrast, when another group of participants was asked, "About how fast were the cars going when they *contacted* each other?" the average estimated speed was only 31.8 miles per hour (Loftus & Palmer, 1974; see Figure 7-10).

The problem of memory reliability becomes even more acute when children are witnesses, because increasing evidence suggests that children's memories are highly vulnerable to the influence of others (Loftus, 1993; Cassel, Roebers, & Bjorklund, 1996). For instance, in one experiment, 5- to 7-year-old girls who had just had a routine physical examination were shown an anatomically explicit doll. The girls were shown the doll's genital area and asked, "Did the doctor touch you here?" Three of the girls who

Figure 7-10 After viewing an accident involving two cars, subjects were asked to estimate the speed of the collision. Estimates varied substantially, depending on the way the question was worded (Loftus & Palmer, 1974).

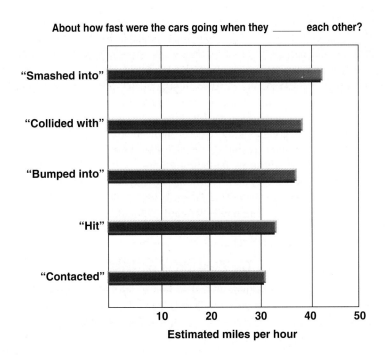

Applying Psychology in the 21st Century

Repressed Memories: Truth or Fiction?

Guilty of murder in the first degree.

That was the jury's verdict in the case of George Franklin, Sr., who was charged with murdering his daughter's playmate. But this case was different from most other murder cases: It was based on memories that had been repressed for twenty years. Franklin's daughter claimed that she had forgotten everything she had once known about her father's crime until two years earlier, when she began to have flashbacks of the event. Gradually, though, the memories became clearer in her mind, until she recalled her father lifting a rock over his head and then seeing her friend lying on the ground, covered with blood. On the basis of her memories, her father was convicted—but then later cleared of the crime following an appeal of the conviction.

Although the prosecutor and jury clearly believed Franklin's daughter, there is good reason to question the validity of *repressed memories,* recollections of events that are initially so shocking that the mind responds by pushing them into the unconscious. Supporters of the notion of repressed memory (who draw on Freud's psychoanalytic theory, first discussed in Chapter 1) suggest that such memories can remain hidden, possibly throughout a person's lifetime, unless they are triggered by some current circumstance, such as the probing that occurs during psychological therapy.

However, memory researcher Elizabeth Loftus (1997, 1998) maintains that so-called repressed memories can well be inaccurate or even wholly false—representing *false memory.* For example, false memories develop when people are unable

As the result of testimony from Eileen Franklin, based on repressed memory, her father was found guilty of murder. The validity of repressed memory, especially in investigating crimes, remains controversial. Can you think of a test to tell whether a recovered memory is accurate or not?

to recall the source of a memory of a particular event about which they have only vague recollections. When the source of the memory becomes unclear or ambiguous, people become confused about whether they actually experienced the event or whether they imagined it. Ultimately, people come to believe that the event actually occurred (Schacter, 1999a; Clancy et al., 2000).

In fact, some therapists have been accused of accidentally encouraging people who come to them with psychological difficulties to recreate false chronicles of childhood sexual experiences. Furthermore, the publicity surrounding well-publicized declarations of supposed repressed memories, such as those of people who claim to be the victims of satanic rituals, makes the possibility of repressed memories seem more legitimate and ultimately might prime people to

recall "memories" of events that never happened (Lynn, 1997).

The controversy regarding the legitimacy of repressed memories is unlikely to be resolved soon. Many psychologists, particularly those who provide therapy, give great weight to the reality of repressed memories. On the other side of the issue are many memory researchers, who maintain that there is no scientific support for the existence of such memories. The challenge for those on both sides of the issue is to distinguish truth from fiction (Brown & Pope, 1996; Pezdek & Banks, 1996; Loftus, 1997; Walcott, 2000).

Can you think of any way to determine which details of a repressed memory are true and which are false? How do you think attorneys and psychologists go about establishing the accuracy or inaccuracy of repressed memories of allegedly criminal actions?

did not have a vaginal or anal exam said that the doctor had in fact touched them in the genital area. And one of those three made up the detail, "The doctor did it with a stick" (Saywitz & Goodman, 1990).

Children's memories are especially susceptible to influence when the situation is highly emotional or stressful. For example, in trials in which there is significant pretrial publicity or where alleged victims are repeatedly questioned, often by untrained interviewers, the memories of alleged victims can be influenced by the type of questions they are asked.

In short, the memories of witnesses are far from reliable, and this is especially true when children are involved (Howe, 1999). The question of the accuracy of memories becomes even more complex, however, when we consider the triggering of memories of events that people at first don't even recall happening. As we discuss in the *Applying Psychology in the 21ˢᵗ Century* box, this issue has raised considerable controversy.

PsychLink

False memory discussion
www.mhhe.com/
feldmanup6-07links

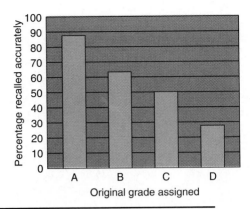

Figure 7-11 We distort memories for unpleasant events. For example, college students are much more likely to accurately recall their good grades, while inaccurately recalling their poor ones (Bahrick, Hall, & Berger, 1996). Now that you know this, how well do you think you can recall your own high school grades?

autobiographical memories: Our recollections of circumstances and episodes from our own lives

Autobiographical Memory: Where Past Meets Present

Your memory of experiences in your own past might well be a fiction—or at least a distortion of what actually occurred. The same constructive processes that act to make us inaccurately recall the behavior of others also reduce the accuracy of autobiographical memories. **Autobiographical memories** are our recollections of circumstances and episodes from our own lives. Autobiographical memories encompass the episodic memories we hold about ourselves (Stein et al., 1997; Rubin, 1999).

For example, we tend to forget information about our past that is incompatible with how we currently see ourselves. One study found that adults who were well adjusted but who had been treated for emotional problems during the early years of their lives tended to forget important but troubling childhood events, such as being in foster care. College students tend to misremember their bad grades—but remember their good ones (see Figure 7-11; Robbins, 1988; Bahrick, Hall, & Berger, 1996; Stein et al., 1996).

It is not just certain kinds of events that are distorted; particular periods of life are remembered more easily than others. For example, when people reach old age, they remember periods of life in which they experienced major transitions, such as attending college or working at their first job, better than their middle-age years (Rubin, 1985; Newcombe et al., 2000).

EXPLORING DIVERSITY

Are There Cross-Cultural Differences in Memory?

Travelers who have visited areas of the world in which there is no written language often have returned with tales of people with phenomenal memories. For instance, storytellers in some preliterate cultures can recount long chronicles that recall the names and activities of people over many generations. These feats initially led experts to argue that people in preliterate societies develop a different, and perhaps better, type of memory than those in cultures that employ a written language. They suggested that in a society that lacks writing, people are motivated to accurately recall information, particularly information relating to tribal histories and traditions that would be lost if they were not passed down orally from one generation to another (Bartlett, 1932; Cole & Gay, 1972; Rubin, 1995).

However, more recent approaches to cultural differences suggest a different conclusion. For one thing, preliterate peoples don't have an exclusive claim on amazing memory feats. For instance, some Hebrew scholars memorize thousands of pages of text and can recall the locations of particular words on the page. Similarly, poetry singers in Yugoslavia can recall thousands of lines of poetry. Even in cultures in which written language exists, then, astounding feats of memory are possible (Neisser, 1982).

Memory researchers now suggest that there are both similarities and differences in memory across cultures. Basic memory processes such as short-term memory capacity and the structure of long-term memory—the "hardware" of memory—are universal and operate similarly in people of all cultures (Wagner, 1981). In contrast, differences can be seen in how information is acquired and rehearsed—the "software" of memory. Culture determines how people frame information initially, how much they practice learning and recalling it, and the strategies they use to try to recall it.

Storytellers in many cultures can recount hundreds of years of history in vivid detail. Research has found that this amazing ability is due less to basic memory processes than to the ways in which they acquire and retain information.

Evaluate

1. While with a group of friends at a dance, Eva bumps into a man she dated last month. When she tries to introduce him to her friends, she cannot remember his name. What is the term for this?

2. _____ is used when a person is asked to retrieve a specific item from memory.

3. Your mother's friend tells you, "I know exactly where I was and what I was doing when I heard that John Lennon died." What phenomenon explains this type of recollection?

4. The same person could probably also accurately describe in detail what she was wearing when she heard about John Lennon's death, right down to the color of her shoes. True or false?

5. _____ are organized bodies of information stored in memory that bias the way new information is interpreted, stored, and recalled.

6. _____ theory states that the more a person analyzes a statement, the more likely he or she is to remember it later.

Rethink

1. How do schemas help people process information during encoding, storage, and retrieval? In what ways are they helpful? Can they contribute to inaccurate autobiographical memories?

2. How might courtroom procedure be improved, based on what you've learned about memory errors and biases?

Answers to Evaluate Questions

1. Tip-of-the-tongue phenomenon 2. Recall 3. Flashbulb memory 4. False; small details probably won't be remembered through flashbulb memory. 5. Schemas 6. Levels-of-processing

Forgetting: When Memory Fails

He could remember, quite literally, nothing—nothing, that is, that had happened since the loss of his brain's temporal lobes and hippocampus during experimental surgery to reduce epileptic seizures. Until that time, his memory had been quite normal. But after the operation he was unable to recall anything for more than a few minutes, and then the memory was seemingly lost forever. He did not remember his address, or the name of the person to whom he was talking. He would read the same magazine over and over again. According to his own description, his life was like waking from a dream and being unable to know where he was or how he got there. (Milner, 1966)

Prepare

Why do we forget information?
What are the biological bases of memory?
What are the major memory impairments?

Organize

Forgetting
   Proactive and Retroactive Interference
   The Biological Bases of Memory
   Memory Dysfunctions

As this case illustrates, a person without a normal memory faces severe difficulties. All of us who have experienced even routine instances of forgetting—such as not remembering an acquaintance's name or a fact on a test—understand the very real consequences of memory failure.

The first attempts to study forgetting were made by German psychologist Hermann Ebbinghaus about a hundred years ago. Using himself as the only participant in his study, he memorized lists of three-letter nonsense syllables—meaningless sets of two consonants with a vowel in between, such as FIW and BOZ. By measuring how easy it was to relearn a given list of words after varying periods of time had passed since initial learning, he found that forgetting occurred systematically, as shown in Figure 7-12. As the figure indicates, the most rapid forgetting occurs in the first nine hours, and particularly in the first hour. After nine hours, the rate of forgetting slows and declines little, even after the passage of many days.

Despite his primitive methods, Ebbinghaus's study had an important influence on subsequent research, and his basic conclusions have been upheld (Wixted & Ebbesen, 1991). There is almost always a strong initial decline in memory, followed by a more gradual drop over time. Furthermore, relearning of previously mastered material is almost always faster than starting from scratch, whether the material is academic information or a motor skill such as serving a tennis ball.

Why do we forget? One reason is that we might not have paid attention to the material in the first place—a failure of *encoding*. For example, if you live in the United States, you have surely been exposed to thousands of pennies during your life. Despite this experience, you probably don't have a clear picture of the details of the coin. (See

Figure 7-12 In his classic work, Ebbinghaus found that the most rapid forgetting occurs in the first nine hours after exposure to new material. However, the rate of forgetting then slows down and declines very little even after many days have passed. (Ebbinghaus, 1885.) Check your own memory: What were you doing exactly two hours ago? What were you doing last Tuesday at 5 P.M.? Which information is easier to retrieve?

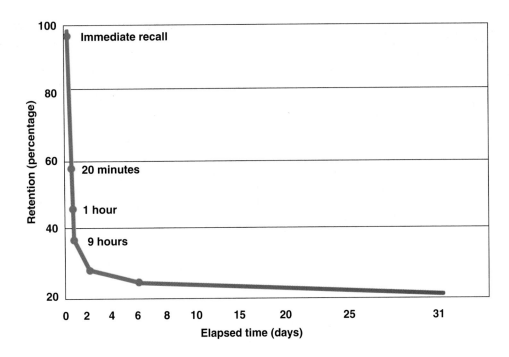

this yourself by looking at Figure 7-13.) Consequently, the reason for your memory failure is that you probably never encoded the information into long-term memory initially. Obviously, if information hasn't been placed in memory initially, there is no way that the information can be recalled.

But what about material that has been encoded into memory and that can't later be remembered? Two major processes account for memory failures: decay and interference.

Decay is the loss of information through nonuse. This explanation for forgetting assumes that when new material is learned, a **memory trace**—a physical change in the brain—appears. In decay, the trace simply fades away with nothing left behind, because of the mere passage of time.

Although there is evidence that decay does occur, this does not seem to be the complete explanation for forgetting. Often there is no relationship between how long ago

decay: The loss of information in memory through its nonuse

memory trace: A physical change in the brain that occurs when new material is learned

Figure 7-13 One of these pennies is the real thing. Can you find it? Why is this task harder than it seems at first? (Nickerson & Adams, 1979.)

If you don't know the answer—and don't have a penny to check against—the correct answer is a.

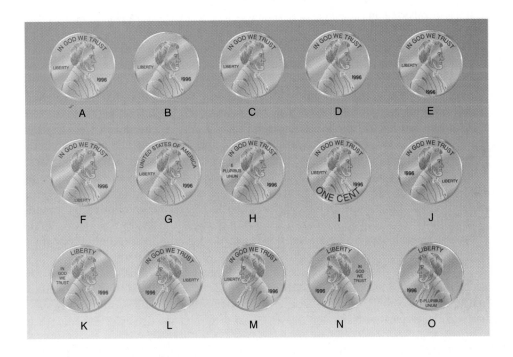

a person was exposed to information and how well it is recalled. If decay explained all forgetting, we would expect that the longer the time between the initial learning of information and our attempt to recall it, the harder it would be to remember it, because there would be more time for the memory trace to decay. Yet people who take several consecutive tests on the same material often recall more of the initial information when taking later tests than they did on earlier tests. If decay were operating, we would expect the opposite to occur (Payne, 1986).

Because decay does not fully account for forgetting, memory specialists have proposed an additional mechanism: **interference.** In interference, information in memory displaces or blocks out other information, preventing its recall.

To distinguish between decay and interference, think of the two processes in terms of a row of books on a library shelf. In decay, the old books are constantly crumbling and rotting away, leaving room for new arrivals. In interference, new books knock the old ones off the shelf, where they become inaccessible.

Most research suggests that interference is the key process in forgetting (Mel'nikov, 1993; Bower, Thompson, & Tulving, 1994). We mainly forget things because new memories interfere with the retrieval of old ones, not because the memory trace has decayed.

interference: The phenomenon by which information in memory displaces or blocks out other information, preventing its recall

Proactive and Retroactive Interference: The Before and After of Forgetting

There are actually two sorts of interference that influence forgetting: proactive and retroactive. In *proactive interference,* information learned earlier interferes with recall of newer material. Suppose, as a student of foreign languages, you first learned French in tenth grade, and then in eleventh grade you took Spanish. When in twelfth grade you took a college achievement test in Spanish, you might have found you had difficulty recalling the Spanish translation of a word because all you could think of was its French equivalent.

On the other hand, *retroactive interference* refers to difficulty in recall of information because of later exposure to different material. If, for example, you have difficulty on a French achievement test because of your more recent exposure to Spanish, retroactive interference is the culprit (see Figure 7-14). One way to remember the difference between proactive and retroactive interference is to keep in mind that *pro*active interference progresses in time—the past interferes with the present—whereas *retro*active interference retrogresses in time, working backward as the present interferes with the past.

Although the concepts of proactive and retroactive interference suggest why material might be forgotten, they still do not explain whether forgetting due to interference is caused by actual loss or modification of information, or by problems in the retrieval of information. Most research suggests that material that has apparently been lost because of interference can eventually be recalled if appropriate stimuli are presented (Tulving & Psotka, 1971; Anderson, 1981), but the question has not been fully answered. In an effort to resolve the issue, some psychologists have begun to study the biological bases of memory in order to better understand what is remembered and what is forgotten—an increasingly important avenue of investigation that we turn to now.

The Biological Bases of Memory

What are the biological foundations of memory? One answer comes from work on *long-term potentiation,* which shows that certain neural pathways become easily excited while a new

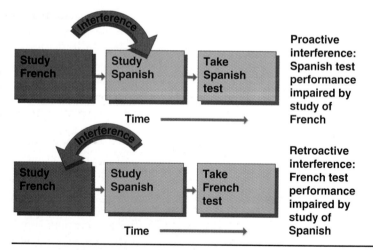

Figure 7-14 Proactive interference occurs when material learned earlier interferes with recall of newer material. In this example, studying French before studying Spanish interferes with performance on a Spanish test. In contrast, retroactive interference exists when material learned after initial exposure to other material interferes with the recall of the first material. In this case, retroactive interference occurs when recall of French is impaired because of later exposure to Spanish.

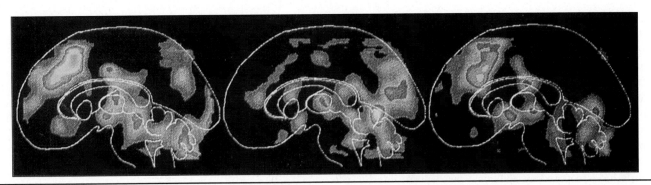

Figure 7-15 PET scans of a subject in an experiment who was first asked to read a list of nouns and produce a related verb (left scan). When asked to repeatedly carry out the task with the same list of nouns, different areas of the brain became active (center). However, when the subject was given a new list of nouns, the regions of the brain that were initially involved became reactivated (right). (Peterson, 1993.)

response is being learned. At the same time, changes occur in the number of synapses between neurons as the dendrites branch out to receive messages. These changes reflect a process called *consolidation,* in which memories become fixed and stable in long-term memory. Long-term memories take some time to stabilize, explaining why events and other stimuli are not suddenly fixed in memory. Instead, consolidation can continue for days and even years (Johnston, 1997; McGaugh, 2000).

Furthermore, the location of *memory traces,* the physical record of memory in the brain, depends on the nature of the material being learned and the specific neural systems that process the information when it is first learned. For a stimulus that contains different sensory aspects, visual, auditory, and other areas of the brain might be simultaneously involved in processing information about that stimulus. Information storage appears to be linked to the sites in which this processing occurs, and is therefore located in the particular areas that initially processed the information in terms of its visual, auditory, and other sensory stimuli.

In short, because several brain processing systems are involved in any learning situation, memory traces are distributed throughout the brain (Desimone, 1992; Squire, 1993; Brewer et al., 1998). Investigators using PET scans, which measure biochemical activity in the brain, also have found that neuronal memory traces are highly specialized. For instance, participants in one experiment were given a list of nouns to read aloud. After reading each noun, they were asked to suggest a related verb. After reading the noun *dog,* for example, they might have proposed the verb *bark.*

Several distinct areas of the brain showed increased neural activity as participants first did the task (see Figure 7-15). However, if they repeated the task with the same nouns several times, the activity in the brain shifted to another area. Most interestingly, if they were given a new list of nouns, the activity in the brain returned to the areas that were initially activated.

The results suggest that a particular part of the brain is involved in the production of words, but another part takes over when the process becomes routine—in other words, when memory comes into play. It also suggests that memory is distributed in the brain not just in terms of its content, but in terms of its function (Horgan, 1993; Corbetta et al., 1993; Petersen & Fiez, 1993).

Certain areas and structures of the brain also seem to specialize in different types of memory-related activities. For example, working memory relating to spatial tasks appears to reside in the frontal cortex. In addition, the *hippocampus,* a small, curved structure that is part of the brain's limbic system (discussed in Chapter 3 and illustrated in Figure 7-16) plays a central role in the consolidation of memories. The hippocampus aids in the initial encoding of information, passing material along to the cerebral cortex of the brain (Smith & Jonides, 1999; Smith, 2000; Tulving & Craik, 2000).

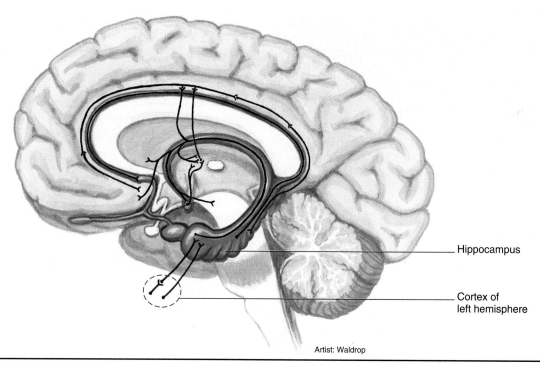

Hippocampus

Cortex of
left hemisphere

Artist: Waldrop

Figure 7-16 The hippocampus, part of the brain's limbic system, plays a central role in the consolidation of memories. (Van De Graff, 2000.)

Memory Dysfunctions: Afflictions of Forgetting

First you notice that you're always misplacing things, or that common nouns are evading you as stubbornly as the names of new acquaintances. Pretty soon you're forgetting appointments and getting flustered when you drive in traffic. On bad days you find you can't hold numbers in your mind long enough to dial the phone. You try valiantly to conceal your lapses, but they become ever more glaring. You crash your car. You spend whole mornings struggling to dress yourself properly. And even as you lose the ability to read or play the piano, you're painfully aware of what's happening to you. (Cowley, 2000, p. 46)

The problem is *Alzheimer's disease,* an illness that includes among its symptoms severe memory problems. Alzheimer's, discussed earlier in this chapter, is the fourth leading cause of death among adults in the United States. One in five people aged 75 to 84, and almost half of those 85 and older, have the disease.

In its initial stages, Alzheimer's symptoms appear as simple forgetfulness of things like appointments and birthdays. As the disease progresses, memory loss becomes more profound, and even the simplest tasks—such as how to dial a telephone—are forgotten. Ultimately, victims can lose their ability to speak or comprehend language, and physical deterioration sets in, leading to death.

The causes of Alzheimer's disease are not fully understood. However, increasing evidence suggests that it results from an inherited susceptibility to a defect in the production of the protein beta amyloid, necessary for the maintenance of nerve cell connections. When the manufacture of beta amyloid goes awry, large clumps of cells grow that trigger inflammation and the deterioration of nerve cells in the brain (Barinaga, 1999; Cowley, 2000; Cooper et al., 2000; see Figure 7-17).

Alzheimer's disease is just one of several memory dysfunctions that plague their victims. Another is *amnesia,* memory loss that occurs without other mental difficulties—the syndrome that affected Terry Dibert, described in the chapter opening prologue. The classic case involves a victim who receives a blow to the head and is unable to remember anything from his or her past. In reality, amnesia of this type, known as retrograde amnesia, is quite rare. In *retrograde amnesia,* memory is lost for occurrences prior to a

⟨⟩ **PsychLink**

Comprehensive Alzheimer's information
www.mhhe.com/
feldmanup6-07links

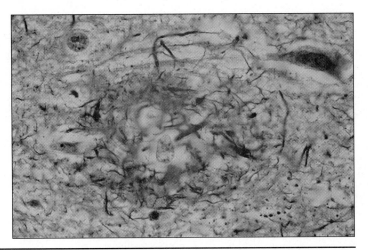

Figure 7-17 These tangles of neurons are characteristic of the damage found in the brains of people with Alzheimer's disease.

certain event. Usually, lost memories gradually reappear, although full restoration can take as long as several years. In certain cases, some memories are lost forever (Eich et al., 1997; Kapur, 1999).

A second type of amnesia is exemplified by people who remember nothing of their current activities. In *anterograde amnesia,* loss of memory occurs for events following an injury. Information cannot be transferred from short-term to long-term memory, resulting in the inability to remember anything other than what was in long-term storage prior to the accident.

Amnesia is also displayed by people who suffer from *Korsakoff's syndrome,* a disease afflicting long-term alcoholics. Although many of their intellectual abilities might be intact, Korsakoff's sufferers display a strange array of symptoms, including hallucinations and repetition of the same story over and over again.

Fortunately, most of us have intact memories, and the occasional failures we do suffer might be preferable to having a perfect memory. Consider, for instance, the case of a man who had total recall. After reading passages of the *Divine Comedy* in Italian—a language he did not speak—he was able to repeat them from memory even some fifteen years later. He could memorize lists of fifty unrelated words and recall them at will more than a decade later. He could even repeat the same list of words backward, if asked (Luria, 1968).

Such a skill might at first seem to be enviable, but it actually presented quite a problem. The man's memory became a jumble of lists of words, numbers, and names, and when he tried to relax, his mind was filled with images. Even reading was difficult, because every word evoked a flood of thoughts from the past that interfered with his ability to understand the meaning of what he was reading. Partially as a consequence of the man's unusual memory, psychologist A. R. Luria, who studied his case, found him to be a "disorganized and rather dull-witted person" (Luria, 1968, p. 65).

We may be grateful, then, that forgetfulness plays a role in our lives.

BECOMING AN INFORMED CONSUMER OF PSYCHOLOGY

Improving Your Memory

 **PsychLink**

Improving memory
www.mhhe.com/
feldmanup6-07links

Apart from the advantages of forgetting, say, a bad date, most of us still would like to find ways to improve our memories. Is it possible to find practical ways to increase our recall of information? Most definitely. Research has revealed a number of strategies that can be used to help us develop better memories (West, 1995; Herrmann et al., 1996; VanLehn, 1996). Among the best:

- *The keyword technique.* Suppose you are taking a foreign language class and need to learn vocabulary words. You can try using the *keyword technique,* in which a foreign word is paired with a common English word that has a similar *sound.* This English word is known as the keyword. For example, to remember the Spanish word for duck (*pato,* pronounced *pot-o*), you might choose the keyword *pot;* for the Spanish word for horse (*caballo,* pronounced *cob-eye-yo*), the keyword might be *eye.*

  Once you have thought of a keyword, imagine the Spanish word "interacting" with the English keyword. For instance, you might envision a duck taking a bath in a pot to remember the word *pato,* or a horse with a large, bulging eye in the center of its head to recall *caballo.* This technique has produced considerably superior results in learning foreign language vocabulary than more traditional techniques involving memorization of the words themselves (Pressley, 1987; Gruneberg & Pascoe, 1996; Carney & Levin, 1998).

- *Encoding specificity.* Some research suggests that we remember information best in an environment that is the same as or similar to where we initially learned it. This

phenomenon is known as *encoding specificity*. You might do better on a test, then, if you study in the classroom where the test will be given. On the other hand, if you must take a test in a different room from the one in which you studied, don't despair: The features of the test itself, such as the wording of the test questions, are sometimes so powerful that they overwhelm the subtler cues relating to the original encoding of the material (Bjork & Richardson-Klarehn, 1989).

- *Organization cues*. Many of life's important recall tasks involve texts that you have read. One proven technique for improving recall of written material is to organize the material in memory as you read it for the first time—one of the rationales for the *P.O.W.E.R. Learning* (prepare-organize-work-evaluate-rethink) system incorporated into this book.

    Organize your reading by using any advance information you have about the content of the material (the *prepare* questions in this book) and about its organization (outlined in the *organize* sections). This activity will enable you to make connections and see relationships among the various facts, and to process the material at a deeper level, which in turn will later aid recall.

- *Effective note-taking*. "Less is more" is perhaps the best advice for taking lecture notes that facilitate recall. Rather than trying to jot down every detail of a lecture, it is better to listen and think about the material, and take down the main points. In effective note taking, thinking about the material initially is more important than writing it down. This is one reason borrowing someone else's notes is a bad proposition, because you will have no framework in memory that you can use to understand them (Feldman, 2000).

- *Practice and rehearse*. Although practice does not necessarily make perfect, it helps. By studying and rehearsing material past initial mastery—a process called *overlearning*—people are able to show better long-term recall than if they stop practicing after their initial learning of the material. Keep in mind that, as research clearly demonstrates, fatigue and other factors prevent long practice sessions from being as effective as distributed practice.

- *Don't believe claims about drugs that improve memory*. Advertisements for One-A-Day vitamins with ginkgo biloba or Quanterra Mental Sharpness Product would have you believe that taking a drug could improve your memory. Not so, according to results of studies. No research has shown that commercial memory enhancers are effective (Meier, 1999). Save your money!

Evaluate

1. If, after learning the history of the Middle East for a class two years ago, you now find yourself unable to recall what you learned, you are experiencing memory _____, caused by nonuse.

2. Difficulty in accessing a memory because of the presence of other information is known as _____.

3. _____ interference occurs when material is difficult to retrieve because of exposure to later material. _____ interference refers to the difficulty in retrieving material due to the interference of previous material.

4. Match the following memory disorders with the correct information:

    1. Affects alcoholics; can result in hallucinations   a. Alzheimer's disease

    2. Memory loss occurring without other mental problems   b. Korsakoff's syndrome

    3. Beta amyloid defect; progressive forgetting and   c. Amnesia
       physical deterioration

Rethink

1. Does the phenomenon of interference help explain the unreliability of autobiographical memory? Why?

2. How might findings on the biological mechanisms of memory aid in the treatment of memory disorders such as amnesia?

Answers to Evaluate Questions

1. decay 2. interference 3. Retroactive; Proactive 4. a-3; b-1; c-2

Looking **Back**

What is memory?

- Memory is the process by which we encode, store, and retrieve information. There are three basic kinds of memory storage: sensory memory, short-term memory, and long-term memory. (p. 198)

Are there different kinds of memory?

- Sensory memory, corresponding to each of the sensory systems, is the first place where information is saved, although the memories are very brief. Despite their brevity, sensory memories are precise, storing a nearly exact replica of each stimulus to which a person is exposed. (p. 199)
- Roughly seven (plus or minus two) chunks of information are capable of being transferred and held in short-term memory. Information in short-term memory is held from fifteen to twenty-five seconds and, if not transferred to long-term memory, is lost. (p. 201)
- Memories are transferred into long-term storage through rehearsal. If memories are transferred into long-term memory, they become relatively permanent. (p. 202)
- Some theorists view short-term memory as a three-part working memory, an active "workspace" in which information is retrieved and manipulated, and held through rehearsal. In this view, there is a central executive, which coordinates the material to focus on during reasoning and decision making, and two subcomponents: the visual store and the verbal store. (p. 204)
- Newer memory models view long-term memory in terms of memory modules, each of which is related to separate memory systems in the brain. For instance, we can distinguish between declarative memory and procedural memory. Declarative memory is further divided into episodic memory and semantic memory. (p. 205)
- Associative models of memory suggest that memory consists of mental representations of clusters of interconnected information. (p. 206)
- Explicit memory refers to intentional or conscious recollection of information. In contrast, implicit memory refers to memories of which people are not consciously aware, but which can affect subsequent performance and behavior. (p. 206)

What causes difficulties and failures in remembering?

- The tip-of-the-tongue phenomenon refers to the experience of trying in vain to remember information that one is certain one knows. A major strategy for successfully recalling information is to use retrieval cues. (p. 208)
- The levels-of-processing approach to memory suggests that the way in which information is initially perceived and analyzed determines the success with which the information is recalled. The deeper the initial processing, the greater the recall of the material. (p. 209)
- Flashbulb memories are memories centered around a specific, important event. Flashbulb memories illustrate the broader point that the more distinctive a memory, the more easily it can be retrieved. (p. 210)
- Memory is a constructive process in which we relate memories to the meaning, guesses, and expectations that we give to the events the memory represents. Specific information is recalled in terms of schemas, organized bodies of information stored in memory that bias the way new information is interpreted, stored, and recalled. (p. 211)
- Eyewitnesses of crimes are apt to make substantial errors when they try to recall details of criminal activity. The problem of memory reliability becomes even more acute when the witnesses are children. (p. 211)
- Autobiographical memory, which refers to memories of circumstances and episodes from our own lives, is influenced by constructive processes. (p. 214)

Why do we forget information?

- Two major processes account for memory failures: decay and interference. Interference seems to be the major cause of forgetting. There are two sorts of interference: proactive interference and retroactive interference. (p. 215)

What are the biological bases of memory?

- Memories are distributed across the brain, relating to different information processing systems involved during the initial exposure to a stimulus. The hippocampus is particularly important in the establishment of memory. (p. 217)

What are the major memory impairments?

- Among the memory dysfunctions are Alzheimer's disease, which leads to a progressive loss of memory, and amnesia, a memory loss that occurs without other mental difficulties and that can take two forms: retrograde amnesia and anterograde amnesia. Korsakoff's syndrome is a disease that afflicts long-term alcoholics, resulting in memory impairment. (p. 219)
- Among the techniques for improving memory are the keyword technique to memorize foreign language vocabulary; using the encoding specificity phenomenon; organizing text material and lecture notes; and practice and rehearsal, leading to overlearning. (p. 220)

Key Terms and Concepts

memory (p. 198)
sensory memory (p. 199)
short-term memory (p. 199)
long-term memory (p. 199)
iconic memory (p. 200)
echoic memory (p. 200)
chunk (p. 201)
rehearsal (p. 202)
working memory (p. 204)
declarative memory (p. 205)
procedural memory (p. 205)
semantic memory (p. 205)
episodic memory (p. 205)
associative models (p. 206)

priming (p. 206)
explicit memory (p. 206)
implicit memory (p. 207)
tip-of-the-tongue phenomenon (p. 209)
levels-of-processing theory (p. 209)
flashbulb memories (p. 210)
constructive processes (p. 211)
schemas (p. 211)
autobiographical memories (p. 214)
decay (p. 216)
memory trace (p. 216)
interference (p. 217)

Psychology on the Web

1. The study of repressed memories can lead down unusual pathways—even more unusual than the criminal investigation pathway we discussed in this chapter. Two other areas in which repressed memories play a large part are alien abduction and reincarnation. Find two sources on the Web that deal with one of these issues— one supportive and one skeptical. Read what they say and relate it to your knowledge of memory. Summarize your findings and indicate which side of the controversy your study of memory leads you to favor.
2. Memory is a topic of serious interest to psychologists, but it is also a source of amusement. Find a website that focuses on the amusing side of memory (such as memory games, tests of recall, or lists of mnemonics; hint: there's even a mnemonics generator out there!). Write down the address of any interesting sites you encounter and summarize what you find there.

Preview

For additional
quizzing and a
variety of interactive
resources, visit the
*Understanding
Psychology* Online
Learning Center at

www.mhhe.com/feldmanup6

Epilogue

In this chapter we have taken a look at memory. We noted that memory comprises the processes of encoding, storage, and retrieval, and we saw that memory can be regarded as having different components. We also encountered several phenomena relating to memory, including the tip-of-the-tongue phenomenon and flashbulb memories. Above all we observed that memory is a constructive process by which interpretations, expectations, and guesses contribute to the nature of our memories.

Before we move on to the next chapter, return briefly to the prologue of this chapter, in which we encountered Terry Dibert and his lost memories of his past. Consider the following questions in light of what you know about memory.

1. Terry Dibert's memory loss is called "retrograde amnesia." What does this mean?
2. What would have been the effects on Dibert's life if his brain cyst had caused anterograde amnesia?
3. Despite his inability to recall recent events, Dibert's memories of older events seemed accurate. Based on what you know about memory, do you believe they were truly accurate? Why or why not?
4. How might investigators use Dibert's case to answer questions about the biological bases of memory? Assuming Dibert gave his consent to PET scans and other means of looking inside his cerebral cortex, what sorts of questions might be explored?

Chapter Eight

Thought and Language

Prologue: House Call in Space

Looking Ahead

Thinking and Reasoning

Mental Images: Examining the Mind's Eye

Concepts: Categorizing the World

Reasoning: Making Up Your Mind

Problem Solving

Preparation: Understanding and Diagnosing the Problem

Production: Generating Solutions

Judgment: Evaluating the Solutions

Impediments to Solutions: Why Is Problem Solving Such a Problem?

Creativity and Problem Solving

Becoming an Informed Consumer of Psychology: Thinking Critically and Creatively

Applying Psychology in the 21st Century: Can Computers Think Creatively?

Language

Grammar: Language's Language

Language Development: Developing a Way with Words

Understanding Language Acquisition: Identifying the Roots of Language

The Influence of Language on Thinking: Do Eskimos Have More Words for Snow Than Texans Have?

Exploring Diversity: Teaching with Linguistic Variety: Bilingual Education

Psychology at Work: Rose Sevcik, Language Researcher

Looking Back

Key Terms and Concepts

Psychology on the Web

OLC Preview

Epilogue

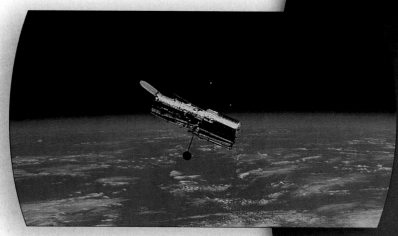

Many situations require problem-solving skills. The repair of the Hubble space telescope, however, demanded an extraordinary degree of problem-solving effort, which eventually led to a triumphant success.

Prologue

House Call in Space

It was a 1.5 billion dollar mistake—a blunder on a grand scale. The finely ground mirror of the Hubble space telescope, designed to provide an unprecedented glimpse into the vast reaches of the universe, was not so finely ground after all.

Despite a variety of quality-control procedures intended to catch any flaws, there was a tiny blemish in the mirror that was not detected until the telescope had been launched into space and started to send back blurry photographs. By then, it seemed too late to fix the mirror.

Or was it? NASA engineers pondered the problem for months, devising and discarding one potential solution after another. Finally, they formulated a daring solution that involved sending a team of astronauts into space. Once there, a space-walking Mr. Goodwrench would install several new mirrors in the telescope, which could refocus the light and compensate for the original flawed mirror.

Although the engineers could not be certain that the $630 million plan would work, it seemed like a good solution, at least on paper. It was not until the first photos were beamed back to earth, though, that NASA knew their solution was A-OK. These photos provided spectacular views of galaxies millions of light years from earth.

cognitive psychology: The branch of psychology that focuses on the study of cognition

thinking: The manipulation of mental representations of information

The repair of the Hubble telescope proved to be a moment of problem-solving triumph for the NASA engineers on the ground, as well as the astronauts in space. Overcoming the obstacles to a solution while working under enormous pressure, the engineers had succeeded in solving a difficult and risky problem. Their success illustrates how thoughtful and painstaking effort can lead to solutions in the face of formidable challenges.

Their accomplishment also raises a number of issues of central importance to psychologists: How do people use and retrieve information to devise innovative solutions to problems? How is such knowledge transformed, elaborated upon, and utilized? More basically, how do people think about, understand, and, through language, describe the world?

In this chapter we focus on **cognitive psychology,** the branch of psychology that focuses on the study of higher mental processes, including thinking, language, memory, problem solving, knowing, reasoning, judging, and decision making. Clearly, the realm of cognitive psychology is broad, and includes the research on memory examined in the previous chapter and much of the work on intelligence that we discuss in the next chapter.

In this chapter we concentrate on three broad topics that are central to the field of cognitive psychology: thinking and reasoning, problem solving and creativity, and language. We first consider concepts, the building blocks of thinking, and various kinds of reasoning. Then we examine different strategies for approaching problems, means of generating solutions, and ways of making judgments about the usefulness and accuracy of solutions. Finally, we consider how language is developed and acquired, its basic characteristics, and the relationship between language and thought.

Prepare

What is thinking?
What processes underlie reasoning and decision making?

Organize

Thinking and Reasoning
    Mental Images
    Concepts
    Reasoning

Thinking and Reasoning

What are you thinking about at this moment?

The mere ability to pose such a question underscores the distinctive nature of the human ability to think. No other species contemplates, analyzes, recollects, or plans as humans do. Understanding what thinking is, however, goes beyond knowing that we think. Philosophers, for example, have argued for generations about the meaning of thinking, with some placing it at the core of human beings' understanding of their own existence.

Psychologists define **thinking** as the manipulation of mental representations of information. The representation may be in the form of a word, a visual image, a sound, or data in any other modality. The function of thinking is to transform that representation of information into new and different forms for the purposes of answering questions, solving problems, or reaching goals.

The work of an architectural engineer demands a high level of thinking—the process of manipulating mental representations of information. Have computers changed these high-level thought processes or just made them easier to use?

Although a clear sense of what specifically occurs when we think remains elusive, the nature of the fundamental elements involved in thinking is becoming increasingly well understood. We begin by considering our use of mental images and concepts, the building blocks of thought.

Mental Images: Examining the Mind's Eye

Think of your best friend.

Chances are that you "see" some kind of visual image when asked to think of her or him, or any other person or object, for that matter. To some cognitive psychologists, such mental images constitute a major part of thinking.

Mental images are representations in the mind in the form of the object or event being represented. They are not just visual representations; our ability to "hear" a tune in our head also relies on a mental image. In fact, it might be that every sensory modality produces corresponding mental images (Paivio, 1971, 1975; Kosslyn et al., 1990; Kosslyn & Shin, 1994).

Research has found that our representations of mental images have many of the properties of the actual perception of objects being represented. For example, it takes longer to scan mental images of large objects than of small ones, just as the eye takes longer to scan an actual large object than an actual small one. Similarly, we are able to manipulate and rotate mental images of objects, just as we are able to manipulate and rotate objects in the real world (Kosslyn, 1981; Cooper & Shepard, 1984; Denis & Greenbaum, 1991; Brandimonte, Hitch, & Bishop, 1992; Sharps, Price, & Williams, 1994; Shepard et al., 2000; see Figure 8-1).

"What do you think I think about what you think I think you've been thinking about?"

 **PsychLink**

Imagery and cognition
www.mhhe.com/
feldmanup6-08links

mental images: Representations in the mind that resemble the object or event being represented

Figure 8-1 Try to mentally rotate one of each pair of patterns to see if it is the same as the other member of the pair. It's likely that the further you have to mentally rotate a pattern, the longer it will take to decide if the patterns match one another. Does this mean that it will take you longer to visualize a map of the world than a map of the United States? Why or why not?

Reprinted with permission from R. Shepard and J. Metzler, "Mental Rotation of Three Dimensional Objects", *Science* 171, 701–703. Copyright 1971 American Association for the Advancement of Science.

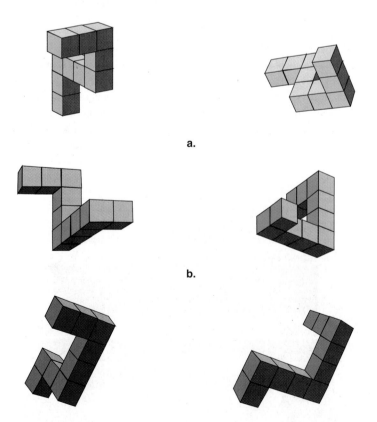

a.

b.

c.

herault, messager
onmongem

Many athletes, such as Reggie Miller (shown here), use mental imagery to focus on a task, a process they call "getting in the zone." What are some other occupations that require the use of strong mental imagery?

concepts: Categorizations of objects, events, or people that share common properties

The production of mental images has been heralded by some as a way to improve various skills. For instance, many athletes use mental imagery in training. Basketball players may try to produce vivid and detailed images of the court, the basket, the ball, and the noisy crowd. They may visualize themselves taking a foul shot, watching the ball, and hearing the swish as it goes through the net (May, 1990; Issac & Marks, 1994). Systematic evaluations of the use of mental imagery by athletes suggest that it provides a means for improving performance in sports (Druckman & Bjork, 1991).

Mental imagery can produce improvements in other types of skills as well. For example, in the realm of music, researcher Alvaro Pascual-Leone taught groups of people to play a five-finger exercise on the piano. One group practiced every day for five days, while a control group played without any training, just hitting the keys at random. Finally, the members of a third group were taught the exercise but were not allowed to actually try it out on the piano. Instead, they rehearsed it mentally, sitting at the piano and looking at the keys, but not actually touching them.

When brain scans of people in the groups were compared, researchers found a distinct difference between those who manually practiced the exercise and those who just randomly hit keys. However, the most surprising finding came from the group that mentally rehearsed: Their brain scans were virtually identical to those of the people who had actually practiced the exercise manually (see Figure 8-2). Apparently, the same network of brain cells involved in carrying out the task was involved in mentally rehearsing it (Chase, 1993; Pascual-Leone et al., 1995). , gronder, quereller

Such research suggests that children whose parents nag them about practicing an instrument, a dance routine, or some other skill that requires practice can now employ a new excuse: They *are* practicing—mentally.

Concepts: Categorizing the World

If someone asked you what was in your kitchen cabinet, you might answer with a detailed list of items ("a jar of peanut butter, three boxes of macaroni and cheese, six unmatched dinner plates," and so forth). More likely, though, you would respond by using some broader categories, such as "food" and "dishes."

The use of such categories reflects the operation of concepts. **Concepts** are categorizations of objects, events, or people that share common properties. By employing concepts, we are able to organize complex phenomena into simpler, and therefore more easily usable, cognitive categories (Margolis & Laurence, 1999).

Concepts allow us to classify newly encountered objects on the basis of our past experience. For example, we can surmise that the small rectangular gadget with buttons that is on the chair near the television is probably a remote control—even if we have never encountered that specific brand before. Ultimately, concepts influence behavior;

Figure 8-2 Compared with the brain scans of people who actually practiced a piano finger exercise, the brain scans of those who only used mental rehearsal but did not touch the piano were nearly identical. The results of the experiment clearly show the value of mental imagery. (Source: Pascual-Leone et al., 1995.)

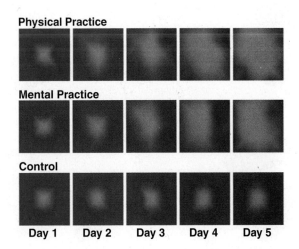

Table 8-1 Prototypes of Common Concepts

Ranking of Prototype from Most to Least Typical	CONCEPT CATEGORY			
	Furniture	Vehicle	Weapon	Vegetable
1—Most Typical	Chair	Car	Gun	Peas
2	Sofa	Truck	Knife	Carrots
3	Table	Bus	Sword	String Beans
4	Dresser	Motorcycle	Bomb	Spinach
5	Desk	Train	Hand grenade	Broccoli
6	Bed	Trolley car	Spear	Asparagus
7	Bookcase	Bicycle	Cannon	Corn
8	Footstool	Airplane	Bow and arrow	Cauliflower
9	Lamp	Boat	Club	Brussels sprouts
10	Piano	Tractor	Tank	Lettuce
11	Cushion	Cart	Tear gas	Beets
12	Mirror	Wheelchair	Whip	Tomato
13	Rug	Tank	Ice pick	Lima beans
14	Radio	Raft	Fists	Eggplant
15—Least Typical	Stove	Sled	Rocket	Onion

Source: Rosch & Mervis, 1975.

we would assume, for instance, that it might be appropriate to pet an animal after determining that it is a dog, but we would make a different assumption after classifying the animal as a wolf.

When cognitive psychologists first studied concepts, they focused on those that were clearly defined by a unique set of properties or features. For example, an equilateral triangle is a closed shape that has three sides of equal length. If an object has these characteristics, it is an equilateral triangle; if it does not, then it is not an equilateral triangle.

Other concepts—including many of those most relevant to our everyday lives— are more ambiguous and difficult to define. For instance, concepts such as "table" or "bird" share a set of general, relatively loose characteristic features, rather than unique, clearly defined properties that distinguish an example of the concept from a nonexample. When we consider these more ambiguous concepts, we usually think in terms of examples called prototypes. **Prototypes** are typical, highly representative examples of a concept. For instance, a prototype of the concept "bird" is a robin; a prototype of "table" is a coffee table. People in a given culture tend to agree on which examples of a concept are prototypes, as well as which examples are not. For instance, most people in Western cultures consider cars and trucks good examples of vehicles, whereas elevators and wheelbarrows are not viewed as very good examples. Consequently, cars and trucks are prototypes of the concept of vehicle (see Table 8-1).

Concepts enable us to think about and understand more readily the complex world we live in. For example, we judge other people's motivations based on how we classify their behavior: we think differently of a person who washes her hands twenty times a day, depending on whether we place her behavior under the concept "health care worker" or "mental patient." Similarly, physicians make diagnoses by drawing upon concepts and prototypes of symptoms that they learned about in medical school. Finally, concepts and

prototypes: Typical, highly representative examples of a concept

How do you view these structures? Whether you categorize them as two houses of workship (left & middle), two similar examples of architecture (middle & right), or simply as three buildings, you are using concepts.

prototypes facilitate our efforts to draw suitable conclusions through the cognitive process we turn to next: reasoning.

Reasoning: Making Up Your Mind

Professors deciding when students' assignments are due.
An employer determining which job applicants to hire.
The president concluding it is necessary to send troops to a foreign nation.

What do these three situations have in common? Each requires *reasoning,* the process by which information is used to draw conclusions and make decisions.

Although philosophers and logicians have considered the foundations of reasoning for centuries, it is only relatively recently that cognitive psychologists have begun to investigate how people reason and make decisions. Together, their efforts have contributed to our understanding of formal reasoning processes as well as the cognitive shortcuts we routinely use—shortcuts that can sometimes lead our reasoning capabilities astray (Evans, Newstead, & Byrne, 1994; Johnson-Laird & Shafir, 1994; Corrigan, 1996).

Syllogistic Reasoning: The Formal Rules of Logic

If you have ever played a card game like poker and tried to figure out what cards your opponent is holding, you have probably used a kind of formal reasoning known as syllogistic reasoning. **Syllogistic reasoning** is formal reasoning in which people draw a conclusion from a set of assumptions. In using syllogistic reasoning, we begin with a general assumption that we believe is true and then derive the implications of the assumption. If the assumption is true, then the conclusions must also be true.

A major technique for studying syllogistic reasoning involves asking people to evaluate a series of statements that present a series of two assumptions, or *premises,* that are used to derive a conclusion. For example, consider the following syllogism:

All men are mortal.	*[premise]*
Socrates is a man.	*[premise]*
Therefore, Socrates is mortal.	*[conclusion]*

Because both premises are true, by applying logic appropriately we come to an accurate conclusion. More abstractly, we can state the syllogism as the following:

All A's are B.	*[premise]*
C is an A.	*[premise]*
Therefore, C is a B.	*[conclusion]*

On the other hand, even if the premises are correct, people might apply logic incorrectly. For example, consider the following syllogism:

syllogistic reasoning: Formal reasoning in which people draw a conclusion from a set of assumptions

 **PsychLink**

Deductive and inductive reasoning
www.mhhe.com/
feldmanup6–08links

All A's are B.	*[premise]*
C is an A.	*[premise]*
Therefore, all A's are C.	*[conclusion]*

Although it might not be immediately apparent, drawing this conclusion is illogical—something seen more readily if we make the syllogism more concrete:

All men are mortal.	*[premise]*
Socrates is a man.	*[premise]*
Therefore, all men are Socrates.	*[conclusion]*

In short, syllogistic reasoning is only as accurate as the truth of the premises and the validity of the logic applied to the premises.

Algorithms and Heuristics

When faced with a decision, we often turn to cognitive shortcuts, known as algorithms and heuristics, to help us. An **algorithm** is a rule that, if applied appropriately, guarantees a solution to a problem. We can use an algorithm even if we cannot understand why it works. For example, you might know that the length of the third side of a right triangle can be found using the formula $a^2 + b^2 = c^2$, although you might not have the foggiest notion of the mathematical principles behind the formula.

For many problems and decisions, however, no algorithm is available. In those instances, we might be able to use heuristics to help us. A **heuristic** is a cognitive shortcut that *might* lead to a solution. Heuristics enhance the likelihood of success in coming to a solution, but, unlike algorithms, they cannot ensure it. For example, when I play tic-tac-toe, I follow the heuristic of placing an *X* in the center squares when I start the game. This tactic doesn't guarantee that I will win, but experience has taught me that it increases my chances of success. Similarly, some students follow the heuristic of preparing for a test by ignoring the assigned textbook reading and studying only their lecture notes—a strategy that might or might not pay off (Nisbett et al., 1993).

Although heuristics often help people solve problems and make decisions, certain kinds of heuristics can lead to inaccurate conclusions. For example, we sometimes use the *availability heuristic:* judging the probability of an event by how easily the event can be recalled from memory. According to this heuristic, we assume that events we remember easily are likely to have occurred more frequently in the past—and are more likely to occur in the future—than those that are harder to remember. For instance, people are usually more afraid of dying in a plane crash than in an auto accident, despite statistics clearly showing that airplane travel is much safer than auto travel. The reason is that plane crashes receive far more publicity than car crashes, and are therefore more easily remembered. The availability heuristic leads people to conclude that they are in greater jeopardy in an airplane than in a car (Slovic, Fischhoff, & Lichtenstien, 1976; Schwarz et al., 1991).

algorithm: A rule that, if applied appropriately, guarantees a solution to a problem

heuristic: A cognitive shortcut that might lead to a solution

⚭ **PsychLink**

Explanation of heuristics
www.mhhe.com/
feldmanup6-08links

Evaluate

1. _____ are representations in the mind that resemble the object or event being represented.
2. _____ are categorizations of objects that share common properties.
3. When you think of the term "chair," you immediately think of a comfortable easy chair. A chair of this type could be thought of as a _____ of the category "chair."
4. When you ask your friend how best to study for your psychology final, he tells you, "I've always found it best to skim over the notes once, then read the book, then go over the notes again." What decision-making tool might this be an example of?

Rethink

1. How might the availability heuristic contribute to prejudices based on race, age, and gender? Can awareness of this heuristic prevent this from happening?
2. In what ways might prototypes for the category "vehicle" differ between members of a tribe living in a rural African village compared with people living in a Western, urban city?

Answers to Evaluate Questions

1. Mental images 2. Concepts 3. prototype 4. Heuristic

Prepare

How do people approach and solve problems?
What are the major obstacles to problem
   solving?

Organize

Problem Solving
   Preparation
   Production
   Judgment
   Impediments to Solutions
   Creativity and Problem Solving

Problem Solving

According to an old legend, a group of Vietnamese monks are guardians of three towers on which sit 64 golden rings. The monks believe that, if they succeed in moving the rings from the first tower to the third according to a series of rigid rules, the world as we know it will come to an end. (Should you prefer that the world remain in its present state, there's no need for immediate concern: The puzzle is so complex that it will take about a trillion years to reach a solution.)

In a simpler version of the task facing the monks, which has come to be known as the Tower of Hanoi puzzle, three disks are placed on three posts in the order shown in Figure 8-3. The goal of the puzzle is to move all three disks to the third post, arranged in the same order, using as few moves as possible. But there are two restrictions: Only one disk can be moved at a time, and no disk can ever cover a smaller one during a move.

Why are cognitive psychologists interested in the Tower of Hanoi problem? The answer is that the way people go about solving this puzzle and simpler ones like it helps illuminate the processes by which people solve complex problems they encounter in school and at work. For example, psychologists have found that problem solving typically involves three major steps: preparation for the creation of solutions, production of solutions, and evaluation of solutions that have been generated (Sternberg & Frensch, 1991).

Preparation: Understanding and Diagnosing the Problem

When approaching a problem like the Tower of Hanoi, most people begin by trying to ensure that they thoroughly understand the problem. If the problem is a novel one, they are likely to pay particular attention to any restrictions placed on coming up with a solution as well as the initial status of the components of the problem. If, on the other hand, the problem is a familiar one, they are apt to spend considerably less time in this stage.

Problems vary from well defined to ill defined (Reitman, 1965; Arlin, 1989). In a *well-defined problem*—such as a mathematical equation or the solution to a jigsaw puzzle—both the nature of the problem itself and the information needed to solve it are available and clear. Thus, straightforward judgments can be made about whether a potential solution is appropriate. With an *ill-defined problem,* such as how to increase morale

Figure 8-3 The goal of the Tower of Hanoi puzzle is to move all three disks from the first post to the last and still preserve the original order of the disks, using the least number of moves possible while following the rules that only one disk at a time can be moved and no disk can cover a smaller one during a move. Try it yourself before you look at the solution, which is listed according to the sequence of moves.

(Solution: Move C to 3, B to 2, C to 2, A to 3, C to 1, B to 3, and C to 3.)

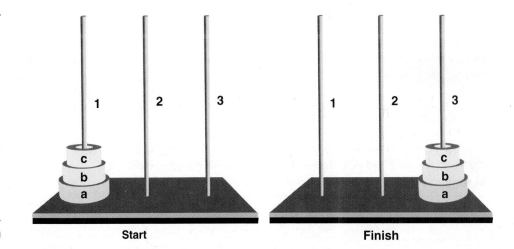

on an assembly line or bring peace to the Middle East, not only might the specific nature of the problem be unclear, but the information required to solve the problem could be even less obvious.

Kinds of Problems

Problems typically fall into one of the three categories exemplified in Figure 8-4: arrangement, inducing structure, and transformation (Greeno, 1978; Spitz, 1987). Solving each type requires somewhat different kinds of psychological skills and knowledge.

Arrangement problems require that a group of elements be rearranged or recombined in a way that will satisfy a certain criterion. Usually several different possible arrangements can be made, but only one or a few of the arrangements will produce a solution. Anagram problems and jigsaw puzzles represent arrangement problems.

In *problems of inducing structure,* a person must identify the relationships that exist among the elements presented and construct a new relationship among them. In such a problem, it is necessary to determine not only the relationships among the elements, but the structure and size of the elements involved. In the example shown in Figure 8-4, a person must first determine that the solution requires the numbers to be considered in pairs (14-24-34-44-54-64). Only after that part of the problem is identified can the solution rule (the first number of each pair increases by one, while the second number remains the same) be determined.

"I don't know about hair care, Rapunzel, but I'm thinking a good cream rinse plus protein conditioner might just solve both our problems."

The Tower of Hanoi puzzle represents a third kind of problem. *Transformation problems* consist of an initial state, a goal state, and a series of methods for changing the initial state into the goal state. In the Tower of Hanoi problem, the initial state is the original configuration; the goal state consists of the three disks on the third peg; and the method consists of the rules for moving the disks.

Whether the problem is one of arrangement, inducing structure, or transformation, the initial stage of understanding and diagnosing is critical in problem solving because it allows us to develop our own cognitive representation of the problem and place it within a personal framework. The problem might be divided into subparts or some information might be ignored as we try to simplify the task. Winnowing out nonessential information is often a critical step in problem solving.

Representing and Organizing the Problem

A crucial aspect of the initial encounter with a problem is how we represent it to ourselves and organize the information presented to us (Brown & Walter, 1993; Davidson, Deuser, & Sternberg, 1994). Consider the following problem:

> A man climbs a mountain on Saturday, leaving at daybreak and arriving at the top near sundown. He spends the night at the top. The next day, Sunday, he leaves at daybreak and heads down the mountain, following the same path he climbed the day before. The question is this: Will there be any time during the second day when he will be at exactly the same point on the mountain as he was at exactly that time on the first day?

If you try to solve this problem by using algebraic or verbal representations, you will have a good deal of trouble. However, if you represent the problem with the kind of simple diagram illustrated in Figure 8-6 on page 238, the solution becomes apparent.

Figure 8-4 The major categories of problems: *(a)* arrangement, *(b)* inducing structure, and *(c)* transformation (Bourne et al., 1986; hobbit problem: Solso, 1991, p. 448; clock problem: Poncini, 1990). For the solutions, see Figure 8-5.

A. Arrangement problems

1. **Anagrams: Rearrange the letters in each set to make an English word:**

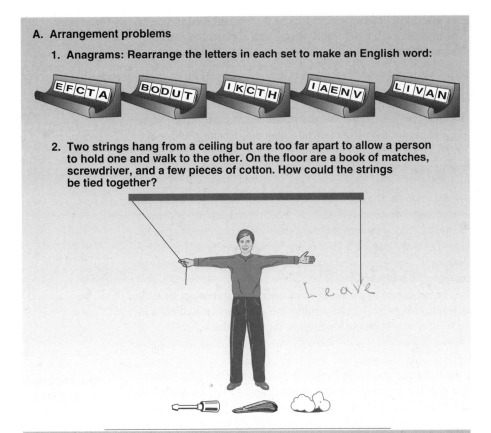

2. **Two strings hang from a ceiling but are too far apart to allow a person to hold one and walk to the other. On the floor are a book of matches, screwdriver, and a few pieces of cotton. How could the strings be tied together?**

B. Problems of inducing structure

1. **What number comes next in the series?**

   1 4 2 4 3 4 4 4 5 4 6 4

2. **Complete these analogies:**

   baseball is to bat as tennis is to _____

   merchant is to sell as customer is to *buy*

3. **The clock faces in each of the three rows are arranged in a logical sequence. Try to find the sequence in each row, and draw the missing hands on the three blank faces, in less than 15 seconds.**

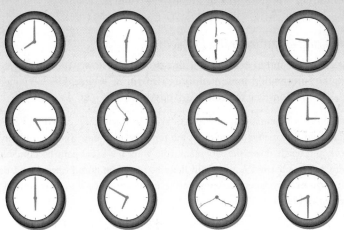

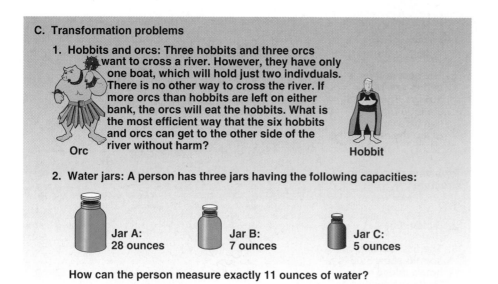

C. Transformation problems

1. **Hobbits and orcs:** Three hobbits and three orcs want to cross a river. However, they have only one boat, which will hold just two indivduals. There is no other way to cross the river. If more orcs than hobbits are left on either bank, the orcs will eat the hobbits. What is the most efficient way that the six hobbits and orcs can get to the other side of the river without harm?

Orc

Hobbit

2. **Water jars:** A person has three jars having the following capacities:

Jar A: 28 ounces

Jar B: 7 ounces

Jar C: 5 ounces

How can the person measure exactly 11 ounces of water?

Our ability to represent a problem—and the kind of solution we eventually come to—is affected by the way a problem is phrased, or *framed.* Suppose, for example, you are a cancer patient having to choose between surgery or radiation, and these options are presented to you in the two ways shown in Figure 8-7 (Tversky & Kahneman, 1987). When framed in terms of the likelihood of survival, only 18 percent of participants in a study chose radiation over surgery. However, when the choice was framed in terms of the likelihood of dying, 44 percent chose radiation over surgery—even though the outcomes are identical in both sets of framing conditions.

Production: Generating Solutions

If a problem is relatively simple, we might already have a direct solution stored in long-term memory, and all we need to do is retrieve the appropriate information. If we can't retrieve or don't know the solution, we must start a process to generate possible solutions and compare them with information in our long- and short-term memory.

At the most primitive level, solutions to problems can be obtained through trial and error. Thomas Edison was able to invent the lightbulb only because he tried thousands of different kinds of materials for a filament before he found one that worked (carbon). The difficulty with trial and error, of course, is that some problems are so complicated it would take a lifetime to try out every possibility. For example, according to one estimate, there are some 10^{120} possible sequences of chess moves.

In place of trial and error, complex problem solving often involves the use of heuristics, which, as we discussed earlier, are cognitive shortcuts that can lead the way to solutions. Probably the most frequently applied heuristic in problem solving is a means-end analysis. In a **means-end analysis,** people repeatedly test for differences between the desired outcome and what currently exists. Consider this simple example (Newell & Simon, 1972):

> I want to take my son to nursery school. What's the difference between what I have and what I want? One of distance. What changes distance? My automobile. My automobile won't work. What is needed to make it work? A new battery. What has new batteries? An auto repair shop . . .

In such a means-end analysis, each step brings the problem-solver closer to a resolution. However, if the problem requires indirect steps that temporarily *increase* the discrepancy between a current state and the solution, a means-end analysis can be counterproductive. For example, sometimes the fastest route to a summit requires a

means-end analysis: Repeated testing for differences between the desired outcome and what currently exists

 **PsychLink**

Means-ends analysis technique
www.mhhe.com/
feldmanup6–08links

Figure 8-5 Solutions to problems posed in Figure 8-4.

From R. L. Solso, *Cognitive Psychology,* 3rd edition. Copyright ©1991 by Allyn & Bacon. Reprinted/ adapted by permission.

A. Arrangement problems

1. **FACET, DOUBT, THICK, NAIVE, ANVIL**

2. **The screwdriver is tied to one of the strings. This makes a pendulum that can be swung to reach the other string.**

B. Problems of inducing structure

1. **7**

2. **racket; buy**

3. **The first blank face should show 5:00 (4½ hours added each time); the second one, 4:30 (45 minutes subtracted each time); the third one, 7:40 (50 minutes added each time).**

C. Transformation problems

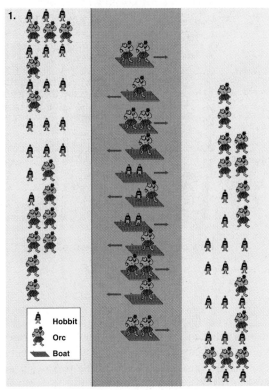

2. **Fill jar A; empty into jar B once and into jar C twice. What remains in jar A is 11 ounces.**

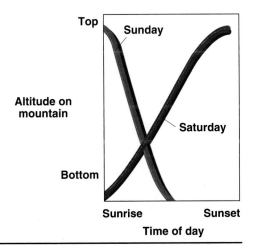

Figure 8-6 You can solve the problem by using a graph. Keep in mind that the goal is not to determine the time, but just to indicate whether an exact time exists. Consequently, the speed at which the traveler is moving is unimportant (Anderson, 1980). Can you think of other approaches that might lead to a solution?

mountain climber to backtrack temporarily; a means-end approach—which implies that the mountain climber should always forge ahead and upward—will be ineffective in such instances.

Furthermore, for some problems, the best approach is working backward, by focusing on the goal rather than the starting point of the problem. Consider, for example, the water lily problem:

> Water lilies are growing on Blue Lake. The water lilies grow rapidly, so that the amount of water surface covered by lilies *doubles* every 24 hours.
>
> On the first day of summer, there was just one water lily. On the 90th day of the summer, the lake was entirely covered. On what day was the lake *half covered*? (Reisberg, 1997)

If you start searching for a solution to the problem by thinking about the initial state on day 1 (one water lily) and move forward from there, you're facing a daunting task of trial-and-error estimation. But try taking a different approach: Start with day 90, where the entire lake was covered with lilies. Given that the lilies double their coverage daily, on the prior day only half the lake was covered. The answer, then, is day 89, a solution found by working backward (Bourne et al., 1986; Hunt, 1994).

Forming Subgoals: Dividing Problems into Their Parts

Another commonly used heuristic is to divide a problem into intermediate steps, or *subgoals,* and to solve each of those steps. For instance, in our modified Tower of Hanoi problem, there are several obvious subgoals that could be chosen, such as moving the largest disk to the third post.

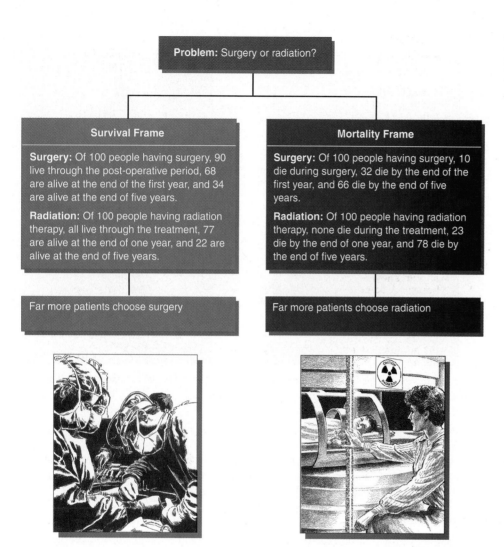

Figure 8-7 Decisions are often affected by the way problems are framed (Tversky & Kahneman, 1987).

If solving a subgoal is a step toward the ultimate solution to a problem, then identifying subgoals is an appropriate strategy. But sometimes subgoals are not all that helpful and can increase the time needed to find a solution (Hayes, 1966; Reed, 1996). For example, some problems cannot be subdivided. Others are so difficult to subdivide that it takes longer to identify the appropriate subdivisions than to solve the problem by other means.

Insight: Sudden Awareness

Some approaches to problem solving focus less on step-by-step processes than on the sudden bursts of comprehension that can come during efforts to solve a problem. Just after World War I, German psychologist Wolfgang Köhler examined learning and problem-solving processes in chimps (Köhler, 1927). In his studies, Köhler exposed chimps to challenging situations in which the elements of the solution were all present; all that was needed was for the chimps to put them together.

For example, in one series of studies, chimps were kept in a cage in which boxes and sticks were strewn about, with a bunch of tantalizing bananas hanging from the ceiling out of reach. Initially, the chimps engaged in a variety of trial-and-error attempts at getting to the bananas: They would throw the sticks at the bananas, jump from one of the boxes, or leap wildly from the ground. Frequently, they would seem to give up in frustration, leaving the bananas dangling temptingly overhead. But then, in what seemed like a sudden revelation, they would abandon whatever activity they were involved in and stand on a box in order to be able to reach the bananas with a stick. Köhler called

 PsychLink

Köhler and insight research
www.mhhe.com/
feldmanup6-08links

insight: A sudden awareness of the relationships among various elements that had previously appeared to be independent of one another

a.

b.

c.

In an impressive display of insight, Sultan, one of the chimpanzees in Köhler's experiments in problem solving, sees a bunch of bananas that is out of his reach (a). He then carries over several crates (b), stacks them, and stands on them to reach the bananas (c).

THE FAR SIDE   By GARY LARSON

the cognitive processes underlying the chimps' behavior **insight,** a sudden awareness of the relationships among various elements that had previously appeared to be unrelated to one another.

Although Köhler emphasized the apparent suddenness with which solutions were revealed, subsequent research has shown that prior experience and initial trial-and-error practice in problem solving are prerequisites for "insight" (Metcalfe, 1986; Ansburg & Dominowski, 2000). One study demonstrated that only chimps who had experience in playing with sticks could successfully solve the problem; inexperienced chimps never made the connection between standing on the box and reaching the bananas (Birch, 1945). Some researchers have suggested that the behavior of the chimps represented little more than the chaining together of previously learned responses, no different from the way a pigeon learns, by trial and error, to peck a key (Epstein et al., 1984; Epstein, 1987, 1996), but it is clear that insight depends on previous experience with the elements involved in a problem.

Judgment: Evaluating the Solutions

The final step in problem solving is judging the adequacy of a solution. Often, this is a simple matter: If there is a clear solution—as in the Tower of Hanoi problem—we will know immediately whether we have been successful.

If the solution is less concrete or if there is no single correct solution, evaluating solutions becomes more difficult. In such instances, we must decide which solution alternative is best. Unfortunately, we are often quite inaccurate in estimating the quality of our own ideas (Johnson, Parrott, & Stratton, 1968). For instance, a team of drug researchers working for a particular company might

feel that their remedy for an illness is superior to all others, overestimating the likelihood of success and belittling the approaches of competing drug companies.

Theoretically, if the heuristics and information we rely on to make decisions are appropriate and valid, we can make accurate choices among problem solutions. However, as we see next, there are several kinds of obstacles to and biases in problem solving that affect the quality of our decisions and judgments.

Impediments to Solutions: Why Is Problem Solving Such a Problem?

Consider the following problem-solving test (Duncker, 1945):

> You are presented with a set of tacks, candles, and matches in small boxes, and told your goal is to place three candles at eye level on a nearby door, so that wax will not drip on the floor as the candles burn [see Figure 8-8]. How would you approach this challenge?

If you have difficulty solving the problem, you are not alone. Most people are unable to solve it when it is presented in the manner illustrated in Figure 8-8, in which the objects are located *inside* the boxes. However, if the objects were presented *beside* the boxes, just resting on the table, chances are you would solve the problem much more readily—which, in case you are wondering, requires tacking the boxes to the door and then placing the candles inside them (see Figure 8-9).

The difficulty you probably encountered in solving the problem stems from its presentation and relates to the fact that you were misled at the initial preparation stage. Actually, significant obstacles to problem solving exist at each of the three major stages. Although cognitive approaches to problem solving suggest that thinking proceeds along fairly rational, logical lines as a person confronts a problem and considers various solutions, a number of factors hinder the development of creative, appropriate, and accurate solutions.

Functional Fixedness and Mental Set

The reason most people experience difficulty with the candle problem is a phenomenon known as **functional fixedness,** the tendency to think of an object only in terms of its typical use. For instance, functional fixedness probably leads you to think of the book

functional fixedness: The tendency to think of an object only in terms of its typical use

Figure 8-8 The problem here is to place three candles at eye level on a nearby door so that the wax will not drip on the floor as the candles burn—using only material in the figure. For a solution, see Figure 8-9.

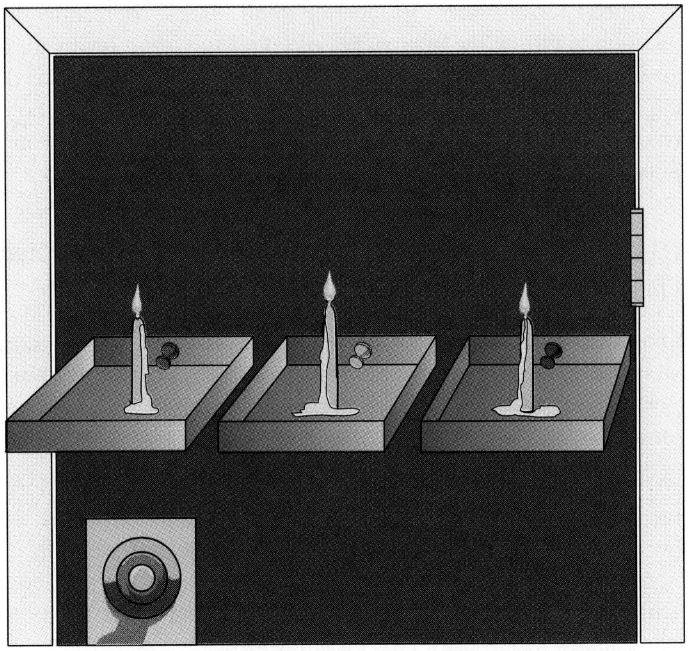

Figure 8-9 A solution to the problem posed in Figure 8-8 involves tacking the boxes to the door and placing the candles in the boxes.

mental set: The tendency for old patterns of problem solving to persist

Given jars with these capacities (in ounces)

	a	b	c	Obtain
1.	21	127	3	100
2.	14	163	25	99
3.	18	43	10	5
4.	9	42	6	21
5.	20	59	4	31
6.	28	76	3	25

Figure 8-10 Try this classic demonstration, which illustrates the importance of mental set in problem solving. The object is to use the jars in each row to measure out the designated amount of liquid. After you figure out the solution for the first five rows, you'll likely have trouble with the sixth row—even though the solution is actually easier. In fact, if you had tried to solve the problem in the sixth row first, you probably would have had no difficulty at all.

before you as something to read and not as a doorstop or as kindling for a fire. In the candle problem, functional fixedness occurs because the objects are first presented inside the boxes, which are then seen simply as containers for the objects they hold rather than as a potential part of the solution.

Functional fixedness is an example of a broader phenomenon known as **mental set,** the tendency for old patterns of problem solving to persist. This phenomenon was demonstrated in a classic experiment carried out by Abraham Luchins (1946). As you can see in Figure 8-10, the object of the task is to use the jars in each row to measure out the designated amount of liquid. (Try it yourself to get a sense of the power of mental set before moving on.)

If you have tried to solve the problem, you know that the first five parts are all solved in the same way: Fill the largest jar (B) and from it fill the middle-size jar (A) once and the smallest jar (C) two times. What is left in B is the designated amount. (Stated as a formula, it is $B - A - 2C$.) The demonstration of mental set comes with the sixth part of the problem, a point at which you probably encountered some difficulty. If you are like most people, you tried the formula and were perplexed when it failed. Chances are, in fact, that you missed the simple (but different) solution to the problem, which merely involves subtracting C from A. Interestingly, those people who were given problem 6 *first* had no difficulty with it at all.

Mental set can also affect perceptions. It can prevent you from seeing your way beyond the apparent constraints of a problem. For example, try to draw four straight lines so that they pass through all nine dots in the grid below—without lifting your pencil from the page.

· · ·
· · ·
· · ·

If you had difficulty with the problem, it was probably because you felt compelled to keep your lines within the grid. If you had gone outside the boundaries, however, you would have succeeded with the solution shown in Figure 8-11. (The phrase "thinking outside the box"—a term commonly used in business today, meant to encourage creativity—stems from research on overcoming the constraining effects of mental set.)

Inaccurate Evaluation of Solutions

When the nuclear power plant at Three Mile Island in Pennsylvania suffered its initial malfunction in 1979, a disaster that almost led to a nuclear meltdown, the plant operators were faced immediately with solving a problem of the most serious kind. Several monitors indicated contradictory information about the source of the problem: One suggested that the pressure was too high, leading to the danger of an explosion; others indicated that the pressure was too low, which could lead to a meltdown. Although the pressure was in fact too low, the supervisors on duty relied on the one monitor—which was faulty—that suggested the pressure was too high. Once they had made their decision and acted upon it, they ignored the contradictory evidence from the other monitors (Wickens, 1984).

One reason for the operators' mistake is *confirmation bias,* in which initial hypotheses are favored and contradictory information supporting alternative hypotheses or solutions is ignored. Even when we find evidence that contradicts a solution we have chosen, we are apt to stick with our original hypothesis.

There are several reasons for the confirmation bias. One is that it takes extra cognitive effort to rethink a problem that appears to be solved already, so we are apt to stick with our first solution. Another is that evidence contradicting an initial solution may present something of a threat to our self-esteem, leading us to hold to the solutions that we have come up with first (Fischoff, 1977; Rasmussen, 1981).

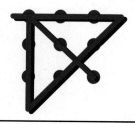

Figure 8-11 Solution to the nine-dot problem requires the use of lines drawn beyond the boundaries of the figure—something that our mental set may prevent us from easily seeing.

Creativity and Problem Solving

Despite obstacles to problem solving, many people are adept at coming up with creative solutions to problems. One of the enduring questions that cognitive psychologists have sought to answer is what factors underlie **creativity,** the combining of responses or ideas in novel ways.

Although identifying the stages of problem solving helps us understand how people approach and solve problems, it does little to explain why some people come up with better solutions than others. For instance, the possible solutions to even the simplest of problems often show wide discrepancies. Consider, for example, how you might respond to the question "How many uses can you think of for a newspaper?"

Now compare your own solution with this one proposed by a 10-year-old boy:

> You can read it, write on it, lay it down and paint a picture on it. . . . You could put it in your door for decoration, put it in the garbage can, put it on a chair if the chair is messy. If you have a puppy, you put newspaper in its box or put it in your backyard for the dog to play with. When you build something and you don't want anyone to see it, put newspaper around it. Put newspaper on the floor if you have no mattress, use it to pick up something hot, use it to stop bleeding, or to catch the drips from drying clothes. You can use a newspaper for curtains, put it in your shoe to cover what is hurting your foot, make a kite out of it, shade a light that is too bright. You can wrap fish in it, wipe windows, or wrap money in it. . . . You put washed shoes in newspaper, wipe eyeglasses with it, put it under a dripping sink, put a plant on it, make a paper bowl out of it, use it for a hat if it is raining, tie it on your feet for slippers. You can put it on the sand if you had no towel, use it for bases in baseball, make paper airplanes with it, use it as a dustpan when you sweep, ball it up for the cat to play with, wrap your hands in it if it is cold. (Ward, Kogan, & Pankove, 1972)

It is obvious that this list shows extraordinary creativity. Unfortunately, it has proved to be considerably easier to identify *examples* of creativity than to determine its causes. Several factors, however, seem to be associated with creativity (Csikszentmihalyi, 1997; Ward, Smith, & Vaid, 1997; Root-Bernstein & Root-Bernstein, 1999).

One of these factors is divergent thinking. **Divergent thinking** refers to the ability to generate unusual, yet nonetheless appropriate, responses to problems or questions. This type of thinking contrasts with **convergent thinking,** which produces responses that are based primarily on knowledge and logic. For instance, someone relying on convergent thinking answers "You read it" to the query "What do you do with a newspaper?" In contrast,

creativity: The combining of responses or ideas in novel ways

divergent thinking: The ability to generate unusual, yet appropriate, responses to problems or questions

convergent thinking: The ability to produce responses that are based primarily on knowledge and logic

Pablo Picasso is considered one of the greatest creative artists of the 20th century. Do you think he relied more on convergent or divergent thinking in his art?

PsychLink

Creativity and innovation
www.mhhe.com/
feldmanup6–08links

"You use it as a dustpan" is a more divergent—and creative— response (Baer, 1993; Runco & Sakamoto, 1993; Finke, 1995).

Another aspect of creativity is *cognitive complexity,* the preference for elaborate, intricate, and complex stimuli and thinking patterns. Similarly, creative people often have a wider range of interests and are more independent and more interested in philosophical or abstract problems than are less creative individuals (Barron, 1990).

One factor that is *not* closely related to creativity is intelligence. Most items on traditional intelligence tests are well defined and have only one acceptable answer: they focus on convergent thinking skills. Highly creative people might therefore find that the tests penalize their divergent thinking. This could explain why researchers consistently find that creativity is only slightly related to school grades and intelligence, when intelligence is measured using traditional intelligence tests (Hong, Milgram, & Gorsky, 1995; Sternberg & O'Hara, 2000).

BECOMING AN INFORMED CONSUMER OF PSYCHOLOGY

Thinking Critically and Creatively

Can we learn to be better thinkers?

Our consideration of cognitive psychology presents a good opportunity to review and expand on some important processes of critical and creative thinking. Cognitive researchers have found that abstract rules of logic and reasoning can be taught and that such training can improve our reasoning about the underlying causes of everyday events in our lives.

In short, research suggests that critical and creative thinkers are made, not born. Consider, for instance, some of these suggestions for increasing critical thinking and creativity (Feldman, Coats, & Schwartzberg, 1994; Halpern, 1998; Levy, 1997):

- *Redefine problems.* Our boundaries and assumptions can be modified by rephrasing problems at either a more abstract or more concrete level.
- *Use fractionation.* In fractionation, an idea or concept is broken down into the parts that make it up. Through fractionation, each part can be examined for new possibilities and approaches, leading to a novel solution for the problem as a whole.
- *Adopt a critical perspective.* Rather than passively accepting assumptions or arguments, we can critically evaluate material, consider its implications, and think about possible exceptions and contradictions.
- *Consider the opposite.* By considering the opposite of a concept we're seeking to understand, we can sometimes make progress. For example, in order to define "good mental health," it might be useful to consider what is meant by "bad mental health."
- *Use analogies.* Analogies provide alternative frameworks for our interpretation of facts and help us uncover new understanding. One particularly effective means of coming up with analogies is to look for examples in the animal kingdom. For instance, architects discovered how to construct the earliest skyscrapers by noting how lily pads on a pond could support the weight of a person (Shouler, 1992; Reisberg, 1997; Getner & Holyoak, 1997).
- *Think divergently.* Instead of thinking in terms of the most logical or common use for an object, consider how it might help your creativity if you were forbidden to use the object in its usual way.

The use of analogies is a characteristic of creativity. Frank Lloyd Wright incorporated into his architecture many analogies to nature, as you can see in this building he designed. How are analogies used by other creative artists?

Applying Psychology in the 21st Century

Can Computers Think Creatively?

To the listening music experts, there was no mistaking who had written the piano piece: Johann Sebastian Bach, the famous, prolific German composer who was born in the seventeenth century.

But the experts were wrong. The supposed Bach composition was created by a computer named EMI by David Cope of the University of California. After a variety of actual Bach pieces were scanned into its memory bank, EMI was able to produce music that was so similar to Bach's actual music that it could fool knowledgeable listeners. And it wasn't just Bach that EMI was able to mimic; composers such as Beethoven, Rachmaninoff, and Chopin also were assessed by EMI and convincingly mimicked in new musical creations (Johnson, 1997).

Such computer mimicry is possible because composers have a particular "signature" that reflects patterns, sequences, and combinations of notes. By employing those "signatures," composers can create compositions that have the full scope and emotional appeal of actual works—and show just as much creativity as those written by the actual composer (Cope, 1998).

But does EMI's success in fooling experts mean that the computer has reached the level of creativity shown by the actual composer? Critics say no, suggesting that there is something unique and special about the human creative process. They suggest that although computers can be programmed to be sensitive to specific, rapid patterns characteristic of a particular composer, they are unable to get the broad, sweeping, "bigger picture" of the works of great composers.

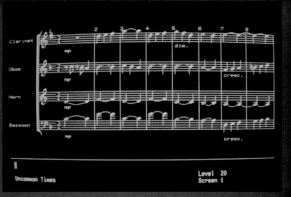

As technology becomes more sophisticated and complex, researchers are exploring the question of whether computers can duplicate human creativity such as that of the composer Bach. What do you think? What test can we use to measure a computer composer's creativity, versus the creativity of a human composer?

We don't know whether the critics are correct. However, it is clear that computers are making significant gains in terms of their abilities to solve problems and carry out some forms of intellectual activities. In fact, the success of computers has led some researchers to consider not only whether computers can compose music, but whether they can be said to actually think in a way that is similar to humans (Chalmers, 1996).

For example, Herbert Simon, a cognitive psychologist and Nobel Prize winner, believed that computers show rudiments of humanlike thinking because of their knowledge of where to look—and where not to look—for an answer to a problem. Simon suggested that the capacity of computer programs (such as those that play winning chess) to evaluate potential moves and to ignore unimportant possibilities gives them thinking ability (Webber, 1996; Wright, 1996).

Many of the questions surrounding the ability of computers to think and behave creatively have not been answered. Still, it is clear that computers are becoming increasingly sophisticated, ever more closely approximating human thought processes. (To listen to a sample of music created by computer, go to the PsychLink listed below.)

Can you think of a human mental task that a computer would have difficulty performing, despite its enormous processing power? Can you think of a task that—like chess playing—could probably be performed "expertly" by a computer? How do the two tasks differ?

- *Take the perspective of another person.* By temporarily adopting the point of view of another person, it may be possible to gain a fresh view of the situation.
- *Use heuristics.* As mentioned earlier, heuristics are cognitive shortcuts that can help bring about a solution to a problem. If the problem has a single correct answer, and a heuristic is available or can be constructed, using the heuristic frequently can help you develop a solution more rapidly and effectively.
- *Experiment with various solutions.* Don't be afraid to use different routes (verbal, mathematical, graphic, even acting out a situation) to find solutions for problems. For instance, try to come up with every conceivable idea you can, no matter how wild or bizarre it might seem at first. After you've come up with a list of solutions, you can review each one and try to think of ways of making what at first appeared impractical seem more feasible.

 PsychLink

Computer-generated music
www.mhhe.com/
feldmanup6-08links

Evaluate

1. Solving a problem by trying to reduce the difference between the current state and the goal state is known as a _____ _____.
2. _____ is the term used to describe the sudden "flash" of revelation that often accompanies the solution to a problem.
3. Thinking of an object only in terms of its typical use is known as _____ _____. A broader, related tendency for old problem-solving patterns to persist is known as a _____ _____.
4. _____ describes the phenomenon of favoring an initial hypothesis and ignoring subsequent competing hypotheses.
5. Generating unusual but appropriate approaches to a question is known as _____.

Answers to Evaluate Questions

1. means-ends analysis 2. Insight 3. functional fixedness; mental set 4. Confirmation bias 5. divergent thinking

Rethink

1. Is the reasoning in the following syllogism correct or incorrect? Why?

   Creative people often have trouble with traditional intelligence tests.

   I have trouble with traditional intelligence tests.

   Therefore, I am a creative person.

2. Are divergent thinking and convergent thinking mutually exclusive or complementary? Why? Are there situations in which one way of thinking is clearly superior? Can the two ways of thinking be combined? How?

Prepare

How do people use language?
How does language develop?

Organize

Language
    Grammar
    Language Development
    Understanding Language Acquisition
    The Influence of Language on Thinking
    Do Animals Use Language?

language: The communication of information through symbols arranged according to systematic rules

grammar: The system of rules that determine how our thoughts can be expressed

phonology: The study of the smallest sound units, called phonemes

phonemes: The smallest basic sound units

Language

> 'Twas brillig, and the slithy toves
> Did gyre and gimble in the wabe:
> All mimsy were the borogoves,
> And the mome raths outgrabe.

Although few of us have ever come face to face with a tove, we have little difficulty in discerning that in Lewis Carroll's (1872) poem "Jabberwocky," the expression *slithy toves* contains an adjective, *slithy,* and the noun it modifies, *toves.*

Our ability to make sense out of nonsense, if the nonsense follows typical rules of language, illustrates both the sophistication of human language capabilities and the complexity of the cognitive processes that underlie the development and use of language. The use of **language**—the communication of information through symbols arranged according to systematic rules—clearly is an important cognitive ability, one that is indispensable for communicating with others. Not only is language central to communication, it is also closely tied to the very ways we think about and understand the world, for there is a crucial link between thought and language. It is not surprising, then, that psychologists have devoted considerable attention to studying the topic of language (Forrester, 1996; Velichkovsky & Rumbaugh, 1996; Barrett, 1999; Owens, 2001).

Grammar: Language's Language

To understand how language develops and its relationship to thought, we first need to review some of the formal elements that constitute language. The basic structure of language rests on grammar. **Grammar** is the system of rules that determine how our thoughts can be expressed.

Grammar deals with three major components of language: phonology, syntax, and semantics. **Phonology** is the study of the smallest basic sound units, called **phonemes,** that affect the meaning of speech, and of the way we use those sounds to form words and produce meaning. For instance, the *a* in *fat* and the *a* in *fate* represent two different phonemes in English (Vihman, 1996; Baddeley, Gathercole, & Pagano, 1998).

Although English speakers use just 42 basic phonemes to produce words, the basic phonemes of other languages range from as few as 15 to as many as 85 (Akmajian, Demers, & Harnish, 1984). Differences in phonemes are one reason people have difficulty learning

other languages: For example, to the Japanese speaker, whose native language does not have an *r* phoneme, English words such as *roar* present some difficulty.

Syntax refers to the rules that indicate how words and phrases can be combined to form sentences. Every language has intricate rules that guide the order in which words may be strung together to communicate meaning. English speakers have no difficulty recognizing that *Radio down the turn* is not an appropriate sequence but *Turn down the radio* is. The importance of appropriate syntax is demonstrated in English by the changes in meaning that are caused by the different word orders in the following three utterances: "John kidnapped the boy," "John, the kidnapped boy," and "The boy kidnapped John" (Lasnik, 1990).

The third major component of language is semantics. **Semantics** refers to the rules governing the meaning of words and sentences (Larson, 1990; Hipkiss, 1995; O'Grady & Dobrovolsky, 1996). Semantic rules allow us to use words to convey the subtlest of nuances. For instance, we are able to make the distinction between "The truck hit Laura" (which we would be likely to say if we had just seen the vehicle hitting Laura) and "Laura was hit by a truck" (which we would probably say if asked why Laura was missing class while she recuperated).

Despite the complexities of language, most of us acquire the basics of grammar without even being aware that we have learned its rules (Pinker, 1994). Moreover, even though we might have difficulty explicitly stating the rules of grammar that we employ, our linguistic abilities are so sophisticated that they enable us to utter an infinite number of different statements. We turn now to a consideration of how such abilities are acquired.

Language Development: Developing a Way with Words

To parents, the sounds of their infant babbling and cooing are music to their ears (except, perhaps, at three o'clock in the morning). These sounds also serve an important function: They mark the first step on the road to the development of language.

Children **babble**—make speechlike but meaningless sounds—from around the age of 3 months through 1 year. While they babble, they might produce, at one time or another, any of the sounds found in all languages, not just the sounds in the languages they are exposed to. Even deaf children display their own form of babbling: Infants who are unable to hear and who are exposed to sign language from birth "babble," but they do it with their hands (Pettito & Marentette, 1991; Pettito, 1993; Meier & Willerman, 1995).

As time goes by, babbling increasingly reflects the specific language that is being spoken in an infant's environment, initially in terms of pitch and tone, and eventually in terms of specific sounds. Some theorists suggest there is a *critical period* for language development early in life, in which a child is particularly sensitive to language cues and during which language is most easily acquired. In fact, if children are not exposed to language during this critical period, they have great difficulty in later overcoming their early deficit (Kuhl et al., 1992; de Boysson-Bardies & Halle, 1994).

By the time the child is approximately 1 year old, sounds that are not in the language to which the infant is exposed disappear. It is then a short step to the production of actual words. In English, these are typically short words that start with a consonant such as *b, d, m, p,* or *t*—which helps explain why *mama* and *dada* are so often among babies' first words. Of course, even before they produce their first words, children are capable of understanding a fair amount of the language they hear. In short, language comprehension precedes language production.

After the age of 1 year, children begin to learn more complicated forms of language. They produce two-word combinations, which become the building blocks of sentences, and the number of different words they are capable of using increases sharply. By the age of 2 years, the average child has a vocabulary of more than fifty words. Just six months later, that vocabulary has grown to several hundred words. At that time, children can produce short sentences, although they use **telegraphic speech**—sentences that sound as if they were part of a telegram, in which words not critical to the message are left out. Rather than saying, "I showed you the book," a child using telegraphic speech

syntax: The rules that indicate how words and phrases can be combined to form sentences

semantics: The rules governing the meaning of words and sentences

babble: Speechlike but meaningless sounds made by children from the ages of around 3 months through 1 year

telegraphic speech: Sentences that sound as if they were part of a telegram, in which words not critical to the message are left out

PsychLink

Language development
www.mhhe.com/
feldmanup6–08links

A syllable in signed language, similar to this, is found in the manual babbling of deaf infants and in the spoken babbling of hearing infants. The similarities in language structure suggest that language has biological roots.

might say, "I show book"; and "I am drawing a dog" might become "Drawing dog." As the child gets older, of course, the use of telegraphic speech declines and sentences become increasingly complex.

By age 3, children learn to make plurals by adding *-s* to nouns and to form the past tense by adding *-ed* to verbs. This ability also leads to errors, because children tend to apply rules too inflexibly. This phenomenon is known as **overgeneralization,** whereby children apply rules even when the application results in an error. Thus, although it is correct to say "walked" for the past tense of *walk,* the *-ed* rule doesn't work quite so well when children say "runned" for the past tense of *run* (Marcus, 1996).

overgeneralization: The phenomenon whereby children apply rules even when their application results in an error

Much of children's acquisition of the basic rules of language is complete by the time they are 5. However, a full vocabulary and the ability to comprehend and use subtle grammatical rules are not attained until later. For example, a 5-year-old boy who is shown a blindfolded doll and asked, "Is the doll easy or hard to see?" would have great difficulty responding to the question. In fact, if he were asked to make the doll easier to see, he would probably try to remove the doll's blindfold. By the time they are 8 years old, children have little difficulty understanding the question, realizing that the doll's blindfold has nothing to do with their own ability to see the doll (Chomsky, 1969).

Understanding Language Acquisition: Identifying the Roots of Language

Anyone who spends even a little time with children will notice the enormous strides they make in language development throughout childhood. However, the reasons for this rapid growth are far from obvious. Two major explanations have been offered, one based on learning theory and the other on innate processes.

The **learning-theory approach** suggests that language acquisition follows the principles of reinforcement and conditioning discussed in Chapter 5. For example, a child who utters "mama" is hugged and praised by her mother, which reinforces the behavior and makes its repetition more likely. This view suggests that children first learn to speak by being rewarded for making sounds that approximate speech. Ultimately, through a process of shaping, language becomes more and more like adult speech (Skinner, 1957).

learning-theory approach: The theory suggesting that language acquisition follows the principles of reinforcement and conditioning

The learning theory approach is supported by research that shows that the more parents speak to their young children, the more proficient the children become in language usage (see Figure 8-12). In addition, higher levels of linguistic sophistication in parents' speech to their young children are related to a greater rate of vocabulary growth, vocabulary usage, and even general intellectual achievement by the time the children are 3 years of age (Hart & Risley, 1997).

The learning-theory approach is less successful when it comes to explaining the acquisition of language rules. Children are reinforced not only when they use proper language, but also when they respond incorrectly. For example, parents answer the child's "Why the dog won't eat?" as readily as they do the correctly phrased question "Why won't the dog eat?" Both sentences are understood equally well. Learning theory, then, has difficulty in providing the full explanation for language acquisition.

Pointing to such problems with learning-theory approaches to language acquisition, Noam Chomsky (1968, 1978, 1991), a linguist, provided a groundbreaking alternative. Chomsky argued that humans are born with an innate linguistic capability that emerges primarily as a function of maturation. According to his analysis, all the world's languages share a similar underlying structure called a **universal grammar.** Chomsky suggests that the human brain has a neural system, the **language acquisition device,** that both permits understanding the structure of language and provides strategies and techniques for learning the unique characteristics of a given native language.

universal grammar: Noam Chomsky's theory that all the world's languages share a similar underlying structure

language acquisition device: A hypothesized neural system of the brain for understanding language

In a sense, then, the brain's hardwired language acquisition device provides the hardware for our acquisition of language; exposure to language in our environment allows us to develop the appropriate software. Chomsky argues that language is a uniquely human phenomenon made possible by the presence of the language acquisition device.

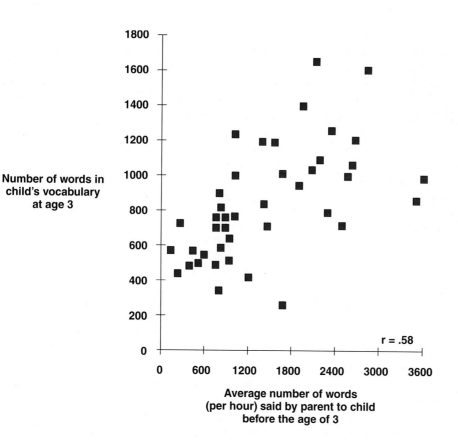

Figure 8-12 The greater the number of words that parents say to their children prior to the age of three, the larger their child's vocabulary. (Hart & Risley, 1997.)

Chomsky's view, as you might suspect, is not without its critics. For instance, learning theorists contend that the apparent ability of animals such as chimpanzees to learn the fundamentals of human language (as we discuss later in this chapter) contradicts the innate view. Thus, the issue of how humans acquire language remains hotly contested (Rice, 1989; Pinker, 1990, 1994; McDonald, 1997; Fromkin, 2000).

PsychLink

Language acquisition
www.mhhe.com/
feldmanup6-08links

The Influence of Language on Thinking: Do Eskimos Have More Words for Snow Than Texans Have?

Do Eskimos living in the frigid Arctic have a more expansive vocabulary for discussing snow than people living in warmer climates?

It makes sense that they would, and arguments that the Eskimo language has many more words than English for snow have been made since the early 1900s. At that time, linguist Benjamin Lee Whorf contended that because snow is so relevant to Eskimos' lives, they had developed a large vocabulary to describe it—considerably larger than what we find in other languages, such as English (Martin & Pullum, 1991; Pinker, 1994).

The contention that the Eskimo language is particularly abundant in snow-related terms led to the *linguistic relativity hypothesis,* the notion that language shapes and, in fact, might determine the way people of a particular culture perceive and understand the world (Whorf, 1956; Lucy, 1992, 1996; Smith, 1996). According to this view, language provides us with categories that we use to construct our view of people and events in the world around us. Consequently, language shapes and produces thought.

Let's consider another possibility, however. Suppose that, instead of language being the *cause* of certain ways of thinking, thought *produces* language. The only reason to expect that Eskimo language might have more words for snow than English is that snow is considerably more relevant to Eskimos than it is to people in other cultures.

Noam Chomsky, who argues that all languages share a universal grammar.

"*He's pretty good at rote categorization and single-object relational tasks, but he's not so hot at differentiating between representational and associational signs, and he's very weak on syntax.*"

Which view is correct? Most recent research refutes the linguistic relativity hypothesis and suggests, instead, that thinking produces language. In fact, new analyses of the Eskimo language suggest that Eskimos have no more words for snow than English speakers, and that if one examines the English language closely, it is hardly impoverished when it comes to describing snow (consider, for example, *sleet, slush, blizzard, dusting,* and *avalanche*). It seems most appropriate to conclude that thought generally influences language—and not the other way around (R. Brown, 1986; Pinker, 1990; McFadyen, 1996).

Do Animals Use Language?

One of the enduring questions that has long puzzled psychologists is whether language is uniquely human or if other animals are able to acquire it as well. Obviously many animals communicate with one another in rudimentary ways: fiddler crabs wave their claws to signal; bees dance to tell their hivemates the direction in which food will be found; certain birds make the sound "zick, zick" during courtship and "kia" when they are about to fly away. But researchers have yet to demonstrate conclusively that these animals use true language, which is characterized in part by the ability to produce and communicate new and unique meanings following a formal grammar.

Psychologists have, however, been able to teach chimps to communicate at surprisingly high levels. For instance, a chimp named Washoe learned to make signs for 132 words and was able to combine signs into simple sentences after four years of training. Even more impressively, Kanzi, a pygmy chimpanzee, has linguistic skills that some psychologists claim are close to those of a 2-year-old human being. Kanzi's trainers suggest that he can create grammatically sophisticated sentences and can even invent new rules of syntax (Gardner & Gardner, 1969; Savage-Rumbaugh et al., 1993).

Despite the skills displayed by primates such as Kanzi, critics contend that the language they use still lacks the grammar and the complex and novel constructions that characterize the realm of human capabilities. Instead, they maintain that the chimps are displaying a skill no different from that of a dog that learns to lie down on command in order to get a reward. Furthermore, firm evidence is lacking that animals are able to recognize and respond to the mental states of others of their species, an important aspect of human communication (Seidenberg & Pettito, 1987; Seyfarth & Cheney, 1992, 1996).

Sue Savage-Rumbaugh with primate friend, Panbanisha. Does the use of sign language by primates indicate true mastery of language?

Most evidence supports the contention that humans are better equipped than animals to produce and organize language in the form of meaningful sentences. But the issue of whether animals are capable of being taught to communicate in a way that resembles human language remains controversial (Gilbert, 1996; Savage-Rumbaugh & Brakke, 1996). (To consider some of the practical implications of work on animal language capabilities, see the *Psychology at Work* box.)

EXPLORING DIVERSITY

Teaching with Linguistic Variety: Bilingual Education

For picture day at New York's P.S. 217, a neighborhood elementary school in Brooklyn, the notice to parents was translated into five languages. That was a nice gesture, but insufficient: More than 40 percent of the children are immigrants whose families speak any one of twenty-six languages, ranging from Armenian to Urdu. (Leslie, 1991, p. 56)

From the biggest cities to the most rural areas, the face—and voice—of education in the United States is changing. Children with last names like Kim, Valdez, and Karachnicoff are becoming increasingly common as the wave of immigration during the 1980s, larger than that of the early 1900s, hits the country's schools. In seven states, including Texas, New York, and Colorado, more that one-quarter of the students are not native English speakers. For some 32 million Americans, English is their second language (see Figure 8-13).

How to deal appropriately and effectively with the increasing number of children who do not speak English is not always obvious. Many educators suggest that *bilingual education* is best. With a bilingual approach, students are taught some subjects in their native language while simultaneously learning English. Proponents of bilingualism maintain that it is necessary for students to develop a sound footing in basic subject areas and that, initially at least, instruction in their native language is the only way to provide them with that foundation. During this same period, they are to learn English, and the eventual goal is to shift all instruction into English.

In contrast, other educators suggest that all instruction ought to be in English from the moment students, including those who speak no English at all, enroll in school. In *immersion programs,* students are immediately plunged into English instruction. The reasoning—endorsed by voters in California in a referendum designed to end bilingual education—is that teaching students in a language other than English simply hinders nonnative English speakers' integration into society and ultimately does them a disservice. Proponents of immersion programs point to evidence that English immersion has led to increases in standardized test scores following the end of bilingual education programs (Wildavsky, 2000).

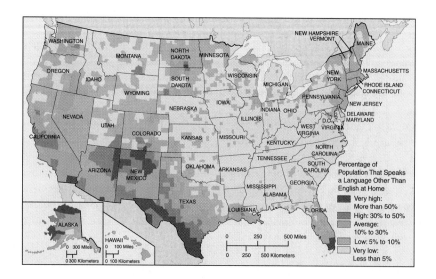

Figure 8-13 The language of diversity. Some 14 percent of people in the United States speak a language other than English at home. The majority of these speak Spanish, with the remainder speaking an astounding variety of different languages. Where are the largest clusters of non-English speakers in the United States, and what do you think explains these concentrations?

Psychology at Work

Rose Sevcik

Language Researcher

Education: A.B., John Carroll University; M.S., University of Connecticut; Ph.D., Georgia State University

Home: Atlanta, Georgia

Rose Sevcik

For years, Sondra's future was considered bleak. Born deaf, mute, and mentally retarded, Sondra appeared to have no hope of ever speaking. Today, though, she is able to make simple requests using a computer-based language.

Sondra's transformation is due to a line of research being pursued by psychologist Rose Sevcik. As a member of a team of researchers seeking to refine our understanding of language development by studying both children and chimpanzees, Sevcik's goal is to develop a language system for children who, due to various disabilities, do not develop speech.

Sevcik began her pursuit of this goal at John Carroll University, a small liberal arts institution in Ohio, which provided the right blend of courses and faculty. "The school offered a lot of undergraduate requirements in all types of disciplines," says Sevcik. "I found a course on research methods quite stimulating because I had the opportunity to learn about the neural sciences, and how the brain influences and affects behavior."

Graduating with an A.B. in psychology, Sevcik went on to the University of Connecticut and obtained a master's degree in experimental physiological psychology, followed by a doctorate in developmental comparative psychology at Georgia State University.

> "We are at work on a long-term project involving the use of microcomputer technology to develop an augmented system for kids who do not develop speech."

At the University of Connecticut, she began to study how children and chimpanzees use and develop language. "I had the experience of taking courses that focused on the relationship between biology and behavior," she notes. "I developed my thesis on the abilities of monkeys to perceive synthesized speech. What really got me into all of this was asking the question, 'Do these animals have any capacity to teach us something about how humans use and develop language?'

"When I came to Atlanta to continue my graduate studies, we used an artificial language developed in a study of how the great apes handle a systematic language system," Sevcik continues. "My doctoral thesis was on how a rare species of infant pygmy chimps would develop a communication system when their only exposure was being shown the language."

Currently, Sevcik works in the mornings with children and in the afternoons with chimps. "We are at work on a long-term project involving the use of microcomputer technology to develop an augmented system for kids who do not develop speech," she says. "We don't just want to look at the kids; we also want them to benefit." For developmentally disabled children such as Sondra, who might learn to communicate effectively for the first time, such work offers real promise.

PsychLink

Bilingual education resources
www.mhhe.com/
feldmanup6-08links

Although the issue is highly controversial, with strong political undercurrents, it is certainly clear that the ability to speak two languages provides significant cognitive benefits compared with speaking only one language. For example, bilingual speakers show more cognitive flexibility and might understand concepts more easily than those who speak only one language. They have more linguistic possibilities at hand for contemplating situations they encounter because of their multiple-language abilities. In turn, this permits them to solve problems with greater creativity and flexibility (Genesee & Gándara, 1999; Hong, 2000; Sanz, 2000).

A related question is this: What is the psychological impact of *biculturalism*, in which a person is a member of two cultures? Some psychologists argue that society should promote an *alternation model* of bicultural competence. In an alternation model, members of minority cultures are supported both in their efforts to maintain their original cultural identity and in their integration into the adopted culture. The model promotes the view that a person can live as part of two cultures, with two cultural identities, without having to choose between them. Whether the alternation model becomes widely adopted remains to be seen (LaFromboise, Coleman, & Gerton, 1995).

Evaluate

1. Match the component of grammar with its definition:

   1. Syntax
   2. Phonology
   3. Semantics

   a. Rules showing how words can be combined into sentences
   b. Rules governing the meaning of words and sentences
   c. The study of the sound units that affect speech

2. Language production and language comprehension develop in infants at about the same time. True or false?

3. _____ refers to the phenomenon in which young children omit nonessential portions of sentences.

4. A child knows that adding -ed to certain words puts them in the past tense. As a result, instead of saying "He came," the child says "He comed." This is an example of _____.

5. _____ theory assumes that language acquisition is based on principles of operant conditioning and shaping.

6. Chomsky argues that language acquisition is an innate ability tied to the structure of the brain. True or false?

Answers to Evaluate Questions

1. 1-a; 2-c; 3-b 2. False; language comprehension precedes language production. 3. Telegraphic speech 4. overgeneralization 5. Learning 6. True

Rethink

1. Why is overgeneralization seen as an argument against a strict learning-theory approach to explaining language acquisition?

2. Do people with two languages, one at home and one at school, automatically have two cultures? Why might people who speak two languages experience cognitive advantages over those who speak only one?

Looking Back

What is thinking?

- Cognitive psychology encompasses the higher mental processes, including the way people know and understand the world, process information, make decisions and judgments, and describe their knowledge and understanding to others. (p. 228)
- Thinking is the manipulation of mental representations of information. Thinking transforms such representations into novel and different forms, permitting people to answer questions, solve problems, or reach goals. (p. 228)
- Mental images are representations in the mind that resemble the object or event being represented. (p. 229)
- Concepts are categorizations of objects, events, or people that share common properties. Prototypes are representative examples of concepts. (p. 230)

What processes underlie reasoning and decision making?

- In syllogistic reasoning, people derive the implications of a set of assumptions that they know to be true. (p. 232)
- Decisions can sometimes (but not always) be improved through the use of algorithms and heuristics. Algorithms are rules that, if applied appropriately, guarantee a solution, whereas heuristics are cognitive shortcuts that might lead to a solution but are not guaranteed to do so. (p. 233)

How do people approach and solve problems?

- Problem solving typically involves three major steps: preparation, production of solutions, and evaluation of solutions that have been generated. (p. 234)
- In arrangement problems, a group of elements must be rearranged or recombined in a way that will satisfy a certain criterion. In problems of inducing structure, a person must identify the relationships among the elements presented and construct a new relationship among them. Finally, transformation problems consist of an initial state, a goal state, and a series of methods for changing the initial state into the goal state. (p. 235)
- A crucial aspect of the preparation stage is the representation and organization of the problem. (p. 235)
- In the production stage, people try to generate solutions. The solutions to some problems may already be in long-term memory. Alternatively, some problems might be solved through simple trial and error, whereas more complex problems require the use of algorithms and heuristics. (p. 237)
- In a means-end analysis, a person will repeatedly test for differences between the desired outcome and what currently exists, trying each time to come closer to the goal. (p. 237)
- Köhler's research with chimpanzees illustrates insight, a sudden awareness of the relationships among elements that had previously seemed unrelated. (p. 239)

What are the major obstacles to problem solving?

- Several factors hinder effective problem solving. Functional fixedness is an example of a broader phenomenon known as mental set. Mental set is the tendency for old patterns of problem solving to persist. The inappropriate use of algorithms and heuristics can also act as an obstacle to the production of solutions. Confirmation bias, in which initial hypotheses are favored, can hinder the accurate evaluation of solutions to problems. (p. 241)
- Creativity is combining responses or ideas in novel ways. Creativity is related to divergent thinking (the ability to respond with unusual, but still appropriate, responses to problems or questions) and cognitive complexity. (p. 243)

How do people use language?

- Language is the communication of information through symbols arranged according to systematic rules. All languages have a grammar—a system of rules that determines how thoughts can be expressed—that encompasses the three major components of language: phonology, syntax, and semantics. (p. 246)

How does language develop?

- Language production, preceded by language comprehension, develops out of babbling, which leads to the production of actual words. After a year, children use two-word combinations and their vocabulary increases, using telegraphic speech, in which words not critical to the message are dropped. By the age of 5, acquisition of language rules is relatively complete. (p. 247)
- Learning theorists suggest that language is acquired through reinforcement and conditioning. In contrast, Chomsky suggests that there is an innate language acquisition device that guides the development of language. (p. 248)
- The linguistic relativity hypothesis suggests that language shapes and might determine the way people think about the world. Most evidence suggests that although language does not determine thought, it does affect the way information is stored in memory and how well it can be retrieved. (p. 249)
- The degree to which language is a uniquely human skill remains controversial. Although some psychologists contend that certain primates communicate at a high level but nonetheless do not use language, others suggest that they truly understand and produce language in much the same way as humans. (p. 250)
- People who speak more than one language might have a cognitive advantage over those who speak only one. (p. 251)

Key Terms and Concepts

cognitive psychology (p. 228)
thinking (p. 228)
mental images (p. 229)
concepts (p. 230)
prototypes (p. 231)
syllogistic reasoning (p. 232)
algorithm (p. 233)
heuristic (p. 233)
means–end analysis (p. 237)
insight (p. 239)
functional fixedness (p. 241)
mental set (p. 242)
creativity (p. 243)
divergent thinking (p. 243)

convergent thinking (p. 243)
language (p. 246)
grammar (p. 246)
phonology (p. 246)
phonemes (p. 246)
syntax (p. 247)
semantics (p. 247)
babble (p. 247)
telegraphic speech (p. 247)
overgeneralization (p. 248)
learning-theory approach (p. 248)
universal grammar (p. 248)
language acquisition device (p. 248)

Psychology on the Web

1. Aside from mental images of sights and sounds, are there mental representations that correspond to the other senses? See if you can answer this question by searching the Web. Summarize your findings in writing.
2. Do animals think? What evidence is there on either side of this question? Find on the Web at least one example of research and/or argument on each side of this question. Summarize your findings and use your knowledge of cognitive psychology to state your position on this question.

Epilogue

The topics in this chapter occupy a central place in the field of psychology. We first examined thinking and reasoning, focusing on the importance of mental images and concepts in our understanding of and interactions with the world. We then turned to problem solving, identifying the three steps commonly involved in problem solving: preparation, production of solutions, and evaluation of generated solutions. Finally, we concluded with a discussion of language, describing the components of grammar and tracing language development in children.

We will continue our focus on cognition in the next chapter, as we turn to the subject of intelligence. Before we proceed, however, turn back to the Prologue, where we looked at the ability of NASA scientists to figure out how to restore vision to the damaged Hubble space telescope. Consider the following questions in light of what you have learned about reasoning, problem solving, and creativity.

1. How might the concepts of functional fixedness and mental set have hindered figuring out a solution to the Hubble problem?
2. Do you believe a computer could have created the solution to the Hubble problem, or is there something special about human problem solving that is superior to computer problem solving? Why?
3. Do you think the concept of insight was involved in finding a way to repair the telescope? How?
4. In what ways do you think divergent and convergent thinking are involved in the processes of problem solving?

Chapter Nine

Intelligence

Prologue: Mindie Crutcher and Greg Smith

Looking Ahead

Defining Intelligent Behavior

Measuring Intelligence

Are There Different Kinds of Intelligence?

Applying Psychology in the 21st Century: When a High IQ Keeps You from Getting a Job: Are You Too Smart for the Job You Want?

The Biological Basis of Intelligence: Finding the Site of IQ

Practical Intelligence and Emotional Intelligence: Toward a More Intelligent View of Intelligence

Becoming an Informed Consumer of Psychology: Scoring Better on Standardized Tests

Variations In Intellectual Ability

Mental Retardation

The Intellectually Gifted

Psychology at Work: Rob Davies, Advocate for the Mentally Retarded

Individual Differences in Intelligence: Hereditary and Environmental Determinants

Exploring Diversity: The Relative Influence of Heredity and of Environment: Nature, Nurture, and IQ

Placing the Heredity-Environment Question in Perspective

Looking Back

Key Terms and Concepts

Psychology on the Web

OLC Preview

Epilogue

Mindie Crutcher and Greg Smith

Prologue

Mindie Crutcher and Greg Smith

When Mindie was born, physicians said she would always be hopelessly retarded, that she would never sit up, never walk, never speak. "She will never know you're her mother," they told 25-year-old Diane Crutcher. "Tell relatives your baby is dead."

Today, the child who would never sit up is a lively seventh-grader. The child who would never talk or know her own mother told a symposium of physicians she was "glad Mom and Dad gave me a chance."

Yet the experts were right about one thing: Mindie does have Down syndrome, a genetic disorder, one of the most common birth defects and the leading physical cause of mental retardation (Turkington, 1987, p. 42).

****

Greg Smith, 10, is so intelligent that while most of his peers are still doing combat with long division, he's off to college.... Last month the 4' 6" youngster arrived at Virginia's Randolph-Macon College to begin his freshman year....

Greg was reeling off names of dinosaurs and their respective periods at age 2. At 4, he was adding sums into the quadrillions. In June, two days after his 10th birthday, he graduated from high school on the same day he lost one of his last baby teeth. And now, three afternoons a week, he excitedly recites theorems in Professor Adrian Rice's Calculus I (Fields-Meyer, 1999, p. 63).

Looking Ahead

Two very different people, with widely different intellectual capabilities and strengths. And yet, at their core, Mindie Crutcher and Greg Smith share basic aspects of humanity and even, one could argue, intelligence, that ultimately make them more similar than different.

In this chapter, we consider intelligence in all its many varieties. Intelligence is a focal point for psychologists intent on understanding how people are able to adapt their behavior to the environment in which they live. It is also a key aspect of how individuals differ from one another in how they learn about and understand the world.

We begin this chapter by considering the challenges involved in defining and measuring intelligence. If you are like most people, you have probably wondered how smart you are. Psychologists, too, have pondered the nature of intelligence. We examine some of their conceptions of intelligence as well as efforts to develop and use standardized tests as a means of measuring intelligence.

We also consider the two groups displaying extremes of individual differences in intelligence: people with mental retardation and the gifted. The special challenges of each population are discussed along with special programs that have been developed to help individuals from both groups reach their full potential.

Finally, we explore what are probably the two most controversial issues surrounding intelligence. After considering the degree to which intelligence is influenced by heredity and by the environment, we discuss whether traditional tests of intelligence are biased toward the dominant cultural groups in society—a difficult issue that has both psychological and social significance.

Prepare

How do psychologists characterize and define intelligence?

What are the major approaches to measuring intelligence?

Organize

Defining Intelligent Behavior

    Measuring Intelligence

    Are There Different Kinds of Intelligence?

    The Biological Basis of Intelligence

    Practical Intelligence and Emotional Intelligence

 **PsychLink**

Evolution of intelligence

www.mhhe.com/
feldmanup6-09links

Defining Intelligent Behavior

It is typical for members of the Trukese, a small tribe in the South Pacific, to sail a hundred miles in open ocean waters. Although their destination may be just a small dot of land less than a mile wide, the Trukese are able to sail unerringly toward it without the aid of a compass, chronometer, sextant, or any of the other sailing tools that are indispensable to modern western navigation. They are able to sail accurately, even when prevailing winds do not allow a direct approach to the island and they must take a zigzag course. (Gladwin, 1964)

How are the Trukese able to navigate so effectively? If you asked them, they could not explain it. They might tell you that they use a process that takes into account the rising and setting of the stars and the appearance, sound, and feel of the waves against the side of the boat. But at any given moment as they are sailing along, they could not identify their position or say why they are doing what they are doing. Nor could they explain the navigational theory underlying their sailing technique.

Some might say the inability of the Trukese to explain in Western terms how their sailing technique works is a sign of primitive or even unintelligent behavior. In fact, if we made Trukese sailors take a Western standardized test of navigational knowledge and theory, or, for that matter, a traditional test of intelligence, they might do poorly on it. Yet, as a practical matter, it is not possible to accuse the Trukese of being unintelligent: Despite their inability to explain how they do it, they are able to navigate successfully through the open ocean waters.

Trukese navigation points out the difficulty in coming to grips with what is meant by intelligence. To a Westerner, traveling in a straight line along the most direct and quickest route, using a sextant and other navigational tools, is likely to represent the most "intelligent" kind of behavior; on the other hand, a zigzag course, based on the "feel" of the waves, would not seem very reasonable. To the Trukese, who are used to their own system of navigation, however, the use of complicated navigational tools might seem so overly complex and unnecessary that they might think of Western navigators as lacking in intelligence.

It is clear that the term *intelligence* can take on many different meanings. Suppose you lived in a remote part of the Australian outback: You might differentiate between

more intelligent and less intelligent people in terms of their hunting skills. Or suppose you lived in the heart of urban Miami: Intelligence might be exemplified to you by being "streetwise" or by business success.

Each of these conceptions of intelligence is reasonable. Each represents an instance in which more intelligent people are better able to use the resources of their environment than less intelligent people, a distinction that is presumably basic to any definition of intelligence. Yet it is also clear that these conceptions represent very different views of intelligence.

That two such different sets of behavior can exemplify the same psychological concept has long posed a challenge to psychologists. For years, they have grappled with the issue of devising a general definition of intelligence that would remain independent of a person's specific culture and other environmental factors. Interestingly, untrained laypersons have fairly clear conceptions of intelligence. For example, in a survey asking people to define what they meant by intelligence, respondents suggested that intelligence encompassed problem-solving ability, verbal abilities, and social competence (Sternberg, 1985b).

The definition of intelligence that psychologists employ contains some of the same elements found in the layperson's conception. To psychologists, **intelligence** is the capacity to understand the world, think rationally, and use resources effectively when faced with challenges (Wechsler, 1975).

Unfortunately, neither the layperson's nor the psychologist's conception of intelligence is of much help when it comes to distinguishing, with any degree of precision, more intelligent people from less intelligent ones. To overcome this problem, psychologists who study intelligence have focused much of their attention on the development of **intelligence tests,** and have relied on such tests to identify a person's level of intelligence. These tests have proven to be of great benefit in identifying students in need of special attention in school, in diagnosing cognitive difficulties, and in helping people make optimal educational and vocational choices. At the same time, their use has proven quite controversial, raising important social and educational issues.

Measuring Intelligence

The forerunner of the modern IQ test was based on an uncomplicated, but completely wrong, assumption: that the size and shape of a person's head could be used as an objective measure of intelligence. The idea was put forward by Sir Francis Galton (1822–1911), an eminent English scientist whose ideas in other domains proved to be considerably better than his notions about intelligence.

Galton's motivation to identify people of high intelligence stemmed from his prejudices. He sought to demonstrate the natural superiority of people of high social class (of which he was one) by showing that intelligence was inherited. He hypothesized that head configuration, being genetically determined, was related to brain size, and therefore related to intelligence.

Galton's theories proved wrong on virtually every count. Head size and shape were not related to intellectual performance, and subsequent research has found little relationship between brain size and intelligence. However, Galton's work did have at least one desirable result: He was the first person to suggest that intelligence could be quantified and measured in an objective manner.

Following Galton's efforts, the first intelligence tests were developed by Alfred Binet (1857–1911). His tests followed a simple premise: If performance on certain tasks or test items improved with *chronological,* or physical, age, then performance could be used to distinguish more intelligent people from less intelligent ones within a particular age group. Using this principle, Binet, a French psychologist, devised the first formal intelligence test, which was designed to identify the "dullest" students in the Paris school system in order to provide them with remedial aid.

intelligence: The capacity to understand the world, think rationally, and use resources effectively when faced with challenges

intelligence tests: Tests devised to identify a person's level of intelligence

PsychLink

Gardner's essay on IQ
www.mhhe.com/
feldmanup6-09links

What does the Trukese people's method of navigation—which is done without maps or instruments—tell us about the nature of intelligence?

Alfred Binet

mental age: The average age of individuals who achieve a particular level of performance on a test

intelligence quotient (IQ): A score that takes into account an individual's mental *and* chronological ages

Binet began by presenting tasks to same-age students who had been labeled "bright" or "dull" by their teachers. If a task could be completed by the bright students but not by the dull ones, he retained the task as a proper test item; otherwise it was discarded. In the end he came up with a test that distinguished between the bright and dull groups, and—with further work—one that distinguished among children in different age groups (Binet & Simon, 1916).

On the basis of the Binet test, children were assigned a score relating to their **mental age,** the average age of individuals who achieve a particular level of performance on a test. For example, if the average 8-year-old answered, say, 45 items correct on a test, anyone who answered 45 items correct would be assigned a mental age of 8 years. Consequently, whether the person taking the test was 20 years old or 5 years old, each would have the same mental age of 8 years.

Assigning a mental age to students provided an indication of their general level of performance. However, it did not allow for adequate comparisons among people of different chronological ages. By using mental age alone, for instance, we might assume that a 20-year-old responding at a 18-year-old's level would be as bright as a 5-year-old answering at a 3-year-old's level, when actually the 5-year-old would be displaying a much greater *relative* degree of slowness.

A solution to the problem came in the form of the **intelligence quotient,** or **IQ,** a score that takes into account an individual's mental *and* chronological ages. To calculate an IQ score, the following formula is used, in which *MA* stands for mental age and *CA* for chronological age:

$$\text{IQ score} = \frac{\text{MA}}{\text{CA}} \times 100$$

Using this formula, we can return to the earlier example of a 20-year-old performing at a mental age of 18 and calculate an IQ score of (18/20) × 100 = 90. In contrast, the 5-year-old performing at a mental age of 3 comes out with a considerably lower IQ score: (3/5) × 100 = 60.

As a bit of trial and error with the formula will show you, anyone who has a mental age equal to his or her chronological age will have an IQ equal to 100. Moreover, people with a mental age that is greater than their chronological age will have IQs that exceed 100.

Although the basic principles behind the calculation of an IQ score still hold, IQ scores are figured in a different manner today and are known as *deviation IQ scores.* First, the average test score for everyone of the same age who takes the test is determined, and this average score is assigned an IQ of 100. Then, with the aid of statistical techniques that calculate the differences (or "deviations") between each score and the average, IQ scores are assigned.

As you can see in Figure 9-1, approximately two-thirds of all individuals fall within 15 IQ points above and below the average score of 100. As scores increase or fall beyond that range, the percentage of people in a category falls considerably.

IQ Tests: Gauging Intelligence

Remnants of Binet's original intelligence test are still with us, although it has been revised in significant ways. Now in its fourth edition and called the *Stanford-Binet IV,* the test consists of a series of items that vary in nature according to the age of the person being tested (Hagan, Sattler, & Thorndike, 1985; Thorndike, Hagan, & Sattler, 1986). For example, young children are asked to copy figures or answer questions about everyday activities. Older people are asked to solve analogies, explain proverbs, and describe similarities that underlie sets of words.

The test is administered orally. An examiner begins by finding a mental age level at which the person is able to answer all questions correctly, and then moves on to successively more difficult problems. When a mental age level is reached at which no items

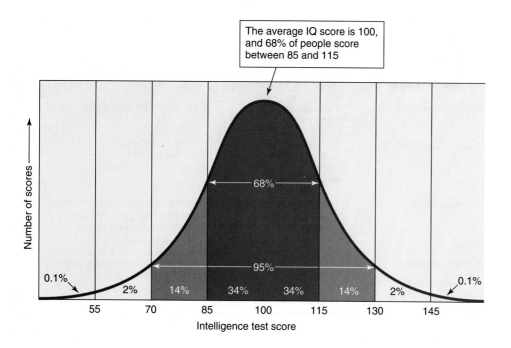

The average IQ score is 100, and 68% of people score between 85 and 115

Number of scores

0.1%

2%

14%

34%

34%

14%

2%

0.1%

68%

95%

55   70   85   100   115   130   145

Intelligence test score

Figure 9-1 The average and most frequent IQ score is 100, and 68 percent of all people are within a 30 point range centered on 100. Some 95 percent of the population have scores that are within 30 points above or below 100, and 99.7 percent have scores that are between 55 and 145.

can be answered, the test is over. By examining the pattern of correct and incorrect responses, the examiner is able to compute an IQ score for the person being tested. In addition, the Stanford-Binet provides separate subscores, providing clues to a test-taker's particular strengths and weaknesses.

The IQ test most frequently used in the United States was devised by psychologist David Wechsler and is known as the *Wechsler Adult Intelligence Scale–III*, or, more commonly, the *WAIS-III*. There is also a children's version, the *Wechsler Intelligence Scale for Children–III*, or *WISC-III*. Both the WAIS-III and the WISC-III have two major parts: a verbal scale and a performance (or nonverbal) scale. As you can see from the sample questions in Figure 9-2, the two scales include questions of very different types. Verbal tasks consist of more traditional kinds of problems, including vocabulary definition and comprehension of various concepts. In contrast, the performance (nonverbal) part involves the timed assembly of small objects and arranging pictures in a logical order. Although an individual's scores on the verbal and performance sections of the test are generally within close range of each other, the scores of a person with a language deficiency or a background of severe environmental deprivation might show a relatively large discrepancy between the two scores. By providing separate scores, the WAIS-III and WISC-III give a more precise picture of a person's specific abilities than other IQ tests (Kaufman & Lichtenberger, 1999).

Because the Stanford-Binet, WAIS-III, and WISC-III all require individualized, one-on-one administration, it is relatively difficult and time-consuming to administer and score them on a large-scale basis. Consequently, there are now a number of IQ tests that allow group administration. Rather than having one examiner ask one person at a time to respond to individual items, group IQ tests are strictly paper-and-pencil measures, in which those taking the tests read the questions and provide their answers in writing. The primary advantage of group tests is their ease of administration (Anastasi & Urbina, 1997).

Now in its fourth edition, the Stanford-Binet test consists of a series of items that vary in nature according to the age of the person being tested. What can we learn about a person from a test of this type?

Figure 9-2 Typical kinds of items found on the verbal and performance scales of the Wechsler Intelligence Scales for Children–III (WISC-III).

Types of Items Found on the Wechsler Intelligence Scales for Children—III (WISC-III)

Name	Goal of Item	Example
Verbal scale		
Information	To assess general information	Where does milk come from?
Comprehension	To test understanding and evaluation of social norms and past experience	Why do we put food in the refrigerator?
Arithmetic	To assess math reasoning through verbal problems	Stacy had two crayons and the teacher gave her two more. How many did she have altogether?
Similarities	To test understanding of how objects or concepts are alike, tapping abstract reasoning	In what way are cows and horses alike?
Performance Scale		
Digit symbol	To assess speed of learning	Match symbols to numbers using the key 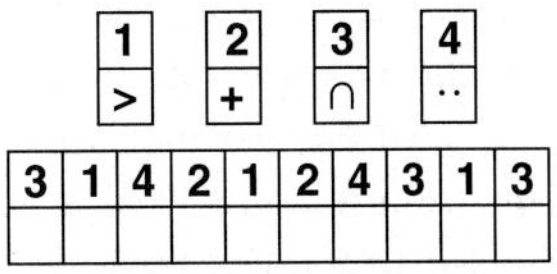
Picture completion	To identify missing parts, testing visual memory and attention	Identify what is missing 
Object assembly	To test understanding of relationship of parts to wholes	Put pieces together to form a whole 

However, group testing involves sacrifices that in some cases can outweigh the benefits. For instance, group tests generally offer fewer kinds of questions than tests administered individually. Furthermore, people might be more motivated to perform at their highest ability level when working on a one-to-one basis with a test administrator than they are in a group. Finally, in some cases it is simply impossible to employ group tests, particularly with young children or people with unusually low IQs (Aiken, 1996).

Achievement and Aptitude Tests

IQ tests are not the only kind of tests that you might have taken during the course of your schooling. Two other kinds of tests, related to intelligence but designed to measure somewhat different phenomena, are achievement tests and aptitude tests. An

achievement test is a test designed to determine a person's level of knowledge in a given subject area. Rather than measuring general ability, as an intelligence test does, an achievement test concentrates on the specific material a person has learned. High school students sometimes take specialized achievement tests in particular areas such as world history or chemistry as a college entrance requirement; lawyers must pass an achievement test (in the form of the bar exam) to practice law.

An **aptitude test** is designed to predict a person's ability in a particular area or line of work. Most of us take one of the best-known aptitude tests in the process of pursuing admission to college: the SAT and ACT. The SAT and ACT are meant to predict how well people will do in college, and the scores have proven over the years to be moderately correlated with college grades.

Although in theory the distinction between aptitude and achievement tests is precise, it is difficult to develop an aptitude test that does not rely at least in part on past achievement. For example, the SAT has been strongly criticized for being less an aptitude test (predicting college success) than an achievement test (assessing prior performance).

Reliability and Validity: Taking the Measure of Tests

When we use a ruler, we expect to find that it measures an inch in the same way as the last time we used it. When we weigh ourselves on the bathroom scale, we hope that the variations we see on the scale are due to changes in our weight and not to errors on the part of the scale (unless the change in weight is in an unwanted direction!).

In the same way, we hope that psychological tests have **reliability**—that they measure consistently what they are trying to measure. We need to be sure that each time we administer the test, a test-taker will achieve the same results—assuming that nothing about the person has changed, relative to what is being measured.

Suppose, for instance, that when you first took the SAT exams you scored a 400 on the verbal section of the test. Then, after taking the test again a few months later, you scored a 700. Upon receiving your new score, you might well stop celebrating for

Thousands of students enroll in courses in an effort to boost their SAT and GRE scores.
Courtesy of Kaplan, Inc.

PsychLink

Reliability and validity
www.mhhe.com/
feldmanup6–09links

achievement test: A test designed to determine a person's level of knowledge in a given subject area

aptitude test: A test designed to predict a person's ability in a particular area or line of work

reliability: A test's measuring consistently what it is supposed to measure

HERE LIES
FREDERICK
JONES

VERBAL — MATH
680   720

validity: A test's actually measuring what it is supposed to measure

a moment to question whether the test is reliable, for it is unlikely that your abilities could have changed enough to raise your score by 300 points.

But suppose your score changed hardly at all, and both times you received a score of about 400. You couldn't complain about a lack of reliability. However, if you knew your verbal skills were above average, you might be concerned that the test did not adequately measure what it was supposed to measure. In sum, the question has now become one of validity rather than reliability. A test has **validity** when it actually measures what it is supposed to measure.

Knowing that a test is reliable is no guarantee that it is also valid. For instance, Sir Francis Galton assumed that skull size was related to intelligence, and he was able to measure skull size with great reliability. However, the measure of skull size was not valid—it had nothing to do with intelligence. In this case, then, we have reliability without validity.

On the other hand, if a test is unreliable, it cannot be valid. Assuming that all other factors—motivation to score well, knowledge of the material, health, and so forth—are similar, if a person scores high the first time he or she takes a specific test and low the second time, the test cannot be measuring what it is supposed to measure. Therefore, the test is both unreliable and not valid.

Test validity and reliability are prerequisites for accurate assessment of intelligence—as well as for any other measurement task carried out by psychologists. Consequently, the measures of personality that we will consider in Chapter 14, clinical psychologists' assessment of psychological disorders discussed in Chapters 16 and 17, and social psychologists' measures of attitudes (Chapter 18) must meet the tests of validity and reliability in order for the results to be meaningful.

norms: Standards of test performance that permit the comparison of one person's score on the test to the scores of others who have taken the same test

Assuming that a test is both valid and reliable, one further step is necessary in order to interpret the meaning of a particular test-taker's score: the establishment of norms. **Norms** are standards of test performance that permit the comparison of one person's score on the test to the scores of others who have taken the same test. For example, a norm permits test-takers to know that they have scored, say, in the top 15 percent of those who have taken the test previously. Tests for which norms have been developed are known as *standardized tests*.

The basic scheme for developing norms is for test designers to calculate the average score achieved by a particular group of people for whom the test is designed. The test designers can then determine the extent to which each person's score differs from the scores of the others who have taken the test in the past. Test-takers are then able to consider the meaning of their raw scores relative to the scores of others who have taken the test, giving them a qualitative sense of their performance.

Obviously, the samples of test-takers who are employed in the establishment of norms are critical to the norming process. The people used to determine norms must be representative of the individuals to whom the test is directed.

Adaptive Testing: Using Computers to Assess Performance

Ensuring that tests are reliable and valid, and are based on appropriate norms, has become even more critical with the introduction of computers to administer standardized tests. The Educational Testing Service (ETS)—the company that devises the SAT and the Graduate Record Examination (GRE), used for college and graduate school admission—is moving to computer administration of all their standardized tests.

In the new computerized version, not only are test questions viewed and answered on a computer, but the test itself is individualized. Using *adaptive testing,* students do not necessarily receive identical sets of test questions. Instead, the computer first presents a randomly selected question of moderate difficulty. If the test-taker answers it correctly, the computer will then present a randomly chosen item of slightly greater difficulty. If the answer is wrong, then the computer will present a slightly easier item. Each question becomes slightly harder or easier than the question preceding it, depending on whether the previous response is correct. Ultimately, the greater the number of difficult questions answered correctly, the higher the score (see Figure 9-3). (For more on how tests are used, see the *Applying Psychology in the 21st Century* box on page 268.)

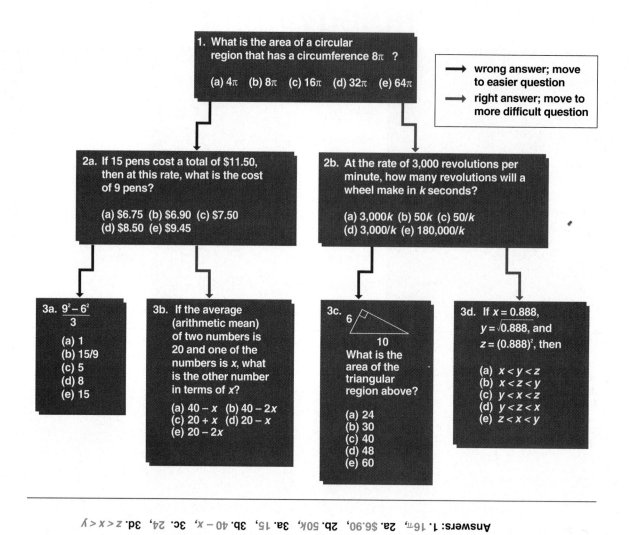

1. What is the area of a circular region that has a circumference 8π ?

(a) 4π (b) 8π (c) 16π (d) 32π (e) 64π

→ wrong answer; move to easier question
→ right answer; move to more difficult question

2a. If 15 pens cost a total of $11.50, then at this rate, what is the cost of 9 pens?

(a) $6.75 (b) $6.90 (c) $7.50
(d) $8.50 (e) $9.45

2b. At the rate of 3,000 revolutions per minute, how many revolutions will a wheel make in k seconds?

(a) $3,000k$ (b) $50k$ (c) $50/k$
(d) $3,000/k$ (e) $180,000/k$

3a. $\dfrac{9^2 - 6^2}{3}$

(a) 1
(b) 15/9
(c) 5
(d) 8
(e) 15

3b. If the average (arithmetic mean) of two numbers is 20 and one of the numbers is x, what is the other number in terms of x?

(a) $40 - x$ (b) $40 - 2x$
(c) $20 + x$ (d) $20 - x$
(e) $20 - 2x$

3c.
6 ╱
    10
What is the area of the triangular region above?

(a) 24
(b) 30
(c) 40
(d) 48
(e) 60

3d. If $x = 0.888$, $y = \sqrt{0.888}$, and $z = (0.888)^2$, then

(a) $x < y < z$
(b) $x < z < y$
(c) $y < x < z$
(d) $y < z < x$
(e) $z < x < y$

Answers: 1. 16π, **2a.** $6.90, **2b.** 50k, **3a.** 15, **3b.** $40 - x$, **3c.** 24, **3d.** $z < x < y$

Figure 9-3 Adaptive testing. In the Graduate Record Examination, the computer randomly selects a first question of medium difficulty. If the test taker answers the question correctly, the computer poses a more difficult question. Once the test taker gives an incorrect answer, he or she is given a question at the next easiest level, as illustrated in this example (*New York Times,* 1993, p. B9). Test takers are graded based on the level of difficulty of the questions they answer correctly, meaning that two test takers who answer the same number of questions correctly can end up with very different scores. What do you think are the drawbacks of adaptive testing of this sort? Do you think such tests may discriminate against test takers who are less familiar with computers compared with those who have easy access to them?

Because the test is able to pinpoint a test-taker's level of proficiency fairly quickly, the total time spent taking the exam is shorter than it is with a traditional exam. Test-takers are not forced to spend a great deal of time answering questions that are either much easier or much harder than they can handle.

Critics of computerized adaptive testing suggest that it can discriminate against test takers who have limited access to computers and thus have less practice with them or be more intimidated by the testing medium (Winerip, 1993). ETS disputes this claim, although some of its own research shows that women and older test-takers show greater anxiety at the beginning of the test. Despite this anxiety, however, their performance ultimately is not affected, and most research suggests that computerized adaptive testing provides scores equivalent to traditional paper-and-pencil measures for most types of testing.

Are There Different Kinds of Intelligence?

Although Binet's procedure for measuring intelligence, exemplified by the modern Stanford-Binet and WAIS-III intelligence tests, remains one of the most frequently employed, some theorists argue that it lacks an underlying conception of what intelligence

Applying Psychology in the 21st Century

When a High IQ Keeps You from Getting a Job: Are You Too Smart for the Job You Want?

Wanted: one not-so-smart police officer.

Although that's not what the advertisement for police officers in New London, Connecticut, said, it might as well have. The official hiring policy prevents people who score too low or too *high* on an employment test administered by the town to be considered for a position as police officer (Allen, 1999).

The hiring standards came to light during a three-year court battle, in which an applicant for a position as police officer was refused even an interview. The reason was he scored 33 out of 50 on an exam used by the police department to screen applicants, and anyone who scored over 27 was considered too skilled to do a good job as a police officer.

The screening test used by the police department has been utilized by 40,000 employers throughout the United States and has been given to 125 million people since it was first devised. It is designed to give a range of scores for people who are likely to be successful in a given profession, with the range depending on the nature of the specific job (see Figure 9-4). Although not a traditional IQ measure, the test gauges learning ability, skill in understanding instructions, and problem-solving potential (Wonderlic, 2000).

The rationale for excluding applicants who score too high, according to the New London police department, is that much police work is routine: highly intelligent police officers become bored and leave the job soon after they have received their expensive initial training.

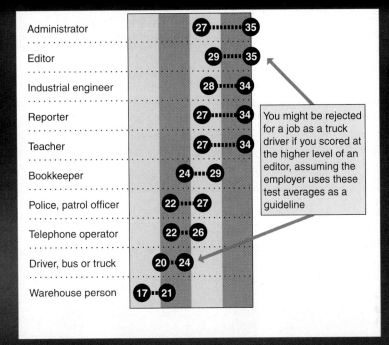

Figure 9-4 Based on a scale from 1 to 50 these are suggested minimum and maximum scores for selected professions as determined by a preemployment test developed by a private human resources firm.
(Source: Wonderlic, Inc., 1999.)

Critics of the police department's position point out that it takes considerable intelligence to deal with complex situations faced by police officers, such as complicated social situations involving families. Furthermore, some decisions must be made instantly and under enormous pressure—situations in which intelligence would clearly be of benefit. Furthermore, one could argue that it is better to have frequent turnover of intelligent workers, rather than be saddled with not-so-intelligent employees for long periods.

Despite these criticisms, courts have ruled that employers have the right to exclude potential workers on the basis of being too skilled, as long as the guidelines are uniformly applied to all job seekers. As a consequence, job applicants have a new worry to add to their anxieties—that they might score too high on a job test.

How do you think employers established that some scores on the tests described above were too high for certain jobs? Do you think it is reasonable to exclude people from certain jobs on the basis of high test scores? Why?

---

is. To Binet and his followers, intelligence was generally conceived of as a direct reflection of a person's score on the test. That was an eminently practical approach, but it depended not on an understanding of the nature of intelligence but primarily on comparing one person's performance with that of others. For this reason, the intelligence tests of Binet and his successors do little to increase our understanding of what intelligence is; they merely measure behavior assumed to exemplify intelligence.

One central question addressed by researchers is whether intelligence is a single, unitary factor, or whether it is made up of multiple components. Early psychologists interested in intelligence assumed that there was a single, general factor for mental ability, which they called **g,** or **g-factor** (Spearman, 1927). This general intelligence factor was thought to underlie performance on every aspect of intelligence, and presumably the g-factor was being measured on tests of intelligence (Jensen, 1998; Mackintosh, 1998).

g or g-factor: The single, general factor for mental ability that was assumed to underlie intelligence in some early theories of intelligence

Fluid and Crystallized Intelligence

More recently, some psychologists have suggested that there are really two different kinds of intelligence: fluid intelligence and crystallized intelligence (Cattell, 1967, 1987). **Fluid intelligence** reflects information-processing capabilities, reasoning, and memory. If we were asked to solve an analogy, group a series of letters according to some criterion, or remember a set of numbers, we would be using fluid intelligence.

In contrast, **crystallized intelligence** is the accumulation of information, skills, and strategies that people have learned through experience and that they can apply in problem-solving situations. We would be likely to rely on crystallized intelligence, for instance, if we were asked to participate in a discussion about the solution to the causes of poverty, a task that allows us to draw upon our own past experiences and knowledge of the world. The differences between fluid and crystallized intelligence become particularly evident in the elderly, who—as we will discuss further in Chapter 13—show declines in fluid, but not crystallized, intelligence (Schaie, 1993, 1994; Schretlen et al., 2000).

Other theoreticians conceive of intelligence as encompassing even more components. For example, Louis Thurstone (1938) suggested there were 7 factors, which he called primary mental abilities, and J. P. Guilford (1985) said there were 150!

Piloting a helicopter requires the use of both fluid intelligence and crystallized intelligence. Which of the two kinds of intelligence do you believe is more important for such a task?

fluid intelligence: Intelligence that reflects information-processing capabilities, reasoning, and memory

crystallized intelligence: The accumulation of information, skills, and strategies learned through experience and that can be applied in problem-solving situations

Gardner's Multiple Intelligences: The Many Ways of Showing Intelligence

In his consideration of intelligence, psychologist Howard Gardner has taken a very different approach from traditional thinking about the topic. Gardner argues that rather than asking "How smart are you," we should be asking a different question: "How are you smart?" In answering the latter question, Gardner has developed a theory of *multiple intelligences* that has become quite influential (Chen & Gardner, 1997).

Gardner argues that we have eight different forms of intelligence (described in Figure 9-5), each relatively independent of the others. He suggests that each of the multiple intelligences is linked to an independent system in the brain (Gardner, 1997, 1999).

Although Gardner illustrates his conception of the specific types of intelligence with descriptions of well-known people, each of us has the same eight kinds of intelligence, although in different degrees. Moreover, although the eight are presented individually, Gardner suggests that these separate intelligences do not operate in isolation. Normally, any activity encompasses several kinds of intelligence working together.

Gardner's theory has led to the development of intelligence tests that include questions in which more than one answer can be correct, providing the opportunity for test-takers to demonstrate creative thinking. These tests are based on the idea that different kinds of intelligence can produce different—but equally valid—responses to the same question.

PsychLink

Multiple intelligences
www.mhhe.com/
feldmanup6-09links

Is Information Processing Intelligence?

One of the newer contributions to understanding intelligence comes from the work of cognitive psychologists. Drawing on the research and theory that we discussed in Chapter 7, cognitive psychologists use an *information-processing approach.* They assert that the way people store material in memory and use the material to solve intellectual tasks provides the most accurate measure of intelligence. Consequently, rather than focusing on the structure of intelligence or its underlying content or dimensions,

"To be perfectly frank, I'm not nearly as smart as you seem to think I am."

1. *Musical intelligence (skills in tasks involving music).* *Case example:*

When he was 3, Yehudi Menuhin was smuggled into the San Francisco Orchestra concerts by his parents. The sound of Louis Persinger's violin so entranced the youngster that he insisted on a violin for his birthday and Louis Persinger as his teacher. He got them both. By the time he was 10 years old, Menuhin was an international performer.

2. *Bodily kinesthetic intelligence (skills in using the whole body or various portions of it in the solution of problems or in the construction of products or displays, exemplified by dancers, athletes, actors, and surgeons). Case example:*

Fifteen-year-old Babe Ruth played third base. During one game, his team's pitcher was doing very poorly and Babe loudly criticized him from third base. Brother Matthias, the coach, called out, "Ruth, if you know so much about it, *you* pitch!" Babe was surprised and embarrassed because he had never pitched before, but Brother Matthias insisted. Ruth said later that at the very moment he took the pitcher's mound, he *knew* he was supposed to be a pitcher.

3. *Logical-mathematical intelligence (skills in problem-solving and scientific thinking). Case example:*

Barbara McClintock won the Nobel Prize in medicine for her work in microbiology. She describes one of her breakthroughs, which came after thinking about a problem for half an hour . . .: "Suddenly I jumped and ran back to the (corn) field. At the top of the field (the others were still at the bottom) I shouted, 'Eureka, I have it!' "

4. *Linguistic intelligence (skills involved in the production and use of language). Case example:*

At the age of 10, T. S. Eliot created a magazine called *Fireside*, to which he was the sole contributor. In a three-day period during his winter vacation, he created eight complete issues.

5. *Spatial intelligence (skills involving spatial configurations, such as those used by artists and architects). Case example:*

Natives of the Caroline Islands navigate at sea without instruments. During the actual trip, the navigator must envision mentally a reference island as it passes under a particular star and from that he computes the number of segments completed, the proportion of the trip remaining, and any corrections in heading.

6. *Interpersonal intelligence (skills in interacting with others, such as sensitivity to the moods, temperaments, motivations, and intentions of others). Case example:*

When Anne Sullivan began instructing the deaf and blind Helen Keller, her task was one that had eluded others for years. Yet, just two weeks after beginning her work with Keller, Sullivan achieved a great success. In her words, "My heart is singing with joy this morning. A miracle has happened! The wild little creature of two weeks ago has been transformed into a gentle child."

7. *Intrapersonal intelligence (knowledge of the internal aspects of oneself; access to one's own feelings and emotions). Case example:*

In her essay "A Sketch of the Past," Virginia Woolf displays deep insight into her own inner life through these lines, describing her reaction to several specific memories from her childhood that still, in adulthood, shock her: "Though I still have the peculiarity that I receive these sudden shocks, they are now always welcome; after the first surprise, I always feel instantly that they are particularly valuable. And so I go on to suppose that the shock-receiving capacity is what makes me a writer."

8. *Naturalist intelligence (ability to identify and classify patterns in nature). Case example:*

During prehistoric times, hunter/gatherers would rely on naturalist intelligence to identify what flora and fauna were edible. Today, people who are sensitive to changes in weather patterns or are adept at distinguishing nuances between large numbers of similar objects may be expressing naturalist intelligence abilities.

Figure 9-5 Howard Gardner believes that there are eight major kinds of intelligences, corresponding to abilities in different domains. In what area does your greatest intelligence reside, and why do you think you have particular strengths in that area? (Adapted from Gardner, 2000.)

information-processing approaches examine the *processes* involved in producing intelligent behavior (Sternberg, 1990; Deary & Stough, 1996; Embretson, 1996).

For example, research shows that people with high IQ scores spend more time on the initial encoding stages of problems, identifying parts of a problem and retrieving relevant information from long-term memory, than do people with lower scores. This initial emphasis on recalling relevant information pays off in the end; those who use this approach are more successful in finding solutions than those who spend relatively less time on the initial stages (Sternberg, 1982, 1990; Deary & Stough, 1996).

Other information-processing approaches examine sheer speed of processing. For example, research shows that the speed with which people are able to retrieve information from memory is related to verbal intelligence. In general, people with higher IQ scores react more quickly on a variety of information-processing tasks, ranging from reactions to flashing lights to distinguishing between letters. The speed of information processing, then, might underlie differences in intelligence (Hunt, 1983; Deary & Stough, 1996; Siegler, 1998).

The Biological Basis of Intelligence: Finding the Site of IQ

You'll recall Sir Francis Galton's misguided efforts to measure head shape in order to assess intelligence. Although he failed, some researchers today have tried, with greater success, to identify the biological basis of intelligence. Using modern-day brain-scanning methods (refer to Chapter 3), researchers have recently identified several areas of the brain that might be the location of the brain's ability to answer IQ test questions.

According to findings of cognitive scientist John Duncan and colleagues, the brains of people completing IQ test–type questions in both verbal and spatial domains show activation in a similar location: the lateral prefrontal cortex (see Figure 9-6). The area is above the outer edge of the eyebrow, about where people rest their heads in the palm of their hands if they were thinking hard about a problem. This area of the brain is critical to juggling many pieces of information simultaneously and solving new problems (Duncan et al., 2000).

The findings suggest that there is a global "workspace" in the brain that organizes and coordinates information, helping to transfer material to other parts of the brain. In this view, the functioning of the workspace represents general intelligence, with the workspace integrating and coordinating specialized processing being carried out in other areas of the brain.

Practical Intelligence and Emotional Intelligence: Toward a More Intelligent View of Intelligence

> An employee who reports to one of your subordinates has asked to talk with you about waste, poor management practices and possible violations of both company policy and the law on the part of your subordinate. You have been in your present position only a year, but in that time you have had no indications of trouble about the subordinate in question. Neither you nor your company has an "open door" policy, so it is expected that employees should take their concerns to their immediate supervisors before bringing a matter to the attention of anyone else. The employee who wishes to meet with you has not discussed this matter with her supervisors because of its delicate nature. (Sternberg, 1998b, p. 17)

Your response to this situation has a lot to do with your future success in a business career, according to its author, psychologist Robert Sternberg. The question is one of a series designed to help give an indication of your intelligence. But it is not traditional intelligence that the question is designed to tap, but rather intelligence of a particular kind: practical intelligence. **Practical intelligence** is intelligence related to overall success in living (Sternberg, 1996, 1998b, 2000; R. K. Wagner, 1997, 2000).

Noting that traditional tests were designed to relate to academic success, Sternberg points to evidence showing that IQ does not relate particularly well to *career* success

practical intelligence: Intelligence related to overall success in living

A. Spatial

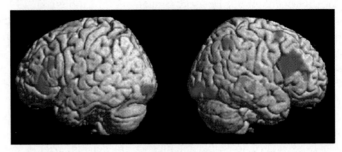

B. Verbal

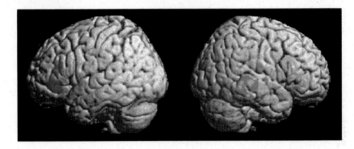

Figure 9-6 The lateral prefrontal cortex is activated when the brain is confronted with problems dealing with both verbal and spatial domains. These results suggest that there is a specific area of the brain that serves as the brain's center for organizing and coordinating information (Duncan et al., 2000).

Major models of intelligence
www.mhhe.com/
feldmanup6–09links

emotional intelligence: The set of skills that underlie the accurate assessment, evaluation, expression, and regulation of emotions

(McClelland, 1993). Specifically, although successful business executives usually score at least moderately well on IQ tests, the rate at which they advance and their ultimate business achievements are only minimally associated with their specific IQ scores.

Sternberg argues that career success requires a very different type of intelligence from academic success. Whereas academic success is based on knowledge of a particular information base obtained from reading and listening, practical intelligence is learned mainly through observation of others' behavior. People who are high in practical intelligence are able to learn general norms and principles and apply them appropriately. Consequently, practical intelligence tests measure the ability to employ broad principles in solving everyday problems (Sternberg et al., 1995; Polk, 1997; see Figure 9-7).

Some psychologists broaden the concept of practical intelligence even further beyond the intellectual realm and consider intelligence involving emotions. **Emotional intelligence** is the set of skills that underlie the accurate assessment, evaluation, expression, and regulation of emotions (Goleman, 1995b; Mayer & Salovey, 1997; Salovey & Sluyter, 1997).

According to psychologist Daniel Goleman (1995b), emotional intelligence underlies the ability to get along well with others. It provides us with the understanding of what other people are feeling and experiencing, and permits us to respond appropriately to others' needs. Emotional intelligence is the basis of empathy for others, self-awareness, and social skills.

Abilities in emotional intelligence might help explain why people with only modest IQ scores can be quite successful, despite their lack of traditional intelligence. High emotional intelligence might enable an individual to tune into others' feelings, permitting a high degree of responsiveness to others.

Although the notion of emotional intelligence makes sense, it has yet to be quantified in a rigorous manner. Furthermore, the view that emotional intelligence is so important that skills related to it should be taught in schools has raised concerns among some educators. They suggest that the nurturance of emotional intelligence is best left to students' families, especially because there is no well-specified set of criteria for what constitutes emotional intelligence (Schulman & Mekler, 1994; Sleek, 1997).

Still, the notion of emotional intelligence reminds us that there are many ways to demonstrate intelligent behavior—just as there are multiple views of the nature of intelligence (Fox & Spector, 2000). Table 9-1 presents a summary of the different approaches used by psychologists.

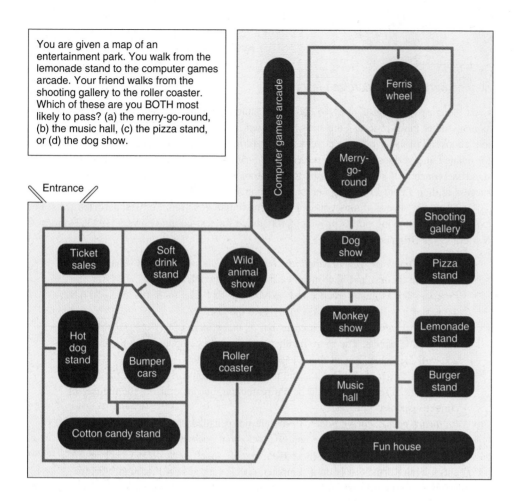

You are given a map of an entertainment park. You walk from the lemonade stand to the computer games arcade. Your friend walks from the shooting gallery to the roller coaster. Which of these are you BOTH most likely to pass? (a) the merry-go-round, (b) the music hall, (c) the pizza stand, or (d) the dog show.

Figure 9-7 Most standard tests of intelligence primarily measure analytical skills, while more comprehensive tests like this measure creative and practical abilities as well. (Sternberg, 2000, p. 389.)

Reprinted with permission from R. J. Sternberg, "The Holey Grail of General Intelligence," *Science*, 289, p. 399–401. Copyright 2000 American Association for the Advancement of Science.

Table 9-1 Major Approaches to Intelligence

Approach	Characteristics
IQ tests	General measures of intelligence
Fluid and crystallized intelligence	Fluid intelligence relates to reasoning, memory, and information-processing capabilities; crystallized intelligence relates to information, skills, and strategies learned through experience.
Gardner's multiple intelligences	Eight independent forms of intelligence
Information-processing approaches	Intelligence is reflected in the ways people store and use material to solve intellectual tasks
Practical intelligence	Intelligence in terms of nonacademic, career, and personal success
Emotional intelligence	Intelligence that provides an understanding of what other people are feeling and experiencing, and permits us to respond appropriately to others' needs

BECOMING AN
INFORMED CONSUMER
OF PSYCHOLOGY

Scoring Better on Standardized Tests

Even though psychologists disagree about the nature of intelligence, intelligence tests—as well as many other kinds of tests—are still widely used in a variety of situations. In school or on the job, almost all of us have had to cope with these formal, standardized tests—tests that have been formulated and verified with large representative samples. And most of us can probably understand the concern of students taking college entrance exams, such as the SAT, who worry that success in their future lives hangs on one morning's test results.

There are several things you can do to maximize your score on standardized tests. For example, the following points provide good advice for test-taking (Powers, 1993; Holmes & Keffer, 1995; Bronner, 1998):

- *Learn as much as you can about the test before you take it.* Know what sections will be on the test and how much each section is worth.
- *Practice.* Try as many practice tests as you can find. The more practice you have, the easier it will be when you actually take the test.
- *If the test is administered on a computer, as many increasingly are, take practice tests on a computer.* The more familiar you are with computers, the more at ease you will feel when you sit down to actually take the test.
- *Time yourself carefully.* Don't spend too much time on early items at the expense of later ones. Your goal should be not perfection, but maximizing the number of correct responses you get.
- *Be aware of the scoring policy.* If you are not penalized for wrong answers, guess. If there are penalties, be more conservative about guessing.
- *If it is a paper-and-pencil test, complete answer sheets accurately.* Check, and check again. If the test is on a computer, check your answer thoroughly before going on to the next question, because you won't be able to go back and change your answer once you've submitted it.

Evaluate

1. _____ is a measure of intelligence that takes into account both a person's chronological and mental ages.
2. _____ tests predict a person's ability in a specific area, while _____ tests determine the specific level of knowledge in an area.
3. Some psychologists make the distinction between _____ intelligence, which reflects reasoning, memory, and information-processing capabilities, and _____ intelligence, which is the information, skills, and strategies that people have learned through experience.
4. Cognitive psychologists use an _____-_____ approach to measure intelligence.

Answers to Evaluate Questions

1. IQ 2. Aptitude; achievement 3. fluid; crystallized 4. information processing

Rethink

1. Job interviews are really a kind of test. In what ways does a job interview resemble an aptitude test? An achievement test? Do you think job interviews can be shown to have validity? Reliability?
2. If fluid and crystallized intelligence do exist, how might they be tested? What applications would each of these types of intelligence have?

Variations in Intellectual Ability

"Hey, hey, hey, Fact Track!" The 11-year-old speaker chose one of his favorite programs. . . .

"What is your name?" appeared on the monitor.

"Daniel Skandera," he typed. A menu scrolled up listing the program's possibilities. Daniel chose multiplication facts, Level 1. . . .

Randomly generated multiplication facts flashed on the screen: "4 × 6," "2 × 9," "3 × 3," "7 × 6." Daniel responded, deftly punching in his answers on the computer's numeric key-pad. . . .

The computer tallied the results. "You completed 20 problems in 66 seconds. You beat your goal. Problems correct = 20. Congratulations Daniel!" And with that the 11-year-old retreated hastily to the TV room. The Lakers and 76ers were about to tip off for an NBA championship game, and Daniel wanted to see the first half before bedtime. (Heward & Orlansky, 1988, p. 100)

Prepare

How can the extremes of intelligence be characterized?

How can we help people reach their full potential?

Organize

Variations in Intellectual Ability
Mental Retardation
The Intellectually Gifted

If you view people with mental retardation as inept and dull, it is time to revise your perceptions. As in the case of Daniel, described above, individuals with deficits of intellectual abilities can lead full, rounded lives and in some cases perform well on certain kinds of academic endeavors.

More than 7 million people in the United States have been identified as having intelligence far enough below average to be regarded as having a serious deficit. Both those individuals with low IQs, known as people with mental retardation, and those with unusually high IQs, referred to as the intellectually gifted, require special attention if they are to reach their full potential.

Mental Retardation

Although sometimes thought of as a rare phenomenon, mental retardation occurs in 1 to 3 percent of the population. There is wide variation among those labeled as mentally retarded, in large part because of the inclusiveness of the definition developed by the American Association on Mental Retardation (AAMR). The association suggests that **mental retardation** exists when there is significantly below-average intellectual functioning, plus limitations in at least two areas of adaptive functioning involving communication skills, self-care, ability to live independently, social skills, community involvement, self direction, health and safety, academics, or leisure and work (AAMR, 1992; Burack, Hodapp, & Zigler, 1998).

Below-average intellectual functioning can be measured in a relatively straightforward manner, using standard IQ tests, but it is more difficult to measure limitations in particular adaptive skill areas. Ultimately, this imprecision leads to a lack of uniformity in how experts apply the label *mental retardation*. Furthermore, it has resulted in significant variation in the abilities of people who are categorized as having mental retardation, ranging from those who can be taught to work and function with little special attention, to those who virtually cannot be trained and must receive institutional treatment throughout their lives (Durkin & Stein, 1996; Negrin & Capute, 1996; Detterman, Gabriel, & Ruthsatz, 2000).

Most people with mental retardation have relatively minor deficits and are classified as having *mild retardation*. These individuals, who have IQ scores ranging from 55 to 69, constitute some 90 percent of all people with mental retardation. Although their development is typically slower than that of their peers, they can function quite independently by adulthood and are able to hold jobs and have families of their own.

At greater levels of retardation—*moderate retardation* (IQs of 40 to 54), *severe retardation* (IQs of 25 to 39), and *profound retardation* (IQs below 25)—the difficulties are more pronounced. For people with moderate retardation, deficits are obvious early, with language and motor skills lagging behind those of peers. Although these individuals can hold simple jobs, they need to have a moderate degree of

mental retardation: Having significantly below-average intellectual functioning and limitations in at least two areas of adaptive functioning

 **PsychLink**

ARC homepage
www.mhhe.com/
feldmanup6-09links

supervision throughout their lives. Individuals with severe and profound mental retardation are generally unable to function independently and typically require care for their entire lives.

PsychLink

NADS homepage
www.mhhe.com/
feldmanup6-09links

Identifying the Roots of Mental Retardation

What are the causes of mental retardation? In nearly one-third of the cases there is an identifiable biological reason. The most common biological cause of retardation is Down syndrome, exemplified by Mindie Crutcher in the prologue of this chapter. *Down syndrome* is caused by the presence of an extra chromosome. In other cases of mental retardation, an abnormality occurs in the structure of a chromosome. Birth complications, such as a temporary lack of oxygen, can also cause retardation (Simonoff, Bolton, & Rutter, 1996; Selikowitz, 1997).

The majority of cases of mental retardation are classified as *familial retardation,* in which no known biological defect exists but there is a history of retardation within the family. Whether the family background of retardation is caused by environmental factors, such as extreme continuous poverty leading to malnutrition, or by some underlying genetic factor, is usually impossible to determine.

Regardless of the cause of mental retardation, important advances in the care and treatment of those with retardation have been made in the last several decades. Much of this change was instigated by the Education for All Handicapped Children Act of 1975 (Public Law 94-142). In this federal law, Congress ruled that people with retardation are entitled to a full education and that they must be educated and trained in the *least restrictive environment.* The law increased the educational opportunities for individuals with mental retardation, facilitating their integration into regular classrooms as much as possible—a process known as *mainstreaming* (Hocutt, 1996; Lloyd, Kameenui, & Chard, 1997).

The philosophy behind mainstreaming suggests that interaction among students with and without mental retardation in regular classrooms will improve educational opportunities for those with retardation, increase their social acceptance, and facilitate their integration into society as a whole. Of course, special education classes still exist; some individuals with retardation function at a level too low to benefit from placement in regular classrooms. Moreover, children with mental retardation mainstreamed into regular classes typically attend special classes for at least part of the day (Guralnick et al., 1996; Phillips-Hershey & Ridley, 1996).

Some educators argue that an alternative to mainstreaming, called full inclusion, might be more effective. *Full inclusion* is the integration of all students, even those with the most severe educational disabilities, into regular classes. Teacher's aides are assigned to help the children with special needs progress. Schools having full inclusion have no separate special education classes. However, full inclusion is a controversial practice, and it is not yet widely applied (Koegel et al., 1996; Hocutt, 1996; Siegel, 1996b).

To read about another application of mainstreaming and full inclusion, in which people with even severe forms of mental retardation are moved from institutions into the community, see the Psychology at Work box.

The Intellectually Gifted

Another group of people—the intellectually gifted—differs from those with average intelligence as much as individuals with mental retardation, although in a different manner. Composing 2 to 4 percent of the population, the **intellectually gifted** have IQ scores greater than 130.

Although the stereotype associated with the gifted suggests that they are awkward, shy, social misfits unable to get along well with peers, most research indicates that just the opposite is true. Like Greg Smith, described in the prologue to this chapter,

intellectually gifted: Having an IQ score above 130; about 2 to 4 percent of the population

the intellectually gifted are most often outgoing, well-adjusted, popular people who are able to do most things better than the average person (Li, 1995; Harden, 2000, Winner, 1997, 2000).

For example, in a long-term study by psychologist Lewis Terman that started in the early 1920s and is still going on, 1,500 children who had IQ scores above 140 were followed and examined periodically over the next sixty years (Terman & Oden, 1947; Sears, 1977). From the start, members of this group were more physically, academically, and socially capable than their nongifted peers. They were generally healthier, taller, heavier, and stronger than average. Not surprisingly, they did better in school as well. They also showed better social adjustment than average. And all these advantages paid off in terms of career success: As a group, the gifted received more awards and distinctions, earned higher incomes, and made more contributions in art and literature than typical individuals. For example, by the time the members of the group were 40 years old, they had collectively written more than 90 books, 375 plays and short stories, and 2,000 articles, and had registered more than 200 patents. Perhaps most important, they reported greater satisfaction in life than the nongifted.

Of course, not every member of the group Terman studied was successful. Furthermore, high intelligence is not a homogeneous quality; a person with a high overall IQ is not necessarily gifted in every academic subject, but might excel in just one or two. A high IQ, then, is no universal guarantee of success (Shurkin, 1992; Winner, 2000).

Although special programs attempting to overcome the deficits of people with mental retardation abound, programs targeted at the intellectually gifted are fewer. This lack of special attention has been due in part to a persistent view that the gifted ought to be able to "make it on their own" ("if they can't, then they really weren't gifted in the first place"). More enlightened approaches, however, have acknowledged that without some form of special attention, the gifted become bored and frustrated with the pace of their schooling and might never reach their potential. Consequently, programs for the gifted are designed to provide enrichment that allow participants' talents to flourish (Harden, 2000; Winner, 2000).

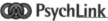 **PsychLink**

Gifted children information
www.mhhe.com/
feldmanup6-09links

Evaluate

1. The term *mental retardation* is applied specifically to people with an IQ below 60. True or false?

2. _____ _____ is a disorder caused by an extra chromosome that is responsible for some cases of mental retardation.

3. _____ is the process by which students with mental retardation are placed in normal classrooms to facilitate learning and reduce isolation.

4. Some forms of retardation can have a genetic basis, and can be passed through families. True or false?

5. People with high intelligence are generally shy and socially withdrawn. True or false?

Answers to Evaluate Questions

1. False: the term is used to describe a wide range of people with various degrees of mental impairment. 2. Down syndrome 3. Mainstreaming 4. True 5. False; the gifted are generally more socially adept than those of lower IQ.

Rethink

1. What advantages and disadvantages do you think full-inclusion programs would present for students with mental retardation? For students without mental retardation?

2. Why do you think negative stereotypes persist of gifted individuals and people with mental retardation, even in the face of contrary evidence? How can these stereotypes be changed?

Psychology at Work

Rob Davies

Advocate for the Mentally Retarded

Education: B.A., State University of New York, New Paltz; M.B.A., State University of New York, Albany

Home: Albany, New York

Rob Davies

Rob Davies has spent his professional life giving the chance to live a better life to those who have had little opportunity. After completing coursework as an undergraduate that included introductory and organizational psychology, he obtained a job working with juvenile delinquents and then ran a group home for individuals with mental retardation. While setting up a recreation program at a sheltered workshop, he realized that people with mental retardation had the potential to control their own lives. "We set up an apartment program for the individuals, and at that time hired homemakers who would teach them to budget, shop, and manage their own household," he says.

That experience ultimately led to his current position at the Bureau of Housing and Family Care for the New York Office of Mental Retardation and Developmental Disabilities, where he helps in the selection of sites for group homes for people with retardation within established neighborhoods. Much of his time is spent in dispelling people's prejudices about individuals with mental retardation.

> "In some ways, *we* are disabled, since we don't have the skills to reach in and pull out the communications. That's the real challenge we have before us."

"We still put limits on human potential," Davies notes. "In the twenty years I've been involved, I have never known anyone to predict human potential. I've heard many professionals say that individuals with mental retardation could never do certain things. But over the years all those predictions have been patently false, if individuals with mental retardation are given the appropriate exposure and stimulation."

Davies recalls a time early in his career when he approached a woman with severe mental retardation lying on a bed in an institution staring at the ceiling. He went over and touched her forehead and noticed an immediate change in her face.

"There was a glow in her eye in which you could almost see her being grateful for being acknowledged. I still see that woman's eyes today," he recalls. "Sometimes seeing people with mental retardation is just recognizing a certain smile or a flicker of the eye. That seeing of people is how we communicate.

"In some ways, *we* are disabled, since we don't have the skills to reach in and pull out the communications. That's the real challenge we have before us," he notes.

Prepare

Are traditional IQ tests culturally biased?
Are there racial differences in intelligence?
To what degree is intelligence influenced by the environment and to what degree by heredity?

Organize

Individual Differences in Intelligence
   Placing the Heredity-Environment Question in Perspective

Individual Differences in Intelligence: Hereditary and Environmental Determinants

Kwang is often washed with a pleck tied to a:

(a) rundel
(b) flink
(c) pove
(d) quirj

If you found this kind of item on an intelligence test, you would probably complain that the test was totally absurd and had nothing to do with your intelligence or anyone else's—and rightly so. How could anyone be expected to respond to items presented in a language that was so unfamiliar?

Yet to some people, even more reasonable questions can appear just as nonsensical. Consider, for example, the child who has been raised in a city who is asked about procedures for milking cows, or someone raised in a rural area who is asked about subway ticketing procedures. Obviously, the previous experience of the test-takers would affect their ability to answer correctly. And if such types of questions were included on an IQ test, a critic could rightly contend that the test had more to do with prior experience than with intelligence.

Although IQ tests nowadays do not include questions that are so clearly dependent on prior knowledge as questions about cows and subways, the background and experiences of test-takers do have the potential to affect results. In fact, the issue of devising fair intelligence tests that measure knowledge unrelated to culture and family background and experience is central to explaining an important and persistent finding: Members of certain racial and cultural groups consistently score lower on traditional intelligence tests than members of other groups (MacKenzie, 1984; Humphreys, 1992). For example, as a group, blacks tend to average 10 to 15 IQ points lower than whites. Does this reflect a true difference in intelligence, or are the questions biased in the kinds of knowledge they test? Clearly, if whites perform better because of their greater familiarity with the kind of information that is being tested, their higher IQ scores are not necessarily an indication that they are more intelligent than members of other groups.

There is good reason to believe that some standardized IQ tests contain elements that discriminate against minority group members whose experiences differ from those of the white majority. Consider the question "What should you do if another child grabbed your hat and ran off with it?" Most white middle-class children answer that they would tell an adult, and this response is scored as correct. On the other hand, a reasonable response might be to chase the person and fight to get the hat back, the answer that is chosen by many urban black children—but one that is scored as incorrect (Miller-Jones, 1989; Aiken, 1996).

Furthermore, tests might include even subtler forms of bias against minority groups. For example, psychologist Janet Helms (1992) argues that assessments of cognitive ability developed in the United States are sometimes constructed to favor responses that implicitly reflect North American or European values, customs, or traditions. At the same time, such tests are biased against African and other cultural value systems.

More specifically, Helms suggests that the traditional Western value of "rugged individualism" means that correct answers to test items can require a test-taker to reason independently of a particular social context. In contrast, the African cultural value of communalism, in which one's group is valued more than individuals, can leave test-takers from that tradition unable to answer a question that provides no information about the social context (Greenfield, 1997).

EXPLORING DIVERSITY

The Relative Influence of Heredity and of Environment: Nature, Nurture, and IQ

In an attempt to produce a **culture-fair IQ test,** one that does not discriminate against members of any minority group, psychologists have tried to devise test items that assess experiences common to all cultures or emphasize questions that do not require language usage. However, test makers have found this difficult to do, because past experiences, attitudes, and values almost always have an impact on respondents' answers. For example, children raised in Western cultures group things based on what they *are* (such as putting *dog* and *fish* into the category of *animal*). In contrast, members of the Kpelle tribe in Africa see intelligence demonstrated by grouping things according to what they *do* (grouping *fish* with *swim*). Similarly, children in the U.S. asked to memorize the position of objects on a chess board perform better than African children living in remote villages if household objects familiar to the U.S. children are used. But if rocks are used instead of household objects, the African children do better. In short, it is difficult to produce a test that is truly culture-fair (Anastasi, 1988; Samuda, 1998; Sandoval et al., 1998).

The efforts of psychologists to produce culture-fair measures of intelligence relate to a lingering controversy over differences in intelligence between members of minority and majority groups. In attempting to identify whether there are differences between such groups, psychologists have had to confront the broader issue of determining the relative contribution to intelligence of genetic factors (heredity) and experience (environment)—the nature-nurture issue that we first discussed in Chapter 1 (Scarr, 1996; Detterman, 1996; Steen, 1996).

culture-fair IQ test: A test that does not discriminate against members of any minority group

 **PsychLink**

The Bell Curve Review
www.mhhe.com/
feldmanup6-09links

heritability: A measure of the degree to which a characteristic is related to genetic, inherited factors

Richard Herrnstein, a psychologist, and Charles Murray, a sociologist, fanned the flames of the debate with the publication of their book, *The Bell Curve,* in the mid 1990s (Herrnstein & Murray, 1994). They argued that an analysis of IQ differences between whites and blacks demonstrated that, although environmental factors played a role, there were also basic genetic differences between the two races. They based their argument on a number of findings. For instance, on average, whites score 15 points higher than blacks on traditional IQ tests even when socioeconomic status (SES) is taken into account. According to Herrnstein and Murray, middle- and upper-SES blacks score lower than middle- and upper-SES whites, just as lower-SES blacks score lower on average than lower-SES whites. Intelligence differences between blacks and whites, they concluded, could not be attributed to environmental differences alone.

Moreover, intelligence in general shows a high degree of **heritability,** a measure of the degree to which a characteristic is related to genetic, inherited factors (e.g., Bouchard et al., 1990; Plomin & Petrill, 1997; Grigorenko, 2000). As can be seen in Figure 9-8, the closer the genetic link between two people, the greater the correspondence of IQ scores. Using data such as these, Herrnstein and Murray argued that differences between races in IQ scores were largely caused by genetically based differences in intelligence.

However, many psychologists reacted strongly to the arguments laid out in *The Bell Curve,* refuting several of the book's contentions (e.g., Nisbett, 1994; Fischer et al., 1996; Neisser et al., 1996). For one thing, even when attempts are made to hold socioeconomic conditions constant, wide variations remain among individual households. Furthermore, no one can convincingly assert that living conditions of blacks and whites are identical even when their socioeconomic status is similar. In addition, as we discussed earlier, there is reason to believe that traditional IQ tests can discriminate against lower-SES urban blacks by asking for information pertaining to experiences they are unlikely to have had.

Moreover, blacks who are raised in economically enriched environments have similar IQ scores to whites in comparable environments. For example, a study by Sandra Scarr and Richard Weinberg (1976) examined black children who had been adopted at an early age by white middle-class families of above-average intelligence. The IQ scores of the children averaged 106—about 15 points above the average IQ scores of unadopted black children in the study. Other research shows that the racial gap in IQ narrows considerably following a college education, and cross-cultural data find that when racial gaps exist in other cultures, it is the economically disadvantaged groups that typically show lower scores. In short, the evidence that genetic factors play the major role in determining racial differences in IQ is not compelling, although the

Figure 9-8 Summary findings on IQ and closeness of genetic relationship. The bars indicate the median correlations found across studies, while the percentages indicate the degree of genetic overlap within the relationship. Note, for example, that the median correlation for unrelated people reared apart is quite low, while the correlation for identical twins reared together is substantially higher. In general, the more similar the genetic and environmental background of two people, the greater the correlation. (Adapted from Bouchard & McGue, 1981.)

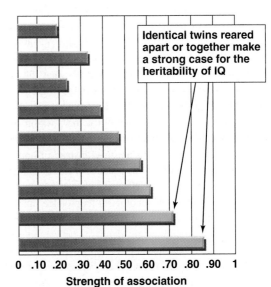

Genetic Overlap	Relationship
0%	Foster parent and child
0%	Unrelated children reared together
50%	Siblings reared apart
50%	Parent and child
50%	Siblings reared together
50%	Fraternal twins, different sex
50%	Fraternal twins, same sex
100%	Identical twins reared apart
100%	Identical twins reared together

Identical twins reared apart or together make a strong case for the heritability of IQ

0 .10 .20 .30 .40 .50 .60 .70 .80 .90 1
Strength of association (median correlations)

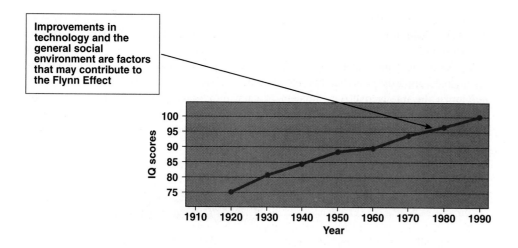

Improvements in technology and the general social environment are factors that may contribute to the Flynn Effect

Figure 9-9 Although average IQ scores have increased steadily during the 1900s—a phenomenon known as the Flynn effect—the reason for the rise is not at all clear. Do you think this trend is likely to continue in the 21st century? (Source: Horgan, 1995, p. 12.)

question still evokes considerable controversy (Ogbu, 1992; Weinberg, Scarr, & Waldman, 1992; Neisser et al., 1996; Myerson et al., 1998).

It is also crucial to remember that IQ scores and intelligence have greatest relevance in terms of individuals, not groups. In fact, considering group *racial* differences presents some conceptually troublesome distinctions. *Race* was originally meant to be a biological concept, referring to classifications based on physical and structural characteristics of a species. Despite its biological origins, however, the term *race* has taken on additional meanings and is used in a variety of ways, ranging from skin color to culture. In short, the concept of "race" is extraordinarily inexact (Betancourt & Lopez, 1993; Yee et al., 1993; Beutler et al., 1996).

Consequently, drawing comparisons between different races on any dimension, including IQ scores, is an imprecise, potentially misleading, and often fruitless venture. By far, the greatest discrepancies in IQ scores occur when comparing *individuals,* and not when comparing mean IQ scores of different *groups*. There are blacks who score high on IQ tests and whites who score low, just as there are whites who score high and blacks who score low. For the concept of intelligence to aid in the betterment of society, we must examine how *individuals* perform, not the groups to which they belong. We need to focus on the degree to which intelligence can be enhanced in a given person, not in members of a particular group (Angoff, 1988).

Other issues make the heredity-versus-environment debate somewhat irrelevant to practical concerns. For example, as we discussed earlier, there are multiple kinds of intelligence, and traditional IQ scores do not tap many of them. Furthermore, IQ scores are often inadequate predictors of ultimate occupational success.

It also appears that intelligence is more flexible and modifiable than originally envisioned. For instance, researchers have been puzzled by data showing a long-term increase in IQ scores since the early 1900s. Because the average person today gets more items correct on IQ tests than the average person several generations ago, scores have risen significantly—a phenomenon known as the *Flynn effect* after its discoverer, James Flynn. The Flynn effect is not trivial, with the performance of the average 20-year-old today measuring some 15 points higher than the performance of the average 20-year-old in 1940 (Neisser, 1998; Flynn, 1999, 2000; see Figure 9-9).

The reason for the Flynn effect is not clear. It could be that increases in technology have made people better at certain skills that IQ tests measure, or it might be that better nutrition, better parenting, or improvements in the general social environment, including education, are the cause. Whatever the cause, the change in IQ scores over the century is not due to genetic changes: The period over which the Flynn effect has occurred is far too short a time for people to have evolved into a more intelligent species (Neisser, 1996; Shea, 1996b).

Placing the Heredity–Environment Question in Perspective

Ultimately, there is no absolute answer to the question of how much intelligence is influenced by heredity or by the environment. We are dealing with an issue for which experiments to unambiguously determine cause and effect cannot be devised. (A

moment's thought about how we might experimentally assign infants to enriched or deprived environments will reveal the impossibility of devising ethically reasonable experiments!)

The more critical question to ask, then, is not whether hereditary or environmental factors primarily underlie intelligence, but whether there is anything we can do to maximize the intellectual development of each individual. If we can find ways to do this, we will be able to make changes in the environment—which might take the form of enriched home and school environments—that can lead each person to reach his or her potential.

Evaluate

1. Intelligence tests might be biased toward the prevailing culture in such a way that minorities are put at a disadvantage when taking these tests. True or false?
2. A_____-_____ test tries to use only questions appropriate to all people taking the test.
3. IQ tests can accurately determine the intelligence of entire groups of people. True or false?
4. Intelligence can be seen as a combination of_____ and_____ factors.

Rethink

1. Why might a test that identifies a disproportionate number of minority group members for special educational services and remedial assistance be considered potentially biased? Isn't the purpose of the test to help persons at risk of falling behind academically? How can a test created for a good purpose be biased?
2. What ideas do you have for explaining the Flynn effect, the steady rise in IQ scores over the past half-century? How would you test your ideas?

Answers to Evaluate Questions

1. True 2. culture-fair 3. False; IQ tests are used to measure individual intelligence. Within any group there are wide variations in individual intelligence. 4. hereditary; environmental

How do psychologists characterize and define intelligence?

- Because intelligence can take many forms, defining it is challenging. One commonly accepted view is that intelligence is the capacity to understand the world, think rationally, and use resources effectively when faced with challenges. (p. 260)

What are the major approaches to measuring intelligence?

- Intelligence tests are used to measure intelligence. Traditionally, such tests have compared a person's mental age and chronological age to yield an IQ, or intelligence quotient, score. (p. 261)
- Specific tests of intelligence include the Stanford-Binet test, the Wechsler Adult Intelligence Scale–III (WAIS-III), and the Wechsler Intelligence Scale for Children–III (WISC-III). Achievement tests and aptitude tests are other types of standardized tests. (p. 262)
- Tests are expected to be both reliable and valid. Reliability refers to the consistency with which a test measures what it is trying to measure. A test has validity when it actually measures what it is supposed to measure. (p. 265)
- The earliest psychologists assumed that there was a general factor for mental ability called g. However, later psychologists disputed the view that intelligence was unidimensional. (p. 268)
- Some researchers suggest that there are two kinds of intelligence: fluid intelligence and crystallized intelligence. Gardner's theory of multiple intelligences proposes that there are eight spheres of intelligence: musical, bodily kinesthetic, logical-mathematical, linguistic, spatial, interpersonal, intrapersonal, and naturalist. (p. 269)
- Information-processing approaches suggest that intelligence should be conceptualized as the way in which people represent and use material cognitively. Rather than focus on the structure of intelligence, this approach examines the processes underlying intelligent behavior. (p. 270)
- Practical intelligence is intelligence related to overall success in living, while emotional intelligence is the set of skills that underlie the accurate assessment, evaluation, expression, and regulation of emotions. (p. 271)

How can the extremes of intelligence be characterized?

- At the two extremes of intelligence are individuals with mental retardation and the intellectually gifted. The levels of mental retardation include mild, moderate, severe, and profound retardation. (p. 275)
- About one-third of the cases of retardation have a known biological cause; Down syndrome is the most common. Most cases, however, are classified as familial retardation, for which there is no known biological cause. (p. 276)
- Two to 4 percent of the population are intellectually gifted, with IQ scores greater than 130. (p. 276)

How can we help people reach their full potential?

- There have been a number of advances in the treatment of both people with mental retardation and the intellectually gifted. In mainstreaming, individuals with mental retardation are integrated into regular education classrooms as much as possible. In full inclusion, all students, even those with the most severe educational disabilities, are integrated into regular classes. (p. 276)

Are traditional IQ tests culturally biased?

- Traditional intelligence tests have frequently been criticized for being biased in favor of the white middle-class population. This controversy has led to attempts to devise culture-fair tests, IQ measures that avoid questions that depend on a particular cultural background. (p. 279)

Are there racial differences in intelligence?

- Issues of race and environmental and genetic influences on intelligence represent major controversies. (p. 279)

To what degree is intelligence influenced by the environment and to what degree by heredity?

- Attempting to distinguish environmental from hereditary factors in intelligence is difficult and ultimately misguided. Because individual IQ scores vary far more than group IQ scores, it is more critical to ask what can be done to maximize the intellectual development of each individual. (p. 281)

Key Terms and Concepts

intelligence (p. 261)

intelligence tests (p. 261)

mental age (p. 262)

intelligence quotient (IQ) (p. 262)

achievement test (p. 265)

aptitude test (p. 265)

reliability (p. 265)

validity (p. 266)

norms (p. 266)

g or g-factor (p. 268)

fluid intelligence (p. 269)

crystallized intelligence (p. 269)

practical intelligence (p. 271)

emotional intelligence (p. 272)

mental retardation (p. 275)

intellectually gifted (p. 276)

culture-fair IQ test (p. 279)

heritability (p. 280)

Psychology on the Web

1. Many sites on the Web permit you to assess your IQ. Take at least two such tests and compare (a) your results, (b) what mental qualities seemed to be tested on the test, and (c) your impression of the reliability and validity of the tests. Write up your conclusions.
2. Find a way to assess at least one other of your multiple intelligences (i.e., one not tested by the IQ tests you took) on the Web. What sort of intelligence was the test supposed to be testing? What sorts of items were included? How valid and reliable do you think it was, both in and of itself and compared with the IQ tests you took? Summarize your findings in writing.

Epilogue

In this chapter, we looked at one of the most controversial areas of psychology—intelligence. Some of the most heated discussions in all of psychology are focused around this topic, engaging educators, policymakers, politicians, and psychologists alike. The issues include the very meaning of intelligence, its measurement, individual extremes of intelligence, and, finally, the heredity–environment question. We saw that the quest of partitioning intelligence into hereditary factors versus environmental factors is generally pointless. In the area of intelligence, the focus of our efforts should

be on making sure that every individual has the opportunity to achieve his or her potential.

Before we leave the topic of intelligence, return to the stories of the two persons of widely different intellectual capabilities discussed in the prologue, Mindie Crutcher and Greg Smith. Consider the following questions on the basis of what you have learned about intelligence in this chapter.

1. Mindie Crutcher's physicians concluded in her infancy that she would never be able to sit up, eat, speak, or recognize her mother. Do you think the physicians' conclusions reflect a kind of aptitude testing, achievement testing, or intelligence testing? Why?

2. In what ways would placing Crutcher in a separate educational program have helped or hurt her chances of reaching her full potential?

3. How might the educational acceleration of Greg Smith help and hinder his later development? Do you think slowing down his educational progress might be beneficial? How?

4. Based on research relating to individuals who have unusually high IQ scores, what do you think Greg's emotional intelligence is like?

Preview

For additional quizzing and a variety of interactive resources, visit the *Understanding Psychology* Online Learning Center at

www.mhhe.com/feldmanup6

Chapter Ten

Motivation and Emotion

Prologue: Tour de Lance

Looking Ahead

Explaining Motivation

Instinct Approaches: Born to Be Motivated

Drive-Reduction Approaches: Satisfying Our Needs

Arousal Approaches: Beyond Drive Reduction

Incentive Approaches: Motivation's Pull

Cognitive Approaches: The Thoughts Behind Motivation

Maslow's Hierarchy: Ordering Motivational Needs

Applying the Different Approaches to Motivation

Human Needs and Motivation: Eat, Drink, and Be Daring

The Motivation Behind Hunger and Eating

Eating Disorders

Becoming an Informed Consumer of Psychology: Dieting and Losing Weight Successfully

The Need for Achievement: Striving for Success

The Need for Affiliation: Striving for Friendship

The Need for Power: Striving for Impact on Others

Understanding Emotional Experiences

The Functions of Emotions

Determining the Range of Emotions: Labeling Our Feelings

The Roots of Emotions

The James-Lange Theory: Do Gut Reactions Equal Emotions?

The Cannon-Bard Theory: Physiological Reactions as the Result of Emotions

The Schachter-Singer Theory: Emotions as Labels

Contemporary Perspectives on Emotion

Applying Psychology in the 21st Century: The Truth About Lies: Do Lie Detectors Work?

Nonverbal Behavior and the Expression of Emotions

Exploring Diversity: Do People in All Cultures Express Emotion Similarly?

The Facial-Feedback Hypothesis: Smile, Though You're Feeling Blue

Looking Back

Key Terms and Concepts

Psychology on the Web

OLC Preview

Epilogue

Prologue

Tour de Lance

When Lance Armstrong completed the final leg of the Tour de France before a cheering crowd of a half million people, it meant more than winning the world's most prestigious cycling race. The moment represented a triumph of human motivation and spirit—with a dash of miracle.

Did the same motivation that drove Lance Armstrong to battle cancer help him win the Tour de France?

Only 33 months earlier, no one would have thought that Armstrong would be the winner of the Tour de France. In fact, the odds were against him ever cycling again. At that time, he learned he had testicular cancer that had spread to his lungs and brain, which contained 12 tumors and two lesions. Doctors gave him a 50–50 chance of surviving.

His treatment was grueling. He suffered through surgery and four rounds of intense chemotherapy, separated by a month each. But he never gave up. Pushing himself, he would ride 20 to 50 miles a day following each of the one-week chemotherapy sessions.

Then the unexpected happened: The cancer disappeared, surprising everyone. And Armstrong picked up where he had left off, training hours each day and entering cycling competitions.

Several years later, Armstrong was crossing the finish line at the Tour de France. It was, he said, a miracle. "Fifteen or 20 years ago, I wouldn't be alive, much less riding a bike or winning the Tour de France. I think it's a miracle" (Abt, 1999, p. D4).

Looking Ahead

What motivation lay behind Armstrong's will to overcome his cancer? Was it the anticipation of the emotional thrill of winning the Tour de France? The potential rewards that would follow if he succeeded? The excitement of participating? The satisfaction of achieving a long-sought goal?

In this chapter, we consider the issues that can help answer such questions, as we address the topic of motivation and the related area of emotion. **Motivation** concerns the factors that direct and energize the behavior of humans and other organisms.

Psychologists who study motivation seek to discover the particular desired goals—the *motives*—that underlie behavior. Motives are exemplified in behavior as basic as drinking to satisfy thirst or as inconsequential as taking a stroll to get exercise. To the psychologist specializing in the study of motivation, underlying motives are assumed to steer one's choice of activities.

The study of motivation, then, consists of identifying why people seek to do the things they do. Psychologists studying motivation ask questions such as these: Why do people choose particular goals for which to strive? What specific motives direct behavior? What individual differences in motivation account for the variability in people's behavior? How can we motivate people to behave in particular ways, such as eating certain foods, quitting smoking, or engaging in safer sexual practices?

Whereas motivation is concerned with the forces that direct future behavior, emotion pertains to the feelings we experience throughout the course of our lives. The study of emotions focuses on our internal experiences at any given moment. Most of us have felt a variety of emotions: happiness at getting an A on a difficult exam, sadness brought about by the death of a loved one, anger at being treated unfairly. Because emotions not only motivate our behavior but can also reflect our underlying motivation, they play an important role in our lives.

We begin this chapter by focusing on the major conceptions of motivation, discussing how the different motives and needs people experience jointly affect behavior. We consider motives that are biologically based and universal in the animal kingdom, such as hunger, as well as motives that are unique to humans, like the needs for achievement, affiliation, and power.

We then turn to the nature of emotional experience. We consider the roles and functions that emotions play in people's lives, discussing a number of theories meant to explain how people understand which emotion they are experiencing at a given moment. Finally, the chapter ends with a look at how emotions are communicated through nonverbal behavior.

motivation: The factors that direct and energize the behavior of humans and other organisms

Prepare

How does motivation direct and energize behavior?

Organize

Explaining Motivation
Instinct Approaches
Drive-Reduction Approaches
Arousal Approaches
Incentive Approaches
Cognitive Approaches
Maslow's Hierarchy
Applying the Different Approaches to Motivation

Explaining Motivation

In just a moment, John Thompson's life changed. That's all it took for him to slip against a piece of farm equipment, which instantly ripped off both his arms.

In the moments following the accident, Thompson demonstrated incredible bravery. Despite his pain and shock, he ran 400 feet to his house. After managing to open the door, he ran inside and dialed for help with a pen gripped in his teeth. When emergency crews arrived 30 minutes later, he told them where to find ice and plastic bags so that his severed arms could be packed for possible surgical reattachment. Thompson's rescuers came none too soon: By the time surgery could start, he had lost half his blood. (Nelson, 1992)

Amazingly, John Thompson's surgery to reattach his arms was a success, and he recovered from his ordeal. But how can we account for his enormous motivation to stay alive?

Like many questions involving motivation, this one has no single answer; biological, cognitive, and social factors combined to fuel his will to survive.

The complexity of motivation has led to the development of a variety of conceptual approaches to its understanding. Although they vary in the degree to which they focus on biological, cognitive, and social factors, all seek to explain the energy that guides people's behavior in particular directions.

Instinct Approaches: Born to Be Motivated

When psychologists first sought to explain motivation, they turned to **instincts,** inborn patterns of behavior that are biologically determined rather than learned. According to instinct approaches to motivation, people and animals are born with preprogrammed sets of behaviors essential to their survival. These instincts provide the energy that channels behavior in appropriate directions. Hence, sex might be explained as a response to an instinct for reproduction, and exploratory behavior might be viewed as motivated by an instinct to examine one's territory.

There are several difficulties with such a conception, however. For one thing, there is no agreement on what, or even how many, primary instincts exist. One early psychologist, William McDougall (1908), suggested that there are 18 instincts. Other theorists came up with even more—with one sociologist (Bernard, 1924) claiming that there are exactly 5,759 distinct instincts!

Furthermore, explanations based on the concept of instincts do not go very far in explaining *why* a specific pattern of behavior, and not others, has appeared in a given species. In addition, although it is clear that a significant amount of animal behavior is based on instincts, the variety and complexity of human behavior, much of which is learned, cannot be seen as instinctual.

As a result of these shortcomings, newer explanations have replaced conceptions of motivation based on instincts. However, instinct approaches still play a role in certain theories, particularly those based on the evolutionary approach we discussed in Chapter 1. Furthermore, in later chapters we will discuss Freud's work, which suggests that instinctual drives of sex and aggression motivate behavior.

Drive-Reduction Approaches: Satisfying Our Needs

After rejecting instinct theory, psychologists first proposed simple drive-reduction theories of motivation in its place (Hull, 1943). **Drive-reduction approaches** suggest that when people lack some basic biological requirement such as water, a drive to obtain that requirement (in this case, the thirst drive) is produced.

To understand this approach, we need to begin with the concept of drive. A **drive** is motivational tension, or arousal, that energizes behavior in order to fulfill some need. Many basic kinds of drives, such as hunger, thirst, sleepiness, and sex, are related to biological needs of the body or of the species as a whole. These are called *primary drives.* Primary drives contrast with *secondary drives,* in which no obvious biological need is being fulfilled. The needs involved in secondary drives are created by prior experience and learning. As we will discuss later, some people have strong needs to achieve academically and in their careers. We can say that their achievement need is reflected in a secondary drive that motivates their behavior.

We usually try to satisfy a primary drive by reducing the need underlying it. For example, we become hungry after not eating for a few hours and might raid the refrigerator, especially if our next scheduled meal is not imminent. If the weather turns cold, we put on extra clothing or raise the setting on the thermostat to keep warm. If our body needs liquids in order to function properly, we experience thirst and seek out water.

Homeostasis

The reason for such behavior is homeostasis, a basic motivational phenomenon underlying primary drives. **Homeostasis** is the body's tendency to maintain a steady internal state. Homeostasis operates through feedback loops that bring deviations in body functioning back to a more optimal state, similar to the way a thermostat and furnace work in a home heating system to maintain a steady temperature (see Figure 10-1). Receptor cells throughout the body constantly monitor factors such as temperature and nutrient levels, and when deviations from the ideal state occur, the body adjusts in an effort to return to an optimal state. Many of our fundamental needs, including the need for food, water, stable body temperature, and sleep, operate via homeostasis.

instincts: Inborn patterns of behavior that are biologically determined rather than learned

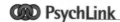 **PsychLink**

Motivation and emotion information
www.mhhe.com/
feldmanup6-10links

drive-reduction approaches to motivation: A theory suggesting that when people lack some basic biological requirement such as water, a drive to obtain that requirement (in this case, the thirst drive) is produced

drive: Motivational tension, or arousal, that energizes behavior in order to fulfill some need

homeostasis: The body's tendency to maintain a steady internal state

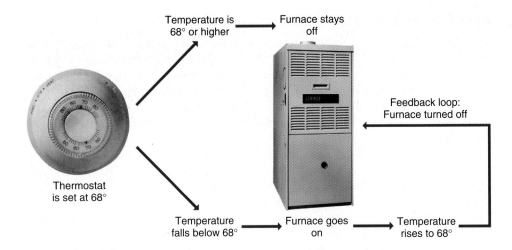

Figure 10-1 Homeostasis operates through a series of feedback loops, similar to the way a thermostat calls for heat from the furnace when the air temperature becomes too cool, and turns off the furnace when the air temperature becomes too warm. Similarly, when our body temperature becomes too low, our blood vessels constrict, causing shivering and making us seek warmth. When body temperature becomes too high, our blood vessels expand, and we sweat as our body tries to lower the temperature. Can you think of other internal systems that operate via homeostasis?

Although drive-reduction theories provide a good explanation of how primary drives motivate behavior, they are inadequate when it comes to explaining behaviors in which the goal is not to reduce a drive, but rather to maintain or even to increase a particular level of excitement or arousal. For instance, some behaviors seem to be motivated by nothing more than curiosity, such as rushing to check e-mail messages. Similarly, many people seek thrills through such activities as riding a roller coaster and steering a raft down the rapids of a river. Such behaviors certainly don't suggest that people seek to reduce drives, as drive-reduction approaches would indicate (Mineka & Hendersen, 1985; Loewenstein, 1994).

Both curiosity and thrill-seeking behavior, then, shed doubt on drive-reduction approaches as a complete explanation for motivation. In both cases, rather than seeking to reduce an underlying drive, people and animals appear to be motivated to *increase* their overall level of stimulation and activity. To explain this phenomenon, psychologists have devised an alternative: arousal approaches to motivation.

Arousal Approaches: Beyond Drive Reduction

Arousal approaches seek to explain behavior in which the goal is to maintain or increase excitement (Berlyne, 1967; Brehm & Self, 1989). According to **arousal approaches to motivation,** each of us tries to maintain a certain level of stimulation and activity. As with the drive-reduction model, if our stimulation and activity levels become too high, we try to reduce them. But in contrast to the drive-reduction model, the arousal model also suggests that if the levels of stimulation and activity are too low, we will try to *increase* them by seeking stimulation.

arousal approaches to motivation: The belief that we try to maintain a certain level of stimulation and activity, increasing or reducing them as necessary

People vary widely in the optimal level of arousal that they seek out, with some people seeking out especially high levels of arousal. For example, psychologists have hypothesized that individuals such as comic John Belushi, daredevil Evel Knievel, and bank robbers Bonnie and Clyde exhibited a particularly high need for arousal. You can get a sense of your own preferred level of stimulation by completing the questionnaire in Table 10-1 (Zuckerman, 1991, 1994; Farley, 1986).

Incentive Approaches: Motivation's Pull

When a luscious dessert is brought to the table after a filling meal, its appeal has little or nothing to do with internal drives or with the maintenance of arousal. Rather, if we choose to eat the dessert, such behavior is motivated by the external stimulus of the dessert itself, which acts as an anticipated reward. This reward, in motivational terms, is an *incentive*.

incentive approaches to motivation: The theory suggesting that motivation stems from the desire to obtain valued external goals, or incentives.

Incentive approaches to motivation suggest that motivation stems from the desire to obtain valued external goals, or incentives. In this view, the desirable properties of external stimuli—be they grades, money, affection, food, or sex—account for a person's motivation.

Table 10-1 Do You Seek Out Sensation?

How much stimulation do you crave in your everyday life? You will have an idea after you complete the following questionnaire, which lists some items from a scale designed to assess your sensation-seeking tendencies. Circle either A or B in each pair of statements.

1. A   I would like a job that requires a lot of travelling.
   B   I would prefer a job in one location.

2. A   I am invigorated by a brisk, cold day.
   B   I can't wait to get indoors on a cold day.

3. A   I get bored seeing the same old faces.
   B   I like the comfortable familiarity of everyday friends.

4. A   I would prefer living in an ideal society in which everyone was safe, secure, and happy.
   B   I would have preferred living in the unsettled days of our history.

5. A   I sometimes like to do things that are a little frightening.
   B   A sensible person avoids activities that are dangerous.

6. A   I would not like to be hypnotized.
   B   I would like to have the experience of being hypnotized.

7. A   The most important goal of life is to live it to the fullest and to experience as much as possible.
   B   The most important goal of life is to find peace and happiness.

8. A   I would like to try parachute jumping.
   B   I would never want to try jumping out of a plane, with or without a parachute.

9. A   I enter cold water gradually, giving myself time to get used to it.
   B   I like to dive or jump right into the ocean or a cold pool.

10. A   When I go on a vacation, I prefer the comfort of a good room and bed.
    B   When I go on a vacation, I prefer the change of camping out.

11. A   I prefer people who are emotionally expressive, even if they are a bit unstable.
    B   I prefer people who are calm and even-tempered.

12. A   A good painting should shock or jolt the senses.
    B   A good painting should give one a feeling of peace and security.

13. A   People who ride motorcycles must have some kind of unconscious need to hurt themselves.
    B   I would like to drive or ride a motorcycle.

Scoring   Give yourself one point for each of the following responses: 1A, 2A, 3A, 4B, 5A, 6B, 7A, 8A, 9B, 10B, 11A, 12A, 13B. Find your total score by adding up the number of points and then use the following scoring key:

0–3 very low sensation seeking

4–5 low

6–9 average

10–11 high

12–13 very high

Keep in mind, of course, that this short questionnaire, for which the scoring is based on the results of college students who have taken it, provides only a rough estimate of your sensation-seeking tendencies. Moreover, as people get older, their sensation-seeking scores tend to decrease. Still, the questionnaire will at least give you an indication of how your sensation-seeking tendencies compare with those of others.

(Source: Zuckerman, 1978, 1994)

Although the theory explains why we might succumb to an incentive (like a mouth-watering dessert) even though internal cues (like hunger) are lacking, it does not provide a complete explanation of motivation, since organisms seek to fulfill needs even when incentives are not apparent. Consequently, many psychologists believe that the internal drives proposed by drive-reduction theory work in tandem with the external incentives of incentive theory to "push" and "pull" behavior, respectively. Thus, at the same time as we seek to satisfy our underlying hunger needs (the push of drive-reduction theory), we are drawn to food that appears particularly appetizing (the pull of incentive theory). Rather than contradicting each other, then, drives and incentives can work together in motivating behavior (Petri, 1996).

Cognitive Approaches: The Thoughts Behind Motivation

Cognitive approaches to motivation suggest that motivation is a product of people's thoughts, expectations, and goals—their cognitions. For instance, the degree to which people are motivated to study for a test is based on their expectation of how well studying will pay off in terms of a good grade (Wigfield & Eccles, 2000).

Cognitive theories of motivation draw a key distinction between intrinsic and extrinsic motivation. *Intrinsic motivation* causes us to participate in an activity for our own enjoyment, rather than for any concrete, tangible reward that it will bring us. In contrast, *extrinsic motivation* causes us to do something for money, a grade, or some other concrete, tangible reward. For example, when a physician works long hours because she loves medicine, intrinsic motivation is prompting her; if she works hard in order to make a lot of money, extrinsic motivation underlies her efforts (Rawsthorne & Elliot, 1999; Ryan & Deci, 2000).

We are more apt to persevere, work harder, and produce work of higher quality when motivation for a task is intrinsic rather than extrinsic. In fact, providing rewards for desirable behavior might cause intrinsic motivation to decline and extrinsic motivation to increase, although this view is controversial (Deci, Koestner, & Ryan, 1999; Eisenberger, Pierce, & Cameron, 1999; Sansone & Harackiewicz, 2000).

In a dramatic demonstration of the differing effects of rewards on motivation, researchers promised a group of nursery school students a reward for drawing with magic markers (an activity for which they had previously shown high motivation). The reward reduced their enthusiasm for the task, for they later showed considerably less zeal for drawing (Lepper & Greene, 1978). It was as if the promise of reward undermined their intrinsic interest in drawing, turning what had been play into work.

Such research suggests the importance of promoting intrinsic motivation and indicates that providing extrinsic rewards (or even just calling attention to them) can undermine the effort and quality of performance. Parents might think twice, then, about offering their children monetary rewards for getting good report cards. Instead, research on intrinsic motivation suggests that better results would come from reminding them of the pleasures that can come from learning and mastering a body of knowledge (Deci, Koestner, & Ryan, 1999: Lepper, Henderlong, & Gingras, 1999).

Maslow's Hierarchy: Ordering Motivational Needs

PsychLink

Maslow's hierarchy explained
www.mhhe.com/
feldmanup6-10links

What do Eleanor Roosevelt, Abraham Lincoln, and Albert Einstein have in common? The common thread, according to a model of motivation devised by psychologist Abraham Maslow, is that each of them fulfilled the highest levels of motivational needs underlying human behavior.

Maslow's model considers different motivational needs to be ordered in a hierarchy, and it suggests that before more sophisticated, higher-order needs can be met, certain primary needs must be satisfied (Maslow, 1970, 1987). The model can be conceptualized as a pyramid (see Figure 10-2) in which the more basic needs are at the bottom and the higher-level needs are at the top. For a particular need to be activated and thereby guide a person's behavior, the more basic needs in the hierarchy must be met first.

The most basic needs are primary drives: needs for water, food, sleep, sex, and the like. To move up the hierarchy, a person must have these basic physiological needs met. Safety needs come next in the hierarchy; Maslow suggests that people need a safe, secure environment in order to function effectively. Physiological and safety needs compose the lower-order needs.

Only when the basic lower-order needs are met can a person consider fulfilling higher-order needs, such as the need for love and a sense of belonging, esteem, and self-actualization. Love and belongingness needs include the need to obtain and give affection and to be a contributing member of some group or society. After these needs are fulfilled, the person strives for esteem. In Maslow's thinking, esteem relates to the need to develop a sense of self-worth by knowing that others are aware of one's competence and value.

SELF-
ACTUALIZATION
A state of self-
fulfillment

ESTEEM
The need to develop a sense
of self-worth

LOVE AND BELONGINGNESS
The need to obtain and give affection

SAFETY NEEDS
The need for a safe and secure environment

PHYSIOLOGICAL NEEDS
The primary drives: needs for water, food, sleep, and sex

Figure 10-2 Maslow's hierarchy shows how our motivation progresses up the pyramid from a basis in the broadest, most fundamental biological needs to higher-order ones. (After Maslow, 1970.) Do you agree that lower-order needs must be satisfied before higher-order needs? Do hermits and monks who attempt to achieve spiritual needs while denying basic physical needs contradict Maslow's hierarchy?

Once these four sets of needs are fulfilled—no easy task—the person is able to strive for the highest-level need, self-actualization. **Self-actualization** is a state of self-fulfillment in which people realize their highest potential in their own unique way. Although at first Maslow suggested that self-actualization occurred in only a few, famous individuals, he later expanded the concept to encompass everyday people. For example, a parent with excellent nurturing skills who raises a family, a teacher who year after year creates an environment that maximizes students' opportunities for success, and an artist who realizes her creative potential might all be self-actualized. The important thing is that people feel at ease with themselves and satisfied that they are using their talents to the fullest. In a sense, achieving self-actualization produces a decline in the striving and yearning for greater fulfillment that marks most people's lives and instead provides a sense of satisfaction with the current state of affairs (Jones & Crandall, 1991).

Although research has been unable to validate the specific ordering of Maslow's stages, and it is difficult to measure self-actualization objectively, Maslow's model is important for two reasons: It highlights the complexity of human needs, and it emphasizes that until more basic biological needs are met, people will be relatively unconcerned with higher-order needs. For example, if people are hungry, their first interest will be in obtaining food; they will not be concerned with such needs as love and self-esteem (Weiss, 1991; Neher, 1991).

self-actualization: A state of self-fulfillment in which people realize their highest potential in their own unique way

 PsychLink
Maslow's self-actualization
www.mhhe.com/
feldmanup6-10links

Applying the Different Approaches to Motivation

The various theories of motivation (summarized in Figure 10-3) provide us with several different perspectives on motivation. Which provides the fullest account of motivation? The answer is that many of the approaches are complementary, rather than contradictory. In fact, it often is useful to employ more than one approach in order to understand motivation in a particular instance.

Approach	Description
Instinct	People and animals are born with preprogrammed sets of behaviors essential to their survival.
Drive reduction	When some basic biological requirement is lacking, a drive is produced.
Arousal	People seek an optimal level of stimulation. If the level of stimulation is too high, they act to reduce it; if it is too low, they act to increase it.
Incentive	External stimuli direct and energize behavior.
Cognitive	Thoughts, expectations, and understanding of the world direct motivation.
Hierarchy of needs	Needs form a hierarchy; before higher-order needs are met, lower-order needs must be fulfilled.

Figure 10–3 The major approaches to motivation.

Consider, for example, John Thompson's brave determination after his farm accident (described earlier in the chapter). From the perspective of instinct theory, John could be seen to have an overwhelming instinct to preserve his life at all costs. From the drive-reduction perspective, he was motivated to get medical help in order to end the pain that followed his accident. And from a cognitive perspective, his expectation that surgeons could reattach his arms led him to take action that would maximize the chances of recovery.

In short, applying multiple approaches to motivation to a given situation provides a broader understanding than we might obtain by employing only a single approach. We'll see this fact again as we proceed to consider specific motives—such as the needs for food, achievement, affiliation, and power—where we will draw upon several of the theories to provide us with the fullest account of what motivates our behavior.

Evaluate

1. _____ are forces that guide a person's behavior in a certain direction.
2. Biologically determined, inborn patterns of behavior are known as_____.
3. Your psychology professor tells you, "Explaining behavior is easy! When we lack something we are motivated to get it." Which approach to motivation does your professor subscribe to?
4. By drinking water after running a marathon, a runner tries to keep his or her body at an optimal level of functioning. This process is called_____.

Rethink

1. Which approaches to motivation are most commonly used in the workplace? How might each approach be used to design employment policies that can sustain or increase motivation?

5. I help an elderly person across the street because doing a good deed makes me feel good. What type of motivation is at work here? What type of motivation would be at work if I were to help an elderly man across the street because he paid me $20?

6. According to Maslow, a person with no job, no home, and no friends can become self-actualized. True or false?

2. A writer who works all day composing copy for an advertising firm has a hard time keeping her mind on her work and continually watches the clock. After work she turns to a collection of stories she is creating and writes long into the night, completely forgetful of the clock. What ideas from your reading on motivation help to explain this phenomenon?

Answers to Evaluate Questions

1. Motives 2. instincts 3. Drive reduction 4. homeostasis 5. Intrinsic; Extrinsic 6. False; lower-order needs must be fulfilled before self-actualization can occur.

Human Needs and Motivation: Eat, Drink, and Be Daring

As a sophomore at the University of California, Santa Cruz, Lisa Arndt followed a menu of her own making: For breakfast she ate cereal or fruit, with 10 diet pills and 50 chocolate-flavored laxatives. Lunch was a salad or sandwich; dinner: chicken and rice. But it was the feast that followed that Arndt relished most. Almost every night at about 9 p.m., she would retreat to her room and eat an entire small pizza and a whole batch of cookies. Then she'd wait for the day's laxatives to take effect. "It was extremely painful," says Arndt of those days in 1992. "But I was that desperate to make up for my bingeing. I was terrified of fat the way other people are afraid of lions or guns." (Hubbard, O'Neill, & Cheakalos, 1999, p. 59)

Lisa was one of the 5 to 10 million females (and 1 million males) who suffer from an eating disorder. These disorders, which usually appear during adolescence, can bring about extraordinary declines in weight and other physical deterioration. They are extremely dangerous, sometimes resulting in death.

Why are Lisa, and others like her, subject to such disordered eating, revolving around the motivation to avoid weight gain at all costs? And why do so many other people engage in overeating, leading to obesity?

To answer these questions, we must consider some of the specific kinds of needs that underlie behavior. In this section, we will examine several of the most important human needs. We'll begin with hunger, the primary drive that has received the most attention from researchers, and then turn to secondary drives—those uniquely human strivings, based on learned needs and past experience, that help explain why people strive to achieve, to affiliate with others, and to seek power over others.

Prepare

What biological and social factors underlie hunger?

How are needs relating to achievement, affiliation, and power motivation exhibited?

Organize

Human Needs and Motivation
The Motivation Behind Hunger and Eating
Eating Disorders
The Need for Achievement
The Need for Affiliation
The Need for Power

The Motivation Behind Hunger and Eating

More than half the people in the United States are overweight, and more than a fifth are so heavy that they have **obesity,** body weight that is more than 20 percent above the average weight for a person of their height. And the rest of the world is not far behind: the prevalence of obesity around the globe is so great that the World Health Organization has said it has reached epidemic proportions (National Center for Health Statistics, 1994; Taubes, 1998).

Perceptions of ideal weight and body shape vary significantly across different cultures and, within Western cultures, from one time period to another. For instance, many contemporary Western cultures stress the importance of slimness in women—a view that is actually relatively recent. In nineteenth-century Hawaii, the most attractive women were those who were the most overweight.

obesity: The state of being more than 20 percent above the average weight for a person of one's height

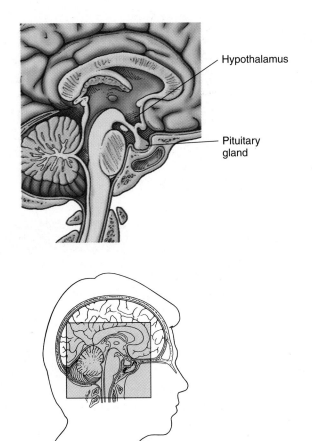

Hypothalamus

Pituitary gland

Figure 10-4 The hypothalamus acts as the brain's "feeding center," being primarily responsible for the monitoring of food intake.

weight set point: The particular level of weight that the body strives to maintain

metabolism: The rate at which food is converted to energy and expended by the body

Furthermore, for most of the twentieth century—except for a period in the 1920s and the most recent decades—the ideal female figure was relatively full. Even today, weight standards differ among different cultural groups. For instance, African Americans generally judge heavier women more positively than whites do (Silverstein et al., 1986; Hebl & Heatherton, 1998; Rosenthal, 1999).

Regardless of societal standards relating to appearance and weight, there is no question that being overweight is a major health risk. However, controlling weight is complicated, because eating behavior involves a variety of mechanisms. In our discussion of what motivates people to eat, we'll start with the biological aspects of eating.

Biological Factors in the Regulation of Hunger

In contrast to human beings, nonhuman species are unlikely to become obese. Internal mechanisms regulate not only the quantity of their food intake, but also the kind of food they desire. For example, rats that have been deprived of particular foods seek out alternatives that contain the specific nutrients their diet is lacking, and animals given the choice of a wide variety of foods choose a well-balanced diet (Rozin, 1977; Bouchard & Bray, 1996; Woods et al., 2000).

The mechanisms by which organisms know whether they require food or should stop eating are complex. It's not just a matter of an empty stomach causing hunger pangs and a full one alleviating hunger. (Even people whose stomachs have been removed still experience the sensation of hunger.) One important factor is changes in the chemical composition of the blood. In particular, changes in levels of glucose, a kind of sugar, regulate feelings of hunger (Inglefinger, 1944; Rodin, 1985; Campfield et al., 1996).

Glucose levels are monitored by the brain's *hypothalamus,* a tiny brain structure we first discussed in Chapter 3 (see Figure 10-4). Increasing evidence suggests that the hypothalamus is the organ primarily responsible for monitoring food intake. Injury to the hypothalamus has radical consequences for eating behavior, depending upon the site of the injury. For example, rats whose *lateral hypothalamus* is damaged might literally starve to death. They refuse food when offered and, unless they are force-fed, eventually die. Rats with an injury to the *ventromedial hypothalamus* display the opposite problem: extreme overeating. Rats with this injury can increase in weight by as much as 400 percent. Similar phenomena occur in humans who have tumors of the hypothalamus (Rolls, 1994; Woods et al., 1998).

Although the hypothalamus clearly plays an important role in regulating food intake, exactly how it operates is still unclear. One hypothesis is that injury to the hypothalamus affects the weight set point by which food intake is regulated. According to this hypothesis, the **weight set point** is the particular level of weight that the body strives to maintain. Acting as a kind of internal weight thermostat, the hypothalamus calls for either greater or less food intake (Nisbett, 1972; Capaldi, 1996; Woods et al., 2000).

In most cases, the hypothalamus does a good job. People who are not monitoring their weight show only minor weight fluctuations, in spite of substantial day-to-day variations in how much they eat and exercise. However, injury to the hypothalamus drastically raises or lowers the weight set point, and the organism then strives to meet its internal goal by increasing or decreasing its food consumption.

The weight set point is determined at least partly by genetic factors. People seem destined through heredity to have a particular **metabolism,** the rate at which food is converted to energy and expended by the body. People with a high metabolic rate are able to eat virtually as much as they want without gaining weight, whereas people with a low metabolic rate might eat literally half as much and yet gain weight readily (Woods et al., 1998).

Cultural influences on eating habits vary tremendously. Grasshoppers, red agave worms, and excamola may be considered a delicacy in Mexico, but most people in the United States would feel differently. Have you ever overcome your culture-based dislike of a food after exposure to another culture's eating habits?

Social Factors in Eating

You've just finished a full meal and are completely stuffed. Suddenly, your host announces with great fanfare that he will be serving his "house specialty" dessert, bananas flambé, and that he has spent the better part of the afternoon preparing it. Even though you are full and don't even like bananas, you accept a serving of his dessert and eat it all.

Clearly, internal biological factors do not provide the full explanation for our eating behavior. External social factors, based on societal rules and conventions and on what we have learned about appropriate eating behavior, also play an important role. Take, for example, the simple fact that people customarily eat breakfast, lunch, and dinner at approximately the same times every day. Because we are accustomed to eating on schedule every day, we tend to feel hungry as the usual hour approaches, sometimes quite independently of what our internal cues are telling us.

Similarly, we tend to put roughly the same amount of food on our plates every day, even though the amount of exercise we may have had, and consequently our need for energy replenishment, varies from day to day. We also tend to prefer particular foods over others. Rats and dogs might be a delicacy in certain Asian cultures, but few people in Western cultures find them appealing, despite their potentially high nutritional value. In sum, cultural influences and our own individual habits play an important role in determining when, what, and how much we eat (Boaks, Popplewell, & Burton, 1987; Rozin, 1990; Booth, 1994; Capaldi, 1996).

Other social factors are related to our eating behavior as well. Some of us head toward the refrigerator after a difficult day, seeking solace in a pint of Heath Bar Crunch ice cream. Why? Perhaps when we were children, our parents gave us food when we were upset. Eventually, we might have learned, through the basic mechanisms of classical and operant conditioning, to associate food with comfort and consolation. Similarly, we might learn that eating, by focusing our attention on immediate pleasures, provides an escape from unpleasant thoughts. As a consequence, we might eat when we experience distress (Heatherton, Herman, & Polivy, 1992; McManus & Waller, 1995; Hill & Peters, 1998).

The Roots of Obesity

Given that eating behavior is influenced by both biological and social factors, determining the causes of obesity has proved to be a challenging task. Researchers have followed several paths.

"Gee, I had no idea you were married to a supermodel."

PsychLink

Information about obesity
www.mhhe.com/
feldmanup6-10links

anorexia nervosa: A severe eating disorder in which people may refuse to eat, while denying that their behavior and appearance—which can become skeletonlike—are unusual

bulimia: A disorder in which a person binges on incredibly large quantities of food, then purges by vomiting or by using laxatives

Some psychologists suggest that obesity is produced by oversensitivity to external eating cues based on social factors, coupled with insensitivity to internal hunger cues. Others argue that overweight people have higher set points than people of normal weight. Because their set points are unusually high, their attempts to lose weight by eating less can make them especially sensitive to external, food-related cues and therefore more apt to eat, perpetuating their obesity (Nisbett, 1968; Schachter, 1971; Hill & Peters, 1998).

But why would some people's weight set points be higher than others? One possible explanation relates to the size and number of fat cells in the body, which increase as a function of weight increase. Because the set-point level appears to reflect the number of fat cells a person has, any increase in weight—which produces a rise in fat cells—might raise the set point. Furthermore, any loss of weight after the age of 2 does not decrease the number of fat cells in the body, although it can make them shrink in size. In short, according to the weight-set-point hypothesis, having too many fat cells can make the set point become "stuck" at a higher level than is desirable. Under such circumstances, losing weight is difficult, because one is constantly at odds with one's own internal set point when dieting (Leibel, Rosenbaum & Hirsch, 1995; Freedman, 1995).

Not everyone agrees with the set point explanation for obesity. Pointing to the rapid rise in obesity over the last several decades in the United States, some researchers suggest that there is no fixed set-point weight that the body attempts to maintain. Instead, they suggest, there is a *settling point,* determined by a combination of our genetic heritage and the nature of the environment in which we live. If high-fat foods are prevalent in our environment, and we are genetically predisposed to obesity, then we settle into an equilibrium that maintains relatively high weight. On the other hand, if our environment is nutritionally healthier, genetic predispositions to obesity will not be triggered, and we will settle into an equilibrium in which our weight is lower (Gibbs, 1996; Comuzzie & Allison, 1998).

Eating Disorders

One of the most devastating weight-related disorders is anorexia nervosa. **Anorexia nervosa** is a severe eating disorder in which people refuse to eat, while denying that their behavior and appearance—which can become skeletonlike—are unusual. Some 10 percent of anorexics literally starve themselves to death.

Anorexia nervosa afflicts mainly females between the ages of 12 and 40, although both men and women of any age can develop it. People with the disorder typically come from stable homes, and they are often successful, attractive, and relatively affluent. The disorder often occurs following serious dieting, which somehow gets out of control. Life begins to revolve around food: Although people with the disorder eat little themselves, they might cook for others, go shopping for food frequently, or collect cookbooks (Lask & Bryant-Waugh, 1999; Rosen, 1999).

A related problem, **bulimia,** from which Lisa Arndt (described earlier) suffered, is a disorder in which people binge on large quantities of food. They might consume an entire gallon of ice cream and a whole pie in a single sitting. Following such a binge, sufferers feel guilt and depression and often induce vomiting or take laxatives to rid themselves of the food—behavior known as purging. Constant bingeing-and-purging cycles and the use of drugs to induce vomiting or diarrhea can lead to heart failure. Often, though, the weight of a person suffering from bulimia remains normal.

Eating disorders are a growing problem: It has been estimated that 1 to 4 percent of high school and college women suffer from either anorexia nervosa or bulimia. As many as 10 percent of women suffer from bulimia at some point in their lives ("Eating Disorders," 1997).

What are the causes of anorexia nervosa and bulimia? Some researchers suspect there is a biological cause such as a chemical imbalance in the hypothalamus or pituitary gland, perhaps brought on by genetic factors. Others believe that these disorders are rooted in societal preference for slenderness and the parallel notion that being obese is undesirable. They maintain that people with anorexia nervosa and bulimia become

Despite looking skeleton-like to others, people with the weight disorder anorexia nervosa see themselves as overweight.

preoccupied with their weight and take to heart the societal view that one can never be too thin. Consistent with such an explanation, as countries become more developed and westernized, and dieting becomes more popular, eating disorders increase. Finally, some psychologists suggest that the disorders occur as a consequence of overdemanding parents or other family problems (Schneider, 1996; Horesh et al., 1996; Walsh & Devlin, 1998).

The complete explanation for anorexia nervosa or bulimia remains elusive. The disorders probably stem from both biological and social causes, and successful treatment is likely to encompass several strategies, including therapy and dietary changes (Walsh & Devlin, 1998; Gilbert, 2000; Miller & Mizes, 2000). If you or a family member or a friend needs advice or help with an eating problem, contact the American Anorexia Bulimia Association at http://www.aabainc.org or at 165 W. 46th Street, Suite 1108, New York, NY 10036; 212-575-6200.

PsychLink

Eating disorders information
www.mhhe.com/
feldmanup6-10links

BECOMING AN INFORMED CONSUMER OF PSYCHOLOGY

Dieting and Losing Weight Successfully

For most of us, dieting is a losing battle: Most people who diet eventually regain the weight they have lost, so they try again and get caught in a seemingly endless cycle of weight loss and gain (Lowe, 1993). Given what we know about the causes of obesity, this is not entirely surprising, because so many factors affect eating behavior and weight.

According to diet experts, there are several things to keep in mind when trying to lose weight (Gurin, 1989; "How to Lose Weight and Keep It Off," 1990; "Dieting and weight loss," 1993):

- *There is no easy route to weight control.* You will have to make permanent changes in your life in order to lose weight without gaining it back. The most obvious strategy, cutting down on the amount of food you eat, is just the first step toward a lifetime commitment to changing your eating habits. You must consider the nutrient content, as well as the overall quantity of food that you consume.

- *Set reasonable goals.* Know how much weight you want to lose before you start to diet. Don't try to lose too much weight too quickly or you may doom yourself to failure.

- *Exercise.* When you exercise, you burn fat stored in your body, which is used as fuel for muscles. As this fat is used, you will probably lose weight. Almost any activity helps burn calories (see Figure 10-5). The weight-set-point hypothesis suggests another advantage to moderate exercise: It might lower your set point. Although there is some dispute about just how much exercise is sufficient to lower weight, most experts recommend at least thirty consecutive minutes of moderate exercise at least three times a week. (If nothing else, the release of endorphins following exercise—discussed in Chapter 3—will make you feel better even if you don't lose weight.)

- *Decrease the influence of external, social stimuli on your eating behavior.* For instance, serve yourself smaller portions of food, and leave the table before you see what is being served for dessert. Don't even buy snack foods such as nachos or potato chips; if they're not readily available in the kitchen cupboard, you're not apt to eat them. Wrap foods in the refrigerator in aluminum foil so you cannot see the contents to avoid being tempted every time you open the refrigerator.

- *Avoid fad diets.* No matter how popular they are at a given time, extreme diets, including liquid diets, usually don't work in the long run and can be dangerous to your health.

- *Maintain good eating habits.* When you have reached your desired weight, maintain the habits built up while dieting to avoid gaining back the weight you have lost.

- *Don't feel guilty!* Above all, don't feel guilty if you don't succeed in losing weight. Given the evidence that obesity may be genetically determined, the inability to lose

Figure 10–5 The ways to burn 150 calories: People can expend 150 calories either by spending more time at a less vigorous activity, or less time at a more vigorous activity. (Adapted from Lertola, 1997.)

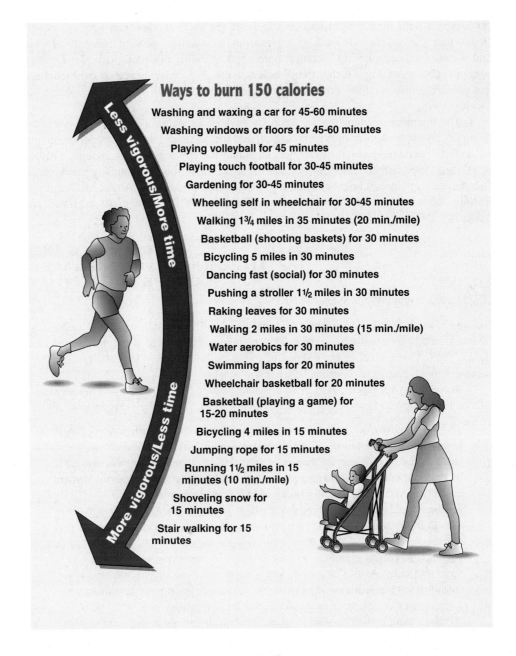

weight should not be seen as a moral failing. Indeed, you are in good company, for some 90 to 95 percent of dieters put back the weight they have lost (Bennett & Gurin, 1982; Fritsch, 1999).

In light of how difficult it can be to lose weight, psychologists Janet Polivy and C. Peter Herman suggest—paradoxically—that the best approach might be to avoid dieting in the first place. They recommend that people eat what they really want to eat, even if this means indulging in candy or ice cream every so often. In turn, this freedom to eat anything can reduce binge eating, which is more likely to occur when people feel that bingeing is their only opportunity to eat what they really wish to eat. Although such an approach might not produce major weight loss, even a relatively small weight loss is better than none: Just a 10- to 15-pound drop in body weight can decrease the major health risks associated with obesity (Polivy & Herman, 1991; Foreyt & Goodrick, 1994; Bruce & Wilfley, 1996).

The Need for Achievement: Striving for Success

Though hunger might be one of the most potent primary drives in our day-to-day lives, we are also motivated by powerful secondary drives that have no clear biological basis (McClelland, 1985; Geen, 1984, 1995). Among the most prominent of these is the need for achievement.

The **need for achievement** is a stable, learned characteristic in which satisfaction is obtained by striving for and attaining a level of excellence (McClelland et al., 1953). People with a high need for achievement seek out situations in which they can compete against some standard—be it grades, money, or winning at a game—and prove themselves successful. But they are not indiscriminate when it comes to picking their challenges: They tend to avoid situations in which success will come too easily (which would be unchallenging) and situations in which success is unlikely. Instead, people high in achievement motivation are apt to choose tasks that are of intermediate difficulty.

In contrast, people with low achievement motivation tend to be motivated primarily by a desire to avoid failure. As a result, they seek out easy tasks, being sure to avoid failure, or they seek out very difficult tasks for which failure has no negative implications because almost anyone would fail at them. People with a high fear of failure will stay away from tasks of intermediate difficulty, because they might fail where others have been successful (Atkinson & Feather, 1966; Sorrentino, Hewitt, & Raso-Knott, 1992; Elliot & Church, 1997).

The outcomes of a high need for achievement are generally positive, at least in a success-oriented society such as our own (Heckhausen, Schmalt, & Schneider, 1985; Spence, 1985). For instance, people motivated by a high need for achievement are more likely to attend college than their low-achievement counterparts, and once in college they tend to receive higher grades in classes that are related to their future careers (Atkinson & Raynor, 1974). Furthermore, high achievement motivation is associated with future economic and occupational success (McClelland, 1985).

Measuring Achievement Motivation

How can we measure a person's need for achievement? The technique used most frequently is to administer a *Thematic Apperception Test (TAT)* (Spangler, 1992). In the TAT, people are shown a series of ambiguous pictures, such as the one in Figure 10-6. They are told to write a story that describes what is happening, who the people are, what led to the situation, what the people are thinking or wanting, and what will happen next. A standard scoring system is then used to determine the amount of achievement imagery in people's stories. For example, someone who writes a story in which the main character is striving to beat an opponent, studying in order to do well at some task, or working hard in order to get a promotion shows clear signs of an achievement orientation. It is assumed that the inclusion of such achievement-related imagery in their stories indicates an unusually high degree of concern with—and therefore a relatively strong need for—achievement.

The Need for Affiliation: Striving for Friendship

Few of us choose to lead our lives as hermits. Why?

One main reason is that most people have a **need for affiliation,** an interest in establishing and maintaining relationships with other people. Individuals with a high need for affiliation write TAT stories that emphasize the desire to maintain or reinstate friendships and show concern over being rejected by friends.

People who are higher in affiliation needs are particularly sensitive to relationships with others. They desire to be with their friends more of the time, and alone less often, than people who are lower in the need for affiliation (O'Connor & Rosenblood, 1996). However, gender is a greater determinant of how much time is actually spent with friends:

need for achievement: A stable, learned characteristic in which satisfaction is obtained by striving for and attaining a level of excellence

need for affiliation: An interest in establishing and maintaining relationships with other people

 **PsychLink**
Discussion of need for achievement
www.mhhe.com/
feldmanup6-10links

Figure 10-6 This ambiguous picture is similar to those used in the Thematic Apperception test to determine people's underlying motivation (© 1943 by the President and Fellows of Harvard College; 1971 by Henry A. Murray.) What do you see? Do you think your response is related to your motivation?

Regardless of their affiliative orientation, female students spend significantly more time with their friends and less time alone than male students do (Wong & Csikszentmihalyi, 1991).

The Need for Power: Striving for Impact on Others

If your fantasies include being elected president of the United States or running Microsoft, they could be reflecting a high need for power. The **need for power**—a tendency to seek impact, control, or influence over others, and to be seen as a powerful individual—is an additional type of motivation (Winter, 1973, 1987).

As you might expect, people with a strong need for power are more apt to belong to organizations and seek office than those low in the need for power. They are also apt to be in professions in which their power needs can be fulfilled, such as business management and—you may or may not be surprised—teaching (Jenkins, 1994). In addition, they seek to display the trappings of power. Even in college, they are more apt to collect prestigious possessions, such as stereos and sports cars.

There are some significant sex differences in the display of need for power. Men who are high in power needs tend to show unusually high levels of aggression, drink heavily, act in a sexually exploitative manner, and participate more frequently in competitive sports—behaviors that collectively represent somewhat extravagant, flamboyant behavior. In contrast, women display their power needs in a more restrained manner, congruent with traditional societal constraints on women's behavior. Women high in the need for power are more apt than men to channel their power needs in a socially responsible manner, such as by showing concern for others or displaying highly nurturant behavior (Winter, 1988).

need for power: A tendency to seek impact, control, or influence over others, and to be seen as a powerful individual

cherifer
1

Evaluate

1. Match the following terms with their definitions:

   1. Hypothalamus
   2. Lateral hypothalamic damage
   3. Ventromedial hypothalamic damage

   a. Leads to refusal of food and starvation
   b. Responsible for monitoring food intake
   c. Causes extreme overeating

2. The_____ _____ _____ is the particular level of weight the body strives to maintain.

3. _____ is the rate at which energy is produced and expended by the body.

4. Julio is the type of person who constantly strives for excellence. He feels intense satisfaction when he is able to master a new task. Julio most likely has a high need for_____.

5. Debbie's Thematic Apperception Test (TAT) story depicts a young girl who is rejected by one of her peers and seeks to regain her friendship. What major type of motivation is Debbie displaying in her story?

   a. Need for achievement
   b. Need for motivation
   c. Need for affiliation
   d. Need for power

Rethink

1. In what ways do societal expectations, expressed by television shows and commercials, contribute to both obesity and excessive concern about weight loss? How could television contribute to better eating habits and attitudes toward weight? Should it be required to do so?

2. Can traits such as need for achievement, need for power, and need for affiliation be used to select workers for jobs? What other criteria, both motivational and personal, would have to be considered when making such a selection?

Answers to Evaluate Questions

1. 1-b; 2-a; 3-c 2. weight set point 3. Metabolism 4. achievement 5. c

Understanding Emotional Experiences

Prepare

What are emotions, and how do we experience them?

What are the functions of emotions?

Organize

Understanding Emotional Experiences
The Functions of Emotions
Determining the Range of Emotions
The Roots of Emotions
The James-Lange Theory
The Cannon-Bard Theory
The Schachter-Singer Theory
Contemporary Perspectives on Emotion

Karl Andrews held in his hands the envelope he had been waiting for. It could be the ticket to his future: an offer of admission to his first-choice college. But what was it going to say? He knew it could go either way; his grades were pretty good, and he had been involved in some extracurricular activities; but his SAT scores had been not-so-terrific. He felt so nervous that his hands shook as he opened the thin envelope (not a good sign, he thought). Here it comes. "Dear Mr. Andrews," it read. "The Trustees of the University are pleased to admit you. . . ." That was all he needed to see. With a whoop of excitement, Karl found himself jumping up and down gleefully. A rush of emotion overcame him as it sank in that he had, in fact, been accepted. He was on his way.

At one time or another, all of us have experienced the strong feelings that accompany both very pleasant and very negative experiences. Perhaps it was the thrill of getting a sought-after job, the joy of being in love, the sorrow over someone's death, or the anguish of inadvertently hurting someone. Moreover, we experience such reactions on a less intense level throughout our daily lives: the pleasure of a friendship, the enjoyment of a movie, or the embarrassment of breaking a borrowed item.

Despite the varied nature of these feelings, they all are emotions. Although everyone has an idea of what an emotion is, formally defining the concept has proved to be an elusive task. We'll use a general definition: **Emotions** are feelings that generally have both physiological and cognitive elements and that influence behavior.

emotions: Feelings that generally have both physiological and cognitive elements and that influence behavior

Think, for example, about how it feels to be happy. First, we obviously experience a feeling that we can differentiate from other emotions. It is likely that we also experience some identifiable physical changes in our body: Perhaps our heart rate increases, or—like Karl Andrews—we find ourselves "jumping for joy." Finally, the emotion probably encompasses cognitive elements: Our understanding and evaluation of the meaning of what is happening prompts our feelings of happiness.

It is also possible, however, to experience an emotion without the presence of cognitive elements. For instance, we might react emotionally to an unusual or novel situation (such as encountering a person who, for no apparent reason, makes us feel uncomfortable, without cognitively understanding why).

Some psychologists argue that there are entirely separate systems governing cognitive responses and emotional responses. One current controversy is whether the emotional response is predominant over the cognitive response or vice versa. Some theorists suggest that we first respond to a situation with an emotional reaction, and later try to understand it (Zajonc, 1985; Zajonc & McIntosh, 1992; Murphy & Zajonc, 1993). For example, we might enjoy a complex modern symphony without at first understanding it or knowing why we like it.

In contrast, other theorists propose that people first develop cognitions about a situation and then react emotionally. This school of thought suggests that it is necessary for us to first think about and understand a stimulus or situation, relating it to what we already know, before we can react on an emotional level (Lazarus, 1991a, 1991b, 1994, 1995).

Both sides of this debate can cite research to support their viewpoints, and so the question is far from resolved. It may be the case that the sequence varies from situation to situation, with emotions predominating in some instances and cognitive processes occurring first in others. What both sides do agree on is that we can experience emotions that involve little or no conscious thought. We might not know why we're afraid of mice, understanding that objectively they represent no danger, but still be frightened out of our wits when we see them (Lewis & Haviland-Jones, 2000).

 **PsychLink**

Emotions and emotional intelligence
www.mhhe.com/
feldmanup6-10links

The Functions of Emotions

Imagine what it would be like if we didn't experience emotion—no depths of despair, no depression, no remorse, but at the same time no happiness, joy, or love. Obviously life might be considerably less satisfying, and even dull, if we lacked the capacity to sense and express emotion.

But do emotions serve any purpose beyond making life interesting? Indeed they do. Psychologists have identified a number of important roles that emotions play in our daily lives (Scherer, 1984, 1994; Averill, 1994; Oatley & Jenkins, 1996). Among the most important daily functions of emotions:

- *Preparing us for action.* Emotions act as a link between events in our environment and our responses. For example, if we see an angry dog charging toward us, the emotional reaction (fear) is associated with physiological arousal of the sympathetic division of the autonomic nervous system (see Chapter 3). The role of the sympathetic division is to prepare us for emergency action, which presumably will get us moving out of the dog's way—quickly.
- *Shaping our future behavior.* Emotions help us learn information that improves our chances of making appropriate responses in the future. For example, the emotional response that occurs when we experience something unpleasant—such as the threatening dog—teaches us to avoid similar circumstances in the future. Similarly, pleasant emotions act as reinforcement for our prior behavior and therefore are apt to lead us to seek out similar situations in the future.
- *Helping us interact more effectively with others.* The emotions we experience are frequently obvious to observers, as they are communicated through our verbal and nonverbal behaviors. These behaviors can act as a signal to observers, allowing them to better understand what we are experiencing and to predict our future behavior. In turn, this promotes more effective and appropriate social interaction.

Determining the Range of Emotions: Labeling Our Feelings

If we were to try to list the words in the English language that have been used for emotions, we would end up with at least 500 examples (Averill, 1975). The list would range from such obvious entries as *happiness* and *fear* to less common ones, such as *adventurousness* and *pensiveness.*

One challenge for psychologists has been to try to sort through this list in order to identify the most important, fundamental emotions. The issue of cataloguing emotions has been hotly contested, and various emotion theorists have come up with different lists, depending on how they define the concept of emotion. In fact, some reject the question entirely, saying that *no* set of emotions should be singled out as most basic, and that emotions are best understood by breaking them down into their component parts. Other researchers argue that it is best to look at emotions in terms of a hierarchy, dividing them into positive and negative categories, and then organizing them into increasingly narrower subcategories (see Fischer, Shaver, & Carnochan, 1990; Carroll & Russell, 1997; Figure 10-7).

Still, most researchers suggest that a list of basic emotions would include, at the minimum, happiness, anger, fear, sadness, and disgust. Other lists are broader, including such emotions as surprise, contempt, guilt, and joy (Plutchik, 1980; Ortony & Turner, 1990; Russell, 1991; Ekman, 1994a; Shweder, 1994).

One difficulty in finding a definitive basic set of emotions is that cultures differ substantially in how they describe emotions. For instance, Germans report experiencing *schadenfreude,* a feeling of pleasure over another person's difficulties, whereas the Japanese experience *hagaii,* a mood of vulnerable heartache colored by frustration. In Tahiti, people experience *musu,* a feeling of reluctance to yield to unreasonable demands made by one's parents.

Finding *schadenfreude, hagaii,* and *musu* in a particular culture doesn't mean that inhabitants of other cultures are incapable of experiencing such emotions, of course. It does suggest, though, that the existence of a linguistic category to describe a particular emotion may make it easier to discuss, contemplate, and perhaps experience the emotion (Russell, 1991; Mesquita & Frijda, 1992; Russell & Sato, 1995).

 **PsychLink**

Culture and emotions
www.mhhe.com/
feldmanup6-10links

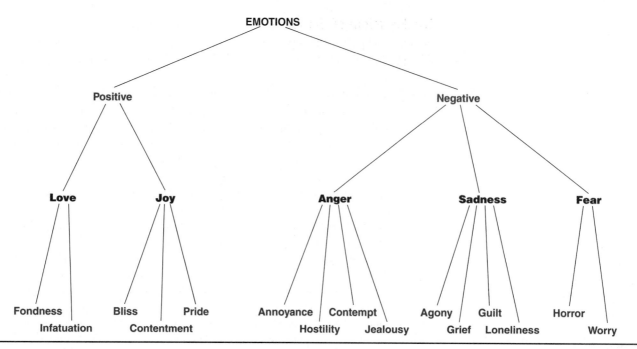

Figure 10-7 One approach to organizing emotions is to use a hierarchy, in which emotions are divided into increasingly narrow subcategories. (Adapted from Fischer, Shaver, & Carnochan, 1990.)

The Roots of Emotions

I've never been so angry before; I feel my heart pounding, and I'm trembling all over. . . . I don't know how I'll get through the performance. I feel like my stomach is filled with butterflies. . . . That was quite a mistake I made! My face must be incredibly red. . . . When I heard the footsteps in the night I was so frightened that I couldn't catch my breath.

If you examine our language, you will find that there are literally dozens of ways to describe how we feel when we experience an emotion, and that the language we use to describe emotions is, for the most part, based on the physical symptoms that are associated with a particular emotional experience (Koveces, 1987).

Consider, for instance, the experience of fear. Pretend that it is late one New Year's Eve. You are walking down a dark road, and you hear a stranger approaching behind you. It is clear that he is not trying to hurry by but is coming directly toward you. You think of what you will do if the stranger attempts to rob you—or worse, hurt you in some way.

While these thoughts are running through your head, something rather dramatic will be happening to your body. The most likely reactions, which are associated with activation of the autonomic nervous system (see Chapter 3), include an increase in your rate of breathing, an acceleration of your heart, a widening of your pupils (to increase visual sensitivity), and a dryness in your mouth as the functioning of your salivary glands, and in fact of your entire digestive system, ceases. At the same time, though, your sweat glands will likely increase their activity, since increased sweating will help you rid yourself of excess heat developed by any emergency activity in which you engage.

Of course, all these physiological changes are likely to occur without your awareness. At the same time, though, the emotional experience accompanying them will be obvious to you: You would most surely report feeling fearful.

Although it is relatively easy to describe the general physical reactions that accompany emotions, the specific role that these physiological responses play in the experience of emotions has proved to be a major puzzle for psychologists. As we shall see, some theorists suggest that there are specific bodily reactions that *cause* us to experience a particular emotion—we experience fear, for instance, *because* our heart is pounding and

we are breathing deeply. In contrast, other theorists suggest that the physiological reaction is the *result* of the experience of an emotion. In this view, we experience fear, and this emotional experience causes our heart to pound and our breathing to deepen.

The James-Lange Theory: Do Gut Reactions Equal Emotions?

To William James and Carl Lange, who were among the first researchers to explore the nature of emotions, emotional experience is, very simply, a reaction to instinctive bodily events that occur as a response to some situation or event in the environment. This view is summarized in James's statement, "we feel sorry because we cry, angry because we strike, afraid because we tremble" (James, 1890).

James and Lange took the view that the instinctive response of crying over a loss leads us to feel sorrow; that striking out at someone who frustrates us results in our feeling anger; that trembling at a menacing threat causes us to feel fear. They suggested that for every major emotion there is an accompanying physiological or "gut" reaction of internal organs—called a *visceral experience.* It is this specific pattern of visceral response that leads us to label the emotional experience.

In sum, James and Lange proposed that we experience emotions as a result of physiological changes that produce specific sensations. In turn, these sensations are interpreted by the brain as particular kinds of emotional experiences (see Figure 10-8). This view has come to be called the **James-Lange theory of emotion** (Izard, 1990; Laird & Bresler, 1990).

The James-Lange theory has some serious drawbacks, however. For the theory to be valid, visceral changes would have to occur at a relatively rapid pace, because we experience some emotions—such as fear upon hearing a stranger rapidly approaching on a dark night—almost instantaneously. Yet emotional experiences frequently occur even before there is time for certain physiological changes to be set into motion. Because of the slowness with which some visceral changes take place, it is hard to see how they could be the source of immediate emotional experience.

The James-Lange theory poses another difficulty: Physiological arousal does not invariably produce emotional experience. For example, a person who is jogging has an increased heartbeat and respiration rate, as well as many of the other physiological changes associated with certain emotions. Yet joggers do not typically think of such changes in terms of emotions. There cannot be a one-to-one correspondence, then, between visceral changes and emotional experience. Visceral changes by themselves may not be sufficient to produce emotion.

Finally, our internal organs produce a relatively limited range of sensations. Although some types of physiological changes are associated with specific emotional experiences (Levenson et al., 1992; Levenson, 1992; Davidson et al., 1994), it is difficult to imagine how the range of emotions that people are capable of experiencing could be the result of unique visceral changes. Many emotions are actually associated with relatively similar sorts of visceral changes, a fact that contradicts the James-Lange theory.

The Cannon-Bard Theory: Physiological Reactions as the Result of Emotions

In response to the difficulties inherent in the James-Lange theory, Walter Cannon, and later Philip Bard, suggested an alternative view. In what has come to be known as the **Cannon-Bard theory of emotion,** they proposed the model illustrated in the second part of Figure 10-8 (Cannon, 1929). The major thrust of the theory is to reject the view that physiological arousal alone leads to the perception of emotion. Instead, the theory assumes that both physiological arousal *and* the emotional experience are produced simultaneously by the same nerve stimulus, which Cannon and Bard suggested emanates from the brain's thalamus.

The theory states that after an emotion-producing stimulus is perceived, the thalamus is the initial site of the emotional response. In turn, the thalamus sends a signal to the autonomic nervous system, thereby producing a visceral response. At the same time, the thalamus communicates a message to the cerebral cortex regarding the nature of the emotion being experienced. Hence, it is not necessary for different emotions to have unique physiological patterns associated with them—as long as the message sent to the cerebral cortex differs according to the specific emotion.

James-Lange theory of emotion: The belief that emotional experience is a reaction to bodily events occurring as a result of an external situation ("I feel sad because I am crying")

Cannon-Bard theory of emotion: The belief that both physiological and emotional arousal are produced simultaneously by the same nerve stimulus

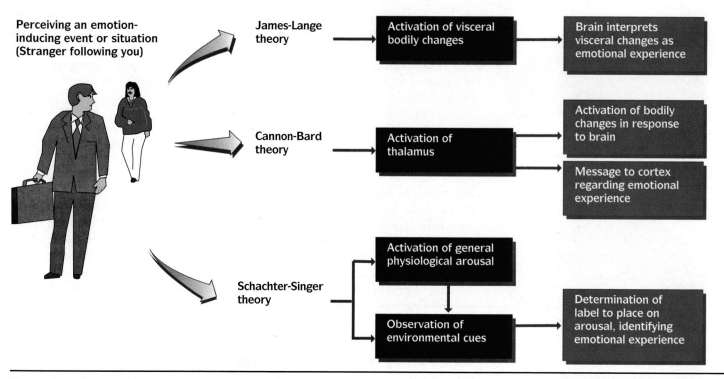

Figure 10-8 A comparison of three models of emotion.

The Cannon-Bard theory seems to have been accurate in its rejection of the view that physiological arousal alone accounts for emotions. However, more recent research has led to some important modifications of the theory. As you may recall from Chapter 3, we now understand that it is the hypothalamus and the limbic system, and not the thalamus, that play a major role in emotional experience. In addition, the simultaneity of the physiological and emotional responses, which is a fundamental assumption of the theory, has yet to be conclusively demonstrated (Pribram, 1984). This ambiguity has allowed room for yet another theory of emotions: the Schachter-Singer theory.

The Schachter-Singer Theory: Emotions as Labels

Suppose that, as you were being followed down a dark street on New Year's Eve, you noticed a man being followed by a shady figure on the other side of the street. Now assume that instead of reacting with fear, the man begins to laugh and act gleeful. Might the reactions of this other individual be sufficient to lay your fears to rest? Might you, in fact, decide there is nothing to fear, and get into the spirit of the evening by beginning to feel happiness and glee yourself?

According to an explanation that focuses on the role of cognition, the **Schachter-Singer theory of emotion,** this might very well happen. This approach to explaining emotions emphasizes that we identify the emotion we are experiencing by observing our environment and comparing ourselves with others (Schachter & Singer, 1962).

A classic experiment found evidence for this hypothesis. In the study, participants were told that they would receive an injection of a vitamin. In reality, they were given epinephrine, a drug that causes an increase in physiological arousal, including higher heart and respiration rates and a reddening of the face, responses that typically occur during strong emotional reactions. Participants in both groups were then individually placed in a situation where a confederate of the experimenter acted in one of two ways. In one condition, he acted angry and hostile, while in the other condition he behaved as if he were exuberantly happy.

The purpose of the experiment was to determine how the participants would react emotionally to the confederate's behavior. When they were asked to describe their own emotional state at the end of the experiment, those participants exposed to the angry confederate reported that they felt angry, whereas those exposed to the happy confederate

This is the high, swaying suspension bridge that was used to increase the physiological arousal of male subjects. What other types of behavior can be explained by the Schachter-Singer theory of emotion?

Schachter–Singer theory of emotion: The belief that emotions are determined jointly by a nonspecific kind of physiological arousal and its interpretation, based on environmental cues

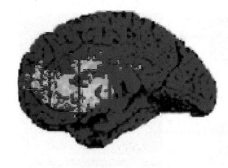

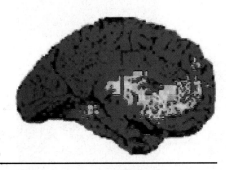

Figure 10-9 Experiencing different emotions activates particular areas of the brain. These scans, showing two views of the brain, indicate brain activity that occurs during the experience of sadness, as compared with situations in which no emotion is being experienced. (Courtesy of Mark George, NIMH)

The emotional brain
www.mhhe.com/
feldmanup6-10links

reported feeling happy. In sum, the results suggest that participants turned to the environment and the behavior of others for an explanation of the physiological arousal they were experiencing.

The results of the Schachter-Singer experiment, then, supported a cognitive view of emotions, in which emotions are determined jointly by a relatively nonspecific kind of physiological arousal *and* the labeling of the arousal based on cues from the environment (refer to the third part of Figure 10-8).

Although later research has found that arousal is not as nonspecific as Schachter and Singer assumed, it is clear that arousal can magnify, and be mistaken for, many emotions. For example, in one experiment, men who crossed a swaying 450-foot suspension bridge spanning a deep canyon were more attracted to a woman they encountered at the other end than those who crossed a stable bridge spanning a shallow stream. Apparently, the men who crossed the frightening bridge attributed their subsequent high arousal to the woman, rather than to the swaying bridge (Dutton & Aron, 1974; Reisenzein, 1983; Leventhal & Tomarken, 1986).

In short, the Schachter-Singer theory of emotions is important because of its suggestion that, at least under some circumstances, emotional experiences are a joint function of physiological arousal and the labeling of that arousal. When the source of physiological arousal is unclear, we may look to our surroundings to determine just what it is we are experiencing.

Contemporary Perspectives on Emotion

When Schachter and Singer carried out their groundbreaking experiment in the early 1960s, they were relatively limited in the ways that they could evaluate the physiology that accompanies emotion. However, advances in the measurement of the nervous system and other parts of the body have allowed researchers to examine more closely the biological responses that are involved in emotion. As a result, contemporary research on emotion is pointing to a revision of earlier views that physiological responses associated with emotions are undifferentiated. Instead, evidence is growing that specific patterns of biological arousal are associated with individual emotions (Davidson, 1994; Levenson, 1994; Franks & Smith, 1999).

For instance, researchers have found that specific emotions produce activation of very different portions of the brain. In one study using PET brain scans, participants were asked to recall either events that made them feel sad, such as deaths and funerals, or events that were happy, such as weddings and births. They also looked at photos of faces that were happy or sad. The results were clear: Happiness was related to a decrease in activity in certain areas of the cerebral cortex, and sadness was associated with increases in activity in particular portions of the cortex (see Figure 10-9). Ultimately, it might be possible to map particular emotions to specific sites in the brain (George et al., 1995).

As new approaches to emotion continue to be developed, it is reasonable to ask why there are so many theories of emotion and, perhaps even more important, which one provides the most complete explanation. But, we have only scratched the surface. There are almost as many explanatory theories of emotion as there are individual emotions (e.g., Izard, 1991; Lazarus, 1991b; Oatley, 1992; Ekman & Davidson, 1994; Strongman, 1996; Averill, 1997).

Why are theories of emotion so plentiful? The answer is that emotions are such complex phenomena, encompassing both biological and cognitive aspects, that no single theory has been able to fully explain all facets of emotional experience. For each of the approaches, there is contradictory evidence of one sort or another, and therefore no theory has proved invariably accurate in its predictions.

This abundance of perspectives on emotion is not a cause for despair—or unhappiness, fear, or any other negative emotion. It simply reflects the fact that psychology is an evolving, developing science. As more evidence is gathered, the specific answers to questions about the nature of emotions will become clearer. Furthermore, even as our understanding of emotions continues to grow, there are ongoing efforts to apply our knowledge of emotions to some practical problems—as you can see in the *Applying Psychology in the 21st Century* box.

Applying Psychology in the 21st Century

The Truth About Lies: Do Lie Detectors Work?

Aldrich Ames was given routine lie detector tests periodically by his employer, the U.S. Central Intelligence Agency. On every occasion he passed the test. Yet at the very same time his truthfulness was being vouched for by the lie detector, he was involved in high-level spying for the Russians.

No surprise, at least among researchers who study the validity of lie detector test results. Repeatedly, lie detectors have proved to be unreliable indicators of lying.

A lie detector, or *polygraph,* is an electronic device designed to expose people who are telling lies. The basic assumption behind the apparatus is straightforward: The autonomic nervous system of people who are not being truthful becomes aroused as their emotionality increases. Polygraphs are designed to detect the physiological changes that are indicative of this arousal.

Actually, a number of separate physiological functions are measured simultaneously by a lie detector, including changes in breathing pattern, heart rate, blood pressure, and sweating. In theory, polygraph operators ask a series of questions, some of which they know will elicit verifiable, truthful responses. For instance, they might ask a person to provide his or her name and address. Then, when more critical questions

are answered, operators can observe the nature of the physiological changes that occur. Answers whose accompanying physiological responses deviate significantly from those accompanying truthful responses are assumed to be false (Reicherter, 1997).

That's the theory, at least. The reality is something different: There is no foolproof technique for assessing the extent of the physiological changes that can indicate a lie. Even truthful responses can elicit physiological arousal, if the question is emotion-laden (Waid & Orne, 1982). How many innocent people accused of a murder, for instance, would *not* respond emotionally when asked whether they committed the crime, since they know that their future may hang in the balance?

One further drawback of lie detector tests is that people are capable of fooling the polygraph. For instance, biofeedback techniques (see Chapter 3) can be employed to produce emotional responses to accompany even truthful statements, meaning that the polygraph operator will be unable to differentiate between honest and dishonest responses. Even biting one's tongue or hiding a tack in a shoe and pressing on it as each question is answered could be sufficient to produce physiological arousal during each response, making truthful and deceptive responses indistinguishable (Honts, Raskin, & Kircher, 1987; Honts & Kircher, 1994; Sleek, 1998).

Because of these sources of error, lie detector operators often make mistakes when trying to judge another person's honesty. The American Psychological Association has adopted a resolution stating that the evidence for the effectiveness of polygraphs "is still unsatisfactory." Even the major proponent of the use of polygraphs—the American Polygraph Association—admits an error rate between 4 and 13 percent, and critics suggest that research has shown that the actual rate is closer to 30 percent. Using such evidence, U.S. federal law bars employers from using polygraphs as screening devices for most jobs (Iacono, 1991; Saxe, 1994; Iacono & Lykken, 1997).

In short, there are good reasons to doubt that polygraph tests can determine accurately whether someone is lying. For now, then, you can be assured that any secrets you might harbor will remain hidden: No one has yet identified a foolproof way to distinguish people who are telling the truth from those who are lying (Saxe, 1994; Alliger, Lilienfeld, & Mitchell, 1996).

Techniques for "fooling" lie detectors focus on artificially elevating emotional responses so that truthful and untruthful responses display similar patterns of emotionality. Do you think a lack of emotional response would therefore indicate truthfulness? Or is it possible to defeat a lie detector by depressing (rather than elevating) one's emotional response?

Evaluate

1. Emotions are always accompanied by a cognitive response. True or false?
2. The _____-_____ theory of emotions states that emotions are a response to instinctive bodily events.
3. According to the _____-_____ theory of emotion, both an emotional response and physiological arousal are produced simultaneously by the same nerve stimulus.
4. Your friend—a psychology major—tells you, "I was at a party last night. During the course of the evening, my general level of arousal increased. Since I was at a party where people were enjoying themselves, I assume I must have felt happy." What theory of emotion does your friend subscribe to?
5. The _____ or "lie detector" is an instrument used to measure physiological responses associated with answers to questions.

Answers to Evaluate Questions

1. False; emotions may occur without a cognitive response. 2. James-Lange 4. Cannon-Bard 5. Schachter-Singer 6. polygraph

Rethink

1. Many people enjoy watching movies, sporting events, and music performances in crowded theaters and arenas more than they like watching them at home alone. Which theory of emotions might help explain this? How?
2. If researchers learned how to control emotional responses so that targeted emotions could be caused or prevented, what ethical concerns might arise? Under what circumstances, if any, should such techniques be used?

Prepare

How does nonverbal behavior relate to the expression of emotions?

Organize

Nonverbal Behavior and the Expression of Emotions
The Facial-Feedback Hypothesis

PsychLink

Facial expressions and occupation
www.mhhe.com/
feldmanup6-10links

Nonverbal Behavior and the Expression of Emotions

Ancient Sanskrit writings speak of someone who, on giving an evasive answer, "rubs the great toe along the ground, and shivers." Shakespeare writes of Macbeth's face as "a place where men may read strange matters." An old love song claims "your eyes are the eyes of a woman in love." Such examples demonstrate how nonverbal behavior has long had the reputation of revealing people's emotions. Only recently, though, have psychologists demonstrated the validity of such claims, finding that nonverbal behavior is an important way we communicate our emotions.

We now know that nonverbal behavior communicates messages simultaneously across several *channels,* paths along which communications flow. For example, facial expressions, eye contact, body movements, tone of voice, and even less obvious behaviors such as the positioning of the eyebrows can each be conceptualized as separate nonverbal channels of communication. Furthermore, each individual channel is capable of carrying a particular message—which might or might not be related to the message being carried by the other channels. Because facial expressions are the primary means of communicating emotional states, we will examine their role in the experience of emotions.

EXPLORING DIVERSITY

Do People in All Cultures Express Emotion Similarly?

Consider, for a moment, the six photos displayed in Figure 10-10. Can you identify the emotions being expressed by the person in each of the photos?

If you are a good judge of facial expressions, you will conclude that six of the basic emotions are displayed: happiness, anger, sadness, surprise, disgust, and fear. These emotions are the ones that are identified in literally hundreds of studies of nonverbal behavior as being consistently distinct and identifiable, even by untrained observers (Ekman & O'Sullivan, 1991).

What is particularly interesting about these six emotions is that they are not limited to members of Western cultures, but rather appear to be the basic emotions expressed universally by members of the human species, regardless of where they have been raised and what learning experiences they have had. This point was demonstrated convincingly by psychologist Paul Ekman, who traveled to New Guinea to study members of an isolated jungle tribe who had had almost no contact with Westerners (Ekman, 1972). The people of the tribe did not speak or understand English, they had never seen a movie, and they had had very limited experience with Caucasians before Ekman's arrival. Yet their nonverbal responses to emotion-evoking stories, as well as their ability to identify basic emotions, were quite similar to those of Westerners.

Because the New Guineans were so isolated, they could not have learned from Westerners to recognize or produce similar facial expressions. Instead, their similar abilities and manner of responding emotionally appear to have been present innately. Although it is possible to argue that similar experiences in both cultures led to the learning of similar types of nonverbal behavior, this appears unlikely, because the two cultures are so very different. The expression of basic emotions, then, seems to be universal (Ekman, 1993, 1994b; Izard, 1994; Scherer & Wallbott, 1994).

The Facial-Affect Program

Why is there similarity in the expression of basic emotions across cultures? One explanation is based on a hypothesis known as the **facial-affect program** (Ekman, 1972).

The facial-affect program—which is assumed to be universally present at birth—is analogous to a computer program that is turned on when a particular

THE FAR SIDE   By GARY LARSON

How to recognize the moods of an Irish setter

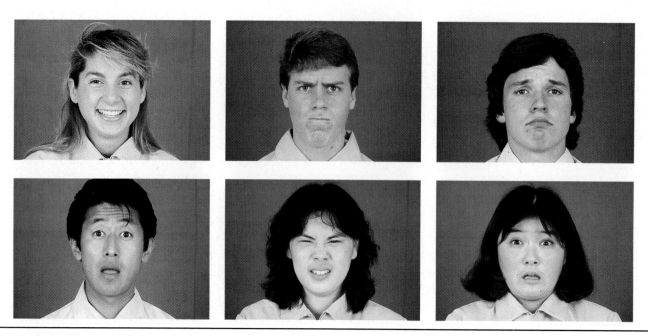

Figure 10-10 These photos demonstrate six of the primary emotions: happiness, anger, sadness, surprise, disgust, and fear.

emotion is experienced. When set in motion, the "program" activates a set of nerve impulses that make the face display an appropriate expression. Each primary emotion produces a unique set of muscular movements, forming the kinds of expressions seen in Figure 10-10. For example, the emotion of happiness is universally displayed by movement of the zygomatic major, a muscle that raises the corners of the mouth—forming what we would call a smile (Ekman, Davidson, & Friesen, 1990).

facial-affect program: The activation of a set of nerve impulses that make the face display the appropriate expression

Display Rules

If you've ever traveled in another culture, you've probably encountered people whose nonverbal behavior is quite different from what you are accustomed to. For instance, perhaps you've been to Japan, where effusive emotional displays tend to be rarer than in Western countries. How do such differences correspond with the evidence showing that the expression of basic emotions is similar across cultures?

The answer resides in display rules. **Display rules** are the guidelines that govern the appropriateness of showing emotion nonverbally. Display rules are learned during childhood, and they act to exaggerate, minimize, or mask emotional expressions (Feldman, 1982, 1991; Halberstadt, 1991).

display rules: The guidelines that govern the appropriateness of showing emotion nonverbally

People are fairly good at using display rules, because we all have a lot of practice. For instance, people who receive an unwanted gift learn to paste a smile on their face, at least in the presence of the gift giver. Similarly, card players learn to avoid gloating when they have a good hand (instead displaying a "poker face").

On the other hand, we're not always successful in masking our true feelings, and subtle indications can give our actual emotions away (Miller & Stiff, 1992). For instance, there is a slight difference in true and sham smiles, as you can see when you compare the photos in Figure 10-11.

The nature of display rules varies considerably from one culture to another. For instance, Asians by and large consider it less desirable to express emotions than people in Mediterranean and Latin cultures (Matsumoto, 1990; Mesquita & Frijda, 1992). Although the evidence is sketchy, some research also suggests that there are display rule differences between whites and African Americans within the United States. For instance, one study suggests that whites show more restrained emotional displays than African Americans. Still, the scope and reliability of such within-culture findings has not been fully established (Hanna, 1984; Manstead, 1991).

Figure 10-11 Which is the real smile? In comparison to a true happy smile *a,* the smiles in the other photos are false. In *b* and *c,* the person is actually experiencing disgust: in *d,* the person is actually feeling sad. (Ekman, Friesen, & O'Sullivan, 1988.)

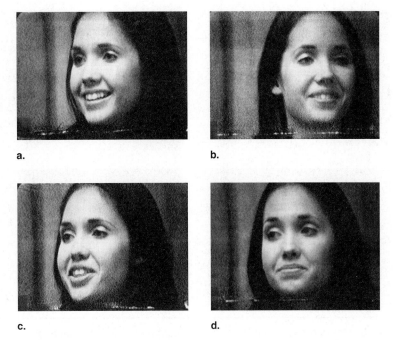

facial-feedback hypothesis: The hypothesis that facial expressions not only *reflect* emotional experience, they also help *determine* how people experience and label emotions

The Facial-Feedback Hypothesis: Smile, Though You're Feeling Blue

If you want to feel happy, try smiling.

That is the implication of an intriguing notion known as the **facial-feedback hypothesis.** According to this hypothesis, facial expressions not only *reflect* emotional experience, they also help *determine* how people experience and label emotions (Izard, 1990). The basic idea is that "wearing" an emotional expression provides muscular feedback to the brain that helps produce an emotion congruent with the expression. For instance, the muscles activated when we smile would send a message to the brain indicating the experience of happiness—even if there is nothing in the environment that would produce that particular emotion. Some theoreticians have gone further, suggesting that facial expressions are *necessary* for an emotion to be experienced (Rinn, 1984, 1991). According to this view, if there is no facial expression present, the emotion cannot be felt.

Support for the facial-feedback hypothesis comes from what has become a classic experiment carried out by psychologist Paul Ekman and colleagues (Ekman, Levenson, & Friesen, 1983). In the study, professional actors were asked to follow very explicit instructions regarding movements of muscles in their faces. You might try this example yourself:

- Raise your brows and pull them together.
- Raise your upper eyelids.
- Now stretch your lips horizontally back toward your ears.

After carrying out these directions—which, as you may have guessed, are meant to produce an expression of fear—the actors showed a rise in heart rate and a decline in body temperature, physiological reactions that are characteristic of fear. Overall, facial expressions representative of the primary emotions produced physiological effects similar to those accompanying the emotions under other circumstances.

Although support for the facial-feedback hypothesis is not firm (Matsumoto, 1987), there is sufficient evidence in its favor to suggest that the old lyric "Smile, though you're feeling blue" might not be far from the mark in its suggestion that you will feel better by putting a smile on your face (Levenson, Ekman, & Friesen, 1990; Larsen, Kasimatis, & Frey, 1992; Laird & Bressler, 1992; Camras, Holland, & Patterson, 1993; Capella, 1993).

Evaluate

1. What are the six primary emotions that can be identified from facial expressions?

2. Viewed as similar to a computer program, the _____-_____ program provides a possible explanation for the universality in the expression of emotions.

3. According to the _____-_____ hypothesis, an emotion cannot be felt without an accompanying facial response.

Answers to Evaluate Questions

1. Surprise, sadness, happiness, anger, disgust, and fear 2. facial-affect 3. facial-feedback

Rethink

1. Do you think there are biological reasons, relating to survival, for the fact that the six basic emotions are associated with universal facial expressions? The facial-affect program is said to be "universally present at birth"; can this be confirmed through experimentation?

2. How might differences in nonverbal display rules between people of different cultures or between racial groups be responsible for misunderstandings during social interaction?

Looking Back

How does motivation direct and energize behavior?

- Motivation relates to the factors that direct and energize behavior. Drive is the motivational tension that energizes behavior to fulfill a need. Primary drives relate to basic biological needs. Secondary drives are those in which no obvious biological need is fulfilled. (p. 288)
- Motivational drives often operate under the principle of homeostasis, the maintenance of a steady internal state. (p. 289)
- A number of broad approaches to motivation move beyond explanations that rely on instincts. Drive-reduction approaches, though useful for primary drives, are inadequate for explaining behavior in which the goal is not to reduce a drive but to maintain or even increase excitement or arousal. In contrast, arousal approaches suggest that we try to maintain a particular level of stimulation and activity. (p. 289)
- Incentive approaches focus on the positive aspects of the environment that direct and energize behavior. Finally, cognitive approaches focus on the role of thoughts, expectations, and understanding of the world in producing motivation. Cognitive approaches draw a distinction between intrinsic and extrinsic motivation. (p. 290)
- Maslow's hierarchy of needs suggests that there are five needs: physiological, safety, love and belongingness, esteem, and self-actualization. Only after the more basic needs are fulfilled is a person able to move toward higher-order needs. (p. 292)

What biological and social factors underlie hunger?

- Eating behavior is subject to homeostasis, because most people's weight stays within a relatively stable range. The brain's hypothalamus is central to the regulation of food intake. (p. 295)
- Social factors, such as mealtimes, cultural food preferences, and other learned habits, also play a role in the regulation of eating, determining when, what, and how much one eats. An oversensitivity to social cues and an insensitivity to internal cues might also be related to obesity. In addition, obesity could be caused by an unusually high weight set point—the weight at which the body attempts to maintain homeostasis—and genetic factors. (p. 297)

How are needs relating to achievement, affiliation, and power motivation exhibited?

- Need for achievement refers to the stable, learned characteristic in which a person strives to attain a level of excellence. Need for achievement is usually measured through the Thematic Apperception Test (TAT), a series of pictures about which a person writes a story. (p. 301)
- The need for affiliation is a concern with establishing and maintaining relationships with others, whereas the need for power is a tendency to seek to exert an impact on others. (p. 301)

What are emotions, and how do we experience them?

- Emotions are broadly defined as feelings that can affect behavior and generally have both a physiological and a cognitive component. There is debate over whether there are separate systems that govern cognitive and emotional responses, and whether one has primacy over the other. (p. 303)

What are the functions of emotions?

- The functions of emotions include preparing us for action, shaping future behavior through learning, and helping us interact more effectively with others. (p. 304)
- Several theories explain emotions. The James-Lange theory suggests that emotional experience is a reaction to bodily, or visceral, changes that occur as a response to an environmental event and are interpreted as an emotional response. (p. 306)
- In contrast, the Cannon-Bard theory contends that both physiological arousal *and* an emotional experience are produced simultaneously by the same nerve stimulus and that the visceral experience itself does not necessarily differ among differing emotions. (p. 306)
- The Schachter-Singer theory suggests that emotions are determined jointly by a relatively nonspecific physiological arousal and the subsequent labeling of that arousal, using cues from the environment to determine how others are behaving in the same situation. (p. 307)
- The most recent approaches to emotions focus on their biological aspects. For instance, it now seems that specific patterns of biological arousal are associated with individual emotions. Furthermore, new scanning techniques have identified the specific parts of the brain that are activated during the experience of particular emotions. (p. 308)

How does nonverbal behavior relate to the expression of emotions?

- Emotions can be revealed through a person's facial expressions. In fact, there are similarities in the way members of different cultures understand the emotional expressions of others. One explanation for this similarity is that an innate facial-affect program activates a set of muscle movements representing the emotion being experienced. (p. 310)
- The facial-feedback hypothesis suggests that facial expressions not only reflect, but also produce emotional experiences. (p. 312)

Key Terms and Concepts

motivation (p. 288)

instincts (p. 289)

drive-reduction approaches to motivation (p. 289)

drive (p. 289)

homeostasis (p. 289)

arousal approaches to motivation (p. 290)

incentive approaches to motivation (p. 290)

cognitive approaches of motivation (p. 292)

self-actualization (p. 293)

obesity (p. 295)

weight set point (p. 296)

metabolism (p. 296)

anorexia nervosa (p. 298)

bulimia (p. 298)

need for achievement (p. 301)

need for affiliation (p. 301)

need for power (p. 302)

emotions (p. 303)

James-Lange theory of emotion (p. 306)

Cannon-Bard theory of emotion (p. 306)

Schachter-Singer theory of emotion (p. 307)

facial-affect program (p. 311)

display rules (p. 311)

facial-feedback hypothesis (p. 312)

Psychology on the Web

1. Find two different websites that deal with nonverbal behavior. One site should present a fairly "academic" discussion of the topic, and the other should be more informal. (Hint: The terms *nonverbal behavior* and *nonverbal communication* might

lead you to more formal discussions of the topic, whereas *body language* might lead you to the less formal discussions.) Compare and contrast your findings from the two sites.

2. Find one or more websites that offer information on polygraphs (lie detectors). The sites should be intended *either* to advertise (i.e., sell) lie detectors or lie detection services *or* to debunk lie detector tests (e.g., by showing how to cheat on them). Evaluate the information on the website(s), using your understanding of lie detection techniques discussed in this chapter. Summarize your findings and conclusions in writing.

Preview

For additional quizzing and a variety of interactive resources, visit the *Understanding Psychology* Online Learning Center at

www.mhhe.com/feldmanup6

Epilogue

In this chapter, we discussed motivation and emotions, two interrelated aspects of psychology. The topic of motivation has spawned a great deal of theory and research in its examination of primary and secondary drives. We then turned to a discussion of emotions, beginning with their functions and proceeding to a review of three major theories that seek to explain what emotions are and how they, and their associated physiological symptoms, emerge in the individual. Finally, we looked at cultural differences in the expression and display of emotions, and discussed the facial-affect program, which seems to be innate and to regulate the nonverbal expression of the basic emotions.

Before we proceed to a discussion of gender and sexuality, return to the scenario in the prologue to this chapter: how cyclist Lance Armstrong overcame cancer and won the Tour de France. Using your knowledge of motivation and emotion, consider the following questions:

1. Which approach or approaches to motivation—instinctual, drive reduction, arousal, incentive, or cognitive—most effectively explain why an athlete like Armstrong will work exceptionally hard over many years to become a competitive cyclist?

2. How might the need for achievement have contributed to Armstrong's decision to continue competitive cycling after his cancer treatment? Would the need for affiliation have played a role? How?

3. What function might Armstrong's emotions have served in helping him overcome his cancer and continue racing competitively?

4. How can Armstrong's comment about his win in the Tour de France ("I think it's a miracle") be interpreted in terms of your understanding of motivation and emotion?

Chapter Eleven

Sexuality and Gender

Prologue: From Boy to Girl and Back

Looking Ahead

Gender and Sex

Gender Roles: Society's Expectations for Women and Men

Gender Differences: More Similar Than Different

Sources of Gender Differences: Where Biology and Society Meet

Understanding Human Sexual Response: The Facts of Life

The Basic Biology of Sexual Behavior

Psychological Aspects of Sexual Excitement: What Turns People On?

The Phases of Sexual Response: The Ups and Downs of Sex

Exploring Diversity: Female Circumcision: A Celebration of Culture—or Genital Mutilation?

The Varieties of Sexual Behavior

Approaches to Sexual Normality

Surveying Sexual Behavior: What's Happening Behind Closed Doors?

Masturbation: Solitary Sex

Heterosexuality

Homosexuality and Bisexuality

Sexual Difficulties: When Sex Goes Wrong

Rape

Psychology at Work: Pat Unger, Crisis Center Counselor

Childhood Sexual Abuse

Sexually Transmitted Diseases (STDs)

Sexual Problems

Becoming an Informed Consumer of Psychology: Lowering the Risks of Date Rape

Applying Psychology in the 21st Century: Bringing Sexual Dysfunction into the Open: The Newest Sexual Revolution

Looking Back

Key Terms and Concepts

Psychology on the Web

OLC Preview

Epilogue

Prologue

From Boy to Girl and Back

It was a gruesome accident. A physician botched the routine circumcision of Bruce Reimer, an 8-month-old infant boy, slicing off his penis.

Bruce or Brenda?

The distraught parents consulted with leading experts, whose predictions were unremittingly grim. Not only could he never have sex, they said, but he could never marry nor live a normal life in any way. The radical solution the experts suggested: The Reimers should turn their son into a daughter.

Following the experts' advice, the Reimers began calling Bruce "Brenda." What was left of his genitals was removed, and he had a series of operations meant to build an artificial vagina. Bruce/Brenda was clothed in dresses and given dolls to play with. He was taught how to be "clean" and "tidy"—in order, it was thought, to be more girl-like. He was given female hormones when he was a teenager to make him develop breasts.

But it never worked. Bruce/Brenda was beset by anxiety and depression growing up, and he didn't feel or even look like a girl. And when he learned the truth about his past when he was 14, he renounced his female identity. He became a boy again (Diamond & Sigmundson, 1997; Colapinto, 2000).

Looking Ahead

Although Bruce Reimer's story is a painful one, his life ultimately turned out well. After plastic surgeons crafted male genitals for him, he married a woman he deeply loved. He has adopted his wife's three children, and leads, by his account, a normal life.

Reimer's experience raises a host of issues. How does heredity account for our sexual identity? How flexible is that identity? What is the relationship between gender (the sense of being male or female) and physical sexual characteristics? How do sex and gender affect our everyday behavior?

Issues like these are central to people's lives. Exemplifying major personal, as well as societal concerns, sex and gender are also key topics for psychologists in a variety of specialties. For instance, psychologists interested in motivation view sexuality in terms of sexual needs, drives, and gratification. Biopsychologists consider sexuality from the perspective of how the brain and nervous system relate to the functioning of the sexual organs. Social psychologists and psychologists who specialize in the study of women focus on society's rules of sexual conduct and the role that sexual behavior plays in interpersonal behavior.

In this chapter, we consider human sexuality from several of these vantage points. We begin by examining gender, discussing differences in societal expectations about how men and women should behave and the impact of those expectations. Next we turn to sexual behavior. We describe the biological aspects of sexual excitement and arousal and then examine the variety of sexual activities in which people engage. We conclude the chapter with a discussion of nonconsenting sex, sexually transmitted diseases, and the psychological aspects of sexual difficulties.

Prepare

What are the major differences between male and female gender roles?

Organize

Gender and Sex
    Gender Roles
    Gender Differences
    Sources of Gender Differences

Gender and Sex

"It's a girl!"
"It's a boy!"

One of these exclamations, or some variant, is typically the first sentence uttered upon the birth of a child. But the consequences of whether we are born with female or male sex organs extend well beyond the moment of birth. Throughout our lives, how others think of us, and even how we view ourselves, is largely based on whether we are labeled as a woman or a man by society—our gender.

Gender is the perception of being male or female. Although there is a good deal of overlap between the concepts of sex and gender, they are not the same: *Sex* typically refers to sexual anatomy and sexual behavior, whereas *gender* refers to the sense of maleness or femaleness related to our membership in a given society.

From the moment of birth, gender differences are defined by outside influences. Is it possible for a family to block these influences completely? Would it be desirable to do so?

Gender Roles: Society's Expectations for Women and Men

Our conclusions about what is or is not "appropriate" behavior for others and ourselves are based on gender roles. **Gender roles** are the set of expectations, defined by a particular society, that indicate what is appropriate behavior for men and women.

If men's and women's gender roles were equivalent, they would have only minor impact upon our lives. However, expectations about men and women differ significantly, which can result in favoritism toward members of one of the sexes. Gender roles can also produce *stereotyping,* judgments about individual members of a group based on their membership in that group. Stereotypes about gender roles are reflected in **sexism,** negative attitudes and behavior toward a person based on that person's gender.

People in Western societies generally hold well-defined stereotypes about men and women that prevail regardless of age, economic status, and social and educational background. Men are more apt to be viewed as having traits involving competence, such as independence,

Table 11-1 Descriptive Adjectives for Men and Women

Adjectives found to apply most to men or most to women in at least 20 of the 25 countries studied in Williams and Best (1990)

ITEMS ASSOCIATED WITH MALES

Active	Daring	Initiative	Robust
Adventurous	Determined	Inventive	Rude
Aggressive	Disorderly	Lazy	Self-confident
Ambitious	Dominant	Logical	Serious
Arrogant	Egotistical	Loud	Severe
Assertive	Energetic	Masculine	Stern
Autocratic	Enterprising	Opportunistic	Stolid
Clear-thinking	Forceful	Progressive	Strong
Coarse	Hardheaded	Rational	Unemotional
Courageous	Hardhearted	Realistic	Wise
Cruel	Independent	Reckless	

ITEMS ASSOCIATED WITH FEMALES

Affected	Dependent	Gentle	Softhearted
Affectionate	Dreamy	Mild	Submissive
Attractive	Emotional	Sensitive	Superstitious
Charming	Fearful	Sentimental	Talkative
Curious	Feminine	Sexy	Weak

objectivity, and competitiveness. In contrast, women tend to be seen as having traits involving warmth and expressiveness, such as gentleness and awareness of others' feelings. Because Western society traditionally values competence more than warmth and expressiveness, the perceived differences between men and women are biased in favor of men (Eagly & Wood, 1999).

What's more, cross-cultural research finds remarkable similarity in the content of gender stereotypes in different societies. For example, a 25-nation study identified a core set of descriptors that were consistently used to describe men and women (Williams & Best, 1990). Women were seen as sentimental, submissive, and superstitious; men were seen as adventurous, forceful, and independent (see Table 11-1).

Stereotypes about women and men have proved to be remarkably enduring. Even though the number of women in the workforce has expanded dramatically in the last few decades, and the feminist movement's influence has been far-reaching, there has been little change in gender stereotypes regarding women's and men's personal characteristics (Allen, 1995; Fan & Marini, 2000).

Sexism on the Job

There are still substantial differences in which occupations are deemed appropriate for men and for women, and members of each gender tend to expect greater success when they enter a profession viewed as appropriate for their gender. Women still tend to be viewed as best suited for traditionally female jobs: secretaries, nurses, bookkeepers, cashiers, and other female-dominated professions that often feature low pay and low status (Crawford & Unger, 1999).

 **PsychLink**

Discussion about gender
www.mhhe.com/
feldmanup6-11links

gender: The perception of being male or female

gender roles: The set of expectations, defined by a particular society, that indicate what is appropriate behavior for women and men

sexism: Negative attitudes and behavior toward a person based on that person's gender

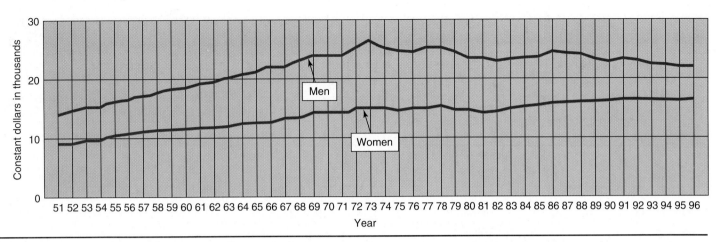

Figure 11-1 The pay gap between men and women has persisted for the past five decades, although the difference has been declining somewhat over the past 20 years. The most recent survey finds that women earn, on average, around three-quarters of what men earn (U.S. Bureau of Labor Statistics, 1999). What are the factors that account for the continuing gap between men's and women's wages?

The extent of gender stereotyping is illustrated by surveys designed to gauge the attitudes of men and women. For example, when women in their first year of college are asked to name a probable career choice, they are much less likely than men to choose careers traditionally dominated by men, such as engineering and computer programming. Women also hold significantly lower expectations than men about their entering salaries and peak salaries. These expectations reflect the reality that women still, on average, earn less than men. Although the gap has been decreasing, women's annual earnings average about three-quarters of men's annual earnings. Furthermore, even when they are in the same professions as men, women generally make less than men in comparable positions (American Council on Education, 1990; Holden, 2000; see Figure 11-1).

Overall, because women tend to enter lower-paying professions than men, women earn an average of 72 cents for every dollar that men earn. And women who are members of minority groups are even worse off: Black women average 62 cents for every dollar men make, and Hispanic women average just 54 cents for every dollar men earn (U.S. Bureau of Labor Statistics, 1999).

Even when women move into upper-level, high-status positions, they can face significant hurdles in their efforts to progress up the corporate ladder, eventually hitting what has come to be called the "glass ceiling." The *glass ceiling* is an invisible barrier within an organization that, because of gender discrimination, can prevent women from being promoted beyond a certain level (Stroh, Brett, & Reilly, 1996; Austin, 2000).

As phenomena such as the glass ceiling make clear, gender stereotypes are typically more positive for men than for women. Although such stereotypes reflect people's perceptions and not necessarily the reality of the world, people often act as if the stereotypes are true, and modify their behavior to match the stereotype. As a result, gender stereotypes limit the behavior of both women and men who conform to them. Furthermore, they ultimately lead to men being treated more favorably than women.

Sexual Harassment

In addition to pay inequity and limited job advancement, women—even those in high-status professions—can face other forms of discrimination from their colleagues. Workplace sexism can result in *sexual harassment:* unwanted sexual attention, the creation of a hostile or abusive environment, or explicit sexual coercion. Sexual harassment is not a minor problem. For instance, one-fifth of women polled say that they have been sexually harassed at work. Some 10 percent of men also report having been sexually harassed on the job (Burgess & Borgida, 1997; Matchen & DeSouza, 2000).

Sexual harassment consists of unwanted sexual attention. How is it possible for men and women to perceive this issue so differently?

Students experiencing each kind of behavior (percent)

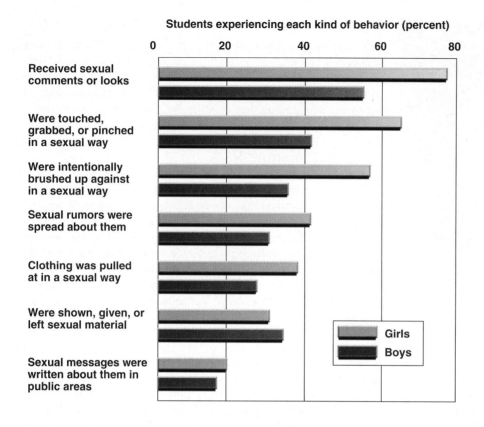

Figure 11-2 Sexual harassment in school. The number of students who report experiencing unwelcomed sexual attention at school is significant (American Association of University Women, 1994).

Sexual harassment is not just a workplace issue. For example, 30 percent of the female graduates of one large California university reported being the recipients of some form of harassment. Such harassment begins earlier in life: In one survey, more than three-quarters of girls in junior and senior high school reported receiving unwelcome sexual comments or looks, and two-thirds said they had without consent been touched, grabbed, or pinched in a sexual way (see Figure 11-2). Although boys also reported being the recipients of similar behavior, it occurred less frequently, and boys perceive the behavior as being considerably less harmful than girls do. For instance, one-third of all girls surveyed react by not wanting to go to school or speak in class. Overall, estimates suggest that one out of every two women will be harassed at some point during her academic or working life (Fitzgerald, 1993; American Association of University Women, 1993).

Sexual harassment often has less to do with sex than with power (which is also the motivation behind many cases of rape, as we will see later in this chapter). In this view, higher-status persons who engage in harassment might be less interested in receiving sexual favors than in demonstrating their power over the victim (Paludi, 1996; O'Donohue, 1997).

In some cases, harassment stems from *benevolent sexism,* attitudes that place women in stereotyped and restrictive roles that appear, on the surface, to be positive. Superficially, benevolent sexism seems to result in consequences that are beneficial to women. For example, a male employer might compliment a woman on her attractiveness, or offer her an easy job so that she won't have to "work so hard." The reality, however, is that such comments can undermine the employee's sense of competence and make her feel that she is not being taken seriously (Glick & Fiske, 1996; Munson, Hulin, & Drasgow, 2000).

Regardless of the motivation behind sexual harassment, the consequences for the victim are clear. Feelings of shame and embarrassment are standard. Because targets of harassment are typically in lower-status positions, such feelings are compounded by a sense of helplessness and powerlessness. People in these situations often suffer emotional and physical consequences, and the quality of their work can decline (Gutek, Cohen, & Tsui, 1996; Jorgenson & Wahl, 2000).

PsychLink

Sexual harassment
www.mhhe.com/
feldmanup6-11links

Research has shown that boys from age 2 tend to be more aggressive than girls, a pattern that continues throughout the life span.

Gender Differences: More Similar Than Different

Not surprisingly, gender stereotyping, combined with other factors, results in actual behavior differences between men and women. Before we consider the nature of gender differences, however, it is important to keep in mind that in most respects, women and men are more similar to one another than they are different. Furthermore, the differences that have been found reflect *average* male and female *group* differences, which tells us nothing about any *individual* female or male (Tavris, 1992; Deaux, 1995).

For example, even if we find that males, on the whole, generally tend to be more talkative than females (as they do, according to research findings), an individual man can be less talkative than most women—just as an individual woman can be more talkative than most men. Generalizations about gender differences should be treated with the same caution as the race differences in IQ we discussed in Chapter 9: when we consider any single person, our focus should remain on the individual rather than on her or his gender group. It is important to take this into account as we examine the findings on gender differences.

Personality Factors

One of the most pronounced differences between men and women is their degree of aggressive behavior. By 2 years of age, boys tend to display more aggression than girls, and this higher level of aggression persists throughout the life span. Furthermore, compared to men, women feel more anxiety and guilt about their aggressiveness and are more concerned about its effects on their victims (Feingold, 1994; Hyde, 1994; Munroe et al., 2000).

Men generally seem to have higher self-esteem than women, although the size of the difference is not great and it is based on different factors. Women's self-esteem is largely influenced by their perception of their sense of interdependence and connection with others. In contrast, men's self-esteem stems from their assessment of their unique characteristics and abilities, traits that help them distinguish themselves from other people (Feingold, 1994; King et al., 1999).

Men and women differ in how positively they view their own abilities and how they estimate the probability of their future success. In general, women evaluate themselves more harshly than men do. One survey of first-year college students compared men's and women's views of whether they were above or below average. As you can see in Figure 11-3, more men than women considered themselves above average in overall academic and mathematical ability, competitiveness, and emotional health (Gabriel, Critelli, & Ee, 1994; Orenstein, 2001).

Women differ from men in their verbal and nonverbal communication styles (McMillan et al., 1977; Feingold, 1994). Women are generally more extraverted and their behavior is typically more nurturing, showing more tenderness and trust than men.

The content of men's and women's speech also differs, with women's speech being more precise. However, women's speech patterns lead others to view them as more tentative and less assertive. They more often raise their pitch at the end of a sentence, and add "tags" at the end of an opinion, rather than stating the opinion outright. For example, instead of saying "It's awfully warm today," a female speaker might say instead "It's awfully warm today, *isn't it?*" thereby appearing less certain of her opinion. When females use such tentative language, they are judged to be less competent and knowledgeable than when they speak assertively (Matlin, 1987; Carli, 1990; Crawford, 1995).

Women's and men's nonverbal behavior also differs in several significant respects. In conversations with people of the opposite sex, women look at their conversation partner significantly more while listening than while speaking, whereas men's levels of looking while speaking and listening are about the same. The effect of the male's pattern is to communicate power and dominance, whereas the woman's pattern is associated with

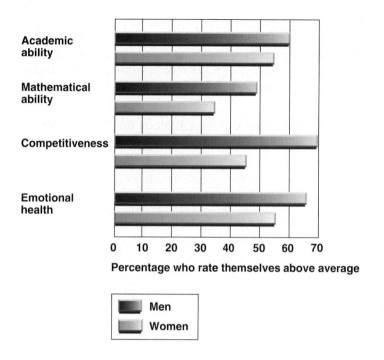

Figure 11-3 Male first-year college students are much more likely than female first-year college students to rate themselves as above average in academic ability, mathematical ability, competitiveness, and emotional health (Dey, Astin, Korn, & Berz, 1990).

lower levels of power. Men are also more likely to touch others; women are more likely to be touched. Women, on the other hand, are better than men at decoding others' facial expressions. In an example of how men's and women's nonverbal behavior is interpreted differently, smiling women are judged to be more competent than nonsmiling women. In contrast, whether a man is smiling makes little difference in how he is judged (Ellyson, Dovidio, & Brown, 1992; Burgoon & Dillman, 1995; Coats & Feldman, 1996).

Cognitive Abilities

No general differences exist between men and women in overall IQ scores, learning, memory, problem solving, and concept-formation tasks. A few differences in more specific cognitive areas have been identified, although the true nature of these differences—and even their existence—has been called into question by more recent research (Halpern, 2000).

In their pioneering study of sex differences, Eleanor Maccoby and Carol Jacklin (1974) concluded that girls outperform boys in verbal abilities, and that boys have superior quantitative and spatial abilities. This conclusion was widely accepted as one of the truisms of the psychological literature.

However, more recent sophisticated analyses have questioned the specific nature and magnitude of these differences. Psychologist Janet Shibley Hyde and colleagues, for instance, examined the mathematical performance of males and females in 100 studies encompassing some 4 million subjects (Hyde, Fennema, & Lamon, 1990). Contrary to traditional wisdom, females slightly outperformed males in math in elementary and middle schools. The finding was reversed in high school, where males scored slightly higher in mathematical problem solving. At all ages, however, the differences were quite small, and they became even smaller when studies of the general adult population were considered. In sum, the differences in mathematical performance between women and men are relatively insignificant, and, if anything, they appear to be declining (Stumpf, 1995; Beller & Gafni, 1996; Benbow, Lubinski, & Hyde, 1997).

Psychologists have drawn a similar conclusion about the extent of gender differences in verbal skills. Despite the earlier view that women show greater verbal abilities than men, a more recent analysis of 165 studies of gender differences in verbal ability, representing the testing of close to 1.5 million subjects, has led to the conclusion that verbal gender differences between men and women are insignificant (Hyde & Linn, 1988; Hedges & Nowell, 1995).

Current evidence suggests, then, that gender differences in cognitive skills are minimal. Meanwhile, particular tests of mathematical and verbal skills do elicit differences in performance, as in the example of the mathematics part of the SAT, where very high scorers are predominantly male. This poses other questions about the nature of cognitive gender differences, which requires additional research (Halpern, 2000).

Sources of Gender Differences: Where Biology and Society Meet

Gender differences
www.mhhe.com/
feldmanup6-11links

If the identification of gender differences has presented a difficult challenge for researchers, the search for their causes has proved to be even more daunting. Given the indisputable fact that sex is a biological variable, it would seem reasonable to look at factors involving biological differences between men and women. It is also true that, from the time they are born, people are treated differently on the basis of their sex. Consequently, we must take into account both biological and social factors when we try to understand the source of gender differences.

Although we'll consider biological and environmental variables separately, neither alone is capable of providing a full explanation for gender differences. Some combination of the two, interacting with each other, will ultimately provide us with an understanding of why women and men might behave differently.

Biological and Evolutionary Factors

Do differences between male and female brains underlie sex and gender differences? This intriguing hypothesis, first discussed in Chapter 3, has been put forward by some psychologists studying brain structure and functioning. For instance, girls who were exposed before birth to unusually high levels of *androgen,* male hormones, because their mothers accidentally took a drug containing the hormone while pregnant, preferred different toys from girls not exposed to androgens. Specifically, they were more likely to play with toys that are stereotypically preferred by boys (such as cars) and less likely to play with toys stereotypically associated with girls (such as dolls). Although you can probably think of several alternative explanations for these results, one possibility is that the exposure to the male hormones affected the development of the girls' brains, making them favor toys that involve certain kinds of skills, such as those relating to spatial abilities (Levine et al., 1999; Mealey, 2000).

Similarly, some evidence suggests that women perform better on tasks involving verbal skill and muscular coordination when their production of the female sex hormone, *estrogen,* is relatively high, compared with when it is low. In contrast, they perform better on tasks involving spatial relationships when their estrogen level is relatively low (Kimura & Hampson, 1988; Kimura, 1999).

Some psychologists take an evolutionary approach to gender differences, arguing that evolutionary forces lead to certain differences between men's and women's behavior. For example, David Buss and colleagues point to differences in the nature of jealousy between men and women. They found that men were more jealous in cases of actual sexual infidelity, as opposed to emotional infidelity in which there was emotional attachment to another man but no actual sexual infidelity. In contrast, women were more jealous in cases of emotional infidelity rather than sexual infidelity (Buss et al., 1992; Buss & Kenrick, 1998).

According to Buss's controversial explanation, the root cause for the differences in jealousy lies in the evolutionary implications of sexual, versus emotional, infidelity for men and women. He argues that for males, sexual infidelity represents a threat to their ability to ensure that their children are actually their own (i.e., have inherited their genes). Knowing that their children are their own allows males to avoid expending scarce resources on others' children, making them more upset over sexual, as opposed to emotional, infidelity.

In contrast, females have no doubt that a child that they carry through pregnancy is their own. However, their major concern is keeping the male involved during child rearing. Thus, to females, maintaining males' emotional attachment is more crucial than ensuring males' sexual fidelity.

Many critics question the assumptions of the evolutionary approach. Rather than assuming the differences are due to evolutionary forces, some psychologists suggest that

differences in males' and females' beliefs about the meaning of infidelity are the actual cause of their jealousy differences. For instance, men might believe that women have sex only when they are in love; they might therefore see sexual infidelity as a sign that a woman is in love with another man, and this could produce more jealousy than emotional infidelity alone. In contrast, women might believe that men are capable of having sex without being in love, and consequently they might find a man's sexual infidelity less bothersome because it does not necessarily mean that he is in love with someone else (DeSteno & Salovey, 1996; Harris & Christenfeld, 1996).

We don't yet know the extent to which biological or evolutionary causes underlie sex differences. However, such factors might explain, at least in part, some of the behavioral differences between men and women (Archer, 1996; Reinisch, 1997; Kimura, 1999).

The Social Environment and Gender Differences

Starting from the moment of birth, with blue blankets for boys and pink ones for girls, most parents and other adults provide environments for children that differ in important respects according to gender. For example, girls and boys are given different kinds of toys, and—until protests brought the practice to an end—items in Toys "R" Us, the largest toy store chain in the United States, were displayed according to gender. Table 11-2 shows how some of their toys were sorted into sections dubbed "Boy's World" and "Girl's World" (Raag & Rackliff, 1998; Bannon, 2000).

How parents interact with their children tends to depend on their sex. Fathers play more roughly with their infant sons than with their daughters. Middle-class mothers tend to talk more to their daughters than to their sons. It is clear that adults frequently treat children differently on the basis of gender (Jacklin & Reynolds, 1993; McHale, Crouter, & Tucker, 1999).

Such differences in behavior (and there are many more) produce different socialization experiences for females and males. *Socialization* is the process by which an individual learns the rules and norms of appropriate behavior. In this case, it refers to learning what society calls appropriate behavior for males and females. According to the processes of social learning theory (discussed in Chapter 6), boys and girls are taught, and rewarded for performing, behaviors that are perceived by society as being appropriate for men or for women, respectively (Philpot, 2000).

It is not just parents, of course, who socialize children. Society as a whole communicates clear messages to children as they are growing up. Children's reading books have traditionally portrayed girls in stereotypically nurturing roles, and boys in more physical and action-oriented roles. Television, too, acts as a particularly influential source of socialization. Despite programs like *E.R.,* which features women in key roles, men

PsychLink

Learning and gender
www.mhhe.com/
feldmanup6-11links

Table 11–2 Gender Labeling of Toys at Toys "R" Us	
Boy's World	**Girl's World**
• Action figures	• Barbie
• Sports collectibles	• Baby dolls
• Radio remote-control cars	• Doll houses
• Tonka trucks	• Collectible horses
• Boy's role play	• Play kitchens
• Walkie-talkies	• Housekeeping toys
	• Girl's dress-up
	• Jewelry
	• Cosmetics
	• Bath and body

Children's reading books have traditionally portrayed girls in stereotypically nurturing roles, while boys have been given more physical and action-oriented roles. Do you think there are cultures in which this is not the case?

gender schema: A mental framework that organizes and guides a child's understanding of information relevant to gender

androgynous: Having psychological and behavioral traits thought typical of both sexes

Androgynous individuals tend to defy stereotypes by combining the psychological and behavioral characteristics thought typical of both sexes.

still outnumber women on television and women are often cast in such stereotypic roles as housewife, secretary, and mother. The potency of television as an agent of socialization is underscored by data indicating that the more television children watch, the more sexist they become (Crabb & Pristash, 1992; Coltraine & Messineo, 2000).

Our educational system also treats girls and boys differently. For example, in elementary school, boys are five times more likely than girls to receive attention from classroom teachers. Boys receive significantly more praise, criticism, and remedial help than girls do. They are also more likely to be praised for the intelligence of their work; girls are more apt to be commended for their neatness. Even in college classes, male students receive more eye contact from their professors than female students, men are called upon more frequently in class, and men are more apt to receive extra help from their professors (Epperson, 1988; American Association of University Women, 1992; Sadker & Sadker, 1994).

According to Sandra Bem (1998), socialization produces a **gender schema,** a mental framework that organizes and guides a child's understanding of information relevant to gender. On the basis of their schemas for appropriate and inappropriate behavior for females and males, children begin to behave in ways that reflect society's gender roles. Hence, a child who goes to summer camp and is offered the opportunity to sew a costume might evaluate the activity not in terms of the intrinsic components of the process (such as the mechanics of using a needle and thread), but in terms of whether the activity is compatible with his or her gender schema (Bem, 1993, 1998).

Bem suggests that one way to decrease the likelihood that children will develop gender schemas is to encourage children to be androgynous. **Androgynous** individuals combine the psychological and behavioral characteristics thought typical of both sexes. Specifically, an androgynous individual might be forceful, assertive, and self-reliant (characteristics typically viewed by society as masculine) under certain circumstances and compassionate, gentle, and soft-spoken (characteristics typically thought of as feminine) when the situation calls for such behavior.

The concept of androgyny does not suggest that there should be no differences between men and women. Far from it: Advocates of androgyny propose that differences should be based on personal choices, freely made, of the best *human* characteristics, and not on an artificially restricted inventory of characteristics deemed by society to be appropriate only for women or only for men.

Evaluate

1. _____ _____ are sets of societal expectations about what is appropriate behavior for men and women.
2. Gender stereotypes seem to be much less prevalent today than they were several decades ago. True or false?
3. Which of the following statements is true about how males and females differ in aggression?
   a. Males are physically more aggressive than females only during childhood.
   b. Sex differences in aggression first become evident during adolescence.
   c. Males are more aggressive than females throughout the life span.
   d. Females and males feel equally anxious about their aggressive acts.
4. _____ _____ are frameworks that organize understanding of gender-specific information.

Answers to Evaluate Questions

1. Gender roles 2. False; they are still prevalent 3. c, 4. Gender schemas

Rethink

1. The U.S. Congress has enacted laws prohibiting women in the armed forces from participating directly in combat, in the interest of keeping them out of harm's way. Do you think such laws are protective or sexist? Is this an example of "benevolent sexism"?
2. If you wished to raise a child in as androgynous a manner as possible, how would you do it? What problems might the child encounter in the everyday world? Do you think this is the best way to raise a child in today's society?

Understanding Human Sexual Response: The Facts of Life

When I started "tuning out," teachers thought I was sick—physically sick that is. They kept sending me to the school nurse to have my temperature taken. If I'd told them I was carrying on with Cindy Crawford in their classes, while supposedly learning my Caesar and my Latin vocabulary, they'd have thought I was—well, delirious. I *was!* I'd even think of Cindy while jogging; I'd have to stop because it'd hurt down there! You can't run and have sex—or can you? (Based on Coles & Stokes, 1985, pp. 18–19)

Prepare

Why, and under what circumstances, do we become sexually aroused?

Organize

Understanding Human Sexual Response
The Basic Biology of Sexual Behavior
Psychological Aspects of Sexual Excitement
The Phases of Sexual Response

Not everyone's sexual fantasies are as consuming as those reported by this teenage boy. Yet sex is an important consideration in most people's lives, for although the physical aspects of human sex are not all that different from those of other species, the meanings, values, and feelings that humans place on sexual behavior elevate it to a special plane. To fully appreciate this difference, however, it will help to understand the basic biology underlying sexual responses.

The Basic Biology of Sexual Behavior

Anyone who has seen two dogs mating knows that sexual behavior has a biological basis. Dogs' sexual behavior appears to occur spontaneously, without much prompting from others. A number of genetically controlled factors influence the sexual behavior of non-human animals. For instance, animal behavior is affected by the presence of certain hormones in the blood, and many female animals are receptive to sexual advances only at certain relatively limited periods of time during the year.

Human sexual behavior, by comparison, is more complicated, although the underlying biology is not all that different from that of related species. In males, for example, the *testes* begin to secrete **androgens,** male sex hormones, at puberty (see Figure 11-4 for the basic anatomy of the male and female **genitals,** or sex organs). Not only do androgens produce male secondary sex characteristics, such as the growth of body hair and a deepening of the voice, they also increase the sex drive. Because the level of androgen production by the testes is fairly constant, males are capable of (and interested in) sexual activities without any regard to biological cycles. Given the proper stimuli leading to arousal, male sexual behavior can occur (Goldstein, 2000).

androgens: Male sex hormones secreted by the testes

genitals: The female and male sex organs

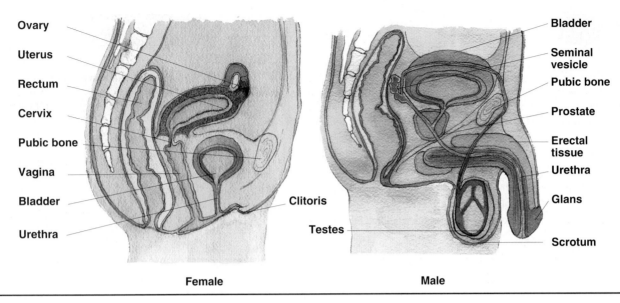

Figure 11-4 Cutaway side views of the female and male sex organs.

estrogen: Female sex hormone
progesterone: Female sex hormone
ovulation: The point at which an egg is released from the ovaries

Females show a different pattern. When they reach maturity at puberty, the two *ovaries* begin to produce **estrogens** and **progesterone,** female sex hormones. However, these hormones are not produced consistently; instead, their production follows a cyclical pattern. The greatest output occurs during **ovulation,** when an egg is released from the ovaries, making the chances of fertilization by a sperm cell highest. In nonhumans, the period around ovulation is the only time the female is receptive to sex, but humans are different: females can be receptive to sex throughout their cycles, depending on the external stimuli they encounter in their environment (Hoon, Bruce, & Kinchloe, 1982).

Though biological factors "prime" people for sex, it takes more than hormones to motivate and produce sexual behavior (McClintock & Herdt, 1996). In animals the presence of a partner who provides arousing stimuli leads to sexual activity. Humans are considerably more versatile; not only other people, but nearly any object, sight, smell, sound, or other stimulus can lead to sexual excitement. Because of prior associations, then, people might be turned on sexually by the smell of Chanel No. 5 or Brut or the sound of a favorite song hummed softly in their ear. The reaction to a specific, potentially arousing stimulus, as we shall see, is highly individual—what turns on one person could do just the opposite for another.

Psychological Aspects of Sexual Excitement: What Turns People On?

If you were to argue that the major human sex organ is the brain, in a sense you would be right. Much of what is considered sexually arousing in our society has little or nothing to do with our genitals, but instead is related to external stimuli that, through a process of learning, have come to be labeled as *erotic,* or sexually stimulating.

erogenous zones: Areas of the body that are particularly sensitive to touch because of the presence of an unusually rich array of nerve receptors

For example, there are no areas of the body that *automatically* produce sexual arousal when touched. Areas of the body, called **erogenous zones,** that have an unusually rich array of nerve receptors are particularly sensitive not just to sexual touch, but to any kind of touch. When a physician touches your breast or penis, the information sent to your brain by your nerve cells is essentially the same as that sent when a lover touches the same spot. What differs is the interpretation you give to the touch. Only when a certain part of the body is touched in what people define as a sexual manner is sexual arousal likely to follow (Gagnon, 1977; Goldstein, 2000).

Although people can learn to respond sexually to almost any stimulus, there is a good deal of agreement within a society or culture about what usually represents an erotic stimulus. In many Western societies, breast size is often the standard by which males measure female appeal, but in many other cultures breast size is irrelevant (Rothblum, 1990).

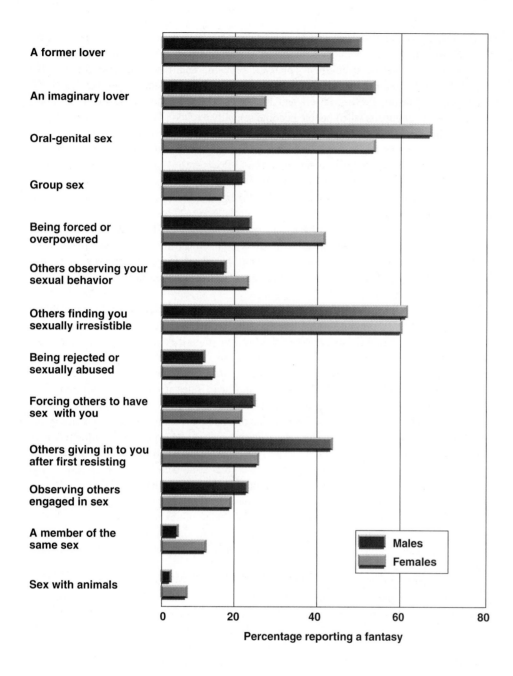

A former lover

An imaginary lover

Oral-genital sex

Group sex

Being forced or overpowered

Others observing your sexual behavior

Others finding you sexually irresistible

Being rejected or sexually abused

Forcing others to have sex with you

Others giving in to you after first resisting

Observing others engaged in sex

A member of the same sex

Sex with animals

■ Males
■ Females

0   20   40   60   80

Percentage reporting a fantasy

Figure 11-5 The kinds of fantasies that men and women have during sexual intercourse are relatively similar (Sue, 1979). Why do you think this is true, and do you think the fantasies are similar in non-Western cultures?

Sexual fantasies also play an important role in producing sexual arousal. Not only do people have fantasies of a sexual nature during their everyday activities, but about 60 percent of all people have fantasies during sexual intercourse. Interestingly, such fantasies often include having sex with someone other than one's partner of the moment.

Men's and women's fantasies differ little from each other in terms of content or quantity (Jones & Barlow, 1990). As you can see in Figure 11-5, thoughts of being sexually irresistible and of engaging in oral-genital sex are most common for both sexes (Sue, 1979; McCauley & Swann, 1980). It is important to note that having a particular fantasy does not mean that one has a desire to fulfill it in the real world. Thus, we should not assume from data of female fantasies that women want to be sexually overpowered, nor should we assume from data of male fantasies that every male desires to force sex on a submissive victim.

The Phases of Sexual Response: The Ups and Downs of Sex

Although the kinds of stimuli that produce sexual arousal are to some degree unique to each of us, we all share some basic aspects of sexual responsiveness. According to pioneering

PsychLink

Sexual fantasies
www.mhhe.com/
feldmanup6-11links

work done by William Masters and Virginia Johnson (1966), who studied sexual behavior in carefully controlled laboratory settings, sexual responses follow a regular pattern consisting of four phases: excitement, plateau, orgasm, and resolution. Although other researchers argue that sexual responses proceed somewhat differently (e.g., Kaplan, 1974; Zilbergeld & Ellison, 1980), Masters and Johnson's research is the most widely accepted account of what happens when people become sexually excited (Masters & Johnson, 1994).

In the **excitement phase,** which can last from just a few minutes to over an hour, an arousing stimulus begins a sequence that prepares the genitals for sexual intercourse. In the male, the *penis* becomes erect when blood flows into it; in the female, the *clitoris* swells with an increase in the blood supply to the area, and the *vagina* becomes lubricated. Women might also experience a "sex flush," a measles-like coloration that typically spreads over the chest and throat.

Next comes the **plateau phase,** the body's preparation for orgasm. During this stage, the maximum level of sexual arousal is attained as the clitoris and penis swell with blood. Women's breasts and vagina expand, heartbeat and blood pressure rises, and breathing rate increases. Muscle tension becomes greater as the body prepares itself for the next stage, orgasm.

Although it is difficult to describe the sensation of **orgasm** beyond saying that it is an intense, highly pleasurable experience, the biological events that accompany the feeling are fairly straightforward. When the orgasm stage is reached, rhythmic muscular contractions occur in the genitals every eight-tenths of a second. In the male, the contractions expel *semen,* a fluid containing sperm, from the penis—a process known as *ejaculation.* For women and men, breathing and heart rates reach their maximum.

Although we can't be sure, the subjective experience of orgasm seems identical for females and males, despite the differences in the organs involved. In one experiment, a group of men and women wrote down their descriptions of how an orgasm felt to them. These descriptions were given to a group of experts, who were asked to identify the sex of each writer. The results showed that the experts were correct at no better than chance levels, suggesting that there is little difference in descriptions of orgasm on the basis of gender (Vance & Wagner, 1976). To get a sense of how people describe orgasms, see Table 11-3.

Following orgasm, people move into the last stage of sexual arousal, the **resolution stage.** The body returns to its normal state, reversing the changes brought about by arousal. The genitals resume their normal size and shape, and blood pressure, breathing, and heart rate return to normal.

Male and female responses differ significantly during the resolution stage; these differences are depicted in Figure 11-6. Women are able to cycle back to the orgasm phase and experience repeated orgasms. Ultimately, of course, females enter the final resolution stage, and they return to their prestimulation state. In contrast, it is generally thought that men enter a refractory period during the resolution stage. During the **refractory period,** men are unable to become aroused and are therefore unable to have another orgasm and ejaculate. The refractory period can last from a few minutes to several hours, although in the elderly it might continue for several days (Goldstein, 2000).

excitement phase: The phase during which an arousing stimulus begins a sequence that prepares the genitals for sexual intercourse

plateau phase: The period in which the maximum level of arousal is attained, the penis and clitoris swell with blood, and the body prepares for orgasm

orgasm: The peak of sexual excitement during which rhythmic muscular contractions occur in the genitals

resolution stage: The interval following orgasm in which the body returns to its normal state, reversing the changes brought about by arousal

refractory period: A temporary period following the resolution stage during which the male cannot be sexually aroused again

EXPLORING DIVERSITY

Female Circumcision: A Celebration of Culture—or Genital Mutilation?

Waris Dirie was just an innocent, unknowing child of 5 when she begged her mother to let her be circumcised like virtually all females in Somalia. "When you've been told over and over that, until this happens, you're filthy and no man would ever marry you, you believe what everybody says," Dirie explains. "I just wanted to be like the other girls."

Months later her awful wish came true. As her mother held down the crying, blindfolded Dirie, a gypsy performed the circumcision using a dirty, dull razor and no anesthetic. She sewed the ragged wound with thorns and thread. "It's not a pain you forget," says Dirie, in a whisper. She was left with only a tiny opening, and urinating became torture. Later, menstruation was so unbearable that Dirie routinely fainted. (Cheakalos & Heyn, 1998, p. 149)

Table 11-3 Orgasm, Male and Female

What does it feel like to have an orgasm? The following ten descriptions were written by men and women in an introductory psychology class. As you read through them, see if you can tell which were written by men and which by women.

1. Your heart pounds more than 100 miles per hour, your body tenses up, you feel an overwhelming sensation of pleasure and joy.

2. An orgasm feels like blood pulsating through my body, rushing essentially to the genital area, a surge of contraction-like waves paired with a rapidly beating heart and strong pulse; my heart feels like someone is squeezing it, painful, and I have trouble breathing deeply.

3. Feels like being plugged into an electrical socket, but pleasurable rather than painful. Nearly indescribable!

4. It's as if every muscle in your body is being charged with intense electricity; your mind is incapable of thinking about anything, and you become totally incoherent. All the nerves in your body tremble, and you have trouble breathing, and get the urge to scream, or yell, or do something wild.

5. An orgasm to me is like the sensations of hot and cold coming together in one throbbing, thrusting, prolonged moment. It is the ultimate excitement of my passion.

6. Like exquisite torture. The sudden release of all the primal urges in the body. The gladness and yet the sadness that the fun is over.

7. An orgasm is that point when you don't care if anyone hears you screaming out your pleasures of ecstasy.

8. It's like all the cells in my brain popping at once and whirling around, while all the muscles in my body heave upward till I reach ultimate sensory bliss.

9. Tingling, throbbing, pleasurable feeling. Breathing is very fast and not rhythmic. Tend to hold my breath at peak. Possible shaking afterward and tightening/contraction of muscles.

10. An orgasm is a heavenly experience. It can be compared to nothing.

If you thought that men and women experience orgasm differently, you may be surprised at how hard it is to tell the difference from these descriptions. The correct answers: 1. Male 2. Female 3. Male 4. Female 5. Female 6. Male 7. Female 8. Male 9. Female 10. Male

a. Male pattern

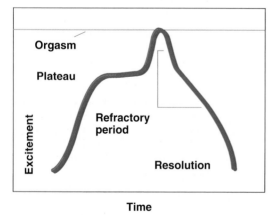

b. Female patterns

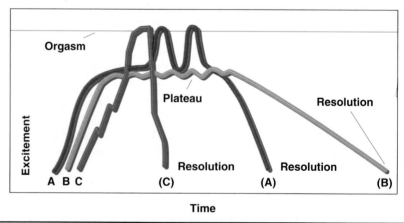

Figure 11-6 A four-stage model of the sexual response cycle for males and females based on the findings of Masters and Johnson (1966). Note how the male pattern *(a)* includes a refractory period. Part *(b)* shows three possible female patterns. In A, the pattern is closest to the male cycle, except that the woman has two orgasms in a row. In B, there is no orgasm, whereas in C orgasm is reached quickly and the woman rapidly returns to an unaroused state (After Masters & Johnson, 1966).

The operation in question—female circumcision—is one of the most controversial sex-related procedures in the world. In such an operation, the clitoris is removed, resulting in a permanent inability to experience sexual pleasure.

Some 80 million women, living mostly in Africa and Asia, have undergone female circumcision. More than 90 percent of Nigerian women have been circumcised during childhood, and more than 90 percent intend to circumcise their daughters. In some cases, the surgery is more extensive; additional parts of the female genitals are removed or are sewn together with catgut or thorns (Ebomoyi, 1987; Rosenthal, 1993; French, 1997).

Those who practice female circumcision say it upholds an ancient societal tradition, no different from other cultural customs. Its purpose, they say, is to preserve virginity before marriage, to keep women faithful to their husbands after marriage, and to enhance a woman's beauty. Proponents believe that it differs little from the common Western practice of male circumcision, in which the foreskin of the penis is surgically removed soon after birth.

Critics, on the other hand, argue that female circumcision is nothing less than female mutilation. Not only does the practice permanently eliminate sexual pleasure, but it can also lead to constant pain and infection, depending on the nature of the surgery. In fact, because the procedure is traditionally conducted in a ritualistic fashion without anesthetic, using a razor blade, saw-tooth knife, or glass, the circumcision itself can be physically traumatic (Dugger, 1996).

The procedure raises some difficult issues, which have been brought to light in various court cases. For instance, a Nigerian immigrant, living temporarily in the United States, went to court to argue that she should be allowed to remain permanently. Her plea: If she and her young daughters were sent back to Nigeria, her daughters would face circumcision upon their return. The court agreed and permitted her to stay indefinitely (Gregory, 1994; Dugger, 1996).

In reaction to the controversy about female circumcision, Congress recently passed laws that make the practice illegal in the United States. Still, some argue that female circumcision is a valued cultural custom, and that no one, particularly someone using the perspective of another culture, should prevent people from carrying out the customs they think are important. In addition, critics point to the practice of *male* circumcision, in which the foreskin of the penis is surgically removed. They suggest that male circumcision provides few significant health benefits, and the decision to have male infants circumcised—an accepted practice in U.S. society—rests on religious, social, and cultural traditions (American Academy of Pediatrics, 1999).

PsychLink

Female circumcision
www.mhhe.com/
feldmanup6-11links

Evaluate

1. Match the phase of sexual arousal with its characteristics.

   1. Excitement phase
   2. Plateau phase
   3. Orgasm phase
   4. Resolution phase

   a. Maximum level of sexual arousal
   b. Erection and lubrication
   c. Rhythmic muscular contractions and ejaculation
   d. Body returns to resting state

2. Men are generally thought to enter a _____ period after sex, in which orgasm is impossible for a period of time.

3. Whereas men are interested in sexual activity regardless of their biological cycles, women are truly receptive to sex only during ovulation, when the production of their sex hormones is greatest. True or false?

4. Men's and women's sexual fantasies are essentially similar to each other. True or false?

Rethink

1. Why do you think humans differ from other species in their year-round receptivity to sex and in the number and variety of sexual stimulants? What evolutionary purpose might this difference serve in humans?

2. How do people learn to be aroused by the stimuli that their society considers erotic? When do they learn this, and where does the message come from?

Answers to Evaluate Questions

1. 1-b; 2-a; 3-c; 4-d 2. refractory 3. False; women are receptive throughout their cycle, depending on the kinds of external stimuli they encounter. 4. True

The Varieties of Sexual Behavior

Prepare

What is "normal" sexual behavior?
How do most people behave sexually?

Organize

The Varieties of Sexual Behavior
   Approaches to Sexual Normality
   Surveying Sexual Behavior
   Masturbation
   Heterosexuality
   Homosexuality and Bisexuality

A boy who practices this habit can never be the best that Nature intended him to be. His wits are not so sharp. His memory is not so good. His power of fixing his attention on whatever he is doing is lessened. . . . A boy like this is a poor thing to look at. . . . [He is] untrustworthy, unreliable, untruthful, and probably even dishonest. (Schofield & Vaughan-Jackson, 1913, pp. 30–42)

The cause of this condition: masturbation—at least according to the authors of the early 1900s sex manual, *What Every Boy Should Know*. The consequences of masturbation for women were considered no less severe. In the words of one nineteenth-century physician, "There is hardly an end to the diseases caused by masturbation: dyspepsia, spinal disease, headache, epilepsy, various kinds of fits . . . impaired eyesight, palpitation of the heart, pain in the side and bleeding at the lungs, spasm of the heart, and sometimes sudden death" (Gregory, 1856).

Such views probably seem bizarre and farfetched to you, as they do to today's experts on human sexual behavior. However, at one time they were considered perfectly sound by people who were otherwise quite reasonable. Indeed, trivia buffs might be interested to learn that cornflakes owe their invention to the belief of one nineteenth-century physician, J. W. Kellogg, that because some foods provoked sexual excitation, an alternative of "unstimulating" grains was needed.

Clearly, sex and sex-related behavior are influenced by expectations, attitudes, beliefs, and the state of medical and biological knowledge of a given period. Today we know that sexual behavior can take a variety of forms and we readily accept what was once seen as "unnatural" and "lewd." Similarly, sexual behavior that is commonplace in one culture is seen as appalling in others. For instance, there are seven societies in which kissing never occurs (Ford & Beach, 1951; Mason, 1994). So it is not easy to distinguish between normal and abnormal sexual behavior, but this certainly hasn't prevented people from trying.

Approaches to Sexual Normality

One approach is to define abnormal sexual behavior in terms of deviation from the average, or typical, behavior. To determine what is abnormal, we simply observe what behaviors are rare and infrequent in a society and label these deviations from the norm as "abnormal."

The difficulty with such an approach, however, is that some behaviors that are statistically unusual hardly seem worthy of concern. Even though most people have sexual intercourse in the bedroom, does the fact that someone prefers sex in the dining room imply abnormality? If some people prefer portly sexual partners, are they abnormal in a society that holds slimness in high esteem? Clearly, the answer to both these questions is no, and so an approach that defines sexual abnormality in terms of deviation from the average is inappropriate. (We'll encounter the same difficulties when we consider definitions of psychological abnormality in Chapter 16.)

An alternative approach would be to compare sexual behavior against some standard or ideal. But here, again, there is a problem: What standard should we use? Some might suggest philosophy, some might turn to the Bible, and some might even consider psychology the ultimate determinant. The trouble is that none of these potential sources of standards is universally acceptable. Furthermore, because standards change radically with shifts in societal attitudes and new knowledge, such an approach is undesirable. For instance, the American Psychiatric Association traditionally listed homosexuality as a mental illness but in 1973 determined that homosexuality was no longer a mental disorder. Obviously the behavior had not changed; the psychiatric profession simply had put a different label on it.

Given the difficulties with other approaches, the most reasonable definition of sexual normality might be one that considers the psychological consequences of the behavior. In this approach, sexual behavior is considered abnormal if it produces a sense of

distress, anxiety, or guilt—or if it is harmful to some other person. According to this view, then, sexual behaviors can be viewed as abnormal only when they have a negative impact on one's own sense of well-being or on others.

It is important to recognize that what is seen as normal and what is seen as abnormal sexual behavior are dictated primarily by societal values, and that there have been dramatic shifts from one generation to another in definitions of appropriate sexual behavior. While people can, and should, make their own personal value judgments about what is appropriate in their own sex lives, there are few universal rights and wrongs.

Surveying Sexual Behavior: What's Happening Behind Closed Doors?

For most of recorded history, the vast variety of sexual practices remained shrouded in ignorance. However, in the late 1930s, biologist Albert Kinsey launched a series of surveys on the sexual behavior of people in the United States. The result was the first comprehensive look at sexual practices, highlighted by the publication of Kinsey's landmark volumes, *Sexual Behavior in the Human Male* (Kinsey, Pomeroy, & Martin, 1948) and *Sexual Behavior in the Human Female* (Kinsey et al., 1953).

Kinsey's efforts represented the first major systematic approach to learning about human sexual behavior. Kinsey and his colleagues interviewed tens of thousands of individuals, and the interview techniques they devised are still regarded as exemplary because of their ability to elicit sensitive information without causing embarrassment.

On the other hand, Kinsey's samples reflected an overrepresentation of college students, young people, well-educated individuals, urban dwellers, and people living in Indiana and the northeast (Kirby, 1977). Furthermore, as with all surveys involving volunteer participants, it is unclear how representative his data are of people who refused to participate in the study. Similarly, because no survey observes behavior directly, it is difficult to assess how accurately people's descriptions of what they do in private match their actual sexual practices.

Kinsey's work set the stage for later surveys, although for political reasons (use of government funding for sex surveys is controversial), surprisingly few comprehensive national surveys have been carried out since Kinsey did his initial work. However, by examining the common results gleaned from different samples of subjects, we now have a reasonably complete picture of contemporary sexual practices—to which we turn next.

Masturbation: Solitary Sex

If you were to listen to physicians fifty years ago, you would have been told that **masturbation**—sexual self-stimulation, often by using the hand to rub the genitals—would lead to a wide variety of physical and mental disorders, ranging from hairy palms to insanity. Had they been correct, however, most of us would be wearing gloves to hide the sight of our hair-covered palms—for masturbation is one of the most frequently practiced sexual activities. Some 94 percent of all males and 63 percent of all females have masturbated at least once, and among college students the frequency ranges from "never" to "several times a day" (Hunt, 1974; Houston, 1981; Michael et al., 1994).

Men and women typically begin to masturbate for the first time at different ages, as you can see in Figure 11-7. Furthermore, men masturbate considerably more often than women, although there are differences in frequency according to age. For instance, male masturbation is most frequent in the early teens and then declines, whereas females both begin and reach a maximum frequency later (Oliver & Hyde, 1993).

Although masturbation is often thought of as an activity to engage in only if no other sexual outlets are available, this is not the reality. Close to three-quarters of married men (age 20 to 40) report masturbating an average of twenty-four times a year, and 68 percent of married women in the same age group masturbate an average of ten times a year (Hunt, 1974; Michael et al., 1994).

Despite the high incidence of masturbation, attitudes toward it still reflect some of the negative views of yesteryear. For instance, one survey found that around 10

PsychLink

History of the Kinsey Institute
www.mhhe.com/
feldmanup6-11links

masturbation: Sexual self-stimulation

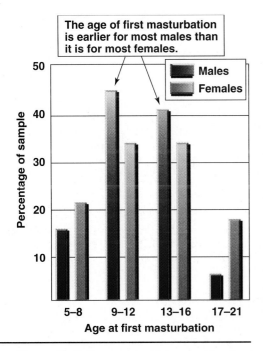

Figure 11-7 The age at which a sample of college students first masturbated. The percentages are based on only those people who had experience with masturbation (Arafat & Cotton, 1974).

percent of the people who masturbated experienced feelings of guilt, and 5 percent of the males and 1 percent of the females considered their behavior perverted (Arafat & Cotton, 1974). Despite these negative attitudes, however, most experts on sex view masturbation not only as a healthy, legitimate—and harmless—sexual activity, but also as a means of learning about one's own sexuality.

Heterosexuality

People often believe that the first time they have sexual intercourse they have achieved one of life's major milestones. However, **heterosexuality**—sexual attraction and behavior directed to the opposite sex—consists of far more than intercourse. Kissing, petting, caressing, massaging, and other forms of sex play are all components of heterosexual behavior. Still, the focus of sex researchers has been on the act of intercourse, particularly in terms of its first occurrence and its frequency.

heterosexuals: People who are sexually attracted to persons of the opposite sex

Premarital Sex

Until fairly recently, premarital sexual intercourse was considered one of the major taboos of our society, at least for women. Traditionally, women have been warned by society that "nice girls don't do it"; men have been told that although premarital sex is OK for them, they should make sure they marry virgins. This view, that premarital sex is permissible for males but not for females, is called the **double standard.**

Although as recently as the 1960s the majority of adult Americans believed that premarital sex was always wrong, since that time there has been a dramatic change in public opinion. For example, as you can see in Figure 11-8, the percentage of middle-aged people who say that sex before marriage is "not wrong at all" has increased considerably over the past thirty years.

Changes in attitudes toward premarital sex were matched by changes in actual rates of premarital sexual activity during the same period. For instance, the most recent figures show that just over one-half of women between the ages of 15 and 19 have had premarital sexual intercourse. These figures are close to double the number of women in the same age range who in 1970 reported having had intercourse. Clearly, the trend over the last several decades has been toward more women engaging in premarital sexual activity (Singh & Carroch, 1999).

double standard: The view that premarital sex is permissible for males but not for females

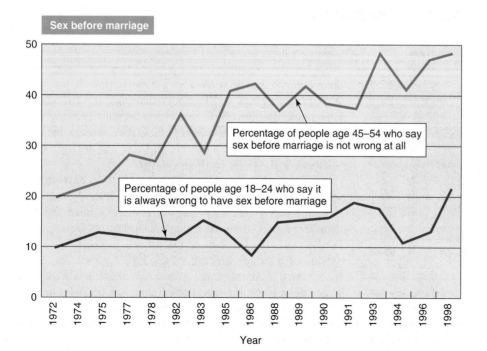

Figure 11-8 The percentage of adults who find that premarital sex is not wrong at all has risen dramatically over the past 25 years, while the percentage of adults who think premarital sex is always wrong has increased only slightly (Gallup Poll News Service, 1998). What changes in society account for this shift in attitudes toward intercourse?

Males, too, are having more premarital sexual intercourse, although the increase has not been as dramatic as for females—probably because the rates for males were higher to begin with. For instance, the first surveys of premarital intercourse carried out in the 1940s showed an incidence of 84 percent across males of all ages; recent figures put the figure at closer to 95 percent. Moreover, the average age of males' first sexual experience has also been declining steadily. Almost half of all males have had sexual intercourse by the age of 18; and 88 percent have had intercourse by the time they reach 20 (Arena, 1984; Centers for Disease Control, 1992; Singh et al., 2000).

What might be most interesting about these patterns is that they show a convergence of male and female attitudes and behavior in regard to premarital sex. But is the change sufficient to signal an end to the double standard?

Probably. For many people, particularly younger individuals, the double standard has been succeeded by a new view: *permissiveness with affection.* According to those holding this view, premarital intercourse is viewed as permissible for both women and men if it occurs within a long-term, committed, or loving relationship (Reiss, 1960; Hyde, 1994; DeGaston, Weed, & Jensen, 1996).

Still, the double standard has not disappeared completely. Where differing standards remain, the attitudes are almost always more lenient toward the male than the female (Peplau, Rubin & Hill, 1977; Sullivan, 1985; Sprecher & Hatfield, 1996). Furthermore, cultures differ substantially in the incidence and acceptability of premarital intercourse. For instance, in Jamaica, the United States, and Brazil, the percentage of males who have had intercourse before age 17 is about 10 times the percentage reported in the Philippines. Furthermore, in some cultures, such as in sub-Saharan Africa, women become sexually active at an earlier age than men—although this could be due to the fact that they marry at a younger age than men (Singh et al., 2000).

extramarital sex: Sexual activity between a married person and someone who is not his or her spouse

Marital Sex

To judge by the number of articles about sex in marriage, one would think that sexual behavior is the number one standard by which marital bliss is measured. Married couples are often concerned that they are having too little sex, too much sex, or the wrong kind of sex (Sprecher & McKinney, 1993).

There are many different dimensions against which sex in marriage is measured, but one is certainly the frequency of sexual intercourse. What is typical? As with most other types of sexual activity, there is no easy answer because there are such wide variations in patterns between individuals. We do know that 43 percent of married couples have sexual intercourse a few times a month, and 36 percent have it two or three times a week. With increasing age and length of marriage, the frequency of intercourse declines. Still, sex continues into late adulthood, with almost half of people reporting they engage in sexual activity at least once a month and that its quality is high (Michael et al., 1994; see Figure 11-9).

Although early research suggested that **extramarital sex** is widespread, apparently this is not true. According to more recent surveys, 85 percent of married women and more than 75 percent of married men are faithful to their spouses. Furthermore, the median number of sex partners, inside and outside of marriage, since the age of 18 for men was 6, and for women 2. Accompanying these numbers is a high, consistent degree of disapproval of extramarital sex, with nine out of ten people saying that it is "always" or "almost always" wrong (Michael et al., 1994; Westera & Bennett, 1994; Calmes, 1998).

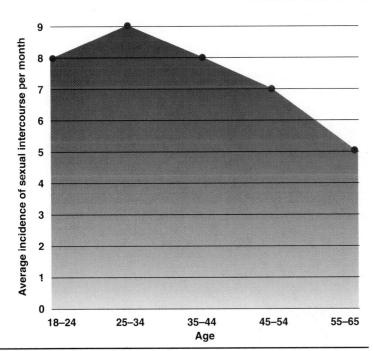

Figure 11-9 Once a couple is past their mid thirties, the average number of times per month they have sexual intercourse declines (Clements, 1994). Why do older couples have intercourse less frequently than younger ones?

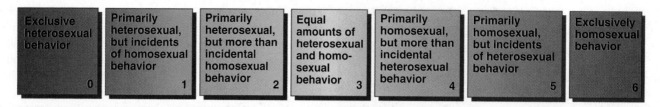

Exclusive heterosexual behavior	Primarily heterosexual, but incidents of homosexual behavior	Primarily heterosexual, but more than incidental homosexual behavior	Equal amounts of heterosexual and homosexual behavior	Primarily homosexual, but more than incidental heterosexual behavior	Primarily homosexual, but incidents of heterosexual behavior	Exclusively homosexual behavior
0	1	2	3	4	5	6

Figure 11-10 The Kinsey scale is designed to define the degree to which sexual orientation is heterosexual, homosexual, or bisexual. Although Kinsey saw people as falling along a continuum, most people believed that they belonged to a specific category.
Source: After Kinsey, Pomeroy, & Martin, 1948.

Homosexuality and Bisexuality

Homosexuals are sexually attracted to people of their own sex; **bisexuals** are sexually attracted to people of the same sex *and* people of the opposite sex. (Many male homosexuals prefer the term *gay* and female homosexuals the label *lesbian*, because they refer to a broader array of attitudes and lifestyle than the term *homosexual*, which focuses on the sexual act.)

The number of people who choose same-sex sexual partners at one time or another is considerable. Estimates suggest that around 20 to 25 percent of males and about 15 percent of females have had at least one homosexual experience during adulthood. The exact number of people who identify themselves as exclusively homosexual has proven difficult to gauge, with some estimates as low as 1.1 percent and some as high as 10 percent. Most experts suggest that between 5 and 10 percent of both men and women are exclusively homosexual during extended periods of their lives (Hunt, 1974; Sells, 1994; Firestein, 1996).

Although many people view homosexuality and heterosexuality as completely distinct sexual orientations, the issue is not that simple. Pioneering sex researcher Alfred Kinsey acknowledged this when he considered sexual orientation in terms of a scale or continuum, with "exclusively homosexual" at one end and "exclusively heterosexual" at the other. In the middle were people who showed both homosexual and heterosexual behavior (see Figure 11-10). Kinsey's approach suggests that sexual orientation is dependent on a person's sexual feelings and behaviors and romantic feelings (Weinberg, Williams, & Pryor, 1991).

What determines people's sexual orientation? Although there are a number of theories, none has proved completely satisfactory. Biological explanations for sexual orientation suggest that there may be genetic or hormonal causes. Evidence for a genetic origin of sexual orientation comes from studies of identical twins, which have found that when one twin identified himself or herself as a homosexual, the occurrence of homosexuality in the other twin was higher than in the general population. This was the case even for twins who were separated early in life and therefore were not necessarily raised in similar social environments (Hamer et al., 1993; Turner, 1995; Bailey et al., 1997).

Furthermore, there is some evidence that differences in brain structures might be related to sexual orientation. For instance, the anterior hypothalamus, an area of the brain that governs sexual behavior, has a different structure in male homosexuals than in male heterosexuals. Similarly, other research shows that, compared with heterosexual men or women, homosexual men have a larger anterior commissure, which is a bundle of neurons connecting the right and left hemispheres of the brain (LeVay, 1991, 1993; Harrison, Everall, & Catalan, 1994; Byne, 1996).

However, research into biological causes for sexual orientation is not conclusive, given that most findings are based on only small samples of individuals. Still, the possibility is real that inherited or biological factors predispose people to their sexual orientations, if certain environmental conditions are met (Bailey & Pillard, 1994; Gladue, 1995; Looy, 1995; Bailey, 1995; Rice et al., 1999).

Other theories of sexual orientation have focused on childhood and family background. Freud believed that homosexuality occurred as a result of inappropriate

homosexuals: Persons who are sexually attracted to people of their own sex
bisexuals: Persons who are sexually attracted to people of the same sex *and* people of the opposite sex

 **PsychLink**

Sexual orientation information
www.mhhe.com/
feldmanup6-11links

Extensive research has found that bisexuals and homosexuals enjoy the same overall degree of mental and physical health as heterosexuals.

identification with the opposite-sex parent during development. He and other psychoanalysts have suggested that the nature of the parent–child relationship can lead to homosexuality, and that male homosexuals frequently have overprotective, dominant mothers and passive, ineffective fathers (Freud, 1922/1959; Bieber et al., 1962; Bailey & Zucker, 1995).

The problem with such theories is that there are probably as many homosexuals who were not subjected to the influence of such family dynamics as there are homosexuals who were. The evidence does not support explanations that rely on child-rearing practices or on the nature of the family structure (Bell & Weinberg, 1978; Isay, 1990).

Another explanation for sexual orientation rests on learning theory (Masters & Johnson, 1979). According to this view, sexual orientation is learned through rewards and punishments in much the same way that we might learn to prefer swimming over tennis. For example, a young adolescent who has an unpleasant heterosexual experience might learn to link unpleasant associations with the opposite sex. If that same person has a rewarding, pleasant homosexual experience, homosexuality might be incorporated into his or her sexual fantasies. If such fantasies are then used during later sexual activities—such as masturbation—they could be positively reinforced through orgasm, and the association of homosexual behavior and sexual pleasure might eventually cause homosexuality to become the preferred form of sexual behavior.

Although the learning theory explanation is plausible, several difficulties rule it out as a definitive explanation. Because our society tends to hold homosexuality in low esteem, one ought to expect that the punishments involved in homosexual behavior would outweigh the rewards attached to it. Furthermore, children growing up with a homosexual parent are statistically unlikely to become homosexual, thus contradicting the notion that homosexual behavior might be learned from others (Victor & Fish, 1995; Golombok, 1995; Golombok & Tasker, 1996).

Given the difficulty in finding a consistent explanation, the majority of researchers reject the notion that any single factor produces sexual orientation. Most experts suspect that a combination of biological and environmental factors is at work (McWhirter, Sanders, & Reinisch, 1990; Greene & Herek, 1994; Bem, 1996).

Although we don't know at this point exactly why people develop a particular sexual orientation, one thing is clear: There is no relationship between sexual orientation and psychological adjustment. Bisexuals and homosexuals enjoy the same overall degree of mental and physical health as heterosexuals do. They hold equivalent ranges and types of attitudes about themselves, independent of sexual orientation. For such reasons, the American Psychological Association and most other mental health organizations have endorsed efforts to reduce discrimination against gays and lesbians, such as efforts to revoke the ban against homosexuals in the military (Herek, 1993; Shawver, 1995; Perez, 2000).

Evaluate

1. The work carried out by _____ in the 1930s was the first systematic study of sexual behavior ever undertaken.
2. Although the incidence of masturbation among young adults is high, once men and women become involved in intimate relationships, they typically cease masturbating. True or false?
3. The increase in premarital sex in recent years has been greater for women than for men. True or false?

Rethink

1. In what ways might a sample of respondents to a survey about sexual practices be biased? How might bias in such a survey be reduced?

4. _____ _____ _____ refers to the view that premarital sex is acceptable within a loving, long-term relationship.

5. Research comparing homosexuals and heterosexuals clearly demonstrates that there is no difference in the level of adjustment or psychological functioning between the two groups. True or false?

2. What societal factors have led to a reduction in the double standard by which sexuality in men and women is regarded differently? Do you think the double standard has completely vanished?

Answers to Evaluate Questions

1. Kinsey 2. False; even people in married relationships show a continued incidence of masturbation. 3. True 4. Permissiveness with affection 5. True

Sexual Difficulties: When Sex Goes Wrong

When sex—an activity that should be pleasurable, joyful, and intimate—is forced on someone, it becomes one of the ultimate acts of aggression and brutality that people are capable of inflicting on one another, and few crimes produce such profound and long-lasting consequences. Similarly, few personal difficulties produce as much anxiety, embarrassment, and even shame as those resulting from sexually transmitted diseases or sexual dysfunctions. We now turn to the major types of problems related to sex.

Rape

Rape occurs when one person forces another to submit to sexual activity such as intercourse or oral-genital sex. Although it usually applies to a male forcing a female, rapes can be said to occur when persons of either sex are forced into sexual activities against their will.

Most people think of rape as a rare crime committed by strangers. Unfortunately, they are wrong on both counts. Rape occurs far more frequently than is commonly thought, and rapists are typically acquaintances of their victims. For instance, a national survey conducted at 35 universities revealed the startling finding that one out of eight women reported having been raped. Of the women who had been raped, about half said the rapists were first dates, casual dates, or romantic acquaintances—a phenomenon called **date rape** (Kilpatrick, Edmunds, & Seymour, 1992; Koss, 1993; Wiehe & Richards, 1995).

Statistically, then, a woman is far more likely to be raped on a date than by a stranger. But whether on a date or alone, a woman's chances of being raped are shockingly high. Although it is hard to obtain reliable estimates, most research suggests that there is a 14 to 25 percent chance that a woman will be the victim of a rape during her lifetime, and there are more than half a million sexual assaults against women each year in the United States (U.S. Bureau of Justice Statistics, 1995).

Women in some segments of society are more at risk for rape than others. Although the likelihood of sexual assault is considerably lower among Latino women in comparison to non-Latino white women, the rate for Black women is slightly higher in comparison to white women. Such racial differences might stem from differing cultural views of women and sexual conduct (Sorenson & Siegel, 1992; Wyatt, 1992; Koss, 1993).

Although on the surface it might appear that rape is primarily a crime of sex, other types of motivation also underlie the behavior. Often the rapist uses sex as a way to demonstrate power and control over the victim. In such cases, there is little that is sexually satisfying about rape to the rapist; instead, the pleasure comes in forcing someone else to be submissive (Hall & Barongan, 1997; Zurbriggen, 2000).

In other cases of rape, the primary motivation is anger. The male rapist uses sexual assault to express his rage at women in general, usually because of some rejection or hurt he believes he suffered in the past. Such rapes are likely to include physical violence and degrading acts against the victim.

Prepare

How prevalent are rape and other forms of nonconsenting sex, and what are their causes?

What are the major sexually transmitted diseases?

What sexual difficulties do people most frequently encounter?

Organize

Sexual Difficulties

Rape

Childhood Sexual Abuse

Sexually Transmitted Diseases (STDs)

Sexual Problems

rape: An act of forcing another person to submit to sexual activity

date rape: Rape in which the rapist is either a date or romantic acquaintance

Psychology at Work

Pat Unger

Crisis Center Counselor

Education: B.A. University of Wisconsin; M.A., Federal City College, Washington, D.C.

Home: Rockville, Maryland, area

Pat Unger

The phone rings at the Sexual Assault Service in Rockville, Maryland. A woman who was raped a few hours earlier haltingly asks for help. It is the job of the person who answers the call to calm the woman, provide immediate guidance on where she can receive help, and start her on the path to recovery—a path that could take months or even years to travel.

Providing such help is a routine part of Pat Unger's job. Unger is clinical supervisor at the Montgomery County Sexual Assault Service in Rockville, Maryland, which provides crisis intervention for victims of sexual assault.

Unger started her journey toward her current position when she obtained a master's degree in counseling psychology. She then took a position in a state prison system, where she worked with prisoners who appeared suicidal, helping them obtain appropriate psychological services. Her experiences there led to her current job.

The work is very demanding, according to Unger. "In providing crisis intervention and ongoing counseling, you're using every theory you've ever learned. You could be working with a woman who has marital problems at home, but then is raped in the parking lot of a supermarket. You end up dealing with a number of problems. You have to look at each individual's situation."

> "There is a lot going on with the crime of rape. You have to take into account the personality variables as well as internal and external dynamics of the survivor and the survivor's surroundings."

The general approach followed in sexual assault cases is first to stabilize the situation. "We will try to get the family to come in and work with the survivor. There is a lot going on with the crime of rape. You have to take into account the personality variables as well as internal and external dynamics of the survivor and the survivor's surroundings," she says.

"We follow up with a plan and enlist the support of the family. At the same time you are working with the victim, you are trying to stabilize her support system," she explains.

"We present ourselves, approach victims, and reach out to them. We call them to see how they are doing, but we don't push them if they don't want to come in. We realize the denial process. We just try to keep the door open."

Unger notes the complexity of a sexual assault and stresses the importance of understanding that there is much more involved than victimization. "These are issues that deserve the attention of a professional because they are so complicated," she says. "You're really pulling on everything you've ever learned from all of the chapters of all the books you've studied."

> "These are issues that deserve the attention of a professional because they are so complicated."

Some rapes *are* based on a desire for sexual gratification. Some men hold the attitude that it is appropriate and desirable for them to actively seek out sex, and that sexual encounters are a form of "war" between the sexes—with winners and losers. These males believe that violence is sometimes an appropriate way to obtain what they want. According to their reasoning, using force to obtain sexual gratification is permissible (Malamuth et al., 1995; Hall, 1996).

Finally, there is a common, although unfounded, societal belief that many women offer token resistance to sex, saying no to sex when they mean yes. A man who holds such a view might inappropriately ignore a woman's protestations that she doesn't want sex (Muehlenhard & Hollabaugh, 1988; Anderson, Cooper, & Okamura, 1997).

The repercussions of rape are devastating for victims. During the rape, the victim experiences fear, terror, and physical pain. Later, victims report shock, disbelief, fear, extreme anxiety, and suspiciousness, and the psychological reactions are no different whether it is date rape or rape by a stranger (Koss & Burkhart, 1989; Golding, 1999). These feelings might sometimes continue for years, even though the victim outwardly appears to have recovered. However, immediate psychological intervention, such as that provided by rape crisis centers, can help diminish the long-term reactions to rape. (To read about a crisis center counselor, see the *Psychology at Work* box.)

Childhood Sexual Abuse

One form of sexual behavior that is surprisingly common, yet little understood, is sexual abuse of children. Although reported cases are low in number and firm data are hard to come by, the frequency of child sexual abuse—instances in which an older person engages in sexual activity with a child—is thought to be relatively high. The reason for the discrepancy between reported and actual cases is that only the most extreme cases are apt to be reported to authorities.

Child abuse is a secret crime in which participants are often motivated, albeit for different reasons, to keep their activities from being discovered. More than 100,000 U.S. children are the victims of childhood sexual abuse each year (NCCAN, 2000).

Who commits child sexual abuse? Usually a relative or an acquaintance; strangers commit only about one-quarter of reported cases of child sexual abuse. The most vulnerable age for being molested is around 10 years old, and abusers tend to be about 20 years older than their victims. Most abusers are male heterosexuals (Finkelhor, 1984; Wolfe, 1999).

The short- and longer-term consequences of childhood sexual abuse are harmful. In terms of initial effects, victims report fear, anxiety, depression, anger, and hostility. Long-term effects can include depression, self-destructive behavior, feelings of isolation, poor self-esteem, substance abuse, and sexual maladjustment. The consequences of childhood sexual abuse are related to the specific nature of the abuse; experiences involving fathers, genital contact, and the use of force are the most damaging (Wolfe, 1999; Berkowitz, 2000; Hawke, Jainchill, & De Leon, 2000).

PsychLink

Child sexual abuse information
www.mhhe.com/
feldmanup6-11links

Sexually Transmitted Diseases (STDs)

Millions of people suffer the discomfort—not to mention the psychological distress—of a **sexually transmitted disease (STD),** a medical condition acquired through sexual contact. It has been estimated that one out of five people in the United States is infected with some form of STD, and at least one out of four will probably contract some STD during their lifetime. The United States has the highest rate of sexually transmitted diseases of all the economically developed countries in the world (Ubell, 1996; Leary, 1996; see Figure 11-11).

The most widespread STD is *chlamydia,* a disease that initially produces no symptoms in women. In men, chlamydia causes a burning sensation during urination and a discharge from the penis. If left untreated, it can lead to pelvic inflammation and even sterility. Chlamydia affects some 4 million women and men each year, but it can be cured with a new antibiotic, azithromycin.

sexually transmitted disease (STD): A disease acquired through sexual contact

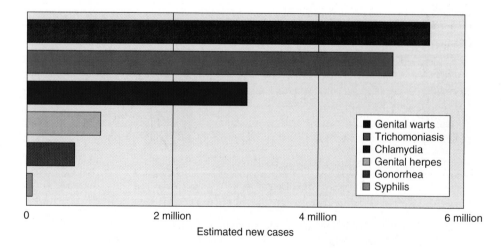

Figure 11-11 Estimates of the numbers of new cases annually of sexually transmitted diseases in the United States. (Source: Kaiser Family Foundation, 1998).

Genital herpes is a virus related to the cold sores that sometimes appear around the mouth. Herpes first appears as small blisters or sores around the genitals, which later break open, causing severe pain. These sores heal after a few weeks, but the disease can and often does reappear, and the cycle repeats itself. There is no cure for genital herpes, and during the active phases of the disease it can be transmitted to sexual partners.

Trichomoniasis is an infection occurring in the vagina or penis. Caused by a parasite, it is often without symptoms, especially in men. Eventually, it can cause painful urination and intercourse, a discharge from the vagina, and an unpleasant odor. The 5 million cases reported each year can be treated with antibiotics.

Gonorrhea and *syphilis* are the two STDs that have been recognized the longest by scientists. Gonorrhea can lead to fertility problems and infection. Syphilis, if untreated, can affect the brain, heart, and a developing fetus, and can even be fatal. Syphilis reveals itself first through a small sore at the point of sexual contact. In its secondary stage, it can include a rash. Both gonorrhea and syphilis can be treated successfully with antibiotics if diagnosed early enough.

Another common STD is *genital warts* (caused by *human papilloma virus*). Genital warts are small, lumpy warts that form on or near the penis or vagina. The warts are easily diagnosed because of their distinctive appearance: they look like small cauliflower bulbs. They usually form about two months after exposure and can be treated with a drug called metronidazole.

In the last two decades, no sexually transmitted disease has had a greater impact on sexual behavior—and society as a whole—than **acquired immune deficiency syndrome (AIDS)**. Although in the United States AIDS at first was found primarily in homosexuals, it has spread to other populations, such as intravenous drug users. In some parts of the world, such as Africa, it mainly affects heterosexuals. In the United States, AIDS is the leading cause of death among men 25 to 44 years of age, and the third leading cause of death among women in that age range. The worldwide figures are even more daunting: Already, 16 million people have died from AIDS, and worldwide there are 34 million people living with the disease (see Figure 11-12).

The extent of the AIDS epidemic has led to significant changes in sexual behavior. Most people are less likely to engage in "casual" sex with new acquaintances, and the use of condoms during sexual intercourse has increased. Nonetheless, the only foolproof

⦾⦾ PsychLink

AIDS virtual library
www.mhhe.com/
feldmanup6-11links

acquired immune deficiency syndrome (AIDS): A fatal, sexually transmitted disease caused by a virus that destroys the body's immune system

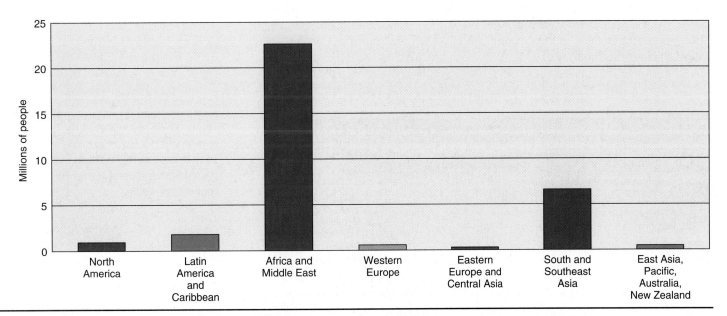

Figure 11-12 The number of people carrying the AIDS virus varies substantially by geographic region. By far the most cases are found in Africa and the Middle East, although the disease is a growing problem in Asia. (Source: United Nations AIDS Program, 1998.)

way to avoid AIDS is celibacy—an option that many people find unrealistic. However, there are several ways to reduce the risk of contracting AIDS (as well as other sexually transmitted diseases); these have come to be called "safer sex" practices (National Institute of Mental Health, 1998; Coates & Collins, 1998).

- *Know your sexual partner—well.* Before entering into a sexual relationship with someone, learn about his or her sexual history.
- *Use condoms.* Condoms are the most reliable way to prevent transmission of the AIDS virus during sex.
- *Do not exchange bodily fluids, particularly semen.* In particular, avoid anal intercourse; the AIDS virus can spread through small tears in the rectum, making anal intercourse without condoms particularly dangerous. Oral sex, once thought relatively safe, is now viewed as potentially dangerous.
- *Practice monogamy.* People in long-term, monogamous relationships with partners who have been faithful are at a lower risk of contracting AIDS.

Sexual Problems

Few of us would feel embarrassed by a case of appendicitis or a broken leg. In contrast, sexual difficulties are often a source of concern and self-consciousness, given the importance that society places on "appropriate" sexual conduct. And such difficulties are surprisingly common: 43 percent of women and 31 percent of men experience problems associated with sexual performance. The following are some of the most widespread disorders (Laumann, Paik, & Rosen, 1999; Goldstein, 2000).

- **Erectile dysfunction** is the inability of a male to achieve or maintain an erection. In rare cases, the male has never been able to have an erection. But in the more common case, the male, though now unable to have an erection, has had at least one in the past. Erectile dysfunction is not an uncommon problem, and it is the rare man who has never experienced it at least once during his lifetime. This is hardly surprising, because the ability to achieve and hold an erection is sensitive to alcohol, drugs, performance fears, anxiety, and a host of other factors. It becomes a more serious problem when it occurs more than occasionally. (To see how drugs such as Viagra have brought about significant advances in the treatment of erectile dysfunction, read the *Applying Psychology in the 21st Century* box on page 347.)

  erectile dysfunction: The inability of a male to achieve or maintain an erection

- In **premature ejaculation,** a male is unable to delay orgasm as long as he wishes. Because "as long as he wishes" is dependent on the man's—and his partner's—attitudes and opinions about how long is appropriate, this is a difficult disorder to diagnose, and sometimes the problem can be resolved simply by having the male redefine how long he wants to delay ejaculation. The reasons for premature ejaculation are most often psychological, rarely physical. One cause could be early sexual learning: Because sexual experiences during adolescence are often accompanied by a fear of being caught, some men learn early in their lives to reach orgasm as quickly as possible.

  premature ejaculation: The inability of a male to delay orgasm as long as he wishes to

- **Inhibited ejaculation** is the opposite problem. In this case, the male is unable to ejaculate when he wants to, if at all. Sometimes men can overcome this difficulty simply by learning general relaxation techniques.

  inhibited ejaculation: The inability of a male to ejaculate when he wants to, if at all

- Some women experience **anorgasmia,** or a lack of orgasm. In *primary orgasmic dysfunction,* the woman has never experienced orgasm; in *secondary orgasmic dysfunction,* the woman is capable of experiencing orgasm only under certain conditions—such as during masturbation but not during sexual intercourse. Because the inability to have an orgasm during sexual intercourse is so common, with some one-third of all women reporting they do not receive sufficient stimulation to reach orgasm during sexual intercourse, some sex researchers suggest that secondary orgasmic dysfunction is not dysfunctional at all, but merely a normal variation of female sexuality.

  anorgasmia (an or GAZ mee uh): A female's lack of orgasm

inhibited sexual desire: A sexual
dysfunction in which the motivation
for sexual activity is restrained or lacking
entirely

- Finally, **inhibited sexual desire** occurs when the motivation for sexual activity is restrained or lacking entirely. When people with inhibited sexual desire find themselves in circumstances that typically would evoke sexual feelings, they begin to turn off sexually and might even experience a kind of "sexual anesthesia." Ultimately they might begin to avoid situations of a sexual nature, thereby forgoing intimacy with others (LoPiccolo, 1980).

Just about everyone experiences one of these problems, at one time or another, during sexual encounters. They're only a cause for concern when they persist, cause undue anxiety, or turn sex into work. Furthermore, treatments for common sexual problems have good success rates (McConaghy, 1993; Masters & Johnson, 1994).

BECOMING AN INFORMED CONSUMER OF PSYCHOLOGY

Lowering the Risks of Date Rape

PsychLink

Date rape information
www.mhhe.com/
feldmanup6-11links

It was a warm Friday evening in autumn, the kind of night that makes a college campus seem a magical place, full of excitement and promise. Exhilarated by her new independence, Casey Letvin, like hundreds of other recently arrived University of Colorado freshmen, was looking for a party. The students milling about the streets of Boulder seemed convivial, and Casey and her roommate thought nothing of stopping four upperclassmen to ask where the parties were. . . . The four young men offered to take them to a nearby off-campus house where about twenty students were gathered. But approximately four hours later, the evening ended in a brutal breach of trust. At 12:30 A.M., Casey Letvin was taken back to her dormitory and raped on her own narrow bed by a man she might never have spoken to had he not been a fellow student. (Freeman, 1990, p. 94)

What happened to Casey Letvin unfortunately is not rare. As we discussed earlier, surveys of college women make clear that a student's greatest danger of rape comes not from an unknown assailant but from a fellow student.

There are ways, however, to reduce the likelihood of date rape. The following suggestions provide some guidance for women and men (American College Health Association, 1989; Jackson, 1996; Shultz, Scherman, & Marshall, 2000):

- Women should clearly believe in their rights to set limits and to communicate those limits clearly, firmly, and early on. They should say no when they mean no.
- Women should be assertive when someone is pressuring them to engage in an activity in which they don't want to engage. They should keep in mind that men might interpret passivity as permission.
- Women should be aware of situations in which they are at risk.
- Women should keep in mind that some men interpret certain kinds of dress as sexually provocative, and that not all men subscribe to the same standards of sex as they do.
- Women should keep close tabs on what they are drinking in social situations; victims of date rape have sometimes been given mind-altering drugs.
- Men should be aware of their dates' views on sexual behavior.
- Men should not hold the view that the goal of dating is to "score."
- The word *no* should be understood to mean no and not be interpreted as an invitation to continue. Men should know that a woman who says no is not rejecting them, but is rejecting a specific act at a specific time.
- Men should not assume that certain kinds of dress or flirtatious behavior are an invitation to sex.
- Both men and women should understand that alcohol and drugs cloud judgment and hinder communication between them.

Applying Psychology in the 21st Century

Bringing Sexual Dysfunction into the Open: The Newest Sexual Revolution

Bob Dole [was] on "The Larry King Show" to discuss his prostate-cancer operation. During a commercial break, so the story goes, King leaned over to ask his old friend, confidentially, how he was dealing with the operation's grimmest side effect, impotence. Dole cheerfully informed the talk-show host that there was a new drug, Viagra, and miraculously, it had cured the problem. King asked Dole if he would discuss it on the air, and Dole said sure, why not?

The world was about to become a very different place. (Hitt, 2000, p. 43)

It was not too long ago that talk of sexual dysfunction was rare even among close friends, let alone on network television. That time has passed as discussions of Viagra have become commonplace, and the drug itself can be ordered almost as easily as aspirin over the World Wide Web. Almost 200,000 prescriptions are filled each week, and 17 million men in the United States have used the drug.

Viagra treats erectile dysfunction by increasing the flow of blood through a man's penis, producing an erection relatively quickly. It is also being used experimentally to treat women's sexual dysfunc-

tion, increasing blood flow to parts of the genitals and improving the chances of reaching orgasm.

Critics of Viagra suggest that the drug might become the Prozac of sex: prescribed indiscriminately and without sufficient consideration for the underlying condition that produced the sexual problem in the first place. In this view, although Viagra might successfully treat the symptoms of erectile dysfunction, it does not address underlying psychological difficulties that might have produced the dysfunction in the first place.

The controversy over Viagra has not stopped pharmaceutical companies from working on the next generation of drugs. They include such possibilities as these:

- *Testosterone patches.* These patches deliver the male hormone testosterone in slow doses, potentially helping men who have inhibited sexual desire.
- *Prostaglandin E-1 cream.* This cream is meant to treat arousal and orgasm dysfunction in women by stimulating blood flow to the genital area.
- *Clitoral blood flow device.* This tiny device nestles, like a thimble, over a woman's clitoris and stimulates blood flow. This produces greater sensitivity and lubrication,

making it easier to have an orgasm (Hitt, 2000).

These products offer the potential of improved treatments for people with sexual dysfunction. All of them, though, address only the biological aspects of sexual behavior. The ultimate effectiveness of treatments for sexual dysfunction that do not take into account psychological issues such as relationship and intimacy considerations remains an open question (Leland, 2000; Weeks & Gambescia, 2000).

Should sex-enhancing drugs such as Viagra be routinely prescribed—or even sold over the counter without a prescription? Why or why not? Is the restricted availability of such drugs an example of medical caution, or is it mainly "puritanical" disapproval of sexuality?

Evaluate

1. A college woman is more likely to be raped by an acquaintance than by a stranger. True or false?
2. Which of the following is unlikely to be a motivation for the act of rape?
   a. Need for power
   c. Desire for sexual gratification
   b. Desire for sexual intimacy
   d. Anger against women in general
3. Which of the following STDs is the most widespread?
   a. Genital herpes
   c. Chlamydia
   b. Gonorrhea
   d. Syphilis
4. Which of the following is not true about changes in sexual behavior as a result of the AIDS epidemic?
   a. The use of condoms has increased.
   b. People are less likely to engage in casual sex.
   c. Many people have found celibacy to be a realistic option.
   d. The risk of contracting AIDS can be reduced by engaging in safer-sex practices.
5. Sexual dysfunctions, even if they occur only once, are cause for considerable concern and should be treated immediately. True or false?

Rethink

1. Should women be free to dress any way they want without concerns about "giving off the wrong signals"? Is it reasonable for men to assume that women sometimes give off signals that indicate that they really want sex even when they say they don't?
2. What responsibilities do people who learn they have a sexually transmitted disease have to their sexual partners?

Answers to Evaluate Questions

1. True 2. b 3. c. 4. c 5. False; sexual dysfunction is experienced by almost everyone at one time or another.

Looking Back

What are the major differences between male and female gender roles?

- Gender is the perception of being male or female. Gender roles are the expectations, defined by society, of what is appropriate behavior for men and women. When gender roles reflect favoritism toward one sex, they lead to stereotyping and produce sexism. (p. 320)
- According to gender-role stereotypes, men have traits related to competence and women have traits related to warmth and expressiveness. Actual sex differences are much less clear, and of smaller magnitude, than the stereotypes suggest. The differences that do exist are produced by a combination of biological and environmental factors. (p. 324)
- Biological causes of sex difference are reflected by evidence of a possible difference in brain structure and functioning between men and women, and might be associated with differential exposure to hormones prior to birth. (p. 326)
- An evolutionary approach explains gender differences in terms of males' and females' different concerns regarding the inheritance of genes and the need for child rearing, but this approach is highly controversial. (p. 326)
- Socialization experiences produce gender schemas, mental frameworks that organize and guide a child's understanding of information relevant to gender. (p. 327)

Why, and under what circumstances, do we become sexually aroused?

- Although biological factors, such as the presence of androgens (male sex hormones) and estrogens and progesterone (female sex hormones) prime people for sex, almost any kind of stimulus can produce sexual arousal, depending on a person's prior experience. (p. 329)
- People's sexual responses follow a regular pattern consisting of four phases: excitement, plateau, orgasm, and resolution. Women can experience multiple orgasms, whereas men enter a refractory period, during which more sex is impossible until a sufficient amount of time has passed. (p. 331)

What is "normal" sexual behavior?

- Approaches to determining normality include deviation from the average, comparison of sexual behavior with some standard or ideal, and consideration of the psychological and physical consequences of the behavior to the person and to others. (p. 335)

How do most people behave sexually?

- The frequency of masturbation is high, particularly for males. Attitudes toward masturbation have traditionally been negative, even though no negative consequences have been detected, but are now becoming increasingly liberal. (p. 336)
- Heterosexuality, or sexual attraction to people of the opposite sex, is the most common sexual orientation. In terms of premarital sex, the double standard, in which premarital sex is thought to be more permissible for men than for women, has declined, particularly among young people. For many people, the double standard has been replaced by endorsement of "permissiveness with affection," the view that premarital intercourse is permissible if it occurs in the context of a loving and committed relationship. (p. 337)

- The frequency of marital sex varies widely. However, younger couples tend to have sexual intercourse more frequently than older couples. In addition, most men and women do not engage in extramarital sex. (p. 338)
- Homosexuals are sexually attracted to people of their own sex; bisexuals are sexually attracted to people of the same sex and people of the opposite sex. No explanation of sexual orientation has been confirmed; possibilities include genetic or biological factors, childhood and family influences, and prior learning experiences and conditioning. However, no relationship exists between sexual orientation and psychological adjustment. (p. 339)

How prevalent are rape and other forms of nonconsenting sex, and what are their causes?

- Rape occurs when one person forces another to submit to sexual activity. Rape does not occur only between strangers; often the victim is acquainted with the rapist. The motivation for rape is only sometimes sexual gratification. More frequently it is power, aggression, or anger. (p. 341)
- Childhood sexual abuse is surprisingly widespread. Most often the perpetrator is an acquaintance or a family member. (p. 343)

What are the major sexually transmitted diseases?

- Acquired immune deficiency syndrome, or AIDS, is a health problem that is profoundly affecting sexual behavior. In the United States, AIDS was first limited largely to homosexuals; now it is found in the heterosexual population and is bringing about changes in casual sex and in people's sexual practices. Other sexually transmitted diseases include chlamydia, genital herpes, trichomoniasis, gonorrhea, syphilis, and genital warts. (p. 343)

What sexual difficulties do people most frequently encounter?

- The major sexual problems reported by males include erectile dysfunction, premature ejaculation, and inhibited ejaculation. For females, the major problem is anorgasmia, or a lack of orgasm. Both men and women can suffer from inhibited sexual desire. (p. 345)

Key Terms and Concepts

gender (p. 321)
gender roles (p. 321)
sexism (p. 321)
gender schema (p. 328)
androgynous (p. 328)
androgens (p. 329)
genitals (p. 329)
estrogen (p. 330)
progesterone (p. 330)
ovulation (p. 330)
erogenous zones (p. 330)
excitement phase (p. 332)
plateau phase (p. 332)
orgasm (p. 332)
resolution stage (p. 332)
refractory period (p. 332)

masturbation (p. 336)
heterosexuality (p. 337)
double standard (p. 337)
extramarital sex (p. 338)
homosexuals (p. 339)
bisexuals (p. 339)
rape (p. 341)
date rape (p. 341)
sexually transmitted disease (STD) (p. 343)
acquired immune deficiency
    syndrome (AIDS) (p. 344)
erectile dysfunction (p. 345)
premature ejaculation (p. 345)
inhibited ejaculation (p. 345)
anorgasmia (p. 345)
inhibited sexual desire (p. 346)

Psychology on the Web

1. Find at least two recent news articles or discussions on the Web about the issue of gender equality in school or the workplace, especially unequal treatment of individuals because of their gender. Summarize in writing what you found, and discuss your own attitudes toward this issue.

2. Find information on the Web about date rape, including guidelines or suggestions published by other colleges for preventing rape among students. Summarize your findings, including recommendations for behavioral or policy changes that might be effective at your college. If your college's policies or publications about this topic could benefit from your findings, bring them to the attention of the appropriate office at your institution and suggest specific changes.

Preview

For additional quizzing and a variety of interactive resources, visit the *Understanding Psychology* Online Learning Center at www.mhhe.com/feldmanup6

Epilogue

We have seen how the subjects of gender and sex are dealt with by psychologists, first with regard to gender roles, gender stereotyping, gender schemas, and sexism. The expectations of society regarding female and male characteristics and behaviors lead to inequities in the treatment of men and women in school, the workplace, and the rest of society—inequities that largely favor men.

With regard to sexuality, we have discussed the nature of the physical processes that surround sexuality and addressed the controversial issue of "normality" in sexual behavior. We have seen the varieties of sexual behavior, and we have discussed premarital sex and marital sex, and sexual orientation (heterosexuality, homosexuality, and bisexuality). We have also examined rape and other forms of nonconsenting sex, including childhood sexual abuse.

Finally, we looked at the sexual problems people can have, including sexually transmitted diseases and sexual dysfunctions. We explored the nature of these problems and discussed ways to treat and deal with them.

Before we turn to the subject of human development in the next few chapters, return to the prologue of this chapter, concerning the case of Bruce Reimer, the boy who was, temporarily, transformed into a girl. Using your knowledge of gender and sex, consider the following questions.

1. What might Bruce's parents have done differently after the accident that cut off Bruce's penis?

2. Is it reasonable to generalize from a single case such as this one to broader issues of sex and gender? Why or why not?

3. "Brenda" was given dolls to play with and taught to be clean and tidy in order to be more like a girl. How were such efforts misguided, and what do they say about society's expectations about male and female behavior?

4. What conclusions can you draw from the lack of success in changing Bruce into Brenda in terms of the relative influence of heredity and environment on sexuality?

Chapter Twelve

Development:
The Beginnings of Life

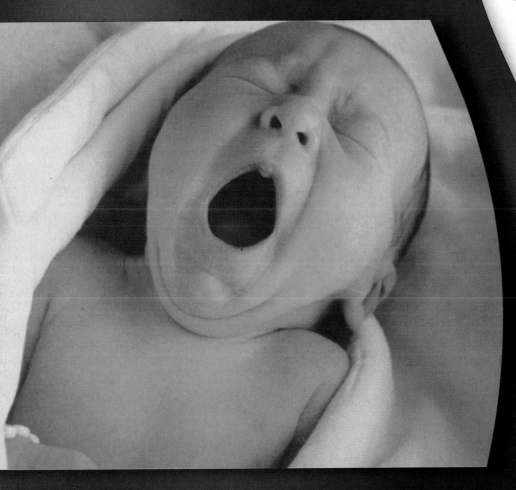

Prologue: The Brave New World of Childhood

Looking Ahead

Nature and Nurture: The Enduring Developmental Issue

Determining the Relative Influences of Nature and Nurture

Specific Research Approaches

Prenatal Development: From Conception to Birth

The Basics of Genetics

Development from Zygote to Birth

Applying Psychology in the 21st Century: Cloning, Gene Therapy, and the Coming Medical Revolution

The Extraordinary Newborn

Reflexes

Development of the Senses: Taking in the World

The Growing Child: Infancy Through Middle Childhood

Physical Development

Development of Social Behavior: Taking on the World

Cognitive Development: Children's Thinking About the World

Psychology at Work: Michael J. Morrier, Preschool Coordinator

Exploring Diversity: Supporting Children's School Achievement: The Asian Success Story

Becoming an Informed Consumer of Psychology: Maximizing Children's Competence

Looking Back

Key Terms and Concepts

Psychology on the Web

OLC Preview

Epilogue

Elizabeth Carr

Prologue

The Brave New World of Childhood

A few years ago, when Elizabeth Carr's class was learning how an egg combines with sperm in the mother's body to create a child, she felt compelled to interrupt.

"I piped up to say that not all babies are conceived like that and explained about sperm and eggs and petri dishes," said Elizabeth . . . , the first child in the United States born through in vitro fertilization.

Because her mother's landmark pregnancy was documented in great detail by a film crew, Elizabeth has seen pictures of the egg and sperm that united to become her, the petri dish where she was conceived, the embryonic blob of cells that grew into the bubbly young woman who now plays field hockey and sings in the school chorus. . . .

Elizabeth . . . said that her parents—whose egg and sperm joined in a petri dish at the Jones Institute for Reproductive Medicine in Norfolk, Virginia—have always made it clear that she was created differently from other children. Although she said she had faced taunts of "test tube baby" or "weirdo" a few times at school, she said she had never felt resentful about her conception. "I'm so grateful that they went through all this to have me" (Rosenthal, 1995, A1, B8).

Now a bubbly teenager, Elizabeth is just "one of a crowd," as her mother predicted when she was born—a crowd of some 60,000 children in the United States who were born only thanks to the technology of in vitro fertilization (Goldberg, 1999).

Welcome to the brave new world of childhood—or rather, one of the brave new worlds. From new ways of conceiving children to learning how to raise children most sensibly, the issues involved in human development touch each of us.

These issues, along with many others, are addressed by **developmental psychology,** the branch of psychology that studies the patterns of growth and change occurring throughout life. In large part, developmental psychologists study the interaction between the unfolding of biologically predetermined patterns of behavior and a constantly changing, dynamic environment. They ask how our genetic background affects our behavior throughout our lives and whether our potential is limited by heredity. Similarly, they are committed to understanding how the environment works with—or against—our genetic capabilities, how the world we live in affects our development, and how we can be encouraged to reach our full potential.

More than other psychologists, developmental psychologists consider the day-to-day patterns and changes in behavior that occur across the life span. This chapter focuses on the early part of the life cycle, beginning with conception, moving through birth and infancy, and ending with childhood. Chapter 13 then explores aspects of development during the remainder of the life cycle—from adolescence to adulthood, and finally to old age and death.

We begin our discussion of development by examining the approaches used to study the environmental and genetic factors—the nature–nurture issue. Then we consider the very start of development, beginning with conception and the nine months of life prior to birth. We describe both genetic and environmental influences on the unborn individual, and how these can affect behavior throughout the remainder of the life cycle.

Next, we examine the remarkable capabilities of newborns, focusing on their inborn reflexes and the rapid development of their senses. Finally, we consider the enormous strides that take place from infancy through middle childhood, focusing on the physical, social, and cognitive advances that mark our journey into adulthood.

developmental psychology: The branch of psychology that studies the patterns of growth and change occurring throughout life

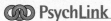 **PsychLink**

Theories of child development
www.mhhe.com/
feldmanup6-12links

Prepare

How do psychologists study the influences of hereditary and environmental factors in development?

What is the nature of development prior to birth?

What factors affect a child during the mother's pregnancy?

Organize

Nature and Nurture

Determining the Relative Influences of Nature and Nurture

Specific Research Approaches

Prenatal Development

The Basics of Genetics

Development from Zygote to Birth

Nature and Nurture: The Enduring Developmental Issue

How many bald, six-foot-six, 250-pound volunteer fire fighters are there in New Jersey who wear droopy mustaches, aviator-style eyeglasses, and a key ring on the right side of the belt?

The answer is: two. Gerald Levey and Mark Newman are identical twins, separated at birth. Each twin did not even know the other existed until they were reunited—in a fire station—by a fellow fire fighter who knew Newman and was startled to see Levey at a fire fighters' convention.

The lives of the twins, although separate, took remarkably similar paths. Levey went to college, studying forestry; Newman planned to study forestry in college but instead took a job trimming trees. Both had jobs in supermarkets. One has a job installing sprinkler systems; the other installed fire alarms.

Both men are unmarried and find the same kind of woman attractive: "tall, slender, long hair." They share similar hobbies, enjoying hunting, fishing, going to the beach, and watching old John Wayne movies and professional wrestling. Both like Chinese food and drink the same brand of beer. Their mannerisms are also similar—for example, each one throws his head back when he laughs. And, of course, there is one more thing: They share a passion for fighting fires.

The similarities we see in twins Gerald Levey and Mark Newman vividly raise one of the fundamental questions posed by developmental psychologists: How can we distinguish between the causes of behavior that are *environmental* (the influence of

parents, siblings, family, friends, schooling, nutrition, and all the other experiences to which a child is exposed) and those causes that are *hereditary* (those based on the genetic makeup of an individual that influence growth and development throughout life)? This question, which we explored when we considered intelligence in Chapter 9, is known as the **nature–nurture issue.** In this context, nature refers to hereditary factors, and nurture to environmental influences.

Although the question was first posed as a nature-*versus*-nurture issue, developmental psychologists today agree that *both* nature and nurture interact to produce specific developmental patterns and outcomes. Consequently, the question has evolved to *how and to what degree* environment and heredity both produce their effects. No one grows up free of environmental influences, nor does anyone develop without being affected by his or her inherited *genetic makeup*. However, the debate over the comparative influence of the two factors remains active, with different approaches and theories of development emphasizing the environment or heredity to a greater or lesser degree (Scarr, 1996; Saudino, 1997; de Waal, 1999).

Gerald Levy and Mark Newman

For example, some developmental theories stress the role of learning in producing changes in behavior in the developing child, relying on the basic principles of learning discussed in Chapter 6. Such theories emphasize the role of environment in accounting for development. In contrast, other approaches emphasize the influence of one's physiological makeup and functioning on development. Such theories stress the role of heredity and *maturation*—the unfolding of biologically predetermined patterns of behavior—in producing developmental change. Maturation can be seen, for instance, in the development of sex characteristics (such as breasts or body hair) that occurs at the start of adolescence. Furthermore, developmental psychologists have been influenced by the work of behavioral geneticists, who study the effects of heredity on behavior, and the theories of evolutionary psychologists, whose goal is to identify behavior patterns that are a result of our genetic inheritance from our ancestors. Both behavioral geneticists and evolutionary psychologists have highlighted the importance of heredity in influencing our behavior (Bjorklund, 1997).

However, developmental psychologists of different theoretical persuasions agree on some points. It seems clear that genetic factors not only provide the potential for particular behaviors or traits to emerge, but also place limitations on the emergence of such behavior or traits. For instance, heredity defines people's general level of intelligence, setting an upper limit which—regardless of the quality of the environment—people cannot exceed. Heredity also provides limits on physical abilities; humans simply cannot run at a speed of 60 miles an hour, nor will they grow to be 10 feet tall, no matter what the quality of their environment (Plomin, 1990; Plomin & McClearn, 1993; Steen, 1996).

Table 12-1 lists some of the characteristics that are most affected by heredity. As you consider these items, keep in mind that these characteristics are not *entirely* determined by heredity, but that environmental factors also play a role.

In fact, in most instances, environmental factors play a critical role in enabling people to develop the capabilities that their genetic background makes possible. Had Albert Einstein received no intellectual stimulation as a child and not been sent to school, it is unlikely that he would have fulfilled his genetic potential for great intellect. Similarly, it is unlikely that the great athlete and basketball star Michael Jordan would have developed outstanding physical skill if he had not been raised in an environment that nurtured his innate talent and gave him the opportunity to train and perfect his natural abilities.

It is clear that the relationship between heredity and environment is far from simple. As a consequence, developmental psychologists typically take an *interactionist* position on the nature–nurture issue, suggesting that a combination of hereditary and environmental

PsychLink

Discussion on nature vs. nurture
www.mhhe.com/
feldmanup6–12links

nature–nurture issue: The issue of the degrees to which environment and heredity influence behavior and development

Table 12-1 Characteristics Influenced Significantly by Genetic Factors

Physical Characteristics	Intellectual Characteristics	Emotional Characteristics and Disorders
Height	Memory	Shyness
Weight	Intelligence	Extraversion
Obesity	Age of language acquisition	Emotionality
Tone of voice	Reading disability	Neuroticism
Blood pressure	Mental retardation	Schizophrenia
Tooth decay		Anxiety
Athletic ability		Alcoholism
Firmness of handshake		
Age of death		
Activity level		

factors influences development. The challenge facing developmental psychologists is to identify the relative strength of each of these influences on the individual, as well as the specific changes that occur over the course of development (Plomin & Neiderhiser, 1992; Wozniak & Fischer, 1993; Saudino & Plomin, 1996).

Determining the Relative Influences of Nature and Nurture

Developmental psychologists use several approaches to determine the relative influence of genetic and environmental factors on behavior. For example, researchers can experimentally control the genetic makeup of laboratory animals by carefully breeding them for specific traits; and by observing animals with identical genetic makeup in varied environments, researchers can ascertain the effects of particular kinds of environmental stimulation. Although generalizing the findings of nonhuman research to a human population must be done only with care, findings from animal research provide important information that, for ethical reasons, could not be obtained by using human participants.

identical twins: Twins who are genetically identical

Human twins also are an important source of information about the relative effects of genetic and environmental factors. If **identical twins** (those who are genetically identical) display different patterns of development, such differences have to be attributed to variations in the environment in which the twins were raised. The most useful data come from identical twins (such as Gerald Levey and Mark Newman) who are adopted at birth by different sets of adoptive parents and raised apart in differing environments. Studies of nontwin siblings who are raised in totally different environments also shed some light on the issue. Because they have relatively similar genetic makeups, siblings who show similarities as adults provide strong evidence for the importance of heredity (Lykken et al., 1993; Gottesman, 1997; McClearn et al., 1997).

It is also possible to take the opposite tack. Instead of concentrating on genetically similar people raised in different environments, we could consider people raised in similar environments who are genetically dissimilar. If we find, for example, that two adopted children—genetically dissimilar but raised in the same family—develop similarly, we have evidence for the importance of environmental influences on development. Moreover, it is possible to carry out research involving genetically dissimilar animals; by experimentally varying the environment in which they are raised, we can determine the influence of environmental factors (independent of heredity) on development (Segal, 1993; Vernon et al., 1997).

Specific Research Approaches

Because of the unique demands of measuring behavioral change across different ages, developmental researchers have designed several unique methodologies. In the most frequently used, **cross-sectional research,** people of different ages are compared at the same point in time. Cross-sectional studies provide information about differences in development between different age groups.

Suppose, for instance, we were interested in the development of intellectual ability in adulthood. To carry out a cross-sectional study, we might compare a sample of 25-, 45-, and 65-year-olds on an IQ test. We then can determine whether average IQ test scores differ in each age group.

Cross-sectional research has limitations, however. For instance, we cannot be sure that the IQ score differences we might find in our example are due to age differences alone. Instead, they might reflect cohort differences in educational attainment. A *cohort* is a group of people who grow up at similar times, in similar places, and under similar conditions. In the case of IQ differences, any age differences we find in a cross-sectional study could reflect educational differences among the cohorts studied: People in the older age group might belong to a cohort that was less likely to attend college than those in the younger groups.

One way around the problem is to employ the second major research strategy used by developmental psychologists: a longitudinal study. In **longitudinal research,** the behavior of one or more participants is traced as the participants age. Longitudinal studies assess *change* in intellectual ability over time, unlike cross-sectional studies, which assess *differences* among groups of people.

For instance, consider how we might investigate intellectual development during adulthood using a longitudinal research strategy. First, we might give IQ tests to a group of 25-year olds. We'd then come back to the same people twenty years later and retest them at age 45. Finally, we'd return to them once more when they were 65 years old and test them again.

By examining changes over several points in time, we can clearly see how individuals develop. Unfortunately, longitudinal research requires an enormous expenditure of time (as the researcher waits for the participants to get older), and participants who begin a study at an early age might drop out, move away, or even die as the research continues. Moreover, participants who take the same test at several points in time can become "testwise" and perform better each time they take it, having become more familiar with the test.

To make up for the limitations in cross-sectional and longitudinal research, investigators have devised an alternative strategy. Known as **cross-sequential research,** it combines cross-sectional and longitudinal approaches by taking a number of different age groups and examining them over several points in time. For example, investigators might use a group of 3-, 5-, and 7-year-olds, examining them every six months for a period of several years. This technique allows the developmental psychologist to tease out the effects of age changes themselves from other possibly influential factors.

cross-sectional research: A research method in which people of different ages are compared at the same point in time

longitudinal research: A research method that investigates behavior as participants age

cross-sequential research: A research method that combines cross-sectional and longitudinal research by considering a number of different age groups and examining them over several points in time

chromosomes: Rod-shaped structures that contain the basic hereditary information

Prenatal Development: From Conception to Birth

Our understanding of the biology of *conception*—when a male's sperm cell penetrates a female's egg cell—makes it no less of a miracle. At that single moment, an individual's genetic endowment is established for the rest of her or his life.

The Basics of Genetics

The one-cell entity that is established at conception contains 23 pairs of **chromosomes,** rod-shaped structures that contain the basic hereditary information. One member of each pair is from the mother and the other is from the father.

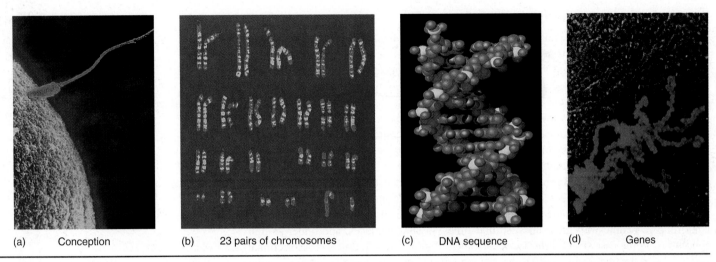

(a)   Conception   (b)   23 pairs of chromosomes   (c)   DNA sequence   (d)   Genes

Figure 12-1 Every individual's characteristics are determined by the individual's specific genetic information. At the moment of conception (a), humans receive 23 pairs of chromosomes (b), half from the mother and half from the father. These chromosomes are made up of coils of DNA (c). Each chromosome contains thousands of genes (d) that "program" the future development of the body.

genes: The parts of the chromosomes through which genetic information is transmitted

PsychLink

Publications on genetics
www.mhhe.com/
feldmanup6-12links

zygote: The new cell formed by the union of an egg and sperm

Each chromosome contains thousands of **genes**—smaller units through which genetic information is transmitted. Either individually or in combination, genes produce the particular characteristics of each person. Composed of sequences of *DNA (deoxyribonucleic acid)* molecules, genes are the biological equivalent of "software" that programs the future development of all parts of the body's hardware. Humans have some 30,000 different genes (see Figure 12-1).

Some genes are responsible for the development of systems common to all members of the human species—the heart, circulatory system, brain, lungs, and so forth; others control the characteristics that make each human unique, such as facial configuration, height, eye color, and the like. The child's sex is also determined by a particular combination of genes. Specifically, a child inherits an X chromosome from its mother, and either an X or Y chromosome from its father. A child with an XX combination is female; a child with an XY combination is male. Male development is triggered by a single gene on the Y chromosome, and without the presence of that specific gene, the individual will develop as a female (illustrated in Figure 12-2 on page 360).

As behavioral geneticists are increasingly discovering, genes are also at least partially responsible for a wide variety of personal characteristics, encompassing cognitive abilities, personality traits, and psychological disorders. Of course, few of these characteristics are determined by a single gene. Instead, most traits are the result of a combination of multiple genes, which operate together with environmental influences (Gilger, 1996; Pillard, 1996; Rieder, Kaufmann, & Knowles, 1996; Funder, 1997).

To better understand how genes influence human characteristics and behavior, scientists have mapped the specific location and sequence of every human gene in the massive, multiyear Human Genome Project (first discussed in Chapter 3). As you can see by reading the *Applying Psychology in the 21st Century* box, the Human Genome Project is likely to produce a revolution in health care, as scientists identify the particular genes that are responsible for various disorders.

Development from Zygote to Birth

When the egg becomes fertilized by the sperm, the result is a one-celled entity called a **zygote** that immediately begins to develop. The zygote starts out as a microscopic speck. Three days after fertilization, though, the zygote increases to around 32 cells,

Applying Psychology in the 21st Century

Cloning, Gene Therapy, and the Coming Medical Revolution

As he chats with the young mother, the doctor flicks a cotton swab into the mouth of her infant son, collecting a small sample of mucus from inside his cheek. In the back room of his office, he inserts the sample into a machine, which extracts DNA from the mucus cells and compares it with the genetic material on a dime-size chip. Minutes later, a computer printer begins to spit out a list of the infant's genes. Fortunately, all but a few of the genes are labeled "normal." It is those few that the doctor discusses as he explains the results to the mother. "Your son's genetic inheritance is generally good," he says, "but he is somewhat predisposed to skin lesions. So starting right away, he should be protected against excessive exposure to the sun." And the doctor warns, "he may well be susceptible to cardiovascular disease later in life. To lessen his risk, after about age two he should begin a lifelong low-fat, high-fiber diet." (Jaroff, 1996, p. 24)

This view of a visit to a pediatrician's office is not so futuristic, for it could become reality within the next few decades. Our increasing understanding of genetics is leading not only to the identification of risk factors in children, but also to the development of new treatments for everything from serious physical illnesses, such as cancer, to psychological disorders like schizophrenia and depression.

This potential medical revolution has been heralded, in part, by an unlikely achievement: the birth of Dolly, a rather ordinary looking sheep with an extraordinary genetic background. Dolly was the first animal to be cloned from the cells of an adult sheep, making her an exact genetic replica of her "parent." Dolly was soon followed by a menagerie of cloned animals, each genetically identical to another member of its species (Pennisi, 1997c; Kolata, 1998).

Dolly, the first adult mammal to be cloned. Is it possible for Dolly to have a different "personality" than her clone?

The ability of scientists to produce clones raises new possibilities of correcting genetic flaws, not only in sheep and other animals, but in humans, and it accelerates the pace of developments in the new field of gene therapy. In *gene therapy*, genes are introduced into existing cells in order to prevent or cure a disorder. For instance, genes targeted to treat a particular disease can be injected into a patient's blood stream. When the genes reach the site of the problem—such as a cancerous tumor—the new genes provide existing cells with a set of new instructions that modify their functioning, thereby potentially curing the disease. It also might be possible to "harvest" defective cells from a child prior to birth. These cells could be treated by gene therapy and reintroduced into the unborn child, thereby repairing the defect (Kmiec, 1999; Levy, 2000; Yan, Kinzler, & Vogelstein, 2000).

Some forms of gene therapy are already in use, and the number of diseases treated by gene therapy is growing. For example, such disorders as AIDS, cystic fibrosis, and rheumatoid arthritis are promising candidates for gene therapy (Begley, 1998; Weiner, 2000).

Cloning advances are likely to continue to raise significant ethical issues. In one radical possibility, cloning might be employed if both a husband and wife were infertile. In such a case, they might consider cloning one or the other of themselves in order to have at least one child who was genetically similar (in this case, genetically identical) to one of them. The ethical and moral issues of such a procedure, of course, are profound—but the rapid advances in cloning and gene therapy suggest they need to be dealt with now (Angier, 1999; Gordon, 1999; Shiels et al., 1999; Wright, 1999).

Would you choose to be genetically tested so that you could know your susceptibility to future genetic diseases? What if you learned that you had a genetic disorder that was likely to shorten your life?

and within a week it has grown to 100 to 150 cells. These first two weeks are known as the *germinal period.*

Two weeks after conception, the developing individual enters the *embryonic period,* which lasts from 2 through 8 weeks, and he or she is now called an **embryo.** As the embryo develops through an intricate, preprogrammed process of cell division, it grows 10,000 times larger by 4 weeks of age, attaining a length of about one-fifth of an inch. At this point it has developed a rudimentary beating heart, brain, and intestinal tract, and a number of other rudimentary organs. Although all these organs are at a primitive stage of development, they are clearly recognizable. Moreover, by 8 weeks, the embryo is about an inch long, and has arms, legs, and a face that are discernible.

From 8 weeks and continuing until birth, the developing individual enters the *fetal period* and is now called a **fetus.** At the start of this period, it begins to respond to touch; it bends its fingers when touched on the hand. At 16 to 18 weeks, its movements

embryo: A developed zygote that has a rudimentary heart, brain, and other organs

fetus: A developing child, from 8 weeks after conception until birth

Figure 12-2 When an ovum and sperm meet at the moment of fertilization, the ovum provides an X chromosome, and the sperm provides either an X or a Y chromosome. If the sperm contributes an X chromosome, the child will have an XX pairing on the 23rd chromosome and will be a girl. If the sperm contributes a Y chromosome, the result will an XY pairing—a boy.

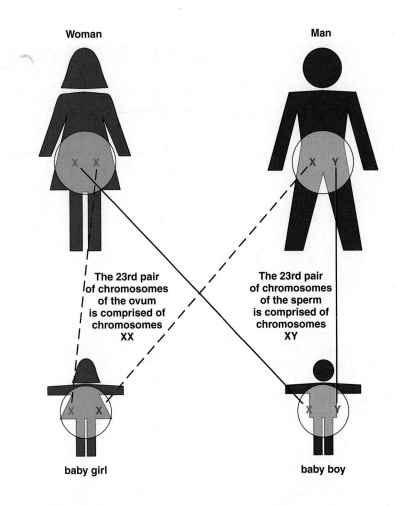

age of viability: The point at which the fetus can survive if born prematurely

become strong enough for the mother to sense the baby's movement. At the same time, hair might begin to grow on the baby's head, and the facial features become similar to those the child will display at birth. The major organs begin functioning, although the fetus could not yet be kept alive outside the mother. In addition, a lifetime's worth of brain neurons are produced—although it is unclear whether the brain is capable of thinking at this early stage.

By 24 weeks, the fetus has many of the characteristics it will display as a newborn. In fact, when an infant is born prematurely at this age, it can open and close its eyes; suck; cry; look up, down, and around; and even grasp objects placed in its hands, although it is still unable to survive for long outside the mother.

The fetus continues to develop prior to birth. It begins to grow fatty deposits under the skin and it gains weight. The fetus reaches the **age of viability,** the point at which it can survive if born prematurely, at about 24 weeks, although through advances in medical technology this crucial age is getting earlier. At 28 weeks, the fetus weighs less than 3 pounds and is about 16 inches long. It might be capable of learning: One study found that the infants of mothers who had repeatedly read aloud the Dr. Seuss story *The Cat in the Hat* prior to birth preferred the sound of that particular story over other stories after they were born (Spence & DeCasper, 1982).

As they develop prior to birth, children pass through several *critical periods,* times during development when specific events have their greatest impact. For example, children are particularly sensitive to environmental influences such as drugs during certain certain critical periods before birth. If they are exposed to the drug before or after the critical period, it might have relatively little impact, but if exposure comes during a critical period, its impact will be maximized. Critical periods can also occur

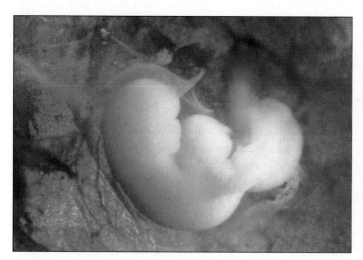
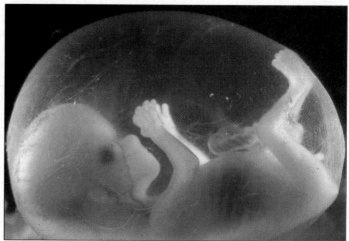

These remarkable photos of live fetuses display the degree of physical development at 4 and 15 weeks.

after birth; some language specialists suggest, for instance, that there is a period where children are particularly receptive to language (Bornstein & Bruner, 1989; Eisen, Field, & Larson, 1991; Shatz, 1992).

In the final weeks of pregnancy, the fetus continues to gain weight and grow. At the end of the normal 38 weeks of pregnancy, the fetus typically weighs around 7 pounds and is about 20 inches in length.

Genetic Influences on the Fetus

The process of fetal growth that we have just described reflects normal development, which occurs in 95 to 98 percent of all pregnancies. Some people are less fortunate, for in the remaining 2 to 5 percent of cases, children are born with serious birth defects. A major cause of such defects is faulty genes or chromosomes. Here are some of the most common genetic and chromosomal difficulties.

- *Phenylketonuria (PKU)*. A child born with the inherited disease phenylketonuria cannot produce an enzyme that is required for normal development. This results in an accumulation of poisons that eventually cause profound mental retardation. The disease is treatable, however, if caught early enough. Most infants today are routinely tested for PKU, and children with the disorder can be placed on a special diet that allows them to develop normally.
- *Sickle-cell anemia*. About 10 percent of the African American population has the possibility of passing on sickle-cell anemia, a disease that gets its name from the abnormal shape of the victims' red blood cells. Children with the disease might have poor appetites, swollen stomachs, and yellowish eyes; they frequently die during childhood.
- *Tay-Sachs disease*. Children born with Tay-Sachs disease, a disorder that most often afflicts Jews of eastern European ancestry, usually die by the age of 3 or 4 because of the body's inability to break down fat. If both parents carry the genetic defect producing the fatal illness, their child has a one in four chance of being born with the disease (Navon & Proia, 1989).
- *Down syndrome*. In Chapter 9, we discussed Down syndrome as a cause of mental retardation. Down syndrome occurs when the zygote receives an extra chromosome at the moment of conception, causing retardation. Down syndrome is often related to the mother's age; mothers over 35 and younger than 18, in particular, stand a higher risk than other women of having a child with the syndrome.

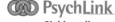

PsychLink

Sickle-cell anemia information
www.mhhe.com/
feldmanup6–12links

Prenatal Environmental Influences

Genetic factors are not the only causes of difficulties in fetal development. Environmental influences—the *nurture* part of the nature–nurture equation—also affect the fetus. Some of the most profound consequences are brought about by **teratogens,** environmental agents such as drugs, chemicals, viruses, or other factors that produce birth defects. Among the major prenatal environmental influences on the fetus:

- *Mother's nutrition and emotional state.* What a mother eats during her pregnancy can have important implications for the health of her baby. Mothers who are seriously undernourished cannot provide adequate nutrition to the growing baby, and they are likely to give birth to underweight babies. Poorly nourished babies are also more susceptible to disease, and a lack of nourishment can adversely affect mental development (Adams & Parker, 1990; Ricciuti, 1993; Sigman, 1995).

  Moreover, the mother's emotional state affects the baby. Mothers who are anxious and tense during the last months of their pregnancies are more apt to have infants who are irritable and who sleep and eat poorly. The reason? One hypothesis is that the autonomic nervous system of the fetus becomes especially sensitive as a result of the chemical changes produced by the mother's emotional state (Kagan, Kearsley, & Zelazo, 1978).

- *Mother's illness.* Several disesases that have a relatively minor effect on the mother's health can have devastating consequences for the developing fetus if contracted during the early part of a woman's pregnancy. For example, rubella (German measles), syphilis, diabetes, and high blood pressure can permanently harm the fetus. The virus that causes AIDS can also be passed from mother to child prior to birth. The virus can also be passed on through breast-feeding after birth (Heyward & Curran, 1988).

- *Mother's use of drugs.* Mothers who take illegal and physically addictive drugs such as cocaine run the risk of giving birth to babies who are similarly addicted. Their newborns suffer painful withdrawal symptoms after birth and sometimes have permanent physical and mental impairment. Even legal drugs taken by pregnant women (who might not know that they have become pregnant) can have a tragic effect. For example, drugs such as the acne medicine Acutane can produce fetal abnormalities (Hannigan et al., 1999; Streissguth et al., 1999; Ikonomidou et al., 2000).

- *Alcohol and nicotine use.* Alcohol and nicotine are dangerous to fetal development. For example, *fetal alcohol syndrome,* a condition resulting in mental and growth retardation, has been found in the children of mothers who consumed heavy or sometimes even moderate amounts of alcohol during pregnancy. Pregnant mothers who smoke also put their children at considerable risk (DiFranza & Lew, 1995; Mills, 1999; Ness et al., 1999).

A number of other environmental factors have an impact upon the child prior to and during birth (see Table 12-2). It is important to keep in mind, however, that although we have been discussing the influences of genetics and environment separately, neither factor works alone. Furthermore, despite the emphasis here on some of the ways development can go wrong, the vast majority of pregnancies develop without difficulty. And in most instances, subsequent child development also proceeds normally, as we discuss next.

teratogens: Environmental agents such as drugs, chemicals, viruses, or other factors that produce birth defects

Table 12-2 Environmental Factors Affecting Prenatal Development

Factor	Possible Effect
Rubella (German measles)	Blindness, deafness, heart abnormalities, stillbirth
Syphilis	Mental retardation, physical deformities, maternal miscarriage
Addictive drugs	Low birth weight, addiction of infant to drug, with possible death, after birth, from withdrawal
Smoking	Premature birth, low birth weight and length
Alcohol	Mental retardation, lower-than-average birth weight, small head, limb deformities
Radiation from X rays	Physical deformities, mental retardation
Inadequate diet	Reduction in growth of brain, smaller-than-average weight and length at birth
Mother's age—younger than 18 at birth of child	Premature birth, increased incidence of Down syndrome
Mother's age—older than 35 at birth of child	Increased incidence of Down syndrome
DES (diethylstilbestrol)	Reproductive difficulties and increased incidence of genital cancer in children of mothers who were given DES during pregnancy to prevent miscarriage
AIDS	Possible spread of AIDS virus to infant; facial deformities; growth failure

Evaluate

1. Developmental psychologists are interested in the effects of both _____ and _____ on development.
2. Environment and heredity both influence development, with genetic potentials generally establishing limits on environmental influences. True or false?
3. By observing genetically similar animals in differing environments, we can increase our understanding of the influences of hereditary and environmental factors in humans. True or false?
4. _____ research studies the same individuals over a period of time, whereas _____-_____ research studies people of different ages at the same time.
5. Match the following terms with their definition:
   1. Zygote
   2. Gene
   3. Chromosome

   a. Smallest unit through which genetic information is passed
   b. Fertilized egg
   c. Rod-shaped structure containing genetic information
6. Specific kinds of growth must take place during a _____ period if the embryo is to develop normally.

Answers to Evaluate Questions

1. heredity (or nature); environment (or nurture), 2. True, 3. True, 4. Longitudinal; cross-sectional, 5. 1-b; 2-a; 3-c, 6. critical

Rethink

1. What sort of policy might you create for notifying persons who have genetically based disorders that can be identified by genetic testing? Would your policy treat potentially fatal disorders differently from less serious ones? Would it make a distinction between treatable and nontreatable disorders?
2. Given the possible effects of the environment on the developing child, do you think expectant mothers should be subject to legal prosecution for their use of alcohol and other drugs that can seriously harm their unborn children? Defend your position.

Prepare

What are the major competencies of newborns?

What are the milestones of physical and social development during childhood?

Organize

The Extraordinary Newborn
    Reflexes
    Development of the Senses
The Growing Child
    Physical Development
    Development of Social Behavior

neonate: A newborn child

PsychLink

Birthing process
www.mhhe.com/
feldmanup6-12links

reflexes: Unlearned, involuntary responses that occur automatically in the presence of certain stimuli

The Extraordinary Newborn

His head was molded into a long melon shape and came to a point at the back. . . . He was covered with a thick greasy white material known as "vernix," which made him slippery to hold. In addition to a shock of black hair on his head, his body was covered with dark, fine hair known as "lanugo." His ears, his back, his shoulders, and even his cheeks were furry. . . . His skin was wrinkled and quite loose. . . . His ears were pressed to his head in unusual positions—one ear was matted firmly forward on his cheek. His nose was flattened and pushed to one side. (Brazelton, 1969, p. 3)

Although the description hardly fits that of the adorable babies seen in advertisements, we are in fact talking about a normal, completely developed child just after the moment of birth. Called a **neonate,** the newborn presents itself to the world in a form that hardly meets the standards of beauty against which we typically measure babies. Yet ask any parent: No sight is more beautiful or exciting than the first glimpse of their newborn.

The neonate's strange appearance is brought about by a number of factors. The trip through its mother's birth canal might have squeezed the incompletely formed bones of the skull together and squashed the nose into the head. *Vernix,* its white, greasy covering, is secreted to protect its skin prior to birth, and it might have *lanugo,* a soft fuzz, over its entire body for a similar purpose. Its eyelids could be puffy with an accumulation of fluids because of its upside-down position during birth.

All this changes during the first two weeks of life as the neonate takes on a more familiar appearance. Even more impressive are the capabilities the neonate begins to display from the time it is born—capabilities that grow at an astounding rate over the ensuing months.

Reflexes

The neonate is born with a number of **reflexes**—unlearned, involuntary responses that occur automatically in the presence of certain stimuli. Many of these reflexes are critical for survival and unfold naturally as a part of an infant's ongoing maturation. The *rooting reflex,* for instance, causes neonates to turn their heads toward things that touch their cheeks—such as the mother's nipple or a bottle. Similarly, a *sucking reflex* prompts the infant to suck at things that touch its lips. Among its other reflexes are a *gag reflex* (to clear its throat); the *startle reflex* (a series of movements in which the infant flings out its arms, fans its fingers, and arches its back in response to a sudden noise); and the *Babinski reflex* (the baby's toes fan out when the outer edge of the sole of its foot is stroked).

These primitive reflexes are lost after the first few months of life and replaced by more complex and organized behaviors. Although at birth the neonate is capable of only jerky, limited voluntary movements, during the first year of life the ability to move independently grows enormously. The typical baby is able to roll over by the age of 3 months; it can sit without support at 6 months, stand alone at about $11\frac{1}{2}$ months, and walk by the time it is just over a year old. Not only does the ability to make large-scale movements improve during this time, but fine-muscle movements also become increasingly sophisticated (as illustrated in Figure 12-3).

Development of the Senses: Taking in the World

When proud parents pick up their neonate and peer into its eyes, is the child able to return their gaze? Although it was thought for some time that newborns could see only a hazy blur, most current

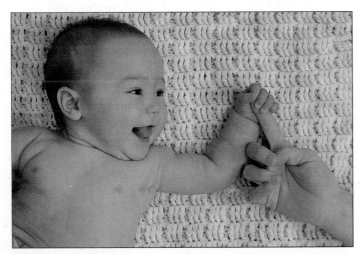

Many of the reflexes that a neonate is born with are critical for survival and unfold naturally as a part of an infant's ongoing maturation. Do you think humans have more or fewer reflexes than other animals?

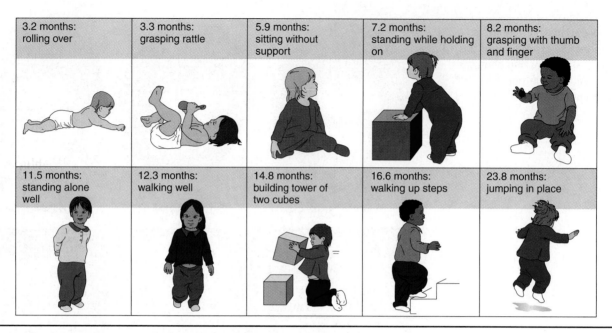

Figure 12–3 Although at birth the neonate is capable of only jerky, limited voluntary movements, during the first year of life the ability to move independently grows enormously. The ages indicate the time when 50 percent of children are able to perform each skill. Remember, however, that when each skill appears varies considerably. For example, 25 percent of children are able to walk well at 11 months, and by 15 months, 90 percent of children are walking well. (Frankenburg et al., 1992.)

findings indicate that the capabilities of neonates are far more impressive. Although their eyes have limited capacity to focus on objects that are not within 7 or 8 inches of their face, neonates are able to follow objects moving within their field of vision. They also show the rudiments of depth perception, as they react by raising their hands when an object appears to be moving rapidly toward the face (Gelman & Au, 1996; Maurer et al., 1999).

You might think that it would be hard to figure out just how well neonates are able to see, given that their lack of both language and reading ability clearly prevents them from saying what direction the *E* on a vision chart is facing. However, a number of ingenious methods, relying on the newborn's biological responses and innate reflexes, have been devised to test perceptual skills (Koop, 1994; Atkinson, 1995).

For instance, infants who are shown a novel stimulus typically pay close attention to it, and, as a consequence, their heart rates increase. But if they are repeatedly shown the same stimulus, their attention to it decreases, as indicated by a return to a slower heart rate. This phenomenon is known as **habituation,** the decrease in the response to a stimulus that occurs after repeated presentations of the same stimulus. By studying habituation, developmental psychologists can tell when a stimulus can be detected and discriminated by a child too young to speak (Peterzell, 1993).

Researchers have developed a number of other methods for measuring neonate and infant perception. One technique involves babies sucking on a nipple attached to a computer. Changes in the rate and vigor of sucking are taken to show that babies can perceive variations in stimuli. Other approaches include examining babies' eye movements and observing which way babies move their heads when presented with a visual stimulus (George, 1999).

Using such research techniques, we now know that infants' visual perception is remarkably sophisticated from birth. At birth, babies show preferences for patterns with contours and edges over less distinct patterns, indicating that they are capable of responding

habituation: The decrease in the response to a stimulus that occurs after repeated presentations of the same stimulus

Figure 12-4 This newborn infant is clearly imitating the expressions of the adult model in these amazing photos. How does this ability contribute to social development?

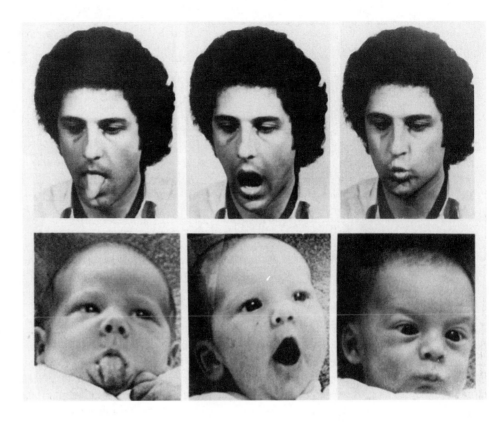

to the configuration of stimuli. Furthermore, even newborns are aware of size constancy, apparently sensitive to the phenomenon that objects stay the same size even though the image on the retina changes size as the distance between the object and the retina varies (Slater, Mattock, & Brown, 1990; Slater, 1996).

In fact, neonates have the ability to discriminate facial expressions—and even to imitate them. As you can see in Figure 12-4, newborns exposed to an adult with a happy, sad, or surprised facial expression are able to produce a good imitation of the adult's expression. Even very young infants, then, can respond to the emotions and moods revealed by their caregivers' facial expressions. This capability provides the foundation for social interactional skills in children (Meltzoff, 1996; Mumme, Fernald, & Herrera, 1996).

Other visual abilities grow rapidly after birth. By the end of their first month, babies can distinguish some colors from others, and after 4 months they can readily focus on near or far objects. By 4 or 5 months, they are able to recognize two- and three-dimensional objects, and they can perceive the gestalt organizing principles that we discussed in Chapter 4. Furthermore, there are rapid improvements in perceptual abilities: Sensitivity to visual stimuli, for instance, becomes three to four times greater at 1 year of age than it was at birth (Slater, 1996; Vital-Durand, Atkinson, & Braddick, 1996).

In addition to vision, infants' other sensory capabilities are quite impressive. Newborns can distinguish different sounds to the point of being able to recognize their own mothers' voices at the age of 3 days. They are also capable of making subtle perceptual distinctions that underlie the language abilities described in Chapter 8. For example, at 2 days of age, infants are able to distinguish between their native tongue and foreign languages, and they can discriminate between such closely related sounds as *ba* and *pa* when they are 4 days old. By 6 months of age, they are capable of discriminating virtually any difference in sound that is relevant to the production of language. Moreover, they are capable of discriminating different tastes and smells at a very early age. There even seems to be something of a built-in sweet tooth: Neonates prefer liquids that have been sweetened with sugar over unsweetened liquids (Bornstein & Arterberry, 1999).

The Growing Child: Infancy Through Middle Childhood

It was during the windy days of March that the problem in the day care center first arose. Its source: 10-month-old Russell Ruud. Otherwise a model of decorum, Russell had somehow learned how to unzip the Velcro chin strap to his winter hat. He would remove the hat whenever he got the urge, seemingly oblivious to the potential health problems that might follow.

But that was just the start of the real difficulty. To the chagrin of the teachers in the day care center, not to speak of the children's parents, soon other children were following his lead, removing their own caps at will.

Russell's mother, made aware of the anarchy at the day care center—and the other parents' distress over Russell's behavior—pleaded innocent. "I never showed Russell how to unzip the Velcro," claimed his mother, Judith Ruud, an economist with the Congressional Budget Office in Washington, D.C. "He learned by trial and error, and the other kids saw him do it one day when they were getting dressed for an outing." (Goleman, 1993a, C10)

At the age of 10 months, Russell is asserting his personality, illustrating the tremendous growth that occurs in a variety of domains during the first year of life. Throughout the remainder of childhood, as children move from infancy into middle childhood and the start of adolescence around age 11 or 12, children develop physically, socially, and cognitively in extraordinary ways. In the remainder of this chapter, we'll consider this development.

Physical Development

The most obvious sign of development is children's physical growth. During the first year of life, children typically triple their weight, and their height increases by about half. This rapid growth slows down as the child gets older—think how gigantic adults would be if that rate of growth were constant—and the average rate of growth from age 3 to the beginning of adolescence, around age 13, is a gain of about 5 pounds and 3 inches a year (see Figure 12-5).

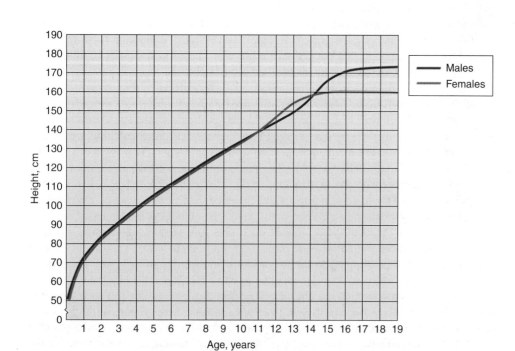

Figure 12-5 The average height growth for males and females in the United States from birth through the age of 19. At what ages are girls heavier and taller than boys, on average?

(From J. M. Tanner, et al., "Standards from Birth to Maturity for Height, Weight, Height Velocity and Weight Velocity: British Children, 1965," *Archives of Disease in Childhood*, 41, 454–471, 613–635, BMJ Publishing Group. Reprinted with permission of BMJ Publishing Group.)

Figure 12-6 As development progresses, the relative size of the head, in relation to the rest of the body, decreases until adulthood is reached. Why do you think the head starts out so large?

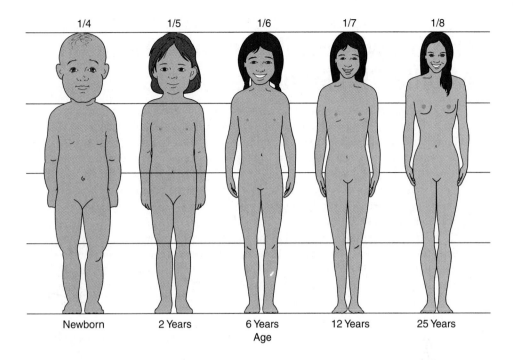

| 1/4 | 1/5 | 1/6 | 1/7 | 1/8 |

| Newborn | 2 Years | 6 Years | 12 Years | 25 Years |

Age

attachment: The positive emotional bond that develops between a child and a particular individual

The physical changes that occur as children develop are not just a matter of increasing growth; the comparative sizes of the various body parts change dramatically as children age. As you can see in Figure 12-6, the head of the newborn is disproportionately large. However, the head soon becomes more proportional in size to the rest of the body as growth occurs mainly in the trunk and legs.

Development of Social Behavior: Taking on the World

As anyone who has seen an infant smiling at the sight of her or his mother can guess, at the same time as infants are growing physically and honing their perceptual abilities, they are also developing socially. The nature of a child's early social development provides the foundation for social relationships that will last a lifetime.

Attachment, the positive emotional bond that develops between a child and a particular individual, is the most important form of social development that occurs during infancy. The earliest studies of attachment were carried out by animal ethologist Konrad Lorenz (1966). Lorenz focused on newborn goslings, who under normal circumstances instinctively follow their mother, the first moving object to which they are exposed after birth. Lorenz found that goslings whose eggs were raised in an incubator and who viewed him immediately after hatching would follow his every movement, as if he were their mother. He labeled this process *imprinting,* behavior that takes place during a critical period and involves attachment to the first moving object that is observed.

Our understanding of attachment made progress when psychologist Harry Harlow, in a classic study, gave infant monkeys the choice of cuddling a wire "mother" that provided milk, or a soft, terry-cloth "mother" that was warm but did not provide milk. Their choice was clear: They spent most of their time clinging to the warm cloth "monkey," although they made occasional forays to the wire monkey to nurse (Harlow & Zimmerman, 1959). It was obvious that the cloth monkey provided greater comfort to the infants; milk alone was insufficient to create attachment (see Figure 12-7).

Building on this pioneering work with nonhumans, developmental psychologists have suggested that human attachment grows through the

Figure 12-7 Although the wire "mother" dispensed milk to the hungry infant monkey, the soft, terry cloth "mother" was preferred (Harry Harlow Primate Laboratory/University of Wisconsin). Do you think human babies would react the same way? What does this tell us about attachment?

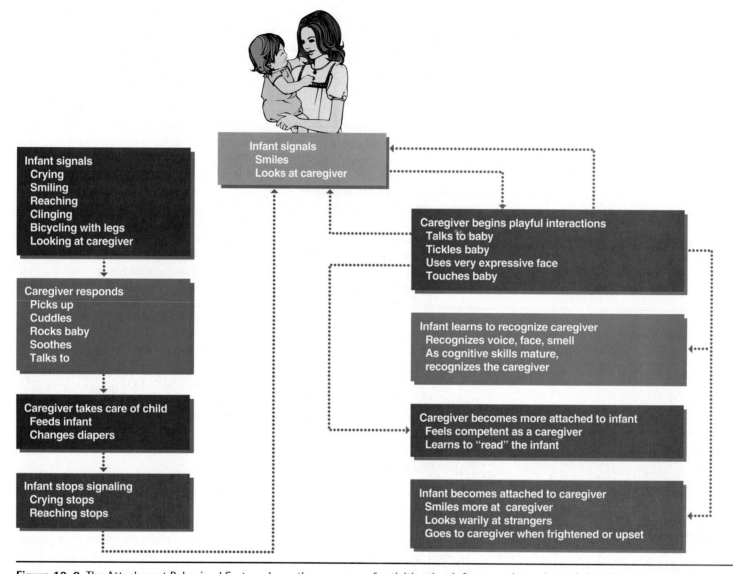

Figure 12–8 The Attachment Behavioral System shows the sequence of activities that infants employ to keep their primary caregivers physically close and to bring about attachment. Early in life, crying is the most effective behavior. Later, though, infants are able to keep the caregiver near through other, more socially appropriate behaviors such as smiling, looking, and reaching. After they are able to walk, children are able to play a more active role in staying close to the caregiver. At the same time, the caregiver's behavior interacts with the baby's activities to promote attachment (Tomlinson-Keasey, 1985).

responsiveness of infants' caregivers to the signals the babies provide, such as cries, smiles, reaching, and clinging. The greater the responsiveness of the caregiver to the child's signals, the more likely it is that the child will become securely attached. Full attachment eventually develops as a result of a complex series of interactions between caregiver and child illustrated in Figure 12-8 (Bell & Ainsworth, 1972). In the course of these interactions, the infant plays as critical and active a role as the caregiver in the formation of the bond. Infants who respond positively to a caregiver produce more positive behavior on the part of the caregiver, which in turn produces an even stronger degree of attachment in the child.

Measuring Attachment

Developmental psychologists have devised a quick and direct way of measuring attachment. Developed by Mary Ainsworth, the *Ainsworth strange situation* consists of a

Attachment theory and research
www.mhhe.com/
feldmanup6-12links

sequence of events involving a child and (typically) his or her mother. Initially, the mother and baby enter an unfamiliar room, and the mother permits the baby to explore while she sits down. An adult stranger then enters the room, after which the mother leaves. The mother then returns, and the stranger leaves. The mother then once again leaves the baby alone, and the stranger returns. Finally, the stranger leaves, and the mother returns (Ainsworth et al., 1978).

Babies' reactions to the experimental situation vary drastically, depending, according to Ainsworth, on their degree of attachment to the mother. One-year-old children who are *securely attached* employ the mother as a kind of home base, exploring independently but returning to her occasionally. When she leaves, they exhibit distress, and they go to her when she returns. *Avoidant* children do not cry when the mother leaves, but they seem to avoid her when she returns, as if they were indifferent to her. *Ambivalent* children display anxiety before they are separated and are upset when the mother leaves, but they might show ambivalent reactions to her return, such as seeking close contact but simultaneously hitting and kicking her. A fourth reaction is *disorganized-disoriented;* these children show inconsistent, often contradictory behavior.

The nature of attachment between children and their mothers has far-reaching consequences for later development. For example, children who are securely attached to their mothers tend to be more socially and emotionally competent than their less securely attached peers, and they are viewed as more cooperative, capable, and playful. Furthermore, research has found that children who are securely attached at age 1 show fewer psychological difficulties when they grow older than do avoidant or ambivalent youngsters (Lewis et al., 1984; Ainsworth & Bowlby, 1991; Greenberg, 1997).

On the other hand, children who lack secure attachment do not always have difficulties later in life, and being securely attached at an early age does not guarantee good adjustment later. Furthermore, some cultures foster higher levels of secure attachment than others. In short, attachment style is related to the social environment that children encounter as they are growing up (Hamilton, 2000; Lewis, Feiring, & Rosenthal, 2000; Waters, Hamilton, & Wienfield, 2000).

The Father's Role

Although early developmental research focused largely on the mother-child relation, more recent research has highlighted the father's role in parenting. With good reason: The number of fathers who are primary caregivers for their children has grown significantly, and fathers play an increasing role in their children's lives. For example, in almost 20 percent of families with children, the father is the parent who stays at home caring for preschoolers (U.S. Bureau of the Census, 1997; Parke, 1996; see Figure 12-9).

When fathers interact with their children, their play is often different from that of mothers. Fathers engage in more physical, rough-and-tumble sorts of activities, whereas

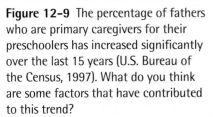

Figure 12-9 The percentage of fathers who are primary caregivers for their preschoolers has increased significantly over the last 15 years (U.S. Bureau of the Census, 1997). What do you think are some factors that have contributed to this trend?

Source: U.S. Bureau of the Census, 1997.

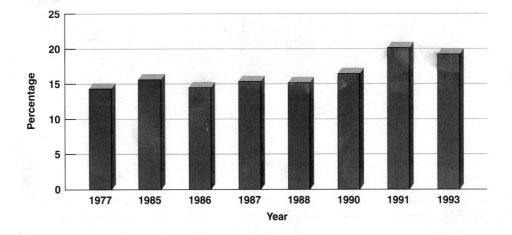

mothers play more verbally oriented and traditional games such as peekaboo. Despite such behavioral differences, attachment between fathers and children can be similar to attachment between mothers and children. In fact, children are capable of forming multiple attachments simultaneously (Lamb, 1982; Larson, Richards, & Perry-Jenkins, 1994; Genuis & Violato, 2000).

Social Relationships with Peers ~similar~

By the time they are 2 years old, children start to become less dependent on their parents and more self-reliant, increasingly preferring to play with friends. Initially, play is relatively independent: Even though they might be sitting side by side, 2-year-olds pay more attention to toys than to one another when playing. Later, however, children actively interact, modifying one another's behavior and later exchanging roles during play (Bukowski, Newcomb, & Hartup, 1996).

As children reach school age, their social interactions begin to follow set patterns, and become more frequent. They might engage in elaborate games involving teams and rigid rules. This play serves purposes other than mere enjoyment. It allows children to become increasingly competent in their social interactions with others. Through play they learn to take the perspective of other people and to infer others' thoughts and feelings, even when these are not directly expressed (Asher & Parker, 1991; Cohen, 1993).

In short, social interaction helps children interpret the meaning of others' behavior and develop the capacity to respond appropriately. Furthermore, children learn physical and emotional self-control: They learn to avoid hitting a playmate who wins at a game, to be polite, and to control their emotional displays and facial expressions (e.g., smiling even when receiving a disappointing gift). Situations that provide children with opportunities for social interaction, then, can enhance their social development (Feldman, 1982, 1993; Crick & Dodge, 1994; Fox, 1994).

The Consequences of Day Care

Research on the importance of social interaction is corroborated by work that examines the benefits of day care, which is an important part of an increasing number of children's lives. For instance, almost 30 percent of preschool children whose mothers work outside the home spend their days in day-care centers. More than 80 percent of infants are cared for by people other than their mothers for part of the day during their first year of life. Most of these infants begin day care before the age of 4 months and are enrolled for almost 30 hours per week (NICHD Early Child Care Research Network, 1997; National Research Council, 2000; see Figure 12-10).

Do out-of-the-home child-care arrangements benefit children's development? If they are of high quality, they can. According to the results of a large study supported by the U.S. National Institute of Child Health and Development (NICHD), children who attend high-quality child-care centers might not only do as well as children who stay at home with their parents, but in some respects might do better. Children in child care are generally more considerate and sociable than other children, and they interact more positively with teachers. They can also be more compliant and regulate their own behavior more effectively, and their mothers show increased sensitivity to their children (Lamb, 1996; NICHD Early Child Care Research Network, 1997, 1998, 1999).

In addition, especially for children from poor or disadvantaged homes, child care in specially enriched environments—those with many toys, books, a variety of children, and high-quality care providers—often is more intellectually stimulating than the home environment. Such child care can lead to increased intellectual achievement, demonstrated in higher IQ scores and better language development. In fact, children in child-care centers are sometimes found to score higher on tests of cognitive abilities than

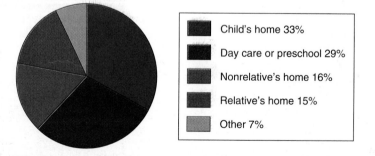

Figure 12-10 Almost 30 percent of children younger than 5 years of age whose mothers work outside the home spend their days in day care or preschool centers, while the remainder are cared for in their own or someone else's home.

Source: U.S. Bureau of the Census, 1997.

Child's home 33%

Day care or preschool 29%

Nonrelative's home 16%

Relative's home 15%

Other 7%

"Please, Jason. Don't you want to grow up to be an autonomous person?"

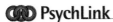

PsychLink

Comprehensive information on parenting
www.mhhe.com/
feldmanup6-12links

authoritarian parents: Parents who are rigid and punitive and value unquestioning obedience from their children

permissive parents: Parents who give their children lax or inconsistent direction and, although warm, require little of them

authoritative parents: Parents who are firm, set clear limits, reason with their children, and explain things to them

uninvolved parents: Parents who show little interest in their children and are emotionally detached from them

children who are cared for by their mothers or by sitters or home day-care providers, and these effects last into adulthood (Wilgoren, 1999; Burchinal et al., 2000).

On the other hand, the outcomes of child care are not universally positive. Children can feel less secure when they are placed in low-quality child care or in multiple child-care arrangements. Furthermore, although the findings are not consistent, some research suggests that infants who are involved in outside care more than twenty hours a week in their first year show less secure attachment to their mothers than those who have not been in day care (Belsky & Rovine, 1988; NICHD Early Child Care Research Network, 1997, 1999).

The key to the success of day care is its quality. High-quality day care produces benefits; low-quality day care provides little or no gain, and can even hinder children's development. In short, significant benefits result from the social interaction and intellectual stimulation provided by high-quality day-care centers—particularly for children from impoverished environments (Harvey, 1999; Burchinal et al., 2000; Campbell, Lamb, & Hwang, 2000).

Parenting Styles and Social Development

Parents' child-rearing practices are critical in shaping their children's social competence. According to classic research by developmental psychologist Diana Baumrind, there are four main parenting styles. **Authoritarian parents** are rigid and punitive and value unquestioning obedience from their children. They have strict standards and discourage expressions of disagreement. **Permissive parents** give their children relaxed or inconsistent direction and, although warm, require little of them. In contrast, **authoritative parents** are firm, setting limits for their children. As the children get older, these parents try to reason with and explain things to them. They also set clear goals and encourage their children's independence. Finally, **uninvolved parents** show little interest in their children. They are emotionally detached, and they view parenting as nothing more than providing food, clothing, and shelter for children. In its most extreme form, uninvolved parents are guilty of neglect, a form of child abuse (Baumrind, 1971, 1980). Table 12-3 summarizes the four parenting styles.

As you might expect, the four parenting styles seem to produce very different kinds of behavior in children (although there are, of course, many exceptions). Children of authoritarian parents tend to be unsociable, unfriendly, and relatively withdrawn. Permissive parents' children tends to be immature, moody, and dependent and have low self-control. The children of authoritative parents fare best: Their social skills are high—they are likable, self-reliant, independent, and cooperative. Worst off are children of uninvolved parents; they feel unloved and emotionally detached, and their physical and cognitive development is impeded (Howes, Galinsky, & Kontos, 1998; Saarni, 1999).

Table 12-3 The Four Main Parenting Styles

Parenting Style	Parent Behavior	Children's Behavior
Authoritarian	Rigid, punitive, strict standards	Unsociable, unfriendly, withdrawn
Permissive	Lax, inconsistent, undemanding	Immature, moody, dependent, low self-control
Authoritative	Firm, sets limits and goals, uses reasoning, encourages independence	Good social skills, likable, self-reliant, independent
Uninvolved	Detached emotionally, sees role as only providing food, clothing, and shelter	Indifferent, rejecting behavior

Source: Baumrind, 1971.

Before we rush to congratulate authoritative parents and condemn authoritarian, permissive, and uninvolved ones, it is important to note that many nonauthoritative parents produce children who are perfectly well adjusted. Moreover, as we'll discuss further in Chapter 14, children are born with a particular **temperament**—a basic, innate disposition. Some children are naturally easy-going and cheerful, whereas others are irritable and fussy. The kind of temperament a baby is born with might tend to elicit a particular parenting style (Goldsmith & Harman, 1994; Kendler, 1996; Chess, 1997).

Furthermore, the findings regarding child-rearing styles apply primarily to U.S. society, with its emphasis on children learning to be independent and not relying too heavily on their parents. In contrast, Japanese parents encourage dependence in order to promote the values of cooperation and community life. These differences in cultural values result in very different philosophies of child rearing. For example, Japanese mothers believe it is a punishment to make a young child sleep alone, so many children sleep next to their mothers throughout infancy and toddlerhood (Kagan, Kearsley, & Zelazo, 1978; Miyake, Chen, & Campos, 1985; Kawasaki et al., 1994).

temperament: Basic, innate disposition

In sum, a child's upbringing is a consequence of the child-rearing philosophy parents hold, the specific practices they use, and the nature of their own and their child's personality. As is the case with other aspects of development, then, behavior is a function of a complex interaction of environmental and genetic factors.

Erikson's Theory of Psychosocial Development

In trying to trace the course of social development, some theorists have considered how society and culture present challenges that change as the individual matures. Following this path, psychoanalyst Erik Erikson developed one of the most comprehensive theories of social development. According to Erikson (1963), the developmental changes occurring throughout our lives can be viewed as a series of eight stages of psychosocial development, of which four occur during childhood. **Psychosocial development** involves changes in our interactions and understanding of one another as well as in our knowledge and understanding of ourselves as members of society.

psychosocial development: Development of individuals' interactions and understanding of each other and of their knowledge and understanding of themselves as members of society

Erikson suggests that passage through each of the stages necessitates resolution of a crisis or conflict. Accordingly, each of Erikson's stages is represented as a pairing of the most positive and most negative aspects of the crisis of the period. Although each crisis is never resolved entirely—life becomes increasingly complicated as we grow older—it needs to be resolved sufficiently so that we are equipped to deal with demands made during the following stage of development.

In the first stage of psychosocial development, the **trust-versus-mistrust stage** (birth to 1½ years), infants develop feelings of trust if their physical requirements and psychological needs for attachment are consistently met and their interactions with the world are generally positive. On the other hand, inconsistent care and unpleasant interactions with others can lead to the development of mistrust and leave the infant unable to meet the challenges required in the next stage of development.

trust-versus-mistrust stage: According to Erikson, the first stage of psychosocial development, occurring from birth to 18 months of age, during which time infants develop feelings of trust or lack of trust

In the second stage, the **autonomy-versus-shame-and-doubt stage** (1½ to 3 years), toddlers develop independence and autonomy if exploration and freedom are encouraged, or they experience shame, self-doubt, and unhappiness if they are overly restricted and protected. According to Erikson, the key to the development of autonomy during this period is for the child's caregivers to provide the appropriate amount of control. If parents provide too much control, children will be unable to assert themselves and develop their own sense of control over their environment; if parents provide too little control, children themselves become overly demanding and controlling.

autonomy-versus-shame-and-doubt stage: The period during which, according to Erikson, toddlers (ages 18 months to 3 years) develop independence and autonomy if exploration and freedom are encouraged, or shame and self-doubt if they are restricted and overprotected

initiative-versus-guilt stage: According to Erikson, the period during which children ages 3 to 6 years experience conflict between independence of action and the sometimes negative results of that action

The next crisis that children face is that of the **initiative-versus-guilt stage** (ages 3 to 6). In this stage, the major conflict is between children's desire to act independently and the guilt that comes from the unintended and unexpected consequences of their behavior. Children in this period come to understand that they are persons in their own right, and they begin to make decisions about their behavior. If parents react positively to their child's attempts at independence, they help their child resolve the initiative-versus-guilt crisis positively.

industry-versus-inferiority stage: According to Erikson, the last stage of childhood, during which children aged 6 to 12 years either develop positive social interactions with others or feel inadequate and become less sociable

The fourth and last stage of childhood is the **industry-versus-inferiority stage** (ages 6 to 12). During this period, successful psychosocial development is characterized by increasing competency in all areas, including social interactions and academic skills. In contrast, difficulties in this stage lead to feelings of failure and inadequacy.

Erikson's theory suggests that psychosocial development continues throughout life, and he proposes that there are four more crises to face past childhood (which we discuss in the next chapter). Although his theory has been criticized on several grounds—such as the imprecision of the concepts he employs and his greater emphasis on male development than female development—it remains influential and is one of the few theories that encompass the entire life span.

Evaluate

1. Researchers studying newborns use _____, or the decrease in the response to a stimulus that occurs after repeated presentations of the same stimulus, as an indicator of a baby's interest.
2. The emotional bond that develops between a child and its caregiver is known as _____.
3. Children develop an attachment to their mothers only; the father's role is important, but children do not become attached to their fathers. True or false?
4. Match the parenting style with its definition:

   1. Permissive
   2. Authoritative
   3. Authoritarian
   4. Uninvolved

   a. Rigid; highly punitive; demand obedience
   b. Give little direction; lax on obedience
   c. Firm but fair; try to explain their decisions
   d. Emotionally detached and unloving

5. Erikson's theory of _____ development involves a series of eight stages, each of which must be resolved in order for a person to develop optimally.

Rethink

1. In what ways might the infant's major reflexes—the rooting, sucking, gagging, startle, and Babinski reflexes—have had survival value, from an evolutionary perspective? Does the infant's ability to mimic the facial expressions of adults have a similar value?

2. Do you think the growing trend toward greater parental involvement by fathers will have effects on the child-rearing styles to which children are exposed? Will it affect attachment? Psychosocial development? Why or why not?

Answers to Evaluate Questions

1. habituation 2. attachment 3. False; attachment to a father can be as strong as attachment to a mother 4. 1-b; 2-c; 3-a; 4-d 5. psychosocial

Prepare

How does cognitive development proceed during childhood?

Organize

Cognitive Development

Cognitive Development: Children's Thinking About the World

Suppose you had two drinking glasses of different shapes—one short and broad, and one tall and thin. Now imagine that you filled the short, broad one with soda about halfway and then poured the liquid from that glass into the tall one. The soda appears to fill about three-quarters of the second glass. If someone asked you whether there was more soda in the second glass than there had been in the first, what would you say?

You might think that such a simple question hardly deserves an answer; of course there is no difference in the amount of soda in the two glasses. However, most 4-year-olds would be likely to say that there is more soda in the second glass. If you then poured the soda back into the short glass, they would say there is now less soda than there was in the taller glass.

Why are young children confused by this problem? The reason is not immediately obvious. Anyone who has observed preschoolers must be impressed by how far they

have progressed from the early stages of development. They speak with ease, know the alphabet, count, play complex games, use tape players, tell stories, and communicate quite ably. Yet, despite this seeming sophistication, there are deep gaps in children's understanding of the world. Some theorists have suggested that children are incapable of understanding certain ideas and concepts until they reach a particular stage of **cognitive development**—the process by which a child's understanding of the world changes as a function of age and experience. In contrast to the theories of physical and social development discussed earlier (such as those of Erikson), theories of cognitive development seek to explain the quantitative and qualitative intellectual advances that occur during development.

Piaget's Theory of Cognitive Development

No theory of cognitive development has had more impact than that of Swiss psychologist Jean Piaget. Piaget (1970) suggested that children throughout the world proceed through a series of four stages in a fixed order. He maintained that these stages differ not only in the *quantity* of information acquired at each stage, but also in the *quality* of knowledge and understanding. Taking an interactionist point of view, he suggested that movement from one stage to the next occurred when the child reached an appropriate level of maturation *and* was exposed to relevant types of experiences. Without such experiences, children were assumed to be incapable of reaching their highest level of cognitive growth.

Piaget's four stages are the sensorimotor, preoperational, concrete operational, and formal operational stages (see Table 12-4). Let's examine each of them and the approximate ages they span.

Sensorimotor Stage: Birth to 2 years During the **sensorimotor stage,** children's understanding of the world is based primarily on touching, sucking, chewing, shaking, and manipulating objects. In the initial part of this stage, children have relatively little competence in representing the environment using images, language, or other kinds of symbols. Consequently, infants have no awareness of objects or people that are not immediately present at a given moment, lacking what Piaget calls **object permanence.** Object permanence is the awareness that objects—and people—continue to exist even if they are out of sight.

How can we know that infants lack object permanence? Although we cannot ask them, we can observe their reactions when a toy that they are playing with is hidden under a blanket. Until the age of about 9 months, children will make no attempt to locate the toy. However, soon after this age they will begin to search actively for the object

cognitive development: The process by which a child's understanding of the world changes as a function of age and experience

PsychLink
Theory of cognitive development
www.mhhe.com/
feldmanup6–12links

sensorimotor stage: According to Piaget, the stage from birth to 2 years, during which a child has little competence in representing the environment using images, language, or other symbols

object permanence: The awareness that objects—and people—continue to exist even if they are out of sight

Table 12-4 Piaget's Stages of Cognitive Development

Stage	Approximate Age Range	Major Characteristics
Sensorimotor	Birth–2 years	Development of object permanence, development of motor skills, little or no capacity for symbolic representation
Preoperational	2–7 years	Development of language and symbolic thinking, egocentric thinking
Concrete operational	7–12 years	Development of conservation, mastery of concept of reversibility
Formal operational	12–adulthood	Development of logical and abstract thinking

Children who have not mastered the principle of conservation assume that the volume of a liquid increases when it is poured from a short, wide container to a tall, thin one. What other tasks might a child under 7 have difficulty comprehending?

preoperational stage: According to Piaget, the period from 2 to 7 years of age which is characterized by language development

egocentric thought: A way of thinking in which the child views the world entirely from his or her own perspective

principle of conservation: The knowledge that the quantity of a substance remains the same even though its shape or other aspects of its physical appearance might change

concrete operational stage: According to Piaget, the period from 7 to 12 years of age, which is characterized by logical thought and a loss of egocentrism

when it is hidden, indicating that they have developed a mental representation of the toy. Object permanence, then, is a critical development during the sensorimotor stage.

Preoperational Stage: 2 to 7 years   The most important development during the **preoperational stage** is the use of language, which we described in more detail in Chapter 8. Children develop internal representational systems that allow them to describe people, events, and feelings. They even use symbols in play, pretending, for example, that a book pushed across the floor is a car.

Although children's thinking is more advanced in this stage than in the earlier sensorimotor stage, it is still qualitatively inferior to that of adults. We see this when we observe the preoperational child using **egocentric thought,** a way of thinking in which the child views the world entirely from her or his own perspective. Preoperational children think that everyone shares their own perspective and knowledge. Thus, children's stories and explanations to adults can be maddeningly uninformative, as they are described without any context. For example, a preoperational child might start a story with "He wouldn't let me go," neglecting to mention who "he" is or where the storyteller wanted to go. Egocentric thinking is also seen when children at the preoperational stage play hiding games. For instance, 3-year-olds frequently hide with their faces against a wall, covering their eyes—although they are still in plain view. It seems to them that if *they* cannot see, no one else will be able to see them, because they assume that others share their view.

Another deficiency of preoperational children is demonstrated by their inability to understand the **principle of conservation,** which is the knowledge that quantity can remain the same when shape and other aspects of physical appearance change. Children who have not mastered this concept do not know, for instance, that the amount or volume of a substance (such as a lump of clay) does not change when its shape or configuration is changed. The question about pouring liquid between two glasses—one short and broad, the other tall and thin—with which we began our discussion of cognitive development illustrates this point quite clearly. Children who do not understand the principle of conservation invariably state that the amount of liquid changes as it is poured back and forth. They cannot comprehend that a transformation in appearance does not imply a transformation in amount. Instead, it seems just as reasonable to the child that there is a change in quantity as it does to the adult that there is no change.

There are a number of other ways, some quite startling, in which their failure to understand the principle of conservation affects children's responses. Research demonstrates that principles that are obvious to and unquestioned by adults can be completely misunderstood by children during the preoperational period, and that it is not until the next stage of cognitive development that children grasp the concept of conservation. (Several examples of conservation are illustrated in Figure 12-11.)

Concrete Operational Stage: 7 to 12 years   The beginning of the **concrete operational stage** is marked by mastery of the principle of conservation. However, there are still some aspects of conservation—such as conservation of weight and volume—that are not fully understood for a number of years.

During the concrete operational stage, children develop the ability to think in a more logical manner, and they begin to overcome some of the egocentrism characteristic of the preoperational period. One of the major principles that children grasp during this stage is reversibility, the idea that some changes can be undone by reversing an earlier action. For example, they can understand that when a ball of clay is rolled into a long sausage shape, it is possible to recreate the original ball by reversing the action. They can even conceptualize this principle in their heads, without having to see the action performed before them.

Although children make important advances in their logical capabilities during the concrete operational stage, there is still one major limitation in their thinking: They are

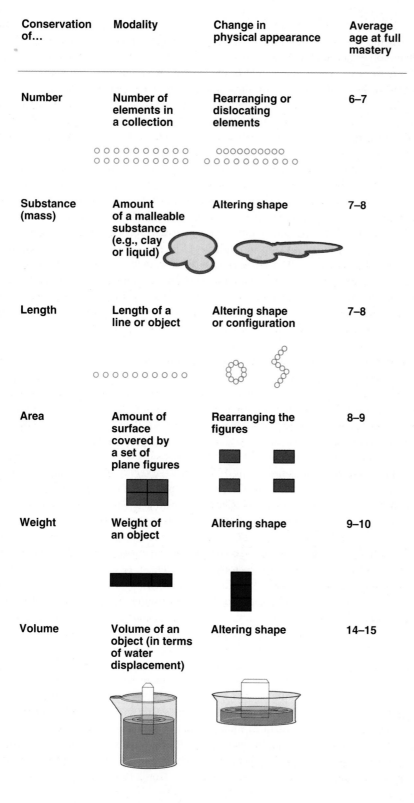

Conservation of...	Modality	Change in physical appearance	Average age at full mastery
Number	Number of elements in a collection	Rearranging or dislocating elements	6–7
Substance (mass)	Amount of a malleable substance (e.g., clay or liquid)	Altering shape	7–8
Length	Length of a line or object	Altering shape or configuration	7–8
Area	Amount of surface covered by a set of plane figures	Rearranging the figures	8–9
Weight	Weight of an object	Altering shape	9–10
Volume	Volume of an object (in terms of water displacement)	Altering shape	14–15

Figure 12-11 These tests are frequently used to assess whether children have learned the principle of conservation across a variety of dimensions (Adapted from Schickendanz, Schickendanz, & Forsyth, 1982). Do you think children in the preoperational stage can be *taught* to avoid conservation mistakes before the typical age of mastery?

From Judith A. Schickendanz, et al., *Understanding children and adolescents*, 4/e © 2001. Copyright © 2001 by Allyn & Bacon. Reprinted by permission.

largely bound to the concrete, physical reality of the world. For the most part, they have difficulty understanding questions of an abstract or hypothetical nature.

Formal Operational Stage: 12 years to adulthood The **formal operational stage** produces a new kind of thinking that is abstract, formal, and logical. Thinking is no longer tied to events observed in the environment but makes use of logical techniques to solve problems.

formal operational stage: According to Piaget, the period from age 12 to adulthood, which is characterized by abstract thought

Jean Piaget

The emergence of formal operational thinking is illustrated by how children approach the "pendulum problem," devised by Piaget (Piaget & Inhelder, 1958). The problem solver is asked to figure out what determines how fast a pendulum swings. Is it the length of the string, the weight of the pendulum, or the force with which the pendulum is pushed? (For the record, the answer is the length of the string.)

Children in the concrete operational stage approach the problem haphazardly, without a logical or rational plan of action. For example, they might simultaneously change the length of the string *and* the weight on the string *and* the force with which they push the pendulum. Because they are varying all factors at once, they are unable to tell which factor is the critical one. In contrast, people in the formal operational stage approach the problem systematically. Acting as if they were scientists conducting an experiment, they examine the effects of changes in just one variable at a time. This ability to rule out competing possibilities is characteristic of formal operational thought.

Although formal operational thought emerges during the teenage years, many individuals use this type of thinking infrequently. Moreover, it appears that many people never reach this stage at all; most studies show that only 40 to 60 percent of college students and adults fully reach it, with some estimates running as low as 25 percent in the general population. In addition, in certain cultures—particularly those that are less technologically sophisticated than most Western societies—almost no one reaches the formal operational stage (Chandler, 1976; Keating & Clark, 1980; Super, 1980).

Stages versus continuous development: Is Piaget right?   No other theorist has given us as comprehensive a theory of cognitive development as Piaget. Still, many contemporary theorists suggest that a better explanation of how children develop cognitively can be provided by theories that do not subscribe to a stage approach. For instance, children are not always consistent in their performance of tasks that—if Piaget's theory were accurate—ought to be performed equally well at a given stage (Siegler, 1994).

Furthermore, some developmental psychologists suggest that cognitive development proceeds in a more continuous fashion than Piaget's stage theory implies. They propose that cognitive development is primarily quantitative in nature, rather than qualitative. They argue that although there are differences in when, how, and to what extent a child is capable of using given cognitive abilities—reflecting quantitative changes—the underlying cognitive processes change relatively little with age (Gelman & Baillargeon, 1983; Case & Okamoto, 1996).

Piaget also underestimated the age at which infants and children are able to understand specific concepts and principles; in fact, they seem to be more sophisticated in their cognitive abilities than Piaget believed. For instance, some evidence suggests that infants as young as 5 months have rudimentary mathematical skills (Wynn, 1995, 2000).

Despite such criticisms, most developmental psychologists agree that, although the processes that underlie changes in cognitive abilities might not unfold in the manner suggested by his theory, Piaget has generally provided us with an accurate account of age-related changes in cognitive development. Moreover, the influence of his theory has been enormous. For example, Piaget suggests that increases in cognitive performance cannot be attained unless both cognitive readiness brought about by maturation *and* appropriate environmental stimulation are present. This view has been influential in determining the nature and structure of educational curricula and how children are taught (see the *Psychology at Work* box on page 380). Piaget's theory and methods have also been used to investigate issues surrounding animal cognition, such as whether primates show object permanence (they seem to; Gagnon & Dore, 1994; Funk, 1996).

Information-Processing Approaches: Charting Children's Mental Programs

If cognitive development does not proceed as a series of stages, as Piaget suggested, what *does* underlie the enormous growth in children's cognitive abilities that is apparent to even the most untutored eye? To many developmental psychologists, changes in **information processing**—the ways people take in, use, and store information—account for cognitive development (Siegler, 1998).

information processing: The way people take in, use, and store information

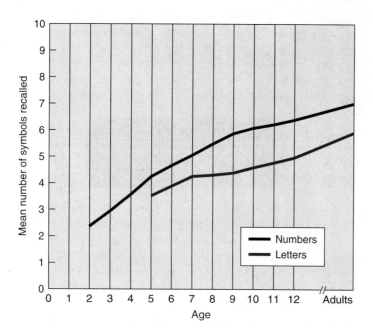

Figure 12-12 Memory span increases with age for both numbers and letters. Source: Adapted from Dempster, 1981.

According to this approach, quantitative changes occur in children's ability to organize and manipulate information. From this perspective, children become increasingly adept at information processing, much as a computer program might become more sophisticated as a programmer modifies it on the basis of experience. Information-processing approaches consider the kinds of "mental programs" children invoke when approaching problems (Reyna, 1997).

Several significant changes occur in children's information-processing capabilities. For one thing, speed of processing increases with age, as some abilities become more automatic. The speed at which stimuli can be scanned, recognized, and compared with other stimuli increases with age. With increasing age, children can pay attention to stimuli longer and discriminate between different stimuli more readily, and they are less easily distracted (Jensen & Neff, 1993; Mayr, Kliegl, & Krampe, 1996; Miller & Vernon, 1997).

Memory also improves dramatically with age. You may recall from Chapter 7 that adults are able to keep seven, plus or minus two, chunks of information in short-term memory. In contrast, preschoolers can hold only two or three chunks; 5-year-olds can hold four; and 7-year-olds can hold five. The size of chunks also grows with age, as does the sophistication and organization of knowledge stored in memory. Still, memory capabilities are impressive at a very early age: Even before they can speak, infants can remember for months events in which they were active participants, according to recent research (Bjorklund, 1985; Rovee-Collier, 1993; Bauer, 1996; see Figure 12-12).

Finally, improvement in information processing is tied to advances in **metacognition**, an awareness and understanding of one's own cognitive processes. Metacognition involves the planning, monitoring, and revising of cognitive strategies. Younger children, who lack an awareness of their own cognitive processes, are often ignorant of their incapabilities. Thus, when they misunderstand others, they might fail to recognize their own errors. It is only later, when metacognitive abilities become more sophisticated, that children are able to know when they *don't* understand. Such increasing sophistication reflects a change in children's *theory of mind,* their knowledge and beliefs about the way the mind operates (Flavell, 1993; Chandler & Lalonde, 1996; Taylor, 1996).

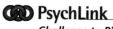 **PsychLink**

Challenge to Piaget's views
www.mhhe.com/
feldmanup6-12links

metacognition: An awareness and understanding of one's own cognitive processes

Vygotsky's View of Cognitive Development: Considering Culture

According to Russian developmental psychologist Lev Vygotsky, the culture in which we are raised has an important influence on our cognitive development. In Vygotsky's

Psychology at Work

Michael J. Morrier

Preschool Coordinator

Education: B.A., psychology, University of Massachusetts at Amherst; M.A., special education, University of Georgia

Home: Decatur, Georgia

Michael J. Morrier

Emory University's Walden Early Childhood Program—one of the premier preschools in the United States—not only prepares young children for primary education, but also provides a means for children with developmental disabilities to become successfully integrated into a school setting, according to Michael Morrier, early childhood and research coordinator for the program.

> "We use their interests as the topics of our teaching and their learning . . . Everything is individualized for each child."

"The program is divided into three sections: the toddler section, which has children from 18 months to 3 years; the preschool, with children aged 3 to 4; and the prekindergarten, with children aged 4 to 5. In each classroom a third of the children are diagnosed with autism, while two-thirds are typically developing children," Morrier explains.

"We use their interests as the topics of our teaching and their learning," he says. "The underlying curriculum is focused on language development, social development, and independence in daily living skills. Everything is individualized for each child."

The Walden program encourages children to interact with one another, according to Morrier. If the children want to go for a snack, they are asked to invite another child to go with them; if they want to play, they ask another child to join in.

"We also are doing research on children's social interests," he notes. "We look at how typical kids develop socially across the age range, and then we look at the group with autism to see what is different.

"Children with autism tend to form three different groups," Morrier explains. "One group avoids interaction entirely; the second group will interact, but only with specific toys, or with toys in general and no people; and the third group appears to want to interact, but the kids in this group don't know what to do, or how to go about it. They want to play, but may end up hitting another child."

When the children leave the program and enter kindergarten they encounter a variety of support systems that differ from the intensive attention they received at Walden. Morrier says, "But all of our students—including the ones with autism—have gone on and have done well."

PsychLink

Discussion of Vygotsky's theory
www.mhhe.com/
feldmanup6-12links

zone of proximal development (ZPD):
According to Vygotsky, the level at which a child can almost, but not fully, comprehend or perform a task on her or his own.

view, which is increasingly influential, the focus on individual performance of both Piagetian and information-processing approaches is misplaced. Instead, Vygotsky holds, we cannot understand cognitive development without taking into account the social aspects of learning (Vygotsky, 1926/1997; Beilin, 1996; Daniels, 1996).

Vygotsky argues that cognitive development occurs as a consequence of social interactions in which children work with others to jointly solve problems. Through such interactions, children increase their cognitive skills and gain the ability to function intellectually on their own. More specifically, children's cognitive abilities increase when they are exposed to information that falls within their zone of proximal development. The **zone of proximal development,** or **ZPD,** is the level at which a child can almost, but not fully, comprehend or perform a task on his or her own. When children encounter information that falls within the ZPD, they are able to increase their understanding or master a new task. On the other hand, if the information lies outside children's ZPD, they will not be able to master it (Blank & White, 1999; see Figure 12-13).

In short, cognitive development occurs when parents, teachers, or skilled peers assist the child by presenting information that is both new and within the ZPD. This type of assistance is called *scaffolding,* the support for learning and problem solving that encourages independence and growth. Vygotsky claims that scaffolding not only promotes the solution of specific problems, it also aids in the development of overall cognitive abilities (Bruner, 1983; Steward, 1995).

More than other approaches to cognitive development, Vygotsky's theory considers how the specific cultural and social context of society affects intellectual growth. How a child understands the world is seen as an outgrowth of interactions with parents, peers, and other members of the child's culture. Furthermore, as we see next, cultural influences on cognitive development also result in significant differences in scholastic success.

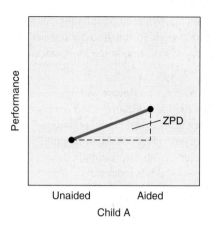

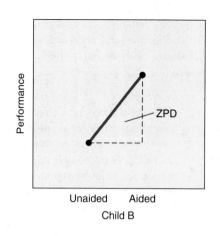

Figure 12-13 While the performances of the two children working at a task without aid are similar, the second child benefits more from aid and thus has a larger zone of proximal development (ZPD).

EXPLORING DIVERSITY

Supporting Children's School Achievement: The Asian Success Story

By the end of public schooling, the average student in Japan achieves at a higher level than the average student in the United States. It doesn't start out that way: In first grade, only minor differences exist between Japanese and American student performance. However, by the fifth grade, the average Japanese student has pulled ahead of her or his American counterpart, and remains ahead through high school (Stevenson & Lee, 1990).

What accounts for the exceptional success of Asian students? One factor is that Asian children face greater cultural pressure to achieve in school. For instance, Japanese and Korean parents spend a great deal of time helping their children with schoolwork, and they stress that academic success is their children's most important task. Asian mothers also hold higher standards for their children's school performance than do mothers in the U.S.

Superior Asian school performance is also due to differences in parental attributions to explain their children's school success. Drawing on the writings of the great Chinese philosopher Confucius, Asian parents stress the importance of effort, hard work, and perseverance in school. At the same time, they minimize the effects of individual abilities. To the Asian parent, then, all children have pretty much the same level of underlying ability; what determines school success is how hard children work. Parents in the U.S. generally take a quite different view: They emphasize the importance of inborn ability, believing that children vary considerably in their abilities and that ability plays a primary role in school performance. At the same time, American parents downplay the role of effort in producing school success.

The impact of this philosophical difference is considerable. When students do not do well in school, parents in the United States might conclude that their children simply don't have sufficient ability. As a result, they do not push their children to work harder. In contrast, Asian children who perform poorly are typically encouraged to work harder, because greater effort is seen as a means to overcome their academic difficulties (Stevenson, 1992; Stevenson, Chen, & Lee, 1992; Chen & Stevenson, 1995; Tuss, Zimmer, & Ho, 1995).

In sum, the apparently superior academic performance of Asian children seems to rest largely on cultural differences in how parents perceive the causes of school performance, in attitudes about the importance of education, and in the ways children are encouraged to succeed. If these cultural standards and values change, so too will the academic performance of students (Tomasello, 2000).

BEING AN
INFORMED CONSUMER
OF PSYCHOLOGY

Maximizing Children's Competence

Are there ways to maximize a child's competence? Although our examination of the nature-nurture issue makes it clear that genetic background plays a critical role in defining the limits on achievement, it is also clear that environmental factors can enhance the probability of an

individual's fulfilling her or his potential. Research carried out by developmental psychologists has identified several child-rearing practices that are important in maximizing competence (Schulman, 1991; Bornstein, 1995; Masten & Coatsworth, 1998). Among the most crucial are these:

- *Be responsive to children, both emotionally and intellectually.* Parents with high-achieving children are interested in their children's lives and encourage and reinforce their efforts. They are warm and supportive, and act as their children's "personal consultants." They allow children to make mistakes, providing consistent support.
- *Let children explore their environment.* Provide children with the maximum opportunity to investigate their surroundings. For instance, if a room can be made safe, a toddler should not be restricted to a playpen.
- *Encourage children to develop close relationships with others.* Provide them with the opportunity to play with a variety of other children.
- *Use descriptive and accurate language when speaking with children.* Avoid "baby talk," and speak *with* children, not *at* them. Ask questions, listen carefully to children's responses, and provide further feedback.
- *Don't push children too hard.* Despite the rigors and demands of modern life, childhood should be a time of enjoyment and not merely a prelude to adulthood. Some psychologists believe that we are producing a society of "hurried children" whose lives revolve around rigid schedules and who are so pressed to succeed that their childhood is filled with stress (Elkind, 1988). Remember that—as in the rest of the life span—it is important to step back and set priorities regarding what is and is not most important.

Evaluate

1. _____ suggested four stages of cognitive development, each of which is dependent on maturational and environmental factors.
2. Match the stage of development with the thinking style characteristic of the stage:

   1. Egocentric thought   a. Sensorimotor
   2. Object permanence   b. Formal operational
   3. Abstract reasoning   c. Preoperational
   4. Conservation; reversibility   d. Concrete operational

3. Current research suggests that child development might proceed in a continuous fashion, rather than in stages as suggested by Piaget. True or false?
4. _____ theories of development suggest that how children handle information is critical to their development.
5. According to Vygotsky, information that is within a child's _____ ____ _____ _____ is most likely to result in cognitive development.

Answers to Evaluate Questions

1. Piaget 2. 1-c; 2-a; 3-b; 4-d 3. True 4. Information-processing 5. zone of proximal development

Rethink

1. According to Piaget's theory, children must reach a certain level of maturity before they can learn particular kinds of information. What might be the pros and cons of exposing a child to more complex material at an early age? What might information-processing theory have to say about this?
2. Do you think the widespread use of IQ testing in the United States contributes to parents' views that their children's academic success is largely due to their children's innate intelligence? Why? Would it be possible (or desirable) to change this view?

How do psychologists study the influences of hereditary and environmental factors in development?

- Developmental psychology is the branch of psychology that studies growth and change throughout life. One fundamental question is how much developmental change is due to heredity and how much is due to environment—the nature-nurture issue. Heredity seems to define the upper limits of our growth and change, whereas the environment affects the degree to which the upper limits are reached. (p. 354)
- Cross-sectional research compares people of different ages with one another at the same point in time. Longitudinal research traces the behavior of one or more participants as the participants become older. Finally, cross-sequential research combines the two methods by taking several different age groups and examining them over several points in time. (p. 357)

What is the nature of development prior to birth?

- At the moment of conception, a male's sperm cell and a female's egg cell unite, with each contributing to the new individual's genetic makeup. The union of sperm and egg produces a zygote, which contains 23 pairs of chromosomes—with one member of each pair coming from the father and the other from the mother. Each chromosome contains genes, through which genetic information is transmitted. Genes, which are composed of DNA sequences, are the "software" that programs the future development of the body's hardware. (p. 357)
- After 2 weeks the zygote becomes an embryo. By 8 weeks, the embryo has become a fetus and is responsive to touch and other stimulation. At about 24 weeks it reaches the age of viability, which means it might survive if born prematurely. A fetus is normally born after 38 weeks of pregnancy, weighing around 7 pounds and measuring about 20 inches. (p. 359)
- Genes affect not only physical attributes but also a wide array of personal characteristics, such as cognitive abilities, personality traits, and psychological disorders. (p. 361)

What factors affect a child during the mother's pregnancy?

- Genetic abnormalities produce birth defects such as phenylketonuria (PKU), sickle-cell anemia, Tay-Sachs disease, and Down syndrome. Among the prenatal environmental influences on fetal growth are the mother's nutrition, illnesses, drug intake, and birth complications. (p. 362)

What are the major competencies of newborns?

- Newborns, or neonates, have rooting, sucking, gag, startle, and Babinski reflexes. (p. 364)
- Sensory abilities also increase rapidly; infants can distinguish color, depth, sound, tastes, and smells relatively soon after birth. (p. 365)

What are the milestones of physical and social development during childhood?

- After birth, physical development is rapid; children typically triple their weight in their first year. (p. 367)
- Social development in infancy is marked by the phenomenon of attachment—the positive emotional bond between a child and a particular individual. Attachment is measured in the laboratory using the Ainsworth strange situation and is related to later social and emotional adjustment. (p. 368)

- As children become older, the nature of their social interactions with peers changes. Initially children play relatively independently, but their play becomes increasingly cooperative. (p. 371)
- The different child-rearing styles include authoritarian, permissive, authoritative, and uninvolved. (p. 372)
- According to Erikson, eight stages of psychosocial development involve people's changing interactions and understanding of themselves and others. During childhood, the four stages are trust versus mistrust (birth to 18 months), autonomy versus shame and doubt (18 months to 3 years), initiative versus guilt (3 to 6 years), and industry versus inferiority (6 to 12 years). (p. 373)

How does cognitive development proceed during childhood?

- Piaget's theory suggests that cognitive development proceeds through four stages in which qualitative changes occur in thinking: the sensorimotor stage (birth to 2 years), the preoperational stage (2 to 7 years), the concrete operational stage (7 to 12 years), and the formal operational period (12 years to adulthood). (p. 375)
- Although Piaget's theory has had an enormous influence, some theorists suggest that development is more continuous and that the changes occurring within and between stages are reflective of quantitative advances in cognitive development rather than qualitative changes in thinking. (p. 378)
- Information-processing approaches suggest that quantitative changes occur in children's ability to organize and manipulate information about the world, such as significant increases in speed of processing, attention span, and memory. In addition, there are advances in metacognition, the awareness and understanding of one's own cognitive processes. (p. 378)
- Vygotsky argued that children's cognitive development occurs as a consequence of social interactions in which children and others work together to solve problems. (p. 379)

Key Terms and Concepts

developmental psychology (p. 354)
nature-nurture issue (p. 355)
identical twins (p. 356)
cross-sectional research (p. 357)
longitudinal research (p. 357)
cross-sequential research (p. 357)
chromosomes (p. 357)
genes (p. 358)
zygote (p. 358)
embryo (p. 359)
fetus (p. 359)
age of viability (p. 360)
teratogens (p. 362)
neonate (p. 364)
reflexes (p. 364)
habituation (p. 365)
attachment (p. 368)
authoritarian parents (p. 372)
permissive parents (p. 372)
authoritative parents (p. 372)

uninvolved parents (p. 372)
temperament (p. 373)
psychosocial development (p. 373)
trust-versus-mistrust stage (p. 373)
autonomy-versus-shame-and-doubt stage (p. 373)
initiative-versus-guilt stage (p. 374)
industry-versus-inferiority stage (p. 374)
cognitive development (p. 375)
sensorimotor stage (p. 375)
object permanence (p. 375)
preoperational stage (p. 376)
egocentric thought (p. 376)
principle of conservation (p. 376)
concrete operational stage (p. 376)
formal operational stage (p. 377)
information processing (p. 378)
metacognition (p. 379)
zone of proximal development (ZPD) (p. 380)

Psychology on the Web

1. On the Web, check out the current status of the Human Genome Project. Find a picture of part of the genetic map the project is creating, download it, and print it out. Summarize the current status of the project.
2. Find information on the Web about cloning. What recent advances in cloning have been made by researchers? What future developments appear to be on the horizon? What ethical issues have been raised regarding the cloning of humans?

 **pilogue**

We have traced major events in the development of children's physical, social, and cognitive abilities in their early years. It is clear that children advance rapidly after birth in all these areas, developing abilities upon which they build further in adolescence and later life, which will be the focus of the next chapter.

As we explored each area of development, we encountered anew the nature–nurture issue, concluding in every significant instance that both nature and nurture contribute to a person's development of skills, personality, and interactions. Specifically, our genetic inheritance—nature—lays down general boundaries within which we can advance and grow, and our environment helps determine the extent to which we take advantage of our potential.

Our consideration of childhood development included a look at the major theories of development, especially Erik Erikson's theory of psychosocial development, Jean Piaget's theory of cognitive development, and Lev Vygotsky's theory of cognitive development. We will reconsider notions and concepts we first encountered in our study of childhood as we turn to adolescence and later life.

Before proceeding to the next chapter, turn once again to the prologue that introduced this one, on Elizabeth Carr, who was conceived using in vitro fertilization. Using your knowledge of childhood development, consider the following questions.

1. Do you think there are any ways Elizabeth Carr's birth, infancy, and development differ from those of her classmates who were not conceived through in vitro fertilization? Why or why not?
2. How would you design a longitudinal study of the development of individuals who were conceived through in vitro fertilization? What sorts of questions would this type of study help you answer?
3. What sorts of questions could you examine through a cross-sectional study? A cross-sequential study?
4. If in the future a girl is *cloned* from her mother, do you think she will turn out to be exactly like her mother, or different in some ways? Why?

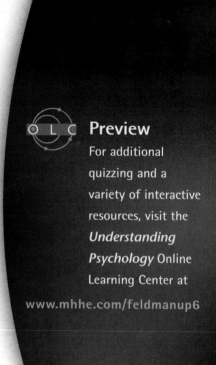

Chapter Thirteen

Development:

Adolescence to the End of Life

Prologue: Life Goes On

Looking Ahead

Adolescence: Becoming an Adult

Physical Development: The Changing Adolescent

Moral and Cognitive Development: Distinguishing Right from Wrong

Social Development: Finding Oneself in a Social World

Exploring Diversity: Rites of Passage: Coming of Age Around the World

Early and Middle Adulthood: The Middle Years of Life

Physical Development: The Peak of Health

Social Development: Working at Life

Marriage, Children, and Divorce: Family Ties

Applying Psychology in the 21st Century: The Changing Institution of Marriage: Is Marriage Declining?

The Later Years of Life: Growing Old

Physical Changes in Late Adulthood: The Aging Body

Cognitive Changes: Thinking About— and During—Late Adulthood

The Social World of Late Adulthood: Old but Not Alone

Becoming an Informed Consumer of Psychology: Adjusting to Death

Looking Back

Key Terms and Concepts

Psychology on the Web

OLC Preview

Epilogue

Sarah and Bessie Delany

Prologue

Life Goes On

"Losing your sister after living together for more than a hundred years, well, it's a pretty terrible thing," wrote Sarah Delany, age 107, whose sister Bessie died peacefully in her sleep at the age of 104. Sarah and Bessie's story is remarkable: Descendants of slaves, they lived long enough to recall "rebby boys" who had fought during the Civil War, and to remember their own efforts to overcome the obstacles that were placed in the paths of African Americans following the transition from slavery to freedom.

And overcome they did. After saving enough money for college, both sisters were accepted by Columbia University, from which they graduated in the mid 1920s. Bessie Delany became the second African American dentist in New York.

Sarah took a different path. Although trained to be a teacher, she knew that school administrators rarely hired African Americans, claiming that their accents could not be understood by white students. To evade this roadblock, Sarah took lessons from a speech coach. After receiving top marks on an exam for prospective teachers, she decided against attending her scheduled job interview, fearing that she would not be hired because of her race. Instead, she wrote a letter to the school, explaining that a mix-up prevented her from attending the interview. She just appeared on the first day of school, and became the first African American home economics teacher in a New York City school.

Sarah wrote of her life without Bessie, "A few days after you left us, Bessie, I started wearing one of your suit coats—you know the gray one you loved so much. It made me feel good, having it wrapped around me. I'm very conscious of being alone. I notice your absence in everything I do. The winter after you left us was the longest, coldest, snowiest one that anyone had ever seen in these parts. It seemed fitting, somehow. But once the spring came I began to feel better. How can you not feel optimistic when the days are longer and warmer? And the birds are singing? The spring reminded me, *Life goes on*" (Delany & Hearth, 1997, p. 127; Delany, 1999).

Apolog

Looking Ahead

The rich lives of the Delany sisters illustrate that even past the age of 100, people continue to change, physically and mentally. The oldest among us continue to hold aspirations and hopes for the future, and must face and adapt to the challenges that are continually present in the course of life. Development, then, extends throughout life, and adolescence and beyond—the greater part of most people's lives—is a period marked by crucial changes that unfold until death.

In this chapter, we examine development from adolescence through young adulthood, middle age, and late adulthood. Our discussion of adolescence focuses on some of the major physical, emotional, and cognitive changes that occur during this transition from childhood to adulthood. Next, we consider early and middle adulthood, stages in which people are at the peak of their physical and intellectual abilities. We discuss the developmental changes people undergo during these periods and their relationship to work, families, and living patterns.

Finally, in our discussion of late adulthood, we examine the kinds of physical, intellectual, and social changes that occur as a consequence of the aging process, and see that aging can bring about both improvements and declines in various kinds of functioning. We end with a discussion of the ways in which people prepare themselves for death.

Prepare

What major physical, social, and cognitive transitions characterize adolescence?

Organize

Adolescence
Physical Development
Moral and Cognitive Development
Social Development

adolescence: The developmental stage between childhood and adulthood

Adolescence: Becoming an Adult

Diana Leary, Age 17: "The school is divided into different groups of kids: the break-dancers, the people who listen to heavy metal, the pretty girls, the ravers and the hip-hop people. But there's no pressure to be in one group or another. If a person is a break-dancer, they can still chill with the ravers. I'm a hip-hopper. We wear baggy jeans and sweatshirts. But if I'm really good friends with a person in the heavy-metal group, I can go chill with them and it's just like, whatever" (Gordon et al., 1999, p. 48).

Trevor Kelson, Age 15: "Keep the Hell Out of My Room!" says a sign on Trevor's bedroom wall, just above an unmade bed, a desk littered with dirty T-shirts and candy wrappers, and a floor covered with clothes. Is there a carpet? "Somewhere," he says with a grin. "I think it's gold" (Fields-Meyer, 1995, p. 53).

Lauren Barry, Age 18: "I went to a National Honor Society induction. The parents were just staring at me. I think they couldn't believe someone with pink hair could be smart. I want to be a high-school teacher, but I'm afraid that, based on my appearance, they won't hire me" (Gordon et al., 1999, p. 47).

Although Diana, Trevor, and Lauren have never met, they share anxieties that are common to adolescence—concerns about friends, parents, appearance, independence, and their futures. **Adolescence,** the developmental stage between childhood and adulthood, is a crucial period. It is a time of profound changes and, occasionally, turmoil. Considerable biological change occurs as adolescents attain sexual and physical maturity. At the same time, these physiological changes are rivaled by important social, emotional, and cognitive changes that occur as adolescents strive for independence and move toward adulthood.

Because many years of schooling precede most people's entry into the workforce in Western societies, the stage of adolescence is a fairly lengthy one, beginning just before the teenage years and ending just after them. No longer children, but considered by society to be not quite adults, adolescents face a

Diana Leary and her mother, Kathryn.

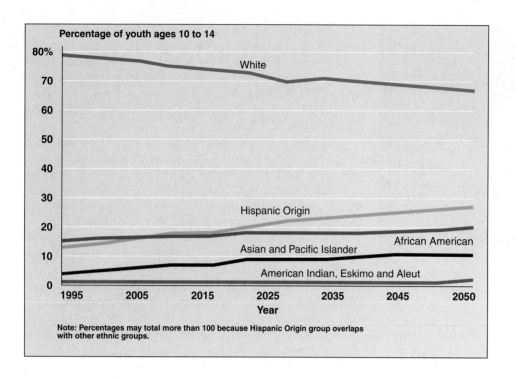

Percentage of youth ages 10 to 14

Note: Percentages may total more than 100 because Hispanic Origin group overlaps with other ethnic groups.

Figure 13-1 By the year 2050, the percentage of U.S. adolescents of nonwhite origin will grow significantly, while the percentage of U.S. whites will decline.

Source: U.S. Bureau of the Census, 1993.

 **puberty:** The period during which maturation of the sexual organs occurs, beginning at about age 11 or 12 for girls and 13 or 14 for boys

period of rapid physical, cognitive, and social change that affects them for the rest of their lives.

Adolescents' development is also being affected by dramatic changes taking place in society. More than half of all children in the United States will spend all or some of their childhood and adolescence in single-parent families. Furthermore, adolescents spend considerably less time with their parents, and more with their peers, than they did several decades ago. Finally, the ethnic and cultural diversity of U.S. adolescents is increasing dramatically. A third of all U.S. adolescents today are of non-European descent, and by the year 2050 the number of adolescents of Hispanic, African American, Native American, or Asian origin will have grown significantly (Carnegie Council on Adolescent Development, 1995; Dreman, 1997; see Figure 13-1).

Physical Development: The Changing Adolescent

If you think back to the start of your own adolescence, it is likely that the most dramatic changes you remember are of a physical nature. A spurt in height, the growth of breasts in girls, deepening voices in boys, the development of body hair, and intense sexual feelings are a source of curiosity, interest, and sometimes embarrassment for individuals entering adolescence.

The physical changes that occur at the start of adolescence are largely a result of the secretion of various hormones (see Chapter 3), and they affect virtually every aspect of the adolescent's life. Not since infancy has development been so dramatic. Weight and height increase rapidly due to a growth spurt that typically begins around age 10 for girls and age 12 for boys. Adolescents might grow as much as 5 inches in one year.

Puberty, the period when the sexual organs mature, begins at about age 11 or 12 for girls and 13 or 14 for boys. However, there are wide variations. For example, some girls begin to menstruate as early as age 8 or 9 or as late as age 16. In both boys and girls, sexual *attraction* to others begins even before the maturation of the sexual organs, at around the age of 10 (see Figure 13-2; Eveleth & Tanner, 1976; Tanner, 1990; McClintock & Herdt, 1996).

PsychLink

Adolescent directory
www.mhhe.com/
feldmanup6-13links

Average male

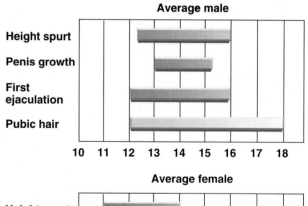

Average female

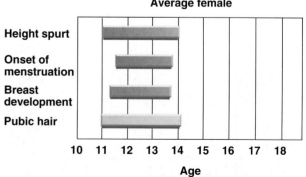

Figure 13-2 The range of ages during which major sexual changes occur during adolescence is shown by the colored bars.

Source: Based on Tanner, 1978.

Although puberty begins around age 11 or 12 for girls and 13 or 14 for boys, there are wide variations. What are some advantages and disadvantages of early puberty?

Significant cultural and situational variations occur in the timing of first menstruation. For example, the average Lumi girl in New Guinea does not begin menstruating until she is 18. In Western cultures, the average age at which adolescents reach sexual maturity has been steadily decreasing over the last century, most likely a result of improved nutrition and medical care (Dreyer, 1982).

The age when they enter puberty has important implications for the way adolescents feel about themselves—as well as how others treat them. Early-maturing boys have a distinct advantage over later-maturing boys. They do better in athletics, are generally more popular with peers, and have more positive self-concepts. On the other hand, they are more likely to have difficulties at school, to commit minor acts of delinquency, and to become involved with alcohol abuse. One reason for such behavior seems to be that early-maturing boys are more likely to become friends with older, and therefore more influential, boys, who might lead them into age-inappropriate activities. On balance, though, the consequences of early maturation for boys are basically positive; early maturers, compared to later maturers, are typically somewhat more responsible and cooperative in later life (Duncan et al., 1985; Peterson, 1985; Anderson & Magnusson, 1990).

The picture is different for girls. Although early-maturing girls are more sought after as dates and have better self-esteem than later-maturing girls, some of the consequences of their early physical maturation can be less positive. For example, early breast development can set them apart from their peers and be a source of ridicule (Simmons & Blyth, 1987; Ge, Conger, & Elder, 1996).

Late maturation can produce certain psychological difficulties for both boys and girls. Boys who are smaller and less coordinated than their more mature peers tend to be ridiculed and seen as less attractive, and in time they might come to view themselves in the same way. Similarly, late-maturing girls are at a disadvantage in junior high and early high school. They hold relatively low social status, and they might be overlooked in dating. On the other hand, late-maturing girls report greater satisfaction with their bodies later in high school and college, because late maturers tend to be relatively tall and slim—closer to the current societal ideal of female beauty (Apter et al., 1981; Clarke-Stewart & Friedman, 1987).

Clearly, the rate at which their physical changes occur can affect the way adolescents are viewed by others and how they view themselves. Just as important as physical changes, however, are the psychological and social changes that unfold during adolescence.

Moral and Cognitive Development: Distinguishing Right from Wrong

In a European country, a woman is near death from a special kind of cancer. The one drug that the doctors think might save her is a medicine that a medical researcher has recently discovered. The drug is expensive to make, and the researcher is charging ten times the cost, or $5000, for a small dose. The sick woman's husband, Henry, approaches everyone he knows in hopes of borrowing money, but he can get together only about $2500. He tells the researcher that his wife is dying and asks him to lower the price of the drug or let him pay later. The researcher says, "No, I discovered the drug and I'm going to make money from it." Henry is desperate and considers stealing the drug for his wife.

What would you tell Henry to do?

Kohlberg's Theory of Moral Development

In the view of psychologist Lawrence Kohlberg, the advice you give Henry is a reflection of your level of moral development. According to Kohlberg, people pass through a series of stages in the evolution of their sense of justice and in the kind of reasoning

Table 13-1 Kohlberg's Levels of Moral Reasoning

	SAMPLE MORAL REASONING OF SUBJECTS	
Level	**In Favor of Stealing the Drug**	**Against Stealing the Drug**
Level 1 Preconventional morality: At this level, the concrete interests of the individual are considered in terms of rewards and punishments.	"If you let your wife die, you will get in trouble. You'll be blamed for not spending the money to save her, and there'll be an investigation of you and the druggist for your wife's death."	"You shouldn't steal the drug because you'll be caught and sent to jail if you do. If you do get away, your conscience will bother you thinking how the police will catch up with you at any minute."
Level 2 Conventional morality: At this level, people approach moral problems as members of society. They are interested in pleasing others by acting as good members of society.	"If you let your wife die, you'll never be able to look anybody in the face again."	"After you steal the drug, you'll feel bad thinking how you've brought dishonor on your family and yourself; you won't be able to face anyone again."
Level 3 Postconventional morality: At this level, people use moral principles which are seen as broader than those of any particular society.	"If you don't steal the drug, and if you let your wife die, you'll always condemn yourself for it afterward. You won't be blamed and you'll have lived up to the outside rule of the law but you won't have lived up to your own standards of conscience."	"If you steal the drug, you won't be blamed by other people, but you'll condemn yourself because you won't have lived up to your own conscience and standards of honesty."

they use to make moral judgments (Kohlberg, 1984). Largely because of the various cognitive limitations that Piaget described (see Chapter 12), preadolescent children tend to think either in terms of concrete, unvarying rules ("It is always wrong to steal" or "I'll be punished if I steal") or in terms of the rules of society ("Good people don't steal" or "What if everyone stole?").

Adolescents, however, are capable of reasoning on a higher plane, having typically reached Piaget's formal operational stage of cognitive development. Because they are able to comprehend broad moral principles, they can understand that morality is not always black and white and that conflict can exist between two sets of socially accepted standards.

Kohlberg (1984) suggests that the changes occurring in moral reasoning can be understood best as a three-level sequence (see Table 13-1). His theory assumes that people move through the levels in a fixed order, and that they are not capable of reaching the highest level until about the age of 13—primarily because of limitations in cognitive development before then. However, many people never reach the highest level of moral reasoning. In fact, Kohlberg found that only a relatively small percentage of adults rise above the second level of his model (Kohlberg & Ryncarz, 1990).

Although Kohlberg's theory has had a substantial influence on our understanding of moral development, the research support is mixed. One difficulty with the theory is that it pertains to moral *judgments,* not moral *behavior.* Knowing right from wrong does not mean that we will always act in accordance with our judgments. In addition, the theory is primarily applicable to Western society and its moral code; cross-cultural research conducted in cultures with different moral systems suggests that Kohlberg's theory is not necessarily relevant there (Kurtines & Gewirtz, 1995; Coles, 1997; Damon, 1999).

Moral Development in Females

One glaring shortcoming of Kohlberg's research is that he used primarily male participants. Furthermore, psychologist Carol Gilligan (1982, 1987, 1993) argues that because of their distinctive socialization experiences, there is a fundamental difference in how women and men view moral behavior. According to Gilligan, men view morality primarily in terms of broad principles, such as justice and fairness. In contrast, women see it in terms of responsibility toward individuals and willingness to make sacrifices to help a specific individual within the context of a particular relationship. Compassion for

PsychLink

Kohlberg's theory of moral development
www.mhhe.com/
feldmanup6-13links

Although moral development generally advances during adolescence, there are significant differences among adolescents in the stage of moral reasoning and behavior that they have achieved.

individuals is a more salient factor in moral behavior for women than it is for men (Gilligan, Ward, & Taylor, 1988; Gilligan, Lyons, & Hanmer, 1990).

Because Kohlberg's model conceives of moral behavior largely in terms of abstract principles such as justice, Gilligan finds it inadequate for describing the moral development of females. She suggests that women's morality is centered on individual well-being and social relationships—a morality of *caring.* In her view, the highest levels of morality are represented by compassionate concern for the welfare of others.

Gilligan's conception of morality is very different from that presented by Kohlberg, and it is clear that gender plays an important role in determining what is seen as moral. Furthermore, their differing conceptions of what constitutes moral behavior can lead women and men to regard the morality of a particular behavior in potentially contradictory ways (Handler, Franz, & Guerra, 1992; Wark & Krebs, 1996).

Social Development: Finding Oneself in a Social World

"Who am I?" "How do I fit into the world?" "What is life all about?"

Questions such as these assume particular significance during the teenage years, as adolescents seek to find their place in the broader social world. As we will see, this quest takes adolescents along several routes.

Erikson's Theory of Psychosocial Development: The Search for Identity

Erikson's theory of psychosocial development, which we first discussed in Chapter 12, emphasizes the search for identity during the adolescent years. As noted earlier, psychosocial development encompasses changes in people's understanding of themselves, one another, and the world around them during the course of development (Erikson, 1963).

The fifth stage of Erikson's theory (summarized, with the other stages, in Table 13-2) is labeled the **identity-versus-role-confusion stage** and encompasses adolescence. This stage is a time of major testing, as people try to determine what is unique and special about themselves. They attempt to discover who they are, what their strengths are, and what kinds of roles they are best suited to play for the rest of their lives—in short, their **identity.** Confusion over the most appropriate role to follow in life can lead to lack of a stable identity, adoption of a socially unacceptable role such as that of a social deviant, or difficulty in maintaining close personal relationships later in life (Kahn et al., 1985; Archer & Waterman, 1994; Kidwell et al., 1995; Brendgen, Vitaro, & Bukowski, 2000).

Erik Erikson

PsychLink

Gilligan vs. Kohlberg
www.mhhe.com/
feldmanup6-13links

identity-versus-role-confusion stage:
According to Erikson, a time in adolescence of major testing to determine one's unique qualities

identity: The distinguishing character of the individual: who each of us is, what our roles are, and what we are capable of

Table 13-2   A Summary of Erikson's Stages

Stage	Approximate Age	Positive Outcomes	Negative Outcomes
1. Trust-vs.-mistrust	Birth–1½ years	Feelings of trust from environmental support	Fear and concern regarding others
2. Autonomy-vs.-shame-and-doubt	1½–3 years	Self-sufficiency if exploration is encouraged	Doubts about self, lack of independence
3. Initiative-vs.-guilt	3–6 years	Discovery of ways to initiate actions	Guilt from actions and thoughts
4. Industry-vs.-inferiority	6–12 years	Development of sense of competence	Feelings of inferiority, no sense of mastery
5. Identity-vs.-role-confusion	Adolescence	Awareness of uniqueness of self, knowledge of role to be followed	Inability to identify appropriate roles in life
6. Intimacy-vs.-isolation	Early adulthood	Development of loving, sexual relationships and close friendships	Fear of relationships with others
7. Generativity-vs.-stagnation	Middle adulthood	Sense of contribution to continuity of life	Trivialization of one's activities
8. Ego-integrity-vs.-despair	Late adulthood	Sense of unity in life's accomplishments	Regret over lost opportunities of life

During the identity-versus-role-confusion period, pressures to identify what one wants to do with one's life are acutely felt. Because these pressures come at a time of major physical changes as well as important changes in what society expects of them, adolescents can find the period particularly difficult. The identity-versus-role-confusion stage has another important characteristic: a decline in reliance on adults for information, with a shift toward using the peer group as a source of social judgments. The peer group becomes increasingly important, enabling adolescents to form close, adultlike relationships and helping them clarify their personal identities. According to Erikson, the identity-versus-role-confusion stage during adolescence marks a pivotal point in psychosocial development, paving the way for continued growth and the future development of personal relationships.

During early adulthood, people enter the **intimacy-versus-isolation stage.** Spanning the period of early adulthood (from post-adolescence to the early thirties), the focus is on developing close relationships with others. Difficulties during this stage result in feelings of loneliness and a fear of relationships with others, but successful resolution of the crises of this stage results in the possibility of forming relationships that are intimate on a physical, intellectual, and emotional level.

During the identity-versus-role confusion stage, adolescents seek to determine what is special and unique about themselves, according to Erikson's theory.

Development continues during middle adulthood as people enter the **generativity-versus-stagnation stage.** Generativity is the ability to contribute to one's family, community, work, and society, assisting the development of the younger generation. Success in this stage results in positive feelings about the continuity of life; difficulties lead to feelings that one's activities are trivial, a sense of stagnation, or feeling that one has done nothing for upcoming generations. In fact, the person who has not successfully resolved the identity crisis of adolescence might still be floundering in middle adulthood to find an appropriate career.

Finally, the last stage of psychosocial development, the period of **ego-integrity-versus-despair,** comprises later adulthood and continues until death. Success in resolving the difficulties presented by this stage of life is signified by a sense of accomplishment; difficulties result in regret over what might have been achieved but was not.

One of the most noteworthy aspects of Erikson's theory is its suggestion that development does not stop at adolescence but continues throughout adulthood, a view that a substantial amount of research now confirms. For instance, a 22-year study by psychologist Susan Whitbourne found considerable support for the fundamentals of Erikson's theory, determining that psychosocial development continues through adolescence and adulthood. In sum, adolescence is not an endpoint but rather a way-station on the path of psychosocial development (Whitbourne et al., 1992; McAdams et al., 1997).

intimacy–versus–isolation stage: According to Erikson, a period during early adulthood that focuses on developing close relationships

generativity–versus–stagnation stage: According to Erikson, a period in middle adulthood during which we take stock of our contributions to family and society

ego-integrity–versus–despair stage: According to Erikson, a period from late adulthood until death during which we review our life's accomplishments and failures

Stormy Adolescence: Myth or Reality?

Does puberty invariably foreshadow a stormy, rebellious period of adolescence?

At one time most children entering adolescence were thought to be beginning a period fraught with stress and unhappiness. However, psychologists

Success in the generativity-versus-stagnation stage results in positive feelings about the continuity of life, while difficulties lead to feelings of triviality regarding one's activities and a sense of stagnation.

THE WORLD'S FIRST GENETICALLY ENGINEERED HUMAN HITS ADOLESCENCE

We buy you the best genes in the world—FOR THIS?

So, I got my nose pierced. So what, man.

I remember checking "genius" on the order form—AND NOW LOOK!

PsychLink
Teenage suicide
www.mhhe.com/
feldmanup6-13links

These students are mourning the deaths of two classmates who committed suicide. The rate of suicide among teenagers has risen significantly over the past few decades. Can you think of any reasons for this phenomenon?

are now finding that this characterization is largely a myth, that most young people pass through adolescence without appreciable turmoil in their lives, and that parents speak easily—and fairly often—with their children about a variety of topics (Steinberg, 1993; Klein, 1998; van Wel, Linssen, & Abma, 2000).

This is not to say that adolescence is completely calm. In most families, there is clearly a rise in the amount of arguing and bickering that goes on. Young teenagers, as part of their search for identity, tend to experience a degree of tension between their attempts to become independent from their parents and their actual dependence on them. They might experiment with a range of behaviors, flirting with a variety of activities that their parents, and even society as a whole, find objectionable. Happily, though, for the majority of families such tensions tend to stabilize during middle adolescence—around age 15 or 16—and eventually decline around age 18 (Eccles, Lord, & Roeser, 1996; Gullotta, Adams, & Markstrom, 1999).

One reason for the increase in discord during adolescence appears to be the protracted period in which children stay at home with their parents. In prior historical periods—and in some nonwestern cultures today—children leave home immediately after puberty and are considered adults. Today, however, sexually mature adolescents might spend as many as seven or eight years with their parents. Current statistics even hint at an extension of the conflicts of adolescence beyond the teenage years for a significant number of people. Some one-third of all unmarried men and one-fifth of unmarried women between the ages of 25 and 34 continue to reside with their parents (Steinberg, 1989; Gross, 1991).

Another source of strife with parents lies in the way adolescents think. Adolescence fosters *adolescent egocentrism,* a state of self-absorption in which adolescents view the world from their own point of view. Egocentrism leads adolescents to be highly critical of authority figures, unwilling to accept criticism, and quick to fault others. It also makes them believe that they are the center of everyone else's attention, leading to considerable self-consciousness. Furthermore, they develop *personal fables,* the view that what happens to them is unique, exceptional, and shared by no one else. Such personal fables can make adolescents feel invulnerable to the risks that threaten others (Elkind, 1967, 1985; Klacynski, 1997).

Adolescence also introduces a variety of stresses outside the home. Typically, adolescents change schools at least twice (from elementary to middle or junior high, then to senior high school), and relationships with friends and peers are particularly volatile. Many adolescents hold part-time jobs, increasing the demands of school, work, and social activities on their time. Such stressors can lead to tensions at home (Steinberg & Dornbusch, 1991; Cotterell, 1996).

Adolescent Suicide

Although the vast majority of teenagers pass through adolescence without major psychological difficulties, some experience unusually severe psychological problems. Sometimes these problems become so extreme that adolescents take their own lives. Suicide is the third leading cause of death for adolescents (after accidents and homicide) in the United States. More teenagers and young adults die from suicide than from cancer, heart disease, AIDS, birth defects, stroke, pneumonia and influenza, and chronic lung disease *combined* (Centers for Disease Control and Prevention [CDC], 2000).

In the United States, a teenager commits suicide every ninety minutes—a rate that has tripled over the last two decades. Furthermore, the reported rate of suicide might be understated, as medical personnel are reluctant to report suicide as a cause of death. Instead, they frequently label a death as an accident in an effort to protect survivors.

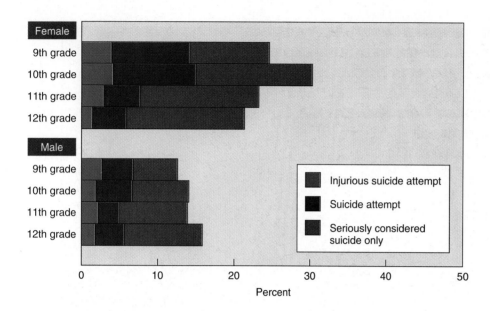

Figure 13-3 Suicide attempts among students in grades 9 to 12 over a 12-month period preceding the 1999 survey (Centers for Disease Control, 2000).

Male adolescents are five times more likely to commit suicide than females, although females *attempt* suicide more often than males. Overall, as many as 200 people might attempt suicide for every person who actually takes his or her own life (Berman & Jobes, 1991; Gelman, 1994; CDC, 2000; see Figure 13-3).

The rate of adolescent suicide is significantly greater among whites than nonwhites. However, the suicide rate for African American males has increased at a considerably higher rate than that of white males over the last two decades. Native Americans have the highest suicide rate of any ethnic group in the United States, and Asians Americans have the lowest rate (National Institute of Mental Health, 1999).

It is not clear why suicide has increased so dramatically over the past few decades. Some psychologists suggest that the amount of stress teenagers experience—in terms of academic and social pressure, alcoholism, drug abuse, and family difficulties—has risen sharply in recent decades, provoking the most troubled adolescents to take their own lives. But that is not the whole story, for the suicide rate for other age groups has remained fairly stable in the last few decades. It is unlikely that stress has increased only for adolescents and not for the rest of the population ("Suicide," 1996).

Although the question of why there has been a rise in adolescent suicide remains unanswered, it is clear that several factors put adolescents at risk. One such factor is depression, characterized by unhappiness, extreme fatigue, and—a variable that seems particularly important—a profound sense of hopelessness. In other cases, adolescents who commit suicide are perfectionists, inhibited socially and prone to extreme anxiety when faced with any social or academic challenge (Schneidman, 1987; Rierdan, 1996; see Figure 13-4).

Family background and adjustment difficulties are also related to suicide. There might be a longstanding history of conflicts between parents and children. These conflicts can lead to adolescent behavior problems, such as delinquency, dropping out of school, and aggressive tendencies. In addition, teenage alcoholics and abusers of other drugs have a relatively high rate of suicide (Wagner, 1997; Stronski et al., 2000).

Several warning signs indicate when a teenager's problems might be severe enough to warrant concern about the possibility of a suicide attempt (Berman & Jobes, 1995). The warning signs include these:

- School problems, such as missing classes, truancy, and a sudden change in grades
- Frequent incidents of self-destructive behavior, such as careless accidents
- Loss of appetite or excessive eating
- Withdrawal from friends and peers

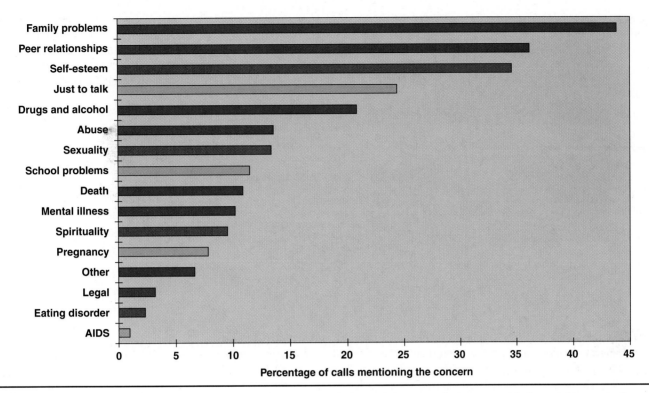

Figure 13-4 According to a review of phone calls to one telephone help line, adolescents who were considering suicide most often mentioned family, peer relationship, and self-esteem problems.

Source: Boehm & Campbell, 1995.

- Sleeping problems
- Signs of depression, tearfulness, or overt indications of psychological difficulties, such as hallucinations
- A preoccupation with death, an afterlife, or what would happen "if I died"
- Putting affairs in order, such as giving away prized possessions or making arrangements for the care of a pet
- An explicit announcement of thoughts of suicide

If you know someone who indicates that suicide is a possibility, urge him or her to seek professional help. You might need to take assertive action, such as enlisting the assistance of family members or friends. Talk of suicide is a serious signal for help, not a confidence to be kept. (For immediate help with a suicide problem, call 800-448-3000.)

EXPLORING DIVERSITY

Rites of Passage: Coming of Age Around the World

It is not easy for male members of the Awa tribe in New Guinea to make the transition from childhood to adulthood. First come whippings, in which the boys are hit with sticks and prickly branches, both for their own past misdeeds and in honor of those tribesmen who were killed in warfare. In the next phase of the ritual, adults jab sharpened sticks into the boys' nostrils. Then they force a 5-foot length of vine into the boys' throats, until they gag and vomit. Finally, tribesmen cut the boys' genitals, causing severe bleeding.

Although the rites that mark the coming-of-age of boys in the Awa sound horrifying to Westerners, they are comparable to those in other cultures. In some cultures, rites require kneeling on hot coals without displaying pain. In others, girls must toss wads of burning cotton from hand to hand and allow themselves to be bitten by hundreds of ants (Selsky, 1997).

Other cultures have less fearsome, although no less important, ceremonies that mark the passage from childhood to adulthood. For instance, when a girl first menstruates in traditional Apache tribes, the event is marked by dawn-to-dusk chanting. Western religions, too, have several types of celebrations, including bar and bat mitzvahs at age 13 for Jewish boys and girls and confirmation ceremonies for children in many Christian denominations (Myerhoff, 1982; Dunham, Kidwell, & Wilson, 1986; Delaney, 1995; Rakoff, 1995).

In most societies, males, but not females, are the focus of coming-of-age ceremonies. The renowned anthropologist Margaret Mead remarked, only partly in jest, that the preponderance of male ceremonies might reflect that "the worry that boys will not grow up to be men is much more widespread than that girls will not grow up to be women" (Mead, 1949, p. 195). Or it might be that men traditionally have higher status than women, and therefore their transition into adulthood is regarded as more important.

However, there is another explanation for why most cultures place greater emphasis on male rites than female rites. For females, the transition from childhood is marked by a definite, biological event: menstruation. For males, no single event pinpoints entry into adulthood, so they are forced to rely on culturally determined rituals to acknowledge that they have become adults (Chodorow, 1978; Bird & Melville, 1994).

Evaluate

1. _____ is the period during which the sexual organs begin to mature.
2. Delayed maturation typically provides both males and females with a social advantage. True or false?
3. _____ proposed a set of three levels of moral development ranging from reasoning based on rewards and punishments to abstract thinking involving concepts of justice.
4. Erikson believed that, during adolescence, people must search for _____, and that during early adulthood the major task is _____.

Answers to Evaluate Questions

1. Puberty 2. False; both male and female adolescents suffer if they mature late. 3. Kohlberg 4. identity; intimacy

Rethink

1. In what ways do school cultures help or hurt teenage students who are going through adolescence? What school policies might benefit early-maturing girls and late-maturing boys? Would same-sex schools help, as some have argued?
2. Many cultures have "rites of passage" that officially recognize young people as adults. Do you think such rites can be beneficial? Does the United States have any such rites? Would setting up an official designation that one has achieved "adult" status have benefits?

Early and Middle Adulthood: The Middle Years of Life

Psychologists generally consider early adulthood to begin around age 20 and last until about age 40 to 45, with middle adulthood beginning then and continuing until around age 65. Despite the enormous importance of these periods of life in terms of both the accomplishments that occur within them and their overall length (together they span some 45 years), they have been studied less than any other stage. One reason is that the physical changes that occur during these periods are less apparent and more gradual than changes during other periods of the life span. In addition, the social changes that arise during this period are so diverse that they defy simple categorization. However, developmental psychologists have recently begun to focus on early and middle adulthood, particularly on the social changes in the family and women's careers.

Prepare

What are the principle kinds of physical, social, and intellectual changes that occur in early and middle adulthood, and what are their causes?

Organize

Early and Middle Adulthood
Physical Development
Social Development
Marriage, Children, and Divorce

Physical Development: The Peak of Health

For most people, early adulthood marks the peak of physical health. From about 18 to 25 years of age, people's strength is greatest, their reflexes are quickest, and their chances of dying from disease are quite slim. Moreover, reproductive capabilities are at their highest level.

Around age 25, the body starts to become slightly less efficient and more susceptible to disease. Overall, however, ill health remains the exception; most people stay remarkably healthy during early adulthood. (Can you think of any machine other than the body that can operate without pause for so long a period?)

During middle adulthood, people gradually become aware of changes in their bodies. Many people begin to put on weight (although this can be avoided through exercise). Furthermore, the sense organs gradually become less sensitive, and it takes more time to react to stimuli. But generally, the physical declines that do occur during middle adulthood are minor and often unnoticeable (DiGiovanna, 1994).

The major biological change during middle adulthood pertains to reproductive capabilities. During their late forties or early fifties, on average, women begin **menopause,** a process in which they stop menstruating and become infertile. Because menopause is accompanied by a significant reduction in the production of estrogen, a female hormone, menopausal women sometimes experience symptoms such as hot flashes, sudden sensations of heat. However, many symptoms can be treated through *estrogen replacement therapy* (ERT), in which the hormones estrogen and progesterone are taken. However, estrogen replacement therapy poses several dangers, such as an increase in the risk of breast cancer. The uncertainties make the routine use of ERT controversial (LaVecchia, 1996; Swan, 1997).

Menopause was once blamed for a variety of psychological symptoms, including depression and memory loss. However, such difficulties, if they do occur, might be caused by women's expectations about reaching an "old" age in a society that highly values youth.

Furthermore, women's reactions to menopause vary significantly across cultures. According to anthropologist Yewoubdar Beyene, the more a society values old age, the less difficulty its women have during menopause. In a study of women in Mayan villages, she found that women looked forward to menopause, because they then stopped having children. In addition, they didn't even experience some of the classic symptoms of menopause; hot flashes, for example, were unheard of. It is clear that a society's attitudes affect how women experience menopause (Ballinger, 1981; Beyene, 1989; Beck, 1992; Figueiras & Marteau, 1995; Mingo, Herman, & Jasperse, 2000).

For men, the aging process during middle adulthood is somewhat subtler. There are no physiological signals of increasing age equivalent to the end of menstruation in women (there is no male menopause). In fact, men remain fertile and are capable of fathering children until well into old age. On the other hand, some gradual physical declines occur: Sperm production decreases and the frequency of orgasm tends to decline. Once again, though, most psychological difficulties associated with these changes are due not so much to physical deterioration as to societal glorification of youthfulness.

Social Development: Working at Life

Whereas physical changes during adulthood reflect development of a quantitative nature, social developmental transitions are more profound. During this period people typically launch themselves into careers, marriage, and families.

The entry into early adulthood is usually marked by leaving one's childhood home and entering the world of work. People envision the accomplishments they desire in life and make career choices. Their lives often become centered on their careers, which form an important part of their identity (Vaillant & Vaillant, 1990; Levinson, 1990, 1992).

In their early forties, however, people might begin to question their lives as they enter a period called the *midlife transition*. The idea that life will end at some point becomes increasingly influential in their thinking, and they might question their past accom-

---

menopause: The point at which women stop menstruating and are no longer fertile

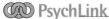

PsychLink

Medical information on menopause
www.mhhe.com/
feldmanup6-13links

Women's reactions to menopause vary significantly across cultures, and, according to one study, the more a society values old age, the less difficulty its women have during menopause. Why do you think this would be the case?

plishments (Gould, 1978). As they face signs of physical aging and feel dissatisfaction with their lives, some individuals experience what has been popularly labeled a *midlife crisis.*

For most people, though, the passage into middle age is relatively calm. Most 40-year-olds view their lives and accomplishments positively enough to proceed relatively smoothly through midlife, and the forties and fifties are often a particularly rewarding period of life. Rather than looking to the future, people concentrate on the present, and their involvement with their families, friends, and other social groups takes on new importance. A major developmental thrust of this period of life is coming to terms with one's circumstances (Whitbourne, 2000).

Finally, during the last stages of adulthood people become more accepting of others and their lives, and less concerned about issues or problems that once bothered them. People come to accept the realization that death is inevitable, and they try to understand their accomplishments in terms of the broader meaning of life. Although people might for the first time begin to label themselves as "old," many also develop a sense of wisdom and feel freer to enjoy life (Gould, 1978; Karp, 1988, 1991).

Marriage, Children, and Divorce: Family Ties

In the typical fairy tale, a dashing young man and a beautiful young woman marry, have children, and live happily ever after. However, such a scenario does not match the realities of love and marriage in the twenty-first century. Today, it is just as likely that the woman and man would first live together, then get married and have children, but ultimately end up getting divorced.

The percentage of unmarried couples in U.S. households has increased dramatically over the last two decades. At the same time, the average age at which marriage takes place is higher than at any time since the turn of the century. As you can see in the *Applying Psychology in the 21st Century* box on page 401, these changes have been dramatic, and they suggest that the institution of marriage has changed considerably from earlier historical periods.

When people do marry, the probability of divorce is high, particularly for younger couples. Even though divorce rates appear to be declining since they peaked in 1981, 60 percent of all first marriages still end in divorce. Two-fifths of children will experience the breakup of their parents' marriage before they are 18 years old. Moreover, the rise in divorce is not just a U.S. phenomenon: The divorce rate has accelerated over the last several decades in most industrialized countries except Japan and Italy (Cherlin, 1993; Ahrons, 1995).

Changes in matrimonial and divorce trends have led to a doubling in the number of single-parent households in the United States over the past two decades. More than one-quarter of all family households are now headed by one parent, compared with 13 percent in 1970, and half of all black children and almost one-third of Hispanic children live in homes with only one parent. Furthermore, in most single-parent families, the children reside with the mother, not the father—a phenomenon that is consistent across racial and ethnic groups throughout the industrialized world (Burns & Scott, 1994; U.S. Bureau of the Census, 1997; see Figure 13-5).

What are the consequences for children living in homes with only one parent? Single-parent families are often economically less well off, diminishing children's opportunities. Many single parents are unable to find good child care, and they feel psychological stress and sometimes guilt over the child-care arrangements they must make for economic reasons. Time is always at a premium in single-parent families

PsychLink

Children and divorce
www.mhhe.com/
feldmanup6-13links

Figure 13-5 For blacks, Hispanics, and whites, the single parent who is living in the home is most often the mother.

Source: U.S. Bureau of the Census, *Census Population Survey,* 1999.

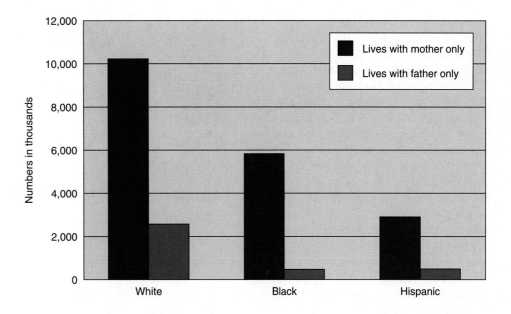

(Hetherington, 1999; Wallerstein, Lewis, & Blakeslee, 2000). Furthermore, for children of divorce, the parents' separation is often a painful experience that can make it difficult for the children to establish close relationships later in life. Children might blame themselves for the breakup or feel pressure to take sides. Most evidence, however, suggests that children from single-parent families are no less well adjusted than those from two-parent families. In fact, children can be more successful growing up in a harmonious single-parent family than in a two-parent family in which the parents are engaged in continuous conflict with one another (Harold et al., 1997; Kelly, 1999; Clarke-Stewart et al., 2000).

In short, the consequences for children of living in a single-parent household are not invariably negative or positive. Certainly, the large number of single-parent households has largely reduced the stigma of such family situations. How children fare, then, depends on a variety of factors, including the family's economic status, the amount of time the parent can devote to the children, and the overall amount of household stress.

The Changing Roles of Men and Women: The Time of Their Lives

One of the major changes in family life in the last two decades has been the evolution of the roles played by men and women. More women than ever before act simultaneously as wives, mothers, and wage earners—in contrast to women in traditional marriages, in which the husband is the sole wage earner and the wife assumes primary responsibility for care of the home and children.

Close to 75 percent of all married women with school-age children are now employed outside the home, and 56 percent of mothers with children under 6 are working. In the mid 1960s, only 17 percent of mothers of 1-year-olds worked full-time; now, more than half are in the labor force (Darnton, 1990; Carnegie Task Force, 1994).

Most married working women are not free of household responsibilities. Even in marriages in which the spouses hold jobs that have similar status and require similar hours, the distribution of household tasks between husbands and wives has not changed substantially. Working wives are still more likely to view themselves as responsible for traditional homemaking tasks such as cooking and cleaning. In contrast, husbands still view themselves as responsible primarily for such household tasks as repairing broken appliances, putting up screens in the summer, and doing yard work (Perry-Jenkins, 1993; Ganong & Coleman, 1999).

The way married men and women spend their time during the average week is also quite different. As you can see in Figure 13-7, although child care represents the biggest

Applying Psychology in the 21st Century

The Changing Institution of Marriage: Is Marriage Declining?

In the United States, by many measures, marriage is a societal institution that is undergoing significant change—and, one could argue, decline. The evidence for such an assertion comes from a variety of measures. Consider these facts (Doyle, 1999; Smock, 2000; Waite & Bachrach, 2000):

- More than half of all marriages—some 56 percent—between 1990 and 1994 were preceded by a couple living together. The comparable figure from 1965 was just 10 percent.

- Living together without marriage often includes the presence of children. Thirty-five percent of never-married couples have children, and half of previously married but now divorced people living together have children.

- During the period of 1890 through 1940, 81 percent of women in the U.S. were married; the comparable figure for 1998 was only 67 percent.

- The decline in the percentage of married women has occurred not only in the United States, but in most western European countries as well (see Figure 13-6).

The decline of marriage—and the increase in the number of couples living together without being married—has occurred for several reasons. First, there is far less stigma in living together and engaging in unmarried sex. In fact, given that more than half of all marriages are preceded by a period of living together, cultural norms are considerably more permissive than earlier.

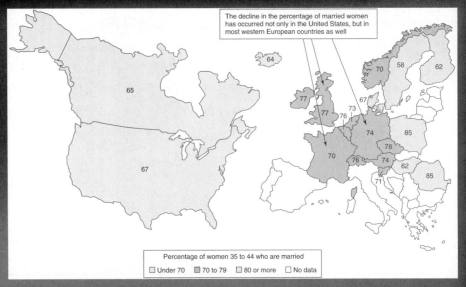

Figure 13-6 The percentage of women who are married has declined in most Western countries over previous decades. (Source: Statistical Office of the European Communities, 1998). What do you think are some of the reasons for the declines, and do you think they will be permanent?

Another factor is money. Certain tax credits can disappear when low-wage earners marry someone who works. And high-income earners are faced with higher combined taxes when both partners earn good salaries and are married than if they were single. Furthermore, many localities provide health-care benefits to domestic partners, not just spouses, eliminating health care as an incentive for marriage. Attitudes about marriage and expectations of success are also less positive. Women especially view marriage with more pessimism than in earlier periods (Doyle, 1999).

Ironically, the decline in marriage comes at a time when research is increasingly demonstrating that marriage has significant benefits. For example, married people have greater financial stability, live longer, have more active and satisfying sex lives, and are less prone to alcohol abuse, compared to those who are not married. Furthermore, most people say they want to get married at some time in their lives, and close to 95 percent eventually do. Even people who divorce are more likely than not to remarry, some of them three or more times—a phenomenon known as serial marriage. In short, marriage remains an important institution in Western cultures, and identifying a mate is a critical issue for most people during adulthood (Rosewicz, 1996; Doyle, 1999; Waite & Bachrach, 2000).

Why do you think that married people live longer than unmarried people and apparently experience greater satisfaction? Should society, through laws, encourage marriage, or should it remain neutral? Why?

time investment for both husbands and wives when they are home, husbands spend much less of their time caring for their children (19 percent), compared to wives (32 percent) (Robinson & Godbey, 1997; Cabrera et al., 2000).

Women's "second shift"   The number of hours put in by working mothers can be staggering. One survey found that employed mothers of children under 3 years of age worked an average of ninety hours per week! Sociologist Arlie Hochschild refers to the additional work experienced by women as the "second shift." According to her analysis of national statistics, employed mothers put in an extra month of 24-hour days during the course of a year. Similar patterns are seen in many developing societies throughout the world, with

Figure 13-7 Although men and women say that child care takes up most of their time when they are not working, women spend considerably more time caring for children than men do (Robinson & Godbey, 1997). Why do you think this is the case? Is it ever likely to change?

Men: 17.4 hours per week

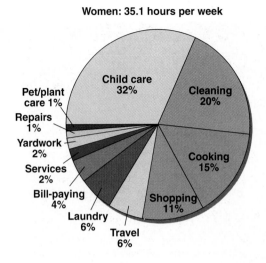

Women: 35.1 hours per week

women working at full-time jobs and also having primary responsibilities for child care (Hochschild, 1990; Hochschild, Machung, & Pringle, 1995; Mednick, 1993).

Consequently, rather than women's careers being a substitute for household work, they usually are an addition to the role of homemaker. It is not surprising that some wives feel resentment toward husbands who spend less time on child care and housework than the wives had expected before the birth of their children (Williams & McCullers, 1983; Ruble et al., 1988; Crouter et al., 1999; Stier & Lewin-Epstein, 2000).

Perhaps surprisingly, many wives are relatively accepting of this unequal distribution. One reason is that traditional societal standards still encourage women to play a dominant role in child care and housework. In addition, for many women the benefits of multiple responsibilities can outweigh the disadvantages. Women who work, particularly those in high-prestige occupations, report feeling a greater sense of mastery, pride, and competence than women who stay at home.

The value of work, then, goes beyond merely earning a salary. Work provides personal satisfaction as well as a sense of contributing to society. In fact, some critics contend that work is valued because it provides an escape from the rigors of a frenetic, stress-filled home life (Schwartzberg & Dytell, 1996; Steil & Hay, 1997; Hochschild, 1997a).

Evaluate

1. Emotional and psychological changes that sometimes accompany menopause are probably not due to menopause itself. True or false?
2. Rob recently turned 40 and surveyed his goals and accomplishments to date. Although he has accomplished a lot, he realized that many of his goals will not be met in his lifetime. This stage is called a _____ _____.
3. It is typically in the best interests of children for their parents to remain in a stormy marriage until the children move away from home. True or false?
4. In households where the partners have similar jobs, the usual division of labor is the same as in "traditional" households where the husband works and the wife stays at home. True or false?

Rethink

1. How do you think popular culture contributes to the midlife crisis experienced by some people as they reach their forties? What sorts of cultural changes might ease the midlife crisis or make the phenomenon less prevalent?
2. Given the current divorce rate and the number of households in which both parents work, do you think it is reasonable to still think in terms of a "traditional" household in which the father is the breadwinner and the wife is a homemaker? What problems might such a definition cause for children whose homes do not match this definition?

Answers to Evaluate Questions

1. True 2. Midlife transition. 3. False; a stable one-parent home is generally preferable to a two-parent home filled with conflict. 4. True

The Later Years of Life: Growing Old

I've always enjoyed doing things in the mountains—hiking or, more recently, active cliff-climbing. When climbing a route of any difficulty at all, it's absolutely necessary to become entirely absorbed in what you're doing. You look for a crack that you can put your hand in. You have to think about whether the foothold over there will leave you in balance or not. Otherwise you can get trapped in a difficult situation. And if you don't remember where you put your hands or feet a few minutes before, then it's very difficult to climb down.

The more difficult the climb, the more absorbing it is. The climbs I really remember are the ones I had to work on. Maybe a particular section where it took two or three tries before I found the right combination of moves that got me up easily—and, preferably, elegantly. It's a wonderful exhilaration to get to the top and sit down and perhaps have lunch and look out over the landscape and be so grateful that it's still possible for me to do that sort of thing (Lyman Spitzer, age 74, quoted in Kotre & Hall, 1990, pp. 358–359).

If you can't quite picture a 74-year-old climbing rocks, some rethinking of your view of old age might well be in order. In spite of the societal stereotype of old age as a time of inactivity and physical and mental decline, *gerontologists*, specialists who study aging, are beginning to paint quite a different portrait of late adulthood.

By focusing on the period of life that starts at around age 65, gerontologists are making important contributions to clarifying the capabilities of older adults. Their work is demonstrating that significant developmental processes continue even during old age. And as life expectancy increases, the number of people who reach older adulthood will continue to grow substantially (see Figure 13-8). Consequently, developing an understanding of late adulthood has become a critical priority for psychologists (Birren, 1996; Moody, 2000).

Physical Changes in Late Adulthood: The Aging Body

Napping, eating, walking, conversing. It probably doesn't surprise you that these relatively nonstrenuous activities represent the typical pastimes of late adulthood. But what is striking about this list is that these activities are identical to the most common leisure activities reported in a survey of college students. Although the students cited more active pursuits—such as sailing and playing basketball—as their favorite activities, in actuality they engaged in such sports relatively infrequently, spending most of their free time napping, eating, walking, and conversing (Harper, 1978).

Although the leisure activities in which older adults engage might not differ all that much from those of younger people, many physical changes are, of course, brought about by the aging process. The most obvious are those of appearance—hair thinning and turning gray, skin wrinkling and folding, and sometimes a slight loss of height as the thickness of the disks between vertebrae in the spine decreases—but there are also subtler changes in the body's biological functioning (DiGiovanna, 1994).

For example, sensory capabilities decrease as a result of aging: Vision, hearing, smell, and taste become less sensitive. Reaction time slows, and there are changes in physical stamina. Because oxygen intake and heart-pumping ability decline, the body is unable to replenish lost nutrients as quickly—and therefore the rebound from physical activity

Prepare

How does the reality of old age differ from the stereotypes about the period?
How can we adjust to death?

Organize

The Later Years of Life
    Physical Changes in Late Adulthood
    Cognitive Changes
    The Social World of Late Adulthood

PsychLink

Information on aging
www.mhhe.com/
feldmanup6-13links

Many people remain active and vigorous during late adulthood, as exemplified by this participant in the Senior Olympics.

Figure 13-8 Projections suggest that by the year 2050, 20 percent of the U.S. population will be over the age of 65. What implications does this statistic carry for U.S. society?

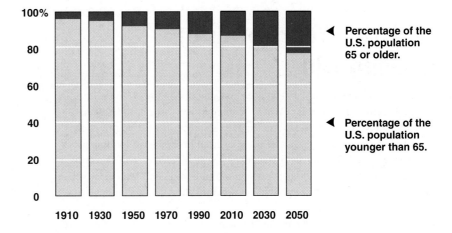

Percentage of the U.S. population 65 or older.

Percentage of the U.S. population younger than 65.

genetic preprogramming theories of aging: Theories that hold that there is a built-in time limit to the reproduction of human cells, and that after a certain time they are no longer able to divide

wear-and-tear theories of aging: Theories that hold that the mechanical functions of the body simply stop working efficiently when we are old

is slower. Of course, none of these changes begins suddenly at age 65. Gradual declines in some kinds of functioning start earlier. In late adulthood, however, these changes become more apparent (Schneider & Rowe, 1996; Whitbourne, 2000).

What are the reasons for these physical declines? **Genetic preprogramming theories of aging** suggest that there is a built-in time limit to the reproduction of human cells. These theories suggest that after a certain time cells stop dividing or become harmful to the body—as if a kind of automatic self-destruct button has been pushed. In contrast, **wear-and-tear theories of aging** suggest that the mechanical functions of the body simply stop working efficiently as people age. Waste by-products of energy production eventually accumulate, and mistakes are made when cells divide. Eventually the body, in effect, wears out, just like an old automobile (Hayflick, 1994; Ly et al., 2000).

Evidence exists to support both the genetic preprogramming view and the wear-and-tear view, and perhaps both processes contribute to natural aging. It is clear, however, that physical aging is not a disease, but rather a natural biological process. Many physical functions do not decline with age. For example, sex remains pleasurable well into old age (although the frequency of sexual activity decreases), and some people report that the pleasure they derive from sex increases during late adulthood (Olshansky, Carnes, & Cassel, 1990; Gelfand, 2000).

Cognitive Changes: Thinking About—and During—Late Adulthood

Three women were talking about the inconveniences of growing old.

"Sometimes," one of them confessed, "when I go to my refrigerator, I can't remember if I'm putting something in or taking something out."

"Oh, that's nothing," said the second woman. "There are times when I find myself at the foot of the stairs wondering if I'm going up or if I've just come down."

"Well, my goodness!" exclaimed the third woman. "I'm certainly glad I don't have any problems like that"—and she knocked on wood. "Oh," she said, starting up out of her chair, "there's someone at the door" (Dent, 1984, p. 38).

At one time, many gerontologists would have agreed with the view—suggested by the story above—that older adults are forgetful and confused. Today, however, most research tells us that this is far from an accurate assessment of older people's capabilities.

One reason for the change in view is the availability of more sophisticated research techniques for studying cognitive changes that occur in late adulthood. For example, if we were to give a group of older adults an IQ test, we might find that the average score is lower than the score achieved by a group of younger people. We might conclude that this signifies a decline in intelligence. Yet if we looked a little closer at the specific test, we might find that such a conclusion is unwarranted. For instance, many IQ tests include portions based on physical performance (such as arranging a group of blocks) or on

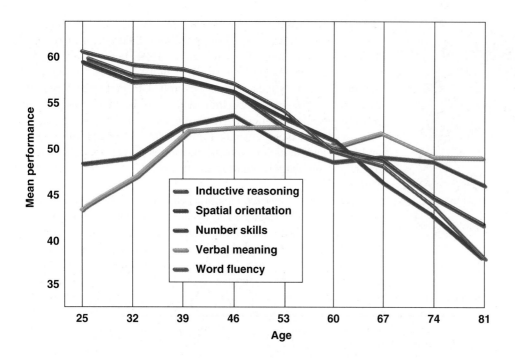

Figure 13-9 Age-related changes in intellectual skills vary according to the specific cognitive ability in question (Schaie, 1994).

speed. In such cases, poorer performance on the IQ test might be due to decrements in reaction time—a physical decline that accompanies old age and has little or nothing to do with the intellectual capabilities of older adults (Schaie, 1991).

Other difficulties hamper research into cognitive functioning during late adulthood. For example, many older people are less healthy than younger ones; when only *healthy* older adults are compared to healthy younger adults, intellectual differences are far less evident. Furthermore, the average number of years in school is often lower in older adults (for historical reasons) than in the younger ones, and older adults can be less motivated to perform well on intelligence tests than younger people. Finally, traditional IQ tests might be inappropriate measures of intelligence in late adulthood. Older adults sometimes perform better on tests of practical intelligence (of the sort we discussed in Chapter 9) than younger individuals do (Cornelius & Caspi, 1987; Willis & Schaie, 1994; Kausler, 1994).

Still, there are some declines in intellectual functioning during late adulthood, although the pattern of age differences is not uniform for different types of cognitive abilities (see Figure 13-9). In general, skills relating to *fluid intelligence* (which involves reasoning, memory, and information processing) do show declines in old age. On the other hand, skills relating to *crystallized intelligence* (intelligence based on the accumulation of information, skills, and problem-solving strategies) remain steady and in some cases actually improve (Schaie, 1993, 1994; Powell & Whitla, 1994; Salthouse, 1996).

Even when changes in intellectual functioning do occur during late adulthood, people often are able to compensate for any decline. They can still learn what they want to; it might just take more time. Furthermore, when older adults learn strategies for dealing with new problems, this can prevent declines in their performance (Willis & Nesselroade, 1990; Coffey et al., 1999).

Memory Changes in Old Age: Are Older Adults Forgetful?

One of the characteristics most frequently attributed to late adulthood is forgetfulness. How accurate is this assumption?

Most evidence suggests that diminished memory is *not* an inevitable part of the aging process. For instance, research shows that in cultures where older adults are held in high esteem, such as in mainland China, older people are less likely to show memory losses than those living in cultures that expect older people's memory to decline.

"As I get older, I find I rely more and more on these sticky notes to remind me."

Similarly, when older people in Western societies are reminded of the advantages of age ("age brings wisdom"), they tend to do better on tests of memory (Levy & Langer, 1994; Levy, 1996).

Even when people do show memory declines during late adulthood, their deficits tend to be limited to particular types of memory. Losses tend to be limited to episodic memories, which relate to specific experiences about our lives. Other types of memories, such as semantic memories (memories of general knowledge and facts) and implicit memories (memories we are not consciously aware of) are largely unaffected by age (Graf, 1990; Russo & Parkin, 1993).

Declines in episodic memories can often be traced to changes in the lives of older adults. For instance, it is not surprising that a retired person who no longer faces the intellectual challenges encountered on the job might well be less practiced in using memory or even be less motivated to remember things, leading to an apparent decline in memory. Even if their long-term memory declines, older adults can usually profit from compensatory efforts. When older adults learn to use the kinds of mnemonic strategies described in Chapter 7, they can not only prevent their long-term memory from deteriorating, but can actually improve it (Kotler-Cope & Camp, 1990; Verhaeghen, Marcoen, & Goossens, 1992; West, 1995).

In the past, older adults with severe cases of memory decline, accompanied by other cognitive difficulties, were viewed as suffering from senility. *Senility* is a broad, imprecise term typically applied to older adults who experience progressive deterioration of mental abilities, including memory loss, disorientation to time and place, and general confusion. Though senility was once thought to be an inevitable state that accompanies aging, the label senile is now viewed by gerontologists as having outlived its usefulness. Rather than senility being the cause of certain symptoms, the symptoms are deemed to be caused by some other factor.

Some cases of memory loss, however, are produced by actual disease. For instance, *Alzheimer's disease* is a progressive brain disorder, discussed in Chapter 7, that leads to a gradual and irreversible decline in cognitive abilities. In other cases, the declines are caused by temporary anxiety and depression, which can be successfully treated, or might even be due to overmedication. The danger is that people suffering such symptoms will be labeled "senile" and left untreated, thereby continuing their decline—even though treatment would have been beneficial (Selkoe, 1997).

disengagement theory of aging: A theory that holds that aging is a gradual withdrawal from the world on physical, psychological, and social levels

In sum, most declines in cognitive functioning in old age are not inevitable. The key to maintaining cognitive skills might lie in intellectual stimulation. Like the rest of us, older adults need a stimulating environment in order to hone and maintain their skills.

The Social World of Late Adulthood: Old but Not Alone

Just as the view that mental declines are an inevitable outcome of old age has proved to be wrong, so has the view that old age inevitably brings loneliness. Most people in late adulthood see themselves as functioning members of society; only a small minority report that loneliness is a serious problem (Binstock & George, 1996).

There is no single way to age successfully. According to the **disengagement theory of aging,** aging produces a gradual withdrawal from the world on physical, psychological, and social

During late adulthood, people can find fulfillment through their contributions to their community and society by working with others.

levels (Cummings & Henry, 1961). But such disengagement serves an important purpose, providing the opportunity for increased reflectiveness and decreased emotional investment in others at a time of life when social relationships will inevitably be ended by death.

An alternative view of aging is presented by the **activity theory of aging,** which suggests that the people who age most successfully are those who maintain the interests, activities, and level of social interaction they experienced during middle adulthood (Blau, 1973). According to activity theory, late adulthood should reflect a continuation, as much as possible, of the activities in which people participated during the earlier part of their lives.

Both disengagement and activity can lead to successful aging. Not all people in late adulthood need a life filled with activities and social interaction to be happy; as in every stage of life, there are those who are just as satisfied leading a relatively inactive, solitary existence. There are vast individual differences in how people cope with the aging process.

Regardless of whether people become disengaged or maintain their activities from earlier stages of life, most engage in a process of **life review,** in which they examine and evaluate their lives. Remembering and reconsidering what has occurred in the past, many people in late adulthood come to a better understanding of themselves, sometimes resolving lingering problems and conflicts, and face their lives with greater wisdom and serenity.

Clearly, people in late adulthood are not just marking time until death. Rather, old age is a time of continued growth and development, as important as any other period of life (Butler et al., 1990; Harlow & Cantor, 1996).

activity theory of aging: A theory that holds that the elderly who age most successfully are those who maintain the interests and activities they had during middle age

life review: The process in which people in late adulthood examine and evaluate their lives

BECOMING AN INFORMED CONSUMER OF PSYCHOLOGY

Adjusting to Death

At some time in our lives, we all face death—certainly our own, as well as the deaths of friends, loved ones, and even strangers. Although there is nothing more inevitable in life, death remains a frightening, emotion-laden topic. Certainly, little is more stressful than the death of a loved one or the contemplation of our own imminent death, and preparing for death is one of our most crucial developmental tasks (Aiken, 2001).

Not too long ago, talk of death was taboo. The topic was never mentioned to dying people, and gerontologists had little to say about it. That changed, however, with the pioneering work of Elisabeth Kübler-Ross (1969), who brought the subject of death into the open with her observation that those facing impending death tend to move through five broad stages:

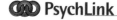 **PsychLink**

Death and dying in America
www.mhhe.com/
feldmanup6-13links

- *Denial.* In this first stage, people resist the idea that they are dying. Even if told that their chances for survival are small, they refuse to admit that they are facing death.
- *Anger.* After moving beyond the denial stage, dying people become angry—angry at people around them who are in good health, angry at medical professionals for being ineffective, angry at God.
- *Bargaining.* Anger leads to bargaining, in which the dying try to think of ways to postpone death. They might decide to dedicate their lives to religion if God saves them; they might say, "If only I can live to see my son married, I will accept death then."
- *Depression.* When dying people come to feel that bargaining is of no use, they move to the next stage: depression. They realize

that their lives really are coming to an end, leading to what Kübler-Ross calls "preparatory grief" for their own death.

- *Acceptance.* In this last stage, people accept impending death. Usually they are unemotional and uncommunicative; it is as if they have made peace with themselves and are expecting death with no bitterness.

It is important to keep in mind that not everyone experiences each of these stages in the same way. In fact, Kübler-Ross's stages pertain only to people who are fully aware that they are dying and have the time to evaluate their impending death. Furthermore, there are vast differences in how specific individuals react to impending death. The specific cause and duration of dying, as well as the person's sex, age, and personality and the type of support received from family and friends, all have an impact on how people respond to death (Zautra, Reich, & Guarnaccia, 1990; Stroebe, Stroebe, & Hansson, 1993).

Few of us enjoy contemplating death. Yet awareness of its psychological aspects and consequences can make its inevitable arrival less anxiety-producing and perhaps more understandable.

Evaluate

1. _____ _____ theories suggest that there is a maximum time limit in which cells are able to reproduce. This time limit explains the eventual breakdown of the body during old age.
2. In contrast to the above theories, _____ - _____ - _____ theories state that the body simply becomes less efficient as time passes.
3. Lower IQ test scores during late adulthood do not necessarily mean a decrease in intelligence. True or false?
4. During old age, a person's _____ intelligence continues to increase, through _____ intelligence might decline.
5. Lavinia feels that, in her old age, she has gradually decreased her social contacts and has become more self-oriented. A proponent of _____ theory interprets the situation as a result of Lavinia's not maintaining her past interests. A supporter of _____ theory views her behavior in a more positive light, suggesting that it is a natural process accompanied by enhanced reflectiveness and declining emotional investment.
6. In Kübler-Ross's _____ stage, people resist the idea of death. In the _____ stage, they attempt to make deals to avoid death, and in the _____ stage, they passively await death.

Rethink

1. Is the possibility that life might be extended for several decades a mixed blessing? What societal consequences might an extended life span bring about?
2. It has been found that people in late adulthood require intellectual stimulation. Does this have implications for the societies in which older people live? In what way might stereotypes about older individuals contribute to their isolation and lack of intellectual stimulation?

Answers to Evaluate Questions

1. Genetic preprogramming 2. wear-and-tear 3. True 4. crystallized; fluid 5. activity; disengagement 6. denial; bargaining; acceptance

Looking **Back**

What major physical, social, and cognitive transitions characterize adolescence?

- Adolescence, the developmental stage between childhood and adulthood, is marked by the onset of puberty, or sexual maturation. The age at which they enter puberty affects how people view themselves and how they are seen by others. (p. 388)
- Moral judgments during adolescence increase in sophistication, according to Kohlberg's three-level model. Although Kohlberg's levels are an adequate description of males' moral judgments, Gilligan suggests that women view morality in terms of caring for individuals rather than in terms of broad, general principles of justice. (p. 390)
- According to Erikson's model of psychosocial development, adolescence can be accompanied by an identity crisis. Adolescence is followed by three stages of psychosocial development that cover the remainder of the life span. (p. 392)

What are the principal kinds of khysical, social, and intellectual changes that occur in early and middle adulthood, and what are their causes?

- Early adulthood marks the peak of physical health. Physical changes occur relatively gradually in men and women during early and middle adulthood. (p. 397)
- One major physical change occurs at the end of middle adulthood for women: They begin menopause, after which they are no longer fertile. (p. 398)
- During middle adulthood, people typically experience a midlife transition in which the notion that life is not unending becomes more important. In some cases this can lead to a midlife crisis, although the passage into middle age is typically relatively calm. (p. 398)
- As aging continues during middle adulthood, people realize in their fifties that their lives and accomplishments are fairly well set, and they try to come to terms with them. (p. 399)
- The most important developmental milestones of adulthood include marriage, family changes, and divorce. Another important determinant of adult development is work. (p. 399)

How does the reality of old age differ from the stereotypes about the period?

- Old age can bring marked physical declines, caused by genetic preprogramming or physical wear and tear. Although the activities of people in late adulthood are not all that different from those of younger people, older adults do experience declines in reaction time, sensory abilities, and physical stamina. (p. 403)
- Intellectual declines are not an inevitable part of aging. Fluid intelligence does decline with age, and long-term memory abilities are sometimes impaired. In contrast, crystallized intelligence shows slight increases with age, and short-term memory remains at about the same level. (p. 404)
- Disengagement theory sees successful aging as a process accompanied by gradual withdrawal from the physical, psychological, and social worlds. In contrast, activity theory suggests that the maintenance of interests and activities from earlier years leads to successful aging. (p. 406)

How can we adjust to death?

- According to Kübler-Ross, dying people move through five stages as they face death: denial, anger, bargaining, depression, and acceptance. (p. 407)

Key Terms and Concepts

adolescence (p. 388)
puberty (p. 389)
identity-versus-role-confusion stage (p. 392)
identity (p. 392)
intimacy-versus-isolation stage (p. 393)
generativity-versus-stagnation stage (p. 393)
ego-integrity-versus-despair stage (p. 393)

menopause (p. 398)
genetic preprogramming theories
    of aging (p. 404)
wear-and-tear theories of aging (p. 404)
disengagement theory of aging (p. 406)
activity theory of aging (p. 407)
life review (p. 407)

Preview

For additional
quizzing and a
variety of interactive
resources, visit the
*Understanding
Psychology* Online
Learning Center at

www.mhhe.com/feldmanup6

Psychology on the Web

1. Should marriage be encouraged by political incentives (such as the movement to eliminate the "marriage penalty" in the U.S. tax code), and should living together (cohabitation) be discouraged? Seek information about the benefits of marriage and/or cohabitation, including financial, emotional, health, legal, spiritual, and other benefits. Examine what you find in terms of the objectivity and credibility of the source. Write a brief summary of your findings.

2. Find different answers to the question "Why do people die?" Search the Web for scientific, philosophical, and spiritual/religious answers. Write a summary in which you compare the different approaches to this question. Does the thinking in any one realm influence the thinking in the others? How?

Epilogue

In this chapter we have examined some of the changes that occur in people's physical, cognitive, moral, and social development as they move through adolescence, early and middle adulthood, and old age. We have noted that many changes are highly likely to occur as people progress through these ages, but that not every change is universal. We have also seen that many preconceptions and stereotypes about these different periods of life are erroneous.

Before we proceed to a consideration of personality, turn back to the prologue of this chapter, about the Delany sisters, and consider these questions.

1. If psychologists had devoted years to the study of individuals from a culture similar to the one in which the Delany sisters grew up, do you think their conclusions about the psychosocial aspects of adolescence would differ from those that are based on the majority culture? In what ways?

2. What sort of identity-versus-role-confusion stage might the Delany sisters—descendants of slaves who were determined to pursue a college education—have faced?

3. Which stage of moral reasoning is exemplified in Sarah Delany's decision to avoid the interview for her first teaching position by pretending that a mix-up prevented her from attending? Why?

4. In what ways does Sarah Delany defy stereotypes about late adulthood?

Chapter Fourteen

Personality

Prologue: Good Guy or Good Fella?

Looking Ahead

Psychoanalytic Approaches to Personality

Freud's Psychoanalytic Theory

The Neo-Freudian Psychoanalysts

Other Major Approaches to Personality: In Search of Human Uniqueness

Trait Approaches: Placing Labels on Personality

Learning Approaches: We Are What We've Learned

Biological and Evolutionary Approaches: Are We Born with Personality?

Applying Psychology in the 21st Century: Can Unjustified High Self-Esteem Lead to Violence?

Humanistic Approaches: The Uniqueness of You

Comparing Approaches to Personality

Assessing Personality: Determining What Makes Us Special

Exploring Diversity: Should Norms Be Based on Race and Ethnicity?

Self-Report Measures of Personality

Projective Methods

Behavioral Assessment

Becoming an Informed Consumer of Psychology: Assessing Personality Assessments

Looking Back

Key Terms and Concepts

Psychology on the Web

OLC Preview

Epilogue

The local police chief stands in front of the house inhabited—and later abandoned—by the man called Tom, who was either a soft-hearted do-gooder or a violent mobster, depending on whom you talked to.

Prologue

Good Guy or Good Fella?

The 60-something man called himself "Tom" and his girlfriend "Helen." He said they were from New York, and they would spend months at a time visiting the Louisiana resort town of Grand Isle.

During his visits, Tom would drive around Grand Isle, offering biscuits to stray dogs. He wept when a dying puppy had to be shot to end its suffering. When he went fishing, he would toss back the small fish. He told a family he befriended how bad it was to permit children to watch violence on television. He bought eyeglasses for a child whose vision needed correction, and bought a family a refrigerator and stove.

"He was a very nice man," said one person who got to know him, and whose children called him "Uncle Tom." "He treated us like family. He was kind. He really had a nice personality. How could you not love him?" (Murphy, 1998, p. A8).

But to criminal investigators at the FBI, he was not so lovable. They said he was a mobster who had run a crime empire that included drug sales and gambling. He was a reputed murderer and bank robber, a man who had held a knife to a banker's throat while extorting $50,000. To the FBI, his pleasant personality was just a front, motivated only by self-interest.

Looking Ahead

Was "Tom" a soft-hearted do-gooder, or, as the FBI contends, a ruthless, greedy mobster, willing to do anything to get ahead?

Many people, like "Tom," have different sides to their personalities, appearing one way to some people and quite differently to others. At the same time, you probably know people whose behavior is so consistent that you can easily predict how they are going to behave, no matter what the situation.

Psychologists who specialize in personality seek to understand the characteristic ways in which people behave. **Personality** is the pattern of enduring characteristics that differentiates a person—those patterns of behaviors that make each of us unique. It is also personality that leads us to act consistently and predictably in different situations and over extended periods of time.

In this chapter we consider a number of approaches to personality. We begin with the broadest and most comprehensive theory: Freud's psychoanalytic theory. Next, we turn to more recent theories of personality. We consider approaches that concentrate on identifying the most fundamental personality traits; on theories that view personality as a set of learned behaviors; on biological and evolutionary perspectives on personality; and on approaches, known as humanistic theories, that highlight the uniquely human aspects of personality. We end our discussion by focusing on how personality is measured and how personality tests can be used.

Prepare

How do psychologists define and use the concept of personality?

What do the theories of Freud and his successors tell us about the structure and development of personality?

Organize

Psychoanalytic Approaches to Personality
    Freud's Psychoanalytic Theory
    The Neo-Freudian Psychoanalysts

personality: The pattern of enduring characteristics that differentiates a person—the patterns of behaviors that make each individual unique

psychoanalytic theory: Freud's theory that unconscious forces act as determinants of personality

unconscious: A part of the personality of which a person is not aware, and which is a potential determinant of behavior

id: The raw, unorganized, inborn part of personality, whose sole purpose is to reduce tension created by primitive drives related to hunger, sex, aggression, and irrational impulses

ego: The part of the personality that provides a buffer between the id and the outside world

superego: According to Freud, the final personality structure to develop; it represents society's standards of right and wrong as handed down by a person's parents, teachers, and other important figures

Psychoanalytic Approaches to Personality

The college student was intent on making a good first impression on an attractive woman he had spotted across a crowded room at a party. As he walked toward her, he mulled over a line he had heard in an old movie the night before: "I don't believe we've been properly introduced yet." To his horror, what came out was a bit different. After threading his way through the crowded room, he finally reached the woman and blurted out, "I don't believe we've been properly seduced yet."

Although this student's error might seem to be merely an embarrassing slip of the tongue, according to one group of personality theorists—*psychoanalysts*—such a mistake is not an error at all (Motley, 1987). Instead, it illustrates one way our behavior is triggered by forces within personality of which we are not aware. These hidden drives, shaped by childhood experiences, play an important role in energizing and directing our everyday behavior.

Freud's Psychoanalytic Theory

Sigmund Freud, an Austrian physician, originated **psychoanalytic theory** in the early 1900s. Freud believed that conscious experience was just the tip of our psychological makeup and experience. In fact, he thought that much of our behavior is motivated by the **unconscious,** a part of the personality of which a person is not aware.

Like the unseen mass of a floating iceberg, the material in the unconscious far surpasses in quantity the information we are aware of. Freud argued that to understand personality, it is necessary to expose what is in the unconscious. But because the unconscious disguises the meaning of the material it holds, the content of the unconscious cannot be observed directly. It is therefore necessary to interpret clues to the unconscious—slips of the tongue, fantasies, and dreams—in order to understand the unconscious processes that direct behavior. A slip of the tongue such as the one quoted earlier (sometimes termed a *Freudian slip*) might be interpreted as revealing the speaker's unconscious sexual desires.

To Freud, much of our personality is determined by our unconscious. Some of the unconscious is made up of the *preconscious,* which contains material that is not threatening and is easily brought to mind, such as the knowledge that $2 + 2 = 4$. But

deeper in the unconscious are instinctual drives, the wishes, desires, demands, and needs that are hidden from conscious awareness because of the conflicts and pain they would cause us if they were part of our everyday lives. The unconscious provides a "safe haven" for our recollections of threatening events.

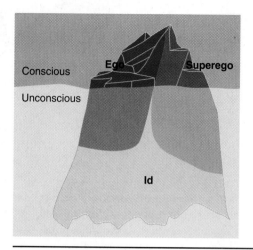

Structuring Personality: Id, Ego, and Superego

To describe the structure of personality, Freud developed a comprehensive theory, which held that personality consists of three separate but interacting components: the id, the ego, and the superego. Freud suggested that the three structures can be diagrammed to show how they are related to the conscious and the unconscious (see Figure 14-1).

Although it might appear that Freud is describing the three components of personality as actual physical structures in the nervous system, they are not. Instead, they represent abstract conceptions of a general *model* of personality that describes the interaction of forces that motivate behavior.

Figure 14-1 In Freud's model of personality, there are three major components: the id, the ego, and the superego. As the iceberg analogy shows, only a small portion of personality is conscious. Why do you think that only the ego and superego have conscious components?

If personality consisted only of primitive, instinctual cravings and longings, it would have just one component: the id. The **id** is the raw, unorganized, inborn part of personality. From the time of birth, the id attempts to reduce tension created by primitive drives related to hunger, sex, aggression, and irrational impulses. These drives are fueled by "psychic energy," or *libido* as Freud called it.

The id operates according to the *pleasure principle,* in which the goal is the immediate reduction of tension and the maximization of satisfaction. However, reality prevents the fulfillment of the demands of the pleasure principle in most cases: We cannot always eat when we are hungry, and we can discharge our sexual drives only when time, place—and partner—are willing. To account for this fact of life, Freud suggested a second component of personality, which he called the ego.

The **ego** strives to balance the desires of the id and the realities of the objective, outside world. In contrast to the pleasure-seeking nature of the id, the ego operates according to the *reality principle,* in which instinctual energy is restrained in order to maintain the safety of the individual and help integrate the person into society. In a sense, then, the ego is the "executive" of personality: It makes decisions, controls actions, and allows thinking and problem solving of a higher order than the id's capabilities permit.

The **superego,** the final personality structure to develop, represents social right and wrong as taught and modeled by a person's parents, teachers, and other significant individuals. The superego has two components, the *conscience* and the *ego-ideal.* The conscience prevents us from behaving in a morally improper way by making us feel guilty if we do wrong, and the ego-ideal, which represents the "perfect person" that we wish we were, motivates us to do what is morally right. The superego helps us control impulses coming from the id, making our behavior less selfish and more virtuous.

The superego and id share an important feature: Both are unrealistic, in that they do not consider the practical realities imposed by society. The superego, if left to operate without restraint, would create perfectionists, unable to make the compromises that life requires. Similarly, an unrestrained id would create a primitive, pleasure-seeking, thoughtless individual, seeking to fulfill every desire without delay. As a result, the ego must compromise between the demands of the superego and the demands of the id.

Freud suggests that the superego, the part of personality that represents the rights and wrongs of society, develops from direct teaching and from the models of parents, teachers, and other significant individuals.

Developing Personality: A Stage Approach

Freud also provided us with a view of how personality develops in childhood through a series of stages. The sequence he proposed is noteworthy because it explains how experiences and difficulties during a particular childhood stage might predict specific characteristics in adult personality. The theory is also unique in focusing each stage on the major biological function that Freud assumed to be the focus of pleasure in that stage (see Table 14-1).

PsychLink

Freud's works
www.mhhe.com/
feldmanup6-14links

oral stage: According to Freud, a stage from birth to 12 to 18 months, in which an infant's center of pleasure is the mouth

fixation: Conflicts or concerns that persist beyond the developmental period in which they first occur

anal stage: According to Freud, a stage from 12 to 18 months to 3 years of age, in which a child's pleasure is centered on the anus

phallic stage: According to Freud, a period beginning around age 3 during which a child's interest focuses on the genitals

Oedipus conflict: A child's sexual interest in his or her opposite-sex parent, typically resolved through identification with the same-sex parent

identification: The process of trying to be like another person as much as possible, imitating that person's behavior and adopting similar beliefs and values

According to Freud, a child goes through the anal stage from 12 to 18 months until 3 years of age. Toilet training is a crucial event at this stage, one that psychoanalytic theory claims directly influences the formation of an individual's personality.

Table 14-1 Freud's Stages of Personality Development

Stage	Age	Major Characteristics
Oral	Birth to 12–18 months	Interest in oral gratification from sucking, eating, mouthing, biting
Anal	12–18 months to 3 years	Gratification from expelling and withholding feces; coming to terms with society's controls relating to toilet training
Phallic	3 to 5–6 years	Interest in the genitals; coming to terms with Oedipal conflict, leading to identification with same-sex parent
Latency	5–6 years to adolescence	Sexual concerns largely unimportant
Genital	Adolescence to adulthood	Reemergence of sexual interests and establishment of mature sexual relationships

In the first stage of development, called the **oral stage,** the baby's mouth is the focal point of pleasure. During the first 12 to 18 months of life, children suck, mouth, and bite anything that will fit into their mouths. To Freud, this behavior suggested that the mouth is the primary site of a kind of sexual pleasure. Infants who are either overly indulged (perhaps by being fed every time they cried) or frustrated in their search for oral gratification might become fixated at this stage. **Fixation** refers to conflicts or concerns that persist beyond the developmental period in which they first occur. Such conflicts can be due to one's needs being either ignored or overly indulged during the earlier period. For example, fixation might occur if an infant's oral needs were constantly immediately gratified at the first sign of hunger. Fixation at the oral stage might produce an adult who is unusually interested in oral activities—eating, talking, smoking—or who shows symbolic sorts of oral interests: being either "bitingly" sarcastic or very gullible ("swallowing" anything).

From around 12 to 18 months until 3 years of age—where the emphasis in Western cultures is on toilet training—the child enters the **anal stage.** At this point, the major source of pleasure changes from the mouth to the anal region, and children obtain considerable pleasure from both retention and expulsion of feces. If toilet training is particularly demanding, the result may be fixation. Freud suggested that adults who are fixated in the anal stage might show unusual rigidity, orderliness, punctuality—or extreme disorderliness or sloppiness.

At about age 3, the **phallic stage** begins, at which point there is another major shift in the primary source of pleasure for the child. This time, interest focuses on the genitals and the pleasures derived from fondling them. This is also the stage of one of the most important points of personality development, according to Freudian theory: the **Oedipus conflict.** As children focus their attention on their genitals, the differences between female and male anatomy become more salient. Furthermore, at this time, according to Freud, the male unconsciously begins to develop sexual interests in his mother, starts to see his father as a rival, and harbors a wish to kill his father—as Oedipus did in the ancient Greek tragedy. But because he views his father as too powerful, he develops a fear of retaliation in the form of "castration anxiety." Ultimately, this fear becomes so powerful that the child represses his desires for his mother and instead identifies with his father. **Identification** is the process of trying to be like another person as much as possible, imitating that person's behavior and adopting similar beliefs and values. By identifying with his father, a son seeks to obtain a woman like his unattainable mother.

For girls, the process is different. Freud reasoned that girls begin to experience sexual arousal toward their fathers and—in a suggestion that was later to bring serious accusations that he viewed women as inferior to men—that they begin to

experience *penis envy:* they wish, said Freud, that they had an anatomical part that, at least to Freud, seems "missing" in girls. Blaming their mothers for their lack of a penis, girls come to believe that their mothers are responsible for their "castration." As with males, though, they find that in order to resolve such unacceptable feelings, they must identify with the same-sex parent by behaving like her and adopting her attitudes and values. In this way, a girl's identification with her mother is completed.

At this point, the Oedipus conflict is said to be resolved, and Freudian theory assumes that both males and females move on to the next stage of development. If difficulties arise during this period, however, all sorts of problems are thought to occur, including improper sex-role behavior and the failure to develop a conscience.

Imitating a person's behavior and adopting similar beliefs and values is part of Freud's concept of identification. How can this concept be applied to the definition of gender roles? Is identification similar in all cultures?

Following the resolution of the Oedipus conflict, typically at around age 5 or 6, children move into the **latency period,** which lasts until puberty. During this period, sexual interests become dormant, even in the unconscious. Then, during adolescence, sexual feelings reemerge, marking the start of the final period, the **genital stage,** which extends until death. The focus during the genital stage is on mature, adult sexuality, which Freud defined as sexual intercourse.

latency period: According to Freud, the period between the phallic stage and puberty during which children temporarily put aside their sexual interests

genital stage: According to Freud, the period from puberty until death, marked by mature sexual behavior (i.e., sexual intercourse)

Defense Mechanisms

Freud's efforts to describe and theorize about the underlying dynamics of personality and its development were motivated by very practical problems that his patients faced in dealing with *anxiety,* an intense, negative emotional experience. According to Freud, anxiety is a danger signal to the ego. Although anxiety can arise from realistic fears—such as seeing a poisonous snake about to strike—it can also occur in the form of *neurotic anxiety,* in which irrational impulses emanating from the id threaten to burst through and become uncontrollable.

Because anxiety, obviously, is unpleasant, Freud believed that people develop a range of defense mechanisms to deal with it. **Defense mechanisms** are unconscious strategies people use to reduce anxiety by concealing its source from themselves and others.

The primary defense mechanism is *repression,* in which unacceptable or unpleasant id impulses are pushed back into the unconscious. Repression is the most direct method of dealing with anxiety; instead of handling an anxiety-producing impulse on a conscious level, one simply ignores it. For example, a college student who feels hatred for her mother might repress these personally and socially unacceptable feelings. The feelings remain lodged within the unconscious, because acknowledging them would provoke anxiety. Similarly, memories of childhood abuse can be repressed (discussed in Chapter 7). Although such memories might not be consciously recalled, they can affect later behavior, and they can be revealed through dreams, slips of the tongue, or symbolically in some other fashion.

defense mechanisms: Unconscious strategies people use to reduce anxiety by concealing the source of the anxiety from themselves and others

If repression is ineffective in keeping anxiety at bay, other defense mechanisms might be used. Freud, and later his daughter Anna Freud (who became a well-known psychoanalyst herself), formulated an extensive list of potential defense mechanisms; the major ones are summarized in Table 14-2 (Cooper, 1989; Conte & Plutchik, 1995; Basch, 1996).

All of us employ defense mechanisms to some degree, according to Freudian theory, and they can serve a useful purpose by protecting us from unpleasant information. Yet some people use them to such an extent that they must constantly direct a large amount of

"Look, call it denial if you like, but I think what goes on in my personal life is none of my own damn business."

Table 14-2 Freud's Defense Mechanisms

Defense Mechanism	Explanation	Example
Repression	Unacceptable or unpleasant impulses are pushed back into the unconscious.	A woman is unable to recall that she was raped.
Regression	People behave as if they were at an earlier stage of development.	A boss has a temper tantrum when an employee makes a mistake.
Displacement	The expression of an unwanted feeling or thought is redirected from a more threatening, powerful person to a weaker one.	A brother yells at his younger sister after a teacher gives him a bad grade.
Rationalization	People distort reality in order to justify something that has happened.	A person who is passed over for an award says she didn't really want it in the first place.
Denial	People refuse to accept or acknowledge an anxiety-producing piece of information.	A student refuses to believe that he has flunked a course.
Projection	People attribute unwanted impulses and feelings to someone else.	A man who is angry at his father acts lovingly to his father but complains that his father is angry with him.
Sublimation	People divert unwanted impulses into socially approved thoughts, feelings, or behaviors.	A person with strong feelings of aggression becomes a soldier.
Reaction formation	Unconscious impulses are expressed as their opposite in consciousness.	A mother who unconsciously resents her child acts in an overly loving way to the child.

psychic energy toward hiding and rechanneling unacceptable impulses. This makes everyday living difficult. The result is a mental disorder produced by anxiety—what Freud called "neurosis" (a term rarely used by psychologists today, although it endures in everyday conversation).

Evaluating Freud's Legacy

Freud's theory has had a significant impact on the field of psychology—and even more broadly on Western philosophy and literature. The ideas of the unconscious, defense mechanisms, and childhood roots of adult psychological difficulties have become accepted by many. Furthermore, Freud's emphasis on the unconscious has been partially supported by current research on dreams (Chapter 5) and implicit memory (Chapter 7), and it has generated an important method of treating psychological disturbances, as we will discuss in Chapter 17 (Westen, 1998; Westen & Gabbard, 1999; Kihlstrom, 1999).

On the other hand, personality psychologists have leveled significant criticisms against the theory. Among the most compelling is the lack of scientific data to support the theory. Although individual case studies *seem* supportive, we lack conclusive evidence showing that the personality is structured and operates along the lines Freud laid out. This is partly due to the fact that Freud's conception of personality is built on unobservable abstract concepts. Moreover, it is difficult to predict how certain developmental difficulties will be displayed in the adult. For instance, a person who is fixated at the anal stage might, according to Freud, be unusually messy—or unusually neat. Freud's theory offers us no way to predict which way the difficulty will be exhibited (Macmillan, 1991; Crews, 1996).

PsychLink

Questioning Freud's theories
www.mhhe.com/
feldmanup6-14links

Finally, Freud made his observations—admittedly insightful ones—and derived his theory from a limited population. His theory was based almost entirely on upper-class Austrian women living in the strict, puritanical era of the early 1900s. How far one can generalize beyond this population is a matter of considerable debate. For instance, in some Pacific Island societies, the role of disciplinarian is played by a mother's oldest brother, not the father. In such a culture, it is unreasonable to argue that the Oedipus conflict would progress in the same way as in Freud's Austrian society, where the father typically was the major disciplinarian. In short, a cross-cultural perspective raises questions about the universality of Freud's view of personality development (Doi, 1990; Brislin, 1993; Altman, 1996).

The Neo-Freudian Psychoanalysts

One important outgrowth of Freud's theorizing was the work done by a series of successors who were trained in traditional Freudian theory but who later rejected some of its major points. These theorists are known as **neo-Freudian psychoanalysts.**

The neo-Freudians placed greater emphasis than Freud on the functions of the ego, suggesting that it had more control than the id over day-to-day activities, and less emphasis on sex as a driving force in people's lives. They also paid greater attention to social factors and the effects of society and culture on personality development.

Jung's Collective Unconscious

One of the most influential neo-Freudians, Carl Jung (pronounced "Yoong"), rejected the notion of the primary importance of unconscious sexual urges. Instead he looked at the primitive urges of the unconscious more positively, suggesting that people had a **collective unconscious,** a set of influences we inherit from our own relatives, the whole human race, and even nonhuman animal ancestors from the distant past. According to Jung, this collective unconscious is shared by everyone and is displayed in behavior that is common across diverse cultures—such as love of mother, belief in a supreme being, and even behavior as specific as fear of snakes.

Jung went on to propose that the collective unconscious contains *archetypes,* universal symbolic representations of a particular person, object, or experience (Jung, 1961). For instance, a mother archetype, which contains reflections of our ancestors' relationships with mother figures, is suggested by the prevalence of mothers in art, religion, literature, and mythology. (Think of the Virgin Mary, Earth Mother, wicked stepmothers of fairy tales, Mother's Day, and so forth!) Jung also suggested that men possess an unconscious feminine archetype affecting how they behave, and that women have a male archetype that colors their behavior.

To Jung, archetypes play an important role in determining our day-to-day reactions, attitudes, and values. For instance, Jung might argue that the popularity of the *Star Wars* movies is due to their use of broad archetypes of good (such as Luke Skywalker) and evil (such as Darth Vader).

Adler and the Other Neo-Freudians

Alfred Adler, another important neo-Freudian psychoanalyst, also considered Freudian theory's emphasis on sexual needs to be misplaced. Adler proposed instead that the primary human motivation is a striving for superiority, not in terms of superiority over others, but as a quest to achieve self-improvement and perfection.

According to Adler, when adults have not been able to overcome the feelings of inferiority that they developed as children, when they were small and limited in their knowledge about the world, they develop an **inferiority complex.** Early social relationships with parents have an important effect on how well children are able to outgrow

neo-Freudian psychoanalysts: Psychoanalysts who were trained in traditional Freudian theory but who later rejected some of its major points

collective unconscious: A set of influences we inherit from our own particular ancestors, the whole human race, and even animal ancestors from the distant evolutionary past

inferiority complex: According to Adler, a complex developed by adults who have not been able to overcome the feelings of inferiority they developed as children, when they were small and limited in their knowledge about the world

PsychLink
Jung's theory
www.mhhe.com/
feldmanup6–14links

In Jungian terms, Darth Vader and Luke Skywalker are archetypes, or universally recognizable symbols of good and evil.

feelings of personal inferiority and instead orient themselves toward attaining more socially useful goals, such as improving society.

Other neo-Freudians, such as Erik Erikson (whose theory we discussed in Chapters 12 and 13), Freud's own daughter Anna Freud, and Karen Horney (1937), also focused less than Freud on inborn sexual and aggressive drives and more on the social and cultural factors behind personality. Horney (pronounced "HORN-eye") was one of the first psychologists to champion women's issues. She suggested that personality develops in terms of social relationships and depends particularly on the relationship between parents and child and how well the child's needs are met. She rejected Freud's suggestion that women have penis envy, asserting that what women envy most in men is not their anatomy but the independence, success, and freedom that women are often denied.

Evaluate

1. _____ theory states that behavior is motivated primarily by unconscious forces.

2. Match each section of the personality (according to Freud) with its description:

   1. Ego
   2. Id
   3. Superego

   a. Determines right from wrong on the basis of cultural standards.

   b. Operates according to the "reality principle"; redirects energy to integrate the person into society.

   c. Seeks to reduce tension brought on by primitive drives.

3. Within the superego, the _____ - _____ motivates us to do what is right, and the _____ restrains us from doing what is unacceptable.

4. Which of the following represents the proper order of personality development according to Freud?

   a. Oral, phallic, latency, anal, genital
   b. Anal, oral, phallic, genital, latency
   c. Oral, anal, phallic, latency, genital
   d. Latency, phallic, anal, genital, oral

5. In the resolution of the _____ complex, Freud believed, boys learn to repress their desire for their mother and identify with their father.

6. _____ - _____ is the term Freud used to describe unconscious strategies used to reduce anxiety.

Answers to Evaluate Questions

1. Psychoanalytic 2. 1–b; 2–c; 3–a 3. ego-ideal; conscience 4. c 5. Oedipus 6. Defense mechanisms

Rethink

1. Can you think of ways in which Freud's theories of unconscious motivations are commonly used in popular culture? How accurately do you think such popular uses of Freudian theories reflect Freud's ideas?

2. What are some examples of archetypes in addition to those mentioned in this chapter? In what ways are archetypes similar to and different from stereotypes?

Other Major Approaches to Personality: In Search of Human Uniqueness

Prepare

What are the major aspects of trait, learning, biological and evolutionary, and humanistic approaches to personality?

Organize

Other Major Approaches to Personality
 Trait Approaches
 Learning Approaches
 Biological and Evolutionary Approaches
 Humanistic Approaches
 Comparing Approaches to Personality

"Tell me about Nelson," said Johnetta.

"Oh, he's just terrific. He's the friendliest guy I know—goes out of his way to be nice to everyone. He hardly ever gets mad. He's just so even-tempered, no matter what's happening. And he's really smart, too. About the only thing I don't like is that he's always in such a hurry to get things done. He seems to have boundless energy, much more than I have."

"He sounds great to me, especially in comparison to Rico," replied Johnetta. "He is so self-centered and arrogant it drives me crazy. I sometimes wonder why I ever started going out with him."

Friendly. Even-tempered. Smart. Energetic. Self-centered. Arrogant.

The interchange above lists a series of trait characterizations of the boyfriends being discussed. In fact, much of our own, personal understanding of the reasons behind others' behavior is based on the premise that people possess certain traits that are consistent across different situations. For example, we generally assume that a person who is outgoing and sociable in one situation will be outgoing and sociable in other situations (Gilbert et al., 1992; Gilbert, Miller, & Ross, 1998).

A number of formal theories of personality employ variations of this approach. We turn now to a discussion of these and other personality approaches, each of which provides an alternative to the psychoanalytic emphasis on unconscious processes in determining behavior.

Trait Approaches: Placing Labels on Personality

If someone were to ask you to characterize another person, it is probable that—like the two people in the conversation just presented—you would come up with a list of that individual's personal qualities, as you see them. But how would you know which of these qualities are most important to an understanding of that person's behavior?

Personality psychologists have asked similar questions themselves. To answer them, they have developed a model of personality known as **trait theory. Traits** are enduring dimensions of personality characteristics along which people differ: Trait theorists do not assume that some people have a trait and others do not; rather, they propose that all people possess certain traits, but that each person possesses a given trait to a given degree that can be quantified, and that people can differ in the degree to which they have a trait. For instance, you might be relatively friendly, whereas I might be relatively unfriendly. We both have a "friendliness" trait, although your degree of "friendliness" might be higher than mine. The major challenge for trait theorists taking this approach has been to identify the specific primary traits necessary to describe personality. As we shall see, different theorists have come up with surprisingly different sets of traits.

trait theory: A model of personality that seeks to identify the basic traits necessary to describe personality

traits Enduring dimensions of personality characteristics along which people differ

Allport's Trait Theory: Identifying the Basics

When personality psychologist Gordon Allport systematically pored over an unabridged dictionary, he came up with some 18,000 separate terms that could be used to describe personality. Although he was able to pare down the list to a mere 4,500 descriptors after eliminating words with the same meaning, he was obviously still left with a problem crucial to all trait approaches: Which of these were the most basic?

Allport answered this question by suggesting that there are three basic categories of traits: cardinal, central, and secondary (Allport, 1961, 1966). A *cardinal trait* is a

single characteristic that directs most of a person's activities. For example, a totally selfless woman might direct all her energy toward humanitarian activities; an intensely power-hungry person might be driven by an all-consuming need for control.

Most people, however, do not develop a single, comprehensive cardinal trait. Instead, they possess a handful of central traits that make up the core of personality. *Central traits,* such as honesty and sociability, are the major characteristics of an individual; most people have five to ten central traits. Finally, *secondary traits* are characteristics that affect an individual's behavior in fewer situations and are less influential than central or cardinal traits. For instance, a reluctance to eat meat or a love of modern art would be considered secondary traits.

Cattell, Eysenck, and the Big Five: Factoring Out Personality

More recent attempts to identify primary traits have centered on a statistical technique known as factor analysis. *Factor analysis* is a method of summarizing the relationships among a large number of variables into fewer, more general patterns. For example, a personality researcher might administer a questionnaire to many participants, asking them to describe themselves by referring to an extensive list of traits. By statistically combining responses and computing which traits are associated with one another in the same person, a researcher can identify the most fundamental patterns or combinations of traits—called factors—that underlie participants' responses.

Using factor analysis, personality psychologist Raymond Cattell (1965) suggested that sixteen pairs of *source traits* represent the basic dimensions of personality. Using these source traits, he developed the Sixteen Personality Factor Questionnaire, or 16 PF, a measure that provides scores for each of the source traits. Figure 14-2 shows the pattern of average scores on each of the source traits for three different groups of participants—airplane pilots, creative artists, and writers (Cattell, Cattell, & Cattell, 1993).

Another trait theorist, psychologist Hans Eysenck (1975, 1994; Eysenck et al., 1992), also used factor analysis to identify patterns of traits, but he came to a very different conclusion about the nature of personality. He found that personality could best

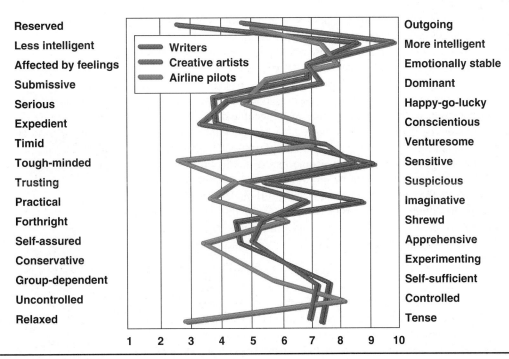

Figure 14–2 Personality profiles for source traits developed by Cattell for three groups of subjects: writers, creative artists, and airline pilots. The average score for the general population is between 4.5 and 6.5 on each scale (Cattell, Eber, & Tatsuoka, 1970). On what traits do airline pilots and writers differ most? How do these differences contribute to their chosen work?

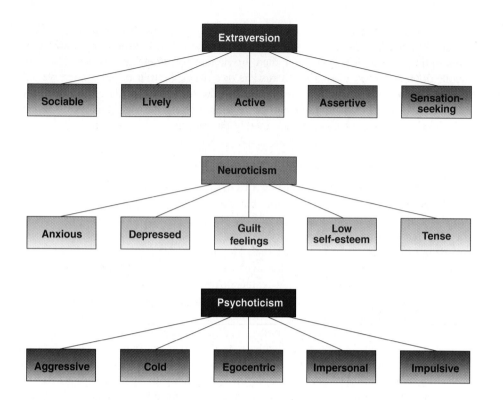

Figure 14-3 According to Eysenck, personality could best be described in terms of just three major dimensions; extraversion, neuroticism, and psychoticism. Eysenck has been able to predict behavior accurately in a variety of types of situations by evaluating people along these three dimensions (Eysenck, 1990). How do you think an airline pilot would score on Eysenck's scale?

be described in terms of just three major dimensions: *extraversion, neuroticism,* and *psychoticism.* The extraversion dimension relates to the degree of sociability; the neurotic dimension encompasses emotional stability; psychoticism refers to the degree to which reality is distorted. By evaluating people along these three dimensions, Eysenck has been able to predict behavior accurately in a variety of types of situations. Figure 14-3 illustrates specific traits associated with each of the dimensions.

The most influential trait approach today contends that five broad trait factors—called the "Big Five"—lie at the core of personality. The five factors are *openness to experience, conscientiousness, extraversion, agreeableness,* and *neuroticism* (emotional stability). (These are described in Table 14-3, and you can remember them using the mnemonic *OCEAN,* representing the first letter of each trait).

The Big Five factors emerge quite consistently in different populations of individuals, including children, college students, older adults, and speakers of different languages. Furthermore, cross-cultural research conducted in countries as diverse as Canada, Finland, Poland, and the Philippines is also supportive. In short, although the evidence is not conclusive, a growing consensus exists that the "Big Five" represent the best description of personality. Still, the debate over the specific number and kinds of traits that are fundamental to personality remains a lively one (McCrae & Costa, 1999; John & Srivastava, 1999; Saggino, 2000).

Evaluating Trait Approaches to Personality

Trait approaches have several virtues. They provide a clear, straightforward explanation of people's behavioral consistencies. Furthermore, traits allow us to readily compare one person with another. Because of these advantages, trait approaches to personality have had an important practical influence on the development of several personality measures discussed later in this chapter (Funder, 1991; Wiggins, 1997).

However, trait approaches also have some drawbacks. For example, we have seen that various trait theories describing personality come to quite different conclusions about which traits are the most fundamental and descriptive. The difficulty in determining which of the theories is most accurate has led some personality psychologists to question the validity of trait conceptions of personality in general.

Table 14-3 The Big Five Personality Factors and Dimensions of Sample Traits

Openness to experience	
Commonplace	Wide interests
Narrow interests	Imaginative
Simple	Intelligent
Shallow	Original

Conscientiousness	
Careless	Organized
Disorderly	Thorough
Frivolous	Planful
Irresponsible	Efficient

Extraversion	
Quiet	Talkative
Reserved	Assertive
Shy	Active
Silent	Energetic

Agreeableness	
Fault-finding	Sympathetic
Cold	Kind
Unfriendly	Appreciative
Quarrelsome	Affectionate

Neuroticism	
Tense	Stable
Anxious	Calm
Nervous	Contented
Moody	Unemotional

Source: Adapted from Pervin (1990), Chapter 3.

Agreeableness is one of the "Big Five" broad trait factors that lie at the core of personality.

social cognitive approaches to personality: The theory that emphasizes the influence of a person's cognitions—thoughts, feelings, expectations, and values—in determining personality

 PsychLink
Self-efficacy and culture
www.mhhe.com/
feldmanup6-14links

Actually, there is an even more fundamental difficulty with trait approaches. Even if we are able to identify a set of primary traits, we are left with little more than a label or description of personality—rather than an explanation of behavior. If we say that someone donates money to charity because he or she has the trait of generosity, we still do not know *why* the person became generous in the first place, or the reasons for displaying generosity in a given situation. In the view of some critics, then, traits do not provide explanations for behavior; they merely describe it.

Learning Approaches: We Are What We've Learned

The psychoanalytic and trait approaches we've discussed concentrate on the "inner" person—the stormy fury of an unobservable but powerful id or a hypothetical but critical set of traits. In contrast, learning approaches to personality focus on the "outer" person. To a strict learning theorist, personality is simply the sum of learned responses to the external environment—internal events such as thoughts, feelings, and motivations are irrelevant. Although they don't deny the existence of personality, learning theorists say that it is best understood by looking at features of a person's environment.

According to the most influential of the learning theorists, B. F. Skinner (whom we discussed first in terms of operant conditioning in Chapter 6), personality is a collection of learned behavior patterns (Skinner, 1975). Similarities in responses across different situations are caused by similar patterns of reinforcement that have been received in such situations in the past. If I am sociable both at parties and at meetings, it is because I have been reinforced previously for displaying social behaviors—not because I am fulfilling some unconscious wish based on experiences during my childhood or because I have an internal trait of sociability.

Strict learning theorists such as Skinner are less interested in the consistencies in behavior across situations, however, than in ways of modifying behavior. Their view is that humans are infinitely changeable through the process of learning new behavior patterns. If one is able to control and modify the patterns of reinforcers in a situation, behavior that other theorists would view as stable and unyielding can be changed and ultimately improved. Learning theorists are optimistic in their attitudes about the potential for resolving personal and societal problems through treatment strategies based on learning theory—methods we will discuss in Chapter 17.

Social Cognitive Approaches to Personality

Not all learning theories of personality take such a strict view in rejecting the importance of what is "inside" the person by focusing solely on the "outside." Unlike other learning approaches to personality, **social cognitive approaches** emphasize the influence of a person's cognitions—thoughts, feelings, expectations, and values—in determining personality. According to Albert Bandura, one of the main proponents of this point of view, people are able to foresee the possible outcomes of certain behaviors in a given setting without actually having to carry them out. This takes place mainly through the mechanism of *observational learning*—viewing the actions of others and observing the consequences (Bandura, 1986, 1999).

For instance, as we first discussed in Chapter 6, children who view a model behaving in, say, an aggressive manner tend to copy the behavior if the consequences of the model's behavior are seen to be positive. If, on the other hand, the model's aggressive behavior has resulted in no consequences or negative consequences, children are considerably less likely to act aggressively. According to social cognitive approaches, personality thus develops by repeated observation of the behavior of others.

Bandura places particular emphasis on the role played by *self-efficacy,* belief in one's own personal capabilities. Self-efficacy underlies people's faith in their ability to carry out a particular behavior or produce a desired outcome. People with high self-efficacy have higher aspirations and greater persistence in working to attain goals, and ultimately achieve greater success, than those with lower self-efficacy (Scheier & Carver, 1992; Bandura, 1997, 1999).

How do we develop self-efficacy? One way is by paying close attention to our prior successes and failures. If we try snowboarding and experience little success, we'll be less likely to try it again. However, if our initial efforts appear promising, we'll be more likely to attempt it again. Direct reinforcement and encouragement from others also play a role in developing self-efficacy (Bandura, 1988; Jenkins & Gortner, 1998).

Compared to other learning theories of personality, social cognitive approaches are distinctive in their emphasis on the reciprocity between individuals and their environment. These approaches assume not only that the environment affects personality, but also that people's behavior and personalities give "feedback" to and modify the environment (Bandura, 1999, 2000).

Our behavior also reflects the view we have of ourselves and our valuations of the various parts of our personality. *Self-esteem* is the component of personality that encompasses our positive and negative self-evaluations. Although people have a general level of self-esteem, it is not unidimensional. Specifically, we could see ourselves positively in one domain but negatively in others. For example, a good student might have high self-esteem in academic domains but more negative self-esteem in athletic areas (Moretti & Higgins, 1990; Baumeister, 1998).

Self-esteem has strong cultural components. For example, having high *relationship harmony*—a sense of success in forming close bonds with other people—is more important to self-esteem in Asian cultures than in more individualistic Western societies (Kwan, Bond, & Singelis, 1997).

Although almost everyone goes through periods of low self-esteem (after, for instance, an undeniable failure), some people are chronically low in self-esteem. For them, failure seems to be an inevitable part of life. Low self-esteem can lead to a cycle of failure, in which past failure breeds future failure. For example, consider students with low self-esteem who are studying for a test. Because of their low self-esteem, they expect to do poorly on the test. In turn, this raises their anxiety level, making it increasingly difficult to study and perhaps even leading them to work less hard. Because of these attitudes, the ultimate outcome is that they do, in fact, do badly on the test. Ultimately, this failure reinforces their low self-esteem, and the cycle is perpetuated, as illustrated in Figure 14-4.

In short, low self-esteem can lead to a self-destructive cycle of failure. On the other hand, high self-esteem can also be of concern. As you can see in the *Applying Psychology in the 21st Century* box on page 427, high self-esteem, particularly if it is unwarranted, can produce problems.

Self-efficacy, the belief in one's own personal capabilities, leads to higher aspirations and greater persistence.

Evaluating Learning Approaches to Personality

Because they ignore the internal processes that are uniquely human, traditional learning theorists such as Skinner have been accused of so oversimplifying personality that the concept becomes meaningless. In the eyes of their critics, reducing behavior to a series

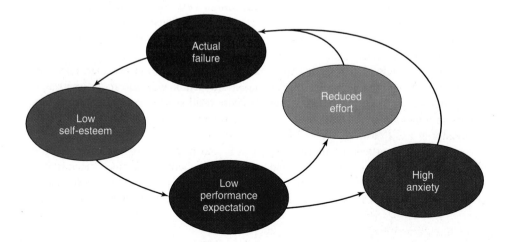

Figure 14-4 The cycle of low self-esteem begins with an individual who has low self-esteem. The person will have low performance expectations and expect to fail a test, thereby producing anxiety and reduced effort. As a result, the person will actually fail, which in turn reinforces the low self-esteem.

of stimuli and responses, and excluding thoughts and feelings from the realm of personality, leaves behaviorists practicing an unrealistic and inadequate form of science.

Of course, some of these criticisms are blunted by social cognitive approaches, which explicitly consider the role of cognitive processes in personality. Still, learning approaches tend to share a highly *deterministic* view of human behavior, seeing it as shaped primarily by forces beyond the control of the individual. According to some critics, determinism disregards our ability to pilot our own courses through life.

On the other hand, learning approaches have had a major impact in a variety of ways. For one thing, they have helped make the study of personality an objective, scientific venture by focusing on observable behavior and environment. In addition, they have produced important, successful means of treating personality disorders. The degree of success these treatments have enjoyed is testimony to the merits of learning theory approaches to personality.

Biological and Evolutionary Approaches: Are We Born with Personality?

Do we inherit our personality?

biological and evolutionary approaches to personality: The theory that important components of personality are inherited

That's the question raised by **biological and evolutionary approaches** to personality, which suggest that important components of personality are inherited. Building on the work of behavioral geneticists (first discussed in Chapter 3), researchers using biological and evolutionary approaches argue that personality is determined at least in part by particular combinations of genes, in much the same way that our height is largely a result of genetic contributions from our ancestors (Plomin & McClearn, 1993; Buss, 1999).

The importance of genetic factors in personality has been illustrated by studies of twins. For instance, personality psychologists Auke Tellegen and colleagues at the University of Minnesota examined the personality traits of pairs of twins who were genetically identical but raised apart from each other (Tellegen et al., 1988). In the study, each of the twins was given a battery of personality tests, including one that measured eleven key personality traits.

The results of the personality tests indicated that in major respects the twins were quite similar in personality, despite having been raised separately from an early age. Moreover, certain traits were more influenced by heredity than others. For example, social potency (the degree to which a person assumes mastery and leadership roles in social situations) and traditionalism (the tendency to follow authority) had particularly strong genetic components, whereas achievement and social closeness had relatively weak genetic components (see Figure 14-5).

temperament: A basic, innate disposition that emerges early in life

Furthermore, it is increasingly clear that the roots of adult personality emerge at the earliest periods of life. Infants are born with a particular **temperament,** a basic, innate disposition. Temperament encompasses several dimensions, including general activity level and mood. For instance, some individuals are quite active, while others are relatively calm; some are relatively easygoing, while others are irritable, easily upset, and difficult to soothe. Temperament is quite consistent, with significant stability from infancy well into adolescence (Caspi et al., 1995; Clark & Watson, 1999; Molfese & Molfese, 2000).

Some researchers believe that specific genes are related to personality. For example, people with a longer version of a dopamine-4 receptor gene are more likely to be thrill seekers than those without such a gene. These thrill seekers tend to be extroverted, impulsive, quick-tempered, and always on the prowl for excitement and novel situations (Benjamin et al., 1996).

Does the identification of specific genes linked to personality, coupled with the discovery that aspects of our temperaments are established before birth, mean that we are destined to have certain types of personalities? Hardly. First, it is unlikely that any single gene is linked to a specific trait. For instance, the dopamine-4 receptor accounts

Applying Psychology in the 21st Century

Can Unjustified High Self-Esteem Lead to Violence?

One societal belief widely held at the start of the twenty-first century is that we should do everything we can to nurture people's self-esteem. High self-esteem is usually viewed as a forerunner of success and accomplishment, and low self-esteem is seen as a problem to be remedied.

But not everyone agrees. According to psychologists Brad Bushman and Roy Baumeister (1998), not only can high self-esteem be psychologically damaging to the person who holds it—it can lead to violence if that self-esteem is unjustified by actual accomplishments. These researchers suggest not only that some people who turn to violence see themselves in a positive light, but that their positive view of themselves is exaggerated. Even in the face of events that would typically lead to lower self-esteem—such as school or work failure—such individuals maintain positive views of themselves, and ultimately this unwarrantedly positive self-esteem leads to violence.

This view of violent personalities suggests that when people with unjustified high self-esteem (a condition known as *narcissism*) feel challenged, or threatened by others, they react vigorously—and often violently—by seeking to maintain their positive view of themselves. In contrast, people with lower self-esteem who are challenged or threatened simply see the challenge or threat as confirming their lower self-esteem; and those with high, but justified, self-esteem are able to ignore challenges and threats (Baumeister, Bushman, & Campbell, 2000).

Results of experiments support this view. For example, Bushman and Baumeister (1998) asked participants in a study to write an essay, which, for some, was greatly criticized. The participants then were asked to play a game that gave them the opportunity to blast loud noise at an opponent—a measure of aggression. The results showed that participants with high unjustified narcissistic self-esteem who had been criticized showed significantly more aggression to their opponents than those with justified high self-esteem.

These findings have direct relevance to social programs that uncritically aim to raise self-esteem. Feel-good messages that seek to instill higher self-esteem in everyone ("We're all special" and "We applaud ourselves") might be off the target, leading people to develop unwarranted high self-esteem. Instead, parents, schools, and community institutions should seek to provide opportunities for people to earn self-esteem through their actual achievements (Begley, 1998b).

Are there particular social groups for which the issue of self-esteem is of particular importance? For example, what might be the consequences if a politician—say, a presidential candidate—had unjustified high self-esteem?

for only about 10 percent of the variation in novelty seeking between different individuals. The rest of the variation is accounted for by other genes and environmental factors (Angier, 1996).

More importantly, genes and the environment never work in isolation. As we saw in our discussions of the heritability of intelligence (Chapter 9) and the nature-nurture issue (Chapter 12), it is impossible to completely divorce genetic factors from environmental factors. Although studies of identical twins raised in different environments are helpful, they are not definitive, because it is impossible to fully assess and control environmental factors. Furthermore, estimates of the influence of genetics are just that—estimates—and they apply to groups, not individuals. Consequently, findings such as those shown in Figure 14-5 must be regarded as approximations.

Finally, even if more genes are found to be linked to specific personality characteristics, genes still cannot be viewed as the sole cause of personality. For one thing, genetically determined characteristics might not be expressed if they are not "turned on" by particular environmental experiences. Furthermore, the appearance of behaviors produced by genes in some ways might create a particular environment. For instance, a cheerful, smiley baby might lead her parents to smile more and act more responsive, thereby creating an environment that is supportive and pleasant. On the other hand, the parents of a cranky, fussy baby might be less inclined to smile at the child, leading to an environment that is less supportive or pleasant. In a sense, then, genes not only influence a person's behavior—they also help produce the environment in which the person is raised (Scarr, 1992, 1993; Plomin & Caspi, 1999).

Although an increasing number of personality theorists are taking biological and evolutionary factors into account, no comprehensive, unified theory that considers biological and evolutionary factors is widely accepted. Still, it is clear that certain personality

Figure 14-5 The roots of personality. The percentages indicate the degree to which eleven personality characteristics reflect the influence of heredity.

Source: Tellegen et al., 1988.

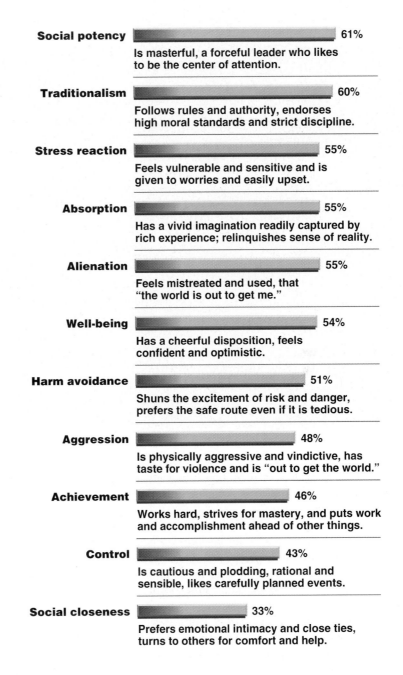

Social potency — 61%
Is masterful, a forceful leader who likes to be the center of attention.

Traditionalism — 60%
Follows rules and authority, endorses high moral standards and strict discipline.

Stress reaction — 55%
Feels vulnerable and sensitive and is given to worries and easily upset.

Absorption — 55%
Has a vivid imagination readily captured by rich experience; relinquishes sense of reality.

Alienation — 55%
Feels mistreated and used, that "the world is out to get me."

Well-being — 54%
Has a cheerful disposition, feels confident and optimistic.

Harm avoidance — 51%
Shuns the excitement of risk and danger, prefers the safe route even if it is tedious.

Aggression — 48%
Is physically aggressive and vindictive, has taste for violence and is "out to get the world."

Achievement — 46%
Works hard, strives for mastery, and puts work and accomplishment ahead of other things.

Control — 43%
Is cautious and plodding, rational and sensible, likes carefully planned events.

Social closeness — 33%
Prefers emotional intimacy and close ties, turns to others for comfort and help.

traits have substantial genetic components and that heredity and environment interact to determine personality (Buss, 1999; Plomin & Caspi, 1999).

Humanistic Approaches: The Uniqueness of You

Where, in all these approaches to personality, is there an explanation for the saintliness of a Mother Teresa, the creativity of a Michelangelo, the brilliance and perseverance of an Einstein? An understanding of such unique individuals—as well as more ordinary sorts of people who share some of the same attributes—comes from humanistic theory.

According to humanistic theorists, all of the approaches to personality that we have discussed share a fundamental misperception in their views of human nature. Instead of seeing people as controlled by unconscious, unseen forces (as do psychoanalytic approaches), a set of stable traits (trait approaches), situational reinforcements and punishments (learning theory), or inherited factors (biological and evolutionary

 **PsychLink**

Humanistic psychology
www.mhhe.com/
feldmanup6-14links

approaches), **humanistic approaches** argue that people are basically good and tend to grow to higher levels of functioning—and that this conscious, self-motivated ability to change and improve, along with people's unique creative impulses, makes up the core of personality.

The major proponent of the humanistic point of view is Carl Rogers (1971). Rogers suggests that people have a need for positive regard that reflects a universal requirement to be loved and respected. Because others provide this positive regard, we grow dependent on them. We begin to see and judge ourselves through the eyes of other people, relying on their values.

According to Rogers, one outgrowth of placing importance on the opinions of others is that there can be a conflict between people's actual experiences and their *self-concepts,* or self-impressions. If the discrepancies are minor, so are the consequences. But great discrepancies will lead to psychological disturbances in daily functioning, such as the experience of frequent anxiety.

Rogers suggests that one way of overcoming the discrepancy between experience and self-concept is through receiving unconditional positive regard from another person—such as a friend, spouse, or therapist. As we will discuss in Chapter 17, **unconditional positive regard** is an attitude of acceptance and respect on the part of an observer, no matter what the other person says or does. This acceptance, says Rogers, allows people the opportunity to evolve and grow both cognitively and emotionally and to develop more realistic self-concepts. You might have experienced the power of unconditional positive regard when you opened up to someone, revealing embarrassing secrets because you knew the listener would still love and respect you, even after hearing the worst about you.

On the other hand, if you receive *conditional positive regard,* others' view of you is dependent on your behavior. Others will withdraw their love and acceptance if you do something they don't approve of. The result is a discrepancy between your true self and what others wish you would be, leading you to feel anxiety and frustration (see Figure 14-6).

To Rogers and other humanistic personality theorists such as Abraham Maslow (whose theory of motivation we discussed in Chapter 10), the ultimate goal of personality growth is self-actualization. **Self-actualization** is a state of self-fulfillment in which people realize their highest potential. To reach this state, people's everyday experience and their self-concept must closely match. People who are self-actualized accept themselves as they are in reality, which enables them to achieve happiness and fulfillment. They are open to new experiences, accepting of others, and independent (Ford, 1991).

"So, while extortion, racketeering, and murder may be bad acts, they don't make you a bad person."

humanistic approaches to personality: The theory that people are basically good and tend to grow to higher levels of functioning

unconditional positive regard: An attitude of acceptance and respect on the part of an observer, no matter what the other person says or does

self-actualization: According to Rogers, a state of self-fulfillment in which people realize their highest potential

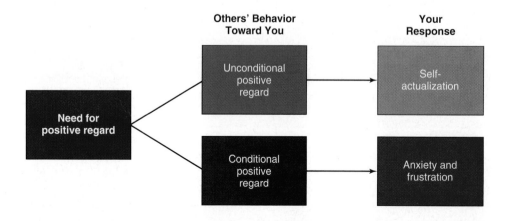

Others' Behavior Toward You	Your Response
Need for positive regard → Unconditional positive regard	→ Self-actualization
Need for positive regard → Conditional positive regard	→ Anxiety and frustration

Figure 14-6 According to the humanistic view of Carl Rogers, people have a basic need to be loved and respected. If you have unconditional positive regard from others, you will develop more realistic self-concepts, but if the response is conditional it may lead to anxiety and frustration.

Evaluating Humanistic Approaches

Although humanistic theories suggest the value of providing unconditional positive regard toward people, unconditional positive regard toward humanistic theories has been less forthcoming. The criticisms have centered on the difficulty of verifying the basic assumptions of the approach, as well as on the question of whether unconditional positive regard does, in fact, lead to greater personality adjustment.

Humanistic approaches have also been criticized for assuming that people are basically "good"—a notion that is unverifiable—and, equally important, for using nonscientific values to build supposedly scientific theories. Still, humanistic theories have been important in highlighting the uniqueness of human beings and in guiding the development of a significant form of therapy designed to alleviate psychological difficulties.

Comparing Approaches to Personality

Given the multiple approaches we have discussed, you could be wondering which of the theories provides the most accurate description of personality. This question cannot be answered precisely. Each theory is built on different assumptions and focuses on somewhat different aspects of personality (see Table 14-4 for a comparison). Given the complexity of every individual, it seems reasonable that personality can be viewed from a number of perspectives simultaneously (Pervin & John, 1999).

Table 14-4 Comparing Approaches to Personality

Theoretical Approach and Major Theorists	Conscious Versus Unconscious Determinants of Personality	Nature (Hereditary Factors) Versus Nurture (Environmental Factors)	Free Will Versus Determinism	Stability Versus Modifiability
Psychoanalytic (Freud)	Emphasizes the unconscious	Stresses innate, inherited structure of personality while emphasizing importance of adulthood experience	Stresses determinism, the view that behavior is directed and caused by factors outside one's control	Emphasizes the stability of characteristics throughout a person's life
Trait (Allport, Cattell, Eysenck)	Disregards both conscious and unconscious	Approaches vary	Stresses determinism, the view that behavior is directed and caused by factors outside one's control	Emphasizes the stability of characteristics throughout a person's life
Learning (Skinner, Bandura)	Disregards both conscious and unconscious	Focuses on the environment	Stresses determinism, the view that behavior is directed and caused by factors outside one's control	Stresses that personality remains flexible and resilient throughout one's life
Biological and Evolutionary (Tellegen)	Disregards both conscious and unconscious	Stresses the innate, inherited determinants of personality	Stresses determinism, the view that behavior is directed and caused by factors outside one's control	Emphasizes the stability of characteristics throughout a person's life
Humanistic (Rogers, Maslow)	Stresses the conscious more than unconscious	Stresses the interaction between both nature and nurture	Stresses the freedom of individuals to make their own choices	Stresses that personality remains flexible and resilient throughout one's life.

Evaluate

1. Carl's determination to succeed is the dominant force in all his activities and relationships. According to Gordon Allport's theory, this is an example of a _____ trait. In contrast, Cindy's fondness for old western movies is an example of a _____ trait.

2. A person who enjoys such activities as parties and hang gliding might be described by Eysenck as high on what trait?

3. Proponents of which approach to personality would be most likely to agree with the statement "Personality can be thought of as learned responses to a person's upbringing and environment"?
   a. Humanistic approaches
   b. Biological and evolutionary approaches
   c. Learning approaches
   d. Trait approaches

4. A person who would make the statement "I know I can't do it" would be rated by Bandura as low on _____-_____.

5. Which approach to personality emphasizes the innate goodness of people and their desire to grow?
   a. Humanistic
   b. Psychoanalytic
   c. Learning
   d. Biological and evolutionary

Answers to Evaluate Questions

1. cardinal; secondary 2. Extraversion 3. c 4. self-efficacy 5. a

Rethink

1. If personality traits are merely descriptive and not explanatory, of what use are they? Can assigning a trait to a person be harmful—or helpful? Why or why not?

2. In what ways are Cattell's 16 source traits, Eysenck's three dimensions, and the "Big Five" factors similar, and in what ways are they different? Which traits seem to appear in all three schemes (under one name or another), and which are unique to one scheme? Is this significant?

Assessing Personality: Determining What Makes Us Special

You have a need for other people to like and admire you.

You have a tendency to be critical of yourself.

You have a great deal of unused potential that you have not turned to your advantage.

Although you have some personality weaknesses, you are generally able to compensate for them.

Relating to members of the opposite sex has presented problems to you.

Although you appear to others to be disciplined and self-controlled, you tend to be anxious and insecure inside.

At times you have serious doubts as to whether you have made the right decision or done the right thing.

You prefer a certain amount of change and variety and become dissatisfied when hemmed in by restrictions and limitations.

You do not accept others' statements without satisfactory proof.

You have found it unwise to be too frank in revealing yourself to others.

If you think these statements provide a surprisingly accurate account of your personality, you are not alone: Most college students think that the descriptions are tailored just to them. In fact, the statements are intentionally designed to be so vague as to apply to just about anyone (Forer, 1949; Russo, 1981).

The ease with which we can agree with such imprecise statements underscores the difficulty in coming up with accurate and meaningful assessments of people's personalities

Prepare

How can we most accurately assess personality?

What are the major types of personality measures?

Organize

Assessing Personality

Self-Report Measures of Personality

Projective Methods

Behavioral Assessment

 **PsychLink**

Personality tests

www.mhhe.com/
feldmanup6-14links

psychological tests: Standard measures devised to assess behavior objectively and used by psychologists to help people make decisions about their lives and understand more about themselves

(Johnson et al., 1985; Prince & Guastello, 1990). Just as trait theorists were faced with the problem of determining the most critical and important traits, psychologists interested in assessing personality must be able to define the most meaningful ways to discriminate between one person's personality and another's. To do this, they use **psychological tests,** standard measures devised to assess behavior objectively. Such tests are used by psychologists to help people make decisions about their lives and understand more about themselves. They are also employed by researchers interested in the causes and consequences of personality (Groth-Marnat, 1990, 1996; Matarazzo, 1992; Kaplan & Saccuzzo, 1997; Aiken, 1997).

Like the intelligence assessments that we discussed in Chapter 9, all psychological tests must have reliability and validity. *Reliability,* you may recall, refers to the measurement consistency of a test. If a test is reliable, it yields the same result each time it is administered to a given person or group. In contrast, unreliable tests give different results each time they are administered.

Tests also must be valid in order to draw meaningful conclusions. Tests have *validity* when they actually measure what they are designed to measure. If a test is constructed to measure sociability, for instance, we need to know that it actually measures sociability and not some other trait.

Finally, psychological tests are based on *norms,* standards of test performance that permit the comparison of one person's score on the test to the scores of others who have taken the same test. For example, a norm permits test-takers who have received a particular score on a test to know that they have scored in the top 10 percent of all those who have taken the test.

Norms are established by administering a particular test to a large number of people and determining the typical scores. It is then possible to compare a single person's score to the scores of the group, providing a comparative measure of test performance against the performance of others who have taken the test.

The establishment of appropriate norms is not a simple endeavor. For instance, the specific group that is employed to determine norms for a test has a profound effect on how an individual's performance is evaluated. In fact, as we discuss next, the process of establishing norms can take on political overtones.

EXPLORING DIVERSITY

Should Norms Be Based on Race and Ethnicity?

The passions of politics can challenge the objectivity of science when test norms are established, at least in the realm of standardized tests that are meant to predict future job performance. In fact, a national controversy has developed around the question of whether different norms should be established for members of various racial and ethnic groups (Kilborn, 1991; Brown, 1994).

At issue is the U.S. government's 50-year-old General Aptitude Test Battery, a test that measures a broad range of abilities, from eye-hand coordination to reading proficiency. The problem that sparked the controversy is that African Americans and Hispanics tend to score lower on the test, on average, than members of other groups. The lower scores are often due to a lack of prior relevant experience and job opportunities, which in turn has been due to prejudice and discrimination.

To promote the employment of minority racial groups, the government developed a separate set of norms for African Americans and Hispanics. Rather than being compared to the pool of all people who took the test, the scores of African American and Hispanic applicants were compared only to the scores of other African Americans and Hispanics. Consequently, a Hispanic who scored in the top 20 percent of the Hispanics taking the test was considered to have performed equivalently to a white job applicant who scored in the top 20 percent of the whites who took the test, even though the absolute score of the Hispanic might be lower than that of the white.

Critics of the adjusted norming system suggest that such a procedure discriminates in favor of certain racial and ethnic groups at the expense of others, thereby fanning the flames of racial bigotry. The practice was challenged in court, and with the passage of the Civil Rights Act in 1991, race norming on the General Aptitude Test Battery was discontinued.

However, proponents of race norming continue to argue that norming procedures that take race into account are an affirmative action tool that simply permits minority job-seekers to be placed on an equal footing with white job-seekers. Furthermore, a panel of the National Academy of Sciences concurred with the practice of adjusting test norms. It suggested that the unadjusted test norms are not terribly useful in predicting job performance, and that they would tend to screen out otherwise qualified minority group members.

Job testing is not the only area in which issues arise regarding norms and the meaning of test scores. As we saw in Chapter 9, when we discussed racial differences in IQ scores, the issue of how to treat racial differences in test scores is both controversial and divisive. Clearly, race norming raises profound and intense feelings that can come into conflict with scientific objectivity, and the controversy is far from over (American Psychological Association, 1993b; Gottfredson, 1994; Sackett & Wilk, 1994; Greenlaw & Jensen, 1996).

The issue of establishing norms for tests is further complicated by the existence of a wide array of personality measures and approaches to assessment. We consider some of these measures, which have a variety of characteristics and purposes, next.

Self-Report Measures of Personality

If someone wanted to assess your personality, one possible approach would be to extensively interview you about the most important events of your childhood, your social relationships, and your successes and failures. Obviously, though, such a technique would be extraordinarily costly in time and effort.

It is also unnecessary. Just as physicians draw only a small sample of your blood to test it, psychologists can utilize **self-report measures** that ask people about a relatively small sample of their behavior. This sampling of self-report data is then used to infer the presence of particular personality characteristics (Conoley & Impara, 1997).

One of the best examples of a self-report measure, and the most frequently used personality test, is the **Minnesota Multiphasic Personality Inventory-2 (MMPI-2).** Although the original purpose of the measure was to differentiate people with specific sorts of psychological difficulties from those without disturbances, it has been found to predict a variety of other behaviors. For instance, MMPI scores have been shown to be good predictors of whether college students will marry within ten years and whether they will get an advanced degree. Police departments use the test to measure whether police officers are prone to use their weapons. Psychologists in Russia administer a modified form of the MMPI to their astronauts and Olympic athletes (Butcher, 1995, 1999; Craig, 1999; Friedman et al., 2000).

The test itself consists of a series of 567 items to which a person responds "true," "false," or "cannot say." The questions cover a variety of issues, ranging from mood ("I feel useless at times") to opinions ("People should try to understand their dreams") to physical and psychological health ("I am bothered by an upset stomach several times a week" and "I have strange and peculiar thoughts").

There are no right or wrong answers. Instead, interpretation of the results rests on the pattern of responses. The test yields scores on ten separate scales, plus three scales meant to measure the validity of the respondent's answers. For example, there is a "lie scale" that indicates when people are falsifying their responses in order to present themselves more favorably (through items such as "I can't remember ever having a bad night's sleep") (Butcher et al., 1990; Butcher, 1999; Graham, 1999).

How did the authors of the MMPI determine what specific patterns of responses indicate? The procedure they used is typical of personality test construction—a process known as **test standardization.** To create the test, groups of psychiatric patients with a specific diagnosis, such as depression or schizophrenia, were asked to complete a large number of items. The test authors then determined which items best differentiated members of these groups from a comparison group of normal participants, and these specific items were included in the final version of the test. By systematically carrying out this procedure on groups with different diagnoses, the test authors were able to devise a number of subscales that identified different forms of abnormal behavior (see Figure 14-7).

self-report measures: A method of gathering data about people by asking them questions about a sample of their behavior

Minnesota Multiphasic Personality Inventory-2 (MMPI-2): A test used to identify people with psychological difficulties as well as to predict such behavior as job performance

PsychLink
MMPI-2
www.mhhe.com/feldmanup6-14links

test standardization: A technique used to validate questions in personality tests by studying the responses of people with known diagnoses

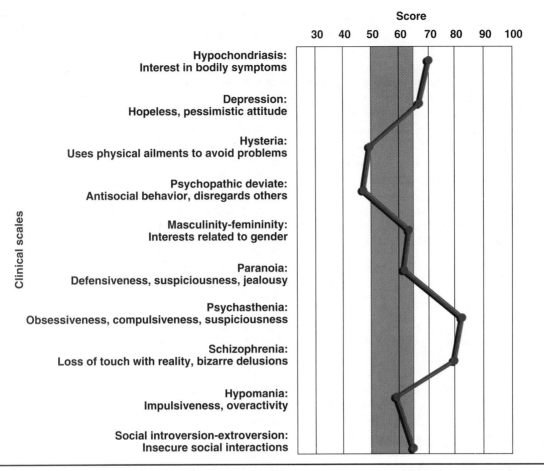

Figure 14-7 A profile on the MMPI-2 of a person who suffers from obsessional anxiety, social withdrawal, and delusional thinking.
Source: Based on data from Halgin & Whitbourne, 1994, p. 72; and Minnesota Multiphasic Personality Inventory-2. Copyright © by the Regents of the University of Minnesota, 1942, 1943 (renewed 1970, 1989).

When the MMPI is used for the purposes for which it was devised—identification of personality disorders—it does a reasonably good job. However, like other personality tests, it can be abused. For instance, employers who use it as a screening tool for job applicants might interpret the results improperly, relying too heavily on the results of individual scales instead of taking into account the overall patterns of results, which require skilled interpretation. Furthermore, critics point out that the individual scales overlap, making their interpretation difficult. In sum, although the MMPI remains the most widely used personality test and has been translated into more than a hundred languages, it must be used with caution (Greene & Clopton, 1994; Graham, 1999; Holden, 2000).

Projective Methods

If you were shown the shape presented in Figure 14-8 and asked what it represented to you, you might not think that your impressions would mean very much. But to a psychoanalytic theoretician, your responses to such an ambiguous figure would provide valuable clues to the state of your unconscious, and ultimately to your general personality characteristics.

The shape in the figure is representative of inkblots used in **projective personality tests,** in which a person is shown an ambiguous stimulus and asked to describe it or tell a story about it. The responses are then considered to be "projections" of what the person is like.

projective personality test: A test in which a person is shown an ambiguous stimulus and asked to describe it or tell a story about it

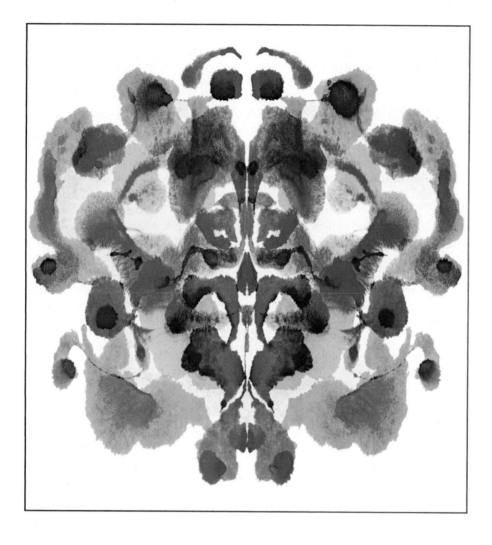

Figure 14–8 This inkblot is similar to the type used in the Rorschach personality test (Alloy, Jacobson, & Acocella, 1999). What do you see in it?

The best-known projective test is the **Rorschach test.** Devised by Swiss psychiatrist Hermann Rorschach (1924), the test consists of showing a series of symmetrical stimuli, similar to the one in Figure 14-8, to people who are then asked what the figures represent to them. Their responses are recorded, and through a complex set of clinical judgments on the part of the examiner, people are classified into different personality types. For instance, respondents who see a bear in one inkblot are thought to have a strong degree of emotional control, according to the rules developed by Rorschach (Aronow, Reznikoff, & Moreland, 1994; Weiner, 1998).

The **Thematic Apperception Test (TAT)** is another well-known projective test. As we noted when we discussed achievement motivation in Chapter 10, the TAT consists of a series of pictures about which a person is asked to write a story. The stories are then used to draw inferences about the writer's personality characteristics (Cramer, 1996; F. D. Kelly, 1997).

Tests with stimuli as ambiguous as the Rorschach and TAT require particular skill and care in their interpretation—too much, in many critics' estimation. The Rorschach, in particular, has been criticized for requiring too much inference on the part of the examiner, and attempts to standardize scoring have frequently failed. Furthermore, many critics complain that the Rorschach does not provide much valid information about underlying personality traits. Despite such problems, both the Rorschach and the TAT are widely used, particularly in clinical settings, and their proponents suggest that their reliability and validity are great enough to provide useful inferences about personality (Bornstein, 1996; Weiner, 1998; Meyer, 2000).

Rorschach test: A test by developed by Swiss psychiatrist Hermann Rorschach that consists of showing a series of symmetrical stimuli to people and then asking them to say what the figures represent to them

Thematic Apperception Test (TAT): A test consisting of a series of ambiguous pictures about which the person is asked to write a story

"Rorschach! What's to become of you?"

Although projective tests such as the Rorschach test and the Thematic Apperception Test (TAT) are frequently employed in testing situations, their reliability and validity have been questioned.

PsychLink

Behavioral assessment
www.mhhe.com/
feldmanup6-14links

behavioral assessment: Direct measures of an individual's behavior used to describe characteristics indicative of personality

Behavioral Assessment

If you were a psychologist subscribing to a learning approach to personality, you would be likely to object to the indirect nature of projective tests. You would instead be more apt to use **behavioral assessment**—direct measures of an individual's behavior used to describe characteristics indicative of personality. As with observational research (discussed in Chapter 2), behavioral assessment can be carried out naturalistically by observing people in their own settings: in the workplace, at home, or in school. It can also be carried out in the laboratory, under controlled conditions in which a psychologist sets up a situation and observes an individual's behavior.

Regardless of the setting in which behavior is observed, an effort is made to ensure that behavioral assessment is carried out objectively, quantifying behavior as much as possible. For example, an observer might record the number of social contacts a person initiates, the number of questions asked, or the number of aggressive acts. Another method is to measure the duration of events: the duration of a temper tantrum in a child, the length of a conversation, the amount of time spent working, or the time spent in cooperative behavior.

Behavioral assessment is particularly appropriate for observing—and eventually remedying—specific behavioral difficulties, such as increasing socialization in shy children. It provides a means of assessing the specific nature and incidence of a problem and subsequently allows psychologists to determine whether intervention techniques have been successful.

Behavioral assessment techniques based on learning theories of personality have also made important contributions to the treatment of certain kinds of psychological difficulties. Indeed, the knowledge of normal personality provided by the theories we have discussed throughout this chapter has led to significant advances in our understanding and treatment of both physical and psychological disorders.

BECOMING AN INFORMED CONSUMER OF PSYCHOLOGY

Assessing Personality Assessments

Wanted: People with "kinetic energy," "emotional maturity," and the ability to "deal with large numbers of people in a fairly chaotic situation."

Although this job description might seem most appropriate for the job of co-host of *Wheel of Fortune,* in actuality it is part of an advertisement for managers for American MultiCinema's theaters (Dentzer, 1986). To find people with such qualities, AMC has developed a battery of personality measures for job applicants to complete. In developing its own tests, AMC joined scores of companies, ranging from General Motors to J. C. Penney, that employ personality tests to help determine who gets hired (Hogan, Hogan, & Roberts, 1996).

Individuals, too, have come to depend on personality testing. Many organizations will—for a hefty fee—administer a battery of personality tests that claim to steer people toward a career for which their personality is particularly suited. When considering the results of such personality testing, either in the role of potential employee, employer, or consumer of testing services, you should keep several points in mind:

- *Understand what the test claims to measure.* Standard personality measures are accompanied by information that discusses how the test was developed, to whom it is most applicable, and how the results should be interpreted. Read any explanations of the test; it will help you understand the meaning of any results.
- *Make no decision based only on the results of any one test.* Test results should be interpreted in the context of other information—academic records, social interests, and home and community activities.
- *Remember that test results are not always accurate.* The results can be in error; the test might be unreliable or invalid. You might, for example, have had a "bad day" when you took the test, or the person scoring and interpreting the test might have

made a mistake. You should not place undue stock in the results of the single administration of any test.

In sum, it is important to keep in mind the complexity of human behavior—particularly your own. No one test can provide an understanding of the intricacies of someone's personality without considering a good deal more information than can be provided in a single testing session.

Evaluate

1. _____ is the consistency of a personality test, while _____ is the ability of a test to actually measure what it is designed to measure.
2. _____ are standards used to compare scores of different people taking the same test.
3. Tests such as the MMPI-2, in which a small sample of behavior is assessed to determine larger trends, are examples of
   a. cross-sectional tests
   b. projective tests
   c. achievement tests
   d. self-report tests
4. A person shown a picture and asked to make up a story about it would be taking a _____ personality test.

Answers to Evaluate Questions

1. Reliability, validity 2. Norms 3. d 4. projective

Rethink

1. What do you think are some of the problems that developers and interpreters of self-report personality tests must deal with in their effort to provide useful information about test-takers? Why is a "lie scale" included on such measures?

2. Should personality tests be used for personnel decisions? Should they be used for other social purposes, such as identifying individuals at risk for certain types of personality disorders? What sorts of policies would you devise to ensure that such tests were used ethically?

Looking Back

How do psychologists define and use the concept of personality?

- Personality is the pattern of enduring characteristics that differentiates a person—those patterns of behaviors that makes each person unique. (p. 414)

What do the theories of Freud and his successors tell us about the structure and development of personality?

- According to psychoanalysts, much behavior is caused by unconscious parts of personality that we are unaware of. (p. 414)
- According to Freud's theory, personality is composed of the id, the ego, and the superego. The id is the unorganized, inborn part of personality whose purpose is to immediately reduce tensions relating to hunger, sex, aggression, and other primitive impulses. The ego restrains instinctual energy in order to maintain the safety of the individual and to help the person to be a member of society. The superego represents social right and wrong and consists of the conscience and the ego-ideal. (p. 415)
- Freud's psychoanalytic theory says that personality develops through a series of stages, each of which is associated with a primary biological function. (p. 415)
- Defense mechanisms are unconscious strategies to reduce anxiety for dealing with anxiety related to impulses from the id. (p. 417)
- Freud's psychoanalytic theory has provoked a number of criticisms, especially focusing on its lack of supportive scientific data, the theory's inadequacy in making predictions, and its reliance on a highly restricted population. (p. 418)
- Neo-Freudian psychoanalytic theorists built on Freud's work, although they placed greater emphasis on the role of the ego and paid greater attention to social factors in determining behavior. (p. 419)

What are the major aspects of trait, learning, biological and evolutionary, and humanistic approaches to personality?

- Trait approaches have tried to identify the most basic and relatively enduring dimensions along which people differ from one another—dimensions known as traits. (p. 421)
- Learning approaches to personality concentrate on observable behavior. To the strict learning theorist, personality is the sum of learned responses to the external environment. (p. 424)
- Social cognitive approaches concentrate on the role of cognitions in determining personality and pay particular attention to how self-efficacy determines behavior.
- Biological and evolutionary approaches to personality focus on the inheritance of personality characteristics. (p. 424)
- Humanistic approaches assume that people are basically good. They consider the core of personality in terms of a person's ability to change and improve. (p. 428)
- The major personality approaches differ substantially from one another, which could reflect both their focus on different aspects of personality and the overall complexity of personality. (p. 430)

How can we most accurately assess personality?

- Psychological tests such as the MMPI are standard assessment tools that are intended to objectively measure behavior. They must be reliable, measuring what they are trying to measure consistently, and valid, measuring what they are supposed to measure. (p. 433)

What are the major types of personality measures?

- Self-report measures ask people about a sample range of their behaviors. These reports are used to infer the presence of particular personality characteristics. (p. 433)
- Projective personality tests (such as the Rorschach and Thematic Apperception Test) present an ambiguous stimulus; the observer's responses are then used to infer information about the observer. (p. 434)
- Behavioral assessment is based on the principles of learning theory. It employs direct measurement of an individual's behavior to determine characteristics related to personality. (p. 436)

Key Terms and Concepts

personality (p. 414)
psychoanalytic theory (p. 414)
unconscious (p. 414)
id (p. 414)
ego (p. 414)
superego (p. 414)
oral stage (p. 416)
fixation (p. 416)
anal stage (p. 416)
phallic stage (p. 416)
Oedipus conflict (p. 416)
identification (p. 416)
latency period (p. 417)
genital stage (p. 417)
defense mechanisms (p. 417)
neo-Freudian psychoanalysts (p. 419)
collective unconscious (p. 419)
inferiority complex (p. 419)
trait theory (p. 421)

traits (p. 421)
social cognitive approaches to personality (p. 424)
biological and evolutionary approaches to personality (p. 426)
temperament (p. 426)
humanistic approaches to personality (p. 429)
unconditional positive regard (p. 429)
self-actualization (p. 429)
psychological tests (p. 432)
self-report measures (p. 433)
Minnesota Multiphasic Personality Inventory-2 (MMPI-2) (p. 433)
test standardization (p. 433)
projective personality test (p. 434)
Rorschach test (p. 435)
Thematic Apperception Test (TAT) (p. 435)
behavioral assessment (p. 436)

Psychology on the Web

1. Sigmund Freud is one of the towering figures of psychology, with an influence far beyond his psychoanalytic work. Find further information on the Web about Freud. Pick one aspect of his work or influence (e.g., on therapy, medicine, literature, film, culture and society, etc.) and summarize in writing what you have found, including your attitude toward your findings.
2. Find a website that links to personality tests and take one or two tests—remembering to take them with skepticism. For each test, summarize in writing the aspects of personality that were tested, the theoretical approach that the test appeared to be based on, and your assessment of the trustworthiness of the information you received.

Epilogue

In this chapter, we have discussed the different ways in which psychologists have interpreted the development and structure of personality. The perspectives we've examined range from Freud's analysis of personality, based primarily on internal, unconscious

factors, to the externally based view of personality as a learned set of traits and actions that is championed by the learning theorists. We have also noted that there are many ways to interpret personality, and that there is no consensus on what are the key traits central to personality.

Before proceeding to the topic of health psychology in the next chapter, return to the prologue of this chapter and consider the case of "Tom," who was—depending on your perspective—either awfully nice or just awful. Use your understanding of personality to consider the following questions.

1. How might a psychoanalytic approach to personality, using the concepts of id, ego, and superego, apply to the apparent two sides to "Tom"?
2. What sort of profile do you think Tom would have displayed if he had been tested in terms of Cattell's sixteen source traits? Where would he fall on Eysenck's major personality dimensions?
3. Would a personality profile of Tom administered during the time he was involved in mob activities have been different from one administered when he was visiting in Grand Isle? Why?
4. How would an advocate of a social cognitive approach to personality interpret and explain Tom's seemingly contradictory behavior? How might the concepts of observational learning and self-efficacy apply to a case like Tom's?

 Preview

For additional quizzing and a variety of interactive resources, visit the *Understanding Psychology* Online Learning Center at

www.mhhe.com/feldmanup6

Chapter Fifteen

Health Psychology:

Stress, Coping, and Well-Being

Prologue: So Much to Do, So Little Time to Do It

Looking Ahead

Stress and Coping

Stress: Reacting to Threat and Challenge

Psychology at Work: Alan Benner, Police Psychologist

Coping with Stress

Becoming an Informed Consumer of Psychology: Effective Coping Strategies

Psychological Aspects of Illness and Well-Being

The A's and B's of Coronary Heart Disease

Psychological Aspects of Cancer

Smoking

Exploring Diversity: Hucksters of Death: Promoting Smoking Throughout the World

Well-Being and Happiness

Applying Psychology in the 21st Century: If You Won the Lottery, Would You Be Happier?

Psychological Factors Related to Physical Illness: Going to the Doctor

Physician–Patient Communication

Complying with Physicians' Recommendations

Becoming an Informed Consumer of Psychology: Speaking with Your Physician

Looking Back

Key Terms and Concepts

Psychology on the Web

OLC Preview

Epilogue

Prologue

So Much to Do, So Little Time to Do It

Susan Reiche, a public policy manager at AT&T in Basking Ridge, N.J., can handle what work throws at her from 9 to 5. It's what life throws at her between 5 and 9 that pushes her to the limit.

After she flips off her office computer, she hurries to a day care center to pick up her 4-year-old son and then rushes across town to fetch her 7-year-old daughter from an after-school program. She makes a quick trip to the store to buy food for dinner, then zips home, where she lets the dog out, makes dinner, referees a fight or two between the children, feeds the dog, says hello to her husband, gives her son a bath, helps her daughter with her spelling words, tosses a load of laundry into the washing machine, plays with her children, reads with them and puts them to bed.

Finally, about 9 P.M., she has a minute to sit down. Whew (Kelly, 1999, p. 18).

Feeling pressured by time and the responsibility of completing a large number of tasks can take both a physical and a psychological toll on one's well-being.

Looking Ahead

health psychology: The branch of psychology that investigates the psychological factors related to wellness and illness, including the prevention, diagnosis, and treatment of medical problems

It's not hard to guess what Susan Reiche was experiencing in the four hours from 5:00 P.M. to 9:00 P.M.: stress. For people like her—and that probably includes most of us—the intensity of juggling multiple roles leads to feelings of never having sufficient time, and, in some cases, takes a toll on both physical and psychological well-being.

Stress, and ways of coping with it, have long been central topics of interest to psychologists. However, in recent years the focus has broadened as psychology has come to view stress in the broader context of a new subfield known as health psychology. **Health psychology** investigates the psychological factors related to wellness and illness, including the prevention, diagnosis, and treatment of medical problems. Health psychologists investigate how illness is influenced by psychological factors such as stress. They examine the psychological principles underlying treatments for disease and illness. They are also concerned with issues of prevention: how health problems such as heart disease and stress can be avoided by more healthful behavior.

Health psychologists take a decisive stand on the enduring mind/body issue that philosophers have debated since the time of the ancient Greeks (a debate that psychologists later joined in on and that we first considered in Chapter 1). In their view, the mind and body are clearly linked, and are not two distinct systems (Sternberg, 2000).

Health psychologists recognize that good health and the ability to cope with illness are affected by psychological factors such as thoughts, emotions, and the ability to manage stress. They have paid particular attention to the *immune system,* the complex of organs, glands, and cells that constitute our body's natural line of defense in fighting disease.

psychoneuroimmunology (PNI): The study of the relationships among psychological factors, the immune system, and the brain

In fact, health psychologists are among the primary investigators in a growing field called (somewhat awkwardly) psychoneuroimmunology. **Psychoneuroimmunology (PNI)** is the study of the relationships among psychological factors, the immune system, and the brain. PNI has led to discoveries such as the existence of an association between one's emotional state and the success of the immune system in fighting disease (Baum, Revenson, & Signer, 2000).

In sum, health psychologists view the mind and the body as two parts of a whole human being that cannot be considered independently. This more recent view marks a sharp departure from earlier thinking. Previously, disease was seen as a purely biological phenomenon, and psychological factors were of little interest to most health care workers. In the early twentieth century, the primary causes of death were short-term infections, from which one either rapidly recovered or died. Now, however, the major causes of death, such as heart disease, cancer, and diabetes, are chronic illnesses that often cannot be cured and that can linger for years, posing significant psychological issues (Delahanty & Baum, 2000).

In this chapter we discuss how psychological factors affect health. We first focus on the causes and consequences of stress and ways of coping with it. Next, we explore the psychological aspects of several major health problems, including heart disease, cancer, and ailments resulting from smoking. Finally, we examine the ways in which patient-physician interactions influence our health, and offer suggestions for increasing people's compliance with behavior that will improve their well-being.

Prepare

How is health psychology a union between medicine and psychology?

What is stress, how does it affect us, and how can we best cope with it?

Organize

Stress and Coping
    Stress
    Coping with Stress

Stress and Coping

Tara Knox's day began badly: She slept through her alarm and had to skip breakfast in order to catch the bus to campus. Then, when she went to the library to catch up on the reading she had to do before taking a test the next day, the article she needed was missing. The librarian told her that replacing it would take 24 hours. Feeling exasperated, she walked to the computer lab to print out the paper she had completed the night before. However, she couldn't get the computer to read her disk. Although she searched for someone to help her, she was unable to find anyone who seemed to know any more than she did.

It was only 9:42 A.M., and all Tara could think about was how much stress she felt.

Stress: Reacting to Threat and Challenge

Most of us need little introduction to the phenomenon of **stress,** the response to events that threaten or challenge a person. Whether it be a paper or exam deadline, a family problem, or even a cumulative series of events such as those faced by Tara Knox, life is full of circumstances and events, known as *stressors,* that produce threats to our well-being. Even pleasant events—such as planning a party or beginning a sought-after job—can produce stress, although negative events result in greater detrimental consequences than positive ones.

All of us face stress in our lives. Some health psychologists believe that daily life actually involves a series of repeated sequences of perceiving a threat, considering ways to cope with it, and ultimately adapting to the threat, with greater or lesser success. Although adaptation is often minor and occurs without our awareness, adaptation requires major effort when stress is more severe or longer lasting. Ultimately, our attempts to overcome stress can produce biological and psychological responses that result in health problems.

The High Cost of Stress

Stress can take its toll in many ways, producing both biological and psychological consequences. Often the most immediate reaction to stress is biological. Exposure to stressors generates a rise in certain hormones secreted by the adrenal glands, an increase in heart rate and blood pressure, and changes in how well the skin conducts electrical impulses. On a short-term basis, these responses can be adaptive because they produce an "emergency reaction" in which the body prepares to defend itself through activation of the sympathetic nervous system (see Chapter 3). These responses can allow more effective coping with the stressful situation (Akil & Morano, 1996; McEwen, 1998).

However, continued exposure to stress results in a decline in the body's overall level of biological functioning due to the constant secretion of stress-related hormones. Over time, stressful reactions can promote deterioration of bodily tissues such as blood vessels and the heart. Ultimately, we become more susceptible to disease as our ability to fight off infection is lowered (Sapolsky, 1996; Shapiro, 1996; McCabe et al., 2000).

In fact, an entire class of physical problems, known as **psychophysiological disorders,** may result from stress. Once referred to as *psychosomatic disorders* (a term dropped because it implied that the disorders were somehow unreal), psychophysiological disorders are actual medical problems influenced by an interaction of psychological, emotional, and physical difficulties. Among the common psychophysiological disorders are headaches, backaches, indigestion, skin problems, and high blood pressure. Stress has even been linked to the common cold (S. Cohen, 1996; Rice, 2000).

On a psychological level, high levels of stress prevent people from adequately coping with life. Their view of the environment can become clouded (e.g., a minor criticism made by a friend is blown out of proportion). Moreover, at the greatest levels of stress, emotional responses can be so extreme that people are unable to act at all. People under a lot of stress also become less able to deal with new stressors. The ability to contend with future stress, then, declines as a result of past stress.

In short, stress affects us in multiple ways. It can increase the risk that we will become ill; it can directly produce illness; it can make us less able to recover from a disease; and it can reduce our ability to cope with future stress. (For a measure of stress in your life, complete the questionnaire in Table 15-1.)

The General Adaptation Syndrome Model: The Course of Stress

The effects of stress are illustrated in a model devised by Hans Selye (pronounced "SELL-yay"), a pioneering stress theorist (Selye, 1976, 1993). This model, the **general adaptation syndrome (GAS),** suggests that the same set of physiological reactions to stress occurs regardless of the particular cause of stress.

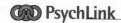 **PsychLink**

Stress management
www.mhhe.com/
feldmanup6-15links

stress: The response to events that are threatening or challenging

psychophysiological disorders: Medical problems influenced by an interaction of psychological, emotional, and physical difficulties

general adaptation syndrome (GAS): A theory developed by Selye that suggests that a person's response to stress consists of three stages: alarm and mobilization, resistance, and exhaustion

Table 15-1 How Stressful Is Your Life?

Test your level of stress by answering these questions, and adding the score from each box. Questions apply to the last month only. A key below will help you determine the extent of your stress.

1 How often have you been upset because of something that happened unexpectedly?

☐ 0=never, 1=almost never, 2=sometimes, 3=fairly often, 4=very often

2 How often have you felt that you were unable to control the important things in your life?

☐ 0=never, 1=almost never, 2=sometimes, 3=fairly often, 4=very often

3 How often have you felt nervous and "stressed"?

☐ 0=never, 1=almost never, 2=sometimes, 3=fairly often, 4=very often

4 How often have you felt confident about your ability to handle your personal problems?

☐ 4=never, 3=almost never, 2=sometimes, 1=fairly often, 0=very often

5 How often have you felt that things were going your way?

☐ 4=never, 3=almost never, 2=sometimes, 1=fairly often, 0=very often

6 How often have you been able to control irritations in your life?

☐ 4=never, 3=almost never, 2=sometimes, 1=fairly often, 0=very often

7 How often have you found that you could not cope with all the things that you had to do?

☐ 0=never, 1=almost never, 2=sometimes, 3=fairly often, 4=very often

8 How often have you felt that you were on top of things?

☐ 4=never, 3=almost never, 2=sometimes, 1=fairly often, 0=very often

9 How often have you been angered because of things that were outside your control?

☐ 0=never, 1=almost never, 2=sometimes, 3=fairly often, 4=very often

10 How often have you felt difficulties were piling up so high that you could not overcome them?

☐ 0=never, 1=almost never, 2=sometimes, 3=fairly often, 4=very often

How You Measure Up:

Stress levels vary among individuals—compare your total score to the averages below:

AGE		GENDER	
18-29	14.2	Men	12.1
30-44	13.0	Women	13.7
45-54	12.6		
55-64	11.9		
65 & over	12.0		

MARITAL STATUS	
Widowed	12.6
Married or living with	12.4
Single or never wed	14.1
Divorced	14.7
Separated	16.6

Source: Cohen, 1999.

PsychLink

General adaptation syndrome
www.mhhe.com/
feldmanup6-15links

As shown in Figure 15-1, the model has three phases. The first stage, the *alarm and mobilization stage,* occurs when people become aware of the presence of a stressor. On a biological level, the sympathetic nervous system (Chapter 3) becomes energized, helping to cope initially with the stressor.

However, if the stressor persists, people move into the next stage of the model. In the *resistance stage,* people prepare themselves to fight the stressor. During resistance, people use a variety of means to cope with the stressor—sometimes successfully—but at a cost of some degree of physical or psychological general well-being.

If resistance is inadequate, people enter the last stage of the model, the *exhaustion stage.* During the exhaustion stage, a person's ability to adapt to the stressor declines to the point where negative consequences of stress appear: physical illness, psychological symptoms in the form of an inability to concentrate, heightened irritability, or, in severe instances, disorientation and a loss of touch with reality. In a sense, people wear out, and their physical reserves are taxed to the limit.

How do people move out of the third stage after they have entered it? Exhaustion sometimes enables people to avoid the stressor. For example, people who become ill from overwork might be excused from their duties for a time, giving them a temporary respite from their responsibilities. At least for a time, then, the immediate stress is reduced.

The GAS model has had a substantial impact on our understanding of stress. By suggesting that the exhaustion of resources in the third stage of the model produces

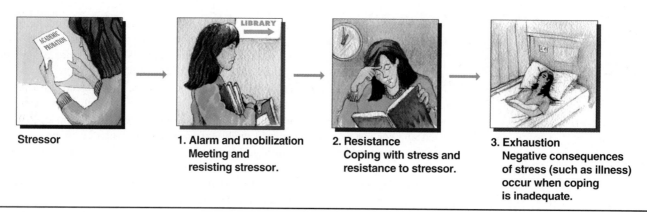

Stressor

1. Alarm and mobilization Meeting and resisting stressor.

2. Resistance Coping with stress and resistance to stressor.

3. Exhaustion Negative consequences of stress (such as illness) occur when coping is inadequate.

Figure 15–1 The general adaptation syndrome (GAS) suggests that there are three major stages to people's response to a stressor.
Source: Selye, 1976.

biological damage, it has provided a specific explanation of how stress can lead to illness. Furthermore, the model can be applied to both people and nonhuman species.

Contemporary health psychologists specializing in PNI (psychoneuroimmunology—the study of the relationships among psychological factors, the immune system, and the brain) have taken a broader approach than the GAS. Focusing on the outcomes of stress, they have identified three main consequences (see Figure 15-2). First, stress has direct physiological results, including an increase in blood pressure, increased hormonal activity, and an overall decline in the functioning of the immune system. Second, stress leads people to engage in behavior that is harmful to their health, including increased use of nicotine, drugs, and alcohol, poor eating habits, and decreased sleep. Finally, stress produces indirect consequences that result in declines in health: a reduction in the likelihood of obtaining health care and decreased compliance with medical advice when it is sought (Baum, 1994; McCabe et al., 2000).

The Nature of Stressors: My Stress Is Your Pleasure

As noted above, the general adaptation syndrome model is useful in explaining how people respond to stress, but it is not specific about what constitutes a stressor for a given person. Although certain kinds of events, such as the death of a loved one or participation in combat during a war, are universally stressful, other situations might or might not be stressful to a particular person (Fleming, Baum, & Singer, 1984; Pledge, 1992; Affleck et al., 1994; Krohne, 1996).

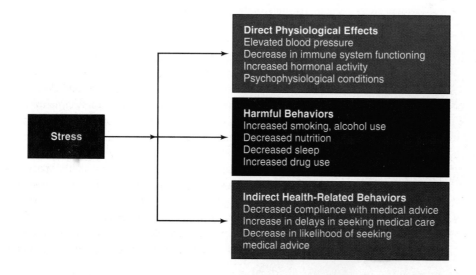

Stress

Direct Physiological Effects
Elevated blood pressure
Decrease in immune system functioning
Increased hormonal activity
Psychophysiological conditions

Harmful Behaviors
Increased smoking, alcohol use
Decreased nutrition
Decreased sleep
Increased drug use

Indirect Health-Related Behaviors
Decreased compliance with medical advice
Increase in delays in seeking medical care
Decrease in likelihood of seeking medical advice

Figure 15–2 Three major types of consequences result from stress: direct physiological effects, harmful behaviors, and indirect health-related behaviors.
Source: Adapted from Baum, 1994.

Consider, for instance, bungee jumping. Some of us would find jumping off a bridge attached to a slender rubber tether extremely stressful. However, there are those who see such an activity as challenging and fun-filled. Whether or not bungee jumping is stressful depends in part, then, on individual perceptions of the activity.

For people to consider an event to be stressful, they must perceive it as threatening and must lack the resources to deal with it effectively (Folkman et al., 1986). Consequently, the same event might at times be stressful and at other times provoke no stressful reaction at all. For instance, a young man might experience stress when he is turned down for a date—if he attributes the refusal to his unattractiveness or unworthiness. But if he attributes it to some factor unrelated to his self-esteem, such as a previous commitment by the person he asked, the experience of being refused might create no stress at all. Hence, our interpretation of events plays an important role in the determination of what is stressful.

The severity of stress is greatest when important goals are threatened, the threat is immediate, or the anticipation of a threatening event extends over a long period. For example, members of minority groups who feel they are potentially the targets of racist behavior experience significant stress (Clark et al., 1999).

Categorizing Stressors

What kinds of events tend to be seen as stressful? There are three general classes of such events: cataclysmic events, personal stressors, and background stressors.

Cataclysmic events are strong stressors that occur suddenly and typically affect many people simultaneously. Disasters such as tornadoes and plane crashes are examples of cataclysmic events that can affect hundreds or thousands of people simultaneously.

Although it might seem that cataclysmic events would produce potent, lingering stress, this is not always true. In fact, cataclysmic events might produce less stress in the long run than events that initially are not as devastating. One reason is that cataclysmic events have a clear resolution. Once they are over and done with, people can look to the future knowing that the worst is behind them. Moreover, the stress induced by cataclysmic events is shared by others who have also experienced the disaster. This permits people to offer one another social support and a firsthand understanding of the difficulties they are all going through (Kaniasty & Norris, 1995; Hobfoll et al., 1996).

On the other hand, some victims of major catastrophes experience **posttraumatic stress disorder** or **PTSD**, in which the original events and the feelings associated with them are reexperienced in vivid flashbacks or dreams. Depending upon what statistics one accepts, between 5 and 60 percent of the veterans of the Vietnam War suffer from PTSD. Even the Persian Gulf War, which ended quickly, produced some cases of PTSD. People who have suffered child abuse or rape, rescue workers facing overwhelming situations, and victims of any sudden natural disaster or accident that produces feelings of helplessness and terror might suffer from the same disorder (Saigh, 1996; Friedman & Marsella, 1996; Ward, 1997; Davidson, 2000; Woods, 2000).

Symptoms of posttraumatic stress disorder include reexperiencing the event, emotional numbing, sleep difficulties, problems relating to others, alcohol and drug abuse, and—in some cases—suicide. For instance, the suicide rate for Vietnam veterans is as much as 25 percent higher than for the general population (Peterson, Prout, & Schwarz, 1991; Wilson & Keane, 1996; Mazza, 2000). (See the *Psychology at Work* box.)

The second major category of stressor is the personal stressor. **Personal stressors** include major life events such as the death of a parent or spouse, the loss of one's job, a major personal failure, or a diagnosis of a life-threatening illness. Typically, personal stressors produce an immediate major reaction that soon tapers off. For example, stress arising from the death

⊖⊖ PsychLink

Posttraumatic stress disorder
www.mhhe.com/
feldmanup6-15links

cataclysmic events: Strong stressors that occur suddenly, affecting many people at once (e.g., natural disasters)

posttraumatic stress disorder (PTSD): A phenomenon in which victims of major catastrophes reexperience the original stress event and associated feelings in vivid flashbacks or dreams

personal stressors: Major life events, such as the death of a family member, that have immediate negative consequences that usually fade with time

Hurricane Andrew, which devastated southern Florida in 1992, was a cataclysmic event that caused severe, though in most cases short-term, stress in thousands of people. Why is this type of stress generally less dangerous than many others?

of a loved one tends to be greatest just after the time of death, but people begin to feel less stress and are better able to cope with the loss after the passage of time.

In some cases, though, the effects of stress are lingering. Victims of rape sometimes suffer consequences long after the event, facing major difficulties in adjustment. Similarly, the malfunction of the Three Mile Island nuclear plant in Pennsylvania in the early 1980s, which exposed people to the stressor of a potential nuclear meltdown, produced emotional, behavioral, and physiological consequences that lasted more than a year and a half (Baum, Cohen, & Hall, 1993; Valentiner et al., 1996).

Standing in a long line at a bank and getting stuck in a traffic jam are examples of the third major category of stressor: **background stressors** or, more informally, *daily hassles*. These are the minor irritations of life that we all face time and time again: delays, noisy cars and trucks, broken appliances, other people's irritating behavior, and so on. Another type of background stressor is a long-term, chronic problem, such as experiencing dissatisfaction with school or job, being in an unhappy relationship, or living in crowded quarters without privacy (Lazarus & Cohen, 1977; van Eck, Nicolson, & Berkhof, 1998).

Everyone confronts daily hassles, or background stressors, at some point. At what point do daily hassles become more than mere irritants?

By themselves, daily hassles do not require much coping or even a response on the part of the individual, although they certainly do produce unpleasant emotions and moods. Yet daily hassles add up—and ultimately they can produce as great a toll as a single, more stressful incident. In fact, the number of daily hassles that people face is associated with psychological symptoms and health problems such as flu, sore throat, and backaches (Chamberlain & Zika, 1990; Roberts, 1995).

The flip side of hassles are **uplifts,** those minor positive events that make one feel good—even if only temporarily. As indicated in Figure 15-3 on page 451, uplifts range from relating well to a companion to finding one's surroundings pleasing. What is especially intriguing about uplifts is that they are associated with people's psychological health in just the opposite way that hassles are: The greater the number of uplifts experienced, the fewer the psychological symptoms people later report.

Learned Helplessness

Have you ever faced an intolerable situation that you just couldn't resolve, where you finally just gave up and accepted things the way they were? This example illustrates one of the possible consequences of being in an environment in which control over a situation is not possible—a state that produces learned helplessness. According to psychologist Martin Seligman, **learned helplessness** occurs when people conclude that unpleasant or aversive stimuli cannot be controlled—a view of the world that becomes so ingrained that they cease trying to remedy the aversive circumstances, even if they actually can exert some influence (Seligman, 1975; Peterson, Maier, & Seligman, 1993). Victims of the phenomenon of learned helplessness have decided that there is no link between the responses they make and the outcomes that occur.

Take, for example, what often happens to elderly persons when they are placed in nursing homes or hospitals. One of the most striking features of their new environment is that they are no longer independent: They do not have control over the most basic activities in their lives. They are told what and when to eat, and told when they may watch TV or participate in recreational activities. In addition, their sleeping schedules are arranged by someone else. It is not hard to see how this loss of control can have negative effects upon people suddenly placed, often reluctantly, in such a situation.

The results of this loss of control and the ensuing stress are frequently poorer health and even a likelihood of earlier death. These outcomes were confirmed in a classic experiment conducted in a nursing home where elderly residents in one group were encouraged

background stressors ("daily hassles"): Everyday annoyances, such as being stuck in traffic, that cause minor irritations that can have long-term ill effects if they continue or are compounded by other stressful events

uplifts: Minor positive events that make one feel good

learned helplessness: A state in which people conclude that unpleasant or aversive stimuli cannot be controlled—a view of the world that becomes so ingrained that they cease trying to remedy their aversive circumstances, even if they actually could exert some influence on them

Psychology at Work

Alan Benner

Police Psychologist

Education: B.A., psychology, San Francisco State University; M.A., organizational psychology, San Francisco State University; Ph.D., psychology, Saybrook Institute, San Francisco, California.

Home: Pacifica, California

Alan Benner

By its very nature, the job of a police officer involves high stress. But because of an innovative program developed by psychologist Alan Benner of the San Francisco Police Department, police officers in that city are better able to cope with stress and other psychological problems.

"In order to be a competent law enforcement officer, you often have to repress normal feelings, such as anger, fear, empathy, and revulsion. After a while the ability to do that becomes habitual and unconscious," says Benner, who has been a police officer for more than 34 years. "The problem is, though, that police officers begin to carry these repressed feelings into their personal lives, and that has negative consequences."

Benner's efforts to help police officers cope with the stress of the job begins with their initial training.

"The first thing we do is provide training at the police academy, where the focus is on getting people to understand their normal reactions to abnormal situations. You try to inoculate them against the traumas they encounter," Benner notes. "You also develop peer support teams and get officers used to talking to other officers."

> "In order to be a competent law enforcement officer, you often have to repress normal feelings, such as anger, fear, empathy, and revulsion."

This training is supported by a program, developed by Benner, called CIRT, or Critical Incident Response Team.

"CIRT is composed of four officers who can be reached by pager 24 hours a day. The officers are trained in post-trauma support, which is designed to help officers who may be involved in a traumatic incident such as a shooting or serious accident," Benner explains. "Psychologists and psychiatrists are used as additional resources."

According to Benner, the rationale for CIRT is that police officers are more likely to talk to a fellow officer than to someone outside of their ranks. The program has proven to be quite successful.

"Since 1993 Critical Incident Response Teams have conducted more than 200 separate debriefings involving more than 1,500 officers," says Benner. "Over time CIRT has changed the organizational climate of the job, making people more aware of the impact of their emotions on other aspects of their lives and better able to deal with them."

> "You also develop peer support teams and get officers used to talking to other officers."

to make more choices and take greater control of their day-to-day activities (Langer & Janis, 1979). As a result, members of the group were more active and happier than a comparison group of residents who were encouraged to let the nursing home staff take care of them. Moreover, an analysis of the residents' medical records revealed that six months after the experiment, the group encouraged to be self-sufficient showed significantly greater health improvement than the comparison group. Even more startling was an examination of the death rate: Eighteen months after the experiment began, only 15 percent of the "independent" group had died—compared with 30 percent of the comparison group.

Other research confirms that learned helplessness has negative consequences, and not just for elderly people. People of all ages report more physical symptoms and depression when they perceive that they have little or no control than when they feel a sense of control over a situation (Rodin, 1986; Joiner & Wagner, 1995; Shnek et al., 1995).

Coping with Stress

Stress is a normal part of life—and not necessarily a completely bad part. For example, without stress, we might not be sufficiently motivated to complete the activities we need to accomplish. However, it is also clear that too much stress can take its toll on both physical and psychological health. How do people deal with stress? Is there a way to reduce its negative effects?

The efforts to control, reduce, or learn to tolerate the threats that lead to stress are known as **coping.** We habitually use certain coping responses to help ourselves deal with stress. Most of the time, we're not aware of these responses—just as we might be unaware of the minor stressors of life until they build up to sufficiently aversive levels (Snyder, 1999).

coping: Efforts to control, reduce, or learn to tolerate the threats that lead to stress

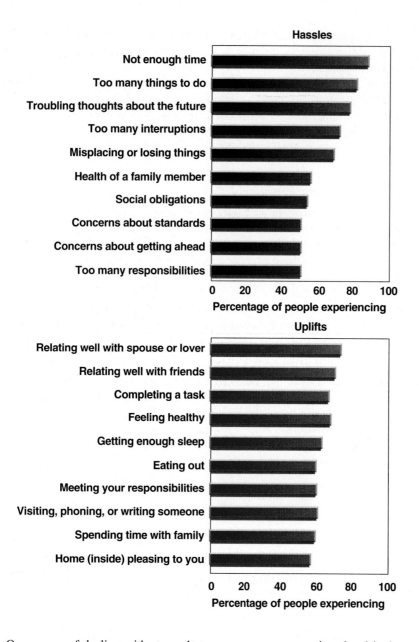

Hassles

Not enough time
Too many things to do
Troubling thoughts about the future
Too many interruptions
Misplacing or losing things
Health of a family member
Social obligations
Concerns about standards
Concerns about getting ahead
Too many responsibilities

0   20   40   60   80   100

Percentage of people experiencing

Uplifts

Relating well with spouse or lover
Relating well with friends
Completing a task
Feeling healthy
Getting enough sleep
Eating out
Meeting your responsibilities
Visiting, phoning, or writing someone
Spending time with family
Home (inside) pleasing to you

0   20   40   60   80   100

Percentage of people experiencing

Figure 15-3 The most common everyday hassles and uplifts (Hassles: Chamberlain & Zika, 1990; uplifts: Kanner et al., 1981). How many of these are part of *your* life, and how do you cope with them?

One means of dealing with stress that occurs on an unconscious level is the use of defense mechanisms. As we discussed in Chapter 14, **defense mechanisms** are reactions that maintain a person's sense of control and self-worth by distorting or denying the actual nature of the situation. For example, one study examined California students who lived in dormitories close to a geological fault. Those who lived in dorms that were rated as being unlikely to withstand an earthquake were significantly more likely to doubt experts' predictions of an impending earthquake than were those who lived in safer structures (Lehman & Taylor, 1988).

Another defense mechanism used to cope with stress is *emotional insulation*, in which a person stops experiencing any emotions at all, thereby remaining unaffected and unmoved by both positive and negative experiences. The problem with defense mechanisms, of course, is that they do not deal with reality but merely hide the problem.

People also use other, more direct and potentially more positive means for coping with stress. Specifically, coping strategies fall into two categories: emotion-focused coping and problem-focused coping. In *emotion-focused coping,* people try to manage their emotions in the face of stress, seeking to change the way they feel about or perceive a problem. Examples of emotion-focused coping include such strategies as accepting sympathy from others or looking at the bright side of a situation. In contrast, *problem-focused coping* attempts to modify the stressful problem or source of the stress.

defense mechanisms: Unconscious strategies people use to reduce anxiety by concealing its source from themselves and others

 **PsychLink**

Coping with stress
www.mhhe.com/
feldmanup6-15links

Problem-focused strategies lead to changes in behavior or to the development of a plan of action to deal with stress. Starting a study group to improve poor classroom performance is an example of problem-focused coping.

In most stressful incidents, people employ *both* emotion-focused and problem-focused strategies. However, they use emotion-focused strategies more frequently when they perceive circumstances as being unchangeable, and problem-focused approaches more often in situations they see as relatively modifiable (Lazarus, 1999; Stanton & Frantz, 1999; Folkman & Moskowitz, 2000).

Coping Style: The Hardy Personality

Most of us cope with stress in a characteristic manner, employing a *coping style* that represents our general tendency to deal with stress in a specific way. For example, you may know people who habitually react to even the smallest amount of stress with hysteria, and others who calmly confront even the greatest stress in an unflappable manner. These kinds of people clearly have quite different coping styles (Taylor, 1991; Gallaher, 1996; Taylor & Aspinwall, 1996).

hardiness: A personality characteristic associated with a lower rate of stress-related illness, consisting of three components: commitment, challenge, and control

Among those who cope with stress most successfully are people with the coping style of **hardiness,** a personality characteristic associated with a lower rate of stress-related illness. It consists of three components (Kobasa, 1979; Gentry & Kobasa, 1984):

- *Commitment.* Commitment is a tendency to throw ourselves into whatever we are doing with a sense that our activities are important and meaningful.
- *Challenge.* Hardy people believe that change, rather than stability, is the standard condition of life. To them, the anticipation of change is an incentive rather than a threat to their security.
- *Control.* Hardy people feel a sense of control—they believe that they can influence the events in their lives.

Hardy individuals approach stress optimistically and take direct action to learn about and deal with stressors, thereby changing stressful events into less threatening ones. As a consequence, hardiness acts as a defense against stress-related illness (Wiebe, 1991; Solcova & Tomanek, 1994; Kobasa et al., 1994).

Social Support: Turning to Others

social support: A mutual network of caring, interested others

Our relationships with others also help us cope with stress. Researchers have found that **social support,** the knowledge that we are part of a mutual network of caring, interested others, enables us to lower our levels of stress and to cope better with the stress we do undergo (Uchino, Uno, & Holt-Lunstad, 1999; McCabe et al., 2000).

The social and emotional support that people provide each other helps in dealing with stress in several ways. For instance, such support demonstrates that the person is an important and valued member of a social network, and other people can provide information and advice about appropriate ways of dealing with stress (Hobfoll et al., 1996; Lepore, Ragan, & Jones, 2000). People who are part of a social support network can also provide actual goods and services to help others in stressful situations: by supplying a person whose house has burned down with temporary living quarters, helping a student who is experiencing stress due to poor academic performance study for a test, and so on (Croyle & Hunt, 1991; Peirce et al., 1996).

Surprisingly, the benefits of social support are not limited to the comfort provided by other humans. One study found that owners of pets were less likely than those without pets to require medical care following exposure to stressors. Dogs, in particular, helped diminish the effects of stress (Siegel, 1990, 1993).

"Today, we examined our life style, we evaluated our diet and our exercise program, and we also assessed our behavioral patterns. Then we felt we needed a drink."

BECOMING AN INFORMED CONSUMER OF PSYCHOLOGY

Effective Coping Strategies

What are the most effective ways to deal with stress? Researchers have made a number of recommendations for dealing with the problem. There is no universal solution, of course, because effective coping depends on the nature of the stressor and the degree to which it is possible to control it. Still, researchers have developed some general guidelines (Holahan & Moos, 1990; McCain & Smith, 1994; Zeidner & Endler, 1996; Aspinwall & Taylor, 1997):

- *Turn threat into challenge.* When a stressful situation might be controllable, the best coping strategy is to treat the situation as a challenge, focusing on ways to control it. For instance, if you experience stress because your car is always breaking down, you might take an evening course in auto mechanics and learn to deal directly with the car's problems.

- *Make a threatening situation less threatening.* When a stressful situation seems to be uncontrollable, a different approach must be taken. It is possible to change your appraisal of the situation, to view it in a different light, and to modify your attitudes toward it. The old truism "Look for the silver lining in every cloud" is supported by research (Silver & Wortman, 1980; Taylor & Aspinwall, 1996; Salovey et al., 2000).

- *Change your goals.* When faced with an uncontrollable situation, a reasonable strategy is to adopt new goals that are practical in view of the particular situation. For example, a dancer who has been in an automobile accident and has lost full use of her legs might abandon her aspiration to a career in dance, replacing it with the goal of becoming a dance instructor.

- *Take physical action.* Changing your physiological reaction to stress can help you cope. For example, biofeedback, discussed in Chapter 3, can alter your basic physiological processes, allowing you to reduce your blood pressure, heart rate, and other consequences of heightened stress. Exercise can also be effective in reducing stress. Regular exercise improves your overall health and can even reduce your risk for certain diseases, such as breast cancer. Finally, exercise can give you a sense of control over your body and a feeling of accomplishment (Thune et al., 1997; Barinaga, 1997; Langreth, 2000).

- *Prepare for stress before it happens.* A final strategy for coping with stress is *proactive coping:* anticipating and preparing for stress *before* you encounter it. Through proactive coping, you can ready yourself for upcoming stressful events and thereby reduce their negative consequences (Aspinwall & Taylor, 1997).

Evaluate

1. _____ is defined as a response to challenging or threatening events.
2. Match each portion of the GAS with its definition
   1. Alarm
   2. Exhaustion
   3. Resistance

   a. The ability to adapt to stress diminishes; symptoms appear
   b. Activation of the sympathetic nervous system
   c. Various strategies are used to cope with a stressor
3. Stressors that affect a single person and produce an immediate major reaction are known as
   a. Personal stressors
   b. Psychic stressors
   c. Cataclysmic stressors
   d. Daily stressors
4. People with the personality characteristic of _____ seem to be more able to successfully combat stressors.

Rethink

1. Why are cataclysmic stressors less stressful in the long run than other types of stressors? Does the reason relate to the coping phenomenon known as social support? How?
2. Given what you know about coping strategies, how would you train people to avoid stress in their everyday lives? How would you use this information with a group of Gulf War veterans suffering from posttraumatic stress disorder?

Answers to Evaluate Questions

1. Stress 2. 1–b; 2–a; 3–c 3. a 4. hardiness

Prepare

How do psychological factors affect such health-related problems as coronary heart disease, cancer, and smoking?

Organize

Psychological Aspects of Illness and Well-Being
The A's and B's of Coronary Heart Disease
Psychological Aspects of Cancer
Smoking
Well-Being and Happiness

Psychological Aspects of Illness and Well-Being

Once a week they meet to talk, to cry, sometimes to laugh together. "Is the pain still worse in the mornings?" Margaret asks Kate today.

A petite, graceful woman in her late forties, Kate shakes her head no. "It's getting bad all the time," she says in a voice raw with worry and fatigue. A few weeks ago she learned that the cancer that began in her breast had spread into her bones. Since then she's hardly slept. She knows, as do the other women in the group, that her prognosis isn't good. "Sometimes I'm afraid I'm not going to do that well because it all came on so fast," she tells them. "It's like being in the ocean and the waves are just coming too fast, and you can't get your breath."

They nod in tacit understanding, eight women sitting in a loose circle of chairs here in a small, sparely furnished room at Stanford University Medical Center. They know. All of them have been diagnosed with recurrent breast cancer. . . .

They gather here each Wednesday afternoon to talk with each other and to listen. It's a chance to discuss their fears and find some small comfort, a time to feel they're not alone. And in some way that no one has been able to explain, it may be keeping them alive. (Jaret, 1992, p. 87)

As recently as two decades ago, most psychologists and health-care providers would have scoffed at the notion that a discussion group could improve a cancer patient's chances of survival. Today, however, such methods have gained increasing respectability.

Growing evidence suggests that psychological factors have a substantial impact, both on major health problems that were once seen in purely physiological terms and on our everyday sense of health, well-being, and happiness. We'll consider the psychological components of three major health problems—heart disease, cancer, and smoking—and then consider the nature of people's well-being and happiness.

The A's and B's of Coronary Heart Disease

Have you ever seethed impatiently at being caught behind a slow-moving vehicle, felt anger and frustration at not finding material you needed at the library, or experienced a sense of competitiveness with almost all your classmates?

Many of us experience these sorts of feelings at one time or another, but for some people they represent a pervasive, characteristic set of personality traits (of the type discussed in Chapter 14) known as the **Type A behavior pattern.** Type A individuals are competitive, show a continual sense of urgency about time, are aggressive, exhibit a driven quality regarding their work, and are hostile, both verbally and nonverbally—especially when interrupted while trying to complete a task. On the other hand, people who show the **Type B behavior pattern** are more cooperative, far less competitive, not especially time-oriented, and not usually aggressive, driven, or hostile. Although people are typically not "pure" Type A's or Type B's, showing instead a combination of both behavior types, they generally do fall into one category or the other (Rosenman, 1990; Strube, 1990; see Table 15-2).

Type A people lead fast-paced, driven lives. They put in longer hours at work than Type B's and are impatient with other people's performance, which they typically perceive as too slow. They also engage in "multitasking," concentrating on several activities simultaneously, such as running on a treadmill while watching television and reading a magazine all at the same time.

The Type A behavior pattern is linked to coronary heart disease. Studies have found that men who display the Type A pattern develop coronary heart disease twice as often and suffer significantly more fatal heart attacks compared with those classified as having

Type A behavior pattern: A pattern of behavior characterized by competitiveness, impatience, tendency toward frustration, and hostility

Type B behavior pattern: A pattern of behavior characterized by cooperation, patience, noncompetitiveness, and nonaggression

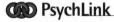 **PsychLink**

Type A personality
www.mhhe.com/
feldmanup6-15links

Table 15-2 Type Yourself

To get an idea of whether you have the characteristics of a Type A or Type B personality, answer the following questions:

1. When you listen to someone talking and this person takes too long to come to the point, how often do you feel like hurrying the person along?
   _____ Frequently
   _____ Occasionally
   _____ Never

2. Do you ever set deadlines or quotas for yourself at work or at home?
   _____ No
   _____ Yes, but only occasionally
   _____ Yes, once a week or more

3. Would people you know well agree that you tend to get irritated easily?
   _____ Definitely yes
   _____ Probably yes
   _____ Probably no
   _____ Definitely no

4. Would people who know you well agree that you tend to do most things in a hurry?
   _____ Definitely yes
   _____ Probably yes
   _____ Probably no
   _____ Definitely no

Scoring: The more frequently your answers reflect affirmative responses, the more Type A characteristics you hold.

Source: Adapted from Jenkins, Zyzanski, & Rosenman, 1978.

the Type B pattern. Moreover, the Type A pattern predicts who is going to develop heart disease at least as well as—and independently of—any other single factor, including age, blood pressure, smoking habits, and cholesterol levels in the body (Roseman et al., 1976, 1994; Wielgosz & Nolan, 2000).

Current research suggests that not every component of the Type A behavior pattern is linked to coronary heart disease. Hostility and anger seem to be the key factors, though other negative emotions, such as depression and low self-esteem, are now also thought to be related to heart attacks (Mittleman et al., 1995; McCabe et al., 2000; Williams, Paton, et al., 2000).

Why is Type A behavior, and hostility and anger in particular, linked to coronary heart disease? The most convincing theory is that the Type A behavior pattern produces excessive physiological arousal in stressful situations. This arousal, in turn, results in increased production of the hormones epinephrine and norepinephrine, as well as increased heart rate and blood pressure. Such exaggerated physiological responsivity ultimately produces an increased incidence of coronary heart disease (Blascovich & Katkin, 1993; Sundin et al., 1995).

It's important to keep in mind that not everyone who displays Type A behaviors is destined to have coronary heart disease. For one thing, a firm association between Type A behaviors and coronary heart disease has not been established for women; most studies have been done on males, not females. Furthermore, the evidence relating Type A behavior and coronary heart disease is correlational. Consequently, as we first discussed in Chapter 2, we cannot say for sure whether Type A behavior

PsychLink

Effects of anger on the heart
www.mhhe.com/
feldmanup6-15links

Most people can be classified as primarily either Type A or Type B. Type A's tend to be competitive, time-oriented, aggressive, driven, and hostile— and to be more vulnerable to coronary heart disease than Type B's. Are there types of careers where Type A personalities are more successful than Type B's? Why?

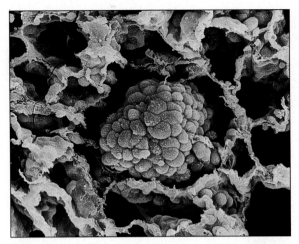

Increasing evidence suggests that the way a cancer patient emotionally deals with the disease may have an impact on its effects and treatment and may slow the growth of cancer cells such as these. Which is the better strategy: stoic acceptance or denial? Why?

causes heart disease or whether, instead, some other factor causes both heart disease and Type A behavior. In fact, rather than focusing on Type A behavior as the cause of heart disease, it might make more sense to ask whether Type B behavior *prevents* heart disease (Powell, Shaker, & Jones, 1993; Orth-Gomér, Chesney, & Wenger, 1996).

Psychological Aspects of Cancer

Hardly any disease is more feared than cancer. Most people think of cancer in terms of lingering pain, and being diagnosed with the disease is typically viewed as receiving a death sentence.

Although a diagnosis of cancer is not as grim as you might at first suspect—several kinds of cancer have a high cure rate if detected early enough—cancer remains the second leading cause of death after coronary heart disease. The precise trigger for the disease is not well understood, but the process by which cancer spreads is straightforward. Certain cells in the body become altered and multiply rapidly and in an uncontrolled fashion. As these cells grow, they form tumors, which, if left unchecked, suck nutrients from healthy cells and bodily tissue, ultimately destroying the body's ability to function properly.

Although the processes involved in the spread of cancer are basically physiological, accumulating evidence suggests that the emotional responses of cancer patients to their disease can have a critical effect on its course. For example, one experiment found that people who adopt a fighting spirit are more likely to recover than those who pessimistically suffer and resign themselves to death (Pettingale et al., 1985). The study analyzed the survival rates of women who had undergone the removal of a breast because of cancer.

The results suggested that the survival rates were related to the psychological response of the women three months after surgery (see Figure 15-4). Women who stoically accepted their fate, trying not to complain, and those who felt the situation was hopeless and that nothing could be done, showed the lowest survival rates; most of these women were dead after ten years. On the other hand, the survival rates of women who showed a fighting spirit (predicting that they would overcome the disease and planning to take steps to prevent its recurrence) and the survival rates of women who (erroneously) denied

Figure 15-4 The relationship between women's psychological response to breast cancer three months after surgery and their survival ten years after the operation (Pettingale et al., 1985). What implications do these findings have for the treatment of people with cancer?

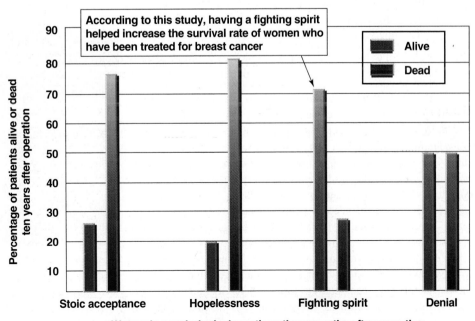

According to this study, having a fighting spirit helped increase the survival rate of women who have been treated for breast cancer

Alive
Dead

Percentage of patients alive or dead ten years after operation

Stoic acceptance   Hopelessness   Fighting spirit   Denial

Women's psychological reactions three months after operation

that they had ever had cancer (saying that the breast removal was merely a preventive step) were significantly higher. In sum, according to this study, cancer patients with a positive attitude were more likely to survive than those with a more negative one.

On the other hand, other research contradicts the notion that the course of cancer is affected by patients' attitudes and emotions. For example, some findings show that although a "fighting spirit" leads to better coping, the long-term survival rate is no better than for patients with a less positive attitude (Watson et al., 1999).

Despite the contradictory evidence, health psychologists believe that patients' emotions might at least partially determine the course of their disease. For example, psychologists specializing in psychoneuroimmunology (PNI) suggest that a patient's emotional state affects the immune system, the body's natural defenses that fight disease. Our bodies produce *lymphocytes,* specialized white blood cells that fight disease, at an extraordinary rate—some 10 million every few seconds—and it is possible that emotions affect this production. In the case of cancer, for instance, it is possible that positive emotional responses might help generate specialized "killer" cells that help control the size and spread of cancerous tumors. Conversely, negative emotions might suppress the ability of the same kinds of cells to fight tumors (Andersen, Kiecolt-Glaser, & Glaser, 1994; Seligman, 1995; Schedlowski & Tewes, 1999).

Other research suggests that "joy"—referring to mental resilience and vigor—is related to the likelihood of survival of patients with recurrent breast cancer. Similarly, cancer patients who are characteristically optimistic report less distress throughout the course of their treatment (Levy et al., 1988; Carver et al., 2000).

Is a particular personality type linked to cancer? Some findings suggest that cancer patients are less emotionally reactive, suppress anger, and lack outlets for emotional release. However, the data are still too tentative and inconsistent to suggest firm conclusions about a link between personality characteristics and cancer. Certainly there is no conclusive evidence that people who develop cancer would not have done so if they had had a different personality or more positive attitudes (Smith, 1988; Zevon & Corn, 1990; Holland, 1996).

What is increasingly clear, however, is that certain types of psychological therapy have the potential to extend the lives of cancer patients. One study found that women with breast cancer who received psychological treatment lived at least a year and a half longer, and experienced less anxiety and pain, than women who did not participate in therapy. Research on patients with other health problems, such as heart disease, also finds that therapy can be beneficial, both psychologically and medically (Spiegel, 1993, 1996a; Galavotti et al., 1997; Frasure-Smith, Lesperance, & Talajic, 2000).

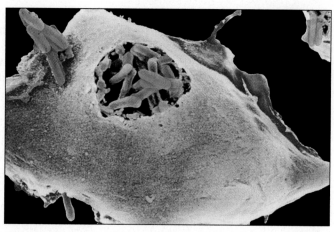

The ability to fight off disease is related to psychological factors. Here a cell from the body's immune system engulfs and destroys disease-producing bacteria.

 **PsychLink**
Stress and cancer
www.mhhe.com/
feldmanup6-15links

Smoking

Would you stroll into a convenience store and buy an item with a label warning you that its use could kill you? Although most of us would probably answer no, millions make such a purchase every day: a pack of cigarettes. Furthermore, they do this despite clear, well-publicized evidence that smoking is linked to cancer, heart attacks, strokes, bronchitis, emphysema, and a host of other serious illnesses. Smoking is the greatest preventable cause of death in the United States. Worldwide, 3 million people die prematurely each year due to the effects of smoking (Heishman, Kozlowki, & Henningfield, 1997; Kawachi et al., 1997; Noble, 1999).

Why do people smoke, despite all the evidence that it is bad for their health? It is not that they are unaware of the link between smoking and disease; surveys show that most *smokers* agree with the statement "Cigarette smoking frequently causes disease and death." And almost three-quarters of the 48 million smokers in the United States say they would like to quit (Centers for Disease Control, 1994; Wetter et al., 1998).

Heredity seems to partly determine whether people will become smokers, how much they will smoke, and how easily they can quit. Genetics also influences how susceptible people are to the harmful effects of smoking. For instance, there is an almost 50 percent higher rate of lung cancer in African American smokers than in white smokers. This difference could be due to genetically produced variations in the efficiency with which enzymes are able to reduce the effects of the cancer-causing chemicals in tobacco smoke (Pomerlau, 1995; Heath & Madden, 1995; Richie, 1994).

On the other hand, although genetics plays a role in smoking, most research suggests that environmental factors are the primary cause of the habit. Smokers might at first see smoking as "cool" or sophisticated, as a rebellious act, or as helping them perform calmly under stressful situations. In addition, smoking a cigarette is sometimes viewed as a "rite of passage" for adolescents, undertaken at the urging of friends and viewed as a sign of growing up (Grube, Rokeach, & Getzlaf, 1990; Boomsma & Koopmans, 1996; Koval et al., 2000; Wagner & Atkins, 2000).

But ultimately smoking becomes a habit. People begin to label themselves smokers, and smoking becomes part of their self-concept. Moreover, they become dependent on the physiological effects of smoking, because nicotine, a primary ingredient of tobacco, is highly addictive. Ultimately, a complex relationship develops among smoking, nicotine levels, and the smoker's emotional state, in which a certain nicotine level becomes associated with a positive emotional state. As a result, people smoke in an effort to regulate *both* emotional states and nicotine levels in the blood (Leventhal & Cleary, 1980; Gilbert, 1995).

Quitting Smoking

Because smoking has both psychological and biological components, few habits are as difficult to break. Long-term successful treatment typically occurs in just 15 percent of those trying to stop smoking, and once smoking becomes a habit, it is as hard to stop as an addiction to cocaine or heroin. In fact, some of the biochemical reactions to nicotine are similar to reactions to cocaine, amphetamines, and morphine. Many people try to quit and fail, as you can see in Figure 15-5 (Glassman & Koob, 1996; Piasecki et al., 1997; National Council on Aging, 2000).

Among the most effective tools for ending the smoking habit are drugs that replace the nicotine found in cigarettes. Whether in the form of gum, patches, nasal sprays, or inhalers, these products provide a dose of nicotine that reduces dependence on cigarettes. Another approach is exemplified by the drug Zyban, which, rather than replacing nicotine, raises dopamine levels in the brain, thereby reducing the desire to smoke (Rock, 1999).

Behavioral strategies that view smoking as a learned habit and concentrate on changing the smoking response can also be effective. Initial "cure" rates of 60 percent

Figure 15-5 The difficulty of quitting smoking is evident in this graph. More than 85 percent of those who tried to quit returned to smoking.

Source: The Harris Poll, 2000.

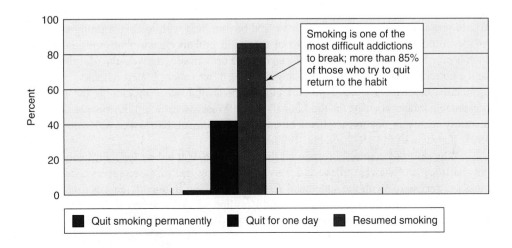

have been reported, and one year after treatment more than half of those who quit have not resumed smoking. Counseling, either individually or in groups, also increases the rate of success in breaking the habit. The best treatment seems to be a combination of nicotine replacement *and* counseling. What doesn't work? Going it alone: Only 5 percent of smokers who quit cold-turkey on their own are successful (Wetter et al., 1998; Rock, 1999; Noble, 1999).

In the long term, the most effective way to reduce smoking could be changes in societal norms and attitudes toward the habit. Many cities and towns have made smoking in public places illegal, and legislation banning smoking in such places as college classrooms and buildings—based on strong popular sentiment—is being passed with increasing frequency (Gibson, 1997; Jacobson, Wasserman, & Anderson, 1997).

The long-term effect of the barrage of information regarding the negative consequences of smoking on people's health has been substantial; overall, smoking has declined over the last two decades, particularly for males. On the other hand, a surge in the availability of discount brands of cigarettes has slowed the decline in smoking that had been occurring over the last decade. In fact, more than one-third of students enrolled in high school are active smokers by the time they graduate. Of these, more than one in six is an active smoker as early as eighth grade (Johnston, Bachman, & O'Malley, 1999; see Figure 15-6).

Changes in society's attitudes, and strong anti-smoking campaigns, can go a long way toward reducing tobacco use.

EXPLORING DIVERSITY

Hucksters of Death: Promoting Smoking Throughout the World

In Dresden, Germany, three women in miniskirts offer passers-by a pack of Lucky Strikes and a leaflet that reads: "You just got hold of a nice piece of America." Says a local doctor, "Adolescents time and again receive cigarettes at such promotions."

A Jeep decorated with the Camel logo pulls up to a high school in Buenos Aires. A woman begins handing out free cigarettes to 15- and 16-year-olds during their lunch recess.

At a video arcade in Taipei, free American cigarettes are strewn atop each game. At a disco filled with high school students, free packs of Salems are on each table (Ecenbarger, 1993, p. 50).

As the number of smokers has declined in the United States, cigarette manufacturers have turned to new markets in an effort to increase the number of people who smoke. In the process, they have employed some dubious marketing techniques.

For instance, in the early 1990s the tobacco company RJ Reynolds developed a new cigarette brand it named "Uptown." The advertising that announced the debut of the cigarette

PsychLink

Smoking and health
www.mhhe.com/
feldmanup6-15links

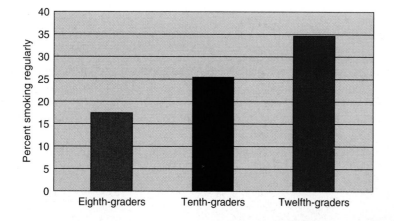

Figure 15-6 Although smoking among teenagers is lower than twenty years ago, a significant number still report smoking regularly (Johnston, Bachman, & O'Malley, 1999). What factors might account for the continued high use of tobacco, despite the increase in anti-smoking advertising?

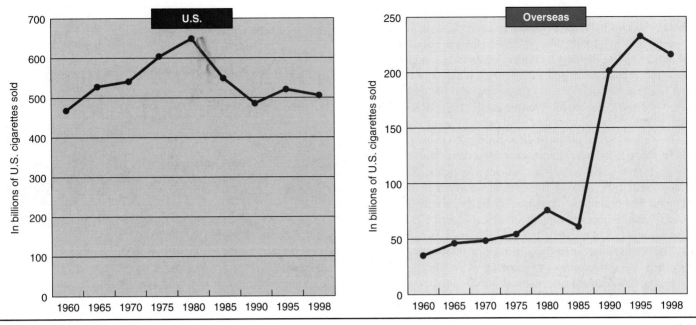

Figure 15-7 Despite the plummeting in sales of cigarettes in the United States, the number sold overseas has dramatically increased.
Source: U.S. Department of Agriculture, 1998.

targeted African Americans (Quinn, 1990; Jhally et al., 1995; Ringold, 1996). Given the questionable ethics of targeting a potentially life-threatening product to a minority population, the product introduction caused considerable controversy. Ultimately, the secretary of the U.S. Department of Health and Human Services condemned the tactic, and the manufacturer stopped distributing the brand soon thereafter.

More recently, cigarette manufacturers have turned their sights to other parts of the world, where they see a fertile market of nonsmokers (Sesser, 1993). Although they must often sell cigarettes more cheaply abroad than in the United States, the number of potential smokers still makes it financially worthwhile for the tobacco companies. For instance, in 1995, China opened its market of 298 million smokers—more than the entire U.S. population—to American brands (Hass, 1994). As can be seen in Figure 15-7, overseas sales have surged since the mid 1980s, as sales in the United States have declined (Bartecchi, MacKenzie, & Schrier, 1995).

Clearly, the push into worldwide markets has been successful. In some Latin American cities, as many as 50 percent of teenagers smoke. Children as young as 7 smoke in Hong Kong. The World Health Organization predicts that smoking will prematurely kill some 200 million of the world's children, and that ultimately 10 percent of the world's population will die due to smoking (Ecenbarger, 1993). Clearly, smoking is one of the world's greatest health problems.

Well-Being and Happiness

What makes for a good life?

Philosophers and theologians have pondered this question for centuries, and now health psychologists are turning their spotlight on it. They are doing so by investigating **subjective well-being,** people's evaluations of their lives in terms of both their thoughts and emotions. Considered another way, subjective well-being is the measure of how happy people are (Diener, 2000).

Research on subjective well-being shows that happy people share several characteristics (Myers & Diener, 1996; Myers, 2000):

subjective well-being: People's evaluations of their lives in terms of both their thoughts and their emotions; how happy people are

Applying Psychology in the 21st Century

If You Won the Lottery, Would You Be Happier?

Probably not.

At least that's the implication of an increasing body of research on subjective well-being. This research shows that although winning the lottery brings an initial surge in happiness, a year later winners' level of happiness seems to return to what it was before. The converse phenomenon occurs for people who have suffered serious injuries in accidents: Despite an initial decline in happiness, most victims return to their prior levels of happiness over time (Diener et al., 1999).

Why is the level of subjective well-being so stable? One explanation is that people have a general "set point" for happiness, a marker that establishes the tone for one's life. Although a particular event (a surprise promotion or a job loss, for example) might temporarily elevate or depress one's mood, ultimately people return to their usual general level of happiness.

Although it is not certain how people's happiness set points are initially established, some evidence suggests that genetic factors play a role. Specifically, identical twins who grow up in widely different circumstances turn out to have quite similar levels of happiness (Diener & Diener, 1996; Lykken & Tellegen, 1996; Kahneman, Diener, & Schwarz, 1998).

Most people's well-being set point is relatively high. For example, some 30 percent

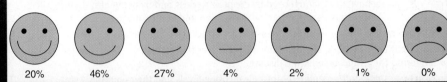

Faces Scale: "Which face comes closest to expressing how you feel about your life as a whole?"

| 20% | 46% | 27% | 4% | 2% | 1% | 0% |

Figure 15-8 Most people in the U.S. rate themselves very happy; only a small percentage indicate that they are not happy.
Source: Myers, 2000.

of people in the United States rate themselves as "very happy," and only one in ten rate themselves as "not too happy." Most people declare themselves to be "pretty happy." Such feelings are graphically confirmed by people asked to place themselves on the measure of happiness illustrated in Figure 15-8. The scale clearly illustrates that most people view their lives quite positively.

Similar results are found when people are asked to compare themselves to others. For example, when asked "Who of the following people do you think is the happiest?" survey respondents answered "Oprah Winfrey" (23 percent), "Bill Gates" (7 percent), "the Pope" (12 percent), "Chelsea Clinton" (3 percent), and "yourself" (49 percent), with 6 percent saying they didn't know (Black & McCafferty, 1998).

Demographic groups don't differ much from each other on this measure. Men and women report being equally happy, and African

Americans are only slightly less likely than white Americans to rate themselves as "very happy." Furthermore, happiness is hardly unique to U.S. culture. Even countries that are far from economically prosperous have, on the whole, happy residents (Myers & Diener, 1996; Mroczek & Kolarz, 1998; Schkade & Kahneman, 1998; Staudinger, Fleeson, & Baltes, 1999; Diener, 2000).

The bottom line: Money does *not* seem to buy happiness. Despite the ups and downs of life, most people tend to be reasonably happy, and they adapt to the trials and tribulations—and joys and delights—of life by returning to a steady-state level of happiness.

Why do you think people consistently rate themselves happier than they rate wealthy and powerful people like Oprah Winfrey and Bill Gates? Do you think Winfrey and Gates would agree?

- *Happy people have high self-esteem.* Particularly in Western cultures, which emphasize the importance of individuality, people who are happy like themselves. They see themselves as more intelligent and better able to get along with others than the average person.
- *Happy people have a firm sense of control.* They feel more in control of events in their lives, unlike people who feel they are the pawns of others and who experience learned helplessness.
- *Happy individuals are optimistic.* Their optimism permits them to persevere at tasks and ultimately to achieve more. Their health is also better (Peterson, 2000).
- *Happy people like to be around other people.* They tend to be extroverted and have a supportive network of close relationships.

Perhaps most important, most people are at least moderately happy most of the time. In both national and international surveys, people living in a wide variety of circumstances report being happy. Furthermore—as we consider in the *Applying Psychology in the 21st Century* box—winning the lottery probably won't make you happy. According to a variety of findings, happiness can't be bought.

Evaluate

1. Type _____ behavior is characterized by cooperativeness and by being easy-going, whereas Type _____ behavior is characterized by aggression and competitiveness.
2. Type A behavior is known to directly cause heart attacks. True or false?
3. A cancer patient's attitude and emotions might affect that person's _____ system, helping or hindering their fight against the disease.
4. Smokers use smoking to regulate both their nicotine levels and their emotional states. True or false?

Answers to Evaluate Questions

1. B; A 2. False; Type A behavior is related to a higher incidence of coronary heart disease, but does not necessarily directly cause it. 3. immune 4. True

Rethink

1. Do you think Type A or Type B behavior is more widely encouraged in the United States? Why?
2. If money doesn't buy happiness, what can you do to make yourself happier? As you answer, consider the research findings on stress and coping, as well as our discussion of emotions in Chapter 9.

Prepare

How do our interactions with physicians affect our health and compliance with medical treatment?

Organize

Psychological Factors Related to Physical Illness
   Physician–Patient Communication
   Complying with Physicians' Recommendations

PsychLink

Physician communication
www.mhhe.com/
feldmanup6-15links

Psychological Factors Related to Physical Illness: Going to the Doctor

When Stuart Grinspoon first noticed the small lump in his arm, he assumed it was just a bruise from the football game he had played the previous week. But as he thought about it more, he considered more serious possibilities and decided that he better get it checked out at the university health service. The visit was less than satisfactory. A shy person, Stuart felt embarrassed talking about his medical condition. Even worse, after answering a string of questions, he couldn't even understand the physician's diagnosis, and was too embarrassed to ask for clarification.

Stuart Grinspoon's attitudes toward health care are shared by many of us. Good medical care does not depend just on physical exams and prescribing a treatment. Several psychological factors are involved in determining the success of a health care provider's effectiveness in diagnosing and treating medical problems.

Physician–Patient Communication

You might be surprised to hear that many patients are reluctant to describe their symptoms to their physicians. But this is a common problem. Many people believe that a skilled physician will easily be able to identify a patient's problems through a thorough physical examination, the way a good mechanic diagnoses car problems. But diagnosing a medical problem is less a science than an art—one in which physicians are not always successful (Leigh & Reiser, 1980; Mentzer & Snyder, 1982; Konrad, 1994).

One source of physician–patient communication difficulties is that physicians have relatively high social prestige and power, which can intimidate patients. Patients might also be reluctant to volunteer information that could cast them in a bad light, and physicians might not be skilled at encouraging their patients to provide information. Physicians often dominate the interview with questions of a technical nature, whereas patients tend to attempt to communicate a personal sense of their illness and the impact it is having on their lives. Add to these communication problems the embarrassment many people feel in discussing personal matters (Beckman & Frankel, 1984; Goleman, 1988).

Patients' reluctance to reveal medical information fully to health care providers and the problems that providers encounter in eliciting information effectively produce major communication difficulties. These factors can prevent providers from understanding the extent of the difficulties that led the patients to seek medical care in the first place (Parrott, Duncan, & Duggan, 2000; see Table 15-3).

The view held by many patients that physicians are "all-knowing" can also result in serious communication problems. For instance, many patients do not understand their treatment, yet fail to ask their physicians for a clearer explanation of a prescribed course of action. About half of all patients are unable to accurately report how long they are to continue taking a medication prescribed for them, and about a quarter do not even know the purpose of the drug. In fact, some patients are not even sure, as they are about to be rolled into the operating room, why they are having surgery (Svarstad, 1976; Atkinson, 1997)!

Another reason for patient–physician communication difficulties is that the information that must be communicated can be too technical for patients who lack fundamental knowledge about the human body and basic medical practices. In response to this problem, some health care providers routinely use baby talk (calling patients "honey" or telling them to go "night-night") and assume that patients are unable to understand even simple information (Whitbourne & Wills, 1993; DiMatteo, 1997; Basset et al., 1998).

Cultural values and expectations also contribute to communication barriers between patients and their physicians, as can language barriers when the patient and the physician do not speak the same native language. Furthermore, medical practices differ between cultures, and medical practitioners need to be familiar with a patient's culture if they are going to be successful in getting the patient to comply with medical recommendations (Bush & Osterweis, 1978; Dressler & Oths, 1997; Whaley, 2000).

Complying with Physicians' Recommendations

One serious major consequence of patient–physician communication difficulties is a lack of compliance with medical advice: Surveys show that perhaps as many as 85 percent of patients do not fully comply with their physician's advice. In fact, some estimates suggest that almost three-quarters of the prescriptions for medicine are not followed properly, at a cost of $100 billion each year (Kaplan, Sallis, & Patterson, 1993; Hammond & Lambert, 1994a, 1994b; Zuger, 1998).

Forms of Patient Noncompliance

Noncompliance can take many forms. Patients might fail to show up for scheduled appointments. They might not follow diets or might not give up smoking. They might discontinue medication during treatment; sometimes, they don't take prescribed medicine at all.

Patients also might practice *creative nonadherence,* in which they modify a treatment prescribed by a physician, relying instead on their own medical judgment and experience. In many cases patients' lack of medical knowledge can be more harmful than helpful (Weintraub, 1976; Taylor, 1995).

Noncompliance is sometimes the result of psychological reactance. **Reactance** is a negative emotional and cognitive reaction to a restriction of one's freedom. People who experience reactance feel hostility and anger. Because of such emotions, they might seek to restore their sense of freedom, but in a self-destructive manner by refusing to accept medical advice and perhaps acting in a way that worsens their medical condition. For instance, a man who develops reactance to a strict diet might eat even more than he did before his diet was restricted (Brehm & Brehm, 1981; Rhodewalt & Fairfield, 1991).

Good health care combines trust on the part of the patient with empathy and understanding on the part of the physician.

reactance: A negative emotional and cognitive reaction to a restriction of one's freedom that can be associated with medical regimens

Table 15-3 A Patient Talks to Her Physician

The following excerpt from a case study used at the Harvard Medical School is an example of poor interviewing technique on the part of the physician.

Patient: I can hardly drink water.
Doctor: Um hum.
Patient: Remember when it started? . . . It was pains in my head. It must have been then.
Doctor: Um hum.
Patient: I don't know what it is. The doctor looked at it . . . said something about glands.
Doctor: Ok. Um hum, aside from this, how have you been feeling?
Patient: Terrible.
Doctor: Yeah.
Patient: Tired . . . there's pains . . . I don't know what it is.
Doctor: Ok. . . . Fevers or chills?
Patient: No.
Doctor: Ok. . . . Have you been sick to your stomach or anything?
Patient: (Sniffles, crying) I don't know what's going on. I get up in the morning tired. The only time I feel good . . . maybe like around suppertime . . . and everything (crying) and still the same thing.
Doctor: Um hum. You're getting the nausea before you eat or after? (Goleman, 1988, p. B16)

Although the frequent "um hums" suggest that the physician is listening to the patient, in fact they do not encourage the patient to disclose more pertinent details. Even more, late in the interview, the physician ignores the patient's emotional distress and coldly continues through the list of questions.

Increasing Compliance

Although compliance with a physician's advice does not guarantee that the patient's medical problems will go away, it does optimize the possibility that the patient's condition will improve. What, then, can physicians do to produce greater compliance on the part of their patients? One strategy is to provide clear instructions to patients regarding drug regimens. Another is for physicians to maintain good, warm relationships with patients (Cramer, 1995; Cheney, 1996).

Physicians who provide clear, honest communication with their patients also produce greater compliance. Patients generally prefer to be well informed, and their degree of satisfaction with their medical care is linked to how well and how accurately physicians convey to them the nature of their medical problems and treatment (Hall, Roter, & Katz, 1988; Haley, Clair, & Saulsberry, 1992).

The ultimate result of enhanced patient satisfaction is not just increased compliance with a physician's advice but more positive treatment outcomes as well. Patients who are well informed and like their physicians have greater confidence in their physician's medical expertise, which in turn leads them to have less anxiety and better medical outcomes. Overall, then, a positive relationship with one's physician brings with it the potential for substantial health benefits (Kaplan, Sallis, & Patterson, 1993; Wyshak & Barsky, 1995).

 **PsychLink**

Physician-patient rapport
www.mhhe.com/
feldmanup6-15links

BECOMING AN INFORMED CONSUMER OF PSYCHOLOGY

Speaking with Your Physician

There are several ways you can improve your communication with your physician (Frishman, 1996; Lown, 1999; Atkinson, 2000):

- *Prepare in advance for your visits with your physician.* Bring a list of the most important symptoms you've been having and the questions you'd like answered.

- *Be precise in what you tell your physician.* Keep careful records of your symptoms, including their frequency, when they occur, how long they last, and what you tried to do to treat them.
- *Take notes.* Either write down what your physician says or bring a tape recorder.
- *Bring a relative or friend.* A social supporter can give you the courage to question your physician more easily.
- *Keep pressing your physician for answers until you feel you understand.* If you don't understand something, ask again—and again, if necessary.
- *Don't be afraid to ask for a second medical opinion.* Good physicians understand that you might want a second source of advice.
- *Educate yourself.* Read, surf the Web, and find out what the newest treatments are, keeping in mind that sources are not all equally reputable.
- *Make sure you understand what your physician wants you to do.* Don't leave a meeting until you are sure you understand what has been prescribed for you, both in medications and in medical tests.

Evaluate

1. Many health psychologists believe that the biggest problem in health care is:
   a. incompetent health care providers.
   b. rising health care costs.
   c. lack of communication between physician and patient.
   d. scarcity of medical research funding.
2. Patients are more likely to comply with a physician's advice if:
   a. they are satisfied with and friendly toward their physician.
   b. the physician is female.
   c. they have a critical illness.
   d. the physician is a specialist as opposed to a general practitioner.
3. A good physician should be able to:
   a. make an accurate diagnosis on the basis of a physical examination alone.
   b. provide information and advice in technical terms.
   c. explain to the patient every decision that is made in her or his care, without considering patient input.
   d. provide good medical skills and sufficient information to the patient.

Answers to Evaluate Questions

1. c 2. a 3. d

Rethink

1. Do you think stress plays a role in communication difficulties between physicians and patients? Why?
2. You are given the job of instructing a group of medical school students on "Physician/Patient Interactions." How would you set up your class, and what kind of information would you provide?

Looking Back

How is health psychology a union between medicine and psychology?

- The field of health psychology considers how psychology can be applied to the prevention, diagnosis, and treatment of medical problems. (p. 444)

What is stress, how does it affect us, and how can we best cope with it?

- Stress is a response to threatening or challenging environmental conditions. People encounter both positive and negative stressors—circumstances that produce stress. (p. 445)
- Stress produces immediate physiological reactions. In the short term, these reactions can be adaptive, but in the long term they can have negative consequences, including the development of psychophysiological disorders. (p. 445)
- The consequences of stress can be explained in part by Selye's general adaptation syndrome (GAS), which suggests that there are three stages in stress responses: alarm and mobilization, resistance, and exhaustion. (p. 445)
- The way a person interprets an environmental circumstance affects whether that person will consider it to be stressful. Still, there are general classes of events that provoke stress: cataclysmic events, personal stressors, and background stressors or daily hassles. (p. 447)
- Stress can be reduced by developing a sense of control over one's circumstances. Some people, though, develop a state of learned helplessness. (p. 449)
- Coping with stress can take a number of forms, including the unconscious use of defense mechanisms and the use of emotion-focused or problem-focused coping strategies. (p. 451)

How do psychological factors affect such health-related problems as coronary heart disease, cancer, and smoking?

- Coronary heart disease is linked to a specific type of behavior pattern known as Type A. Type A individuals tend to be competitive, show a sense of time urgency and hurriedness, be hostile and aggressive, and be driven. (p. 454)
- There is increasing evidence that a patient's attitudes and emotional responses can affect the course of that patient's disease through links to the immune system. (p. 456)
- Smoking, the leading preventable cause of health problems, has proved to be difficult to control, even though most smokers are aware of the dangerous consequences of smoking. (p. 457)
- Subjective well-being, the measure of how happy people are, is highest in people with high self-esteem, a sense of control, optimism, and a supportive network of close relationships. (p. 460)

How do our interactions with physicians affect our health and compliance with medical treatment?

- Although patients often expect physicians to make a diagnosis from only a physical examination, communicating one's problem to the physician is equally critical. (p. 462)
- Many patients find it difficult to communicate openly with their physicians because of the high social prestige of physicians and the technical nature of medical information. (p. 463)

Key Terms and Concepts

health psychology (p. 444)

psychoneuroimmunology (PNI) (p. 444)

stress (p. 445)

psychophysiological disorders (p. 445)

general adaptation syndrome (GAS) (p. 445)

cataclysmic events (p. 448)

posttraumatic stress disorder (PTSD) (p. 448)

personal stressors (p. 448)

background stressors (p. 449)

uplifts (p. 449)

learned helplessness (p. 449)

coping (p. 450)

defense mechanisms (p. 451)

hardiness (p. 452)

social support (p. 452)

Type A behavior pattern (p. 454)

Type B behavior pattern (p. 454)

subjective well-being (p. 460)

reactance (p. 463)

Preview

For additional quizzing and a variety of interactive resources, visit the *Understanding Psychology* Online Learning Center at

www.mhhe.com/feldmanup6

Psychology on the Web

1. Find three or more websites that deal with stress reduction. Gather at least five techniques for reducing stress and summarize them. Write a critique and evaluation of these techniques, using the information you learned about stress in this chapter. Which ones seem to have a sound basis in psychological theory and/or research?

2. Are you a Type A personality or a Type B? Find two websites offering tests that claim to provide the answer. Summarize in writing the nature of each test and compare the results you received from each one.

Epilogue

In this chapter we have explored an important area in which psychology and physiology intersect. We've seen how the emotional and psychological experience of stress can lead to physical symptoms of illness, how personality factors can be related to major health problems, and how psychological factors can interfere with effective communications between physician and patient. We've also looked at the other side of the coin, noting that some relatively simple strategies can help us control stress, affect our illness, and improve our interactions with our physicians.

Turn back to the prologue of this chapter, about Susan Reiche and her hectic after-work schedule, and use your understanding of health psychology and stress to consider these questions.

1. Based on the description of Susan Reiche's day, which of her stressors are personal and which are background stressors? What might happen to "elevate" the stress level of a background stressor to a more serious level? Are there likely to be any uplifts in Reiche's day?

2. How does the general adaptation syndrome (GAS) apply to Reiche's situation? How might events in her life move her along the three stages of the model?

3. What steps would you advise Reiche to take to keep her level of stress under control? How might others in her life be involved in such an effort?

4. Does Reiche appear more likely to have a Type A or a Type B personality? Why?

Chapter Sixteen

Psychological Disorders

Prologue: Lori Schiller

Looking Ahead

Normal Versus Abnormal: Making the Distinction

Defining Abnormality

Psychology at Work: Margaret H. Coggins, Senior Research Psychologist

Perspectives on Abnormality: From Superstition to Science

Classifying Abnormal Behavior: The ABCs of the *DSM*

Major Disorders

Anxiety Disorders

Somatoform Disorders

Applying Psychology in the 21st Century: Internet Addiction: Real or Virtual?

Dissociative Disorders

Mood Disorders

Schizophrenia

Personality Disorders

Beyond the Major Disorders: Abnormal Behavior in Perspective

Exploring Diversity: The DSM and Culture—and the Culture of the DSM

The Prevalence of Psychological Disorders: The Mental State of the Union

Becoming an Informed Consumer of Psychology: Deciding When You Need Help

Looking Back

Key Terms and Concepts

Psychology on the Web

OLC Preview

Epilogue

Lori Schiller, who suffered from schizophrenia, is now a peer counselor at a mental health center and a member of the Board of Directors of the National Alliance for the Mentally Ill.

Prologue

Lori Schiller

Lori Schiller thinks it all began one night at summer camp when she was 15.

Suddenly, she was hearing voices. "You must die! Die! Die!" they screamed. The voices drove her from her bunk, out into the dark, where she thought she could escape. Camp officials found her jumping frantically on a trampoline, screaming. "I thought I was possessed," says Ms. Schiller, now 33. Terrified, she told no one about the voices when she first heard them. The camp sent her home sick. Says Nancy Schiller, her mother: "We thought she had the flu...."

Voices had begun sliding down the telephone wire; they were assaulting her from the TV screen. "The people on TV were telling me it was my responsibility to save the world, and if I didn't I would be killed," she says....

Her behavior became erratic, wilder. On a whim one day, she hopped into her car, drove four hours home to Scarsdale, changed her mind and drove back. She went sky diving. She got stopped by police for speeding. She had fits of hysterical laughter....

As time went on, Lori had more and more trouble concentrating, and more difficulty in controlling her impulses, one of which was to commit suicide. "I used to sit in the library, up all these stairs, and think about jumping," she recalls. Finally, in her senior year, she told her parents she "had problems" and asked to see a counselor (Bennett, 1992, pp. A1, A10).

Looking Ahead

Although she initially managed to hide her disorder from everyone, Lori Schiller was losing her grip on reality. Less than a year after she graduated from college, her parents convinced her to get treatment. She would spend the next decade in and out of institutions, suffering from schizophrenia, one of the most severe psychological disorders.

Happily, today Schiller is a leader in the mental health field. But her case raises several questions. What caused her disorder? Were genetic factors involved, or were stressors in her life primarily responsible? Were there signs that others should have noticed earlier? Could her schizophrenia have been prevented? What were the specific symptoms of her psychological disorder? And, more generally, how do we distinguish normal from abnormal behavior, and how can Lori's behavior be categorized and classified to pinpoint the specific nature of her problem?

We address some of the issues raised by Lori Schiller's case in this and the following chapter. We begin by discussing the subtle distinctions between normal and abnormal behavior. We examine the various approaches that have been used to explain psychological disorders, ranging from explanations based on superstition to those based on more scientific approaches.

The heart of the chapter consists of a description of the various types of psychological disorders. Using a classification system employed by mental health practitioners, we examine the most significant kinds of disorders. The chapter also includes a discussion of how you can evaluate your own behavior to determine whether it is advisable for you to seek help from a mental health professional.

Prepare

How can we distinguish normal from abnormal behavior?

What are the major perspectives on psychological disorders used by mental health professionals?

What classification system is used to categorize psychological disorders?

Organize

Normal Versus Abnormal

Defining Abnormality

Perspectives on Abnormality

Classifying Abnormal Behavior

 **PsychLink**

Information on disorders
www.mhhe.com/
feldmanup6-16links

Normal Versus Abnormal: Making the Distinction

Universally that person's acumen is esteemed very little perceptive concerning whatsoever matters are being held as most profitable by mortals with sapience endowed to be studied who is ignorant of that which the most in doctrine erudite and certainly by reason of that in them high mind's ornament deserving of veneration constantly maintain when by general consent they affirm that other circumstances being equal by no exterior splendour is the prosperity of a nation. . . .

It would be easy to conclude that these words were the musings of a madman. The passage does not seem to make any sense at all. But literary scholars would disagree. This passage is from James Joyce's classic *Ulysses* (Joyce, 1934, p. 377), which has beeen hailed as one of the major works of twentieth-century literature.

As this example illustrates, a casual examination of a person's writing is insufficient to determine the degree to which he or she is "normal." But even when we consider more extensive samples of a person's behavior, we find that there might be only a fine line between behavior that is considered normal and that which is considered abnormal.

Defining Abnormality

Because of the difficulty in distinguishing normal from abnormal behavior, psychologists have struggled to devise a precise, scientific definition of "abnormal behavior." For instance, consider the following definitions, each of which has its advantages and disadvantages:

- *Abnormality as deviation from the average.* To employ this statistics-based approach, we simply observe what behaviors are rare or infrequent in a given society or culture and label these deviations from the norm "abnormal."

  The difficulty with such a definition is that some behaviors that are statistically rare clearly do not lend themselves to classification as abnormal. If most people prefer to have cornflakes for breakfast, but you prefer raisin bran, this hardly makes your behavior abnormal. Similarly, based on such a concept of abnormality

a person who has an unusually high IQ would be categorized as abnormal simply because a high IQ is statistically rare. A definition of abnormality that rests on deviation from the average, then, is insufficient.

- *Abnormality as deviation from the ideal.* An alternative approach considers abnormality in relation to the standard toward which most people are striving—the ideal. This sort of definition considers behavior abnormal if it deviates enough from some kind of ideal or cultural standard. However, because society has so few standards on which people agree, and the standards that do arise tend to change over time and vary across cultures, the deviation-from-the-ideal approach is inadequate.

- *Abnormality as a sense of personal discomfort.* A more useful definition concentrates on the psychological consequences of the behavior for the individual. In this approach, behavior is considered abnormal if it produces a sense of personal distress, anxiety, or guilt in an individual—or if it is harmful to others in some way.

  Even a definition that relies on personal discomfort has its drawbacks, though. For instance, people with some particularly severe forms of mental disturbance report feeling wonderful, even though their behavior seems bizarre to others. Most of us would consider their behavior abnormal even though they feel a personal state of well-being.

- *Abnormality as the inability to function effectively.* Most people are able to feed themselves, hold a job, get along with others, and in general live as productive members of society. Yet there are those who are unable to adjust to the demands of society or function effectively.

  According to this view of abnormality, people who are unable to function effectively and adapt to the demands of society are abnormal. For example, an unemployed, homeless woman living on the street might be considered unable to function effectively, so her behavior would be viewed as abnormal even if she had chosen to live this way. Her inability to adapt to the requirements of society is what makes her "abnormal," according to this approach.

- *Abnormality as a legal concept.* According to the jury that heard his case, mass murderer Jeffery Dahmer was perfectly sane when he killed his victims. Although you might question this view, it is a reflection of how the law defines abnormal behavior. To the judicial system, the distinction between normal and abnormal behavior rests on the definition of *insanity,* which is a legal, but not a psychological, term. The definition of insanity varies from one jurisdiction to another. In some states, insanity simply means that a defendant could not understand the difference between right and wrong at the time when he or she committed a criminal act. Other states consider whether defendants are substantially incapable of understanding the criminality of their behavior or unable to control themselves. And some jurisdictions do not allow any pleas of insanity (Steadman et al., 1993; Weiner & Wettstein, 1993).

PsychLink

Insanity defense
www.mhhe.com/
feldmanup6–16links

Identifying Normal and Abnormal Behavior: Drawing the Line on Psychological Disorders

Clearly, none of the previous definitions is broad enough to cover all instances of abnormal behavior. Consequently, the distinction between normal and abnormal behavior often remains ambiguous even to trained professionals. Furthermore, what is viewed as abnormal behavior depends largely on cultural expectations for "normal" behavior in a particular society (Scheff, 1999).

Probably the best way to deal with this imprecision is to view abnormal and normal behavior as marking two ends of a continuum rather than as absolute states. Behavior would then be evaluated in terms of gradations, ranging from completely normal functioning to extremely abnormal behavior. Behavior typically falls somewhere between these two extremes. (To learn about someone who deals with life-and-death issues involving the potential of disordered behavior, see the *Psychology at Work* box.)

A person who is unable to function effectively in day-to-day life may be regarded as psychologically abnormal; yet the courts deemed Jeffrey Dahmer, who confessed to a series of gruesome murders, sane and deserving of legal punishment. Why are psychological and legal definitions of abnormality so different? Should they be?

Psychology at Work

Margaret H. Coggins

Senior Research Psychologist, United States Secret Service

Education: B.A., psychology, Dickinson College; M.A., Ph.D., psychology, Catholic University

Home: Reston, Virginia

Margaret H. Coggins

Protecting the president of the United States is the responsibility of the Secret Service, whose agents must be ready at an instant to aid and defend the U.S. leader. And while many agents are literally at the president's side every moment, others—such as psychologist Margaret Coggins—work for his or her safety in the background.

Coggins works closely with agents in the field and with mental health professionals to ensure the safety of U.S. leaders.

"The nature of my work consists of research, liaison, and training and educational work. All are tied to the Secret Service's protective mission," Coggins explained.

"The research program is designed to help the agency better understand the risk factors for violence that may be directed toward the people we protect, as well as helping to prevent and minimize any risk that is out there," she said.

Agents in the field not only must be vigilant in watching people, but must also be knowledgeable about the state of mind of people wishing to harm U.S. leaders or their families. Coggins works to identify the motivations and behaviors of those who are potentially threatening.

"Many of the individuals who come to the attention of the Secret Service are those who have active symptoms of a psychiatric disorder or are found to have a history of mental disorder," she said. "We conduct research on the cases that come to the attention of the Secret Service so we can get a better grasp on the types of behaviors, threats, and motivations. Some people communicate threats but are not likely to do harm, while a few others do pose serious threats."

Bringing together law enforcement with mental health and behavioral science is a major commitment for Coggins. As a result, her staff works closely with mental health specialists to manage the treatment of clients whose behavior could be threatening to people under Secret Service protection.

"One main area of our research has to do with the general understanding and awareness in the mental health community about our protective mission," she noted. "We share some of the same goals, and we have to make the right decisions."

> "We conduct research on the cases that come to the attention of the Secret Service so we can get a better grasp on the types of behaviors, threats, and motivations."

Perspectives on Abnormality: From Superstition to Science

For much of the past, abnormal behavior was linked to superstition and witchcraft. People displaying abnormal behavior were accused of being possessed by the devil or some sort of demonic god. Authorities felt justified in "treating" abnormal behavior by attempting to drive out the source of the problem. This typically involved whipping, immersion in hot water, starvation, or other forms of torture in which the cure was often worse than the affliction (Howells & Osborn, 1984; Berrios, 1996).

Contemporary approaches take a more enlightened view. Today, there are six major perspectives on psychological disorders. These perspectives suggest not only different causes of abnormal behavior but also, as we shall see in the next chapter, different treatment approaches. Furthermore, some are more applicable to particular disorders than others. Table 16-1 summarizes the perspectives and how each can be applied to the case of Lori Schiller described in the Prologue.

The Medical Perspective

When people display the symptoms of tuberculosis, we generally find the tuberculin germ in their body tissue. In the same way, the **medical perspective** suggests that when an individual displays symptoms of abnormal behavior, the fundamental cause will be found in a physical examination of the individual, which might reveal a hormonal imbalance, a chemical deficiency, or a brain injury. Indeed, when we speak of mental "illness," "symptoms" of abnormal behavior, and mental "hospitals," we are using terminology associated with the medical perspective.

Because many abnormal behaviors have been linked to biological causes, the medical perspective is a reasonable approach. Yet serious criticisms have been leveled against

medical perspective: The perspective that the root cause of abnormal behavior will be found in a physical examination of the individual, which might reveal a hormonal imbalance, a chemical deficiency, or a brain injury

Table 16-1 Perspectives on Psychological Disorder

In considering the case of Lori Schiller, discussed in the prologue to this chapter, we can employ each of the different perspectives on abnormal behavior. Note, however, that given the nature of her psychological disorder, some of the perspectives are more applicable than others.

Perspective	Description	Possible Application of Perspective to Schiller's Case
Medical perspective	Assumes that physiological causes are at the root of psychological disorders	Examine Schiller for medical problems, such as brain tumor, chemical imbalance in the brain, or disease
Psychoanalytic perspective	Argues that psychological disorders stem from childhood conflicts	Seek out information about Schiller's past, considering possible childhood conflicts
Behavioral perspective	Assumes that abnormal behaviors are learned responses	Concentrate on rewards and punishments for Schiller's behavior, and identify environmental stimuli that reinforce her behavior
Cognitive perspective	Assumes that cognitions (people's thoughts and beliefs) are central to psychological disorders	Focus on Schiller's perceptions of herself and her environment
Humanistic perspective	Emphasizes people's responsibility for their own behavior and the need to self-actualize	Consider Schiller's behavior in terms of her choices and efforts to reach her potential
Sociocultural perspective	Assumes that behavior is shaped by family, society, and culture	Focus on how societal demands contributed to Schiller's disorder

it. For one thing, there are many forms of abnormal behavior for which no biological cause has been identified. In addition, some critics have argued that the use of the term *illness* implies that people displaying abnormal behavior are not responsible for their actions (Szasz, 1982, 1994).

Still, recent advances in our understanding of the biological bases of behavior have supported the importance of considering physiological factors in abnormal behavior. For instance, we'll see later in this chapter that some of the most severe forms of psychological disturbance, such as major depression and schizophrenia, are influenced by genetic factors and neurotransmitters (Resnick, 1992; Brunner et al., 1993; Crow, 1995; Petronis & Kennedy, 1995).

The Psychoanalytic Perspective

Whereas the medical perspective suggests that biological causes are at the root of abnormal behavior, the **psychoanalytic perspective** holds that abnormal behavior stems from childhood conflicts over opposing wishes regarding sex and aggression. As we discussed in Chapter 10, Freud believed that children pass through a series of stages in which sexual and aggressive impulses take different forms and produce conflicts that require resolution—and that if these childhood conflicts are not dealt with successfully, they remain unresolved in the unconscious and eventually bring about abnormal behavior during adulthood.

To understand the roots of people's disordered behavior, the psychoanalytic perspective scrutinizes their early life history. However, because there is no conclusive way of linking people's childhood experiences with the abnormal behaviors they display as adults, we can never be sure that the causes suggested by psychoanalytic theory are accurate. Moreover, psychoanalytic theory paints a picture of people as having relatively little control over their behavior, because much of it is taken to be guided by unconscious impulses.

On the other hand, the contributions of psychoanalytic theory have been significant. More than any other approach to abnormal behavior, this perspective highlights the fact that people can have a rich, involved inner life and that prior experiences can have a profound effect on current psychological functioning (Horgan, 1996).

psychoanalytic perspective: The perspective that abnormal behavior stems from childhood conflicts over opposing wishes regarding sex and aggression

The Behavioral Perspective

behavioral perspective: The perspective that looks at the behavior itself as the problem

Both the medical and psychoanalytic perspectives look at abnormal behaviors as *symptoms* of some underlying problem. In contrast, the **behavioral perspective** looks at the behavior itself as the problem. Using the principles of learning theory discussed in Chapter 5, behavioral theorists see both normal and abnormal behaviors as responses to a set of stimuli, responses that have been learned through past experience and that are guided in the present by stimuli in the individual's environment. To explain why abnormal behavior occurs, one must analyze how an abnormal behavior has been learned and observe the circumstances in which it is displayed.

The emphasis on observable behavior is both the greatest strength and the greatest weakness of the behavioral approach to abnormal behavior. The behavioral perspective is the most precise and objective approach for examining behavioral displays of particular disorders, such as attention deficit hyperactivity disorder (ADHD), which we'll consider later in this chapter. At the same time, though, critics charge that the perspective ignores the rich inner world of thoughts, attitudes, and emotions that can contribute to abnormal behavior.

The Cognitive Perspective

cognitive perspective: The perspective that people's thoughts and beliefs are a central component of abnormal behavior

The medical, psychoanalytic, and behavioral perspectives view people's behavior as being caused by factors largely beyond their control. To many critics, however, people's thoughts cannot be ignored.

In response to such concerns, some psychologists employ a **cognitive perspective.** Rather than considering only external behavior, as in traditional behavioral approaches, the cognitive approach assumes that *cognitions* (people's thoughts and beliefs) are central to a person's abnormal behavior. A primary goal of treatment using the cognitive perspective is to explicitly teach new, more adaptive ways of thinking.

For instance, suppose that whenever she takes an exam, a student forms the erroneous cognition "Doing well on this exam is crucial to my entire future." Through therapy, such a person might be taught to hold the more realistic, and less anxiety-producing, thought: "My entire future is not dependent on this one exam." By changing cognitions in this way, psychologists working within a cognitive framework seek to help people free themselves from thoughts and behaviors that are potentially maladaptive.

The Humanistic Perspective

humanistic perspective: The perspective that emphasizes people's responsibility for their own behavior, even when such behavior is abnormal

Psychologists who subscribe to the **humanistic perspective** emphasize the responsibility that people have for their own behavior, even when such behavior is seen as abnormal. The humanistic perspective—growing out of the work of Rogers and Maslow (see Chapter 14)—concentrates on what is uniquely human, viewing people as basically rational, oriented toward a social world, and motivated to seek self-actualization (Rogers, 1980).

Humanistic approaches focus on the relationship between the individual and society, considering how people view themselves in relation to others and see their place in the world. People are viewed as having an awareness of life and of themselves that leads them to search for meaning and self-worth. Rather than assuming that a "cure" is required, the humanistic perspective suggests that individuals can, by and large, set their own limits of what is acceptable behavior. As long as they are not hurting others and do not feel personal distress, people should be free to choose what behaviors to engage in.

Although the humanistic perspective has been criticized for its reliance on unscientific, unverifiable information and its vague, almost philosophical, formulations, it offers a distinctive view of abnormal behavior. The perspective stresses the unique aspects of being human and provides a number of important suggestions for helping those with psychological problems.

The Sociocultural Perspective

The **sociocultural perspective** assumes that people's behavior—both normal and abnormal—is shaped by the kind of family group, society, and culture in which they live. According to this view, one's relationships with others can support abnormal behaviors and even cause them to occur. Consequently, the kinds of stresses and conflicts people experience as part of their daily interactions with others in their environment can promote and maintain abnormal behavior.

Statistical support for the position that sociocultural factors shape abnormal behavior can be found in the fact that some kinds of abnormal behavior are far more prevalent among certain social classes than among others. For instance, there tend to be more diagnoses of schizophrenia among members of lower socioeconomic groups than among members of more affluent groups. Proportionally more African Americans than whites are involuntarily hospitalized for psychological disorders. Furthermore, poor economic times tend to be linked to general declines in psychological functioning, and social problems such as homelessness are associated with psychological disorders (Kiesler, 1999; López & Guarnaccia, 2000).

On the other hand, alternative explanations abound for the association between abnormal behavior and social factors. For example, poorer people might be less likely than wealthier people to seek help, and therefore might be more likely to develop symptoms that are severe and warrant a more serious diagnosis. Furthermore, sociocultural explanations provide relatively little specific guidance for the treatment of individuals showing mental disturbance, because the focus is on broader societal factors (Paniagua, 2000).

"First off, you're not a nut. You're a legume."

sociocultural perspective: The perspective that people's behavior—both normal and abnormal—is shaped by the kind of family group, society, and culture in which they live

Classifying Abnormal Behavior: The ABCs of the DSM

Crazy. Whacked. Mental. Loony. Insane. Neurotic. Psycho. Strange. Demented. Odd. Possessed.

Society has long placed labels on people who display abnormal behavior. Unfortunately, most of the time these labels have reflected intolerance and have been used with little thought to what the label signifies.

Providing appropriate and specific names and classifications for abnormal behavior has presented a major challenge to psychologists. It is not too hard to understand why, given the difficulties discussed earlier in simply distinguishing normal from abnormal behavior. Yet classification systems are necessary in order to be able to describe and ultimately to diagnose abnormal behavior.

The DSM-IV: *Determining Diagnostic Distinctions*

Over the years many different classification systems have been used. Some have been more useful than others, and some have been more accepted than others by mental health workers. Today, however, one standard system, devised by the American Psychiatric Association, has emerged in the United States; it is employed by most professionals to diagnose and classify abnormal behavior. This classification system is presented in the ***Diagnostic and Statistical Manual of Mental Disorders*, fourth edition (*DSM-IV*).**

The *DSM-IV* presents comprehensive and relatively precise definitions for more than 200 diagnostic categories. By following the criteria presented in the system, diagnosticians can clearly describe the specific problem an individual is experiencing. (Table 16-2 provides a brief outline of the major diagnostic categories.)

One noteworthy feature of the *DSM-IV* is that it is designed to be primarily descriptive and tries to avoid suggesting an underlying cause for an individual's behavior and problems. Hence, the term *neurotic*—a label that is commonly used by people in their

Diagnostic and Statistical Manual of Mental Disorders, Fourth Edition (DSM-IV): The manual of the American Psychiatric Association that presents the diagnostic system used by most U.S. mental health professionals to diagnose and classify abnormal behavior

Table 16-2 Major *DSM-IV* Diagnostic Categories

The following list of disorders represents the major categories from the *DSM-IV*. This is only a partial list of the over 200 disorders found in the *DSM-IV*.

Disorder	Subcategories
Anxiety (problems in which anxiety impedes daily functioning)	Generalized anxiety disorder, panic disorder, phobic disorder, obsessive-compulsive disorder, post-traumatic stress disorder
Somatoform (psychological difficulties displayed through physical problems)	Hypochondriasis, conversion disorder
Dissociative (the splitting apart of crucial parts of personality that are usually integrated)	Dissociative identity disorder (multiple personality), dissociative amnesia, dissociative fugue
Mood (emotions of depression or euphoria that are so strong they intrude on everyday living)	Major depression, bipolar disorder
Schizophrenia (declines in functioning, thought and language disturbances, perception disorders, emotional disturbances, and withdrawal from others)	Disorganized, paranoid, catatonic, undifferentiated, residual
Personality (problems that create little personal distress but that lead to an inability to function as a normal member of society)	Antisocial (sociopathic) personality disorder, narcissistic personality disorder
Sexual (problems related to sexual arousal from unusual objects or problems related to sexual functioning)	Paraphilia, sexual dysfunction
Substance-related (problems related to drug dependence and abuse)	Alcohol, cocaine, hallucinogens, marijuana
Delirium, dementia, amnesia, and other cognitive disorders	

everyday descriptions of abnormal behavior—is not listed as a *DSM-IV* category. The reason is that the term *neurotic* comes directly from Freud's theory of personality. Because the term refers to problems associated with a specific cause and theoretical approach, neurosis is no longer listed as a category.

The *DSM-IV* has the advantage, then, of providing a descriptive system that does not specify a cause or reason behind the problem. Instead, it paints a picture of the behavior that is being displayed. Why should this be important? For one thing, it allows communication between mental health professionals of diverse backgrounds and approaches. In addition, precise descriptive classification enables researchers to make progress in exploring the causes of a problem. If displays of an abnormal behavior cannot be reliably described, researchers will be hard-pressed to find ways of investigating the disorder. Finally, the *DSM-IV* provides a kind of conceptual shorthand through which professionals can describe the behaviors that tend to occur together in an individual (Frances, First, & Pincus, 1995; Halling & Goldfarb, 1996).

Conning the Classifiers: The Shortcomings of the DSM-IV

When clinical psychologist David Rosenhan and eight colleagues sought admission to separate mental hospitals across the United States in the 1970s, each stated that they were hearing voices—"unclear voices" that said "empty," "hollow," and "thud"—and each was immediately admitted to the hospital (Rosenhan, 1973).

However, the truth was that they were conducting a study, and none of them was actually hearing voices. Aside from these misrepresentations, *everything* else they did and said was their true behavior, including the responses they gave during extensive

PsychLink

Symptoms of disorders
www.mhhe.com/
feldmanup6-16links

admission interviews and answers to the battery of tests they were asked to complete. In fact, as soon as they were admitted, they said they no longer heard any voices. In short, each of the pseudo-patients acted in a "normal" way.

We might assume that Rosenhan and his colleagues would be quickly discovered as the impostors they were, but they were not. Instead, each of them was diagnosed as severely abnormal on the basis of observed behavior. Most were labeled as suffering from schizophrenia, and they were kept in the hospital from 3 to 52 days, with the average stay being 19 days. Even when they were discharged, most of the "patients" left with the label *schizophrenia—in remission,* implying that the abnormal behavior had only temporarily subsided and could recur at any time. Most disturbing of all, none of the pseudo-patients was identified by the staff of the hospitals as an impostor—although some of the real patients figured out the ruse.

The results of Rosenhan's classic study illustrate the fact that labeling individuals powerfully influences how their actions are perceived and interpreted. It also points out that determining who is psychologically disordered is not always a clear-cut, accurate process.

Although the *DSM-IV* was developed to provide more accurate and consistent determinations of psychological disorders, it has not been entirely successful. For instance, critics charge that it relies too much on the medical perspective on psychological disorders. It was drawn up by psychiatrists—who are physicians—and some condemn it for viewing psychological disorders primarily in terms of symptoms of some underlying physiological disorder. Moreover, critics suggest that the *DSM-IV* sorts people into inflexible, all-or-none categories, ignoring the degree to which a person displays psychologically disordered behavior.

Other concerns with the *DSM-IV* are more subtle, but equally important. For instance, some critics argue that labeling an individual "abnormal" attaches a lifetime stigma to that person that is dehumanizing. Furthermore, after an initial diagnosis is made, other diagnostic possibilities might be overlooked by mental health professionals, who concentrate on the initial diagnostic category (Szasz, 1961, 1994; Kirk, 1992).

Still, despite the drawbacks inherent in any labeling system, the *DSM-IV* has had an important influence on how mental health professionals approach psychological disorders. It has increased both the reliability and the validity of diagnostic categorization, and it gives us a logical way to organize our examination of the major types of mental disturbance, to which we turn next.

Evaluate

1. One problem in defining abnormal behavior is that:
   a. statistically rare behavior might not be abnormal.
   b. not all abnormalities are accompanied by feelings of discomfort.
   c. cultural standards are too general to use as a measuring tool.
   d. all of the above.

2. If abnormality is defined as experiencing personal discomfort or causing harm to others, which of the following people is most likely to need treatment?
   a. An executive who is afraid to accept a promotion because it would require moving from his ground-floor office to the top floor of a tall office building.
   b. A woman who decides to quit her job and chooses, with great pleasure, to live on the street in order to live a "simpler life."
   c. A man who believes that friendly spacemen visit his house every Thursday, and is glad for their company.
   d. A photographer who enjoys living with nineteen cats in a small apartment.

3. Virginia's mother thinks that Virginia's behavior is clearly abnormal because, despite being offered admission to medical school, Virginia decides to become a waitress instead. What approach is Virginia's mother using to define abnormal behavior?

Rethink

1. Imagine that an acquaintance of yours was recently arrested for shoplifting a $3 pen. What sorts of questions and issues would be raised by proponents of *each* of these perspectives on abnormality: medical, psychoanalytic, behavioral, cognitive, humanistic, and sociocultural?

2. Do you agree or disagree that the *DSM* should be updated every several years? What makes abnormal behavior so variable? Why can't there be one, unchanging definition of abnormal behavior?

4. Which of the following is a strong argument against the medical perspective?

   a. Physiological abnormalities are almost always impossible to identify.

   b. There is no conclusive way to link past experience and behavior.

   c. The medical perspective rests too heavily on the effects of nutrition.

   d. Assigning behavior to a physical problem takes responsibility away from the individual for changing his or her behavior.

5. Cheryl is painfully shy. According to the behavioral perspective, the best way to deal with her "abnormal" behavior is to

   a. treat the underlying physical problem.

   b. use the principles of learning theory to modify her shy behavior.

   c. express a great deal of caring.

   d. uncover her negative past experiences through hypnosis.

Answers to Evaluate Questions

1. d 2. a 3. Deviation from the ideal 4. d 5. b

Prepare

What are the major psychological disorders?

Organize

Major Disorders
    Anxiety Disorders
    Somatoform Disorders
    Dissociative Disorders

Major Disorders

Sally experienced her first panic attack out of the blue, 3 weeks after completing her senior year in college. She had just finished a job interview and was meeting some friends for dinner. In the restaurant, she began to feel dizzy. Within a few seconds, her heart was pounding, and she was feeling breathless, as though she might pass out. Her friends noticed that she did not look well and offered to drive her home. Sally suggested they stop at the hospital emergency room instead. Although she felt better by the time they arrived at the hospital, and tests indicated nothing wrong, Sally experienced a similar episode a week later while at a movie. . . .

Her attacks became more and more frequent. Before long, she was having several attacks per week. In addition, she constantly worried about having attacks. She began to avoid exercise and other activities that produced physical sensations. She also noticed the attacks were worse when she was alone. She began to avoid driving, shopping in large stores, and eating in all restaurants. Some weeks she avoided leaving the house completely (Antony, Brown, & Barlow, 1992, p. 79).

Sally suffered from panic disorder, one of the specific psychological disorders we'll be considering in the remainder of this chapter. Keep in mind that although we'll be discussing these disorders in a dispassionate manner, each represents a very human set of difficulties that influence, and in some cases considerably disrupt, people's lives.

Anxiety Disorders

All of us, at one time or another, experience *anxiety,* a feeling of apprehension or tension, in reaction to stressful situations. There is nothing "wrong" with such anxiety. As we discussed in Chapter 15, anxiety is a normal reaction to stress that often helps, rather than hinders, our daily functioning. Without some anxiety, for instance, most of us probably would not be terribly motivated to study hard, undergo physical exams, or spend long hours at our jobs.

But some people experience anxiety for no clear reason. When anxiety occurs without external justification and begins to affect a person's daily functioning, it is considered a psychological problem known as an **anxiety disorder.** We'll discuss four types of anxiety disorders: phobic disorder, panic disorder, generalized anxiety disorder, and obsessive-compulsive disorder.

anxiety disorder: Anxiety with no obvious external cause that impairs daily functioning

478

Table 16-3 Giving Fear a Proper Name

Phobia	Trigger	Phobia	Trigger
Acrophobia	Heights	Herpetophobia	Reptiles
Aerophobia	Flying	Hydrophobia	Water
Agoraphobia	Entering public spaces	Mikrophobia	Germs
Ailurophobia	Cats	Murophobia	Mice
Amaxophobia	Vehicles, driving	Mysophobia	Dirt or germs
Anthophobia	Flowers	Numerophobia	Numbers
Anthrophobia	People	Nyctophobia	Darkness
Aquaphobia	Water	Ochlophobia	Crowds
Arachnophobia	Spiders	Ophidiophobia	Snakes
Astraphobia	Lightning	Ornithophobia	Birds
Brontophobia	Thunder	Phonophobia	Speaking out loud
Claustrophobia	Closed spaces	Pyrophobia	Fire
Cynophobia	Dogs	Thanatophobia	Death
Dementophobia	Insanity	Trichophobia	Hair
Gephyrophobia	Bridges	Xenophobia	Strangers

Phobic Disorder

Claustrophobia. Acrophobia. Xenophobia. Although these sound like characters in a Greek tragedy, they are actually members of a class of psychological disorders known as phobias. **Phobias** are intense, irrational fears of specific objects or situations. For example, claustrophobia is a fear of enclosed places, acrophobia is a fear of high places, and xenophobia is a fear of strangers. Although the objective danger posed by an anxiety-producing stimulus (which can be just about anything, as you can see from the list in Table 16-3) is typically small or nonexistent, to the individual suffering from the phobia the danger is great, and a full-blown panic attack can follow exposure to the stimulus. Phobic disorders differ from generalized anxiety disorders and panic disorders in that there is a specific, identifiable stimulus that sets off the anxiety reaction.

Phobias might have only a minor impact if those who suffer from them can avoid the stimuli that trigger the fear. If one is not a professional firefighter or tightrope walker, for example, a fear of heights might have little impact on one's daily life. On the other hand, a fear of strangers presents a more serious problem. In one extreme case, a Washington woman suffering from xenophobia left her home just three times in thirty years—once to visit her family, once for a medical operation, and once to purchase ice cream for a dying companion (Adler, 1984).

Panic Disorder

In another type of anxiety disorder, **panic disorder,** *panic attacks* occur that last from a few seconds to several hours. Unlike phobias, which are brought about by specific objects or situations, panic disorders are not triggered by any identifiable stimulus.

phobias: Intense, irrational fears of specific objects or situations

panic disorder: Anxiety that reveals itself in the form of panic attacks that last from a few seconds to as long as several hours

Agoraphobia, the fear of being in a place from which escape is difficult, is one complication that can result from panic disorder. What sort of behavior modification approaches might be used to deal with agoraphobia?

Instead, during an attack, such as the ones experienced by Sally in the case described earlier, anxiety suddenly—and often without warning—rises to a peak, and the individual feels a sense of impending, unavoidable doom. Although symptoms differ from person to person, they might include heart palpitations, shortness of breath, unusual amounts of sweating, faintness and dizziness, an urge to urinate, gastric sensations, and—in extreme cases—a sense of imminent death. After such an attack, it is no wonder that people tend to feel exhausted (Rachman & deSilva, 1996; Pollack & Marzol, 2000).

Panic attacks seemingly come out of nowhere and are unconnected to any specific stimulus. Because they don't know what triggers their feelings of panic, victims of panic attacks can become fearful of going places. In fact, some people with panic disorder develop a complication called *agoraphobia,* the fear of being in a situation in which escape is difficult, and in which help for a possible panic attack would not be available. People with extreme cases of agoraphobia never leave their homes (Langs et al., 2000).

Generalized Anxiety Disorder

generalized anxiety disorder: Long-term, persistent anxiety and worry

People with **generalized anxiety disorder** experience long-term, persistent anxiety and worry. Sometimes their concerns are directed toward identifiable issues involving such things as family, money, work, and health. In other cases, though, people with the disorder feel that something dreadful is about to happen but can't identify what it is, experiencing "free-floating" anxiety.

Because of their persistent anxiety, they cannot concentrate, cannot set their worry and fears aside, and their lives become centered around their worry. Their anxiety can eventually result in medical problems. Because of heightened muscle tension and arousal, individuals with generalized anxiety disorder can begin to experience headaches, dizziness, heart palpitations, or insomnia. The most frequent symptoms are listed in Figure 16-1.

Obsessive-Compulsive Disorder

obsessive-compulsive disorder: A disorder characterized by obsessions or compulsions
obsession: A persistent, unwanted thought or idea that keeps recurring

People with **obsessive-compulsive disorder** are plagued by unwanted thoughts (obsessions) or feel that they must carry out some actions (compulsions) against their will.

An **obsession** is a persistent, unwanted thought or idea that keeps recurring. For example, a student might be unable to stop thinking that she has neglected to put her name on a test and might think about it constantly for the two weeks it takes to get the paper back. A man might go on vacation and wonder the whole time whether he locked his house. A woman might hear the same tune running through her head over and over again. In each case, the thought or idea is unwanted and difficult to put out of mind. Of course, many of us suffer from mild obsessions from time to time, but usually such thoughts persist only for a short period. For people with serious obsessions, however, the thoughts persist for days or months and can consist of bizarre, troubling images.

compulsion: An irresistible urge to repeatedly carry out some act that seems strange and unreasonable

As part of an obsessive-compulsive disorder, people might also experience **compulsions,** irresistible urges to repeatedly carry out some act that seems strange and unreasonable, even to them. Whatever the compulsive behavior, these people experience extreme anxiety if they cannot carry it out, even if it is something they want to stop. The acts involved could be relatively trivial, such as repeatedly checking the stove to make sure all the burners are turned off, or more unusual, such as continuously washing oneself (Rachman & Hodgson, 1980; Carter, Pauls, & Leckman, 1995). For example, consider this case report of a 27-year-old woman with a cleaning ritual:

> Bess would first remove all of her clothing in a preestablished sequence. She would lay out each article of clothing at specific spots on her bed, and examine each one for any indications of "contamination." She would then thoroughly scrub her body, starting at her feet and working meticulously up to the top of her head, using certain washcloths for certain areas of her body. Any articles of clothing that appeared to have been "contaminated" were thrown into the laundry. Clean clothing was put in the spots that were vacant. She would then dress herself in the opposite order from which she took the clothes off. (Meyer & Osborne, 1987, p. 156)

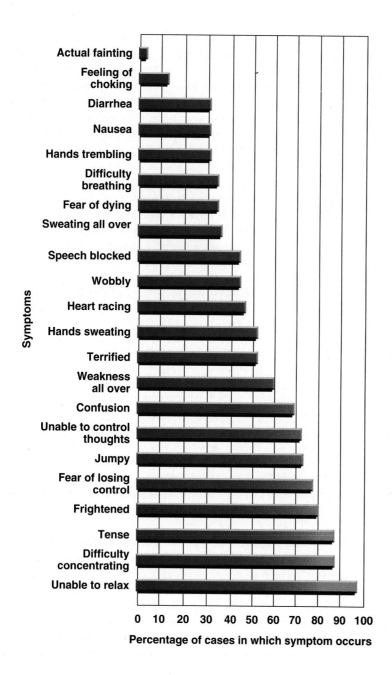

Figure 16-1 Frequency of symptoms in cases of generalized anxiety disorder.
Source: Adapted from Beck & Emery, 1985, pp. 87–88.

Unfortunately for those experiencing an obsessive-compulsive disorder, little or no reduction in anxiety results from carrying out a compulsive ritual. People with severe cases lead lives filled with unrelenting tension (Goodman, Rudorfer, & Maser, 1999).

The Causes of Anxiety Disorders

No one cause fully explains all cases of anxiety disorders, and each of the perspectives on abnormal behavior that we discussed earlier has something to say about their causes. However, the medical, behavioral, and cognitive perspectives have been particularly influential in psychologists' thinking about anxiety disorders.

Biological approaches, derived from the medical perspective, have shown that genetic factors play a role in anxiety disorders. For example, if one identical twin has panic disorder, there is a 30 percent chance that the other twin will have it also. Furthermore, recent research shows that a person's characteristic level of anxiety is related to a specific gene that is involved in the production of the neurotransmitter serotonin.

PsychLink

Causes of anxiety disorders
www.mhhe.com/
feldmanup6-16links

This work is consistent with findings indicating that certain chemical deficiencies in the brain appear to produce some kinds of anxiety disorder (Lesch et al., 1996; Rieder, Kaufmann, & Knowles, 1996).

Psychologists employing the behavioral perspective have taken a different approach, emphasizing environmental factors. They consider anxiety to be a learned response to stress. For instance, suppose a young girl is bitten by a dog. When she next sees a dog, she is frightened and runs away—a behavior that relieves her anxiety and thereby reinforces her avoidance behavior. After repeated encounters with dogs in which she is reinforced for her avoidance behavior, she might develop a full-fledged phobia regarding dogs.

Finally, the cognitive perspective suggests that anxiety disorders are an outgrowth of inappropriate and inaccurate cognitions about circumstances in the person's world. For example, a person with an anxiety disorder might view any friendly puppy as a ferocious and savage pit bull, or might see an air disaster looming whenever she or he is in the vicinity of an airplane. According to the cognitive perspective, people's maladaptive thoughts about the world are at the root of anxiety disorders. (For a potentially new form of anxiety disorder, see the *Applying Psychology in the 21st Century* box.)

Somatoform Disorders

Somatoform disorders are psychological difficulties that take on a physical (somatic) form, but for which there is no medical cause. Even though an individual with a somatoform disorder reports physical symptoms, no biological cause exists, or, if there is a medical problem, the person's reaction is greatly exaggerated.

One type of somatoform disorder is **hypochondriasis,** in which people have a constant fear of illness and a preoccupation with their health, taking everyday aches and pains to be symptoms of some dread disease. The "symptoms" are not faked; instead, hypochondriasis is the misinterpretation of these ordinary sensations as evidence of some dread disease—often in the face of inarguable medical evidence to the contrary (Noyes et al., 1993; Cantor & Fallon, 1996).

Another somatoform disorder is conversion disorder. Unlike hypochondriasis, in which there is no actual physical problem, **conversion disorders** involve an actual physical disturbance—such as the inability to see or hear, or to move an arm or leg—but the *cause* of the physical disturbance is purely psychological. There is no biological reason for the problem. Some of Freud's classic cases involved conversion disorders. For instance, one patient of Freud's was suddenly unable to use her arm, without any apparent physiological cause. Later, just as abruptly, she regained its use.

Conversion disorders often have a rapid onset. People wake up one morning blind or deaf, or they experience numbness that is restricted to a certain part of the body. Someone's hand, for example, might become entirely numb, while an area above the wrist, controlled by the same nerves, remains sensitive to touch—something that is biologically implausible. Such a condition is referred to as "glove anesthesia," because the area that is numb is the part of the hand that would be covered by a glove, and not a region related to pathways of the nervous system (see Figure 16-2).

One of the most surprising characteristics of people with conversion disorders is their lack of concern over symptoms that most of us would find very anxiety-producing. Most sighted people would be panic-stricken if they suddenly went blind. For a person in good health to suddenly go blind and react to this with bland dispassion (with *"la belle indifference,"* a French phrase meaning "beautiful indifference") hardly seems appropriate.

somatoform disorder: Psychological difficulties that take on a physical (somatic) form, but for which there is no medical cause

hypochondriasis: A disorder involving having a constant fear of illness and a preoccupation with one's health

conversion disorder: A major somatoform disorder that involves an actual physical disturbance, such as the inability to use a sensory organ or the complete or partial inability to move an arm or leg

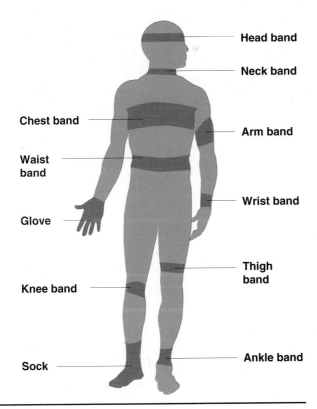

Figure 16-2 Conversion disorders sometimes produce numbness in particular isolated areas of the body (indicated by the shaded areas of the figure). For instance, in glove anesthesia, the area of the body covered by a glove is numb. However, the condition is biologically implausible because of the nerves involved, suggesting that the problem is the result of a psychological disorder rather than actual nerve damage.

Applying Psychology in the 21st Century

Internet Addiction: Real or Virtual?

When Michael Ian Campbell, a would-be actor, was brought before a jury on charges of threatening to "finish what began" at the Columbine High School shootings, his defense was a novel one: Internet addiction. According to his lawyer, who put forward the legal theory, Campbell was so immersed in the world of the Internet that he could not tell fact from fiction. His threat, said his lawyer, was a virtual one, and not made with criminal intent (Janofsky, 2000).

Whether such "Internet addiction" defenses will be effective in court remains to be seen, but it is clear that the jury is out on whether Internet addiction is an actual, rather than merely "virtual," psychological disorder.

Clearly, some people spend hours each day on the Internet, developing behavior that borders on the compulsive. Some high-use individuals feel anxiety when they are away from a computer, and some try, with little success, to reduce their use of computers and the Internet.

These people report that they are unable to stop thinking about computers and the Internet, and some spend increasing amounts of time on line, to the neglect of their friends and family. In one court case involving a divorce and custody suit, the husband asserted that his wife spent 10 hours a day on the Internet, neglecting their children. The court supported the husband's claims and awarded him custody of the children. The judge further agreed that the wife's use of the Internet amounted to abnormal behavior (Orzack, 1999).

Who is most vulnerable to compulsive use of the Internet? People who are easily bored, lonely and shy, or depressed appear most vulnerable, along with people who use the Internet as an escape from everyday life and their problems. Ironically, as people use the Internet more, they report becoming less socially engaged with others and more lonely and depressed (Kiesler & Kraut, 1999; Orzack, 1999; Greenfield, 1999).

Although there is evidence that some people use the Internet compulsively, the findings are far from definitive. No specific disorder of Internet addiction or compulsion has been identified

by clinical psychologists. In fact, some researchers argue that Internet use itself is not addictive but is instead simply a vehicle that permits people to pursue preexisting obsessions. For example, people using the Internet at very high levels tend to be primarily interested in sex, gambling, trading, and shopping; only a few compulsive users merely surf the Web (Kaiser, 1999; DeAngelis, 2000).

Whether excessive Internet use will eventually be seen as a psychological disorder remains to be seen. Furthermore, it is far from clear whether defendants (such as Michael Ian Campbell) will be able to successfully use an Internet addiction defense in court.

Do you think "Internet addiction" is more than a fascination with new technology? Do you think an "addiction" to television would have been observed when that technology was introduced? How about movies or radio? Are there features of the Internet that make it more addictive than other new technologies? Do you think it is reasonable to argue that such an addiction should excuse antisocial or dangerous behavior?

Dissociative Disorders

The topic of the classic movie *The Three Faces of Eve* and the book *Sybil* (about a girl who allegedly had sixteen personalities) represents a class of disorders that are among the most dramatic: dissociative disorders. **Dissociative disorders** are characterized by the separation (or dissociation) of critical parts of personality that are normally integrated and work together. People who dissociate key parts of their personality are able to prevent disturbing memories or perceptions from reaching their conscious awareness, thereby reducing their anxiety (Ross et al., 1990; Putnam, 1995a; Spiegel, 1996b).

There are several dissociative disorders, and all are rare. A person with **dissociative identity disorder** (or **multiple personality**) displays characteristics of two or more distinct personalities. Each personality has a unique set of likes and dislikes and its own reactions to situations. Some people with multiple personalities even carry several pairs of glasses because their vision changes with each personality. Moreover, each individual personality can be well adjusted when considered on its own (Ross, 1996; Kluft, 1996).

The problem, of course, is that there is only one body available to the various personalities, forcing the personalities to take turns. Because there can be strong variations in personalities, the person's behavior—considered as a whole—can appear very inconsistent. For instance, in the famous case portrayed in *The Three Faces of Eve*, the meek, bland Eve White provided a stunning contrast to the dominant and carefree Eve Black (Sizemore, 1989).

A person with **dissociative amnesia** has significant, selective memory loss. Dissociative amnesia is unlike simple amnesia, which, as we discussed in Chapter 7, involves an actual loss of information from memory, typically due to a physiological cause. In cases of dissociative amnesia, the "forgotten" material is still present in

PsychLink

Dissociative disorders
www.mhhe.com/
feldmanup6-16links

dissociative disorder: Psychological dysfunctions characterized by the separation of critical personality facets that are normally integrated; this reduces anxiety by repressing disturbing thoughts or memories

dissociative identity disorder (multiple personality): A disorder in which a person displays characteristics of two or more distinct personalities

dissociative amnesia: A disorder in which the person has significant, selective memory loss

"Jane Doe," who suffered from dissociative amnesia, was found wandering in a Florida park, unable to recall who she was or anything about her past.

dissociative fugue: A form of amnesia in which people take sudden, impulsive trips, sometimes assuming a new identity

memory—it simply cannot be recalled. The term *repressed memories* is sometimes used to describe the lost memories of dissociative amnesia.

In the most severe forms, individuals cannot recall their names, are unable to recognize parents and other relatives, and do not know their addresses. In other respects, though, they might appear quite normal. Apart from an inability to remember certain facts about themselves, they might be able to recall skills and abilities that they developed earlier. For instance, a chef might not remember where he grew up or received training, but might still be able to prepare gourmet meals.

In some cases of dissociative amnesia, the memory loss is quite profound. For example, a woman—dubbed Jane Doe by her rescuers—was found by a Florida park ranger in the early 1980s. Incoherent, thin, and only partially clothed, Doe was unable to recall her name, her past, and even how to read and write. On the basis of her accent, authorities thought the woman was from Illinois, and interviews conducted while she was given tranquilizing drugs revealed that she had had a Catholic education. However, the childhood memories she revealed were so universal that her background could not be further pinpointed. In a desperate attempt to rediscover her identity, she appeared on the television show *Good Morning America,* and ultimately a couple from Roselle, Illinois, whose daughter had moved to Florida, stepped forward, saying that they were her parents. However, Jane Doe never regained her memory (Carson, Butcher, & Coleman, 1992).

A more unusual form of amnesia is a condition known as **dissociative fugue.** In this state, people take sudden, impulsive trips, sometimes assuming a new identity. After a period of time—days, months, or sometimes even years—they suddenly realize that they are in a strange place and completely forget the period that they had spent wandering. Their last memories are from the time just before they entered the fugue state.

What the dissociative disorders have in common is that they allow people to escape from some anxiety-producing situation. Either the person produces a new personality to deal with stress, or the situation that caused the stress is forgotten or left behind as the individual journeys to some new—and perhaps less anxiety-producing—environment (Spiegel & Cardena, 1991; Putnam, 1995b).

Evaluate

1. Kathy is terrified of elevators. She is likely to be suffering from
   a. an obsessive-compulsive disorder
   b. a phobic disorder
   c. a panic disorder
   d. a generalized anxiety disorder
2. Carmen described an incident in which her anxiety suddenly rose to a peak and she felt a sense of impending doom. Carmen had experienced a(n) _____ _____.
3. Troubling thoughts that persist for days or months are known as
   a. obsessions
   b. compulsions
   c. rituals
   d. panic attacks
4. An overpowering urge to carry out a strange ritual is called a(n) _____.
5. In what major way does conversion disorder differ from hypochondriasis?
6. The separation of the personality, providing escape from stressful situations, is the key factor in _____ disorders.

Rethink

1. What cultural factors might contribute to the rate of anxiety disorders found in a culture? What perspectives on psychological disorders would best explain cultural contributions to anxiety disorders?
2. Do you think the behavioral perspective would be effective in dealing with dissociative disorders? Why or why not? Which perspective do you think would be most promising for this type of disorder?

Answers to Evaluate Questions

1. b 2. panic attack 3. a 4. compulsion 5. In conversion disorder, an actual physical disturbance is present. 6. dissociative

Mood Disorders

imagine

> I do not care for anything. . . . I do not care to walk, for walking is too strenuous. I do not care to lie down, for I should either have to remain lying, and I do not care to do that, or I should have to get up again, and I do not care to do that either. . . . I do not care at all.

We all experience mood swings. Sometimes we are happy, perhaps even euphoric; at other times we feel upset, saddened, or depressed. Such changes in mood are a normal part of everyday life. In some people, however, moods are so pronounced and lingering—like the feelings described above by philosopher Søren Kierkegaard—that they interfere with the ability to function effectively. In extreme cases a mood can become life-threatening, and in others it can cause the person to lose touch with reality. Situations such as these represent **mood disorders,** disturbances in emotional feelings strong enough to impair everyday living.

Major Depression

President Abraham Lincoln. Queen Victoria. Mark Twain. The common link among these people? Each suffered from periodic attacks of **major depression,** one of the most common mood disorders. Some 15 million people in the United States suffer from major depression, and at any one time, between 6 and 10 percent of the U.S. population is clinically depressed. Almost one in five people in the United States experience major depression at some point in their lives. The cost of depression to society approaches $50 *billion* a year (Cronkite, 1994; Rich, 1997).

Women are twice as likely as men to experience major depression; approximately one-fourth of all females will experience it at some point in their lives. Furthermore, although no one is quite sure why, the rate of depression is going up throughout the world. Results of in-depth interviews conducted in the United States, Puerto Rico, Taiwan, Lebanon, Canada, Italy, Germany, and France indicate that the incidence of depression has increased significantly over previous rates in every area. In fact, in some countries, the likelihood that individuals will suffer major depression at some point in their lives is three times higher than it was for earlier generations. In addition, people are developing major depression at increasingly early ages (Compas, Ey, & Grant, 1993; Weissman & Olfson, 1995; Beckham & Leber, 1997; Culbertson, 1997).

When psychologists speak of major depression, they do not mean the sadness that comes from experiencing one of life's disappointments, something that we have all experienced. Some depression is normal following the breakup of a long-term relationship, the death of a loved one, or the loss of a job. It is even normal following less serious problems, like doing badly on a test or finding that a romantic partner has forgotten one's birthday.

People who suffer from major depression experience similar sorts of feelings, but with much greater severity. They might feel useless, worthless, and lonely and might despair over the future. Moreover, they might experience such feelings for months or even years. They might cry uncontrollably or have sleep disturbances, and they are at risk for suicide. The depth of such behavior and the length of time it lasts are the hallmarks of major depression. (Table 16-4 provides an assessment for depression.)

Mania and Bipolar Disorders

↳ exaltation, gaité

Depression leads to the depths of despair; mania leads to emotional heights. **Mania** is an extended state of intense, wild elation. People experiencing mania feel intense happiness, power, invulnerability, and energy. They might become involved in wild schemes, believing that they will succeed at anything they attempt. Consider, for example, the following description of an individual who experienced a manic episode:

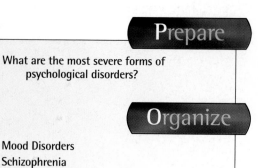

Prepare

What are the most severe forms of psychological disorders?

Organize

Mood Disorders
Schizophrenia
Personality Disorders

mood disorder: Disturbances in emotional feelings strong enough to interfere with everyday living

major depression: A severe form of depression that interferes with concentration, decision making, and sociability

PsychLink

Major depressive disorders
www.mhhe.com/
feldmanup6-16links

mania: An extended state of intense, wild elation

Table 16-4 A Test for Depression

This test was distributed by mental health organizations during National Depression Screening Day in the early 1990s, a nationwide event that sought to identify people who suffered from depression severe enough to warrant psychological intervention. On the day of the screening, the organizations received some 30,000 inquiries (Hill, 1992).

To complete the questionnaire, count the number of statements with which you agree:

1. I feel downhearted, blue, and sad.

2. I don't enjoy the things that I used to.

3. I feel that others would be better off if I were dead.

4. I feel that I am not useful or needed.

5. I notice that I am losing weight.

6. I have trouble sleeping through the night.

7. I am restless and can't keep still.

8. My mind isn't as clear as it used to be.

9. I get tired for no reason.

10. I feel hopeless about the future.

Scoring If you agree with at least five of the statements, including either item 1 or 2, and if you have had these symptoms for at least two weeks, help from a professional is strongly recommended. If you answer yes to number 3, you should get help immediately.

Mr. O'Reilly took a leave of absence from his civil service job. He purchased a large number of cuckoo clocks and then an expensive car, which he planned to use as a mobile showroom for his wares, anticipating that he would make a great deal of money. He proceeded to "tear around town" buying and selling clocks and other merchandise, and when he was not out, he was continuously on the phone making "deals." He rarely slept and, uncharacteristically, spent every evening in neighborhood bars drinking heavily and, according to him, "wheeling and dealing.". . . He was $3000 in debt and had driven his family to exhaustion with his excessive activity and talkativeness. He said, however, that he felt "on top of the world" (Spitzer et al., 1983, p. 115).

bipolar disorder: A disorder in which a person alternates between periods of euphoric feelings of mania and periods of depression

A person who sequentially experiences periods of mania and depression has **bipolar disorder** (or, as it used to be known, manic-depressive disorder). The swings between highs and lows might occur as frequently as a few days apart or they might alternate over a period of years. The periods of depression usually are longer than the periods of mania.

Ironically, some of society's most creative individuals have suffered from bipolar disorder. The imagination, drive, excitement, and energy of their manic periods fuel their creativity. For instance, historical analysis of his music shows that composer Robert Schumann was most prolific during his periodic episodes of mania. His output dropped off drastically during his periods of depression (see Figure 16-3). On the other hand, the high output associated with mania does not necessarily lead to higher quality: Schumann created some of his greatest works when he was not manic (Jamison, 1995; Week & James, 1995; Ludwig, 1996).

Despite the creative fires that can be lit by mania, persons who experience this disorder often show a recklessness that produces self-injury—emotionally and sometimes physically. They might alienate others with their talkativeness, inflated self-esteem, and indifference to the needs of others.

PsychLink

Bipolar disorder
www.mhhe.com/
feldmanup6-16links

Causes of Mood Disorders

Because they are a major mental health problem, mood disorders—and, in particular, depression—have received a good deal of study. Several approaches have been used to explain mood disorders. Psychoanalytic approaches, for example, see depression as the

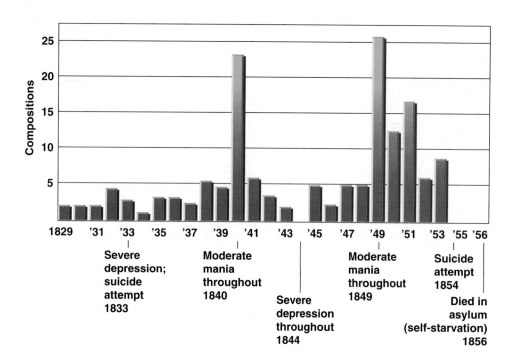

Figure 16–3 The number of pieces written by composer Robert Schumann in a given year is related to his periods of depression and mania (Slater & Meyer, 1959; reprinted in Jamison, 1993). Why do you think mania might be associated with creative productivity in some people?

result of feelings of loss (real or potential) or of anger directed at oneself. One psychoanalytic approach sees depression as produced by the loss or threatened loss of a parent early in life; another sees depression as caused by people feeling responsible for the bad things that happen to them and directing their anger inward.

On the other hand, convincing evidence has been found that both bipolar disorder and major depression may have genetic and biochemical roots. Heredity is known to play a role in bipolar disorder: the affliction clearly runs in some families. Furthermore, several neurotransmitters, including serotonin and norepinephrine, appear to play a role in depression (Delgado & Moreno, 2000; Leonard, 2000; Vogel, 2000).

Some explanations for mood disorders are based on cognitive factors. For example, psychologist Martin Seligman suggests that depression is largely a response to learned helplessness. As discussed in Chapter 15, *learned helplessness* is a learned expectation that one cannot control the events in one's life and that there is no escape from one's situation. People with these expectations simply give up fighting negative events and submit to them, and develop depression. Other theorists go a step further, suggesting that depression is a result of *hopelessness,* a combination of learned helplessness and an expectation that negative outcomes in one's life are inevitable (Peterson, Maier, & Seligman, 1993; Nunn, 1996; Alloy, Abramson, & Francis, 1999).

Clinical psychologist Aaron Beck has proposed that faulty cognitions underlie people's depressed feelings. Specifically, his cognitive theory of depression suggests that depressed individuals typically view themselves as life's losers, blaming themselves whenever anything goes wrong. By focusing on the negative side of situations, they feel inept and unable to act constructively to change their environment. In sum, their negative cognitions lead to feelings of depression (Sacco & Beck, 1995; Wright & Beck, 1996).

The most recent explanation of depression is drawn from evolutionary psychology. In this view, depression is an adaptive response to pursuing goals that are unattainable. When people fruitlessly pursue an ever-elusive goal, depression kicks in, ending pursuit of the goal. Ultimately, when the depression lifts,

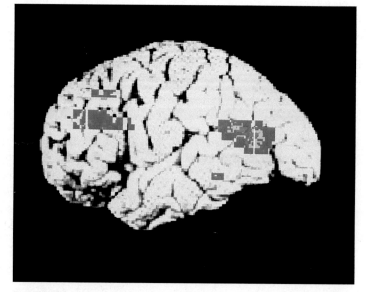

The functioning of several areas of the brain is involved in producing the symptoms of depression.

people can turn to other, more reasonable goals. In this view, depression serves a positive function, in the long run increasing the chances of survival for particular individuals, who can then pass the behavior to their offspring. Such reasoning, of course, is highly speculative (Nesse, 2000).

The various theories of depression have still not provided a complete answer to an elusive question that has dogged researchers: Why is the incidence of depression twice as high for women as for men? One explanation is that women experience more stress than men at certain points in their lives—such as when a woman must simultaneously earn a living and be the primary caregiver for her children. In addition, women have a higher risk for physical and sexual abuse, typically earn lower wages than men, report greater unhappiness with their marriages, and generally experience chronic negative circumstances (Joiner & Coyne, 1999; Nolen-Hoeksema, Larson, & Grayson, 1999).

But biological factors could also explain some women's depression. For example, 25 to 50 percent of women who take oral contraceptives report symptoms of depression, and depression that occurs following the birth of a child is linked to hormonal changes (Strickland, 1992).

As yet, researchers have discovered no definitive solutions to the puzzle of depression. Many alternative explanations are offered, and most likely mood disorders are caused by a complex interaction of several factors.

Schizophrenia

I'm a doctor, you know . . . I don't have a diploma, but I'm a doctor. I'm glad to be a mental patient, because it taught me how to be humble. I use Cover Girl creamy natural makeup. Oral Roberts has been here to visit me. . . . This place is where *Mad* magazine is published. The Nixons make Noxon metal polish. When I was a little girl, I used to sit and tell stories to myself. When I was older, I turned off the sound on the TV set and made up dialogue to go with the shows I watched. . . . I'm a week pregnant. I have schizophrenia—cancer of the nerves. My body is overcrowded with nerves. This is going to win me the Nobel Prize for medicine. I don't consider myself schizophrenic anymore. There's no such thing as schizophrenia, there's only mental telepathy. I once had a friend named Camilla Costello. She was Abbot and Costello's daughter. . . . I'm in the Pentecostal Church, but I'm thinking of changing my religion. I have a dog at home. I love instant oatmeal. When you have Jesus, you don't need a diet. Mick Jagger wants to marry me. I want to get out of the revolving door. With Jesus Christ, anything is possible. I used to hit my mother. It was the hyperactivity from all the cookies I ate. I'm the personification of Casper the Friendly Ghost. I used to go outside asking the other kids to be my friend when I was little. California's the most beautiful state in the Union. I've been there once, by television. My name is Jack Warden, and I'm an actress (Sheehan, 1982, pp. 72–73).

This excerpt shows the efforts of a woman with schizophrenia, one of the most severe forms of mental disturbance, to hold a conversation. People with schizophrenia make up by far the largest percentage of people hospitalized for mental disorders. They are also in many respects the least likely to recover from their psychological difficulties.

Schizophrenia refers to a class of disorders involving severe distortions of reality. Thinking, perception, and emotion might deteriorate; there might be a withdrawal from social interaction; and there might be displays of bizarre behavior. Although several types of schizophrenia have been observed (see Table 16-5), the distinctions between them are not always clear-cut (Bentall, 1992; Cannon, 1998). Moreover, the symptoms displayed by persons with schizophrenia can vary considerably over time, and people with schizophrenia can have significantly different symptoms even though they are labeled with the same diagnostic category. Nonetheless, a number of characteristics reliably distinguish schizophrenia from other disorders:

- *Decline from a previous level of functioning.* The individual can no longer carry out activities he or she was once able to do.

PsychLinks
Schizophrenia
www.mhhe.com/
feldmanup6-16links

schizophrenia: A class of disorders involving severe distortions of reality

Table 16-5 The Major Types of Schizophrenia

Type	Symptoms
Disorganized (hebephrenic) schizophrenia	Inappropriate laughter and giggling, silliness, incoherent speech, infantile behavior, strange and sometimes obscene behavior
Paranoid schizophrenia	Delusions and hallucinations of persecution or of greatness, loss of judgment, erratic and unpredictable behavior
Catatonic schizophrenia	Major disturbances in movement; in some phases, loss of all motion, with patient frozen into a single position, remaining that way for hours and sometimes even days; in other phases, hyperactivity and wild, sometimes violent, movement
Undifferentiated schizophrenia	Variable mixture of major symptoms of schizophrenia; classification used for patients who cannot be typed into any of the more specific categories
Residual schizophrenia	Minor signs of schizophrenia following a more serious episode

- *Disturbances of thought and language.* People with schizophrenia use logic and language in peculiar ways. Their thinking often does not make sense, and their information processing is frequently faulty. They also do not follow conventional linguistic rules (Penn et al., 1997). Consider, for example, the following response to the question "Why do you think people believe in God?"

> Uh, let's, I don't know why, let's see, balloon travel. He holds it up for you, the balloon. He don't let you fall out, your little legs sticking down through the clouds. He's down to the smokestack, looking through the smoke trying to get the balloon gassed up you know. Way they're flying on top that way, legs sticking out. I don't know, looking down on the ground, heck, that'd make you so dizzy you just stay and sleep you know, hold down and sleep there. I used to be sleep outdoors, you know, sleep outdoors instead of going home. (Chapman & Chapman, 1973, p. 3)

As this selection illustrates, although the basic grammatical structure may be intact, the substance of thinking characteristic of schizophrenia is illogical, garbled, and lacking in meaningful content (see Figure 16-4).

- *Delusions.* People with schizophrenia often have *delusions,* firmly held, unshakable beliefs with no basis in reality. Most commonly, they believe that they are being controlled by someone else, that they are being persecuted by others, or that their thoughts are being broadcast so that others are able to know what they are thinking.

- *Perceptual disorders.* People with schizophrenia do not perceive the world as most other people do. They might see, hear, or smell things differently than others do (see Figure 16-5), and they do not have a normal sense of their bodies. For instance, they could have difficulty determining where their own bodies stop and the rest of the world begins (Ritzler & Rosenbaum, 1974). They might also have *hallucinations,* perceiving things that do not actually exist (McGuire, Shah, & Murray, 1993; Ruppin, Reggia, & Horn, 1996; Reichman & Rabins, 1996).

- *Emotional disturbances.* People with schizophrenia sometimes show a bland lack of emotional response to even the most dramatic events. Or they might display

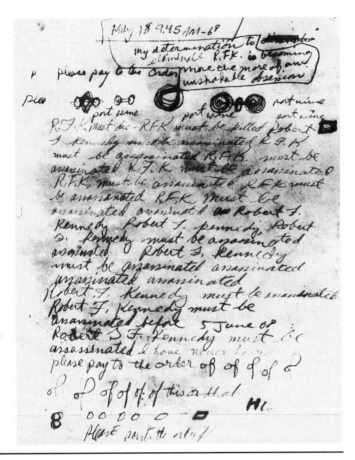

Figure 16–4 This is an excerpt from the diary of the killer of Senator Robert Kennedy who, like his brother President John Kennedy, was assassinated in the 1960s (World Wide Photos). It shows disturbances of thought and language characteristic of schizophrenia. Kennedy's killer is still in prison, but is seeking parole on the grounds that his schizophrenia is no longer a problem. Would you permit him to go free?

emotion that is inappropriate to a situation. For example, a person with schizophrenia might laugh uproariously at a funeral or might react with anger when being helped by someone.

- *Withdrawal.* People with schizophrenia tend to have little interest in others. They tend not to socialize or hold real conversations with others, although they might talk *at* another person. In the most extreme cases they do not even acknowledge the presence of other people, appearing to be in their own isolated world.

The symptoms of schizophrenia follow two primary courses. In *process schizophrenia,* the symptoms develop relatively early in life, slowly and subtly. There could be a gradual withdrawal from the world, excessive daydreaming, and a blunting of emotion, until eventually the disorder reaches the point where others cannot overlook it. In other cases, known as *reactive schizophrenia,* the onset of symptoms is sudden and conspicuous. The treatment outlook for reactive schizophrenia is relatively favorable; process schizophrenia has proved to be much more difficult to treat.

A relatively recent addition to the classifications for schizophrenia distinguishes *positive-symptom schizophrenia* from *negative-symptom schizophrenia* (Fenton & McGlashan, 1994; Tandon, 1995; Hafner & Maurer, 1995). Positive-symptom schizophrenia is indicated by the presence of disordered behavior such as hallucinations, delusions, and extremes of emotionality. In contrast, negative-symptom schizophrenia involves an absence or loss of normal functioning, such as social withdrawal or blunted emotions. The distinction is becoming increasingly important because it suggests that two different underlying processes might explain the roots of schizophrenia—which remains one of the greatest mysteries facing psychologists who deal with disordered behavior (Fenton & McGlashan, 1991b; Heinrichs, 1993).

Solving the Puzzle of Schizophrenia: Biological Causes

Although it is clear that schizophrenic behavior departs radically from normal behavior, its causes are less apparent. It does appear, however, that schizophrenia has both biological and environmental origins.

Let's first consider the evidence pointing to a biological cause of schizophrenia. Because schizophrenia is more common in some families than in others, genetic factors seem to be involved in producing at least a susceptibility to or readiness for developing schizophrenia. For example, research has shown that the closer the genetic link between a person with schizophrenia and another individual, the higher the likelihood that the other person will develop schizophrenia (see Table 16-6; Gottesman & Moldin, 1998; Brzustowicz et al., 2000).

On the other hand, if genetics alone were responsible, the chance that the identical twin of a schizophrenic would have schizophrenia would be 100 percent instead of 48 percent (Table 16-6), because identical twins are genetically identical. Moreover, research that has sought to find a link between schizophrenia and a particular gene has been only partly successful. Apparently schizophrenia is produced by more than genetic factors alone (Franzek & Beckmann, 1996; Lenzenweger & Dworkin, 1998).

One of the most intriguing biological hypotheses to explain schizophrenia is that the brains of victims harbor either a biochemical imbalance or a structural abnormality. For example, the *dopamine hypothesis* is that schizophrenia occurs when there is excess activity in the areas of the brain that use dopamine as a neurotransmitter. This hypothesis came to light after the discovery that drugs that block dopamine action in

Figure 16-5 These drawings of cats were made by an artist who suffered from schizophrenia.

brain pathways can be highly effective in reducing the symptoms of schizophrenia. Other research suggests that dopamine might operate in conjunction with other neurotransmitters such as serotonin (Seeman, 1993; Kapur & Remington, 1996; Abi-Dargham et al., 1997).

Some biological explanations propose that there are structural abnormalities in the brains of people with schizophrenia, perhaps due to exposure to a virus during prenatal development. For example, some research has found abnormal neural circuits in the cortex and limbic system of individuals with schizophrenia. Consistent with such research, different brain functioning has been found in people with schizophrenia compared to those without the disorder (Andreasen et al., 1994; Akbarian et al., 1996; Brown et al., 1996; Lenzenweger & Dworkin, 1998; see Figures 16-6 and 16-7).

Environmental Perspectives on Schizophrenia

Although biological factors provide some pieces of the puzzle of schizophrenia, we still need to consider past and current experiences in the environments of people who develop the disturbance. For instance, psychoanalytic approaches suggest that schizophrenia is a form of regression to earlier experiences and stages of life. Freud believed that people

Table 16-6 Risk of Developing Schizophrenia, Based on Genetic Relatedness to a Person with Schizophrenia

Relationship	Genetic Relatedness, %	Risk of Developing Schizophrenia, %
Identical twin	100	48
Child of two schizophrenic parents	100	46
Fraternal twin	50	17
Offspring of one schizophrenic parent	50	17
Sibling	50	9
Nephew or niece	25	4
Spouse	0	2
Unrelated person	0	1

Source: Gottesman, 1991.

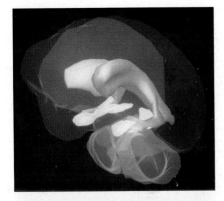

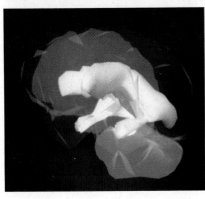

Figure 16-6 Structural changes in the brain have been found in people with schizophrenia. In the first MRI reconstruction of the brain of a patient with schizophrenia, the hippocampus (yellow) is shrunken, and the ventricles (gray) are enlarged and fluid-filled. In contrast, the lower MRI of a brain of a person without the disorder appears structurally different.

Source: N.C. Andreasen, University of Iowa.

with schizophrenia lack strong enough egos to cope with their unacceptable impulses. They regress to the oral stage—a time in which the id and ego are not yet separated. In this view, individuals suffering from schizophrenia essentially lack an ego and act out impulses without concern for reality.

Although this reasoning is theoretically plausible, there is little evidence to support psychoanalytic explanations. Somewhat more convincing are theories that look to the emotional and communication patterns of families of people with schizophrenia. For instance, some researchers suggest that schizophrenia is a result of high levels of expressed emotion. *Expressed emotion* is an interaction style characterized by criticism, hostility, and emotional intrusiveness by family members. Other researchers suggest that faulty communication patterns lie at the heart of schizophrenia (Weisman et al., 1993; Mueser et al., 1993; Bayer, 1996; Linszen et al., 1997).

Psychologists who take a cognitive perspective on schizophrenia look for cognitive causes for disordered schizophrenic thinking. Some suggest that schizophrenia is the result of *overattention* to stimuli in the environment. Rather than being able to screen out unimportant or inconsequential stimuli and focus on the most important things in the environment, people with schizophrenia might be excessively receptive to virtually everything in their environment. This overloads their information-processing capabilities, which eventually break down. Other cognitivists argue that schizophrenia is the result of *underattention* to certain stimuli: people with schizophrenia fail to focus on important stimuli sufficiently, and pay attention to other, less important information in their surroundings (Braff, 1993).

Although it is plausible that overattention and underattention are related to different forms of schizophrenia, these phenomena do not explain the origins of such information-processing disorders. Consequently, cognitive approaches—like other environmental explanations—are not the full explanation of the disorder.

The Multiple Causes of Schizophrenia

We have seen that several different biological and environmental factors are related to schizophrenia. It is likely, then, that not just one but several causes jointly explain the onset of the disorder. The predominant approach used today, the *predisposition model of schizophrenia,* considers a number of factors simultaneously. This model suggests that individuals might inherit a predisposition or an inborn sensitivity to schizophrenia that makes them particularly vulnerable to stressful factors in the environment. The stressors can vary—social rejection or dysfunctional family communication patterns—but if they are strong enough and are coupled with a genetic predisposition, the result will be the onset of schizophrenia. Similarly, if the genetic predisposition is strong enough, schizophrenia can occur even when the environmental stressors are relatively weak.

In short, schizophrenia is associated with several kinds of biological and environmental factors and is produced by a combination of interrelated variables (Lenzenweger & Dworkin, 1998; McDonald & Murray, 2000; Meltzer, 2000).

Personality Disorders

I had always wanted lots of things; as a child I can remember wanting a bullet that a friend of mine had brought in to show the class. I took it and put it into my school bag and when my friend noticed it was missing, I was the one who stayed after school with him and searched the room, and I was the one who sat with him and bitched about the other kids and how one of them took his bullet. I even went home with him to help him break the news to his uncle, who had brought it home from the war for him.

But that was petty compared with the stuff I did later. I wanted a Ph.D. very badly, but I didn't want to work very hard—just enough to get by. I never did the experiments I reported; hell, I was smart enough to make up the results. I knew enough about statistics to make anything look plausible. I got my master's degree without even spending one hour in a laboratory. I mean, the professors believed

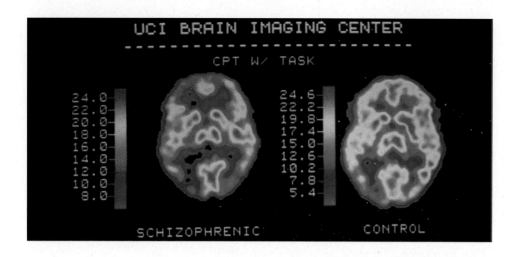

Figure 16-7 Compare these PET scans, which show differences in functioning between two people, one of who has been diagnosed with schizophrenia. Both are performing a vigilance task. In the nonschizophrenic, the task increases prefrontal cortex metabolism (*left*). For the person with schizophrenia, however, this does not occur (*right*).

Source: M.S. Buchsbaum, University of California–Irvine.

anything. I'd stay out all night drinking and being with my friends, and the next day I'd get in just before them and tell 'em I'd been in the lab all night. They'd actually feel sorry for me. (Duke & Nowicki, 1979, pp. 309–310)

This excerpt provides a graphic first-person account of a person with a personality disorder. **Personality disorders** are different from the other problems we have discussed in this chapter, because people with these psychological maladjustments feel little personal distress. In fact, people with personality disorders frequently lead seemingly normal lives. However, just below the surface lies a set of inflexible, maladaptive personality traits that do not permit them to function appropriately as members of society (Clarkin & Lenzenweger, 1996; Millon & Davis, 1996; Millon & Davis, 1999).

The best-known type of personality disorder is **antisocial personality disorder** (sometimes referred to as sociopathic personality). Individuals with this disturbance show no regard for the moral and ethical rules of society or the rights of others. Although they are intelligent and likable (at least at first), upon closer examination they turn out to be manipulative and deceptive. Moreover, they lack any feelings of guilt or anxiety over their wrongdoings. When people with antisocial personality disorder injure others, they understand intellectually that they have caused the harm but feel no remorse (Lykken, 1995).

People with antisocial personalities are often impulsive, and they are unable to tolerate frustration. They can be extremely manipulative. They also can have excellent social skills, being charming, engaging, and highly persuasive. Some of the best con men have antisocial personalities.

What causes such an unusual constellation of problems? Many factors have been suggested, ranging from a biologically induced inability to appropriately experience emotions to problems in family relationships. For example, many people with antisocial behavior come from a home in which a parent has died or left, or where they have been treated with a lack of affection, a lack of consistency in discipline, or outright rejection. Other explanations concentrate on sociocultural factors, because an unusually high proportion of people with antisocial personalities come from lower socioeconomic groups. Still, no one has been able to pinpoint the specific causes of antisocial personalities, and it is likely that some combination of factors is responsible (Nigg & Goldsmith, 1994; Hare, Hart, & Harpur, 1991; Rosenstein & Horowitz, 1996).

People with **borderline personality disorder** have difficulty developing a secure sense of who they are. As a consequence, they tend to rely on relationships with others to define their identity. The problem with this strategy is that rejections are devastating. People with this disorder are distrustful of others and have difficulty controlling their anger, and their emotional volatility leads them to impulsive and self-destructive behavior. Individuals with borderline personality disorder often feel empty

personality disorder: A mental disorder characterized by a set of inflexible, maladaptive personality traits that keep a person from functioning properly in society

antisocial personality disorder: A disorder in which individuals tend to display no regard for the moral and ethical rules of society or the rights of others

PsychLink
Antisocial personality
www.mhhe.com/
feldmanup6-16links

borderline personality disorder: A disorder in which individuals have difficulty developing a secure sense of who they are

narcissistic personality disorder: A personality disturbance characterized by an exaggerated sense of self-importance

and alone. They might form intense, sudden, one-sided relationships, demanding the attention of another person and then feeling angered when they don't receive it (Horwitz et al., 1996).

Another example of a personality disturbance is **narcissistic personality disorder,** characterized by an exaggerated sense of self-importance. People with this disorder expect special treatment from others, and at the same time disregard others' feelings. One of the main attributes of the narcissistic personality is an inability to experience empathy for other people.

There are several other categories of personality disorder, ranging in severity from individuals who might simply be regarded by others as eccentric, obnoxious, or difficult, to people who criminally endanger others. Although they are not out of touch with reality in the way that people with schizophrenia are, people with personality disorders live on the fringes of society (Millon et al., 2000).

Attention Deficit Hyperactivity Disorder (ADHD)

attention deficit hyperactivity disorder (ADHD): A learning disability marked by inattention, impulsiveness, a low tolerance for frustration, and a great deal of inappropriate activity

You'll find one in almost every elementary school classroom: a student who can't sit still, has trouble concentrating, and is constantly fidgeting. The cause, quite often, is **attention deficit hyperactivity disorder,** or **ADHD,** a disorder marked by inattention, impulsiveness, a low tolerance for frustration, and generally a great deal of inappropriate activity. Although all children show such behavior some of the time, it is so frequent in children diagnosed with ADHD that it interferes with their everyday functioning (Barkley, 1998b; Silver, 1999; Brown, 2000).

ADHD is a surprisingly common disorder; it has been estimated that 3 to 5 percent of the school-age population—or some 3.5 million children under the age of 18—in the United States have ADHD. Children diagnosed with the disorder are often exhausting to parents and teachers, and even their peers find them difficult to deal with.

The cause of ADHD is not known, although most experts feel that it is produced by dysfunctions in the nervous system. For example, one theory suggests that ADHD is caused by unusually low levels of arousal in the central nervous system. To compensate, children with ADHD seek out stimulation in order to increase their arousal. Still, such theories are speculative. Furthermore, because many children occasionally show behaviors characteristic of ADHD, it is often misdiagnosed. It is the frequency and persistence of the symptoms of ADHD that allow for a correct diagnosis, which can only be done by a trained professional (Hinshaw et al., 1997; Barkley, 1998a, 1998b).

Evaluate

1. States of extreme euphoria and energy paired with severe depression characterize _____ disorder.
2. _____ schizophrenia is characterized by symptoms that are sudden and of easily identifiable onset, whereas _____ schizophrenia develops gradually over a person's lifespan.
3. The _____ _____ states that schizophrenia might be caused by an excess of certain neurotransmitters in the brain.
4. Which of the following theories states that schizophrenia is caused by the combination of a genetic predisposition and environmental stressors?
   a. Learned inattention theory
   b. Predisposition model
   c. Learned helplessness theory

Answers to Evaluate Questions

1. bipolar 2. Reactive; process 3. dopamine hypothesis 4. b

Rethink

1. Do any of the explanations of schizophrenia offer the promise of a treatment or cure of the disorder? Do any of the explanations permit us to predict who will be affected by the disorder? How is explanation different from treatment and prediction?

2. Personality disorders are often not apparent to others, and many people with these problems seem to live basically normal lives without being a threat to others. If these people can function well in society, why should they be considered psychologically disordered?

Beyond the Major Disorders: Abnormal Behavior in Perspective

Prepare

What indicators signal a need for the help of a mental health practitioner?

Organize

Beyond the Major Disorders
The Prevalence of Mental Disorders

The various forms of abnormal behavior described in the *DSM-IV* cover much wider ground than we have been able to discuss in this chapter. Some we have considered in earlier chapters, such as *psychoactive substance-use disorder,* in which problems arise from the abuse of drugs (Chapter 4); *eating disorders* (Chapter 9); and *sexual disorders,* in which one's sexual activity is unsatisfactory (Chapter 11). Another important class of disorders that we have previously touched upon is *organic mental disorders.* These are problems that have a purely biological basis. There are other disorders we have not mentioned at all, and each of the classes we have discussed can be divided into several subcategories.

Keep in mind that the specific natures of the disorders included in the *DSM-IV* are reflections of today's Western cultures. The classification system is a snapshot of how its authors viewed mental disorder when the *DSM-IV* was published in 1994. In fact, the development of the latest version of the *DSM* was a source of great debate, in part reflecting social issues.

For example, two disorders were particularly controversial during the revision process. One, the category "self-defeating personality disorder," was ultimately removed from the appendix, where it had appeared in the previous revision. The label *self-defeating personality disorder* was meant to apply to people who neither leave nor take other action regarding relationships in which they receive unpleasant and demeaning treatment. It was typically applied to people who remained in abusive relationships. Although some clinicians argued that it was a valid category, applicable to patients they observed in their clinical practice, it lacked adequate research support. Furthermore, some critics complained that use of the label condemned targets of abuse for their plight—a blame-the-victim phenomenon. For these reasons, the category was removed from the manual.

A second and even more controversial category was "premenstrual dysphoric disorder": severe, incapacitating mood changes or depression related to a woman's menstrual cycle. Some critics argued that the classification simply labeled normal female behavior as a disorder. Former U.S. Surgeon General Antonia Novello suggested that what "in women is called PMS [premenstrual syndrome, a similar classification] in men is called healthy aggression and initiative" (Cotton, 1993, p. 13). Advocates for including the disorder prevailed, however, and "premenstrual dysphoric disorder" appears in the appendix of *DSM-IV* (Hartung & Widiger, 1998).

Such controversies underline the fact that our understanding of abnormal behavior is a reflection of the society and culture in which we live. Future revisions of *DSM* might include a different catalog of disorders. Even now, other cultures might well include a list of disorders that look very different from the list that appears in the current *DSM,* as we discuss next.

PsychLink
PMS vs. PMDD
www.mhhe.com/
feldmanup6-16links

EXPLORING DIVERSITY

The DSM *and Culture—and the Culture of the* DSM

In most people's estimation, a person who hears voices of the recently deceased is probably a victim of some psychological disturbance. Yet some Plains Indians routinely hear the voices of the dead calling to them from the afterlife.

This is but one example of the role culture plays in the labeling of behavior as "abnormal." In fact, of all the major adult disorders identified in the *DSM,* just four are found across all cultures of the world: schizophrenia, bipolar disorder, major depression, and anxiety disorders. *All* the rest are particular to North America and western Europe (Kleinman, 1996; López & Guarnaccia, 2000; Cohen, Slomkowski, & Robins, 1999).

Take, for instance, anorexia nervosa, first discussed in Chapter 9. Anorexia nervosa is a disorder in which people, particularly young women, develop inaccurate views of their body appearance, become obsessed with their weight, and refuse to eat, sometimes starving to death. This disorder appears only in cultures holding the societal standard that slender female bodies are most desirable. Most of the world does not have this standard, and likewise does not have anorexia nervosa. Interestingly, there is no anorexia nervosa in all of Asia, with two exceptions: the upper and upper-middle classes of Japan and Hong Kong, where Western influence tends to be great. It is also noteworthy that anorexia nervosa is a fairly recent disorder even in Western cultures. In the 1600s and 1700s it did not occur because the ideal female body in Western cultures at that time was plump.

PsychLink
Dissociative identity disorder
www.mhhe.com/
feldmanup6-16links

Similarly, dissociative identity disorder (multiple personality) makes sense as a problem only in societies where a sense of self is fairly concrete. In India, the self is based more on external factors that are relatively independent of the person. There, when an individual displays symptoms of what people in a Western society would call dissociative identity disorder, it is assumed that the person is possessed either by demons (and has a malady) or by gods (and does not need treatment).

Furthermore, even though such disorders as schizophrenia are found throughout the world, the particular symptoms of the disorder are influenced by cultural factors. Hence, catatonic schizophrenia, in which unmoving patients appear to be frozen in the same position, sometimes for days, is rare in North America and Western Europe. In contrast, in India, 80 percent of those with schizophrenia are catatonic.

Other cultures have disorders that do not appear in the West. For example, in Malaysia, a behavior called "amok" is characterized by a wild outburst in which a person, usually quiet and withdrawn, kills or severely injures another. "Koro" is a condition in Southeast Asian males who develop an intense panic that their penis is about to withdraw into their abdomen. Some West African men develop a disorder when they first attend college they call "brain frag"; it includes feelings of heaviness or heat in the head, as well as depression and anxiety. Finally, *ataque de nervios* is a disorder found most often among Latinos from the Caribbean, characterized by trembling, crying, uncontrollable screams, and incidents of verbal or physical aggression (Stix, 1996; Cohen, Slomkowski, & Robins, 1999; López & Guarnaccia, 2000).

In sum, we should not assume that the *DSM* provides the final word on psychological disorders. The disorders it includes are very much a creation and function of Western cultures at a particular moment in time, and its categories should not be seen as universally applicable.

The Prevalence of Psychological Disorders: The Mental State of the Union

How common are the kinds of psychological disorders we've been discussing? Here's one answer: Every second person you meet in the United States is likely to suffer, at some point in his or her life, from a psychological disorder.

At least that's the conclusion drawn from a massive study on the prevalence of psychological disorders. In the study, researchers conducted face-to-face interviews with more than 8,000 women and men of ages 15 to 54 years. The sample was designed to be representative of the population of the United States. According to results of the study, 48 percent of those interviewed had experienced a disorder at some point in their lives. In addition, 30 percent had experienced a disorder in any given year (Kessler et al., 1994).

The most common disorder was depression; 17 percent of those surveyed reported having had a major episode at least once in their lifetime (see Figure 16-8). Ten percent of those surveyed had suffered from depression during the current year. The next most frequent disorder was alcohol dependence, which occurred at a lifetime incidence rate of 14 percent. In addition, 7 percent of those interviewed had experienced alcohol dependence during the last year. Other frequently occurring psychological disorders were drug dependence, disorders involving panic (such as an overwhelming fear of talking to strangers or terror of heights), and posttraumatic stress disorder.

The study also found some unexpected gender differences. For example, 12 percent of women experienced posttraumatic stress disorder—a rate twice as high as for

men. The researchers concluded that posttraumatic stress disorder, which occurs follow-ing a sudden, severe psychological shock, is a major psychological risk for women.

The results of the study highlight the extent of the need for mental health services. For example, some 14 percent of those interviewed reported having had three or more psy-chological disorders at some time during their lives. Statistically, the people making up this group, which is the segment of the population most in need of psychological services, tend to be low-income, urban, poorly educated white women in their twenties and thirties.

These findings are supported by survey research conducted over the past 40 years, which shows that the number of people who experienced a "nervous breakdown"—admittedly a crude and imprecise term—had increased from 19 percent in 1957 to 26 percent in the mid 1990s (Swindle et al., 2000).

It is important to keep in mind that the findings are representative only of people living in the United States, and that results in other cultures differ significantly. For instance, cross-cultural surveys show that the incidence of major depression varies sig-nificantly from one culture to another. The probability of suffering at least one episode of depression is only 1.5 percent in Taiwan and 2.9 percent in Korea, compared to 11.6 percent in New Zealand and 16.4 percent in France. Such notable differences underscore the importance of considering the cultural context of psychological disorders (Weissman et al., 1996).

The prevalence figures for the United States suggest that psychological disorders are far from rare, and yet significant prejudice and discrimination are directed toward people with psychological disorders. The stigma (a label that leads people to be seen as different and therefore defective) against people who experience a psychological disor-der remains real.

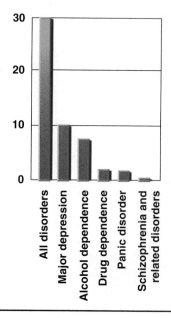

Figure 16-8 The percentage of people in the United States who reported a psychological disorder in the preceding year (Kessler et al., 1994). Are you surprised by the prevalence of psychological disorders?

BECOMING AN INFORMED CONSUMER OF PSYCHOLOGY

Deciding When You Need Help

After you consider the range and variety of psychological disturbances that can afflict people, it would not be surprising if you began to feel that you are suffering from one (or more) of the problems we have discussed. In fact, there is a name for this perception: *medical student's dis-ease*. Although in the present case it might more aptly be labeled "psychology student's disease," the basic symptoms are the same: feeling that you suffer from the problems you are studying.

Most often, of course, your concerns will be unwarranted. As we have discussed, the dif-ferences between normal and abnormal behavior are often so fuzzy that it is easy to jump to the conclusion that one has the symptoms that are involved in serious forms of mental disturbance.

Before coming to such a conclusion, though, it is important to reflect on the fact that over time we all experience a wide range of emotions, and it is not unusual to feel deeply unhappy, to fantasize about bizarre situations, or to feel anxiety about the circumstances of one's life. It is the persistence, depth, and consistency of such behavior that set abnormal reactions apart from nor-mal ones. If you have not previously had serious doubts about the normality of your behavior, reading about others' psychological disorders is probably not a strong reason for you to reevalu-ate your earlier self-confidence.

On the other hand, many people do have problems that merit concern, and it is important for them to consider the possibility that they might need professional help. Following is a list of symptoms that can arise when the normal problems of everyday living escalate beyond your abil-ity to deal with them yourself (Engler & Goleman, 1992):

- Long-term feelings of distress that interfere with your sense of well-being, competence, and ability to function effectively in daily activities
- Occasions in which you experience overwhelmingly high stress, accompanied by feelings of inability to cope with the situation
- Prolonged depression or feelings of hopelessness, particularly when they do not have any clear cause (such as the death of someone close)
- Withdrawal from other people

- A chronic physical problem for which no physical cause can be determined
- A fear or phobia that prevents you from engaging in everyday activities
- Feelings that other people are out to get you or are talking about and plotting against you
- The inability to interact effectively with others, preventing the development of friendships and loving relationships

This list offers a rough set of guidelines for determining when you might need to seek professional help. In such situations, the least reasonable approach would be to pore over the psychological disorders we have discussed in an attempt to pigeonhole yourself into a specific category. A more reasonable strategy is to consider seeking professional help—a possibility that we discuss in the next chapter.

Evaluate

1. The latest version of the DSM is considered to be the conclusive guideline on defining mental disorders. True or False?

2. _____ _____ _____, characterized by severe, incapacitating mood changes or depression related to a woman's menstrual cycle, was eventually added to the appendix of the DSM-IV despite controversy surrounding its inclusion.

3. Match the disorder with the culture in which it is most common:

   1. amok   a. India
   2. anorexia nervosa   b. Malaysia
   3. brain frag   c. United States
   4. catatonic schizophrenia   d. West Africa

4. Recent research on the prevalence of psychological disorders has found that _____ is the most common disorder, with 17 percent of those surveyed reporting having had a major episode at least once in their lifetime.

Answers to Evaluate Questions

1. False; the development of the latest version of the DSM was a source of great controversy, in part reflecting issues that divide society. 2. Premenstrual dysphoric disorder 3. 1b, 2c, 3d, 4a 4. depression

Rethink

1. Why is inclusion in the DSM-IV of "borderline" disorders such as self-defeating personality disorder and premenstrual dysphoric disorder so controversial and political? What disadvantages does inclusion bring? Does inclusion bring any benefits?

2. What societal changes would have to occur for psychological disorders to be regarded as the equivalent of appendicitis or another treatable physical disorder? Do you think a person who has been treated for a psychological disorder could become president of the United States? Should such a person become president?

How can we distinguish normal from abnormal behavior?

- Definitions of abnormality include deviation from the average, deviation from the ideal, abnormality as a sense of personal discomfort, inability to function effectively, and legal conceptions. (p. 470)
- No single definition is totally adequate, suggesting that abnormal and normal behavior should be considered in terms of a continuum. (p. 471)

Looking Back

What are the major perspectives on psychological disorders used by mental health professionals?

- The medical perspective views abnormality as a symptom of an underlying disease that requires a cure. (p. 472)
- Psychoanalytic perspectives see abnormal behavior as caused by conflicts in the unconscious produced by past experience. (p. 473)
- Behavioral approaches view abnormal behavior not as a symptom of some underlying problem, but as the problem itself. To resolve the problem, one must change the behavior. (p. 474)
- The cognitive approach sees abnormal behavior as the result of faulty cognitions. In this view, abnormal behavior can be remedied through a change in cognitions (thoughts and beliefs). (p. 474)
- Humanistic approaches view people as rational and motivated to get along with others; abnormal behavior is seen as a result of difficulty in fulfilling one's needs. (p. 474)
- Sociocultural approaches view abnormal behavior in terms of difficulties arising from family and other social relationships. (p. 475)

What classification system is used to categorize psychological disorders?

- In the United States, the most widely used system for classifying psychological disorders is the *DSM-IV—the Diagnostic and Statistical Manual of Mental Disorders,* fourth edition. (p. 475)

What are the major psychological disorders?

- Anxiety disorders are present when a person experiences so much anxiety that it affects daily functioning. Specific types of anxiety disorders include phobic disorder, panic disorder, generalized anxiety disorder, and obsessive-compulsive disorder. (p. 478)
- Somatoform disorders are psychological difficulties that take on a physical (somatic) form, but for which there is no medical cause. Examples are hypochondriasis and conversion disorders. (p. 482)
- Dissociative disorders are marked by the separation, or dissociation, of crucial parts of personality that are usually integrated. The major kinds of dissociative disorders are dissociative identity disorder (multiple personality), dissociative amnesia, and dissociative fugue. (p. 483)

What are the most severe forms of psychological disorders?

- Mood disorders are characterized by emotional states of depression or euphoria so strong that they intrude on everyday living. They include major depression and bipolar disorder. (p. 485)

- Schizophrenia is one of the severest forms of mental illness. Symptoms of schizophrenia include declines in functioning, thought and language disturbances, perceptual disorders, emotional disturbance, and withdrawal from others. (p. 488)
- Strong evidence links schizophrenia to genetic, biochemical, and environmental factors. According to the predisposition model, interactions among these kinds of factors produce the disorder. (p. 490)
- People with personality disorders feel little or no personal distress, but they do suffer from an inability to function as normal members of society. The best-known types of personality disorders are antisocial personality disorder, borderline personality disorder, and narcissistic personality. (p. 492)
- Attention deficit hyperactivity disorder (ADHD), which is marked by inattention, impulsiveness, a low tolerance for frustration, and inappropriate activity, has become a commonly diagnosed (and sometimes misdiagnosed) disorder, particularly among schoolchildren. (p. 494)

What indicators signal a need for the help of a mental health practitioner?

- There are many other categories of disorders, including sexual disorders, psychoactive substance-use disorders, and organic mental disorders. There are significant cultural differences in the nature and prevalence of psychological disorders. (p. 495)
- Students of psychology are susceptible to the same sort of "disease" that afflicts medical students: the perception that they suffer from the problems they are studying. (p. 497)
- The signals that indicate a need for professional help include long-term feelings of psychological distress, feelings of inability to cope with stress, withdrawal from other people, prolonged feelings of hopelessness, chronic physical problems with no apparent causes, phobias and compulsions, paranoia, and an inability to interact with others. (p. 497)

Key Terms and Concepts

medical perspective (p. 472)
psychoanalytic perspective (p. 473)
behavioral perspective (p. 474)
cognitive perspective (p. 474)
humanistic perspective (p. 474)
sociocultural perspective (p. 475)
Diagnostic and Statistical Manual of Mental Disorders, fourth edition (DSM-IV) (p. 475)
anxiety disorder (p. 478)
phobias (p. 479)
panic disorder (p. 479)
generalized anxiety disorder (p. 480)
obsessive-compulsive disorder (p. 480)
obsession (p. 480)
compulsion (p. 480)
somatoform disorder (p. 482)
hypochondriasis (p. 482)

conversion disorder (p. 482)
dissociative disorder (p. 483)
dissociative identity disorder (multiple personality) (p. 483)
dissociative amnesia (p. 483)
dissociative fugue (p. 484)
mood disorder (p. 485)
major depression (p. 485)
mania (p. 485)
bipolar disorder (p. 486)
schizophrenia (p. 488)
personality disorder (p. 493)
antisocial personality disorder (p. 493)
borderline personality disorder (p.493)
narcissistic personality disorder (p. 494)
attention deficit hyperactivity disorder (ADHD) (p. 494)

Psychology on the Web

1. On the Web, consulting at least two sources, research the insanity defense as it is used in U.S. courts of law. Summarize your findings, evaluating them against the psychological perspectives you read about in this chapter. Are there differences

between legal and psychological interpretations of "sanity"? Do you think such differences are appropriate?

2. Find information on the Web about the controversy surrounding dissociative (or multiple) personality disorder. Summarize both sides of the controversy. Using your knowledge of psychology, state your own opinions on the matter.

Epilogue

In this chapter, we discussed a few of the many types of psychological disorders to which people are prone, noting the difficulty that psychologists and physicians have in clearly differentiating normal from abnormal behavior, and looking at some of the approaches that have been taken to explain and treat psychological disorders. We took note of what is currently the most commonly used classification scheme (the *DSM-IV*), and we examined some of the most prevalent forms of psychological disorders. To gain a perspective on the topic of psychological disorders, we discussed the surprisingly broad incidence of psychological disorders in U.S. society and the cultural nature of such disorders.

Before we proceed to focus on treatment of such disorders, turn back to the Prologue, where you read about Lori Schiller. Using the knowledge you gained from this chapter, consider the following questions.

1. Schiller was diagnosed as suffering from schizophrenia. What elements of her behavior seem to fit the description of schizophrenia provided by the *DSM-IV* (and summarized in Table 16-2)?

2. From which type of schizophrenia (disorganized, paranoid, catatonic, undifferentiated, or residual; see Table 16-5) do you think Schiller was probably suffering? Why?

3. Which perspective (medical, psychoanalytic, behavioral, cognitive, humanistic, or sociocultural) do you think provides the best explanation of Schiller's case? Could two or more approaches be used together?

4. Were there signs of psychological disorder in Schiller's actions during adolescence? Why do you think Schiller's family failed to notice that she needed help? Why do you think it took so long for Schiller to tell her parents she had problems?

Preview

For additional quizzing and a variety of interactive resources, visit the *Understanding Psychology* Online Learning Center at

www.mhhe.com/feldmanup6

Chapter Seventeen

Treatment of Psychological Disorders

Prologue: Breaking the Silence

Looking Ahead

Psychotherapy: Psychological Approaches to Treatment

Psychodynamic Approaches to Therapy

Behavioral Approaches to Therapy

Cognitive Approaches to Therapy

Humanistic Approaches to Therapy

Group Therapy

Evaluating Psychotherapy: Does Therapy Work?

Applying Psychology in the 21st Century: Virtual Therapy: Is the World Wide Web a Good Place to Get Treatment?

Exploring Diversity: Racial and Ethnic Factors in Treatment: Should Therapists Be Color-Blind?

Biomedical Therapy: Biological Approaches to Treatment

Drug Therapy

Electroconvulsive Therapy (ECT)

Psychosurgery

Biomedical Therapies in Perspective: Can Abnormal Behavior Be Cured?

Community Psychology: A Focus on Prevention

Becoming an Informed Consumer of Psychology: Choosing the Right Therapist

Looking Back

Key Terms and Concepts

Psychology on the Web

OLC Preview

Epilogue

Correspondent Mike Wallace is one of many people who are benefiting from new drugs that help people cope with depression.

Prologue

Breaking the Silence

In his living room on Martha's Vineyard, . . . CBS newsman Mike Wallace sat and listened to his friend, the author William Styron, talk about how depressed he was. He was so low, remembers Wallace, "I was worried about him taking his life." But Wallace, who had landed in a New York hospital for depression just months before, didn't say a word about his private agonies. "I was still in the closet," he says, "even with my friends" (Biddle et al., 1996, p. 20).

Ten years later, Wallace was in Washington, D.C., testifying about his mental illness. No longer hiding the fact of his depression, he was there acclaiming the benefits of the drug that ended his depression and changed his life. "I will take Zoloft every day for the rest of my life. And I'm quite content to do it" (Biddle et al., 1996, p. 20; Buchman, 2000).

Looking Ahead

The drug that helped Mike Wallace emerge from the darkness of depression represents just one of the literally hundreds of new treatment approaches that in the last few decades have revolutionized how psychological disorders are treated. Although treatment approaches vary considerably, ranging from one-meeting informal counseling sessions to long-term drug therapy, all have a common objective: relief from a psychological disorder, with the ultimate aim of enabling individuals to achieve rich, meaningful, and fulfilling lives.

In this chapter, we explore a number of basic issues related to the treatment of abnormal behavior: How do we treat people with psychological disorders? Who is the most appropriate person to provide treatment? Is one form of therapy better than others?

Most of this chapter focuses on the various approaches used by providers of treatment for psychological disturbances. Despite their diversity, these approaches fall into two main categories: psychologically based therapy and biologically based therapy. Psychologically based therapy, or **psychotherapy**, is treatment in which a trained professional—a therapist—uses psychological techniques to help someone overcome psychological difficulties and disorders, resolve problems in living, or bring about personal growth. In psychotherapy, the goal is to produce psychological change in a person (called a "client" or "patient") as a result of discussions and interactions with the therapist. In contrast, **biomedical therapy** relies on drugs and other medical procedures to improve psychological functioning.

As we describe the various approaches to therapy, keep in mind that although the distinctions might seem clear-cut, there is a good deal of overlap among the classifications and procedures employed. In fact, many therapists today use a variety of methods with a given person, in what is referred to as an *eclectic approach to therapy*. Assuming that psychological disorders are often the product of both psychological and biological processes, eclectic therapists will draw from several perspectives simultaneously, in an effort to address both the psychological and the biological aspects of a person's problems (Wachtel & Messer, 1997; Nathan & Gorman, 1997).

Prepare

What are the goals of psychologically and biologically based treatment approaches?
What are the basic kinds of psychotherapies?

Organize

Psychotherapy
  Psychodynamic Approaches to Therapy
  Behavioral Approaches to Therapy
  Cognitive Approaches to Therapy

psychotherapy: Treatment in which a trained professional—a therapist—uses psychological techniques to help someone overcome psychological difficulties and disorders, resolve problems in living, or bring about personal growth
biomedical therapy: Therapy that relies on drugs and other medical procedures to improve psychological functioning
psychodynamic therapy: First suggested by Freud, therapy based on the premise that the primary sources of abnormal behavior are unresolved past conflicts and the possibility that unacceptable unconscious impulses will enter consciousness

Psychotherapy: Psychological Approaches to Treatment

There are some 400 different varieties of psychotherapy, approaches to therapy that focus on psychological factors. Although diverse in many respects, all psychological approaches see treatment as a way of solving psychological problems by modifying people's behavior and helping them gain a better understanding of themselves and their past, present, and future.

Given the variety of psychological approaches, it is not surprising that the people who provide therapy vary considerably in their educational backgrounds and training (see Table 17-1). Many have doctoral degrees in psychology (meaning that they have attended graduate school, learned clinical and research techniques, and held an internship). But therapy is also provided by people in fields allied with psychology, such as psychiatry and social work.

Regardless of their specific training, almost all psychotherapists employ one of four major approaches to therapy—psychodynamic, behavioral, cognitive, and humanistic—each of which is based on the models of personality and abnormal behavior discussed in Chapters 14 and 16. We'll consider each in turn.

Psychodynamic Approaches to Therapy

Psychodynamic therapy is based on the premise, first suggested by Freud in his psychoanalytic approach to personality, that the primary sources of abnormal behavior are unresolved past conflicts and the possibility that unacceptable unconscious impulses might enter consciousness. To guard against this anxiety-provoking possibility, individuals employ *defense mechanisms*, psychological strategies to protect themselves from these unconscious impulses (see Chapter 14).

Table 17-1 Getting Help from the Right Person

Clinical psychologists

Ph.D. or Psy.D. who have also completed a postgraduate internship. They specialize in assessment and treatment of psychological difficulties

Counseling psychologists

Psychologists with Ph.D. or Ed.D. who typically treat day-to-day adjustment problems, often in a university mental health clinic

Psychiatrists

M.D.s with postgraduate training in abnormal behavior. Because they can prescribe medication, they often treat the most severe disorders

Psychoanalysts

Either M.D.s or psychologists who specialize in psychoanalysis, the treatment technique first developed by Freud

Clinical or **Psychiatric Social Workers**

Professionals with a master's degree and specialized training who may provide therapy, usually regarding common family and personal problems

Each of these trained professionals could be expected to give helpful advice and direction. However, the nature of the problem a person is experiencing may make one or another more appropriate. For example, a person who is suffering from a severe disturbance and who has lost touch with reality will typically require some sort of biologically based drug therapy. In that case, a psychiatrist—who is a physician—would be the professional of choice. On the other hand, those suffering from milder disorders, such as difficulty in adjusting to the death of a family member, have a broader choice that might include any of the professionals listed above. The decision can be made easier by initial consultations with professionals in mental health facilities in communities, colleges, and health organizations, who can provide guidance in selecting an appropriate therapist.

The most common defense mechanism is repression, in which threatening conflicts and impulses are pushed back into the unconscious. However, because unacceptable conflicts and impulses can never be completely buried, some of the anxiety associated with them can produce abnormal behavior in the form of what Freud called *neurotic symptoms*.

How does one rid oneself of the anxiety produced by unconscious, unwanted impulses and drives? To Freud, the answer was to confront the conflicts and impulses by bringing them out of the unconscious part of the mind and into the conscious part. Freud assumed that this technique would reduce anxiety stemming from past conflicts and that the patient could then participate in his or her daily life more effectively.

The challenge facing a psychodynamic therapist, then, is to find a way to assist patients' attempts to explore and understand their unconscious. The technique that has evolved has a number of components, but basically it consists of leading patients to consider and discuss their past experiences from the time of their first memories, in explicit detail. This process assumes that patients will eventually stumble upon long-hidden crises, traumas, and conflicts that are producing anxiety in their adult lives. They will then be able to "work through"—understand and rectify—these difficulties.

Psychoanalysis: Freud's Therapy

Classic Freudian psychodynamic therapy, called **psychoanalysis,** tends to be a lengthy and expensive affair. Patients typically meet with their therapists for an hour a day, four to six days a week, for several years. In their sessions, they often use a technique developed by Freud called *free association*. Patients are told to say aloud whatever comes to mind, regardless of its apparent irrelevance or senselessness, and analysts attempt to recognize and label the connections between what is being said and the

 **PsychLink**

What is psychotherapy?
www.mhhe.com/
feldmanup6-17links

psychoanalysis: Psychodynamic therapy that involves frequent sessions and can last for many years

Freud's psychoanalytic therapy is an intensive, lengthy process that includes techniques such as free association and dream interpretation. What are some advantages and disadvantages of psychoanalysis compared to other approaches?

patient's unconscious. Therapists also use *dream interpretation,* examining dreams to find clues to unconscious conflicts and problems (first discussed in Chapter 5). Moving beyond the surface description of a dream (the *manifest content*), therapists seek to find its underlying meaning (the *latent content*), thereby revealing the true unconscious meaning of the dream (Galatzer-Levy & Cohler, 1997).

The processes of free association and dream interpretation do not always move forward easily. The same unconscious forces that initially produced repression can work to keep past difficulties out of the conscious, producing resistance. *Resistance* is an inability or unwillingness to discuss or reveal particular memories, thoughts, or motivations. Resistance can be expressed in a number of ways. For instance, patients might be discussing a childhood memory and suddenly forget what they were saying, or they might completely change the subject. It is the therapist's job to pick up instances of resistance and to interpret their meaning, as well as to ensure that patients return to the subject—which is likely to hold difficult or painful memories for them.

Because of the close, almost intimate interaction between patient and psychoanalyst, the relationship between the two often becomes emotionally charged and takes on a complexity unlike most others. Patients might eventually perceive the analyst as symbolic of significant others in their past, perhaps a parent or a lover, and apply some of their feelings for that person to the analyst—a phenomenon known as *transference* (Mann, 1997).

Transference can be used by a therapist to help the patient recreate past relationships that were psychologically difficult. For instance, if a patient undergoing transference views her therapist as symbolic of her father—with whom she had a difficult relationship—the patient and therapist might "redo" an earlier interaction, this time including more positive aspects. Through this process, conflicts regarding the real father might be resolved—something that is beginning to happen in the following therapy session:

> Sandy: My father . . . never took any interest in any of us. . . . It was my mother—
>   rest her soul—who loved us, not our father. He worked her to death. Lord, I miss
>   her. . . . I must sound angry at my father. Don't you think I have a right to be
>   angry?
> Therapist: Do you think you have a right to be angry?
> Sandy: Of course, I do! Why are you questioning me? You don't believe me, do
>   you?
> Therapist: You want me to believe you.
> Sandy: I don't care whether you believe me or not. . . . I know what you're
>   thinking—you think I'm crazy—you must be laughing at me—I'll probably be a
>   case in your next book! You're just sitting there—smirking—making me feel like
>   a bad person—thinking I'm wrong for being mad, that I have no right to be mad.
> Therapist: Just like your father.
> Sandy: Yes, you're just like my father.—Oh my God! Just now—I—I—thought I
>   was talking to him (Sue, Sue, & Sue, 1990, pp. 514–515).

Contemporary Alternatives to Psychoanalysis

Few people have the time, money, or patience required for years of traditional psychoanalysis. Moreover, no conclusive evidence shows that psychoanalysis, as originally conceived by Freud, works better than other, more contemporary versions of psychodynamic therapy. Today, for instance, psychodynamic therapy tends to be shorter, usually lasting no longer than three months or twenty sessions. The therapist takes a more active role than Freud would have liked, controlling the course of therapy and prodding and advising the patient with considerable directness. Finally, there

is less emphasis on a patient's past history and childhood. Instead, the therapist concentrates on an individual's current relationships and specific complaints ("Brief Psychodynamic Therapy," 1994).

Even with its current modifications, psychodynamic therapy has its critics. In its longer versions, it can be relatively time-consuming and expensive, especially in comparison with other forms of psychotherapy that we will discuss later. Furthermore, patients who are less articulate might not do as well as those who are more verbal.

Ultimately, the most important concern about psychodynamic treatment is whether it actually works, and here we find no simple answer. Psychodynamic treatment techniques have been controversial since Freud introduced them. Part of the problem is the difficulty in establishing whether or not patients have improved following psychodynamic therapy. One must depend on reports from the therapist or the patients themselves, reports that are obviously open to bias and subjective interpretation.

Critics have questioned the entire theoretical basis of psychodynamic theory, maintaining that there is no proof that such constructs as the unconscious exist. Despite the considerable criticism, though, the psychodynamic treatment approach has remained viable. To proponents, it not only provides effective treatment in many cases of psychological disturbance, but also permits the potential development of an unusual degree of insight into one's life (Barber & Lane, 1995; Clay, 2000).

Behavioral Approaches to Therapy

Perhaps, as a child, you were rewarded by your parents with an ice cream cone when you were especially good . . . or sent to your room if you misbehaved. As we saw in Chapter 6, the principles behind such a child-rearing strategy are valid: Good behavior is maintained by reinforcement, and unwanted behavior can be eliminated by punishment.

These principles represent the basic underpinnings of **behavioral treatment approaches.** Building upon the basic processes of learning (see Chapter 6), behavioral treatment approaches make this fundamental assumption: Both abnormal behavior and normal behavior are *learned*. People who display abnormal behavior have either failed to learn the skills needed to cope with the problems of everyday living or have acquired faulty skills and patterns that are being maintained through some form of reinforcement. To modify abnormal behavior, then, behavioral approaches propose that people must learn new behavior to replace the faulty skills they have developed and unlearn their maladaptive behavior patterns (Bergin & Garfield, 1994; Agras & Berkowitz, 1996).

To behavioral psychologists, it is not necessary to delve into people's pasts or their psyches. Rather than viewing abnormal behavior as a symptom of some underlying problem, they consider the abnormal behavior itself as the problem in need of modification. Changing people's behavior to allow them to function more effectively solves the problem—with no need for concern about the underlying cause. In this view, then, if you can change abnormal behavior, you've cured the problem.

Aversive Conditioning Techniques

Suppose you bite into your favorite candy bar and find that it is not only infested with ants, but that you've swallowed a bunch of them. You immediately become sick to your stomach and throw up. Your long-term reaction? You never eat that kind of candy bar again, and it might be months before you eat any type of candy.

This simple example demonstrates how classical conditioning might be used to modify behavior. Recall from our discussion in Chapter 6 that when a stimulus that naturally evokes a negative response (such as an unpleasant taste or a puff of air in the face) is paired with a previously neutral stimulus (such as

⚭ PsychLink

Benefits of psychotherapy
www.mhhe.com/
feldmanup6–17links

behavioral treatment approaches:
Treatment approaches that build upon the basic processes of learning, such as reinforcement and extinction

Behavioral approaches to treatment would seek to modify the behavior of this couple, rather than focusing on the underlying causes of the behavior.

Table 17-2 Producing the Relaxation Response

Step 1. Pick a focus word or short phrase that's firmly rooted in your personal belief system. For example, a nonreligious individual might choose a neutral word like *one* or *peace* or *love*. A Christian person desiring to use a prayer could pick the opening words of Psalm 23. *The Lord is my shepherd;* a Jewish person could choose *Shalom.*

Step 2. Sit quietly in a comfortable position.

Step 3. Close your eyes.

Step 4. Relax your muscles.

Step 5. Breathe slowly and naturally, repeating your focus word or phrase silently as you exhale.

Step 6. Throughout, assume a passive attitude. Don't worry about how well you're doing. When other thoughts come to mind, simply say to yourself, "Oh, well," and gently return to the repetition.

Step 7. Continue for 10 to 20 minutes. You may open your eyes to check the time, but do not use an alarm. When you finish, sit quietly for a minute or so, at first with your eyes closed and later with your eyes open. Then do not stand for one or two minutes.

Step 8. Practice the technique once or twice a day.

the sound of a tone), the neutral stimulus can come to elicit a similar negative reaction by itself. Using this procedure, we can create unpleasant reactions to stimuli that an individual previously enjoyed—possibly to excess. The technique, known as *aversive conditioning,* has been used to treat alcoholism, drug abuse, and smoking.

The basic procedure in aversive conditioning is relatively straightforward. For example, a person with a drinking problem might be given an alcoholic drink along with a drug that causes severe nausea and vomiting. After these two are paired a few times, the alcohol alone becomes associated with the vomiting and becomes less appealing.

Although aversion therapy works reasonably well to inhibit substance-abuse problems such as alcoholism and certain kinds of sexual disorders, its long-term effectiveness is questionable. There are also important ethical concerns about aversion techniques that employ such potent stimuli as electric shock, which are used only in the most extreme cases, such as self-mutilation. It is clear, though, that aversion therapy is an important procedure for eliminating maladaptive responses for some period of time— a respite that provides, even if only temporarily, the opportunity to encourage more adaptive behavior patterns (Yuskauskas, 1992).

Systematic Desensitization

The most successful treatment based on classical conditioning is systematic desensitization. **Systematic desensitization** is a technique in which gradual exposure to an anxiety-producing stimulus is paired with relaxation in order to extinguish the response of anxiety (Wolpe, 1990; St. Onge, 1995a).

Suppose, for instance, you were extremely afraid of flying. The very thought of being in an airplane made you begin to sweat and shake, and you'd never even been able to get yourself near enough to an airport to know how you'd react if you actually had to fly somewhere. If systematic desensitization were used to treat your problem, you would first be trained in relaxation techniques by a behavior therapist (see Table 17-2), learning to relax your body fully—a highly pleasant state, as you might imagine.

The next step would involve the construction of a *hierarchy of fears*—a list, in order of increasing severity, of the things that are associated with your fears. For instance, your hierarchy might resemble this one:

systematic desensitization: A behavioral technique in which gradual exposure to anxiety-producing stimuli is paired with relaxation in order to extinguish the response of anxiety

These participants in a systematic desensitization program have worked to overcome their fear of flying and are about to "graduate" by taking a brief flight. In what ways is this approach based on classical conditioning?

1. Watching a plane fly overhead
2. Going to an airport
3. Buying a ticket
4. Stepping into the plane
5. Seeing the plane door close
6. Having the plane taxi down the runway
7. Taking off
8. Being in the air

Once this hierarchy had been developed and you had learned relaxation techniques, the two sets of responses would be associated with each other. To do this, your therapist might ask you to put yourself into a relaxed state and then to imagine yourself in the first situation identified in your hierarchy. After you were able to consider that first step while remaining relaxed, you would move on to the next situation, eventually moving up the hierarchy in gradual stages until you could imagine yourself being in the air without experiencing anxiety. Ultimately, you would be asked to make a visit to an airport and later to take a flight.

Systematic desensitization has proved to be an effective treatment for a number of problems, including phobias, anxiety disorders, and even impotence and fear of sexual contact. In short, we *can* learn to enjoy the things we once feared (Mendez & Garcia, 1996).

Operant Conditioning Techniques

Behavioral approaches using operant conditioning techniques (which demonstrate the effects of rewards and punishments on future behavior) are based on the notion that we should reward people for carrying out desirable behavior and extinguish behavior that we wish to eliminate, by either ignoring it or punishing it (Kazdin, 1994).

One example of the systematic application of operant conditioning principles is the *token system,* whereby a person is rewarded for desired behavior with a token such as a poker chip or some kind of play money. Although it is most frequently employed in institutional settings for individuals with relatively serious problems, the system is not unlike what parents do when they give children money for being well behaved—money that they can later exchange for something they want. The desired behavior might range from such simple things as keeping one's room neat to personal grooming or interacting with other people. In institutions, tokens can be exchanged for some object or activity, such as snacks, new clothes, or, in extreme cases, being able to sleep in one's own bed rather than on the floor.

PsychLink

Treating fear of flying
www.mhhe.com/
feldmanup6-17links

A "fearless peer" who models appropriate and effective behavior can help children overcome their fears.

Contingency contracting, a variant of the more extensive token system, has proved quite effective in producing behavior modification. In *contingency contracting,* a written agreement is drawn up between therapist and client (or teacher and student, or parent and child). The contract states a series of behavioral goals that the client hopes to achieve. It also specifies the positive consequences for the client if the goals are reached—usually some explicit reward such as money or additional privileges. Contracts frequently state negative consequences if the goals are not met. For example, clients who are trying to quit smoking might write out a check to a cause they have no interest in supporting (for instance, the National Rifle Association if they are strong gun control supporters). If the client smokes on a given day, the therapist would mail the check.

Behavior therapists also make use of *observational learning,* the process in which the behavior of other people is modeled, to systematically teach people new skills and ways of handling their fears and anxieties. For example, modeling helps teach basic social skills such as maintaining eye contact during conversation or acting assertively. Similarly, children with dog phobias have been able to overcome their fears by watching another child—called the "Fearless Peer"—repeatedly walk up to a dog, touch it, pet it, and finally play with it. Modeling, then, can play an effective role in resolving some kinds of behavior difficulties, especially if the model is rewarded for her or his behavior (Bandura, Grusec, & Menlove, 1967; St. Onge, 1995b).

How Does Behavior Therapy Stack Up?

Behavior therapy works particularly well for phobias and compulsions, for establishing control over impulses, and for learning complex social skills to replace maladaptive behavior. More than any of the other therapeutic techniques, it has produced methods that can be employed by nonprofessionals to change their own behavior. Moreover, it tends to be economical in terms of time, because it is directed toward the solution of carefully defined problems (Wilson & Agras, 1992).

Behavior therapy has its disadvantages. It is not particularly successful in treating deep depression or personality disorders (Brody, 1990). And, because it emphasizes changing external behavior, people do not necessarily gain insight into their thoughts and expectations that might be fostering their maladaptive behavior. Finally, behavior therapy has less success in the long term than in the short term. Because of such concerns, some psychologists have turned to cognitive approaches.

Cognitive Approaches to Therapy

If you assumed that faulty, maladaptive cognitions lie at the heart of psychological disorders, wouldn't the most direct treatment route be to teach people new, more adaptive modes of thinking? The answer is yes, according to psychologists who take a cognitive approach to treatment.

cognitive treatment approaches:
Approaches to treatment that teach people to think in more adaptive ways by changing their dysfunctional cognitions about the world and themselves

cognitive-behavioral approach: An approach used by cognitive therapists that attempts to change the way people think through the use of basic principles of learning

Cognitive treatment approaches teach people to think in more adaptive ways by changing their dysfunctional cognitions about the world and themselves. Unlike behavior therapists, who focus on modifying external behavior, cognitive therapists also attempt to change the way people think. Because they often use basic principles of learning, the methods they employ are sometimes referred to as the **cognitive-behavioral approach** (Beck, 1991; McCullough, 1999).

Cognitive treatment approaches take many forms, but they all assume that anxiety, depression, and negative emotions develop from maladaptive thought processes. Accordingly, cognitive treatments seek to change the thought patterns that lead to getting "stuck" in dysfunctional ways of thinking. During therapy, people are systematically taught to challenge their assumptions and adopt new approaches to old problems.

Cognitive therapy is relatively short-term, usually lasting a maximum of twenty sessions. Therapy tends to be highly structured and focused on concrete problems. Therapy often begins with the therapist teaching the theory behind the approach, and

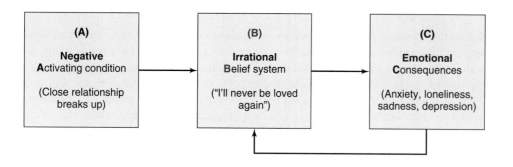

Figure 17-1 In the A-B-C model of rational-emotive behavior therapy, negative activating conditions (A) lead to the activation of an irrational belief system (B), that leads to emotional consequences (C). Those emotional consequences then feed back and support the belief system. At what steps in the model could change occur due to rational-emotive behavior therapy?

therapists continue to take an active role throughout the course of therapy, acting as a combination of teacher, coach, and partner.

One of the best examples of cognitive treatment is rational-emotive behavior therapy. **Rational-emotive behavior therapy** attempts to restructure a person's belief system into a more realistic, rational, and logical set of views. According to psychologist Albert Ellis (1999), many people lead unhappy lives and suffer from psychological disorders because they harbor such irrational, unrealistic ideas as these:

- That it is necessary to have the love or approval of virtually every significant other person for everything we do
- That we should be thoroughly competent, adequate, and successful in all possible respects if we are to consider ourselves worthwhile
- That it is horrible when things don't turn out the way we want them to

Such irrational beliefs trigger negative emotions, which in turn support the irrational beliefs, leading to a self-defeating cycle. Ellis calls it the A-B-C model, in which negative activating conditions (A) lead to the activation of an irrational belief system (B), that in turn leads to emotional consequences (C). For example, if a person goes through the breakup of a close relationship (A) and holds the irrational belief (B) "I'll never be loved again," this triggers negative emotions (C) that in turn feed back into support of the irrational belief (see Figure 17-1).

The goal of rational-emotive behavior therapy is to help clients eliminate the maladaptive cognitions and adopt more effective thinking. To accomplish this goal, therapists take an active, directive role during therapy, openly challenging patterns of thought that appear to be dysfunctional. Consider this example:

Martha: The basic problem is that I'm worried about my family. I'm worried about money. And I never seem to be able to relax.

Therapist: Why are you worried about your family? . . . What's to be concerned about? They have certain demands which you don't want to adhere to.

Martha: I was brought up to think that I mustn't be selfish.

Therapist: Oh, we'll have to knock that out of your head!

Martha: My mother feels that I shouldn't have left home—that my place is with them. There are nagging doubts about what I should—

Therapist: Why are there doubts? Why *should* you?

Martha: I think it's a feeling I was brought up with that you always have to give of yourself. If you think of yourself, you're wrong.

Therapist: That's a *belief*. Why do you have to keep believing that—at *your* age? You believed a lot of superstitions when you were younger. Why do you have to retain them? Your parents indoctrinated you with this nonsense, because that's *their* belief. . . . Who needs that philosophy? All it's gotten you, so far, is guilt. (Ellis, 1974, pp. 233–286)

By poking holes in Martha's reasoning, the therapist is attempting to help her adopt a more realistic view of herself and her circumstances (Ellis & Dryden, 1997; Dryden, 1999).

Another form of therapy that builds on a cognitive perspective is that of Aaron Beck (Beck, 1991, 1995). Like rational-emotive behavior therapy, the basic goal of

rational-emotive behavior therapy: A form of therapy that attempts to restructure a person's belief system into a more realistic, rational, and logical set of views

 **PsychLink**

Rational-emotive therapy discussion
www.mhhe.com/
feldmanup6-17links

"To this day, I can hear my mother's voice—harsh, accusing. 'Lost your mittens? You naughty kittens! Then you shall have no pie!'"

Beck's *cognitive therapy* is to change people's illogical thoughts about themselves and the world. However, cognitive therapy is considerably less confrontational and challenging than rational-emotive behavior therapy. Instead of the therapist actively arguing with clients about their dysfunctional cognitions, cognitive therapists are more apt to play the role of teacher. Clients are urged to obtain information on their own that will lead them to discard their inaccurate thinking. During the course of treatment, clients are helped to discover ways of thinking more appropriately about themselves and others (Alford & Beck, 1997; Greenberg, 2000; Rosen, 2000).

Cognitive approaches to therapy have proved successful in dealing with a broad range of disorders. The ability to incorporate additional treatment approaches (e.g., combining cognitive and behavioral techniques in cognitive behavioral therapy) has made cognitive therapy a particularly effective form of treatment (McMullin, 2000).

Evaluate

1. Match the following kinds of mental health practitioners with the appropriate description

   1. Psychiatrist

   2. Clinical psychologist

   3. Counseling psychologist

   4. Psychoanalyst

   a. Ph.D. specializing in treatment of psychological disorders

   b. Professional specializing in Freudian therapy techniques

   c. M.D. trained in abnormal behavior

   d. Ph.D. specializing in adjustment of day-to-day problems

2. According to Freud, people use _____ _____ to ensure that unwanted impulses will not intrude on conscious thought.

3. In dream interpretation, a psychoanalyst must learn to distinguish between the _____ content of a dream, which is what appears on the surface, and the _____ content, its underlying meaning.

4. Which of the following treatments deals with phobias by gradual exposure to the item producing the fear?

   a. Systematic desensitization

   b. Partial reinforcement

   c. Behavioral self-management

   d. Aversion therapy

Answers to Evaluate Questions

1. 1-c; 2-a; 3-d; 4-b 2. defense mechanisms 3. manifest; latent 4. a

Rethink

1. In what ways are psychoanalysis and cognitive therapy similar, and how do they differ?

2. How might you examine the reliability of dream interpretation?

Prepare

What are humanistic approaches to treatment?

How does group therapy differ from individual types of therapy?

How effective is therapy, and which kind of therapy works best in a given situation?

Organize

Humanistic Approaches to Therapy

Group Therapy

Evaluating Psychotherapy

Humanistic Approaches to Therapy

As you know from your own experience, it is impossible to master the material covered in a course without some hard work, no matter how good the teacher and the textbook are. *You* must take the time to study, to memorize the vocabulary, to learn the concepts. Nobody else can do it for you. If you choose to put in the effort, you'll succeed; if you don't, you'll fail. The responsibility is primarily yours.

Humanistic therapy draws upon this philosophical perspective of self-responsibility in developing treatment techniques. The many different types of therapy that fit into this category have a similar rationale: We have control of our own behavior; we can make choices about the kinds of lives we want to live; and it is up to us to solve the difficulties that we encounter in our daily lives.

Instead of being the directive figures seen in some psychodynamic and behavioral approaches, humanistic therapists view themselves as guides or

facilitators. Therapists using humanistic techniques seek to lead people to realizations about themselves and help them find ways to come closer to the ideal they hold for themselves. In this view, psychological disorders are the result of people's inability to find meaning in life and of feeling lonely and unconnected to others.

Humanistic approaches have produced a number of therapeutic techniques. Among the most important are client-centered therapy and gestalt therapy.

Client-Centered Therapy

Consider the following therapy session excerpt:

> Alice: I was thinking about this business of standards. I somehow developed a sort of a knack, I guess, of—well—habit—of trying to make people feel at ease around me, or to make things go along smoothly. . . .
>
> Therapist: In other words, what you did was always in the direction of trying to keep things smooth and to make other people feel better and to smooth the situation.
>
> Alice: Yes. I think that's what it was. Now the reason why I did it probably was—I mean, not that I was a good little Samaritan going around making other people happy, but that was probably the role that felt easiest for me to play. . . .
>
> Therapist: You feel that for a long time you've been playing the role of kind of smoothing out the frictions or differences or what not. . . .
>
> Alice: M-hm.
>
> Therapist: Rather than having any opinion or reaction of your own in the situation. Is that it? (Rogers, 1951, pp. 152–153)

The therapist's comments are not interpretations or answers to questions that the client has raised. Instead, they tend to clarify or reflect back what the client has said (e.g., "In other words, what you did . . ."; "You feel that . . ."; "Is that it?"). This therapeutic technique is known as *nondirective counseling*. Nondirective counseling is at the heart of client-centered therapy, which was first practiced by Carl Rogers (Rogers, 1951, 1980; Raskin & Rogers, 1989).

The goal of **client-centered therapy** is to enable people to reach their potential for self-actualization. By providing a warm and accepting environment, therapists hope to motivate clients to air their problems and feelings. In turn, this enables clients to make realistic and constructive choices and decisions about the things that bother them in their current lives.

Instead of directing choices that clients make, therapists provide what Rogers calls *unconditional positive regard*—expressing acceptance and understanding, regardless of the feelings and attitudes the client expresses. In doing so, therapists hope to create an atmosphere in which clients are able to come to decisions that can improve their lives (Farber, Brink, & Raskin, 1996).

Furnishing unconditional positive regard does not mean that therapists must approve of everything their clients say or do. Rather, the assumption is that therapists need to communicate that they are caring, nonjudgmental, and *empathetic*—understanding of a client's emotional experience (Fearing & Clark, 2000).

It is relatively rare for client-centered therapy to be used today in its purest form. Contemporary approaches are apt to be somewhat more directive, with therapists nudging clients toward insights rather than merely reflecting back their statements. However, clients' insights are still seen as central to the therapeutic process.

Gestalt Therapy

Have you ever thought back to some childhood incident in which you were treated unfairly and again felt the rage that you experienced at that time? To therapists working in a gestalt perspective, the healthiest thing for you to do psychologically might be to act out that rage—by hitting a pillow, kicking a chair, or yelling in frustration. This sort

 PsychLink

Gestalt therapy
www.mhhe.com/
feldmanup6–17links

of activity is an important part of what goes on in gestalt therapy sessions, in which the client is encouraged to act out past conflicts and difficulties.

The rationale for this treatment approach is the idea that people need to integrate their thoughts, feelings, and behaviors into a *gestalt,* the German term for "whole" (as we discussed in reference to perception in Chapter 4). In **gestalt therapy,** people are led to examine their earlier experiences and complete any "unfinished business" from their past that might still affect and color present-day relationships. Gestalt therapy typically includes reenactments of specific conflicts that clients experienced earlier. For instance, a client might first play the part of his angry father and then play himself when his father yelled at him. Such reenactments are assumed to promote better understanding of the source of psychological disorders, as clients broaden their perspective on their situation. Ultimately, the goal of gestalt therapy is to experience life in a more unified and complete way (Perls, 1970; Perls, Hefferline, & Goodman, 1994; Serok, 2000).

Humanistic Approaches in Perspective

The notion that psychological disorders are the consequence of restricted growth potential is philosophically appealing to many people. Furthermore, humanistic therapists' acknowledgment that the freedom we possess can lead to psychological difficulties provides an unusually supportive environment for therapy. In turn, this atmosphere can help clients find solutions to difficult psychological problems.

On the other hand, the lack of specificity of the humanistic treatments has troubled critics. Humanistic approaches are not very precise and are probably the least scientifically and theoretically developed type of treatment. Moreover, this form of treatment is best suited for the same type of highly verbal client who profits most from psychoanalytic treatment.

Group Therapy

Although most treatment takes place between a single individual and a therapist, some forms of therapy involve groups of people seeking treatment. In **group therapy,** several unrelated people meet with a therapist to discuss some aspect of their psychological functioning.

People typically discuss their problems with the group, which is often centered around a common difficulty, such as alcoholism or a lack of social skills. The other members of the group provide emotional support and describe how they have coped effectively with similar problems (Yalom, 1997; Free, 2000).

Groups vary greatly in terms of the particular model they employ; there are psychoanalytic groups, humanistic groups, and groups corresponding to the other therapeutic approaches. Furthermore, groups also differ in the degree of guidance the therapist provides. In some, the therapist is quite directive; in others, the members of the group set their own agenda and determine how the group will proceed (Spira, 1997; Early, 1999).

Because several people are treated simultaneously in group therapy, it is a much more economical means of treatment than individual psychotherapy. On the other hand, critics argue that group settings do not afford the individual attention inherent in one-to-one therapy, and that in a group setting especially shy and withdrawn individuals might not receive the attention they need.

Family Therapy

One specialized form of group therapy is family therapy. As the name implies, **family therapy** involves two or more members of the same family, one (or more) of whose problems led to

gestalt therapy: An approach to therapy that attempts to integrate a client's thoughts, feelings, and behavior into a unified whole

group therapy: Therapy in which people discuss problems in a group

family therapy: An approach that focuses on the family and its dynamics

In group therapy, people with psychological difficulties meet with a therapist to discuss their problems.

treatment. But rather than focusing simply on members of the family who present the initial problem, family therapists consider the family as a whole unit, to which each member contributes. By meeting with the entire family simultaneously, family therapists attempt to obtain a sense of how the family members interact with one another (Rolland & Walsh, 1996; Cooklin, 2000).

Family therapists view the family as a "system," and they assume that the separate individuals in the family cannot improve without understanding the conflicts that are to be found in the interactions of the family members. Thus each member is expected to contribute to the resolution of the problem being addressed.

Many family therapists assume that family members fall into rigid roles or set patterns of behavior, with one person acting as the scapegoat, another as a bully, and so forth. In their view, family disturbances are perpetuated by this system of roles. One goal of this type of therapy, then, is to get the family members to adopt new, more constructive roles and patterns of behavior (Minuchin & Nichols, 1992; Sprenkle & Moon, 1996).

In family therapy, the family system as a whole—not just one family member identified as the "problem"—is treated. Why is this advantageous?

Evaluating Psychotherapy: Does Therapy Work?

Your best friend, Ben, comes to you because he just hasn't been feeling right about things lately. He's upset because he and his girlfriend aren't getting along, but his difficulties go beyond that. He can't concentrate on his studies, has a lot of trouble getting to sleep, and—this is what really bothers him—he's begun to think that people are ganging up on him, talking about him behind his back. It just seems that no one really cares about or understands him or makes any effort to see why he's become so miserable.

Ben is aware that he ought to get *some* kind of help, but he is not sure where to turn. He is fairly skeptical of psychologists, thinking that a lot of what they say is just mumbo-jumbo, but he's willing to put his doubts aside and try anything to feel better. He also knows there are many different types of therapy, and he doesn't have a clue as to which would be best for him. He turns to you for advice, because he knows you are taking a psychology course. He asks, "Which kind of therapy works best?"

Is Therapy Effective?

Such a question requires a complex response, for there is no easy answer. In fact, identifying which form of treatment is most appropriate is a controversial, and still unresolved, task for psychologists specializing in psychological disorders. For example, even before considering whether any one form of therapy works better than another, we need to determine whether therapy in *any* form is effective in alleviating psychological disturbances.

Until the 1950s, most people simply assumed that therapy was effective. But in 1952 psychologist Hans Eysenck published what became a classic article that challenged this assumption. He claimed that people who received psychodynamic treatment and related therapies were no better off at the end of treatment than people who were placed on a waiting list for treatment but never received it. According to his analysis, about two-thirds of the people who reported suffering from "neurotic" symptoms believed that those symptoms had disappeared after two years, regardless of whether or not they had been in therapy. Eysenck concluded that people would go into **spontaneous remission,** recovery without treatment, if they were simply left alone—certainly a cheaper and simpler process.

Although Eysenck's conclusions were quickly challenged, his review stimulated a continuing stream of better controlled, more carefully crafted studies on the effectiveness of psychotherapy, and today most psychologists agree: Therapy does work. Several comprehensive reviews indicate that therapy brings about greater improvement than no treatment at all, with the rate of spontaneous remission being fairly low. In most cases, then, the symptoms of abnormal behavior do not go away by themselves if left untreated—although the issue continues to be hotly debated (Bergin & Garfield, 1994; Seligman, 1996; Sohn, 1996).

 **PsychLinks**

Effectiveness of psychotherapy
www.mhhe.com/
feldmanup6-17links

spontaneous remission: Recovery without treatment

Figure 17-2 Estimates of the effectiveness of different types of treatment, in comparison to control groups of untreated people (Smith, Glass, & Miller, 1980). The percentile score shows how much more effective a particular type of treatment is for the average patient than is no treatment. For example, people given psychodynamic treatment score, on average, more positively on outcome measures than about three-quarters of untreated people.

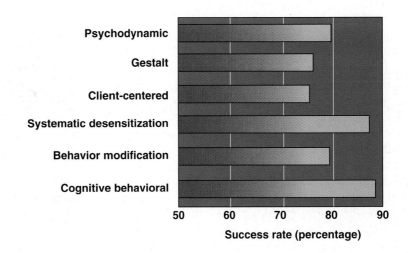

Success rate (percentage)

Which Kind of Therapy Works Best?

Although most psychologists feel confident that psychotherapeutic treatment *in general* is more effective than no treatment at all, the question of whether any specific form of treatment is superior to any other has yet to be answered definitively (Barber & Lane, 1995; Pratt & Moreland, 1996).

For instance, one classic study comparing the effectiveness of various approaches found that although there is some variation among the success rates of the various treatment forms, most treatments have about the same success rate. As Figure 17-2 indicates, the success rates ranged from about 70 to 85 percent greater success for treated than for untreated individuals. There was a slight tendency for behavioral approaches and cognitive approaches to be more successful, but this result might have been due to differences in the severity of cases treated (Smith, Glass, & Miller, 1980; Orwin & Condray, 1984).

Other research, relying on *meta-analysis,* in which data from a large number of studies are statistically combined, yields similar general conclusions. Furthermore, a large-scale survey of 186,000 individuals found that although survey respondents felt they had benefited substantially from psychotherapy (see Figure 17-3), there was little difference in "consumer satisfaction" based on the specific type of treatment they had received ("Mental Health," 1995; M.E.P. Seligman, 1995; Strupp, 1996).

In short, converging evidence allows us to draw several conclusions about the effectiveness of psychotherapy (Strupp & Binder, 1992; Seligman, 1996):

- *For most people, psychotherapy is effective.* This conclusion holds over different lengths of treatment, specific kinds of psychological disorders, and types of treatment. Thus, the question "Does psychotherapy work?" appears to be convincingly answered: It does (Lipsey & Wilson, 1993; Seligman, 1996; Spiegel, 1999).
- *On the other hand, psychotherapy doesn't work for everyone.* As many as 10 percent of people show no improvement or actually deteriorate following treatment (Lambert, Shapiro, & Bergin, 1986; Luborsky, 1988).
- *Certain specific types of treatments are somewhat, although not invariably, better for specific types of problems.* For example, cognitive therapy works particularly well for panic disorders, and systematic desensitization relieves specific phobias quite effectively. However, there are many exceptions, and often the differences in success rates for different types of treatment are not substantial (Hubble, Duncan, & Miller, 1999; Miller & Magruder, 1999).
- *No single form of therapy works best on every problem.* Consequently, there is no definitive answer to the question "Which therapy works best?"— nor will one be found soon, due to the difficulties in sorting out the various

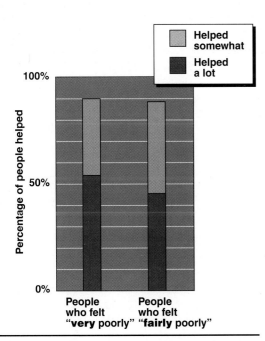

Figure 17-3 A large-scale survey of 186,000 individuals found that while the respondents had benefited substantially from psychotherapy, there was little difference in "consumer satisfaction" based on the specific type of treatment they had received.

Source: "Mental Health: Does Therapy Help?" 1995.

Applying Psychology in the 21st Century

Virtual Therapy: Is the World Wide Web a Good Place to Get Treatment?

When the mayor of a small Midwestern town and his wife decided they needed marriage counseling, they were wary of seeking out a local therapist, for fear of gossip. So without ever leaving their home, they turned to the place where millions of anonymous business and personal transactions take place each day: the Internet.

The couple's cybersearch eventually landed them in the All Rivers Online Christian Counseling Center, where they plugged in their credit card number and began engaging in e-mail counseling with a psychologist who billed himself as "Dr. Ralph." (Almer, 2000, p. A1)

With people increasingly comfortable turning to the World Wide Web to find everything from new CDs to new friends, why not a therapist?

Although the number of people who are being treated today using online therapy is small, it is a growing trend. And as various technologies become more advanced and affordable, including the development of inexpensive, high-quality two-way video links over the Web (something that likely will occur in the next few years), experts predict that incidence of online therapy will grow (Jerome et al., 2000).

Most online therapy occurs primarily through e-mail. Therapists and patients exchange messages, which are sometimes supplemented with telephone calls. For people like the town mayor and his wife, online therapy can provide the treatment they need, without risking their privacy.

Proponents of virtual therapy suggest it will open new avenues of treatment to people with psychological disorders. Those who live in remote areas can receive treatment, as can those who are disabled, concerned with privacy, or too embarrassed to seek out local providers ("Advances in Telepsychology/Telehealth," 2000; Jerome et al., 2000).

Despite its potential advantages, e-mail therapy has many critics. Because therapists are unable to see and hear those coming for therapy, they lack the valuable information provided by clients' nonverbal behavior. Furthermore, virtual clients can misrepresent themselves more easily than they could in face-to-face communication. Although the advent of video links will reduce the possibility of such deception, it will remain a problem when patients are physically distant from their therapist. Finally, privacy concerns are real; no one is able to guarantee that highly personal information shared on the Web will not be open to computer hackers (Almer, 2000).

An even greater problem for people seeking therapy online is that there is no procedure for licensing individuals who decide to provide treatment. *Anyone* can call himself or herself a therapist and start providing therapy—and collecting money—from potential patients. In addition, no large-scale research studies have found that online therapy is effective, and research is only now being conducted to answer the question (Sleek, 1995; Grohol, 1997; Rabasca, 2000).

Despite these drawbacks, online therapy in one form or another is likely to become a common option for people seeking treatment for psychological disorders. Whether it becomes routine—and is as effective as traditional face-to-face therapy—remains to be seen.

Do you think people are likely to be more honest or less honest when discussing their problems with an online therapist, as compared with an in-person therapist? What kinds of patients do you think are most likely to find online therapy appealing? Why?

factors that enter into the success of therapy. Furthermore, new types of therapy continue to emerge (see, for example, the *Applying Psychology in the 21st Century* box for a discussion of online therapy), making it difficult to draw sweeping conclusions about treatment effectiveness.

Because no one type of psychotherapy is invariably effective, eclectic approaches to therapy have become increasingly popular. In an **eclectic approach to therapy,** a therapist uses a variety of techniques, integrating several perspectives, to treat a person's problems. The eclectic therapist can choose a mix of treatment procedures appropriate to the specific needs of the individual. Furthermore, therapists with certain personal characteristics might work better with particular individuals and types of treatments, and—as we consider next—even racial and ethnic factors might be related to the success of treatment (Roth & Fonagy, 1996; Cheston, 2000).

eclectic approach to therapy: An approach to therapy that uses techniques taken from a variety of treatment methods, rather than just one method

EXPLORING DIVERSITY

Racial and Ethnic Factors in Treatment: Should Therapists Be Color-Blind?

Consider the following description, written by a school counselor about Jimmy Jones, a 12-year-old student who was referred to a counselor because of his disinterest in schoolwork:

Jimmy does not pay attention, daydreams often, and frequently falls asleep during class. There is a strong possibility that Jimmy is harboring repressed rage that needs to be ventilated and dealt with. His inability to directly express his anger had led him to

Treatment for psychological disorders must take into account the individual's environmental, cultural, and socioeconomic background. What are the potential dangers in not considering these factors when providing treatment?

PsychLinks

Minorities and psychotherapy
www.mhhe.com/
feldmanup6-17links

adopt passive aggressive means of expressing hostility, i.e., inattentiveness, daydreaming, falling asleep. It is recommended that Jimmy be seen for intensive counseling to discover the basis of the anger. (Sue & Sue, 1990, p. 44)

The counselor was wrong, however. Rather than suffering from "repressed rage," Jimmy lived in a poverty-stricken and disorganized home. Because of the overcrowding at his house, he did not get enough sleep and consequently was tired in the daytime. Frequently, he was also hungry. In short, his problems were due largely to the stresses arising from his environment and not to any deep-seated psychological disturbances.

This incident underscores the importance of taking people's environmental and cultural backgrounds into account during treatment for psychological disorders. In particular, members of racial and ethnic minority groups, especially those who are also poor, might behave in ways that help them deal with a society that discriminates against them. As a consequence, behavior that might signal psychological disorder in middle- and upper-class whites might simply be adaptive among people of other racial and socioeconomic groups. For instance, people who are characteristically suspicious and distrustful might be displaying a survival strategy to protect themselves from psychological and physical injury, rather than suffering from a psychological disturbance (Sue & Sue, 1990; Aponte & Wohl, 2000).

In fact, some of the most basic assumptions of psychotherapy must be questioned when dealing with members of racial, ethnic, and cultural minority groups. For example, compared with the dominant U.S. culture, Asian and Latino cultures typically place much greater emphasis on the group, family, and society. When critical decisions are to be made, the family helps make them—suggesting that family members should play a role in psychological treatment. Similarly, when traditional Chinese men and women feel depressed or anxious, they are urged by others to avoid thinking about whatever is upsetting them. Consider how this advice contrasts with the view of treatment approaches that emphasize the value of insight (Okun, 1996; Kleinman & Cohen, 1997; Ponterotto et al., 2001).

Consequently, therapists *cannot* be "color-blind." Instead, they must take into account the racial, ethnic, cultural, and social class backgrounds of their clients in determining the nature of a psychological disorder and the course of treatment (Sue, 1998; Ariel, 1999; Aponte & Wohl, 2000).

Evaluate

1. Match each of the following treatment strategies with the statement you might expect to hear from a therapist using that strategy.

   1. Gestalt therapy

   2. Group therapy

   3. Unconditional positive regard

   4. Behavioral therapy

   5. Nondirective counseling

   a. "In other words, you don't get along with your mother because she hates your girlfriend, is that right?"

   b. "I want you all to take turns talking about why you decided to come, and what you hope to gain from therapy."

   c. "I can understand why you wanted to wreck your friend's car after she hurt your feelings. Now, tell me more about the accident."

   d. "That's not appropriate behavior. Let's work on replacing it with something else."

   e. "Remember the anger you felt and scream until you feel better."

2. _____ therapies assume people should take responsibility for their lives and the decisions they make.

3. _____ therapy emphasizes the integration of thoughts, feelings, and behaviors.

4. One of the major criticisms of humanistic therapies is that:

   a. they are too imprecise and unstructured.

   b. they treat only the symptom of the problem.

   c. the therapist dominates the patient-therapist interaction.

   d. it works well only on clients of lower socioeconomic status.

5. In a controversial study, Eysenck found that some people go into _____ _____, or recovery without treatment, if they are simply left alone instead of treated.

6. Treatments that combine techniques from all the theoretical approaches are called _____ procedures.

Answers to Evaluate Questions

1. 1–e; 2–b; 3–c; 4–d; 5–a 2. Humanistic 3. Gestalt 4. a 5. spontaneous remission 6. eclectic

Rethink

1. How can people be successfully treated in group therapy when individuals with the "same" problem are so different? What advantages might group therapy offer over individual therapy?

2. List some examples of behavior that might be considered abnormal by members of one cultural or economic group and normal by members of a different cultural or economic group. Suppose that most therapies had been developed by psychologists from minority culture groups and lower socioeconomic status; how might they differ from current therapies?

Biomedical Therapy: Biological Approaches to Treatment

If you get a kidney infection, you're given an antibiotic and, with luck, about a week later your kidney is as good as new. If your appendix becomes inflamed, a surgeon removes it and soon your body functions normally once more. Could a comparable approach, focusing on the body's physiology, be taken with psychological disturbances?

According to biological approaches to treatment, the answer is yes. Biomedical therapies are used routinely. The approach suggests that rather than focusing on a patient's psychological conflicts or past traumas, or on environmental factors that might produce abnormal behavior, it can be more appropriate to focus treatment on brain chemistry and other neurological factors directly. This can be done through the use of drugs, electric shock, or surgery.

Prepare

How are drug, electroconvulsive, and psychosurgical techniques used today in the treatment of psychological disorders?

Organize

Biomedical Therapy
Drug Therapy
Electroconvulsive Therapy (ECT)
Psychosurgery
Biomedical Therapies in Perspective
Community Psychology

Drug Therapy

Drug therapy, the control of psychological disorders through drugs, works by altering the operation of neurotransmitters and neurons in the brain. Some drugs operate by inhibiting neurotransmitters or receptor neurons, thus reducing activity at particular

drug therapy: Control of psychological problems through drugs

Table 17-3 Drug Treatments

Class of Drug	Effects of Drug	Primary Action of Drug	Examples
ANTIPSYCHOTIC DRUGS	Reduction in loss of touch with reality, agitation	Block dopamine receptors	Chlorpromazine (Thorazine) Clozapine (Clozaril)
ANTIDEPRESSANT DRUGS			
Tricyclic antidepressants	Reduction in depression	Permits rise in neurotransmitters such as norepinepherine	Trazodone (Desyrel), Amitriptyline (Elavil), Desipramine (Norpamin)
MAO inhibitors	Reduction in depression	Prevent MAO from breaking down neurotransmitters	Phenelzine (Nardil)
Selective serotonin reuptake inhibitors	Reduction in depression	Inhibit reuptake of serotonin	Fluoxetine (Prozac), Luvox, Paxil, Celexa, Zoloft, Nefazodone (Serzone)
MOOD STABILIZERS			
Lithium	Mood stabilizer	Can alter transmission of impulses within neurons	Lithium (Lithonate), Depakote, Tegretol
ANTIANXIETY DRUGS	Reduction in anxiety	Increase activity of neurotransmitter GABA	Benzodiazepines (Valium, Xanax)

synapses, the sites where nerve impulses travel from one neuron to another (as first discussed in Chapter 3). Other drugs do just the opposite: They increase the activity of certain neurotransmitters or neurons, allowing particular neurons to fire more frequently. The major drugs are described below and summarized in Table 17-3.

Antipsychotic Drugs

Probably no greater change has occurred in mental hospitals than the successful introduction in the mid 1950s of **antipsychotic drugs**—drugs used to reduce severe symptoms of disturbance, such as loss of touch with reality and agitation. Previously, the typical mental hospital fulfilled all the stereotypes of the insane asylum, with screaming, moaning, clawing patients displaying the most bizarre behaviors. Suddenly, in just a matter of days, the hospital wards became considerably calmer environments in which professionals could do more than just try to get the patients through the day without causing serious harm to themselves or others.

This dramatic change was brought about by the introduction of a drug called *chlorpromazine.* This drug, and others of a similar nature, rapidly became the most popular and successful treatment for schizophrenia. Today drug therapy is the preferred treatment for most cases of severely abnormal behavior and, as such, is used for most hospitalized patients with psychological disorders. For instance, the drug *clozapine* represents the current generation of antipsychotics (Wallis & Willwerth, 1992; Rosenheck et al., 1997).

How do antipsychotic drugs work? Most operate by blocking the dopamine receptors at the brain's synapses. Some newer drugs, like clozapine, increases dopamine levels in certain parts of the brain, such as those related to planning and goal-directed activity (Mrzljak et al., 1996; Moghaddam & Adams, 1998).

Despite the effectiveness of antipsychotic drugs, they do not produce a "cure" in the same way that, say, penicillin cures an infection. As soon as the drug is withdrawn, the original symptoms tend to reappear. Furthermore, such drugs can have long-term side effects, such as dryness of the mouth and throat, dizziness, and sometimes tremors and loss of muscle control that might continue even after drug treatments are stopped (Shriqui & Annable, 1995).

antipsychotic drugs: Drugs that temporarily reduce psychotic symptoms such as agitation, overactivity, hallucinations, and delusions

PsychLink
Information on medications
www.mhhe.com/
feldmanup6-17links

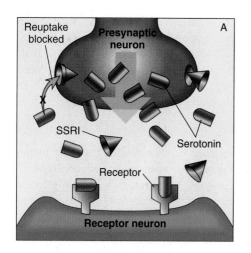
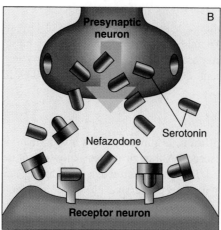

Figure 17-4 In *(a)*, selective serotonin reuptake inhibitors (SSRIs) reduce depression by permitting the neurotransmitter serotonin to remain in the synapse. In *(b)*, a newer antidepressant, Nefazodone (Serzone), operates more selectively, blocking serotonin at certain sites but not others, helping to reduce the side effects of the drug.

From "Antidepressants: Choices and Controversy," by D. Mischoulon. Copyright © 2000, Massachusetts Medical Society. All rights reserved.

Antidepressant Drugs

As you might guess from the name, **antidepressant drugs** are a class of medications used in cases of severe depression to improve patients' mood. They were discovered quite by accident: It was found that patients suffering from tuberculosis who were given the drug iproniazid suddenly became happier and more optimistic. When the same drug was tested on people suffering from depression, a similar result occurred, and drugs became an accepted form of treatment for depression (Shuchter, Downs, & Zisook, 1996).

Most antidepressant drugs work by changing the concentration of particular neurotransmitters. For example, *tricyclic drugs* increase the availability of norepinepherine at the synapses of neurons, whereas *MAO inhibitors* prevent the enzyme monoamine oxidase (MAO) from breaking down neurotransmitters. Newer antidepressants, *selective serotonin reuptake inhibitors (SSRIs),* target the neurotransmitter serotonin, permitting it to linger at the synapse. One of the latest antidepressants, Nefazodone (Serzone), blocks serotonin at some receptor sites but not others (see Figure 17-4; Berman, Krystal, & Charney, 1996; J.W. Williams et al., 2000).

Although antidepressant drugs can produce side effects such as drowsiness and faintness, their overall success rate is quite good. Unlike antipsychotic drugs, antidepressants can produce lasting, long-term recoveries from depression. In many cases, even after patients stop taking the drugs, their depression does not return (Spiegel, 1989; Julien, 1995; Zito, 1993).

Antidepressant drugs have become some of the most heavily prescribed of all drugs. Billions of dollars are spent each year on antidepressants, and sales are increasing at a rate of more than 20 percent a year. In particular, the antidepressant *Fluoxetine,* sold under the trade name *Prozac,* has been highlighted on magazine covers and been the topic of best-sellers.

Does Prozac deserve its acclaim? In some respects, yes. Despite its high cost— each daily dose costs more than $2—it has significantly improved the lives of thousands of depressed individuals. Compared to other antidepressants, Prozac (along with its cousins Luvox, Paxil, Celexa, and Zoloft) has relatively few side effects. Furthermore, many people who do not respond to other types of antidepressants do well on Prozac. On the other hand, like all drugs, Prozac does not agree with everyone. For example, 20 to 30 percent of users report experiencing nausea and diarrhea, and a smaller percentage report sexual dysfunctions (Kramer, 1993; Glenmullen, 2000).

Another drug that has received a great deal of publicity is *St. John's wort,* an herb that has been likened to a "natural" antidepressant. Widely used in Europe for the treatment of depression, the substance is considered a dietary supplement in the United States and therefore is available without a prescription.

antidepressant drugs: Medication that improves a depressed patient's mood and feeling of well-being

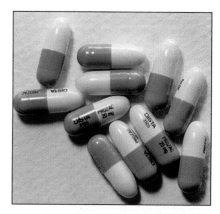

Prozac is a widely prescribed—but still controversial—antidepressant.

Despite its popularity, the jury is still out on the effectiveness of St. John's wort. Although the American College of Physicians has supported the use of the herb in treating mild, short-term depression, the most recent and carefully-designed study found the drug useless in treating depression, making its use problematic (Nierenberg, 1998b; Maidment, 2000; J.W. Williams et al., 2000; Shelton et al., 2001).

Lithium

lithium: A mineral salt used to treat bipolar disorders

Lithium, a mineral salt, is a drug that has been used very successfully to treat bipolar disorder. Although no one knows definitely why, it and other drugs such as *Depakote* and *Tegretol* are effective in reducing manic episodes. However, they are not effective in treating depressive phases of bipolar disorder, and antidepressants are usually prescribed during these phases (Dubovsky, 1999).

Lithium and drugs similar to it have a quality that sets them apart from other drug treatments: They can be a *preventive* treatment, blocking future episodes of bipolar disorder. Many people who have had episodes of bipolar disorder in the past can prevent a recurrence of their symptoms by taking a daily dose of lithium. In contrast, most other drugs are useful only after symptoms of psychological disturbance occur.

Antianxiety Drugs

antianxiety drugs: Drugs that can reduce a person's level of anxiety, essentially by reducing excitability and increasing feelings of well-being

As the name implies, **antianxiety drugs** reduce the level of anxiety a person experiences and increasing feelings of well-being. They are used not only to reduce general tension in people who are experiencing temporary difficulties but also to aid in the treatment of more serious anxiety disorders (Zito, 1993).

Antianxiety drugs such as Xanax and Valium are among the medications most frequently prescribed by physicians. In fact, more than half of all U.S. families have someone who has taken such a drug at one time or another.

Although the popularity of antianxiety drugs suggests that they hold few risks, they can produce a number of potentially serious side effects. For instance, they can cause fatigue, and long-term use can lead to dependence. Moreover, taken in combination with alcohol, some antianxiety drugs can become lethal. But a more important issue concerns their use to suppress anxiety. Almost every therapeutic approach to psychological disturbance views continuing anxiety as a signal of some sort of problem. Thus, drugs that mask anxiety can simply be hiding difficulties. Consequently, people who use antianxiety drugs might simply be hiding from, rather than confronting, their underlying problems.

◯◯ PsychLink

Information on ECT
www.mhhe.com/
feldmanup6-17links

Electroconvulsive Therapy (ECT)

Martha Manning had contemplated all kinds of suicide—by pills, hanging, even guns. Her depression was so deep that she lived each minute "afraid I [wouldn't] make it to the next hour." But she balked when her therapist recommended electroconvulsive therapy, commonly known as "shock treatment." Despite her training and practice as a clinical psychologist, Manning immediately flashed to scenes from *One Flew Over the Cuckoo's Nest,* "with McMurphy and the Chief jolted with electroshock, their bodies flailing with each jolt" (Guttman, 1995, p. 16).

The reality, it turned out, was quite different. Although it did produce some memory loss and temporary headaches, the procedure also brought Manning back from the brink of suicide.

electroconvulsive therapy (ECT): A procedure in which an electric current of 70 to 150 volts is briefly administered to a patient's head, causing a loss of consciousness and often seizures

First introduced in the 1930s, **electroconvulsive therapy (ECT)** is a procedure in which an electric current of 70 to 150 volts is briefly administered to a patient's head, causing a loss of consciousness and often seizures. Usually the patient is sedated and receives muscle relaxants prior to administration of the current, to reduce the intensity of muscle contractions produced during ECT. The typical patient receives about ten such

treatments in the course of a month, but some patients continue with maintenance treatments for months afterward (Nierenberg, 1998a; Fink, 1999).

ECT is a controversial technique. Apart from the obvious distastefulness of a treatment that evokes images of electrocution, ECT has frequent side effects. For instance, following treatment patients often experience disorientation, confusion, and sometimes memory loss that can last for months. Furthermore, many patients fear ECT, even though they are anesthetized during the treatment and thus experience no pain. Finally, we still do not know why ECT works, and critics suggest that the treatment can produce permanent brain damage (Fisher, 1985; Valente, 1991).

Given the drawbacks to ECT, why is it used at all? The basic reason is that for many severe cases of depression it is the only quickly effective treatment. For instance, it can prevent depressed, suicidal individuals from committing suicide, and it can act more quickly than antidepressive medications. In fact, the use of ECT has risen in the last decade, with more than 100,000 people undergoing ECT each year. Still, ECT tends to be used only when other treatments have proved ineffective (APA Task Force, 1990; Sackheim et al., 1996; Fink, 2000).

Psychosurgery

If ECT strikes you as a questionable procedure, the use of **psychosurgery**—brain surgery in which the object is to reduce symptoms of mental disorder—is likely to appear even more so. A technique that is used only rarely today, psychosurgery was first introduced as a "treatment of last resort" in the 1930s.

The first form of psychosurgery, *prefrontal lobotomy,* consisted of surgically destroying or removing parts of a patient's frontal lobes that were thought to control emotionality. In the 1930s and 1940s, the procedure was performed on thousands of patients, often with little precision. For example, in one common technique, a surgeon would jab an ice pick under a patient's eyeball and swivel it back and forth (Miller, 1994).

Such psychosurgery often did improve a patient's behavior—but not without drastic side effects. For along with remission of symptoms of mental disorder, some patients suffered personality changes, becoming bland, colorless, and unemotional. Other patients became aggressive and unable to control their impulses. In the worst cases, treatment killed the patient.

With the introduction of effective drug treatments—and the obvious ethical questions regarding the appropriateness of forever altering someone's personality—psychosurgery became nearly obsolete. However, it is still used in very rare cases when all other procedures have failed and the patient's behavior presents a high risk to self and others. Today, a more precise form of psychosurgery called a *cingulotomy* is sometimes employed in rare cases of obsessive-compulsive disorder. Psychosurgery is also occasionally used in dying patients with severe, uncontrollable pain. Still, even these cases raise important ethical issues, and psychosurgery remains a highly controversial treatment (Miller, 1994; Baer et al., 1995; Jenike, 1998).

Biomedical Therapies in Perspective: Can Abnormal Behavior Be Cured?

In some respects, there has been no greater revolution in the field of mental health than that represented by the biological approaches to treatment. As previously violent, uncontrollable patients have been calmed by the use of drugs, mental hospitals have been able to concentrate more on actually helping patients and less on custodial functions. Similarly, patients whose lives have been disrupted by depression or bipolar episodes have been able to function normally, and other forms of drug therapy have also shown remarkable results.

On the other hand, biomedical therapies are not without their detractors. For one thing, critics charge that they merely provide relief from the *symptoms* of mental disorder; as soon as the drugs are withdrawn, the symptoms return. Although it is considered a major step in the right direction, biomedical treatment might not solve the underlying problems that led a patient to therapy in the first place. Moreover, biomedical therapies

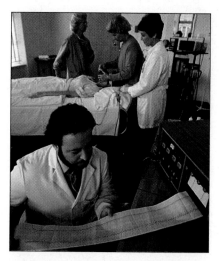

Dr. Richard B. Weiner of Duke University Medical Center reads a patient's electroencephalogram as technicians administer electroconvulsive therapy. ECT is a controversial treatment, but it does help some people whose severe depression has not responded to other approaches.

psychosurgery: Brain surgery once used to reduce symptoms of mental disorder but rarely used today

While deinstitutionalization has had many successes, it has also contributed to the release of mental patients into the community with little or no support. As a result many have become homeless.

community psychology: A branch of psychology that focuses on the prevention and minimization of psychological disorders in the community

deinstitutionalization: The transfer of former mental patients from institutions into the community

can produce side effects, ranging from physical reactions to the development of *new* symptoms of abnormal behavior. For these reasons, then, biologically based treatment approaches are not a cure-all for psychological disorders.

Community Psychology: A Focus on Prevention

Each of the treatments that we have reviewed in this chapter has a common element: It is a "restorative" treatment, aimed at alleviating psychological difficulties that already exist. However, an approach known as **community psychology** is geared toward a different aim: to prevent or minimize the incidence of psychological disorders.

Community psychology came of age in the 1960s, when plans were developed for a nationwide network of community mental health centers. These centers were meant to provide low-cost mental health services, including short-term therapy and community educational programs. Moreover, during the last three decades the population of mental hospitals has plunged, as drug treatments have made physical restraint of patients unnecessary. The movement of former mental patients out of institutions and into the community—a process known as **deinstitutionalization**—further spurred the community psychology movement. Proponents of deinstitutionalization were concerned with ensuring not only that deinstitutionalized patients received proper treatment but also that their civil rights were maintained (Melton & Garrison, 1987).

Unfortunately, the goals of community psychology have not been met. Deinstitutionalization has failed in significant ways. What started as a worthy attempt to move people out of mental institutions into the community ended, in many cases, with former patients being dumped into the community without any real support. Many became homeless, and some became involved in illegal acts, such as robberies, caused by their disorders. In short, many people who need treatment do not get it, and in some cases care for people with psychological disorders has simply shifted from one type of treatment site to another (Kiesler & Simpkins, 1993; Torrey, 1996, 1997).

On the other hand, the community psychology movement has had some positive outcomes. Telephone "hot lines" are now common. At any time of the day or night, people experiencing acute stress can call a trained, sympathetic listener who can provide immediate—although obviously limited—treatment (Boehm et al., 1995; Blewett, 2000).

College and high school crisis centers are another innovation that grew out of the community psychology movement. Modeled after suicide prevention hot-line centers (places for potential suicide victims to call and speak to someone about their difficulties), crisis centers provide callers with the opportunity to discuss life crises with a sympathetic listener, who is often a volunteer.

BECOMING AN INFORMED CONSUMER OF PSYCHOLOGY

Choosing the Right Therapist

If you make the decision to seek therapy, you're faced with a daunting task. Choosing a therapist is no simple matter. One place to start the process of identifying a therapist is at the "Help Center" of the American Psychological Association at http://helping.apa.org/, or at 1-800-964-2000. And if you start therapy, the following general guidelines can help you determine whether you've made the right choice:

- *You and your therapist should agree on the goals for treatment.* They should be clear, specific, and attainable.
- *You should feel comfortable with your therapist.* You should not be intimidated by, or in awe of, a therapist. Instead, you should trust the therapist and feel free to discuss even the most personal issues without fearing a negative reaction. In sum, the "personal chemistry" should feel right.
- *Therapists should have appropriate training and credentials and should be licensed by appropriate state and local agencies.* Check therapists' membership in national

"Looking good!"

and state professional associations. In addition, the cost of therapy, billing practices, and other business matters should be clear at the outset. It is no breach of etiquette to get these matters out on the table during an initial consultation.

- *You should feel that you are making progress after therapy has begun, despite occasional setbacks.* If you have no sense of improvement after repeated visits, this issue should be frankly discussed. Although there is no set timetable, the most obvious changes resulting from therapy tend to occur relatively early in the course of treatment. For instance, half of patients in psychotherapy improve by the eighth session and three-fourths by the twenty-sixth session (see Figure 17-5). The average number of sessions with college students is just five (Crits-Cristoph, 1992; Brief Psychodynamic Therapy, 1994; Lazarus, 1997).

You should be aware that you will have to put in a great deal of effort in therapy. Although ours is a culture that promises quick cures for any problem, the reality is that solving difficult problems is not easy. People must be committed to making therapy work and should know that it is they, and not the therapist, who must do most of the work to resolve their problems. The potential is there for the effort to pay off handsomely—therapy can lead to a more positive, fulfilling, and meaningful life.

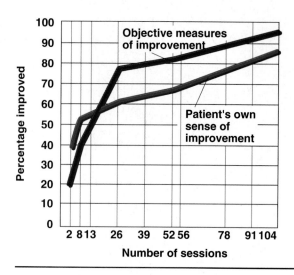

Figure 17-5 For most patients improvements in psychological functioning occur relatively early after therapy has begun.

Source: Howard et al., 1986.

PsychLink

Choosing a therapist
www.mhhe.com/
feldmanup6-17links

Evaluate

1. Antipsychotic drugs have provided effective, long-term, and complete cures for schizophrenia. True or false?
2. One of the most effective biomedical treatments for psychological disorders, used mainly to arrest and prevent manic-depressive episodes, is
   a. chlorpromazine.
   b. lithium.
   c. Librium.
   d. Valium.
3. Psychosurgery has grown in popularity as a method of treatment as surgical techniques have become more precise. True or false?
4. The trend toward releasing more patients from mental hospitals into the community is known as _____.

Answers to Evaluate Questions

1. False; schizophrenia can be controlled, but not cured, by medication. 2. b 3. False; psychosurgery is now used only as a treatment of last resort. 4. deinstitutionalization

Rethink

1. One of the main criticisms of biological therapies is that they treat the symptoms of mental disorders without uncovering and treating the underlying problems from which people are suffering. Do you agree with this criticism or not? Why?
2. If a dangerously violent person could be "cured" of violence through a new psychosurgical technique, would you approve the use of this technique? Suppose the person agreed to—or requested—the technique? What sort of policy would you develop for the use of psychosurgery?

Looking Back

What are the goals of psychologically and biologically based treatment approaches?

- Psychotherapy (psychologically based therapy) and biomedical therapy (biologically based therapy) share the goal of resolving psychological problems by modifying people's thoughts, feelings, expectations, evaluations, and ultimately their behavior. (p. 504)

What are the basic kinds of psychotherapies?

- Psychoanalytic treatment, based on Freud's psychodynamic theory, seeks to bring unresolved past conflicts and unacceptable impulses from the unconscious into the conscious, where the problems can be dealt with more effectively. This involves using techniques such as free association and dream interpretation. (p. 505)
- Behavioral approaches to treatment view abnormal behavior itself as the problem, rather than viewing the behavior as a symptom of some underlying cause. To bring about a "cure," according to this view, the outward behavior must be changed. To do this, behavioral approaches use aversive conditioning, systematic desensitization, observational learning, token systems, and contingency contracting. (p. 507)
- Cognitive approaches to treatment see the goal of therapy as a restructuring of a person's belief system into a more realistic, rational, and logical view of the world. (p. 510)

What are humanistic approaches to treatment?

- Humanistic therapy is based on the premise that people have control over their behavior, that they can make choices about their lives, and that it is up to them to solve their own problems. Humanistic therapies, which take a nondirective approach, include client-centered therapy and gestalt therapy. (p. 512)

How does group therapy differ from individual types of therapy?

- In group therapy, several people meet with a therapist to discuss some aspect of their psychological functioning, often centering on a common problem. (p. 514)

How effective is therapy, and which kind of therapy works best in a given situation?

- Most research suggests that, in general, therapy is more effective than no therapy, although how much more effective is not known. (p. 515)
- The answer to the more difficult question of which therapy works best is even less clear. However, particular kinds of therapy are more appropriate for some problems than for others. (p. 516)

How are drug, electroconvulsive, and psychosurgical techniques used today in the treatment of psychological disorders?

- Biological treatment approaches focus on the physiological causes of abnormal behavior, rather than considering psychological factors. Drug therapy, the best example of biomedical treatments, has dramatically reduced the symptoms of mental disturbance. (p. 519)
- Antipsychotic drugs such as chlorpromazine are very effective in reducing psychotic symptoms. Antidepressant drugs, such as Prozac, reduce depression so successfully that they are very widely used. The antianxiety drugs, or minor tranquilizers, are among the most frequently prescribed medications. (p. 520)

- In electroconvulsive therapy (ECT), used only in severe cases of depression, an electric current of 70 to 150 volts is briefly administered to a patient. (p. 522)
- Psychosurgery consists of surgically destroying parts of the brain. (p. 523)
- Community psychology was the stimulus for deinstitutionalization, in which previously hospitalized mental patients were released into the community. (p. 524)

Key Terms and Concepts

psychotherapy (p. 504)
biomedical therapy (p. 504)
psychodynamic therapy (p. 504)
psychoanalysis (p. 505)
behavioral treatment approaches (p. 507)
systematic desensitization (p. 508)
cognitive treatment approaches (p. 510)
cognitive-behavioral approach (p. 510)
rational-emotive behavior therapy (p. 511)
humanistic therapy (p. 513)
client-centered therapy (p. 513)
gestalt therapy (p. 514)
group therapy (p. 514)

family therapy (p. 514)
spontaneous remission (p. 515)
eclectic approach to therapy (p. 517)
drug therapy (p. 519)
antipsychotic drugs (p. 520)
antidepressant drugs (p. 521)
lithium (p. 522)
antianxiety drugs (p. 522)
electroconvulsive therapy (ECT) (p. 522)
psychosurgery (p. 523)
community psychology (p. 524)
deinstitutionalization (p. 524)

Preview

For additional quizzing and a variety of interactive resources, visit the *Understanding Psychology* Online Learning Center at

www.mhhe.com/feldmanup6

Psychology on the Web

1. Find out more about computer-assisted psychotherapy on the Web. Locate (1) a computerized therapy program, such as ELIZA, that offers "therapy" over the Internet, and (2) a report on "cybertherapy," by which therapists use the Web to interact with patients. Compare the two, describing how each one works.
2. Find more information on the Web about deinstitutionalization. Try to find pro and con arguments for it and summarize the arguments, including your judgment of the effectiveness and advisability of deinstitutionalization.

Epilogue

In this chapter we have examined how psychological professionals treat people with psychological disorders. We considered a range of approaches, including both psychologically based and biologically based therapies. It is clear that substantial progress has been made in recent years, both in terms of treating the symptoms of mental disorders and in understanding their underlying causes.

Before we leave the topic of psychological disorders, turn back to the Prologue, which describes Mike Wallace's liberation from his depression, and consider the following questions.

1. Are people who must take drugs for the rest of their lives in order to avoid the symptoms of depression truly cured? Why or why not?
2. How and why has the social climate changed so that people who suffer from depression, like Mike Wallace, no longer feel compelled to hide the fact that they are taking drugs for the disorder?
3. Do you think that the fact that the rates of depression are considerably higher for women than men contributed to Wallace's initial reluctance to admit to his disorder?
4. Do you think that people who recover from depression can easily reenter the world and take up their lives as if nothing had happened to them? What sorts of adjustments might people have to make?

Chapter Eighteen

Social
Psychology

Prologue: A Modern Lynching

Looking Ahead

Attitudes and Social Cognition

Persuasion: Changing Attitudes

Psychology at Work: Ann Altman, Advertising Executive

Social Cognition: Understanding Others

Exploring Diversity: Attributions in a Cultural Context: How Fundamental Is the Fundamental Attribution Error?

Social Influence

Conformity: Following What Others Do

Compliance: Submitting to Direct Social Pressure

Obedience: Obeying Direct Orders

Applying Psychology in the 21st Century: Reading Your Mind, Reaching Your Wallet: Using Computer Technology to Increase Compliance

Prejudice and Discrimination

The Foundations of Prejudice

Working to End Prejudice and Discrimination

Positive and Negative Social Behavior

Liking and Loving: Interpersonal Attraction and the Development of Relationships

Aggression and Prosocial Behavior: Hurting and Helping Others

Becoming an Informed Consumer of Psychology: Dealing with Anger Effectively

Looking Back

Key Terms and Concepts

Psychology on the Web

OLC Preview

Epilogue

Prologue

A Modern Lynching

Ross Byrd, left, and Renee Mullins, children of murder victim James Byrd, Jr., mourn his loss.

When police in a small Texas town responded to a report of a dead body, first they found James Byrd's headless torso. Then, following a trail of blood, they found his head a mile away, and then his right arm, and then other parts of his body.

Byrd—by all accounts a gentle and peaceful soul—had taken a ride through hell, in which he was chained to the back of a pickup truck and dragged for miles by three white supremacists. Pathologists would later report that Byrd had probably been conscious for the start of his journey, until his head was torn from his body.

Byrd's crime, in the eyes of his killers: He was African American.

Looking Ahead

The hatred and violence shown by Byrd's killers are extreme examples of prejudice and discrimination. Yet many people are the targets of verbal and physical aggression, as well as other forms of discrimination, simply because of their race, ethnicity, sexual preference, physical disability, or other characteristics that somehow set them apart from others.

Why do some people develop, and act on, prejudice? What processes shape the development of such attitudes? How can we improve social conditions to help people live together in harmony?

Each of these questions can be answered only by taking into account findings from the field of social psychology, the branch of psychology that focuses on those aspects of human behavior that unite—and separate—us from one another. **Social psychology** is the study of how people's thoughts, feelings, and actions are affected by others. Social psychologists consider the nature and causes of individual behavior in social situations.

The broad scope of social psychology is conveyed by the kinds of questions social psychologists ask, such as these: How can we convince people to change their attitudes or to adopt new ideas and values? How do we come to understand what others are like? How are we influenced by what others do and think? Why do some people display such violence, aggression, and cruelty toward others that people throughout the world live in fear of annihilation at their hands? And why, on the other hand, do some people place their own lives at risk to help others?

In this chapter, we explore social psychological approaches to these and other issues. Not only do we examine the processes that underlie social behavior, we also discuss strategies for confronting and solving a variety of problems and issues that all of us face—ranging from achieving a better understanding of persuasive tactics to forming more accurate impressions of others.

We begin with a look at how our attitudes shape our behavior, and how we form judgments about others. We'll discuss how we are influenced by others, and we will consider prejudice and discrimination, focusing on their roots and how they can be reduced. After examining what social psychologists have learned about the ways people form friendships and relationships, the chapter concludes with a look at the determinants of aggression and helping.

social psychology: The study of how people's thoughts, feelings, and actions are affected by others

attitudes: Learned predispositions to respond in a favorable or unfavorable manner to a particular person, behavior, belief, or thing

Prepare

What are attitudes and how are they formed, maintained, and changed?

How do we form impressions of what others are like and of the causes of their behavior?

What biases influence how we view others' behavior?

Organize

Attitudes and Social Cognition
  Persuasion
  Social Cognition

 **PsychLink**

Attitudes
www.mhhe.com/
feldmanup6-18links

Attitudes and Social Cognition

What do Tiger Woods, Rosie O'Donnell, and Bill Cosby have in common?

Each appears in television commercials designed to mold or change our attitudes. Such commercials are part of the barrage of messages we receive each day—from sources as varied as politicians, sales staff in stores, and celebrities—all meant to influence us.

Persuasion: Changing Attitudes

Persuasion is the process of changing attitudes, one of the central concepts of social psychology. **Attitudes** are learned predispositions to respond in a favorable or unfavorable manner to a particular person, behavior, belief, or thing (Eagly & Chaiken, 1993, 1995).

The ease with which attitudes can be changed depends on a number of factors, including these:

- *Message source.* The characteristics of a person who delivers a persuasive message, known as the *attitude communicator,* have a major impact on the effectiveness of that message. Communicators who are physically and socially attractive produce greater attitude change than those who are less attractive. Moreover, the expertise and trustworthiness of a communicator are related to the impact of a message—except when the communicator is believed to have an ulterior motive (Hovland, Janis, & Kelly, 1953; Priester & Petty, 1995).

- *Characteristics of the message.* It is not just *who* delivers a message but *what* the message is like that affects attitude and behavior change. One-sided arguments—in which only the communicator's side is presented—are probably best if the communicator's message is initially viewed favorably by the target (recipient) of the message. But if the target receives a message presenting an unpopular viewpoint, two-sided messages—which include both the communicator's position and the one he or she is arguing against—are more effective, probably because they are seen as more precise and thoughtful. In addition, fear-producing messages ("If you don't practice safer sex, you'll get AIDS") are generally effective, although not always. For instance, if the fear aroused is too strong, such messages can arouse people's defense mechanisms and be ignored (Karlins & Abelson, 1979; Perloff, 1993; L. H. Rosenthal, 1997).
- *Characteristics of the target.* Once a message has been communicated, characteristics of the *target* of the message can determine whether the message will be accepted. For example, intelligent people are more resistant to persuasion than those who are less intelligent. There also seem to be gender differences in persuasibility. Women are somewhat more easily persuaded than men, particularly when they have less knowledge of the message topic. However, the magnitude of the difference between men and women is not large (Eagly, 1989; Rhodes & Wood, 1992; Wood & Stagner, 1994).

Companies use sports stars like Tiger Woods to persuade consumers to buy their products. Can celebrities really affect the purchasing habits of consumers? How?

Whether recipients will be receptive to persuasive messages depends on the type of information processing they use. Social psychologists have discovered two primary information-processing routes to persuasion: central-route and peripheral-route processing. **Central-route processing** occurs when the recipient thoughtfully considers the issues and arguments involved in persuasion. **Peripheral-route processing,** in contrast, occurs when people are persuaded on the basis of factors unrelated to the nature or quality of the content of a persuasive message. Instead, they are influenced by factors that are irrelevant or extraneous to the attitude topic or issue, such as who is providing the message or how long the arguments are (Petty & Cacioppo, 1986; Petty et al., 1994).

In general, central-route processing occurs when targets are highly involved and motivated to comprehend the message. However, if central-route processing is not employed because the target is uninvolved, unmotivated, bored, or distracted, then the nature of the message becomes less important, and peripheral factors more critical (see Figure 18-1). Although both central-route and peripheral-route processing lead to attitude change, central-route processing generally leads to stronger, more lasting attitude change.

Are some people more likely than others to use central-route processing rather than peripheral-route processing? The answer is yes. People who are high in the *need for cognition,* a person's habitual level of thoughtfulness and cognitive activity, are more likely

central-route processing: Message interpretation characterized by thoughtful consideration of the issues and arguments used to persuade

peripheral-route processing: Message interpretation characterized by consideration of the source and related general information rather than of the message itself

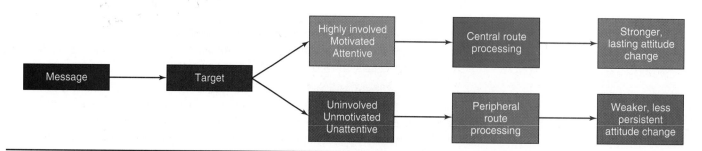

Figure 18-1 Routes to persuasion. Targets who are highly involved, motivated, and attentive use central route processing when considering a persuasive message, and central route processing leads to more lasting attitude change. In contrast, uninvolved, unmotivated, and inattentive targets are more likely to use peripheral route processing, and attitude change is likely to be less enduring. Can you think of particular advertisements that try to produce central route processing?

Table 18-1 The Need for Cognition

Which of the following statements apply to you?

1. I really enjoy a task that involves coming up with new solutions to problems.

2. I would prefer a task that is intellectual, difficult, and important to one that is somewhat important but does not require much thought.

3. Learning new ways to think doesn't excite me very much.

4. The idea to rely on thought to make my way to the top does not appeal to me.

5. I think only as hard as I have to.

6. I like tasks that require little thought once I've learned them.

7. I prefer to think about small, daily projects rather than long-term ones.

8. I would rather do something that requires little thought than something that is sure to challenge my thinking abilities.

9. I find little satisfaction in deliberating hard and for long hours.

10. I don't like to be responsible for a situation that requires a lot of thinking.

Scoring: The more you agree with statements 1 and 2, and disagree with the rest, the greater the likelihood that you have a high need for cognition.

Source: Adapted from Cacioppo et al., 1996.

 **PsychLink**

Dual process persuasion
www.mhhe.com/
feldmanup6-18links

to employ central-route processing. Consider the statements shown in Table 18-1. People who agree with the first two statements, and disagree with the rest, have a relatively high need for cognition (Cacioppo et al., 1996).

People who are high in the need for cognition enjoy thinking, philosophizing, and pondering about the world. As a consequence, they tend to reflect more on persuasive messages using central-route processing, and they are likely to be persuaded by complex, logical, and detailed messages. In contrast, those who are low in the need for cognition become impatient when forced to spend too much time thinking about an issue. Consequently, they are more likely to use peripheral-route processing and to be more persuaded by factors other than the quality and detail of messages (Haugtvedt, Petty, & Cacioppo, 1992). (To consider attitude change from the vantage point of the advertising industry, see the *Psychology at Work* box on page 534.)

The Link Between Attitudes and Behavior

Not surprisingly, attitudes influence behavior. The strength of the link between particular attitudes and behavior varies, of course, but generally people strive for consistency between their attitudes and their behavior. Furthermore, people are fairly consistent in their attitudes. You would probably not hold the attitude that eating meat is immoral and still have a positive attitude toward hamburgers (Kraus, 1995).

Interestingly, not only do our attitudes influence our behavior, but sometimes our behavior shapes our attitudes. Consider, for instance, the following situation:

You've just spent what you feel is the most boring hour of your life, turning pegs for a psychology experiment. Just as you're finally finished and about to leave, the experimenter asks you to do him a favor. He tells you that he needs a helper for future experimental sessions to introduce subsequent participants to the peg-turning task. Your specific job would be to tell them that turning the pegs is an interesting, fascinating experience. Each time you tell this tale to another participant, you'll be paid $1.

If you agree to help out the experimenter, you could be setting yourself up for a state of psychological tension that is known as cognitive dissonance. According to a

major social psychologist, Leon Festinger (1957), **cognitive dissonance** occurs when a person holds two attitudes or thoughts (referred to as *cognitions*) that contradict each other.

A participant in the situation just described is left with two contradictory thoughts: (1) I believe the task is boring; and (2) I said it was interesting with little justification ($1). This should arouse dissonance. How can such dissonance be reduced? One cannot deny having said that the task was interesting without breaking with reality. Relatively speaking, it is easier to change one's attitude toward the task—and thus the theory predicts that participants will reduce dissonance by adopting more positive attitudes toward the task (Johnson, Kelly, & LeBlanc, 1995).

This prediction was confirmed in a classic experiment (Festinger & Carlsmith, 1959). The experiment followed essentially the same procedure outlined earlier. A participant was offered $1 to describe a boring task as interesting. In addition, as a control, other participants were offered $20 to say that the task was interesting. The reasoning behind this condition was that $20 was so much money that participants in this condition had a good reason to be conveying incorrect information; dissonance would *not* be aroused, and *less* attitude change would be expected. The results supported this notion. Participants who were paid $1 changed their attitudes more (becoming more positive toward the peg-turning task) than participants who were paid $20.

We now know that dissonance explains a number of everyday occurrences involving attitudes and behavior. For example, a smoker who knows that smoking leads to lung cancer holds contradictory cognitions: (1) I smoke; and (2) Smoking leads to lung cancer. The theory predicts that these two thoughts will lead to a state of cognitive dissonance. More important, it predicts that the individual will be motivated to reduce such dissonance by one of the following methods: (1) modifying one or both of the cognitions; (2) changing the perceived importance of one cognition; (3) adding cognitions; or (4) denying that the two cognitions are related to each other. Hence the smoker might decide that he really doesn't smoke all that much (modifying the cognition), that the evidence linking smoking to cancer is weak (changing the importance of a cognition), that the amount of exercise he gets compensates for the smoking (adding cognitions), or that there is no evidence linking smoking and cancer (denial). Whatever technique is used, the result is a reduction in dissonance (see Figure 18-2).

cognitive dissonance: The conflict that occurs when a person holds two attitudes or thoughts (referred to as *cognitions*) that contradict each other

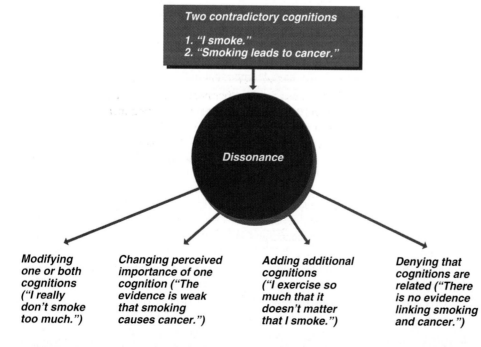

Figure 18-2 The simultaneous presence of two contradictory cognitions ("I smoke" and "Smoking leads to cancer") produces cognitive dissonance, which can be reduced through several methods. What are additional ways that dissonance can be reduced?

Psychology at Work

Ann Altman

Advertising Executive

Education: B.A., psychology/philosophy, University of Florida at Gainesville; M.A., clinical psychology, University of Florida at Gainesville; further work toward an M.B.A., Florida State University

Home: Palm Harbor, Florida

Ann Altman

It is not surprising that over the years the field of advertising has looked to psychology as an important source of ideas for fine-tuning its promotion of products and services and for communicating with potential customers. Nor is it surprising to find people with psychology backgrounds becoming interested in and pursuing careers in advertising. Such is the case with Ann Altman.

Initially Altman pursued a doctorate, spending time in Holland researching the development of language in children with epilepsy. Eventually her interest in communication led her to the international business world of advertis-

> "Interestingly enough, my psychology background has given me the ability to step back and analyze what the client is truly saying, and to understand what the client needs."

ing, where her academic background and strengths in research have proved highly useful in the 15 years she has spent as an advertising executive.

"I apply psychology to everything I do," says Altman, who is the founder and president of the Altman Meder Lawrence Hill Advertising firm. "Advertising is a field of communication that mediates an essential interaction between a company and the audience it is trying to reach. Interestingly enough, my psychology background has given me the ability to step back and analyze what the client is truly saying, and to understand what the client needs."

Altman cites as an example a West German

Social Cognition: Understanding Others

Regardless of his personal transgressions and his impeachment trial, many Americans genuinely *liked* President Bill Clinton, and his popularity remained high through the end of his second term. Cases like this illustrate the power of our impressions and attest to the importance of determining how people develop an understanding of others. One of the dominant areas of study in social psychology during the last few years has focused on learning how we come to understand what others are like and how we explain the reasons underlying others' behavior (Fiske & Taylor, 1991; Kunda, 1999).

Understanding What Others Are Like

Consider for a moment the enormous amount of information about other people to which we are exposed. How are we able to decide what is important and what is not, and to make judgments about the characteristics of others? Social psychologists interested in this question study **social cognition**—the processes that underlie our understanding of the social world. They have learned that individuals have highly developed **schemas,** sets of cognitions about people and social experiences (see Chapter 7). These schemas organize information stored in memory, represent in our minds the way the social world operates, and give us a framework to categorize, store, remember, and interpret information relating to social stimuli (Fiske & Taylor, 1991; Fiske, 1992a, 1992b).

We typically hold schemas for particular types of people. Our schema for "teacher," for instance, generally consists of a number of characteristics: knowledge of the subject matter he or she is teaching, a desire to impart that knowledge, and an awareness of the student's need to understand what is being said. Our schema for "mother" might include the characteristics of warmth, nurturance, and caring. Regardless of their accuracy, schemas are important because they organize the way in which we recall, recognize, and categorize information about others. Moreover, they allow us to predict what others are like on the basis of relatively little information, because we tend to fit people into schemas even if we don't have much concrete evidence to go on (Bargh et al., 1995).

social cognition: The processes that underlie our understanding of the social world

schemas: Sets of cognitions about people and social experiences

pharmaceutical company that approached her firm needing help in promoting a natural toothpaste in the United States. The company had tried and failed several times to bring the product to the U.S. market, according to Altman.

"We began by establishing focus groups around the product, involving dental professionals, general users, and other groups we thought would be our target audience. We began to see certain patterns," she notes. "We found that the audience of greatest interest was female, aged 35 to 40, and of a certain educational level. Based on that finding, we set up targeted television, newspaper, and direct mail promotions.

"In the first research we did, 9 out of 10 people who tried the product said they would never touch it again because it wasn't foamy or sweet, but we were able to turn that around by finding

out more about our participants' expectations and reactions," says Altman. "We have to be accountable to our clients in establishing effective communications between them and their potential customers. Research—practical and targeted, but psychological research nonetheless—plays a big role. It is important that we know what our typical buyers are thinking and expecting. Then we have to prepare them for what we are delivering."

> "Research—practical and targeted, but psychological research nonetheless plays a big role. It is important that we know what our typical buyers are thinking and expecting."

Impression Formation

How do we decide that Sayreeta is a flirt, Jacob is obnoxious, or Hector is a really nice guy? The earliest work on social cognition was designed to examine *impression formation,* the process by which an individual organizes information about another person to form an overall impression of that person. In one classic study, for instance, students were told that they were about to hear a guest lecturer (Kelley, 1950). One group of students was told that the lecturer was "a rather warm person, industrious, critical, practical, and determined"; a second group was told that he was "a rather cold person, industrious, critical, practical, and determined."

The simple substitution of "cold" for "warm" was responsible for drastic differences in the way the students in each group perceived the lecturer, even though he gave the same talk in the same style in each condition. Students who had been told he was "warm" rated him considerably more positively than students who had been told he was "cold."

The findings from this experiment led to additional research on impression formation that focused on how people pay particular attention to certain unusually important traits—known as **central traits**—to help them form overall impressions of others. According to this work, the presence of a central trait alters the meaning of other traits. Hence the description of the lecturer as "industrious" presumably meant something different according to which central trait it was associated with—"warm" or "cold" (Asch, 1946; Widmeyer & Loy, 1988).

Other work on impression formation has used information-processing approaches (see Chapter 8) to develop mathematically oriented models of how individual personality traits are combined to create an overall impression. Generally, the results of this research suggest that in forming an overall judgment of a person, we use a psychological "average" of the individual traits we see, in a manner that is analogous to finding the mathematical average of several numbers (Kaplan, 1975; Anderson, 1996).

Of course, as we gain more experience with people and observe them in a variety of situations, our impressions of them become more complex. But, because there usually are gaps in our knowledge of others, we still tend to fit them into personality schemas that represent particular "types" of people. For instance, we might have a schema of

 **PsychLink**
Impression formation
www.mhhe.com/
feldmanup6-18links

central traits: The major traits considered in forming impressions of others

"gregarious person" that includes the traits of friendliness, aggressiveness, and openness. The presence of just one or two of the associated traits might be sufficient to make us assign a person to a particular schema (Anderson & Klatzky, 1987; Sherman & Klein, 1994).

However, our schemas are susceptible to error. For example, our mood affects how we perceive others. People who are happy form more favorable impressions and make more positive judgments than people who are in a bad mood (Kenny, 1994; Bernieri et al., 1994).

Even when schemas are not entirely accurate, they serve an important function: They allow us to develop expectations about how others will behave. These expectations permit us to plan our interactions with others more easily, and they simplify a complex social world.

attribution theory: The theory of personality that seeks to explain how we decide, on the basis of samples of an individual's behavior, what the specific causes of that person's behavior are

situational causes (of behavior): A perceived cause of behavior that is based on environmental factors

dispositional causes (of behavior): A perceived cause of behavior that is based on internal traits or personality factors

Attribution Processes: Understanding the Causes of Behavior

Consider the following case:

> When Barbara Washington, a new employee at the Ablex Computer Company, completed a major staffing project two weeks early, her boss, Yolanda, was delighted. At the next staff meeting, she announced how pleased she was with Barbara and explained that *this* was an example of the kind of performance she was looking for in her staff. The other staff members looked on resentfully, trying to figure out why Barbara had worked night and day to finish the project not just on time, but two weeks early. She must be an awfully compulsive person, they decided.

Most of us, at one time or another, have puzzled over another person's behavior. Perhaps it was in a situation similar to the one above, or it may have been under more formal circumstances, such as serving as a judge on a student judiciary board in a cheating case. In contrast to work on social cognition, which describes how people develop an overall impression about others' personality traits, **attribution theory** seeks to explain how we decide, on the basis of samples of an individual's behavior, what the specific causes of that person's behavior are (Weiner, 1985a, 1985b; Jones, 1990; White, 1992).

The general process we use to determine the causes of behavior and other social occurrences proceeds in several steps, illustrated in Figure 18-3. After first noticing that a behavioral event has occurred, we must interpret the meaning of the event. This leads to the formulation of an initial explanation. Depending on the time available, the cognitive resources on hand (such as the attention we can give to the matter), and our motivation (determined in part by how important the event is to us), we might choose to accept our initial explanation or seek to modify it. If we have the time, cognitive resources, and motivation, the event becomes the trigger for deliberate problem solving as we seek a fuller explanation. During the problem formulation and resolution stage, we might try out several possibilities before determining that we have reached a solution (Krull & Anderson, 1997).

In seeking an explanation for behavior, one central question we must answer is whether the cause is situational or dispositional (Heider, 1958). **Situational causes** are elements of the environment. For instance, someone who knocks over a quart of milk and then cleans it up is probably doing so not because he or she is necessarily a terribly neat person, but because the *situation* requires it. In contrast, a person who spends hours shining the kitchen floor is probably doing so because he or she *is* a neat person—hence, the behavior has a **dispositional cause,** prompted by the person's disposition (her or his internal traits or personality characteristics).

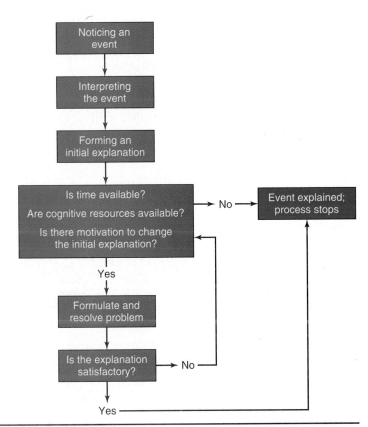

Figure 18-3 The general process we use to determine the causes of others' behavior and social occurrences proceeds in several steps. The kind of explanation we come up with depends on the time available to us, our cognitive resources, and our degree of motivation to come up with an accurate explanation. If time, cognitive resources, and motivation are limited, we'll make use of our first impression, which can be inaccurate.

Source: Adapted from Krull & Anderson, 1997, p. 2.

In our example involving Barbara, her fellow employees attributed her behavior to her disposition rather than to the situation. But from a logical standpoint, it is equally plausible that there was something about the situation that caused the behavior. If asked, Barbara might attribute her accomplishment to situational factors, explaining that she had so much other work to do that she just had to get the project out of the way, or that the project was not all that difficult and so it was easy to complete ahead of schedule. To her, then, the reason for her behavior might not be dispositional at all; it could be situational.

Biases in Attribution: To Err Is Human

If we always processed information in the rational manner that attribution theory suggests, the world might run a lot more smoothly. Unfortunately, although attribution theory generally makes accurate predictions, people do not always process information about others in such a logical fashion. In fact, research reveals consistent biases in the ways people make attributions. Among the most typical are these:

- *The fundamental attribution error.* One of the most common biases in people's attributions is the tendency to over-attribute others' behavior to dispositional causes, and the corresponding failure to recognize the importance of situational causes. Known as the **fundamental attribution error,** this tendency is quite prevalent in Western cultures. We tend to exaggerate the importance of personality characteristics (dispositional causes) in producing others' behavior, minimizing the influence of the environment (situational factors). For example, we are more likely to jump to the conclusion that someone who is often late to work is too lazy to take an earlier bus (a dispositional cause) than to assume that the cause is due to situational factors, such as the bus always running late.

  Why should the fundamental attribution error be so common? One reason pertains to the nature of the information that is available to the people making an attribution. When we view the behavior of another person in a particular setting, the information that is most conspicuous is the person's behavior itself. Because the individual's immediate surroundings are relatively unchanging, the person whose behavior we're considering is the center of our attention; the person's environment is less attention-grabbing. Consequently, we are more likely to make attributions based on personal, dispositional factors and less likely to make attributions relating to the situation (Ross, 1977; Ross & Nisbett, 1991; Gilbert & Malone, 1995).

- *The halo effect.* Harry is intelligent, kind, and loving. Is he also conscientious? If you were to guess, your response probably would be yes. Your guess reflects the **halo effect,** a phenomenon in which an initial understanding that a person has positive traits is used to infer other uniformly positive characteristics. The opposite would also hold true. Learning that Harry is unsociable and argumentative would probably lead you to assume he is lazy as well. However, few people have uniformly positive or uniformly negative traits, so the halo effect leads to misperceptions of others (Petzold, 1992; Larose & Standing, 1998).

- *Assumed-similarity bias.* How similar to you—in terms of attitudes, opinions, and likes and dislikes—are your friends and acquaintances? Most people believe that their friends and acquaintances are fairly similar to themselves. But this feeling goes beyond just people we know; there is a general tendency—known as the **assumed-similarity bias**—to think of people as being similar to oneself, even

fundamental attribution error: A tendency to attribute others' behavior to dispositional causes and the tendency to minimize the importance of situational causes

halo effect: A phenomenon in which an initial perception of a person as having positive traits produces the expectation that the person has other uniformly positive characteristics

assumed-similarity bias: The tendency to think of people as being similar to oneself, even when meeting them for the first time

Is this youngster shy or is he just taking a break from a vigorous game of basketball? In the fundamental attribution error, people over-attribute behavior to dispositional causes, and minimize the importance of situational causes. Do you think something similar can occur between nations?

Many students in Asian societies perform exceptionally well in school, in part because the culture emphasizes academic success and perseverance.

when meeting them for the first time. Given the range of people in the world, this means we're often wrong (Ross, Greene, & House, 1977; Hoch, 1987; Marks & Miller, 1987).

EXPLORING DIVERSITY

Attributions in a Cultural Context: How Fundamental Is the Fundamental Attribution Error?

Not everyone is susceptible to attribution biases in the same way. The kind of culture in which we are raised clearly plays a role in the attributions we make about others' behavior.

Take, for example, the fundamental attribution error, the tendency to overestimate the importance of personal, dispositional factors and underattribute situational causes when determining the causes of others' behavior. The error is pervasive in Western cultures but not in Asian societies.

Specifically, social psychologist Joan Miller (1984) found that adult experimental participants in India were more likely to use situational attributions than dispositional ones in explaining events. These findings are the opposite of those based on experimental participants in the United States, and they contradict the fundamental attribution error.

Miller suggested that we can discover the reason for these results by examining the norms and values of Indian society, which emphasize social responsibility and societal obligations to a greater extent than these traits are emphasized in Western societies. She also suggested that the particular language spoken in a culture can lead to different sorts of attributions. For instance, a tardy person using English might say "I am late," suggesting a personal, dispositional cause ("I am a tardy person"). In contrast, users of Spanish who are late say, "The clock caused me to be late." Clearly, the statement in Spanish implies that the cause is a situational one (Zebrowitz-McArthur, 1988).

Cultural differences in attributions can have profound implications. As we first discussed in Chapter 12, for example, parents in Asia tend to attribute good academic performance to effort and hard work (situational factors). In contrast, parents in Western cultures tend to deemphasize the role of effort and to attribute school success to innate ability (a dispositional factor). As a result, Asian students tend to strive harder to achieve and ultimately outperform U.S. students in school (Stevenson, Chen, & Lee, 1993a; Lee, Hallahan, & Herzog, 1996).

Evaluate

1. A learned predisposition to respond in a favorable or an unfavorable manner to a particular object is called a(n) _____.
2. One brand of peanut butter advertises its product by describing its taste and nutritional value. It is hoping to persuade customers through _____-route processing. In ads for a competing brand, a popular actor happily eats the product—but does not describe it. This approach hopes to persuade customers through _____-route processing.
3. Cognitive dissonance theory suggests that we commonly change our behavior to keep it consistent with our attitudes. True or false?
4. Sopan was happy to lend his textbook to a fellow student who seemed bright and friendly. He was surprised when his classmate did not return it. His assumption that the bright and friendly student would also be responsible reflects the _____ effect.

Rethink

1. Suppose you were assigned to develop a full advertising campaign for a product, including television, radio, and print ads. How might the theories in this chapter guide your strategy to suit the different media?
2. Joan sees Annette, a new coworker, act in a way that seems abrupt and curt. Joan concludes that Annette is unkind and unsociable. The next day Joan sees Annette acting kindly to another worker. Is Joan likely to change her impression of Annette? Why or why not? Finally, Joan sees several friends of hers laughing and joking with Annette, treating her in a very friendly fashion. Is Joan likely to change her impression of Annette? Why or why not?

Answers to Evaluate Questions

1. attitude 2. central; peripheral 3. False; we typically change our attitudes, not our behavior, to reduce cognitive dissonance. 4. halo

Social Influence

You have just transferred to a new college and are attending your first class. When the professor enters, your fellow classmates instantly rise, bow to the professor, and then stand quietly, with their hands behind their backs. You've never encountered such behavior, and it makes no sense to you. Is it more likely that you will (1) jump up to join the rest of the class or (2) remain seated?

Based on what research has told us about **social influence,** the process by which the actions of an individual or group affect the behavior of others, the answer to the question would almost always be the first option. As you undoubtedly know from your own experience, pressures to conform can be painfully strong, and they can bring about changes in behavior that, when considered in perspective, otherwise never would have occurred.

Conformity: Following What Others Do

Conformity is a change in behavior or attitudes brought about by a desire to follow the beliefs or standards of other people. The classic demonstration of pressure to conform comes from a series of studies carried out in the 1950s by Solomon Asch (Asch, 1951). In the experiments, participants thought they were participating in a test of perceptual skills with a group of six other participants. The participants were shown one card with three lines of varying length and a second card that had a fourth line that matched one of the first three (see Figure 18-4). The task was seemingly straightforward: The participants had to announce aloud which of the first three lines was identical in length to a "standard" line. Because the correct answer was always obvious, the task seemed easy to the participants.

Indeed, since the participants all agreed on the first few trials, the procedure appeared to be quite simple. But then something odd began to happen. From the perspective of the participant in the group who got to answer last, all of the first six participants' answers seemed to be wrong—in fact, unanimously wrong. And this pattern persisted. Over and over again, the first six participants provided answers that contradicted what the last participant believed to be correct. The dilemma that this situation posed for the last participant was whether to follow his or her own perceptions or to follow the group and repeat the answer that everyone else was giving.

As you might have guessed, this experiment was more contrived than it first appeared. The first six participants were actually confederates (paid employees of the experimenter) and had been instructed to give unanimously erroneous answers in many of the trials. And the study had nothing to do with perceptual skills. Instead, the issue under investigation was conformity.

What Asch found was that in about one-third of the trials, participants conformed to the unanimous but erroneous group answer, with about 75 percent of all participants conforming at least once. However, there were strong individual differences. Some participants conformed nearly all the time, whereas others never did so.

Since Asch's pioneering work, literally hundreds of studies have examined the factors affecting conformity, and we now know a great deal about the phenomenon (Moscovici, 1985; Tanford & Penrod, 1984; Wood et al., 1994). Among the most important variables producing conformity are the following:

- *The characteristics of the group.* The more attractive a group is to its members, the greater its ability to produce conformity (Hogg & Hardie, 1992). Furthermore, a person's relative **status,** the social rank held within a group, is critical: The lower a person's status in the group, the greater the power of the group over that person's behavior.
- *The situation in which the individual is responding.* Conformity is considerably higher when people must make a response publicly than when they can respond privately, as our founding fathers noted when they authorized secret ballots in voting.

Prepare

What are the major sources and tactics of social influence?

Organize

Social Influence
Conformity
Compliance
Obedience

social influence: The process by which the actions of an individual or group affect the behavior of others

conformity: A change in behavior or attitudes brought about by a desire to follow the beliefs or standards of other people

status: Social rank within a group

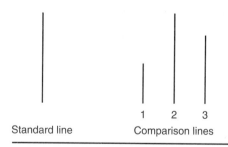

Figure 18-4 Which of the three comparison lines is the same length as the "standard" line? In Asch's conformity experiment, there was always a clear, correct answer, yet participants often conformed to the answers of the other group members. What are some ways that participants in the study could have avoided being influenced by the pressure from the group?

- *The kind of task.* People working on tasks and questions that are ambiguous (having no clear answer) are more susceptible to social pressure. Asked to give an opinion, such as on what type of clothing is fashionable, a person is more likely to yield to conformist pressures than if asked a question of fact. In addition, tasks at which an individual is less competent relative to the group create conditions in which conformity is more likely.
- *Unanimity of the group.* Conformity pressures are most pronounced in groups that are unanimous in their support of a position. But what of the case in which people with dissenting views have an ally in the group, known as a **social supporter,** who agrees with them? Having just one person present who shares the unpopular point of view is sufficient to reduce conformity pressures (Allen, 1975; Levine, 1989).

social supporter: A person who shares an unpopular opinion or attitude of another group member, thereby encouraging nonconformity

Groupthink: Caving in to Conformity

Although we usually think of conformity in terms of interpersonal effects, conformity pressures can sometimes lead to disastrous decisions with long-term consequences. For instance, consider NASA's decision to launch the space shuttle *Challenger* on the morning after a night of subfreezing temperatures. Despite a recommendation from engineers involved in the manufacture of the shuttle that extreme temperatures could make a set of rubber seals so brittle that they could deteriorate, leading to potential disaster, a consensus formed to proceed with the launch. In fact, NASA officials were so eager to get the shuttle off the ground that they ordered the engineers to rethink their recommendation. Ultimately, the individual who made the final decision was not even informed of the engineers' concerns; subordinate members of the launch team sought to "protect" him from dissenting information. We now know that that the engineers were correct: The rubber seals did fail, leading to the disastrous rocket explosion that killed all seven astronauts on board.

With the clarity of hindsight, it is clear that NASA's decision was wrong. How could such a poor decision have been made?

A phenomenon known as groupthink provides an explanation. *Groupthink* is a type of thinking in which group members share such a strong motivation to achieve consensus that they lose the ability to critically evaluate alternative points of view. Groupthink is most likely to occur when there is a popular or powerful leader who is surrounded by people of lower status—obviously the case with any U.S. president and his or her advisors, but also true in a variety of other organizations (Janis, 1972, 1989; 'T Hart, 1990; Manz & Sims, 1992; Neck & Moorhead, 1995; Pratkanis & Turner, 1999).

The phenomenon of groupthink is likely to occur in situations with these characteristics (McCauley, 1989):

- There is an illusion that the group is invulnerable and cannot make major errors in judgment.
- Information that is contradictory to the dominant group view tends to be ignored, discounted, or minimized.
- Group members are pressured to conform to the majority view—although the pressures might be relatively subtle.
- The pressure to conform discourages minority viewpoints from being brought before the group. Consequently, there *appears* to be unanimity in the group, even if this is not really the case.
- There is an illusion of morality. Because the group views itself as representing something just and moral, members assume that any judgment that the group reaches will be just and moral as well.

The consequences of groupthink are almost always negative. Groups tend to limit their list of possible solutions to just a few, and they spend relatively little time considering any alternatives once the leader seems to be leaning toward a particular solution. In fact, they might completely ignore information that challenges a developing

consensus. Historical research shows that many disastrous decisions reflect groupthink, so it is important for groups to be on guard (Tetlock et al., 1992, 1993; Cline, 1994; Schafer & Crichlow, 1996).

Compliance: Submitting to Direct Social Pressure

Conformity is a phenomenon in which the social pressure is subtle or indirect. But in some situations social pressure is much more obvious, and there is direct, explicit pressure to endorse a particular point of view or to behave in a certain way. Social psychologists call the type of conforming behavior that occurs in response to direct social pressure **compliance.**

Several specific sales tactics are intended to gain compliance. The following are some of the most common:

- *The foot-in-the-door technique.* A salesperson comes to your door and asks you to accept a small sample. You agree, thinking you have nothing to lose. A little later comes a larger request, which, because you have already agreed to the first one, you have a harder time turning down.

  The salesperson in this case is employing a tried-and-true strategy that social psychologists call the *foot-in-the-door technique:* You first ask a person to agree to a small request and later ask them to comply with a more important one; compliance with the later request increases significantly when the person first agrees to the smaller favor.

  The foot-in-the-door phenomenon was first demonstrated in a study in which a number of experimenters went door-to-door asking residents to sign a petition in favor of safe driving (Freedman & Fraser, 1966). Almost everyone complied with this small, benign request. However, a few weeks later, different experimenters contacted the residents again and made a much larger request: that the residents erect a huge sign reading "Drive Carefully" on their front lawns. The results were clear: 55 percent of those who had signed the petition agreed to the request, whereas only 17 percent of people in a control group who had not been asked to sign the petition agreed.

  Why does the foot-in-the-door technique work? One reason is that involvement with the small request leads to an interest in an issue, and taking an action—any action—makes the individual more committed to the issue, thereby increasing the likelihood of future compliance. Another explanation revolves around people's self-perceptions. By complying with the initial request, individuals might come to see themselves as the kind of person who provides help when asked. Then, when confronted with the larger request, they agree in order to maintain the kind of consistency in attitudes and behavior that we described earlier. Although we don't know which of these two explanations is more accurate, it is clear that the foot-in-the-door strategy is effective (Burger, 1999).

- *The door-in-the-face technique.* A fund raiser asks for a $500 contribution. You laughingly refuse, telling her that the amount is way out of your league. She then asks for a $10 contribution. What do you do? If you are like most people, you'll probably be a lot more compliant than if she hadn't asked for the huge contribution first. The reason lies in the *door-in-the-face technique,* in which a large request, refusal of which is expected, is followed by a smaller one. This strategy, which is the opposite of the foot-in-the-door approach, has also proved to be effective (Dillard, 1991; Reeves et al., 1991; Abrahams & Bell, 1994).

  One example of its success was shown in a field experiment in which college students were stopped on the street and asked to agree to a substantial favor—acting as unpaid counselors for juvenile delinquents two hours a week for two years (Cialdini et al., 1975). Not surprisingly, no one agreed to make such an enormous commitment.

 **PsychLink**

Persuasion and control
www.mhhe.com/
feldmanup6–18links

compliance: Conforming behavior that occurs in response to direct social pressure

"It's macaroni. We call it pasta as a marketing ploy."

But when they were later asked the considerably smaller favor of taking a group of delinquents on a two-hour trip to the zoo, half the people complied. In comparison, only 17 percent of a control group of participants who had not first received the larger request agreed.

The use of this technique is widespread. You may have used it at some point yourself, perhaps by asking your parents for a very large increase in your allowance and later settling for less. Similarly, television writers sometimes sprinkle their scripts with obscenities that they know will be cut by network censors, hoping to keep other key phrases intact (Cialdini, 1988).

- *The that's-not-all technique.* In this technique, you're offered a deal at an inflated price. But immediately following the initial offer, the salesperson offers an incentive, discount, or bonus to clinch the deal.

  Although it sounds transparent, such a practice can be quite effective. In one study, the experimenters set up a booth and sold cupcakes for 75 cents each. In one condition, customers were told directly that the price was 75 cents. But in another condition, they were told the price was $1, but had been reduced to 75 cents. As the that's-not-all technique would predict, more cupcakes were sold at the "reduced" price—even though it was identical to the price in the other experimental condition (Burger, 1986).

- *The not-so-free sample.* If you're ever given a free sample, keep in mind that it comes with a psychological cost. Salespeople provide samples to potential customers in order to instigate the norm of reciprocity. The *norm of reciprocity* is the well-accepted societal standard dictating that we should treat other people as they treat us. Receiving a not-so-free sample, then, suggests the need for reciprocation—in the form of a purchase, of course (Cialdini, 1988).

The techniques devised by social psychologists for promoting compliance are often used by companies seeking to sell their products to consumers, but they are also used by employers to bring about compliance and raise productivity of employees in the workplace. In fact, a branch of psychology, **industrial-organizational (I/O) psychology,** considers such issues as worker motivation, satisfaction, safety, and productivity. I/O psychologists also focus on the operation and design of organizations, asking such questions as how can decision making be improved in large organizations, and how can the fit between workers and their jobs be maximized. Furthermore, as we discuss in the *Applying Psychology in the 21st Century* box, one of the newest frontiers for industrial-organizational psychologists is tracking and targeting consumers virtually.

industrial-organizational (I/O) psychology: The branch of psychology that focuses on work and job-related issues, including productivity, job satisfaction, decision making, and consumer behavior

Obedience: Obeying Direct Orders

Compliance techniques try to gently lead people toward agreement with a request. In some cases, however, requests are geared toward producing **obedience,** a change in behavior in response to the commands of others. Although obedience is considerably less common than conformity and compliance, it does occur in several specific kinds of relationships. For example, we might show obedience to our boss, teacher, or parent, merely because of the power they hold to reward or punish us.

obedience: Conforming behavior in reaction to the commands of others

To acquire an understanding of obedience, consider for a moment how you might respond if a stranger said to you:

> I've devised a new way of improving memory. All I need is for you to teach people a list of words and then give them a test. The test procedure requires only that you give learners a shock each time they make a mistake on the test. To administer the shocks you will use a "shock generator" that gives shocks ranging from 30 to 450 volts. You can see that the switches are labeled from "slight shock" through

Applying Psychology in the 21st Century

Reading Your Mind, Reaching Your Wallet: Using Computer Technology to Increase Compliance

Jennifer Zweben has a weakness: she loves to buy CDs. Her studio apartment in San Jose, California, is littered with new purchases, everything from hip-hop to alternative, classical to techno. She's also a frequent online shopper, usually ringing up an order for CDs or books at least once a month. Indeed, just the other day, Zweben dropped by www.cdnow.com, an online music store, to check the price for her latest must-have. . . . While reading about the album, she noticed that the Web site had generated a list of other CDs for her to consider. One stood out: "Mermaid Avenue" by Billy Bragg and Wilco. Zweben, Webmaster at IBM Research, had heard a few songs from the album on the radio and liked them. "I'm always scouting for new music," she says, "but I wouldn't have remembered to look for this title on my own." She . . . plunked "Mermaid Avenue" into her virtual shopping cart (Lach, 1998, p. 39).

Welcome to the world of virtual persuasion, where compliance pressures are carefully addressed to the specific attitudes and prior behavior of individuals like Jennifer Zweben. Such targeting of website visitors represents the newest use by industrial-organization psychologists of psychographics, a technique that divides people into lifestyle profiles related to purchasing patterns. Psychographics considers such characteristics as a target's age, race, ethnicity, religion, income, marital status, and buying patterns. The technique also examines leisure activities of consumers of particular products. For instance, auto manufacturers know that buyers of minivans are more likely to participate in conversations with friends, go to family gatherings, read, and attend church functions than owners of sport utility vehicles. On the other hand, sport utility vehicle owners are more likely to go to sporting events, work out, hunt, and go out to clubs than minivan owners (Bradsher, 2000; Binkley, 2000).

Web-based persuasion techniques employ past purchasing history and previously stated preferences to build profiles of individuals, permitting sellers to target offers that are most likely to be of interest to given individuals. For example, if someone expresses an interest online

in a new 'N Sync CD, a Web supplier might search its database to see what other CDs were purchased by those who bought 'N Sync CDs. Once it has found this information, it will create a screen on the computer, offering a list of CDs of potential interest—a process called *collaborative filtering*.

Such technology might well move beyond the Web and spawn other persuasion techniques. Consider this scenario: you load up your shopping cart at the supermarket with a week's worth of groceries. After scanning your purchases into the cash register, the clerk reads a message that pops up on a computer screen and says to you, "Do you need dog food today?" You nod and rush back for the dog food, knowing that your buying habits—and the fact that you buy dog food every month or so—lie in the database of the supermarket's computers (Lach, 1998).

Do you think psychographics and collaborative filtering are basically helpful tools for consumers, or are they invasions of privacy? Is there any downside to being led to make purchases that are entirely consistent with what you and others with similar purchasing habits have bought in the past?

"danger: severe shock" at the top level, where there are three red X's. But don't worry; although the shocks may be painful, they will cause no permanent damage.

Presented with this situation, you would be likely to think that neither you nor anyone else would go along with the stranger's unusual request. Clearly, it lies outside the bounds of what we consider good sense.

Or does it? Suppose the stranger asking for your help were a psychologist conducting an experiment. Or suppose it were your teacher, your employer, or your military commander—all people in authority with some seemingly legitimate reason for their request.

If you still believe it unlikely that you would comply—think again. For the situation presented above describes a now-classic experiment conducted by social psychologist Stanley Milgram in the 1960s (Milgram, 1974). In the study, participants were placed in a situation in which they were told by an experimenter to give increasingly stronger shocks to another person as part of a study on learning (see Figure 18-5). In reality, the experiment had nothing to do with learning; the real issue under consideration was the degree to which participants would comply with the experimenter's requests. In fact, the "learner" supposedly receiving the shocks was actually a confederate who never really received any shocks.

Most people who hear a description of the experiment feel that it is unlikely that *any* participant would give the maximum level of shock—or, for that matter, any shock

Perils of obedience
www.mhhe.com/
feldmanup6-18links

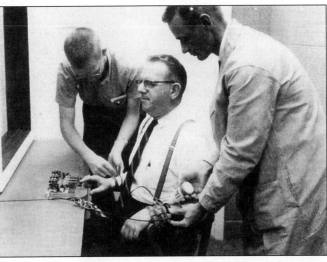

Figure 18-5 This impressive looking "shock generator" was used to lead participants to believe they were administering electric shocks to another person, who was connected to the generator by electrodes that were attached to the skin.

at all. Even a group of psychiatrists to whom the situation was described predicted that fewer than 2 percent of the participants would fully comply and administer the strongest shocks.

However, the actual results contradicted both experts' and nonexperts' predictions. Some 65 percent of the participants eventually used the highest setting on the shock generator, 450 volts, to shock the learner. This obedience occurred even though the learner, who had mentioned at the start of the experiment that he had a heart condition, demanded to be released, screaming "Let me out of here! Let me out of here! My heart's bothering me. Let me out of here!" Still, despite the learner's pleas, most participants continued to administer the shocks.

Why did so many individuals comply with the experimenter's demands? Extensive interviews were carried out with participants following the experiment. They showed that participants were obedient primarily because they believed that the experimenter would be responsible for any potential ill effects that befell the learner. The experimenter's orders were accepted, then, because the participants thought that they personally could not be held accountable for their actions—they could always blame the experimenter (Darley, 1995; Blass, 1996).

The Milgram experiment has been criticized for creating an extremely trying set of circumstances for the participants, thereby raising serious ethical concerns. (Undoubtedly, the experiment could not be conducted today because of ethical considerations.) Other critics have suggested that the conditions in Milgram's experiment did not mirror real-world obedience (Miller, Collins, & Brief, 1995; Blass, 2000).

Despite these concerns, Milgram's research remains one of the strongest laboratory demonstrations of obedience. We need only consider actual instances of obedience to authority to witness some frightening real-life parallels. For instance, a major defense offered after World War II by Nazi officers to excuse their participation in atrocities during the war was that they were "only following orders." Milgram's experiment, which was motivated in part by his desire to explain the behavior of everyday Germans during World War II, forces each of us to ask ourselves this question: Would we be able to withstand the intense power of authority?

Evaluate

1. A _____ _____, or person who agrees with the dissenting viewpoint, is likely to reduce conformity.

2. Who pioneered the study of conformity?
   a. Skinner
   b. Asch
   c. Milgram
   d. Fiala

3. Which of the following techniques asks a person to comply with a small initial request to enhance the likelihood that the person will later comply with a larger request?
   a. Door-in-the-face
   b. Foot-in-the-door
   c. That's-not-all
   d. Not-so-free sample

4. The _____-_____-_____-_____ technique begins with an outrageous request which then makes a smaller request seem reasonable.

5. _____ is a change in behavior that is due to another person's orders.

Answers to Evaluate Questions

1. social supporter 2. b 3. b 4. door-in-the-face 5. Obedience

Rethink

1. Given that persuasive techniques like those described in this section are so powerful, should there be laws against the use of such techniques? Should people be taught defenses against such techniques? Is the use of such techniques ethically and morally defensible?

2. Why do you think the Milgram experiment is so controversial? What sorts of effects might the experiment have had on participants? Do you think the experiment would have had similar results if it had been conducted not in a laboratory setting, but among members of a social group (such as a fraternity or sorority) with strong pressures to conform?

Prejudice and Discrimination

What do you think of when someone says, "He's African American" or "She's Chinese" or "woman driver"?

If you're like most people, you'll probably automatically jump to some sort of impression of what that individual is like. Such views represent **stereotypes,** generalized beliefs and expectations about social groups and their members. Stereotypes, which can be negative or positive, are the outgrowth of our tendency to categorize and organize the vast amount of information we encounter in our everyday lives. All stereotypes oversimplify the world: We view individuals not in terms of their individual characteristics, but in terms of their membership in a particular group (Jussim et al., 1996; Macrae, Stangor, & Hewstone, 1996).

Stereotypes can lead to **prejudice,** the negative (or positive) evaluations of groups and their members. For instance, racial prejudice occurs when a member of a racial group is evaluated in terms of race and not because of her or his own characteristics or abilities.

The most common stereotypes and forms of prejudice have to do with racial, religious, and ethnic categorizations. Over the years, various groups have been called "lazy" or "shrewd" or "cruel" with varying degrees of regularity by members of other groups. Stereotypes remain, even today, despite major progress toward the reduction of legally sanctioned manifestations of prejudice such as school segregation (Katz & Braly, 1933; Johnston, 1996).

Although usually backed by little or no evidence, stereotypes often have harmful consequences. When people act on negative stereotypes, the result is **discrimination**—negative behavior toward members of a particular group. Discrimination can lead to exclusion from jobs, neighborhoods, or educational opportunities, and can result in members of particular groups receiving lower salaries and benefits.

Prepare

What are stereotypes, prejudice, and discrimination?
How can we reduce prejudice and discrimination?

Organize

Prejudice and Discrimination
    The Foundations of Prejudice
    Working to End Prejudice
        and Discrimination

stereotypes: Generalized beliefs and expectations about social groups and their members

prejudice: The negative (or positive) evaluations of groups and their members

discrimination: Negative behavior toward members of a particular group

Stereotyping not only leads to overt discrimination; it can actually *cause* members of stereotyped groups to behave in ways that reflect the stereotype, through a phenomenon known as the *self-fulfilling prophecy.* Self-fulfilling prophecies are expectations about the occurrence of a future event or behavior that act to increase the likelihood that the event or behavior *will* occur. For example, if people think that members of a particular group lack ambition, they might treat them in a way that diminishes their ambition (Harris-Kern & Perkins, 1995; Madon, Jussim, & Eccles, 1997).

The Foundations of Prejudice

No one has ever been born disliking a particular racial, religious, or ethnic group. People learn to hate, in much the same way that they learn the alphabet.

According to *social learning approaches* to stereotyping and prejudice, people's feelings about members of various groups are shaped by the behavior of parents, other adults, and peers. For instance, bigoted parents might commend their children for expressing prejudices. Likewise, young children learn prejudice by imitating the behavior of adult models. Such learning starts at an early age; children as young as 3 years of age begin to show preferences for members of their own race (Katz, 1976; Yenerall, 1995).

The mass media also provide a major source of information about stereotypes, not just for children, but for adults as well. Even today, some television shows and movies portray Italians as Mafia-like mobsters, Jews as greedy bankers, and African Americans as promiscuous or lazy. When such inaccurate portrayals are the primary source of information about minority groups, they can lead to the development and maintenance of unfavorable stereotypes (Herrett-Skjellum & Allen, 1996; Coltraine & Messineo, 2000).

Other explanations of prejudice and discrimination focus on how being a member of a particular group can magnify our self-esteem. According to *social identity theory,* we use group membership as a source of pride and self-worth. Slogans such as "Gay pride" and "Black is beautiful" exemplify the argument that group membership gives us self-respect (Tajfel, 1982; Rowley et al., 1998).

However, there is an unfortunate outcome of the use of group membership to provide social respect. In an effort to maximize our sense of self-esteem, we might come to think that our own group is *better* than others. Consequently, we inflate the positive aspects of our own group—and, devalue groups to which we do not belong. Ultimately, we come to view members of other groups as inferior to members of our own (Turner et al., 1992). The end result is prejudice toward members of groups of which we are not a part.

Neither social learning nor social identity approaches provide the full story of stereotyping and prejudice. For instance, some psychologists argue that prejudice results when there is perceived competition for scarce societal resources. Thus, when they must compete for jobs or housing, members of majority groups might perceive (however unjustly or inaccurately) minority group members as hindering their efforts to attain their goals, which can lead to prejudice (Simpson & Yinger, 1985). Other explanations for prejudice emphasize human cognitive limitations that lead us to categorize people on the basis of visually conspicuous physical features such as race, sex, and ethnic group. Such categorization can lead to stereotypes and, ultimately, to discriminatory behavior (Fiske & Morling, 1996; Fiske, 1998).

Working to End Prejudice and Discrimination

How can we diminish the effects of prejudice and discrimination? Psychologists have developed several strategies that have proven effective, including these:

PsychLink

Testing hidden prejudice
www.mhhe.com/
feldmanup6-18links

Like father, like son: Social learning approaches to stereotyping and prejudice suggest that attitudes and behaviors toward members of minority groups are learned through the observation of parents and other individuals. How can this cycle be broken?

- *Increasing contact between the target of stereotyping and the holder of the stereotype.* Research has shown that increasing the amount of interaction between people from different groups can reduce negative stereotyping. But only certain kinds of contact are likely to foster a reduction in prejudice and discrimination. Situations where there is relatively intimate contact, where the individuals are of equal status, or where participants must cooperate with one another or are dependent on one another are most likely to reduce stereotyping (Gaertner et al., 1996; Pettigrew, 1997; Oskamp, 2000).

- *Making positive values and norms against prejudice more conspicuous.* It is not always necessary to rely on contact to reduce prejudice and discrimination. Another approach is to demonstrate to people the inconsistencies between values they hold regarding equality and fair treatment of others, and negative stereotyping. For instance, people who are made to understand that their values regarding equality and fairness are inconsistent with their negative perceptions of minority group members are more likely to work actively against prejudice in the future. Similarly, people who hear others vehemently condemn racism are subsequently more likely to strongly condemn racism (Rokeach, 1971; Blanchard, Lilly, & Vaughn, 1991).

- *Providing information about the objects of stereotyping.* Probably the most direct way to change stereotypical and discriminatory attitudes is through education: teaching people to be more aware of the positive characteristics of targets of stereotyping. For instance, when the meaning of puzzling behavior is explained to people holding stereotypes, they might come to appreciate its true significance—even though it might still appear foreign and perhaps even threatening. Furthermore, training in statistical reasoning, which illustrates various logical fallacies, can inhibit the formation of certain stereotypes (Langer, Bashner, & Chanowitz, 1985; Landis et al., 1976; Schaller et al., 1996).

- *Reducing stereotype vulnerability.* Social psychologist Claude Steele suggests that many African Americans suffer from *stereotype vulnerability,* obstacles to performance that stem from awareness of society's stereotypes regarding minority group members. He argues that African American students who receive instruction from teachers who doubt their abilities and who set up special remedial programs to assist them can come to accept society's stereotypes and believe that they are prone to fail (Steele, 1992, 1997).

  Such beliefs can have devastating effects. When confronted with an academic task, African American students might fear that their performance will simply confirm society's negative stereotypes. The immediate consequence of this fear is anxiety that hampers performance. But the long-term consequences can be even worse: Faced with doubts about their ability to perform successfully in academic environments, African Americans might decide that the risks of failure are so great that it is not worth the effort even to attempt to do well. Ultimately, they might "disidentify" with academic success by minimizing the importance of academic endeavors (Steele & Aronson, 1995; Steele, 1997; Stone et al., 1999).

  However, Steele's analysis suggests that it might be possible to overcome the predicament in which African Americans may find themselves. Specifically, intervention programs can train minority group members about their vulnerability to stereotypes and illustrate that the stereotypes are inaccurate. If they can be convinced that they have the potential to be academically successful, members of minority groups might well become immune to the potentially treacherous consequences of negative stereotypes.

 **PsychLink**

Teaching tolerance project
www.mhhe.com/
feldmanup6-18links

Evaluate

1. Any expectation—positive or negative—about an individual based solely on that person's membership in a group can be a stereotype. True or false?

2. A negative (or positive) evaluation of a group and its members is called:

   a. stereotyping

   b. prejudice

   c. self-fulfilling prophecy

   d. discrimination

3. Paul is a store manager who does not expect women to succeed in business. He therefore offers important, high-profile responsibilities only to men. If the female employees fail to move up in the company, this could be an example of a _____-_____ prophecy.

Answers to Evaluate Questions

1. True 2. b 3. self-fulfilling

Rethink

1. How are stereotypes, prejudice, and discrimination related? In a society committed to equality, which of the three should be changed first? Why?

2. Do you think women can be victims of stereotype vulnerability? In what topical areas might this occur? Can men be victims of stereotype vulnerability?

Prepare

Why are we attracted to certain people, and what progression do social relationships generally follow?

What factors underlie aggression and prosocial behavior?

Organize

Positive and Negative Social Behavior

    Liking and Loving

    Aggression and Prosocial Behavior

interpersonal attraction (or close relationships): Positive feelings for others; liking and loving

Positive and Negative Social Behavior

Are people basically good or bad?

Like philosophers and theologians, social psychologists have pondered the basic nature of humanity. Is it represented by the violence and cruelty we see throughout the world, or is there something special about human nature that permits loving, considerate, unselfish, and even noble behavior?

We turn to two routes that social psychologists have followed in seeking answers to these questions. We first consider what they have learned about the sources of our attraction to others, and we end this chapter with a look at two sides of the coin of human behavior: aggression and helping.

Liking and Loving: Interpersonal Attraction and the Development of Relationships

There is nothing more central in most people's lives than their feelings for others, and consequently it is not surprising that liking and loving have become a major focus of interest for social psychologists. Known more formally as the study of **interpersonal attraction** or **close relationships,** this area addresses the factors that lead to positive feelings for others.

How Do I Like Thee? Let Me Count the Ways

By far the greatest amount of research has focused on liking, probably because it is easier for investigators conducting short-term experiments to produce states of liking for strangers one has just met than to instigate and observe loving relationships over long periods of time. Hence traditional studies have given us a good deal of knowledge about the factors that initially attract two people to each other (Berscheid, 1985; Simpson & Harris, 1994). Among the most important factors considered by social psychologists are the following:

- *Proximity.* If you live in a dormitory or an apartment, consider the friends you made when you first moved in. Chances are you became friendliest with those who lived geographically closest to you. In fact, this is one of the most firmly established findings in the interpersonal attraction literature: *Proximity* leads to liking (Festinger, Schachter, & Back, 1950; Nahome & Lawton, 1975).

- *Mere exposure.* Repeated exposure to a person is often sufficient to produce attraction. Interestingly, repeated exposure to *any* stimulus—a person, picture, compact disc, or virtually anything—usually makes us like the stimulus more. Becoming familiar with a stimulus can evoke positive feelings; the positive feelings stemming from familiarity are then transferred to the stimulus itself. There are exceptions, though. When the initial interactions are strongly negative, repeated exposure is unlikely to cause us to like another person more. Instead, the more we are exposed to him or her, the more we might dislike the individual (Bornstein & D'Agostino, 1994; Kruglanski, Freund, & Bar Tal, 1996).

- *Similarity.* Folk wisdom tells us that birds of a feather flock together. Unfortunately, it also maintains that opposites attract. Social psychologists have come up with a clear verdict regarding which of the two statements is correct: We tend to like those who are similar to us. Discovering that others are similar to us in terms of attitudes, values, or traits promotes our liking them. Furthermore, the more similar others are, the more we like them (Byrne, 1969; Glaman, Jones, & Rozelle, 1996).

    One reason similarity increases the likelihood of interpersonal attraction is that we assume that people with similar attitudes will evaluate us positively. Because there is a strong **reciprocity-of-liking effect** (a tendency to like those who like us), our knowledge that another person evaluates us positively promotes our attraction to that person. In addition, we assume that when we like someone else, that person likes us in return (Condon & Crano, 1988; Metee & Aronson, 1974; Tagiuri, 1958).

- *Physical attractiveness.* For most people, the equation *beautiful = good* is quite true. As a result, people who are physically attractive are more popular than those who are physically unattractive, if all other factors are equal. This finding, which contradicts the values that most people say they hold, is apparent even in childhood—with nursery-school-age children rating popularity on the basis of attractiveness—and continues into adulthood. Indeed, physical attractiveness might be the single most important element promoting initial liking in college dating situations, although its influence eventually decreases when people get to know each other better (Keller & Young, 1996; Langlois et al., 2000; Sangrador & Yela, 2000).

The factors we have discussed are not, of course, the only constituents of liking. For example, surveys have sought to identify the factors critical in friendships. In a questionnaire answered by some 40,000 respondents, the qualities that were most valued in a friend were the ability to keep confidences, loyalty, and warmth and affection, followed closely by supportiveness, frankness, and a sense of humor (Parlee, 1979). The results are summarized in Figure 18-6.

How Do I Love Thee? Let Me Count the Ways

Whereas our knowledge of what makes people like one another is extensive, our understanding of love is more limited in scope and recently acquired. For some time, many social psychologists believed that love was a phenomenon too difficult to observe and study in a controlled, scientific way. However, love is such a central issue in most people's lives that, in time, social psychologists could not resist its allure and became infatuated with the topic (Aron et al., 1997).

As a first step, researchers tried to identify the characteristics that distinguish between mere liking and full-blown love. They discovered that love is not simply liking of a greater quantity, but a qualitatively different psychological state. For instance, at least in its early stages, love includes relatively intense physiological arousal, an all-encompassing interest in another individual, fantasizing about the other, and relatively rapid swings of emotion. Similarly, love, unlike liking, includes elements of passion,

"I'm attracted to you, but then I'm attracted to me, too."

 **PsychLink**

Study of relationships
www.mhhe.com/
feldmanup6-18links

reciprocity-of-liking effect: A tendency to like those who like us

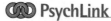 **PsychLink**

Definition of love
www.mhhe.com/
feldmanup6-18links

Figure 18-6 These are the key qualities looked for in a friend according to some 40,000 respondents to a questionnaire.

Keeping confidences, loyalty, and warmth and affection are among the most important qualities people look for in a friend

closeness, fascination, exclusiveness, sexual desire, and intense caring. Partners are idealized; we exaggerate their good qualities and minimize their imperfections (Murray & Holmes, 1997).

Other researchers have theorized that there are two main types of love: passionate love and companionate love. **Passionate (or romantic) love** is a state of intense absorption in another person. It includes intense physiological arousal, psychological interest, and caring for the needs of the other. In contrast, **companionate love** is the strong affection we have for those with whom our lives are deeply involved. The love we feel for our parents, other family members, and even some close friends falls into the category of companionate love (Singelis, Choo, & Hatfield, 1995; Baumeister & Bratslavsky, 1999; Regan, 2000).

According to psychologist Robert Sternberg (1986, 1988), an even finer differentiation between types of love is in order. He proposes that love is made up of three components: an *intimacy component,* encompassing feelings of closeness and connectedness; a *passion component,* made up of the motivational drives relating to sex, physical closeness, and romance; and a *decision/commitment component,* encompassing the initial cognition that one loves someone and the longer-term feelings of commitment to maintain love. These three components combine to produce the possible different types of love (see Figure 18-7).

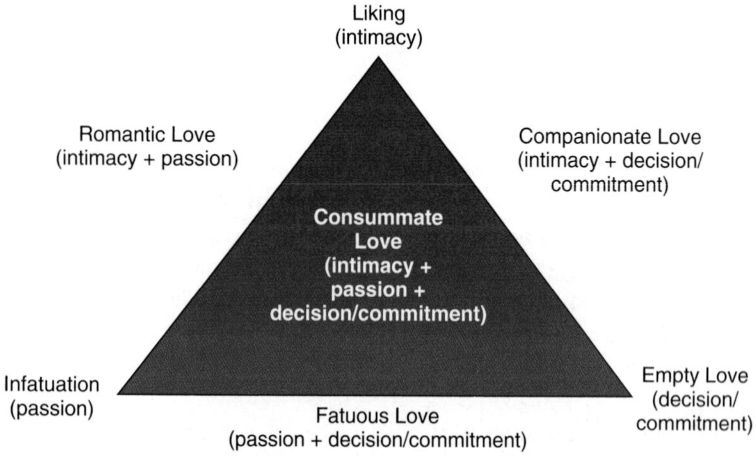

Is love a necessary ingredient of a good marriage? Yes, if you live in United States. On the other hand, it's considerably less important in other cultures. Although mutual attraction and love are the most important characteristics desired in a mate for women and men in the United States, men in China rated good health as most important, and women there rated emotional stability and maturity as most important. In Zulu South Africa, women rated dependable character first and men rated emotional stability first (Buss et al., 1990; see Table 18-2).

passionate (or romantic) love: A state of intense absorption in someone that includes intense physiological arousal, psychological interest, and caring for the needs of another

companionate love: The strong affection we have for those with whom our lives are deeply involved

Figure 18-7 According to Sternberg, there are three main components of love: intimacy, passion, and decision/commitment. Different combinations of these components can create other various types of love. Nonlove contains none of the components.

Table 18-2 Rank Ordering of Desired Characteristics in a Mate

	UNITED STATES		CHINA		SOUTH AFRICAN ZULU	
	Females	Males	Females	Males	Females	Males
Mutual attraction—love	1	1	8	4	5	10
Emotional stability and maturity	2	2	1	5	2	1
Dependable character	3	3	7	6	1	3
Pleasing disposition	4	4	16	13	3	4
Education and intelligence	5	5	4	8	6	6
Good health	9	6	3	1	4	5
Good looks	13	7	15	11	16	14
Sociability	8	8	9	12	8	11
Desire for home and children	7	9	2	2	9	9
Refinement, neatness	12	10	10	7	10	7
Ambition and industriousness	6	11	5	10	7	8
Similar education	10	12	12	15	12	12
Good cook and housekeeper	16	13	11	9	15	2
Favorable social status or rating	14	14	13	14	14	17
Similar religious background	15	15	18	18	11	16
Good financial prospect	11	16	14	16	13	18
Chastity (no prior sexual intercourse)	18	17	6	3	18	13
Similar political background	17	18	17	17	17	15

Source: Buss et al., 1990.

Aggression and Prosocial Behavior: Hurting and Helping Others

Drive-by shootings, carjackings, and abductions are just some of the examples of violence that seem all too common today. Yet we also find examples of generous, unselfish, thoughtful behavior that suggest a more optimistic view of humankind. Consider, for instance, people like Mother Teresa, who ministered to the poor in India. Or contemplate the simple kindnesses of life: lending a valued compact disc, stopping to help a child who has fallen off her bicycle, or merely sharing a candy bar with a friend. Such instances of helping are no less characteristic of human behavior than the distasteful examples of aggression. In this last part of the chapter, we explore how social psychologists have sought to explain instances of aggressive behavior and helping behavior (A. G. Miller, 1999).

Hurting Others: Aggression

We need look no farther than our daily paper or the nightly news to be bombarded with examples of aggression, both on a societal level (war, invasion, assassination) and on an individual level (crime, child abuse, and the many petty cruelties that humans are capable of inflicting on one another). Is such aggression an inevitable part of the human condition? Or is aggression primarily a product of particular circumstances that, if changed, could lead to its reduction?

The difficulty of answering such knotty questions becomes quickly apparent as soon as we consider how best to define the term *aggression*. Depending on the definition, examples of inflicted pain or injury might or might not qualify as aggression

PsychLink

Driver aggression/road rage
www.mhhe.com/
feldmanup6-18links

Table 18-3 Is This Aggression?

To see for yourself the difficulties involved in defining aggression, consider each of the following acts and determine whether it represents aggressive behavior—according to your own definition of aggression.

1. A spider eats a fly.

2. Two wolves fight for the leadership of the pack.

3. A soldier shoots an enemy at the front line.

4. The warden of a prison executes a convicted criminal.

5. A man viciously kicks a cat.

6. A man, while cleaning a window, knocks over a flower pot, which, in falling, injures a pedestrian.

7. Mr. X, a notorious gossip, speaks disparagingly of many people of his acquaintance.

8. A man mentally rehearses a murder he is about to commit.

9. An angry son purposely fails to write to his mother, who is expecting a letter and will be hurt if none arrives.

10. An enraged boy tries with all his might to inflict injury on his antagonist, a bigger boy, but is not successful in doing so. His efforts simply amuse the bigger boy.

11. A senator does not protest the escalation of bombing to which she is morally opposed.

12. A farmer beheads a chicken and prepares it for supper.

13. A hunter kills an animal and mounts it as a trophy.

14. A physician gives a flu shot to a screaming child.

15. A boxer gives his opponent a bloody nose.

16. A Girl Scout tries to assist an elderly woman but trips her by accident.

17. A bank robber is shot in the back while trying to escape.

18. A tennis player smashes her racket after missing a volley.

19. A person commits suicide.

20. A cat kills a mouse, parades around with it, and then discards it.

Source: Adapted from Benjamin, 1985, p. 41.

(see Table 18-3). It is clear, for instance, that a rapist is acting with aggression toward his victim. On the other hand, it is less certain that a physician who causes extreme pain to a patient by carrying out an emergency medical procedure with no available anesthetic should be considered aggressive.

Most social psychologists define aggression in terms of the intent and purpose behind the behavior. **Aggression** involves intentionally inflicting injury or harm on another person (Berkowitz, 1993). Under this definition, it is clear that the rapist in our example is acting aggressively, whereas the physician causing pain during a medical procedure is not.

We turn now to several explanations for aggressive behavior developed by social psychologists (Berkowitz, 1993; Geen & Donnerstein, 1998).

Instinct approaches: Aggression as a release   If you have ever punched an adversary in the nose, you might have experienced a certain satisfaction, despite your better judgment. Instinct theories, noting the prevalence of aggression not only in humans but in animals as well, propose that aggression is primarily the outcome of innate—inborn—urges.

Sigmund Freud was one of the first to suggest, as part of his theory of personality, that aggression is a primary instinctual drive (see Chapter 14). Konrad Lorenz, an

aggression: The intentional infliction of injury or harm on another person

ethologist (a scientist who studies animal behavior), expanded on Freud's notions by arguing that humans, along with members of other species, have a fighting instinct, which in earlier times ensured protection of food supplies and weeded out the weaker of the species (Lorenz, 1966, 1974). The controversial notion arising from Lorenz's instinct approach is that aggressive energy is constantly being built up within an individual until it is finally discharged in a process called **catharsis.** The longer the energy is built up, says Lorenz, the greater will be the amount of the aggression displayed when it is discharged.

> **catharsis:** The process of discharging built-up aggressive energy

Probably the most controversial idea to come out of instinct theories of aggression is Lorenz's proposal that society ought to provide acceptable means of catharsis through, for instance, participation in sports and games, in order to prevent its discharge in less socially desirable ways. Although the notion makes logical sense, there is no possible way to devise an adequate experiment to test it. Relatively little support exists for instinct theories in general, because of the difficulty in finding evidence for any kind of pent-up reservoir of aggression (Berkowitz, 1993; Geen & Donnerstein, 1983). Most social psychologists suggest that we should look to other approaches to explain aggression.

Frustration-aggression approaches: Aggression as a reaction to frustration

Suppose you've been working on a paper that is due for a class early the next morning, and your printer runs out of ink just before you can print out the paper. You rush to the store to buy a new ink cartridge, only to find the salesclerk locking the door for the day. Even though the clerk can see you gesturing and literally begging him to open the door, he refuses, shrugging his shoulders and pointing to a sign that indicates when the store will open the next day. At that moment, the feelings you experience toward the salesclerk probably place you on the verge of real aggression, and you are undoubtedly seething inside.

Frustration-aggression theory tries to explain aggression in terms of events like this one. When first put forward, the theory said flatly that frustration *always* leads to aggression of some sort, and that aggression is *always* the result of some frustration, where **frustration** is defined as the thwarting or blocking of some ongoing, goal-directed behavior (Dollard et al., 1939). More recent formulations, however, have modified the original one, suggesting instead that frustration produces anger, leading to a *readiness* to act aggressively. Whether or not actual aggression occurs depends on the presence of *aggressive cues,* stimuli that have been associated in the past with actual aggression or violence and that will trigger aggression again (Berkowitz, 1984). In addition, frustration is assumed to produce aggression only to the extent that the frustration produces negative feelings (Berkowitz, 1989, 1990).

> **frustration:** The thwarting or blocking of some ongoing, goal-directed behavior

What kinds of stimuli act as aggressive cues? They can range from the most overt, such as the presence of weapons, to the subtlest, such as the mere mention of the name of an individual who has behaved violently in the past. For example, in one experiment, angered participants behaved significantly more aggressively when in the presence of a rifle and revolver than in a comparable situation in which no guns were present (Berkowitz & LePage, 1967). Similarly, frustrated participants in an experiment who had viewed a violent movie were more physically aggressive toward a confederate with the same name as the star of the movie than toward a confederate with a different name (Berkowitz & Geen, 1966). It appears, then, that frustration does lead to aggression, at least when aggressive cues are present (Carlson, Marcus-Newhall, & Miller, 1990).

Observational learning approaches: Learning to hurt others

Do we learn to be aggressive? The observational learning (sometimes called social learning) approach to aggression says we do. Taking a view almost the opposite of instinct theories, which focus on innate explanations of aggression, observational learning theory (see Chapter 6) emphasizes that social and environmental conditions can teach individuals to be aggressive. Aggression is seen not as inevitable, but rather as a learned response that can be understood in terms of rewards and punishments.

Observational learning theory pays particular attention not only to direct rewards and punishments that individuals themselves receive, but to the rewards and punishments that models—individuals who provide a guide to appropriate behavior—receive for their aggressive behavior. According to observational learning theory, people observe the behavior of models and the subsequent consequences of the behavior. If the consequences are positive, the behavior is likely to be imitated when observers find themselves in a similar situation.

Suppose, for instance, that a girl hits her younger brother when he damages one of her new toys. Whereas instinct theory would suggest that the aggression had been pent up and was now being discharged, and frustration-aggression theory would examine the girl's frustration at no longer being able to use her new toy, observational learning theory would look to previous situations in which the girl had viewed others being rewarded for their aggression. For example, perhaps she had watched a friend get to play with a toy after he painfully twisted it out of the hand of another child.

Observational learning theory has received wide research support. For example, nursery-school-age children who have watched an adult model behave aggressively and then receive reinforcement for the aggression later display similar behavior themselves, if they have been angered, insulted, or frustrated after exposure (Bandura, 1973, 1983; Anderson & Dill, 2000).

Helping Others: The Brighter Side of Human Nature

prosocial behavior: Helping behavior

Turning away from aggression, we move now to the opposite—and brighter—side of the coin of human nature: helping behavior. Helping behavior, or **prosocial behavior** as it is more formally known, has been considered under many different conditions. However, the question that psychologists have looked at most closely relates to bystander intervention in emergency situations. What are the factors that lead someone to help a person in need?

diffusion of responsibility: The tendency for people to feel that responsibility for acting is shared, or diffused, among those present

As we noted in Chapter 2 in the case of Kitty Genovese, one critical factor is the number of others present. When more than one person is witness to an emergency situation, a sense of diffusion of responsibility can arise among bystanders. **Diffusion of responsibility** is the tendency for people to feel that responsibility for acting is shared, or diffused, among those present. The more people present in an emergency, then, the less personally responsible each of them feels—and therefore the less help they provide (Latané & Nida, 1981; Kalafat, Elias, & Gara, 1993; Bickman, 1994; Markey, 2000).

Although the majority of research on helping behavior supports the diffusion-of-responsibility formulation, other factors are clearly involved in helping behavior. According to a model developed by Latané and Darley (1970), the process of helping involves four basic steps (see Figure 18-8):

- *Noticing a person, event, or situation that might require help.*
- *Interpreting the event as one that requires help.* Even if an event is noticed, it could be sufficiently ambiguous to be interpreted as a nonemergency situation (Shotland, 1985; Harrison & Wells, 1991). It is here that the presence of others first affects helping behavior. The presence of inactive others could indicate to the observer that a situation does not require help—a judgment the observer might not necessarily make if she or he were the lone observer.
- *Assuming responsibility for taking action.* It is at this point that diffusion of responsibility is likely to occur if others are present. Moreover, a bystander's particular expertise is likely to play a role in determining whether she or he helps. For instance, if people with training in medical aid or lifesaving techniques are present, untrained bystanders are less likely to intervene because they feel they have less expertise. This point was well illustrated in a study by Jane and Irving Piliavin (1972), who conducted a field experiment in which an individual seemed to collapse in a subway car with blood trickling out of the corner of his mouth. The results of the experiment showed that bystanders were

Figure 18-8 The basic steps of helping.
Source: Based on Latané & Darley, 1970.

less likely to help when a person (actually a confederate) appearing to be an intern was present than when the "intern" was not present.

- *Deciding on and implementing the form of assistance.* After an individual assumes responsibility for helping, he or she must decide how to provide assistance. Helping can range from very indirect forms of intervention, such as calling the police, to more direct forms, such as giving first aid or taking the victim to a hospital. Most social psychologists use a *rewards-costs approach* to predict the nature of assistance a bystander will choose to provide. The general notion is that the rewards of helping, as perceived by the bystander, must outweigh the costs if helping is to occur, and most research tends to support this notion (Bell et al., 1995).

After the nature of assistance is determined, one step remains: the actual implementation of the assistance. A rewards-costs analysis suggests that the least costly form of implementation is the most likely to be used. However, this is not always the case: In some situations, people behave altruistically. **Altruism** is helping behavior that is beneficial to others but clearly requires self-sacrifice. For example, an instance in which a person runs into a burning house to rescue a stranger's child might be considered altruistic, particularly when compared with the alternative of simply calling the fire department (Batson, 1991; Shapiro & Gabbard, 1994).

Some research suggests that people who intervene in emergency situations tend to possess certain personality characteristics that differentiate them from nonhelpers. For example, helpers are more self-assured, sympathetic, and emotionally understanding, and they have greater *empathy* (a personality trait in which someone observing another person experiences the emotions of that person) than nonhelpers (Batson et al., 1995; Sibicky, Schroeder, & Dovidio, 1995).

Still, most social psychologists agree that no single set of attributes differentiates helpers from nonhelpers. For the most part, temporary situational factors (such as the mood we're in) determine whether we will intervene in a situation requiring aid (Eisenberg, 1991; Knight et al., 1994; Bersoff, 1999).

Altruism is often the only bright side of a natural disaster. In response to the massive flooding that hit the U.S. Midwest, thousands of volunteers came from other areas of the country to pile sandbags, distribute donated food, and otherwise lend a helping hand.

altruism: Helping behavior that is beneficial to others but clearly requires self-sacrifice

BECOMING AN INFORMED CONSUMER OF PSYCHOLOGY

Dealing with Anger Effectively

At one time or another, almost everyone feels angry. The anger might result from a frustrating situation, or it could be due to the behavior of another individual. How we deal with such anger might determine the difference between a promotion and a lost job or a broken relationship and one that mends itself.

Social psychologists who have studied the topic suggest that there are several good ways to deal with anger, strategies that maximize the potential for positive consequences (Deffenbacher, 1988, 1996; Bass, 1996; Nelson & Finch, 2000). Among the most useful strategies are the following:

- *Look again at the anger-provoking situation from the perspective of others.* By taking others' point of view, you might be able to understand the situation better, and with increased understanding you might become more tolerant of the apparent shortcomings of others.
- *Minimize the importance of the situation.* Does it really matter that someone is driving too slowly and that you'll be late to an appointment as a result? Reinterpret the situation in a way that is less bothersome.
- *Fantasize about getting even—but don't act on it.* Fantasy provides a safety valve. In your fantasies, you can yell at that unfair professor all you want and suffer no consequences at all. However, don't spend too much time brooding: Fantasize, but then move on.

- *Relax.* By teaching yourself the kind of relaxation techniques used in systematic desensitization (see Table 17-2 in the previous chapter), you can help reduce your reactions to anger. In turn, your anger might dissipate.

No matter which of these strategies you try, above all, don't ignore your anger. People who always strive to suppress their anger can experience a variety of unhappy consequences, such as self-condemnation, frustration, and even physical illness (Engebretson & Stoney, 1995; Sharma, Ghosh, & Spielberger, 1995).

Evaluate

1. We tend to like people who are similar to us. True or false?
2. Which of the following sets are the three components of love proposed by Sternberg?
   a. Passion, closeness, sexuality
   b. Attraction, desire, complementarity
   c. Passion, intimacy, decision/commitment
   d. Commitment, caring, sexuality
3. Based on the research evidence, which of the following might be the best way to reduce the amount of fighting a young boy does?
   a. Take him to the gym and let him work out on the boxing equipment.
   b. Take him to see *The Matrix* several times in the hope that it will provide catharsis.
   c. Reward him if he doesn't fight during a certain period.
   d. Ignore it and let it die out naturally.
4. If a person in a crowd does not help in an apparent emergency situation because many other people are present, that person is falling victim to the phenomenon of _____ ___ _____.

Answers to Evaluate Questions

1. True 2. c 3. c 4. diffusion of responsibility

Rethink

1. Can love be studied scientifically? Is there an elusive quality to love that makes it at least partially unknowable? How would you define "falling in love"? How would you study it?
2. How would the aggression of a Timothy McVeigh, convicted of blowing up a federal building in Oklahoma City, be interpreted by the three main approaches to the study of aggression: instinct approaches, frustration-aggression approaches, and observational learning approaches? Do you think any of these approaches fits the McVeigh case more closely than the others?

What are attitudes and how are they formed, maintained, and changed?

- Social psychology is the study of the ways in which people's thoughts, feelings, and actions are affected by others, and the nature and causes of individual behavior in social situations. (p. 530)
- Attitudes are learned predispositions to respond in a favorable or unfavorable manner to a particular object. (p. 532)
- Cognitive dissonance occurs when two cognitions—attitudes or thoughts—contradict each other and are held simultaneously by an individual. To resolve the contradiction, the person might modify the cognition, change its importance, or deny a link, thereby bringing about a reduction in dissonance. (p. 533)

How do we form impressions of what others are like and of the causes of their behavior?

- Social cognition involves the processes that underlie our understanding of the social world. Schemas help us organize information about people and social experiences in memory and allow us to interpret and categorize information about others. (p. 534)
- People form impressions of others in part through the use of central traits, personality characteristics that are given unusually heavy weight when an impression is formed. (p. 535)
- Information-processing approaches have found that we tend to average sets of traits to form an overall impression. (p. 535)
- Attribution theory tries to explain how we understand the causes of behavior, particularly with respect to situational or dispositional factors. (p. 536)

What biases influence how we view others' behavior?

- Even though logical processes are involved, attribution is still prone to error. For instance, the fundamental attribution error is the tendency to over-attribute others' behavior to dispositional causes, and the corresponding failure to recognize the importance of situational causes. (p. 537)
- Other biases include the halo effect and the assumed-similarity bias. (p. 537)

What are the major sources and tactics of social influence?

- Social influence is the area of social psychology concerned with situations in which the actions of an individual or group affect the behavior of others. (p. 539)
- Conformity refers to changes in behavior or attitudes that occur as the result of a desire to follow the beliefs or standards of others. (p. 539)
- Compliance is behavior that occurs as a result of direct social pressure. Tactics for eliciting compliance include the foot-in-the-door, door-in-the-face, that's-not-all, and not-so-free-sample techniques. (p. 541)
- Obedience is a change in behavior in response to the commands of others. (p. 542)

What are stereotypes, prejudice, and discrimination?

- Stereotypes are generalized beliefs and expectations about social groups and their members. (p. 545)
- Prejudice is the negative (or positive) evaluation of groups and their members. (p. 545)
- Stereotyping and prejudice can lead to discrimination, negative behavior toward members of a particular group. (p. 545)

- Self-fulfilling prophecies are expectations about the occurrence of future events or behaviors that increase the likelihood that the events or behaviors will actually occur. (p. 546)
- According to social learning approaches, people learn stereotyping and prejudice by observing the behavior of parents, other adults, and peers. Social identity theory suggests that group membership is used as a source of pride and self-worth, which can lead people to think of their own group as better than others. (p. 546

How can we reduce prejudice and discrimination?

- Ways to reduce prejudice and discrimination include increasing contact, making positive values against prejudice apparent, and providing information about the target of the attribution or stereotype. (p. 546)
- Stereotype vulnerability relates to the obstacles to performance for minority group members that stem from their awareness of society's stereotypes. (p. 547)

Why are we attracted to certain people, and what progression do social relationships generally follow?

- Among the primary determinants of liking are proximity, mere exposure, similarity, and physical attractiveness. (p. 548)
- Loving is distinguished from liking by the presence of intense physiological arousal, an all-encompassing interest in the other, fantasies about the other, rapid swings of emotion, fascination, sexual desire, exclusiveness, and strong feelings of caring. (p. 549)
- Love can be categorized into two types (passionate and companionate). In addition, the components of love—intimacy, passion, and decision/ commitment—combine to form seven different types of love. (p. 550)

What factors underlie aggression and prosocial behavior?

- Aggression is intentional infliction of injury or harm on another person. (p. 552)
- Explanations of aggression include instinct approaches, frustration-aggression theory, and observational learning. (p. 551)
- Helping behavior in emergencies is determined in part by the phenomenon of diffusion of responsibility, which results in a lower likelihood of helping when more people are present. (p. 554)
- Deciding to help is the outcome of a four-stage process consisting of noticing a possible need for help, interpreting the situation as requiring aid, assuming responsibility for taking action, and deciding on and implementing a form of assistance. (p. 554)

Key Terms and Concepts

social psychology (p. 530)
attitudes (p. 530)
central-route processing (p. 531)
peripheral-route processing (p. 531)
cognitive dissonance (p. 533)
social cognition (p. 534)
schemas (p. 534)
central traits (p. 535)
attribution theory (p. 536)
situational causes (of behavior) (p. 536)
dispositional causes (of behavior) (p. 536)

fundamental attribution error (p. 537)
halo effect (p. 537)
assumed-similarity bias (p. 537)
social influence (p. 539)
conformity (p. 539)
status (p. 539)
social supporter (p. 540)
compliance (p. 541)
industrial-organizational (I/O) psychology (p. 542)
obedience (p. 542)

stereotypes (p. 545)

prejudice (p. 545)

discrimination (p. 545)

interpersonal attraction
   (or close relationships) (p. 548)

reciprocity-of-liking effect (p. 549)

passionate (or romantic) love (p. 550)

companionate love (p. 550)

aggression (p. 552)

catharsis (p. 553)

frustration (p. 553)

prosocial behavior (p. 554)

diffusion of responsibility (p. 554)

altruism (p. 555)

Psychology on the Web

1. Find examples on the Web of advertisements or other persuasive messages using central-route processing and peripheral-route processing. What type of persuasion appears to be more prevalent on the Web? For what type of persuasion does the Web appear to be most suited? Is there a difference between Web-based advertising and other forms of advertising?

2. Is "hate crimes legislation" a good idea? Use the Web to find at least two discussions of hate crimes legislation—one in favor and one opposed—and summarize in writing the main issues and arguments presented. Using your knowledge of prejudice and aggression, evaluate the arguments for and against hate crimes legislation. State your opinion about whether this type of legislation is advisable.

pilogue

In this chapter we have touched on some of the major ideas, research topics, and experimental findings of social psychology. We have examined how people form, maintain, and change attitudes; and how they form impressions of others and assign attributions to them. We have also seen how groups, through conformity and tactics of compliance, can influence individuals' actions and attitudes. Finally, we discussed interpersonal relationships, including both liking and loving, and we looked at the two sides of a coin that represent the extremes of social behavior: aggression and prosocial behavior.

Turn back to the prologue of this chapter, which describes the death of James Byrd, who was killed because of his race. Use your understanding of social psychology to consider the following questions.

1. What factors would a social psychologist consider in examining why Byrd's killers initially formed negative attitudes toward African Americans?

2. How would an instinct approach account for the aggression displayed by Byrd's killers? a frustration-aggression approach? an observational learning approach? Which approach appears to you to be most useful in this situation? Why?

3. The public reaction to Byrd's death was horror and outrage. Anger was directed not only at the three killers, but at white supremacists in general. Do you think anger should be directed at the person who harbors prejudice and commits a crime or at the prejudice itself? What difference does that make and why?

Appendix

Going by the Numbers: Statistics in Psychology

Prologue: Selma Vorwerk

Looking Ahead

Descriptive Statistics

The Mean: Finding the Average

The Median: Finding the Middle

The Mode: Finding What Is Most Frequent

Comparing the Three M's: Mean Versus Median Versus Mode

Measures of Variability

The Range: Highest Minus Lowest

The Standard Deviation: Differences from the Mean

Using Statistics to Answer Questions: Inferential Statistics and Correlation

The Correlation Coefficient: Measuring Relationships

Looking Back

Key Terms and Concepts

Prologue

Selma Vorwerk

As the boat moved nearer to shore, the outline of the Statue of Liberty was plainly visible in the distance. Closer and closer it came, sending a chill down the spine of Selma Vorwerk. A symbol of America, the statue represented the hopes she carried from her native Europe in the early 1900s—hopes for liberty, for success, for a life free of economic and social strain.

Yet as the boat sailed closer to Ellis Island, the first point of arrival in the United States, Vorwerk did not realize that her hopes—and those of the other thousands of immigrants seeking their fortune in a land of opportunity—were threatened. A strong political movement was growing in the country on which she was pinning her hopes. This movement sought to stem the flow of immigrants through "scientific" analysis of data, using information collected by psychologists.

The major claim of this group was that a flood of "mentally deficient" immigrants was poisoning the intellectual capital of the United States. Supporters of this view believed that drastic measures must be taken to prevent Western civilization from collapsing from a lack of intelligence.

To support this view, Lathrop Stoddard, a member of the anti-immigration movement, reported the results of a study of intelligence in which tests were administered to a group of 82 children and 400 adults. On the basis of these test results, he concluded that the average mental age of people in the U.S. was only 14 years—proof to him that unlimited immigration had already produced a serious decline in the country's intelligence.

Fortunately for immigrants such as Selma Vorwerk, observers in favor of immigration pointed out the fallacy of using data from a relatively small sample—when a considerably larger set of intelligence test data was available. Specifically, the Army had been collecting intelligence data for years and had the test scores of 1.7 million men available. When these scores were analyzed, it was immediately apparent that the claim that the average mental age of American adults was 14 years was completely without merit.

A debate reminiscent of this earlier one rages today, as some observers suggest that an unrestrained flow of immigrants—this time from Latin America and Asia—will seriously damage the United States. This time, though, the debate is based more on analyses of social and economic statistics, with opponents of immigration suggesting that the social fabric of the country will be changed and that longer-term residents are losing jobs to the influx of immigrants. Equally vehement proponents of immigration suggest that the relevant statistics are being misinterpreted, and that *their* analyses of the situation result in a quite different conclusion.

Statistics, the branch of mathematics concerned with collecting, organizing, analyzing, and drawing conclusions from numerical data, is a part of all of our lives. For instance, we are all familiar with the claims and counterclaims regarding the effects of smoking. The U.S. government requires that cigarette manufacturers include on every package of cigarettes and in all their advertisements a warning that smoking is dangerous to people's health. The government's data show clear statistical links between smoking and disease. At the same time, the tobacco industry has long minimized the negative effects of smoking.

Statistics also lie at the heart of a considerable number of debates within the field of psychology. How do we determine the nature and strength of the effects of heredity on behavior? What is the relationship between learning and schedules of reinforcement? How do we know if the "double standard" for male and female sexual practices has shifted over time? These questions, and most others of interest to psychologists, cannot be answered without a reliance on statistics.

In this appendix, we consider the basic approaches to statistical measurement. We first discuss approaches to summarizing data that allow us to describe sets of observations. Next, we consider techniques for deciding how different one set of scores is from another. Finally, we examine approaches to measuring the relationship between two sets of scores.

statistics: The branch of mathematics concerned with collecting, organizing, analyzing, and drawing conclusions from numerical data

descriptive statistics: The branch of statistics that provides a means of summarizing data

frequency distribution: An arrangement of scores from a sample that indicates how often a particular score is present

histogram: Bar graph

Descriptive Statistics

Suppose, as an instructor of college psychology, you wanted to evaluate your class's performance on its first exam. Where might you begin?

You would probably start by using **descriptive statistics,** the branch of statistics that provides a means of summarizing data, presenting it in a usable and convenient form. For instance, you might first simply list the scores the pupils had received on the test:

$$72 \quad 78 \quad 78 \quad 92 \quad 69 \quad 73$$
$$85 \quad 49 \quad 86 \quad 86 \quad 72 \quad 59$$
$$58 \quad 85 \quad 89 \quad 80 \quad 83 \quad 69$$
$$78 \quad 90 \quad 90 \quad 96 \quad 83$$

Viewed in this way, the scores are a jumble of numbers and it is difficult to make any sense of them. However, there are several methods by which you could begin to organize the scores in a more meaningful way. For example, you might sort them in order of highest to lowest score, as is done in Table A-1. By indicating the number of people who obtained each score, you would have produced what is called a **frequency distribution,** an arrangement of scores from a sample that indicates how often a particular score is present.

Another way of summarizing the scores is to consider them visually. For example, you could construct a **histogram** or bar graph, shown in Figure A-1. In the histogram, the number of people obtaining a given score is represented pictorially. The

"Meaningless statistics were up one-point-five per cent this month over last month."

Table A-1 A Sample Frequency Distribution

Test Score	Number of Students Attaining That Score
96	1
92	1
90	2
89	1
86	2
85	2
83	2
80	1
78	3
73	1
72	2
69	2
59	1
58	1
49	1

central tendency: An index of the central location within a distribution of scores; the most representative score in a distribution of scores (the mean, median, and mode are measures of central tendency)

mean: The average of all scores, arrived at by adding all scores together and dividing by the total number of scores

scores are ordered along one dimension of the graph, and the number of people obtaining each score along the other dimension.

Arranging the scores from the highest to the lowest allows us to visually inspect the data. Most often, however, visual inspection is insufficient. For one thing, there may be so many scores in a sample that it is difficult to construct a meaningful visual representation. For another, as the research we discussed in Chapter 4 suggests, our perceptions of the meaning of stimuli are often biased and inaccurate; more precise, mathematically based measures would seem to be preferable. In cases in which a precise means of summarizing the data is desirable, psychologists turn to measures of central tendency. **Central tendency** is an index of the central location within a distribution of scores. There are three major measures of central tendency: the mean, the median, and the mode.

The Mean: Finding the Average

The most familiar measure of central tendency is the mean. **Mean** is the technical term for an average, which is simply the sum of all the scores in a set, divided by the number of scores making up the set. For example, to calculate the mean of the sample we have been using, begin by adding each of the numbers (96 + 92 + 90 + 90 + 89 + · · · and so forth). When you have the total, divide this sum by the number of scores, which is 23. This calculation, 1800/23 = 78.26, produces a mean score, or average, for our sample.

In general, the mean is an accurate reflection of the central score in a set of scores; as you can see from the histogram in Figure A-1, our mean of 78.26 falls roughly in the center of the distribution of scores. Yet the mean does not always provide the best measure of central tendency. For one thing, the mean is very sensitive to extreme scores. As an example, imagine that we added two scores of 20 and 22 to our sample scores. The mean would now become 1842/25, or 73.68, a drop of almost five points. Because of its sensitivity to extreme scores, then, the mean can sometimes present a deceptive picture of a set of scores, especially where the mean is based on a relatively small number of scores.

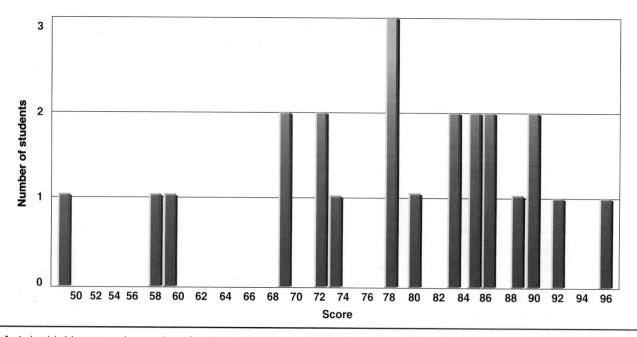

Figure A-1 In this histogram, the number of students obtaining each score is represented by a bar.

The Median: Finding the Middle

A measure of central tendency that is less sensitive to extreme scores than the mean is the median. The **median** is the point in a distribution of scores that divides the distribution exactly in half. If we arranged all the scores in order from the highest to the lowest, the median lies in the middle of the distribution.

For example, consider a distribution of five scores: 10, 8, 7, 4, and 3. The point that divides the distribution exactly in half is the score 7: Two scores in the distribution lie above the 7 score, while two scores lie below it. If there are an even number of scores in a distribution—in which case there would be no score lying in the middle—the two middle scores would be averaged. If our distribution consisted of scores of 10, 8, 7, 6, 4, and 3, then, we would average the two middle scores of 7 and 6 to form a median of 7 + 6 divided by 2, or 13/2 = 6.5.

In our original sample test scores, there are 23 scores. The score that divides the distribution exactly in half will be the 12th score in the frequency distribution of scores, because the 12th score has 11 scores above it and 11 below it. If you count down to the 12th score in the distribution depicted in Table A-1 you will see the score is 80. Therefore, the median of the distribution is 80.

One feature of the median as a measure of central tendency is that it is insensitive to extreme scores. For example, adding the scores of 20 and 22 to our distribution would change the median no more than adding scores of 48 and 47 to the distribution. The reason is clear: The median divides a set of scores in half, and the magnitude of the scores is of no consequence in this process.

The median is often used instead of the mean when extreme scores might be misleading. For example, government statistics on income are typically presented using the median as the measure of central tendency, since the median corrects for the small number of extreme cases of very wealthy individuals, whose high incomes might otherwise inflate the mean income.

median: The point in a distribution of scores that divides the distribution exactly in half when the scores are listed in numerical order

The Mode: Finding What Is Most Frequent

The final measure of central tendency is the mode. The **mode** is the most frequently occurring score in a set of scores. If you return to the distribution in Table A-1, you can see that three people scored 78, and the frequency of all of the other scores is either 2 or 1. The mode for the distribution, then, is 78.

Some distributions, of course, might have more than one score occurring most frequently. For instance, we could imagine that if the distribution had an additional score of 86 added to the two that are already there, there would be two most frequently occurring categories: 78 and now 86. In this instance, we would say there are two modes—a case known as a *bimodal distribution.*

The mode is often used as a measure of preference or popularity. For instance, if teachers wanted to know who was the most popular child in their elementary school classrooms, they might develop a questionnaire which asked the students to choose someone with whom they would like to participate in some activity. After the choices were tallied, the mode would probably provide the best indication of which child was most popular.

mode: The most frequently occurring score in a set of scores

normal distribution: A distribution of scores that produces a bell-shaped, symmetrical curve

Comparing the Three M's: Mean Versus Median Versus Mode

If a sample is sufficiently large, there is generally little difference between the mean, median, and mode. The reason is that with large samples, scores typically form what is called a normal distribution. A **normal distribution** is a distribution of scores that produces the bell-shaped curve displayed in Figure A-2, in which the right half mirrors the left half.

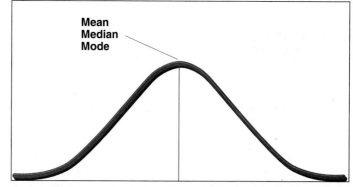

Figure A-2 In a normal distribution, the mean, median, and mode are identical, falling at the center of the distribution.

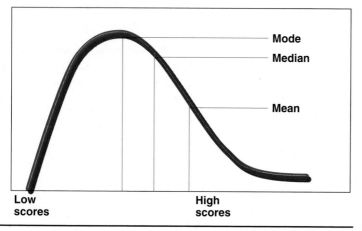

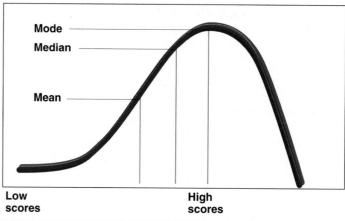

Figure A-3 In this skewed distribution, most scores are low.

Figure A-4 In this example of a skewed distribution, there tend to be more high scores than low scores.

Most large distributions, those containing many scores, produce a normal curve. For instance, if you asked a large number of students how many hours a week they studied, you might expect to find that most studied within a similar range of hours, while there would be a few who studied many, many hours, and some very few who studied not at all. There would be many scores hovering around the center of the distribution of scores, then, and only a few at the extremes—producing a normal distribution. Many phenomena of interest to psychologists produce a normal curve when graphed. For example, if you turn to Figure 9-1 in Chapter 9, where the distribution of intelligence scores is given, you can see the pattern of scores falls into a normal distribution.

The mean, median, and mode fall at exactly the same point in a normal distribution. This means that in a normal distribution of scores, the mean score will divide the distribution exactly in half (the median), and it will be the most frequently occurring score in the distribution (the mode).

The mean, median, and mode differ, however, when distributions are not normal. In cases in which the distributions are *skewed,* or not symmetrical, there is a "hump" at one end or the other (see Figures A-3 and A-4). For instance, if we gave a calculus exam to a group of students enrolled in an elementary algebra class, we would expect that most students would fail the test, leading to low scores being overrepresented in the distribution, as in Figure A-3. On the other hand, if we gave the same students a test of elementary addition problems, the scores would probably form a distribution in which high scores predominated, such as in Figure A-4. Both distributions are skewed, although in opposite directions, and the mean, median, and mode are different from one another.

Evaluate

1. A frequency distribution of numbers could be displayed pictorially by constructing a bar graph, or _____.
2. Match each item in the left-hand column with the corresponding item in the right-hand column.
   1. Mean = 10.0
   2. Median = 11
   3. Mode = 12

   a. 2, 8, 10, 12, 13, 18
   b. 4, 5, 10, 10, 15, 16
   c. 4, 5, 12, 12, 12, 16
3. The mean, median, and mode are measures of _____ _____.

Rethink

1. Government statistics on family income are presented in a variety of ways. What would be the most useful way of providing a summary of family incomes across the country: the mean, median, or mode? Why might only providing the mean be misleading?

4. Professor Garcia explains to the class that most of the forty exam scores fell within a B range, but there were two extremely high scores. Should she report the median or the mean as a measure of central tendency?

5. The mean, median, and mode will differ in a normal distribution. True or false?

Measures of Variability

Although measures of central tendency provide us with information about where the center of a distribution lies, often this information is insufficient. For example, suppose a psychologist is interested in determining the nature of people's eye movements while they are reading in order to perfect a new method to teach reading. It would not be enough to know how *most* people move their eyes (information that a measure of central tendency would provide); it would also be important to know how much individual people's eye movements differ or vary from one another.

A second important characteristic of a set of scores provides this information: variability. **Variability** is the spread, or dispersion, of scores in a distribution. Figure A-5 contains two distributions of scores that have identical means, but that differ in variability. Measures of variability provide a means of describing the spread of scores in a distribution.

The Range: Highest Minus Lowest

The simplest measure of variability is the range. A **range** is the difference between the highest score in a distribution and the lowest score. In the set of scores presented in Table A-1 the distribution has a range of 47 (96 − 49 = 47).

The fact that a range is simple to calculate is about its only virtue. The problem with this particular measure of variability is that it is based entirely on extreme scores, and a single score that is very different from the others in a distribution can distort the picture of the distribution as a whole. For example, the addition of a score of 20 to the test score distribution in Table A-1 (on page A.2) would almost double the range measure, even though the variability of the remaining scores in the distribution has not changed at all.

The Standard Deviation: Differences from the Mean

The most frequently used method of characterizing the variability of a distribution of scores is the standard deviation. The standard deviation bears a conceptual relationship to a mean. You will recall that the mean is the average score in a distribution of scores.

Prepare

How can we assess the variability of a set of data?

Organize

Measures of Variability
The Range
The Standard Deviation

variability: The spread, or dispersion, of scores in a distribution

range: The difference between the highest and lowest score in a distribution

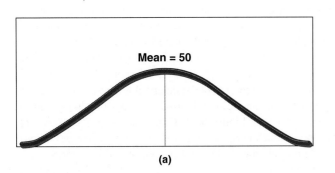

Mean = 50

(a)

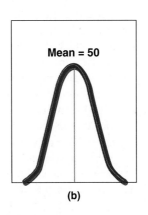

Mean = 50

(b)

Figure A–5 Although the mean is identical in these two distributions, the variability, or spread of scores, is very different. Specifically, the variability is considerably greater in *(a)* than in *(b)*.

A.5

Table A-2 Calculating a Standard Deviation

1. The calculation of a standard deviation begins with the calculation of the mean of distribution. In the following distribution of scores on a psychology student's weekly quizzes, the mean is 84.5: 82, 88, 71, 86, 96, 84. (As you recall, the mean is the sum of the scores divided by the number of scores in the distribution, or 507 ÷ 6 = 84.5.)

2. The next step is to produce a deviation score for each score in the distribution. A deviation score is simply an original score minus the mean of all the scores in a distribution. This has been done in the second column below:

Original Score	Deviation Score*	Deviation Score Squared
82	−2.5	6.25
88	3.5	12.25
71	−13.5	182.25
86	1.5	2.25
96	11.5	132.25
84	−.5	.25

3. In the third step, the deviation scores are squared (multiplied by themselves) to eliminate negative numbers. This has been carried out in the third column above.

4. The squared deviation scores are then added together, and this sum is divided by the number of scores. In the example above, the sum of the squared deviation scores is 6.25 + 12.25 + 182.25 + 2.25 + 132.25 + .25 = 335.50, and 335.50 ÷ 6 = 55.916.

5. The final step is to take the square root of the resulting number. The square root of 55.916 is 7.4777—which is the standard deviation of the distribution of scores.

6. To summarize, the standard deviation is calculated using the formula

$$\sqrt{\frac{\Sigma(\text{score}-\text{mean})^2}{N}}$$

*Original score minus the mean of 84.5

(Note: Because this formula provides the standard deviation for a sample, the sum of the deviation scores is divided by the number of scores, N. However, in some cases, in which we might wish to generalize beyond the specific sample to a larger population, the standard deviation is calculated by using the number of scores minus 1, or $N - 1$.)

standard deviation: An index of the average deviation of a set of scores from the center of the distribution

A **standard deviation** is an index of the average deviation of a set of scores from the center of the distribution.

Consider, for instance, the distributions in Figure A-5. The distribution on the left is widely dispersed, and on the average an individual score in the distribution can be thought of as deviating quite a bit from the center of the distribution. Certainly the scores in the distribution on the left are going to deviate more from the center of the distribution than those in the distribution on the right.

On the other hand, in the distribution on the right, the scores are closely packed together and there is little deviation of a typical score from the center of the distribution. Based on this analysis, then, it would be expected that a good measure of variability would yield a larger value for the distribution on the left than it would for the one on the right—and, in fact, a standard deviation would do exactly this by indicating how far away a typical score lies from the center of the distribution.

In a normal distribution, 68 percent of the scores fall within one standard deviation of the mean (34 percent on either side of it), 95 percent of scores fall within two standard deviations, and 99.7 percent fall within three standard deviations. As noted in Chapter 9, IQ scores of intelligence fall into a normal distribution, and they have a mean of 100 and a standard deviation of 15 (see Figure 9-1). Consequently, an IQ score of 100 does not deviate from the mean, but an IQ score that is three standard deviations above the mean (or 145) is very unusual (higher than 99 percent of all IQ scores).

The calculation of the standard deviation follows the logic of calculating the difference of individual scores from the mean of the distribution. (The exact technique is presented in Table A-2.) Not only does the standard deviation provide an excellent indicator of the variability of a set of scores, it provides a means for converting initial scores on standardized tests such as the SAT into the scales used to report results. In this way, it is possible to make a score of 585 on the verbal section of the SAT exam, for example, equivalent from one year to the next, even though the specific test items differ from year to year.

Evaluate

1. A measure of variability based solely on the distance between the most extreme scores is the
   a. spread
   b. standard deviation
   c. deviation score
   d. range

2. By simply eyeing the following sets of numbers, predict which will have a higher standard deviation and explain why:
   a. 6, 8, 10, 10, 11, 12, 13
   b. 2, 5, 8, 11, 16, 17, 18

3. Calculate the mean and standard deviation for sets **a** and **b** in the previous question.

Answers to Evaluate Questions

1. d 2. b, because the numbers are more widely dispersed. 3. Set A: Mean = 10, standard deviation = 2.20; Set B: mean = 11, standard deviation = 5.80

Rethink

1. If you want to know how many people live below the poverty line in the United States, why might the range and standard deviation provide you with a better answer than measures of central tendency (the mean, median, and mode) alone?

Using Statistics to Answer Questions: Inferential Statistics and Correlation

Prepare

How do we generalize from data?
How can we determine the nature of a relationship, and the significance of differences, between two sets of scores?

Organize

Using Statistics to Answer Questions
The Correlation Coefficient

Suppose you were a psychologist who was interested in whether there was a relationship between smoking and anxiety. Would it be reasonable to simply look at a group of smokers and measure their anxiety using some rating scale? Probably not. It clearly would be more informative if you compared their anxiety to the anxiety exhibited by a group of nonsmokers.

Once you had decided to observe anxiety in two groups of people, you would have to determine just who would be your subjects. In an ideal world with unlimited resources, you might contact *every* smoker and nonsmoker, because these are the two populations with which you are concerned. A **population** consists of all the members of a group of interest. Obviously, however, this would be impossible, given the enormous sizes of the two groups; instead, you would limit your subjects to a sample of smokers and nonsmokers. A **sample,** in formal statistical terms, is a subgroup of a population of interest that is intended to be representative of the larger population. Once you had identified samples representative of the population of interest to you, it would be possible to carry out your study, yielding two distributions of scores—one from the smokers and one from the nonsmokers.

The obvious question is whether the two samples differ in the degree of anxiety displayed by their members. The statistical procedures that we discussed earlier are helpful in answering this question, because each of the two samples can be examined in terms of central tendency and variability. The more important question, though, is whether the

population: All the members of a group of interest

sample: A subgroup of a population of interest

magnitude of difference between the two distributions is sufficient to conclude that the distributions truly differ from one another, or if, instead, the differences are attributable merely to chance.

To answer the question of whether samples are truly different from one another, psychologists use inferential statistics. **Inferential statistics** is the branch of statistics that uses data from samples to make predictions about a larger population, permitting generalizations to be drawn. To take a simple example, suppose you had two coins that were each flipped 100 times. Suppose further that one coin came up heads 49 times and the other came up heads 65 times. Are both coins fair? We know that a fair coin should come up heads about 50 times in 100 flips. But a little thought would also suggest that it is unlikely that even a fair coin would come up heads exactly 50 times in 100 flips. The question is, then, how far a coin could deviate from 50 heads before the coin would be considered unfair.

Questions such as this—as well as whether the results found are due to chance or represent unexpected, nonchance findings—revolve around how "probable" certain events are. Using coin flipping as an example, 53 heads in 100 flips would be a highly probable outcome because it departs only slightly from the expected outcome of 50 heads. In contrast, if a coin were flipped 100 times and 90 of those times it came up heads, it would be a highly improbable outcome. In fact, 90 heads out of 100 flips should occur by chance only once in 2 million trials of 100 flips of a fair coin. Ninety heads in 100 flips, then, is an extremely improbable outcome; if 90 heads did appear, the odds would be that the coin or the flipping process was rigged.

Inferential statistics are used to mathematically determine the probability of observed events. By using inferential statistics to evaluate the result of an experiment, psychologists are able to calculate the likelihood of whether the difference is a reflection of a true difference between populations. For example, suppose we find that the mean on an anxiety scale is 68 for smokers, and 48 for nonsmokers. Inferential statistical procedures allow us to determine whether this difference is really meaningful, or whether we might expect the same difference to occur merely because of chance factors.

Results of inferential statistical procedures are described in terms of measures of significance. To a psychologist, a **significant outcome** is one in which the observed outcome would be expected to occur by chance less than 5 times out of 100. Put another way, a significant difference between two means says that there is only a 5 percent probability that the difference an experimenter has found is due to chance, rather than to an actual difference between the means.

Obtaining a significant outcome in a study does not necessarily imply that the results of an experiment have real-world importance. An experiment might demonstrate that two groups differ significantly from one another, but the meaning of the differences in terms of what occurs outside the laboratory might be limited. Still, finding a significant outcome tells us something important: The differences a researcher has found are overwhelmingly likely to be true differences, and not due only to chance.

The Correlation Coefficient: Measuring Relationships

How do we know if television viewing is related to aggression, if reading romance novels is related to sexual behavior, or if mothers' IQs are related to their daughters' IQs?

Each of these questions revolves around the issue of the degree of relationship between two variables. One way of answering them is to draw a *scatterplot,* a graphical illustration of the relationship between two variables. We would first collect two sets of paired measures and assign one score to the horizontal axis (variable *x*) and the other score to the vertical axis (variable *y*). Then we would draw a dot at the place where the two scores meet on the graph. The first two scatterplots illustrated in Figure A-6 present typical situations. In (a) and (b), there is a **positive relationship,** in which high values of variable *x* are associated with high values of variable *y* and low values of *x* are associated with low values of *y*. In (c) and (d), there is a **negative relationship:** As values of variable *x* increase, the values of variable *y* decrease. In (e), no clear relationship exists between variable *x* and variable *y*.

inferential statistics: The branch of statistics that uses data from samples to make predictions about the larger population from which the sample is drawn

significant outcome: An outcome expected to occur by chance less than 5 percent of the time

positive relationship: A relationship established by data that shows high values of one variable corresponding with high values of another, and low values of the first variable corresponding with low values of the other

negative relationship: A relationship established by data that shows high values of one variable corresponding with low values of the other

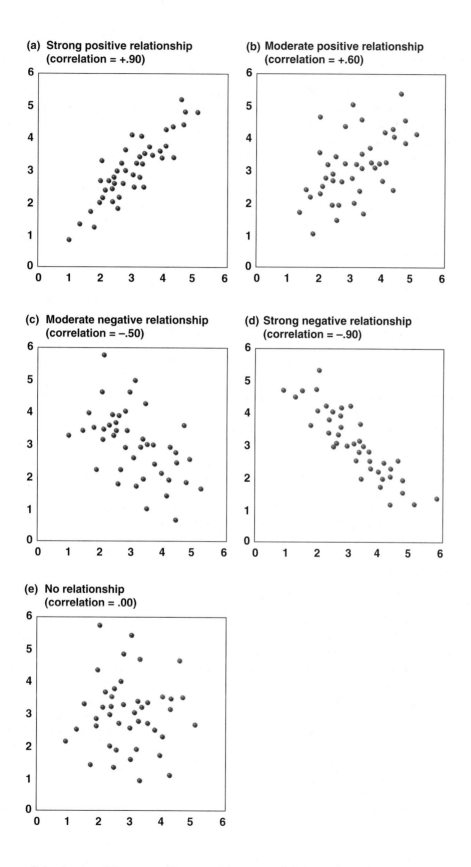

Figure A-6 These scatterplots show relationships of different strengths. In (a) and (b), the relationships are positive, although in (a) the relationship is considerably stronger than in (b). In contrast, the relationships in (c) and (d) are negative, with (d) representing a stronger negative relationship. Finally, (e) illustrates a case where no systematic relationship exists between the variables.

It is also possible to consider scores in terms of their mathematical relationship to one another, rather than simply the way they appear on a scatterplot. Suppose, for example, that a psychologist is interested in the degree to which a daughter's IQ is related to the mother's IQ—specifically, whether mothers with a high IQ tend to have daughters

Table A–3 IQ Scores of Mothers and Daughters

Mother's IQ	Daughter's IQ
135	122
128	130
125	110
120	132
114	100
110	116
102	108
96	89
90	84
86	92

correlation coefficient: A numerical measure that indicates the relationship between two variables

who have a high IQ, and whether mothers with a low IQ tend to have daughters with a low IQ. To examine the issue, suppose the psychologist measures the IQs of ten mothers and daughters and arranges their IQs as presented in Table A-3.

Looking at the data in the table, it is obvious that mothers and daughters do not have identical IQs. Moreover, they do not even have IQs that are rank-ordered the same in the two columns. For example, the mother with the highest IQ does not have the daughter with the highest IQ, and the mother with the lowest IQ does not have the daughter with the lowest IQ. It is apparent, then, that there is not a *perfect* relationship between the IQ of the mother and the IQ of the daughter. However, it would be a mistake to conclude that there is a *zero,* or no, relationship between the IQs of the mothers and daughters, because it is clear that there is a tendency for mothers who have high IQs to have daughters with high IQs, and for mothers with low IQs to have daughters with low IQs.

The statistic that provides a precise mathematical index of the degree to which two variables are related is the correlation coefficient. A **correlation coefficient** is a numerical measure that indicates the extent of the relationship between two variables. It ranges in value from $+1.00$ to -1.00. A value of $+1.00$ indicates that two variables have a perfect positive relationship with one another, meaning that the highest score on one variable is associated with the highest score on the other variable, the second highest score on the first variable is associated with the second highest score on the second variable, and so on. A value of -1.00 indicates that there is a perfect negative relationship between the two variables; the highest score on the first variable is associated with the lowest score on the second variable, the second highest score is associated with the second lowest score, and so forth.

Correlation coefficients around zero indicate that there is no relationship between the two variables. In such cases, there is no tendency for high values on one variable to be associated with either high or low values on the second variable.

Correlation coefficients that range between zero and ± 1.00 reflect varying degrees of relationship between the two variables. For instance, a value of $+.20$ or $-.20$ would indicate that there is a slight relationship between the two variables, a value of around $+.50$ or $-.50$ would indicate a moderate relationship, and a value of $+.80$ or $-.80$ would indicate a relatively strong relationship between the variables. As an example, if we were to calculate the correlation of the two sets of variables in Table A-3, we would find a correlation that is quite strong: The coefficient is $+.86$.

It is important to note that finding a strong correlation between two variables does *not* in any way indicate that one variable *causes* changes in another—only that they are associated with one another. Although it might seem plausible to us, for example, that it is the mother's intelligence that causes higher intelligence in a daughter, it is just as possible that a daughter's intelligence affects how the mother performs on an IQ test. (Perhaps the daughter's behavior affects the general home environment, affecting the mother's performance on IQ tests.) It is even plausible that some other unmeasured— and previously unconsidered—third variable is causing both mother's and daughter's IQs to increase or decrease simultaneously. Here is a clear example: Even if we find that ice cream sales and violent crimes are positively correlated with one another (as they happen to be), we would not presume that they were causally related. In this case, it is likely they are both influenced by a third factor—the weather.

The crucial point is that even if we find a perfect correlation between two sets of variables, we would not be able to say that the two variables were linked causally—only that they are strongly related to one another.

Evaluate

1. Researchers would like to estimate the level of stress for college freshmen for a given year at a large university. A stress index is given to a randomly assigned group of 500 freshmen. The class size is 6,000 for that year. In this example the group of 500 is known as a _____, and the entire class of freshmen is known as the _____.

2. Dr. Sanders states that the results of his experiment show a difference between the two groups, and that there is a 90 percent probability that the results are due to a true difference between the groups and not to chance. Are his results statistically significant?

3. A hypothetical set of data drawn from a sample of college sophomores at a university found that as the rate of caffeine consumption increases, amount of sleep decreases. The scatterplot for these data is apt to show a _____ relationship.

4. What would the value of the correlation coefficient be for

   a. a perfect negative relationship?

   b. a perfect positive relationship?

   c. no relationship?

5. If we observe a correlation coefficient of −.90 in Question 3, we would probably be safe in saying that caffeine consumption *causes* lack of sleep in college students. True or false? _____

6. The researchers in Question 3 decide to generalize the findings they obtain from their sample of college sophomores to all adults. Would you accept their generalization? Why or why not?

Answers to Evaluate Questions

1. sample; population 2. No, at least not at the .05 level. 3. negative 4. a. −1.00; b. +1.00; c. 0 5. False; we cannot assume a causal relation, only an association. 6. No, the sample (freshmen) does not represent the population (all college students).

Rethink

1. For many years, cigarette manufacturers argued that because the data linking smoking and disease is correlational, one cannot infer that there is a causal connection between them and therefore there is no reason not to smoke. Did the manufacturers have a valid argument? How could you refute their argument?

Looking Back

What measures can we use to summarize sets of data?

- Statistics is concerned with collecting, organizing, analyzing, and drawing conclusions from numerical data. (p. A.1)
- Descriptive statistics provides a means of summarizing data and presenting it in a usable and convenient form. (p. A.1)
- A frequency distribution arranges scores from a sample by indicating how often a particular score is presented. A histogram, or bar graph, presents the same data pictorially. (p. A.1)
- Central tendency is the most representative score in a distribution of scores. The mean (or average) is generally the best measure of central tendency. The median is the point or score in a distribution that divides the distribution in half, so that half the scores are higher and half are lower. The third measure of central tendency is the mode, the most frequently occurring score in a distribution of scores. (p. A.2)

How can we assess the variability of a set of data?

- The range and standard deviation are two measures of variability, which is the spread, or dispersion, of scores in a distribution. The range is the distance between the largest score in a distribution minus the smallest score. The standard deviation is an index of the extent to which the average score in a distribution deviates from the center of the distribution. (p. A.5)

How do we generalize from data?

- Inferential statistics, techniques that use data from samples to make predictions about a larger population, are useful in deciding whether differences between distributions of data are attributable to real differences or to chance variation. (p. A.7)

How can we determine the nature of a relationship, and the significance of differences, between two sets of scores?

- Measures of relationship provide a numerical index of the extent to which two variables are related. The correlation coefficient ranges in value from +1.00 to −1.00, with +1.00 indicating a perfect positive relationship and −1.00 a perfect negative relationship. Correlations close to or at zero indicate there is little or no relationship between two variables. (p. A.8)

Key Terms and Concepts

statistics (p. A.1)

descriptive statistics (p. A.1)

frequency distribution (p. A.1)

histogram (p. A.1)

central tendency (p. A.2)

mean (p. A.2)

median (p. A.3)

mode (p. A.3)

normal distribution (p. A.3)

variability (p. A.5)

range (p. A.5)

standard deviation (p. A.6)

population (p. A.7)

sample (p. A.7)

inferential statistics (p. A.8)

significant outcome (p. A.8)

positive relationship (p. A.8)

negative relationship (p. A.8)

correlation coefficient (p. A.10)

Glossary

a

absolute threshold   The smallest intensity of a stimulus that must be present for the stimulus to be detected (Ch. 4)

achievement test   A test designed to determine a person's level of knowledge in a given subject area (Ch. 9)

acquired immune deficiency syndrome (AIDS)   A fatal, sexually transmitted disease caused by a virus that destroys the body's immune system (Ch. 11)

action potential   An electric nerve impulse that travels through a neuron when it is set off by a "trigger," changing the neuron's charge from negative to positive (Ch. 3)

activation-synthesis theory   Hobson's theory that the brain produces random electrical energy during REM sleep that stimulates memories lodged in various portions of the brain (Ch. 5)

activity theory of aging   A theory that holds that the elderly who age most successfully are those who maintain the interests and activities they had during middle age (Ch. 13)

adaptation   An adjustment in sensory capacity following prolonged exposure to stimuli (Ch. 4)

addictive drugs   Drugs that produce a biological or psychological dependence in the user; withdrawal from them leads to a craving for the drug that in some cases can be nearly irresistible (Ch. 5)

adolescence   The developmental stage between childhood and adulthood (Ch. 13)

age of viability   The point at which the fetus can survive if born prematurely (Ch. 12)

aggression   The intentional infliction of injury or harm on another person (Ch. 18)

algorithm   A rule that, if applied appropriately, guarantees a solution to a problem (Ch. 8)

all-or-none law   The rule that neurons are either on or off (Ch. 3)

altruism   Helping behavior that is beneficial to others but clearly requires self-sacrifice (Ch. 18)

anal stage   According to Freud, a stage from 12 to 18 months to 3 years of age, in which a child's pleasure is centered on the anus (Ch. 14)

androgen   Male sex hormones secreted by the testes (Ch. 11)

androgynous   Having psychological and behavioral traits thought typical of both sexes (Ch. 11)

anorexia nervosa   A severe eating disorder in which people may refuse to eat, while denying that their behavior and appearance—which can become skeletonlike—are unusual (Ch. 10)

anorgasmia (an or GAZ mee uh)   A female's lack of orgasm (Ch. 11)

antianxiety drugs   Drugs that can reduce a person's level of anxiety, essentially by reducing excitability and increasing feelings of well-being (Ch. 17)

antidepressant drugs   Medication that improves a depressed patient's mood and feeling of well-being (Ch. 17)

antipsychotic drugs   Drugs that temporarily reduce psychotic symptoms such as agitation, overactivity, hallucinations, and delusions (Ch. 17)

antisocial personality disorder   A disorder in which individuals tend to display no regard for the moral and ethical rules of society or the rights of others (Ch. 16)

anxiety disorder   Anxiety with no obvious external cause that impairs daily functioning (Ch. 16)

aptitude test   A test designed to predict a person's ability in a particular area or line of work (Ch. 9)

archival research   Research in which existing data, such as census documents, college records, or newspaper clippings, are examined to test a hypothesis (Ch. 2)

arousal approaches to motivation   The belief that we try to maintain a certain level of stimulation and activity, increasing or reducing them as necessary (Ch. 10)

association areas   One of the major areas of the brain; the site of the higher mental processes such as thought, language, memory, and speech (Ch. 3)

associative models of memory   Models of memory as consisting of mental representations of clusters of interconnected information (Ch. 7)

assumed-similarity bias   The tendency to think of people as being similar to oneself, even when meeting them for the first time (Ch. 18)

attachment   The positive emotional bond that develops between a child and a particular individual (Ch. 12)

attention deficit hyperactivity disorder (ADHD)   A learning disability marked by inattention, impulsiveness, a low tolerance for frustration, and a great deal of inappropriate activity (Ch. 16)

attitudes   Learned predispositions to respond in a favorable or unfavorable manner to a particular person, behavior, belief, or thing (Ch. 18)

attribution theory   The theory of personality that seeks to explain how we decide, on the basis of samples of an individual's behavior, what the specific causes of that person's behavior are (Ch. 18)

authoritarian parents   Parents who are rigid and punitive and value unquestioning obedience from their children (Ch. 12)

authoritative parents   Parents who are firm, set clear limits, reason with their children, and explain things to them (Ch. 12)

autobiographical memories   Our recollections of circumstances and episodes from our own lives (Ch. 7)

autonomic division   The part of the nervous system that controls involuntary movement (the actions of the heart, glands, lungs, and other organs) (Ch. 3)

autonomy-versus-shame-and-doubt stage   The period during which, according to Erikson, toddlers (ages 18 months to 3 years) develop independence and autonomy if exploration and freedom are encouraged, or shame and self-doubt if they are restricted and overprotected (Ch. 12)

axon   The part of the neuron that carries messages destined for other neurons (Ch. 3)

b

babble   Speechlike but meaningless sounds made by children from the ages of around 3 months through 1 year (Ch. 8)

background stressors ("daily hassles")   Everyday annoyances, such as being stuck in traffic, that cause minor irritations that can have long-term ill effects if they continue or are compounded by other stressful events (Ch. 15)

basilar membrane   A vibrating structure that runs through the center of the cochlea, dividing it into an upper and a lower chamber, and containing sense receptors for sound (Ch. 4)

behavior modification   A formalized technique for promoting the frequency of desirable behaviors and decreasing the incidence of unwanted ones (Ch. 6)

behavioral assessment   Direct measures of an individual's behavior used to describe characteristics indicative of personality (Ch. 14)

behavioral genetics   The study of the effects of heredity on behavior (Ch. 3)

behavioral perspective   The perspective that looks at the behavior itself as the problem (Ch. 1, 16)

behavioral treatment approaches   Treatment approaches that build upon the basic processes of learning, such as reinforcement and extinction (Ch. 17)

biofeedback   A procedure in which a person learns to control through conscious thought internal physiological processes such as blood pressure, heart and respiration rate, skin temperature, sweating, and constriction of particular muscles (Ch. 3)

biological and evolutionary approaches to personality   The theory that important components of personality are inherited (Ch. 14)

biological perspective   The approach that views behavior from the perspective of biological functioning (Ch. 1)

biomedical therapy   Therapy that relies on drugs and other medical procedures to improve psychological functioning (Ch. 17)

biopsychologists (or behavioral neuroscientists)   Psychologists who specialize in considering the ways in which biological structures and functions of the body affect behavior (Ch. 3)

bipolar disorder   A disorder in which a person alternates between periods of euphoric feelings of mania and periods of depression (Ch. 16)

bisexuals   Persons who are sexually attracted to people of the same sex and people of the opposite sex (Ch. 11)

borderline personality disorder   A disorder in which individuals have difficulty developing a secure sense of who they are (Ch. 16)

bottom-up processing   Perception that consists of recognizing and processing information about the individual components of the stimuli (Ch. 4)

bulimia   A disorder in which a person binges on incredibly large quantities of food, then purges by vomiting or by using laxatives (Ch. 10)

C

Cannon-Bard theory of emotion   The belief that both physiological and emotional arousal are produced simultaneously by the same nerve stimulus (Ch. 10)

case study   An in-depth, intensive investigation of an individual or small group of people (Ch. 2)

cataclysmic events   Strong stressors that occur suddenly, affecting many people at once (e.g., natural disasters) (Ch. 15)

catharsis   The process of discharging built-up aggressive energy (Ch. 18)

central core   The "old brain," which controls such basic functions as eating and sleeping and is common to all vertebrates (Ch. 3)

central nervous system (CNS)   The system that includes the brain and spinal cord (Ch. 3)

central-route processing   Message interpretation characterized by thoughtful consideration of the issues and arguments used to persuade (Ch. 18)

central tendency   An index of the central location within a distribution of scores; the most representative score in a distribution of scores (the mean, median, and mode are measures of central tendency) (App.)

central traits   The major traits considered in forming impressions of others (Ch. 18)

cerebellum (ser uh BELL um)   The part of the brain that controls bodily balance (Ch. 3)

cerebral cortex   The "new brain," responsible for the most sophisticated information processing in the brain; contains the lobes (Ch. 3)

chromosomes   Rod-shaped structures that contain the basic hereditary information (Ch. 12)

chunk   A meaningful grouping of stimuli that can be stored as a unit in short-term memory (Ch. 7)

circadian rhythms   Biological processes that occur repeatedly on approximately a twenty-four-hour cycle (Ch. 5)

classical conditioning   A type of learning in which a neutral stimulus comes to bring about a response after it is paired with a stimulus that naturally brings about that response (Ch. 6)

client-centered therapy   Therapy in which the goal is to reach one's potential for self-actualization (Ch. 17)

cochlea (KOKE lee uh)   A coiled tube in the ear filled with fluid that vibrates in response to sound (Ch. 4)

cognitive approaches of motivation   The theory suggesting that motivation is a product of people's thoughts and expectations—their cognitions (Ch. 10)

cognitive-behavioral approach   An approach used by cognitive therapists that attempts to change the way people think through the use of basic principles of learning (Ch. 17)

cognitive development   The process by which a child's understanding of the world changes as a function of age and experience (Ch. 12)

cognitive dissonance   The conflict that occurs when a person holds two attitudes or thoughts (referred to as cognitions) that contradict each other (Ch. 18)

cognitive map   A mental representation of spatial locations and directions (Ch. 6)

cognitive perspective   The approach that focuses on how people think, understand, and know about the world (Ch. 1)

cognitive perspective   The perspective that people's thoughts and beliefs are a central component of abnormal behavior (Ch. 16)

cognitive psychology   The branch of psychology that focuses on the study of cognition (Ch. 8)

cognitive-social learning theory   The study of the thought processes that underlie learning (Ch. 6)

cognitive treatment approaches   Approaches to treatment that teach people to think in more adaptive ways by changing their dysfunctional cognitions about the world and themselves (Ch. 17)

collective unconscious   A set of influences we inherit from our own particular ancestors, the whole human race, and even animal ancestors from the distant evolutionary past (Ch. 14)

community psychology   A branch of psychology that focuses on the prevention and minimization of psychological disorders in the community (Ch. 17)

companionate love   The strong affection we have for those with whom our lives are deeply involved (Ch. 18)

compliance   Conforming behavior that occurs in response to direct social pressure (Ch. 18)

compulsion   An irresistible urge to repeatedly carry out some act that seems strange and unreasonable (Ch. 16)

concepts   Categorizations of objects, events, or people that share common properties (Ch. 8)

concrete operational stage   According to Piaget, the period from 7 to 12 years of age, which is characterized by logical thought and a loss of egocentrism (Ch. 12)

conditioned response (CR)   A response that, after conditioning, follows a previously neutral stimulus (e.g., salivation at the ringing of a bell) (Ch. 6)

conditioned stimulus (CS)   A once-neutral stimulus that has been paired with an unconditioned stimulus to bring about a response formerly caused only by the unconditioned stimulus (Ch. 6)

cones   Cone-shaped, light-sensitive receptor cells in the retina that are responsible for sharp focus and color perception, particularly in bright light (Ch. 4)

conformity   A change in behavior or attitudes brought about by a desire to follow the beliefs or standards of other people (Ch. 18)

consciousness   The awareness of the sensations, thoughts, and feelings being experienced at a given moment (Ch. 5)

constructive processes   Processes in which memories are influenced by the meaning we give to events (Ch. 7)

continuous reinforcement schedule   Reinforcement of behavior every time it occurs (Ch. 6)

control group   A group that receives no treatment in an experiment (Ch. 2)

convergent thinking   The ability to produce responses that are based primarily on knowledge and logic (Ch. 8)

conversion disorder   A major somatoform disorder that involves an actual physical disturbance, such as the inability to use a sensory organ or the complete or partial inability to move an arm or leg (Ch. 16)

coping   Efforts to control, reduce, or learn to tolerate the threats that lead to stress (Ch. 15)

correlation coefficient   A numerical measure that indicates the relationship between two variables (App.)

correlational research   Research that examines the relationship between two sets of variables to determine whether they are associated, or "correlated" (Ch. 2)

creativity   The combining of responses or ideas in novel ways (Ch. 8)

cross-sectional research   A research method in which people of different ages are compared at the same point in time (Ch. 12)

cross-sequential research   A research method that combines cross-sectional and longitudinal research by considering a number of different age groups and examining them over several points in time (Ch. 12)

crystallized intelligence   The accumulation of information, skills, and strategies learned through experience and that can be applied in problem-solving situations (Ch. 9)

culture-fair IQ test A test that does not discriminate against members of any minority group (Ch. 9)

d

date rape Rape in which the rapist is either a date or romantic acquaintance (Ch. 11)

daydreams Fantasies that people construct while awake (Ch. 5)

decay The loss of information in memory through its nonuse (Ch. 7)

declarative memory Memory for factual information: names, faces, dates, and the like (Ch. 7)

defense mechanisms Unconscious strategies people use to reduce anxiety by concealing the source of the anxiety from themselves and others (Ch. 14, 15)

deinstitutionalization The transfer of former mental patients from institutions into the community (Ch. 17)

dendrites A cluster of fibers at one end of a neuron that receive messages from other neurons (Ch. 3)

dependent variable The variable that is measured and is expected to change as a result of changes caused by the experimenter's manipulation (Ch. 2)

depressants Drugs that slow down the nervous system (Ch. 5)

descriptive statistics The branch of statistics that provides a means of summarizing data (App.)

developmental psychology The branch of psychology that studies the patterns of growth and change occurring throughout life (Ch. 12)

Diagnostic and Statistical Manual of Mental Disorders, Fourth Edition (DSM-IV) The manual of the American Psychiatric Association that presents the diagnostic system used by most U.S. mental health professionals to diagnose and classify abnormal behavior (Ch. 16)

difference threshold The smallest level of stimulation required to sense that a change in stimulation has occurred (Ch. 4)

diffusion of responsibility The tendency for people to feel that responsibility for acting is shared, or diffused, among those present (Ch. 18)

discrimination Negative behavior toward members of a particular group (Ch. 18)

disengagement theory of aging A theory that holds that aging is a gradual withdrawal from the world on physical, psychological, and social levels (Ch. 13)

display rules The guidelines that govern the appropriateness of showing emotion nonverbally (Ch. 10)

dispositional causes (of behavior) A perceived cause of behavior that is based on internal traits or personality factors (Ch. 18)

dissociative amnesia A disorder in which the person has significant, selective memory loss (Ch. 16)

dissociative disorder Psychological dysfunctions characterized by the separation of critical personality facets that are normally integrated, allowing stress avoidance by escape (Ch. 16)

dissociative fugue A form of amnesia in which people take sudden, impulsive trips, sometimes assuming a new identity (Ch. 16)

dissociative identity disorder (multiple personality) A disorder in which a person displays characteristics of two or more distinct personalities (Ch. 16)

divergent thinking The ability to generate unusual, yet appropriate, responses to problems or questions (Ch. 8)

double standard The view that premarital sex is permissible for males but not for females (Ch. 11)

dreams-for-survival theory The theory that dreams permit information that is critical for our daily survival to be reconsidered and reprocessed during sleep (Ch. 5)

drive Motivational tension, or arousal, that energizes behavior in order to fulfill some need (Ch. 10)

drive-reduction approaches to motivation A theory suggesting that when people lack some basic biological requirement such as water, a drive to obtain that requirement (in this case, the thirst drive) is produced (Ch. 10)

drug therapy Control of psychological problems through drugs (Ch. 17)

e

eardrum The part of the ear that vibrates when sound waves hit it (Ch. 4)

echoic memory Memory of auditory information coming from the ears (Ch. 7)

eclectic approach to therapy An approach to therapy that uses techniques taken from a variety of treatment methods, rather than just one method (Ch. 17)

ego The part of the personality that provides a buffer between the id and the outside world (Ch. 14)

egocentric thought A way of thinking in which the child views the world entirely from his or her own perspective (Ch. 12)

ego-integrity-versus-despair stage According to Erikson, a period from late adulthood until death during which we review our life's accomplishments and failures (Ch. 13)

electroconvulsive therapy (ECT) A procedure in which an electric current of 70 to 150 volts is briefly administered to a patient's head, causing a loss of consciousness and often seizures (Ch. 17)

embryo A developed zygote that has a rudimentary heart, brain, and other organs (Ch. 12)

emotional intelligence The set of skills that underlie the accurate assessment, evaluation, expression, and regulation of emotions (Ch. 9)

emotions Feelings that generally have both physiological and cognitive elements and that influence behavior (Ch. 10)

endocrine system A chemical communication network that sends messages throughout the nervous system via the bloodstream (Ch. 3)

episodic memory Memory for the biographical details of our individual lives (Ch. 7)

erectile dysfunction The inability of a male to achieve or maintain an erection (Ch. 11)

erogenous zones Areas of the body that are particularly sensitive to touch because of the presence of an unusually rich array of nerve receptors (Ch. 11)

estrogen Female sex hormone (Ch. 11)

evolutionary psychology The branch of psychology that seeks to identify behavior patterns that result from our genetic inheritance from our ancestors (Ch. 3)

excitatory message A chemical message that makes it more likely that a receiving neuron will fire and an action potential will travel down its axons (Ch. 3)

excitement phase The phase during which an arousing stimulus begins a sequence that prepares the genitals for sexual intercourse (Ch. 11)

experiment The investigation of the relationship between two (or more) variables by deliberately producing a change in one variable in a situation and observing the effects of that change on other aspects of the situation (Ch. 2)

experimental bias Factors that distort how the independent variable affects the dependent variable in an experiment (Ch. 2)

experimental group Any group receiving a treatment in an experiment (Ch. 2)

experimental manipulation The change that an experimenter deliberately produces in a situation (Ch. 2)

explicit memory Intentional or conscious recollection of information (Ch. 7)

extinction The decrease in frequency, and eventual disappearance, of a previously conditioned response; one of the basic phenomena of learning (Ch. 6)

extramarital sex Sexual activity between a married person and someone who is not his or her spouse (Ch. 11)

f

facial-affect program The activation of a set of nerve impulses that make the face display the appropriate expression (Ch. 10)

facial-feedback hypothesis The hypothesis that facial expressions not only *reflect* emotional experience, they also help *determine* how people experience and label emotions (Ch. 10)

family therapy An approach that focuses on the family and its dynamics (Ch. 17)

feature analysis A theory of perception according to which we perceive a shape, pattern, object, or scene by reacting first to the individual elements that make it up (Ch. 4)

feature detection   The activation of neurons in the cortex by visual stimuli of specific shapes or patterns (Ch. 4)

fetus   A developing child, from 8 weeks after conception until birth (Ch. 12)

fixation   Conflicts or concerns that persist beyond the developmental period in which they first occur (Ch. 14)

fixed-interval schedule   A schedule that provides reinforcement for a response only if a fixed time period has elapsed, making overall rates of response relatively low (Ch. 6)

fixed-ratio schedule   A schedule whereby reinforcement is given only after a certain number of responses are made (Ch. 6)

flashbulb memories   Memories of a specific, important, or surprising event that are so vivid, they are like a snapshot of the event (Ch. 7)

fluid intelligence   Intelligence that reflects information-processing capabilities, reasoning, and memory (Ch. 9)

formal operational stage   According to Piaget, the period from age 12 to adulthood, which is characterized by abstract thought (Ch. 12)

frequency distribution   An arrangement of scores from a sample that indicates how often a particular score is present (App.)

frequency theory of hearing   The theory that the entire basilar membrane acts like a microphone, vibrating as a whole in response to a sound (Ch. 4)

frustration   The thwarting or blocking of some ongoing, goal-directed behavior (Ch. 18)

functional fixedness   The tendency to think of an object only in terms of its typical use (Ch. 8)

functionalism   An early approach to psychology that concentrated on what the mind does—the functions of mental activity—and the role of behavior in allowing people to adapt to their environments (Ch. 2)

fundamental attribution error   A tendency to attribute others' behavior to dispositional causes and the tendency to minimize the importance of situational causes (Ch. 18)

g

g or g-factor   The single, general factor for mental ability that was assumed to underlie intelligence in some early theories of intelligence (Ch. 9)

gate-control theory of pain   The theory that particular nerve receptors lead to specific areas of the brain related to pain (Ch. 4)

gender   The perception of being male or female (Ch. 11)

gender roles   The set of expectations, defined by a particular society, that indicate what is appropriate behavior for women and men (Ch. 11)

gender schema   A mental framework that organizes and guides a child's understanding of information relevant to gender (Ch. 11)

general adaptation syndrome (GAS)   A theory developed by Selye that suggests that a person's response to stress consists of three stages: alarm and mobilization, resistance, and exhaustion (Ch. 15)

generalized anxiety disorder   Long-term, persistent anxiety and worry (Ch. 16)

generativity-versus-stagnation stage According to Erikson, a period in middle adulthood during which we take stock of our contributions to family and society (Ch. 13)

genes   The parts of the chromosomes through which genetic information is transmitted (Ch. 12)

genetic preprogramming theories of aging Theories that hold that there is a built-in time limit to the reproduction of human cells, and that after a certain time they are no longer able to divide (Ch. 13)

genital stage   According to Freud, the period from puberty until death, marked by mature sexual behavior (i.e., sexual intercourse) (Ch. 14)

genitals   The female and male sex organs (Ch. 11)

gestalt (geh SHTALLT) psychology   An approach to psychology that focuses on the organization of perception and thinking in a "whole" sense, rather than on the individual elements of perception (Ch. 1)

gestalt laws of organization   A series of principles that describe how we organize bits and pieces of information into meaningful wholes (Ch. 4)

gestalt therapy   An approach to therapy that attempts to integrate a client's thoughts, feelings, and behavior into a unified whole (Ch. 17)

grammar   The system of rules that determine how our thoughts can be expressed (Ch. 8)

group therapy   Therapy in which people discuss problems in a group (Ch. 17)

h

habituation   The decrease in the response to a stimulus that occurs after repeated presentations of the same stimulus (Ch. 12)

hair cells   Tiny cells covering the basilar membrane that, when bent by vibrations entering the cochlea, transmit neural messages to the brain (Ch. 4)

hallucinogen   A drug that is capable of producing hallucinations, or changes in the perceptual process (Ch. 5)

halo effect   A phenomenon in which an initial perception of a person as having positive traits produces the expectation that the person has other uniformly positive characteristics (Ch. 18)

hardiness   A personality characteristic associated with a lower rate of stress-related illness, consisting of three components: commitment, challenge, and control (Ch. 15)

health psychology   The branch of psychology that investigates the psychological factors related to wellness and illness,

including the prevention, diagnosis, and treatment of medical problems (Ch. 15)

hemispheres   The two symmetrical left and right halves of the brain; each controls the side of the body opposite to it (Ch. 3)

heritability   A measure of the degree to which a characteristic is related to genetic, inherited factors (Ch. 9)

heterosexuality   Sexual attraction and behavior directed to the opposite sex (Ch. 11)

heuristic   A cognitive shortcut that might lead to a solution (Ch. 8)

histogram   Bar graph (App.)

homeostasis   The body's tendency to maintain a steady internal state (Ch. 10)

homosexuals   Persons who are sexually attracted to people of their own sex (Ch. 11)

hormones   Chemicals that circulate through the blood and affect the functioning or growth of other parts of the body (Ch. 3)

humanistic approaches to personality   The theory that people are basically good and tend to grow to higher levels of functioning (Ch. 14)

humanistic perspective   The approach that suggests that all individuals naturally strive to grow, develop, and be in control of their lives and behavior (Ch. 1)

humanistic perspective   The perspective that emphasizes people's responsibility for their own behavior, even when such behavior is abnormal (Ch. 16)

humanistic therapy   Therapy in which the underlying assumption is that people have control of their behavior, can make choices about their lives, and are essentially responsible for solving their own problems (Ch. 17)

hypnosis   A trancelike state of heightened susceptibility to the suggestions of others (Ch. 5)

hypochondriasis   A disorder involving having a constant fear of illness and a preoccupation with one's health (Ch. 16)

hypothalamus   A tiny part of the brain, located below the thalamus of the brain, that maintains homeostasis and produces and regulates vital, basic behavior such as eating, drinking, and sexual behavior (Ch. 3)

hypothesis   A prediction, stemming from a theory, stated in a way that allows it to be tested (Ch. 2)

i

iconic memory   Memory of information from our visual system (Ch. 7)

id   The raw, unorganized, inborn part of personality, whose sole purpose is to reduce tension created by primitive drives related to hunger, sex, aggression, and irrational impulses (Ch. 14)

identical twins   Twins who are genetically identical (Ch. 12)

identification   The process of trying to be like another person as much as possible, imitating that person's behavior and adopting similar beliefs and values (Ch. 14)

identity The distinguishing character of the individual: who each of us is, what our roles are, and what we are capable of (Ch. 13)

identity-versus-role-confusion stage According to Erikson, a time in adolescence of major testing to determine one's unique qualities (Ch. 13)

implicit memory Memories people are not consciously aware of, but that can affect their subsequent performance and behavior (Ch. 7)

incentive approaches to motivation The theory suggesting that motivation stems from the desire to obtain valued external goals, or incentives (Ch. 10)

independent variable The variable that is manipulated by an experimenter (Ch. 2)

industrial-organizational (I/O) psychology The branch of psychology that focuses on work and job-related issues, including productivity, job satisfaction, decision making, and consumer behavior (Ch. 18)

industry-versus-inferiority stage According to Erikson, the last stage of childhood, during which children aged 6 to 12 years either develop positive social interactions with others or feel inadequate and become less sociable (Ch. 12)

inferential statistics The branch of statistics that uses data from samples to make predictions about the larger population from which the sample is drawn (App.)

inferiority complex According to Adler, a complex developed by adults who have not been able to overcome the feelings of inferiority they developed as children, when they were small and limited in their knowledge about the world (Ch. 14)

information processing The way people take in, use, and store information (Ch. 12)

informed consent A document signed by participants affirming that they have been told the basic outlines of a research study and are aware of what their participation will involve (Ch. 2)

inhibited ejaculation The inability of a male to ejaculate when he wants to, if at all (Ch. 11)

inhibited sexual desire A sexual dysfunction in which the motivation for sexual activity is restrained or lacking entirely (Ch. 11)

inhibitory message A chemical message that prevents a receiving neuron from firing (Ch. 3)

initiative-versus-guilt stage According to Erikson, the period during which children ages 3 to 6 years experience conflict between independence of action and the sometimes negative results of that action (Ch. 12)

insight A sudden awareness of the relationships among various elements that had previously appeared to be independent of one another (Ch. 8)

instincts Inborn patterns of behavior that are biologically determined rather than learned (Ch. 10)

intellectually gifted Having an IQ score above 130; about 2 to 4 percent of the population (Ch. 9)

intelligence The capacity to understand the world, think rationally, and use resources effectively when faced with challenges (Ch. 9)

intelligence quotient (IQ) A score that takes into account an individual's mental and chronological ages (Ch. 9)

intelligence tests Tests devised to identify a person's level of intelligence (Ch. 9)

interference The phenomenon by which information in memory displaces or blocks out other information, preventing its recall (Ch. 7)

interneurons Neurons that connect sensory and motor neurons, carrying messages between the two (Ch. 3)

interpersonal attraction (or close relationships) Positive feelings for others; liking and loving (Ch. 18)

intimacy-versus-isolation stage According to Erikson, a period during early adulthood that focuses on developing close relationships (Ch. 13)

introspection A procedure used to study the structure of the mind, in which subjects are asked to describe in detail what they are experiencing when they are exposed to a stimulus (Ch. 1)

j

James-Lange theory of emotion The belief that emotional experience is a reaction to bodily events occurring as a result of an external situation ("I feel sad because I am crying") (Ch. 10)

just noticeable difference The minimum stimulation required to detect the difference between two stimuli (Ch. 4)

l

language The communication of information through symbols arranged according to systematic rules (Ch. 8)

language acquisition device A hypothesized neural system of the brain for understanding language (Ch. 8)

latency period According to Freud, the period between the phallic stage and puberty during which children temporarily put aside their sexual interests (Ch. 14)

latent content of dreams According to Freud, the "disguised" or real meanings of dreams, hidden by more obvious subjects (Ch. 5)

latent learning Learning in which a new behavior is acquired but is not demonstrated until reinforcement is provided (Ch. 6)

lateralization The dominance of one hemisphere of the brain in specific functions (Ch. 3)

learned helplessness A state in which people conclude that unpleasant or aversive stimuli cannot be controlled—a view of the world that becomes so ingrained that they cease trying to remedy their aversive circumstances, even if they actually could exert some influence on them (Ch. 15)

learning A relatively permanent change in behavior brought about by experience (Ch. 6)

learning-theory approach The theory suggesting that language acquisition follows the principles of reinforcement and conditioning (Ch. 8)

levels-of-processing theory The theory of memory that emphasizes the degree to which new material is mentally analyzed (Ch. 7)

life review The process in which people in late adulthood examine and evaluate their lives (Ch. 13)

limbic system The part of the brain located outside the "new brain" that controls eating, aggression, and reproduction (Ch. 3)

lithium A mineral salt used to treat bipolar disorders (Ch. 17)

lobes The four major sections of the cerebral cortex: frontal, parietal, temporal, and occipital (Ch. 3)

longitudinal research A research method that investigates behavior as participants age (Ch. 12)

long-term memory Memory that stores information on a relatively permanent basis, although it might be difficult to retrieve (Ch. 7)

m

major depression A severe form of depression that interferes with concentration, decision making, and sociability (Ch. 16)

mania An extended state of intense, wild elation (Ch. 16)

manifest content of dreams According to Freud, the overt story line of dreams (Ch. 15)

masturbation Sexual self-stimulation (Ch. 11)

mean The average of all scores, arrived at by adding scores together and dividing by the number of scores (App.)

means-end analysis Repeated testing for differences between the desired outcome and what currently exists (Ch. 8)

median The point in a distribution of scores that divides the distribution exactly in half when the scores are listed in numerical order (App.)

medical perspective The perspective that the root cause of abnormal behavior will be found in a physical examination of the individual, which might reveal a hormonal imbalance, a chemical deficiency, or a brain injury (Ch. 16)

meditation A learned technique for refocusing attention that brings about an altered state of consciousness (Ch. 5)

memory trace A physical change in the brain that occurs when new material is learned (Ch. 7)

memory The process by which we encode, store, and retrieve information (Ch. 7)

menopause The point at which women stop menstruating and are no longer fertile (Ch. 13)

mental age The average age of individuals who achieve a particular level of performance on a test (Ch. 9)

mental images   Representations in the mind that resemble the object or event being represented (Ch. 8)

mental retardation   Having significantly below-average intellectual functioning and limitations in at least two areas of adaptive functioning (Ch. 9)

mental set   The tendency for old patterns of problem solving to persist (Ch. 8)

metabolism   The rate at which food is converted to energy and expended by the body (Ch. 10)

metacognition   An awareness and understanding of one's own cognitive processes (Ch. 12)

Minnesota Multiphasic Personality Inventory-2 (MMPI-2)   A test used to identify people with psychological difficulties as well as to predict such behavior as job performance (Ch. 14)

mode   The most frequently occurring score in a set of scores (App.)

mood disorder   Disturbances in emotional feelings strong enough to interfere with everyday living (Ch. 16)

motivation   The factors that direct and energize the behavior of humans and other organisms (Ch. 10)

motor (efferent) neurons   Neurons that communicate information from the nervous system to muscles and glands of the body (Ch. 3)

motor area   The part of the cortex that is largely responsible for the voluntary movement of particular parts of the body (Ch. 3)

myelin sheath   Specialized cells of fat and protein that wrap themselves around the axon, providing a protective coating (Ch. 3)

n

narcissistic personality disorder   A personality disturbance characterized by an exaggerated sense of self-importance (Ch. 16)

narcotics   Drugs that increase relaxation and relieve pain and anxiety (Ch. 15)

naturalistic observation   Research in which an investigator simply observes some naturally occurring behavior and does not make a change in the situation (Ch. 2)

nature-nurture issue   The issue of the degrees to which environment and heredity influence behavior and development (Ch. 12)

need for achievement   A stable, learned characteristic in which satisfaction is obtained by striving for and attaining a level of excellence (Ch. 10)

need for affiliation   An interest in establishing and maintaining relationships with other people (Ch. 10)

need for power   A tendency to seek impact, control, or influence over others, and to be seen as a powerful individual (Ch. 10)

negative reinforcer   An unpleasant stimulus whose removal leads to an increase in the probability that a preceding response will occur again in the future (Ch. 6)

negative relationship   A relationship established by data that shows high values of one variable corresponding with low values of the other (App.)

neo-Freudian psychoanalysts   Psychoanalysts who were trained in traditional Freudian theory but who later rejected some of its major points (Ch. 14)

neonate   A newborn child (Ch. 12)

neurons   Nerve cells, the basic elements of the nervous system (Ch. 3)

neurotransmitters   Chemicals that carry messages across the synapse to the dendrite (and sometimes the cell body) of a receiver neuron (Ch. 3)

neutral stimulus   A stimulus that, before conditioning, does not naturally bring about the response of interest (Ch. 6)

normal distribution   A distribution of scores that produces a bell-shaped, symmetrical curve (App.)

norms   Standards of test performance that permit the comparison of one person's score on the test to the scores of others who have taken the same test (Ch. 9)

o

obedience   Conforming behavior in reaction to the commands of others (Ch. 18)

obesity   The state of being more than 20 percent above the average weight for a person of one's height (Ch. 10)

object permanence   The awareness that objects—and people—continue to exist even if they are out of sight (Ch. 12)

observational learning   Learning through observing the behavior of another person called a model (Ch. 6)

obsession   A persistent, unwanted thought or idea that keeps recurring (Ch. 16)

obsessive-compulsive disorder   A disorder characterized by obsessions or compulsions (Ch. 16)

Oedipus conflict   A child's sexual interest in his or her opposite-sex parent, typically resolved through identification with the same-sex parent (Ch. 14)

operant conditioning   Learning in which a voluntary response is strengthened or weakened, depending on its favorable or unfavorable consequences (Ch. 6)

operationalization   The process of translating a hypothesis into specific, testable procedures that can be measured and observed (Ch. 2)

opponent-process theory of color vision   The theory that receptor cells are linked in pairs, working in opposition to each other (Ch. 4)

optic nerve   A bundle of ganglion axons that carry visual information (Ch. 4)

oral stage   According to Freud, a stage from birth to 12 to 18 months, in which an infant's center of pleasure is the mouth (Ch. 14)

orgasm   The peak of sexual excitement during which rhythmic muscular contractions occur in the genitals (Ch. 11)

otoliths   Tiny, motion-sensitive crystals within the semicircular canals that sense body acceleration (Ch. 4)

overgeneralization   The phenomenon whereby children apply rules even when their application results in an error (Ch. 8)

ovulation   The point at which an egg is released from the ovaries (Ch. 11)

p

panic disorder   Anxiety that reveals itself in the form of panic attacks that last from a few seconds to as long as several hours (Ch. 16)

parasympathetic division   The part of the autonomic division of the nervous system that acts to calm the body after the emergency situation is resolved (Ch. 3)

partial reinforcement schedule   Reinforcement of behavior some but not all of the time (Ch. 6)

passionate (or romantic) love   A state of intense absorption in someone that includes intense physiological arousal, psychological interest, and caring for the needs of another (Ch. 18)

perception   The sorting out, interpretation, analysis, and integration of stimuli involving our sense organs and brain (Ch. 4)

peripheral nervous system   The part of the nervous system that includes the autonomic and somatic subdivisions; made up of long axons and dendrites, it branches out from the spinal cord and brain and reaches the extremities of the body (Ch. 3)

peripheral-route processing   Message interpretation characterized by consideration of the source and related general information rather than of the message itself (Ch. 18)

permissive parents   Parents who give their children lax or inconsistent direction and, although warm, require little of them (Ch. 12)

personal stressors   Major life events, such as the death of a family member, that have immediate negative consequences that usually fade with time (Ch. 15)

personality   The pattern of enduring characteristics that differentiates a person— the patterns of behaviors that make each individual unique (Ch. 14)

personality disorder   A mental disorder characterized by a set of inflexible, maladaptive personality traits that keep a person from functioning properly in society (Ch. 16)

phallic stage   According to Freud, a period beginning around age 3 during which a child's interest focuses on the genitals (Ch. 14)

phobias   Intense, irrational fears of specific objects or situations (Ch. 16)

phonemes   The smallest basic sound units (Ch. 8)

phonology   The study of the smallest sound units, called phonemes (Ch. 8)

pituitary gland   The "master gland," the major component of the endocrine system, which secretes hormones that control growth (Ch. 3)

place theory of hearing The theory that different areas of the basilar membrane respond to different frequencies (Ch. 4)

placebo A false treatment, such as a pill, "drug," or other substance, that has no significant chemical properties or active ingredient (Ch. 2)

plateau phase The period in which the maximum level of arousal is attained, the penis and clitoris swell with blood, and the body prepares for orgasm (Ch. 11)

population All the members of a group of interest (App.)

positive reinforcer A stimulus added to the environment that brings about an increase in a preceding response (Ch. 6)

positive relationship A relationship established by data that shows high values of one variable corresponding with high values of another, and low values of the first variable corresponding with low values of the other (App.)

posttraumatic stress disorder (PTSD) A phenomenon in which victims of major catastrophes reexperience the original stress event and associated feelings in vivid flashbacks or dreams (Ch. 15)

practical intelligence Intelligence related to overall success in living (Ch. 9)

prejudice The negative (or positive) evaluations of groups and their members (Ch. 18)

premature ejaculation The inability of a male to delay orgasm as long as he wishes to (Ch. 11)

preoperational stage According to Piaget, the period from 2 to 7 years of age which is characterized by language development (Ch. 12)

priming A phenomenon in which exposure to a word or concept (called a prime) later makes it easier to recall related information, even when one has no conscious memory of the word or concept (Ch. 7)

principle of conservation The knowledge that the quantity of a substance remains the same even though its shape or other aspects of its physical appearance might change (Ch. 12)

procedural memory Memory for skills and habits, such as riding a bike or hitting a baseball, sometimes referred to as "nondeclarative memory" (Ch. 7)

progesterone Female sex hormone (Ch. 11)

projective personality test A test in which a person is shown an ambiguous stimulus and asked to describe it or tell a story about it (Ch. 14)

prosocial behavior Helping behavior (Ch. 18)

prototypes Typical, highly representative examples of a concept (Ch. 8)

psychoactive drugs Drugs that influence a person's emotions, perceptions, and behavior (Ch. 5)

psychoanalysis Psychodynamic therapy that involves frequent sessions and can last for many years (Ch. 17)

psychoanalytic perspective The perspective that abnormal behavior stems from childhood conflicts over opposing wishes regarding sex and aggression (Ch. 16)

psychoanalytic theory Freud's theory that unconscious forces act as determinants of personality (Ch. 14)

psychodynamic perspective The approach based on the belief that behavior is motivated by unconscious inner forces over which the individual has little control (Ch. 1)

psychodynamic therapy First suggested by Freud, therapy based on the premise that the primary sources of abnormal behavior are unresolved past conflicts and the possibility that unacceptable unconscious impulses will enter consciousness (Ch. 17)

psychological tests Standard measures devised to assess behavior objectively and used by psychologists to help people make decisions about their lives and understand more about themselves (Ch. 14)

psychology The scientific study of behavior and mental processes (Ch. 1)

psychoneuroimmunology (PNI) The study of the relationships among psychological factors, the immune system, and the brain (Ch. 15)

psychophysics The study of the relationship between the physical aspects of stimuli and our psychological experience of them (Ch. 4)

psychophysiological disorders Medical problems influenced by an interaction of psychological, emotional, and physical difficulties (Ch. 15)

psychosocial development Development of individuals' interactions and understanding of each other and of their knowledge and understanding of themselves as members of society (Ch. 12)

psychosurgery Brain surgery once used to reduce symptoms of mental disorder but rarely used today (Ch. 17)

psychotherapy Treatment in which a trained professional—a therapist—uses psychological techniques to help someone overcome psychological difficulties and disorders, resolve problems in living, or bring about personal growth (Ch. 17)

puberty The period during which maturation of the sexual organs occurs, beginning at about age 11 or 12 for girls and 13 or 14 for boys (Ch. 13)

punishment A stimulus that decreases the probability that a previous behavior will occur again (Ch. 6)

r

random assignment to condition A procedure in which participants are assigned to different experimental groups or "conditions" on the basis of chance and chance alone (Ch. 2)

range The difference between the highest and lowest score in a distribution (App.)

rape An act of forcing another person to submit to sexual activity (Ch. 11)

rapid eye movement (REM) sleep Sleep occupying 20 percent of an adult's sleeping time, characterized by increased heart rate, blood pressure, and breathing rate; erections; eye movements; and the experience of dreaming (Ch. 5)

rational-emotive behavior therapy A form of therapy that attempts to restructure a person's belief system into a more realistic, rational, and logical set of views (Ch. 17)

reactance A negative emotional and cognitive reaction to a restriction of one's freedom that can be associated with medical regimens (Ch. 15)

reciprocity-of-liking effect A tendency to like those who like us (Ch. 18)

reflexes Automatic, involuntary responses to incoming stimuli (Ch. 3)

reflexes Unlearned, involuntary responses that occur automatically in the presence of certain stimuli (Ch. 12)

refractory period A temporary period following the resolution stage during which the male cannot be sexually aroused again (Ch. 11)

rehearsal The repetition of information that has entered short-term memory (Ch. 7)

reinforcement The process by which a stimulus increases the probability that a preceding behavior will be repeated (Ch. 6)

reinforcer Any stimulus that increases the probability that a preceding behavior will occur again (Ch. 6)

reliability A test's measuring consistently what it is supposed to measure (Ch. 9)

replication The repetition of research, sometimes using other procedures, settings, and other groups of participants, in order to increase confidence in prior findings (Ch. 2)

resolution stage The interval following orgasm in which the body returns to its normal state, reversing the changes brought about by arousal (Ch. 11)

resting state The state in which there is a negative electrical charge of about −70 millivolts within the neuron (Ch. 3)

reticular formation The part of the brain from the medulla through the pons made up of groups of nerve cells that can immediately activate other parts of the brain to produce general bodily arousal (Ch. 3)

retina The part of the eye that converts the electromagnetic energy of light into useful information for the brain (Ch. 4)

reuptake The reabsorption of neurotransmitters by a terminal button (Ch. 3)

rods Thin, cylindrical receptor cells in the retina that are highly sensitive to light (Ch. 4)

Rorschach test A test by developed by Swiss psychiatrist Hermann Rorschach that consists of showing a series of symmetrical stimuli to people and then asking them to say what the figures represent to them (Ch. 14)

s

sample A subgroup of a population of interest (App.)

Schachter-Singer theory of emotion   The belief that emotions are determined jointly by a nonspecific kind of physiological arousal and its interpretation, based on environmental cues (Ch. 10)

schedules of reinforcement   The frequency and timing of reinforcement following desired behavior (Ch. 6)

schemas   Organized bodies of information stored in memory that bias the way new information is interpreted, stored, and recalled (Ch. 7)

schemas   Sets of cognitions about people and social experiences (Ch. 18)

schizophrenia   A class of disorders involving severe distortions of reality (Ch. 16)

scientific method   The approach used by psychologists to systematically acquire knowledge and understanding about behavior and other phenomena of interest (Ch. 2)

self-actualization   A state of self-fulfillment in which people realize their highest potential in their own unique way (Ch. 10)

self-actualization   According to Rogers, a state of self-fulfillment in which people realize their highest potential (Ch. 14)

self-report measures   A method of gathering data about people by asking them questions about a sample of their behavior (Ch. 14)

semantic memory   Memory for general knowledge and facts about the world, as well as memory for the rules of logic that are used to deduce other facts (Ch. 7)

semantics   The rules governing the meaning of words and sentences (Ch. 8)

semicircular canals   Three tubelike structures of the inner ear containing fluid that sloshes through them when the head moves, signaling rotational or angular movement to the brain (Ch. 4)

sensation   The processes by which our sense organs receive information from the environment (Ch. 4)

sensorimotor stage   According to Piaget, the stage from birth to 2 years, during which a child has little competence in representing the environment using images, language, or other symbols (Ch. 12)

sensory (afferent) neurons   Neurons that transmit information from the perimeter of the body to the central nervous system (Ch. 3)

sensory area   The site in the brain of the tissue that corresponds to each of the senses, with the degree of sensitivity relating to the amount of tissue (Ch. 3)

sensory memory   The initial, momentary storage of information, lasting only an instant (Ch. 7)

sexism   Negative attitudes and behavior toward a person based on that person's gender (Ch. 11)

sexually transmitted disease (STD)   A disease acquired through sexual contact (Ch. 11)

shaping   The process of teaching a complex behavior by rewarding closer and closer approximations to the desired behavior (Ch. 6)

short-term memory   Memory that holds information for 15 to 25 seconds (Ch. 7)

significant outcome   Meaningful results that make it possible for researchers to feel confident that they have confirmed their hypotheses (Ch. 2)

significant outcome   An outcome expected to occur by chance less than 5 percent of the time (App.)

situational causes (of behavior)   A perceived cause of behavior that is based on environmental factors (Ch. 18)

skin senses   The senses that include touch, pressure, temperature and pain (Ch. 4)

social cognition   The processes that underlie our understanding of the social world (Ch. 18)

social cognitive approaches to personality   The theory that emphasizes the influence of a person's cognitions—thoughts, feelings, expectations, and values—in determining personality (Ch. 14)

social influence   The process by which the actions of an individual or group affect the behavior of others (Ch. 18)

social psychology   The study of how people's thoughts, feelings, and actions are affected by others (Ch. 18)

social support   A mutual network of caring, interested others (Ch. 15)

social supporter   A person who shares an unpopular opinion or attitude of another group member, thereby encouraging nonconformity (Ch. 15)

sociocultural perspective   The perspective that people's behavior—both normal and abnormal—is shaped by the kind of family group, society, and culture in which they live (Ch. 16)

somatic division   The part of the nervous system that specializes in the control of voluntary movements and the communication of information to and from the sense organs (Ch. 3)

somatoform disorder   Psychological difficulties that take on a physical (somatic) form, but for which there is no medical cause (Ch. 16)

sound   The movement of air molecules brought about by the vibration of an object (Ch. 4)

spinal cord   A bundle of nerves that leaves the brain and runs down the length of the back and is the main means for transmitting messages between the brain and the body (Ch. 3)

split-brain patient   A person who suffers from independent functioning of the two halves of the brain, as a result of which the sides of the body work in disharmony (Ch. 3)

spontaneous recovery   The reemergence of an extinguished conditioned response after a period of rest (Ch. 6)

spontaneous remission   Recovery without treatment (Ch. 17)

stage 1 sleep   The state of transition between wakefulness and sleep, characterized by relatively rapid, low-voltage brain waves (Ch. 5)

stage 2 sleep   A sleep deeper than that of stage 1, characterized by a slower, more regular wave pattern, along with momentary interruptions of "sleep spindles" (Ch. 5)

stage 3 sleep   A sleep characterized by slow brain waves, with greater peaks and valleys in the wave pattern (Ch. 5)

stage 4 sleep   The deepest stage of sleep, during which we are least responsive to outside stimulation (Ch. 5)

standard deviation   An index of the average deviation of a set of scores from the center of the distribution (App.)

statistics   The branch of mathematics concerned with collecting, organizing, analyzing, and drawing conclusions from numerical data (App.)

status   Social rank within a group (Ch. 18)

stereotypes   Generalized beliefs and expectations about social groups and their members (Ch. 18)

stimulants   Drugs that affect the central nervous system by causing a rise in heart rate, blood pressure, and muscular tension (Ch. 5)

stimulus   Energy that produces a response in a sense organ (Ch. 4)

stimulus discrimination   The ability to differentiate between stimuli (Ch. 6)

stimulus generalization   A response to a stimulus that is similar to but different from a conditioned stimulus; the more similar the two stimuli, the more likely generalization is to occur (Ch. 6)

stress   The response to events that are threatening or challenging (Ch. 15)

structuralism   Wundt's approach, which focuses on the basic elements that form the foundation of thinking, consciousness, emotions, and other kinds of mental states and activities (Ch. 1)

subjective well-being   People's evaluations of their lives in terms of both their thoughts and their emotions; how happy people are (Ch. 15)

superego   According to Freud, the final personality structure to develop; it represents society's standards of right and wrong as handed down by a person's parents, teachers, and other important figures (Ch. 14)

survey research   Research in which people chosen to represent some larger population are asked a series of questions about their behavior, thoughts, or attitudes (Ch. 2)

syllogistic reasoning   Formal reasoning in which people draw a conclusion from a set of assumptions (Ch. 8)

sympathetic division   The part of the autonomic division of the nervous system that acts to prepare the body in stressful emergency situations, engaging all the organism's resources to respond to a threat (Ch. 3)

synapse The space between two neurons where the axon of a sending neuron communicates with the dendrites of a receiving neuron using chemical messages (Ch. 3)

syntax The rules that indicate how words and phrases can be combined to form sentences (Ch. 8)

systematic desensitization A behavioral technique in which gradual exposure to anxiety-producing stimuli is paired with relaxation in order to extinguish the response of anxiety (Ch. 17)

t

telegraphic speech Sentences that sound as if they were part of a telegram, in which words not critical to the message are left out (Ch. 8)

temperament A basic, innate disposition that emerges early in life (Ch. 12, 14)

teratogens Environmental agents such as drugs, chemicals, viruses, or other factors that produce birth defects (Ch. 12)

terminal buttons Small bulges at the end of axons that send messages to other neurons (Ch. 3)

test standardization A technique used to validate questions in personality tests by studying the responses of people with known diagnoses (Ch. 14)

thalamus The part of the brain located in the middle of the central core that acts primarily as a busy relay station, mostly for information concerning the senses (Ch. 3)

Thematic Apperception Test (TAT) A test consisting of a series of ambiguous pictures about which the person is asked to write a story (Ch. 14)

theories Broad explanations and predictions concerning phenomena of interest (Ch. 2)

thinking The manipulation of mental representations of information (Ch. 8)

tip-of-the-tongue phenomenon The inability to recall information that one realizes one knows—a result of the difficulty of retrieving information from long-term memory (Ch. 7)

top-down processing Perception that is guided by higher-level knowledge, experience, expectations, and motivations (Ch. 4)

trait theory A model of personality that seeks to identify the basic traits necessary to describe personality (Ch. 14)

traits Enduring dimensions of personality characteristics along which people differ (Ch. 14)

treatment In an experiment, the manipulation implemented by the experimenter (Ch. 2)

trichromatic theory of color vision The theory that there are three kinds of cones in the retina, each of which responds primarily to a specific range of wavelengths (Ch. 4)

trust-versus-mistrust stage According to Erikson, the first stage of psychosocial development, occurring from birth to 18 months of age, during which time infants develop feelings of trust or lack of trust (Ch. 12)

Type A behavior pattern A pattern of behavior characterized by competitiveness, impatience, tendency toward frustration, and hostility (Ch. 15)

Type B behavior pattern A pattern of behavior characterized by cooperation, patience, noncompetitiveness, and nonaggression (Ch. 15)

u

unconditional positive regard An attitude of acceptance and respect on the part of an observer, no matter what the other person says or does (Ch. 14)

unconditioned response (UCR) A response that is natural and needs no training (e.g., salivation at the smell of food) (Ch. 6)

unconditioned stimulus (UCS) A stimulus that brings about a response without having been learned (Ch. 6)

unconscious wish fulfillment theory Sigmund Freud's theory that dreams represent unconscious wishes that dreamers desire to fulfill (Ch. 5)

unconscious A part of the personality of which a person is not aware, and which is a potential determinant of behavior (Ch. 14)

uninvolved parents Parents who show little interest in their children and are emotionally detached from them (Ch. 12)

universal grammar Noam Chomsky's theory that all the world's languages share a similar underlying structure (Ch. 8)

uplifts Minor positive events that make one feel good (Ch. 15)

V

validity A test's actually measuring what it is supposed to measure (Ch. 9)

variability The spread, or dispersion, of scores in a distribution (App.)

variable-interval schedule A schedule whereby the time between reinforcements varies around some average rather than being fixed (Ch. 6)

variable-ratio schedule A schedule whereby reinforcement occurs after a varying number of responses rather than after a fixed number (Ch. 6)

variables Behaviors, events, or other characteristics that can change, or vary, in some way (Ch. 2)

visual illusions Physical stimuli that consistently produce errors in perception (Ch. 4)

W

wear-and-tear theories of aging Theories that hold that the mechanical functions of the body simply stop working efficiently when we are old (Ch. 13)

Weber's law One of the basic laws of psychophysics, that a just noticeable difference is in constant proportion to the intensity of an initial stimulus (Ch. 4)

weight set point The particular level of weight that the body strives to maintain (Ch. 10)

working memory An active "workspace" in which information is retrieved and manipulated, and in which information is held through rehearsal (Ch. 7)

Z

zone of proximal development (ZPD) According to Vygotsky, the level at which a child can almost, but not fully, comprehend or perform a task on her or his own (Ch. 12)

zygote The new cell formed by the union of an egg and sperm (Ch. 12)

References

Abi-Dargham, A., Laruelle, M., Aghajanian, G. K., Charney, D., et al. (1997). The role of serotonin in the pathophysiology and treatment of schizophrenia. *Journal of Neuropsychiatry and Clinical Neurosciences, 9,* 1–17.

Abrahams, M. F., & Bell, R. A. (1994). Encouraging charitable contributions: An examination of three models of door-in-the-face compliance. *Communication Research, 21,* 131–153.

Abt, S. (1999, July 26). Armstrong wins tour and journey. *New York Times,* pp. D1, D4.

Adams, B., & Parker, J. D. (1990). Maternal weight gain in women with good pregnancy outcome. *Obstetrics and Gynecology, 76,* 1–7.

Adler, J. (1984, April 23). The fight to conquer fear. *Newsweek,* pp. 66–72.

Adler, P. A., & Adler, P. (1994). Observational techniques. In N. K. Denzin & Y. S. Lincoln (Eds.), *Handbook of qualitative research.* Thousand Oaks, CA: Sage.

Advances in telepsychology/telehealth. (2000). *Professional Psychology: Research and Practice, 31* (2).

Affleck, G., Tennen, H., Urrows, S., & Higgins, P. (1994). Person and contextual features of daily stress reactivity: Individual differences in relations of undesirable daily events with mood disturbance and chronic pain intensity. *Journal of Personality and Social Psychology, 66,* 329–340.

Aghajanian, G. K. (1994). Serotonin and the action of LSD in the brain. *Psychiatric Annals, 24,* 137–141.

Agras, W. S., & Berkowitz, R. I. (1996). Behavior therapy. In R. E. Hales & S. C. Yudofsky (Eds.), *The American Psychiatric Press synopsis of psychiatry.* Washington, DC: American Psychiatric Press.

Ahissar, M., Ahissar, E., Bergman, H., & Vaadia, E. (1992). Encoding of sound-source location and movement: Activity of single neurons and interactions between adjacent neurons in the monkey auditory cortex. *Journal of Neurophysiology, 67,* 203–215.

Ahrons, C. (1995). *The good divorce: Keeping your family together when your marriage comes apart.* New York: HarperPerennial.

Aiken, L. R. (1996). *Assessment of intellectual functioning* (2nd ed.). New York: Plenum Press.

Aiken, L. R. (1997). *Psychological testing and assessment* (9th ed.). Boston: Allyn & Bacon.

Aiken, L. R. (2001). *Dying, death, and bereavement* (4th ed.). Mahwah, NJ: Erlbaum.

Ainsworth, M. D. S., Blehar, M. C., Waters, E., & Wall, S. (1978). *Patterns of attachment: A psychological study of the strange situation.* Hillsdale, NJ: Erlbaum.

Ainsworth, M. D. S., Bowlby, J. (1991). An ethological approach to personality development. *American Psychologist, 46,* 333–341.

Akbarian, S., Kim, J. J., Potkin, S. G., Hetrick, W. P., et al. (1996). Maldistribution of interstitial neurons in prefrontal white matter of the brains of schizophrenic patients. *Archives of General Psychiatry, 53,* 425–436.

Akil, H., & Morano, M. I. (1996). The biology of stress: From periphery to brain. In S. J. Watson (Ed.), *Biology of schizophrenia and affective disease.* Washington, DC: American Psychiatric Press.

Akmajian, A., Demers, R. A., & Harnish, R. M. (1984). *Linguistics.* Cambridge, MA: MIT Press.

Akutsu, P. D., Sue, S., Zane, N. W. S., & Nakamura, C. Y. (1989). Ethnic differences in alcohol consumption among Asians and Caucasians in the United States: An investigation of cultural and physiological factors. *Journal of Studies on Alcohol, 50,* 261–267.

Alford, B. A., & Beck, A. T. (1997) *The integrative power of cognitive therapy.* New York: Guilford Press.

Allen, M. (1999, September 19). Help wanted: The not-too-high-Q standard. *New York Times,* p. 3.

Allen, V. L. (1965). Situational factors in conformity. In L. Berkowitz (Ed.), *Advances in experimental social psychology* (Vol. 1). New York: Academic Press.

Allen, V. L. (1975). Social support for nonconformity. In L. Berkowitz (Ed.), *Advances in experimental and social psychology* (Vol. 8). New York: Academic Press.

Alliger, G. M., Lilienfeld, S. O., & Mitchell, K. E. (1996). The susceptibility of overt and covert integrity tests to coaching and faking. *Psychological Science, 7,* 32–39.

Alloy, L. B., Abramson, L. Y., & Francis, E. L. (1999). Do negative cognitive styles confer vulnerability to depression? *Current Directions in Psychological Science, 8,* 128–132.

Alloy, L. B., Jacobson, N. S., & Acocella, J. (1999). *Abnormal psychology* (8th ed.). New York: McGraw-Hill.

Allport, G. W. (1961). *Pattern and growth in personality.* New York: Holt, Rinehart & Winston.

Allport, G. W. (1966). Traits revisited. *American Psychologist, 21,* 1–10.

Allport, G. W., & Postman, L. J. (1958). The basic psychology of rumor. In E. D. Maccoby, T. M. Newcomb, & E. L. Hartley (Eds.), *Readings in social psychology* (3rd ed.). New York: Holt, Rinehart & Winston.

Almer, E. (2000, April 22). Online therapy: An arm's length approach. *New York Times,* pp. A1, A11.

Altman, N. (1996). The accommodation of diversity in psychoanalysis. In R. P. Foster, M. Moskowitz, & R. A. Javier (Eds.), *Reaching across boundaries of culture and class: Widening the scope of psychotherapy.* Northvale, NJ: Jason Aronson.

American Academy of Pediatrics. (1999a, July 26). *Circumcision: Information for parents.* Available on the World Wide Web at http://www.aap.org/family/circ.htm.

American Academy of Pediatrics. (1999b). Media education (RE9911). *Pediatrics, 104,* 341–343.

American Association on Mental Retardation (AAMR). (1992). *Mental retardation: Definition, classification, and systems of support.* Washington, DC: Author.

American Association of University Women (AAUW). (1992). *How schools shortchange women: The A.A.U.W. Report.* Washington, DC: AAUW Educational Foundation.

American Association of University Women (AAUW). (1993). *Hostile hallways.* Washington, DC: AAUW Educational Foundation.

American College Health Association. (1989). *Guidelines on acquaintance rape.* Washington, DC: Author.

American Council on Education, Cooperative Institutional Research Program. (1990). *The American freshman: National norms for fall 1990.* Los Angeles: Author.

American Psychiatric Association, Task Force on Electroconvulsive Therapy. (1990). *The practice of electroconvulsive therapy: Recommendations for treatment, training, and privileging.* Washington, DC: American Psychiatric Association.

American Psychiatric Association. (1994). *Diagnostic and statistical manual of mental disorders* (4th ed.). Washington, DC: Author.

American Psychological Association (APA). (1988). *Behavioral research with animals.* Washington, DC: Author.

American Psychological Association (APA). (1992). *Ethical principles of psychologists and code of conduct.* Washington, DC: Author.

American Psychological Association (APA). (1993, January/February). Subgroup norming and the Civil Rights Act. *Psychological Science Agenda, 5,* 6.

American Psychological Association (APA). (1996). *Psychology careers for the twenty-first century.* Washington, DC: Author.

American Psychological Association (APA). (1999). *Talk to someone who can help.* Washington, DC: American Psychological Association.

Anastasi, A. (1988). *Psychological testing* (6th ed.). New York: Macmillan.

Anastasi, A. (1996). *Psychological testing* (7th ed.). New York: Macmillan.

Anastasi, A., & Urbina, S. (1997). *Psychological testing* (7th ed.). Englewood Cliffs, NJ: Prentice Hall.

Anderson, B. F. (1980). *The complete thinker: A handbook of techniques for creative and critical problem solving.* Englewood Cliffs, NJ: Prentice Hall.

Andersen, B. L., Kiecolt-Glaser, J.K., & Glaser, R. (1994). A biobehavioral model of cancer stress and disease course. *American Psychologist, 49,* 389–404.

Anderson, C. A., & Dill, K. E. (2000). Video games and aggressive thoughts, feelings, and behavior in the laboratory and in life. *Journal of Personality and Social Psychology, 78,* 772–790.

Anderson, J. (1988). Cognitive styles and multicultural populations. *Journal of Teacher Education, 39,* 2–9.

Anderson, J. A., & Adams, M. (1992). Acknowledging the learning styles of diverse student populations: Implications for instructional design. *New Directions for Teaching and Learning, 49,* 19–33.

Anderson, J. R. (1981). Interference: The relationship between response latency and response accuracy. *Journal of Experimental Psychology: Human Learning and Memory, 7,* 311–325.

Anderson, J. R., & Bower, G. H. (1972). Recognition and retrieval processes in free recall. *Psychological Review, 79,* 97–123.

Anderson, K. B., Cooper, H., & Okamura, L. (1997). Individual differences and attitudes toward rape: A meta-analytic review. *Personality and Social Psychology Bulletin, 23,* 295–315.

Anderson, N. H. (1996). *A functional theory of cognition.* Mahwah, NJ: Erlbaum.

Anderson, S. M., & Klatzky, R. L. (1987). Traits and social stereotypes: Levels of categorization in person perception. *Journal of Personality and Social Psychology, 53,* 235–246.

Anderson, T., & Magnusson, D. (1990). Biological maturation in adolescence and the development of drinking habits and alcohol abuse among young males: A prospective longitudinal study. *Journal of Youth and Adolescence, 19,* 33–42.

Andreasen, N. C., Arndt, S., Swayze II, V., Cizadlo, T., Flaum, M., O'Leary, D., Ehrhardt, J. C., & Yuh, W. T. C. (1994, October 14). Thalamic abnormalities in schizophrenia visualized through magnetic resonance image averaging. *Science, 266,* 294–298.

Angier, N. (1991, January 22). A potent peptide prompts an urge to cuddle. *New York Times,* p. C1.

Angier, N. (1996, Nov. 1). Maybe gene isn't to blame for thrill-seeking manner. *New York Times,* p. A12.

Angier, N. (1999, May 16). Baby in a box. *New York Times Magazine,* p. 86.

Angoff, W. H. (1988). The nature-nurture debate, aptitudes, and group differences. *American Psychologist, 43,* 713–720.

Ansburg, P. I., & Dominowski, R. L. (2000). Promoting insightful problem solving. *Journal of Creative Behavior, 34,* 30–60.

Antony, M. M., Brown, T. A., & Barlow, D. H. (1992). Current perspectives on panic and panic disorder. *Current Directions in Psychological Science, 1,* 79–82.

Aponte, J. F., & Wohl, J. (2000). *Psychological intervention and cultural diversity.* Needham Heights, MA: Allyn & Bacon.

Apter, A., Galatzer, A., Beth-Halachmi, N., & Laron, Z. (1981). Self-image in adolescents with delayed puberty and growth retardation. *Journal of Youth and Adolescence, 10,* 501–505.

Arafat, I., & Cotton, W. L. (1974). Masturbation practices of males and females. *Journal of Sex Research, 10,* 293–307.

Archambault, D. L. (1992). Adolescence: A physiological, cultural, and psychological no man's land. In G. W. Lawson, & A. W. Lawson (Eds.), *Adolescent substance abuse: Etiology, treatment, and prevention.* Gaithersburg, MD: Aspen.

Archer, J. (1996). Sex differences in social behavior: Are the social role and evolutionary explanations compatible? *American Psychologist, 51,* 909–917.

Archer, S. L., & Waterman, A. S. (1994). Adolescent identity development: Contextual perspectives. In C. B. Fisher & R. M. Lerner (Eds.), *Applied developmental psychology.* New York: McGraw-Hill.

Arena, J. M. (1984, April). A look at the opposite sex. *Newsweek on Campus,* p. 21.

Ariel, S. (1999). *Culturally competent family therapy: A general model.* Westport, CT: Greenwood Press.

Arlin, P. K. (1989). The problem of the problem. In J. D. Sinnott (Ed.), *Everyday problem solving: Theory and applications.* New York: Praeger.

Aron, A., Melinat, E., Aronon, E. N., Vallone, R. D., & Bator, R. J. (1997). The experimental generation of interpersonal closeness: A procedure and some preliminary findings. *Personality and Social Psychology Bulletin, 23,* 363–377.

Aronow, E., Reznikoff, M., & Moreland, K. (1994). *The Rorschach technique: Perceptual basics, content interpretation, and applications.* Boston: Longwood.

Aronson, E. (1988). *The social animal* (3rd ed.). San Francisco: Freeman.

Asch, S. E. (1946). Forming impressions of personality. *Journal of Abnormal and Social Psychology, 41,* 258–290.

Asch, S. E. (1951). Effects of group pressure upon the modification and distortion of judgments. In H. Guetzkow (Ed.), *Groups, leadership, and men.* Pittsburgh: Carnegie Press.

Asher, S. R., & Parker, J. G. (1991). Significance of peer relationship problems in childhood. In B. H. Schneider, G. Attili, J. Nadel, & R. P. Weissberg (Eds.), *Social competence in developmental perspective.* Amsterdam: Kluwer Academic.

Aspinwall, L. G., & Taylor, S. E. (1997). A stitch in time: Self-regulation and proactive coping. *Psychological Bulletin, 121,* 417–436.

Atkinson, H. (Ed.). (1997, January 21). Understanding your diagnosis. *HealthNews,* p. 3.

Atkinson, H. G. (2000, February). Decision-making dialogue. *HealthNews,* pp. 4–5.

Atkinson, J. (1995). Through the eyes of an infant. In R. L. Gregory, J. Harris, P. Heard, & D. Rose (Eds.), *The artful eye.* Oxford: Oxford University Press.

Atkinson, J. W., & Feather, N. T. (1966). *Theory of achievement motivation.* New York: Krieger.

Atkinson, J. W., & Raynor, J. O. (Eds.). (1974). *Motivation and achievement.* Washington, DC: Winston.

Atkinson, J. W., & Shiffrin, R. M. (1971, August). The control of short-term memory. *Scientific American,* pp. 82–90.

Atkinson, R. C., & Shiffrin, R. M. (1968). Human memory: A proposed system and its control processes. In K. W. Spence and J. T. Spence (Eds.), *The psychology of learning and motivation: Advances in research and theory* (Vol. 2, pp. 80–195). New York: Academic Press.

Austin, L. S. (2000). *What's holding you back?: Eight critical choices for women's success.* New York: Basic Books.

Averill, J. R. (1975). A semantic atlas of emotional concepts. *Catalog of Selected Documents in Psychology, 5,* 330.

Averill, J. R. (1994). Emotions are many splendored things. In P. Ekman & R. J. Davidson (Eds.), *The nature of emotion: Fundamental questions.* New York: Oxford University Press.

Averill, J. R. (1997). The emotions: An integrative approach. In R. Hogan, J. Johnson, & S. Briggs (Eds.), *Handbook of personality psychology.* Orlando: Academic Press.

Aycan, Z. (2000). Cross-cultural industrial and organizational psychology: Contributions, past developments, and future directions. *Journal of Cross-Cultural Psychology, 31,* 110–128.

Baddeley, A. D. (1992, January 31). Working memory. *Science, 255,* 556–559.

Baddeley, A. D. (1993). Working memory and conscious awareness. In A. F. Collins, S. E. Gathercole, M. A. Conway, & P. E. Morris (Eds.), *Theories of memory.* Hillsdale, NJ: Erlbaum.

Baddeley, A. D. (1995a). The psychology of memory. In A. D. Baddeley, B. A. Wilson, & F. N. Watts (Eds.), *Handbook of memory disorders.* Chichester, England: John Wiley.

Baddeley, A. D. (1995b). Working memory. In M. S. Gazzaniga (Ed.), *The cognitive neurosciences.* Cambridge, MA: MIT Press.

Baddeley, A. D. (1996). Exploring the central executive. *Quarterly Journal of Experimental Psychology, Human Experimental Psychology, 49A,* 5–28.

Baddeley, A. D., Gathercole, S., & Papagno, C. (1998). The phonological loop as a language learning device. *Psychological Review, 105,* 158–173.

Baddeley, A. D., & Wilson, B. (1985). Phonological coding and short-term memory in patients without speech. *Journal of Memory and Language, 24,* 490–502.

Baer, J. (1993). *Creativity and divergent thinking: A task-specific approach.* Hillsdale, NJ: Erlbaum.

Baer, L., Rauch, S. L., Callantine, T., Martuza, R., et al. (1995). Cingulotomy for intractable obsessive-compulsive disorder: Prospective long-term follow-up of 18 patients. *Archives of General Psychiatry, 52,* 384–392.

Bahrick, H. P., Hall, L. K., & Berger, S. A. (1996). Accuracy and distortion in memory for high school grades. *Psychological Science, 7,* 265–269.

Bailey, J. M. (1995). Biological perspectives on sexual orientation. In A. R. D'Augelli & C. J. Patteson (Eds.), *Lesbian, gay, and bisexual identities over the lifespan: Psychological perspectives.* New York: Oxford University Press.

Bailey, M., & Pillard, R. C. (1994, January). The innateness of homosexuality. *Harvard Mental Health Letter, 10,* pp. 4–6.

Bailey, J. M., Pillard, R. C., Kitzinger, C., & Wilkinson, S. (1997). Sexual orientation: Is it determined by biology? In M. R. Walsh (Ed.), *Women, men, and gender: Ongoing debates.* New Haven, CT: Yale University Press.

Bailey, J. M., & Zucker, K. J. (1995). Childhood sex-typed behavior and sexual orientation: A conceptual analysis and quantitative review. *Developmental Psychology, 31,* 43–55.

Baird, J. C. (1997). *Sensation and judgment: Complementarity theory of psychophysics.* Mahwah, NJ: Erlbaum.

Baker, R. A. (1998, February). A view of hypnosis. *Harvard Mental Health Letter,* pp. 5–6.

Baker, S. P., Lamb, M. W., Li, G., & Dodd, R. S. (1993). Human factors in crashes of commuter airplanes. *Aviation, Space, and Environmental Medicine, 64,* 63–68.

Ball, E. M., Simon, R. D., Tall, A. A., Banks, M. B., Nino-Murcia, G., & Dement, W. C. (1997, February 24). Diagnosis and treatment of sleep apnea within the community. *Archive of Internal Medicine, 157,* 419–424.

Ballinger, C. B. (1981). The menopause and its syndromes. In J. G. Howells (Ed.), *Modern perspectives in the psychiatry of middle age* (pp. 279–303). New York: Brunner/Mazel.

Bandura, A. (1973). *Aggression: A social learning analysis.* Englewood Cliffs, NJ: Prentice Hall.

Bandura, A. (1977). *Social learning theory.* Englewood Cliffs, NJ: Prentice Hall.

Bandura, A. (1983). Psychological mechanisms of aggression. In R. G. Geen & E. I. Donnerstein (Eds.), *Aggression: Theoretical and empirical reviews, Vol. 1: Theoretical and methodological issues.* New York: Academic Press.

Bandura, A. (1986). *Social foundations of thought and action: A social cognitive theory.* Englewood Cliffs, NJ: Prentice Hall.

Bandura, A. (1988). Self-regulation of motivation and action through goal systems. In V. Hamilton & H. Gordon (Eds.), *Cognitive perspectives on emotion and motivation.* Dordrecht, Netherlands: Kluwer Academic.

Bandura, A. (1994). Social cognitive theory of mass communication. In J. Bryant & D. Zillmann (Eds.), *Media effects: Advances in theory and research.* Hillsdale, NJ: Erlbaum.

Bandura, A. (1997). *Self-efficacy: The exercise of control.* New York: W. H. Freeman.

Bandura, A. (1999). Social cognitive theory of personality. In D. Cervone & Y. Shod (Eds.), *The coherence of personality.* New York: Guilford.

Bandura, A. (2000). Self-efficacy: The foundation of agency. In W. J. Perrig & A. Grob (Eds.), *Control of human behavior, mental processes, and consciousness: Essays in honor of the 60th birthday of August Flammer.* Mahwah, NJ: Erlbaum.

Bandura, A., Grusec, J. E., & Menlove, F. L. (1967). Vicarious extinction of avoidance behavior. *Journal of Personality and Social Psychology, 5,* 16–23.

Bandura, A., Ross, D., & Ross, S. (1963a). Imitation of film-mediated aggressive models. *Journal of Abnormal and Social Psychology, 66,* 3–11.

Bandura, A., Ross, D., & Ross, S. (1963b). Vicarious reinforcement and imitative learning. *Journal of Abnormal and Social Psychology, 67,* 601–607.

Banich, T., & Heller, W. (1998). Evolving perspectives on lateralization of function. *Current Directions in Psychological Science, 7,* 1–2.

Bannon, L. (2000, February 14). Why boys and girls get different toys. *Wall Street Journal,* pp. B1, B4.

Barber, J. (Ed.). (1996). *Hypnosis and suggestion in the treatment of pain: A clinical guide.* New York: W. W. Norton.

Barber, S., & Lane, R. C. (1995). Efficacy research in psychodynamic therapy: A critical review of the literature. *Psychotherapy in Private Practice, 14,* 43–69.

Bargh, J., & Pietromonaco, P. (1982). Automatic information processing and social perception: The influence of trait information presented outside of conscious awareness on impression formation. *Journal of Personality and Social Psychology, 43,* 437–449.

Bargh, J. A., Raymond, P., Pryor, J. B., & Strack, F. (1995). Attractiveness of the underling: An automatic power sex association and its consequences for sexual harassment and aggression. *Journal of Personality and Social Psychology, 68,* 768–781.

Baringa, M. (1997, May 30). How much pain for cardiac gain? *Science, 276,* 1324–1327.

Baringa, M. (1999, July 23). Mapping smells in the brain. *Science, 285,* 508.

Barkley, R. A. (1998a, September). Attention-deficit hyperactivity disorder. *Scientific American,* pp. 66–71.

Barkley, R. A. (1998b). *Attention-deficit hyperactivity disorder: A handbook for diagnosis and treatment.* New York: Guilford Press.

Barnard, N. D., & Kaufman, S. R. (1997, February). Animal research is wasteful and misleading. *Scientific American,* pp. 80–82.

Barrett, M. (1999). *The development of language.* Philadelphia: Psychology Press.

Barron, F. (1990). *Creativity and psychological health: Origins of personal vitality and creative freedom.* Buffalo, NY: Creative Education Foundation.

Bartecchi, C. E., MacKenzie, T. D., & Schrier, R. W. (1995, May). The global tobacco epidemic. *Scientific American,* pp. 44–51.

Bartoshuk, L. (2000, July/August). The bitter with the sweet. *APS Observer, 11,* 33.

Bartoshuk, L., & Beauchamp, G. K. (1994). Chemical senses. *Annual Review of Psychology, 45,* 419–449.

Bartoshuk, L., & Drewnowski, A. (1997, February). Symposium presented at the annual meeting of the American Association for the Advancement of Science, Seattle.

Bartoshuk, L., & Lucchina, L. (1997, January 13). Are you a supertaster? *U.S. News & World Report,* pp. 58, 59.

Basch, M. F. (1996). Affect and defense. In D. L. Nathanson (Ed.), *Knowing feeling: Affect, script, and psychotherapy.* New York: W. W. Norton.

Bass, A. (1996, April 21). Is anger good for you? *Boston Globe Magazine,* pp. 20–41.

Batista, A. P., Buneo, C. A., Snyder, L. H., & Anderson, R. A. (1999, July 9). Reach plans in eye-centered coordinates. *Science, 285,* 257–260.

Batson, C. D. (1991). *The altruism question: Toward a social-psychological answer.* Hillsdale, NJ: Erlbaum.

Batson, C. D., Batson, J. G., Todd, R. M., & Brummett, B. H. (1995). Empathy and the collective good: Caring for one of the others in a social dilemma. *Journal of Personality and Social Psychology, 68,* 619–631.

Bauer, P. J. (1996). What do infants recall of their lives? Memory for specific events by one- to two-year-olds. 102nd Annual Convention of the American Psychological Association. (1994, Los Angeles, California, US) *American Psychologist, 51,* 29–41.

Baum, A. (1994). Behavioral, biological, and environmental interactions in disease processes. In S. Blumenthal, K. Matthews, and S. Weiss (Eds.), *New research frontiers in behavioral medicine: Proceedings of the National Conference.* Washington, DC: NIH Publications.

Baum, A., Cohen, L., & Hall, M. (1993). Control and instrusive memories as possible determinants of chronic stress. *Psychosomatic Medicine, 55,* 274–286.

Baum, A. S., Revenson, R. A., & Singer, J. E. (Eds.). (2000). *Handbook of health psychology.* Mahwah, NJ: Erlbaum.

Baumeister, R. F. (1998). The self. In D. T. Gilbert & S. T. Fiske (Eds.), *The handbook of social psychology* (4th ed., Vol. 1). New York: McGraw-Hill.

Baumeister, R., & Bratslavsky, E. (1999). Passion, intimacy, and time: Passionate love as a function of change in intimacy. *Personality and Social Psychology Review, 3,* 49–67.

Baumeister, R. F., Bushman, B. J., & Campbell, W. K. (2000). Self-esteem, narcissism, and aggression: Does violence result from low self-esteem or from threatened egotism? *Current Directions in Psychological Science, 9,* 26–29.

Baumrind, D. (1971). Current patterns of parental authority. *Developmental Psychology Monographs, 4* (1, pt. 2).

Baumrind, D. (1980). New directions in socialization research. *Psychological Bulletin, 35,* 639–652.

Bayer, D. L. (1996). Interaction in families with young adults with a psychiatric diagnosis. *American Journal of Family Therapy, 24,* 21–30.

Baynes, K., Eliassen, J. C., Lutsep, H. L., & Gazzaniga, M. S. (1998, May 8). Modular organization of cognitive systems marked by interhemispheric integration. *Science, 280,* 902–905.

Bazell, B. (1998, August 25). Back pain goes high-tech. *Slate.msn.com,* 1–4.

Bear, M. F., Connors, B. W., & Paradiso, M. A. (2000). *Neuroscience: Exploring the brain.* Philadelphia: Lippincott Williams & Wilkins.

Beatty, J. (2000). *The human brain: Essentials of behavioral neuroscience.* Thousand Oaks, CA: Sage.

Beck, A. T. (1991). Cognitive therapy: A 30-year perspective. *American Psychologist, 46,* 368–375.

Beck, A. T. (1995). Cognitive therapy: Past, present, and future. In M. J. Mahoney (Ed.), *Cognitive and constructive psychotherapies: Theory, research, and practice.* New York: Springer.

Beck, A. T., & Emery, G., with Greenberg, R. L. (1985). *Anxiety disorders and phobias: A cognitive perspective.* New York: Basic Books.

Beck, M. (1992, May 25). Menopause. *Newsweek,* pp. 71–79.

Beckham, E. E., & Leber, W. R. (Eds.). (1997). *Handbook of depression* (2nd ed.). New York: Guilford Press.

Beckman, H. B., & Frankel, R. M. (1984). The effect of physician behavior on the collection of data. *Annals of Internal Medicine, 101,* 692–696.

Bedard, W. W., & Persinger, M. A. (1995). Prednisolone blocks extreme intermale social aggression in seizure-induced, brain-damaged rats: Implications for the amygdaloid central nucleus, corticotrophin-releasing factor, and electrical seizures. *Psychological Reports, 77,* 3–9.

Begley, S. (1998a). Homework. In *How to help your child succeed in school* (pp. 48–52). New York: Newsweek/Score.

Begley, S. (1998b, July 13). You're OK, I'm terrific: "Self-esteem" backfires. *Newsweek,* p. 69.

Begley, S. (2000, April 10). Decoding the human body. *Newsweek,* pp. 50–62.

Beilin, H. (1996). Mind and meaning: Piaget and Vygotsky on causal explanation. *Human Development, 39,* 277–286.

Bell, A., & Weinberg, M. S. (1978). *Homosexuality: A study of diversities among men and women.* New York: Simon & Schuster.

Bell, J., Grekul, J., Lamba, N., & Minas, C. (1995). The impact of cost on student helping behavior. *Journal of Social Psychology, 135,* 49–56.

Bell, S. M., & Ainsworth, M. D. S. (1972). Infant crying and maternal responsiveness. *Child Development, 43,* 1171–1190.

Bellack, A. S., Hersen, M., & Kazdin, A. E. (1990). *International handbook of behavior modification and therapy.* New York: Plenum Press.

Beller, M., & Gafni, N. (1996). 1991 International assessment of educational progress in mathematics and sciences: The gender differences perspective. *Journal of Educational Psychology, 88,* 365–377.

Bellezza, F. S., Six, L. S., & Phillips, D. S. (1992). A mnemonic for remembering long strings of digits. *Bulletin of the Psychonomic Society, 30,* 271–274.

Belsky, J., & Rovine, M. (1988). Nonmaternal care in the first year of life and infant-parent attachment security. *Child Development, 59,* 157–167.

Bem, D. J. (1996). Exotic becomes erotic: A developmental theory of sexual orientation. *Psychological Review, 103,* 320–335.

Bem, D. J., & Honorton, C. (1994). Does psi exist? Replicable evidence for an anomalous process of information transfer. *Psychological Bulletin, 115,* 4–18.

Bem, S. L. (1993). *Lenses of gender.* New Haven, CT: Yale University Press.

Bem, S. L. (1998). *An unconventional family.* New Haven, CT: Yale University Press.

Benbow, C. P., Lubinski, D., & Hyde, J. S. (1997). Mathematics: Is biology the cause of gender differences in performance? In M. R. Walsh (Ed.), *Women, men, and gender: Ongoing debates.* New Haven, CT: Yale University Press.

Benjamin, J., Li, L., Patterson, C., Greenberg, B. D., Murphy, D. L., & Hamer, D. H. (1996). Population and familial association between the D4 dopamine receptor gene and measures of novelty seeking. *Nature and Genetics, 12,* 81–84.

Benjamin, L. T., Jr. (1985, February). Defining aggression: An exercise for classroom discussion. *Teaching of Psychology, 12* (1), 40–42.

Benjamin, L. T., Jr. (1997). The psychology of history and the history of psychology: A historiographical introduction. In L. T. Benjamin (Ed.), *A history of psychology: Original sources and contemporary research* (2nd ed.). New York: McGraw-Hill.

Benjamin, L. T., Jr., & Shields, S. A. (1990). Foreword. In H. Hollingworth, *Leta Stetter Hollingworth: A biography.* Bolton, MA: Anker.

Bennett, A. (1992, October 14). Lori Schiller emerges from the torments of schizophrenia. *Wall Street Journal,* pp. A1, A10.

Bennett, M. R. (2000). The concept of transmitter receptors: 100 years on. *Neuropharmacology, 39,* 523–546.

Bennett, W., & Gurin, J. (1982). *The dieter's dilemma: Eating less and weighing more.* New York: Basic Books.

Benson, H. (1993). The relaxation response. In D. Goleman & J. Guerin (Eds.), *Mind-body medicine: How to use your mind for better health.* Yonkers, NY: Consumer Reports.

Benson, H., & Friedman, R. (1985). A rebuttal to the conclusions of Davis S. Holme's article, "Meditation and somatic arousal reduction." *American Psychologist, 40,* 725–726.

Benson, H., Kornhaber, A., Kornhaber, C., LeChanu, M. N., et al. (1994). Increases in positive psychological characteristics with a new relaxation-response curriculum in high school students. *Journal of Research and Development in Education, 27,* 226–231.

Bentall, R. P. (1992). The classification of schizophrenia. In D. J. Kavanagh (Ed.), *Schizophrenia: An overview and practical handbook.* London: Chapman & Hall.

Bergin, A. E., & Garfield, S. L. (1994). (Eds.). *Handbook of psychotherapy and behavior change* (4th ed.). New York: Wiley.

Berkowitz, C. D. (2000). The long-term medical consequences of sexual abuse. In R. M. Reece, et al. (Ed.), *Treatment of child abuse: Common ground for mental health, medical, and legal practitioners.* Baltimore: Johns Hopkins University Press.

Berkowitz, L. (1984). Aversive conditioning as stimuli to aggression. In R. J. Blanchard & C. Blanchard (Eds.), *Advances in the study of aggression* (Vol. 1). New York: Academic Press.

Berkowitz, L. (1989). Frustration-aggression hypothesis. *Psychological Bulletin, 106,* 59–73.

Berkowitz, L. (1990). On the formation and regulation of anger and aggression: A cognitive-neoassociationistic analysis. *American Psychologist, 45,* 494–503.

Berkowitz, L. (1993). *Aggression: Its causes, consequences, and control.* New York: McGraw-Hill.

Berkowitz, L., & Geen, R. G. (1966). Film violence and the cue properties of available targets. *Journal of Personality and Social Psychology, 3,* 525–530.

Berkowitz, L., & LePage, A. (1967). Weapons as aggression-eliciting stimuli. *Journal of Personality and Social Psychology, 7,* 202–207.

Berkowitz, L., & LePage, A. (1996). Weapons as aggression-eliciting stimuli. In S. Fein & S. Spencer (Eds.), *Readings in social psychology: The art and science of research.* Boston: Houghton Mifflin.

Berlyne, D. (1967). Arousal and reinforcement. In D. Levine (Ed.), *Nebraska symposium on motivation.* Lincoln: University of Nebraska Press.

Berman, A. L., & Jobes, D. A. (1991). *Adolescent suicide: Assessment and intervention.* Washington, DC: American Psychological Association.

Berman, A. L., & Jobes, D. A. (1995). Suicide prevention in adolescents (age 12–18). In M. M. Silverman & R. W. Maris (Eds.), *Suicide prevention: Toward the year 2000.* New York: Guilford Press.

Berman, R. M., Krystal, J. H., & Charney, D. S. (1996). Mechanism of action of antidepressants: Monoamine hypotheses and beyond. In S. J. Watson (Ed.), *Biology of schizophrenia and affective disease.* Washington, DC: American Psychiatric Press.

Bernard, J. (1982). *The future of marriage* (2nd ed.). New York: Bantam Books.

Bernard, L. L. (1924). *Instinct: A study in social psychology.* New York: Holt.

Bernieri, F. J., Zuckerman, M., Koestner, R., & Rosenthal, R. (1994). Measuring person perception accuracy: Another look at self-other agreement. *Personality and Social Psychology Bulletin, 20,* 367–378.

Berquier, A., & Ashton, R. (1992). Characteristics of the frequent nightmare sufferer. *Personality and Social Psychology, 101,* 246–250.

Berrettini, W. H. (2000). Genetics of psychiatric disease. *Annual Review of Medicine, 51,* 465–479.

Berrios, G. E. (1996). *The history of mental symptoms: Descriptive psychopathology since the nineteenth century.* Cambridge, England: Cambridge University Press.

Berscheid, E. (1985). Interpersonal attraction. In G. Lindzey & E. Aronson (Eds.), *Handbook of social psychology* (3rd ed.). New York: Random House.

Bersoff, D. N. (1995). *Ethical conflicts in psychology.* Washington, DC: American Psychological Association.

Bersoff, D. N. (1999). Why good people sometimes do bad things: Motivated reasoning and unethical behavior. *Personality and Social Psychology Bulletin, 25,* 28–39.

Betancourt, H., & Lopez, S. R. (1993). The study of culture, ethnicity, and race in American psychology. *American Psychologist, 48,* 1586–1596.

Beutler, L. E., Brown, M. T., Crothers, L., Booker, K., et al. (1996). The dilemma of factitious demographic distinctions in psychological research. *Journal of Consulting and Clinical Psychology, 64,* 892–902.

Beyene, Y. (1989). *From menarche to menopause: Reproductive lives of peasant women in two cultures.* Albany: State University of New York Press.

Bickman, L. (1994). Social influence and diffusion of responsibility in an emergency. In B. Puka (Ed.), *Reaching out: Caring, altruism, and prosocial behavior. Moral development: A compendium, Vol. 7.* New York: Garland.

Bieber, I., et al. (1962). *Homosexuality: A psychoanalytic study.* New York: Basic Books.

Biederman, I. (1981). On the semantics of a glance at a scene. In M. Kubovy and J. R. Pomerangtz (Eds.), *Perceptual organization.* Hillsdale, NJ: Erlbaum.

Biederman, I. (1987). Recognition-by-components: A theory of human image understanding. *Psychological Review, 94,* 115–147.

Biederman, I. (1990). Higher-level vision. In D. N. Osherson, S. Kosslyn, & J. Hollerbach (Eds.), *An invitation to cognitive science: Visual cognition and action.* Cambridge, MA: MIT Press.

Bigler, E. D. (Ed.). (1996). *Neuroimaging.* New York: Plenum Press.

Binet, A., & Simon, T. (1916). *The development of intelligence in children (the Binet-Simon scale).* Baltimore: Williams & Wilkins.

Binkley, C. (2000, May 4). Casion chain mines data on its gamblers, and strikes pay dirt. *Wall Street Journal,* pp. A1, A10.

Binstock, R., & George, L. K. (Eds.). (1996). *Handbook of aging and the social sciences* (4th ed.). San Diego: Academic Press.

Birbaumer, N., Ghanayim, N., Hinterberger, T., Iversen, I., Kotchoubey, B., Kubler, A., Perelmouter, J., Taub, E., & Flor, H. (1999, March 25). A spelling device for the paralysed [letter]. *Nature, 398,* 297–298.

Birch, H. G. (1945). The role of motivation factors in insightful problem solving. *Journal of Comparative Psychology, 38,* 295–317.

Bird, G., & Melville, K. (1994). *Families and intimate relationships.* (1994). New York: McGraw-Hill.

Birren, J. E. (Ed.). (1996). *Encyclopedia of gerontology: Age, aging and the aged.* San Diego: Academic Press.

Bjork, D. W. (1993). *B. F. Skinner: A life.* New York: Basic Books.

Bjork, E. L., & Bjork, R. A. (Eds.). (1996). *Memory.* New York: Academic Press.

Bjork, R. A., & Richardson-Klarehn, A. (1989). On the puzzling relationship between environmental context and human memory. In C. Izawa (Ed.), *Current issues in cognitive processes: The Tulane-Floweree symposium on cognition.* Hillsdale, NJ: Erlbaum.

Bjorklund, D. F. (1985). The role of conceptual knowledge in the development of organization in children's memory. In C. J. Brainerd & M. Pressley (Eds.), *Basic process in memory development.* New York: Springer-Verlag.

Bjorklund, D. F. (1997). In search of a metatheory for cognitive development (or, Piaget is dead and I don't feel so good myself). *Child Development, 68,* 144–148.

Blakeslee, S. (1992, August 11). Finding a new messenger for the brain's signals to the body. *New York Times,* p. C3.

Blakeslee, S. (2000, January 4). A decade of discovery yields a shock about the brain. *New York Times,* D1.

Blanchard, F. A., Lilly, R., & Vaughn, L. A. (1991). Reducing the expression of racial prejudice. *Psychological Science, 2,* 101–105.

Blanck, P. D. (Ed.). (1993). *Interpersonal expectations: Theory, research and applications.* Cambridge, England: Cambridge University Press.

Blank, M., & White, S. J. (1999). Activating the zone of proximal development in school: Obstacles and solutions. In P. Lloyd & C. Fernyhough (Eds.), *Lev Vygotsky: Critical assessments: The zone of proximal development, Vol. 3.* New York: Routledge.

Blascovich, J. J., & Katkin, E. S. (Eds.) (1993). *Cardiovascular reactivity to psychological stress and disease.* Washington, DC: American Psychological Association.

Blass, T. (1996). Attribution of responsibility and trust in the Milgram obedience experiment. *Journal of Applied Social Psychology, 26,* 1529–1535.

Blass, T. (Ed.). (2000). *Obedience to authority: Current perspectives on the Milgram paradigm.* Mahwah, NJ: Erlbaum.

Blau, Z. S. (1973). *Old age in a changing society.* New York: New Viewpoints.

Blewett, A. E. (2000). Help cards for patients. *Psychiatric Bulletin, 24,* 276.

Blume, S. B. (1998, March). Alcoholism in women. *Harvard Mental Health Letter,* pp. 5–7.

Boakes, R. A., Popplewell, D. A., & Burton, M.J. (Eds.). (1987). *Eating habits: Food, physiology, and learned behaviour.* New York: Wiley.

Boehm, K. E., & Campbell, N. B. (1995). Suicide: A review of calls to an adolescent peer listening phone service. *Child Psychiatry and Human Development, 26,* 61–66.

Boehm, K. E., Schondel, C. K., Marlowe, A. L., & Rose, J. S. (1995). Adolescents calling a peer-listening phone service: Variations in calls by gender, age, and season of year. *Adolescence, 30,* 863–871.

Bolla, K. I., Cadet, J. L., & London, E. D. (1998). The neuropsychiatry of chronic cocaine abuse. *Journal of Neuropsychiatry and Clinical Neurosciences, 10,* 280–289.

Booth, D. A. (1994). *Psychology of nutrition.* London: Taylor & Francis.

Borbely, A. (1996). *Secrets of sleep.* New York: Basic Books.

Bornstein, M. H. (Ed.). (1995). *Handbook of parenting: Vol. 4. Applied and practical parenting.* Mahwah, NJ: Erlbaum.

Bornstein, M. H. & Arterberry, M. (1999). Perceptual development. In M. Bornstein & M. Lamb, *Developmental psychology.* Mahwah, NJ: Erlbaum.

Bornstein, M. H., & Bruner, J. S. (Eds.). (1989). *Interaction on human development: Crosscurrents in contemporary psychology services.* Hillsdale, NJ: Erlbaum.

Bornstein, R. F. (1996). Construct validity of the Rorschach Oral Dependency Scale: 1967–1995. *Psychological Assessment, 8,* 200–205.

Bornstein, R. F., & D'Agostino, P. R. (1994). The attribution and discounting of perceptual fluency: Preliminary tests of a perceptual fluency/attributional model of the mere exposure effect. *Social Cognition, 12,* 103–128.

Botting, J. H., & Morrison, A. R. (1997, February). Animal research is vital to medicine. *Scientific American, 276,* 83–86.

Botvin, G. J., & Botvin, E. M. (1992). Adolescent tobacco, alcohol, and drug abuse: Prevention strategies, empirical findings, and assessment issues. *Journal of Developmental and Behavioral Pediatrics, 13,* 290–301.

Botvin, G. J., Schinke, S. P. Epstein, J. A., & Diaz, T. (1994). Effectivenenss of culturally focused and generic skills training approaches to alcohol and drug abuse prevention among minority youths. *Psychology of Addictive Behaviors, 8,* 116–127.

Botvin, G. J., Schinke, S. P., Epstein, J. A., Diaz, T., et al. (1995). Effectiveness of culturally focused and generic skills training approaches to alcohol and drug abuse prevention among minority adolescents: Two-year follow-up results. *Psychology of Addictive Behaviors, 9,* 183–194.

Bouchard, C., & Bray, G. A. (Eds.). (1996). *Regulation of body weight: Biological and behavioral mechanisms.* New York: Wiley.

Bouchard, C., Tremblay, A., Despres, J. P., Nadeau, A., et al. (1990, May 24). The response to long-term overfeeding in identical twins. *New England Journal of Medicine, 322,* 1477–1482.

Bouchard, T. J., & McGue, M. (1981). Familial studies of intelligence: A review. *Science, 212,* 1055–1059.

Bourne, L. E., Dominowski, R. L., Loftus, E. F., & Healy, A. F. (1986). *Cognitive processes* (2nd ed.). Englewood Cliffs, NJ: Prentice Hall.

Bower, G. H., Thompson, S. S., & Tulving, E. (1994). Reducing retroactive interference: An interference analysis. *Journal of Experimental Psychology Learning, Memory, and Cognition, 20,* 51–66.

Bradsher, K. (2000, July 17). Was Freud a minivan or S.U.V. kind of guy? *New York Times,* pp. A1, A16.

Braff, D. L. (1993). Information processing and attention dysfunctions in schizophrenia. *Schizophrenia Bulletin, 19,* 233–259.

Brand, D. (1987, August 31). The new whiz kids. *Time,* pp. 42–51.

Brandimonte, M. A., Hitch, G. J., & Bishop, D. V. (1992). Manipulation of visual mental images in children and adults. *Journal of Experimental Child Psychology, 53,* 300–312.

Braun, A. R., Balkin, T. J., Wesensten, N. J., Gwadry, F., Carson, R. E., Varga, M., Baldwin, P., Belenky, G., & Herscovitch, P. (1998). Dissociated pattern of activity in visual cortices and their projections during human rapid eye movement sleep. *Science, 279,* 91–95.

Brazelton, T. B. (1969). *Infants and mothers: Differences in development.* New York: Dell.

Brehm, J. W., & Self, E. A. (1989). The intensity of motivation. *Annual Review of Psychology, 40,* 109–131.

Brehm, S. S., & Brehm, J. W. (1981). *Psychological reactance.* New York: Academic Press.

Breland, K., & Breland, M. (1961). Misbehavior of organisms. *American Psychologist, 16,* 681–684.

Brendgen, M., Vitaro, F., & Bukowski, W. M. (2000). Deviant friends and early adolescents' emotional and behavioral adjustment. *Journal of Research on Adolescence, 10,* 173–189.

Brewer, J. B., Zhao, Z., Desmond, J. E., Glover, G. H., & Gabrieli, J. D. E. (1998, August 21). Making memories: Brain activity that predicts how well visual experience will be remembered. *Science, 281,* 1185–1187.

Brief psychodynamic therapy, Part I. (1994, March). *Harvard Mental Health Letter,* p. 10.

Brislin, R. (1993). *Understanding culture's influence on behavior.* Fort Worth, TX: Harcourt Brace Jovanovich.

Brody, J. E. (1987, November 19). Encouraging news for the absent-minded: Memory can be improved, with practice. *New York Times,* p. C-1.

Brody, N. (1990). Behavior therapy versus placebo: Comment on Bowers and Clum's meta-analysis. *Psychological Bulletin, 107,* 106–109.

Bromm, B., & Desmedt, J. E. (Eds.). (1995). *Pain and the brain: From nociception to cognition.* New York: Raven Press.

Bronner, E. (1998, November 24). Study casts doubt on the benefits of S.A.T. coaching courses. *New York Times,* p. A19.

Brookhiser, R. (1997, January 13). Lost in the weed. *U.S. News and World Report,* p. 9.

Broota, K. D. (1990). *Experimental design in behavioral research.* New York: Wiley.

Brown, A. S., Susser, E. S., Butler, P. D., Andrews, R. R., et al. (1996). Neurobiological plausibility of prenatal nutritional deprivation as a risk factor for schizophrenia. *Journal of Nervous and Mental Disease, 184,* 71–85.

Brown, D. C. (1994). Subgroup norming: Legitimate testing practice or reverse discrimination? *American Psychologist, 49,* 927–928.

Brown, L. S., & Pope, K. S. (1996). *Recovered memories of abuse: Assessment, therapy, forensics.* Washington, DC: American Psychological Association.

Brown, M. B. (2000). Diagnosis and treatment of children and adolescents with attention-deficit/hyperactivity disorder. *Journal of Counseling and Development, 78,* 195–203.

Brown, P. K., & Wald, G. (1964). Visual pigments in single rod and cones of the human retina. *Science, 144,* 45–52.

Brown, R. (1958). How shall a thing be called? *Psychological Review, 65,* 14–21.

Brown, R. (1986). *Social psychology* (2nd ed.). New York: Macmillan.

Brown, S. I., & Walter, M. I. (Eds.). (1993). *Problem posing: Reflections and applications.* Hillsdale, NJ: Erlbaum.

Bruce, B., & Wilfley, D. (1996). Binge eating among the overweight population: A serious and prevalent problem. *Journal of the American Dietetic Association, 96,* 58–61.

Bruce, V., Green, P. R., & Georgeson, M. (1997). *Visual perception: Physiology, psychology and ecology* (3rd ed.). Mahwah, NJ: Erlbaum.

Bruner, J. (1983). *Child's talk: Learning to use language.* Oxford: Oxford University Press.

Brunner, H. G., Nelen, M., Breakefield, X. O., Ropers, H. H., & van Oost, B. A. (1993, October 22). Abnormal behavior associated with a point mutation in the structural gene for monoamine oxidase A. *Science, 262,* 578–580.

Brzustowicz, L. M., Hodgkinson, K. A., Chow, E. W. C., Honer, W. G., & Bassett, A. S. (2000, April 28). Location of major susceptibility locus for familial schizophrenia on chromosome 1q21-q22. *Science, 288,* 678–682.

Buck, L., & Axel, R. (1991, April 5). A novel multigene family may encode odorant receptors: A molecular basis for odor recognition. *Cell, 65,* 167–175.

Buckhout, R. (1974). Eyewitness testimony. *Scientific American,* pp. 23–31.

Bukowski, W. M., Newcomb, A. F., & Hartup, W. W. (Eds.). (1996). *The company they keep: Friendship in childhood and adolescence.* New York: Cambridge University Press.

Burack, J. A., Hodapp, R. M., & Zigler, E. (Eds.). (1998). *Handbook of mental retardation and development.* New York: Cambridge University Press.

Burchinal, M. R., Roberts, J. E., Riggins, R., Jr., Zeisel, S. A., Neebe, E., & Bryant, D. (2000). Relating quality of center-based child care to early cognitive and language development longitudinally. *Child Development, 71,* 338–357.

Burger, J. M. (1986). Increasing compliance by improving the deal: The that's-not-all technique. *Journal of Personality and Social Psychology, 51,* 277–283.

Burger, J. M. (1999). The foot-in-the-door compliance procedure: A multiple-process analysis and review. *Personality and Social Psychology Review, 3,* 303–325.

Burgess, D., & Borgida, E. (1997). Sexual harassment: An experimental test of sex-role spillover theory. *Personality and Social Psychology Bulletin, 23,* 63–75.

Burgoon, J. K., & Dillman, L. (1995). Gender, immediacy, and nonverbal communication. In P. J. Kalbfleisch & M. J. Cody (Eds.), *Gender, power, and communication in human relationships. LEA's communication series.* Hillsdale, NJ: Erlbaum.

Burnham, D. K. (1983). Apparent relative size in the judgment of apparent distance. *Perception, 12,* 683–700.

Bush, P. J., & Osterweis, M. (1978). Pathways to medicine use. *Journal of Health and Social Behavior, 19,* 179–189.

Bushman, B. J. (1993). Human aggression while under the influence of alcohol and other drugs: An integrative research review. *Current Directions in Psychological Science, 2,* 148–152.

Bushman, B. J., & Baumeister, R. F. (1998). Threatened egotism, narcissism, self-esteem, and direct and displaced aggression: Does self-love or self-hate lead to violence? *Journal of Personality and Social Psychology, 75,* 219–229.

Buss, D. M. (1999). Human nature and individual differences: The evolution of human personality. In L. A. Pervin & O. P. John (Eds.), *Handbook of personality: Theory and research* (2nd ed.). New York: Guilford Press.

Buss, D. M., & Kenrick, D. T. (1998). Evolutionary social psychology. In D. T. Gilbert, S. T. Fiske, & G. Lindzey (Eds.), *The handbook of social psychology* (4th ed., Vol. 2). New York: McGraw-Hill.

Buss, D. M., Larsen, R. J., Westen, D., & Semmelroth, J. (1992). Sex differences in jealousy: Evolution, physiology, and psychology. *Psychological Science, 3,* 251–255.

Butcher, J. N. (1995). Interpretation of the MMPI-2. In L. E. Beutler & M. R. Berren (Eds.), *Integrative assessment of adult personality.* New York: Guilford Press.

Butcher, J. N. (1999). *A beginner's guide to the MMPI-2.* Washington, DC: American Psychological Association.

Butcher, J. N., Graham, J. R., Dahlstrom, W. G., & Bowman, E. (1990). The MMPI-2 with college students. *Journal of Personality Assessment, 54,* 1–15.

Butler, R., Oberlink, M. R., & Schechter, M. (Eds.). (1990). *The promise of productive aging: From biology to social policy.* New York: Springer.

Byne, W. (1996). Biology and homosexuality: Implications of neuroendocrinological and neuroanatomical studies. In R. P. Cabaj & T. S. Stein (Eds.), *Textbook of homosexuality and mental health.* Washington, DC: American Psychiatric Press.

Byrne, D. (1969). Attitudes and attraction. In L. Berkowitz (Ed.), *Advances in experimental social psychology* (Vol. 4, pp. 35–89). New York: Academic Press.

Cabrera, N. J., Tamis-LeMonda, C. S., Bradley, R. H., Hofferth, S., & Lamb, M. E. (2000). Fatherhood in the twenty-first century. *Child Development, 71,* 127–136.

Calmes, J. (1998, March 5). Americans retain puritan attitudes on matters of sex. *Wall Street Journal,* p. A12.

Campbell, J. J., Lamb, M. E., & Hwang, C. P. (2000). Early child-care experiences and children's social competence between 1.5 and 15 years of age. *Applied Developmental Science, 4,* 166–175.

Campfield, L. A., Smith, F. J., Rosenbaum, M., & Hirsch, J. (1996). Human eating: Evidence for a physiological basis using a modified paradigm. [Special Issue: Society for the Study of Ingestive Behavior, Second Independent Meeting.] *Neuroscience and Biobehavioral Reviews, 20,* 133–137.

Camras, L. A., Holland, E. A., & Patterson, M. J. (1993). Facial expression. In M. Lewis & J. M. Haviland (Eds.), *Handbook of emotions.* New York: Guilford Press.

Cannon, T. D. (1998). Genetic and perinatal influences in the etiology of schizophrenia: A neurodevelopmental model. In M. F. Lenzenweger & R. H. Dworkin (Eds.), *The origins and development of schizophrenia: Advances in experimental psychopathology.* Washington, DC: American Psychological Association.

Cannon, W. B. (1929). Organization for physiological homeostatics. *Physiological Review, 9,* 280–289.

Cantor, C., & Fallon, B. A. (1996). *Phantom illness: Shattering the myth of hypochondria.* Boston: Houghton Mifflin.

Capaldi, E. D. (Ed.) (1996). *Why we eat what we eat: The psychology of eating.* Washington, DC: American Psychological Association.

Cappella, J. N. (1993). The facial feedback hypothesis in human interaction: Review and speculation. [Special Issue: Emotional communication, culture, and power.] *Journal of Language and Social Psychology, 12,* 13–29.

Carli, L. L. (1990). Gender, language, and influence. *Journal of Personality and Social Psychology, 59,* 941–951.

Carlson, M., Marcus-Newhall, A., & Miller, N. (1990). Effects of situational aggression cues: A quantitative review. *Journal of Personality and Social Psychology, 58,* 622–633.

Carnegie Council on Adolescent Development. (1995). *Great transitions: Preparing adolescents for a new century.* New York: Carnegie Corporation.

Carnegie Task Force on Meeting the Needs of Young Children. (1994). *Starting points: Meeting the needs of our youngest children.* New York: Carnegie Corporation.

Carney, R. N., & Levin, J. R. (1998). Coming to terms with the keyword method in introductory psychology: A "neuromnemonic" example. *Teaching of Psychology, 25,* 132–135.

Carney, R. N., Levin, J. R., Levin, M. E. & Schoen, L. M. (2000). Improving memory. In M. E. Ware & D. E. Johnson et al. (Eds.), *Handbook of demonstrations and activities in the teaching of psychology: Physiological-comparative, perception, learning, cognitive, and developmental* (2nd ed., Vol. 2). Mahwah, NJ: Erlbaum.

Carroll, J. M., & Russell, J. A. (1997). Facial expressions in Hollywood's portrayal of emotion. *Journal of Personality and Social Psychology, 72,* 164–176.

Carson, R. C., Butcher, J. N., & Coleman, J. C. (1992). *Abnormal psychology and modern life* (9th ed.). New York: HarperCollins.

Carter, A. S., Pauls, D. L., & Leckman, J. F. (1995). The development of obsessionality: Continuities and discontinuities. In D. Cicchetti & D. J. Cohen (Eds.), *Developmental psychopathology: Vol. 2. Risk, disorder, and adaptation.* New York: Wiley.

Carver, C. S., Harris, S. D., Lehman, J. M., Durel, L. A., Antoni, M. H., Spencer, S. M., & Pozo-Kaderman, C. (2000). How important is the perception of personal control? Studies of early stage breast cancer patients. *Personality and Social Psychology Bulletin, 26,* 139–149.

Case, R., & Okamoto, Y. (1996). The role of central conceptual structures in the development of children's thought. *Monographs of the Society for Research in Child Development, 61,* v-265.

Caspi, A., Henry, B., McGee, R. O., Moffitt, T. E., & Silva, P. A. (1995). Temperamental origins of child and adolescent behavior problems: From age three to age fifteen. *Child Development, 66,* 55–68.

Cassel, W. S., Roebers, C. E. M., & Bjorklund, D. F. (1996). Developmental patterns of eyewitness responses to repeated and increasingly suggestive questions. *Journal of Experimental Child Psychology, 61,* 116–133.

Cattell, R. B. (1965). *The scientific analysis of personality.* Chicago: Aldine.

Cattell, R. B. (1967). *The scientific analysis of personality.* Baltimore: Penguin.

Cattell, R. B. (1987). *Intelligence: Its structure, growth, and action.* Amsterdam: North-Holland.

Cattell, R. B., Cattell, A. K., & Cattell, H. E. P. (1993). *Sixteen personality factor questionnaire (16PF)* (5th ed.). San Antonio: Harcourt Brace.

Cattell, R. B., Eber & Tatsuoka (1970). *Handbook for the 16PF.* Champaign, IL: Institute for Personality and Ability Testing.

Center on Addiction and Substance Abuse. (1996). *Gender and drug and alcohol abuse.* New York: Author.

Centers for Disease Control. (1992). *Most students sexually active: Survey of sexual activity.* Atlanta: Author.

Centers for Disease Control and Prevention. (1994). Cigarette smoking among adults—United States, 1993. *Morbidity and Mortality Weekly Report, 43,* 925–930.

Centers for Disease Control and Prevention. (2000a). *Health, United States, 2000: Adolescent Health Chartbook.* Atlanta: Author.

Centers for Disease Control and Prevention. (2000b). *Suicide prevention fact sheet, National Center for Injury Prevention and Control.* Atlanta: Author.

Chalmers, D. (1996). *The conscious mind.* New York: Oxford University Press.

Chamberlain, K., & Zika, S. (1990). The minor events approach to stress: Support for the use of daily hassles. *British Journal of Psychology, 81,* 469–481.

Chamberlin, J. (1998, June). Help for students of color. *APA Monitor,* p. 37.

Chandler, M. J. (1976). Social cognition and life-span approaches to the study of child development. In H. W. Reese & L. P. Lipsitt (Eds.), *Advances in child development and behavior* (Vol. 11). New York: Academic Press.

Chandler, M., & Lalonde, C. (1996). Shifting to an interpretive theory of mind: 5- to 7-year-olds' changing conceptions of mental life. In A. J. Sameroff & M. M. Haith (Eds.), *The five to seven year shift: The age of reason and responsibility.* Chicago: University of Chicago Press.

Chao, R. K. (2000). Cultural explanations for the role of parenting in the school success of Asian-American children. In R. D. Taylor & M. C. Wang (Eds.), *Resilience across contexts: Family, work, culture, and community* (pp. 333–363). Mahwah, NJ: Erlbaum.

Chapman, L. J., & Chapman, J. P. (1973). *Disordered thought in schizophrenia.* New York: Appleton-Century-Crofts.

Chase, M. (1993, October 13). Inner music: Imagination may play role in how the brain learns muscle control. *Wall Street Journal,* pp. A1, A6.

Chastain, G., & Landrum, R. E. (Eds.). (1999). *Protecting human subjects: Departmental subject pools and institutional review boards.* Washington, DC: American Psychological Association.

Cheakalos, C., & Heyn, E. (1998, November 2). Mercy mission. *People Weekly,* pp. 149–150.

Chen, C., & Stevenson, H. W. (1995). Motivation and mathematics achievement: A comparative study of Asian-American, Caucasian-American, and East Asian high school students. *Child Development, 66,* 1215–1234.

Chen, J., & Gardner, H. (1997). Alternative assessment from a multiple intelligences theoretical perspective. In D. P. Flanagen, J. L. Genshaft, & P. L. Harrison (Eds.), *Contemporary intellectual assessment: Theories, tests, and issues.* New York: Guilford Press.

Cheney, C. D. (1996). Medical nonadherence: A behavior analysis. In J. R. Cautela & W. Ishaq (Eds.), *Contemporary issues in behavior therapy: Improving the human condition: Applied clinical psychology.* New York: Plenum Press.

Cheng, H., Cao, Y., & Olson, L. (1996, July 26). Spinal cord repair in adult paraplegic rats: Partial restoration of hind limb function. *Science, 273,* 510–513.

Cherlin, A. (1993). *Marriage, divorce, remarriage.* Cambridge, MA: Harvard University Press.

Cherry, B. J., Buckwalter, J. G., & Henderson, V. W. (1996). Memory span procedures in Alzheimer's disease. *Neuropsychology, 10,* 286–293.

Chess, S. (1997, November). Temperament: Theory and clinical practice. *Harvard Mental Health Letter,* pp. 5–7.

Cheston, S. E. (2000). A new paradigm for teaching counseling theory and practice. *Counselor Education and Supervision, 39,* 254–269.

Chi-Ching, Y., & Noi, L. S. (1994). Learning styles and their implications for cross-cultural management in Singapore. *Journal of Social Psychology, 134,* 593–600.

Chin, S. B., & Pisoni, D. B. (1997). *Alcohol and speech.* New York: Academic Press.

Cho, A. (2000, June 16). What's shakin' in the ear? *Science, 288,* 1954–1955.

Chodorow, N. (1978). *The reproduction of mothering.* Berkeley: University of California Press.

Chomsky, N. (1968). *Language and mind.* New York: Harcourt Brace Jovanovich.

Chomsky, N. (1969). *The acquisition of syntax in children from five to ten.* Cambridge, MA: MIT Press.

Chomsky, N. (1978). On the biological basis of language capacities. In G. A. Miller & E. Lennenberg (Eds.), *Psychology and biology of language and thought* (pp. 199–220). New York: Academic Press.

Chomsky, N. (1991). Linguistics and cognitive science: Problems and mysteries. In A. Kasher (Ed.), *The Chomskyan turn.* Cambridge, MA: Blackwell.

Churchland, P. S., & Ramachandran, V. S. (1995). Filling in: Why Dennett is wrong. In B. Dahlbom (Ed.), *Dennett and his critics: Demystifying mind: Philosophers and their critics.* Oxford, England: Basil Blackwell.

Cialdini, R. B. (1988). *Influence: Science and practice* (2nd ed.). Glenview, IL: Scott, Foresman.

Cialdini, R. B. (1997). Professionally responsible communication with the public: Giving psychology a way. *Personality and Social Psychology Bulletin, 31,* 206–215.

Cialdini, R. B., Schaller, M., Houlihan, D., Arps, K., Fultz, J., & Beaman, A. L. (1975). Reciprocal concessions procedure for inducing compliance: The door-in-the-face technique. *Journal of Personality and Social Psychology, 31,* 206–215.

Clancy, S. A., Schacter, D. L., McNally, R. J, & Pitman, R. K. (2000). False recognition in women reporting recovered memories of sexual abuse. *Psychological Science. 11,* 26–31.

Clark, L., & Watson, R. (1999). Temperament. In L. A. Pervin & O. P. John (Eds.), *Handbook of personality: Theory and research* (2nd ed.). New York: Guilford Press.

Clark, R., Anderson, N. B., Clark, V. R., & Williams, D. R. (1999). Racism as a stressor for African Americans: A biopsychosocial model. *American Psychologist, 54,* 805–816.

Clark, R. E., & Squire, L. R. (1998, April 3). Classical conditioning and brain systems: The role of awareness. *Science, 280,* 77–81.

Clarke-Stewart, K. A., & Friedman, S. (1987). *Child development: Infancy through adolescence.* New York: Wiley.

Clarke-Stewart, K. A., Vandell, D. L., McCartney, K., Owen, M. T., & Booth, C. (2000). Effects of parental separation and divorce on very young children. *Journal of Family Psychology, 14,* 304–326.

Clarkin, J. F., & Lenzenweger, M. F. (Ed.). (1996). *Major theories of personality disorder.* New York: Guilford Press.

Clay, R. A. (January, 2000). Psychotherapy *is* cost effective. *Monitor on Psychology,* pp. 39–41.

Clayton, R. R., Leukefeld, C. G., Harrington, N. G., & Cattarello, A. (1996). DARE (Drug Abuse Resistance Education): Very popular but not very effective. In C. B. McCoy & L. R. Metsch (Eds.), *Intervening with drug-involved youth.* Thousand Oaks, CA: Sage.

Clements, M. (1994, August 7). Making love: How old, how often. *Parade Magazine,* p. 5.

Cline, R. J. W. (1994). Groupthink and the Watergate cover-up: The illusion of unanimity. In L. R. Frey (Ed.), *Group communication in context: Studies of natural groups.* Hillsdale, NJ: Erlbaum.

Cloud, J. (2000, June 5). The lure of ecstasy. *Time,* pp. 60–68.

Coates, T. J., & Collins, C. (1998, July). Preventing HIV infection. *Scientific American,* pp. 96–97.

Coats, E. J., & Feldman, R. S. (1996). Gender differences in nonverbal correlates of social status. *Personality and Social Psychology Bulletin, 22,* 1014–1022.

Coats, E. J., Feldman, R. S., & Schwartzberg, S. (1994). *Critical thinking: General principles and case studies.* New York: McGraw-Hill.

Coffey, C. E., Saxton, J. A., Ratcliff, G., Bryan, R. N., & Lucke, J. F. (1999). Relation of education to brain size in normal aging: Implications for the reserve hypothesis. *Neurology, 53,* 198–207.

Coffey, C. E., Saxton, J. A., Ratcliff, G., Bryan, R. N., & Lucke, J. F. (1999). Relation of education to brain size in normal aging: Implications for the reserve hypothesis. *Neurology, 53,* 189–196.

Cohen, D. (1993). *The development of play* (2nd ed.). London: Routledge.

Cohen, D. (1996). Law, social policy, and violence: The impact of regional cultures. *Journal of Personality and Social Psychology, 70,* 961–978.

Cohen, P., Slomkowski, C., & Robins, L. N. (Eds.). (1999). *Historical and geographical influences on psychopathology.* Mahwah, NJ: Erlbaum.

Cohen, S. (1996, June). Psychological stress, immunity, and upper respiratory infections. *Current Directions in Psychological Science, 5,* 86–90.

Colapinto, J. (2000). *As nature made him: The boy who was raised as a girl.* New York: HarperCollins.

Cole, M., & Gay, J. (1972). Culture and memory. *American Anthropologist, 74,* 1066–1084.

Coles, R. (1997). *The moral intelligence of children.* New York: Random House.

Coles, R., & Stokes, G. (1985). *Sex and the American teenager.* New York: Harper & Row.

Collins, A. F., Gathercole, S. E., Conway, M. A. & Morris, P. E. (Eds.). (1993). *Theories of memory.* Hillsdale, NJ: Erlbaum.

Collins, A. M., & Loftus, E. F. (1975). A spreading-activation theory of semantic processing. *Psychological Review, 82,* 407–428.

Collins, A. M., & Quillian, M. R. (1969). Retrieval times from semantic memory. *Journal of Verbal Learning and Verbal Behavior, 8,* 240–247.

Coltraine, S., & Messineo, M. (2000). The perpetuation of subtle prejudice: Race and gender imagery in 1990s television advertising. *Sex Roles, 42,* 363–389.

Compas, B. E., Ey, S., & Grant, K. E. (1993). Taxonomy, assessment, and diagnosis of depression during adolescence. *Psychological Bulletin, 114,* 323–344.

Comuzzie, A. G., & Allison, D. B. (1998, May 29). The search for human obesity genes. *Science, 280,* 1374–1377.

Condon, J. W., & Crano, W. D. (1988). Inferred evaluation and the relation between attitude similarity and interpersonal attraction. *Journal of Personality and Social Psychology, 54,* 789–797.

Conoley, J. C., & Impara, J. C. (Eds.). (1997). *The 12th mental measurements yearbook.* Lincoln, NE: Buros Institute.

Conte, H. R., & Plutchik, R. (Eds.). (1995). *Ego defenses: Theory and measurement.* New York: Wiley.

Conway, M. A. (Ed.). (1997). *Cognitive models of memory.* Cambridge, MA: MIT Press.

Cooklin, A. (2000). Therapy, the family and others. In H. Maxwell (Ed.), *Clinical psychotherapy for health professionals.* London: Whurr.

Cooper, J., & Mackie, D. (1986). Video games and aggression in children. *Journal of Applied Social Psychology, 16,* 726–744.

Cooper, L. A., & Shepard, R. N. (1984, December). Turning something over in the mind. *Scientific American.* pp. 106–114.

Cooper, N. R., Kalaria, R. N., McGeer, P. L., & Rogers, J. (2000). Key issues in Alzheimer's disease inflammation. *Neurobiology of Aging, 21,* 451–453.

Cooper, S. H. (1989). Recent contributions to the theory of defense mechanism: A comparative view. *Journal of the American Psychoanalytic Association, 37,* 865–892.

Cope, D. (1998). *New directions in music* (6th ed.). Prospect Heights, IL: Waveland Press.

Corbetta, M., Miezin, F. M., Shulman, G. L., & Petersen, S. E. (1993, March). A PET study of visuospatial attention. *Journal of Neuroscience, 13,* 1202–1226.

Coren, S. (1992). The moon illusion: A different view through the legs. *Perceptual and Motor Skills, 75,* 827–831.

Coren, S., & Aks, D. J. (1990). Moon illusion in pictures: A multimechanism approach. *Journal of Experimental Psychology: Human Perception and Performance, 16,* 365–380.

Coren, S., Porac, C., & Ward, L. M. (1984). *Sensation and perception* (2nd ed). New York: Academic Press.

Coren, S., & Ward, L. M. (1989). *Sensation and perception* (3rd ed.). San Diego: Harcourt Brace Jovanovich.

Cornelius, S. W., & Caspi, A. (1987). Everyday problem solving in adulthood and old age. *Psychology and Aging, 2,* 144–153.

Cornell, T. L., Fromkin, V. A., & Mauner, G. (1993). A linguistic approach to language processing in Broca's aphasia: A paradox resolved. *Current Directions in Psychological Science, 2,* 47–52.

Corrigan, P. W. (1996). Models of "normal" cognitive functioning. In P. W. Corrigan & S. C. Yudofsky (Eds.), *Cognitive rehabilitation for neuropsychiatric disorders.* Washington, DC: American Psychiatric Press.

Cotterell, J. (1996). *Social networks and social influences in adolescence.* London: Routledge.

Cotton, P. (1993, July 7). Psychiatrists set to approve DSM-IV. *Journal of the American Medical Association, 270,* 13–15.

Cowley, G. (2000, January 31). Alzheimer's: Unlocking the mystery. *Time,* pp. 46–54.

Crabb, P. B., & Pristash, D. (1992, June). *Gender-typing of material culture in children's books, 1937–1989.* Paper presented at the annual meeting of the American Psychological Society, San Diego.

Craig, I. W., McClay, J., Plomin, R., & Freeman, B. (2000). Chasing behaviour genes into the next millennium. *Trends in Biotechnology, 18,* 22–26.

Craig, R. J. (1999). *Interpreting personality tests: A clinical manual for the MMPI-2, MCMI-III, CPI-R, and 16PF.* New York: Wiley.

Craik, F. I. (1990). Levels of processing. In M. E. Eysenck (Ed.), *The Blackwell dictionary of cognitive psychology,* London: Blackwell.

Craik, F. I., & Lockhart, R. S. (1972). Levels of processing: A framework for memory research. *Journal of Verbal Behavior, 11,* 671–684.

Cramer, J. A. (1995). Optimizing long-term patient compliance. *Neurology, 45,* s25–s28.

Cramer, P. (1996). *Storytelling, narrative, and the Thematic Apperception Test.* New York: Guilford Press.

Crapo, L. (1985). *Hormones, the messengers of life.* New York: Freeman.

Crawford, M. (1995). *Talking difference: On gender and language.* Thousand Oaks, CA: Sage.

Crawford, M., & Unger, R. K. (1999). *Women and gender: A feminist psychology* (3rd ed.). New York: McGraw-Hill.

Crews, F. (1996). The verdict on Freud. *Psychological Science, 7,* 63–68.

Crick, N. R., & Dodge, K. A. (1994). A review and reformulation of social information-processing mechanisms in children's social adjustment. *Psychological Bulletin, 115,* 74–101.

Crits-Christoph, P. (1992). The efficacy of brief dynamic psychotherapy: A meta-analysis. *American Journal of Psychiatry, 149,* 151–158.

Crits-Cristoph, P., Siqueland, L., Blaine, J., et al. (1999). Psychosocial treatments for cocaine dependence: National Institute on Drug Abuse Collaborative Cocaine Treatment Study. *Archives of General Psychiatry, 56,* 493–502.

Cronkite, K. (1994). *On the edge of darkness: Conversations about depression.* New York: Doubleday.

Crouter, A. C., Bumpus, M. F., Maguire, M. C., & McHale, S. M. (1999). Linking parents' work pressure and adolescents' well-being: Insights into dynamics in dual-earner families. *Developmental Psychology, 35,* 1453–1461.

Crow, T. J. (1995). A theory of the evolutionary origins of psychosis. *European Neuropsychopharmacology, 5,* 59–63.

Croyle, R. T., & Hunt, J. R. (1991). Coping with health threat: Social influence processes in reactions to medical test results. *Journal of Personality and Social Psychology, 60,* 382–389.

Csikszentmihalyi, M. (1997). *Creativity: Flow and the psychology of discovery and invention.* New York: Basic Books.

Culbertson, F. M. (1997, January). Depression and gender: An international review. *American Psychologist, 52,* 25–31.

Cummings, E., & Henry, W. E. (1961). *Growing old.* New York: Basic Books.

Cwikel, J., Behar, L., & Rabson-Hare, J. (2000). A comparison of a vote count and a meta-analysis review of intervention research with adult cancer patients. *Research on Social Work Practice, 10,* 139–158.

Czeisler, C. A., Duffy, J. F., Shanahan, T. L., Brown, E. N., Mitchell, J. F., Rimmer, D. W., Ronda, J. M., Silva, E. J., Allan, J. S., Emens, J. S., Dijk, D. J., & Kronauer, R. E. (1999, June 25). Stability, precision, and near-24-hour period of the human circadian pacemaker. *Science, 284,* 2177–2181.

Damasio, A. (1999). *The feeling of what happens: Body and emotion in the making of consciousness.* New York: Harcourt Brace.

Damasio, H., Grabowski, T., Frank, R., Galaburda, A. M., & Damasio, A. R. (1994, May 20). The return of Phineas Gage: Clues about the brain from the skull of a famous patient. *Science, 264,* 1102–1105.

Damon, W. (1999, August). The moral development of children. *Scientific American,* pp. 72–78.

Daniels, H. (Ed.). (1996). *An introduction to Vygotsky.* London: Routledge.

Darley, J. M. (1995). Constructive and destructive obedience: A taxonomy of principal-agent relationships. *Journal of Social Issues, 51,* 125–154.

Darnton, N. (1990, June 4). Mommy vs. Mommy. *Newsweek,* pp. 64–67.

Darwin, C. J., Turvey, M. T., & Crowder, R. G. (1972). An auditory analogue of the Sperling partial-report procedure: Evidence for brief auditory storage. *Cognitive Psychology, 3,* 255–267.

Davidson, J. E., Deuser, R., & Sternberg, R. J. (1994). The role of metacognition in problem solving. In J. Metcalfe & A. P. Shimamura (Eds.), *Metacognition: Knowing about knowing.* Cambridge, MA: MIT Press.

Davidson, J. R. T. (2000). Trauma: The impact of post-traumatic stress disorder. *Journal of Psychopharmacology, 14,* S5–S12.

Davidson, R. J. (1994). Complexities in the search for emotion-specific physiology. In P. Ekman & R. J. Davidson (Eds.), *The nature of emotion.* New York: Oxford University Press.

Davidson, R. J., Gray, J. A., LeDoux, J. E., Levenson, R. W., Panksepp, J., & Ekman, P. (1994). Is there emotion-specific physiology? In P. Ekman & R. J. Davidson (Eds.), *The nature of emotion.* New York: Oxford University Press.

DeAngelis, T. (1991, June). DSM being revised but problems remain. *APA Monitor,* p. 14.

DeAngelis, T. (2000, April). Is Internet addiction real? *APA Monitor,* pp. 24–27.

Deary, I. J., & Stough, C. (1996). Intelligence and inspection time: Achievements, prospects, and problems. *American Psychologist, 51,* 599–608.

Deaux, K. (1995). How basic can you be? The evolution of research on gender stereotypes. *Journal of Social Issues, 51,* 11–20.

de Boysson-Bardies, B., & Halle, P. A. (1994). Speech development: Contributions of cross-linguistic studies. In A. Vyt, H. Bloch, & M. H. Bornstein (Eds.), *Early child development in the French tradition: Contributions from current research.* Hillsdale, NJ: Erlbaum.

deCharms, R. C., Blake, D. T., & Merzenich, M. M. (1998, May 29). Optimizing sound features for cortical neurons. *Science, 280,* 1439–1440.

Deci, E. L., Koestner, R., & Ryan, R. M. (1999). A meta-analytic review of experiments examining the effects of extrinsic rewards on intrinsic motivation. *Psychological Bulletin, 125,* 627–668.

Deffenbacher, J. L. (1988). Cognitive relaxation and social skills treatments of anger: A year later. *Journal of Consulting Psychology, 35,* 309–315.

Deffenbacher, J. L. (1996). Cognitive-behavioral approaches to anger reduction. In K. S. Dobson & K. D. Craig (Eds.), *Advances in cognitive-behavioral therapy* (Vol. 2). Thousand Oaks, CA: Sage.

DeGaton, J. F., Week, S., & Jensen, L. (1996). Understanding gender differences in adolescent sexuality. *Adolescence, 31,* 217–231.

de Gelder, B. (2000, August 18). More to seeing than meets the eye. *Science, 289,* 1148–1149.

deGroot, A. D. (1966). Perception and memory versus thought: Some old ideas and recent findings. In B. Kleinmuntz (Ed.), *Problem solving: Research, method, and theory,* New York: Wiley.

Delahanty, D., & Baum, A. (2000). Stress and breast cancer. In A. S. Baum, R. A. Revenson, & J. E. Singer (Eds.), *Handbook of health psychology.* Mahwah, NJ: Erlbaum.

Delaney, C. H. (1995). Rites of passage in adolescence. *Adolescence, 30,* 891–897.

Delany, S. (1999). *Having our say: The Delany sisters' first 100 years.* Burnsville, MN: Econo-Clad Books.

Delany, S., & Hearth, H. (1997). *Having our say: The Delaney sisters' first 100 years.* New York: Delta.

Delgado, P. L., & Moreno, F. A. (2000). Role of norepinephrine in depression. *Journal of Clinical Psychiatry, 61,* 5–12.

Della Sala, S., Baddeley, A. D., Papagno, C., & Spinnler, H. (1995). Dual-task paradigm: A means to examine the central executive. In J. Grafman, K. J. Holyoak, & F. Boller (Eds.), *Structure and functions of the human prefrontal cortex.* [Annals of the New York Academy of Sciences, Vol. 769.] New York: New York Academy of Sciences.

Delprato, D. J., & Midgley, B. D. (1992). Some fundamentals of B. F. Skinner's behaviorism. *American Psychologist, 47,* 1507–1520.

Dement, W. C. (1976). *Some must watch while some must sleep.* New York: Norton.

Dement, W. C. (1979). Two kinds of sleep. In D. Goleman & R. J. Davidson (Eds.), *Consciousness: Brain, states of awareness, and mysticism* (pp. 72–75). New York: Harper & Row.

Dement, W. C. (1989). Circadian rhythms and sleeping cycles. In D. F. Dinges and R. J. Broughton (Eds.), *Sleep and alertness: Chrono-biological, behavioral and medical aspects of napping.* New York: Lippincott, Williams & Wilkins.

Dement, W. C., & Wolpert, E. A. (1958). The relation of eye movements, body mobility, and external stimuli to dream content. *Journal of Experimental Psychology, 55,* 543–553.

Dempster, F. N. (1981). Memory span: Sources of individual and developmental differences. *Psychological Bulletin, 89,* 63–100.

Denis, M., & Greenbaum, C. (Trans.). (1991). *Image and cognition.* London, England: Harverster Wheatsheaf.

Denmark, G. L., & Fernandez, L. C. (1993). Historical development of the psychology of women. In F. L. Denmark & M. A. Paludi (Eds.), *A handbook of issues and theories.* Westport, CT: Greenwood Press.

Dent, J. (1984, March). *Reader's Digest,* p. 38.

Dentzer, S. (1986, May 5). Can you pass the job test? *Newsweek,* pp. 46–53.

Deregowski, J. B. (1973). Illusion and culture. In R. L. Gregory & G. H. Combrich (Eds.), *Illusion in nature and art* (pp. 161–192). New York: Scribner's.

Desimone, R. (1992, October 9). The physiology of memory: Recordings of things past. *Science, 258,* 245–255.

DeSteno, D. A., & Salovey, P. (1996). Evolutionary orgins of sex differences in jealousy? Questioning the "fitness" of the model. *Psychological Science, 7,* 367–372.

Detterman, D. K. (Ed.). (1996). *The environment.* Norwood, NJ: Ablex.

Detterman, D. K., Gabriel, L. T., & Ruthsatz, J. M. (2000). Intelligence and mental retardation. In R. J. Sternberg et al. (Eds.), *Handbook of intelligence.* New York: Cambridge University Press.

de Valois, R. L., & de Valois, K. K. (1993). A multi-stage color model. *Vision Research, 33,* 1053–1065.

de Waal, F. B. M. (1999, December). The end of nature versus nurture. *Scientific American,* pp. 94–99.

Diamond, M., & Simundson, H. K. (1997). Sex reassignment at birth: Long-term review and clinical implications. *Archives of Pediatrics and Adolescent Medicine, 15,* 298–304.

Diaz-Guerrero, R. (1979). Culture and personality revisited. *Annals of the New York Academy of Sciences, 285,* 119–130.

DiChiara, T. J., & Reinhart, P. H. (1997). Redox modulation of hslo Ca^{2+}-activated K^+ channels. *Journal of Neuroscience, 17,* 4942–4955.

Diener, E. (2000). Subjective well-being: The science of happiness and a proposal for a national index. *American Psychologist, 55,* 34–43.

Diener, E., & Diener, C. (1996). Most people are happy. *Psychological Science, 7,* 181–185.

Diener, E., Suh, E. M., Lucas, R. E., & Smith, H. L. (1999). Subjective well-being: Three decades of progress. *Psychological Bulletin, 125,* 276–302.

Dietz, T. L. (1998). An examination of violence and gender role portrayals in video games: Implications for gender socialization and aggressive behavior. *Sex Roles, 38,* 425–442.

DiFranza, J. R., & Lew, R. A. (1995, April). Effect of maternal cigarette smoking on pregnancy complications and sudden infant death syndrome. *Journal of Family Practice, 40,* 385–394.

DiGiovanna, A. G. (1994). *Human aging: Biological perspectives.* New York: McGraw-Hill.

Dillard, J. P. (1991). The current status of research on sequential-request compliance techniques. [Special issue: Meta-analysis in personality and social psychology.] *Personality and Social Psychology Bulletin, 17,* 283–288.

Dillman, D. A. (2000). *Mail and internet surveys: The tailored design method.* New York: Wiley.

DiMatteo, M. R. (1997). Health behaviors and care decisions: An overview of professional-patient communications. In D. S. Gochman (Ed.), *Handbook of health behavior research.* New York: Plenum Press.

Dinges, D. F., Pack, F., Williams, K., Gillen, K. A., Powell, J. W., Ott, G. E., Aptowicz, C., & Pack, A. I. (1997). Cumulative sleepiness, mood disturbance, and psychomotor vigilance performance decrements during a week of sleep restricted to 4–5 hours per night. *Sleep, 20,* 267–273.

Dishman, R. K. (1997, January). Brain monoamines, exercise, and behavioral stress: animal models. *Medical Science Exercise, 29,* 63–74.

Dobbins, A. C., Jeo, R. M., Fiser, J., & Allman, J. M. (1998, July 24). Distance modulation of neural activity in the visual cortex. *Science, 281,* 552–555.

Dobelle, W. H. (2000). Artificial vision for the blind by connecting a television camera to the visual cortex. *ASAIO Journal, 46,* 3–9.

Doi, T. (1990). The cultural assumptions of psychoanalysis. In J. W. Stigler, R. A. Shweder, & G. Herdt (Eds.), *Cultural psychology: Essays on comparative human development.* New York: Cambridge University Press.

Dollard, J., Doob, L., Miller, N., Mower, O. H., & Sears, R. R. (1939). *Frustration and aggression.* New Haven, CT: Yale University Press.

Domhoff, G. W. (1996). *Finding meaning in dreams: A quantitative approach.* New York: Plenum Press.

Dorion, A. A., Chantome, M., Hasboun, D., Zouaoui, A., Marsault, C., Capron, C., & Duyme, M. (2000). Hemispheric asymmetry and corpus callosum morphometry: A magnetic resonance imaging study. *Neuroscience Research, 36,* 9–13.

Dortch, S. (1996, October). Our aching heads. *American Demographics,* pp. 4–8.

Doty, R. L., Green, P. A., Ram, C., & Yankell, S. L. (1982). Communication of gender from human breath odors: Relationship to perceived intensity and pleasantness. *Hormones and Behavior, 16,* 13–22.

Doyle, R. (1999, December). The decline of marriage. *Scientific American,* pp. 36–37.

Dreman, S. (1997). *The family on the threshold of the 21st century.* Mahwah, NJ: Erlbaum.

Dressler, W. W., & Oths, K. S. (1997). Cultural determinants of health behavior. In D. S. Gochman (Ed.), *Handbook of health behavior research.* New York: Plenum Press.

Dreyer, P. H. (1982). Sexuality during adolescence. In B. B. Wolman (Ed.), *Handbook of developmental psychology.* Englewood Cliffs, NJ: Prentice Hall.

Druckman, D., & Bjork, R. A. (1991). *In the mind's eye: Enhancing human performance.* Washington, DC: National Academy Press.

Druckman, D., & Bjork, R. A. (Eds.). (1994). *Learning, remembering, believing: Enhancing human performance.* Washington, DC: National Academy Press.

Drummond, D. C., Tiffany, S. T., Glautier, S., & Remington, B. (Eds.). (1995). *Addictive behaviour: Cue exposure theory and practice.* Chichester, England: Wiley.

Dryden, W. (1999). *Rational emotive behavior therapy: A training manual.* New York: Springer.

Dubovsky, S. (1999, February 25). Tuning in to manic depression. *HealthNews, 5,* p. 8.

Dugger, C. W. (1996, December 28). Tug of taboos: African genital rite vs. U.S. law. *New York Times,* pp. 1, 9.

Dugger, C. W. (2001, February 1). Snatched from the grave. *New York Times,* A1.

Duke, M., & Nowicki, S., Jr. (1979). *Abnormal psychology: Perspectives on being different.* Monterey, CA: Brooks/Cole.

Duncan, J., Seitz, R. J., Kolodny, J., Bor, D., Herzog, H., Ahmed, A., Newell, F. N., & Emslie H. (2000, July 21). A neural basis for general intelligence. *Science,* 457–460.

Duncan, P. D., et al. (1985). The effects of pubertal timing on body image, school behavior, and deviance. [Special Issue: Time of maturation and psychosocial functioning in adolescence: I.] *Journal of Youth and Adolescence, 14,* 227–235.

Duncker, K. (1945). On problem solving. *Psychological Monographs, 58* (5, whole no. 270).

Dunham, R. M., Kidwell, J. S., & Wilson, S. M. (1986). Rites of passage at adolescence: A ritual process paradigm. *Journal of Adolescent Research, 1,* 139–153.

Dupre, D., Miller, N., Gold, M., & Rospenda, K. (1995). Initiation and progression of alcohol, marijuana, and cocaine use among adolescent abusers. *American Journal on Addictions, 4,* 43–48.

Durkin, M. S., & Stein, Z. A. (1996). Classification of mental retardation. In J. W. Jacobson & J. A. Mulick (Eds.), *Manual of diagnosis and professional practice in mental retardation.* Washington, DC: American Psychological Association.

Dusenbury, L., & Botvin, G. J. (1992). Substance abuse prevention: Competence enhancement and the development of positive life options. *Journal of Addictive Diseases, 11,* 29–45.

Dutton, D. G., & Aron, A. P. (1974). Some evidence for heightened sexual attraction under conditions of high anxiety. *Journal of Personality and Social Psychology, 30,* 510–517.

Eagly, A. (1989, May). *Meta-analysis of sex differences.* Paper presented at the annual conference on adversity, University of Massachusetts, Amherst.

Eagly, A. H., & Chaiken, S. (1993). *The psychology of attitudes.* Fort Worth, TX: Harcourt Brace Jovanovich.

Eagly, A. H., & Chaiken, S. (1995). Attitude strength, attitude structure, and resistance to change. In R. E. Petty & J. A. Krosnick (Eds.), *Attitude strength: Antecedents and consequences.* Mahwah, NJ: Erlbaum.

Earley, J. (1999). *Interactive group therapy: Integrating interpersonal, action-oriented and psychodynamic approaches.* New York: Brunner/Mazel.

Eating disorders, Part II. (1997, November). *Harvard Mental Health Letter,* pp. 1–5.

Ebbinghaus, H. (1885/1913). *Memory: A contribution to experimental psychology* (H. A. Roger & C. E. Bussenius, Trans.). New York: Columbia University Press.

Ebomoyi, E. (1987). Prevalence of female circumcision in two Nigerian communities. *Sex Roles, 17,* 13–152.

Eccles, J. S., Lord, S. E., & Roeser, R. W. (1996). Round holes, square pegs, rocky roads, and sore feet: The impact of stage-environment fit on young adolescents' experiences in schools and families. In D. Cicchetti & S. L. Toth (Eds.), *Adolescence: Opportunities and challenges.* Rochester, NY: University of Rochester Press.

Eccleston, C., & Crombez, G. (1999). Pain demands attention: A cognitive-affective model of the interruptive function of pain. *Psychological Bulletin, 125,* 356–366.

Ecenbarger, W. (1993, April 1). America's new merchants of death. *Reader's Digest,* p. 50.

Ecklund, A. (1999, July 12). Now hear this! Deaf since childhood, a TV actress celebrates the gift of hearing. *People Weekly,* pp. 67+.

Edgette, J. H., & Edgette, J. S. (1995). *The handbook of hypnotic phenomena in psychotherapy.* New York: Brunner/Mazel.

Egeth, H. E., & Yantis, S. (1997). Visual attention: Control, representation, and time course. *Annual Review of Psychology, 48,* 269–297.

Eich, E., Macaulay, D., Loewenstein, R. J., & Dihle, P. H. (1997). Memory, amnesia, and dissociative identity disorder. *Psychological Science, 8,* 417–421.

Eichenbaum, H. (1993, August 20). Thinking about brain cell assemblies. *Science, 261,* 993–994.

Eichenbaum, H. (1997). Declarative memory: Insights from cognitive neurobiology. *Annual Review of Psychology, 48,* 547–572.

Eisen, L., Field, T. M., & Larson, S. K. (1991). Environmental effects on the fetus: The examples of alcohol, cocaine, and exercise. In L. Diamant (Ed.), *Mind-body maturity: Psychological approaches to sports, exercise, and fitness.* New York: Hemisphere.

Eisenberg, A. (1999, June 24). Blind people with eye damage may someday use chips to see. *New York Times,* p. D1.

Eisenberg, N. (1991). Meta-analytic contributions to the literature on prosocial behavior. *Personality and Social Psychology Bulletin, 17,* 273–282.

Eisenberger, R., Pierce, W. D., & Cameron, J. (1999). Effects of reward on intrinsic motivation—negative, neutral, and positive: Comment on Deci, Koestner, and Ryan (1999). *Psychological Bulletin, 125,* 677–691.

Ekman, P. (1972). Universals and cultural differences in facial expressions of emotion. In J. Cole (Ed.), *Darwin and facial expression: A century of research in review* (pp. 169–222). New York: Academic Press.

Ekman, P. (1993). Facial expression and emotion. *American Psychologist, 48,* 384–392.

Ekman, P. (1994a). All emotions are basic. In P. Ekman & R. J. Davidson (Eds.), *The nature of emotion: Fundamental questions.* New York: Oxford University Press.

Ekman, P. (1994b). Strong evidence for universals in facial expressions: A reply to Russell's mistaken critique. *Psychological Bulletin, 115,* 268–287.

Ekman, P., & Davidson, R. J. (1994). *The nature of emotion: Fundamental questions.* New York: Oxford University Press.

Ekman, P., Friesen, W. V., & O'Sullivan, M. (1988). Smiles when lying. *Journal of Personality and Social Psychology, 54,* 414–420.

Ekman, P., Davidson, R. J., & Friesen, W. V. (1990). Emotional expression and brain physiology: II. The Duchenne smile. *Journal of Personality and Social Psychology, 58,* 342–353.

Ekman, P., Levenson, R. W., & Friesen, W. V. (1983, September 16). Autonomic nervous system activity distinguishes among emotions. *Science, 223,* 1208–1210.

Ekman, P., & O'Sullivan, M. (1991). Facial expression: Methods, means, and moues. In R. S. Feldman & B. Rimé (Eds.), *Fundamentals of nonverbal behavior.* Cambridge, England: Cambridge University Press.

Elkind, D. (1967). Egocentrism in adolescence. *Child Development, 38,* 1025–1034.

Elkind, D. (1985). Cognitive development and adolescent disabilities. *Journal of Adolescent Health Care, 6,* 84–89.

Elkind, D. (1988). *Miseducation.* New York: Knopf.

Elkins, I. J., McGue, M., & Iacono, W. G. (1997). Genetic and environmental influences on parent-son relationships: Evidence for increasing genetic influence during adolescence. *Developmental Psychology, 33,* 351–363.

Elliot, A. J., & Church, M. A. (1997). A hierarchical model of approach and avoidance achievement motivation. *Journal of Personality and Social Psychology, 72,* 218–232.

Ellis, A. (1974). *Growth through reason.* Hollywood, CA: Wilshire Books.

Ellis, A. (1999). Why rational emotive to rational emotive behavior therapy? *Psychotherapy, 36,* 154–159.

Ellis, A., & Dryden, W. (1997). *The practice of rational emotive behavior therapy* (2nd ed.). New York: Springer.

Ellyson, S. L., Dovidio, J. F., & Brown, C. E. (1992, April). *Visual dominance of behavior in mixed-sex interaction: A meta-analysis.* Paper presented at the annual meeting of the Eastern Psychological Association, Boston.

Embretson, S. E. (1996). Multidimensional latent trait models in measuring fundamental aspects of intelligence. In I. Dennis & P. Tapsfield (Eds.), *Human abilities: Their nature and measurement.* Mahwah, NJ: Erlbaum.

Engebretson, T. O., & Stoney, C. M. (1995). Anger expression and lipid concentrations. *International Journal of Behavioral Medicine, 2,* 281–298.

Engen, T. (1987, September-October). Remembering odors and their names. *American Scientist, 75,* 497–503.

Engle-Friedman, M., Baker, A., & Bootzin, R. R. (1985). Reports of wakefulness during EEG identified stages of sleep. *Sleep Research, 14,* 152.

Engler, J., & Goleman, D. (1992). *The consumer's guide to psychotherapy.* New York: Simon & Schuster.

Enserink, M. (1999, April 9). Can the placebo be the cure? *Science, 284,* 238–240.

Enserink, M. (2000a, April 21). Are placebo-controlled drug trials ethical? *Science, 288,* 416.

Enserink, M. (2000b, July 28). The violence of the lambs. *Science, 289,* 580–581.

Epstein, R. (1987). The spontaneous interconnection of four repertoires of behavior in a pigeon. *Journal of Comparative Psychology, 101,* 197–201.

Epstein, R. (1996). *Cognition, creativity, and behavior: Selected essays.* Westport, CT: Praeger/Greenwood.

Epstein, R., Kirshnit, C. E., Lanza, R. P., & Rubin, L. C. (1984). Insight in the pigeon: Antecedents and determinants of intelligent performance. *Nature, 308,* 61–62.

Erickson, M. H., Hershman, S., & Secter, I. I. (1990). *The practical application of medical and dental hypnosis.* New York: Brunner/Mazel.

Erikson, E. H. (1963). *Childhood and society* (2nd ed.). New York: W. W. Norton.

Erlandson, D. A., Harris, E. L., Skipper, B. L., & Allen, S. D. (1993). *Doing naturalistic inquiry: A guide to methods.* Newbury Park, CA: Sage.

Estes, W. K. (1991). Cognitive architectures from the standpoint of an experimental psychologist. *Annual Review of Psychology, 42,* 1–28.

Estes, W. K. (1997). Significance testing in psychological research: Some persisting issues. *Psychological Science, 8,* 18–19.

Evans, J. S. B. T., Newstead, S. E., & Byrne, R. M. E. (1994). *Human reasoning: The psychology of deduction.* Hillsdale, NJ: Erlbaum.

Eveleth, P., & Tanner, J. (1976). *World-wide variation in human growth.* New York: Cambridge University Press.

Eysenck, H. H. (1975). *Eysenck on extroversion.* New York: Wiley.

Eysenck, H. J. (1990). Biological dimensions of personality. In L. A. Pervin (Ed.), *Handbook of personality: Theory and research* (p. 246). New York: Guilford Press.

Eysenck, H. J. (1994a). The Big Five or giant three: Criteria for a paradigm. In C. F. Halverson, Jr., G. A. Kohnstamm, & R. P. Martin (Eds.), *The developing structure of temperament and personality from infancy to adulthood.* Hillsdale, NJ: Erlbaum.

Eysenck, H. J. (1994b). Cancer, personality and stress: Prediction and prevention. *Advances in Behaviour Research and Therapy, 16,* 167–215.

Eysenck, H. J., Barrett, P., Wilson, G., & Jackson, C. (1992). Primary trait measurement of the 21 components of the P-E-N system. *European Journal of Psychological Assessment, 8,* 109–117.

Falk, D., Forese, N., Sade, D. S., & Dudek, B. C. (1999). Sex differences in brain/body relationships of Rhesus monkeys and humans. *Journal of Human Evolution, 36,* 233–238.

Fan, P., & Marini, M. M. (2000). Influences on gender-role attitudes during the transition to adulthood. *Social Science Research, 29,* 258–283.

Farber, B. A., Brink, D. C., & Raskin, P. M. (Eds.). (1996). *The psychotherapy of Carl Rogers: Cases and commentary.* New York: Guilford Press.

Farley, F. (1986, May). The big T in personality. *Psychology Today,* pp. 44–52.

Fearing, V. G., & Clark, J. (Eds.). (2000). *Individuals in context: A practical guide to client-centered practice.* Chicago: Slack.

Feingold, A. (1994). Gender differences in personality: A meta-analysis. *Psychological Bulletin, 116,* 429–456.

Feldman, R. S. (Ed.). (1982). *Development of nonverbal behavior in children.* New York: Springer-Verlag.

Feldman, R. S. (Ed.). (1993). *Applications of nonverbal behavioral theories and research.* Hillsdale, NJ: Erlbaum.

Feldman, R. S., Coats, E. J., & Schwartzberg, S. (1994). *Case studies and critical thinking about psychology.* New York: McGraw-Hill.

Fenton, W. S., & McGlashan, T. H. (1991). Natural history of schizophrenia subtypes: II. Positive and negative symptoms and long-term course. *Archives of General Psychiatry, 48,* 978–986.

Fenton, W. S., & McGlashan, T. H. (1994). Antecedents, symptom progression, and long-term outcome of the deficit syndrome in schizophrenia. *American Journal of Psychiatry, 151,* 351–356.

Festinger, L. (1957). *A theory of cognitive dissonance.* Stanford, CA: Stanford University Press.

Festinger, L., & Carlsmith. J. M. (1959). Cognitive consequences of forced compliance. *Journal of Abnormal and Social Psychology, 58,* 203–210.

Festinger, L., Schachter, S., & Back, K. W. (1950). *Social pressure in informal groups.* New York: Harper.

Fields-Meyer, T. (1995, September 25). Having their say. *People,* pp. 50–60.

Fields-Meyer, T. (1999, October 25). The whiz kids. *People,* pp. 59–63.

Figueiras, M. J., & Marteau, T. M. (1995). Experiences of the menopause: A comparison between Portugal and the United Kingdom. *Analise Psicologica, 13,* 163–171.

Fine, L. (1994). Personal communication on cultural rituals.

Fink, A. & Kosecoff, J. (1998). *How to conduct surveys: A step-by-step guide.* Thousand Oaks, CA: Sage.

Fink, M. (1999). *Electroshock: Restoring the mind.* New York: Oxford University Press.

Fink, M. (2000). Electroshock revisited. *American Scientist, 88,* 162–167.

Finke, R. A. (1995). Creative insight and preinventive forms. In R. J. Sternberg & J. E. Davidson (Eds.), *The nature of insight.* Cambridge, MA: MIT Press.

Finkelhor, D. (1984). *Child sexual abuse: New theory and research.* New York: Free Press.

Firestein, B. A. (Ed.). (1996). *Bisexuality: The psychology and politics of an invisible minority.* Thousand Oaks, CA: Sage.

Fischer, C. S., Hout, M., Jankowksi, M. S., Lucas, S. R., Swidler, A., & Voss, K. (1996). *Inequality by design: Cracking the bell curve myth.* Princeton, NJ: Princeton University Press.

Fischer, K. W., Shaver, P. R., & Carnochan, P. (1990). How emotions develop and how they organize development. *Cognition and Emotion, 4,* 81–127.

Fischoff, B. (1977). Perceived informativeness of facts. *Journal of Experimental Psychology: Human Perception and Performance, 3,* 349–358.

Fisher, C. B., & Fyrberg, D. (1994). Participant partners: College students weigh the costs and benefits of deceptive research. *American Psychologist, 49,* 417–427.

Fisher, K. (1985, March). ECT: New studies on how, why, who. *APA Monitor,* pp. 18–19.

Fiske, S. T. (1992a). Stereotypes work . . . but only sometimes: Comment on how to motivate the "unfinished mind." *Psychological Inquiry, 3,* 161–162.

Fiske, S. T. (1992b). Thinking is for doing: Portraits of social cognition from daguerreotype to laserphoto. *Journal of Personality and Social Psychology, 63,* 877–889.

Fiske, S. T. (1998). Stereotyping, prejudice, and discrimination. In D. T. Gilbert, S. T. Fiske, & G. Lindzey (Eds.), *The handbook of social psychology* (4th ed.). New York: McGraw-Hill.

Fiske, S. T., & Morling, B. (1996). Stereotyping as a function of personal control motives and capacity constraints: The odd couple of power and anxiety. In R. M. Sorrentino & E. T. Higgins (Eds.), *Handbook of motivation and cognition: Vol. 3. The interpersonal context.* New York: Guilford Press.

Fiske, S. T., & Taylor, S. E. (1991). *Social cognition* (2nd ed.). New York: McGraw-Hill.

Flam, F. (1991, June 14). Queasy riders. *Science, 252,* 1488.

Flavell, J. H. (1993). Young children's understanding of thinking and consciousness. *Current Directions in Psychological Science, 2,* 40–43.

Fleming, R., Baum, A., & Singer, J. E. (1984). Toward an integrative approach to the study of stress. *Journal of Personality and Social Psychology, 46,* 939–949.

Flynn, J. R. (1999). Searching for justice: The discovery of IQ gains over time. *American Psychologist, 54,* 5–20.

Flynn, J. R. (2000). IQ gains and fluid g. *American Psychologist, 55,* 543.

Folkman, S., Lazarus, R. S., Dunkel-Schetter, C., DeLongis, A., & Green, R. J. (1986). Dynamics of a stressful encounter: Cognitive appraisal, coping, and encounter outcome. *Journal of Personality and Social Psychology, 50,* 992–1003.

Folkman, S., & Moskowitz, J. T. (2000). Stress, positive emotion, and coping. *Current Directions in Psychological Science, 9,* 115–118.

Ford, C. S., & Beach, F. A. (1951). *Patterns of sexual behavior.* New York: Harper.

Ford, J. G. (1991). Rogers's theory of personality: Review and perspectives. *Journal of Social Behavior and Personality, 6,* 19–44.

Forer, B. (1949). The fallacy of personal validation: A classroom demonstration of gullibility. *Journal of Abnormal and Social Psychology, 44,* 118–123.

Foreyt, J. P., & Goodrick, G. K. (1994). *Living without dieting.* New York: Warner.

Forrester, M. A. (1996). *Psychology of language: A critical introduction.* Thousand Oaks, CA: Sage.

Fox, R. E. (1994). Training professional psychologists for the twenty-first century. *American Psychologist, 49,* 200–206.

Fox, S., & Spector, P. E. (2000). Relations of emotional intelligence, practical intelligence, general intelligence, and trait affectivity with interview outcomes: It's not all just 'G'. *Journal of Organizational Behavior, 21,* 203–220.

Frances, A., First, M. B., & Pincus, H. A. (1995). *DSM-IV guidebook.* Washington, DC: American Psychiatric Press.

Frankenberg, W. K. et al., 1992. *Denver II training manual.* Denver: Denver Developmental Materials.

Franks, D. D., & Smith, T. S. (Eds.). (1999). *Mind, brain, and society: Toward a neurosociology of emotion* (Vol. 5). Stamford, CT: Jai Press.

Franks, D. D., & Smith, T. S. (2000). *Mind, brain, and society: Toward a neurosociology of emotion.* Stamford, CT: JAI Press.

Franzek, E., & Beckmann, H. (1996). Gene-environment interaction in schizophrenia: Season-of-birth effect reveals etiologically different subgroups. *Psychopathology, 29,* 14–26.

Frasure-Smith, N., Lesperance, F., & Talajic, M. (2000). The prognostic importance of depression, anxiety, anger, and social support following myocardial infarction: Opportunities for improving survival. In P. M. McCabe, N. Schneiderman. T. M. Field, & A. R. Wellens (Eds.), *Stress, coping, and cardiovascular disease.* Mahwah, NJ: Erlbaum.

Free, M. L. (2000). *Cognitive therapy in groups: Guidelines and resources for practice.* New York: Wiley.

Freedman, D. S. (1995). The importance of body fat distribution in early life. *American Journal of the Medical Sciences, 310,* S72–S76.

Freedman, J. L., & Fraser, S. C. (1966). Compliance without pressure: The foot-in-the-door technique. *Journal of Personality and Social Psychology, 4,* 195–202.

Freeman, P. (1990, December 17) Silent no more. *People Weekly,* pp. 94–104.

French, H. W. (1997, February 2). Africa's culture war: Old customs, new values. *New York Times,* pp. 1E, 4E.

Freud, S. (1922/1959). *Group psychology and the analysis of the ego.* London: Hogarth Press.

Freud, S. (1990). *The interpretation of dreams.* New York: Basic Books.

Friedman, A. F., Lewak, R., Nichols, D. S., & Webb, J. T. (2000). *Psychological assessment with the MMPI-2.* Mahwah, NJ: Erlbaum.

Friedman, M. J., & Marsella, A. J. (1996). Posttraumatic stress disorder: An overview of the concept. In A. J. Marsella, M. J. Friedman, E. T. Gerrity, & R. M. Scurfield (Eds.), *Ethnocultural aspects of posttraumatic stress disorder: Issues, research, and clinical applications.* Washington, DC: American Psychological Association.

Frishman, R. (1996). Don't be a wimp in the doctor's office. *Harvard Health Letter, 21,* 1–2.

Fritsch, J. (1999, October 5). Scientists unmask diet myth: Willpower. *New York Times,* pp. D1, D9.

Fromkin, V. A. (2000). On the uniqueness of language. In K. Emmorey & H. Lane, et al. (Eds.), *The signs of language revisited: An anthology to honor Ursula Bellugi and Edward Klima.* Mahwah, NJ: Erlbaum.

Fromm, E., & Nash, M. (Eds.). (1992). *Contemporary hypnosis research.* New York: Guilford Press.

Funder, D. C. (1991). Global traits: A neo-Allportian approach to personality. *Psychological Science, 2,* 31–39.

Funder, D. C. (1997). *The personality puzzle.* New York: W. W. Norton.

Funk, M. S. (1996). Development of object permanence in the New Zealand parakeet *(Cyanoramphus auriceps). Animal Learning and Behavior, 24,* 375–383.

Furnham, A. (1995). The relationship of personality and intelligence to cognitive learning style and achievement. In D. H. Saklofske & M. Zeidner (Eds.), *International handbook of personality and intelligence: Perspectives on individual differences.* New York: Plenum Press.

Furst, P. T. (1977). "High states" in culture-historical perspective. In N. E. Zinberg (Ed.), *Alternate states of consciousness.* New York: Free Press.

Gabriel, M. T., Critelli, J. W., & Ee, J. S. (1994). Narcissistic illusions in self-evaluations of intelligence and attractiveness. *Journal of Personality, 62,* 143–155.

Gaertner, S. L., Rust, M. C., Dovidio, J. F., Bachman, B. A., et al. (1996). The contact hypothesis: The role of a common ingroup identity on reducing intergroup bias among majority and minority group members. In J. L. Nye & A. M. Brower (Eds.), *What's social about social cognition? Research on socially shared cognition in small groups.* Thousand Oaks, CA: Sage.

Gagnon, G. H. (1977). *Human sexualities.* Glenview, IL: Scott, Foresman.

Gagnon, S., & Dore, F. X. (1994). Cross-sectional study of object permanence in domestic puppies *(Canis familiaris). Journal of Comparative Psychology, 108,* 220–232.

Galanter, E. (1962). Contemporary psychophysics. In R. Brown, E. Galanter, E. Hess, & G. Maroler (Eds.), *New directions in psychology* (pp. 87–157). New York: Holt.

Galanter, M. (Ed.). (1995). *Recent developments in alcoholism: Vol. 12. Alcoholism and women.* New York: Plenum Press.

Galanter, M., & Kleber, H. D. (Eds.). (1999). *The American Psychiatric Press textbook of substance abuse: Abuse treatment* (2nd ed.). Washington, DC: American Psychiatric Press.

Galatzer-Levy, R. M., & Cohler, B. J. (1997). *Essential psychoanalysis: A contemporary introduction.* New York: Basic Books.

Galavotti, C., Saltzman, L. E., Sauter, S. L., & Sumartojo, E. (1997, February). Behavioral science activities at the Center for Disease Control and Prevention: A selected overview of exemplary programs. *American Psychologist, 52,* 154–166.

Gale, N., Golledge, R. G., Pellegrino, J. W., & Doherty, S. (1990). The acquisition and integration of route knowledge in an unfamiliar neighborhood. *Journal of Environmental Psychology, 10,* 3–25.

Gallagher, J. J. (1994). Teaching and learning: New models. *Annual Review of Psychology, 45,* 171–195.

Gallagher, M., & Rapp, R. R. (1997). The use of animal models to study the effects of aging on cognition. *Annual Review of Psychology, 48,* 339–370.

Gannon, P. J., Holloway, R. L., Broadfield, D. C., & Braun, A. R. (1998, January 9). Asymmetry of chimpanzee planum temporale: Humanlike pattern of Wernicke's brain language area homolog. *Science, 279,* 220–222.

Ganong, L. H. & Coleman, M. (1999). *Changing families, changing responsibilities: Family obligations following divorce and remarriage.* Mahwah, NJ: Erlbaum.

Gao, J., Parsons, L. M., Bower, J. M., Xiong, J., Li, J., & Fox, P. T. (1996, April 26). Cerebellum implicated in sensory acquisition and discrimination rather than motor control. *Science, 272,* 545–547.

Garcia, J. (1990). Learning without memory. *Journal of Cognitive Neuroscience, 2,* 287–305.

Garcia, J., Hankins, W. G., & Rusiniak, K. W. (1974). Behavioral regulation of the milieu intern in man and rat. *Science, 185,* 824–831.

Garcia-Andrade, C., Wall, T. L., & Ehlers, C. L. (1997). The firewater myth and response to alcohol in Mission Indians. *Journal of Psychiatry, 154,* 983–988.

Gardner, H. (1975). *The shattered mind: The person after brain damage.* New York: Knopf.

Gardner, H. (1997). *Extraordinary minds.* New York: Basic Books.

Gardner, H. (1999). *Intelligence reframed: Multiple intelligences for the 21st century.* New York: Basic Books.

Gardner, R. A., & Gardner, B. T. (1969). Teaching sign language to a chimpanzee. *Science, 165,* 664–672.

Garling, T. (1989). The role of cognitive maps in spatial decisions. *Journal of Environmental Psychology, 9,* 269–278.

Garrison, D. W., & Foreman, R. D. (1994). Decreased activity of spontaneous and noxiously evoked dorsal horn cells during transcutaneous electrical nerve stimulation (TENS). *Pain, 58,* 309–315.

Gass, C. S., Luis, C. A., Meyers, T. L., & Kuljis, R. O. (2000). Familial Creutzfeldt-Jakob disease: A neuropsychological case study. *Archives of Clinical Neuropsychology, 15,* 165–175.

Gatchel, R. J., & Baum, A. (1983). *An introduction to health psychology.* Reading, MA: Addison-Wesley.

Gatchel, R. J., & Turk, D. C. (Eds.). (1996). *Psychological Approaches to Pain Management: A Practitioner's Handbook.* New York: Guilford Press.

Gatchel, R. J., & Weisberg, J. N. (Eds.). (2000). *Personality characteristics of patients with pain.* Washington, DC: American Psychological Association.

Gathercole, S. E., & Baddeley, A. D. (1993). *Working memory and language processing.* Hillsdale, NJ: Erlbaum.

Gawin, F. H. (1991, March 29). Cocaine addiction: Psychology and neurophysiology. *Science, 251,* 1580–1586.

Gazzaniga, M. S. (1998, July). The split brain revisited. *Scientific American,* pp. 50–55.

Ge, X., Conger, R. D., & Elder, G. H., Jr. (1996). Coming of age too early: Pubertal influences on girls' vulnerability to psychological distress. *Child Development, 67,* 3386–3400.

Geary, D. C., & Bjorklund, D. F. (2000). Evolutionary developmental psychology. *Child Development, 71,* 57–65.

Geen, R. G. (1984). Human motivation: New perspectives on old problems. In A. M. Rogers & C. J. Scheirer (Eds.), *The G. Stanley Hall Lecture Series* (Vol. 4). Washington, DC: American Psychological Association.

Geen, R. G. (1995). *Human motivation: A social psychological approach.* Pacific Grove, CA: Brooks/Cole.

Geen, R. G., & Donnerstein, E. (1983). *Aggression: Theoretical and empirical reviews.* New York: Academic Press.

Geen, R. G., & Donnerstein, E. (Eds.). (1998). *Human aggression: Theories, research and implications for social policy.* Orlando, FL: Academic Press.

Geiselman, R. E., Fisher, R. P., MacKinnon, D. P., & Holland, H. L. (1985). Eyewitness memory enhancement in the police interview: Cognitive retrieval mnemonics versus hypnosis. *Journal of Applied Psychology, 70,* 401–412.

Gelfand, M. M. (2000). Sexuality among older women. *Journal of Women's Health and Gender-Based Medicine, 9* (Suppl. 1), S15–S20.

Gelman, D. (1994, April 18). The mystery of suicide. *Newsweek,* pp. 44–49.

Gelman, R., & Au, T. K.-F. (Eds.). (1996). *Perceptual and cognitive development.* New York: Academic Press.

Gelman, R., & Baillargeon, R. (1983). A review of some Piagetian concepts. In J. H. Flavell & E. M. Markman (Eds.). *Handbook of child psychology: Vol. 3. Cognitive development* (4th ed.). New York: Wiley.

Genesse, F., & Gándara, P. (1999). Bilingual education programs: A cross-national perspective. *Journal of Social Issues, 55,* 665–685.

Gentry, W. D., & Kobasa, S. C. O. (1984). Social and psychological resources mediating stress-illness relationships in humans. In W. D. Gentry (Ed.), *Handbook of behavioral medicine.* New York: Guilford Press.

Genuis, M., & Violato, C. (2000). Attachment security to mother, father, and the parental unit. In C. Violato & E. Oddone-Paolucci (Eds.), *The changing family and child development.* Aldershot, England: Ashgate.

George, M. S., Wassermann, E. M., Williams, W. A., Callahan, A., et al. (1995). Daily repetitive transcranial magnetic stimulations (rTMS) improves mood in depression. *Neuroreport: An International Journal for the Rapid Communication of Research in Neuroscience, 6,* 1853–1856.

George, T. P. (1999). Design, measurement, and analysis in developmental research. In M. Bornstein & M. Lamb, *Developmental psychology.* Mahwah, NJ: Erlbaum.

Gescheider, G. A. (1997). *Psychophysics: The fundamentals* (3rd ed.). Mahwah, NJ: Erlbaum.

Getner, D., & Holyoak, K. J. (1997, January). Reasoning and learning by analogy. *American Psychologist, 52,* 32–34.

Gibbons, A. (1990, July 13). New maps of the human brain. *Science, 249,* 122–123.

Gibbs, M. E., O'Dowd, B. S., Hertz, L., Robinson, S. R., et al. (1996). Inhibition of glutamine synthetase activity prevents memory consolidation. *Cognitive Brain Research, 4,* 57–64.

Gibbs, W. W. (1996, August). Gaining on fat. *Scientific American,* pp. 88–94.

Gibson, B. (1997). Smoker-nonsmoker conflict: Using a social psychological framework to understand a current social controversy. *Journal of Social Issues, 53,* 97–112.

Gibson, H. B. (1995). A further case of the misuse of hypnosis in a police investigation. *Contemporary Hypnosis, 12,* 81–86.

Gilbert, B. (1996). New ideas in the air at the National Zoo. *Smithsonian,* pp. 32–43.

Gilbert, D. G. (1995). *Smoking: Individual differences, psychopathology, and emotion.* Philadelphia: Taylor & Francis.

Gilbert, D. T., & Malone, P. S. (1995). The correspondence bias. *Psychological Bulletin, 117,* 21–38.

Gilbert, D. T., McNulty, S. E., Guiliano, T. A., & Benson, J. E. (1992). Blurry words and fuzzy deeds: The attribution of obscure behavior. *Journal of Personality and Social Psychology, 62,* 18–25.

Gilbert, D. T., Miller, A. G., & Ross, L. (1998). Speeding with Ned: A personal view of the correspondence bias. In J. M. Darley & J. Cooper (Eds.), *Attribution and social interaction: The legacy of Edward E. Jones.* Washington, DC: American Psychological Association.

Gilbert, P. (2000). Varieties of submissive behavior as forms of social defense: Their evolution and role in depression. In L. Sloman & P. Gilbert (Eds.), *Subordination and defeat: An evolutionary approach to mood disorders and their therapy.* Mahwah, NJ: Erlbaum.

Gilger, J. W. (1996). How can behavioral genetic research help us understand language development and disorders? In M. L. Rice (Ed.), *Toward a genetics of language.* Mahwah, NJ: Erlbaum.

Gilligan, C. (1982). *In a different voice: Psychological theory and women's development.* Cambridge, MA: Harvard University Press.

Gilligan, C. (1987). Adolescent development reconsidered. *New Directions for Child Development, 37,* 63–92.

Gilligan, C. (1993). Woman's place in man's life cycle. In A. Dobrin (Ed.), *Being good and doing right: Readings in moral development.* Lanham, MD: University Press of America.

Gilligan, C., Lyons, N. P., & Hanmer, T. J. (Eds.). (1990). *Making connections.* Cambridge, MA: Harvard University Press.

Gilligan, C., Ward, J. V., & Taylor, J. M. (Eds.). (1988). *Mapping the moral domain: A contribution of women's thinking to psychological theory and education.* Cambridge, MA: Harvard University Press.

Gillyatt, P. (1997, February). When the nose doesn't know. *Harvard Health Letter,* pp. 6–7.

Gladue, B. A. (1995). The biopsychology of sexual orientation. *Current Directions in Psychological Science, 3,* 150–154.

Gladwin, T. (1964). Culture and logical process. In N. Goodenough (Ed.), *Explorations in cultural anthropology: Essays in honor of George Peter Murdoch.* New York: McGraw-Hill.

Glaman, J. M., Jones, A. P., & Rozelle, R. M. (1996). The effects of co-worker similarity on the emergence of affect in work teams. *Group and Organization Management, 21,* 192–215.

Glassman, A. H., & Koob, G. F. (1996, February 22). Neuropharmacology: Psychoactive smoke. *Nature, 379,* 677–678.

Glenmullen, J. (2000). *Prozac backlash: Overcoming the dangers of Prozac, Zoloft, Paxil, and other antidepressants with safe, effective alternatives.* New York: Simon & Schuster.

Glick, P., & Fiske, S. T. (1996). The Ambivalent Sexism Inventory: Differentiating hostile and benevolent sexism. *Journal of Personality and Social Psychology, 70,* 491–512.

Gobet, F., & Simon, H. A. (1996). Recall of random and distorted chess positions: Implications for the theory of expertise. *Memory and Cognition, 24,* 493–503.

Goldberg, C. (1999, October 27). Just another girl, unlike any other. *New York Times,* p. A14.

Golding, J. M. (1999). Sexual-assault history and long-term physical health problems: Evidence from clinical and population epidemiology. *Current Directions in Psychological Science, 8,* 191–193.

Goldsmith, H. H., & Harman, C. (1994). Temperament and attachment: Individuals and relationships. *Current Directions in Psychological Science, 3,* 53–56.

Goldstein, E. B. (1984). *Sensation and perception* (2nd ed.). Pacific Grove, CA: Brooks/Cole.

Goldstein, G., Beers, S. R., Longmore, S., & McCue, M. (1996). Efficacy of memory training: A technological extension and replication. *Clinical Neuropsychologist, 10,* 66–72.

Goldstein, I. (2000, August). Male sexual circuitry. *Scientific American,* pp. 70–75.

Goleman, D. (1988, January 21). Physicians may bungle key part of treatment: The medical interview. *New York Times,* p. B16.

Goleman D. (1993, July 21). "Expert" babies found to teach others. *New York Times,* p. C10.

Goleman, D. (1995). *Emotional intelligence: Why it can matter more than IQ.* New York: Bantam Books.

Golledge, R. G., Klatzyy, R. L., Loomis, J. L., Speigle, J., & Tietz, J. (1998). A geographical information system for a GPS based personal guidance system. *International Journal of Geographical Information Science, 12,* 727–749.

Golombok, S., & Tasker, F. (1996). Do parents influence the sexual orientation of their children? Findings from a longitudinal study of lesbian families. *Developmental Psychology, 32,* 3–11.

Goode, E. (1999a, October 19). "Fighting spirit" little help in cancer fight. *New York Times,* p. D10.

Goode, E. (1999b, April 13). If things taste bad, "phantoms" may be at work. *New York Times,* pp. C1–C2.

Goodglass, H. (1993). *Understanding aphasia.* San Diego: Academic Press.

Goodman, W. K., Rudorfer, M. V., & Maser, J. D. (1999). *Obsessive-compulsive disorder: Contemporary issues in treatment.* Mahwah, NJ: Erlbaum.

Goodwin, C. J. (1999). *Research and psychology: Methods and design* (2nd ed.). New York: Wiley.

Gordon, J. W. (1999, March 26). Genetic enhancement in humans. *Science, 283,* 2023–2024.

Gottesman, I. I. (1991). *Schizophrenia genesis: The origins of madness.* New York: Freeman.

Gottesman, I. I. (1997, June 6). Twin: En route to QTLs for cognition. *Science, 276,* 1522–1523.

Gottesman, I. I., & Moldin, S. O. (1998). Genotypes, genes, genesis, and pathogenesis in schizophrenia. In M. F. Lenzenweger & R. H. Dworkin (Eds.), *The origins and development of schizophrenia: Advances in experimental psychopathology.* Washington, DC: American Psychological Association.

Gottfredson, L. S. (1994). The science of politics and race-norming. *American Psychology, 49,* 955–963.

Gould, E., Reeves, A. J., Graziano, M. S. A., & Gross, C. G. (1999, October 15). Neurogenesis in the neocortex of adult primates. *Science,* pp. 548–552.

Gould, R. L. (1978). *Transformations.* New York: Simon & Schuster.

Gouras, P. (1991). Color vision. In E. R. Kandel, J. H. Schwartz, & T. M. Jessell (Eds.), *Principles of neural science* (3rd ed.). New York: Elsevier.

Graf, P. (1990). Life-span changes in implicit and explicit memory. *Bulletin of the Psychonomic Society, 28,* 353–358.

Graf, P., & Masson, M. E. J. (Eds.). (1993). *Implicit memory: New directions in cognition, development, and neuropsychology.* Hillsdale, NJ: Erlbaum.

Graffin, N. F., Ray, W. J., & Lundy, R. (1995). EEG concomitants of hypnosis and hypnotic susceptibility. *Journal of Abnormal Psychology, 104,* 123–131.

Graham, J. R. (1999). *MMPI-2: Assessing personality and psychopathology* (3rd ed.). New York: Oxford University Press.

Graham, S. (1992). "Most of the subjects were white and middle class": Trends in published research on African Americans in selected APA journals, 1970–1989. *American Psychologist, 47,* 629–639.

Grammer, K. (1996, June). *Sex and olfaction.* Paper presented at the annual meeting of the Human Behavior and Evolution Society, Evanston, Illinois.

Greenberg, R. L. (2000). The creative client in cognitive therapy. *Journal of Cognitive Psychotherapy, 14,* 163–174.

Greenberg, S. H. (1997, Spring/Summer). The loving ties that bond. *Newsweek,* pp. 68–72.

Greene, B., & Herek, G. (1994). *Lesbian and gay psychology: Theory, research, and clinical applications.* Newbury Park, CA: Sage.

Greene, R. L., & Clopton, J. R. (1994). Minnesota Multiphasic Personality Inventory–2. In M. E. Maruish (Ed.), *The use of psychological tests for treatment planning and outcome assessment.* Hillsdale, NJ: Erlbaum.

Greenfield, D. N. (1999, August). *Nature of Internet addiction: Psychological factors in compulsive Internet use.* Paper presented at the annual meeting of the American Psychological Association, Boston.

Greenfield, P. M. (1997). You can't take it with you. Why ability assessments don't cross cultures. *American Psychologist, 52,* 1115–1124.

Greenlaw, P. S., & Jensen, S. S. (1996). Race-norming and the Civil Rights Act of 1991. *Public Personnel Management, 25,* 13–24.

Greeno, J. G. (1978). Natures of problem-solving abilities. In W. K. Estes (Ed.), *Handbook of learning and cognitive processes.* Hillsdale, NJ: Erlbaum.

Greenwald, A. G., Draine S. C., & Abrams, R. L. (1996, September 20). Three cognitive markers of unconscious semantic activation. *Science, 272,* 1699–1702.

Greenwald, A. G., Spangenberg, E. R., Pratkanis, A. R., & Eskenzai, J. (1991). Double-blind tests of subliminal self-help audiotapes. *Psychological Science, 2,* 119–122.

Greenwood, C. R., Carta, J. J., Hart, B., Kamps, D., Terry, B., Arreaga-Mayer, C., Atwater, J., Walker, D., Risley, T., & Delquadri, J. C. (1992). Out of the laboratory and into the community: 26 years of applied behavior analysis at the Juniper Gardens children's project. *American Psychologist, 47,* 1464–1474.

Gregory, R. L. (1978). *The psychology of seeing* (3rd ed.). New York: McGraw-Hill.

Gregory, S. (1856). *Facts for young women.* Boston.

Gregory, S. S. (1994, March 21). At risk of mutilation. *Time,* pp. 45–46.

Greig, G. L. (1990). On the shape of energy-detection ROC curves. *Perception and Psychophysics, 48,* 77–81.

Greist-Bousquet, S., & Schiffman, H. R. (1986). The basis of the Poggendorff effect: An additional clue for Day and Kasperczyk. *Perception and Psychophysics, 39,* 447–448.

Griffith, R. M., Miyago, O., & Tago, A. (1958). The universality of typical dreams: Japanese vs. Americans. *American Anthropologist, 60,* 1173–1179.

Griffiths, M. (1997). Video games and aggression. *Psychologist, 10,* 397–401.

Grigorenko, E. L. (2000). Heritability and intelligence. In R. J. Sternberg et al. (Eds.), *Handbook of intelligence.* New York: Cambridge University Press.

Grillner, S. (1996, January). Neural networks for vertebrate locomotion. *Scientific American,* pp. 64–69.

Grimsley, D. L., & Karriker, M. W. (1996). Bilateral skin temperature, handedness, and the biofeedback control of skin temperature. *Journal of Behavioral Medicine, 19,* 87–94.

Grimson, W. E. L., Kikinis, R., Jolesz, F. A., & Black, P. M. (1999, June). Image-guided surgery. *Scientific American,* pp. 62–69.

Grohol, J. M. (1997). *The insider's guide to health resources online.* New York: Guilford Press.

Gross, J. (1991, June 16). More young single men hang onto apron strings. *New York Times,* pp. 1, 18.

Grossi, G., Samenza, C., Corazza, S., & Volterra, V. (1996). Hemispheric specialization for sign language. *Neuropsychologia, 34,* 737–740.

Groth-Marnat, G. (1990). *Handbook of psychological assessment* (2nd ed.). New York: Wiley.

Groth-Marnat, G. (1996). *Handbook of psychological assessment* (3rd ed.). Somerset, NJ: Wiley.

Grube, J. W., Rokeach, M., & Getzlaf, S. B. (1990). Adolescents' value images of smokers, ex-smokers, and nonsmokers. *Addictive Behaviors, 15,* 81–88.

Gruneberg, M. M., & Pascoe, K. (1996). The effectiveness of the keyword method for receptive and productive foreign vocabulary learning in the elderly. *Contemporary Educational Psychology, 21,* 102–109.

Guilford, J. P. (1985). *The analysis of intelligence.* New York: McGraw-Hill.

Gullotta, T., Adams, G., & Markstrom, C. (1999). *The adolescent experience.* Orlando, FL: Academic Press.

Gur, R. C. (1996, March). Paper presented at the annual meeting of the American Association for the Advancement of Science, Baltimore, Maryland.

Gur, R. C., Gur, R. E., Obrist, W. D., Hungerbuhler, J. P., Younkin, D., Rosen, A. D., Skilnick, B. E., & Reivich, M. (1982). Sex and handedness differences in cerebral blood flow during rest and cognitive activity. *Science, 217,* 659–661.

Gur, R. C., Mozley, L. H., Mozley, P. D., Resnick, S. M., Karp, J. S., Alavi, A., Arnold, S. E., & Gur, R. E. (1995, January 27). Sex differences in regional cerebral glucose metabolism during a resting state. *Science, 267,* 528–531.

Gur, R. C., Turetsky, B. I., Matsui, M., Yan, M., Bilker, W., Hughett, P., & Gur, R. E. (1999). Sex differences in brain gray and white matter in healthy young adults: Correlations with cognitive performance. *Journal of Neuroscience, 19,* 4065–4072.

Guralnick, M. J., Connor, R. T., Hammond, M., Gottman, J. M., et al. (1996). Immediate effects of mainstreamed settings on the social interactions and social integration of preschool children. *American Journal on Mental Retardation, 100,* 359–377.

Gurin, J. (1989, July). Leaner, not lighter. *Psychology Today,* pp. 32–36.

Gurman, E. B. (1994). Debriefing for all concerned: Ethical treatment of human subjects. *Psychological Science, 5,* 139.

Gustavson, C. R., Garcia, J., Hankins, W. G., & Rusniak, K. W. (1974). Coyote predation control by aversive conditioning. *Science, 184,* 581–583.

Gutek, B. A., Cohen, A. G., & Tsui, A. (1996). Reactions to perceived sex discrimination. *Human Relations, 49,* 791–813.

Guthrie, R. V. (1998). *Even the rat was white: A historical view of psychology* (2nd ed.). Needham Heights, MA: Allyn & Bacon.

Guttman, M. (1995, March 3–5). She had electroshock therapy. *USA Weekend,* p. 16.

Gwynn, M. I., & Spanos, N. P. (1996). Hypnotic responsiveness, nonhypnotic suggestibility, and responsiveness to social influence. In R. G. Kunzendorf, N. P. Spahos, & B. Wallace (Eds.), *Hypnosis and imagination.* Amityville, NY: Baywood.

Haber, R. N. (1983). Stimulus information processing mechanisms in visual space perception. In J. Beck, B. Hope, & A. Rosenfeld (Eds.), *Human and machine vision.* New York: Academic Press.

Hafner, H., & Maurer, K. (1995). Epidemiology of positive and negative symptoms in schizophrenia. In C. L. Shriqui & H. A. Nasrallah (Eds.), *Contemporary issues in the treatment of schizophrenia.* Washington, DC: American Psychiatric Press.

Hagen, E., Sattler, J. M., & Thorndike, R. L. (1985). *Stanford-Binet test.* Chicago: Riverside.

Haimov, I., & Lavie, P. (1996). Melatonin: A soporific hormone. *Current Directions in Psychological Science, 5,* 106–111.

Halberstadt, A. G. (1991). Toward an ecology of expressiveness: Family socialization in particular and a model in general. In R. S. Feldman & B. Rimé (Eds.), *Fundamentals of nonverbal behavior.* Cambridge, England: Cambridge University Press.

Haley, W. E., Clair, J. M., & Saulsberry, K. (1992). Family caregiver satisfaction with medical care of their demented relatives. *Gerontologist, 32,* 219–226.

Hall, G. C. N. (1996). *Theory-based assessment, treatment, and prevention of sexual aggression.* New York: Oxford University Press.

Hall, G. C. N., & Barongan, C. (1997). Prevention of sexual aggression: Sociocultural risk and protective factors. *American Psychologist, 52,* 5–14.

Hall, J. A., Roter, D. L., & Katz, N. R. (1988). Task versus socioemotional behaviors in physicians. *Medical Care, 25,* 399–412.

Hall, P. (Ed.). (1997). *Race, ethnicity, and multiculturalism.* Hamden, CT: Garland.

Halling, S., & Goldfarb, M. (1996). The new generation of diagnostic manuals (*DSM-III, DSM-III-R,* and *DSM-IV*): An overview and a phenomenologically based critique. *Journal of Phenomenological Psychology, 27,* 49–71.

Halpern, D. F. (1998). Teaching critical thinking for transfer across domains. *American Psychologist, 53,* 449–455.

Halpern, D. F. (2000). *Sex differences in cognitive abilities* (3rd ed.). Mahwah, NJ: Erlbaum.

Hamer, D. H., Hu, S., Magnuson, V. L., Hu, N., & Pattatucci, A. M. L. (1993, July 16). A linkage between DNA markers on the X chromosome and male sexual orientation. *Science, 261,* 321–327.

Hamilton, C. E. (2000). Continuity and discontinuity of attachment from infancy through adolescence. *Child Development, 71,* 690–694.

Hammond, S. L., & Lambert, B. L. (1994a). Communicating about medications: Directions for research [Special Issue: Communicating with patients about their medications]. *Health Communication, 6,* 247–251.

Hammond, S. L., & Lambert, B. L. (Eds.). (1994b). *Communicating with patients about their medications.* Mahwah, NJ: Erlbaum.

Handler, A., Franz, C. E., & Guerra, M. (1992, April). *Sex differences in moral orientation in midlife adults: A longitudinal study.* A paper presented at the meetings of the Eastern Psychological Association, Boston.

Hanna, J. L. (1984). Black/white nonverbal differences, dance, and dissonance: Implications for desegregation. In A. Wolfgang (Ed.), *Nonverbal behavior: Perspectives, applications, intercultural insights.* Lewiston, NY: Hogrefe.

Hannigan, J. H., Spear, L. P., Spear, N. E., & Goodlett, C. R. (Eds.). (1999). *Acohol and alcoholism: Effects on brain and development.* Mahwah, NJ: Erlbaum.

Harden, B. (2000, January 9). Very young, smart, and restless. *New York Times Education Life,* pp. 28–31.

Hare, R. D., Hart, S. D., & Harpur, T. J. (1991). Psychopathy and the *DSM-IV* criteria for antisocial personality disorder. *Journal of Abnormal Psychology, 100,* 391–398.

Harlow, H. F., Harlow, M. K., & Meyer, D. R. (1950). Learning motivated by a manipulation drive. *Journal of Experimental Psychology, 40,* 228–234.

Harlow, H. F., & Zimmerman, R. R. (1959). Affectional responses in the infant monkey. *Science, 130,* 421–432.

Harlow, J. M. (1869). Recovery from the passage of an iron bar through the head. *Massachusetts Medical Society Publication, 2,* 329–347.

Harlow, R. E., & Cantor, N. (1996). Still participating after all these years: A study of life task participation in later life. *Journal of Personality and Social Psychology, 71,* 1235–1249.

Harold, G. T., Fincham, F. D., Osborne, L. N., & Conger, R. D. (1997). Mom and dad are at it again: Adolescent perceptions of marital conflict and adolescent psychological distress. *Developmental Psychology, 33,* 333–350.

Harper, T. (1978, November 15). It's not true about people 65 or over. *Green Bay Press-Gazette.* (Wisconsin), p. D1.

Harris, C. R., & Christenfeld, N. (1996). Gender, jealousy, and reason. *Psychological Science, 7,* 364–366.

Harris-Kern, M. J., & Perkins, R. (1995). Effects of distraction on interpersonal expectancy effects: A social interaction test of the cognitive busyness hypothesis. *Social Cognition, 13,* 163–182.

Harris Poll. (2000 February 2). *The power of tobacco addiction.* New York: Harris Interactive.

Harrison, J. A., & Wells, R. B. (1991). Bystander effects on male helping behavior: Social comparison and diffusion of responsibility. *Representative Research in Social Psychology, 19,* 53–63.

Harrison, P. J., Everall, I. P., & Catalan, J. (1994). Is homosexual behaviour hard-wired? Sexual orientation and brain structure. *Psychological Medicine, 24,* 811–816.

Hart, B., & Risley, T. R. (1997). *Use of language by three-year-old children.* Courtesy of Drs. Betty Hart, University of Kansas, Lawrence, and Todd Risley, University of Alaska, Anchorage.

Hartmann, E. (1967). *The biology of dreaming.* Springfield, IL: Thomas.

Hartmann, W. M. (1993). On the origin of the enlarged melodic octave. *Journal of the Acoustical Society of America, 93,* 3400–3409.

Hartung, C. M., & Widiger, T. A. (1998). Gender differences in the diagnosis of mental disorders: Conclusions and controversies of the *DSM-IV. Psychological Bulletin, 123,* 260–278.

Harvey, E. (1999). Short-term and long-term effects of early parental employment on children of the National Longitudinal Survey of Youth. *Developmental Psychology, 35,* 445–459.

Haseltine, W. A. (1997, March). Discovering genes for new medicines. *Scientific American,* pp. 92–97.

Hass, N. (1994, March 21). Fighting and switching. *Newsweek,* pp. 52–53.

Haugtvedt, C. P., Petty, R. E., & Cacioppo, J. T. (1992). Need for cognition and advertising: Understanding the role of personality variables in consumer behavior. *Journal of Consumer Psychology, 1,* 239–260.

Hauri, P. J. (Ed.). (1991). *Case studies in insomnia.* New York: Plenum Press.

Haviland-Jones, J., & Chen, D. (1999, April 17). *Human olfactory perception.* Paper presented at the Association for Chemoreception Sciences, Sarasota, Florida.

Hawke, J. M., Jainchill, N., & De Leon, G. (2000). The prevalence of sexual abuse and its impact on the onset of drug use among adolescents in therapeutic community drug treatment. *Journal of Child and Adolescent Substance Abuse, 9,* 35–49.

Hayes, J. R. (1966). Memory, goals, and problem solving. In B. Kleinmuntz (Ed.), *Problem solving: Research, method, and theory.* New York: Wiley.

Hayflick, L. (1994). *How and why we age.* New York: Ballantine.

Heath, A. C., & Madden, P. A. F. (1995). Genetic influences on smoking behavior. In J. R. Turner, L. R. Cardon & J. K. Hewitt (Eds.), *Behavior genetic approaches in behavioral medicine: Perspectives on individual differences.* New York: Plenum Press.

Heatherton, T. F., Herman, C. P., & Polivy, J. (1992). Effects of distress on eating: The importance of ego-involvement. *Journal of Personality and Social Psychology, 62,* 801–803.

Hebl, M. R. & Hetherton, T. F. (1998). The stigma of obesity in women: The difference is black and white. *Personality and Social Psychology Bulletin, 24,* 417–426.

Heckhausen, H., Schmalt, H. D., & Schneider, K. (1985). *Achievement motivation in perspective* (M. Woodruff & R. Wicklund, Trans.). Orlando, FL: Academic Press.

Hedges, L. V., & Nowell, A. (1995, July 7). Sex differences in mental test scores, variability, and numbers of high-scoring individuals. *Science, 269,* 41–45.

Heider, F. (1958). *The psychology of interpersonal relations.* New York: Wiley.

Heinrichs, R. W. (1993). Schizophrenia and the brain: Conditions for neuropsychology of madness. *American Psychologist, 48,* 221–233.

Heishman, S. J., Kozlowski, L. T., & Henningfield, J. E. (1997). Nicotine addiction: Implications for public health policy. *Journal of Social Issues, 53,* 13–33.

Helms, J. E. (1992). Why is there no study of cultural equivalence in standardized cognitive ability testing? *American Psychologist, 47,* 1083–1101.

Helmuth, L. (2000, August 25). Synapses shout to overcome distance. *Science, 289,* 1273.

Herek, G. M. (1993). Sexual orientation and military service: A social science perspective. *American Psychologist, 48,* 538–549.

Herholz, K. (1995). FDG PET and differential diagnosis of dementia. *Alzheimer Disease & Associated Disorders, 9,* 6–16.

Hermann, C., Kim, M., & Blanchard, E. B. (1995). Behavioral and prophylactic pharmacological intervention studies of pediatric migraine: An exploratory meta-analysis. *Pain, 60,* 239–255.

Herrett-Skjellum, J., & Allen, M. (1996). Television programming and sex stereotyping: A meta-analysis. In B. R. Burleson (Ed.), *Communication yearbook* (Vol. 19). Thousand Oaks, CA: Sage.

Hermann, D., McEvoy, C., Hertzog, C., Hertel, P., & Johnson, M. (Eds.). (1996). *Basic and applied research. Volume 1: Theory and context. Volume 2: Practical applications.* Mahwah, NJ: Erlbaum.

Herrnstein, R. J., & Murray, C. (1994). *The bell curve: Intelligence and class structure in American life.* New York: Free Press.

Hetherington, E. M. (Ed.). (1999). *Coping with divorce, single parenting, and remarriage: A risk and resiliency perspective.* Mahwah, NJ: Erlbaum.

Heward, W. L., & Orlansky, M. D. (1988). *Exceptional children* (3rd ed.). Columbus, OH: Merrill.

Heyward, W. L., & Curran, J. W. (1988, October). The epidemiology of AIDS in the U.S. *Scientific American,* pp. 72–81.

Hilgard, E. R. (1975). Hypnosis. *Annual Review of Psychology, 26,* 19–44.

Hill, J. O., & Peters, J. C. (1998). Environmental contributions to the obesity epidemic. *Science, 280,* 1371–1374.

Hill, W. (1992). Personal communication. Public Affairs Network Coordinator for the American Psychiatric Association.

Hinshaw, S. P., Zupan, B. A., Simmel, C., Nigg, J. T., & Melnick, S. (1997). Peer status in boys with and without attention-deficit hyperactivity disorder: Predictions from overt and covert antisocial behavior, social isolation, and authoritative parenting beliefs. *Child Development, 68,* 880–896.

Hipkiss, R. A. (1995). *Semantics: Defining the discipline.* Mahwah, NJ: Erlbaum.

Hirsh, I. J., & Watson, C. S. (1996). Auditory psychophysics and perception. *Annual Review of Psychology, 47,* 461–484.

Hitt, J. (2000, February 20). The second sexual revolution. *New York Times Magazine,* pp. 34–62.

Hobfoll, S. E., Freedy, J. R., Green B. L., & Solomon, S. D. (1996). Coping in reaction to extreme stress: The roles of resource loss and resource availability. In M. Zeidner & N. S. Endler (Eds.), *Handbook of coping: Theory, research, applications.* New York: Wiley.

Hobson, J. A. (1989). *Sleep.* New York: Scientific American Library.

Hobson, J. A. (1996, February). How the brain goes out of its mind. *Harvard Mental Health Letter,* pp. 3–5.

Hobson, J. A., & Silverstri, L. (1999, February). Parasomnias. *Harvard Mental Health Letter,* pp. 3–5.

Hoch, S. J. (1987). Perceived consensus and predictive accuracy: The pros and cons of projection. *Journal of Personality and Social Psychology, 53,* 221–234.

Hochberg, J. E. (1978). *Perception.* Englewood Cliffs, NJ: Prentice Hall.

Hochschild, A. R. (1990). The second shift: Employed women and putting in another day of work at home. *Utne Reader, 38,* 66–73.

Hochschild, A. R. (1997a, April 20). There's no place like work. *New York Times Magazine,* pp. 51–84.

Hochschild, A. R. (1997b). *The time bind: When work becomes home and home becomes work.* New York: Henry Holt.

Hochschild, A. R., Machung, A., & Pringle, R. (1995). The architecture of gender: Women, men, and inequality. In D. M. Newman (Ed.), *Sociology: Exploring the architecture of everyday life: Readings.* Thousand Oaks, CA: Sage.

Hocutt, A. M. (1996). Effectiveness of special education: Is placement the critical factor? *Future of Children, 6,* 77–102.

Hoeller, K. (Ed.). (1990). *Readings in existential psychology and psychiatry.* Seattle: Review of Existential Psychology and Psychiatry.

Hogan, R., Hogan, J., & Roberts, B. W. (1996). Personality measurement and employment decisions: Questions and answers. *American Psychologist, 51,* 469–477.

Hogg, M. A., & Hardie, E. A. (1992). Prototypicality, conformity and depersonalized attraction: A self-categorization analysis of group cohesiveness. *British Journal of Social Psychology, 31,* 41–56.

Holahan, C. J., & Moos, R. H. (1990). Life stressors, resistance factors, and improved psychological functioning: An extension of the stress resistance paradigm. *Journal of Personality and Social Psychology, 58,* 909–917.

Holden, C. (2000, July 21). Parity as a goal sparks bitter battle. *Science, 289,* 380.

Holden, R. R. (2000). Are there promising MMPI substitutes for assessing psychopathology and personality? Review and prospect. In R. H. Dana (Ed.), *Handbook of cross-cultural and multicultural personality assessment.* Mahwah, NJ: Erlbaum.

Holland, J. C. (1996, September). Cancer's psychological challenges. *Scientific American,* pp. 158–161.

Hollingworth, H. L. (1943/1990). *Leta Stetter Hollingworth: A biography.* Boston: Anker.

Hollis, K. L. (1984). The biological function of Pavlovian conditioning: The best defense is a good offense. *Journal of Experimental Psychology: Animal Behavior Processes, 10,* 413–425.

Hollis, K. L. (1997, September). Contemporary research on Pavlovian conditioning: A "new" functional analysis. *American Psychologist, 52,* 956–965.

Holmes, C. T., & Keffer, R. L. (1995). A computerized method to teach Latin and Greek root words: Effect on verbal SAT scores. *Journal of Educational Research, 89,* 47–50.

Holmes, D. S. (1985). To meditate or rest? The answer is rest. *American Psychologist, 40,* 728–731.

Holroyd, J. (1996). Hypnosis treatment of clinical pain: Understanding why hypnosis is useful. *International Journal of Clinical and Experimental Hypnosis, 44,* 33–51.

Holy, T. E., Dulac, C., & Meister, M. (2000, September 1). Responses of vomeronasal neurons to natural stimuli. *Science, 289,* 1569–1572.

Hong, E., Milgram, R. M., & Gorsky, H. (1995). Original thinking as a predictor of creative performance in young children. *Roeper Review, 18,* 147–149.

Honts, C. R., & Kircher, J. C. (1994). Mental and physical countermeasures reduce the accuracy of polygraph tests. *Journal of Applied Psychology, 79,* 252–259.

Honts, C. R., Raskin, D. C., & Kircher, J. C. (1987). Effects of physical countermeasure and their electromyographic detection during polygraphy tests for deception. *Journal of Psychophysiology, 1,* 241–247.

Hoon, P. W., Bruce, K., & Kinchloe, B. (1982). Does the menstrual cycle play a role in sexual arousal? *Psychophysiology, 19,* 21–26.

Horesh, N., Apter, A., Ishai, J., Danziger, Y., et al. (1996). Abnormal psychosocial situations and eating disorders in adolescence. *Journal of the American Academy of Child and Adolescent Psychiatry, 35,* 921–927.

Horgan, J. (1993, December). Fractured functions: Does the brain have a supreme integrator? *Scientific American,* pp. 36–37.

Horgan, J. (1995, November). Get smart, take a test. *Scientific American,* pp. 12–14.

Horgan, J. (1996, December). Why Freud isn't dead. *Scientific American,* pp. 106–111.

Horney, K. (1937). *Neurotic personality of our times.* New York: Norton.

Horwitz, L., Gabbard, G. O., Allen, J. G., Frieswyk, S. H., Colson, D. B., Newsom, G. E., & Coyne, L. (1996). *Borderline personality disorder: Tailoring the psychotherapy to the patient.* Washington, DC: American Psychiatric Press.

Houston, L. N. (1981). Romanticism and eroticism among black and white college students. *Adolescence, 16,* 263–272.

Hovland, C., Janis, I., & Kelly, H. H. (1953). *Communication and persuasion.* New Haven, CT: Yale University Press.

Howard, A., Pion, G. M., Gottfredson, G. D., Flattau, P. E., Oskamp, S., Pfafflin, S. M., Bray, D. W., & Burstein, A. D. (1986). The changing face of American psychology: A report from the committee on employment and human resources. *American Psychologist, 41,* 1311–1327.

Howe, M. L. (1999). *The fate of early memories: Developmental science and the retention of childhood experiences.* Washington, DC: American Psychological Association.

Howells, J. G., & Osborn, M. L. (1984). *A reference companion to the history of abnormal psychology.* Westport, CT: Greenwood Press.

Howes, C., Galinsky, E., & Kontos, S. (1998). Child care caregiver sensitivity and attachment. *Social Development, 7,* 25–36.

How to lose weight and keep it off. (1990, February). *Consumer Reports Health Letter, 2,* 9–11.

Hubbard, K., O'Neill, A., & Cheakalos, C. (1999, April 12). Out of control. *People,* pp. 52–72.

Hubble, M. A., Duncan, B. L., & Miller, S. D. (Eds.). (1999). *The heart and soul of change: What works in therapy.* Washington, DC: American Psychological Association.

Hubel, D. H., & Wiesel, T. N. (1979). Brain mechanisms of vision. *Scientific American,* pp. 150–162.

Hudson, W. (1960). Pictorial depth perception in subcultural groups in Africa. *Journal of Social Psychology, 52,* 183–208.

Huesmann, L. R., & Moise, J. (1996, June). Media violence: A demonstrated public health threat to children. *Harvard Mental Health Letter,* pp. 5–7.

Hull, C. L. (1943). *Principles of behavior.* New York: Appleton-Century-Crofts.

Human Genome Project. (2000, January 19). *http://www.ornl.gov/hgmis/* or *http://www.ornl.gov/hgmis/project/about.html.*

Humphreys, G. W., & Müller, H. (2000). A search asymmetry reversed by figure-ground assignment. *Psychological Science, 11,* 196–200.

Humphreys, L. G. (1992). Commentary: What both critics and users of ability tests need to know. *Psychological Science, 3,* 271–274.

Hunt, E. (1983). On the nature of intelligence. *Science, 219,* 141–146.

Hunt, E. (1994). Problem solving. In R. J. Sternberg (Ed.), *Thinking and problem solving: Handbook of perception and cognition* (2nd ed.). San Diego: Academic Press.

Hunt, M. (1974). *Sexual behaviors in the 1970s.* New York: Dell.

Hunt, M. (1999). *How science takes stock: The story of meta-analysis.* New York: Russell Sage Foundation.

Hyde, J. S. (1994). *Understanding human sexuality* (5th ed.). New York: McGraw-Hill.

Hyde, J. S., Fennema, E., & Lamon, S. J. (1990). Gender differences in mathematics

performance: A meta-analysis. *Psychological Bulletin, 107,* 139–155.

Hyde, J. S., & Linn, M. C. (1988). Gender differences in verbal ability: A meta-analysis. *Psychological Bulletin, 104,* 53–69.

Hyman, R. (1994). Anomaly or artifact? Comments on Bem and Honorton. *Psychological Bulletin, 115,* 19–24.

Iacono, W. G. (1991). Can we determine the accuracy of polygraph tests? In P. K. Ackles, J. R. Jennings, & M. G. H. Coles (Eds.), *Advances in psychophysiology* (Vol. 4). Greenwich, CT: JAI Press.

Iacono, W. G., & Lykken, D. T. (1997). The validity of the lie detector: Two surveys of scientific opinion. *Journal of Applied Psychology, 82,* 426–433.

Ikonomidou, C., Bittigau, P., Ishimaru, M. J., Wozniak, D. F., et al. (2000, February 11). Ethanol-induced apoptotic neurodegeneration and fetal alcohol syndrome. *Science, 287,* 1056–1060.

Inglefinger, F. J. (1944). The late effects of total and subtotal gastrectomy. *New England Journal of Medicine, 231,* 321–377.

Isay, R. A. (1990). *Being homosexual: Gay men and their development.* New York: Avon.

Issac, A. R., & Marks, D. F. (1994). Individual differences in mental imagery experience: Developmental changes and specialization. *British Journal of Psychology, 85,* 479–500.

Iversen, L. L. (2000). *The science of marijuana.* Oxford, England: Oxford University Press.

Izard, C. E. (1990). Facial expressions and the regulation of emotions. *Journal of Personality and Social Psychology, 58,* 487–498.

Izard, C. E. (1991). *The psychology of emotions.* New York: Plenum Press.

Izard, C. E. (1994). Innate and universal facial expressions: Evidence from developmental and cross-cultural research. *Psychological Bulletin, 115,* 288–299.

Jacklin, C. N., & Reynolds, C. (1993). Gender and childhood socialization. In A. E. Beall & R. J. Sternberg (Eds.), *The psychology of gender.* New York: Guilford Press.

Jackson, T. L. (Ed.). (1996). *Acquaintance rape: Assessment, treatment, and prevention.* Sarasota, FL: Professional Resource Press/Professional Resource Exchange.

Jacobson, P. D., Wasserman, J., & Anderson, J. R. (1997). Historical overview of tobacco legislation and regulation. *Journal of Social Issues, 53,* 75–95.

James, J. E. (1997). *Understanding caffeine: A biobehavioral analysis.* Newbury Park, CA: Sage.

James, W. (1890). *The principles of psychology.* New York: Holt.

Jamison, K. R. (1993). *Touched with fire: Manic depressive illness and the artistic temperament.* New York: Free Press.

Jamison, K. R. (1995, February). Manic-depressive illness and creativity. *Scientific American,* pp. 62–67.

Janis, I. (1972). *Victims of groupthink: A psychological study of foreign policy decisions and fiascoes.* Boston: Houghton Mifflin.

Janis, I. L. (1989). *Crucial decisions: Leadership in policy-making management.* New York: Free Press.

Janofsky, M. (2000, January 13). Defense cites an addiction to the Internet in threat case. *New York Times,* p. A18.

Jaret, P. (1992, November/December). Mind over malady. *Health,* pp. 87–94.

Jaroff, L. (1996, Fall). Keys to the kingdom. *Time* [Special issue: The frontiers of medicine], pp. 24–29.

Jenike, M.A. (1998). Neurosurgical treatment of obsessive-compulsive disorder. *British Journal of Psychiatry, 173,* 79–90.

Jenkins, C. D., Zyzanski, S. J., & Rosenman, R. H. (1978). Coronary-prone behavior: One pattern or several? *Psychosomatic Medicine, 40,* 25–43.

Jenkins, L. S., & Gortner, S. R. (1998). Correlates of self-efficacy expectation and prediction of walking behavior in cardiac surgery elders. *Annals of Behavioral Medicine, 20,* 99–103.

Jenkins, S. R. (1994). Need for power and women's careers over 14 years: Structural power, job satisfaction, and motive change. *Journal of Personality and Social Psychology, 66,* 155–165.

Jensen, A. R. (1998). *The g factor: The science of mental ability.* Wesport, CT: Praeger.

Jensen, J. K., & Neff, D. L. (1993). Development of basic auditory discrimination in preschool children. *Psychological Science, 4,* 104–107.

Jerome, L., DeLeon, P., James, L., & Gedney, J. (2000). The coming of age of telecommunications in psychological research practice. *American Psychologist, 55,* 128–133.

Jevning, R., Anand, R., Biedebach, M., & Fernando, G. (1996). Effects on regional cerebral blood flow of transcendental meditation. *Physiological Behavior, 59,* 399–402.

Jhally, S., Goldman, R., Cassidy, M., Katula, R., et al. (1995). Advertising. In G. Dines & J. M. Humez (Eds.), *Gender, race, and class in media: A text-reader.* Thousand Oaks, CA: Sage.

John, O. P., & Srivastava, R. S. (1999). The big five trait taxonomy: History, measurement, and theoretical perspectives. In L. A. Pervin & O. P. John (Eds.), *Handbook of personality: Theory and research* (2nd ed.). New York: Guilford.

Johnson, D. M., Parrott, G. R., & Stratton, R. P. (1968). Production and judgment of solutions to five problems. *Journal of Educational Psychology Monograph Supplement, 59* (6, pt. 2).

Johnson, J. T., Cain, L. M., Falke, T. L., Hayman, J., & Perillo, E. (1985). The "Barnum Effect" revisited: Cognitive and motivational factors in the acceptance of personality descriptions. *Journal of Personality and Social Psychology, 49,* 1378–1391.

Johnson, R. W., Kelly, R. J., & LeBlanc, B. A. (1995). Motivational basis of dissonance: Aversive consequences of inconsistency. *Personality and Social Psychology Bulletin, 21,* 850–855.

Johnson-Laird, P. N., & Shafir, E. (Eds.). (1994). *Reasoning and decision making.* New York: Blackwell.

Johnston, D. (1997, October 17). A missing link: LTP and learning. *Science, 278,* 401–402.

Johnston, L. (1996). Resisting change: Information-seeking and stereotype change. *European Journal of Social Psychology, 26,* 799–825.

Joiner, T. E., & Coyne, J. C. (Eds.). (1999). *The interactional nature of depression: Advances in interpersonal approaches.* Washington, DC: American Psychological Association.

Joiner, T. E., & Wagner, K. D. (1995). Attribution style and depression in children and adolescents: A meta-analytic review. *Clinical Psychology Review, 15,* 777–798.

Jones, A., & Crandall, R. (Eds.). (1991). Handbook of self-actualization. *Journal of Social Behavior and Personality, 6,* 1–362.

Jones, E. E. (1990). *Interpersonal perception.* New York: Freeman.

Jones, J. C., & Barlow, D. H. (1990). Self-reported frequency of sexual urges, fantasies, and masturbatory fantasies in heterosexual males and females. *Archives of Sexual Behavior, 19,* 269–279.

Jones, J. M. (1994). Our similarities are different: Toward a psychology of affirmative diversity. In E. J. Trickett, R. J. Watts, & D. Birman (Eds.), *Human diversity: Perspectives on people in context.* San Francisco: Jossey-Bass.

Jorgenson, L. M., & Wahl, K. M. (2000). Workplace sexual harassment: Incidence, legal analysis, and the role of the psychiatrist. *Harvard Review of Psychiatry, 8,* 94–98.

Joseph, R. (1996). *Neuropsychiatry, neuropsychology, and clinical neuroscience: Emotion, evolution, cognition, language, memory, brain damage, and abnormal behavior* (2nd ed.). Baltimore: Williams & Wilkins.

Josephs, R. A., & Steele, C. M. (1990). The two faces of alcohol myopia: Attentional mediation of psychological stress. *Journal of Abnormal Psychology, 99,* 115–126.

Joyce, J. (1934). *Ulysses.* New York: Random House.

Julien, R. M. (1995). *Prime of drug action* (7th ed.). New York: Freeman.

Jung, C. G. (1961). *Freud and psychoanalysis.* New York: Pantheon.

Jussim, L., Fleming, C. J., Coleman, L., & Kohberger, C. (1996). The nature of stereotypes: II. A multiple-process model of evaluations. *Journal of Applied Social Psychology, 26,* 283–312.

Kagan, J., Kearsley, R., & Zelazo, P. R. (1978). *Infancy: Its place in human development.* Cambridge, MA: Harvard University Press.

Kahn, R. S., Davidson, M., & Davis, K. L. (1996). Dopamine and schizophrenia revisited. In S. J. Watson (Ed.), *Biology of schizophrenia and affective disease.* Washington, DC: American Psychiatric Press.

Kahn, S., Zimmerman, G., Csikszentmihalyi, M., & Getzels, J. W. (1985). Relations between identity in young adulthood and intimacy at midlife. *Journal of Personality and Social Psychology, 49,* 1316–1322.

Kahneman, D., Diener, E., & Schwarz, N. (1998). *Well-being: The foundations of hedonic psychology.* New York: Russell Sage Foundation.

Kaiser, J. (1999, September 3). Hold the clicks, they may be addictive. *Science, 285,* 1455.

Kakei, S., Hoffman, D. S., & Strick, P. L. (1999, September 24). Muscle and movement representations in the primary motor cortex. *Science, 285,* 2136–2139.

Kakigi, R., Matsuda, Y., & Kuroda, Y. (1993). Effects of movement-related cortical activities on pain-related somatosensory evoked potentials following CO-sub-2 laser stimulation in normal subjects. *Acta Neurologica Scandinavica, 88,* 376–380.

Kalafat, J., Elias, M., & Gara, M. A. (1993). The relationship of bystander intervention variables to adolescents' responses to suicidal peers. *Journal of Primary Prevention, 13,* 231–244.

Kaniasty, K., & Norris, F. H. (1995, June). Mobilization and deterioration of social support following natural disasters. *Current Directions in Psychological Science, 4,* 94–98.

Kanner, A. D., Coyne, J. C., Schaefer, C., & Lazarus, R. (1981). Comparison of two modes of stress measurement: Daily hassles and uplifts versus major life events. *Journal of Behavioral Medicine, 4,* 14.

Kaplan, H. S. (1974). *The new sex therapy.* New York: Brunner-Mazel.

Kaplan, J. R., & Manuck, S. B. (1989). The effect of propranolol on behavioral interactions among adult male cynomolgus monkeys *(Macaca fascicularis)* housed in disrupted social groupings. *Psychosomatic Medicine, 51,* 449–462.

Kaplan, M. F. (1975). Information integration in social judgment: Interaction of judge and informational components. In M. Kaplan & S. Schwartz (Eds.), *Human development and decision processes.* New York: Academic Press.

Kaplan, R. M., & Saccuzzo, D. P. (1997). *Psychological testing: Principles, applications, and issues* (4th ed.). Pacific Grove, CA: Brooks/Cole.

Kaplan, R. M., Sallis, J. F., Jr., & Patterson, T. L. (1993). *Health and human behavior.* New York: McGraw-Hill.

Kapur, N. (1999). Syndromes of retrograde amnesia: A conceptual and empirical synthesis. *Psychological Bulletin, 125,* 800–825.

Kapur, S., & Remington, G. (1996). Serotonin-dopamine interaction and its relevance to schizophrenia. *American Journal of Psychiatry, 153,* 466–476.

Karlins, M., & Abelson, H. I. (1979). *How opinions and attitudes are changed.* New York: Springer-Verlag.

Karni, A., Tanne, D., Rubenstein, B. S., Askenazy, J. J. M., & Sagi, D. (1992, October). No dreams—no memory: The effect of REM sleep deprivation on learning a new perceptual skill. *Society for Neuroscience Abstracts, 18,* 387.

Karni, A., Tanne, D., Rubenstein, B. S., Askenasy, J. J. M., & Sagi, D. (1994, July 29). Dependence on REM sleep of overnight improvement of a perceptual skill. *Science, 265,* 679–682.

Karp, D. A. (1988). A decade of remembrances: Changing age consciousness between fifty and sixty years old. *Gerontologist, 28,* 727–738.

Karp, D. A. (1991). A decade of reminders: Changing age consciousness between fifty and sixty years old. In B. B. Hess & E. W. Markson (Eds.), *Growing old in America* (4th ed.). New Brunswick, NJ: Transaction.

Katz, A. N. (1989). Autobiographical memory as a reconstructive process: An extension of Ross's hypothesis. *Canadian Journal of Psychology, 43,* 512–517.

Katz, D., & Braly, K. W. (1933). Racial stereotypes of 100 college students. *Journal of Abnormal and Social Psychology, 4,* 280–290.

Katz, P. A. (Ed.). (1976). *Towards the elimination of racism.* New York: Pergamon Press.

Kaufman, A. S., & Lichtenberger, E. O. (1999). *Essentials of WISC-III and WPPSI-R assessment.* New York: Wiley.

Kausler, D. H. (1994). *Learning and memory in normal aging.* San Diego: Academic Press.

Kawachi, I., Colditz, G. A., Speizer, F. E., Manson, J. E., Stampger, M. J., Willett, W. C., & Hennekens, C. H. (1997). A prospective study of passive smoking and coronary heart disease. *Circulation, 95,* 2374–2379.

Kawasaki, C., Nugent, J. K., Miyashita, H., Miyahara, H., et al. (1994). The cultural organization of infants' sleep [Special issue: Environments of birth and infancy]. *Children's Environment, 11*, 135–141.

Kazdin, A. E. (1994). *Behavior modification in applied settings* (5th ed.). Pacific Grove, CA: Brooks/Cole.

Keating, D. P., & Clark, L. V. (1980). Development of physical and social reasoning in adolescence. *Developmental Psychology, 16*, 23–30.

Keefe, F. J., & France, C. R. (1999). Pain: Biopsychosocial mechanisms and management. *Current Directions in Psychological Science, 8*, 137–141.

Keehn, J. D. (1996). *Master builders of modern psychology: From Freud to Skinner.* New York: New York University Press.

Keller, M. C., & Young, R. K. (1996). Mate assortment in dating and married couples. *Personality and Individual Differences, 21*, 217–221.

Kelley, H. (1950). The warm-cold variable in first impressions of persons. *Journal of Personality and Social Psychology, 18*, 431–439.

Kelly, A. L. (1999, June 13). For employed moms, the pinnacle of stress comes after work ends. *New York Times*, p. 18.

Kelly, D. D. (1991b). Sexual differentiation of the nervous system. In E. R. Kandel, J. H. Schwartz, & T. M. Jessell (Eds.), *Principles of neural science* (3rd ed.). New York: Elsevier.

Kelly, F. D. (1997). *The assessment of object relations phenomena in adolescents: TAT and Rorschach measures.* Mahwah, NJ: Erlbaum.

Kempermann, G., & Gage, F. H. (1999, May). New nerve cells for the adult brain. *Scientific American*, 48–53.

Kendler, K. S. (1996). Parenting: A genetic-epidemiologic perspective. *American Journal of Psychiatry, 153*, 11–20.

Kenny, D. A. (1994). *Interpersonal perception.* New York: Guilford Press.

Kenshalo, R. (1968). *The skin senses.* Springfield, IL: Charles C. Thomas.

Kessler, R. C., McGonagle, K. A., Zhao, S., Nelson, C. B., Hughes, M., Eshleman, S., Wittchen, H., & Kendler, K. S. (1994). Lifetime and 12-month prevalence of *DSM-III-R* psychiatric disorders in the United States. *Archives of General Psychiatry, 51*, 8–19.

Kidwell, J. S., Dunham, R. M., Bacho, R. A., Pastorino, E., et al. (1995). Adolescent identity exploration: A test of Erikson's theory of transitional crisis. *Adolescence, 30*, 785–793.

Kienker, P. K., Sejnowski, T. J., Hinton, G. E., & Schumacher, L. E. (1986). Separating figure from ground with a parallel network. *Perception, 15*, 197–216.

Kiesler, C. A., & Simpkins, C. G. (1993). *The unnoticed majority in psychiatric inpatient care.* New York: Plenum Press.

Kiesler, D. J. (1999). *Beyond the disease model of mental disorders.* Westport, CT: Praeger.

Kiesler, S., & Kraut, R. (1999, September). Internet use and ties that bind. *American Psychologist, 15*, 783–784.

Kihlstrom, J. F. (1999). Unconscious. In L. A. Pervin & O. P. John (Eds.), *Handbook of personality: Theory and research* (2nd ed.). New York: Guilford Press.

Kihlstrom, J. F., Schacter, D. L., Cork, R. C., Hurt, C. A., & Behr, S. E. (1990). Implicit and explicit memory following surgical anesthesia. *Psychological Science, 1*, 303–306.

Kilborn, P. T. (1991, May 15). "Race norming" tests become a fiery issue. *New York Times*, B1.

Kilpatrick, D. G., Edmunds, C. S., & Seymour, A. K. (1992, November 13). *Rape in America: A report to the nation.* Arlington, VA: National Victims Center and Medical University of South Carolina.

Kimble, G. A. (1989). Psychology from the standpoint of a generalist. *American Psychologist, 44*, 491–499.

Kimmel, A. J. (1996). *Ethical issues in behavioral research: A survey.* Oxford, England: Blackwell.

Kimura, D. (1992, September). Sex differences in the brain. *Scientific American*, pp. 119–125.

Kimura, D. (1999). *Sex and cognition.* Cambridge, MA: MIT Press.

Kimura, D., & Hampson, E. (1988). Reciprocal effects of hormonal fluctuations on human motor and perceptual-spatial skills. *Behavioral Neuroscience, 102*, 456–459.

King, G. R., & Logue, A. W. (1990). Humans' sensitivity to variation in reinforcer amount: Effects of the method of reinforcer delivery. *Journal of the Experimental Analysis of Behavior, 53*, 33–46.

King, K. C., Hyde, J. S., Showers, C. J., & Buswell, B. N. (1999). Gender differences in self-esteem: A meta-analysis. *Psychological Bulletin, 125*, 470–500.

King, S. H. (1993). The limited presence of African-American teachers. *Review of Educational Research, 63*, 114–149.

Kinsey, A. C., Pomeroy, W. B., & Martin, C. E. (1948). *Sexual behavior in the human male.* Philadelphia: Saunders.

Kinsey, A. C., Pomeroy, W. B., Martin, C. E., & Gebhard, P. H. (1953). *Sexual behavior in the human female.* Philadelphia: Saunders.

Kirby, D. (1977). The methods and methodological problems of sex research. In J. S. DeLora & C. A. B. Warren (Eds.), *Understanding sexual interaction.* Boston: Houghton Mifflin.

Kirk, S. A. (1992). *The selling of DSM: The rhetoric of science in psychiatry.* Hawthorne, New York: Aldine de Gruyter.

Kirsch, I. (Ed.). (1999). *How expectancies shape experience.* Washington, DC: American Psychological Association.

Kirsch, I., & Lynn, S. J. (1995). The altered state of hypnosis: Changes in the theoretical landscape. *American Psychologist, 50*, 846–858.

Kirsch, I., & Lynn, S. J. (1998). Dissociating the wheat from the chaff in theories of hypnosis: Reply to Kihlstrom (1998) and Woody and Sadler (1998). *Psychological Bulletin, 123*, 198–202.

Kirshner, H. S. (1995). Alexias. In H. S. Kirshner (Ed.), *Handbook of neurological speech and language disorders: Neurological disease and therapy* (Vol. 33). New York: Marcel Dekker.

Kitterle, F. L. (Ed.). (1991). *Cerebral laterality: Theory and research.* Hillsdale, NJ: Erlbaum.

Klein, M. (1998, February). Family chats. *American Demographics*, p. 37.

Kleinman, A. (1996). How is culture important for *DSM-IV*? In J. E. Mezzich, A. Kleinman, H. Fabrega, Jr., & D. L. Parron (Eds.), *Culture and psychiatric diagnosis: A DSM-IV perspective.* Washington, DC: American Psychiatric Press.

Kleinman, A., & Cohen, A. (1997, March). Psychiatry's global challenge. *Scientific American*, pp. 86–89.

Klinke, R., Kral, A., Heid, S., Tillein, J., & Hartmann, R. (1999, September 10). Recruitment of the auditory cortex in congenitally deaf cats by long-term cochlear electrostimulation. *Science, 285*, 1729–1733.

Klinkenborg, V. (1997, January 5). Awakening to sleep. *New York Times*, pp. 26–31, 41, 51, 55.

Kluft, R. P. (1996). Dissociative identity disorder. In L. K. Michelson & W. J. Ray (Eds.), *Handbook of dissociation: Theoretical, empirical, and clinical perspectives.* New York: Plenum Press.

Kmiec, E. B. (1999). Gene therapy. *American Scientist, 87*, 240–247.

Knight, G. P., Johnson, L. G., Carlo, G., & Eisenberg, N. (1994). A multiplicative model of the dispositional antecedents of prosocial behavior: Predicting more of the people more of the time. *Journal of Personality and Social Psychology, 66*, 178–183.

Kobasa, S. C. (1979). Stressful life events, personality, and health: An inquiry into hardiness. *Journal of Personality and Social Psychology, 37*, 1–11.

Kobasa, S. C. O., Maddi, S. R., Puccetti, M. C., & Zola, M. A. (1994). Effectiveness of hardiness, exercise and social support as resources against illness. In A. Steptoe & J. Wardle (Eds.), *Psychosocial processes and health: A reader.* Cambridge, England: Cambridge University Press.

Koegel, L. K., Koegel, R. L., Kellegrew, D., & Mullen, K. (1996). Parent education for prevention and reduction of severe problem behaviors. In L. K. Koegel, R. L. Koegel, et al. (Eds.), *Positive behavioral support: Including people with difficult behavior in the community.* Baltimore: Paul H. Brookes.

Kohlberg, L. (1984). *The psychology of moral development: Essays on moral development* (Vol. 2). San Francisco: Harper & Row.

Kohlberg, L., & Ryncarz, R. A. (1990). Beyond justice reasoning: Moral development and consideration of a seventh stage. In C. N. Alexander & E. J. Langer (Eds.), *Higher stages of human development: Perspectives on adult growth.* New York: Oxford University Press.

Köhler, W. (1927). *The mentality of apes.* London: Routledge & Kegan Paul.

Kolata, G. (1998). *Clone: The road to Dolly and the path ahead.* New York: William Morrow.

Konishi, M. (1993, April). Listening with two ears. *Scientific American*, pp. 66–73.

Konrad, W. (1994, April). Ten things your doctor won't tell you. *Smart Money*, p. 76.

Koocher, G. P., & Keith-Spiegel, P. (1998). *Ethics in psychology: Professional standards and cases* (2nd ed.). New York: Oxford University Press.

Koop, C. B. (1994). Infant assessment. In C. B. Fisher & R. M. Lerner (Eds.), *Applied developmental psychology.* New York: McGraw-Hill.

Kosambi, D. D. (1967). Living prehistory in India. *Scientific American*, p. 105.

Koss, M. P. (1993). Rape: Scope, impact, interventions, and public policy responses. *American Psychologist, 48*, 1062–1069.

Koss, M. P., & Burkhart, B. R. (1989). A conceptual analysis of rape victimization. *Psychology of Women Quarterly, 13*, 27–40.

Kosslyn, S. M. (1981). The medium and the message in mental imagery. *Psychological Review, 88*, 46–66.

Kosslyn, S. M., & Shin, L. M. (1994). Visual mental images in the brain: Current issues. In M. J. Farah & G. Ratcliff (Eds.), *The neuropsychology of high-level vision: Collected tutorial essays.* Hillsdale, NJ: Erlbaum.

Kotler-Cope, S., & Camp, C. J. (1990). Memory interventions in aging populations. In E. A. Lovelace (Ed.), *Aging and cognition: Mental processes, self-awareness, and interventions.* Amsterdam, Netherlands: North-Holland.

Kotre, J., & Hall, E. (1990). *Seasons of life.* Boston: Little, Brown.

Koval, J. J., Pederson, L. L., Mills, C. A., McGrady, G. A., & Carvajal, S. C. (2000). Models of the relationship of stress, depression, and other psychosocial factors to smoking behavior: A comparison of a cohort of students in Grades 6 and 8. *Preventive Medicine, 30,* 463–477.

Koveces, Z. (1987). *The container metaphor of emotion.* Paper presented at the University of Massachusetts, Amherst.

Kramer, P. (1993). *Listening to Prozac.* New York: Viking.

Kraus, S. J. (1995, January). Attitudes and the prediction of behavior: A meta-analysis of the empirical literature. *Personality and Social Psychology Bulletin, 21,* 58–75.

Kravitz, E. A. (1988). Hormonal control of behavior: Amines and the biasing of behavioral output in lobsters. *Science, 241,* 1775–1782.

Kremer, J. M. D., & Scully, D. M. (1994). *Psychology in sport.* London, England: Taylor & Francis.

Kreuger, L. E. (1989). *The world of touch.* Hillsdale, NJ: Erlbaum.

Kriz, J. (1995). Naturwissenschaftliche Konzepte in der gegenwartigen Diskussion zum Problem der Ordnung (The contribution of natural science concepts to the current discussion of order). *Gestalt Theory, 17,* 153–163.

Krohne, H. W. (1996). Individual differences in coping. In M. Zeidner & N. S. Endler (Eds.), *Handbook of coping: Theory, research, applications.* New York: Wiley.

Kruglanski, A. W., Freund, T., & Bar Tal, D. (1996). Motivational effects in the mere-exposure paradigm. *European Journal of Social Psychology, 26,* 479–499.

Krull, D. S., & Anderson, C. A. (1997). The process of explanation. *Current Directions in Psychological Science, 6,* 1–5.

Kübler-Ross, E. (1969). *On death and dying.* New York: Macmillan.

Kuhl, P. K., Williams, K. A., Lacerda, F., Stevens, K. N., & Lindblom, B. (1992, January 31). Linguistic experience alters phonetic perception in infants by 6 months of age. *Science, 255,* 606–608.

Kulynych, J. J., Vladar, K., Jones, D. W., & Weinberger, D. R. (1994). Gender differences in the normal lateralization of the supratemporal cortex: MRI surface-rendering morphometry of Heschl's gyrus and the planum temporale. *Cerebral Cortex, 4,* 107–118.

Kunda, Z. (1999). *Social cognition: Making sense of people.* Cambridge, MA: MIT Press.

Kupfer, D. J., Reynolds, C. F., III. (1997, January 30). Management of insomnia. *New England Journal of Medicine, 336,* 341–346.

Kurtines, W., & Gewirtz, J. (1995). *Moral development: An introduction.* Boston: Allyn & Bacon.

Kvale, S. (1996). *Interviews: An introduction to qualitative research interviewing.* Newbury Park, CA: Sage.

Kwan, V. S. Y., Bond, M. H., & Singelis, T. M. (1997). Pancultural explanations for life satisfaction: Adding relationship harmony to self-esteem. *Journal of Personality and Social Psychology, 73,* 1038–1051.

Lach, J. (1998, November). Reading your mind, reaching your wallet. *American Demographics,* pp. 39–42.

LaFromboise, T., Coleman, H. L. K., & Gerton, J. (1995). Psychological impact of biculturalism: Evidence and theory. In N. R. Goldberger & J. B. Veroff (Eds.), *The culture and psychology reader.* New York: New York University Press.

Laird, J. D., & Bresler, C. (1992). The process of emotional experience: A self-perception theory. In M. S. Clark (Ed.), *Review of personality and social psychology.* Newbury Park, CA: Sage.

Lamb, M. (1982). The bonding phenomenon: Misinterpretations and their implications. *Journal of Pediatrics, 101,* 555–557.

Lamb, M. E. (1996). Effects of nonparental child care on child development: An update. *Canadian Journal of Psychiatry, 41,* 330–342.

Lambert, M. J., Shapiro, D. A., & Bergin, A. E. (1986). The effectiveness of psychotherapy. In S. L. Garfield & A. E. Bergin (Eds.), *Handbook of psychotherapy and behavior change* (3rd ed.). New York: Wiley.

Landis, D., Day, H. R., McGrew, P. L., Thomas, J. A., & Miller, A. B. (1976). Can a black "culture assimilator" increase racial understanding? *Journal of Social Issues, 32,* 169–183.

Landry, D. W. (1997, February). Immunotherapy for cocaine addiction. *Scientific American,* pp. 41–45.

Langer, E., Bashner, R. S., & Chanowitz, B. (1985). Decreasing prejudice by increasing discrimination. *Journal of Personality and Social Psychology, 49,* 113–120.

Langer, E., & Janis, I. (1979). *The psychology of control.* Beverly Hills, CA: Sage.

Langlois, J. H., Kalakanis, L., Rubenstein, A. J., Larson, A., Hallam, M., & Smoot, M. (2000). Maxims or myths of beauty? A meta-analytic and theoretical review. *Psychological Bulletin, 126,* 390–423.

Langreth, R. (1996, August 20). Science yields powerful new therapies for pain. *Wall Street Journal,* pp. B1, B4.

Langreth, R. (2000, May 1). Every little bit helps: How even moderate exercise can have a big impact on your health. *Wall Street Journal,* p. R5.

Langs, G., Quehenberger, F., Fabisch, K., Klug, G., Fabisch, H., & Zapotoczky, H. G. (2000). The development of agoraphobia in panic disorder: A predictable process? *Journal of Affective Disorders, 58,* 43–50.

Larose, H., & Standing, L. (1998). Does the halo effect occur in the elderly? *Social Behavior and Personality, 26,* 147–150.

Larsen, R. J., Kasimatis, M., & Frey, K. (1992). Facilitating the furrowed brow: An unobtrusive test of the facial feedback hypothesis applied to unpleasant affect. *Cognition and Emotion, 6,* 321–338.

Larson, R. K. (1990). Semantics. In D. N. Osherson & H. Lasnik (Eds.). *Language.* Cambridge, MA: MIT Press.

Larson, R. W., Richards, M. H., & Perry-Jenkins, M. (1994). Divergent worlds: The daily emotional experience of mothers and fathers in the domestic and public spheres. *Journal of Personality and Social Psychology, 67,* 1034–1046.

Lask, B., & Bryant-Waugh, R. (Eds.). (1999). *Anorexia nervosa and related eating disorders in childhood and adolescence.* New York: Brunner/Mazel.

Lasnik, H. (1990). Syntax. In D. N. Osherson & H. Lasnik (Eds.), *Language,* Cambridge, MA: MIT Press.

Latané, B., & Darley, J. M. (1970). *The unresponsive bystander: Why doesn't he help?* New York: Appleton-Century-Crofts.

Latané, B., & Nida, S. (1981). Ten years of research on group size and helping. *Psychological Bulletin, 89,* 308–324.

Laumann, E. O., Paik, A., & Rosen, R. C. (1999, February 10). Sexual dysfunction in the United States: Prevalence and predictors. *Journal of the American Medical Association, 281,* 537–544.

Lazarus, A. A. (1997). *Brief but comprehensive psychotherapy: The multimodal way.* New York: Springer.

Lazarus, R. S. (1991a). Cognition and motivation in emotion. *American Psychologist, 46,* 352–367.

Lazarus, R. S. (1991b). *Emotion and adaptation.* New York: Oxford University Press.

Lazarus, R. S. (1994). Appraisal: The long and short of it. In P. Ekman & R. J. Davidson (Eds.), *The nature of emotion: Fundamental questions.* New York: Oxford University Press.

Lazarus, R. S. (1995). Emotions express a social relationship, but it is an individual mind that creates them. *Psychological Inquiry, 6,* 253–265.

Lazarus, R. S. (1999). *Stress and emotion: A new synthesis.* New York: Springer.

Lazarus, R. S., & Cohen, J. B. (1977). Environmental stress. In I. Altman & J. F. Wohlwill (Eds.), *Human behavior and the environment: Current theory and research* (Vol. 2). New York: Plenum Press.

Leary, W. E. (1996, November 20). U.S. rate of sexual diseases highest in developed world. *New York Times,* p. C1.

Lee, F., Hallahan, M., & Herzog, T. (1996). Explaining real-life events: How culture and domain shape attributions. *Personality and Social Psychology Bulletin, 22,* 732–741.

Lehman, D. R., Lempert, R. O., & Nisbett, R. E. (1988). The effects of graduate training on reasoning: Formal discipline and thinking about everyday-life events. *American Psychologist, 43,* 431–442.

Lehman, D. R., & Taylor, S. E. (1988). Date with an earthquake: Coping with a probable, unpredictable disaster. *Personality and Social Psychology Bulletin, 13,* 546–555.

Lehrer, P. M. (1996). Recent research findings on stress management techniques. In Editorial Board of Hatherleigh Press, *The Hatherleigh guides series.* Vol. 4: *The Hatherleigh guide to issues in modern therapy.* New York: Hatherleigh Press.

Leibel, R. L., Rosenbaum, M., & Hirsch, J. (1995, March 9). Changes in energy expenditure resulting from altered body. *New England Journal of Medicine, 332,* 621–628.

Leibovic, K. N. (Ed.). (1990). *Science of vision.* New York: Springer-Verlag.

Leigh, H., & Reiser, M. F. (1980). *The patient.* New York: Plenum Press.

Leland, J. (2000, May 29). The science of women and sex. *Newsweek,* pp. 48–54.

Lenzenweger, M. F. & Dworkin, R. H. (Eds.). (1998). *The origins and development of schizophrenia: Advances in experimental psychopathology.* Washington, DC: American Psychological Association.

Leonard, B. E. (2000). Evidence for a biochemical lesion in depression. *Journal of Clinical Psychiatry, 61,* 12–17.

Leong, F. L, & Blustein, D. L. (2000). Toward a global vision of counseling psychology. *Counseling Psychologist, 28*, 5–9.

Lepore, S. J., Ragan, J. D., & Jones, S. (2000). Talking facilitates cognitive-emotional processes of adaptation to an acute stressor. *Journal of Personality and Social Psychology, 78*, 499–508.

Lepper, M. R., & Greene, D. (Eds.). (1978). *The hidden costs of reward.* Hillsdale, NJ: Erlbaum.

Lepper, M. R., Henderlong, J., & Gingras, I. (1999). Understanding the effects of extrinsic rewards on intrinsic motivation—Uses and abuses of meta-analysis: Comment on Deci, Koestner, and Ryan (1999). *Psychological Bulletin, 125*, 669–676.

Lerner, R. M., Fisher, C. B., & Weinberg, R. A. (2000). Toward a science for and of the people: Promoting civil society through the application of developmental science. *Child Development, 71*, 11–20.

Lertola, J. (1997, February 10). The ways to burn 150 calories. *Time*, p. 36.

Lesch, K.-P., Bengel, D., Heils, A., Sabol, S. Z., Greenberg, B. D., Petri, S., Benjamin, J., Muller, C. R., Hamer, D. H., & Murphy, D. L. (1996, November 29). Association of anxiety-related traits with a polymorphism in the serotonin transporter gene regulatory region. *Science, 274*, 1527–1531.

Leslie, C. (1991, February 11). Classrooms of Babel. *Newsweek*, pp. 56–57.

LeVay, S. (1991) A difference in hypothalamic structure between heterosexual and homosexual men. *Science, 253*, 1034–1037.

Levenson, R. W. (1992). Autonomic nervous system differences among emotions. *Psychological Science, 3*, 23–27.

Levenson, R. W. (1994). The search for autonomic specificity. In P. Ekman & R. J. Davidson (Eds.), *The nature of emotion: Fundamental questions.* New York: Oxford University Press.

Levenson, R. W., Ekman, P., & Friesen, W. V. (1990). Voluntary facial expression generates emotion-specific nervous system activity. *Pschophysiology, 27*, 363–384.

Levenson, R. W., Ekman, P., Heider, K., & Friesen, W. V. (1992). Emotion and autonomic nervous system activity in the Minangkabau of West Sumatra. *Journal of Personality and Social Psychology, 62*, 972–988.

Leventhal, H., & Cleary, P. D. (1980). The smoking problem: A review of the research and theory in behavioral risk modification. *Psychological Bulletin, 88*, 370–405.

Leventhal, H., & Tomarken, A. J. (1986). Emotion: Today's problems. *Annual Review of Psychology, 37*, 565–610.

Levine, J. M. (1989). Reaction to opinion deviance in small groups. In P. B. Paulus (Ed.), *Psychology of group influence* (2nd ed.). Hillsdale, NJ: Erlbaum.

Levine, M. W., & Shefner, J. M. (1991). *Fundamentals of sensation and perception* (2nd ed.). Pacific Grove, CA: Brooks/Cole.

Levine, S. C., Huttenlocher, J., Taylor, A., & Langrock, A. (1999). Early sex differences in spatial skill. *Developmental Psychology, 35*, 940–949.

Levinson, D. J. (1990). A theory of life structure development in adulthood. In C. N. Alexander & E. J. Langer (Eds.), *Higher stages of human development: Perspectives on adult growth.* New York: Oxford University Press.

Levy, B. (1996). Improving memory in old age through implicit self-stereotyping. *Journal of Personality and Social Psychology, 71*, 1092–1107.

Levy, B. L., & Langer, E. (1994). Aging free from negative stereotypes: Successful memory in China and among the American deaf. *Journal of Personality and Social Psychology, 66*, 989–997.

Levy, D. H. (2000, August 20). Are you ready for the genome miracle? *Parade*, pp. 8–10.

Levy, S. (1997, May 19). Big Blue's hand of God. *Newsweek*, p. 72.

Levy, S. M., Lee, J., Bagley, C., & Lippman, M. (1988). Survival hazards analysis in first recurrent breast cancer patients: Seven-year follow-up. *Psychosomatic Medicine, 50*, 520–528.

Lewis, M., Feiring, C., McGuffog, C., & Jaskir, J. (1984). Predicting psychopathology in six-year-olds from early social relations. *Child Development, 55*, 123–136.

Lewis, M., Feiring, C., & Rosenthal, S. (2000). Attachment over time. *Child Development, 71*, 707–720.

Lewis, M., & Haviland-Jones, J. M. (2000). *Handbook of emotions* (2nd ed.). New York: Guilford Press.

LeWitt, P. A. (2000). The challenge of managing mild Parkinson's disease. *Pharmacotherapy, 20*, 2S–7S.

Li, S. (1995). (A comparative study of personality in supernormal children and normal children.) *Psychological Science—China, 18*, 184–186.

Li, Y., Xu, J., Shi, X., & Yan, Y. (1999). Intelligence, memory, and event-related potential in patients with motor neuron disease. *Chinese Mental Health Journal, 13*, 180–181.

Liebert, R. M., & Sprafkin, J. (1988). *The early window: Effects of television on children and youth* (3rd ed.). New York: Pergamon Press.

Lindsay, P. H., & Norman, D. A. (1977). *Human information processing* (2nd ed.). New York: Academic Press.

Linscheid, T. R., Iwata, B. A., Ricketts, R. W., Williams, D. E., & Griffin, J. C. (1990). Clinical evaluation of the self-injurious behavior inhibiting system (SIBIS). *Journal of Applied Behavior Analysis, 23*, 53–78.

Linszen, D. H., Dingemans, P. M., Nugter, M. A., Van der Does, A. J. W., et al. (1997). Patient attributes and expressed emotion as risk factors for psychotic relapse. *Schizophrenia Bulletin, 23*, 119–130.

Lipsey, M. W., & Wilson, D. B. (1993). The efficacy of psychological, educational, and behavioral treatment: Confirmation from meta-analysis. *American Psychologist, 48*, 1181–1209.

Lloyd, J. W., Kameenui, E. J., & Chard, D. (Eds.). (1997). *Issues in educating students with disabilities.* Mahwah, NJ: Erlbaum.

Loewenstein, G. (1994). The psychology of curiosity: A review and reinterpretation. *Psychological Bulletin, 116*, 75–98.

Loftus, E. F. (1993). Psychologists in the eyewitness world. *American Psychologist, 48*, 550–552.

Loftus, E. F. (1997). Memory for a past that never was. *Current Directions in Psychological Science, 6*, 60–65.

Loftus, E. F. (1998, November). The memory police. *APA Observer*, pp. 3, 14.

Loftus, E. F., Loftus, G. R., & Messo, J. (1987). Some facts about "weapon focus." *Law and Human Behavior, 11*, 55–62.

Loftus, E. F., & Palmer, J. C. (1974). Reconstruction of automobile destruction: An example of the interface between language and memory. *Journal of Verbal Learning and Verbal Behavior, 13*, 585–589.

Logie, R. H., & Gilhooly, K. J. (1998). *Working memory and thinking.* Philadelphia: Psychology Press.

Long, A. (1987, December). What is this thing called sleep? *National Geographic, 172*, 786–821.

Long, G. M., & Beaton, R. J. (1982). The case for peripheral persistence: Effects of target and background luminance on a partial-report task. *Journal of Experimental Psychology: Human Perception and Performance, 8*, 383–391.

Loomis, J. M., Golledge, R. G., & Klatzky, R. L. (in press). Navigation system for the blind: Auditory display modes and guidance. In *Presence: Teleoperators and Virtual Environments.*

Loomis, J. M., Klatzky, R. L., Golledge, R. G., Cicinelli, J. G., Pellegrino, J. W., & Fry, P. A. (1993). Nonvisual navigation by blind and sighted: Assessment of path integration ability. *Journal of Experimental Psychology: General, 122*, 73–91.

Looy, H. (1995). Born gay? A critical review of biological research on homosexuality. *Journal of Psychology and Christianity, 14*, 197–214.

López, S. R., & Guarnaccia, P. J. J. (2000). Cultural psychopathology: Uncovering the social world of mental illness. *Annual Review of Psychology, 51*, 571–598.

LoPiccolo, L. (1980). Low sexual desire. In S. R. Leiblum & L. A. Pervin (Eds.), *Principles and practice of sex therapy.* New York: Guilford Press.

Lorenz, K. (1966). *On aggression.* New York: Harcourt Brace Jovanovich.

Lorenz, K. (1974). *Civilized man's eight deadly sins.* New York: Harcourt Brace Jovanovich.

Lovaas, O. I., & Koegel, R. (1973). Behavior therapy with autistic children. In C. Thoreson (Ed.), *Behavior modification and education.* Chicago: University of Chicago Press.

Lowe, M. R. (1993). The effects of dieting on eating behavior: A three-factor model. *Psychological Bulletin, 114*, 100–121.

Lown, B. (1999). *The lost art of healing.* New York: Ballantine.

Luborsky, L. (1988). *Who will benefit from psychotherapy?* New York: Basic Books.

Luce, R. D. (1993). *Sound and hearing.* Hillsdale, NJ: Erlbaum.

Lucy, J. A. (1992). *Language diversity and thought: A reformulation of the linguistic relativity hypothesis.* Cambridge, England: Cambridge University Press.

Lucy, J. A. (1996). The scope of linguistic relativity: An analysis and review of empirical research. In J. J. Gumperz & S. C. Levinson (Eds.), *Rethinking linguistic relativity. Studies in the social and cultural foundations of language*, No. 17. Cambridge, England: Cambridge University Press.

Ludwig, A. M. (1969). Altered states of consciousness. In C. T. Tart (Ed.), *Altered states of consciousness.* New York: Wiley.

Ludwig, A. M. (1996, March). Mental disturbances and creative achievement. *Harvard Mental Health Letter*, pp. 4–6.

Luria, A. R. (1968). *The mind of a mnemonist.* Cambridge, MA: Basic Books.

Ly, D. H., Lockhart, D. J., Lerner, R. A., & Schultz, P. G. (2000, March 31). Mitotic misregulation and human aging. *Science, 287,* 2486–2492.

Lykken, D. T. (1995). *The antisocial personalities.* Mahwah, NJ: Erlbaum.

Lykken, D. T., & Tellegen, A. (1996). Happiness is a stochastic phenomenon. *Psychological Science, 7,* 181–185.

Lyman, D. R., Milich, R., Zimmerman, R., Novak, S. P., Logan, T. K., Martin, C., Leukefeld, M. C., & Clayton, R. (1999). Project DARE: No effects at 10-year follow-up. *Journal of Consulting and Clinical Psychology, 67,* 590–593.

Lynn, S. J., Lock, T. G., Myers, B., & Payne, D. G. (1997). Recalling the unrecallable: Should hypnosis be used to recover memories in psychotherapy? *Current Directions in Psychological Science, 6,* 79–83.

Lynn, S. J., Neufeld, V., Green, J. P., Sandberg, D., et al. (1996). Daydreaming, fantasy, and psychopathology. In R. G. Kunzendorf, N. P. Spanos, & B. Wallace (Eds.), *Hypnosis and imagination.* Amityville, NY: Baywood.

Lynn, S. J., & Rhue, J. W. (1988). Fantasy-proneness: Hypnosis, developmental antecedents, and psychopathology. *American Psychologist, 43,* 35–44.

Macaluso, E., Frith, C. D., & Driver, J. (2000, August 18). Modulation of human visual cortex by crossmodal spatial attention. *Science, 289,* 1206–1208.

Maccoby, E. E., & Jacklin, C. N. (1974). *The psychology of sex differences.* Stanford, CA: Stanford University Press.

MacKenzie, B. (1984). Explaining race differences in IQ: The logic, the methodology, and the evidence. *American Psychologist, 39,* 1214–1233.

Mackintosh, N. J. (1998). *IQ and human intelligence.* Cambridge, England: Oxford University Press.

Macmillan, M. (1991). *Freud evaluated: The competed arc.* Amsterdam: North-Holland.

Macrae, C. N., Stangor, C., & Hewstone, M. (1996). *Stereotypes and stereotyping.* New York: Guilford Press.

Madon, S., Jussim, L., & Eccles, J. (1997). In search of the powerful self-fulfilling prophecy. *Journal of Personality and Social Psychology, 72,* 791–809.

Maidment, I. (2000). The use of St John's Wort in the treatment of depression. *Psychiatric Bulletin, 24,* 232–234.

Mairs, D. A. E. (1995). Hypnosis and pain in childbirth. *Contemporary Hypnosis, 12,* 111–118.

Malamuth, N. M., Linz, D., Heavey, C. L., & Barnes, G. (1995). Using the confluence model of sexual aggression to predict men's conflict with women: A 10-year follow-up study. *Journal of Personality and Social Psychology, 69,* 353–369.

Malina, R. M. (1975). *Growth and development: The first twenty years in man.* Minneapolis: Burgess.

Malott, R. W., Whaley, D. L., & Malott, M. E. (1993). *Elementary principles of behavior* (2nd ed.). Englewood Cliffs, NJ: Prentice Hall.

Mann, D. (1997). *Psychotherapy: An erotic relationship.* New York: Routledge.

Manstead, A. S. R. (1991). Expressiveness as an individual difference. In R. S. Feldman & B. Rime (Eds.), *Fundamentals of nonverbal behavior.* Cambridge, England: Cambridge University Press.

Manz, C. C., & Sims, H. P., Jr. (1992). The potential for "groupthink" in autonomous work groups. In R. Glaser (Ed.), *Classic readings in self-managing teamwork: 20 of the most important articles.* King of Prussia, PA: Organization Design and Development.

Mapes, G. (1990, April 10). Beating the clock: Was it an accident Chernobyl exploded at 1:23 in the morning? *Wall Street Journal,* pp. A1, A16.

Marcus, G. F. (1996). Why do children say "breaked"? *Current Directions in Psychological Science, 5,* 81–85.

Marcus, M. B. (1998, March 30). The next miracles: Microchips for the blind and cartilage for the lame. *U.S. News & World Report,* pp. 74–79.

Margolis, E., & Laurence, S. (Eds.). (1999). *Concepts: Core readings.* Cambridge, MA: MIT Press.

Marijuana as medicine: How strong is the science? (May, 1997). *Consumer Reports,* pp. 62–63.

Markey, P. M. (2000). Bystander intervention in computer-mediated communication. *Computers in Human Behavior, 16,* 183–188.

Marks, G., & Miller, N. (1987). Ten years of research on the false-consensus effect: An empirical and theoretical review. *Psychological Bulletin, 102,* 72–90.

Martin, A., Haxby, J. V., Lalonde, F. M., Wiggs, C. L., & Ungerleider, L. G. (1995, October 6). Discrete cortical regions associated with knowledge of color and knowledge of action. *Science, 270,* 102–105.

Martin, L., & Pullum, G. K. (1991). *The great Eskimo vocabulary hoax.* Chicago: University of Chicago Press.

Martindale, C. (1981). *Cognition and consciousness.* Homewood, IL: Dorsey.

Maslow, A. H. (1970). *Motivation and personality* (2nd ed.). New York: Harper & Row.

Maslow, A. H. (1987). *Motivation and personality* (3rd ed.). New York: Harper & Row.

Mason, M. (1994). *The making of Victorian sexual attitudes* (Vol. 2). New York: Oxford University Press.

Masten, A. S., & Coatsworth, J. D. (1998). The development of competence in favorable and unfavorable environments: Lessons from research on successful children. *American Psychologist, 53,* 205–220.

Masters, W. H., & Johnson, V. E. (1966). *Human sexual response.* Boston: Little, Brown.

Masters, W. H., & Johnson, V. E. (1979). *Homosexuality in perspective.* Boston: Little, Brown.

Masters, W. H., & Johnson, V. E. (1994). *Heterosexuality.* New York: HarperCollins.

Mastropieri, M. A., & Scruggs, T. E. (1991). *Teaching students ways to remember: Strategies for learning mnemonically.* Cambridge, MA: Brookline Books.

Matarazzo, J. D. (1992). Psychological testing and assessment in the 21st century. *American Psychologist, 47,* 1007–1018.

Matchen, J., & De Souza, E. (2000). The sexual harassment of faculty members by students. *Sex Roles, 42,* 295–306.

Matlin, M. M. (1987). *The psychology of women.* New York: Holt.

Matsumoto, D. (1987). The role of facial response in the experience of emotion: More methodological problems and a meta-analysis. *Journal of Personality and Social Psychology, 52,* 769–774.

Matsumoto, D. (1990). Cultural similarities and differences in display rules. *Motivation and Emotion, 14,* 195–214.

Matthews, D. B., Best, P. J., White, A. M., Vandergriff, J. L., & Simson, P. E. (1996). Ethanol impairs spatial cognitive processing: New behavioral and electrophysiological findings. *Current Directions in Psychological Science, 5,* 111–115.

Matute, H. (1994). Learned helplessness and superstitious behavior as opposite effects of uncontrollable reinforcement in humans. *Learning and Motivation, 25,* 216–232.

Matute, H. (1995). Human reactions to uncontrollable outcomes: Further evidence for superstitions rather than helplessness. *Quarterly Journal of Experimental Psychology Comparative and Physiological Psychology, 48,* 142–157.

Mauro, R., Sato, K., & Tucker, J. (1992). The role of appraisal in human emotions: A cross-cultural study. *Journal of Personality and Social Psychology, 62,* 301–317.

Mayer, J. D., & Salovey, P. (1997). What is emotional intelligence? In P. Salovey & D. J. Sluyter (Eds.), *Emotional development and emotional intelligence.* New York: Basic Books.

Mayr, U., Kliegl, R., & Krampe, R. T. (1996). Sequential and coordinative processing dynamics in figural transformations across the life span. *Cognition, 59,* 61–90.

Mays, V. M., Rubin, J., Sabourin, M., & Walker, L. (1996). Moving toward a global psychology: Changing theories and practice to meet the needs of a changing world. *American Psychologist, 51,* 485–487.

Mazza, J. J. (2000). The relationship between posttraumatic stress symptomatology and suicidal behavior in school-based adolescents. *Suicide and Life-Threatening Behavior, 30,* 91–103.

McAdams, D. P., Diamond, A., de St. Aubin, E., & Mansfield, E. (1997). Stories of commitment: The psychosocial construction of generative lives. *Journal of Personality and Social Psychology, 72,* 678–694.

McCabe, P. M., Schneiderman, N., Field, T., & Wellens, A. R. (Eds.). (2000). *Stress, coping, and cardiovascular disease.* Mahwah, NJ: Erlbaum.

McCain, N. L., & Smith, J. (1994). Stress and coping in the context of psychoneuroimmunology: A holistic framework for nursing practice and research. *Archives of Psychiatric Nursing, 8,* 221–227.

McCann, U. D., Mertl, M., Eligulashvili, V., & Ricaurte, G. A. (1999). Cognitive performance in (±) 3,4-methylenedioxymethamphetamine (MDMA, "Ecstasy") users: A controlled study. *Psychopharmacology, 143,* 417–425.

McCauley, C. (1989). The nature of social influence in groupthink: Compliance and internalization. *Journal of Personality and Social Psychology, 57,* 250–260.

McCauley, C., & Swann, C. P. (1980) Sex differences in the frequency and functions of fantasies during sexual activity. *Journal of Research in Personality, 14,* 400–411.

McClearn, G. E., Johansson, B., Berg, S., Pedersen, N. L., Ahern, F., Petrill, S. A., & Plomin, R. (1997, June 6). Substantial genetic influence on cognitive abilities in twins 80 or more years old. *Science, 276,* 1560–1583.

McClelland, D. C. (1985). How motives, skills, and values determine what people do. *American Psychologist, 40,* 812–825.

McClelland, D. C. (1993). Intelligence is not the best predictor of job performance. *Current Directions in Psychological Research, 2,* 5–8.

McClelland, D. C., Atkinson, J. W., Clark, R. A., & Lowell, E. L. (1953). *The achievement motive.* New York: Appleton-Century-Crofts.

McClintock, M. K., & Herdt, G. (1996). Rethinking puberty: The development of sexual attraction. *Current Directions in Psychological Science, 5,* 178–183.

McConaghy, N. (1993). *Sexual behavior: Problems and management.* New York: Plenum Press.

McCrae, R. R., & Costa, P. T., Jr. (1990). *Personality in adulthood.* New York: Guilford Press.

McCrae, R. R., & Costa, P. T., Jr. (1999). A five-factor theory of personality. In L. A. Pervin & O. P. John (Eds.), *Handbook of personality: Theory and research* (2nd ed.). New York: Guilford Press.

McCullough, J. P., Jr. (1999). *Treatment for chronic depression: Cognitive behavioral analysis system of psychology (CBASP).* New York: Guilford Press.

McDonald, C., & Murray, R. M. (2000). Early and late environmental risk factors for schizophrenia. *Brain Research Reviews, 31,* 130–137.

McDonald, H. E., & Hirt, E. R. (1997). When expectancy meets desire: Motivational effects in reconstructive memory. *Journal of Personality and Social Psychology, 72,* 5–23.

McDonald, J. L. (1997). Language acquisition: The acquisition of linguistic structure in normal and special populations. *Annual Review of Psychology, 48,* 215–241.

McDonald, J. W. (1999, September). Repairing the damaged spinal cord. *Scientific American,* pp. 65–73.

McDougall, W. (1908). *Introduction to social psychology.* London: Methuen.

McDowell, D. M., & Spitz, H. I. (1999). *Substance abuse.* New York: Brunner/Mazel.

McEwen, B. S. (1998, January 15). Protective and damaging effects of stress mediators [Review article]. *New England Journal of Medicine, 338,* 171–179.

McFadyen, R. G. (1996). Gender, status and "powerless" speech: Interactions of students and lectures. *British Journal of Social Psychology, 35,* 353–367.

McGaugh, J. L. (2000, January 14). Memory—A century of consolidation. *Science, 287,* 248–251.

McGaugh, J. L., Weinberger, N. M., & Lynch, G. (Eds.). (1990). *Brain organization and memory: Cells, systems, and circuits.* New York: Oxford University Press.

McGue, M. (1999). The behavioral genetics of alcoholism. *Current Directions in Psychological Science, 8,* 109–115.

McGuire, P. K., Shah, G. M. S., & Murray, R. M. (1993, September 18). Increased blood flow in Broca's area during auditory hallucinations in schizophrenia. *Lancet, 342,* 703–706.

McGuire, W. J. (1997). Creative hypothesis generating in psychology: Some useful heuristics. *Annual Review of Psychology, 48,* 1–30.

McHale, S. M., Crouter, A. C., & Tucker, C. (1999). Family context and gender role socialization in middle childhood: Comparing girls to boys and sisters to brothers. *Child Development, 70,* 990–1004.

McLaughlin, S., & Margolskee, R. F. (1994). The sense of taste: The internal molecular workings of the taste bud help it distinguish the bitter from the sweet. *American Scientist, 82,* 538–454.

McManus, F., & Waller, G. (1995). A functional analysis of binge-eating. *Clinical Psychology Review, 15,* 845–863.

McMillan, J. R., et al. (1977). Women's language: Uncertainty or interpersonal sensitivity and emotionality? *Sex Roles, 3,* 545–560.

McMullin, R. E. (2000). *The new handbook of cognitive therapy techniques.* New York: Norton.

McWhirter, D. P., Sanders, S., & Reinisch, J. M. (1990). *Homosexuality, heterosexuality: Concepts of sexual orientation.* New York: Oxford University Press.

Mead, M. (1949). *Male and female.* New York: Morrow.

Mealey, L. (2000). *Sex differences: Developmental and evolutionary strategies.* Orlando, FL: Academic Press.

Mednick, A. (1993). World's women familiar with a day's double shift. *APA Monitor,* p. 32.

Meier, R. P., & Willerman, R. (1995). Prelinguistic gesture in deaf and hearing infants. In K. Emmorey & J. S. Reilly (Eds.), *Language, gesture, and space.* Hillsdale, NJ: Erlbaum.

Mel'nikov, K. S. (1993, October–December). (On some aspects of the mechanistic approach to the study of processes of forgetting.) *Vestnik Moskovskogo Universiteta Seriya 14 Psikhologiya,* 64–67.

Melton, G. B., & Garrison, E. G. (1987). Fear, prejudice, and neglect: Discrimination against mentally disabled persons. *American Psychologist, 42,* 1007–1026.

Meltzer, H. Y. (2000). Genetics and etiology of schizophrenia and bipolar disorder. *Biological Psychiatry, 47,* 171–173.

Meltzoff, A. N. (1996). The human infant as imitative generalist: A 20-year progress report on infant imitation with implications for comparative psychology. In C. M. Heyes & B. G. Galef, Jr. (Eds.), *Social learning in animals: The roots of culture.* San Diego: Academic Press.

Mendez, F. J., & Garcia, M. J. (1996). Emotive performances: A treatment package for children's phobias. *Child and Family Behavior Therapy, 18,* 19–34.

Mental health: Does therapy help? (1995, November). *Consumer Reports,* pp. 734–739.

Mentzer, S. J., & Snyder, M. L. (1982). The doctor and the patient: A psychological perspective. In G. S. Sanders and J. Suls (Eds.), *Social psychology of health and illness* (pp. 161–181). Hillsdale, NJ: Erlbaum.

Merlin, D. (1993). Origins of the modern mind: Three stages in the evolution of culture and cognition. *Behavioral and Brain Sciences, 16,* 737–791.

Mesquita, B., & Frijda, N. H. (1992). Cultural variations in emotions: A review. *Psychological Bulletin, 112,* 179–204.

Metcalfe, J. (1986). Premonitions of insight predict impending error. *Journal of Experimental Psychology: Learning, Memory, and Cognition, 12,* 623–634.

Metee, D. R., & Aronson, E. (1974). Affective reactions to appraisal from others. In T. L. Huston (Ed.), *Foundations of interpersonal attraction* (pp. 235–283). New York: Academic Press.

Meyer, G. J. (2000). Incremental validity of the Rorschach Prognostic Rating scale over the MMPI Ego Strength Scale and IQ. *Journal of Personality Assessment, 74,* 356–370.

Meyer, R. G., & Osborne, Y. V. H. (1987). *Case studies in abnormal behavior* (2nd ed.). Boston: Allyn & Bacon.

Michael, R. T., Gagnon, J. H., Laumann, E. O., & Kolata, G. (1994). *Sex in America: A definitive survey.* Boston: Little, Brown.

Middlebrooks, J. C., Clock, A. E., Xu, L., & Green, D. M. (1994, May 6). A panoramic code for sound location by cortical neurons. *Science, 264,* 842–844.

Middlebrooks, J. C., & Green, D. M. (1991). Sound localization by human listeners. *Annual Review of Psychology, 42,* 135–159.

Mifflin, L. (1998, January 14). Study finds a decline in TV network violence. *New York Times,* p. A14.

Mikamo, K., Takao, Y., Wakutani, Y., & Nishikawa, S. (1994). Effects of mecobalamin injection at acupoints on intractable headaches. *Current Therapeutic Research, 55,* 1477–1485.

Miles, R. (2000, January 14). Diversity in inhibition. *Science, 287,* 244–246.

Milgram, R. M., Dunn, R. S., & Price, G. E. (Eds.). (1993). *Teaching and counseling gifted and talented adolescents: An international learning style perspective.* Westport, CT: Praeger/Greenwood.

Milgram, S. (1974). *Obedience to authority.* New York: Harper & Row.

Miller, A. G. (1999). Harming other people: Perspectives on evil and violence. *Personality and Social Psychology Review, 3,* 176–178.

Miller, A. G., Collins, B. E., & Brief, D. E. (1995). Perspectives on obedience to authority: The legacy of the Milgram experiments. *Journal of Social Issues, 51,* 1–19.

Miller, D. W. (2000, February 25). Looking askance at eyewitness testimony. *Chronicle of Higher Education,* pp. A19–A20.

Miller, G. A. (1956). The magical number seven, plus or minus two: Some limits on our capacity for processing information. *Psychology Review, 63,* 81–97.

Miller, G. R., & Stiff, J. B. (1992). Applied issues in studying deceptive communication. In R. S. Feldman (Ed.), *Applications of nonverbal behavioral theories and research.* Hillsdale, NJ: Erlbaum.

Miller, J. G. (1984). Culture and the development of everyday social explanation. *Journal of Personality and Social Psychology, 46,* 961–978.

Miller, J. G. (1999). Cultural psychology: Implications for basic psychological theory. *Psychological Science, 10,* 85–91.

Miller, K. J., & Mizes, J. S. (Eds.). (2000). *Comparative treatments for eating disorders.* New York: Springer.

Miller, L. T., & Vernon, P. A. (1997). Developmental changes in speed of information processing in young children. *Developmental Psychology, 33,* 549–554.

Miller, M. W. (1994, December 1). Brain surgery is back in a limited way to treat mental ills. *Wall Street Journal,* pp. A1, A12.

Miller, N. E. (1985, February). Rx: Biofeedback. *Psychology Today,* pp. 54–59.

Miller, N. E., & Magruder, K. M. (Eds.). (1999). *Cost-effectiveness of psychotherapy: A guide for practitioners, researchers, and policymakers.* New York: Oxford University Press.

Miller-Jones, D. (1989). Culture and testing. *American Psychologist, 44,* 360–366.

Millon, T., & Davis, R. (1996). *Disorders of personality: DSM-IV and beyond* (2nd ed.). New York: Wiley.

Millon, T., & Davis, R. (1999). *Personality disorders in modern life.* New York: Wiley.

Millon, T., Davis, R., Millon, C., Escovar, L., & Meagher, S. (2000). *Personality disorders in modern life.* New York: Wiley.

Mills, J. L. (1999). Cocaine, smoking, and spontaneous abortion. *New England Journal of Medicine, 340,* 380–381.

Milner, B. (1966). *Amnesia following operation on temporal lobes.* In C. W. M. Whitty & P. Zangwill (Eds.), *Amnesia.* London: Butterworth.

Milton, J., & Wiseman, R. (1999). Does psi exist? Lack of replication of an anomalous process of information transfer. *Psychological Bulletin, 125,* 387–391.

Mind over matter. (1999). *Discover, 20,* p. 2.

Mineka, S., & Henderson, R. W. (1985). Controllability and predictability in acquired motivation. *Annual Review of Psychology, 36,* 495–529.

Mingo, C., Herman, C. J., & Jasperse, M. (2000). Women's stories: Ethnic variations in women's attitudes and experiences of menopause, hysterectomy, and hormone replacement therapy. *Journal of Women's Health and Gender-Based Medicine, 9* (Suppl. 2), S27–S38.

Minuchin, S., & Nichols, M. P. (1992). *Family healing.* New York: Free Press.

Miserando, M. (1991). Memory and the seven dwarfs. *Teaching of Psychology, 18,* 169–171.

Miyake, K., Chen, S., & Campos, J. J. (1985). Infant temperament, mother's mode of interaction, and attachment in Japan: An interim report. *Monographs of the Society for Research in Child Development, 50,* 276–297.

Miyashita, Y. (1995, June 23). How the brain creates imagery: Projection to primary visual cortex. *Science, 268,* 1719–1720.

Moghaddam, B., & Adams, B. W. (1998, August 28). Reversal of phencyclidine effects by a group II metabotropic glutamate receptor agonist in rats. *Science, 281,* 1349–1352.

Molfese, V. J. & Molfese, D. L. (2000). *Temperament and personality development across the life span.* Mahwah, NJ: Erlbaum.

Moore-Ede, M. (1993). *The twenty-four hour society.* Boston: Addison-Wesley.

Moretti, M. M., & Higgins, E. T. (1990). The development of self-system vulnerabilities: Social and cognitive factors in developmental psychopathology. In R. J. Sternberg & J. Kolligian, Jr. (Eds.), *Competence considered.* New Haven, CT: Yale University Press.

Morrow, J., & Wolff, R. (1991, May). Wired for a miracle. *Health,* pp. 64–84.

Moscovici, S. (1985). Social influence and conformity. In G. Lindzey & E. Aronson (Eds.), *Handbook of social psychology* (3rd ed.). New York: Random House.

Motley, M. T. (1987, February). What I meant to say. *Psychology Today,* pp. 25–28.

Moutoussis, K., & Zeki, S. (1997). A direct demonstration of perceptual asynchrony in vision. *Proceedings of the Royal Society of London, B., Biological Sciences, 264,* 393–399.

Movshon, J. A., & Newsome, W. T. (1992). Neural foundations of visual motion perception. *Current Directions in Psychological Science, 1,* 35–39.

Mroczek, D. K., & Kolarz, C. M. (1998). The effect of age on positive and negative affect: A developmental perspective on happiness. *Journal of Personality and Social Psychology, 75,* 1333–1349.

Mrzljak, L., Bergson, C., Pappy, M., Huff, R., et al. (1996). Localization of dopamine D4 receptors in GABAergic neurons of the primate brain. *Nature, 381,* 245–248.

Muehlenhard, C. L., & Hollabaugh, L. C. (1988). Do women sometimes say no when they mean yes? The prevalence and correlates of women's token resistance to sex. *Journal of Personality and Social Psychology, 54,* 872–879.

Mueser, K. T., Bellack, A. S., Wade, J. H., Sayers, S. L., Tierney, A., & Haag, G. (1993). Expressed emotion, social skill, and response to negative affect in schizophrenia. *Journal of Abnormal Psychology, 102,* 339–351.

Mufson, M. J. (1999, September). What is the role of psychiatry in the management of chronic pain? *Harvard Mental Health Letter,* pp. 8–10.

Mukerjee, M. (1997, February). Trends in animal research. *Scientific American,* pp. 86–93.

Mumme, D. L., Fernald, A., & Herrera, C. (1996). Infants' responses to facial and vocal emotional signals in a social referencing paradigm. *Child Development, 67,* 3219–3237.

Munroe, R. L., Hulefeld, R., Rodgers, J. M., Tomeo, D. L., & Yamazaki, S. K. (2000). Aggression among children in four cultures. *Cross-Cultural Research, 34,* 3–25.

Munson, L. J., Hulin, C., & Drasgow, F. (2000). Longitudinal analysis of dispositional influences and sexual harassment: Effects on job and psychological outcomes. *Personnel Psychology, 53,* 21–46.

Murphy, S. (1998, January 4). Whitey Bulger's life on the run. *Boston Globe,* pp. A1, A8–A9.

Murphy, S. T., & Zajonc, R. B. (1993). Affect, cognition, and awareness: Affective priming with optimal and suboptimal stimulus exposures. *Journal of Personality and Social Psychology, 64,* 723–739.

Murray, J. B. (1990). Nicotine as a psychoactive drug. *Journal of Psychology, 125,* 5–25.

Murray, J. B. (1995). Evidence for acupuncture's analgesic effectiveness and proposals for the physiological mechanisms involved. *Journal of Psychology, 129,* 43–461.

Murray, S. L., & Holmes, J. G. (1997). A leap of faith? Positive illusions in romantic relationships. *Personality and Social Psychology Bulletin, 23,* 586–604.

Myerhoff, B. (1982). Rites of passage: Process and paradox. In V. Turner (Ed.), *Celebration: Studies in festivity and ritual.* Washington, DC: Smithsonian Institution Press.

Myers, D. G. (2000). The funds, friends, and faith of happy people. *American Psychologist, 55,* 56–67.

Myers, D. G., & Diener, E. (1996, May). The pursuit of happiness: New research uncovers some anti-intuitive insights into how many people are happy—And why. *Scientific American,* pp. 70–72.

Myerson, J., Rank, M. R., Raines, F. Q., & Schnitzler, M. A. (1998). Race and general cognitive ability: The myth of diminishing returns to education. *Psychological Science, 9,* 139–142.

Nahome, L., & Lawton, M. P. (1975). Similarity and propinquity in friendship formation. *Journal of Personality and Social Psychology, 32,* 205–213.

Nathan, P. E., & Gorman, J. M. (Eds.). (1997). *A guide to treatments that work.* New York: Oxford University Press.

Nathans, J., Davenport, C. M., Maumenee, I. H., Lewis, R. A., et al. (1989, August 25). Molecular genetics of human blue cone monochromacy. *Science, 245,* 831–838.

National Center for Health Statistics (1994). *Report on obesity in the United States.* Washington, DC: Author.

National Center on Addiction and Substance Abuse. (1996, June). *Substance abuse and the American woman.* New York: Author.

National Clearinghouse on Child Abuse and Neglect. (2000). *Child maltreatment 1998.* Washington, DC: Author.

National Institute of Mental Health, Multisite HIV Prevention Trial Group. (1998, June 19). The NIMH multisite HIV prevention trial: Reducing HIV sexual risk behavior. *Science, 280,* 1889–1894.

National Institute on Alcohol Abuse and Alcoholism (NIAAA). (1990). *Alcohol and health.* Washington, DC: U.S. Government Printing Office.

National Institute on Drug Abuse. (1991). *National survey results on drug use.* Washington, DC: U.S. Department of Health and Human Services.

National Research Council. (2000). *From neurons to neighborhoods: The science of early childhood development.* Washington, DC: National Academy Press.

Navon, R., & Proia, R. L. (1989, March 17). The mutations in Ashkenazi Jews with adult G(M2) Gangliosidosis, the adult form of Tay-Sachs disease. *Science, 243,* 1471–1474.

Neck, C. P., & Moorhead, G. (1995). Groupthink remodeled: The importance of leadership, time pressure, and methodical decision-making procedures. *Human Relations, 48,* 537–557.

Negrin, G., & Capute, A. J. (1996). Mental retardation. In R. H. A. Haslam & P. J. Valletutti (Eds.). *Medical problems in the classroom: The teacher's role in diagnosis and management* (3rd ed.). Austin, TX: PRO-ED.

Neher, A. (1991). Maslow's theory of motivation: A critique. *Journal of Humanistic Psychology, 31,* 89–112.

Neisser, U. (1982). *Memory observed.* San Francisco: Freeman.

Neisser, U. (1996, April). *Intelligence on the rise: Secular changes in IQ and related measures.* Paper presented at a conference at Emory University, Atlanta.

Neisser, U. (Ed.). (1998). *The rising curve: Long-term gains in IQ related measures.* Washington, DC: American Psychological Association.

Neisser, U., Boodoo, G., Bouchard, T. J., Jr., Boykin, A. W., et al. (1996). Intelligence: Knowns and unknowns. *American Psychologist, 51,* 77–101.

Neitz, J., Neitz, M., & Kainz, P. M. (1996, November 1). Visual pigment gene structure and the severity of color vision defects. *Science, 274,* 801–804.

Nelson, M. (1992, February 3). Too tough to die. *People Weekly,* pp. 30–33.

Nelson, W. M., III, & Finch, A. J., Jr. (2000). Managing anger in youth: A cognitive-behavioral intervention approach. In P. C.

Kendall (Ed.), *Child and adolescent therapy: Cognitive-behavioral procedures* (2nd ed.). New York: Guilford Press.

Ness, R. B., Grisso, J. A., Hirschinger, N., Markovic, N., Shaw, L. M., Day, N. L., & Kline, J. (1999). Cocaine and tobacco use and the risk of spontaneous abortion. *New England Journal of Medicine, 340,* 333–339.

Nesse, R. M. (2000). Is depression an adaptation? *Archives of General Psychiatry, 57,* 14–20.

A new approach to test-taking. (1994, November 15). *New York Times,* p. B9.

Newcombe, N. S., Drummey, A. B., Fox, N. A., Lie, E., & Ottinger-Alberts, W. (2000). Remembering early childhood: How much, how, and why (or why not). *Current Directions in Psychological Science, 9,* 55–58.

Newell, A., & Simon, H. (1972). *Human problem solving.* Englewood Cliffs, NJ: Prentice Hall.

NICHD Early Child Care Research Network. (1997). The effects of infant care on infant-mother attachment security: Results of the NICHD study of early child care. *Child Development, 68,* 860–879.

NICHD Early Child Care Research Network. (1999). Child care and mother-child interaction in the first 3 years of life. *Developmental Psychology, 35,* 1399–1413.

Nickerson, R. S., & Adams, M. J. (1979). Long-term memory for a common object. *Cognitive Psychology, 11,* 287–307.

Nierenberg, A. (1998a, February 17). The physician's perspective. *HealthNews,* pp. 3–4.

Nierenberg, A. (1998b, April 20). Should you take St. John's Wort? *HealthNews,* p. 4.

Nigg, J. T., & Goldsmith, H. H. (1994). Genetics of personality disorders: Perspectives from personality and psychopathology research. *Psychological Bulletin, 115,* 346–380.

Nikles, C. D., II, Brecht, D. L., Klinger, E., & Bursell, A. L. (1998). The effects of current concern- and nonconcern-related waking suggestions on nocturnal dream content. *Journal of Personality and Social Psychology, 75,* 242–255.

Nisbett, R. E. (1968). Taste, deprivation, and weight determinants of eating behavior. *Journal of Personality and Social Psychology, 10,* 107–116.

Nisbett, R. E. (1972). Hunger, obesity and the ventromedial hypothalamus. *Psychological Review, 79,* 433–453.

Nisbett, R. E. (1994, October 31). Blue genes. *New Republic, 211,* 15.

Nisbett, R. E., Krantz, D. H., Jepson, D., & Kunda, Z. (1993). The use of statistical heuristics in everyday reasoning. In R. E. Nisbett (Ed.), *Rules for reasoning.* Hillsdale, NJ: Erlbaum.

Noble, H. B. (1999, March 12). New from the smoking wars: Success. *New York Times,* pp. D1–D2.

Nolen-Hoeksema, S., Larson, J., & Grayson, C. (1999). Explaining the gender differences in depressive symptoms. *Journal of Personality and Social Psychology, 77,* 1061–1072.

Novak, M. A., & Petto, A. J. (1991). *Through the looking glass: Issues of psychological well-being in captive nonhuman primates.* Washington, DC: American Psychological Association.

Noyes, R., Kathol, R. G., Fisher, M. M., Phillips, B. M., et al. (1993). The validity of *DSM-III-R* hypochondriasis. *Archives of General Psychiatry, 50,* 961–970.

Nunn, K. P. (1996). Personal hopefulness: A conceptual review of the relevance of the perceived future to psychiatry. *British Journal of Medical Psychology, 69,* 227–245.

Nyberg, L., & Tulving, E. (1996). Classifying human long-term memory: Evidence from converging dissociations. *European Journal of Cognitive Psychology, 8,* 163–183.

Oatley, K. (1992). *Best laid schemes: The psychology of emotions.* Cambridge, MA: Cambridge University Press.

Oatley, K., & Jenkins, J. M. (1996). *Understanding emotions.* Oxford, England: Blackwell.

O'Connor, S. C., & Rosenblood, L. K. (1996). Affiliation motivation in everyday experience: A theoretical comparison. *Journal of Personality and Social Psychology, 70,* 513–522.

O'Donohue, W. (Ed.). (1997). *Sexual harassment: Theory, research, and treatment.* Boston: Allyn & Bacon, Inc.

Ogbu, J. (1992). Understanding cultural diversity and learning. *Educational Researcher, 21,* 5–14.

Ogilvie, R., & Harsh, J. (Eds.). (1994). *Sleep onset: Normal and abnormal processes.* Washington, DC: American Psychological Association.

O'Grady, W. D., & Dobrovolsky, M. (Eds.). (1996). *Contemporary linguistic analysis: An introduction* (3rd ed.). Toronto: Copp Clark Pitman.

O'Hare, D., & Roscoe, S. (1990). *Flightdeck performance: The human factor.* Ames: Iowa State University Press.

Okun, B. F. (1996). *Understanding diverse families: What practitioners need to know.* New York: Guilford Press.

Olds, J., & Milner, P. (1954). Positive reinforcement produced by electrical stimulation of septal area and other regions of rat brain. *Journal of Comparative and Physiological Psychology, 47,* 411–427.

Olds, M. E., & Fobes, J. L. (1981). The central basis of motivation: Intracranial self-stimulation studies. *Annual Review of Psychology, 32,* 123–129.

Oliver, M. B., & Hyde, J. S. (1993). Gender differences in sexuality: A meta-analysis. *Psychological Bulletin, 114,* 29–51.

Olshansky, S. J., Carnes, B. A., & Cassel, C. (1990, November 2). In search of Methuselah: Estimating the upper limits to human longevity. *Science, 250,* 634–639.

O'Neil, J. (1999, July 27). For the disabled, special dogs assume special duties. *New York Times,* p. D6.

Oren, D. A., & Terman, M. (1998, January 16). Tweaking the human circadian clock with light. *Science, 279,* 333–334.

Orenstein, P. (2001). Unbalanced equations: Girls, math, and the confidence gap. In R. Satow (Ed.), *Gender and social life.* Boston: Allyn & Bacon.

Ornstein, R. (1998). *The right mind: Making sense of the hemispheres.* New York: Harcourt Brace.

Orth-Gomer, K., & Schneiderman, N. (Eds.). (1995). *Behavioral medicine approaches to cardiovascular disease prevention.* Mahwah, NJ: Erlbaum.

Ortony, A., & Turner, T. J. (1990). What's basic about basic emotions? *Psychological Review, 97,* 315–331.

Orwin, R. G., & Condray, D. S. (1984). Smith and Glass' psychotherapy conclusions need further probing: On Landman and Dawes' re-analysis. *American Psychologist, 39,* 71–72.

Orzack, M. S. (1999). Computer addiction: Is it real or virtual? *Harvard Mental Health Letter,* p. 8.

Oskamp, S. (Ed.) (2000). *Reducing prejudice and discrimination.* Mahwah, NJ: Erlbaum.

Oster, M. I. (1994). Psychological preparation for labor and delivery using hypnosis. *American Journal of Clinical Hypnosis, 37,* 12–21.

Owens, R. E., Jr. (2001). *Language development: An introduction* (5th ed.). Boston: Allyn & Bacon.

Paivio, A. (1971). *Imagery and verbal processes.* New York: Holt, Rinehart & Winston.

Paivio, A. (1975). Perceptual comparison through the mind's eye. *Memory and Cognition, 3,* 635–647.

Paludi, M. A. (Ed.). (1996). *Sexual harassment on college campuses: Abusing the ivory power.* Albany: State University of New York Press.

Paniagua, F. A. (2000). *Diagnosis in a multicultural context: A casebook for mental health professionals.* Thousand Oaks, CA: Sage.

Parlee, M. B. (1979, October). The friendship bond. *Psychology Today,* pp. 43–45.

Parrott, R., Duncan, V., & Duggan, A. (2000). Promoting patients' full and honest disclosure during conversations with health caregivers. In S. Petronio (Ed.), *Balancing the secrets of private disclosures.* Mahwah, NJ: Erlbaum.

Pascual-Leone, A., et al. (1995). Modulation of muscle responses evoked by transcranial magnetic stimulation during the acquisition of new fine motor skills. *Journal of Neurophysiology, 74,* 1037–1045.

Patzwahl, D. R., Zanker, J. M., & Altenmuller, E. O. (1994). Cortical potentials reflecting motion processing in humans. *Visual Neuroscience, 11,* 1135–1147.

Pavlides, C., & Winson, J. (1989). Influences of hippocampal place cell firing in the awake state on the activity of these cells during subsequent sleep episodes. *Journal of Neuroscience, 9,* 2907–2918.

Pavlov, I. P. (1927). *Conditioned reflexes.* London: Oxford University Press.

Pawlik, K., & d'Ydewalle, G. (1996). Psychology and the global commons: Perspectives of international psychology. *American Psychologist, 51,* 488–495.

Payne, D. G. (1986). Hyperamnesia for pictures and words: Testing the recall level hypothesis. *Journal of Experimental Psychology: Learning, Memory, and Cognition, 12,* 16–29.

Peirce, R. S., Frone, M. R., Russell, M., & Cooper, M. L. (1996). Financial stress, social support, and alcohol involvement: A longitudinal test of the buffering hypothesis in a general population survey. *Health Psychology, 15,* 38–47.

Penn, D. L., Corrigan, P. W., Bentall, R. P., Racenstein, J. M., & Newman, L. (1997). Social cognition in schizophrenia. *Psychological Bulletin, 121,* 114–132.

Penney, J. B., Jr. (2000). Synopsis of neuropsychiatry. In B. S. Fogel, R. B. Schiffer, et al. (Eds.). *Neurochemistry.* Philadelphia: Lippincott-Raven.

Pennisi, E. (1997a, October 24). Enzyme linked to alcohol sensitivity in mice. *Science, 278,* 573.

Pennisi, E. (1997b, August 15). Schizophrenia clues from monkeys. *Science, 277,* 900.

Pennisi, E. (1997c, August 1). Transgenic lambs from cloning lab. *Science, 277,* 631.

Pennisi, E. (2000, May 19). And the gene number is . . . ? *Science, 288,* 1146–1147.

Peplau, L. A., Rubin, Z., & Hill, C. T. (1977). Sexual intimacy in dating relationships. *Journal of Social Issues, 2,* 86–109.

Perez, R. M., DeBord, K. A., & Bieschke, K. J. (Eds.). (2000). *Handbook of counseling and psychotherapy with lesbian, gay, and bisexual clients.* Washington, DC: American Psychological Association.

Perkins, D. N. (1983). Why the human perceiver is a bad machine. In J. Beck, B. Hope, & A. Rosenfeld (Eds.), *Human and machine vision.* New York: Academic Press.

Perlmutter, M., & Mitchell, D. B. (1986). The appearance and disappearance of age differences in adult memory. In I. M. Craik & S. Trehub (Eds.), *Aging and cognitive processes,* New York: Plenum Press.

Perloff, R. M. (1993). *The dynamics of persuasion.* Hillsdale, NJ: Erlbaum.

Perls, F. S. (1967). Group vs. individual therapy. *ETC: A Review of General Semantics, 34,* 306–312.

Perls, F. S. (1970). *Gestalt therapy now: Therapy, techniques, applications.* Palo Alto, CA: Science & Behavior Books.

Perls, F. S., Hefferline, R., & Goodman, P. (1994). *Gestalt therapy: Excitement and growth in the human personality* (2nd ed.). New York: New York Journal Press.

Perry-Jenkins, M. (1993). Family roles and responsibilities: What has changed and what has remained the same? In J. Frankel (Ed.), *The employed mother and the family context.* New York: Springer.

Pervin, L. A. & John, O. P. (Eds.) (1999). *Handbook of personality: Theory and research* (2nd ed.) New York: Guilford Press.

Petersen, S. E., & Fiez, J. A. (1993). The processing of single words studied with positron emission tomography. *Annual Review of Neuroscience, 16,* 509–530.

Peterson, A. (1985). Pubertal development as a cause of disturbance: Myths, realities, and unanswered questions. *Genetic, Social and General Psychology Monographs, 111,* 205–232.

Peterson, C. (2000). The future of optimism. *American Psychologist, 55,* 44–55.

Peterson, C., Maier, S. F., & Seligman, M. E. P. (1993). *Learned helplessness: A theory for the age of personal control.* New York: Oxford University Press.

Peterson, K. C., Prout, M. F., & Schwarz, R. A. (1991). *Post-traumatic stress disorder: A clinician's guide.* New York: Plenum Press.

Peterson, L. R., & Peterson, M. J. (1959). Short-term retention of individual items. *Journal of Experimental Psychology, 58,* 193–198.

Peterson, S. E. (1993, December). Fractured functions: Does the brain have a supreme integrator? *Scientific American,* p. 36.

Peterzell, D. H. (1993). Individual differences in the visual attention of human infants: Further evidence for separate sensitization and habituation processes. *Developmental Psychobiology, 26,* 207–218.

Petri, H. L. (1996). *Motivation: Theory, research, and applications* (4th ed.). Pacific Grove, CA: Brooks/Cole.

Petronis, A., & Kenedy, J. L. (1995). Unstable genes—unstable mind? *American Journal of Psychiatry, 152,* 164–172.

Pettigrew, T. F. (1997, February). Generalized intergroup contact effects on prejudice.

Personality and Social Psychology Bulletin, 23, 173–185.

Pettingale, K. W., Morris, T., Greer, S., & Haybittle, J. L. (1985). Mental attitudes to cancer: An additional prognostic factor. *Lancet,* p. 750.

Pettito, L. A. (1993). On the ontogenetic requirements for early language acquisition. In B. de Boysson-Bardies, S. de Schonen, P. W. Jusczyk, P. McNeilage, & J. Morton (Eds.), *Developmental neurocognition: Speech and face processing in the first year of life.* Dordrecht, Netherlands: Kluwer Academic.

Pettito, L. A., & Marentette, P. F. (1991, March 22). Babbling in the manual mode: Evidence for the ontogeny of language. *Science, 251,* 1493–1496.

Petty, R. E., & Cacioppo, J. T. (1986). The elaboration likelihood model of persuasion. In L. Berkowitz (Ed.), *Advances in experimental social psychology* (Vol. 10). New York: Academic Press.

Petty, R. E., Cacioppo, J. T., Strathman, A. J., & Priester, J. R. (1994). To think or not to think: Exploring two routes to persuasion. In S. Savitt & T. C. Brock (Eds.), *Persuasion: Psychological insights and perspectives.* Boston: Allyn & Bacon.

Petzold, P. (1992). Context effects in judgments of attributes: An information-integration approach. In H. G. Geissler, S. W. Link, & J. T. Townsend (Eds.), *Cognition, information processing, and psychophysics: Basic issues.* Scientific psychology series. Hillsdale, NJ: Erlbaum.

Pezdek, K., & Banks, W. P. (Eds.). (1996). *The recovered memory/false memory debate.* New York: Academic Press.

Phillips-Hershey, E. H., & Ridley, L. (1996). Strategies for acceptance of diversity of students with mental retardation. *Elementary School Guidance and Counseling, 30,* 282–291.

Philpot, C. L. (2000). Socialization of gender roles. In W. C. Nichols, M. A. Pace-Nichols, et al. (Eds.), *Handbook of family development and intervention.* New York: Wiley.

Phinney, J. S. (1996). When we talk about American ethnic groups, what do we mean? *American Psychologist, 51,* 918–927.

Piaget, J. (1970). Piaget's theory. In P. H. Mussen (Ed.), *Carmichael's manual of child psychology* (3rd ed., Vol. 1). New York: Wiley.

Piaget, J., & Inhelder, B. (1958). *The growth of logical thinking from childhood to adolescence* (A. Parsons & S. Seagrin, Trans.). New York: Basic Books.

Piasecki, T. M., Kenford, S. L., Smith, S. S., Fiore, M. C., & Baker, T. B. (1997). Listening to nicotine: Negative affect and the smoking withdrawal conundrum. *Psychological Science, 8,* 184–189.

Pich, E. M., Pagliusi, S. R., Tessari, M., Talabot-Ayer, D., Hooft van Huijsduijnen, R., & Chiamulera, C. (1997, January 3). Common neural substrates for the addictive properties of nicotine and cocaine. *Science, 275,* 83–86.

Pihlgren, E. M., Gidycz, C. A., & Lynn, S. J. (1993). Impact of adulthood and adolescent rape experiences on subsequent sexual fantasies. *Imagination, Cognition and Personality, 12,* 321–339.

Piliavin, J. A., & Piliavin, I. M. (1972). Effect of blood on reactions to a victim. *Journal of Personality and Social Psychology, 23,* 353–362.

Pillard, R. C. (1996). Homosexuality from a familial and genetic perspective. In R. P. Cabaj

& T. S. Stein (Eds.), *Textbook of homosexuality and mental health.* Washington, DC: American Psychiatric Press.

Pinker, S. (1990). Language acquisition. In D. N. Osherson & H. Lasnik (Eds.), *Language.* Cambridge, MA: MIT Press.

Pinker, S. (1994). *The language instinct.* New York: William Morrow.

Pion, G. M., Mednick, M. T., Astin, H. S., Hall, C. C. I., Kenkel, M. B., Keita, G. P., Kohout, J. L., & Kelleher, J. C. (1996). The shifting gender composition of psychology: Trends and implications for the discipline. *American Psychologist, 51,* 509–528.

Pledge, D. S. (1992). Marital separation/divorce: A review of individual responses to a major life stressor. *Journal of Divorce and Remarriage, 17,* 151–181.

Plomin, R. (1990, April 13). The role of inheritance in behavior. *Science, 248,* 183–188.

Plomin, R., & Caspi, R. (1999). Behavioral genetics and personality. In L. A. Pervin & O. P. John (Eds.), *Handbook of personality: Theory and research* (2nd ed.). New York: Guilford Press.

Plomin, R., & McClearn, G. E. (Eds.) (1993). *Nature, nurture and psychology.* Washington, DC: American Psychological Association.

Plomin, R., & Neiderhiser, J. M. (1992). Genetics and experience. *Current Directions in Psychological Science, 1,* 160–163.

Plomin, R., & Petrill, S. A. (1997). Genetics and intelligence: What's new? *Intelligence, 24,* 53–77.

Plous, S. (1996a). Attitudes toward the use of animals in psychological research and education: Results from a national survey of psychologists. *American Psychologist, 51,* 1167–1180.

Plous, S. (1996b). Attitudes toward the use of animals in psychological research and education: Results from a national survey of psychology majors. *Psychological Science, 7,* 352–358.

Plumert, J. M., Carswell, C., De Vet, K., & Ihrig, D. (1995). The content and organization of communication about object locations. *Journal of Memory and Language, 34,* 477–498.

Plummer, W., & Pick, G. (1996, October 10). Beating the blitz. *People Weekly,* pp. 129–132.

Plutchik, R. (1980). *Emotion: A psychorevolutionary synthesis.* New York: Harper & Row.

Polivy, J., & Herman, C. P. (1991). Good and bad dieters: Self-perception and reaction to a dietary challenge. *International Journal of Eating Disorders, 10,* 91–99.

Polk, N. (1997, March 30). The trouble with school testing systems. *New York Times,* p. CN3.

Pollack, A. (2000, May 30). Neural cells, grown in labs, raise hopes on brain disease. *New York Times,* pp. D1, D6.

Pollack, M. H., & Marzol, P. C. (2000). Panic: Course, complications and treatment of panic disorder. *Journal of Psychopharmacology, 14,* S25–S30.

Pomerlau, O. F. (1995). Individual differences in sensitivity to nicotine: Implications of genetic research on nicotine dependence [Special Issue: Genetic, environmental, and situational factors mediating the effects of nicotine]. *Behavior Genetics, 25,* 161–177.

Poncini, M. (1990). *Brain fitness.* New York: Random House.

Ponterotto, J. G., Casas, J. M., Suzuki, L. A., & Alexander, C. M. (Eds.). (2001). *Handbook of multicultural counseling.* Thousand Oaks, CA: Sage.

Porkka-Heiskanen, T., Strecker, R. E., Thakkar, M., Bjorkum, A. A., Greene, R. W., & McCarley, R. W. (1997, May 23). Adenosine: A mediator of the sleep-inducing effects of prolonged wakefulness. *Science, 276,* 1265–1268.

Porte, H. S., & Hobson, J. A. (1996). Physical motion in dreams: One measure of three theories. *Journal of Abnormal Psychology, 105,* 329–335.

Porter, R. H., Cernich, J. M., & McLaughlin, F. J. (1983). Maternal recognition of neonates through olfactory cues. *Physiology and Behavior, 30,* 151–154.

Potheraju, A., & Soper, B. (1995). A comparison of self-reported dream themes for high school and college students. *College Student Journal, 29,* 417–420.

Pottieger, A. E., Tressell, P. A., Inciardi, J. A., & Rosales, T. A. (1992). Cocaine use patterns and overdose. *Journal of Psychoactive Drugs, 24,* 399–410.

Powell, D. H., & Whitla, D. K. (1994, February). Normal cognitive aging: Toward empirical perspectives. *Current Directions in Psychological Science, 3,* 27–31.

Powell, L. H., Shaker, L. A., & Jones, B. A. (1993). Psychosocial predictors of mortality in 83 women with premature acute myocardial infarction. *Psychosomatic Medicine, 55,* 426–433.

Powers, D. E. (1993). Coaching for the SAT: A summary of the summaries and an update. *Educational Measurement Issues and Practice, 12,* 24–30, 39.

Pratkanis, A. R., & Turner, M. E. (1999). Groupthink and preparedness for the Loma Prieta earthquake: A social identity maintenance analysis of causes and preventions. In R. Wageman (Ed.), *Groups in context: Vol. 2. Research on managing groups and teams.* Stamford, CT: Jai Press.

Pratt, S. I., & Moreland, K. L. (1996). Introduction to treatment outcome: Historical perspectives and current issues. In S. I. Pfeiffer (Ed.), *Outcome assessment in residential treatment.* New York: Haworth Press.

Pressley, M. (1987). Are keyword method effects limited to slow presentation rates? An empirically based reply to Hall and Fuson (1986). *Journal of Educational Psychology, 79,* 333–335.

Pressman, M. R., & Orr, W. C. (1997). *Understanding sleep: The evaluation and treatment of sleep disorders.* Washington, DC: American Psychological Association.

Pribram, K. H. (1984). Emotion: A neurobehavioral analysis. In K. R. Scherer & P. Ekman (Eds.), *Approaches to emotion.* Hillsdale, NJ: Erlbaum.

Price, D. D. (2000, June 9). Psychological and neural mechanisms of the affective dimension of pain. *Science, 288,* 1769–1772.

Priester, J. R. & Petty, R. E. (1995). Source attributions and persuasion: Perceived honesty as a determinant of message scrutiny. *Personality and Social Psychology Bulletin, 21,* 637–654.

Prince, R. J., & Guastello, S. J. (1990). The Barnum effect in a computerized Rorschach interpretation system. *Journal of Personality, 124,* 217–222.

Pulvirenti, L., & Koob, G. F. (1994). Lisuride reduces intravenous cocaine self-administration in rats. *Pharmacology, Biochemistry and Behavior, 47,* 819–822.

Purves, D., Augustine, G. J., Fitzpatrick, D., Katz, L. C., LaMantia, A., & McNamara, J. O. (Eds.). (1997). *Neuroscience.* Sunderland, MA: Sinauer.

Putnam, F. W. (1995a). Development of dissociative disorders. In D. Cicchetti & D. J. Cohen (Eds.), *Developmental psychopathology: Vol. 2. Risk, disorder, and adaptation.* New York: Wiley.

Putnam, F. W. (1995b). Traumatic stress and pathological dissociation. In G. P. Chrousos, R. McCarty, et al. (Eds.), *Stress: Basic mechanisms and clinical implications.* New York: New York Academy of Sciences.

Quinn, M. (1990, January 29). Don't aim that pack at us. *Time,* p. 60.

Raag, T., & Rackliff, C. L. (1998). Preschoolers' awareness of social expectations of gender: Relationships to toy choices. *Sex Roles, 38,* 685–700.

Rachman, S., & deSilva, P. (1996). *Panic disorder.* Oxford, England: Oxford University Press.

Rachman, S., & Hodgson, R. (1980). *Obsessions and compulsions.* Englewood Cliffs, NJ: Prentice Hall.

Rakoff, V. M. (1995). Trauma and adolescent rites of initiation. In R. C. Marohn & S. C. Feinstein (Eds.), *Adolescent psychiatry: Developmental and clinical studies.* Hillsdale, NJ: Analytic Press.

Ramachandran, V. S. (1995). Filling in gaps in logic: Reply to Durgin et al. *Perception, 24,* 841–845.

Raskin, N. J., & Rogers, C. R. (1989). Person-centered therapy. In R. J. Corsini & D. Wedding (Eds.), *Current psychotherapies* (4th ed.). Itasca, IL: F. E. Peacock.

Rasmussen, J. (1981). Modeis of mental strategies in process control. In J. Rasmussen & W. Rouse (Eds.), *Human detection and diagnosis of system failures.* New York: Plenum Press.

Ratcliff, R., & McKoon, G. (1989). Memory models, text processing, and cue-dependent retrieval. In H. L. Roediger III & F. I. M. Craik (Eds.), *Varieties of memory and consciousness: Essays in honour of Endel Tulving.* Hillsdale, NJ: Erlbaum.

Ratner, H. H., Schell, D. A., Crimmins, A., Mittelman, D., et al. (1987). Changes in adults' prose recall: Aging or cognitive demands? *Developmental Psychology, 23,* 521–525.

Rau, H., Weitkunat, R., Brody, S., Buhrer, M., et al. (1996). Biofeedback of R-wave to pulse interval produces differential learning of blood pressure control. *Scandinavian Journal of Behaviour Therapy, 25,* 17–25.

Rawsthorne, L. J., & Elliot, A. J. (1999). Achievement goals and intrinsic motivation: A meta-analytic review. *Personality and Social Psychology Review, 3,* 326–344.

Ray, W. J. (2000). *Methods: Toward a science of behavior and experience* (6th ed.). Belmont, CA: Wadsworth.

Redding, G. M., & Hawley, E. (1993). Length illusion in fractional Müller-Lyer stimuli: An object-perception approach. *Perception, 22,* 819–828.

Reed, S. K. (1996). *Cognition: Theory and applications* (4th ed.). Pacific Grove, CA: Brooks/Cole.

Rees, G., Frith, C. D., & Lavie, N. (1998). Modulating irrelevant motion perception by varying attentional load in an unrelated task. *Science, 278,* 1616–1619.

Reeves, R. A., Baker, G. A., Boyd, J. G., & Cialdini, R. B. (1991). The door-in-the-face technique: Reciprocal concessions vs. self-presentational explanations. *Journal of Social Behavior and Personality, 6,* 545–558.

Regan, P. C. (2000). Love relationships. In L. T. Szuchman & F. Muscarella (Eds.), *Psychological perspectives on human sexuality.* New York: Wiley.

Reichman, W. E., & Rabins, P. V. (1996). Schizophrenia and other psychotic disorders. In W. E. Reichman & P. R. Katz (Eds.), *Psychiatric care in the nursing home.* New York: Oxford University Press.

Reinisch, J. M., Rosenblum, L. A., Rubin, D. B., Schulsinger, M. F., et al. (1997). Biological causation: Are gender differences wired into our biology? In M. R. Walsh (Ed.), *Women, men, and gender: Ongoing debates.* New Haven, CT: Yale University Press.

Reisberg, D. (1997). *Cognition: Exploring the science of the mind.* New York: W. W. Norton.

Reisenzein, R. (1983). The Schachter theory of emotion: Two decades later. *Psychological Bulletin, 94,* 239–264.

Reiss, I. L. (1960). *Premarital sexual standards in America.* New York: Free Press.

Reitman, J. S. (1965). *Cognition and thought.* New York: Wiley.

Rescorla, R. A. (1988). Pavlovian conditioning: It's not what you think it is. *American Psychologist, 43,* 151–160.

Resnick, S. M. (1992). Positron emission tomography in psychiatric illness. *Current Directions in Psychological Science, 1,* 92–98.

Reyna, V. F. (1997). Conceptions of memory development with implications for reasoning and decision making. In R. Vasta (Ed.), *Annals of child development: A research annual* (Vol. 12, pp. 87–118). London: Kingsley.

Reynolds, R. I., & Takooshian, H. (1988, January). Where were you August 8, 1985? *Bulletin of the Psychonomic Society, 26,* 23–25.

Rhodes, N., & Wood, W. (1992). Self-esteem and intelligence affect influenceability: The mediating role of message reception. *Psychological Bulletin, 111,* 156–171.

Rhodewalt, F., & Fairfield, M. (1991). An alternative approach to Type A behavior and health: Psychological reactance and medical noncompliance. In M. J. Strube (Ed.), *Type A behavior.* Newbury Park, CA: Sage.

Rhue, J. W., Lynn, S. J., & Kirsch, I (Eds.). (1993). *Handbook of clinical hypnosis.* Washington, DC: American Psychological Association.

Ricciuti, H. N. (1993). Nutrition and mental development. *Current Directions in Psychological Science, 2,* 43–46.

Rice, G., Anderson, C., Risch, N., & Ebers, G. (1999, April 23). Male homosexuality: Absence of linkage to microsatellite markers at Xq28. *Science, 284,* 665–667.

Rice, M. L. (1989). Children's language acquisition. *American Psychologist, 44,* 149–156.

Rice, V. H. (Ed.). (2000). *Handbook of stress, coping and health.* Thousand Oaks, CA: Sage.

Rich, F. (1997, May 1). Harnisch's perfect pitch. *New York Times,* p. A35.

Richie, J. (1994, April). Paper presented at the annual meeting of the American Association for Cancer Research, San Francisco.

Rieder, R. O., Kaufmann, C. A., & Knowles, J. A. (1996). Genetics. In R. E. Hales & S. C. Yudofsky (Eds.), *The American Psychiatric Press synopsis of psychiatry.* Washington, DC: American Psychiatric Press, Inc.

Riefer, D. M., Keveri, M. K., & Kramer, D. L. F. (1995). Name that tune: Eliciting the tip-of-the-tongue experience using auditory stimuli. *Psychological Reports, 77,* 1379–1390.

Rierdan, J. (1996). Adolescent suicide: One response to adversity. In R. S. Feldman (Ed.), *The psychology of adversity.* Amherst: University of Massachusetts Press.

Ringold, D. J. (1996). Social criticisms of target marketing: Process or product? In R. P. Hill (Ed.), *Marketing and consumer research in the public interest.* Thousand Oaks, CA: Sage.

Rinn, W. E. (1984). The neuropsychology of facial expression: A review of neurological and psychological mechanisms for producing facial expressions. *Psychological Bulletin, 95,* 52–77.

Rinn, W. E. (1991). Neuropsychology of facial expression. In R. S. Feldman & B. Rimé (Eds.), *Fundamentals of nonverbal behavior.* Cambridge, England: Cambridge University Press.

Risch, N., & Merikangas, K. (1996, September 13). The future of genetic studies of complex human diseases. *Science, 273,* 1516–1517.

Risley, R. C., & Rescorla, R. A. (1972). Associations in higher order conditioning and sensory pre-conditioning. *Journal of Comparative and Physiological Psychology, 81,* 1–11.

Ritzler, B., & Rosenbaum, G. (1974). Proprioception in schizophrenics and normals: Effects of stimulus intensity and interstimulus interval. *Journal of Abnormal Psychology, 83,* 106–111.

Robbins, T. W. (1988). Arresting memory decline. *Nature, 336,* 207–208.

Roberts, S. M. (1995). Applicability of the goodness-of-fit hypothesis to coping with daily hassles. *Psychological Reports, 77,* 943–954.

Robertson, L. C., & Ivry, R. (2000). Hemispheric asymmetries: Attention to visual and auditory primitives. *Current Directions in Psychological Science, 9,* 59–63.

Robins, R. W., Gosling, S. D., & Craik, K. H. (1999). An empirical analysis of trends in psychology. *American Psychologist, 54,* 117–128.

Robinson, J., & Godbey, G. (1997). *Time for life.* University Park, PA: Pennsylvania State University Press.

Rock, A. (1999, January). Quitting time for smokers. *Money,* pp. 139–141.

Rodin, J. (1985). Insulin levels, hunger, and food intake: An example of feedback loops in body-weight regulation. *Health Psychology, 4,* 1–18.

Rodin, J. (1986, September 19). Aging and health: Effects of the sense of control. *Science, 233,* 1271–1276.

Roffwarg, H. P., Muzio, J. N., & Dement, W. C. (1966). Ontogenic development of the human sleep-dream cycle. *Science, 152,* 604–619.

Rogers, C. R. (1951). *Client-centered therapy,* Boston: Houghton-Mifflin.

Rogers, C. R. (1971). A theory of personality. In S. Maddi (Ed.), *Perspectives on personality.* Boston: Little, Brown.

Rogers, C. R. (1980). *A way of being.* Boston: Houghton Mifflin.

Rogers, P., & Eftimiades, M. (1995, July 24). Abner Louima. *People Weekly,* pp. 42–43.

Rogler, L. H. (1999). Methodological sources of cultural insensitivity in mental health research. *American Psychologist, 54,* 424–433.

Rokeach, M. (1971). Long-range experimental modification of values, attitudes, and behavior. *American Psychologist, 26,* 453–459.

Rolland, J. S., & Walsh, F. (1996). Family therapy: Systems approaches to assessment and treatment. In R. E. Hales & S. C. Yudofsky (Eds.), *The American Psychiatric Press synopsis of psychiatry.* Washington, DC: American Psychiatric Press.

Rolls, E. T. (1994). Neural processing related to feeding in primates. In C. R. Legg & D. A. Booth (Eds.). *Appetite: Neural and behavioural bases.* Oxford, England: Oxford University Press.

Root-Bernstein, R., & Root-Bernstein, M. (1999). *Sparks of genius: The thirteen thinking tools of the world's most creative people.* New York: Houghton Mifflin.

Rorschach, H. (1924). *Psychodiagnosis: A diagnostic test based on perception.* New York: Grune & Stratton.

Rosch, E., & Mervis, B. (1975). Family resemblances: Studies in the internal structure of categories. *Cognitive-Psychology, 7,* 573–605.

Roseman, I. J., Wiest, C., & Swartz, T. S. (1994). Phenomenology, behaviors, and goals differentiate discrete emotions. *Journal of Personality and Social Psychology, 67,* 206–221.

Rosen, D. (1999, May 10). Dieting disorder: A physician's perspective. *Harvard Mental Health Newsletter,* p. 4.

Rosen, H. (2000). The creative evolution of the theoretical foundations for cognitive therapy. *Journal of Cognitive Psychotherapy, 14,* 123–134.

Rosenberg, D., & Bai, M. (1997, October 13). Drinking and dying. *Newsweek,* p. 69.

Rosenhan, D. L. (1973). On being sane in insane places. *Science, 179,* 250–258.

Rosenheck, R., Cramer, J., Xu, W., Thomas, J., Henderson, W., Frisman, L., Fye, C., & Charney, D. (1997). A comparison of clozapine and haloperidol in hospitalized patients with refractory schizophrenia. *New England Journal of Medicine, 337,* 809–815.

Rosenman, R. H. (1990). Type A behavior pattern: A personal overview. *Journal of Social Behavior and Personality, 5,* 1–24.

Rosenman, R. H., Brand, R. J., Sholtz, R. I., & Friedman, M. (1976). Multivariate prediction of coronary heart disease during 8.5 year follow-up in the Western collaborative group study. *American Journal of Cardiology, 37,* 903–910.

Rosenstein, D. S., & Horowitz, H. A. (1996). Adolescent attachment and psychopathology. *Journal of Consulting and Clinical Psychology, 64,* 244–253.

Rosenthal, A. M. (1993, July 27). The torture continues. *New York Times,* p. A13.

Rosenthal, E. (1999, December 9). China's chic wasitline: Convex to concave. *New York Times,* pp. A1, A4.

Rosenthal, L. H. (1997). *A new perspective on the relation between fear and persuasion: The application of dual-process models.* Unpublished doctoral dissertation, Dept. of Psychology. University of Massachusetts, Amherst.

Rosenzweig, M. R. (2000). Continuity and change in the development of psychology around the world. *American Psychologist, 54,* 252–259.

Rosewicz, B. (1996, September) Here comes the bride . . . for the umpteenth time. *Wall Street Journal,* p. B1.

Rosnow, R. L., & Rosenthal, R. (1997). *Turn away influences that undermine scientific experiments.* New York: Freeman.

Rosnow, R. L., Rotheram-Borus, M. J., Ceci, S. J., Blanck, P. D., & Koocher, G. P. (1993). The institutional review board as a mirror of scientific and ethical standards. *American Psychologist, 48,* 821–826.

Ross, C. A. (1996). *Dissociative identity disorder: Diagnosis, clinical features, and treatment of multiple personality.* Somerset, NJ: Wiley.

Ross, C. A., Miller, S. D., Reagor, P., Bjornson, L., Fraser, G. A., & Anderson, G. (1990). Structured interview data on 102 cases of multiple personality disorder from four centers. *American Journal of Psychiatry, 147,* 596–601.

Ross, L. (1977). The intuitive psychologist and his shortcomings: Distortions in the attribution process. In L. Berkowitz (Ed.), *Advances in experimental social psychology* (Vol. 10, pp. 174–221). New York: Academic Press.

Ross, L., Greene, D., & House, P. (1977). The false consensus effect: An egocentric bias in social perception and attribution processes. *Journal of Experimental Social Psychology, 13,* 279–301.

Ross, L., & Nisbett, R. E. (1991). *The person and the situation.* New York: McGraw-Hill.

Ross, M., & Newby, I. R. (1996). Distinguishing memory from fantasy. *Psychological Inquiry, 7,* 173–177.

Roth, A., & Fonagy, P. (1996). *What works for whom? A critical review of psychotherapy research.* New York: Guilford Press.

Rothblum, E. D. (1990). Women and weight: Fad and fiction. *Journal of Psychology, 124,* 5–24.

Roush, W. (1995, September 1). Can "resetting" hormonal rhythms treat illness? *Science, 269,* 1220–1221.

Routtenberg, A., & Lindy, J. (1965). Effects of the availability of rewarding septal and hypothalamic stimulation on bar pressing for food under conditions of deprivation. *Journal of Comparative and Physiological Psychology, 60,* 158–161.

Rovee-Collier, C. (1993). The capacity for long-term memory in infancy. *Current Directions in Psychological Science, 2,* 130–135.

Rowe, J. B., Toni, I., Josephs, O., Frackowiak, R. S. J., & Passingham, R. E. (2000, June 2). The prefrontal cortex: Response selection or maintenance within working memory? *Science, 288,* 1656–1660.

Rowley, S. J., Sellers, R. M., Chavous, T. M., & Smith, M. A. (1998). The relationship between racial identity and self-esteem in African American college and high school students. *Journal of Personality and Social Psychology, 74,* 715–724.

Rozin, P. (1977). The significance of learning mechanisms in food selection: Some biology, psychology and sociology of science. In L. M. Barker, M. R. Best, & M. Donijan (Eds.), *Learning mechanisms in food selection.* Waco, TX: Baylor University Press.

Rozin, P. (1990). The importance of social factors in understanding the acquisition of food habits. In E. D. Capaldi & T. L. Powley (Eds.), *Taste, experience, and feeding.* Washington, DC: American Psychological Association.

Rubenstein, C. (1982, July). Psychology's fruit flies. *Psychology Today,* pp. 83–84.

Rubin, D. C. (1985, September). The subtle deceiver: Recalling our past. *Psychology Today,* pp. 39–46.

Rubin, D. C. (1995). *Memory in oral traditions.* New York: Oxford University Press.

Rubin, D. C. (1999). *Remembering our past: Studies in autobiographical memory.* New York: Cambridge University Press.

Ruble, D. N., Fleming, A. S., Hackel, L. S., & Stangor, C. (1988). Changes in the marital relationship during the transition to first-time motherhood: Effects of violated expectations concerning division of household labor. *Journal of Personality and Social Psychology, 55,* 78–87.

Runco, M. A. (1991). *Divergent thinking.* Norwood, NJ: Ablex.

Runco, M. A., & Sakamoto, S. O. (1993). Reaching creatively gifted students through their learning styles. In R. M. Milgram, R. S. Dunn, & G. E. Price (Eds.), *Teaching and counseling gifted and talented adolescents: An international learning style perspective.* Westport, CT: Praeger/Greenwood.

Ruppin, E., Reggia, J. A., & Horn, D. (1996). Pathogenesis of schizophrenic delusions and hallucinations: A neural model. *Schizophrenia Bulletin, 22,* 105–123.

Russell, J. A. (1991). Culture and the categorization of emotion. *Psychological Bulletin, 110,* 426–450.

Russell, J. A., & Sato, K. (1995). Comparing emotion words between languages. *Journal of Cross Cultural Psychology, 26,* 384–391.

Russo, N. (1981). In L. T. Benjamin, Jr., & K. D. Lowman (Eds.), *Activities handbook for the teaching of psychology.* Washington, DC: American Psychological Association.

Russo, R., & Parkin, A. J. (1993). Age differences in implicit memory: More apparent than real. *Memory & Cognition, 21,* 73–80.

Ryan, R. M., & Deci, E. L. (1996). When paradigms clash: Comments on Cameron and Pierce's claim that rewards do not undermine intrinsic motivation. *Review of Educational Research, 66,* 33–38.

Rychlak, J. (1997). *In defense of human consciousness.* Washington, DC: American Psychological Association.

Saarni, C. (1999). *The development of emotional competence.* New York: Guilford Press.

Sacco, W. P., & Beck, A. T. (1995). Cognitive theory and therapy. In E. E. Beckham & W. R. Leber (Eds.), *Handbook of depression* (2nd ed.). New York: Guilford Press.

Sack, R. L., Lewy, A. J., White, D. M., Singer, C. M., Fireman, M. J., & Vandiver, R. (1990). Morning vs. evening light treatment for winter depression: Evidence that the therapeutic effects of light are mediated by circadian phase shift. *Archives of General Psychiatry, 47,* 343–351.

Sackett, P. R., & Wilk, S. L. (1994). Within-group norming and other forms of score adjustment in preemployment testing. *American Psychologist, 49,* 929–954.

Sackheim, H. A., Luber, B., Katzman, G. P., et al. (1996, September). The effects of electroconvulsive therapy on quantitative electroencephalograms. *Archives of General Psychiatry, 53,* 814–824.

Sadker, M., & Sadker, D. (1994). *Failing at fairness: How America's schools cheat girls.* New York: Scribners.

Saggino, A. (2000). The Big Three or the Big Five? A replication study. *Personality and Individual Differences, 28,* 879–886.

Saigh, P. A. (1996). Posttraumatic stress disorder among children and adolescents: An introduction. *Journal of School Psychology, 34,* 103–105.

Salovey, P., Rothman, A. J., Detweiler, J. B., & Steward, W. T. (2000). Emotional states and physical health. *American Psychologist, 55,* 110–121.

Salovey, P., & Sluyter, D. J. (Eds.). (1997). *Emotional development and emotional intelligence.* New York: Basic Books.

Salthouse, T. A. (1996, July). The processing-speed theory of adult age differences in cognition. *Psychological Review, 103,* 403–428.

Sams, M., Hari, R., Rif, J., & Knuutila, J. (1993). The human auditory memory trace persists about 10 sec: Neuromagnetic evidence. *Journal of Cognitive Neuroscience, 5,* 363–370.

Samuda, R. J. (1998). *Psychological testing of American minorities: Issues and consequences.* Thousand Oaks, CA: Sage.

Sandoval, J., Frisby, C. L., Geisinger, K. F., Scheuneman, J. D., & Grenier, J. R. (Eds.). (1998). *Test interpretation and diversity: Achieving equity in assessment.* Washington, DC: American Psychological Association.

Sanes, J. N., Donoghue, J. P., Thangaraj, V., Edelman, R. R., & Warach, S. (1995, June 23). Shared neural substrates controlling hand movements in human motor cortex. *Science, 268,* 1775–1777.

Sangrador, J. L., & Yela, C. (2000). "What is beautiful is loved": Physical attractiveness in love relationships in a representative sample. *Social Behavior and Personality, 28,* 207–218.

Sansone, C., & Harackiewicz, J. M. (Eds.). (2000). *Intrinsic and extrinsic motivation.* Orlando, FL: Academic Press.

Sanz, C. (2000). Bilingual education enhances third language acquisition: Evidence from Catalonia. *Applied Psycholinguistics, 21,* 33–44.

Sapolsky, R. M. (1996, August 9). Why stress is bad for your brain. *Science, 273,* 749–750.

Saudino, K. J. (1997). Moving beyond the heritability question: New directions in behavioral genetic studies of personality. *Current Directions in Psychological Science, 6,* 86–90.

Saudino, K. J., & Plomin, R. (1996). Personality and behavioral genetics: Where have we been and where are we going? *Journal of Research in Personality, 30,* 335–347.

Savage-Rumbaugh, E. S., Murphy, J., Sevcik, R. A., Williams, S., Brakke, K., & Rumbaugh, D. M. (1993). Language comprehension in ape and child. *Monographs of the Society for Research in Child Development, 58* (3, 4).

Savage-Rumbaugh, S., & Brakke, K. E. (1996). Animal language: Methodological and interpretive issues. In M. Bekoff & D. Jamieson (Eds.), *Readings in animal cognition.* Cambridge, MA: MIT Press.

Saxe, L. (1994). Detection of deception: Polygraphy and integrity tests. *Current Directions in Psychological Science, 3,* 69–73.

Sayette, M. A. (1993). An appraisal disruption model of alcohol's effects on stress responses in social drinkers. *Psychological Bulletin, 114,* 459–476.

Saywitz, K., & Goodman, G. (1990). [Unpublished study reported in D. Goleman (1990,

November 6). Doubts rise on children as witnesses. *New York Times,* pp. C1, C6.]

Scarr, S. (1992). Developmental theories for the 1990s: Development and individual differences. *Child Development, 63,* 1–19.

Scarr, S. (1993). Genes, experience, and development. In D. Magnusson, P. Jules, & M. Casaer (Eds.), *Longitudinal research on individual development: Present status and future perspectives.* Cambridge, England: Cambridge University Press.

Scarr, S. (1996). Behavior genetics and social-ization theories of intelligence: Truce and reconciliation. In R. J. Sternberg & E. Grigorenko (Eds.), *Intelligence, heredity, and environment.* New York: Cambridge University Press.

Scarr, S., & Weinberg, R. A. (1976). I.Q. test performance of black children adopted by white families. *American Psychologist, 31,* 726–739.

Schab, F. R. (1991). Odor memory: Taking stock. *Psychological Bulletin, 109,* 242–251.

Schab, F. R., & Crowder, R. G. (Eds.). (1995). *Memory for odors.* Mahwah, NJ: Erlbaum.

Schacter, D. L. (1994). Implicit knowledge: New perspectives on unconscious processes. In O. Sporns & G. Tononi (Eds.), *Selectionism and the brain. International review of neurobiology, Vol. 37.* San Diego: Academic Press.

Schacter, D. L. (1995). Implicit memory: A new frontier for cognitive neuroscience. In M. S. Gazzaniga (Ed.), *The cognitive neurosciences.* Cambridge, MA: MIT Press.

Schacter, D. L. (1998, April 3). Memory and awareness. *Science, 280,* 59–60.

Schacter, D. L., Chiu, C.-Y. P., & Ochsner, K. N. (1993). Implicit memory: A selective review. *Annual Review of Neuroscience, 16,* 159–182.

Schacter, D. L., Wagner, A. D., & Buckner, R. L. (2000). Memory systems of 1999. In E. Tulving, F. I. Craik, I. M. Fergus, et al. (Eds.). *The Oxford handbook of memory.* New York: Oxford University Press.

Schachter, S. (1971). Some extraordinary facts about obese humans and rats. *American Psychologist, 26,* 129–144.

Schachter, S., & Singer, J. E. (1962). Cognitive, social, and physiological determinants of emotional state. *Psychological Review, 69,* 379–399.

Schafer, M., & Crichlow, S. (1996). Antecedents of groupthink: A quantitative study. *Journal of Conflict Resolution, 40,* 415–435.

Schaie, K. W. (1991). Developmental designs revisited. In S. H. Cohen & H. W. Reese (Eds.), *Life-span developmental psychology: Methodological innovations.* Hillsdale, NJ: Erlbaum.

Schaie, K. W. (1993). The Seattle longitudinal studies of adult intelligence. *Current Directions in Psychological Science, 2,* 171–175.

Schaie, K. W. (1994). The course of adult intellectual development. *American Psychologist, 49,* 304–313.

Schaller, M., Asp, C. H., Rosell, M. C., & Heim, S. J. (1996). Training in statistical reasoning inhibits the formation of erroneous group stereotypes. *Personality and Social Psychology Bulletin, 22,* 829–844.

Schapira, A. H. V. (1999). Clinical review: Parkinson's disease. *British Medical Journal, 318,* 311–314.

Scharf, M. (1999, October 1). A new option for insomnia. *HealthNews,* p. 4.

Schatz, R. T., & Fiske, S. T. (1992). International reactions to the threat of nuclear war: The rise and fall of concern in the eighties. *Political Psychology, 13,* 1–29.

Schedlowski, M., & Tewes, U. (Eds.) (1999). *Psychoneuroimmunology: An interdisciplinary introduction.* New York: Plenum Press.

Scheff, T. J. (1999). *Being mentally ill: A sociological theory* (3rd ed.). Hawthrone, NY: Aldine de Gruyter.

Scheier, M. F., & Carver, C. S. (1992). Effects of optimism on psychological and physical well-being: Theoretical overview and empirical update. [Special issue: Cognitive perspectives in health psychology.] *Cognitive Therapy and Research, 16,* 201–228.

Scherer, K. R. (1984). Les motions: Fonctions et composantes. [Emotions: Functions and components.] *Cahiers de psychologie cognitive, 4,* 9–39.

Scherer, K. R. (1994). Emotion serves to decouple stimulus and response. In P. Ekman & R. J. Davidson (Eds.), *The nature of emotion: Fundamental questions.* New York: Oxford University Press.

Scherer, K. R., & Wallbott, H. G. (1994). Evidence for universality and cultural variation of differential emotion response patterning. *Journal of Personality and Social Psychology, 66,* 310–328.

Schkade, D. A., & Kahneman, D. (1998). Does living in California make people happy? A focusing illusion in judgments of life satisfaction. *Psychological Science, 9,* 340–346.

Schmidt, D. (1999). Stretched dream science: The essential contribution of long-term naturalistic studies. *Dreaming, 9,* 43–69.

Schmolck, H., Buffalo, E. A., & Squire, L. R. (2000). Memory distortions develop over time: Recollections of the O. J. Simpson trial verdict after 15 and 32 months. *Psychological Science, 11,* 39–45.

Schneider, E. L., & Rowe, J. W. (Eds.). (1996). *Handbook of the biology of aging* (4th ed.). San Diego: Academic Press.

Schneider, K. S. (1996, June 3). Mission impossible. *People,* pp. 65–74.

Schneider, K. S., & Gold, T. (1998, December 7). After the tears. *People,* pp. 126–136.

Schneider, W., Gruber, H., Gold, A., & Opwis, K. (1993). Chess expertise and memory for chess positions in children and adults. *Journal of Experimental Child Psychology, 56,* 328–349.

Schneidman, E. S. (1987). A psychological approach to suicide. In G. R. VandenBos & B. K. Bryant (Eds.), *Cataclysms, crises, and catastrophes: Psychology in action.* Washington, DC: American Psychological Association.

Schoen, L. M. (1996). Mnemopoly: Board games and mnemonics. *Teaching of Psychology, 23,* 30–32.

Schofield, W., & Vaughan-Jackson, P. (1913). *What a boy should know.* New York: Cassell.

Schretlen, D., Pearlson, G. D., Anthony, J. C., Aylward, E. H., Augustine, A. M., Davis, A., & Barta, P. (2000). Elucidating the contributions of processing speed, executive ability, and frontal lobe volume to normal age-related differences in fluid intelligence. *Journal of the International Neuropsychological Society, 6,* 52–61.

Schulman, M. (1991). *The passionate mind: Bringing up an intelligent and creative child.* New York: Free Press.

Schulman, M., & Mekler, E. (1994). *Bringing up a moral child.* New York: Morrow.

Schwartz, M. S., & Schwartz, N. M. (1993). Biofeedback: Using the body's signals. In D. Goleman & J. Gurin (Eds.), *Mind-body medicine.* Yonkers, NY: Consumer Reports Books.

Schwartzberg, N. S., & Dytell, R. S. (1996). Dual-earner families: The importance of work stress and family stress for psychological well-being. *Journal of Occupational Health Psychology, 1,* 211–223.

Schwarz, N. (1999). Self-reports: How the questions shape the answers. *American Psychologist, 54,* 93–105.

Schwarz, N., Bless, H., Strack, F., Klumpp, G., et al. (1991). Ease of retrieval as information: Another look at the availability heuristic. *Journal of Personality and Social Psychology, 61,* 195–202.

Searleman, A., & Herrmann, D. (1994). *Memory from a broader perspective.* New York: McGraw-Hill.

Sears, D. O. (1986). College sophomores in the laboratory: Influences of a narrow data base on social psychology's view of human nature. *Journal of Personality and Social Psychology, 51,* 515–530.

Sears, R. R. (1977). Sources of life satisfaction of the Terman gifted men. *American Psychologist, 32,* 119–128.

Sebel, P. S., Bonke, B., & Winograd, E. (Eds.). (1993). *Memory and awareness in anesthesia.* Englewood Cliffs, NJ: Prentice Hall.

Seeman, P. (1993). Schizophrenia as a brain disease: The dopamine receptor story. *Archives of Neurology, 50,* 1093–1095.

Segal, N. L. (1993). Twin, sibling, and adoption methods: Tests of evolutionary hypotheses. *American Psychologist, 48,* 943–956.

Segall, M. H., Campbell, D. T., & Herskovits, M. J. (1966). *The influence of culture on visual perception.* New York: Bobbs-Merrill.

Seidenberg, M. S., & Pettitto, L. A. (1987). Communication, symbolic communication, and language: Comment on Savage-Rumbaugh, McDonald, Sevcik, Hopkins, & Rupert (1986). *Journal of Experimental Psychology: General, 116,* 279–287.

Seligman, L. (1995). *Promoting a fighting spirit: Psychotherapy for cancer patients, survivors, and their families.* San Francisco: Jossey-Bass.

Seligman, M. E. P. (1975). *Helplessness: On depression, development, and death.* San Francisco: Freeman.

Seligman, M. E. P. (1995, December). The effectiveness of psychotherapy: The *Consumer Reports* study. *American Psychologist, 50,* 965–974.

Seligman, M. E. P. (1996, October). Science as an ally of practice. *American Psychologist, 51,* 1072–1079.

Selikowitz, M. (1997). *Down syndrome: The facts* (2nd ed.). New York: Oxford University Press.

Selkoe, D. J. (1997, January 31). Alzheimer's disease: Genotypes, phenotype, and treatments. *Science, 275,* 630–631.

Sells, R. (1994, August). *Homosexuality study.* Paper presented at the annual meeting of the American Statistical Association, Toronto.

Selsky, A. (1997, February 16). African males face circumcision rite. *Boston Globe,* p. C7.

Seltzer, L. (1986). *Paradoxical strategies in psychotherapy.* New York: Wiley.

Selye, H. (1976). *The stress of life.* New York: McGraw-Hill.

Selye, H. (1993). History of the stress concept. In L. Goldberger & S. Breznitz (Eds.), *Handbook of stress: Theoretical and clinical aspects* (2nd ed.). New York: Free Press.

Seppa, N. (1996, May). A multicultural guide to less spanking and yelling. *APA Monitor,* p. 37.

Seppa, N. (1997, June). Children's TV remains steeped in violence. *APA Monitor,* p. 36.

Serok, S. (2000). *Innovative applications of gestalt therapy.* New York: Krieger.

Sesser, S. (1993, September 13). Opium war redux. *New Yorker,* pp. 78–89.

Seyfarth, R. M., & Cheney, D. L. (1992, December). Meaning and mind in monkeys (vocalizations and intent). *Scientific American, 267,* 122–128.

Seyfarth, R. M., & Cheney, D. L. (1996). Inside the mind of a monkey. In M. Bekoff & D. Jamieson (Eds.), *Readings in animal cognition.* Cambridge, MA: MIT Press.

Shadish, W. R., Cook, T. D., & Campbell, D. T. (2002). *Experimental and quasi-experimental designs for generalized causal inference.* New York: Houghton Mifflin.

Shapiro, A. P. (1996). *Hypertension and stress: A unified concept.* Mahwah, NJ: Erlbaum.

Shapiro, Y., & Gabbard, G. O. (1994). A reconsideration of altruism from an evolutionary and psychodynamic perspective. *Ethics and Behavior, 4,* 23–42.

Sharma, J., Angelucci, A., & Sur, M. (2000). Induction of visual orientation modules in auditory cortex. *Nature, 404,* 841–847.

Sharma, S., Ghosh, S. N., & Spielberger, C. D. (1995). Anxiety, anger expression and chronic gastric ulcer. *Psychological Studies, 40,* 187–191.

Sharps, M. J., Price, J. L., & Williams, J. K. (1994). Spatial cognition and gender: Instructional and stimulus influences on mental image rotation performance. *Psychology of Women Quarterly, 18,* 413–425.

Shatz, C. J. (1992, September). The developing brain. *Scientific American,* pp. 60–67.

Shaughnessy, J. J., Zechmeister, E. B., & Zechmeister, J. S. (2000). *Research methods in psychology* (5th ed.). New York: McGraw-Hill.

Shawver, L. (1995). *And the flag was still there: Straight people, gay people, and sexuality in the U.S. military.* New York: Harrington Park Press/Haworth Press.

Shaywitz, B. A., Shaywitz, S. E., Pugh, K. R., Constable, R. T., et al. (1995). Sex differences in the functional organization of the brain for language. *Nature, 373,* 607–609.

Shea, C. (1996a, January 12). New students uncertain about racial preferences. *Chronicle of Higher Education,* p. A33.

Shea, C. (1996b, September 27). Researchers try to understand why people are doing better on IQ tests. *Chronicle of Higher Education,* p. A18.

Shear, J. (Ed.). (1997). *Explaining consciousness: The hard problem.* Cambridge, MA: MIT Press.

Sheehan, S. (1982). *Is there no place on earth for me?* Boston: Houghton Mifflin.

Shelton, R. C., Keller, M. B., Gelenberg, A., Dunner, D. L., Hirschfeld, R., Thase, M. E., Russell, J., Lydiard, B., Crits-Cristoph, P., Gallop, R., Todd, L., Hellerstein, D., Goodnick, P., Keitner, G., Stahl, S. M., & Halbreich, U. (2001, April 18). Effectiveness of St. John's Wort in major depression. *Journal of the American Medical Association, 285,* 1978–1986.

Shepard, R., & Metzler, J. (1971). Mental rotation of three dimensional objects. *Science, 171*, 701–703.

Shepard, R. N., Metzler, J., Bisiach, E., Luzzati, C., Kosslyn, S. M., Thompson, W. L., Kim, I., & Alpert, N. M. (2000). Part IV: Imagery. In M. S. Gazzaniga et al. (Eds.), *Cognitive neuroscience: A reader.* Malden, MA: Blackwell.

Sherman, J. W., & Klein, S. B. (1994). Development and representation of personality impressions. *Journal of Personality and Social Psychology, 67*, 972–983.

Sherman, M. (1999, July 13). The man who vanished into his past. *New York Times,* p. F8.

Shiels, P. G., Kind, A. J., Campbell, K. H., Waddington, D., Wilmut, I., Colman, A., & Schnieke, A. E. (1999, May 27). Analysis of telomere lengths in cloned sheep [letter]. *Nature, 399*, 316–317.

Shier, D., Butler, J., & Lewis, R. (2000). *Hole's essentials of human anatomy and physiology* (7th ed.). New York: McGraw-Hill.

Shnek, Z. M., Foley, F. W., LaRocca, N. G., Smith, C. R., et al. (1995). Psychological predictors of depression in multiple sclerosis. *Journal of Neurologic Rehabilitation, 9*, 15–23.

Shotland, R. L. (1985, June). When bystanders just stand by. *Psychology Today,* pp. 50–55.

Shoulder, K. (1992, August). The empire returns. *Sky,* pp. 40–44.

Shrique, C. L., & Annable, L. (1995). Tardive dyskinesia. In C. L. Shriqui & H. A. Nasrallah (Eds.), *Contemporary issues in the treatment of schizophrenia.* Washington, DC: American Psychiatric Press.

Shuchter, S. R., Downs, N., & Zisook, S. (1996). *Biologically informed psychotherapy for depression.* New York: Guilford Press.

Shultz, S. K., Scherman, A., & Marshall, L. J. (2000). Evaluation of a university-based date rape prevention program: Effect on attitudes and behavior related to rape. *Journal of College Student Development, 41*, 193–201.

Shurkin, J. N. (1992). *Terman's kids: The groundbreaking study of how the gifted grow up.* Boston: Little, Brown.

Shweder, R. A. (1994). "You're not sick, you're just in love": Emotion as an interpretive system. In P. Ekman & R. J. Davidson (Eds.), *The nature of emotion: Fundamental questions.* New York: Oxford University Press.

Sibicky, M. E., Schroeder, D. A., & Dovidio, J. F. (1995). Empathy and helping: Considering the consequences of intervention. *Basic and Applied Social Psychology, 16*, 435–453.

Siegel, B. (1996a). Is the emperor wearing clothes? Social policy and the empirical support for full inclusion of children with disabilities in the preschool and early elementary grades. *Social Policy Report, 10*, pp. 2–17.

Siegel, B. (1996b). *The world of the autistic child: Understanding and treating autistic spectrum disorders.* New York: Oxford University Press.

Siegel, J. M. (1990). Stressful life events and use of physician services among the elderly: The moderating role of pet ownership. *Journal of Personality and Social Psychology, 58*, 1081–1086.

Siegel, J. M. (1993). Companion animals: In sickness and in health. *Journal of Social Issues, 49*, 157–167.

Siegel, J. M. (2000, January). Narcolepsy. *Scientific American,* pp. 76–81.

Siegel, R. K. (1989). *Life in pursuit of artificial paradise.* New York: Dutton.

Siegler, R. S. (1994). Cognitive variability: A key to understanding cognitive development. *Current Directions in Psychological Science, 3*, 1–5.

Siegler, R. S. (1998). *Children's thinking* (3rd ed.). Upper Saddle River, NJ: Prentice Hall.

Sigman, M. (1995). Nutrition and child development: More food for thought. *Current Directions in Psychological Science, 4*, 52–55.

Silver, L. B. (1999). *Attention-deficit/hyperactivity disorder: A clinical guide to diagnosis and treatment for health and mental health professionals.* Washington, DC: American Psychiatric Press.

Silver, R. L., & Wortman, C. B. (1980). Coping with undesirable life events. In J. Barber & M. E. P. Seligman (Eds.), *Human helplessness: Theory and application.* New York: Academic Press.

Silverman, K., Evans, S. M., Strain, E. C., & Griffiths, R. R. (1992, October 15). Withdrawal syndrome after the double-blind cessation of caffeine consumption. *New England Journal of Medicine, 327*, 1109–1114.

Silverman, K., Mumford, G. K., & Griffiths, R. R. (1994). Enhancing caffeine reinforcement by behavioral requirements following drug ingestion. *Psychopharmacology, 114*, 424–432.

Silverstein, B., Perdue, L., Peterson, B., Vogel, L., et al. (1986). Possible causes of the thin standard of bodily attractiveness for women. *International Journal of Eating Disorders, 5*, 907–916.

Simmons, R., & Blyth, D. (1987). *Moving into adolescence.* New York: Aldine de Gruyter.

Simonoff, E., Bolton, P., & Rutter, M. (1996). Mental retardation: Genetic findings, clinical implications and research agenda. *Journal of Child Psychology and Psychiatry and Allied Disciplines, 37*, 259–280.

Simpson, G. E., & Yinger, J. M. (1985). *Racial and cultural minorities: An analysis of prejudice and discrimination* (5th ed.). New York: Harper & Row.

Simpson, J. A., & Harris, B. A. (1994). Interpersonal attraction. In A. L. Weber & J. H. Harvey (Eds.), *Perspectives on close relationships.* Boston: Allyn & Bacon.

Sinclair, J. D. (1990). Drugs to decrease alcohol drinking. *Annals of Medicine, 22*, 357–362.

Singelis, T., Choo, P., & Hatfield, E. (1995). Love schemas and romantic love. *Journal of Social Behavior and Personality, 10*, 15–36.

Singer, J. L. (1975). *The inner world of daydreaming.* New York: Harper & Row.

Sizemore, C. C. (1989). *A mind of my own: The woman who was known as Eve tells the story of her triumph over multiple personality disorder.* New York: Morrow.

Skinner, B. F. (1957). *Verbal behavior.* New York: Appleton-Century-Crofts.

Skinner, B. F. (1975). The steep and thorny road to a science of behavior. *American Psychologist, 30*, 42–49.

Slater, A. (1996). The organization of visual perception in early infancy. In F. Vital-Durand, J. Atkinson, & O. J. Braddick (Eds.), *Infant vision.* Oxford, England: Oxford University Press.

Slater, A., Mattock, A., & Brown, E. (1990). Size constancy at birth: Newborn infants' responses to retinal and real size, *Journal of Experimental Child Psychology, 49*, 314–322.

Slater, E., & Meyer, A. (1959). Contributions to a pathography of the musicians. *Confinia Psychiatrica.* Reprinted in K. R. Jamison,

Touched with fire: Manic-depressive illness and the artistic temperament. New York: Free Press.

Sleek, S. (1995, November). Online therapy services raise ethical question. *APA Monitor,* p. 9.

Sleek, S. (1997, June). Can "emotional intelligence" be taught in today's schools? *APA Monitor,* p. 25.

Sleek, S. (1998, June). Psychologists debate merits of the polygraph. *APA Monitor,* p. 30.

Sloan, E. P., Hauri, P., Bootzin, R., Morin, C., et al. (1993). The nuts and bolts of behavioral therapy for insomnia. *Journal of Psychosomatic Research, 37* (Suppl), 19–37.

Slovic, P., Fischoff, B., & Lichenstein, S. (1976). Cognitive processes and societal risk taking. In J. S. Carroll & J. W. Payne (Eds.), *Cognition and social behavior.* Mahwah, NJ: Erlbaum.

Smith, E. (1988, May). Fighting cancerous feelings. *Psychology Today,* pp. 22–23.

Smith, E. E. (2000). Neural bases of human working memory. *Current Directions in Psychological Science, 9*, 45–49.

Smith, E. E., & Jonides, J. (1999, March 12). Storage and executive processes in the frontal lobes. *Science, 283*, 1657–1661.

Smith, K. A., Williams, C., & Cowen, P. J. (2000). Impaired regulation of brain serotonin function during dieting in women recovered from depression. *British Journal of Psychiatry, 176*, 72–75.

Smith, M. L., Glass, G. V., & Miller, T. J. (1980). *The benefits of psychotherapy.* Baltimore: Johns Hopkins.

Smith, M. V. (1996). Linguistic relativity: On hypotheses and confusions. *Communication and Cognition, 29*, 65–90.

Smith, M., & Lin, K. M. (1996). Gender and ethnic differences in the pharmacogenetics of psychotropics. In M. F. Jensvold, U. Halbreich, & J. A. Hamilton, (Eds.), *Psychopharmacology and women: Sex, gender, and hormones.* Washington, DC: American Psychiatric Press.

Smith, S. M. (1994). Frustrated feelings of imminent recall: On the tip of the tongue. In J. Metcalfe & A. P. Shimamura (Eds.), *Metacognition: Knowing about knowing.* Cambridge, MA: MIT Press.

Smock, P. J. (2000). Cohabitation in the United States: An appraisal of research themes, findings, and implications. *Annual Review of Sociology, 26*, 1–20.

Snyder, C. R. (1999). *Coping: The psychology of what works.* New York: Oxford University Press.

Snyder, F. (1970). The phenomenology of dreaming. In L. Madow & L. H. Snow (Eds.), *The psychodynamic implications of the physiological studies on dreams.* Springfield, IL: Thomas.

Social Health Association. (1998). *Estimates of the numbers of new cases annually of sexually transmitted diseases in the United States.* Paper prepared for the Kaiser Family Foundation of America by the American Social Health Association.

Sohn, D. (1996). Publication bias and the evaluation of psychotherapy efficacy in reviews of the research literature. *Clinical Psychology Review, 16*, 147–156.

Solcova, I., & Tomanek, P. (1994). Daily stress coping strategies: An effect of hardiness. *Studia Psychologica, 36*, 390–392.

Solomon, C. (1993, December 21). Having nightmares? Chances are, they are about your job. *Wall Street Journal,* pp. A1, A4.

Solso, R. L. (1991). *Cognitive psychology* (3rd ed.). Boston: Allyn & Bacon.

Sommer, B. B., & Sommer, R. (1997). *A practical guide to behavioral research: Tools and techniques* (4th ed.). New York: Oxford University Press.

Sommerhof, G. (2000). *Understanding consciousness: Its function and brain processes*. Thousand Oaks, CA: Sage.

Sorenson, S. B., & Siegel, J. M. (1992). Gender, ethnicity, and sexual assault: Findings from a Los Angeles study. *Journal of Social Issues, 48*, 93–104.

Sorrentino, R. M., Hewitt, E. C., & Raso-Knott, P. A. (1992). Risk-taking in games of chance and skill: Informational and affective influences on choice behavior. *Journal of Personality and Social Psychology, 62*, 522–533.

Spangler, W. D. (1992). Validity of questionnaire and TAT measures of need for achievement: Two meta-analyses. *Psychological Bulletin, 112*, 140–154.

Spanos, N. P., Burgess, C. A., Roncon, V., Wallace-Capretta, S., et al. (1993). Surreptitiously observed hypnotic responding in simulators and in skill-trained and untrained high hypnotizables. *Journal of Personality and Social Psychology, 65*, 391–398.

Spearman, C. (1927). *The abilities of man*. London: Macmillan.

Spence, J. T. (1985, August). *Achievement American style: The rewards and costs of individualism*. Presidential address, 93rd annual convention of the American Psychological Association, Los Angeles.

Spence, M. J., & DeCasper, A. J. (1982, March). *Human fetuses perceive maternal speech*. Paper presented at the meeting of the International Conference on Infant Studies, Austin, TX.

Sperling, G. (1960). The information available in brief visual presentation. *Psychology Monographs, 74* (whole no. 498).

Sperry, R. (1982). Some effects of disconnecting the cerebral hemispheres. *Science, 217*, 1223–1226.

Spiegel, D. (1993). Social support: How friends, family, and groups can help. In D. Goleman & J. Gurin (Eds.), *Mind-body medicine*. Yonkers, NY: Consumer Reports Books.

Spiegel, D. (1996a, July). Cancer and depression. *British Journal of Psychiatry, 168*, 109–116.

Spiegel, D. (1996b). Dissociative disorders. In R. E. Hales & S. C. Yudofsky (Eds.), *The American Psychiatric Press synopsis of psychiatry*. Washington, DC: American Psychiatric Press, Inc.

Spiegel, D. (1996c). Hypnosis. In R. E. Hales & S. C. Yudofsky (Eds.), *The American Psychiatric Press synopsis of psychiatry*. Washington, DC: American Psychiatric Press.

Spiegel, D. (Ed.). (1999). *Efficacy and cost-effectiveness of psychotherapy*. New York: American Psychiatric Press.

Spiegel, D., & Cardena, E. (1991). Disintegrated experience: The dissociative disorders revisited. *Journal of Abnormal Psychology, 100*, 366–378.

Spiegel, D., Frischholz, E. J., Fleiss, J. L., & Spiegel, H. (1993). Predictors of smoking abstinence following a single-session restructuring intervention with self-hypnosis. *American Journal of Psychiatry, 150*, 1090–1097.

Spiegel, R. (1989). *Psychopharmacology: An introduction*. New York: Wiley.

Spielman, D. A., & Staub, E. (2000). Reducing boys' aggression: Learning to fulfill basic needs constructively. *Journal of Applied Developmental Psychology, 21*, 165–181.

Spillmann, L., & Werner, J. (Eds.). (1990). *Visual perception: The neurophysiological foundations*. San Diego: Academic Press.

Spira, J. (Ed.). (1997). *Group therapy for medically ill patients*. New York: Guilford Press.

Spitz, H. H. (1987). Problem-solving processes in special populations. In J. G. Borkowski & J. D. Day (Eds.), *Cognition in special children: Comparative approaches to retardation, learning disabilities, and giftedness*. Norwood, NJ: Ablex.

Spitzer, R. L., Skodol, A. E., Gibbon, M., & Williams, J. B. W. (1983). *Psychopathology: A case book*. New York: McGraw-Hill.

Sprecher, S., & Hatfield, E. (1996). Premarital sexual standards among U.S. college students: Comparison with Russian and Japanese students. *Archives of Sexual Behavior, 25*, 261–288.

Sprecher, S., & McKinney, K. (1993). *Sexuality*. Newbury Park, CA: Sage.

Sprenkle, D. H., & Moon, S. M. (Eds.). (1996). *Research methods in family therapy*. New York: Guilford Press.

Squire, L. R. (1993). The hippocampus and spatial memory. *Trends in Neurosciences, 6*, 56–57.

St. Onge, S. (1995a). Modeling and role-playing. In M. Ballou (Ed.), *Psychological interventions: A guide to strategies*. Westport, CT: Praeger/Greenwood.

St. Onge, S. (1995b). Systematic desensitization. In M. Ballou (Ed.), *Psychological interventions: A guide to strategies*. Westport, CT: Praeger/Greenwood.

Stake, R. E. (1995). *The art of case study research*. Newbury Park, CA: Sage.

Stanton, A. L., & Franz, R. (1999). Focusing on emotions: An adaptive coping strategy? In C. R. Snyder (Ed.), *Coping: The psychology of what works*. New York: Oxford University Press.

Stanton, H. E. (1994). Sports imagery and hypnosis: A potent mix. *Australian Journal of Clinical and Experimental Hypnosis, 22*, 119–124.

Statistical Office of the European Communities. (1998). *Marriage statistics*. Paris: Author.

Staub, E. (1996). Cultural-societal roots of violence. *American Psychologist, 51*, 117–132.

Staudinger, U. M., Fleeson, W., & Baltes, P. B. (1999). Predictors of subjective physical health and global well-being: Similarities and differences between the United States and Germany. *Journal of Personality and Social Psychology, 76*, 305–319.

Steadman, H., McGreevy, M. A., Morrissey, J. P., et al. (1993). *Before and after Hinckley: Evaluating insanity defense reform*. New York: Guilford Press.

Steblay, N. M. (1992). A meta-analytic review of the weapon focus effect. *Law and Human Behavior, 16*, 413–424.

Steele, C. M. (1992, April). Race and the schooling of Black America. *Atlantic Monthly*, pp. 37–53.

Steele, C. M. (1997). A threat in the air: How stereotypes shape intellectual identity and performance. *American Psychologist, 52*, 613–629.

Steele, C. M., & Aronson, J. (1995). Stereotype threat and the intellectual test performance of African Americans. *Journal of Personality and Social Psychology, 69*, 797–811.

Steele, C. M., & Josephs, R. A. (1990). Alcohol myopia: Its prized and dangerous effects. *American Psychologist, 45*, 921–933.

Steele, C. M., & Southwick, L. (1985). Alcohol and social behavior I: The psychology of drunken excess. *Journal of Personality and Social Psychology, 48*, 18–34.

Steen, R. G. (1996). *DNA and destiny: Nature and nurture in human behavior*. New York: Plenum Press.

Steil, J. M., & Hay, J. L. (1997, April). Social comparison in the workplace: A study of 60 dual-career couples. *Personality and Social Psychology Bulletin, 23*, 427–438.

Stein, N. L., Brainerd, C., Ornstein, P. A., & Tversky, B. (Eds.). (1996). *Memory for everyday and emotional events*. Mahwah, NJ: Erlbaum.

Stein, N. L., Ornstein, P. A., Tversky, B., & Brainerd, C. (Eds.). (1997). *Memory for everyday and emotional events*. Mahwah, NJ: Erlbaum.

Steinberg, L. (1989). *Adolescence* (2nd ed.). New York: Knopf.

Steinberg, L. (1993). *Adolescence* (3rd ed.). New York: McGraw-Hill.

Steinberg, L., & Dornbusch, S. (1991). Negative correlates of part-time employment during adolescence: Replication and elaboration. *Developmental Psychology, 27*, 304.

Stern, R. M., & Koch, K. L. (1996). Motion sickness and differential susceptibility. *Current Directions in Psychological Science, 5*, 115–120.

Sternberg, J. (2000, July 21). The holey grail of general intelligence. *Science, 289*, 499–501.

Sternberg, R. J. (1982). Reasoning, problem solving, and intelligence. In R. J. Sternberg (Ed.), *Handbook of human intelligence* (pp. 225–307). New York: Cambridge University Press.

Sternberg, R. J. (1985). Implicit theories of intelligence, creativity, and wisdom. *Journal of Personality and Social Psychology, 49*, 607–627.

Sternberg, R. J. (1986). Triangular theory of love. *Psychological Review, 93*, 119–135.

Sternberg, R. J. (1988). Triangulating love. In R. J. Sternberg & M. J. Barnes (Eds.), *The psychology of love*. New Haven, CT: Yale University Press.

Sternberg, R. J. (1990). *Metaphors of mind: Conceptions of the nature of intelligence*. New York: Cambridge University Press.

Sternberg, R. J. (1995). Theory and measurement of tacit knowledge as a part of practical intelligence. *Zeitschrift für Psychologie, 203*, 319–334.

Sternberg, R. J. (1998). *Successful intelligence: How practical and creative intelligence determine success in life*. New York: Plume.

Sternberg, R. J. (2000). Intelligence and wisdom. In R. J. Sternberg (Ed.), *Handbook of intelligence*. New York: Cambridge University Press.

Sternberg, R. J., & Beall, A. E. (1991). How can we know what love is? An epistemological analysis. In G. J. O. Fletcher & F. D. Fincham (Eds.), *Cognition in close relationships*. Hillsdale, NJ: Erlbaum.

Sternberg, R. J., & Frensch, P. A. (1991). *Complex problem solving: Principles and mechanisms*. Hillsdale, NJ: Erlbaum.

Sternberg, R. J., & Grigorenko, E. (1997). Are cognitive styles still in style? *American Psychologist, 52*, 700–712.

Sternberg, R. J., & O'Hara, L. A. (2000). Intelligence and creativity. In R. J. Sternberg (Ed.), *Handbook of intelligence*. New York: Cambridge University Press.

Stevens, G., & Gardner, S. (1982). *The women of psychology: Pioneers and innovators* (Vol. 1). Cambridge, MA: Schenkman.

Stevenson, H. W. (1992, December). Learning from Asian schools. *Scientific American*, pp. 70–75.

Stevenson, H. W., Chen, C., & Lee, S. Y. (1993). A comparison of the parent-child relationship in Japan and the United States. In J. L. Roopnarine & D. B. Carter (Eds.), *Parent-child socialization in diverse cultures*. Norwood, NJ: Ablex.

Stevenson, H. W., & Lee, S. Y. (1990). Contexts of achievement: A study of American, Chinese, and Japanese children. *Monographs of the Society for Research in Child Development*, no. 221, *55*, nos. 1–2.

Steward, E. P. (1995). *Beginning writers in the zone of proximal development*. Hillsdale, NJ: Erlbaum.

Stewart, D. W., & Kamins, M. A. (1993). *Secondary research: Information sources and methods.* (2nd ed.). Newbury Park, CA: Sage.

Stier, H., & Lewin-Epstein, N. (2000). Women's part-time employment and gender inequality in the family. *Journal of Family Issues, 21*, 390–410.

Stix, G. (1996, January). Listening to culture. *Scientific American*, pp. 16–17.

Stone, J., Lynch, C. I., Sjomeling, M., & Darley, J. M. (1999). Stereotype threat effects on black and white athletic performance. *Journal of Personality and Social Psychology, 77*, 1213–1227.

Stone, R., & Kelner, K. (2000, July 28). Violence: No silver bullet. *Science, 289*, 569.

Strauss, E. (1998, May 8). Writing, speech separated in split brain. *Science, 280*, 827.

Streissguth, A. P., Barr, H. M., Bookstein, F. L., Sampson, P. D., & Olson, H. C. (1999). The long-term neurocognitive consequences of prenatal alcohol exposure: A 14-year study. *Psychological Science, 10*, 186–190.

Strickland, B. R. (1992). Women and depression. *Current Directions in Psychological Science, 1*, 132–135.

Stroebe, M. S., Stroebe, W., & Hansson, R. O. (Eds.). (1993). *Handbook of bereavement: Theory, research, and intervention*. Cambridge, England: Cambridge University Press.

Stroh, L. K., Brett, J. M., & Reilly, A. H. (1996). Family structure, glass ceiling, and traditional explanations for the differential rate of turnover of female and male managers. *Journal of Vocational Behavior, 49*, 99–118.

Strongman, K. T. (1996). *The psychology of emotion: Theories of emotion in perspective* (4th ed.). Chichester, England: Wiley.

Stronski, S. M., Ireland, M., Michaud, P., Narring, F., & Resnick, M. D. (2000). Protective correlates of stages in adolescent substance use: A Swiss national study. *Journal of Adolescent Health, 26*, 420–427.

Strube, M. (Ed.). (1990). Type A behavior [Special issue] *Journal of Social Behavior and Personality, 5*.

Strupp, H. H. (1996, October). The tripartite model and the *Consumer Reports* study. *American Psychologist, 51*, 1017–1024.

Strupp, H. H., & Binder, J. L. (1992). Current developments in psychotherapy. *Independent Practitioner, 12*, 119–124.

Stumpf, H. (1995). Gender differences in performance on tests of cognitive abilities: Experimental design issues and empirical results [Special Issue: Psychological and psychobiological perspectives on sex differences in cognition: I. Theory and research]. *Learning and Individual Differences, 7*, 275–287.

Sue, D. (1979). Erotic fantasies of college students during coitus. *Journal of Sex Research, 15*, 299–305.

Sue, D. W., & Sue, D. (1990). *Counseling the culturally different: Theory and practice* (2nd ed.). New York: Wiley.

Sue, D. W., Sue, D., & Sue, S. (1990). *Understanding abnormal behavior* (3rd ed.). Boston: Houghton-Mifflin.

Sue, S. (1998). In search of cultural competence in psychotherapy and counseling. *American Psychologist, 53*, 440–448.

Suicide. (1996, November). *Harvard Mental Health Letter*, pp. 1–5.

Sullivan, B. (1985). *Double standard.* Paper presented at the annual meeting of the Society for the Scientific Study of Sex, San Diego.

Sulzer-Azaroff, B., & Mayer, R. (1991). *Behavior analysis and lasting change*. New York: Holt.

Sundin, O., Ohman, A., Palm, T., & Strom, G. (1995). Cardiovascular reactivity, Type A behavior, and coronary heart disease: Comparisons between myocardial infarction patients and controls during laboratory-induced stress. *Psychophysiology, 32*, 28–35.

Super, C. M. (1980). Cognitive development: Looking across at growing up. In C. M. Super & S. Harakness (Eds.), *New directions for child development: Anthropological perspectives on child development* (pp. 59–69). San Francisco: Jossey-Bass.

Suzuki, K. (1991). Moon illusion simulated in complete darkness: Planetarium experiment reexamined. *Perception and Psychophysics, 49*, 349–354.

Svarstad, B. (1976). Physician-patient communication and patient conformity with medical advice. In D. Mechanic (Ed.), *The growth of bureaucratic medicine*. New York: Wiley.

Swan, S. W. (1997). Hormone replacement therapy and the risk of reproductive cancers. *Journal of Psychosomatic Obstetrics and Gynecology, 18*, 165–174.

Swets, J. A., & Bjork, R. A. (1990). Enhancing human performance: An evaluation of "new age" techniques considered by the U.S. Army. *Psychological Science, 1*, 85–96.

Swindle, R., Jr., Heller, K., Pescosolido, B., & Kikuzawa, S. (2000). Responses to nervous breakdowns in America over a 40-year period. *American Psychologist, 55*, 740–749.

Szasz, T. S. (1961). *The myth of mental illness.* New York: Harper & Row.

Szasz, T. S. (1994). *Cruel compassion: Psychiatric control of society's unwanted.* New York: Wiley.

Tabakoff, B., & Hoffman, P. L. (1996). Effect of alcohol on neurotransmitters and their receptors and enzymes. In H. Begleiter & B. Kissin (Eds.), *The pharmacology of alcohol and alcohol dependence. Alcohol and alcoholism, No. 2*. New York: Oxford University Press.

Tagiuri, R. (1958). Social preference and its perception. In R. Tagiuri & L. Petrullo (Eds.), *Person, perception, and interpersonal behavior* (pp. 316–336). Stanford, CA: Stanford University Press.

Tajfel, H. (1982). *Social identity and intergroup relations.* London: Cambridge University Press.

Tan, V. L., & Hicks, R. A. (1995). Type A-B behavior and nightmare types among college students. *Perceptual and Motor Skills, 81*, 15–19.

Tandon, R. (1995). Neurobiological substrate of dimensions of schizophrenic illness. *Journal of Psychiatric Research, 29*, 255–260.

Tanford, S., & Penrod, S. (1984). Social influence model: A formal integration of research on majority and minority influence processes. *Psychological Bulletin, 95*, 189–225.

Tanner, J. M. (1978). *Education and physical growth* (2nd ed.). New York: International Universities Press.

Tanner, J. M. (1990). *Foetus into man: Physical growth from conception to maturity (rev. ed.).* Cambridge, MA: Harvard University Press.

Taubes, G. (1998, May 29). Weight increases worldwide? *Science, 280*, 1368.

Tavris, C. (1992). *The mismeasure of woman.* New York: Simon & Schuster.

Taylor, A. (1991, April 8). Can Iacocco fix Chrysler—again? *Fortune*, pp. 50–54.

Taylor, H. (2000, January 29). *Harris Poll #5: Political trends.* New York: Harris Poll Interactive.

Taylor, M. (1996). A theory of mind perspective on social cognitive development. In R. Gelman & T. K-F. Au (Eds.), *Perceptual and cognitive development: Handbook of perception and cognition* (2nd ed.). San Diego: Academic Press.

Taylor, S. E. (1995). Quandary at the crossroads: Paternalism versus advocacy surrounding end-of-treatment decisions. *American Journal of Hospital Palliatory Care, 12*, 43–46.

Taylor, S. E., & Aspinwall, L. G. (1996). Mediating and moderating processes in psychosocial stress: Appraisal, coping, resistance, and vulnerability. In H. B. Kaplan (Ed.), *Psychosocial stress: Perspectives on structure, theory, life-course, and methods.* San Diego: Academic Press.

Tellegen, A., Lykken, D. T., Bouchard, T. J., Jr., Wilcox, K. J., Segal, N. L., & Rich, S. (1988). Personality similarity in twins reared apart and together. *Journal of Personality and Social Psychology, 54*, 1031–1039.

Terman, L. M., & Oden, M. H. (1947). *Genetic studies of genius, IV: The gifted child grows up.* Stanford, CA: Stanford University Press.

Tetlock, P. E., Hoffmann, S., Janis, I. L., Stein, J. G., Kressel, N. J., & Cohen, B. C. (1993). The psychology of international conflict. In N. J. Kressel (Ed.), *Political psychology: Classic and contemporary readings*. New York: Paragon House.

Tetlock, P. E., Peterson, R. S., McGuire, C., Chang, S., & Feld, P. (1992). Assessing political group dynamics: A test of the groupthink model. *Journal of Personality and Social Psychology, 63*, 403–425.

Tharp, R. G. (1989). Psychocultural variables and constants: Effects on teaching and learning in schools. [Special issue: Children and their development: Knowledge base, research agenda, and social policy application.] *American Psychologist, 44*, 349–359.

'tHart, P. (1991). Groupthink, risk-taking and recklessness: Quality of process and outcome in policy decision making. *Politics and the Individual, 1*, 67–90.

Thombs, D. L. (1999). *Introduction to addictive behaviors* (2nd ed.). New York: Guilford Press.

Thomson, A.M. (1997, January 10). More than just frequency detectors? *Science, 275*, 179–180.

Thorndike, E. L. (1932). *The fundamentals of learning.* New York: Teachers College Press.

Thorndike, R. L., Hagen, E., & Sattler, J. (1986). *Stanford-Binet* (4th ed.). Chicago: Riverside Press.

Thune, I., Brenn, T., Lund, E., & Gaard, M. (1997, May 1). Physical activity and the risk of breast cancer. *New England Journal of Medicine, 336*, 1269–1275.

Thurstone, L. L. (1938). *Primary mental abilities.* Chicago: University of Chicago Press.

Tolman, E. C., & Honzik, C. H. (1930). Introduction and removal of reward and maze performance in rats. *University of California Publications in Psychology, 4*, 257–275.

Tomasello, M. (2000). Culture and cognitive development. *Current Directions in Psychological Science, 9*, 37–40.

Tomes, H. (1998, December). Diversity: Psychology's life depends on it. *APA Monitor*, p. 28.

Torrey, E. F. (1996). *Out of the shadows: Confronting America's mental illness crisis.* New York: Wiley.

Torrey, E. F. (1997, June 13). The release of the mentally ill from institutions: A well-intentioned disaster. *Chronicle of Higher Education,* pp. B4–B5.

Toth, J. P., & Reingold, E. M. (1996). *Beyond perception: Conceptual contributions to unconscious influences of memory.* Oxford, England: Oxford University Press.

Treisman, A. (1988). Features and objects: The Fourteenth Bartlett Memorial Lecture. *Quarterly Journal of Experimental Psychology, 40*, 201–237.

Treisman, A. (1993). The perception of features and objects. In A. D. Baddeley & L. Weiskrantz (Eds.), *Attention: Selection, awareness, and control: A tribute to Donald Broadbent.* Oxford, England: Oxford University Press.

Tsunoda, T. (1985). *The Japanese brain: Uniqueness and universality.* Tokyo: Taishukan.

Tucker, J. A., Donovan, D. M., & Marlatt, G. A. (Eds.). (1999). *Changing addictive behavior: Bridging clinical and public health strategies.* New York: Guilford Press.

Tulving, E. (1993). What is episodic memory? *Current Directions in Psychological Science, 2*, 67–70.

Tulving, E. (2000). Concepts of memory. In E. Tulving & F. I. M. Craik (Eds.), *The Oxford handbook of memory.* New York: Oxford University Press.

Tulving, E., & Craik, F. M. (2000). *The Oxford handbook of memory.* Cambridge, England: Oxford University Press.

Tulving, E., & Psotka, J. (1971). Retroactive inhibition in free recall: Inaccessibility of information available in the memory store. *Journal of Experimental Psychology, 87*, 1–8.

Tulving, E., & Schacter, D. L. (1990, January 19). Priming and human memory systems. *Science, 247*, 301–306.

Tulving, E., & Thompson, D. M. (1973). Encoding specificity and retrieval processes in episodic memory. *Psychological Review, 80*, 352–373.

Turk, D. C. (1994). Perspectives on chronic pain: The role of psychological factors. *Current Directions in Psychological Science, 3*, 45–49.

Turk, D. C., & Nash, J. M. (1993). Chronic pain: New ways to cope. In D. Goleman & J. Guerin (Eds.), *Mind-body medicine: How to use your mind for better health.* Yonkers, NY: Consumer Reports.

Turkewitz, G. (1993). The origins of differential hemispheric strategies for information processing in the relationships between voice and face perception. In B. de Boysson-Bardies et al. (Eds.), *Developmental neurocognition: Speech and face processing in the first year of life.* Dordrecht, Netherlands: Kluwer Academic.

Turkington, C. (1987, September). Special talents. *Psychology Today*, pp. 38–49.

Turner, M. E., Pratkanis, A. R., Probasco, P., & Leve, C. (1992). Threat, cohesion, and group effectiveness: Testing a social identity maintenance perspective on groupthink. *Journal of Personality and Social Psychology, 63*, 781–796.

Turner, W. J. (1995). Homosexuality, Type 1: An Xq28 phenomenon. *Archives of Sexual Behavior, 24*, 109–134.

Tuss, P., Zimmer, J., & Ho, H. Z. (1995). Causal attributions of underachieving fourth grade students in China, Japan, and the United States. *Journal of Cross Cultural Psychology, 26*, 408–425.

Tversky, A., & Kahneman, D. (1987). Rational choice and the framing of decisions. In R. Hogarth & M. Reder (Eds.), *Rational choice: The contrast between economics and psychology.* Chicago: University of Chicago Press.

Ubell, E. (1993, January 10). Could you use more sleep? *Parade*, pp. 16–18.

Ubell, E. (1996, September 15). Are you at risk? *Parade*, pp. 20–21.

Uchino, B. N., Uno, D., & Holt-Lunstad, J. (1999). Social support, physiological processes, and health. *Current Directions in Psychological Science, 8*, 145–148.

Udolf, R. (1981). *Handbook of hypnosis for professionals.* New York: Van Nostrand.

Ullman, S. (1996). *High-level vision: Object recognition and visual cognition.* Cambridge, MA: MIT Press.

Underwood, G. D. M. (Ed.). (1996). *Implicit cognition.* Oxford, England: Oxford University Press.

United Nations AIDS Program. (1998). *AIDS around the world.* Geneva: United Nations.

U.S. Bureau of the Census. (1993a). Household and family characteristics. *Current population reports.* Washington, DC: Author.

U.S. Bureau of the Census. (1993b). *The top 25 languages.* Washington, DC: Author.

U.S. Bureau of the Census. (1997). *Primary caregivers at home.* Washington, DC: Author.

U.S. Bureau of the Census. (1999). *Census population survey.* Washington, DC: Author.

U.S. Bureau of Justice Statistics. (1995). *National crime victimization survey.* Washington, DC: U.S. Department of Justice.

U.S. Department of Agriculture. (1998). *Sales of cigarettes in the United States and abroad.* Washington, DC: Author.

Vaillant, G. E., & Vaillant, C. O. (1990). Natural history of male psychological health: XII. A 45-year study of predictors of successful aging at age 65. *American Journal of Psychiatry, 147*, 31–37.

Valente, S. M. (1991). Electroconvulsive therapy. *Archives of Psychiatric Nursing, 5*, 223–228.

Valentiner, D. P., Foa, E. B., Riggs, D. S., & Gershuny, B. S. (1996). Coping strategies and posttraumatic stress disorder in female victims of sexual and nonsexual assault. *Journal of Abnormal Psychology, 105*, 455–458.

Van Biema, D. (1996, November 11). Just say life skills. *Time*, p. 70.

Vance, E. B., & Wagner, N. W. (1976). Written descriptions of orgasm: A study of sex differences. *Archives of Sexual Behavior, 5*, 87–98.

Van De Graaff, K. (2000). *Human anatomy* (5th ed.). New York: McGraw-Hill.

van Eck, M., Nicolson, N. A., & Berkhof, J. (1998). Effects of stressful daily events on mood states: Relationship to global perceived stress. *Journal of Personality and Social Psychology, 75*, 1572–1585.

Van Ginkel, R. (1990). Fishermen, taboos, and ominous animals: A comparative perspective. *Anthrozoos, 4*, 73–81.

VanLehn, K. (1996). Cognitive skill acquisition. *Annual Review of Psychology, 47*, 513–539.

van Wel, F., Linssen, H., & Abma, R. (2000). The parental bond and the well-being of adolescents and young adults. *Journal of Youth and Adolescence, 29*, 307–318.

Velichkovsky, B. M., & Rumbaugh, D. M. (Eds.). (1996). *Communicating meaning: The evolution and development of language.* Mahwah, NJ: Erlbaum.

Velmans, M. (2000). *Understanding consciousness.* New York: Psychology Press.

Verhaeghen, P., Marcoen, A., & Goossens, L. (1992). Improving memory performance in the aged through mnemonic training: A meta-analytic study. *Psychology and Aging, 7*, 242–251.

Vernon, P. A., Jang, K. L., Harris, J. A., & McCarthy, J. M. (1997). Environmental predictors of personality differences: A twin and sibling study. *Journal of Personality and Social Psychology, 72*, 177–183.

Victor, S. B., & Fish, M. C. (1995). Lesbian mothers and the children: A review for school psychologists. *School Psychology Review, 24*, 456–479.

Vihman, M. M. (1996). *Phonological development: The origins of language in the child.* London, England: Blackwell.

Vital-Durand, F., Atkinson, J., & Braddick, O. J. (Eds.). (1996). *Infant vision.* Oxford, England: Oxford University Press.

Vogel, G. (13 October, 2000). New brain cells prompt new theory of depression. *Science, 290*, 258–259.

von Restorff, H. (1933). Über die wirking von bereichsbildungen im Spurenfeld. In W. Kohler & H. von Restorff, *Analyse von vorgangen in Spurenfeld: I. Psychologische forschung, 18*, 299–342.

Vygotsky, L. S. (1926/1997). *Educational psychology.* Delray Beach, FL: St. Lucie Press.

Wachtel, P. L., & Messer, S. B. (Eds.). (1997). *Theories of psychotherapy: Origins and evolution.* Washington, DC: American Psychological Association.

Wagner, B. M. (1997). Family risk factors for child and adolescent suicidal behavior. *Psychological Bulletin, 121*, 246–298.

Wagner, D. A. (1981). Culture and memory development. In H. C. Triandis & A. Heron (Eds.), *Handbook of cross-cultural psychology: Vol. 4. Developmental psychology.* Boston: Allyn & Bacon.

Wagner, E. F., & Atkins, J. H. (2000). Smoking among teenage girls. *Journal of Child and Adolescent Substance Abuse, 9*, 93–110.

Wagner, R. K. (1997). Intelligence, training, and employment. *American Psychologist, 52,* 1059–1069.

Wagner, R. K. (2000). Practical intelligence. In R. J. Sternberg (Ed.), *Handbook of intelligence.* New York: Cambridge University Press.

Waid, W. M., & Orne, M. T. (1982). The physiological detection of deception. *American Scientist, 70,* 402–409.

Waite, L. J., & Bachrach, C. (Eds.). (2000) *The ties that bind: Perspectives on marriage and cohabitation.* New York: Aldine De Gruyter.

Walcott, D. M. (2000). Repressed memory still lacks scientific reliability. *Journal of the American Academy of Psychiatry and the Law, 28,* 243–244.

Waldrop, M. W. (1989, September 29). NIDA aims to fight drugs with drugs. *Science, 245,* 1443–1444.

Wall, P. D., & Melzack, R. (1989). *Textbook of pain* (2nd ed.). New York: Churchill Livingstone.

Wallace, R. K., & Benson, H. (1972, February). The physiology of meditation. *Scientific American,* pp. 84–90.

Wallerstein, J. S., Lewis, J., Blakeslee, S., & Lewis, J. (2000). *The unexpected legacy of divorce.* New York: Hyperion.

Wallis, C., & Willwerth, J. (1992, July 6). Schizophrenia: A new drug brings patients back to life. *Time,* pp. 52–57.

Walsh, B. T., & Devlin, M. J. (1998, May 29). Eating disorders: Progress and problems. *Science, 280,* 1387–1390.

Walsh, D. M., Liggett, C., Baxter, D., & Allen, J. M. (1995). A double-blind investigation of the hypoalgesic effects of transcutaneous electrical nerve stimulation upon experimentally induced ischaemic pain. *Pain, 61,* 39–45.

Walter, H. J., Vaughan, R. D., & Wynder, E. L. (1994). Primary prevention of cancer among children: Changes in cigarette smoking and diet after six years of intervention. In A. Steptoe & J. Wardle (Eds.), *Psychosocial processes and health: A reader.* Cambridge, England: Cambridge University Press.

Walters, J. M., & Gardner, H. (1986). The theory of multiple intelligences: Some issues and answers. In R. J. Sternberg & R. K. Wagner (Eds.), *Practical intelligence.* Cambridge, England: Cambridge University Press.

Ward, T. (1997, April 15). Resolving Gulf War syndrome. *HealthNews,* p. 4.

Ward, T. B., Smith, S. M., & Vaid, J. (1997). *Creative thought: An investigation of conceptual structures and processes.* Washington, DC: American Psychological Association.

Ward, W. C., Kogan, N., & Pankove, E. (1972). Incentive effects in children's creativity. *Child Development, 43,* 669–677.

Wark, G. R., & Krebs, D. L. (1996). Gender and dilemma differences in real-life moral judgement. *Developmental Psychology, 32,* 220–230.

Wasserman, E. A., & Miller, R. R. (1997). What's elementary about associative learning? *Annual Review of Psychology, 48,* 573–607.

Waters, E., Hamilton, C. E., & Weinfield, N. S. (2000). The stability of attachment security from infancy to adolescence and early adulthood: General introduction. *Child Development, 71,* 678–683.

Waters, M. (2000, July/August). Bringing minorities into the research fold. *Monitor on Psychology,* pp. 44–47.

Watson, J. B. (1924). *Behaviorism.* New York: Norton.

Watson, J. B., & Rayner, R. (1920). Conditioned emotional reactions. *Journal of Experimental Psychology, 3,* 1–14.

Watson, M., Haviland, J. S., Greer, S., Davidson, J., & Bliss, J. M. (1999, October 16). Influence of psychological response on survival in breast cancer: A population-based cohort study. *Lancet, 354,* 1331–1336.

Wauquier, A., McGrady, A., Aloe, L., Klausner, T., et al. (1995). Changes in cerebral blood flow velocity associated with biofeedback-assisted relaxation treatment of migraine headaches are specific for the middle cerebral artery. *Headache, 35,* 358–362.

Webb, W. B. (1992). *Sleep: The gentle tyrant* (2nd ed.). Boston: Anker.

Webber, B. (1996, February 19). A mean chess-playing computer tears at the meaning of thought. *New York Times,* pp. A1, B6.

Wechsler, D. (1975). Intelligence defined and undefined. *American Psychologist, 30,* 135–139.

Wechsler, H., Davenport, A., Dowdall, G., Moeykens, B., & Castillo, S. (1994). Health and behavioral consequences of binge drinking in college: A national survey of students at 140 campuses. *Journal of the American Medical Association, 272,* 1672–1677.

Wechsler, H., Kelley, K., Weitzman, E. R., San Giovanni, J. P., & Seibring, M. (2000). What colleges are doing about student binge drinking: A national survey of college administrators. *Journal of American College Health, 48,* 219–226.

Week, D., & James, J. (1995). *Eccentrics: A study of sanity and strangeness.* New York: Villard Books.

Weeks, G. R., & Gambescia, N. (2000). *Erectile dysfunction: Integrating couple therapy, sex therapy, and medical treatment.* New York: W. W. Norton.

Weinberg, M. S., Williams, C. J., & Pryor, D. W. (1991, February 27). Personal communication. Indiana University, Bloomington.

Weinberg, R. A., Scarr, S., & Waldman, I. D. (1992). The Minnesota Transracial Adoption Study: A follow-up of IQ test performance at adolescence. *Intelligence, 16,* 117–135.

Weiner, B. (1985a). *Human motivation.* New York: Springer-Verlag.

Weiner, B. (1985b). "Spontaneous" casual thinking. *Psychological Bulletin, 97,* 74–84.

Weiner, B. A., & Wettstein, R. (1993). *Legal issues in mental health care.* New York: Plenum Press.

Weiner, I. B. (1998). *Principles of Rorschach interpretation.* Mahwah, NJ: Erlbaum.

Weiner, J. (2000, February 7). Curing the incurable. *New Yorker,* pp. 64–73.

Weintraub, M. (1976). Intelligent noncompliance and capricious compliance. In L. Lasagna (Ed.), *Patient compliance.* Mt. Kisco, NY: Futura.

Weisberg, H. F., Krosnick, J. A., & Bowen, B. D. (1996). *An introduction to survey research, polling, and data analysis.* Newbury Park, CA: Sage.

Weisman, A., Lopez, S. R., Karno, M., & Jenkins, J. (1993). An attributional analysis of expressed emotion in Mexican-American families with schizophrenia. *Journal of Abnormal Psychology, 102,* 601–606.

Weiss, A. S. (1991). The measurement of self-actualization: The quest for the test may be as challenging as the search for the self. *Journal of Social Behavior and Personality, 6,* 265–290.

Weissman, M. M., Bland, R. C., Canino, G. J., et al. (1996, July 24–31). Cross-national epidemiology of major depression and bipolar disorder. *Journal of the American Medical Association, 276,* 293–299.

Weissman, M. W., & Olfson, M. (1995, August 11). Depression in women: Implications for health care research. *Science, 269,* 799–801.

Weitzenhoffer, A. M. (1999). *The practice of hypnotism* (2nd ed.). New York: Wiley.

Wells, G. L., Malpass, R. S., Lindsay, R. C. L., Fisher, R. P., Turtle, J. W., & Fulero, S. M. (2000). From the lab to the police station: A successful application of eyewitness research. *American Psychologist, 55,* 581–598.

"We're sorry": A case of mistaken identity. (1982, October 4). *Time,* p. 45.

Wertheimer, M. (1923). Untersuchungen zur Lehre von der Gestalt. II. *Psychol. Forsch., 5,* 301–350. In Beardsley and M. Wertheimer (Eds.), *Readings in perception* (New York: Van Nostrand, 1958).

West, R. L. (1995). Compensatory strategies for age-associated memory impairment. In A. D. Baddeley, B. A. Wilson, & F. N. Watts (Eds.), *Handbook of memory disorders.* Chichester, England: Wiley.

Westen, D. (1998). The scientific legacy of Sigmund Freud: Toward a psychodynamically informed psychological science. *Psychological Bulletin, 124,* 333–371.

Westen, D., & Gabbard, G. O. (1999). Psychoanalytic approaches to personality. In L. A. Pervin & O. P. John (Eds.), *Handbook of personality: Theory and research* (2nd ed.). New York: Guilford Press.

Westera, D. A., & Bennett, L. R. (1994). Population-focused research: A broad-based survey of teens' attitudes, beliefs, and behaviours. *International Journal of Nursing Studies, 31,* 521–531.

Wetter, D. W., Fiore, M. C., Gritz, E. R., Lando, H. A., Stitzer, M. L., Hasselblad, V., & Baker, T. B. (1998). The Agency for Health Care Policy and Research. Smoking cessation clinical practice guideline: Findings and implications for psychologists. *American Psychologist, 53,* 657–669.

Whaley, B. B. (Ed.). (2000). *Explaining illness: Research, theory, and strategies.* Mahwah, NJ: Erlbaum.

Whitbourne, S. K. (1999). Physical changes. In J. C. Cavanaugh & S. K. Whitbourne (Eds.), *Gerontology: An interdisciplinary perspective.* New York: Oxford University Press.

Whitbourne, S. K., & Wills, K. (1993). Psychological issues in institutional care of the aged. In S. B. Goldsmith (Ed.), *Long-term care.* Gaithersburg, MD: Aspen Press.

Whitbourne, S. K., Zuschlag, M. K., Elliot, L. B., & Waterman, A. S. (1992). Psychosocial development in adulthood: A 22-year sequential study. *Journal of Personality and Social Psychology, 63,* 260–271.

White, P. A. (1992). The anthropomorphic machine: Causal order in nature and the world view of common sense. *British Journal of Psychology, 83,* 61–96.

Whorf, B. L. (1956). *Language, thought, and reality.* New York: Wiley.

Wickelgren, I. (1998a, September 11). The cerebellum: The brain's engine of agility. *Science, 281,* 1588–1590.

Wickelgren, I. (1998b, June 26). Teaching the brain to take drugs. *Science, 280,* 2045–2047.

Wickens, C. D. (1984). *Engineering psychology and human performance*. Columbus, OH: Merrill.

Widiger, T. A., Frances, A. J., Pincus, H. A., & Davis, W. W. (1990). *DSM-IV* literature reviews: Rationale, process, and limitations. *Journal of Psychopathology and Behavioral Assessment, 12,* 189–202.

Widmeyer, W. N., & Loy, J. W. (1988). When you're hot, you're hot! Warm-cold effects in first impressions of persons and teaching effectiveness. *Journal of Educational Psychology, 80,* 118–121.

Wiebe, D. J. (1991). Hardiness and stress moderation: A test of proposed mechanisms. *Journal of Personality and Social Psychology, 60,* 89–99.

Wiehe, V. R., & Richards, A. L. (1995). *Intimate betrayal: Understanding and responding to the trauma of acquaintance rape.* Thousand Oaks, CA: Sage.

Wielgosz, A. T., & Nolan, R. P. (2000). Biobehavioral factors in the context of ischemic cardiovascular diseases. *Journal of Psychosomatic Research, 48,* 339–345.

Wigfield, A., & Eccles, J. S. (2000). Expectancy-value theory of achievement motivation. *Contemporary Educational Psychology, 25,* 68–81.

Wiggins, J. S. (1997). In defense of traits. In R. Hogan, J. Johnson, & S. Briggs, (Eds.), *Handbook of personality psychology.* Orlando, FL: Academic Press.

Wildavsky, B. (2000, September 4). A blow to bilingual education. *U.S. News and World Report,* 22–28.

Wilgoren, J. (1999, October 22). Quality day care, early, is tied to achievements as an adult. *New York Times,* p. A16.

Williams, J. E., & Best, D. L. (1990). *Measuring sex stereotypes: A multinational study.* Newbury Park, CA: Sage.

Williams, J. E., Paton, C. C., Siegler, I. C., Eigenbrodt, M. L., Nieto, F. J., & Tyroler, H. A. (2000). Anger proneness predicts coronary heart disease risk: Prospective analysis from the Atherosclerosis Risk in Communities (ARIC) study. *Circulation, 101,* 2034–2039.

Williams, J. W., Mulrow, C. D., Chiquette, E., Noel, P. H., Aguilar, C., & Cornell, J. (2000). A systematic review of newer pharmacotherapies for depression in adults: Evidence report summary. *Annals of Internal Medicine, 132,* 743–756.

Williams, S. W., & McCullers, J. C. (1983). Personal factors related to typicalness of career and success in active professional women. *Psychology of Women Quarterly, 7,* 343–357.

Willis, S. L., & Nesselroade, C. S. (1990). Long-term effects of fluid ability training in old-old age. *Developmental Psychology, 26,* 905–910.

Willis, S. L., & Schaie, K. W. (1994). In C. B. Fisher & R. M. Lerner (Eds.), *Applied developmental psychology.* New York: McGraw-Hill.

Wilson, G. T., & Agras, W. S. (1992). The future of behavior therapy. *Psychotherapy, 29,* 39–43.

Wilson, J. P., & Keane, T. M. (Eds.). (1996). *Assessing psychological trauma and PTSD.* New York: Guilford Press.

Windholz, G. (1997, September). Ivan P. Pavlov: An overview of his life and psychological work. *American Psychologist, 52,* 941–946.

Winerip, M. (1993, November 15). No. 2 pencil fades as graduate exam moves to computer. *New York Times,* pp. A1, B9.

Winkler, K. J. (1997, July 11). Scholars explore the blurred lines of race, gender, and ethnicity. *Chronicle of Higher Education,* pp. A11–A12.

Winner, E. (1997). *Gifted children: Myths and realities.* New York: Basic Books.

Winner, E. (2000). The origins and ends of giftedness. *American Psychologist, 55,* 159–169.

Winningham, R. G., Hyman, I. E., Jr., & Dinnel, D. L. (2000). Flashbulb memories? The effects of when the initial memory report was obtained. *Memory, 8,* 209–216.

Winson, J. (1990, November). The meaning of dreams. *Scientific American,* pp. 86–96.

Winter, D. G. (1973). *The power motive.* New York: Free Press.

Winter, D. G. (1987). Leader appeal, leader performance, and the motive profile of leaders and followers: A study of American presidents and elections. *Journal of Personality and Social Psychology, 52,* 196–202.

Winter, D. G. (1988). The power motive in women—and men. *Journal of Personality and Social Psychology, 54,* 510–519.

Witelson, S. F. (1995). Neuroanatomical bases of hemispheric functional specialization in the human brain: Possible developmental factors. In F. L. Kitterle (Ed.), *Hemispheric communication: Mechanisms and models.* Hillsdale, NJ: Erlbaum.

Witt, G. E. (1998, December). Vote early and often. *American Demographics,* p. 23.

Wixted, J. T., & Ebbesen, E. B. (1991). On the form of forgetting. *Psychological Science, 2,* 409–415.

Wolfe, D. A. (1999). *Child abuse: Implications for child development and psychopathology.* Thousand Oaks, CA: Sage.

Wolpe, J. (1990). *The practice of behavior therapy.* Boston: Allyn & Bacon.

Wolters, G. (1995). Het geheugen. Functie, structuur en processen (Memory: Its function, structure, and processes). *Psycholoog, 30,* 369–374.

Wonderlic. (1999). *Pre-employment test scores for various professions.* Wonderlic: Libertyville, IL.

Wonderlic. (2000, March 7). Wonderlic Personnel Test. Available on the World Wide Web at *http://www.wonderlic.com/wpt.html.*

Wong, M. M., & Csikszentmihalyi, M. (1991). Affiliation motivation and daily experience: Some issues on gender differences. *Journal of Personality and Social Psychology, 60,* 154–164.

Wood, J. M., & Bootzin, R. (1990). The prevalence of nightmares and their independence from anxiety. *Journal of Abnormal Psychology, 99,* 64–68.

Wood, W., Lundgren, S., Ouellette, J. A., Busceme, S., & Blackston, T. (1994). Minority influence: A meta-analytic review of social influence processes. *Psychological Bulletin, 115,* 323–345.

Wood, W., & Stagner, B. (1994). Why are some people easier to influence than others? In S. Savitt & T. C. Brock (Eds.), *Persuasion: Psychological insights and perspectives.* Boston: Allyn & Bacon.

Woodruff-Pak, D. S. (1999). New directions for a classical paradigm: Human eyeblink conditioning. *Psychological Science, 10,* 1–7.

Woods, S. C., Schwartz, M. W., Baskin, D. G., & Seeley, R. J. (2000). Food intake and the regulation of body weight. *Annual Review of Psychology, 51,* 255–277.

Woods, S. C., Seeley, R. J., Porte, D., Jr., & Schwartz, M. W. (1998, May 29). Signals that regulate food intake and energy homeostasis. *Science, 280,* 1378–1383.

Woods, S. J. (2000). Prevalence and patterns of posttraumatic stress disorder in abused and postabused women. *Issues in Mental Health Nursing, 21,* 309–324.

Wozniak, R. H., & Fischer, K. W. (Eds.). (1993). *Development in context: Acting and thinking in specific environments.* Hillsdale, NJ: Erlbaum.

Wright, J. H., & Beck, A. T. (1996). Cognitive therapy. In R. E. Hales & S. C. Yudofsky (Eds.), *The American Psychiatric Press synopsis of psychiatry.* Washington, DC: American Psychiatric Press.

Wright, R. (1996, March 25). Can machines think? *Time,* pp. 50–56.

Wright, S. J. (1999). Human embryonic stem-cell research: Science and ethics. *American Scientist, 87,* 352–361.

Wyatt, G. E. (1992). The sociocultural context of African American and White American women's rape. *Journal of Social Issues, 48,* 77–92.

Wynn, K. (2000). Addition and subtraction by human infants. In D. Muir & A. Slater (Eds.), *Infant development: The essential readings.* Malden, MA: Blackwell.

Wyshak, G., & Barsky, A. (1995). Satisfaction with and effectiveness of medical care in relation to anxiety and depression: Patient and physician ratings compared. *General Hospital Psychiatry, 17,* 108–114.

Yalom, I. D. (1997). *The Yalom reader: On writing, living, and practicing psychotherapy.* New York: Basic Books.

Yan, H., Kinzler, K. W., & Vogelstein, B. (2000, September 15). Genetic testing—present and future. *Science, 289,* 1890–1892.

Yee, A. H., Fairchild, H. H., Weizmann, F., & Wyatt, G. E. (1993). Addressing psychology's problem with race. *American Psychologist, 48,* 1132–1140.

Yenerall, J. D. (1995). College socialization and attitudes of college students toward the elderly. *Gerontology and Geriatrics Education, 15,* 37–48.

Yost, W. A. (1992). Auditory perception and sound source determination. *Current Directions in Psychological Science, 1,* 179–184.

Young, M. W. (2000, March). The tick-tock of the biological clock. *Scientific American,* 64–71.

Zaidel, D. W. (1994). Worlds apart: Pictorial semantics in the left and right cerebral hemispheres. *Current Directions in Psychological Science, 3,* 5–8.

Zajonc, R. B. (1985). Emotion and facial efference: A theory reclaimed. *Science, 228,* 15–21.

Zajonc, R. B., & McIntosh, D. N. (1992). Emotions research: Some promising questions and some questionable promises. *Psychological Science, 3,* 70–74.

Zamarra, J. W., Schneider, R. H., Besseghini, I., Robinson, D. K., & Salerno, J. W. (1996). Usefulness of the transcendental meditation program in the treatment of patients with coronary artery disease. *American Journal of Cardiology, 77,* 867–870.

Zautra, A. J., Reich, J. W., & Guarnaccia, C. A. (1990). Some everyday life consequences of disability and bereavement for older adults. *Journal of Personality and Social Psychology, 59,* 550–561.

Zebrowitz-McArthur, L. (1988). Person perception in cross-cultural perspective. In M. H. Bond (Ed.), *The cross-cultural challenge to social psychology.* Newbury Park, CA: Sage.

Zeidner, M., & Endler, N. S. (Eds.). (1996). *Handbook of coping: Theory, research, applications.* New York: Wiley.

Zevon, M., & Corn, B. (1990). Paper presented at the annual meeting of the American Psychological Association, Boston.

Zhdanova, I. V., Lynch, H. J., & Wurtman, R. J. (1997). Melatonin: A sleep-promoting hormone. *Sleep, 20,* 899–907.

Zhdanova, I., Wurtman, R., & Green, C. H. (1996, June). How does melatonin affect sleep? *Harvard Mental Health Letter,* p. 8.

Zilbergeld, B., & Ellison, C. R. (1980). Desire discrepancies and arousal problems in sex therapy. In S. R. Leiblum & L. A. Pervin (Eds.), *Principles and practices of sex therapy.* New York: Guilford Press.

Zito, J. M. (1993). *Psychotherapeutic drug manual* (3rd ed., rev.). New York: Wiley.

Zuckerman, M. (1978). The search for high sensation. *Psychology Today,* pp. 30–46.

Zuckerman, M. (1991). One person's stress is another person's pleasure. In C. D. Spielberger, I. G. Sarason, Z. Kulczar, & G. L. Van Heck (Eds.), *Stress and emotion: Anxiety, anger, and curiosity.* New York: Hemisphere.

Zuckerman, M. (1994). *Behavioral expression and biosocial expression of sensation seeking.* Cambridge, England: Cambridge University Press.

Zuger, A. (1998, June 2). The "other" drug problem: Forgetting to take them. *New York Times,* pp. C1, C5.

Zurbriggen, E. L. (2000). Social motives and cognitive power-sex associations: Predictors of aggressive sexual behavior. *Journal of Personality and Social Psychology, 78,* 559–581.

Acknowledgments

Chapter 1

Figure 1-1: From 1997 Survey of Doctorate Recipients, National Research Council and National Science Foundation. Compiled by APA Research Office. Reprinted with permission. **Figure 1-2:** American Psychological Association, 1991.

Chapter 2

Figure 2-4: From J.M. Darley & B. Latané, "Bystanders Intervention in Emergencies," Journal of Personality & Social Psychology, 8, 377–383. Copyright © 1968, by the American Psychological Association. Reprinted with permission. **Cartoon by Roz Chast, page 31:** © The New Yorker Collection 1998 Roz Chast from cartoonbank.com. All rights reserved. **Cartoon, page 34:** © The New Yorker Collection 1993 J.B. Handelsman from cartoonbank.com. All rights reserved. **Cartoon by Donald Reilly, page 47:** © The New Yorker Collection 1993 Donald Reilly from cartoonbank.com. All rights reserved.

Chapter 3

Figure 3-1: From *Human Anatomy, 5th edition*, by K. Van De Graaff, p. 339. Copyright © 2000 by The McGraw-Hill Companies, Inc. **Figure 3-2:** From C.F. Stevens, "The Neuron," *Scientific American*, September 1979, page 56. Reprinted with permission of Carol Donner. **Figure 3-4a:** From *Human Biology, 6th edition*, by S. Mader, p. 250. Copyright © 2000 by The McGraw-Hill Companies, Inc. **Figure 3-4b:** From *The Living World, 2nd edition*, by G.B. Johnson and T. Emmel, p. 600. Copyright © 2000 by The McGraw-Hill Companies, Inc. **Figure 3-6:** From *Psychology, 4th edition*, by E. Loftus and C. Wortmann, p. 63. Copyright © 1989 by The McGraw-Hill Companies, Inc. **Figure 3-9:** From *Anatomy & Physiology, 5th edition*, by R. Seeley, T. Stephens, and P. Tate, p. 384. Copyright © 2000 by The McGraw-Hill Companies, Inc. **Figure 3-10:** From *The Living World, 2nd edition*, by G.B. Johnson and T. Emmel, p. 606. Copyright © 2000 by The McGraw-Hill Companies, Inc. **Figure 3-11a:** From *Elements of Physiological Psychology*, by A.M. Schneider and B. Tarshis. Copyright © 1995 by The McGraw-Hill Companies, Inc. **Figure 3-11b:** Courtesy of Dr. Robert B. Livingston, University of California-San Diego, and Philip J. Mercurio, Neurosciences Institute. **Figure 3-14:** Reprinted with permission of Dr. Peter Fox, Research Imaging Center, University of Texas Health Science Center. **Figure 3-16:** From *Human Biology, 6th edition*, by S. Mader, p. 297. Copyright © 2000 by The McGraw-Hill Companies, Inc.

Chapter 4

Figure 4-1: From *Anatomy & Physiology, 5th edition*, by R. Seeley, T. Stephens, and P. Tate, p. 477. Copyright © 2000 by The McGraw-Hill Companies, Inc. **Figure 4-3:** From *Hole's Essentials of Human Anatomy and Physiology, 7th edition*, by D. Shier, J. Butler, and R. Lewis, p. 283. Copyright © 2000 by The McGraw-Hill Companies, Inc. **Figure 4-5:** From *Human Biology, 6th edition*, by S. Mader, p. 282. Copyright © 2000 by The

McGraw-Hill Companies, Inc. **Figure 4-8:** From *Anatomy & Physiology, 5th edition*, by R. Seeley, T. Stephens, and P. Tate, p. 490. Copyright © 2000 by The McGraw-Hill Companies, Inc. **Figure 4-9:** From *Anatomy & Physiology, 5th edition*, by R. Seeley, T. Stephens, and P. Tate, p. 477. Copyright © 2000 by The McGraw-Hill Companies, Inc. **Figure 4-10:** Adapted from S. Brownlee and T. Watson, "The Senses," *US News & World Report*, January 13, 1997, pp. 51–59. Reprinted with permission of Linda M. Bartoshuk. **Figure 4-11:** From Kenshalo, *The Skin Senses*, 1968. Courtesy of Charles C. Thomas, Publisher, Ltd., Springfield, Illinois. **Figure 4-12c:** From *Mind Sights* by Roger N. Shepard © 1990 by Roger N. Shepard. Used with the permission of W.H. Freeman and Company. **Figure 4-15:** From *Sensation & Perception, 2nd edition*, by E. Goldstein © 1984. Reprinted with permission of Wadsworth, an imprint of the Wadsworth Group, a division of Thomson Learning. Fax: 800-730-2215. **Figure 4-16:** I. Biederman, *Higher Level Vision*. In D.N. Osherson, S. Kosslyn and J. Hollerbach (eds.), *An Invitation to Cognitive Science: Visual Cognition and Action*, 1990. Reprinted with permission of MIT Press. **Figure 4-18:** Figure from *Sensation and Perception, Third Edition*, by Stanley Coren and Lawrence M. Ward, copyright 1989 by Harcourt, Inc., reproduced by permission of the publisher. **Figure 4-19:** Figure from *Sensation and Perception, Second Edition*, by Stanley Coren, Clare Porac and Lawrence M. Ward, copyright 1989 by Harcourt, Inc., reproduced by permission of the publisher. **Figure 4-20a:** Figure from *Sensation and Perception, Second Edition*, by Stanley Coren, Clare Porac and Lawrence M. Ward, copyright 1989 by Harcourt, Inc., reproduced by permission of the publisher. **Figure 4-23:** From Gregory & Gombrich, *Illusion in Nature and Art*, Figure 5-16. Copyright © 1973, by permission of Gerald Duckworth & Co. Ltd. **Table 4-1:** From Better Hearing Institute, 1998. *Decibel Levels*. Washington, DC: Better Hearing Institute. **Cartoon by Ian Falconer, page 114:** © The New Yorker Collection 1996 Ian Falconer from cartoonbank.com. All rights reserved.

Chapter 5

Figure 5-1: From *Sleep* by J. Allen Hobson © 1989 by J. Allan Hobson. Used with the permission of W.H. Freeman and Company. **Figure 5-2:** From E. Hartmann, *The Biology of Dreaming*, 1967. Courtesy of Charles C. Thomas, Publisher, Ltd., Springfield, Illinois. **Figure 5-3:** From *Secrets of Sleep* by Alexander Borbely. English translation copyright © 1986 by Basic Books, Inc. Copyright © 1984 by Deutsche Verlag-Anstalt GmbH, Stuttgart. Reprinted by permission of Basic Books, a member of Perseus Books, L.L.C. **Figure 5-4:** Reprinted with permission from H.P. Roffwarg, J.N. Munzio and W.C. Dement, "Ontogenic Development of the Human Sleep-Dream Cycle," *Science*, 152, 1996, p. 604–619. Copyright 1996 American Association for the Advancement of Science. **Figure 5-5:** Griffith, Otoya & Tago, "The Universality of Typical Dreams: Japanese vs. American," *American Anthropologist*, 60:6, pt.1. December 1958.

Figure 5-6: Dr. Allen R. Braun, N.I.D.C.D., N.I.H. **Figure 5-7:** From D.F. Dinges and R.J. Broughton (eds.), *Sleep and Alertness: Chronobiological, Behavioral, and Medical Aspects of Napping*, 1990. Copyright © 1990 Lippincott, Williams, and Wilkins. **Figure 5-8:** From *The Relaxation Response* by Herbert Benson, M.D., with Miriam Z. Klipper. Copyright © 1975 by William Morrow & Company, Inc. Reprinted by permission of HarperCollins Publishers, Inc. **Figure 5-9:** Monitoring the Future Study, 1999. University of Michigan. **Figure 5-10:** From *Human Biology, Sixth Edition*, by S. Mader, p. 282. Copyright © 2000 by The McGraw-Hill Companies, Inc. **Figure 5-11:** Copyright © 1991 by the New York Times Co. Reprinted by permission. **Figure 5-12:** From F.H. Gawin and H.D. Kleber, *Archives of General Psychiatry*, 42, 1986, pp. 107–113. Copyright 1986 American Medical Association. **Figure 5-13:** H. Wechsler, et al., 2000, *Student Survey on Binge Drinking*, Harvard University. Reprinted with permission of Henry Wechsler. **Figure 5-15:** Monitoring the Future Study, 1999. University of Michigan. **Quote, page 151:** Just Say No—to Dare? Finding Anti-Drug Programs That Work: From D. Van Blema, "Just Say Life Skills," *Time*, November 11, 1996, p. 70. Copyright © 1996 Time, Inc. Used by permission. **Cartoon, page 137:** THE FAR SIDE © 1983 FARWORKS, INC. All rights reserved. **Cartoon by Mascha Richter, page 147:** © The New Yorker Collection 1993 Mascha Richter from cartoonbank.com. All rights reserved.

Chapter 6

Figure 6-5: E.C. Tolman and C.H. Honzik, 1930, *Introduction and Removal of Reward and Maze Performance in Rats*, University of California Publications in Psychology, 4, 257–275. **Cartoon by Tom Cheney, page 175:** © The New Yorker Collection 1993 Tom Cheney from cartoonbank.com. All rights reserved. **Cartoon by Gahan Wilson, page 184:** © The New Yorker Collection 1995 Gahan Wilson from cartoonbank.com. All rights reserved.

Chapter 7

Figure 7-2: Figure from "Human Memory: A Proposed System and Its Control Processes," by R.C. Atkinson and R.M. Shiffrin, from *The Psychology of Learning and Motivation: Advances in Research and Theory*, Volume 2, edited by K.W. Spence and J.T. Spence, copyright © 1968 by Academic Press, reproduced by permission of the publisher. **Figure 7-3:** From "Perception and Memory Versus Thought: Some Old Ideas and Recent Findings," by A.D. deGroot in *Problem Solving: Research, Method & Theory*, by B. Kleinmuntz (ed.). Copyright © 1966 John Wiley & Sons, Inc. Reprinted by permission of John Wiley & Sons, Inc. **Figure 7-4:** Adapted from S.E. Gathercole and A.D. Baddeley, 1993, *Working Memory and Language Processing*, Taylor and Francis, Inc. **Figure 7-6:** Figure from "Retrieval Times from Semantic Memory," by A.M. Collins and M.R. Quillian in *Journal of Verbal Learning and Verbal Behavior*, Volume 8, 240–247, copyright © 1969 by Academic Press, reproduced by permission of the publisher. **Figure 7-9:** From D.C. Rubin,

"The Subtle Deceiver Recalling," *Psychology Today,* September 1995. Reprinted with permission from *Psychology Today* Magazine. Copyright 1995 Sussex Publishers, Inc. **Figure 7-10:** Figure from "Reconstruction of Automobile Destruction," by E.F. Loftus and J.C. Palmer in *Journal of Verbal Learning and Verbal Behavior,* Volume 13, 585–589, copyright © 1974 by Academic Press, reproduced by permission of the publisher. **Figure 7-11:** From H.P. Bahrick, L.K. Hall, and S.A. Berger, "Accuracy and Distortion in Memory for High School Grades," *Psychological Science,* 7, 1996, 265–269. Reprinted with permission of Blackwell Publishers. **Figure 7-13:** Figure from R.S. Nickerson and M.J. Adams, *Cognitive Psychology,* Volume 11, page 297. Copyright © 1979 by Academic Press, reproduced by permission of the publisher. **Figure 7-15:** Courtesy of Dr. Steven E. Peterson, Washington University. **Figure 7-16:** From *Human Anatomy, Fifth Edition,* by K. Van De Graaff. Copyright © 2000 by The McGraw-Hill Companies, Inc. **Cartoon by Roz Chast, page 203:** © The New Yorker Collection 1994 Roz Chast from cartoonbank.com. All rights reserved. **Cartoon by Mick Stevens, page 217:** © The New Yorker Collection 1998 Mick Stevens from cartoonbank.com. All rights reserved.

Chapter 8

Figure 8-1: Reprinted with permission from R. Shepard and J. Metzler, "Mental Rotation of Three Dimensional Objects," *Science,* 171, 701–703. Copyright 1971 American Association for the Advancement of Science. **Figure 8-2:** Republished with permission of American Physiological Society, from *Journal of Neurophysiology,* by Alvaro Pascual-Leone, September 1995; permission conveyed through Copyright Clearance Center, Inc. **Figure 8-5:** From R.L. Solso, *Cognitive Psychology, Third Edition.* Copyright © 1991 by Allyn & Bacon. Reprinted/adapted by permission. **Figure 8-6:** Barry F. Anderson, *The Complete Thinker,* 1980. Reprinted with permission of Barry F. Anderson. **Figure 8-12:** Courtesy of Drs. Betty Hart and Todd Risley, 1997. **Figure 8-13:** From *Time* Magazine, January 30, 1995. Copyright © 1995 Time, Inc. Reprinted by permission. **Table 8-1:** Table from "Family Resemblances: Studies in the Internal Structure of Categories," by E. Rosch and C. Mervis in *Cognitive Psychology,* Volume 7, 573–605, copyright © 1975 by Academic Press, reproduced by permission of the publisher. **Cartoon by Michael Maslin, page 229:** © The New Yorker Collection 1996 Michael Maslin from cartoonbank.com. All rights reserved. **Cartoon by Michael Maslin, page 235:** © The New Yorker Collection 2000 Michael Maslin from cartoonbank.com. All rights reserved. **Cartoon, page 240:** THE FAR SIDE © 1981 FARWORKS, INC. All rights reserved. **Cartoon by James Stevenson, page 250:** © The New Yorker Collection 1989 James Stevenson from cartoonbank.com. All rights reserved.

Chapter 9

Figure 9-1: Data from "A Neural Basis for General Intelligence," by Duncan, *Science,* 289, July 21, 2000, p. 399. **Figure 9-2:** Adaptation of sample items from *Weschler Intelligence Scales for Children (WISC-III).* The Psychological Corporation. **Figure 9-3:** Reprinted with permission of Wonderlic, Inc., Libertyville, Illinois. **Figure 9-4:** Copyright © 1994 by the New York Times Co. Reprinted

by permission. **Figure 9-5:** From J.M. Walters and H. Gardner, in Robert J. Sternberg and Richard K. Wagner (eds.), *Practical Intelligence: Nature and the Origins of Competence,* 1986, pp. 167–173. Reprinted with the permission of Cambridge University Press. **Figure 9-7:** Reprinted with permission from R.J. Sternberg, "The Holy Grail of General Intelligence," *Science,* 289, pp. 399–401. Copyright 2000 American Association for the Advancement of Science. **Figure 9-8:** Adapted from "Familial Studies of Intelligence: A Review," by T.J. Bouchard and M. McGue, Science, 212, 1981, pp. 1055–1059. **Figure 9-9:** From J. Horgan, "Get Smart, Take a Test," *Scientific American,* November 1995, pp. 12–14. Reprinted with permission of Dimitry Schildovsky. **Cartoon by Roz Chast, page 265:** © The New Yorker Collection 1998 Roz Chast from cartoonbank.com. All rights reserved. **Cartoon by W.B. Park, page 269:** © The New Yorker Collection 1983 W.B. Park from cartoonbank.com. All rights reserved.

Chapter 10

Figure 10-2: *Motivation and Personality,* by A. Maslow, © 1998. Reprinted by permission of Prentice-Hall, Inc., Upper Saddle River, NJ. **Figure 10-4:** From *Anatomy & Physiology, Fifth Edition,* by R. Seeley, T. Stephens, and P. Tate. Copyright © 2000 by The McGraw-Hill Companies, Inc. **Figure 10-5:** From *Time* Magazine, July 22, 1997. Copyright © 1997 Time, Inc. Reprinted by permission. **Figure 10-7:** K.W. Fischer, P.R. Shaver, and P. Carnochan, "How Emotions Develop and How They Organize Development," *Cognition and Emotion,* 1990. Reprinted by permission of Psychology Press Limited, Hove, UK. **Table 10-1:** From M. Zuckerman, "The Search for High Sensation," *Psychology Today,* February 1978. Reprinted with permission from *Psychology Today* Magazine, Copyright © 1978 Sussex Publishers, Inc. **Quote, page 287:** S. Abt, "Armstrong Wins Tour and Journey," *New York Times,* July 26, 1999, p. D4. **Cartoon by Michael Maslin, page 297:** © The New Yorker Collection 1999 Michael Maslin from cartoonbank.com. All rights reserved. **Cartoon, page 310:** THE FAR SIDE © 1992 FARWORKS, INC. All rights reserved.

Chapter 11

Figure 11-1: US Department of Labor, 1999. **Figure 11-2:** *Hostile Hallways: The AAUW Survey on Sexual Harassment in American Schools,* 1993. Reprinted with permission of the American Association of University Women Educational Foundation. **Figure 11-3:** From Dey, Astin, Korn & Berz, *The American Freshman: National Norms for Fall,* 1990. Reprinted with permission of Higher Education Research Institute. **Figure 11-5:** Republished with permission of Society for the Scientific Study of Sexuality, from *Journal of Sex Research,* D. Sue, "Erotic Fantasies of College Students During Coitus," 1979; permission conveyed through Copyright Clearance Center, Inc. **Figure 11-6:** W.H. Masters and V.E. Johnson, 1966, *Human Sexual Response.* Boston: Little, Brown. **Figure 11-7:** Republished with permission of Society for the Scientific Study of Sexuality, from *Journal of Sex Research,* Arafat and Cotton, "Masturbation Practices of Males and Females," 1974; permission conveyed through Copyright Clearance Center, Inc. **Figure 11-8:** Gallup News Service, 1998. **Figure 11-9:** M. Clements, "Making Love, How Old, How Often." *Parade* Magazine, August 7, 1994, p. 5.

Figure 11-10: From Kinsey, Pomeroy and Martin, *Sexual Behavior in the Human Male,* 1948. Reprinted with permission of W.B. Saunders Company. **Figure 11-11:** Prepared for the Kaiser Family Foundation of America by American Social Health Association, 1998. **Figure 11-12:** UN AIDS Program, 1999. **Table 11-1:** From J.E. Williams and D.L. Best, *Measuring Sex Stereotypes: A Multinational Study.* Copyright © 1990 by Sage Publications. Reprinted by Permission of Sage Publications, Inc. **Table 11-2:** Republished with permission of *The Wall Street Journal,* from February 14, 2000; permission conveyed through Copyright Clearance Center, Inc. **Table 11-3:** E.E. Vance and N.W. Wagner, "Written Descriptions of Orgasm: A Study of Sex Differences," *Archives of Sexual Behavior,* 6, 1976, 87–98. Reprinted with permission of Kluwer Academic/Plenum Publishers.

Chapter 12

Figure 12-3: Reproduced with permission from *Pediatrics,* Vol. 89, pages 91–97, 1992. **Figure 12-5:** From J.M. Tanner, et al., "Standards from Birth to Maturity for Height, Weight, Height Velocity and Weight Velocity: British Children, 1965," *Archives of Disease in Childhood,* 41, 454–471, 613–635, BMJ Publishing Group. Reprinted with permission of BMJ Publishing Group. **Figure 12-6:** Adapted from W.J. Robbins, 1929. *Growth,* New Haven, CT: Yale University Press. **Figure 12-8:** Adapted from S.M. Bell, & M.D.S. Ainsworth, 1972, "Infant Crying and Maternal Responsiveness," *Child Development,* 43, pp. 1171–1190, and C. Tomlinson-Keasey, 1985, *Child Development: Psychological, Sociological, and Biological Factors.* Homewood, IL: Dorsey. **Figure 12-9:** US Bureau of Census 1995. **Figure 12-10:** US Bureau of Census 1997. **Figure 12-11:** From Judith A. Schickedanz, et al., *Understanding Children and Adolescents, Fourth Edition.* Copyright © 2001 by Allyn & Bacon. Reprinted by permission. **Figure 12-12:** Adapted from F.N. Dempster, "Memory Span: Sources for Individual and Developmental Differences," *Psychological Bulletin,* 89, 63–100. Copyright © 1981, by the American Psychological Association. Adapted with permission. **Cartoon by Roz Chast, page 373:** © The New Yorker Collection 1995 Roz Chast from cartoonbank.com. All rights reserved. **Cartoon by Lee Lorenz, page 372:** © The New Yorker Collection 1985 Lee Lorenz from cartoonbank.com. All rights reserved.

Chapter 13

Figure 13-1: US Bureau of the Census 1993. **Figure 13-2:** Reprinted from *Education and Physical Growth,* by J.M. Tanner. By permission of International Universities Press, Inc. Copyright 1978 by International Universities Press, Inc. **Figure 13-3:** US Department of Health and Human Services, Centers for Disease Control: *Health, United States, 2000 Adolescent Health Chartbook.* **Figure 13-4:** K.E. Boehm and N.B. Campbell, "Suicide: A Review of Calls to an Adolescent Peer Listening Phone Service," *Child Psychiatry and Human Development,* 1996, 26, 61–66. Reprinted with permission of Kluwer Academic/Plenum Publishers. **Figure 13-5:** US Bureau of Census. Census Population Survey, 1999. **Figure 13-6:** Statistical Office of the European Communities, 1998. **Figure 13-7:** From John P. Robinson and Geoffrey Godbey, *Time for Life,* 1997, University Park: The Pennsylvania State University Press, 1997. Copyright 1997 by The Pennsylvania State University Press. Reproduced by permission of the publisher. **Figure 13-8:** US Bureau of the Census. Census Population Survey, 1999. **Figure 13-9:** From K.W. Schaie, "The Course of Adult Intellectual Development," *American Psychologist,* 49, 304–313. Copyright © 1994 by the American Psychological Association. Reprinted with permission. **Table 13-1:** From L. Kohlberg, "State and Sequence: The Cognitive-Developmental Approach to Socialization." In D. Goslin (ed.) *Handbook of Socialization Theory and Research,* 1969. Reprinted with permission of D. Goslin. **Cartoon by Roz Chast, page 394:** © The New Yorker Collection 1993 Roz Chast from cartoonbank.com. All rights reserved. **Cartoon by Michael Crawford, page 399:** © The New Yorker Collection 1991 Michael Crawford from cartoonbank.com. All rights reserved. **Cartoon by Arnie Levin, page 406:** © The New Yorker Collection 1996 Arnie Levin from cartoonbank.com. All rights reserved. **Cartoon by Roz Chast, page 407:** © The New Yorker Collection 1993 Roz Chast from cartoonbank.com. All rights reserved.

Chapter 14

Figure 14-2: Catell, Eber & Tatsuoka, 1970, *Handbook for the 16PF.* Institute for Personality and Ability Testing. Printed with permission. **Figure 14-3:** From H.J. Eysenck, "Biological Dimensions of Personality," In L.A. Pervin (ed.) *Handbook of Personality: Theory & Research,* 1990, p. 246. Reprinted with permission of Guilford Press. **Figure 14-5:** From Tellegen, Lykken, Bouchard, Wilcox, Segal & Rich, "Personality Similarity in Twins Reared Apart and Together," *Journal of Personality and Social Psychology,* 54, 1031–1039. Copyright © 1988 by the American Psychological Association. Reprinted with permission. **Figure 14-7:** Based on R.P. Halgin and S.K. Whitbourne, 1994, *Abnormal Psychology,* Fort Worth, TX: Harcourt Brace, and *Minnesota Multiphasic Personality Inventory 2,* University of Minnesota. **Table 14-3:** From L.A. Pervin (ed.), *Handbook of Personality: Theory & Research,* 1990, Chapter 3. Reprinted with permission of Guilford Press. **Quote, page 413:** From "Whitney Bulger's Life on the Run," by Shelly Murphy, January 4, 1998, p. A8. Reprinted courtesy of The Boston Globe. **Cartoon by Sidney Harris, page 415:** Copyright © 2001 by Sidney Harris. **Cartoon by Robert Mankoff, page 417:** © The New Yorker Collection 2000 Robert Mankoff from cartoonbank.com. All rights reserved. **Cartoon by Robert Mankoff, page 429:** © The New Yorker Collection 1991 Robert Mankoff from cartoonbank.com. All rights reserved. **Cartoon by Sidney Harris, page 435:** Copyright © 2001 by Sidney Harris.

Chapter 15

Figure 15-1: From *The Stress of Life,* by H. Selye. Copyright © 1975 by The McGraw-Hill Companies, Inc. **Figure 15-2:** Adapted from Baum, A., "Behavioral, Biological and Environmental Interactions in Disease Processes," In S. Blumenthal, K. Matthews, and S. Weiss (eds) *New Research Frontiers in Behavioral Medicine: Proceedings of the National Conference,* NIH Publications, 1994. **Figure 15-3: Hassles –** From Kerry Chamberlain and Sheryl Zika, "The Minor Events Approach to Stress: Support for the Use of Daily Hassles," *British Journal of Psychology,* Volume 81, Part 4 (November 1990), pp. 469–481, Copyright © The British Psychological Society. **Uplifts –** Kanner, Coyne, Schaefer, & Lazarus, "Comparison of Two Modes of Stress Measurement: Daily Hassles and Uplifts Versus Major Life Events," *Journal of Behavioral Medicine,* 4, 14, 1981. Reprinted with permission of Kluwer Academic/Plenum Publishers. **Figure 15-4:** K.W. Pettingale, T. Morris, S. Greer, and J. L. Haybittle, "Mental Attitudes to Cancer: An Additional Prognostic Factor," *Lancet,* 750. Copyright © 1985 The Lancet, Ltd. **Figure 15-5:** *Morbidity and Mortality Weekly Report,* July 9, 1993. Centers for Disease Control. **Figure 15-6:** *Monitoring the Future Study,* 1999, University of Michigan. **Figure 15-7:** US Department of Agriculture, 1998. **Figure 15-8:** F.M. Andrews and S.B. Withey, *Social Indicators of Well-Being: Americans' Perceptions of Life Quality,* 1976, pp. 207 and 306. Reprinted with permission of Kluwer Academic/Plenum Publishers. **Table 15-1:** Perceived Stress Scale from "A Global Measure of Perceived Stress," by S. Cohen, T. Kamarck, and R. Mormelstein, 1983, *Journal of Health and Social Behavior,* 24, p. 385–396. Reprinted with permission of American Sociological Association. **Table 15-2:** From Jenkins, Zyzndki & Rosenman, "Coronary-Prone Behavior: One Pattern or Several?" *Psychosomatic Medicine,* 40, 25–43, 1979. Reprinted with permission of Lippincott, Williams & Wilkins. **Table 15-3:** Copyright © 1988 by the New York Times Co. Reprinted by permission. **Quote, page 443:** Copyright © 1999 by the New York Times Co. Reprinted with permission. **Quote, page 454:** By Peter Jaret, "Mind Over Malady," *Health,* November/December 1992, p. 87. Reprinted with permission from Health, © 1992. **Cartoon by Edward Koren, page 452:** © The New Yorker Collection 1995 Edward Koren from cartoonbank.com. All rights reserved.

Chapter 16

Figure 16-1: From *Anxiety Disorders and Phobias* by Aaron T. Beck and Gary Emery, with Ruth L. Greenberg. Copyright © 1985 by Aaron T. Beck, MD & Gary Emery, PhD. Reprinted by permission of Basic Books, a member of Perseus Books, L.L.C. **Figure 16-3:** Copyright © 1993 by the New York Times Co. Reprinted by permission. **Figure 16-6:** Reprinted with permission of Nancy C. Andreasen, University of Iowa Hospitals and Clinics. **Table 16-4:** Personal communication with W. Hill, 1992. Public Affairs Network Coordinator for the American Psychiatric Association. **Table 16-6:** From *Schizophrenia Genesis* by Irving I. Gottesman © 1991 by Irving I. Gottesman. Used with permission of W.H. Freeman and Company. **Quote, page 469:** Republished with permission of *Wall Street Journal,* from "Lori Schiller Emerges From the Torments of Schizophrenia," by A. Bennett, October 14, 1992; permission conveyed through Copyright Clearance Center, Inc. **Quote, page 478:** From M.M. Antony, T.A. Brown, and D.H. Barlow, "Current Perspectives on Pain and Panic Disorder," *Current Directions in Psychological Science,* 1, 1992, page 79. Reprinted with permission of Blackwell Publishers. **Quote, page 488:** Excerpt from *Is There No Place on Earth For Me?* By Susan Sheehan. Copyright © 1982 by Susan Sheehan. This material originally appeared in slightly different form in *The New Yorker,* Spring 1981. Reprinted by permission of Houghton Mifflin Company. All rights reserved. **Quote, pages 492–493:** "Personality disorders," From *Abnormal Psychology, First Edition,* by M. Duke and S. Nowicki © 1979. Reprinted with permission of Wadsworth Group, a division of Thomson Learning. Fax: 800-730-2215. **Cartoon by Arnie Levin,**

pages 475: © The New Yorker Collection 2000 Arnie Levin from cartoonbank.com. All rights reserved.

Chapter 17

Figure 17-2: Smith, Mary Lee, Gene V. Glass, and Thomas I. Miller, *The Benefits of Psychotherapy,* © 1980 Johns Hopkins University Press. Reprinted with permission of The Johns Hopkins University Press. **Figure 17-3:** "Mental Health: Does Therapy Help?" © 1995 by Consumers Union of U.S., Inc. Yonkers, NY 10703-1057, a nonprofit organization. Reprinted with permission from the November 1995 issue of CONSUMER REPORTS ® for educational purposes only. No commercial use or photocopying/transmitting permitted. To subscribe, call 1-800-234-1645 or log on to www.ConsumerReports.org. **Figure 17-4:** From "Antidepressants: Choices and Controversy," by D. Mischoulon. Copyright © 2000, Massachusetts Medical Society. All rights reserved. **Figure 17-5:** From Howard, et al., "The Changing Face of American Psychology: A Report from the Committee on Employment and Human Resources," *American Psychologist,* 41, 1311–1327. Copyright © 1986 by the American Psychological Association. Reprinted with permission. **Table 17-2:** Reprinted by permission of Dr. Herbert Benson, Beth Israel Deaconess Medical Center, Boston, MA. **Cartoon by Donald Reilly, page 511:** © The New Yorker Collection 1994 Donald Reilly from cartoonbank.com. All rights reserved. **Cartoon by Gahan Wilson, page 524:** © The New Yorker Collection 1994 Gahan Wilson from cartoonbank.com. All rights reserved.

Chapter 18

Figure 18-3: From Anderson, Krull & Weiner, "Explanations: Processes and Consequences," in Higgins & Kruglanski (eds.) *Social Psychology: Handbook of Basic Principles,* 1996, p. 274. Adapted with permission of Guilford Press. **Figure 18-6:** From M.B. Parlee, "The Friendship Bond," *Psychology Today,* October 1979. Reprinted with permission from Psychology Today Magazine. Copyright 1979 Sussex Publishers, Inc. **Figure 18-7:** From R.J. Sternberg, "A Triangular Theory of Love," *Psychological Review,* 93, 119–135. Copyright © 1986 by the American Psychological Association. Reprinted with permission. **Figure 18-8:** Based on B. Latané and J.M. Darley, 1970. *The Unresponsive Bystander: Why Doesn't He Help?* New York: Appleton-Century-Crofts, from Feldman, *Understanding Psychology, Fifth Edition,* p. 642. **Table 18-1:** Adapted from Cacioppo, Bernston and Crites, "Social Neuroscience: Principles of Psychophysiological Arousal and Response," in Higgins and Kruglanski (eds.), *Social Psychology: Handbook of Basic Principles,* 1996, Guilford Press. **Table 18-2:** From D.M. Buss, et al., "International Preferences in Selecting Mates: A Study of 37 Cultures," *Journal of Cross-Cultural Psychology,* 21, pp. 5–47. Copyright © 1990 by Sage Publications. Reprinted by permission of Sage Publications, Inc. **Table 18-3:** From "Defining Aggression: An Exercise for Classroom Discussion," by L.T. Benjamin, Jr., February 1985, *Teaching of Psychology* 12, 1, p. 40–42. Reprinted with permission of Lawrence Erlbaum Associates, Inc. **Quote, page 543:** Reprinted with permission from American Demographics. Copyright © 1998 by Intertec Publishing, a PRIMEDIA Company. **Cartoon by Robert Weber, page 541:** © The New Yorker Collection 1989 Robert Weber from cartoonbank.com. All rights reserved. **Cartoon by Richard Cline, page 549:** © The New Yorker Collection 1999 Richard Cline from cartoonbank.com. All rights reserved.

Appendix

Cartoon by Dana Fradon, page A.1: © The New Yorker Collection 1977 Dana Fradon from cartoonbank.com. All rights reserved.

PHOTOS

Chapter 1

Opener: © Jon Riley/STONE; **p. 3:** © AP/Wide World Photos; **p. 7(top):** © Laura Dwight/Photo Edit; **p. 7 (bottom):** © Ann Chwatsky/Phototake/PictureQuest; **p. 10:** Courtesy, Carolyn Copper; **p. 12:** © Bettmann/Corbis Images; **p. 13:** © The Granger Collection; **p. 14:** Courtesy, Wellesley College Archives. Photographed by Notman; **p. 15:** © Bettmann/Corbis Images; **p. 16:** © Culver Pictures; **p. 17:** © TimePix; **p. 20 (left):** © Richard T. Nowitz/National Geographic Image Collection; **p. 20 (right):** © Frank Herholdt/STONE

Chapter 2

Opener: © Bob Daemmrich/Image Works; **p. 29:** © Corbis-Sygma; **p. 34:** © Robert I. M. Campbell/National Geographic Image Collection; **p. 35:** ©Hulton-Deutsch Collection/Corbis Images; **p. 37:** © Bill Aron/Photo Edit; **p. 38:** ©James Wilson/Woodfin Camp; **p. 39 (top):** Courtesy, Bibb Latane; **p. 39 (bottom):** Courtesy, John Darley, Princeton University; **p. 44:** Courtesy, Mary Garrett; **p. 45 (top):** © Tom Stewart/Stock Market; **p. 45 (bottom):** © Dan McCoy/Rainbow; **p. 46:** © Douglas Faulkner/Photo Researchers

Chapter 3

Opener: © Alexander Tsiaras/Stock Boston; **p. 53:** © AP/Wide World Photos; **p. 57:** © John D. Cunningham/Visuals Unlimited; **p. 66:** From Deloukas, et al. October 23, 1998. "A physical map of 30,000 human genes." Science 282(5389), 744–746. © 1998 American Association for the Advancement of Science. http://www.ncbi.nlm.nih.gov/genemap; **p. 68 (top):** © Leonard Lessin/Peter Arnold; **Fig. 3.8 a-b:** © SPL/Science Source/Photo Researchers; **Fig. 3.8c:** © Mehau Kulyk/SPL/Photo Researchers; **Fig. 3.8d:** © Dan McCoy/Rainbow; **Fig. 3.8e:** © Roger Ressmeyer/Corbis Images; **p. 69:** Artificial Intelligence Laboratory, MIT. Image courtesy of Michael Leventon; **p. 71:** © Gavin Smith/FSP/Liaison Agency; **Fig. 3.13:** Courtesy, Trustees of the British Museum, Natural History; **p. 75 (bottom):** From: Damasio H, Grabowski, T, Frank R, Galaburda AM, Damasio AR. 1994. "The return of Phineas Gage: Clues about the brain from the skull of a famous patient." Science, 264:1102–1105, 1994. ©1994 American Association for the Advancement of Science. Department of Neurology and Image Analysis Facility, University of Iowa; **Fig. 3.14:** Courtesy, Peter T. Fox and Jack L. Lancaster, Research Imaging Center, UTHSCSA; **Fig. 3.15:** B.A. Shaywitz et al., 1995. NMR/Yale Medical School; **Fig. 3.17:** Courtesy, Neal Miller

Chapter 4

Opener: © Martine Mouchy/STONE; **p. 89:** © Everett Collection; **p. 91:** © Curtis Myers/Stock Connection/Picturequest; **p. 94 (left):** ©Biophoto Associates/Photo Researchers; **p. 94 (right):** © Biophoto Associates/Photo Researchers; **Fig. 4.6 a-c:** © Joe Epstein/Design Conceptions; **p. 101:** © AP/Wide World Photos; **p. 104:** © VideoSurgery/Photo Researchers; **p. 108 (top):** © Prof. P. Motta/Dept. of Anatomy/University "La Sapienza", Rome/SPL/Photo Researchers; **p. 108 bottom:** © Omikron/Photo Researchers; **p. 110:** Courtesy, Julie Mennella; **p. 111:** © Lisa M. McGeady/Corbis Images; **Fig. 4.17:** Courtesy, Bela Julesz; **p. 118:** © Cary Wolinsky/Stock Boston; **p. 119:** © Jeff Greenberg/Stock Boston; **Fig. 4.19:** ©John G. Ross/Photo Researchers; **Fig. 4.21 b-c:** © Innervisions

Chapter 5

Opener: © Nicholas Devore III/Network Aspen; **p. 131:** © AP/Wide World Photos; **p. 135:** © Ted Spagna/Photo Researchers; **p. 139:** © Stock Portfolio/Stock Connection/PictureQuest; **p. 143:** © Jose Carrillo/Stock Boston; **p. 145:** © AP, Midland Daily News/Wide World Photos; **p. 151:** Courtesy, Princeton Health Press; **p. 152 (left):** © Pictor International/PictureQuest; **p. 152 (right):** © Corbis Images; **p. 154:** © Dr. Dennis Kunkel/PhotoTake; **p. 155 (left):** © Bob Daemmrich/Stock Boston; **p. 155 (right):** © IT Int'l/eStock Photography/PictureQuest; **p. 158:** © Lawrence Migdale/Stock Boston; **p. 159:** © Kal Muller/Woodfin Camp

Chapter 6

Opener: © Joanna B. Penneo/Aurora/PictureQuest; **p. 165:** © AP/Wide World Photos; **p. 167:** © Culver Pictures; **p. 170:** © Pictor International/PictureQuest; **p. 172 (all):** © Stuart Ellins; **p. 174:** © Nina Leen/TimePix; **p. 180:** © Chris Stanford/Allsport; **p. 182:** Courtesy, Lynn Calero; **p. 181:** Courtesy, Dr. Marian Bailey; **p. 185:** © Spencer Grant/Stock Boston; **p. 186 (top):** From Meltzhoff, A.N. (1988). Imitation of Televised Models by Infants. Child Development, 59, 1221–1229. Photos Courtesy of A.N. Meltzhoff & M. Hanak; **p. 186 (bottom):** Courtesy, Albert Bandura; **p. 187:** © Michael Newman/Photo Edit

Chapter 7

Opener: © Steve Raymer/Corbis Images; **p. 197:** © Mary Ann McDonald/Corbis Images; **p. 200:** © Bob Wallace/Stock Boston; **p. 201:** © F. Dewey Webster/Sovfoto/Eastfoto/PictureQuest; **p. 205:** © Arthur Tilley/FPG; **p. 206:** © Susan Werner/PictureQuest; **p. 208:** © Tom McCarthy/Index Stock Imagery; **Fig. 7.7:** © Disney Enterprises, Inc; **p. 213:** © Shahn Kermani/Liaison Agency; **p. 214:** © Joseph Nettis/Photo Researchers; **Fig. 7.15:** © Dr. Steven E. Peterson/Washington University. From Scientific American, 12/93; **Fig. 7.17:** © Cecil Fox/Science Source/Photo Researchers

Chapter 8

Opener: © Dwayne Newton/Photo Edit; **p. 227:** NASA; **p. 228:** © Jeff Greenberg/eStock Photography/PictureQuest; **p. 229:** © AP/Wide World Photos; **p. 232 (left):** © Greg Girard/Contact Press Images/PictureQuest; **p. 232 (center):** © Tom McHugh/Photo Researchers; **p. 232 (right):** © Stephen Studd/STONE; **p. 240 (all):** © Superstock; **p. 244 (top):** © Roberto Otero/Black Star; **p. 244 (bottom):** © Bob Schatz/Liaison Agency; **p. 245 (left):** © The Granger Collection; **p. 245 (right):** © Kevin Fleming/Corbis Images; **p. 247:** Courtesy, Dr. Laura Ann Petitto © 1991/ photo by

Chapter 9

Opener: © AP/Wide World Photos; **p. 259 (left):** © James S. Douglass; **p. 259 (right):** © Yunghi Kim/Contact Press Images; **p. 261:** © David Hiser/Network Aspen; **p. 262:** © Roger Viollet/Liaison Agency; **p. 263:** © M. Siluk/Image Works; **p. 265:** © 2001 Kaplan, Inc. Photo: eStock Photography/Leo de Wys; **p. 269:** © Bob Daemmrich/Image Works; **Fig. 9.5(1):** © TimePix; **Figs. 9.5(2), 9.5(4), 9.5(6):** © Bettmann/Corbis Images; **Fig. 9.5(8):** © Corbis Digital Stock; **Fig. 9.6 a-b:** From Duncan, J., et al. July 21, 2000. "A neural basis for general intelligence." Science 289: 459. ©2000 American Association for the Advancement of Science. Photo courtesy John Duncan; **p. 265:** © 2001 Kaplan, Inc. Photo: eStock Photography/Leo de Wys; **p. 269:** © Bob Daemmrich/Image Works; **p. 278:** Courtesy, Rob Davies

Chapter 10

Opener: © Michael Schwarz/Liaison Agency; **p. 287:** © AP/Wide World Photos; **Fig. 10.1a:** © PhotoDisc; **Fig. 10.1b:** Courtesy, Lennox Industries; **p. 297:** © Peter Menzel/Stock Boston; **p. 298:** © Tony Freeman/PhotoEdit; **Fig. 10.6:** Reprinted by permission of the publisher from THEMATIC APPERCEPTION TEST by Henry A. Murray, Cambridge, Mass.: Harvard University Press, Copyright © 1943 by the Presidents and Fellows of Harvard College, © 1971 by Henry A. Murray; **p. 307:** © Donald G. Dutton; **Fig. 10.9:** George, M.S., et al. "Brain activity during transient sadness and happiness in healthy women." American Journal of Psychiatry, 152:341–351, 1995. © 1995 The American Psychiatric Association. Reprinted by permission; **Fig. 10.10 (all):** Matsumoto & Ekman, 1988; **Fig. 10.11 a-d:** From "Smiles when Lying." Ekman, Friesen, & O'Sullivan, 1988

Chapter 11

Opener: © Esbin-Anderson/Photo Network/PictureQuest; **p. 319:** © Mark Newman/Photo Network/PictureQuest; **p. 320:** © Pete Winkel/Focus Group/PictureQuest; **p. 322, 324:** © Bob Daemmrich/Stock Boston; **p. 328 (top):** © David Young-Wolff/Photo Edit; **p. 328 (bottom left):** © Laura Dwight/Stock Connection/PictureQuest; **p. 328 (bottom right):** © Mark Gibson/Photo 20-20/PictureQuest; **p. 340:** © Bob Daemmrich/Stock Boston; **p. 342:** Courtesy, Pat Unger; **p. 347:** © Bob Daemmrich/Stock Boston

Chapter 12

Opener: © Look GMBH/eStock Photography/PictureQuest; **p. 353:** © Evan Richman/New York Times Pictures; **p. 355:** © Peter Byron; **Fig. 12.1a:** © D.W. Fawcett/Photo Researchers; **Fig. 12.1b:** © L. Willatt, East Anglian Regional Genetics Service/SPL/Photo Researchers; **Fig. 12.1c:** © Kenneth Eward/Photo Researchers; **Fig. 12.1d:** © Biophoto Associates/Science Source/Photo Researchers; **p. 359:** © AP/Wide World Photos; **p. 361 (left):** © Lennart Nilsson/Albert Bonniers Forlag AB/*A Child is Born*/Dell Publishing; **p. 361 (right):** © Petit Format/Science Source/Photo Researchers; **p. 364:** © Charles Gupton/Stock Boston; **Fig. 12.4 (all):** From: A.N. Meltzhoff & M.K. Moore. 1977. "Imitation of facial and manual gestures by human neonates." *Science*, 198: 75–78. © 1977 American Association for the Advancement of Science; **Fig. 12.7:** Harlow Primate Laboratory, University of Wisconsin; **p. 376:** © Laura Dwight/Peter Arnold; **p. 378:** © Farrell Grehan/Corbis Images; **p. 380:** Courtesy, Michael Morrier

Chapter 13

Opener: © Tom Prettyman/PhotoEdit; **p. 387:** Having Our Say by Sara and A. Elizabeth Delany with Amy Hill Hearth, 1993 Kodansha America, Inc. © Amy Hill Hearth, Sara Louise Delany and Annie Elizabeth Delany; **p. 403:** © Bob Daemmrich/Stock Boston; **p. 388:** © Najlah Feanny/Saba; **p. 390:** © Danny Lehman/Corbis Images; **p. 391:** © David Young Wolff/STONE; **p. 392:** © Olive Pierce/Black Star; **p. 393 (top):** © C/B Productions/Stock Market; **p. 393 (bottom left):** © Lawrence Migdale/Stock Boston; **p. 393 (bottom right):** © Julie Houck/Stock Boston; **p. 394:** © AP/Wide World Photos; **p. 398:** © Stephen Simpson/FPG; **p. 406:** © Lori Grinker/Contact Press Images/PictureQuest

Chapter 14

Opener: © Jill Sabella/FPG; **p. 413:** Republished with permission of Globe Newspaper Company, Inc., from the 1/4/98 issue of The Boston Globe, © 1998; **p. 415:** © Tom Stewart/Stock Market;

p. 416: © Guy Gillette/Photo Researchers; **p. 417:** © Tony Freeman/Photo Edit; **p. 419 (both):** © Kobal Collection/LucasFilm/20th Century Fox; **p. 424:** © Meritt Vincent/Photo Edit; **p. 425:** © AP/Wide World Photos; **p. 436:** © Laura Dwight/Corbis Images

Chapter 15

Opener: © Seth Resnick/Stock Boston; **p. 443:** ©Jonathon Nourok/STONE; **p. 448:** © Frank Siteman/Index Stock Imagery; **p. 449:** © Corbis Digital Stock; **p. 450:** Courtesy, Alan Benner; **p. 455:** © Bob Daemmrich/Stock Boston; **p. 456:** © Moredun Animal Health Ltd./SPL/Photo Researchers; **p. 457:** © Prof. S.H.E. Kaufmann & Dr. J.R. Golecki/SPL/Photo Researchers; **p. 459:** © 2001 Buttout.com; **p. 463:** © David Toerge/Black Star

Chapter 16

Opener: © Vanessa Vick/Photo Researchers; **p. 469:** Courtesy, Lori Schiller; **p. 471:** © AP/Wide World Photos; **p. 472:** Courtesy, Margaret Coggins; **p. 479:** © Owen Franken/Corbis Images; **p. 484:** © Susan Greenwood/Liaison Agency; **p. 487:** © Wellcome Dept. of Cognitive Neurology/SPL/Photo Researchers; **Fig. 16.4:** © AP/Wide World Photos; **Fig. 16.5 (all):** © Derek Bayes/TimePix; **Fig. 16.6 (both):** Courtesy, Nancy Andreasen,

University of Iowa Hospitals & Clinics; **Fig. 16.7:** Monte S. Buchsbaum, M.D., Mt. Sinai School of Medicine, New York, NY

Chapter 17

Opener: © Zigy Kaluzny/STONE; **p. 503:** © AP/Wide World Photos; **p. 506:** © Bruce Ayres/STONE; **p. 507:** © Jonathan Nourok/PhotoEdit; **p. 509:** © Rick Freedman/Black Star; **p. 510:** © Michael Newman/Photo Edit; **p. 514:** © Jon Bradley/STONE; **p. 515:** © David Young-Wolff/PhotoEdit; **p. 518 (left):** © Tony Freeman/Photo Edit; **p. 518 (right):** © Paul Chesley/Photographers/Aspen/PictureQuest; **p. 521:** © Custom Medical Stock Photo; **p. 523:** © Will & Deni McIntyre/Photo Researchers; **p. 524:** © Phyllis Picard/Stock South/PictureQuest

Chapter 18

Opener: © AP/Wide World Photos; **p. 529, 531:** © AP/Wide World Photos; **p. 534:** Courtesy, Ann Altman; **p. 537:** © Myrleen Ferguson/Photo Edit; **p. 538:** © Mark Wexler/Woodfin Camp; **Fig. 18.5 (both):** From the film OBEDIENCE © 1965 by Stanley Milgram and distributed by Penn. State Media Sales. Permission granted by Alexandra Milgram; **p. 546:** © Barbara Burnes/Photo Researchers; **p. 555:** © AP/Wide World Photos.

Name Index

Abelson, H. I., 531
Abi-Dargham, A., 491
Abma, R., 394
Abrahams, M. F., 541
Abrams, R. L., 123
Abramson, L. Y., 487
Abt, S., 287
Acocella, J., 435
Adams, B., 362
Adams, B. W., 520
Adams, G., 394
Adams, M., 188
Adams, M. J., 216
Adler, J., 479
Adler, P. A., 34
Affleck, G., 447
Aghajanian, G. K., 159
Agras, W. S., 507, 510
Ahissar, M., 107
Ahrons, C., 399
Aiken, L. R., 264, 279, 407, 432
Ainsworth, M. D. S., 369, 370
Akbarian, S., 491
Akil, H., 445
Akmajian, A., 246
Aks, D. J., 118
Akutsu, P. D., 156
Alford, B. A., 512
Allen, M., 268, 546
Allen, V. L., 540
Alliger, G. M., 309
Allison, D. B., 298
Alloy, L. B., 435, 487
Allport, G. W., 211, 421
Almer, E., 517
Altenmuller, E. O., 97
Altman, N., 419
Anastasi, A., 263, 279
Andersen, B. L., 457
Anderson, B. F., 238
Anderson, C., 187
Anderson, C. A., 554
Anderson, J., 188
Anderson, J. R., 209, 217, 459
Anderson, K. B., 342
Anderson, N. H., 535
Anderson, S. M., 536
Anderson, T., 390
Andreasen, N. C., 491
Andrews, M., xxviii
Angelucci, A., 66, 73
Angier, N., 82, 359, 427
Angoff, W. H., 281
Ansburg, P. I., 240
Antony, M. M., 478
Aponte, J. F., 518
Apter, A., 390
Arafat, I., 336, 337
Archambault, D. L., 159
Archer, J., 327

Archer, S. L., 392
Arena, J. M., 338
Ariel, S., 518
Arlin, P. K., 234
Aron, A., 308, 549
Aronow, E., 435
Aronson, E., 42, 549
Aronson, J., 547
Arterberry, M., 366
Asch, S. E., 535, 539
Asher, S. R., 371
Ashton, R., 137
Aspinwall, L. G., 452, 453
Astin, H. S., 325
Atkins, J. H., 458
Atkinson, H. G., 463, 464
Atkinson, J. W., 199, 301, 365, 366
Au, T. K.-F., 365
Austin, L. S., 322
Averill, J. R., 304, 308
Axel, R., 108
Aycan, Z., 7

Bachman, B. A., 149, 154, 158, 459
Bachrach, C., 401
Back, K. W., 548
Baddeley, A. D., 201, 204, 246
Baer, J., 244
Baer, L., 523
Bahrick, H. P., 214
Bai, M., 131
Baiardo, R., xxvii, xxviii
Bailey, J. M., 339, 340
Baillargeon, R., 378
Baird, J. C., 91
Baker, A., 141
Baker, R. A., 146
Baker, S. P., 121
Ball, E. M., 141
Ballinger, C. B., 398
Baltes, P. B., 461
Bandaret, L., xxviii
Bandura, A., 185, 424, 425, 510, 554
Banich, T., 78
Banks, W. P., 213
Bannon, L., 327
Barber, J., 146
Barber, S., 507, 516
Bargh, J., 123, 534
Barinaga, M., 219, 453
Barkley, R. A., 494
Barlow, D. H., 331, 478
Barnard, N. D., 46
Barongan, C., 17, 341
Barrett, M., 246
Barron, F., 244
Barsky, A., 464
Bar Tal, D., 549
Bartecchi, C. E., 460

Bartoshuk, L., 107, 108, 109
Basch, M. F., 417
Bashner, R. S., 547
Bass, A., 555
Batista, A. P., 74
Batson, C. D., 555
Batt, C., xxviii
Bauer, P. J., 379
Baum, A., 447, 449
Baumeister, R., 425, 427, 550
Bayer, D. L., 492
Bayer, M., xxvii
Baynes, K., 80
Bazell, B., 82, 111
Beach, F. A., 335
Beall, A. E., 31
Bear, M. F., 55
Beaton, R. J., 200
Beatty, J., 54
Beauchamp, G. K., 107
Beck, A. T., 487, 510, 511, 512
Beck, M., 398
Beckham, E. E., 485
Beckman, H. B., 462
Beckmann, H., 490
Bedard, W. W., 71
Begley, S., 66, 359
Behar, L., 41
Beilin, H., 380
Bell, A., 340
Bell, J., 555
Bell, R. A., 541
Bell, S. M., 369
Bellack, A. S., 190
Beller, M., 325
Bellezza, F. S., 203
Belsky, J., 372
Bem, D. J., 123, 340
Bem, S. L., 328
Benbow, C. P., 325
Benjamin, J., 426
Benjamin, L. T., Jr., 14
Bennett, A., 469
Bennett, L. R., 338
Bennett, M. R., 60
Bennett, W., 300
Benson, H., 147
Bentall, R. P., 488
Berger, S. A., 214
Bergin, A. E., 507, 515, 516
Berkhof, J., 449
Berkowitz, C. D., 343
Berkowitz, L., 187, 552, 553
Berkowitz, R. I., 507
Berlyne, D., 290
Berman, A. L., 395
Berman, R. M., 521
Berman, S. L., xxviii
Bernard, L. L., 289
Bernieri, F. J., 536

Berquier, A., 137
Berrettini, W. H., 66
Berrios, G. E., 472
Berscheid, E., 548
Bersoff, D. N., 44, 555
Best, D. L., 321
Betancourt, H., 21, 281
Beutler, L. E., 281
Bey, K., xxvii, xxviii
Beyene, Y., 398
Bickman, L., 554
Bieber, I., 340
Biederman, I., 116, 117
Binder, J. L., 516
Binet, A., 262
Binkley, C., 543
Binstock, R., 406
Birbaumer, N., 69
Birch, H. G., 240
Bird, G., 397
Birren, J. E., 403
Bishop, D. V., 229
Bjork, D. W., 174
Bjork, E. L., 207
Bjork, R. A., 123, 166, 207, 221, 230
Bjorklund, D. F., xxvii, 8, 212, 355, 379
Black, P. M., 461
Blake, D. T., 74
Blakeslee, S., 77, 400
Blanchard, E. B., 112
Blanchard, F. A., 547
Blanck, P. D., 47
Blank, M., 380
Blascovich, J. J., 455
Blass, T., 544
Blau, Z. S., 407
Blewett, A. E., 524
Blume, S. B., 156
Blustein, D. L., 21
Blyth, D., 390
Boehm, K. E., 524
Bolla, K. I., 152
Bolton, P., 276
Bond, M. H., 425
Bonke, B., 206
Booth, D. A., 297
Bootzin, R., 137, 141
Borden, D., xxviii
Borgida, E., 322
Bornstein, M. H., 361, 366, 382
Bornstein, R. F., 435, 549
Botting, J. H., 46
Botts, T., xxvii
Bouchard, C., 296
Bouchard, T. J., 280
Bourne, L. E., 236, 238
Bowen, B. D., 34
Bower, G. H., 209, 217
Bowlby, J., 370
Braddick, O. J., 366
Bradsher, K., 543
Brakke, K., 251
Braly, K. W., 545
Brandimonte, M. A., 229
Bratslavsky, E., 550
Braun, A. R., 140
Bray, G. A., 296

Brazelton, T. B., 364
Brehm, J. W., 290, 463
Brehm, S. S., 463
Breland, K., 181
Breland, M., 181
Brendgen, M., 392
Bresler, C., 306
Brett, J. M., 322
Brewer, J. B., 218
Brief, D. E., 544
Brilhl, D., xxviii
Brink, D. C., 513
Brislin, R., 419
Brody, N., 510
Bromm, B., 111
Bronner, E., 274
Brookhiser, R., 159
Brown, A. S., 491
Brown, C. E., 325
Brown, D. C., 432
Brown, E., 366
Brown, L. S., 213
Brown, M. B., 494
Brown, P. K., 99
Brown, R., 203, 250
Brown, S. I., 235
Brown, T. A., 478
Brucato, D., xxvii
Bruce, B., 300
Bruce, K., 330
Bruce, V., 98, 119
Bruner, J., 361, 380
Brunner, H. G., 473
Bryant-Waugh, R., 298
Brzustowicz, L. M., 490
Buck, L., 108
Buckhout, R., 212
Buckner, R. L., 205
Buckwalter, J. G., 204
Buffalo, E. A., 211
Bukowski, W. M., 371, 392
Burack, J. A., 275
Burchinal, M. R., 372
Burger, J. M., 541, 542
Burgess, D., 322
Burgoon, J. K., 325
Burkhart, B. R., 342
Burnham, D. K., 119
Bush, P. J., 463
Bushman, B. J., 156, 427
Buss, D. M., 326, 426, 428, 550
Butcher, J. N., 433, 484
Butler, J., 96
Butler, R., 407
Byne, W., 339
Byrne, D., 549
Byrne, R. M. E., 232

Cabrera, N. J., 401
Cacioppo, J. T., 531, 532
Cadet, J. L., 152
Calmes, J., 338
Cameron, J., 292
Camp, C. J., 406
Campbell, D. T., 121
Campbell, J. J., 372

Campbell, W. K., 427
Campfield, L. A., 296
Campos, J. J., 373
Camras, L. A., 312
Cannon, T. D., 488
Cannon, W. B., 306
Cantor, C., 482
Cantor, N., 407
Cao, Y., 77
Capaldi, E. D., 296, 297
Capute, A. J., 275
Cardena, E., 484
Carli, L. L., 324
Carlson, M., 553
Carnes, B. A., 404
Carney, R. N., 203, 220
Carnochan, P., 304, 305
Carroll, J. M., 304
Carson, R. C., 484
Carter, A. S., 480
Carver, C. S., 424, 457
Case, R., 378
Caspi, A., 405, 426
Caspi, R., 427, 428
Cassel, C., 404
Cassel, W. S., 212
Catalan, J., 339
Cattell, R. B., 269, 422
Catterson, S., xxvii
Cavasina, R., xxviii
Cernich, J. M., 108
Chalmers, D., 245
Chamberlain, K., 449, 451
Chamberlin, J., 10
Chandler, M., 378, 379
Chanowitz, B., 547
Chao, R. K., 20
Chaparro, L., xxvii
Chapman, J. P., 489
Chapman, L. J., 489
Chard, D., 276
Charney, D., 521
Chase, M., 230
Chastain, G., 44
Cheakalos, C., 295, 332
Chen, C., 20, 381, 538
Chen, D., 108
Chen, J., 269
Chen, S., 373
Cheney, C. D., 464
Cheney, D. L., 250
Cheng, H., 77
Cherlin, A., 399
Cherry, B. J., 204
Chess, S., 373
Cheston, S. E., 517
Chi-Ching, Y., 188
Chin, S. B., 156
Chiu, C.-Y. P., 207
Cho, A., 103
Chodorow, N., 397
Chomsky, N., 248
Choo, P., 550
Christenfeld, N., 327
Church, M. A., 301
Churchland, P. S., 97
Cialdini, R. B., 21, 541, 542

Clair, J. M., 464
Clancy, S. A., 213
Clark, J., 513
Clark, L., 426
Clark, L. V., 378
Clark, R., 448
Clark, R. E., 171
Clarke-Stewart, K. A., 390, 400
Clarkin, J. F., 493
Clay, R. A., 507
Clayton, R., 151
Cleary, P. D., 458
Clements, M., 338
Cline, R. J. W., 541
Clopton, J. R., 434
Cloud, J., 159
Coates, T. J., 345
Coats, E. J., 21, 244, 325
Coatsworth, J. D., 382
Coffey, C. E., 405
Cohen, A., 518
Cohen, A. G., 323
Cohen, C., xxvii
Cohen, D., 187, 371
Cohen, J. B., 449
Cohen, L., 449
Cohen, P., 495, 496
Cohen, S., 445
Cohler, B. J., 506
Colapinto, J., 319
Cole, M., 214
Coleman, H. L. K., 252
Coleman, J. C., 484
Coleman, M., 400
Coles, R., 329, 391
Collins, A. M., 206, 207
Collins, B. E., 544
Collins, C., 345
Coltraine, S., 328, 546
Compas, B. E., 485
Comuzzie, A. G., 298
Condon, J. W., 549
Condray, D. S., 516
Conger, R. D., 390
Conkright, B., xxvii
Connors, B. W., 55
Conoley, J. C., 433
Conte, H. R., 417
Conway, M. A., 207
Cooklin, A., 515
Cooper, H., 342
Cooper, J., 187
Cooper, L. A., 229
Cooper, N. R., 219
Cooper, S. H., 417
Cope, D., 245
Corbetta, M., 218
Coren, S., 93, 117, 118, 120, 121
Corn, B., 457
Cornelius, S. W., 405
Cornell, T. L., 76
Corrigan, P. W., 232
Costa, P. T., Jr., 423
Cotterell, J., 394
Cotton, P., 495
Cotton, W. L., 336, 337
Cowen, P. J., 61

Cowley, G., 219
Coyne, J. C., 488
Crabb, P. B., 328
Craig, I. W., 66
Craig, R. J., 433
Craik, F. I., 203, 209
Craik, F. M., 218
Craik, K. H., 14, 21
Cramer, J., 435, 464
Crandall, R., 293
Crano, W. D., 549
Crapo, L., 80
Crawford, M., 321, 324
Crews, F., 418
Crichlow, S., 541
Crick, N. R., 371
Critelli, J. W., 324
Crits-Christoph, P., 152, 525
Crombez, G., 110
Cronkite, K., 485
Crouter, A. C., 327, 402
Crow, T. J., 473
Crowder, R. G., 200, 209
Croyle, R. T., 452
Csikszentmihalyi, M., 243, 302
Culbertson, F. M., 485
Cummings, E., 407
Curran, J. W., 362
Cwikel, J., 41
Czeisler, C. A., 142

D'Agostino, P. R., 549
Damasio, A., 132
Damasio, H., 76
Damon, W., 391
Daniels, H., 380
Darley, J. M., 31, 41, 544, 554
Darnton, N., 400
Darwin, C. J., 200
Davidson, J. E., 235, 306
Davidson, J. R. T., 448
Davidson, M., 61
Davidson, R. J., 308, 311
Davis, K. L., 61
Davis, R., 493
DeAnda, N., xxvii, xxviii
DeAngelis, T., 483
Deary, I. J., 271
Deaux, K., 324
De Boysson-Bardies, B., 247
DeCasper, A. J., 360
DeCharms, R. C., 74
Deci, E. L., 292
Deffenbacher, J. L., 555
DeGroot, A. D., 202
Delaney, C. H., 387, 397
De Leon, G., 343
Delgado, P. L., 487
Della Sala, S., 204
Delprato, D. J., 174
Dement, W. C., 135, 136, 137, 139, 142
Demers, R. A., 246
Denis, M., 229
Denmark, G. L., 14
Dent, J., 404
Dentzer, S., 436

Deregowski, J. B., 122, 123
DeSilva, P., 480
Desimone, R., 218
Desmedt, J. E., 111
DeSteno, D. A., 327
Detterman, D. K., 275, 279
Deuser, R., 235
De Valois, K. K., 100
De Valois, R. L., 100
Devlin, M. J., 299
De Waal, F. B. M., 355
Diaz, G., xxvii
Diaz-Guerrero, R., 148
DiChiara, T. J., 159
Diener, C., 461
Diener, E., 460, 461
Dietz, T. L., 187
DiFranza, J. R., 362
DiGiovanna, A. G., 398, 403
Dill, K. E., 17, 187, 554
Dillard, J. P., 541
Dillman, D. A., 35
Dillman, L., 325
DiMatteo, M. R., 463
Dinges, D. F., 137
Dinnel, D. L., 211
Dishman, R. K., 61
Dobbins, A. C., 119
Dobelle, W. H., 101
Dobrovolsky, M., 247
Dodge, K. A., 371
Doi, T., 419
Dollard, J., 553
Domhoff, G. W., 138, 139
Dominowski, R. L., 240
Donnerstein, E., 552, 553
Donovan, D. M., 150
Dore, F. X., 378
Dorion, A. A., 78
Dornbusch, S., 394
Dortch, S., 149
Doty, R. L., 108
Douglas, K. T., xxvii, xxviii
Dovidio, J. F., 325, 555
Downs, N., 521
Doyle, R., 401
Draine, S. C., 123
Drasgow, F., 323
Dreman, S., 389
Dressler, W. W., 463
Drewnowski, A., 108
Dreyer, P. H., 390
Driver, J., 98
Druckman, D., 166, 230
Drummond, D. C., 170
Dryden, W., 511
Dubovsky, S., 522
Duggan, A., 463
Dugger, C. W., 3, 334
Duke, M., 493
Dulac, C., 108
Duncan, B. L., 516
Duncan, J., 271, 272
Duncan, P. D., 390
Duncan, V., 463
Duncker, K., 241
Dunham, R. M., 397

Dunn, R. S., 188
Dupre, D., 150
Durkin, M. S., 275
Dusenbury, L., 151
Dutton, D. G., 308
Dworkin, R. H., 490, 491, 492
Dytell, R. S., 402

Eagly, A., 321, 530, 531
Ebbesen, E. B., 215
Ebbinghaus, H., 216
Ebomoyi, E., 334
Eccles, J., 292, 394, 546
Eccleston, C., 110
Ecenbarger, W., 459, 460
Ecklund, A., 89
Edgette, J. H., 146
Edgette, J. S., 146
Edmunds, C. S., 341
Ee, J. S., 324
Eftimiades, M., 30
Egeth, H. E., 117
Ehlers, C. L., 156
Eich, E., 220
Eichenbaum, H., 62, 205
Eisen, L., 361
Eisenberg, A., 101
Eisenberg, N., 555
Eisenberger, R., 292
Ekman, P., 304, 308, 310, 311, 312
Elder, G. H., Jr., 390
Elias, M., 554
Elkind, D., 382, 394
Elkins, I. J., 66
Elliot, A. J., 292, 301
Ellis, A., 511
Ellison, C. R., 332
Ellyson, S. L., 325
Embretson, S. E., 271
Endler, N. S., 453
Engebretson, T. O., 556
Engen, T., 107, 108
Engle-Friedman, M., 141
Engler, J., 497
Enserink, M., 17, 47
Epstein, R., 240
Erickson, M. H., 146
Erikson, E. H., 373, 392
Erlandson, D. A., 34
Estes, W. K., 41, 62
Evans, J. S. B. T., 232
Eveleth, P., 389
Everall, I. P., 339
Ey, S., 485
Eysenck, H. H., 422
Eysenck, H. J., 423

Fairfield, M., 463
Falk, D., 78
Fallon, B. A., 482
Fan, P., 321
Farber, B. A., 513
Farley, F., 290
Farrar, T., xxviii
Fearing, V. G., 513

Feather, N. T., 301
Feingold, A., 324
Feiring, C., 370
Feldman, R. S., 21, 221, 244, 311, 325, 371
Fennema, E., 325
Fenton, W. S., 490
Fernald, A., 366
Fernandez, L. C., 14
Festinger, L., 533, 548
Field, T., 361
Fielder, A., xxviii
Fields-Meyer, T., 259, 388
Fiez, J. A., 218
Figueiras, M. J., 398
Finch, A. J., Jr., 555
Fine, L., 148
Fink, A., 34
Fink, M., 523
Finke, R. A., 244
Finkelhor, D., 343
Firestein, B. A., 339
First, M. B., 476
Fischer, C. S., 280
Fischer, K. W., 304, 305, 356
Fischoff, B., 233, 243
Fish, M. C., 340
Fisher, C. B., 21, 44
Fisher, K., 523
Fiske, S. T., 21, 323, 534, 546
Fitch, S. K., xxviii
Flam, F., 107
Flavell, J. H., 379
Fleeson, W., 461
Fleming, R., 447
Flickinger, L., xxviii
Flynn, J. R., 281
Foat, C., xxviii
Fobes, J. L., 71
Folkman, S., 448, 452
Fonagy, P., 517
Ford, C. S., 335
Ford, J. G., 429
Foreman, R. D., 112
Forer, B., 431
Foreyt, J. P., 300
Forrester, M. A., 246
Forte, T., xxviii
Fox, R. E., 371
Fox, S., 272
France, C. R., 111
Frances, A., 476
Francis, E. L., 487
Frankel, R. M., 462
Franks, D. D., 308
Franz, C. E., 392
Franzek, E., 490
Fraser, S. C., 541
Frasure-Smith, N., 457
Free, M. L., 514
Freedman, D. S., 298
Freedman, J. L., 541
Freeman, P., 346
French, H. W., 334
Frensch, P. A., 234
Freud, S., 340
Freund, T., 549
Frey, K., 312

Friedman, A. F., 433
Friedman, M. J., 448
Friedman, R., 147
Friedman, S., 390
Friesen, W. V., 311, 312
Frijda, N. H., 304, 311
Frishman, R., 464
Frith, C. D., 98, 117
Fritsch, J., 300
Fromkin, V. A., 76, 249
Fromm, E., 146
Frost, C., xxviii
Funder, D. C., 66, 358, 423
Funk, M. S., 378
Furnham, A., 188
Furst, P. T., 148
Fyrberg, D., 44

Gabbard, G. O., 418, 555
Gabriel, L. T., 275
Gabriel, M. T., 324
Gaertner, S. L., 547
Gafni, N., 325
Gage, F. H., 80
Gagnon, G. H., 330
Gagnon, S., 378
Galanter, E., 91
Galanter, M., 156
Galatzer-Levy, R. M., 506
Galavotti, C., 457
Gale, N., 184
Galinsky, E., 372
Gallagher, J. J., 189
Gallagher, M., 46
Gannon, P. J., 75
Ganong, L. H., 400
Gao, J., 70
Gara, M. A., 554
Garcia, J., 171
Garcia, M. J., 509
Garcia-Andrade, C., 156
Gardner, B. T., 250
Gardner, H., 76, 269, 270
Gardner, R. A., 250
Gardner, S., 14
Garfield, S. L., 507, 515
Garling, T., 184
Garrison, D. W., 112
Garrison, E. G., 524
Gass, C. S., 34
Gatchel, R. J., 110, 111
Gathercole, S., 204, 246
Gawin, F. H., 154
Gay, J., 214
Gazzaniga, M. S., 80
Ge, X., 390
Geary, D. C., 8
Geen, R. G., 301, 552, 553
Geiselman, R. E., 146
Gelfand, M. M., 404
Gelman, D., 395
Gelman, R., 365, 378
Gentry, W. D., 452
George, L. K., 406
George, M. S., 308
George, T. P., 365

Georgeson, M., 98, 119
Gerton, J., 252
Gescheider, G. A., 91
Getner, D., 244
Getzlaf, S. B., 458
Gewirtz, J., 391
Ghosh, S. N., 556
Gibbons, A., 73
Gibbs, M. E., 60
Gibson, B., 459
Gibson, H. B., 146
Gidycz, C. A., 143
Gilbert, B., 251
Gilbert, D. G., 458
Gilbert, D. T., 421, 537
Gilbert, P., 299
Gilger, J. W., 358
Gilhooly, K. J., 204
Gilligan, C., 391, 392
Gillis, R., xxviii
Gillyatt, P., 107
Gingras, I., 292
Gladue, B. A., 339
Gladwin, T., 260
Glaman, J. M., 549
Glaser, R., 457
Glass, G. V., 516
Glassman, A. H., 458
Glenmullen, J., 521
Glick, P., 323
Gobet, F., 202
Godbey, G., 401
Gold, T., 53
Goldberg, C., 354
Goldfarb, M., 476
Golding, J. M., 342
Goldsmith, H. H., 373, 493
Goldstein, E. B., 115
Goldstein, G., 203
Goldstein, I., 329, 330, 332, 345
Goleman, D., 272, 367, 462, 464, 497
Golledge, R. G., 101
Golombok, S., 340
Goode, E., 107
Goodglass, H., 76
Goodman, G., 213
Goodman, P., 514
Goodman, W. K., 481
Goodrick, G. K., 300
Goodwin, C. J., 33
Goossens, L., 406
Gordon, A., xxviii
Gordon, J. W., 359, 388
Gorman, J. M., 504
Gorsky, H., 244
Gortner, S. R., 425
Gosling, S. D., 14, 21
Gottesman, I. I., 356, 490
Gottfredson, L. S., 433
Gould, E., 80
Gould, R. L., 399
Gouras, P., 100
Graf, P., 207, 406
Graffin, N. F., 146
Graham, J. R., 433, 434
Graham, S., 45
Grammer, K., 108

Grant, K. E., 485
Grayson, C., 488
Green, D. M., 102
Green, P. R., 98, 119
Greenbaum, C., 229
Greenberg, R. L., 512
Greenberg, S. H., 370
Greene, B., 340
Greene, D., 292, 538
Greene, R. L., 434
Greenfield, D. N., 483
Greenfield, P. M., 279
Greenlaw, P. S., 433
Greeno, J. G., 235
Greenwald, A. G., 123
Greenwood, C. R., 191
Gregory, R. L., 121
Gregory, S. S., 334, 335
Greist-Bousquet, S., 121
Griffith, R. M., 138
Griffiths, M., 187
Griffiths, R. R., 152
Grigorenko, E., 188, 280
Grillner, S., 66
Grimsley, D. L., 82
Grimson, W. E. L., 69
Grohol, J. M., 517
Gross, J., 394
Grossi, G., 78
Groth-Marnat, G., 432
Grube, J. W., 458
Gruneberg, M. M., 220
Grusec, J. E., 185, 510
Guarnaccia, C. A., 408
Guastello, S. J., 432
Guerra, M., 392
Guilford, J. P., 269
Gullotta, T., 394
Gur, R. C., 78, 79
Guralnick, M. J., 276
Gurin, J., 300
Gurman, E. B., 44
Gustavson, C. R., 172
Gutek, B. A., 323
Guthrie, R. V., 45
Guttman, M., 522
Gwynn, M. I., 145

Haber, R. N., 113
Hafner, H., 490
Haimov, I., 144
Halberstadt, A. G., 311
Haley, W. E., 464
Hall, E., 402
Hall, G. C. N., 17, 341, 342
Hall, J. A., 464
Hall, L. K., 214
Hall, M., 449
Hall, P., 20
Hallahan, M., 538
Halle, P. A., 247
Halling, S., 476
Halpern, D. F., 244, 325, 326
Hamer, D. H., 339
Hamilton, C. E., 370
Hammond, S. L., 463

Hampson, E., 326
Hanak, J., xxviii
Handler, A., 392
Hankins, W. G., 171
Hanmer, T. J., 392
Hanna, J. L., 311
Hannigan, J. H., 362
Hansson, R. O., 408
Harackiewicz, J. M., 292
Harden, B., 277
Hardie, E. A., 539
Hare, R. D., 493
Harlow, H. F., 368
Harlow, J. M., 75
Harlow, R. E., 407
Harman, C., 373
Harnish, R. M., 246
Harold, G. T., 400
Harper, T., 403
Harpur, T. J., 493
Harris, B. A., 548
Harris, C. R., 327
Harris-Kern, M. J., 546
Harrison, D., xxviii
Harrison, P. J., 339
Harrison, S. H., xxviii, xxix
Hart, B., 248, 249
Hart, S. D., 493
Hartmann, E., 135
Hartung, C. M., 495
Hartup, W. W., 371
Harvey, E., 372
Haseltine, W. A., 66
Hass, N., 460
Hatcher, M., xxviii
Hatfield, E., 338, 550
Haugtvedt, C. P., 532
Hauri, P., 141
Haviland-Jones, J., 108, 303
Hawke, J. M., 343
Hawley, E., 121
Hay, J. L., 402
Hayes, J. R., 239
Hayflick, L., 404
Haynes, T., xxviii
Hearth, H., 387
Heath, A. C., 458
Heatherton, T. F., 296, 297
Hebl, M. R., 296
Heckhausen, H., 301
Hedges, L. V., 325
Hefferline, R., 514
Hegar, A., xxviii
Heinrichs, R. W., 490
Heishman, S. J., 457
Heller, W., 78
Helms, J. E., 279
Helmuth, L., 60
Henderlong, J., 292
Henderson, V. W., 204
Henningfield, J. E., 457
Henry, L. M., xxix
Henry, W. E., 407
Herdt, G., 330, 389
Herek, G., 340
Herholz, K., 75
Herman, C. J., 398

Herman, C. P., 297, 300
Hermann, C., 112
Hernstein, R. J., 280
Herrera, C., 366
Herrett-Skjellum, J., 546
Herrmann, D., 207, 220
Hersen, M., 190
Hershman, S., 146
Herskovits, M. J., 121
Herzog, T., 538
Hetherington, E. M., 400
Heward, W. L., 275
Hewitt, E. C., 301
Hewstone, M., 545
Heyn, E., 332
Heyward, W. L., 362
Hicks, R. A., 137
Higgins, E. T., 425
Hilgard, E. R., 146
Hill, C. T., 338
Hill, J. O., 297, 298
Hill, W., 486
Hinkel, K., xxviii
Hipkiss, R. A., 247
Hirsch, J., 298
Hirsh, I. J., 107
Hirt, E. R., 211
Hitch, G. J., 229
Hitt, J., 347
Ho, H. Z., 381
Hobfoll, S. E., 448, 452
Hobson, J. A., 134, 140, 141
Hoch, S. J., 538
Hochschild, A. R., 402
Hocutt, A. M., 276
Hodapp, R. M., 275
Hodgson, R., 480
Hoeller, K., 19
Hoffman, D. S., 74
Hoffman, P. L., 61
Hogan, J., 436
Hogan, R., 436
Hogg, M. A., 539
Holahan, C. J., 453
Holden, C., 434
Holland, E. A., 312
Holland, J. C., 457
Hollingworth, H. L., 14
Hollis, K. L., 171, 181
Holmes, D. S., 147
Holmes, J. G., 550
Holroyd, J., 112
Holt-Lunstad, J., 452
Holy, T. E., 108
Holyoak, K. J., 244
Hong, E., 244, 252
Honorton, C., 123
Honts, C. R., 309
Honzik, C. H., 183, 184
Hoon, P. W., 330
Horesh, N., 299
Horgan, J., 218, 281, 473
Horn, D., 489
Horney, K., 14, 420
Horowitz, H. A., 493
Horowitz, J. M., xxix
Horwitz, L., 494

House, P., 538
Houston, L. N., 336
Hovland, C., 530
Howe, M. L., 213
Howells, J. G., 472
Howes, C., 372
Hren, W., xxviii
Hubbard, K., 295
Hubble, M. A., 516
Hubel, D. H., 97
Hudson, W., 122
Huesmann, L. R., 187
Huffman, L., xxix
Hulin, C., 323
Hull, C. L., 289
Humphreys, G. W., 114
Humphreys, L. G., 279
Hunt, E., 238, 271
Hunt, J. R., 452
Hunt, M., 42, 336, 339
Hutchinson, R., xxviii
Hwang, C. P., 372
Hyde, J. S., 324, 325, 336, 338
Hyman, I. E., Jr., 211
Hyman, R., 123
Hynes, R., xxix

Iacono, W. G., 66, 309
Ikonomidou, C., 362
Impara, J. C., 433
Inglefinger, F. J., 296
Inhelder, B., 378
Isay, R. A., 340
Issac, A. R., 230
Iversen, L. L., 159
Ivry, R., 78
Izard, C. E., 306, 308, 310, 312

Jacklin, C. N., 325, 327
Jackson, T. L., 346
Jacobson, N. S., 435
Jacobson, P. D., 459
Jainchill, N., 343
James, J., 486
James, J. E., 152
James, W., 306
Jamison, K. R., 486, 487
Janis, I., 450, 530, 540
Janofsky, M., 483
Jaret, P., 454
Jaroff, L., 359
Jasperse, M., 398
Jenike, M. A., 523
Jenkins, J. M., 304
Jenkins, L. S., 425
Jenkins, S. R., 302
Jensen, A. R., 268
Jensen, J. K., 379
Jensen, S. S., 433
Jenses, R., xxix
Jerome, L., 517
Jevning, R., 147
Jhally, S., 460
Jobes, D. A., 395
John, O. P., 423, 430
Johnson, D. M., 240

Johnson, J. T., 432
Johnson, R. W., 533
Johnson, V., 332
Johnson, V. E., 333, 340, 346
Johnson-Laird, P. N., 232
Johnston, D., 218
Johnston, L., 545
Joiner, T. E., 450, 488
Jones, A., 293
Jones, A. P., 549
Jones, B. A., 456
Jones, E. E., 536
Jones, J. C., 331
Jones, J. M., 21
Jones, S., 452
Jonides, J., 218
Jorgenson, L. M., 323
Joseph, R., 66
Josephs, R. A., 156
Joyce, J., 470
Julien, R. M., 159, 521
Jussim, L., 545, 546

Kagan, J., 362, 373
Kahn, R. S., 61
Kahn, S., 392
Kahneman, D., 237, 239, 461
Kainz, P. M., 99
Kaiser, J., 483
Kakei, S., 74
Kakigi, R., 111
Kalafat, J., 554
Kameenui, E. J., 276
Kamins, M. A., 33
Kaniasty, K., 448
Kanner, A. D., 451
Kaplan, H. S., 332
Kaplan, M. F., 535
Kaplan, R. M., 432, 463, 464
Kapur, N., 220
Kapur, S., 491
Karlins, M., 531
Karni, A., 140
Karp, D. A., 399
Karriker, M. W., 82
Kasimatis, M., 312
Katkin, E. S., 455
Katz, A. N., 211
Katz, D., 545
Katz, N. R., 464
Katz, P. A., 546
Kaufman, A. S., 263
Kaufman, S. R., 46
Kaufmann, C. A., 358, 482
Kausler, D. H., 405
Kawachi, I., 457
Kawasaki, C., 373
Kazdin, A. E., 190, 509
Keane, T. M., 448
Kearsley, R., 362, 373
Keating, D. P., 378
Keefe, F. J., 111
Keehn, J. D., 174
Keffer, R. L., 274
Keith-Spiegel, P., 44
Keller, M. C., 549

Kelley, H., 535
Kelly, A. L., 400, 443
Kelly, D. D., 136
Kelly, F. D., 435
Kelly, H. H., 530
Kelly, R. J., 533
Kelner, K., 17
Kempermann, G., 80
Kendler, K. S., 373
Kenny, D. A., 536
Kenrick, D. T., 326
Kenshalo, R., 110
Kessler, R. C., 497
Keveri, M. K., 208
Kidwell, J. S., 392, 397
Kiecolt-Glaser, J. K., 457
Kienker, P. K., 113
Kiesler, C. A., 524
Kiesler, D. J., 475
Kiesler, S., 483
Kihlstrom, J. F., 206, 418
Kilborn, P. T., 432
Kilpatrick, D. G., 341
Kim, M., 112
Kimble, G. A., 19
Kimmel, A. J., 44
Kimura, D., 78, 326, 327
Kinchloe, B., 330
King, G. R., 178
King, K. C., 324
King, S. H., 10
Kinney, N. E., xxix
Kinsey, A. C., 336
Kinzler, K. W., 359
Kirby, D., 336
Kircher, J. C., 309
Kirk, S. A., 477
Kirsch, I., 47, 145, 146
Kirshner, H. S., 76
Kitterle, F. L., 78
Klatzky, R. L., 101, 536
Kleber, H. D., 156
Klein, M., 394, 536
Kleinman, A., 495, 518
Kliegl, R., 379
Klinke, R., 74
Klinkenborg, V., 141
Kluft, R. P., 483
Kmiec, E. B., 359
Knight, G. P., 555
Knowles, J. A., 358, 482
Kobasa, S. C., 452
Koch, K. L., 107
Koegel, L. K., 276
Koegel, R., 177
Koestner, R., 292
Kogan, N., 243
Kohlberg, L., 391
Köhler, W., 239
Kolarz, C. M., 461
Kolata, G., 359
Konishi, M., 102
Konrad, W., 462
Kontos, S., 372
Koob, G. F., 158, 458
Koocher, G. P., 44
Koop, C. B., 365

Kosambi, D. D., 111
Kosecoff, J., 34
Koss, M. P., 17, 341, 342
Kosslyn, S. M., 229
Kotler-Cope, S., 406
Kotre, J., 403
Koval, J. J., 458
Koveces, Z., 305
Kozlowski, L. T., 457
Krail, W. R., xxix
Kramer, D. L. F., 208
Kramer, P., 521
Krampe, R. T., 379
Kraus, S. J., 532
Kraut, R., 483
Kravitz, E. A., 80
Krebs, D. L., 392
Kremer, J. M. D., 61
Kreuger, L. E., 109
Kriz, J., 114
Krohne, H. W., 447
Krosnick, J. A., 34
Kruglanski, A. W., 549
Krull, D. S., 536
Krystal, J. H., 521
Kübler-Ross, E., 407
Kuhl, P. K., 247
Kulynych, J. J., 78
Kunda, Z., 534
Kupfer, D. J., 143
Kuroda, Y., 111
Kurtines, W., 391
Kvale, S., 34
Kwan, V. S. Y., 425

Lach, J., 543
LaFromboise, T., 252
Laird, J. D., 306, 312
Lalonde, C., 379
Lamb, M. E., 371, 372
Lambert, B. L., 463
Lambert, M. J., 516
Lamon, S. J., 325
Landis, D., 547
Landrum, R. E., 44
Landry, D. W., 152
Lane, R. C., 507, 516
Langer, E., 406, 450, 547
Langreth, R., 109, 453
Langs, G., 480
Larose, H., 537
Larsen, L., xxix
Larsen, R. J., 312
Larson, J., 488
Larson, R. K., 247
Larson, R. W., 371
Larson, S. K., 361
Lask, B., 298
Lasnik, H., 247
Latané, B., 31, 41, 554
Laumann, E. O., 345
Laurence, S., 230
Lavie, N., 117
Lavie, P., 144
Lawton, M. P., 548
Lazarus, A. A., 525

Lazarus, R. S., 303, 308, 449, 452
Leary, W. E., 343
Leber, W. R., 485
LeBlanc, B. A., 533
Leckman, J. F., 480
Lee, S. Y., 381, 538
Lehman, D. R., 451
Leibel, R. L., 298
Leibovic, K. N., 100
Leigh, H., 462
Lenzenweger, M. F., 490, 491, 492, 493
Leonard, B. E., 487
Leong, F. L., 21
LePage, A., 187, 553
Lepore, S. J., 452
Lepper, M. R., 292
Lerner, R. M., 21
Lertola, J., 300
Lesch, K.-P., 482
Leslie, C., 251
Lesperance, F., 457
LeVay, S., 339
Levenson, R. W., 306, 308, 312
Leventhal, H., 308, 458
Levin, J. R., 220
Levine, J. M., 540
Levine, S. C., 326
Levinson, D. J., 398
Levy, B. L., 406
Levy, D. H., 359
Levy, S., 244
Levy, S. M., 457
Lew, R. A., 362
Lewin-Epstein, N., 402
Lewis, J., 400
Lewis, M., 303, 370
Lewis, R., 96
Li, S., 277
Li, Y., 60
Lichenstein, S., 233
Lichtenberger, E. O., 263
Liebert, R. M., 186
Lilienfeld, S. O., 309
Lilly, R., 547
Lin, K. M., 156
Lindsay, P. H., 206
Lindy, J., 71
Linn, M. C., 325
Linscheid, T. R., 177
Linssen, H., 394
Linszen, D. H., 492
Lipsey, M. W., 516
Lloyd, J. W., 276
Lockhart, R. S., 203, 209
Loewenstein, G., 290
Loftus, E. F., 206, 212, 213
Loftus, G. R., 212
Logie, R. H., 204
Logue, A. W., 178
London, E. D., 152
Long, A., 133
Long, G. M., 200
Loomis, J. M., 101
Looy, H., 339
López, S. R., 21, 281
LoPiccolo, L., 346
Lord, S. E., 394

Lorenz, K., 368, 553
Lovaas, O. I., 177
Lowe, M. R., 299
Lown, B., 464
Loy, J. W., 535
Lubinski, D., 325
Lucchina, L., 109
Luce, R. D., 107
Lucy, J. A., 249
Ludwig, A. M., 132, 486
Lundy, R., 146
Luria, A. R., 220
Lusk, B., xxviii
Ly, D. H., 404
Lykken, D. T., 309, 356, 461, 493
Lynch, G., 62
Lynch, H. J., 144
Lynn, S. J., 143, 145, 146, 213
Lyons, N. P., 392

Macaluso, E., 98
Maccoby, E. E., 325
Machung, A., 402
MacKenzie, B., 279
MacKenzie, T. D., 460
Mackie, D., 187
Mackintosh, N. J., 268
Macmillan, M., 418
Macrae, C. N., 545
Madden, P. A. F., 458
Madon, S., 546
Magnusson, D., 390
Magruder, K. M., 516
Maidment, I., 522
Maier, S. F., 449, 487
Mairs, D. A. E., 146
Malamuth, N. M., 342
Malone, P. S., 537
Malott, M. E., 190
Malott, R. W., 190
Manganello, J., xxix
Mann, D., 506
Manstead, A. S. R., 311
Manz, C. C., 540
Mapes, G., 142
Marcoen, A., 406
Marcus, G. F., 248
Marcus, M. B., 101
Marcus-Newhall, A., 553
Marentette, P. F., 247
Margolis, E., 230
Margolskee, R. F., 108
Marini, M. M., 321
Markey, P. M., 554
Markham, M. R., xxix
Marks, D. F., 230
Marks, G., 538
Markstrom, C., 394
Marlatt, G. A., 150
Marsella, A. J., 448
Marshall, L. J., 346
Marteau, T. M., 398
Martin, A., 75
Martin, C. E., 336
Martin, L. R., xxviii, xxix, 249
Martindale, C., 132

Marzol, P. C., 480
Maser, J. D., 481
Maslow, A. H., 292, 293
Mason, M., 335
Masson, M. E. J., 207
Masten, A. S., 382
Mastenbrook, J., xxix
Masters, W. H., 332, 333, 340, 346
Mastropieri, M. A., 203
Matarazzo, J. D., 432
Matchen, J., 322
Matlin, M. M., 324
Matsuda, Y., 111
Matsumoto, D., 311, 312
Matthews, D. B., 156
Mattock, A., 366
Matute, H., 180
Mauner, G., 76
Maurer, K., 365, 490
Mayer, J. D., 272
Mayer, R., 177, 190
Mayr, U., 379
McAdams, D. P., 393
McCabe, P. M., 445, 447, 452, 455
McCain, N. L., 453
McCann, U. D., 159
McCauley, C., 331, 540
McClearn, G. E., 355, 356, 426
McClelland, D. C., 272, 301
McClintock, M. K., 330, 389
McConaghy, N., 346
McCrae, R. R., 423
McCullers, J. C., 402
McCullough, J. P., Jr., 510
McDonald, C., 492
McDonald, H. E., 211
McDonald, J. L., 249
McDonald, J. W., 77
McDougall, W., 289
McDowell, D. M., 150
McEwen, B. S., 445
McFadyen, R. G., 250
McGaugh, J. L., 62, 218
McGlashan, T. H., 490
McGue, M., 66, 156, 280
McGuire, P. K., 489
McGuire, W. J., 31
McHale, S. M., 327
McIntosh, D. N., 303
McKinney, K., 338
McKoon, G., 208
McLaughlin, F. J., 108
McManus, F., 297
McMillan, J. R., 324
McMullin, R. E., 512
McWhirter, D. P., 340
Mead, M., 397
Mealey, L., 326
Mednick, A., 402
Meier, R. P., 221, 247
Meister, M., 108
Mekler, E., 272
Melton, G. B., 524
Meltzer, H. Y., 492
Meltzoff, A. N., 366
Melville, K., 397
Melzack, R., 111

Mendez, F. J., 509
Menlove, F. L., 185, 510
Mentzer, S. J., 462
Mercer, D. L., xxix
Merikangas, K., 66
Merlin, D., 65
Merzenich, M. M., 74
Mesquita, B., 304, 311
Messer, S. B., 504
Messineo, M., 328, 546
Messo, J., 212
Metcalfe, J., 240
Metee, D. R., 549
Metzler, J., 229
Meyer, A., 487
Meyer, G. J., 435
Meyer, R. G., 480
Michael, R. T., 336, 338
Middlebrooks, J. C., 102, 107
Midgley, B. D., 174
Mifflin, L., 186
Mikamo, K., 61
Miles, M., xxviii
Miles, M., xxix
Miles, R., 60
Milgram, R. M., 188, 244
Milgram, S., 543
Miller, A. G., 186, 421, 544, 551
Miller, D. W., 212
Miller, G. A., 201
Miller, G. R., 311
Miller, J. G., 7, 21, 538
Miller, K. J., 299
Miller, L. T., 379
Miller, M. W., 523
Miller, N., 538, 553
Miller, N. E., 82
Miller, R., xxix
Miller, R. R., 169
Miller, T. J., 516
Miller-Jones, D., 279
Millon, T., 493, 494
Mills, J. L., 362
Milner, B., 72, 203, 215
Milner, P., 71
Milton, J., 123
Mineka, S., 290
Mingo, C., 398
Minuchin, S., 515
Miserando, M., 209
Miserendino, M., xxix
Mitchell, K. E., 309
Miyago, O., 138
Miyake, K., 373
Miyashita, Y., 75
Mizes, J. S., 299
Moghaddam, B., 520
Moise, J., 187
Moldin, S. O., 490
Molfese, D. L., 426
Molfese, V. J., 426
Moon, S. M., 515
Moore-Ede, M., 142
Moorhead, G., 540
Moos, R. H., 453
Morano, M. I., 445
Moreland, K., 435, 516

Moreno, F. A., 487
Moretti, M. M., 425
Morling, B., 546
Morrison, A. R., 46
Morrow, J., 82
Moscovici, S., 539
Moskowitz, J. T., 452
Motley, M. T., 414
Moutoussis, K., 98
Movshon, J. A., 119
Mroczek, D. K., 461
Mrzljak, L., 520
Muehlenhard, C. L., 342
Mueser, K. T., 492
Mufson, M. J., 112
Mukerjee, M., 46
Muller, C. R., 114
Mumford, G. K., 152
Mumme, D. L., 366
Munroe, R. L., 324
Munson, L. J., 323
Murdock, G., xxviii
Murphy, S. T., 303, 413
Murray, C., 280
Murray, J. B., 61, 111, 152
Murray, R. M., 489, 492
Murray, S. L., 550
Musgrove, G. J., xxviii, xxix
Myerhoff, B., 397
Myers, D. G., 460, 461
Myerson, J., 281

Nahome, L., 548
Nash, J. M., 112
Nash, M., 146
Nathan, P. E., 504
Nathans, J., 99
Navon, R., 361
Neck, C. P., 540
Neff, D. L., 379
Negrin, G., 275
Neher, A., 293
Neiderhiser, J. M., 356
Neisser, U., 214, 280, 281
Neitz, J., 99
Neitz, M., 99
Nelson, M., 288
Nelson, W. M., III, 555
Ness, R. B., 362
Nesse, R. M., 488
Nesselroade, C. S., 405
Newby, I. R., 211
Newcomb, A. F., 371
Newcombe, N. S., 214
Newell, A., 237
Newell, J., xxix
Newsome, W. T., 119
Newstead, S. E., 232
Nichols, M. P., 515
Nickerson, R. S., 216
Nichols, G., xxviii
Nicolson, N. A., 449
Nida, S., 554
Nierenberg, A., 522, 523
Nieves, S., xxviii
Nigg, J. T., 493

Nikles, C. D., II, 139
Nisbett, R. E., 233, 280, 296, 298, 537
Noble, H. B., 457, 459
Noi, L. S., 188
Nolan, R. P., 455
Nolen-Hoeksema, S., 488
Norman, D. A., 206
Norris, F. H., 448
Novak, M. A., 46
Nowell, A., 325
Nowicki, S., Jr., 493
Noyes, R., 482
Nunn, K. P., 487
Nyberg, L., 205

Oatley, K., 304, 308
Ochsner, K. N., 207
O'Connor, S. C., 301
Oden, M. H., 277
O'Donohue, W., 323
Ogbu, J., 189, 281
O'Grady, W. D., 247
O'Hara, L. A., 244
O'Hare, D., 121
Okamoto, Y., 378
Okamura, L., 342
Okun, B. F., 518
Olds, J., 71
Olfson, M., 485
Oliver, M. B., 336
Olshansky, S. J., 404
Olson, G., xxix
Olson, L., 77
O'Neil, J., 165
O'Neill, A., 295
Oren, D. A., 142
Orenstein, P., 324
Orlansky, M. D., 275
Orne, M. T., 309
Ornstein, R., 78
Orr, W. C., 141
Ortony, A., 304
Orwin, R. G., 516
Orzack, M. S., 483
Osborn, M. L., 472
Osborne, Y. V. H., 480
Oskamp, S., 547
Oster, M. I., 146
Osterweis, M., 463
O'Sullivan, M., 310, 312
Oths, K. S., 463
Owens, R. E., Jr., 246

Paik, A., 345
Paivio, A., 229
Palmer, J. C., 212
Paludi, M. A., 323
Paniagua, F. A., 475
Pankove, E., 243
Paradiso, M. A., 55
Parker, J. D., 362
Parker, J. G., 371
Parkin, A. J., 406
Parlee, M. B., 549
Parrott, G. R., 240
Parrott, R., 463

Pascoe, K., 220
Pascual-Leone, A., 230
Paton, C. C., 455
Patterson, M. J., 312
Patterson, T. L., 463, 464
Patzwahl, D. R., 97
Pauls, D. L., 480
Pavlides, C., 140
Pavlov, I. P., 167
Payne, D. G., 217
Peirce, R. S., 452
Penn, D. L., 489
Penney, J. B., Jr., 60
Pennisi, E., 66, 156, 359
Penrod, S., 539
Peplau, L. A., 338
Perez, R. M., 340
Perkins, D. N., 121
Perkins, R., 546
Perloff, R. M., 531
Perls, F. S., 514
Perry-Jenkins, M., 371, 400
Pervin, L. A., 423, 430
Peters, J. C., 297, 298
Petersen, S. E., 218
Peterson, A., 390
Peterson, C., 449, 487
Peterson, K. C., 448
Peterson, L. R., 203
Peterson, M. J., 203
Peterson, S. E., 218
Peterzell, D. H., 365
Petri, H. L., 291
Petrill, S. A., 280
Petronis, A., 473
Pettigrew, T. F., 547
Pettingale, K. W., 456
Pettito, L. A., 247, 250
Petto, A. J., 46
Petty, R. E., 530, 531, 532
Petzold, P., 537
Pezdek, K., 213
Phillips, D. S., 203
Phillips-Hershey, E. H., 276
Philpot, C. L., 327
Phinney, J. S., 21
Piaget, J., 375, 378
Piasecki, T. M., 458
Pich, E. M., 152
Pick, G., 149
Pierce, W. D., 292
Pietromonaco, P., 123
Pihlgren, E. M., 143
Piliavin, I. M., 554
Piliavin, J. A., 554
Pillard, R. C., 339, 358
Pincus, H. A., 476
Pinker, S., 247, 249, 250
Pisoni, D. B., 156
Pledge, D. S., 447
Plomin, R., 280, 355, 356, 426, 427, 428
Plous, S., 46
Plumert, J. M., 184
Plummer, W., 149
Plutchik, R., 304, 417
Polivy, J., 297, 300
Polk, N., 272

Pollack, A., 77
Pollack, M. H., 480
Pomerlau, O. F., 458
Pomeroy, W. B., 336
Poncini, M., 236
Ponday, C., xxviii
Ponterotto, J. G., 518
Pope, K. S., 213
Porac, C., 121
Porkka-Heiskanen, T., 136
Porte, H. S., 140
Porter, R. H., 108
Postman, L. J., 211
Potheraju, A., 138
Pottieger, A. E., 152
Powell, D. H., 405
Powell, L. H., 456
Powers, D. E., 274
Pratkanis, A. R., 540
Pratt, S. I., 516
Pressley, M., 220
Pressman, M. R., 141
Pribram, K. H., 307
Price, B., xxviii
Price, D. D., 109
Price, G. E., 188
Price, J. L., 229
Priester, J. R., 530
Prince, R. J., 432
Pringle, R., 402
Pristash, B., 328
Proia, R. L., 361
Prout, M. F., 448
Pryor, D. W., 339
Psotka, J., 208, 217
Pullum, G. K., 249
Pulvirenti, L., 158
Purves, D., 60
Putnam, F. W., 17, 483, 484

Quillian, M. R., 206, 207
Quinn, D., xxix
Quinn, M., 460

Raag, T., 327
Rabins, P. V., 489
Rabson-Hare, J., 41
Rachman, S., 480
Rackliff, C. L., 327
Radigan, B., xxix
Ragan, J. D., 452
Rakoff, V. M., 397
Ramachandran, V. S., 97
Randall, C. K., xxix
Rapp, R. R., 46
Raskin, D. C., 309
Raskin, N. J., 513
Rasmussen, J., 243
Raso-Knott, P. A., 301
Ratcliff, R., 208
Rau, H., 82
Rawsthorne, L. J., 292
Ray, W. J., 33, 146
Raynor, J. O., 169, 301
Rector, K., xxviii
Redding, G. M., 121

Reed, S. K., 239
Rees, G., 117
Reeves, R. A., 541
Regan, P. C., 550
Reggia, J. A., 489
Reich, J. W., 408
Reichman, W. E., 489
Reilly, A. H., 322
Reingold, E. M., 206
Reinisch, J. M., 327, 340
Reisberg, D., 238, 244
Reisenzein, R., 308
Reiser, M. F., 462
Reiss, I. L., 338
Reitman, J. S., 234
Remington, G., 491
Rescorla, R. A., 169, 171
Resnick, S. M., 473
Reyna, V. F., 379
Reynolds, C., 327
Reynolds, C. F., III, 143
Reynolds, R. I., 206
Reznikoff, M., 435
Rhodes, N., 531
Rhodewalt, F., 463
Rhue, J. W., 143, 145, 146
Ricciuti, H. N., 362
Rice, G., 339
Rice, M. L., 249
Rice, V. H., 445
Rich, F., 485
Richards, A. L., 341
Richards, M. H., 371
Richardson-Klarehn, A., 221
Richie, J., 458
Riday, G., xxviii
Ridley, L., 276
Rieder, R. O., 358, 482
Riefer, D. M., 208
Rierdan, J., 395
Ringold, D. J., 460
Rinn, W. E., 312
Risch, N., 66
Risley, T., 248, 249
Ritzler, B., 489
Rizley, R. C., 171
Robbins, M., xxviii
Robbins, T. W., 214
Roberts, B. W., 436
Roberts, S. M., 449
Robertson, L. C., 78
Robins, L. N., 495, 496
Robins, R. W., 14, 21
Robinson, J., 401
Rock, A., 458, 459
Rodin, J., 296, 450
Roebers, C. E. M., 212
Roeser, R. W., 394
Rogers, C. R., 429, 474, 513
Rogers, P., 30
Rogler, L. H., 45
Rokeach, M., 458, 547
Rolland, J. S., 515
Rolls, E. T., 296
Root-Bernstein, M., 243
Root-Bernstein, R., 243
Rorschach, H., 435

Roscoe, S., 121
Roseman, I. J., 455
Rosen, D., 298
Rosen, H., 512
Rosen, R. C., 345
Rosenbaum, G., 489
Rosenbaum, M., 298
Rosenberg, D., 131
Rosenblood, L. K., 301
Rosenhan, D. L., 476
Rosenheck, R., 520
Rosenstein, D. S., 493
Rosenthal, A. M., 334
Rosenthal, E., 296
Rosenthal, L. H., 531
Rosenthal, R., 47
Rosenthal, S., 370
Rosenzweig, M. R., 7, 21
Rosewicz, B., 401
Rosnow, R. L., 44, 47
Ross, C. A., 483
Ross, D., 185
Ross, L., 421, 537, 538
Ross, M., 211
Ross, S., 185
Roter, D. L., 464
Roth, A., 517
Rothblum, E. D., 330
Roush, W., 142
Routtenberg, A., 71
Rovee-Collier, C., 379
Rovine, M., 372
Rowe, J. B., 75
Rowe, J. W., 404
Rowley, S. J., 546
Rozelle, R. M., 549
Rozin, P., 296, 297
Rubenstein, C., 44
Rubin, D. C., 210, 214
Rubin, Z., 338
Ruble, D. N., 402
Rudorfer, M. V., 481
Rumbaugh, D. M., 246
Runco, M. A., 244
Ruppin, E., 489
Rusiniak, K. W., 171
Russell, J. A., 304
Russo, N., 431
Russo, R., 406
Ruthsatz, J. M., 275
Rutter, M., 276
Ryan, R. M., 292
Rychlak, J., 132
Ryncarz, R. A., 391

Saarni, C., 372
Sacco, W. P., 487
Saccuzzo, D. P., 432
Sack, R. L., 142
Sackett, P. R., 433
Sackheim, H. A., 523
Sadker, D., 328
Sadker, M., 328
Saenz, K. P., xxix
Saggino, A., 423
Saigh, P. A., 448

St. Onge, S., 508, 510
Sakamoto, S. O., 244
Sallis, J. F., Jr., 463, 464
Salovey, P., 272, 327, 453
Salthouse, T. A., 405
Sams, M., 200
Samuda, R. J., 279
Sanders, S., 340
Sandoval, J., 279
Sanes, J. N., 74
Sangrador, J. L., 549
Sansone, C., 292
Sanz, C., 252
Sapolsky, R. M., 445
Saterfield, H., xxviii
Sato, K., 304
Saudino, K. J., 355, 356
Saulsberry, K., 464
Savage-Rumbaugh, E. S., 250
Savage-Rumbaugh, S., 251
Saxe, L., 309
Sayette, M. A., 156
Saywitz, K., 213
Scarr, S., 279, 281, 355, 427
Schab, F. R., 107, 209
Schachter, S., 298, 307, 548
Schacter, D. L., 205, 206, 207
Schafer, M., 541
Schaie, K. W., 269, 405
Schaller, M., 547
Schapira, A. H. V., 61
Scharf, M., 143
Schedlowski, M., 457
Scheff, T. J., 471
Scheier, M. F., 424
Scherer, K. R., 304, 310
Scherman, A., 346
Schiffman, H. R., 121
Schkade, D. A., 461
Schmalt, H. D., 301
Schmolck, H., 211
Schneider, E. L., 404
Schneider, K. S., 53, 299, 301
Schneidman, E. S., 395
Schnopp-Wyatt, N., xxix
Schoen, L. M., 203
Schofield, W., 335
Schorr, n., xxix
Schretlen, D., 269
Schrier, R. W., 460
Schroeder, D. A., 555
Schulman, M., 272, 382
Schwartzberg, N. S., 402
Schwartzberg, S., 22, 244
Schwarz, N., 34, 233, 461
Schwarz, R. A., 448
Scott, B., xxviii
Scott, S., xxviii, xxix
Scruggs, T. E., 203
Scully, D. M., 61
Searleman, A., 207
Sears, D. O., 45
Sears, R. R., 277
Sebel, P. S., 206
Secter, I. I., 146
Seeley, R. J., 70, 103
Seeman, P., 491

Segal, N. L., 356
Segall, M. H., 121
Seidenberg, M. S., 250
Self, E. A., 290
Seligman, L., 457
Seligman, M. E. P., 449, 487, 515, 516
Selikowitz, M., 276
Selkoe, D. J., 60, 406
Sells, R., 339
Selsky, A., 396
Seltzer, L., 144
Selye, H., 445
Seppa, N., 17, 177
Serok, S., 514
Seyfarth, R. M., 250
Seymour, A. K., 341
Shafir, E., 232
Shah, G. M. S., 489
Shaker, L. A., 456
Shapiro, A. P., 445
Shapiro, D. A., 516
Shapiro, Y., 555
Sharma, J., 66, 73
Sharma, S., 556
Sharps, M. J., 229
Shatz, C. J., 361
Shaughnessy, J. J., 33
Shaver, A., xxix
Shaver, P. R., 304, 305
Shaw, E., xxviii
Shawver, L., 340
Shaywitz, B. A., 78, 79
Shea, C., 35, 281
Shear, J., 132
Sheehan, S., 488
Shepard, R., 229
Sherman, J. W., 536
Sherman, M., 197
Shields, S. A., 14
Shiels, P. G., 359
Shier, D., 96
Shiffrin, R. M., 199
Shin, L. M., 229
Shnek, Z. M., 450
Shuchter, S. R., 521
Shultz, S. K., 346
Shurkin, J. N., 277
Shweder, R. A., 304
Sibicky, M. E., 555
Siegel, B., 177, 276
Siegel, J. M., 141, 341, 452
Siegel, R. K., 148
Siegler, R. S., 271, 378
Sigman, M., 362
Silver, L. B., 494
Silver, R. L., 453
Silverman, K., 152
Silverstein, B., 296
Silverstri, L., 141
Simmons, R., 390
Simon, C., xxviii
Simon, H. A., 202, 237
Simon, T., 262
Simonoff, E., 276
Simpkins, C. G., 524
Simpson, G. E., 546
Simpson, J. A., 548

Sims, H. P., Jr., 540
Sinclair, J. D., 158
Singelis, T., 425, 550
Singer, J. E., 307, 447
Singer, J. L., 143
Sinha, D., xxix
Six, L. S., 203
Sizemore, C. C., 483
Skinner, B. F., 248, 424
Slater, A., 366
Slater, E., 487
Slaughter, N., xxix
Sleek, S., 272, 517
Sloan, E. P., 144
Slomkowski, C., 495, 496
Slovic, P., 233
Sluyter, D. J., 272
Smith, E., 457
Smith, E. E., 218
Smith, J., 453
Smith, K. A., 61
Smith, M., 156
Smith, M. L., 516
Smith, M. V., 249
Smith, S. M., 208, 243
Smith, T. S., 308
Smock, P. J., 401
Snyder, C. R., 450
Snyder, F., 137
Snyder, M. L., 462
Sohn, D., 515
Solcova, I., 452
Solomon, C., 138
Solso, R. L., 236
Sommer, B. B., 34
Sommer, R., 34
Sommerhof, G., 132
Soper, B., 138
Sorenson, S. B., 341
Sorrentino, R. M., 301
Southwick, L., 156
Spangler, W. D., 301
Spanos, N. P., 145, 146
Spaulding, Jean, xxviii
Spaulding, Jeanne, xxix
Spear, M. H., xxviii
Spearman, C., 268
Spector, P. E., 272
Spence, J. T., 301
Spence, M. J., 360
Sperling, G., 200
Sperry, R., 80
Spiegel, D., 112, 146, 457, 483, 484
Spiegel, R., 521
Spielberger, C. D., 556
Spielman, D. A., 17
Spillane, B., xxviii
Spillmann, L., 115
Spira, J., 514
Spitz, H. H., 235
Spitz, H. I., 150
Spitzer, R. L., 486
Sprafkin, J., 186
Sprecher, S., 338
Sprenkle, D. H., 515
Squire, L. R., 171, 211, 218
Srivastava, R. S., 423
Stagner, B., 531

Standing, L., 537
Stangor, C., 545
Stanton, H. E., 146
Staub, E., 17
Staudinger, U. M., 461
Steadman, H., 471
Steblay, N. M., 212
Steele, C. M., 156, 547
Steen, R. G., 279, 355
Steil, J. M., 402
Stein, N. L., 214
Stein, Z. A., 275
Steinberg, L., 394
Stephenson, P., xxviii
Stern, R. M., 107
Sternberg, J., 273
Sternberg, R. J., 31, 234, 235, 244, 261, 271,
  550
Stevens, G., 14
Stevenson, H. W., 20, 381, 538
Steward, E. P., 380
Stewart, D. W., 33
Stier, H., 402
Stiff, J. B., 311
Stix, G., 496
Stokes, G., 329
Stone, J., 547
Stone, R., 17
Stoney, C. M., 556
Stough, C., 271
Stratton, R. P., 240
Strauss, E., 80
Streissguth, A. P., 362
Strick, P. L., 74
Strickland, B. R., 488
Stroebe, M. S., 408
Stroebe, W., 408
Stroh, L. K., 322
Strongman, K. T., 308
Stronski, S. M., 395
Strupp, H. H., 516
Stubbs, J., xxviii
Stumpf, H., 325
Sue, D. W., 506, 518
Sue, S., 506
Sullivan, B., 338
Sulzer-Azaroff, B., 177, 190
Sundin, O., 455
Super, C. M., 378
Sur, M., 66, 73
Suzuki, K., 118
Svarstad, B., 463
Swan, S. W., 398
Swann, C. P., 331
Swets, J. A., 123
Swindle, R., Jr., 497
Szasz, T. S., 473, 477

Tabakoff, B., 61
Tagiuri, R., 549
Tago, A., 138
Tajfel, H., 546
Takooshian, H., 206
Talajic, M., 457
Tan, V. L., 137
Tandon, R., 490

Tanford, S., 539
Tanner, J., 367, 389
Tasker, F., 340
Taubes, G., 295
Tavris, C., 324
Taylor, A., 452
Taylor, H., 17
Taylor, J. M., 392
Taylor, M., 379
Taylor, S. E., 451, 453, 463, 534
Tellegen, A., 426, 461
Templeton, R., xxviii
Terman, L. M., 277
Terman, M., 142
Tetlock, P. E., 541
Tewes, U., 457
Tharp, R. G., 187, 188
Thombs, D. L., 150
Thompson, D. M., xxviii, 208
Thompson, S. S., 217
Thomson, A. M., 60
Thorndike, E. L., 174, 262
Thune, I., 453
Thurstone, L. L., 269
Tinnin, J., xxviii
Tolman, E. C., 183, 184
Tomanek, P., 452
Tomarken, A. J., 308
Tomasello, M., 381
Tomes, H., 9
Torrey, E. F., 524
Toth, J. P., 206
Townsend, R., xxviii
Treisman, A., 116
Tsui, A., 323
Tsunoda, T., 79
Tucker, C., 327
Tucker, J. A., 150
Tulving, E., 205, 206, 207, 208, 217, 218
Turk, D. C., 110, 111, 112
Turkewitz, G., 78
Turkington, C., 259
Turner, B., xxviii
Turner, M. E., 540, 546
Turner, T. J., 304
Turner, W. J., 339
Turvey, M. T., 200
Tuss, P., 381
Tversky, A., 237

Ubell, E., 144, 343
Uchino, B. N., 452
Udolf, R., 146
Ullman, S., 115
Underwood, G. D. M., 207
Unger, R. K., 321
Uno, D., 452
Urbina, S., 263

Vaid, J., 243
Vaillant, G. E., 398
Valente, S. M., 523
Valentiner, D. P., 449
Vallacher, R., xxviii
Van Biema, D., 151
Vance, E. B., 332

Van Eck, M., 449
Van Ginkel, R., 180
VanLehn, K., 220
Van Wel, F., 394
Vasquez, W., xxix
Vaughan, R. D., 190, 547
Vaughan-Jackson, P., 335
Velichkovsky, B. M., 246
Velmans, M., 132
Verhaeghen, P., 406
Vernon, P. A., 356, 379
Verschoor, C., xxix
Victor, S. B., 340
Vihman, M. M., 246
Vital-Durand, F., 366
Vitaro, F., 392
Vogel, G., 487
Vogelstein, B., 359
Volckmann, J., xxviii
Von Restorff, H., 211
Vygotsky, L. S., 380

Wachtel, P. L., 504
Wagner, A. D., 205
Wagner, B. M., 395
Wagner, D. A., 214
Wagner, E. F., 458
Wagner, K. D., 450
Wagner, N. W., 332
Wagner, R. K., 271
Wahl, K. M., 323
Waid, W. M., 309
Waite, L. J., 401
Walcott, D. M., 213
Wald, G., 99
Waldman, I. D., 281
Waldrop, M. W., 158
Walker, G., xxviii
Wall, P. D., 111
Wall, T. L., 156
Wallace, R. K., 147
Wallbott, H. G., 310
Waller, G., 297
Wallerstein, J. S., 400
Wallis, C., 520
Walsh, B. T., 299
Walsh, D. M., 112
Walsh, F., 515
Walter, H. J., 190
Walter, M. I., 235
Walters, J. M., 270
Ward, J. V., 392
Ward, L. M., 93, 117, 120, 121
Ward, T., 448
Ward, W. C., 243
Wark, G. R., 392
Wasserman, E. A., 169
Wasserman, J., 459
Waterman, A. S., 392
Waters, E., 370
Waters, M., 9
Watson, C. S., 107
Watson, J. B., 16, 169
Watson, M., 457
Watson, R., 426
Webb, W. B., 136, 137

Webber, B., 245
Wechsler, D., 261
Wechsler, H., 155
Week, D., 486
Weinberg, M. S., 339, 340
Weinberg, R. A., 21, 280, 281
Weinberger, N. M., 62
Weiner, B., 536
Weiner, B. A., 471
Weiner, I. B., 435
Weiner, J., 359
Weinfield, N. S., 370
Weintraub, M., 463
Weisberg, H. F., 34
Weisberg, J. N., 110, 111
Weisman, A., 492
Weiss, A. S., 293
Weissman, M. M., 497
Weissman, M. W., 485
Weitzenhoffer, A. M., 145
Wells, G. L., 212
Werner, J., 115
Wertheimer, M., 114
West, R. L., 220, 406
Westen, D., 418
Westera, D. A., 338
Wetter, D. W., 457, 459
Wettstein, R., 471
Whaley, B. B., 463
Whaley, D. L., 190
Whitbourne, S. K., 393, 404, 463
White, P. A., 536
White, S. J., 380
Whitla, D. K., 405
Whorf, B. L., 249
Wickelgren, I., 70, 150
Widiger, T. A., 495
Widmeyer, W. N., 535
Wiebe, D. J., 452
Wiehe, V. R., 341
Wielgosz, A. T., 455
Wiesel, T. N., 97
Wigfield, A., 292
Wiggins, J. S., 423
Wilcox, S. G., xxviii, xxix

Wildavsky, B., 251
Wilfley, D., 300
Wilgoren, J., 372
Wilk, S. L., 433
Willerman, R., 247
Williams, C., 61
Williams, C. J., 339
Williams, J. B. W., 521, 522
Williams, J. E., 321, 455
Williams, J. K., 229
Williams, S. W., 402
Willis, S. L., 405
Wills, K., 463
Willwerth, J., 520
Wilson, B., 201
Wilson, D. B., 516
Wilson, G. T., 510
Wilson, J. P., 448
Wilson, S. M., 397
Windholz, G., 167
Winerip, M., 267
Winkler, K. J., 21
Winner, E., 277
Winningham, R. G., 211
Winslow, M. P., xxix
Winson, J., 140
Winter, D. G., 302
Wiseman, R., 123
Witelson, S. F., 78
Witt, G. E., 35
Wixted, J. T., 215
Wohl, J., 518
Wolfe, D. A., 343
Wolpe, J., 508
Wolpert, E. A., 135, 139
Wolters, G., 207
Wong, M. M., 302
Wood, J. M., 137
Wood, W., 531, 539
Woodruff-Pak, D. S., 170, 171
Woods, S. C., 296, 448
Wortman, C. B., 453
Wozniak, R. H., 356
Wright, J. H., 487
Wright, R., 245

Wright, S. J., 359
Wurst, S., xxviii
Wurtman, R., 144
Wyatt, G. E., 341
Wynder, E. L., 190
Wynn, K., 378
Wyshak, G., 464

Yalom, I. D., 514
Yan, H., 359
Yantis, S., 117
Yee, A. H., 281
Yela, C., 549
Yenerall, J. D., 546
Yinger, J. M., 546
Yost, W. A., 102
Young, M. W., 142
Young, R. K., 549

Zabel, A., xxviii, xxix
Zajonc, R. B., 303
Zamarra, J. W., 147
Zanker, J. M., 97
Zautra, A. J., 408
Zebrowitz-McArthur, L., 538
Zechmeister, E. B., 33
Zechmeister, J. S., 33
Zeidner, M., 453
Zeki, S., 98
Zelazo, P. R., 362, 373
Zevon, M., 457
Zhdanova, I., 144
Zigler, E., 275
Zika, S., 449, 451
Zilbergeld, B., 332
Zimmer, J., 381
Zimmerman, R. R., 368
Zisook, S., 521
Zito, J. M., 521, 522
Zucker, K. J., 340
Zuckerman, M., 290, 291
Zuger, A., 463
Zurbriggen, E. L., 341

Subject Index

Abnormal behavior, 470–478
Absolute threshold, 91–92
Accommodation, 94, 102
Acetylcholine (AC), 60–61
Achievement, need for, 301–302
Achievement tests, 264–265, 274
Acid, 159
Acquired immune deficiency
    syndrome (AIDS),
    344–345
    prenatal development, 363
Acquisition of language, 248–249
Action potential, 57–58
Activation-synthesis theory, 140
Activity theory of aging, 407–408
Acupuncture, 111
Adaptation, 92–93
Adaptive testing, 266–267
Addiction, 150
Addictive drugs, 150
Adjectives for men and
    women, 321
Adler, neo-Freudians, 419–420
Adolescence, 13, 388–397
Adolescent egocentrism, 394
Adolescent suicide, 394–396
Adrenal gland, 81
Advertising executives, 534–535
Advocate for the mentally
    retarded, 278
Afferent neurons, 62
Affiliation, need for, 301–302
African Americans
    adolescence, 389
    culture generally. See Culture
    diversity generally. See
        Diversity
    influencing behavior, 21
    single parents, 400
Afterimage, 99–100
Age, mental, 262
Age of mother, prenatal
    development, 363
Age of viability, 360
Aggression, 37, 551–556
Aggressive cues, 553
Aging, activity theory of,
    407–408
Aging, information on, 403–404
Aging population, 404
Agoraphobia, 480
Agreeableness, 423
AIDS, 344–345
    prenatal development, 363
Ainsworth strange situation,
    369–370
Alarm and mobilization stage,
    stress, 446
Alcohol, 154–157
    binge drinking, 131–132, 155

identifying alcohol problems,
    159–160
    prenatal development, 362–363
Alcoholics, 156
Algorithms, 233
All-or-none law, 57
Allport's trait theory, 421–422, 430
Altered state of consciousness, 132
Alternation model of bicultural
    competence, 252
Altruism, 555
Alzheimer's disease, 219, 406
Ambivalent children, 370
American Indians
    culture generally. See Culture
    diversity generally. See
        Diversity
    influencing behavior, 21
Amnesia, 219
Amphetamines, 153–154
Amygdala, 71
Anal stage of personality
    development, 416
Analogies, 244
Analytical style to learning, 188
Anatomy of the eye, 94–98
Androgen, 326, 329
Androgynous, 328
Anger, 311, 313
    heart disease, 455
Animal research, 46, 48–49
Animal spirits, 12
Animals, use of language, 250–251
Anorexia nervosa, 298
Anorgasmia, 345
Anterograde amnesia, 220
Antianxiety drugs, 520, 522
Antidepressant drugs, 520–522
Antidrug programs, 151
Antipsychotic drugs, 520
Antisocial personality
    disorder, 493
Anvil, ear, 103
Anxiety, 417
Anxiety disorders, 478–482
Aphasia, 76
Apraxia, 76
Aptitude tests, 264–265, 274
ARC, 275
Archetypes, 419
Architectural engineer, 228
Archival research, 33, 42–43, 49
Armstrong, Lance, 287
Arousal approaches to motivation,
    290, 294
Arrangement problems, 235–238
Asch's conformity experiment, 539
Asian success story, school
    achievement, 381
Assessing personality, 431–437

Association areas of the cortex,
    75–76
Associative models of memory,
    206–208
Assumed-similarity bias, 537
Ataturk, Mustafa Kemal, 35
Athletes, hypnosis, 146
Attachment, 368–370, 374
Attachment behavioral system, 369
Attention deficit hyperactivity
    disorder (ADHD), 494
Attitude communicator, 530
Attitudes and social cognition,
    530–538
Attraction, interpersonal, 548–551
Attraction, sexual, 389, 549
Attribution theory, 536
Auditory area of the cortex, 74
Auditory canal, 103, 112
Authoritarian parents, 372
Authoritative parents, 372
Autism, 177
Autobiographical memory, 214
Autonomic division of nervous
    system, 63–65, 67
Autonomy-versus-shame-and-
    doubt stage of development,
    373, 392
Aversive conditioning techniques,
    507–508
Avoidant children, 370
Axons, 55, 57, 62

Babble, 247
Babinski reflex, 364
Bach and computer creativity, 245
Background stressors, 449, 451
Balance, inner ear, 107
Bandura and observational
    learning, 186
Barbiturates, 156
Basics of sleep behavior, 136
Basilar membrane, 103
Bedtime, sleeping better, 143
Beginning researchers, guide
    for, 30
Behavior analysis, 189–191
Behavior modification,
    189–191, 516
Behavioral assessment, 436
Behavioral genetics, 66–67
Behavioral neuroscientists, 54
Behavioral perspective, 15–16,
    18, 24
    abnormality, 473–474
    conscious versus unconscious
        causes of behavior, 19
    free will versus determinism,
        19

individual differences versus
    universal principles, 19–20
nature versus nurture, 19
observable behavior versus
    internal mental processes,
    19, 23
Behavioral treatment approaches,
    507–510, 516
Behaviorism, 13
Bell curve, 280
Benevolent sexism, 323
Bias, experimental, 47, 49
Biases in attribution, 537–538
Big five personality factors,
    422–423
Bilingual education, 251–252
Bimodal distribution in statistics,
    A.5
Binet and measuring intelligence,
    262
Binge drinking, 131–132, 155
Binocular disparity, 119, 124
Biofeedback, 82
    pain management, 112
Biological and evolutionary
    approaches to personality,
    426, 430
Biological bases of memory,
    217–218
Biological basis of intelligence,
    271
Biological causes of schizophrenia,
    490–491
Biological constraints on learning,
    181
Biological factors in gender
    differences, 326–327
Biological factors in the regulation
    of hunger, 295
Biologically based addictions, 150
Biology of sexual behavior,
    329–330
Biomedical therapy, 519–525
Biopsychologists (behavioral
    neuroscientists), 54
Biopsychology, 14–15, 24
    conscious versus unconscious
        causes of behavior, 19
    free will versus determinism,
        19
    individual differences versus
        universal principles, 19–20
    nature versus nurture, 19
    observable behavior versus
        internal mental
        processes, 19
    subfields of psychology,
        5–6, 11
Bipolar cells, 96
Bipolar disorder, 486, 494

Bisexuality, 339–340
Bisexuals, 339
Blacks. *See* African Americans
Blind spot, 95, 97
Blood alcohol levels, 157
Blue-yellow color blindness, 99
Bodily kinesthetic intelligence, 270
Borderline personality disorder, 493–494
Bottom-up processing, 117, 124
Brain, 63, 64, 67–72
   depression, 487
   drug use, 150
   emotion, 308
   messages to the eye, 96–97
   motivation, 296
   organizing and coordinating information, 272
   rapid eye movement (REM) sleep, 141
Brain scans, 68, 72–73
   mental imagery, 230
Brain stimulation, pain management, 112
Brain-wave patterns, 134
Brain waves overcoming physical limitations, 69
BrainMap, 76
Breast cancer, 456–457
Bridging the gap between neurons, 58–60
Broca's aphasia, 76
Bulimia, 298
Burning calories, 300

Caffeine, 150–151
   sleeping better, 143
Calero, Lynn, 182
Calkins, Mary, 14
   timeline, 12
Calories, burning, 300
Cancer, 456–457
Cannon-Bard theory of emotion, 306–307, 309
Cardinal trait, 421–422, 431
Case study, 34, 36, 42–43, 49
Cataclysmic events, 448
Catatonic schizophrenia, 489
Catharsis, 553
Cattell personality theory, 422–423
Caucasian. *See* Whites
Causes of anxiety disorders, 481–482
Causes of mood disorders, 486–488
Centenarians, 387–388
Central core of the brain, 69–73
Central nervous system (CNS), 62–65
Central tendency in statistics, A.4, A.7
Central traits, 422
   impression formation, 535
Central-route processing, persuasion, 531, 538
Cerebellum, 70–71

Cerebral cortex, 70, 73–76
   visual area, primary, 98
Challenge, coping styles, 452
Changes in behavior, 7
Chess and chunks, 201–202
Child care, 371–372, 401–402
Child competence, maximizing, 381–382
Child vocabulary, 249
Childhood sexual abuse, 343
Children, 399–402
Chimpanzees, insight, 240
Chlamydia, 343
Chlorpromazine, 520
Chomsky and universal grammar, 248–249
Chromosomes, 357–358, 360
Chunks, 201–202, 208
Cingulotomy, 523
Circadian rhythms, 142, 144
Circumcision, 332–334
Classical conditioning, 167–172
Classifying abnormal behavior, 475–477
Client-centered therapy, 13, 513, 516
Clinical neuropsychology, 6, 8
   timeline, 13
Clinical psychologists, 505
Clinical psychology, 6–7, 11
Clinical social workers, 505
Clitoris, 332
Cloning, 359
Close relationships, 548–551
Closure, gestalt laws of organization, 114
Clozapine, 520
Cocaine, 152–154
Cochlea, 103
Cochlear implant, 105
Cognition, need for, 531–532
Cognitive abilities, gender differences, 325–326
Cognitive approaches to motivation, 292, 294
Cognitive complexity, 244
Cognitive development, 374–382
   adolescence, 390–392
   late adulthood, 404–406
Cognitive dissonance, 533
Cognitive map, 184
Cognitive perspective on abnormality, 473–474
Cognitive psychology, 6, 11, 15–16, 24, 228
   conscious *versus* unconscious causes of behavior, 19
   free will *versus* determinism, 19
   individual differences *versus* universal principles, 19–20
   language. *See* Language
   nature *versus* nurture, 19
   observable behavior *versus* internal mental processes, 19
   problem solving, 234–246
      Hubble space telescope, 227

   thinking and reasoning, 228–233
   language, 249
   timeline, 13
Cognitive restructuring, pain management, 112
Cognitive treatment approaches, 510–512
Cognitive-behavior approach to treatment, 510, 516
Cognitive-social approaches to learning, 183–191
Cognitive-social learning theory, 183, 189, 191
Cohort, 357
Collective unconscious, 419
College students as experiment participants, 44–45, 49
College students' drinking habits, 155
Color blindness, 98–100
Commitment
   coping styles, 452
   love, 550
Common dreams, 138
Community psychology, 524
Companionate love, 550
Compensation gap between men and women, 322
Compliance in social influence, 541–543
Compulsion, 480, 484
Computerized axial tomography (CAT), 68
Computers and compliance, 543
Computers and creativity, 245
Computers and testing, 266–267
Conception to birth, development, 357–363
Concepts, 230–233
Concrete stage of cognitive development, 375–376
Conditional positive regard, 429
Conditioned response (CR), 169, 172
Conditioned stimulus (CS), 168
Cones of the eye, 95–96
Confirmation bias, 243, 246
Conformity, 539–540
Conscience, 415, 420
Conscientiousness, 423
Conscious *versus* unconscious causes of behavior, 19
Consciousness, 131–163
   drug use, 149–160
   hypnosis and meditation, 145–148
   sleep and dreams, 133–144
Consent, informed, 44, 48
Consolidation, memory, 218
Constructive processes in memory, 211
Consumers of psychology, 22–23
   alcohol problems, 159–160
   anger, 555–556
   behavior analysis and modification, 189–191

   biofeedback, 82
   child competence, 381–382
   coping with stress, 453
   date rape, 346
   death, adjusting to, 407–408
   dieting, 299–300
   disorders, 497–498
   drug problems, 159–160
   memory, 220–221
   pain management, 111–112
   personality assessments, 436–437
   physician-patient communication, 464–465
   research, 47–48
   sleeping better, 143–144
   standardized tests, 274
   therapist, choosing, 524–525
   thinking critically and creatively, 244–245
Contingency contracting, operant conditioning techniques, 510
Continuous reinforcement, 177, 183
Control
   coping styles, 452
   persuasion, 541
Control group, 38, 43, 49
Convergent thinking, 243–244
Conversion disorders, 482, 484
Coping styles, 452
Coping with depression, Mike Wallace, 503
Coping with stress, 450–453
Cornea, 94–95, 102
Coronary heart disease, 454–456
Corpus callosum, 70
   gender, 78
Correlation coefficient, A.9–A.13
Correlational research, 36, 41, 49
Counseling psychologists, 505
Counseling psychology, 6–7, 11
Courtrooms, memory in, 211–213
Creative nonadherence to physician recommendations, 463
Creativity in problem solving, 243–244
Crisis center counselors, 342
Critical period for language development, 247
Critical periods prior to birth, 360, 363
Critical perspective, 244
Cross-cultural psychology, 6–7, 21, 24
Cross-sectional research, 357, 363
Cross-sequential research, 357
Crutcher and intelligence, 259
Crystallized intelligence, 269, 273–274
   late adulthood, 405, 408
Culture, 20–21
   adolescence, 389
   altered states of consciousness, 147–148

Asian success story, school achievement, 381
deaf culture, 105
Diagnostic and Statistical Manual of Mental Disorders (DSM-IV), 495–496
discrimination, 545–548
eating, 297
emotions, 304, 310–311
female circumcision, 332–334
fundamental attribution error, 538
IQ tests, 279–282
learning, 187–189
memory, 214
norms, 432–433
perception, 121–122
rites of passage, 396–397
self-efficacy, 424
smoking, 459–460
teaching with linguistic variety, 251–252
treatment of disorders, 517
Trukese people, 261
Vygotsky's view of cognitive development, 379–381
Curvature of the spine, 82

Daily hassles, 449, 451
D.A.R.E., 151
Dark adaptation, 96
Darley, John, 39–42
Date rape, 341, 346
Date rape drug, 156
Day care, 371–372
Daydreams, 143
Deaf culture, 105
Death, adjusting to, 407–408
Decay, 216, 221
Decibels, 105–106
Decision, love, 550
Declarative memory, 205–207
Deductive reasoning, 232
Defense mechanisms, 417, 420
psychodynamic therapy, 504, 512
stress, 451
Defense of insanity, 471
Defining intelligent behavior, 260–274
Definition of psychology, 4, 24
Deinstitutionalization, 524–525
Delusion, schizophrenia, 489
Dendrites, 55, 57, 62
Denial, 418
Depakote, 522
Dependent variable, 38, 43, 49
Depressants, 153–154
Depression, major, 485–487, 498
antidepressant drugs, 520–522
Wallace, Mike, 503
Depth perception, 118–119, 124
DES (diethylstilbestrol), prenatal development, 363
Descartes, 12
Descriptive adjectives for men and women, 321

Descriptive statistics, A.3–A.7
Determinism *versus* free will, 19
Development
adolescence, 388–397
adolescence to the end of life, 387–408
beginnings of life, 353–382
cognitive development, 374–382
infancy through middle childhood, 367–374
language, 247–248
later years of life, 403–408
middle years of life, 397–402
nature and nurture, 354–357
newborns, 364–366
prenatal development, 357–363
Developmental psychology, 6–7, 11, 24, 354
Devil's tuning fork, 122
Diagnostic and Statistical Manual of Mental Disorders, fourth edition *(DSM-IV)*, 475–477, 498
Dieting, 299–300
Difference thresholds, 92
Diffusion of responsibility, 31, 554, 556
Direct physiological effects of stress, 447
Discrimination, 545–548
stimulus, 171–172, 180
Disengagement theory of aging, 406–408
Disgust, 311, 313
Disorders, 469–498
biomedical therapy, 519–525
major disorders, 478–494
normal *versus* abnormal, 470–478
prevalence of mental disorders, 495–498
psychotherapy, 504–519
treatment, 503–525
Disorganized schizophrenia, 489
Disorganized-disoriented children, 370
Displacement, 418
Display rules, 311
Dispositional causes of behavior, 536
Dissociative amnesia, 483–484
Dissociative disorders, 483–484
Dissociative fugue, 484
Dissociative identity disorder (multiple personality), 483
Divergent thinking, 243–246
Diversity, 20–21
adolescence, 389
altered states of consciousness, 147–148
Asian success story, school achievement, 381
brain, 78–80
Diagnostic and Statistical Manual of Mental Disorders, 495–496

discrimination, 545–548
eating, 297
emotions, 304, 310–311
female circumcision, 332–334
fundamental attribution error, 538
IQ tests, 279–282
learning, 187–189
memory, 214
norms, 432–433
perception, 121–122
research participants, 44–45
rites of passage, 396–397
self-efficacy, 424
smoking, 459–460
teaching with linguistic variety, 251–252
timeline, 13
treatment of disorders, 517
Trukese people, 261
Vygotsky's view of cognitive development, 379–381
Dividing problems into their parts, 238–239
Divorce, 399–402
DNA, 358
Dogs and learning, 165, 167–169
Dolphin research, 182
Door-in-the-face technique, compliance, 541, 545
Dopamine (DA), 61
Dopamine hypothesis to schizophrenia, 490–491, 494
Double standard, 337
Double-blind procedure, 47–49
Down syndrome, 276–277, 361
Dreams, 133–144
day dreams, 143
function of dreams, 137–141
meaning of dreams, 137–141, 506
Dreams without sleep, 143
Dreams-for-survival theory, 139–140
Drinking habits of college students, 155
Drinking to excess, 131–132, 155
Drive, 289
Drive reduction approaches to motivation, 289–290, 294–295
Driver aggression, 551
Drug therapy, 519–522
Drug use
consciousness, 149–160
identifying alcohol problems, 159–160
memory, 221
prenatal development, 362–363
Dual process persuasion, 532
Dysfunctions, memory, 219–220

Eardrum, 103–104
Early adulthood, 396–402
Earthquakes, 3
Eating, 295–300
Eating disorders, 298–299

Ebbinghaus and forgetting, 216
Echoic memory, 200
Ecklund, Amy, 89
Eclectic approach to therapy, 517, 519
Ecstasy, 159
Education of a psychologist, 10–11
Educational psychology, 6, 11
Efferent neurons, 62
Ego, 414–415
Egocentric thought, 376
adolescent egocentrism, 394
Ego-ideal, 415, 420
Ego-integrity-*versus*-despair stage of late adulthood, 392–393
Ejaculation, 332
Elaborative rehearsal, 203
Electroconvulsive therapy (ECT), 522–523
Electroencephalogram (EEG), 68, 134
Embryo, 359
Embryonic period, 359
Emotional insulation, 451
Emotional intelligence, 271–273, 303
Emotion-focused coping, 451
Emotions, 303–313
contemporary perspectives, 308
expression, 310–313
functions of, 304
genetic influences, 356
range of, 304
roots of, 305–309
schizophrenia, 489
Empathy, 555
Encoding of memory, 198–208, 215
Encoding specificity, 220–221
Endocrine system, 80–83
Endorphins, 61
Environment *versus* heredity, 18–19
development, 354–357, 363
intelligence, 278–282
personality, 426–428, 430
Environmental factors in gender differences, 327–329
Environmental influences in prenatal development, 362–363
Environmental perspectives on schizophrenia, 491–492
Environmental psychology, 6
Episodic memory, 205
Erectile dysfunction, 345
Erikson's theory of psychosocial development, 373–374
adolescence, 392–393
Erogenous zones, 330
Erotic, 330
Estrogen, 326, 330
Estrogen replacement therapy (ERT), 398
Ethics of research, 43–44, 48
animal research, 46

Ethnicity
adolescence, 389
discrimination, 545–548
influencing behavior, 20–21
norms, 432–433
single parents, 400
treatment of disorders, 517
Evaluating solutions, 240–241, 243
Evolution of intelligence, 260
Evolution of the nervous
system, 65
Evolutionary approach to
personality, 426, 430
Evolutionary factors in gender
differences, 326–327
Evolutionary psychology, 6, 8,
65, 67
timeline, 13
Excitatory messages, 60
Excitement phase of sexual
response, 332–333
Exercise
dieting, 299
sleeping better, 143
Exhaustion stage, stress, 446
Expectations in experiments,
47–49
Experimental bias, 47, 49
Experimental group, 38, 49
Experimental manipulation, 38, 49
Experimental psychology, 6–7, 11
Experimental research, 37–45
Experimenter expectations, 47–49
Experimenting with solutions, 245
Experiments, 37–38
Explicit memory, 205–207
Expressed emotion, schizophrenia,
492
Expression of emotions, 310–313
Extinction, 170, 172
Extramarital sex, 338
Extrasensory perception (ESP),
123–124
Extraversion, 423, 431
Extrinsic motivation, 292, 295
Eye, structure of, 94–98
Eyewitness testimony, 211–213
Eysenck personality theory,
422–423, 430

Facial expressions, 310–313
Facial-affect program, 310–311
Facial-feedback hypothesis,
312–313
Factor analysis, 422
Facts of life, 329–334
Fading dot, 92
Failures of memory, 198
False memory, 213
Familial retardation, 276
Family therapy, 514–515
Fantasies, sexual, 331
Father's role in parenting, 370–371
Fear, 311, 313
systematic desensitization,
508–510
Feature analysis, 114–116

Feature detection, 97
Female circumcision, 332–334
Female moral development,
391–392
Female sex organs, 329–330
Festinger, Leon, 13
Fetal alcohol syndrome, 362
Fetal period, 359
Fetus, 359, 361
Firing the neuron, 57–58
Fixation, 416
Fixed-interval schedules, 178–179
Fixed-ratio schedule, 178–179
Flashbulbs memories,
210–211, 215
Fluid intelligence, 269, 273–274
late adulthood, 405, 408
Fluoxetine, 521
Flying, fear of, 509
Flynn effect, IQ, 281
Focused-attention stage, 116
Foot-in-the-door technique,
compliance, 541
Forebrain, 70
Forensic psychology, 6
Forgetting, 215–221
Formal operational stage of
cognitive development,
375, 377–378
Forming subgoals, 238–239
Fornix, 71
Fossey, Dian, 34
Fovea, 95
Fox, Michael, 53
Fractionation, 244
Framing problems, 237, 239
Free association, 505
Free will versus determinism, 19
Frequency, 104, 112
Frequency distribution, A.3–A.4
Frequency theory of hearing, 106
Freud, Sigmund, 15
dreams, 138–139
personality, 414–419
psychoanalysis, 505–507
timeline, 12
Freudian slip, 414
Friendship, 301–302
Frontal lobe, 73–74
Frontiers of psychology, 7–8
Frustration and aggression, 553
Full inclusion, 276
Function of the brain, 67–69
Functional fixedness,
241–242, 246
Functionalism, 12–13, 24
Fundamental attribution error, 537
Future of psychology, 21, 23–24

Gage, Phineas, 75–76
Gamma-amino butyric acid
(GABA), 60–61
Ganglion cells, 96
Gardner's essay on IQ, 261
Gardner's multiple intelligences,
269–270, 273
Garrett, Mary, 44

Gate-control theory of pain,
111–112
Gays, 339–340
Gender, 319–329
brain, 78–80
endocrine system, 81
Gender differences, 324–329
Gender labeling of toys, 327
Gender roles, 320–323, 329
Gender schema, 328–329
Gene therapy, 359
General adaptation syndrome
(GAS), 445–447
Generalization, stimulus, 170–172
Generalized anxiety disorder,
480–481
Generativity-versus-stagnation
stage of middle adulthood,
392–393
Genes, 358
behavioral genetics, 66
IQ, 12–13
schizophrenia, 491
Genetic preprogramming theories
of aging, 404, 408
Genetics, 357–359
behavioral genetics, 66–67
human behavioral genetic
data, 66
Genital herpes, 344
Genital mutilation, 332–334
Genital stage of personality
development, 416–417
Genital warts, 344
Genitals, 329–330
Genome, 66
German measles, 363
Gerontologists, 403
Gestalt laws of organization,
113–115
Gestalt psychology, 14, 18, 24
timeline, 13
Gestalt therapy, 513–514, 516, 519
G-factor, 268
Gifted intellectually, 276–277
Glass ceiling, 322
Glial cells, 55
Glucagon, 81
Glutamate, 60–61
Gonorrhea, 344
Gorillas, 34
Grammar, 246–247
GRE, 265, 267
Group therapy, 514–515
Groupthink, 540–541
Guess that Sound, 89
Guide for beginning
researchers, 30
Guiding Light, 89
Gustation. See Taste

Habituation, 365, 374
Hagaii, 304
Hair cells, 103
Hallucinogens, 153, 158–159
Halo effect, 537–538
Hammer, ear, 103

Happiness, 311, 313, 460–462
Harassment, sexual, 322–323
Hardiness, 452–453
Harmful behaviors, stress, 447
Health psychology, 6–7, 11,
24, 444
Hearing, 102–107
absolute threshold, 91
Hearing loss, 105
Heart disease, 454–456
Hebephrenic schizophrenia, 489
Height, averages, 367
Helping others, 554–555
Hemispheres of the brain,
77–78, 80
Heredity versus environment,
18–19
development, 354–357, 363
intelligence, 278–282
personality, 426–428, 430
Heritability, intelligence, 280
Heroin, 157–158
Herpes, 344
Heterosexuality, 337–339
Heterosexuals, 337
Heuristics, 233, 245
Hierarchical organization, nervous
system, 65
Hierarchy of fears, systematic
desensitization, 508
Hierarchy of needs, 292–294
High self-esteem, 425, 427
Hindbrain, 69
Hippocampus, 71
memory, 218–219
Hippocrates, 12
Hispanic
adolescence, 389
culture generally. See Culture
diversity generally. See
Diversity
influencing behavior, 21
single parents, 400
Histogram, A.3–A.4, A.7
History, 11–18, 24
Homeostasis, 71, 289–290, 295
Homosexuality, 339–340
Homosexuals, 339
Hopelessness, mood disorders, 487
Hormones, 80–81
Hours of sleep needed, 136
Hubbel space telescope, 227
Hubel, David, 13
Human behavioral genetic data, 66
Human genome project, 66
Human papilloma virus, 344
Humanistic approaches to
personality, 430
Humanistic perspective, 15–16,
18, 24
abnormality, 473–474
conscious versus unconscious
causes of behavior, 19
free will versus determinism,
19
individual differences versus
universal principles, 19–20

nature *versus* nurture, 19
observable behavior *versus* internal mental processes, 19
personality, 428–430
Humanistic therapy, 512–514, 519
Hunger, 295–300
Hypnosis, 145–146, 148
pain management, 112, 146
Hypochondriasis, 482
Hypothalamus, 70–71, 73
endocrine system, 81
hunger, 296
Hypothesis, 32, 49

Iconic memory, 200
Id, 414–415
Identical twins, 356
schizophrenia, 491
Identification, 416–417
Identifying the roots of language, 248–249
Identity, 392, 397
Identity-*versus*-role-confusion stage of adolescence, 392
Ill-defined problems, 234
Illusion, perception, 120–121
Imagery and cognition, 229–230
Imitation in newborns, 366
Immersion programs, bilingual education, 251
Impediments to solutions, 241–243
Implicit memory, 207
Impression formation, 535–536
Imprinting, 368
Improving memory, 220
In vitro fertilization, 353
Inaccurate evaluation of solutions, 243
Incentive approaches to motivation, 290–291, 294
Independent variable, 38, 43, 49
India, 3
Indirect health-related behaviors, stress, 447
Individual differences in intelligence, 278–282
Individual differences *versus* universal principles, 19–20
Inducing structure, problems of, 235–238
Inductive reasoning, 232
Industrial/organizational (I/O) psychology, 6, 8, 11, 542
Industry-*versus*-inferiority stage of development, 374, 392
Ineffability, 132
Infancy, 367–374
Inferential statistics and correlation, A.9–A.13
Inferiority complex, 419–420
Information-processing approach to cognitive development, 378–379, 382
Information-processing approach to intelligence, 269, 271, 273–274

Informed consent, 44, 48–49
Informed consumers of psychology. *See* Consumers of psychology
Inhibited ejaculation, 345
Inhibited sexual desire, 346
Inhibitory messages, 60
Initiative-*versus*-guilt stage of development, 374, 392
Inkblot test, 435–436
Innovation, 244
Insanity defense, 471
Insight, 239–240, 246
Insomnia, 141
Instincts, 289, 294–295
aggression, 552–553
Insulin, 81
Intellectually gifted, 276–277
Intelligence, 259–282
defining intelligent behavior, 260–274
genetic influences, 356
individual differences, 278–282
variations in intellectual ability, 275–277
Intelligence quotient. *See* IQ
Intelligence testing, 12–13, 261–264, 273
culture fair tests, 279–282
jobs, 268
scoring better on, 274
Intensity of sound, 104
Interactionist position on nature-nurture issue, 355–356
Interference, 217, 221
Internal mental processes *versus* observable behavior, 19
International Society for Psychophysics, 91
Internet addiction, 483
Interneurons, 62
Interpersonal attraction, 548–551
Interpersonal intelligence, 270
Interpretation of dreams, 139
Intimacy in love, 550
Intimacy-*versus*-isolation stage of early adulthood, 392–393
Intoxication
binge drinking, 131–132, 155
depressants, 154
Intrapersonal intelligence, 270
Intrinsic motivation, 292, 295
Introspection, 13, 18
IQ, 12–13, 261–264, 273
culture fair tests, 279–282
Gardner's essay on IQ, 261
jobs, 268
scoring better on, 274
Iris, 94–95

James, William, 12–13
James-Lange theory of emotion, 306–307, 309
Jet lag, 142
Job, sexism on the, 321–322
Job tests, 268
Josef, Franz, 12

Journal of Applied Behavior Analysis, 189
Judgment, 240–241
Jung's collective unconscious, 419
Just noticeable difference, 92
Just say no, 151

Keyword techniques to memory improvement, 220
Kinds of problems, 235
Kinsey institute, 336, 341
Kinsey scale, 339
Kohlberg's theory of moral development, 390–391, 397
Kohler and insight, 239–240
Korsakoff's syndrome, 220

Language, 246–253
Language acquisition device, 248
Language development, 247–248
Language researcher, 252
Lanugo, 364
Latane, Bibb, 39–42
Late adulthood, 403–408
Latency period of personality development, 416–417
Latent content of dreams, 138, 506, 512
Latent learning, 183–184, 191
Lateral hypothalamus and hunger, 296
Lateralization, 78
Latino
adolescence, 389
culture generally. *See* Culture
diversity generally. *See* Diversity
influencing behavior, 21
single parents, 400
Law enforcement, hypnosis, 146
Learned helplessness, 449–450
mood disorders, 487
Learning, 6, 165–191
classical conditioning, 167–172
cognitive-social approaches, 183–189
gender, 327
limbic system, 72
operant conditioning, 173–182
Pavlov, Ivan, 12
personality, 424–426, 430
Learning styles, 188
Learning through imitation, 185–186, 191
Learning-theory approach to language, 248, 253
Least restrictive environment, 276
Left visual field, 98
Lens, 102
Lesbians, 339–340
Levels-of-processing theory, 209, 215
Libido, 415
Lie detectors, 309
Life cycles, 142
Life review, 407

Life Skills Training, 151
Light adaptation, 96
Limbic system, 71–72
Linear perspective, 119
Linguistic intelligence, 270
Linguistic relativity hypothesis, 249
Lithium, 522
Lobes, 73–74
Locke, John, 12
Logic, formal rules of, 232–233
Logical-mathematical intelligence, 270
Longitudinal research, 357, 363
Long-term memory, 199–200, 203
Long-term memory modules, 205–206
Long-term potentiation, 217
Losing weight successfully, 299–300
Lottery and happiness, 461
Louima, Abner, 29
Love, 549–551
Low self-esteem, 425, 427
LSD, 159
Lymphocytes, 457

Magnetic resonance imaging (MRI), 68–69
gender, 79
Mainstreaming, 276–277
Major depression, 485–487, 498
antidepressant drugs, 520–522
Wallace, Mike, 503
Major disorders, 478–494
Male sex organs, 329–330
Managing pain, 111–112
Mania, 485
Manifest content of dreams, 138, 506, 512
Mantra, 147–148
MAO inhibitors, 521
Marijuana, 158–159
Marital sex, 338
Marriage, 399–402
Maslow, Abraham, 13
hierarchy of needs, 292–294
Master gland, 70, 81
Masturbation, 336–337, 341
Maturation, 166
nature-nurture, 355
MDMA (ecstasy), 159
Mean in statistics, A.4–A.5, A.7, A.9
Means-ends analysis technique, 237, 246
Measures of variability, A.7–A.9
Measuring achievement motivation, 301
Measuring attachment, 369–370
Measuring intelligence, 261–267
Median in statistics, A.5, A.7
Medical perspective on abnormality, 472–473
Medication, pain management, 111
Meditation, 147–148
Medulla, 69–70

Memory, 12, 189–221
  encoding, storage and retrieval, 198–208
  forgetting, 215–221
  late adulthood, 405–406
  limbic system, 72
  recalling long-term memories, 208–215
Memory dysfunctions, 219–220
Memory storehouses, 199–203
Memory traces, 216, 218
Mending the brain, 76–77
Mennello, Julia, 110
Menopause, 398
Mental age, 262
Mental health, 7
Mental images, 229–230, 233
Mental retardation, 275–278
Mental set, 241–242, 246
Mental state of the union, 496–497
Meta-analysis, 42
  therapy, 516
Metabolic rate, 81
Metabolism, 296, 302
Metacognition, 379
Methadone, 158, 160
Midbrain, 70
Middle adulthood, 397–402
Middle childhood, 367–374
Middle ear, 103
Middle years of life, 397–402
Midlife crisis, 399
Midlife transition, 398, 402
Mild retardation, 275
Milk, sleeping better, 143
Miller and mental imagery, 230
Minnesota Multiphasic Personality Inventory-2 (MMPI-2), 433–434
MIT, binge drinking, 131
Mnemonics, 203, 208
Mode in statistics, A.5
Model, learning through imitation, 185, 191
Moderate retardation, 275
Monocular cues, 119
Mood disorders, 485–488
Moral development, 390–392
Morphine, 157
Motion parallax, 119
Motion perception, 119–120
Motivation, 287–302
  achievement, 301–302
  affiliation, 301–302
  arousal approaches, 290, 294
  cognitive approaches, 292, 294
  drive reduction approaches, 289–290, 294–295
  eating, 295–300
  friendship, 301–302
  incentive approaches, 290–291, 294
  instincts, 289, 294
  Maslow's hierarchy, 292–294
  power, 302
  success, 301–302
Motivation and Personality, 13

Motive, 288, 295
Motor area of the cortex, 73–74, 83
Motor (efferent) neurons, 62
Movies and violence, 186–187
Muller-Lyer illusion, 121–122
Multiculturalism, 20–21
  timeline, 13
Multiple intelligences, 269–270, 273
Multiple personality disorder, 483
Musical intelligence, 270
Musu, 304
Myelin project, 58
Myelin sheath, 55, 62

Narcissism, 427
Narcissistic personality disorder, 494
Narcolepsy, 141
Narcotics, 153, 157–158
NASA's Hubble space telescope, 227
Native Americans
  culture generally. *See* Culture
  diversity generally. *See* Diversity
  influencing behavior, 21
Naturalistic observation, 34, 42–43, 49
Nature *versus* nurture, 18–19
  development, 354–357, 363
  intelligence, 278–282
  personality, 426–428, 430
Need for achievement, 301–302
Need for affiliation, 301–302
Need for cognition, 531–532
Need for power, 302
Negative correlation, 36, 43
Negative punishment, 176
Negative reinforcers, 175
Negative relationship, correlation coefficient, A.10–A.11, A.13
Negative social behavior, 548–555
Negative-symptom schizophrenia, 490
Neo-Freudian psychoanalysts, 419–420
Neonates, 364–366
Nerve stimulation, pain management, 112
Nervous system, 62–67
  drug use, 150
Networks, social, 7
Neurons, 55–62
Neuropsychology, 54
Neuroscientists, 54
Neurotic, 475–476
  psychodynamic therapy, 504
Neuroticism, 423
Neurotransmitters, 58–62
Neutral stimulus, 167
"New" brain, 70, 73–76
Newborns, 364–366
Nicotine, 152
  prenatal development, 362
Nightmares, 137

Nondirective counseling, client-centered therapy, 513
Non-REM (NREM) sleep, 135, 137
Nonverbal behavior, 310–313
Norm of reciprocity, compliance, 542
Normal distribution in statistics, A.5
Normal *versus* abnormal behavior, 470–478
Norms, tests, 266
  psychological tests, 432, 437
Note-taking and memory, 221
Not-so-free technique, compliance, 542
Nutrition in prenatal development, 362

Obedience, 542–545
Obesity, 295, 297–298
Object performance, 375
Observable behavior *versus* internal mental processes, 19
Observational learning, 185–186, 191, 424
  aggression, 553–554
  operant conditioning techniques, 510
Obsession, 480
Obsessive-compulsive disorder, 480–481
Occipital lobes, 73–74
Oedipus conflict, 416, 420
"Old" brain, 69–73
Olfaction, 107–108
  absolute threshold, 91
Olfactory cells, 108
Ongoing research, links to, 47
Openness to experiences, 423
Operant conditioning, 173–182
Operant conditioning techniques, 509–510
Operationalization, 33, 42, 49
Opponent-process theory of color vision, 100
Opposite, considering, 244
Optic chiasm, 97–98
Optic nerve, 95, 97–98
Optic tract, 98
Optical illusions, 120–121
Oral stage of personality development, 416
Organization home pages, 4
Organizational/industrial psychology, 6, 8, 11
Organizing problems, 235–237
Orgasm, 332–333
Otoliths, 107
Outer ear, 102
Oval window, 103, 112
Ovaries, 81, 330
Overattention, schizophrenia, 492
Overgeneralization, 248, 253
Overlearning, 221
Ovulation, 330

Pain
  gate-control theory of pain, 111
  managing pain, 111–112
Pancreas, 81
Panic attacks, 479–480, 484
Panic disorder, 479–480
Paranoid schizophrenia, 489
Paraplegia, 62
Parasympathetic division of nervous system, 64–65
Parathyroid gland, 81
Parenting styles, 372–373
Parietal lobes, 73–74
Parkinson's disease, 53
Parthenon, 120
Partial reinforcement, 177, 183
Participants in experiments, 39
  diversity, 44–45
  expectations, 47–49
Passion in love, 550
Passionate love, 550
Pavlov, Ivan, 12
Pay gap between men and women, 322
Peers, social relationships, 371
Penis, 332
Penis envy, 417
Perception, 6, 90, 93, 113–124
  depth perception, 118–119, 124
  extrasensory perception (ESP), 123–124
  illusions, 120–121
  motion perception, 119–120
  schizophrenia, 489
  subliminal perception, 123–124
Perception demonstrations, 90
Perceptual constancy, 118, 124
Peripheral nervous system, 62–65
Peripheral vision, 96
Peripheral-route processing, persuasion, 531, 538
Permissive parents, 372
Permissiveness with affection, 338, 341
Personal fables, 394
Personal stressors, 448
Personality, 413–437
  assessing personality, 431–437
  non-psychoanalytic approaches, 421–431
  psychoanalytic approaches, 414–420, 430
Personality disorders, 492–494
Personality factors, gender differences, 324–325
Personality psychology, 6–7, 11, 24
Personality tests, 431–437
Perspective of another, taking, 245
Perspectives on psychology, 14–18
Persuasion, 530–532, 541
Phallic stage of personality development, 416
Phases of sexual response, 331–333
Phenylketonuria (PKU), 361
Pheromones, 108

Phobias, 479
Phobic disorder, 479
Phonemes, 246
Phonology, 246
Phrenology, 12
Physical aspects of sound, 104–105
Physical attractiveness, 389, 549
Physical characteristics influenced by genetics, 356
Physical development, 367–368
adolescence, 389–390
early and middle adulthood, 398
late adulthood, 403–404
Physical health, 7
going to the doctor, 462–465
Physical limitations, brain waves overcoming, 69
Physician recommendations, complying with, 463–464
Physician-patient communication, 462–465
Piaget, Jean, 13
cognitive development theory, 375–378, 382
Picasso and convergent and divergent thinking, 244
Pitch, 104
Pituitary gland, 70, 81
hunger, 296
Place theory of hearing, 106
Placebo, 47, 49
Plateau phase of sexual response, 332–333
Pleasure, limbic system, 72
Pleasure principle, 415
Poggendorf illusion, 121
Police hypnosis, 146
Police psychologist, 450
Polygraph tests, 309
Pons, 69–70
Population, age of, 404
Population in statistics, A.9, A.13
Positive correlation, 36
Positive punishment, 176
Positive reinforcers, 175
Positive relationship, correlation coefficient, A.10–A.11
Positive social behavior, 548–555
Positive-symptom schizophrenia, 490
Positron emission tomography (PET), 68–69
memory, 218
schizophrenia, 493
Posttraumatic stress disorder (PTSD), 448
Power, need for, 302
Practical intelligence, 271–273
Practice, memory, 221
Preattentive stage, 116
Preconscious, 414
Predisposition model of schizophrenia, 492
Prefrontal lobotomy, 523
Prejudice, 545–548

Premarital sex, 337–338
Premature ejaculation, 345
Premenstrual dysphoric disorder, 495, 498
Prenatal development, 357–363
Preoperational stage of cognitive development, 375–376
Preparation, problem understanding and diagnosing, 234–237
Preschool, 371–372
Preschool coordinators, 380
Prevalence of mental disorders, 496–497
Prevention in community psychology, 524
Primary drives, 289
Primary orgasmic dysfunction, 345
Primary reinforcer, 175
Prime, subliminal perception, 123
Priming, 206
Principle of conservation, 376–377
Principles of Psychology, 12
Proactive interference, 217, 221
Problem solving, 234–246
Hubble space telescope, 227
Problem-focused coping, 451
Procedural memory, 205–206
Process schizophrenia, 490, 494
Processing the visual message, 97–98
Production, solution generation, 237–240
Profound retardation, 275
Progesterone, 330
Program evaluation, 6
Projection, 418
Projective personality test, 434, 437
Prosocial behavior, 554–556
Prototypes, 231, 233
Proximity, gestalt laws of organization, 114
Prozac, 521
Pseudo-psychology distinguished, 22–23
Psychiatric social workers, 505
Psychiatrists, 505
Psychoactive drugs, 149, 160
Psychoanalysis, 505–507
Psychoanalysts, 505
Psychoanalytic approaches to personality, 414–420, 430
Psychoanalytic perspective on abnormality, 473
Psychodynamic approaches to therapy, 504–507, 516
Psychodynamic perspective, 12, 15, 18, 24
conscious versus unconscious causes of behavior, 19, 23
free will versus determinism, 19
individual differences versus universal principles, 19–20
nature versus nurture, 19
observable behavior versus internal mental processes, 19

Psychological disorders. See Disorders
Psychological tests, 432, 437
Psychologically based addictions, 150
Psychology at work. See Working at psychology
Psychology defined, 4, 24
Psychology organization home pages, 4
Psychoneuroimmunology (PNI), 444
Psychophysics, 91
Psychophysiological disorders, 445
Psychosocial development, 373–374
Psychosomatic disorders, 445
Psychosurgery, 523, 525
Psychotherapy, 504–519
Psychoticism, 423
Puberty, 389–390, 397
Punishment, 176–177
Pupil, 94–95, 102

Quadriplegia, 62
Quitting smoking, 458–459

Race
African Americans. See African Americans
Asian success story, school achievement, 381
culture generally. See Culture
discrimination, 545–548
diversity generally. See Diversity
influencing behavior, 20–21
norms, 432–433
treatment of disorders, 517
Radiation in prenatal development, 363
Random assignment to condition, 39, 49
Range in statistics, A.7
Rape, 341–342
Rapid eye movement (REM) sleep, 135–137, 141, 144
Rapid eye movement (REM) sleep behavior disorder, 133
Rational-emotive behavior therapy, 511
Rationalization, 418
Reactance, 463
Reaction formation, 418
Reactive schizophrenia, 490, 494
Reality principle, 415
Reasoning, 232–233
Rebound effect, REM sleep, 136
Recalling long-term memories, 208–215
Recalls, 209, 215
Reciprocity-of-liking effect, 549
Recognition, 209
Redefining problems, 244
Red-green color blindness, 99
Reduction of violence, 17

Reflexes, 62, 67, 364–365
Refraction, 94
Refractory stage of sexual response, 332–334
Regression, 418
Rehearsal, 202–203, 221
Reinforcement, 175–179
Reinforcement schedules, 177–179
Reinforcer, 175
Relational style to learning, 188
Relationship harmony, 425
Relative size, 119
Relaxation response, 508
Relaxation techniques (pain management), 112
Reliability of tests, 265
psychological tests, 432, 437
Replication, 42
Representing problems, 235–237
Repressed memories, 213, 484
Repression, 417–418
Research, 29–51
animal research, 46, 48–49
archival research, 33, 42–43, 49
case study, 34, 36, 42–43, 49
challenges, 43–47
correlational research, 36, 41
developmental research, 357, 363
experimental research, 37–45
naturalistic observation, 34, 42–43, 49
scientific method to, 30–32
strategies, 41
survey research, 34–35, 42–43
Research challenges, 43–47
Research psychologists, 472
Residual schizophrenia, 489
Resistance, psychoanalysis, 506
Resistance stage, stress, 446
Resolution stage of sexual response, 332–333
Resting state, 57
Reticular function, 70
Retina, 95–96, 102
Retrieval of memory, 198–208
Retroactive interference, 217, 221
Retrograde amnesia, 219
Reuptake, 60
Rhodopsin, 96
Right visual field, 98
Rites of passage, 396–397
Road rage, 551
Rods of the eye, 95–96
Rogers, Carl, 13
personality, 429–430
Rohypnol, 156
Romantic love, 550
Rooting reflex, 364
Roots of language, 248–249
Rorschach test, 435–436
Rubella, 363

Sadness, 311, 313
St. John's wort, 521–522
Salary gap between men and women, 322

Salt taste, 109
Sampling, 34, 48, A.9, A.13
San Francisco State College,
    working at psychology, 44
SAT, 265
Scaffolding, 380
Schachter-singer theory of
    emotion, 307–309
Schadenfreude, 304
Schedules of reinforcement,
    177–179
Schemas, 211, 215
    social cognition, 534
Schizophrenia, 469, 488–493
School achievement, Asians, 381
School psychology, 6, 11
School sexual harassment, 323
Science and Human Behavior, 13
Scientific method to research,
    30–32, 49
Seasonal affective disorder, 142
Secondary drives, 289
Secondary orgasmic dysfunction,
    345
Secondary reinforcer, 175
Secondary traits, 422, 431
Securely attached children, 370
Selective serotonin reuptake
    inhibitors (SSRIs), 521
Self-actualization, 13
    motivation, 293
    personality, 429
Self-concepts, 429
Self-defeating personality disorder,
    495
Self-efficacy, 424–425, 431
Self-esteem, 425, 427
    happiness, 461
Self-fulfilling prophecy, 546, 548
Self-preservation, limbic system,
    72
Self-report measures of
    personality, 433–434
Semantic memory, 205, 207–208
Semantics, 247
Semen, 332
Semicircular canals, 107, 112
Senior Olympics, 403
Sensation, 90–93
    hearing, 102–107
    perception. See Perception
    skin senses, 108–111
    smell, 107–108
    taste, 108
    vision, 93–102
Sensation seekers, 291
Senses, 6
    development, 365–366
Sensing sound, 102–104
Sensorimotor stage of cognitive
    development, 375–376
Sensory adaptation, 92–93
Sensory (afferent) neurons, 62
Sensory area of the cortex, 74–75
Sensory illusions, 120–121
Sensory memory, 199–201
Serotonin, 61

Settling point, obesity, 298
Seveik, language researcher, 252
Severe retardation, 275
Sex before marriage, 337–338
Sex, extramarital, 338
Sex, marital, 338
Sex organs, 329–330
Sexism, 321–322
    benevolent sexism, 323
Sexual abuse, 343
Sexual attraction, 389, 549
Sexual behavior, 335–341
Sexual difficulties, 341–347
Sexual fantasies, 331
Sexual harassment, 322–323
Sexual normality, approaches to,
    335–336
Sexual orientation, 339–340
Sexual problems, 345–347
Sexual response, 329–334
    adolescence, 389–390
Sexually transmitted diseases
    (STDs), 343–345
Shaping, 180–181
Short-term memory, 199–200,
    201–202
Sickle cell anemia, 361
Sight
    absolute threshold, 91
    for the blind, 101
    perception. See Perception
Sign language, 247
    primates, 250
Significant outcome, 41
    statistics, A.10
Similarity
    attraction, 549
    gestalt laws of organization,
        114
Simplicity, gestalt laws of
    organization, 114
Single parents, 400
Situational causes of behavior,
    536
Skewed distribution in statistics,
    A.6
Skin senses, 108–111
Skin sensitivity, 110
Skinner, B. F., 13, 174
Skinner box, 174
Sleep and dreams, 133–144
    amount of sleep necessary,
        136–137
    better sleeping, 143–144
    circadian rhythms, 142
    day dreams, 143
    disturbances, sleep, 141
    function of dreams, 137–141
    meaning of dreams, 137–141
    REM sleep, 135–136
    stages of sleep, 134–135
    why we sleep, 136–137
Sleep apnea, 141
Sleep disturbances, 141–142
Sleep spindles, 134
Sleeping pills, 144
Slumbering problems, 141–142

Smell, 107–108
    absolute threshold, 91
Smiles, 312–313
Smith, Greg, 259
Smoking, 457–460
    hypnosis, 146
    prenatal development, 363
Social behavior, development of,
    368–374
    adolescence, 392–396
    early and middle adulthood,
        398–399
    late adulthood, 406–407
Social cognition, 534–538
Social cognitive approaches to
    personality, 424
Social factors in eating, 297
Social factors in gender
    differences, 327–329
Social influence, 539–545
Social learning theory, 185
    prejudice, 546
Social networks, 7
Social psychology, 6–7, 11, 24,
    529–556
    attitudes and social cognition,
        530–538
    positive and negative social
        behavior, 548–555
    prejudice and discrimination,
        545–548
    social influence, 539–545
Social support, coping with
    stress, 452
Social supporter, 540, 545
Socialization, 327
Sociocultural perspective to
    abnormality, 473, 475
Solitary sex, 336–337, 341
Solution generation, 237–240
Somatic division of nervous
    system, 63–64, 67
Somatoform disorders, 482
Somatosensory area of the cortex,
    74–75
Sound, 102–107
Sound localization, 102
Sound waves, 104–105
Source traits, 422
Spatial intelligence, 270
Specialties in the field of
    psychology, 5–8, 24
Spicy taste, 109
Spinal cord, 62, 67, 70
Spine, curvature of, 82
Split-brain patient, 80
Spontaneous recovery, 170
Spontaneous remission, 515, 519
Sport psychology, 6
Sports, hypnosis, 146
Stability in behavior, 7
Stage 1 sleep, 134–135
Stage 2 sleep, 134–135
Stage 3 sleep, 134–135
Stage 4 sleep, 134–135
Stages of personality development,
    Freud, 415–416

Stages of sleep, 134–135
Standard deviation in statistics,
    A.7–A.9
Standardized tests, 266, 273
Stanford-Binet test, 263
States of consciousness. See
    Consciousness
Statistical portrait of psychologists,
    9
Statistics, A.2–A.13
    descriptive statistics, A.3–A.7
    inferential statistics and
        correlation, A.9–A.13
    measures of variability, A.7–A.9
Status, conformity, 539
Stereotypes, 545
    gender roles, 320
Stetter, Leta, 13
Stimulants, 150–153
Stimulus, 91
Stimulus control training, 180
Stimulus discrimination,
    171–172, 180
Stimulus generalization,
    170–172, 180
Stirrup, ear, 103
Storage of memory, 198–208
Strategies, research, 41
Stress and coping, 443–453
    cancer, 457
    coping with stress, 450–453
    reacting to threat and challenge,
        445–450
Stress defined, 445
Stress management, 445
Stress test, 446
Stressors, 445
    categorizing, 448–449
    nature of, 447–448
Structuralism, 12–13, 18, 24
Structure of the brain, 67–69
Structure of the eye, 94–98
Structure of the neuron, 55–57
Student sexual harassment, 323
Students as experiment
    participants, 44–45, 49
Styles of parenting, 372–373
Subfields of psychology, 5–8, 24
Subgoals, forming, 238–239
Subjective well-being, 460
Subjects of experiments, 39
Sublimation, 418
Subliminal perception, 123–124
Subtance P, 109
Success, striving for, 301–302
Sucking reflex, 364
Sudden awareness, 239–240
Sudden infant death syndrome
    (SIDS), 141
Sugar metabolism, 81
Suicide, 394–396
Sultan, insight, 240
Superconducting quantum
    interface device
    (SQUID), 68
Superego, 414–415
Superstitious behavior, 180

Surgery, pain management, 112
Surprise, 311, 313
Survey research, 34–35, 42–43
Surveying sexual behavior, 336
Sweet taste, 109
Syllogistic reasoning, 232–233
Symbolism in dreams, 139
Sympathetic division of nervous
    system, 64–65
Symptoms of disorders, 476
Synapses, 58–59, 62
Syntax, 247
Syphilis, 344, 363
Systematic desensitization, 170,
    508–509, 516

Tabula rasa, 12
Taste, 108–109
    absolute threshold, 91
Taste buds, 108–109
Taste researcher, 110
Tay-Sachs disease, 361
Teaching Tolerance Project, 547
Teaching with linguistic variety,
    251–252
Technology, blindness, 101
Teenage drug use, 149
Teenage smoking, 459
Teenage suicide, 394–396
Tegretol, 522
Telegraphic speech, 247, 253
Television viewing, 37
    violence, 186–187, 554
Temperament, 373, 426
Temporal lobes, 73–74
Teratogens, 362
Terminal buttons, 55
Test standardization, 433
Testing, adaptive, 266–267
Testing, intelligence, 12–13,
    261–264, 273
    culture fair tests, 279–282
    jobs, 268
    scoring better on, 274
Tests, achievement, 264–265, 274
Tests, aptitude, 264–265, 274
Tests, personality, 431–437
Tests, psychological, 432, 437
Tests, stress, 446
Thalamotomy, 53
Thalamus, 70–71
That's-not-all technique,
    compliance, 542
Thematic apperception test (TAT),
    301, 435–436
Theories generally, 31–32, 49
Theories of sound, 105–107
Theories on learning, 166
Theory of cognitive development,
    374–382

Theory of Cognitive Dissonance,
    13
Theory of sensory memory, 200
Therapist, choosing, 524–525
Thinking and reasoning, 228–233
    language, 249
Thorndike's law of effect, 173–174
Thought, 6
Threats to experiments, 47
Three systems of memory, 199–203
Three-dimensional, perception,
    118–119
Thymus, 81
Thyroid gland, 81
Timeline of major landmarks in the
    development of psychology,
    12–13
Tip-of-the-tongue processing,
    209, 215
Token system, operant
    conditioning techniques,
    509
Top-down processing,
    116–117, 124
Touch, absolute threshold, 91
Tour de France, 287
Tower of Hanoi, 234
Toys, gender labeling, 327
Toys "R" US, gender labeling, 327
Trait approaches to personality,
    421–424, 430
Trait theory, 421
Traits, 421
Transcendental meditation
    research, 147
Transcutaneous electrical nerve
    stimulation (TENS), 112
Transference, psychoanalysis, 506
Transformation problems, 235–238
Treatment, 38
Trephining, 12
Trichomoniasis, 344
Trichromatic theory of color
    vision, 99, 102
Tricyclic drugs, 521
Trukese people, 261
Trust-versus-mistrust stage of
    development, 373, 392
Twins, 356
    schizophrenia, 491
Two-dimensional, perception,
    118–119
Two-group randomized
    experiment, 38
Type a behavior pattern, heart
    disease, 454–456, 462
Type b behavior pattern, heart
    disease, 454–456, 462

Unconditional positive regard, 429
    client-centered therapy, 513

Unconditioned response (UCR),
    168, 172
Unconditioned stimulus (UCS),
    168, 172
Unconscious, 414
Unconscious causes of behavior
    versus conscious, 19
Unconscious wish fulfillment
    theory, 138–140, 144
Understanding language
    acquisition, 248–249
Undifferentiated schizophrenia,
    489
Uninvolved parents, 372
Universal grammar, 248
Universal principles versus
    individual differences,
    19–20
Uplifts, 449, 451
U.S. government, working at
    psychology, 10

Vagina, 332
Validity of tests, 266
    psychological tests, 432, 437
Variability, measures of, A.7–A.9
Variable-interval schedules,
    178–179
Variable-ratio schedule,
    178–179, 183
Variables, 36, 43
Variations in intellectual ability,
    275–277
Ventromedial hypothalamus,
    hunger, 296
Vernix, 364
Viagra, 347
Violence and high self-esteem, 427
Violence on television and in
    movies, 186–187, 554
Violence, reduction of, 17
Virtual aggression, 187
Virtual therapy, 517
Visceral experiences, 306
Vision, 93–102
    optical illusions, 120–121
Vision cells in the brain, 13
Visual area of the cortex, 75
Visual illusions, 120–121
Visual perception, 93–102
Visual spectrum, 93–94
Vocabulary, 249
Vorwerk, Selma, A.2–A.3
Vygotsky's view of cognitive
    development, 379–381

Waking consciousness, 132
Wallace, Mike, 503
Warm milk, sleeping better, 143
Watson, John, 16
    timeline, 13

Wear-and-tear theories of aging,
    404, 408
Web surveys, 35
Weber's law, 92
Wechsler Adult Intelligence
    Scale-III (WAIS-III), 263
Wechsler Intelligence Scale for
    Children-III (WISC-III),
    263–264
Weight set point, 296, 302
Well-being and happiness,
    460–462
Well-defined problems, 234
Wernicke's aphasia, 76
Whites
    adolescence, 389
    culture generally. See Culture
    diversity generally. See
        Diversity
    influencing behavior, 21
    single parents, 400
Wiesel, Torsten, 13
Women and breast cancer,
    456–457
Women in psychology, founding
    mothers, 14
Women, moral development,
    391–392
Women, psychology of, 6
Women, sexism at work, 321–322
Women's "second shift," 401
Woods, Tiger, 531
Work, sexism at, 321–322
Working at psychology, 5, 24
    advertising executive,
        534–535
    advocate for the mentally
        retarded, 278
    crisis center counselor, 342
    dolphin research, 182
    global concentration of
        psychologists, 9
    help wanted ads, 8
    language researcher, 252
    police psychologist, 450
    preschool coordinator, 380
    research psychologist, 472
    San Francisco State College, 44
    taste researcher, 110
    U.S. government, 10
    where U.S. psychologists work,
        8–9
Working memory, 204
Wundt, William, 12, 18, 24

X-rays, prenatal development, 363

Zone of proximal development
    (ZPD), 380, 382
Zygotes, 358–359